DIRECTORY OF BOOK PUBLISHERS, DISTRIBUTORS AND WHOLESALERS 1993

Cornell University Press
124 Roberts Place
Ithaca, NY 14850

The Univ
Chicago Press

The
BOOKSELLERS ASSOCIATION
of Great Britain & Ireland

First published, 1954, twenty second edition 1993
© 1993 The Booksellers Association of Great Britain and Ireland.

Distributed by:
Booksellers Association Service House Ltd,
Minster House,
272 Vauxhall Bridge Road,
London SW1V 1BA.

ISBN 0-907972-61-6

All rights reserved. No part of this publication may be reproduced, stored in a retrieval system, or transmitted in any form or by any means, electronic, mechanical, photocopying, recording or otherwise, without prior permission of the publisher and copyright owner.

Not available for resale to libraries or the public.

Data processing and computer typesetting by:
BPCC Whitefriars Ltd, Tunbridge Wells, and printed and bound in Great Britain by BPCC Wheatons Ltd, Exeter

CONTENTS

	PAGE
Preface	v
How To Use The Directory	vii
Useful Addresses	ix
Country Codes	xv
Companies & Imprints Index	1
PUBLISHERS & DISTRIBUTORS	91
Distributor, Sales Agency & Wholesaler Specialisations	737
UK & IRISH WHOLESALERS	742
FOREIGN WHOLESALERS	783
AUDIO BOOK SUPPLIERS	785
REMAINDER DEALERS	801
Subject Category Index	813
Amendments Forms	833 & 835
Order Form	837

QUALITY: TAKEN AS READ!

BPCC Journals and Reference Books Ltd are proud to have typeset, printed and bound your copy of *The Directory of Book Publishers, Distributors & Wholesalers*

PRODUCTS
- Catalogues
- Books
- Journals
- Directories
- Magazines
- Yearbooks
- Looseleaf

SERVICES
- Typesetting
- DTP Bureau Service
- Web & Sheet-fed Printing
- Cased & Limp Binding
- Looseleaf Production
- Mailing & Distribution

Please call Iain Littlejohn on 0892 544366 to find out how our service will meet your needs

BPCC Journals & Reference Books Ltd
12 Spa Industrial Park, Longfield Road,
Tunbridge Wells TN2 3EN
Tel 0892 544366 Fax 0892 544267

PREFACE

Keeping up with developments in the book industry is, like painting the Forth Bridge, a never ending task. Each year this Directory is completely overhauled to keep pace with the many takeovers, mergers, movements and newly emerging companies.

Following last year's decision to bring the database in house, we have been able to speed up production, which we hope will keep the inevitable changes from collection of data to publication to an absolute minimum, thus increasing the currency of the Directory. This investment has also enabled us to introduce basic information on an additional three hundred plus smaller publishers and we will continue to expand the database in this area. The other major new initiative this year, is the information tabled in the Distributor, Sales Agency and Wholesaler Specialisations section. Booksellers looking for new sources of supply in specific subject categories and publishers seeking help in distribution or sales and marketing will, we hope, find this a useful starting point. Further details on the information contained in the entries can be found at the beginning of each section or in the How To Use The Directory section.

All the data in this publication comes, needless to say, from the companies themselves. Every company has had an opportunity to check their entry, and every effort has been made to ensure its accuracy. Sometimes, however, especially with handwritten forms, misunderstandings and errors do slip through and, inevitably, we find that in certain cases the information supplied by the companies has changed after the Directory has gone to press. Please use the amendments form at the back to inform us of any misprints, errors or omissions.

Details of trade terms in the Directory should serve as a guide, enabling booksellers to achieve the highest possible gross margins, which, in the current economic climate, is obviously of great importance. Further notes on small order surcharges and payment methods should also assist booksellers in providing the best service with the minimum cost. The actual discount received is, of course, a matter for negotiation between the individual bookseller and supplier, but as the terms shown are basic terms, booksellers should not hesitate in requesting additional discounts if it is believed to be justified.

The production of such a publication is an enormous task for a small organisation. I am grateful to my colleagues in the Booksellers Association for their invaluable help in producing this new edition. We hope that with each new edition we have improved on the last. However, we always welcome ideas from users of the Directory, so please do not hesitate to send in your suggestions.

Sydney Davies
Trade Practice Executive

The Booksellers Association of Great Britain and Ireland

- *The Booksellers Association represents over 3,300 bookshops. Our members range from large chains to small independent booksellers.*

- *The BA provides a wide range of services and all are designed to assist members in the smooth and efficient running of their bookshops.*

- *As a member of the BA you will be able to trade in Book Tokens, just one of the many benefits of membership.*

- *To receive a free membership information pack, and find out how we can help make your business prosper, contact us now!*

Membership Department,
The Booksellers Association,
Minster House, 272 Vauxhall Bridge Road, London, SW1V 1BA.
Tel: 071-834 5477. Fax: 071-834 8812.

Terms
The terms of supply listed apply to retail booksellers in the UK and Ireland only and have no reference to arrangements with wholesalers or overseas booksellers. More and more publishers are using independent distributors and, where the distributor's terms apply, this is indicated. Reference should then be made to the distributor's entry. Information on whether orders for more than one publisher on a distributor's list may be bulked to avoid surcharges has also been included.

Reference to net terms, net books, and net prices, in the Directory refers to books issued to the trade, subject to the Publishers Association Standard Conditions of Sale of Net Books, under the Net Book Agreement 1957.

Credit Cards
Companies have been asked to state whether or not they will accept payment by credit card (at normal trade terms) in order to avoid the need for pro-forma invoices. The majority of those indicating that they do accept credit cards will accept Visa or Access, and some will also accept other credit or charge cards, such as Amex or Diners Club. Some will also accept additional cards and booksellers are advised to check with the company if they have 'Other' listed.

Distributor, Sales Agency & Wholesaler Specialisations
UK & Irish Wholesalers
Foreign Wholesalers
Audio Book Suppliers
Remainder Dealers

Notes on the lists precede the entries.

Subject Category Index
Publishers weree asked to inform us from a list provided, areas in which they *specialise*. It is therefore not necessarily totally comprehensive, but we hope it will at least serve as a useful indicator. The list of subjects precedes the index.

Updating Entries
While every care has been taken to ensure the accuracy of the information contained in the Directory, the Booksellers Association does not accept responsibility for any possible errors, or omissions, or the refusal of companies to supply any particular bookseller at the terms indicated herein.

Please note that the names of companies who failed to submit updated information for publication in this edition are listed in the index. We have attempted to contact all of them several times before reluctantly omitting them.

Every effort is made to include changes in company ownership and distribution as late as possible, but inevitably there are some situations where the position is not clear at the time of going to press. These will be corrected in the next edition.

We would be grateful for notification of any obvious omissions or misprints, which will be immediately corrected. Please use the form at the back of the Directory.

USEFUL ADDRESSES

Book Trade Services . Carriers . Government Agencies
Trade Associations & Agencies . Trade Journals

Activair Ltd
Unit 11/13 Lidall Way
Horton Road, West Drayton
Middlesex UB7 8PG
Tel: 0895 441541
Fax: 0895 445515

AIM UK
The Old Vicarage
Haley Hill, Halifax
West Yorkshire HX3 6DR
Tel: 0422 359161
Fax: 0422 355604

American Booksellers Association
560 White Plains Road
Tarrytown, New York 10591 USA
Tel: (914) 631 7800
Fax: (914) 631 8391

Antiquarian Booksellers Association
The Secretary
Suite 2, 26 Charing Cross Road
London WC2H 0DG
Tel: 071-379 3041
Fax: 071-497 2114

Article Number Association (UK) Ltd
11 Kingsway
London WC2B 6AR
Tel: 071-240 2912
Fax: 071-240 8149

Arts Council of Great Britain
Literature Director
14 Great Peter Street
London SW1P 3NQ
Tel: 071-333 0100
Fax: 071-973 6590

Association of Mail Order Publishers
- Direct Marketing Association (UK) Ltd

Association of Publishers Educational Representatives
Mr S W Hall
88 Haven Chase, Cookridge
Leeds LS16 6SG
Tel: 0532 673956
Fax: No Fax

Association of Subscription Agents
Mr J B Merriman, Secretary
Thames Gardens, Charlbury
Oxford OX7 3QH
Tel: 0608 810375
Fax: 0993 778879

Attache du Livre
Cultural Department
French Embassy
21-23 Cromwell Road
London SW7 2EN
Tel: 071-581 5292
Fax: 071-823 8956

Book Data Ltd
Northumberland House
2 King Street, Twickenham
Middlesex TW1 3RZ
Tel: 081-892 2272
Fax: 081-892 9109

Book House
45 East Hill, Wandsworth
London SW18 2QZ
Tel: 081-870 9055
Fax: 081-874 4790
also
Book House Training Centre
Fax: 081-870 8985
also
Book Information Service
also
Book Trust
also
Childrens Book Foundation

Book Industry Communication
39-41 North Road
London N7 9DP
Tel: 071-607 0021
Fax: 071-607 0415

Book Marketing Ltd
7A Bedford Square
London WC1B 3RA
Tel: 071-580 7282
Fax: 071-580 7236

Book Packagers Association
93A Blenheim Crescent
London W11 2EQ
Tel: 071-221 9089
Fax: No Fax
also
Directory Publishers Association

Book Publishers Representatives Assn
Brian Darton
137 First Avenue
Bush Hill Park
Enfield
Middlesex EN1 1BP
Tel: 081-363 2765
Fax: 081-364 5553

Book Shippers Association Inc
Unit A
Hanworth Lane Trading Estate
Hanworth Lane, Chertsey
Surrey KT16 9JX
Tel: 0932 570083
Fax: 0932 570090

Book Tokens Ltd
- The Booksellers Association of
  Great Britain and Ireland

Book Trade Benevolent Society
Ann Brown (Executive Secretary)
Dillon Lodge, The Retreat
Kings Langley
Hertfordshire WD4 8LT
Tel: 0923 263128
Fax: 0923 270732

Book Trade Improvements Ltd
- The Booksellers Association
  of Great Britain and Ireland

Book Trust
- Book House

Book Trust (Scotland)
The Scottish Book Centre
137 Dundee Street
Edinburgh EH11 1BG
Tel: 031-229 3663
Fax: 031-228 4293

'Books'
- Publishing News

'Books for Keeps'
- School Bookshop Association

Books In Print
- J Whitaker & Sons Ltd

'The Bookseller'
- J Whitaker & Sons Ltd

**The Booksellers Association
of Great Britain and Ireland**
272 Vauxhall Bridge Road
London SW1V 1BA
Tel: 071-834 5477
Fax: 071-834 8812
also
Booksellers Assn Service House
'Bookselling'
also
Book Tokens Ltd
Book Trade Improvements Ltd
Booksellers Clearing House
Tel: 071-834 5488
Fax: 071-834 8781
Answer Service For Orders:
Tel: 071-834 8815

Booksellers Order Dist Ltd (BOD)
49 Victoria Road
Aldershot
Hampshire GU11 1SJ
Tel/Fax: 0252 20697

'Bookselling'
- The Booksellers Association
  of Great Britain and Ireland

Bookwatch Ltd
15-Up East Street, Lewin's Yard
Chesham, Bucks HP5 1HQ
Tel: 0494 792269
Fax: 0494 784850

The British Council
Medlock Street
Manchester M15 4PR
Tel: 061-957 7000
Fax: 061-957 7168
Telex: 8952201 BRICON G

'British Book News'
The British Council
10 Spring Gardens
London SW1A 2BN
Tel: 071-930 8466
Fax: 071-839 6347

**British Library
National Bibliographic Services**
Boston Spa, Wetherby
West Yorkshire LS23 7BQ
Tel: 0937 546585
Fax: 0937 546586

British Printing Industries Federation
11 Bedford Row
London WC1R 4DX
Tel: 071-242 6904
Fax: 071-405 7784

British Retail Consortium
Bedford House
69-79 Fulham High Street
London SW6 3JW
Tel: 071-371 5185
Fax: 071-371 0529

Childrens Book Foundation
- Book House

Christian Book Promotion Trust
The Market House, Cantelupe Road
East Grinstead
West Sussex RH19 3BH
Tel: 0342 312750/715889

Christian Booksellers Association
Grampian House, 144 Deansgate
Manchester M3 3ED
Tel: 061-833 2848
Fax: 061-835 3000

Christian Booksellers Convention
41 Dace Road
London E3 2NG
Tel: 081-986 0178
Fax: 081-986 1531

Cle (Cumann Leabharfhoilsitheoiri Eireann)
PO Box 9534
Dublin 1
Tel: 01-283 5552

Copyright Licensing Agency Ltd
90 Tottenham Court Road
London W1P 9HE
Tel: 071-436 5931
Fax: 071-436 3986

**Council of Academic and
Professional Publishers**
- The Publishers Association

Direct Marketing Association (UK) Ltd
Haymarket House
1 Oxendon Street
London SW1Y 4EE
Tel: 071-321 2525
Fax: 071-321 0191

Directory Publishers Association
- Book Packagers Association

Edinburgh Book Festival
- Scottish Publishers Association

Educational Publishers Council
- The Publishers Association

Educational Low-Priced Book Scheme
- International Book Development

'European Bookseller'
Advertising/Circulation
Byron House
112A Shirland Road
London W9 2EQ
Tel: 071-266 1986
Fax: 071-586 2429
Editorial
19 Baskerville Road
London SW18 3RW
Tel/Fax: 081-874 9189

Federal Express (Europe) Inc
Sutherland House, Matlock Road
Foleshill, Coventry CV1 4JQ
Tel: 0203 637637
Fax: 0203 637851/637866

Federation of European Publishers
92 Avenue de Tervuren
B-1040 Bruxelles
Belgium
Tel: 322 736 3616
Fax: 322 736 1987

Federation of Radical Booksellers
Lifespan, Townhead
Dunford Bridge, Sheffield S30 6TG
Tel: No Tel/Fax

First Edition EDI Services Ltd
44 Dartford Road
Sevenoaks
Kent TN13 3TQ
Tel: 0732 740192
Fax: 0732 457542

GALC
(Booksellers Associations Group in the EC)
Ter Borchtlaan 75
B/2650 Edegem
Belgium
Tel: 32344 93730
Fax: 32344 93730

IBIS Information Services Ltd
Waterside, Lowbell Lane
London Colney, St Albans
Hertfordshire AL2 1DX
Tel: 0727 82520950
Fax: 0727 826461

Independent Publishers Guild
25 Cambridge Road
Hampton
Middlesex TW12 2JL
Tel/Fax: 081-979 0250

**Institute of Translation
& Interpreting**
377 City Road
London EC1V 1NA
Tel: 071-713 7600
Fax: 071-713 7650

International Book Development
10 Barley Mow Passage
London W4 4PH
Tel: 081-994 6477
Fax: 081-747 8715

International Booksellers Federation
Grosser Hirschgraben 17-21
D-6000 Frankfurt am Main 1
Germany
Tel: 069/1306 318
Fax: 069/1306 309

International Map Dealers Association
European Division
5 Spinacre, Becton Lane
Barton-on-Sea
Hants BH25 7DF
Tel & Fax: 0425 620532

**Irish Book Publishers' Association
- Cle**

ISSN Agency
UK National Serials Data Centre
The British Library
Boston Spa, Wetherby
West Yorkshire LS23 7BY
Tel: 0937 546958/9
Fax: 0937 546979

The Library Association
7 Ridgmount Street
London WC1E 7AE
Tel: 071-636 7543
Fax: 071-436 7218

**Local Authorities Co-ordinating Body
on Trading Standards (LACOTS)**
PO Box 6, Token House
1A Robert Street
Croydon, Surrey CR9 1LG
Tel: 081-688 1996
Fax: 081-680 1509

London International Book Fair
Oriel House, 26 The Quadrant
Richmond, Surrey TW9 1DL
Tel: 081-948 9800
Fax: 081-948 9930

Lynx Express Delivery Network
Fountain House
Great Cornbow, Halesowen
West Midlands B63 3BS
Tel: 021-550 7676
Fax: 021-501 1058

The Mail Order Traders Association
100 Old Hall Street
Liverpool L3 9TD
Tel: 051-227 4181
Fax: 051-227 2584

Mail Users Association Ltd
3 Pavement House, The Pavement
Hay-on-Wye, Hereford HR3 5BU
Tel: 0497 821357
Fax: 0497 821360

Music Publishers Association Ltd
3rd Floor, Strandgate
18/20 York Buildings
London WC2N 8JU
Tel: 071-839 7779
Fax: 071-839 7776

National Acquisitions Group
Westfield House, North Road
Horsforth, Leeds LS18 5HG
Tel/Fax: 0532 591447

Office of Fair Trading
Publications, Field House
15-25 Breams Building
London EC4A 1PR
Tel: 071-242 2858
Fax: 071-269 8800

Office of the Data Protection Registrar
Wycliffe House, Water Lane
Wilmslow
Cheshire SK9 5AF
Tel: 0625 535777 (Enquiries)
Tel: 0625 535711 (Admin)
Fax: 0625 524510

Out of Print Book Services
13 Pantbach Road
Birchgrove
Cardiff CF4 1TU
Tel: 0222 627703
Fax: No Fax

Parceline Ltd
Commercial & Marketing
Head Office, Royal House
Vine Street, Uxbridge
Middlesex UB8 1HW
Tel: 0895 272999
Fax: 0895 270760

The Performing Right Society
29/33 Berners Street
London W1P 4AA
Tel: 071-580 5544
Fax: 071-631 4138

Periodical Publishers Association
Imperial House
15-19 Kingsway
London WC2B 6UN
Tel: 071-379 6268
Fax: 071-379 5661

Poetry Society
22 Betterton Street
London WC2H 9BU
Tel: 071-240 4810
Fax: 071-240 4818

Post-a-Book
Postal Supply Department
11 Maylands Avenue
Hemel Hempstead
Herts HP2 4SF
Tel: 0442 213611
Fax: 0442 61813

Provincial Fair Booksellers Association
Secretary Administrator
Mrs Gina Dolan
The Old Coach House, 16 Melbourn Street
Royston, Herts SG8 7BZ
Tel: 0763 248400
Fax: 0763 248921

The Publishers Association
(Council of Academic &
Professional Publishers,
Educational Publishers Council
International Department/BDC
Publishing, Management & Technology)
19 Bedford Square
London WC1B 3HJ
Tel: 071-580 6321/5
Fax: 071-636 5375
Telex: 26716 PUBASS G

Publishers Publicity Circle
Christina Thomas (Secretary)
48 Crabtree Lane
London SW6 6LW
Tel/Fax: 071-385 3708

'Publishing News'
43 Museum Street
London WC1A 1LY
Tel: 071-404 0304
Fax: 071-242 0762
also
'Books'

'The Radical Bookseller'
265 Seven Sisters Road
London N4 2DE
Tel: 081-802 8773
Fax: 081-802 3835

Royal Mail Parcelforce
Headquarters, Solaris Court
Davy Avenue, Knowl Hill
Milton Keynes MK5 8PP
Tel: 0908 687000
Fax: 0908 687333

School Bookshop Association
6 Brightfield Road
London SE12 8QF
Tel: 081-852 4953
Fax: No Fax
also
'Books For Keeps'

School Library Association
Liden Library
Barrington Close
Liden, Swindon
Wiltshire SN3 6HF
Tel: 0793 617838
Fax: No Fax

Scottish Publishers Association
Scottish Book Centre
137 Dundee Street
Edinburgh EH11 1BG
Tel: 031-228 6866
Fax: 031-228 3220
also
Edinburgh Book Festival
Tel: 031-228 5444
Fax: 031-228 4333

Securicor Omega Express
Sutton Park House
15 Carshalton Road
Sutton
Surrey SM1 4LE
Tel: 0345 200345
Fax: 081-643 1059

Small Press Group of Britain
BM Bozo
London WC1N 3XX
Tel: 0234 211606
Small Press Centre Tel: 081-362 6058

Society of Authors
84 Drayton Gardens
London SW10 9SB
Tel: 071-373 6642
Fax: 071-373 5768

Society of Indexers
Mrs Elizabeth Wallis
25 Leybourne Park
Kew Gardens, Richmond
Surrey TW9 3HB
Tel: 081-940 4771
Fax: No Fax

Society of Young Publishers
- J Whitaker & Sons Ltd

Standard Address Numbering Agency
- J Whitaker & Sons Ltd

Standard Book Numbering Agency
- J Whitaker & Sons Ltd

Teleordering Ltd
3 The Windmills
St Mary's Close, Turk Street
Alton, Hampshire, GU34 1EF
Tel: 0420 544177 (Gen Enq)
    0420 544355 (Help Desk)
Fax: 0420 543930

Union of Welsh Publishers and Booksellers
(Undeb Cyhoeddwyr a Llyfrewerthwyr Cymraeg)
c/o Gomer Press
Llandysul
Dyfed SA44 4BQ
Tel: 0559 362371
Fax: 0559 363758

United Carriers
Turnells Mill Lane
Wellinborough
Northants NN8 2QQ
Tel: 0933 440400
Fax: 0933 441241

Video Trade Association
54D High Street
Northwood
Middlesex HA6 1BL
Tel: 0923 829122
Fax: 0923 835980

Welsh Books Council
(Cyngor Llyfrau Cymraeg)
Castell Brychan
Aberystwyth
Dyfed SY23 2JB
Tel: 0970 624151
Fax: 0970 625385

J Whitaker & Sons Ltd
12 Dyott Street
London WC1A 1DF
Tel: 071-836 8911
Fax: 071-836 2909
also
'The Bookseller'
Fax: 071-836 6381
Society of Young Publishers
Standard Address Numbering Agency
Standard Book Numbering Agency
Fax: 071-836 4342
Women in Publishing

Wages Inspectorate
Department of Employment

London
Clifton House, 83-117 Euston Rd
London NW1 2RA
Tel: 071-387 2511
Fax: 071-383 7318
Midlands
Cumberland Hse, 200 Broad St
Birmingham B15 1TD
Tel: 021-631 3300
Fax: 021-643 2863
North Western
2nd Floor, Alexandra House
14-22 Parsonage Gardens
Manchester M3 2JS
Tel: 061-832 6506
Fax: 061-834 7515
Northern
Broadacre House
Market Street East
Newcastle-Upon-Tyne NE1 6HH
Tel: 091-232 1881
Fax: 091-230 4197
Scotland
127-129 George Street
Edinburgh EH2 4JN
Tel: 031-220 2777
Fax: 031-225 5482
South West
The Pithay
Bristol BS1 2NQ
Tel: 0272 273710
Fax: 0272 256605
Yorkshire and Humberside
City House, New Station Street
Leeds LS1 4JD
Tel: 0532 438232
Fax: 0532 444898

COUNTRY CODES

AF	Afghanistan	HA	Haiti	PA	Panama
AG	Algeria	HG	Hungary	PG	Portugal
AL	Albania	HK	Hong Kong	PH	Philippines
AR	Arab Emirates	HN	Honduras	PK	Pakistan
AS	Austria			PL	Poland
AT	Argentina	IA	Iran	PN	Papua New Guinea
AU	Australia	IC	Iceland	PR	Peru
		ID	Indonesia	PU	Puerto Rico
BA	Bahamas	IN	India	PY	Paraguay
BB	Barbados	IQ	Iraq		
BG	Belgium	IR	Ireland	RM	Romania
BH	Bangladesh	IS	Israel	RU	Russia & CIS
BL	Boliva	IT	Italy		
BM	Burma				
BO	Botswana	JD	Jordan	SA	South Africa
BU	Bulgaria	JM	Jamaica	SD	Saudia Arabia
BZ	Brazil	JP	Japan	SG	Senegal
				SI	Singapore
CA	Canada			SL	Sri Lanka
CB	Cuba	KN	Korea (North)	SP	Spain
CH	China	KS	Korea (South)	SW	Sweden
CL	Chile	KY	Kenya	SX	Swaziland
CM	Cameroon			SY	Syria
CO	Colombia	LA	Latvia	SZ	Switzerland
CR	Costa Rica	LB	Lebanon		
CY	Cyprus	LE	Lesotho	TA	Taiwan
CZ	Czechoslovakia	LI	Liechtenstein	TH	Thailand
		LT	Lithuania	TK	Turkey
DN	Denmark	LX	Luxembourg	TN	Tunisia
		LY	Libya	TT	Trinidad & Tobago
EA	Estonia			TZ	Tanzania
EC	Ecuador	MA	Malawi		
EG	Egypt	MC	Morocco	UG	Uganda
ES	El Salvador	ML	Malaysia	UR	Uruguay
ET	Ethiopia	MU	Mauritius	US	USA
		MX	Mexico		
FN	Finland			VZ	Venezuela
FR	France	NA	Namibia		
		NC	Nicaragua	YG	Former Yugoslavia
GA	Guyana	NG	Nigeria		
GE	Germany	NP	Nepal	ZB	Zimbabwe
GH	Ghana	NT	Netherlands	ZM	Zambia
GR	Greece	NW	Norway		
GU	Guatamala	NZ	New Zealand		

Novel Insurance Solutions from Willis Corroon

The Booksellers Association insurance schemes are now in the capable hands of Willis Corroon, providing exclusive protection for member companies.

As the largest corporate insurance broker in the United Kingdom, Willis Corroon is able to offer you the benefits of bulk buying on behalf of the Booksellers Association, combined with personal attention and advice from experienced insurance professionals.

As the insurance market cycle turns and premiums rise, now is a good time to review your existing policies. If you are interested in obtaining a quotation on general business insurance or motor insurance, or some advice on any risk management or insurance issues, contact our dedicated team:

Charlotte Bibb 071 787 6590
Simon Sadler   071 787 6277
Simon Marsh   071 787 6561.

Willis Corroon London Limited
Willis Corroon House, Wood Street,
Kingston upon Thames,
Surrey, KT1 1UG.

WILLIS CORROON

Companies and Imprints Index

A Capella (US) — D: TURNAROUND
AA Publishing — D: EXEL LOGISTICS
AA PUBLISHING
AAB BRITISH BOOK SEARCH
AB ACADEMIC PUBLISHERS
Abacus — I: LITTLE BROWN & CO
Abacus — D: TIPTREE BOOK SERV
Abacus Software Inc (US) — D: COMPUTER BOOKSHOPS
Abage Publications (Partial) (US) — D: HILMARTON MANOR
Abaris Books Inc (US) — D: ART BOOK DIST CO
Abbeville Press (US) — D: JOHN MURRAY PUB LTD
Abbeville Press (US) — D: GRANTHAM BOOK SERV
Abbey Press - St Meinrad (Partial) (US) — D: ANTHONY CLARKE PUB
ABC Clio (US) — D: CLIO PRESS LTD
ABC Verlag (Partial) (SZ) — D: S HENEAGE DIST
ABC/All Books for Children — D: PLYMBRIDGE DIST LTD
ABC/All Books for Children — A: DEREK SEARLE ASS LTD
ABC/ALL CHILDRENS COMPANY
ABCO DESIGN LTD
Abelard-Schuman — BLACKIE imprint no longer used
Abercastle Publications (Partial) — D: WELSH BOOKS COUNCIL
ABERDEEN & NE SCOTLAND FAMILY HISTORY SOC
Aberdeen UP — In receivership
Abhinav Publications (IN) — D: BOOKS FROM INDIA
Abingdon Press (US) — D: SPCK
Abington Publishing — I: WOODHEAD PUBLISHING
ABJAD (US) — D: ALIF INTERNATIONAL
Ablex Publishing Corporation (US) — D: LAWRENCE ERLBAUM ASS
Aborignial Culture Abroad (AU) — D: MILLBANK BOOKS LTD
Abradale Press — I: HARRY N ABRAMS INC
ABRAMS INC, HARRY N
Absolute Classics — I: ABSOLUTE PRESS
Absolute Press — D: CENTRAL BOOKS
ABSOLUTE PRESS
ABSON BOOKS
ACADEMIC & UNIVERSITY PUBLISHERS GROUP
ACADEMIC BOOK ASSOCIATES
Academic Press — I: HARCOURT BRACE JOVAN
Academic Therapy Publications (Part only) (US) — D: ANN ARBOR PUBLISHERS
Academic University Publishers Group — D: BIBLIOS PUB DIST
Academy Books — D: VINE HOUSE DIST
ACADEMY BOOKS LTD
Academy Chicago Pub Ltd (US) — D: GAZELLE BOOK SERVICE
Academy Editions — I: ACADEMY GROUP LTD
Academy Editions — I: VCH PUB (UK) LTD
ACADEMY GROUP LTD
Academy Science Publishers (KY) — D: AFRICAN BOOKS COLL
ACADEMY SOUND & VISION — A
ACAIR LTD
Accelerated Development Inc (US) — D: GAZELLE BOOK SERVICE
ACCENT EDUCATIONAL PUBLISHERS LTD
Access Press (US) — I: HARPERCOLLINS GENREF
ACCOUNTANCY BOOKS
Accountancy Books (ICAEW) — A: ROGER BAYLISS
Accountants Publishing Co, The — I: ICAS
ACE — I: WOLFHOUND PRESS
ACE Books — D: BOOKPOINT LIMITED
ACE BOOKS
Ache Comics — D: COMBINED BOOK SERV
Achiasat (IS) — D: KUPERARD LTD
ACI (US) — A: AMERICAN TECH PUB
Acme Publications — D: CENTRAL BOOKS
Acorn Books — D: ROY YATES BOOKS
Acorn Books (SA) — D: LAKESIDE PUBNS
Acorn Editions — I: JAMES CLARKE & CO
Acorn Series — I: JAY BOOKS
ACR (FR) — D: S HENEAGE DIST
Acrobat Books Publishers (US) — D: GAZELLE BOOK SERVICE

1

Acropolis Books — I: ANNESS PUBLISHING
Acropolis Books Ltd (US) — D: GAZELLE BOOK SERVICE
ACS Publications (US) — D: AIRLIFT BOOK CO
ACT 3 PUBLISHING
Actinic Press — I: CRESSRELLES PUB LTD
Activities Press Ltd — D: BOOKPOINT LIMITED
Activity Digest, The — I: PRINTFORCE LTD
Acts/Initiatives Publishers (KY) — D: LEISHMAN & TAUSSIG
Actual Size Press — No reply 92/93
Ad Lib — I: SCHOLASTIC PUB LTD
Adam Editions (GR) — D: CENTRAL BOOKS
Adamantine Press (US) — D: EDS
Adams Inc, Bob — D: BOOKPOINT LIMITED
ADAMSON BOOKS
Addington Press — I: RSCM
Addison-Wesley — D: SOUTHPORT BOOK DIST
ADDISON-WESLEY PUBLISHERS
Addor et Associes, Henry (Partial) (FR) — D: HILMARTON MANOR
Adelphi Press — I: EXCALIBUR PRESS
Adizes Institute (US) — D: EVENLODE BOOK DIST
Adlard Coles Nautical — I: A & C BLACK LTD
Adlard Coles Nautical (Ireland only) — A: BLACKSTAFF PRESS LTD
Ad-Lib Publications (US) — D: GAZELLE BOOK SERVICE
ADT — I: PHAIDON PRESS LTD
Adtech Book Co Ltd — I: ARTECH HOUSE
ADULT LITERACY & BASIC SKILLS UNIT
Advaita Publications — D: ELEMENT BOOKS LTD
Advance Memory Research (US) — D: GAZELLE BOOK SERVICE
Adventure Unlimited (US) — D: SPRINGFIELD BOOKS
ADVISORY CENTRE FOR EDUCATION
ADVISORY UNIT FOR MICROTECHNOLOGY IN EDUCATION
Adyar T P H (IN) — D: THEOSOPHICAL PUB LTD
Aedes Gallery (GE) — D: ART DATA
AEDIFICAMUS PRESS
Aeolian Press (AU) — D: PETER MOORE BOOKS
Aerofax Inc (US) — D: MIDLAND COUNTIES LTD
AEROSPACE PROFILES
Aerospace Publishing — D: AIRLIFE PUBLISHING
AESCULUS PRESS
Affiliated East-West Press (IN) — D: BOOKS FROM INDIA
Affinity Press (US) — D: EVENLODE BOOK DIST
Affirmation Books (US) — D: COLUMBA BOOK SERVICE
AFRICA CHRISTIAN PRESS
African American Images (US) — D: GAZELLE BOOK SERVICE
AFRICAN BOOKS COLLECTIVE
African Contemporary Record — I: BOOK REP & DIST LTD
Africana Publishing — I: BOOK REP & DIST LTD
Afroworld — D: CENTRAL BOOKS
After the Battle — I: BATTLE OF BRITAIN
Age Concern England — ACE BOOKS
AGE CONCERN SCOTLAND
AGENDA & EDITIONS CHARITABLE TRUST
Agneau 2 — I: ALLARDYCE BARNETT
AGORA BOOKS
AGRICOLA TRAINING
AGS PUBLICATIONS
Ahmadiyya Ishaat Islam Lahore (US) — D: GAZELLE BOOK SERVICE
AIKEN, ALEX
Aimari Publishing (US) — D: EVENLODE BOOK DIST
Aims Corp (JP) — I: BLENHEIM ONLINE
Air Research — D: FOUNTAIN PRESS LTD
AIR-BRITAIN HISTORIANS
Aird Books Pty Ltd (AU) — D: GAZELLE BOOK SERVICE
AIRLIFE PUBLISHING
AIRLIFT BOOK COMPANY
Aisan Humanities (US) — D: WISDOM BOOKS
Ajanta Books (IN) — D: BOOKS FROM INDIA
AJK LTD
AK DISTRIBUTION
AK Press — D: AK DISTRIBUTION
Akademie Verlag — I: VCH PUB (UK) LTD
Akros Publications — No reply 92/93
Aktok — D: CENTRAL BOOKS
Al Fresco Publications — D: BREWIN BOOK DIST
Al Saqi Books (Partial) — A: P M LLEWELLYN CO
ALADDIN BOOKS LTD
Alamo Square Press (US) — D: TURNAROUND
Alaska Northwest Books (Partial) (US) — D: CORDEE
ALASTAIR PRESS, THE
Alaw — D: WELSH BOOKS COUNCIL
Albatross Books (AU) — D: LION PUBLISHING PLC
Albert House Press — D: VINE HOUSE DIST

Alberta Univ Press (CA) — D: LAVIS MARKETING
Albion Scott — CALVIN MORGAN BOOKSELLERS
Albright-Knox Gallery (US) — D: ART DATA
ALBSU — D: AVANTI BOOKS
ALBSU — I: ALBSU
Alda Publishers — D: ASHFORD BUCHAN
Aldwych Press — DISTROPA LTD
Aldwych Press (US) — D: EDS
ALECTO HISTORICAL EDITIONS
Alemany Press — I: SIMON & SCHUSTER INT
ALEMBIC PRESS
ALEXIUS PRESS
Al-Hoda — D: ALIF INTERNATIONAL
Alianza (SP) — D: EUROPEAN SCHOOLBOOKS
Alibaba Verlag (GE) — D: ROY YATES BOOKS
ALIF INTERNATIONAL
ALKIN BOOKS
All Boys — D: INT MUSIC PUB
Allan Group Ltd, Ian — D: BOOKPOINT LIMITED
Allan, Philip — I: SIMON & SCHUSTER INT
ALLAN PUBLISHING, IAN
ALLARDYCE BARNETT PUBLISHERS
Allen & Co Ltd, J A — D: SHEED & WARD LTD
Allen & Unwin (Partial List) (AU) — D: QUARTET BOOKS LTD
Allen & Unwin Pty Ltd (AU) — D: UCL PRESS LTD
ALLEN LTD, J A
ALLEN PUBLISHING CO
Allen, W H — VIRGIN PUBLISHING
ALLENHOLME PRESS
Allenson — I: JAMES CLARKE & CO
Allhems (Partial) (SW) — D: HAN SHAN TANG LTD
ALLIANCE BOOK SERVICES
Allison & Busby — I: VIRGIN PUBLISHING
ALLOWAY PUBLISHING LTD
Allright-Knox Art Gallery — I: SIMON & SCHUSTER INT
Allured Published (US) — D: FOOD TRADE PRESS LTD
Allweather Charts — I: BARNACLE MARINE LTD
Allworth Press (US) — D: GAZELLE BOOK SERVICE
Allworth (US) — A: H I MARKETING
Allworth (US) — D: TIPTREE BOOK SERV
Allyn & Bacon — I: SIMON & SCHUSTER INT
Alma Books — A: VERULAM PUB LTD
Almond Press (US) — D: SHEFFIELD ACD PRESS
Alouette Josef (GE) — D: GAZELLE BOOK SERVICE
Alphabooks — I: A & C BLACK LTD
Alpine Club, The — D: CORDEE
ALPINE FINE ARTS COLLECTION
Alpine (Fine Arts) Ltd — A: JOHN WILSON BOOKS
Alpine Garden Society — I: AGS PUBLICATIONS LTD
Al-Saadawi Publications (US) — D: ALIF INTERNATIONAL
ALSTON BOOKS
Altan Publishing (US) — D: EVENLODE BOOK DIST
Al-Tawhid Institute — D: ALIF INTERNATIONAL
ALTERNATIVE BOOKS — W
Alternative Press — I: BRAINWAVE
Alton Douglas Books — I: BREWIN BOOK DIST
Altos Designs — D: CORDEE
Alun Books — D: WELSH BOOKS COUNCIL
Alyson Publications Inc (US) — D: GMP PUBLISHERS LTD
AMACOM (American Management Assn) (US) — D: MERCURY BOOKS
Amacom (US) — D: BIBLIOS PUB DIST
Amaising Publishing House — D: VINE HOUSE DIST
AMAISING PUBLISHING HOUSE
AMALGAMATED BOOK SERVICES
AMALGAMATED PAPERBACKS UK — W
Amana Books (US) — D: ALIF INTERNATIONAL
AMATE PRESS, THE
Amateur Yacht Society — No reply 92/93
Amazing Colossal Press, The — I: A TWIST IN THE TALE
Ambassador Productions — D: EVANGELICAL PR WALES
AMBASSADOR PRODUCTIONS LTD
AMBASSADOR PRODUCTIONS LTD — A
AMBER LANE PRESS LTD
Amberco (Partial) (US) — D: CORDEE
Ambit — D: CENTRAL BOOKS
AMC (US) — D: ROGER LASCELLES
AMCD (PUBLISHERS) LTD
American Alpine Club (US) — D: CORDEE
American Association of Neurosurgeons (US) — D: MCGRAW HILL BOOK CO
American Association of Cereal Chemists (US) — D: FOOD TRADE PRESS LTD
American Association of Petroleum Geologists (US) — D: GEOLOGICAL SOCIETY
American Association of Clinical Chemistry (US) — D: CLARKE ASSOCIATES

American Automobile Association — I: MAXWELL MACMILLAN
American Chamber of Commerce (Partial) — D: ALFRED WALLER LTD
American Chemical Society (US) — D: TURPIN DISTRIBUTION
American College of Physicians (US) — D: BMJ PUBLISHING GROUP
American College of Radiology (US) — D: CLARKE ASSOCIATES
American Early Medieval Studies (US) — D: OXBOW BOOKS
American Enterprise Institute (US) — D: EDS
American Federation of Astrologers (US) — D: L N FOWLER & CO LTD
American Institute of Architects Press (US) — D: BOOKS CONTINENTAL
American Institute of Bakers (US) — D: FOOD TRADE PRESS LTD
American Library Association (US) — D: EDS
American Map Corporation (US) — D: ROGER LASCELLES
American Mathematical Society (US) — D: OXFORD UNI PRESS DIS
American Medical Assoc (Partial List) (US) — D: PHARMACEUTICAL PRESS
American Oil Chemists Society (US) — D: FOOD TRADE PRESS LTD
American Pharmaceutical Assoc (US) — D: PHARMACEUTICAL PRESS
American Physiological Society — D: OXFORD UNI PRESS DIS
American Planning Association (US) — A: UNI PRESSES MARKETNG
American Psychiatric Press (US) — D: PLYMBRIDGE DIST LTD
AMERICAN PSYCHIATRIC PRESS
American Psychological Association (US) — D: EDS
American Public Health Association (US) — D: CHAPMAN & HALL
American Society of Civil Engineers (US) — D: CLARKE ASSOCIATES
American Survey of Mechanical Engineers (US) — D: MECHANICAL ENG PUB
American Technical Publishers (US) — D: GAZELLE BOOK SERVICE
AMERICAN TECHNICAL PUBLISHERS
American University Press (US) — D: EDS
American Welding Society (USA) — D: WOODHEAD PUBLISHING
Amethyst Books (US) — D: ASHGROVE PRESS
Amethyst (US) — D: TURNAROUND
AMG — A: JOHN RITCHIE LTD
AMG Publishers (US) — D: B MCCALL BARBOUR
Amgueddfa Genedlaethol Cymru — D: WELSH BOOKS COUNCIL
Amherst Media (US) — D: TURNAROUND
Amnesty International — D: CENTRAL BOOKS
AMNESTY PUBLICATIONS
Amok Books (US) — D: AK DISTRIBUTION
Amok (Partial) (US) — D: TEMPLE PRESS LTD
Amok (US) — D: TURNAROUND
AMP — D: SEND THE LIGHT
AMPERSAND PRESS LTD
Amphoto (US) — A: PHAIDON PRESS LTD
AMRA IMPRINT
AMS Press (Originals, not reprints) (US) — D: EDS
AMSCO Publications — I: OMNIBUS PRESS
An Comlacht Oideachais — I: EDUC CO OF IRELAND
AN PUBLICATIONS
An Taisce — NATIONAL TRUST FOR IRELAND
Anabas (GE) — D: TURNAROUND
Anatomical Chart Co (US) — D: GAZELLE BOOK SERVICE
Anatomical Charts (US) — D: QUEST MERIDIEN LTD
Anaya Publishers — D: FABER BOOK SERVICES
ANAYA PUBLISHERS
Anchor Press (Partial) (US) — D: ASHGROVE PRESS
Anchorage Press Inc (US) — D: CRESSRELLES PUB LTD
Ancient City Press (Partial) (US) — D: CORDEE
And All That (CA) — D: ACCENT EDUCATIONAL
Andersen Press — A: RANDOM HOUSE UK LTD
Andersen Press — D: TIPTREE BOOK SERV
ANDREW PUBLISHING, PETER
ANDREWS PHOTOGRAPHIC ART, CHRIS
Angel Books — D: AIRLIFT BOOK CO
Angel Press — I: GOODAY STUDIOS LTD
Angell Editions — A: WORLD LEISURE MKTG
Angell Editions — D: PLYMBRIDGE DIST LTD
Anglia Young Books (AYB) — D: MINIMAX BOOKS LTD
Anglican Book Centre (CA) — D: HYMNS ANCIENT & MOD
Angling Publications — D: VINE HOUSE DIST
Anglo Catalan Society — D: DOLPHIN BOOK CO LTD
ANGLO ISRAEL ASSOCIATION
Anglo Soviet Music Press Ltd — I: BOOSEY & HAWKES LTD
Anglo-Catalan Society — D: SHEFFIELD ACD PRESS
Anglo-German Foundation — D: POLICY STUDIES INST
ANGLO-GERMAN FOUNDATION
Angus & Robertson — I: HARPERCOLLINS TRADE
Angus and Robertson Publishers (Partial) (AU) — D: GAZELLE BOOK SERVICE
Anna Livia (IR) — D: TURNAROUND
ANNESS PUBLISHING
Annick Press Ltd (Partial) (CA) — D: RAGGED BEARS LTD
Annick Press Ltd (Pb only) (CA) — D: ROY YATES BOOKS
Annihilation Press — I: CREATION PRESS
Annual Concepts — D: BOOKPOINT LIMITED

ANNUAL CONCEPTS
Annual Concepts Ltd — A: JOHN WILSON BOOKS
Annwn — D: WELSH BOOKS COUNCIL
Anodyne Publishing Services — D: L N FOWLER & CO LTD
Ansay Pty Ltd (AU) — D: GAZELLE BOOK SERVICE
ANSI (US) — A: AMERICAN TECH PUB
Antef Institute, The — I: KARNAK HOUSE
Anthroposophic Press (US) — D: RUDOLF STEINER PRESS
Anti Slavery Society — D: TURNAROUND
ANTIQUE COLLECTORS CLUB
Antique Publications (US) — D: LISTER ART BOOKS
Antler — D: MARLBOROUGH BOOKS
ANVIL BOOKS LTD
Anvil (Dublin) (IR) — D: TURNAROUND
Anvil Press Poetry — D: PASSWORD (BOOKS) LTD
ANVIL PRESS POETRY
Anvil Press (ZB) — D: LEISHMAN & TAUSSIG
ANWB (NT) — D: IMRAY LAURIE & NORIE
Anzea Publishers (AU) — D: SCRIPTURE UNION PUB
AP Information Services — A: MERCURY BOOKS
AP INFORMATION SERVICES
Aperture (US) — D: ROBERT HALE LTD
APEX BOOKS CONCERN
Apex Press — I: ZED BOOKS LTD
Apex Press (US) — D: ZED BOOKS LTD
Apollo Books (Partial) (US) — D: HILMARTON MANOR
Apollo Press — D: NOVELLO & CO LTD
Apollo Press — D: BIBLIOS PUB DIST
APOLLO PRESS
Apollos — I: INTERVARSITY PRESS
Aporia Press — I: COUNTER PRODUCTIONS
Aporia Press — D: AK DISTRIBUTION
Appalachian Mountain Club (US) — D: CORDEE
Appalachian Trail Conference (US) — D: CORDEE
Apparitions Press — I: STRIDE PUBLICATIONS
Applause (US) — D: COMBINED BOOK SERV
Apple Press — D: D SERVICES
APPLE PRESS, THE
APPLEFORD PUBLISHING GROUP
Appleton & Lange — I: SIMON & SCHUSTER INT
APPLETREE PRESS LTD
APPLIED MARKET INFORMATION
Appraisal Institute (Partial) (US) — D: RICS BOOKS
APRA Press — D: HEART OF ALBION
Apria (FR) — D: FOOD TRADE PRESS LTD
Aquarian Press — I: HARPERCOLLINS THORS
Aquila Books — D: VINE HOUSE DIST
ARBOR PUBLISHERS, ANN
Arbor Science, Ann — I: BUTTERWORTH-HEINEMAN
Arbor Science, Ann — D: REED BOOK SERVICES
Arc Publications — I: LITTLEWOOD ARC
Arcade (Free Market & Europe) — I: LITTLE BROWN & CO
Arcadia (IT) — D: ART DATA
Arcadia (Partial) (IT) — D: S HENEAGE DIST
Arcaedizioni (IT) — D: S HENEAGE DIST
Arcania Press (US) — D: ASHGROVE PRESS
Archer, J P T — D: DEEP BOOKS LTD
Archifdy Gwynedd — D: WELSH BOOKS COUNCIL
Archipelago Press (SI) — D: MILLBANK BOOKS LTD
Architects for Peace — D: CENTRAL BOOKS
ARCHITECTURAL ASSOCIATION PUBLICATIONS
Architectural Book Pub Co Inc (US) — D: GAZELLE BOOK SERVICE
Architectural Design — I: ACADEMY GROUP LTD
Architectural Monographs — I: ACADEMY GROUP LTD
Architecture Design and Technology Press — I: PHAIDON PRESS LTD
Architecture Technology Corporation (US) — D: ELSEVIER SCIENCE PUB
ARCHIVAL FACSIMILES
Archive Editions — I: ARCHIVE RESEARCH LTD
ARCHIVE RESEARCH LTD
Archives Press (US) — D: AIRLIFT BOOK CO
Archivos (SP) — D: DOLPHIN BOOK CO LTD
Archon (US) — D: CLIO PRESS LTD
Arco — I: SIMON & SCHUSTER INT
ARCTURUS PRESS
Ardis (Stockists) (US) — A: THORNTON'S OF OXFORD
Are Press — D: DEEP BOOKS LTD
ARE Press (US) — D: ELEMENT BOOKS LTD
Argentina, Barry (AT) — D: BOOSEY & HAWKES LTD
Argus Books — I: ARGUS PUBLICATIONS
Argus Books — A: CHRIS LLOYD SALES
ARGUS PUBLICATIONS
Argyll Publishing — D: CLAN BOOKS

ARIAN PUBLICATIONS
Aris & Phillips Ltd — D: LA HAULE BOOKS LTD
ARIS & PHILLIPS LTD
Arista Editions (FR) — D: L N FOWLER & CO LTD
Ark Paperbacks — I: ROUTLEDGE
Arkana/Penguin — D: WISDOM BOOKS
ARKLETON TRUST
Arlington Books — D: BIBLIOS PUB DIST
Armada — I: HARPERCOLLINS CHILD
Arms & Armour Press — I: CASSELL PLC
Armstrong, Alan — DAWSON UK
Army Museum Ogilby Trust — D: PICTON PUBLISHING
Arnold — I: NOVELLO & CO LTD
Arnold, Edward — I: HODDER & STOUGHTON
Arnolfini Gallery — D: ART DATA
Aronson Publishers, Jason (US) — D: EDS
Aronson Publishers, Jason (US) (Jewish Interest) — D: KUPERARD LTD
Arpel (US) — D: AIRLIFT BOOK CO
ARRL (US) — D: RADIO SOCIETY OF GB
Arrow Books — I: RANDOM HOUSE (ARROW)
Arrow Books — D: TIPTREE BOOK SERV
Arsenal Pulp Press Ltd (CA) — D: GAZELLE BOOK SERVICE
Arsenale (IT) — D: S HENEAGE DIST
Art & Design — I: ACADEMY GROUP LTD
ART BOOK DISTRIBUTION COMPANY
Art Books International — I: S HENEAGE DIST
ART DATA
Art Gallery of New South Wales (AU) — D: ART DATA
Art Guides — I: A & C BLACK LTD
Art Institute of Chicago (US) — D: ART DATA
Art Media (Partial) (US) — D: HAN SHAN TANG LTD
Art Metropole (US) — D: ART DATA
Art Random (JP) — D: ART DATA
ART SALES INDEX
ART TRADE PRESS
ARTECH HOUSE
Artemis London Ltd — D: BOOKPOINT LIMITED
Artemis Press — I: VISION PRESS LTD
Artemis Press — D: VINE HOUSE DIST
Artery Publications — D: CORDEE
Artificio (IT) — D: S HENEAGE DIST
Artisan Sales (Partial) (US) — D: COVENANT PUB CO LTD
Artists Bookworks — D: ART DATA
Artlines — No reply 92/93
Artmusique Publishing — Ceased trading 92
Arts Council — D: AN PUBLICATIONS
Arts Media Group — D: CENTRAL BOOKS
Artspace (US) — D: SERPENT'S TAIL
Artulen (FR) — D: BIBLIOS PUB DIST
Artways (AU) — D: SPRINGFIELD BOOKS
Artwork Publishing — POMEGRANATE EUROPE
ASA SWIMMING ENTERPRISES LTD
Ash Tree Publishing (US) — D: EVENLODE BOOK DIST
Ashanti Publishing (SA) — D: LAKESIDE PUBNS
Ashbourne Editions — D: MOORLAND PUB CO LTD
Ashbourne Editions — A: WORLD LEISURE MKTG
Ashfield Press (US) — D: EDS
Ashford — I: ASHFORD BUCHAN
ASHFORD BUCHAN & ENRIGHT
Ashford Press (Partial) — A: P M LLEWELLYN CO
Ashford Press Publishing — I: ASHFORD BUCHAN
ASHGATE PUBLISHING GROUP
ASHGROVE DISTRIBUTION
Ashgrove Press Ltd — D: ASHGROVE PRESS
Ashley Books Inc (US) — D: GAZELLE BOOK SERVICE
Ashley Courtenay — D: D SERVICES
Ashmolean Museum — D: GAZELLE BOOK SERVICE
Ashmolean Museum — D: OXFORD UNI PRESS DIS
ASHMOLEAN MUSEUM PUBLICATIONS
Ashton Scholastic (AU) — D: SCHOLASTIC PUB LTD
Ashton Scholastic (NZ) — D: SCHOLASTIC PUB LTD
Asia Labour Monitor (HK) — D: CENTRAL BOOKS
Asia Publishing House — I: BOOKS FROM INDIA
Asian Education Press — I: BOOKS FROM INDIA
Asian Humanities Press (US) — D: ELEMENT BOOKS LTD
Aslan Publishing (US) — D: EVENLODE BOOK DIST
ASLIB — A: MERCURY BOOKS
ASLIB
ASM International (US) — A: AMERICAN TECH PUB
ASOR (US) — D: SHEFFIELD ACD PRESS
ASR Books — Ceased trading 92
ASR RESOURCES

Assemblies of God — D: SEND THE LIGHT
Assn Assistant Librarians — No reply 93
Assn Clinical Research — No reply 93
Associated University Presses — I: GOLDEN COCKEREL
Association for a Peoples Carnival — D: NEW BEACON BOOKS LTD
Association for Bahai Studies (CA) — D: BAHAI PUBLISHING
Association for Computing Machinery (US) — D: CLARKE ASSOCIATES
ASSOCIATION FOR THE EXPORT OF CANADIAN BOOKS (CA) — W
Association of American University Presses (US) — A: UNI PRESSES MARKETNG
Association of Christian Teachers of Wales — D: EVANGELICAL PR WALES
Association of Commonwealth Universities — D: SHEED & WARD LTD
ASSOCIATION OF COMMONWEALTH UNIVERSITIES
ASSOCIATION OF CRICKET STATISTICIANS
Association of Germany Engineers (VDI) (GE) (Eng Lang Only) — D: WOODHEAD PUBLISHING
ASSOCIATION OF METROPOLITAN AUTHORITIES
Astic Research Associates — I: GWASG GWENFFRWD
ASTM (US) — A: AMERICAN TECH PUB
Aston Publications — D: SPRINGFIELD BOOKS
Astrolabe (FR) — D: ROGER LASCELLES
ATC Foulks Lynch — I: ATC PUBLICATIONS LTD
ATC PUBLICATIONS
Atheneum Publishers — I: MAXWELL MACMILLAN
Atheneum Publishers — D: MARSTON BOOKS SERV
Athlone Press Ltd — D: BMS LTD
ATHLONE PRESS LTD
Atlantic — D: IAN ALLAN PUBLISHING
ATLANTIC EUROPE PUBLISHING
Atlantic Large Print Books — I: CHIVERS PRESS LTD
Atlantic Publishing — D: BOOKPOINT LIMITED
ATLAS
Atlas Press — D: AIRLIFT BOOK CO
Atma Press — D: DEEP BOOKS LTD
Atomeka Press — D: COMBINED BOOK SERV
Atomic Weapons Establishment — D: HMSO BOOKS
Attack International — D: AK DISTRIBUTION
ATTIC BOOKS
Attic (Dublin) (IR) — D: TURNAROUND
Attic Press — D: GILL & MACMILLAN LTD
Auburn House (US) — D: EDS
Audel — I: MAXWELL MACMILLAN
Audel — D: MARSTON BOOKS SERV
Audio Literature (US) — D: AIRLIFT BOOK CO
Audio Press (US) — D: AIRLIFT BOOK CO
Audio-Forum — I: SUSSEX PUBLICATIONS
Augsburg Fortress (US) — D: CONCORDIA PUB LTD
Augsburg Publishing House (US) — D: SCM PRESS LTD
AUGUSTINE PUBLISHING CO
AUKANA TRUST
AUM Publications — D: ELEMENT BOOKS LTD
Aunt Lute Books (US) — D: AIRLIFT BOOK CO
Aurora Metro — D: BOOKSPEED
Aurora (Northern Classics) — I: ORKNEY PRESS LTD
Aurora Press (US) — D: AIRLIFT BOOK CO
Aurora Publishing Co (US) — D: GAZELLE BOOK SERVICE
Aurora (SU) — D: CENTRAL BOOKS
Aurum — A: PEGASUS PUB SERV
Aurum Press — D: EXEL LOGISTICS
AURUM PRESS LTD
AUSTICKS PUBLICATIONS
Australian Bureau of Statistics (AU) — D: BOOKS EXPRESS
Australian Centre of Egyptology (AU) — A: ARIS & PHILLIPS LTD
AUSTRALIAN CONSOLIDATED PRESS
Australian Doll Digest (AU) — D: GAZELLE BOOK SERVICE
Australian Women's Weekly Home Library — I: AUSTRALIAN CON PRESS
Author-Publisher Enterprise — I: JOHN DAWES PUB
AUTODATA LTD
Automotive — I: WINDROW & GREENE
Autonomedia (US) — D: AK DISTRIBUTION
Autonomedia/Semiotext — D: COUNTER PRODUCTIONS
Autumn House — I: STANBOROUGH PRESS
Auvidis (FR) — D: EUROPEAN SCHOOLBOOKS
Avant Books (US) — D: GAZELLE BOOK SERVICE
AVANTI BOOKS
Avebury — I: ASHGATE PUB GROUP
Avero Publications (Partial) — D: CHADWYCK-HEALEY LTD
Avery Publishing Co (AU) — D: ROY YATES BOOKS
Avery (West Point Military History Series) (US) — D: SPA BOOKS LTD
Avis, F C — Ceased trading 92
Avon Paperbacks (US) — D: COMBINED BOOK SERV
Avon-Anglia — I: KINGSMEAD PRESS
AWARD PUBLICATIONS
AWARD PUBLICATIONS — R

AYLESFORD PRESS
AZIMUTH EDITIONS
b small publishing — A: VERULAM PUB LTD
Baardwell Press — D: LAVIS MARKETING
Baba Books, Meher — D: ELEMENT BOOKS LTD
BABANI LTD, BERNARD
Back to the Bible Broadcast — D: HUGHES & COLEMAN LTD
Backus Books (US) — D: EVANGELICAL PRESS
BACSA
Bad Blood — I: CREATION PRESS
Bad Taste Books — I: SILVEY-JEX PUB LTD
Badger Books — D: WEST COUNTRY BOOKS
BADGER PUBLISHING
Badger Publishing (Partial) — D: ROUNDHOUSE PUB LTD
Bahai Canada Publications (CA) — D: BAHAI PUBLISHING
Bahai Publications (AU) — D: BAHAI PUBLISHING
BAHAI PUBLISHING
Bahai Publishing Trust (IN) — D: BAHAI PUBLISHING
Bahai Publishing Trust (JP) — D: BAHAI PUBLISHING
Bahai Publishing Trust (ML) — D: BAHAI PUBLISHING
Bahai Publishing Trust (TA) — D: BAHAI PUBLISHING
Bahai Publishing Trust (US) — D: BAHAI PUBLISHING
Bahai Verlag (GE) — D: BAHAI PUBLISHING
Bailey Bros & Swinfen — D: SHELWING LTD
BAILEY DISTRIBUTION LTD
Bailey's African Photo Archive (SA) — D: CENTRAL BOOKS
Bailliere Tindall — I: HARCOURT BRACE JOVAN
BAIRSTOW, MARTIN
Bakenwell & Wye Valley Press — COUNTRY BOOKSTORE
BAKER & TAYLOR INTERNATIONAL (US) — W
Baker Book House (Partial) — D: SEND THE LIGHT
Baker Book House (US) — D: EVANGELICAL PRESS
Baker Books — I: ROY YATES BOOKS
Baker Books — No reply 93
Baker's Plays (US) — D: SAMUEL FRENCH LTD
Balch Institute Press — I: GOLDEN COCKEREL
Balcony Books — D: CENTRAL BOOKS
BALDWIN, M & M
Balearic Islands Publishing (SP) — D: BARNACLE MARINE LTD
Balkema, A A (NT) — A: MOMENTA PUB CO LTD
BALL PRESS, JOHN
Ballantine (US) — D: RANDOM HOUSE (ARROW)
Balloon Books — I: LADYBIRD BOOKS LTD
BALNAIN BOOKS
Baltimore Museum of Art (US) — D: ART DATA
Bamboo Publishing — I: HAN SHAN TANG LTD
Bamboo Publishing — A: ANTIQUE COLLECTORS
Bamboo Publishing (Partial) — D: WELLSWEEP PRESS
BANKERS BOOKS LTD
Banking Technology — I: IBC PUBLISHING LTD
Banmar Inc (US) — D: GAZELLE BOOK SERVICE
Banned Books (US) — D: AIRLIFT BOOK CO
Banner of Truth Trust — D: INTERVARSITY PRESS
BANNER OF TRUTH TRUST
Bantam — I: TRANSWORLD PUB
BANTON PRESS
Baobab Books — D: AFRICAN BOOKS COLL
Baobab Books (ZB) — D: LEISHMAN & TAUSSIG
BARBARA BOOKS LTD — R
Barbican Gallery (Partial) — D: S HENEAGE DIST
Barbour Books (US) — D: NOVA DISTRIBUTION
Barebones Books — I: PICTON PUBLISHING
BARKER & HOWARD LTD
BARMARICK PUBLICATIONS
BARN DANCE PUBLICATIONS
BARN DANCE PUBLICATIONS — A
BARNACLE MARINE LTD
Barnes, P — D: DALENNAU
BARNICOAT LTD, J — W
BARNY BOOKS
Baron Birch — I: QUOTES LTD
Barracuda Books — QUOTES imprint no longer used
Barrie & Jenkins — I: RANDOM HOUSE UK LTD
Barrie & Jenkins — D: TIPTREE BOOK SERV
Barron's Educational Series Inc (US) — D: D SERVICES
Bartholomew — I: HARPERCOLLINS BARTH
Bartholomew Clyde — I: HARPERCOLLINS BARTH
Bartholomew Holiday Maps — I: HARPERCOLLINS BARTH
Barton House — D: ASHGROVE PRESS
BARTON HOUSE PUBLISHING
Barton Publishers — D: B T BATSFORD LTD
BARTON PUBLISHERS

Basic Books — I: HARPERCOLLINS INTER
Basic Books (US) (Jewish Interest) — D: KUPERARD LTD
Bateman, David Ltd (NZ) — D: VERULAM PUB LTD
BATSFORD LTD, B T
BATTLE OF BRITAIN
Bauhaus Archive (GE) — D: ART DATA
BAXTER PHOTOGRAPHY, COLIN
Baxter Photography Ltd, Colin — D: BOOKPOINT LIMITED
Baxter Photography Ltd, Colin (England & Ireland) — A: DEREK SEARLE ASS LTD
BAY FOREIGN LANGUAGE BOOKS
Bay View Books — D: CHRIS LLOYD SALES
BAY VIEW BOOKS LTD
Bayard Press (FR) — D: ROY YATES BOOKS
BAYLISS, ROGER
BBC Books — D: EXEL LOGISTICS
BBC BOOKS
BBC English — D: BEBC DISTRIBUTION
BBC Radio Collection — D: BBC BOOKS
BBC RADIO COLLECTION — A
BBC Radio Sussex — D: COUNTRYSIDE BOOKS
BBC TELEVISION TRAINING
BCC Publications — CCBI PUBLICATIONS
Beacon Press (US) — D: AIRLIFT BOOK CO
BEACONSFIELD PUBLISHERS LTD
BEAN PUBLISHERS, RUTH
Bear & Co (US) — D: AIRLIFT BOOK CO
BEATTIE PUBLISHING, DEREK
Beaufort Press — D: AIRLIFE PUBLISHING
BEBC DISTRIBUTION
Beckett Sterling (NZ) — D: PLYMBRIDGE DIST LTD
Bedford Square Press — I: NCVO PUBLICATIONS
Bedford Square Press — D: PLYMBRIDGE DIST LTD
Bedford Way Series — I: INST OF EDUCATION
BEE BOOKS NEW & OLD
BEECH PUBLISHING
Beechwood Publishing — I: BARN DANCE PUB LTD
Beehive Books — I: VERITAS PUBLICATIONS
Beekay Publishers — D: HUGO'S LANGUAGE BOOK
Beginners Series (Unwin Hyman) — D: NORTHCOTE HOUSE PUB
Behr's Verlag (GE) — D: FOOD TRADE PRESS LTD
Beil, Frederic C Publisher Inc (US) — D: GAZELLE BOOK SERVICE
BELDAM COLLECTION, GEORGE
Beldam Collection, The George — D: VINE HOUSE DIST
Belgrove Publishing — D: VINE HOUSE DIST
Belhaven Press — I: PINTER PUBLISHERS
Belhue Press (US) — D: TURNAROUND
Believers Bookshelf Inc — D: CHAPTER TWO
Belin (FR) — D: EUROPEAN SCHOOLBOOKS
Belitha — A: JOHN WILSON BOOKS
Belitha Press Ltd — D: BAILEY DIST LTD
Belknap — I: HARVARD UNIV PRESS
Bellevue Books — D: GAZELLE BOOK SERVICE
BELLEVUE BOOKS
BELLEW PUBLISHING
Bellew Publishing Ltd — D: PLYMBRIDGE DIST LTD
Bellew Publishing (Partial) — D: ALIF INTERNATIONAL
Belser (GE) — A: PHAIDON PRESS LTD
Belvedere Fine Publishing — D: GAZELLE BOOK SERVICE
BE-MA (IT) — D: S HENEAGE DIST
Benacci (Travel), Thomas — D: KUPERARD LTD
BENARDOUT, RAYMOND
BENEDICT BOOKS
Benedikt Taschen (GE) — D: BOOK BARGAINS LTD
Benedikt Taschen (GE) — D: COMBINED BOOK SERV
Benjamin/Cummings Pub Co Inc — I: ADDISON-WESLEY PUB
Benjamins, John BV (NT) — D: BEBC DISTRIBUTION
BENN BUSINESS INFORMATION SERVICES
Benn, Ernest — I: A & C BLACK LTD
Benn Technical Books — I: TOLLEY PUBLISHING CO
BENNET BOOKS, DAVID
Bennett Books (US) — D: ELEMENT BOOKS LTD
BENNETT TRAINING SYSTEMS, JIM
Benteli Verlag (SZ) — D: ART DATA
BEREAN PUBLISHING TRUST
BERG PUBLISHERS LTD
Bergin & Garvey (US) — D: EDS
Bergli Books AG (SZ) — D: GAZELLE BOOK SERVICE
Berko (Partial) (BG) — D: S HENEAGE DIST
Berkshire House Publishers (US) — D: GAZELLE BOOK SERVICE
Berkswell — D: MARLBOROUGH BOOKS
Berlitz — D: CHARLES LETTS & CO
BERLITZ PUBLISHING

BERLITZ PUBLISHING — A
Berllan Books — D: DALENNAU
Bernan Press (US) — D: GAZELLE BOOK SERVICE
Bernard Galerie, Claude (FR) — D: ART DATA
Berndtson & Berndtson (GE) (Maps) — D: KUPERARD LTD
Berol Limited — D: BOOKPOINT LIMITED
BERTIE RAMIFICATIONS
BERTRAM BOOKS LTD — W
BERTRAM ROTA LTD
Berwick Publishers (IR) — D: COLIN SMYTHE LTD
Beshara Publications — D: ELEMENT BOOKS LTD
BESHARA PUBLICATIONS
Best Guides (Eden Cross) (NT) — D: GMP PUBLISHERS LTD
Bestseller — STUDIO EDITIONS
Bethany House (US) — D: NOVA DISTRIBUTION
Be'that Foundation (IA) — D: ALIF INTERNATIONAL
BETTER BOOKS
Betterway Publications Inc (US) — D: GAZELLE BOOK SERVICE
Beyond The Pale Publications — D: CENTRAL BOOKS
Beyond Words — D: DEEP BOOKS LTD
BFI PUBLISHING
BFP Books — D: B T BATSFORD LTD
BFP BOOKS
Bibal Press (US) — D: SHEFFIELD ACD PRESS
Bibby Books, John — I: QED
Bible Distributors — I: CHAPTER TWO
Bible Reading Fellowship — D: LION PUBLISHING PLC
BIBLE READING FELLOWSHIP
Bible Societies BFBS — I: BIBLE SOCIETY
BIBLE SOCIETY
BIBLE SOCIETY — A
Bible Temple — D: NEW WINE MINISTRIES
Bible Truth Publishers — D: CHAPTER TWO
BIBLIAGORA
Bibliographical Society of London — D: OXFORD UNI PRESS DIS
Bibliographisches Institut (Duden) (GE) — D: EUROPEAN SCHOOLBOOKS
Bibliopolis (Eng Lang) (IT) — D: LAVIS MARKETING
BIBLIOS PUBLISHERS DISTRIBUTION
Bibliotheque des Arts (Partial) (SZ) — D: HILMARTON MANOR
Biblotheque des Arts (Partial) (FR) — D: HILMARTON MANOR
Bicycle Books Inc (US) — D: CHRIS LLOYD SALES
Biddulph, Joseph — I: LANGUAGE INFO CENTRE
Big Time — I: GOLDEN COCKEREL
Bildibok (SW) — D: CENTRAL BOOKS
Billboard Books — I: OMNIBUS PRESS
Billboard (Partial) (US) — D: GUINNESS PUBLISHING
BIMH (British Inst of Mental Handicapped) — D: MULTILINGUAL MATTERS
Bingley, Clive — I: LIBRARY ASSN PUB LTD
Biochemical Society — I: PORTLAND PRESS LTD
BIOS (Non-Trade Only) — D: PORTLAND PRESS LTD
BIOS Scientific Publishers (Labfax Series) — D: BLACKWELL SCIENTIFIC
Birchard Summy (US) — D: INT MUSIC PUB
Birds Farm Books — D: ASHFORD BUCHAN
Birkhauser Verlag (SZ) — A: MOMENTA PUB CO LTD
Birmingham & Midland Institute — D: BREWIN BOOK DIST
Birmingham Library Services — D: BREWIN BOOK DIST
BIRMINGHAM SETTLEMENT
Birmingham University Semetics Study Aids — D: SHEFFIELD ACD PRESS
Biro, Adam (Partial) (FR) — D: S HENEAGE DIST
Birth of the Theotokos Monastery (GR) — D: ELEMENT BOOKS LTD
BISHOPGATE PRESS LTD
Black, A & C (Ireland only) — A: BLACKSTAFF PRESS LTD
Black & Red — D: COUNTER PRODUCTIONS
Black and Red (US) — D: AK DISTRIBUTION
Black Butterfly (US) — D: AIRLIFT BOOK CO
Black Cat Press (2 Titles Only) (IR) — D: CALDER PUB LTD
Black Dagger Crime Reprints — I: CHIVERS PRESS LTD
BLACK FROG PRESS
BLACK LTD, A & C
Black Moss (CA) — D: TURNAROUND
Black Pudding Press — D: CENTRAL BOOKS
Black Rose (CA) — D: AK DISTRIBUTION
Black Rose Press (CA) — D: CENTRAL BOOKS
Black Sheep Press (SZ) — D: CENTRAL BOOKS
Black Sparrow Press (US) — D: AIRLIFT BOOK CO
Black Spring Press — D: AIRLIFT BOOK CO
BLACK SPRING PRESS
Black Sun Pub — No reply 93
Black Swan — I: TRANSWORLD PUB
BLACK SWAN PRESS, THE
Black Woman Talk — D: AIRLIFT BOOK CO
Blackberry Books — D: CENTRAL BOOKS

Blackheath Court Press — I: EXECUTIVE GRAPEVINE
Blackie (Academic & Professional) — I: CHAPMAN & HALL
BLACKIE (ACADEMIC & PROF)
Blackie (Childrens Books) — I: PENGUIN BOOKS LTD
Blackie Educational — I: THOMAS NELSON & SONS
Blackstaff Press — D: BIBLIOS PUB DIST
Blackstaff Press — A: MAINSTREAM PUB CO
BLACKSTAFF PRESS LTD
Blackstone Press — A: ROGER BAYLISS
BLACKSTONE PRESS LTD
BLACKWATER PRESS
Blackwater Press (IR) — D: TURNAROUND
Blackwell Business — I: BLACKWELL PUB LTD
Blackwell Education — I: SIMON & SCHUSTER INT
Blackwell Publishers — D: MARSTON BOOKS SERV
BLACKWELL PUBLISHERS
Blackwell Scientific Publications Ltd — D: MARSTON BOOKS SERV
BLACKWELL SCIENTIFIC PUBLICATIONS
Blair Press — I: SIMON & SCHUSTER INT
Blake Publishing Ltd — D: BOOKPOINT LIMITED
BLAKE PUBLISHING LTD
Blake Publishing (US) — D: GAZELLE BOOK SERVICE
BLAKETON HALL LTD
Blandford Press — I: CASSELL PLC
Blast Books (US) — D: TURNAROUND
BLAY (FR) — D: ROGER LASCELLES
BLENHEIM ONLINE
BLEWBURY PRESS
Blob — D: AK DISTRIBUTION
Bloc Marine (FR) — D: IMRAY LAURIE & NORIE
BLOODAXE BOOKS
BLOOM LTD, ROY — R
Bloomsbury Publishing — D: EXEL LOGISTICS
BLOOMSBURY PUBLISHING LTD
Blubber Head Press (AU) — D: PETER MOORE BOOKS
Blue & Gold Maps — A: WORLD LEISURE MKTG
Blue Dolphin (US) — D: ELEMENT BOOKS LTD
Blueprint — I: CHAPMAN & HALL
Blueprint — I: INT THOMSON PUB SERV
Blueprint Extra's (Overseas Orders Only) — D: ARCHITECTURAL ASSN
Blueprint Monographs — I: FOURTH ESTATE
Bluffer's Guides — I: RAVETTE BOOKS LTD
Bluston, H S — I: ENERGY CONSULTANCY
BMJ PUBLISHING GROUP
BMS LTD
BNA INTERNATIONAL PLC
Board of the Faculty of Oriental Studies, Univ of Oxford — D: OXFORD UNI PRESS DIS
Boatswain Press Ltd — I: KENNETH MASON PUB
Bobcat Books — I: OMNIBUS PRESS
BODLEAIN LIBRARY
Bodley Head Children's Books, The — I: RANDOM HOUSE UK LTD
Bodley Head Children's Books, The — D: TIPTREE BOOK SERV
Bodley Head, The — I: RANDOM HOUSE UK LTD
Bodley Head, The — D: TIPTREE BOOK SERV
BODMIN BOOKS
Boing Boing — D: COUNTER PRODUCTIONS
Bold Strummer, The (Partial List) (US) — D: KAHN & AVERILL
Bonacci (IT) — D: EUROPEAN SCHOOLBOOKS
BOND STREET MUSIC — A
Bondhus, S (US) — D: LISTER ART BOOKS
Bonechi - Edizioni Il Turismo (IT) — D: EUROPEAN SCHOOLBOOKS
Bonfini — I: CLEMATIS PRESS
Bonnie Gaunt (US) — D: COVENANT PUB CO LTD
Bonus Books Inc (US) — D: GAZELLE BOOK SERVICE
BOOK BARGAINS LTD
BOOK BARGAINS LTD — R
BOOK CASTLE LTD
Book Connections — I: GRANTA EDITIONS
Book Distribution Center (US) — D: ALIF INTERNATIONAL
BOOK GUILD LTD
Book Guild Ltd, The — D: BAILEY DIST LTD
Book House Training Centre — D: SPA BOOKS LTD
Book Law — A: IAN ALLAN PUBLISHING
BOOK MARKETING ASSOCIATES INTERNATIONAL
Book of Words Series — I: CARCANET PRESS
Book Production Consultants — I: GRANTA EDITIONS
Book Publishing Co (US) — D: AIRLIFT BOOK CO
BOOK REPRESENTATION & DISTRIBUTION LTD
Book Systems Plus Ltd — A: ACADEMIC BOOK ASSOC
BOOKMARK INTERNATIONAL — R
.Bookmarks — A: TURNAROUND
BOOKMARKS

Bookmarks Publishing Co-op — I: BOOKMARKS
BOOKMART LIMITED — R
BOOKPOINT LIMITED
Books Americana Inc (US) — D: GAZELLE BOOK SERVICE
BOOKS & TOYS LTD — R
BOOKS CONTINENTAL
BOOKS EXPRESS
BOOKS FROM INDIA
BOOKSCENE LTD — W
BOOKSELLERS ASSOCIATION
BOOKSPEED
BOOKSPEED — W
BOOKWORLD WHOLESALE — W
BOOSEY & HAWKES LTD
Booth Clibborn Editions — I: INTERNOS BOOKS
Bordas (Children's Only) (FR) — D: ROY YATES BOOKS
Bordas et fils, Pierre (Partial) (FR) — D: ACCENT EDUCATIONAL
Bordas (FR) — D: EUROPEAN SCHOOLBOOKS
Borgo Press (Selected Titles) (US) — D: PAUPERS' PRESS
Borradaile Press — D: FOUNTAIN PRESS LTD
BORTHWICK INSTITUTE PUBLIUCATIONS
BOSSINEY BOOKS
Bostid (US) — D: INTERMEDIATE TEC PUB
Bote & Bock — D: NOVELLO & CO LTD
Boulevard Books — I: IMPACT BOOKS
Bounty Books — D: REED BOOK SERVICES
Bowker, R R — I: BOWKER-SAUR LTD
Bowker, R R (Partial List) (US) — D: BUTTERWORTH & CO LTD
Bowker-Saur — D: BUTTERWORTH & CO LTD
BOWKER-SAUR LTD
Boxtree Ltd — D: LITTLEHAMPTON BK SVC
BOXTREE LTD
BOYARS PUBLISHERS, MARION
Boyd & Fraser (US) — D: INT THOMSON PUB SERV
BOYDELL & BREWER
Boydell Press — I: BOYDELL & BREWER LTD
BPL REMAINDERS — R
BPP PUBLISHING LTD
BPS Books — I: BRITISH PSYCH SOC
Bra Books — D: CENTRAL BOOKS
BRACEWELL-MILNES, DR
Brachot Galerie, Isy (FR) — D: ART DATA
Bracken Books — I: STUDIO EDITIONS LTD
Bradford Books — I: MIT PRESS LTD
BRADFORD LIBRARIES
Bradshaw Society, Henry — D: BOYDELL & BREWER LTD
Bradt Publications — D: SPRINGFIELD BOOKS
BRADT PUBLICATIONS
Brady Publishing — I: SIMON & SCHUSTER INT
BRAINIAC BOOKS LTD
BRAINWAVE
Brampton Publications — A: SB PUBLICATIONS
Branden Publishing Co (US) — D: GAZELLE BOOK SERVICE
Brandon Book Publishers — D: GILL & MACMILLAN LTD
Brandon (IR) — D: TURNAROUND
Braniac Books — D: TURNAROUND
Brash Pte Ltd, Graham (SI) — D: GAZELLE BOOK SERVICE
BRASS WIND PUBLICATIONS
Brassey's (UK & US) — I: MAXWELL MACMILLAN
Brassey's (UK) Ltd — D: MARSTON BOOKS SERV
BRASSEY'S (UK) LTD
Brassey's (US) — D: MARSTON BOOKS SERV
Braus (GE) — D: ART DATA
Braziller, George — D: ANTIQUE COLLECTORS
BREALEY PUBLISHING, NICHOLAS
Brearley, Nicholas — D: BOOKPOINT LIMITED
Brearly Publishers, Nicholas — A: JOHN WILSON BOOKS
Breedon — D: D SERVICES
BREEDON BOOKS
Breese Books — I: MARTIN BREESE PUB
BREESE PUBLICATIONS, MARTIN
Breese Publishing, Martin — D: CLIPPER DIST SERVICE
BREFI PRESS
Brefi Press (Partial) — D: WELSH BOOKS COUNCIL
BRENTHAM PRESS
BRESLICH & FOSS
Brewer, D S — I: BOYDELL & BREWER LTD
Brewer Publishing, Michael — D: COMBINED BOOK SERV
Brewers' Society, The — D: HOTEL & CATERING CO
BREWIN BOOK DISTRIBUTION SERVICES
Brewin Books — I: BREWIN BOOK DIST
BRIAN & O'KEEFFE LTD, MARTIN

BRIDGE BOOK COMPANY LTD — R
Bridge House Publications — I: FIRST TIME PUB
Bridge Publishing Inc (US) — A: SHARON PUBLICATIONS
Bridge Street Books — I: LEARNING DEV AIDS
Bridges of Britain Magazines — I: KINGSCLERE PUB LTD
Briggs Associates, Robert (Selected titles) (US) — D: PAUPERS' PRESS
BRIGHT BOOKS
Brilliance Books — D: CENTRAL BOOKS
BRIMAX BOOKS LTD
Bristol Classical Press — I: GERALD DUCKWORTH
Bristol Papers — D: WHITING & BIRCH LTD
Bristol Publishing Enterprises (US) — D: GAZELLE BOOK SERVICE
Britannia Crest International Ltd — D: BOOKPOINT LIMITED
Britannia Press — D: EAST WEST PUB LTD
Britannica Software — I: ENCYC BRITANNICA LTD
British Academic Press — I: I B TAURIS & CO LTD
BRITISH ACADEMY, THE
British Academy, The (Pre-1986) — D: OXBOW BOOKS
British Academy, The (Published since 1986) — D: OXFORD UNI PRESS DIS
British Agencies for Adoption & Fostering — D: B T BATSFORD LTD
British Antartic Survey — D: TURPIN DISTRIBUTION
British Association For American Studies — D: RYBURN DISTRIBUTION
British Association for Local History — D: PHILLIMORE & CO LTD
BRITISH ASSOCIATION FOR COMMERCIAL & INDUSTRIAL EDUCATION
British Association of Libertarian Feminists — D: LIBERTARIAN ALLIANCE
British Association of Nature Conservationist — D: PACKARD PUB LTD
British Association of Social Workers — I: VENTURE PRESS
British Association Ski Instructors — D: CORDEE
BRITISH ATLETICS FEDERATION
British Bankers' Association — D: PROBUS EUROPE
British Canoe Union — D: CORDEE
BRITISH CERAMIC RESEARCH
BRITISH COUNCIL, THE
British Dental Journal — D: BMJ PUBLISHING GROUP
BRITISH ENTOMOLOGICAL & NATURAL HISTORY SOCIETY
British Film Institute — D: PLYMBRIDGE DIST LTD
British Food Manufacturing Industries Research Association — D: FOOD TRADE PRESS LTD
BRITISH HORSE SOCIETY
British Hospitality Association — A: WORLD LEISURE MKTG
British Inst of Management — INST OF MANAGEMENT FOUNDATION
British Institute in East Africa, The — D: OXBOW BOOKS
British Institute of Radiology — D: VINE HOUSE DIST
BRITISH LIBRARY DOCUMENT SUPPLY CENTRE
BRITISH LIBRARY MARKETING & PUBLISHING
BRITISH LIBRARY NATIONAL BIBLIOGRAPHIC SERVICE
BRITISH LIBRARY NATIONAL SOUND ARCHIVE — A
British Medical Association — I: BMJ PUBLISHING GROUP
British Medical Journal Publications — A: MOMENTA PUB CO LTD
British Mountaineering Council — D: CORDEE
British Museum (Jewish Interest) — D: KUPERARD LTD
BRITISH MUSEUM PRESS
British Museum Publications Ltd — D: THAMES & HUDSON LTD
British North American Committee — I: BRITISH NTH AMER RES
BRITISH NORTH AMERICAN RESEARCH ASSOCIATION
British Nuclear Energy Society — D: THOMAS TELFORD LTD
British Orienteering Federation — A: HARVEY MAP SERVICES
British Psychological Society — D: ROUTLEDGE
British Psychological Society — A: BOOK REP & DIST LTD
BRITISH PSYCHOLOGICAL SOCIETY
Briubasi (IN) — D: HAN SHAN TANG LTD
BROAD OAK PRESS
Broadcast Books — I: ELEMENT BOOKS LTD
Broadman (US) — D: NOVA DISTRIBUTION
BROADSIDE
Broadside Books — WORLD SERVICE PUBLICATIONS
Brockhaus (GE) — D: EUROPEAN SCHOOLBOOKS
Brodies Notes — I: MACMILLAN DIST LTD
Bronant — I: GWASG GWENFFRWD
Brookes, Paul H (US) — A: JESSICA KINGSLEY PUB
Brookes, Paul H (US) — D: KOGAN PAGE LTD
Brookings Institution Press, The (US) — D: INT BOOK DIST
Brookings Institution Press, The (US) — A: UNI PRESSES MARKETNG
Brooklyn Museum of Art (US) — D: ART DATA
BROOKS BOOKS
Brooks Cole (US) — D: INT THOMSON PUB SERV
Brookside Press — I: VILLIERS PUB LTD
Brotherhood of Life (US) — D: C W DANIEL CO LTD
BROWN ASSOCIATES, TREVOR
BROWN, DAVID
Brown Packaging — A: VERULAM PUB LTD
Brown Publishing, John — D: BOOKPOINT LIMITED
BROWN PUBLISHING, W C

BROWN SON & FERGUSON
Brown, Trevor — D: INT BOOK DIST
Brown, W C (US) — D: INT BOOK DIST
BROWN WATSON LTD
Brownstone Books (Selected Titles) (US) — D: PAUPERS' PRESS
Brundish Books — D: JARROLD PUBLISHING
Bruno Gmunder Verlag (GE) — D: GMP PUBLISHERS LTD
Bruschettini Foundation (US) — D: OXFORD UNI PRESS DIS
Bruton, Eric — D: TIPTREE BOOK SERV
BRYNMILL PRESS, THE
BSP Books — D: PLYMBRIDGE DIST LTD
Buchan & Enright — I: ASHFORD BUCHAN
Buchu Books (SA) — D: LEISHMAN & TAUSSIG
BUCKLEBURY PRESS, THE
Bucknell U P — I: GOLDEN COCKEREL
Buddhist Publication Group — D: WISDOM BOOKS
Buddhist Publication Society (SL) — D: WISDOM BOOKS
BUDDHIST PUBLISHING GROUP
Buddhist Society — D: WISDOM BOOKS
BUILDING BLOCKS EDUCATIONAL
BUILDING SOCIETIES ASSOCIATION
Bulfinch — I: LITTLE BROWN & CO
BUNAC — D: ROGER LASCELLES
Bundesamt Fut Landestopographie (Partial) (SZ) — D: CORDEE
BURALL FLORAPRINT
Bureau of Business Practice — I: SIMON & SCHUSTER INT
BURGESS PUBLICATIONS, JOHN
Burke Books — I: W & R CHAMBERS LTD
Burke, Edmund (IR) — D: CENTRAL BOOKS
BURKE'S PEERAGE
Burke's Peerage Press — D: BOOKPOINT LIMITED
Burlington — I: GOLDEN COCKEREL
Burlington Editions — D: BIBLIOS PUB DIST
Burlington Publishing Ltd — D: BMS LTD
BURN, GRAHAM
Burnier/Vamos (FR) — D: CORDEE
Burns & Oates — A: SPCK
Burns & Oates Ltd — I: SEARCH PRESS LIMITED
Burns & Oates/Search — D: VERITAS PUBLICATIONS
BURSTON DISTRIBUTION SERVICES
Bus Enthusiast Publishing Company — D: PLATFORM 5 PUB LTD
Bush Press — D: BAY FOREIGN BOOKS
Business Education — D: HLT PUBLICATIONS
BUSINESS EDUCATION PUBLISHERS
Business Foundation (PL) — A: ASLIB
Business Int — No reply 93
Business One Irwin (US) — D: ADDISON-WESLEY PUB
Butterfly Books (AU) — D: ELEMENT BOOKS LTD
BUTTERWORTH & CO LTD
Butterworth Architecture — I: BUTTERWORTH-HEINEMAN
Butterworth Architecture — D: REED BOOK SERVICES
BUTTERWORTH IRELAND
Butterworth Ireland (IR) — D: BUTTERWORTH & CO LTD
Butterworth Legal — D: BUTTERWORTH & CO LTD
Butterworth Medical — I: BUTTERWORTH-HEINEMAN
Butterworth Medical — D: REED BOOK SERVICES
Butterworth Scientific — I: BUTTERWORTH-HEINEMAN
Butterworth Scientific — D: REED BOOK SERVICES
Butterworth Tax — D: BUTTERWORTH & CO LTD
Butterworth-Heinemann — D: REED BOOK SERVICES
BUTTERWORTH-HEINEMANN
Buzz Books — I: REED CONS MANDARIN
Bygone Kent — I: MERESBOROUGH BOOKS
BYRONIC BOOKS
CAB INTERNATIONAL
Caddy Planner — D: BOOKPOINT LIMITED
Caddy Planner — A: DEREK SEARLE ASS LTD
CADOGAN BOOKS
Cadogan Books Ltd — A: WORLD LEISURE MKTG
Cadogan Guides — I: CADOGAN BOOKS
Cadogan Guides — D: GRANTHAM BOOK SERV
Caduceus Press — I: J A ALLEN LTD
Cadw (Partial) — D: WELSH BOOKS COUNCIL
CADW:WELSH HISTORIC MONUMENTS
Cairn Press, The — A: BOOK MARKETING ASSOC
Cairns Publications, Francis — No reply 92/93
Caissa Books (US) — D: THE CHESS PLAYER
Calabria — D: AK DISTRIBUTION
Calder & Boyers Ltd — I: CALDER PUB LTD
Calder Educational Trust — D: COMBINED BOOK SERV
CALDER PUBLICATIONS LTD
Calder (Publishers), John — I: CALDER PUB LTD

CALEDONIAN BOOKS
California Culinary Academic (The Cole Group) — D: FOUNTAIN PRESS LTD
California State, Long Beach University Press (US) — D: EDS
CALOUSTE GULBENKIAN FOUNDATION
Calvert's Press — D: WORLDLY GOODS
Cambridge Adult Education Co — I: SIMON & SCHUSTER INT
Cambridge Bibles — D: B MCCALL BARBOUR
Cambridge Book Co — D: COMBINED BOOK SERV
Cambridge Book Co — No reply 93
CAMBRIDGE UNIVERSITY PRESS
Camden House Inc (US) — D: BOYDELL & BREWER LTD
CAMDEN PRESS
Camera Austria (AS) — D: CENTRAL BOOKS
Camera Obscura (Partial) (SZ) — D: HILMARTON MANOR
Camerapix International — D: GRANTHAM BOOK SERV
Camerapix International — A: WORLD LEISURE MKTG
Camerapix Publishers International (KY) — D: LEISHMAN & TAUSSIG
Camerawork — D: CENTRAL BOOKS
Campaign Against The Arms Trade — D: CENTRAL BOOKS
Campbell Books — D: TIPTREE BOOK SERV
CAMPBELL BOOKS
CAMPBELL MATTHEWS & CO
Campden Food & Drink Research Association — D: FOOD TRADE PRESS LTD
CAMPUS PUBLISHING
CAMRA (Campaign For Real Ale) — A: VERULAM PUB LTD
Canada Communications Group - Publishing (CA) — D: BOOKS EXPRESS
Canadian Institute of Ukrainian Studies (CA) — D: ORBIS BOOKS LTD
Canadian Museum of Civilization (CA) — A: UNI PRESSES MARKETNG
CANAL PUBLISHING COMPANY
Canary Press — D: HOUSMANS BOOKSHOP
Canary Press — D: AK DISTRIBUTION
Cancioneros Reales (SP) — D: DOLPHIN BOOK CO LTD
Candle — I: TRITON PUB CO LTD
Candle Books Ltd — D: SEND THE LIGHT
Canolfan Adnoddau Aberystwyth (Partial) — D: WELSH BOOKS COUNCIL
Canolfan Genedlaethol Addysg Grefyddol (Partial) — D: WELSH BOOKS COUNCIL
Canongate Classic — I: CANONGATE PRESS PLC
Canongate Ltd — D: BOOKPOINT LIMITED
CANONGATE PRESS PLC
Canterbury & York Society — D: BOYDELL & BREWER LTD
Canterbury Press — A: SPCK
Canterbury Press Norwich — I: HYMNS ANCIENT & MOD
Canto — I: CAMBRIDGE UNIV PRESS
CANTO PUBLICATIONS — A
CAPABILITY PUBLISHING
Cape Children's Books, Jonathan — I: RANDOM HOUSE UK LTD
Cape Children's Books, Jonathan — D: TIPTREE BOOK SERV
Cape, Jonathan — I: RANDOM HOUSE UK LTD
Cape, Jonathan — D: GRANTHAM BOOK SERV
CAPITAL PLANNING INFORMATION
CAPITAL TRANSPORT PUBLISHING
Carcanet Pleiade — I: CARCANET PRESS
CARCANET PRESS
Carcanet Press Ltd — A: CASSELL PLC
Carcanet Press Ltd — D: LITTLEHAMPTON BK SVC
Cardoza (US) — D: OLDCASTLE BOOKS LTD
Care Concern — I: HAWKER PUBLICATIONS
Careers & Occupational Information Centre — D: BIBLIOS PUB DIST
Careerscope — I: HAMILTON HOUSE PUB
Carey Publications — D: EVANGELICAL PRESS
CARGATE PRESS
Carleton University Press — D: OXFORD UNI PRESS DIS
Carleton University Press (CA) — D: DUNDURN DISTRIBUTION
Carlsen (GE) — D: EUROPEAN SCHOOLBOOKS
CARLTON BOOKS
Carn Publishing — D: ALLOWAY PUB LTD
Carnegie Press — D: COUNTYVISE LTD
CARNEGIE PUBLISHING LTD
Carnell (Jewish Interest) — D: KUPERARD LTD
Carnival — I: HARPERCOLLINS CHILD
Carolina Biological Supply Co (Partial) (US) — D: PACKARD PUB LTD
Carolrhoda Books — D: TURNAROUND
Carpenter Publishing, Jon — D: CENTRAL BOOKS
CARPENTER PUBLISHING, JON
CARR, J L
CARR, RD & JM
Carreg Gwalch — D: DALENNAU
CARRICK MEDIA
Carrick Wholesale — BOOKSPEED
Carrs Maps — I: RD & JM CARR
Carswell (CA) — A: HAMMICKS MAIL ORDER
Cartographia (Partial) (HG) — D: CORDEE

Casa Editrice Bonechi (IT) — D: EUROPEAN SCHOOLBOOKS
Casariego (Partial) (SP) — D: DOLPHIN BOOK CO LTD
CASDEC LTD
CASS & CO LTD, FRANK
Cass, Frank — D: BIBLIOS PUB DIST
Cass, Frank (Jewish Interest) — D: KUPERARD LTD
Cassandra Press (US) — D: AIRLIFT BOOK CO
Cassell ELT — I: SIMON & SCHUSTER INT
CASSELL PLC
Cassell Publishing London (Scotland only) — A: MAINSTREAM PUB CO
Cassell Religious Titles (Ireland Only) — D: COLUMBA BOOK SERVICE
Cassells — D: VERITAS PUBLICATIONS
Castalia (SP) — D: EUROPEAN SCHOOLBOOKS
CASTEBERG
Castellanos (US) — D: DOLPHIN BOOK CO LTD
Casterman (Except Tin Tin) (BG) — D: ROY YATES BOOKS
Casterman (FR) — D: EUROPEAN SCHOOLBOOKS
CASTLE BOOKS
Castle Kent Associates — D: GAZELLE BOOK SERVICE
Castle Mountain (US) — D: EVENLODE BOOK DIST
Castlemead — A: THE BOOK CASTLE LTD
Castlemead Publications — I: WARD'S PUB SERVICES
Catbird (US) — D: TURNAROUND
Catedra (SP) — D: EUROPEAN SCHOOLBOOKS
Cathie Ltd, Kyle — A: CASSELL PLC
Cathie Ltd, Kyle — D: LITTLEHAMPTON BK SVC
CATHIE LTD, KYLE
Catholic Institute for International Relations — D: CENTRAL BOOKS
CATHOLIC INSTITUTE FOR INTERNATIONAL RELATIONS
CATHOLIC TRUTH SOCIETY
Catholic University of America Press (US) — D: EDS
CATT EDUCATIONAL LTD, JOHN
Catt Ltd, John — D: HUGO'S LANGUAGE BOOK
Causeway Language Centre (Not N Ireland) — D: ACCENT EDUCATIONAL
CAUSEWAY PRESS LTD
CAVE ASSOCIATES, GODFREY — R
CAVE PUBLICATIONS LTD, PAUL
CAVENDISH PUBLISHING
CBD RESEARCH LTD
CBHT Ed — D: CHAPTER TWO
CBPT — I: CHRISTIAN BOOK PROMO
CBSI — I: CBSI
CCBI PUBLICATIONS
CCH EDITIONS
CDIUPA (FR) — D: FOOD TRADE PRESS LTD
Cectal — D: SHEFFIELD ACD PRESS
Cedar — I: REED CONS MANDARIN
CEDAR TREE HOUSE
Celebration Music (US) — D: CELEBRATION SERV LTD
Celebration Records — I: MCCRIMMON PUBLISHING
CELEBRATION SERVICES LTD
Celestial Arts (US) — D: AIRLIFT BOOK CO
Centaur Books — I: OLD VICARAGE PUB
CENTAUR PRESS LTD
Center for Creative Photography (US) — D: ART DATA
Center for Traditional Acupuncture (US) — D: ELEMENT BOOKS LTD
Center Publications (US) — D: WISDOM BOOKS
CENTRAAL BOEKHUIS BV (NT) — W
Central Africana (MA) — D: LEISHMAN & TAUSSIG
CENTRAL BOOKS
CENTRAL BUREAU FOR EDUCATIONAL VISITS
Central Bureau (Travel) — D: KUPERARD LTD
Central Law Publishing — I: CENTRAL LAW TRAINING
CENTRAL LAW TRAINING
Centre D'Arts Plastiques Contemporains (FR) — D: ART DATA
CENTRE D'EXPORTATION DU LIVRE FRANCAIS (FR) — W
Centre for Applied Research in Education (CARE) — I: SIMON & SCHUSTER INT
CENTRE FOR BUSINESS RESEARCH
Centre for European Policy Studies — I: BRASSEY'S (UK) LTD
Centre for European Policy Studies — D: MARSTON BOOKS SERV
CENTRE FOR INDEPENDENT TRANSPORT RESEARCH IN LONDON
CENTRE FOR INFORMATION ON LANGUAGE TEACHING & RESEARCH
CENTRE FOR JEWISH EDUCATION
Centre for North West Regional Studies — D: CARNEGIE PUB LTD
Centre for Policy on Ageing — D: BAILEY DIST LTD
CENTRE FOR POLICY ON AGEING
Centre for Social Research (MA) — D: AFRICAN BOOKS COLL
Centre for Study Language Information (US) — A: UNI PRESSES MARKETNG
Centre For Travel & Tourism — D: BUSINESS EDUC PUB
CENTRE FOR URBAN & REGIONAL RESEARCH
Centre Georges Pompidou (FR) — D: ART DATA
Centreprise — D: TURNAROUND

CENTRO DE EXPORTACION DE LIBROS ESPANOLES (SP) — W
Centurion Books — A: DEREK SEARLE ASS LTD
Centurion Books Ltd — D: BOOKPOINT LIMITED
Centurion (FR) — D: ROY YATES BOOKS
Century — I: RANDOM HOUSE UK LTD
Century — D: TIPTREE BOOK SERV
Century Business — I: RANDOM HOUSE UK LTD
Century Business — D: TIPTREE BOOK SERV
Cerebus — I: SIMON & SCHUSTER INT
CESARA PUBLICATIONS
Chadwyck Healey (US) — D: BRITISH LIB NAT BIB
CHADWYCK-HEALEY LTD
Chahine, Richard (LB) — D: S HENEAGE DIST
CHALCOMBE PUBLICATIONS
Chalcott Marketing — D: CENTRAL BOOKS
Chalice Guild (SZ) — D: ELEMENT BOOKS LTD
Chalkface — D: HAMILTON HOUSE PUB
CHALKSOFT LTD
Chambers & Partners Publishing — I: ORBACH & CHAMBERS
Chambers & Partners Publishing — D: BIBLIOS PUB DIST
CHAMBERS LTD, W & R
Chambers, Oswald Pub Ltd — D: NOVA DISTRIBUTION
Chameleon Publications — No reply 92/93
Champion Enterprises (CA) — D: PAUL H CROMPTON LTD
Chanakya Publications (IN) — D: BOOKS FROM INDIA
Chancellor Press — I: REED CONS BOUNTY
Chancery Law Publishing — I: JOHN WILEY & SONS
Chand & Co, S (IN) — D: BOOKS FROM INDIA
CHANGE PUBLICATIONS
Channel View Books — I: MULTILINGUAL MATTERS
Chansitor Publications — I: HYMNS ANCIENT & MOD
CHAPMAN
Chapman & Hall — D: INT THOMSON PUB SERV
CHAPMAN & HALL
Chapman, Geoffrey — I: CASSELL PLC
Chapman, Geoffrey (Ireland Only) — D: COLUMBA BOOK SERVICE
Chapman (Partial) (AU) — D: CORDEE
Chapman Publications — I: CHAPMAN
Chapman Publishing, Paul — D: PLYMBRIDGE DIST LTD
CHAPMAN PUBLISHING, PAUL
Chapmans — A: MACMILLAN DIST LTD
CHAPMANS PUBLISHERS LTD
CHAPTER TWO
Chapter Two Christian Media — I: CHAPTER TWO
CHAR — D: TURNAROUND
Charis Communications — No reply 92/93
Charisma Publications — D: BOOKPOINT LIMITED
CHARLES PUBLICATIONS, DEBORAH
Charlesbridge Publishing (US) — D: GAZELLE BOOK SERVICE
Chartac (up to April 1991) — I: ACCOUNTANCY BOOKS
CHARTERED BUILDING SOCIETIES INSTITUTE
Chartered Institute of Bankers — A: ROGER BAYLISS
CHARTERED INSTITUTE OF PURCHASING & SUPPLY
Chartered Insurance Institute Publications — D: GRANTA EDITIONS
CHARTWELL-BRATT
Chatham House Publishers (US) — A: ROUNDHOUSE PUB LTD
Chatham House (US) — D: COMBINED BOOK SERV
Chatsworth Library — I: AIRLIFE PUBLISHING
Chatto & Windus — I: RANDOM HOUSE UK LTD
Chatto & Windus — D: GRANTHAM BOOK SERV
CHEATLE PRESS, ZELDA
CHECKMATE PUBLICATIONS
Cheerman Ltd — D: CENTRAL BOOKS
Chelsea House Publishers (US) — D: LUTTERWORTH PRESS
Chelsea House Publishers (US) — A: ACADEMIC & UNIV PUB
Chemical Publishing (US) — D: FOOD TRADE PRESS LTD
Cherry Lane (US) — D: INT MUSIC PUB
Cherrytree Books — I: CHIVERS PRESS LTD
Chess Digest (US) — D: THE CHESS PLAYER
CHESS PLAYER, THE
Chetham Society — D: CARNEGIE PUB LTD
CHEVERELL PRESS, THE
Chicago University Press (US) — D: INT BOOK DIST
Chicago University Press (US) — A: UNI PRESSES MARKETNG
CHICHESTER, FRANCIS
Child Poverty Action Group — D: CENTRAL BOOKS
Childrens Book Trust (IN) — D: BOOKS FROM INDIA
Childrens Poolbeg — I: POOLBEG PRESS LTD
CHILDREN'S SOCIETY
Children's Universe — I: RIZZOLI INT PUBNS
CHILD'S PLAY
CHILD'S PLAY — A

Child's Play (Ireland Only) — D: ISLAND PUBLICATIONS
Chilton Book Co (US) — D: B T BATSFORD LTD
CHILTON DESIGNS PUBLISHERS
China Books & Periodicals (Partial) (US) — D: MILLBANK BOOKS LTD
Chiriotti (IT) — D: FOOD TRADE PRESS LTD
Chiron Publications — D: ELEMENT BOOKS LTD
CHIVERS PRESS LTD
CHIVERS PRESS LTD — A
Chockstone Press (US) — D: CORDEE
Choice Magazines — D: COMBINED BOOK SERV
Choose Your Own Adventure — I: TRANSWORLD PUB
Chopsticks Publications Ltd (HK) — D: GAZELLE BOOK SERVICE
CHRISTADELPHIAN MAGAZINE & PUBLISHING ASSOCIATION
CHRISTCHURCH PUBLISHERS LTD
CHRISTIAN BOOK PROMOTION TRUST
Christian Bookshop Network — D: WORD PUBLISHING
CHRISTIAN BOOKSTALL MANAGERS ASSOCIATION
Christian Classics Inc (Partial) (US) — D: SHEED & WARD LTD
CHRISTIAN FOCUS PUBLICATIONS
Christian Life Publications — D: MOORLEY'S PRINT PUB
Christian Literature Association (MA) — D: LEISHMAN & TAUSSIG
CHRISTIAN LITERATURE CRUSADE
CHRISTIAN LITERATURE CRUSADE — W
Christian Medical Fellowship — D: INTERVARSITY PRESS
CHRISTIAN MUSIC MINISTRIES
CHRISTIAN SCIENCE PUBLISHING SOCIETY
Christian Socialist Movement — D: CENTRAL BOOKS
Christie's (Partial) — D: S HENEAGE DIST
CHRISTIE'S WINE PUBLICATIONS
Chronicle Books (US) — A: H I MARKETING
Chronicle Books (US) — D: TIPTREE BOOK SERV
Chronicle Communications — I: RANDOM HOUSE UK LTD
Chronicle Communications — D: TIPTREE BOOK SERV
Chronimed Inc (US) — D: GAZELLE BOOK SERVICE
Chronos Publications — D: AK DISTRIBUTION
CHTHONIOS BOOKS
Church Growth/Resources Books (Selected) — D: BIBLE SOCIETY
Church House Publications — D: HYMNS ANCIENT & MOD
CHURCH HOUSE PUBLISHING
CHURCH LITERATURE ASSOCIATION
Church Music Society — D: RSCM
CHURCH PASTORAL AID SOCIETY
CHURCH SOCIETY
Church Times — I: HYMNS ANCIENT & MOD
CHURCHILL LIVINGSTONE
CIB Publications — I: BANKERS BOOKS LTD
CIBA Collection of Medical Illustrations (Netter Atlases) — D: FARRAND PRESS
CIBA-Geigy Pharmaceuticals — D: FARRAND PRESS
Cicerone — A: WORLD LEISURE MKTG
CICERONE PRESS
Ciclo Editorial (SP) — D: EUROPEAN SCHOOLBOOKS
Cienfuegos Press — D: AK DISTRIBUTION
Cilgwyn Publications — I: GREENCROFT BOOKS
CIM Ltd — I: SIMON & SCHUSTER INT
CIMTECH LTD
Cin-Dav Inc (US) — D: GAZELLE BOOK SERVICE
Cinefix (BG) — D: CENTRAL BOOKS
Circle Books — A: VERULAM PUB LTD
CIS Educational (AU) — D: ACCENT EDUCATIONAL
Cistercian Publications — D: THE FRIENDLY PRESS
Citadel Film Library (US) — D: VIRGIN PUBLISHING
Cito Plan (FR) — D: MCCARTA LTD
Cito Town Maps — A: WORLD LEISURE MKTG
City Guides — I: LONELY PLANET PUB
City Lights Books (US) — D: AIRLIFT BOOK CO
CITY MUSEUM & ART GALLERY
City of Bristol Museums & Art Gallery — D: KINGSMEAD PRESS
CITY PRESS LTD
CIVIC TRUST
Civil Liberties Trust — D: CENTRAL BOOKS
CJE — I: CENTRE JEWISH EDUC
Claire Publications — I: JONATHAN PRESS
CLAN BOOKS
CLAN BOOKS — W
Clare Books, John — No reply 92/93
Clarendon Press — I: OXFORD UNIV PRESS
Claridge Press — D: BAILEY DIST LTD
CLARIDGE PRESS
Clarion Books (IN) — D: BOOKS FROM INDIA
Clarity (US) — D: TURNAROUND
CLARK LTD, T & T
Clark, Robin — I: QUARTET BOOKS LTD

Clarke & Co, James — A: H I MARKETING
CLARKE & CO, JAMES
CLARKE ASSOCIATES
Clarke, I.E. (US) — D: CRESSRELLES PUB LTD
CLARKE PUBLISHERS, ANTHONY
Class Publishing — D: PLYMBRIDGE DIST LTD
CLASS PUBLISHING
Class War — D: AK DISTRIBUTION
CLASSEY LTD, E W
Classic Words & Image — I: ELITE WORDS & IMAGE
Classica Entomologica — I: E W CLASSEY LTD
Classical Association — D: OXFORD UNI PRESS DIS
Claymont Communications (US) — D: ELEMENT BOOKS LTD
CLB PUBLISHING
CLE International (FR) — D: EUROPEAN SCHOOLBOOKS
Clear Light Publishers (US) — D: BIBLIOS PUB DIST
Cleis Press (US) — D: AIRLIFT BOOK CO
CLEMATIS PRESS
Clement Books — I: CLEMENT PUBS LTD
CLEMENT PUBLISHERS LTD
Cliff College Publications — I: MOORLEY'S PRINT PUB
Cliffs Notes Inc (US) — D: GAZELLE BOOK SERVICE
Climbers Club, The — D: CORDEE
Clinical Neuroscience Press — A: ROGER BAYLISS
Clinical Press — D: GAZELLE BOOK SERVICE
Clio (Montessori) — D: KUPERARD LTD
CLIO PRESS LTD
CLIO PRESS LTD — A
CLIPPER DISTRIBUTION SERVICES
Clo Chailleann — D: GAIRM PUBLICATIONS
Clo Iar-Chonnachta - Teenage Book List (IR) — D: EDUC CO OF IRELAND
Cloudcap (US) — D: CORDEE
CLOVER PUBLICATIONS
Cloverleaf — I: EVANS BROTHERS LTD
Clowes Publishers Ltd, William — D: HYMNS ANCIENT & MOD
Clubman Books — D: AK DISTRIBUTION
Clyde Marine Press — D: IMRAY LAURIE & NORIE
Clydeside Press — D: AK DISTRIBUTION
CMA Publications — D: BOOSEY & HAWKES LTD
CMC Publishing (US) — D: GAZELLE BOOK SERVICE
CMP Publications — No reply 92/93
Cockbird Press — A: COLLINS & BROWN
Cockbird Press — D: COLLINS & BROWN
Cocky's Circle Children's Books — I: AUSTRALIAN CON PRESS
CODESRIA (SG) — D: AFRICAN BOOKS COLL
Colchester Archaeological Trust — D: OXBOW BOOKS
COLD TONNAGE BOOKS
Cole & Whurr Ltd — I: WHURR PUBLISHERS LTD
COLE, LLOYD
Colebrooke Map Service, Stephen — ELSTEAD MAPS
Colegio de Espana (SP) — D: EUROPEAN SCHOOLBOOKS
Coleman Books, Bruce — D: NATURAL HIST BOOK SV
COLEMAN PUBLISHING, FRANK
Coleman's SARC, Neville — D: BAY FOREIGN BOOKS
Colin (FR) — D: EUROPEAN SCHOOLBOOKS
Colleagues Press (US) — D: BOYDELL & BREWER LTD
Collector Books (Partial) (US) — D: MILLBANK BOOKS LTD
Collector Books (US) — D: LISTER ART BOOKS
Collector Grade Publications (CA) — D: SPA BOOKS LTD
College Board — I: MAXWELL MACMILLAN
College Hill (Partial) (US) — D: TURPIN DISTRIBUTION
COLLEGE OF ESTATE MANAGEMENT
College Press (SA) — D: LAKESIDE PUBNS
College Press (ZB) — D: LEISHMAN & TAUSSIG
COLLETS PUBLISHERS
Collie Books — SANDPIPER BOOKS
Collier Paperbacks — I: MAXWELL MACMILLAN
Collier Paperbacks — D: MARSTON BOOKS SERV
COLLIN PUBLISHING LTD, PETER
Collin Publishing, Peter — D: BEBC DISTRIBUTION
Collin Publishing, Peter — A: BOOK REP & DIST LTD
Collins — D: VERITAS PUBLICATIONS
Collins — I: HARPERCOLLINS GENREF
Collins — I: HARPERCOLLINS BARTH
Collins & Brown — D: BIBLIOS PUB DIST
COLLINS & BROWN
Collins Bibles — I: HARPERCOLLINS RELIG
Collins Bibles — D: B MCCALL BARBOUR
Collins Cobuild — I: HARPERCOLLINS GENREF
Collins Dove (AU) — I: HARPERCOLLINS RELIG
Collins Dove (AU) — D: GILL & MACMILLAN LTD
Collins Educational — I: HARPERCOLLINS EDUC

Collins ELT — I: THOMAS NELSON & SONS
Collins English Dictionaries — I: HARPERCOLLINS GENREF
Collins English Library — I: HARPERCOLLINS GENREF
Collins Gems — I: HARPERCOLLINS GENREF
Collins Gift Classics — I: HARPERCOLLINS GENREF
Collins Liturgical Books — I: HARPERCOLLINS RELIG
Collins Longman — I: HARPERCOLLINS BARTH
Collins Willow — I: HARPERCOLLINS GENREF
COLLINSON, JOHN — W
CollinsSanFrancisco — I: HARPERCOLLINS INTER
Colorado Fiber Center (Craft Books only) (US) — D: ALISON HODGE PUB
Colorcards — I: WINSLOW PRESS
Colour Library Books — I: CLB PUBLISHING
Colt Archaeological Institute (US) — D: LA HAULE BOOKS LTD
COLT BOOKS
COLUMBA BOOK SERVICE
Columba Press Dominican Publications — D: COLUMBA BOOK SERVICE
Columbia University Press (US) — A: UNI PRESS CALIFORNIA
Columbia University Press (US) — D: JOHN WILEY & SONS
Columbus Globus (GE) — D: MCCARTA LTD
COMBINED BOOK SERVICES
Combustion — D: AK DISTRIBUTION
Come Learn — I: GO TEACH PUB
Comedia Publications — D: CENTRAL BOOKS
Comerford, Miller & Associates — D: CENTRAL BOOKS
CommEd — A: JOHN WILEY & SONS
Commer International — D: IMAGES DISTRIBUTION
COMMERCE BUSINESS COMMUNICATIONS
Commission for Racial Equality — D: LAVIS MARKETING
COMMISSION FOR RACIAL EQUALITY
Common Courage Press (US) — D: AK DISTRIBUTION
Common Ground — D: WORLDLY GOODS
COMMONWEALTH SECRETARIAT
Commonword — D: TURNAROUND
Commune-a-Key (US) — D: EVENLODE BOOK DIST
Communes Network — D: BOOKSPEED
COMMUNITY DEVELOPMENT FOUNDATION
Community Health Foundation — D: CENTRAL BOOKS
Community Service Volunteers — CSV EDUCATION
Company's Coming Publishing Ltd (CA) — D: GAZELLE BOOK SERVICE
Compass Services — D: HOTEL & CATERING CO
CompCare Publishers (US) — D: GAZELLE BOOK SERVICE
Compton's Learning Company — I: ENCYC BRITANNICA LTD
COMPUTATIONAL MECHANICS PUBLICATIONS
Compute Publishing (US) — D: COMPUTER BOOKSHOPS
COMPUTER BOOKSHOPS
Computer Guides, The — I: BRIAN GOOCH LTD
Computer Publishing Enterprises — D: BOOKPOINT LIMITED
Computer Publishing Enterprises (US) — D: CHARLES LETTS & CO
Computer Science Press — I: W H FREEMAN & CO LTD
COMPUTER STEP LTD
Computer Technology Research Corporation (US) — D: ELECTRONICA BOOKS
Computer Weekly — D: BUTTERWORTH-HEINEMAN
Computer Weekly — D: REED BOOK SERVICES
Conari Press (US) — D: AIRLIFT BOOK CO
Concept Media — Ceased trading 92
CONCORD BOOKS — W
Concord Publications (HK) — D: WINDROW & GREENE
CONCORDIA PUBLISHING HOUSE LTD
Condie Publications, Allan T — D: MIDLAND COUNTIES LTD
CONDIE PUBLICATIONS, ALLAN T
Condor — I: SOUVENIR PRESS LTD
CONFEDERATION OF BRITISH INDUSTRY
Congden Weed (US) — D: GAZELLE BOOK SERVICE
Congress of South African Writers (SA) — D: LEISHMAN & TAUSSIG
Connoisseurs Choice — A: DEREK SEARLE ASS LTD
Connolly Association — D: CENTRAL BOOKS
Conran Octopus — I: REED CONSUMER TRADE
Conran Octopus — D: REED BOOK SERVICES
CONSERVATIVE CENTRAL OFFICE
Constable — D: TIPTREE BOOK SERV
CONSTABLE & COMPANY LTD
Constable (Ireland only) — A: BLACKSTAFF PRESS LTD
Constitutional Comments — I: MOZAMBIQUE INSTITUTE
Consultants Bureau — I: PLENUM PUBLISHING CO
Consumers Association — D: HODDER & STOUGHTON
Consumers Association (ML) — D: CENTRAL BOOKS
Contemporary Books Inc (US) — D: GAZELLE BOOK SERVICE
Contemporary Drama (US) — D: HANBURY PLAYS
Continuum Publishing (Partial) — D: ROUNDHOUSE PUB LTD
Contour — I: WINSLOW PRESS
Contour Designs (Scotland Only) — D: CLAN BOOKS

Conway Maritime Press Ltd — D: MARSTON BOOKS SERV
CONWAY MARITIME PRESS LTD
Cook, David C (US) — D: NOVA DISTRIBUTION
Cook Publications, Thomas — D: ALAN SUTTON PUB LTD
COOK PUBLISHING, THOMAS
Cook, Thomas — D: ROGER LASCELLES
Coombe Springs Press — D: ELEMENT BOOKS LTD
Cooper Hewitt Museum (US) — A: UNI PRESSES MARKETNG
Cooper, Leo — D: AIRLIFE PUBLISHING
Cooper, Leo — I: PEN & SWORD BOOKS
CO-OPERATIVE UNION
Copp Clark Pitman (CA) — D: LONGMAN GROUP UK LTD
COPPER BEECH PUBLISHING LTD
Corbett Publishing, Ivan (Partial) — D: WELSH BOOKS COUNCIL
CORDEE
CORDEE — W
Cordillera Press (US) — D: CORDEE
Core Business Studies (Mitchell Beazley) — D: NORTHCOTE HOUSE PUB
Corgi — I: TRANSWORLD PUB
Cork Publishing (IR) — D: PROFESSIONAL BK SALE
CORK PUBLISHING LTD
CORK UNIVERSITY PRESS
Cork University Press (IR) — D: CENTRAL BOOKS
Cormorant (CA) — D: TURNAROUND
Cornell University Press (US) — A: TREVOR BROWN ASSOC
Cornerhouse — A: TURNAROUND
CORNERHOUSE PUBLICATIONS
Cornerstone House — D: SEND THE LIGHT
Cornerstone Press (Partial) (US) — D: STRIDE PUBLICATIONS
Corning Museum of Glass Press — I: GOLDEN COCKEREL
Cornish Connection — D: ASHGROVE PRESS
Cornish Language Board — D: DYLLANSOW TRURAN
Cornwall Books — I: GOLDEN COCKEREL
Cornwall Books — D: WEST COUNTRY BOOKS
Coronet — I: HODDER & STOUGHTON
CORTNEY PUBLICATIONS
Corwin Press — I: SAGE PUBLICATIONS
Cosmic Resources (US) — D: EVENLODE BOOK DIST
Costello — I: D J COSTELLO PUB LTD
COSTELLO PUBLISHERS LTD, D J
COUNCIL FOR BRITISH ARCHAELOGY
Council of Europe (FR) — D: HMSO BOOKS
Council of Mortgage Lenders — BUILDING SOC ASSN
COUNTER PRODUCTIONS
COUNTRY BOOKSTORE — W
Country House — D: GILL & MACMILLAN LTD
Countryman Press Inc (US) — D: GAZELLE BOOK SERVICE
COUNTRYSIDE BOOKS
COUNTYVISE LTD
Courtenay — I: APPLEFORD PUB GROUP
COVENANT PUBLISHING CO LTD
Covent Garden Books — I: DORLING KINDERSLEY
Cover to Cover Cassettes Ltd — D: BOOKPOINT LIMITED
COVER TO COVER LTD — A
COWARD, RICHARD & ERIKA
Cowley Publications (US) — D: SPCK
COX & SON LTD, T — W
CPC Guidebooks — I: CANAL PUBLISHING CO
CPC Publishing (US) — D: ART DATA
CPL Press — I: CPL SCIENTIFIC LTD
CPL SCIENTIFIC LTD
CPP Belwin (US) — D: INT MUSIC PUB
CRABTREE PUBLISHING
Crabtree Publishing (CA) — D: LAVIS MARKETING
CRAC — I: HOBSONS PUBLISHING
Crack Editions — I: KNOCKABOUT COMICS
CRAFTS COUNCIL
Craftsman House — D: SCI & TECH BOOK SVCE
Craftsman House (AU) — D: S HENEAGE DIST
Cramer Music — D: BOOSEY & HAWKES LTD
CRANE PRESS
Crane Russak — I: TAYLOR & FRANCIS LTD
CRANSWICK PRESS
Crawford's — I: ECONOMIST BOOKS
Crazy Horse Press (CA) — D: CORDEE
CRC Press Inc (US) — D: MOSBY-YEARBOOK EUR
CRCS Publications (US) — D: AIRLIFT BOOK CO
CRCS (US) — D: L N FOWLER & CO LTD
Creation House (US) — A: SHARON PUBLICATIONS
Creation Press — D: COMBINED BOOK SERV
CREATION PRESS
CREATIVE BOOKS INTERNATIONAL

Creative Bound Inc (CA) — D: GAZELLE BOOK SERVICE
Creative Education (US) — D: MELIA PUB SERVICES
CREATIVE MONOCHROME
Creative Publications — D: JONATHAN PRESS
Creative Publishing — D: SEND THE LIGHT
Creatures at Large Press (US) — D: GAZELLE BOOK SERVICE
Creel Publishing — D: BIBLIOS PUB DIST
CRESCENT MOON PUBLISHING
CRESSRELLES PUBLISHING COMPANY LTD
CRESTA PUBLISHING COMPANY
Crime Club — I: HARPERCOLLINS TRADE
Crocodile Books (US) — D: ROY YATES BOOKS
CROMPTON LTD, PAUL H
Crompton, Paul H — D: AIRLIFT BOOK CO
Cromwell Editions — I: ALPINE FINE ARTS
Cromwell Editions — A: JOHN WILSON BOOKS
Cromwell Publications — No reply 92/93
CRONER PUBLICATIONS
Croom Helm — I: ROUTLEDGE
Cross Publishing, Maggie — D: ASHFORD BUCHAN
Crossing Press (US) — D: AIRLIFT BOOK CO
Crossroad Publishing House (US) — D: SCM PRESS LTD
Crossway Books — D: SEND THE LIGHT
Crossway Books (Partial) (US) — D: SEND THE LIGHT
Crown — I: RAMBORO BOOKS
Crown (US) — D: EUROPEAN PRESS SERV
Crowood Press Ltd — D: BOOKPOINT LIMITED
Crowood Press (Partial) — A: P M LLEWELLYN CO
CROWOOD PRESS, THE
CROWTHER, G L
CRS RECORDS — A
Crucible — I: HARPERCOLLINS THORS
Cruising Guide Publications (Part) (US) — D: BARNACLE MARINE LTD
Crystal Clarity Publications (US) — D: ELEMENT BOOKS LTD
CRYSTAL PALACE FOUNDATION
CSA Publishers (US) — D: L N FOWLER & CO LTD
CSA Telltapes — D: BIBLIOS PUB DIST
CSA TELLTAPES — A
CSV — D: AVANTI BOOKS
CSV EDUCATION
CT PROJECTS
CTFA Inc (US) — D: MICELLE PRESS
CTI Publications (US) — D: FOOD TRADE PRESS LTD
CTS Publications — I: CATHOLIC TRUTH SOC
Cube Publications — D: COUNTRYSIDE BOOKS
Cuisenaire Co of America — D: JONATHAN PRESS
Culinary Arts (US) — D: EVENLODE BOOK DIST
Cultural Atlas Series — I: FACTS ON FILE
Cummins, James (US) — D: DAWSON UK LTD
CURLEW PUBLISHING COMPANY
Currency Press Pty Ltd (AU) — D: GAZELLE BOOK SERVICE
CURRENT SCIENCE LTD
Currey Publishers, James — D: PLYMBRIDGE DIST LTD
Curtis — I: RAC PUBLISHING
Curtis, John — I: HODDER & STOUGHTON
Curwen Books — I: HARLEY BOOKS
Curzon Press — D: BIBLIOS PUB DIST
CURZON PRESS LTD
Custom House Group — D: VINE HOUSE DIST
Customs Co-operation Council (BG) — D: HMSO BOOKS
Cwmni Cyhoeddi Gwynn — D: WELSH BOOKS COUNCIL
CWR
Cyd-bwyllgor Addysg Cymru — D: WELSH BOOKS COUNCIL
Cygnet Press (AU) — D: PETER MOORE BOOKS
Cygnet Press (Partial) — D: S HENEAGE DIST
Cyhoeddiadau Barddas — D: WELSH BOOKS COUNCIL
Cyhoeddiadau Mei — D: WELSH BOOKS COUNCIL
Cyhoeddiadau Modern Cymreig — D: WELSH BOOKS COUNCIL
Cymdeithas Lyfrau Ceredigion — D: WELSH BOOKS COUNCIL
Cyngor Llyfrau Cymraeg — WELSH BOOKS COUNCIL
CYPRESS BOOK COMPANY
D & S (Partial List) (US) — D: BUTTERWORTH & CO LTD
D SERVICES
Da Capo Press Paperbacks & Reprints (US) — D: EDS
Daily & Sunday Express — I: ANNUAL CONCEPTS LTD
Daily Mail Crossword Books — D: BIBLIOS PUB DIST
Daily Star — I: ANNUAL CONCEPTS LTD
Daily Telegraph Map Series — D: ROGER LASCELLES
Daimon Verlag (SZ) — D: AIRLIFT BOOK CO
DAISY BOOKS
Dake Bible Sales Inc (US) — D: B MCCALL BARBOUR
Dale Seymour Publications — D: JONATHAN PRESS

Dalebank Books — D: BIBLIOS PUB DIST
Dalebrook Publications — I: TRENT VALLEY PUB
DALENNAU
Dales Large Print — I: MAGNA LARGE PRINT
Dalesman (Partial) — D: CORDEE
DALESMAN PUBLISHING COMPANY LTD
Dalkey Archive Press (US) — D: TURNAROUND
Dallas Institute (US) — D: ELEMENT BOOKS LTD
DALTON LTD, TERENCE
DALTON WATSON FINE BOOKS
DANCE BOOKS LTD
Dance Horizons (US) — D: DANCE BOOKS LTD
Dance Horizons (US) — D: DANCE BOOKS LTD
Dangaroo Press — D: PASSWORD (BOOKS) LTD
Dangaroo Press — No reply 93
Daniel Co Ltd, C W — D: L N FOWLER & CO LTD
DANIEL COMPANY LTD, C W
DANIELS PUBLISHING
Dar Al Saqi — I: SAQI BOOKS
Dar Al Taqwa (Partial) — A: P M LLEWELLYN CO
Dar es Salaam University Press (TZ) — D: AFRICAN BOOKS COLL
Dar es Salaam University Press (TZ) — D: LEISHMAN & TAUSSIG
DARF PUBLISHERS LTD
Darf Publishers (Partial) — A: P M LLEWELLYN CO
Dark Star — D: AK DISTRIBUTION
DARLOW, J — W
Dartmouth — I: ASHGATE PUB GROUP
Darton, Longman & Todd (Bibles & Testaments) — D: BIBLE SOCIETY
DARTON LONGMAN TODD
Darwen Finlayson — I: PHILLIMORE & CO LTD
DATA CONSULTANCY
DATA NETWORK PUBLISHING LTD
Data Packs — I: E J MORTEN PUB
David & Charles — D: EXEL LOGISTICS
DAVID & CHARLES PLC
DAVIES BOOKS, MIKE — R
DAVIES PUBLISHERS, CHRISTOPHER
Davis Books, Michael (FR) — A: WORDSWORTH EDITIONS
Davis Books, Michael (NT) — A: WORDSWORTH EDITIONS
Davis Books, Michael (NW) — A: WORDSWORTH EDITIONS
Davis Books, Michael (SW) — A: WORDSWORTH EDITIONS
Davis, F A — I: WILLIAMS & WILKINS
Davis Press (CA) — D: LAVIS MARKETING
Davis Publications Inc (US) — D: GAZELLE BOOK SERVICE
DAWES PUBLICATIONS, JOHN
Dawn Horse Press (US) — D: REAL BOOKS
DAWSON UK LTD
Dayal (Ravi) Publishers (IN) — D: SANGAM BOOKS LTD
Daybreak — I: DARTON LONGMAN TODD
Daycare Trust — D: CENTRAL BOOKS
Dayspring (US) — D: NOVA DISTRIBUTION
Daytons Guides (partial) — D: ASHFORD BUCHAN
DBI (Partial) (US) — D: CASSELL PLC
DCI (US) — D: INT MUSIC PUB
De Haske (NT) — D: BOOSEY & HAWKES LTD
De Muiderkring (NT) — D: PC PUBLISHING
Deaconess Press (US) — D: GAZELLE BOOK SERVICE
Deans — I: REED CONS BOUNTY
Dearborn (US) — D: KOGAN PAGE LTD
Debrett's Peerage — A: DEREK SEARLE ASS LTD
Debrett's Peerage Ltd — D: BOOKPOINT LIMITED
DEBRETTS PEERAGE LTD
Decadence from Dedalus — I: DEDALUS LTD
December Press (US) — D: CEDAR TREE HOUSE
Decker Inc, B C (US) — D: MOSBY-YEARBOOK EUR
Decopoulos, John (Partial) (GR) — D: OLD VICARAGE PUB
Decorative Stained Glass — D: SEND THE LIGHT
Dedalus — D: CENTRAL BOOKS
DEDALUS LTD
Dedalus Press (IR) — D: PASSWORD (BOOKS) LTD
DEDALUS PRESS (IR), THE
DEE BOOKS — W
Dee, Ivan R Inc (US) — D: GAZELLE BOOK SERVICE
DEEP BOOKS LTD
Defiant Books — D: CENTRAL BOOKS
Degremont — D: INTERCEPT LTD
Dekker Inc, Marcel — A: ACADEMIC BOOK ASSOC
Dekker, Marcel (SZ) — D: EUROPEAN PRESS SERV
Delacroix Press (AU) — D: LA HAULE BOOKS LTD
DELAMARE PUBLISHING
Delectation Books — I: DELECTUS BOOKS
DELECTUS BOOKS

Delfino Editore, Antonio (Partial) (IT) — D: MICELLE PRESS
Delft University Press (NT) — D: ART DATA
Delightful — I: RAMBORO BOOKS
Dell — I: TRANSWORLD PUB
Delmar (US) — D: INT THOMSON PUB SERV
DeLorme Mapping (Partial) (US) — D: CORDEE
Delos Inc (US) — D: AIRLIFT BOOK CO
Delpa Edition (FR) — D: CEDAR TREE HOUSE
Delpha Editions (FR) — D: EUROPEAN SCHOOLBOOKS
Delpha Editions (FR) — D: BOOKS CONTINENTAL
DELTA — W
Delta (Partial) — D: PARFITTS BOOK SERV
DELTA PRESS LTD
Demast Books — I: QED
Deneway Guides — D: SPRINGFIELD BOOKS
Denny Publications — No reply 92/93
Dent, J M — I: ORION PUBLISHING
Dent, J M — D: LITTLEHAMPTON BK SVC
Dept of Land Economy Publications — D: GRANTA EDITIONS
Design Council — D: SHEED & WARD LTD
DESIGN COUNCIL BOOKS
Destino (SP) — D: EUROPEAN SCHOOLBOOKS
Destiny Books (US) — D: AIRLIFT BOOK CO
DEUTSCH, ANDRE
Deutsch, Andre (Ireland only) — A: BLACKSTAFF PRESS LTD
Deutsch Childrens' Books, Andre — I: SCHOLASTIC PUB LTD
Deutsch Ltd, Andre — A: CASSELL PLC
Deutsch Ltd, Andre — D: LITTLEHAMPTON BK SVC
Deutscher Taschenbuch Verlag (GE) — D: EUROPEAN SCHOOLBOOKS
DEVELOPMENT EDUCATION PROJECT
Devon Books — D: WEST COUNTRY BOOKS
Devorss & Co (US) — D: L N FOWLER & CO LTD
Devyn Press Inc (US) — D: GAZELLE BOOK SERVICE
Dewey (DDC) Publications — I: OCLC EUROPE
Dharma Books (US) — D: ELEMENT BOOKS LTD
Dharma Drum (US) — D: WISDOM BOOKS
Dharmafarer Enterprises (ML) — D: WISDOM BOOKS
Diadem — I: HODDER & STOUGHTON
Diamond Books — D: COMBINED BOOK SERV
Diapofilm (FR) — D: EUROPEAN SCHOOLBOOKS
DICKSON LTD, KEN
DICKSON PRICE PUBLISHERS
Dictation Disc Co (US) — D: COMPUTER BOOKSHOPS
Didasko — No reply 92/93
Didier & Richard Maps (Partial) (FR) — D: CORDEE
Didier (FR) — D: EUROPEAN SCHOOLBOOKS
Didier Maps, Richard — A: WORLD LEISURE MKTG
Didier Richard (FR) — D: MCCARTA LTD
Diesterweg (GE) — D: EUROPEAN SCHOOLBOOKS
Digital Press — I: SIMON & SCHUSTER INT
Dignon, Lesley — A: NEWS PRODUCTIONS
Dimi Publishing (US) — D: EVENLODE BOOK DIST
Diodex — A: WORLD LEISURE MKTG
Diogenes (GE) — D: EUROPEAN SCHOOLBOOKS
Direct Distribution — LAWRENCE ERLBAUM ASSOCIATES
Director Books — A: WOODHEAD-FAULKNER
Directors Guild Publishers (US) — D: GAZELLE BOOK SERVICE
Directory of Social Change — D: AN PUBLICATIONS
Directory of Social Change — D: TURNAROUND
Directory of Training — I: TRAINING INFO LTD
Dis Voir (FR) — D: GAZELLE BOOK SERVICE
Disability Alliance — D: CENTRAL BOOKS
Discovery Books — A: JARROLD PUBLISHING
Disney — I: LADYBIRD BOOKS LTD
Disney Press (Free Market & Europe) — D: LITTLE BROWN & CO
Distribution & Management Services — EXEL LOGISTICS
Distribution Book Co — No reply 93
DISTRIBUTION BOOK COMPANY
DISTROPA LTD
Divyanand Verlag GmbH (GE) — D: EAST WEST PUB LTD
Diwan Press (AU) — D: ELEMENT BOOKS LTD
DK Today Ltd — D: BAY FOREIGN BOOKS
DLF PUBLICATIONS
DLT — D: VERITAS PUBLICATIONS
DMS DISTRIBUTION LTD — W
DNDS Records (SZ) — D: ELEMENT BOOKS LTD
DOBSON BOOKS LTD
Dobson, Dennis — I: DOBSON BOOKS LTD
Doctor Who — I: VIRGIN PUBLISHING
DOD'S PARLIAMENTARY
D'Offay Gallery, Anthony — D: ART DATA
Dog Eared Press — D: AK DISTRIBUTION

Dolmen Press — I: COLIN SMYTHE LTD
DOLPHIN BOOK CO LTD
Dolphin Computer Books — I: MANUTIUS PRESS
Domino Books (Partial) — D: WELSH BOOKS COUNCIL
Domino Books (Wales) (Partial) — A: P M LLEWELLYN CO
Donald Publishers, John — A: DEREK SEARLE ASS LTD
DONALD PUBLISHERS LTD, JOHN
Donemus — D: NOVELLO & CO LTD
DONHEAD PUBLISHING
Dorling Kindersley — D: TIPTREE BOOK SERV
DORLING KINDERSLEY
Dorling Kindersley Family Library — D: BIBLIOS PUB DIST
Dorling Kindersley Marketing Services — D: BIBLIOS PUB DIST
Dorset Books — D: WEST COUNTRY BOOKS
Dorset House (US) — A: JOHN WILEY & SONS
DORSET PUBLISHING COMPANY
Dos Tejedoras (Craft Books only) (US) — D: ALISON HODGE PUB
DOT PUBLICATIONS
Doubleday — I: TRANSWORLD PUB
Doubleday (US) — D: VERITAS PUBLICATIONS
Doubleday (US) — D: EUROPEAN PRESS SERV
Dovecote Press — D: COUNTRYSIDE BOOKS
DOVECOTE PRESS LTD
Dovehouse Editions (CA) — D: LIVERPOOL UNIV PRESS
Dover — D: TIPTREE BOOK SERV
Dover (Ireland only) — A: BLACKSTAFF PRESS LTD
Dover Publications Inc (US) — D: CONSTABLE & CO LTD
Down East Books (Craft Books only) (US) — D: ALISON HODGE PUB
DOWNLANDER PUBLISHING
DP PUBLICATIONS LTD
Dr Watson Computer Learning Series — I: ABCO DESIGN LTD
Dragon Door Publications (US) — D: GAZELLE BOOK SERVICE
Dragon's World — D: GRANTHAM BOOK SERV
Dragons World — A: PEGASUS PUB SERV
DRAGONS WORLD LTD
Drake, A J — D: CORDEE
DRAKE AV VIDEO — A
Drake Marketing Services — D: BAILEY DIST LTD
DRAKE PUBLISHING SERVICES
Drama Book Publishers (US) — D: GAZELLE BOOK SERVICE
Dramaline Publications (US) — D: GAZELLE BOOK SERVICE
Dramco Publishers (Partial) — D: HERLADRY TODAY
Dref Wen — D: DALENNAU
Dresser Publications Ltd, Julian — D: BOOKPOINT LIMITED
Dressler (GE) — D: EUROPEAN SCHOOLBOOKS
Drew Publishing Ltd, Richard — I: W & R CHAMBERS LTD
Drew, Richard — W & R CHAMBERS
Droemer Knaur (GE) — D: EUROPEAN SCHOOLBOOKS
Dryad Press — I: B T BATSFORD LTD
Dryden Press — I: HARCOURT BRACE JOVAN
Du Mont — A: PALLAS ATHENE
DUCKWORTH & COMPANY, GERALD
Duculot (BG) — D: ROY YATES BOOKS
Duculot (FR) — D: EUROPEAN SCHOOLBOOKS
Duke of Edinburgh's Award — D: CORDEE
Duke University Press (US) — A: ACADEMIC & UNIV PUB
DUN & BRADSTREET LTD
DUNDURN DISTRIBUTION
Dundurn Distribution (CA) — D: LAVIS MARKETING
Dundurn Press (CA) — D: DUNDURN DISTRIBUTION
Dunitz Ltd, Martin — D: WILLIAMS & WILKINS
Dunitz Ltd, Martin — D: BOOKPOINT LIMITED
DUNITZ LTD, MARTIN
Dunod (FR) — D: EUROPEAN SCHOOLBOOKS
DUNROD PRESS
Dupuis (FR) — D: EUROPEAN SCHOOLBOOKS
Durr & Kessler (GE) — D: EUROPEAN SCHOOLBOOKS
Dwyer (AU) — D: VERITAS PUBLICATIONS
Dwyer, E J (AU) — D: COLUMBA BOOK SERVICE
Dyllansow Truran — D: DALENNAU
DYLLANSOW TRURAN
Dzuka Publishing Co (MA) — D: MALLORY INT
Dzuka Publishing Co (MA) — D: LEISHMAN & TAUSSIG
Eagle — I: INTER PUB SERVICE
EAGLE BOOKS LTD
Eagle Publishing — D: SEND THE LIGHT
Early English Text Society — D: OXFORD UNI PRESS DIS
Ears & Eyes — I: BOOSEY & HAWKES LTD
Earth Heart (US) — D: EVENLODE BOOK DIST
EARTH RESOURCES RESEARCH LTD
Earth Spirit Inc — D: DEEP BOOKS LTD
Earthscan Publications — I: KOGAN PAGE LTD

EASON & SON LTD
EASON & SON LTD — W
EASON & SON (NI) LTD — W
East African Educational Publishers (KY) — D: LEISHMAN & TAUSSIG
East African Publishing House (KY) — D: LEISHMAN & TAUSSIG
East Herts Publishing — D: BOOKPOINT LIMITED
East West Express (SI) — D: GAZELLE BOOK SERVICE
EAST WEST PUBLICATIONS LTD
Eastern Africa Pubs (inc EALB) (TZ) — D: LEISHMAN & TAUSSIG
Eastman Kodak — D: NEWPRO UK LTD
East-West Publications — D: ASHGROVE PRESS
Ebenezer Press — D: WINDSOR BOOKS INT
EBJLA (AT) — D: BAHAI PUBLISHING
Ebury Press — I: RANDOM HOUSE UK LTD
Ebury Press — D: TIPTREE BOOK SERV
Ecclesia Services — D: ARTHUR JAMES LTD
Ecclesiastical Architects & Surveyors Assn — D: RIBA PUBLICATIONS
ECM Maps — A: WORLD LEISURE MKTG
ECONOMIC & SOCIAL RESEARCH COUNCIL
ECONOMIST BOOKS
Economist Books Ltd, The — D: MARSTON BOOKS SERV
Economist Publications — A: WOODHEAD-FAULKNER
Eddington Hook — COMBINED BOOK SERVICES
EDELSA (SP) — D: EUROPEAN SCHOOLBOOKS
Eden Grove Editions — D: AIRLIFT BOOK CO
Ediciones Atrium (SP) — D: S HENEAGE DIST
Ediciones Ekare (VZ) — D: ROY YATES BOOKS
Ediciones Poligrafa (SP) — D: W & G FOYLE LTD
Edicoes Peregrino — I: EVANGELICAL PRESS
Edinburgh Publishing Company — A: DEREK SEARLE ASS LTD
Edinburgh University, Dept of Archaeology — D: OXBOW BOOKS
EDINBURGH UNIVERSITY PRESS
Edisud (FR) — D: ROGER LASCELLES
Edisud (Partial) (FR) — D: CORDEE
Editio Musica Budapest (HG) — D: BOOSEY & HAWKES LTD
Edition Belvedere (IT) — D: BIBLIOS PUB DIST
Edition Cantz (GE) — D: ART DATA
Edition Hansjorg Mayer (GE) — D: ART DATA
Edition 'M' (Partial) (SZ) — D: HILMARTON MANOR
Edition Marzona (GE) — D: ART DATA
Edition Mycologia Lucerne (SZ) — D: RICHMOND PUB CO LTD
Edition Stemmle (GE) — D: ART DATA
Editions Aubrey Walter — D: GMP PUBLISHERS LTD
Editions Beauchesne (Partial) — D: BAY FOREIGN BOOKS
Editions de l'Ocean Indien — D: AFRICAN BOOKS COLL
Editions de l'Ocean Indien (MU) — D: LEISHMAN & TAUSSIG
Editions Delta (BG) — D: CEDAR TREE HOUSE
Editions Du Regard (FR) — D: ROY YATES BOOKS
Editions Du Seuil (FR) — D: ROY YATES BOOKS
Editions Franck (Partial) (FR) — D: CORDEE
Editions Georgraphiques Generales (FR) — D: EUROPEAN SCHOOLBOOKS
Editions Graphocartes France (Partial) (FR) — D: BARNACLE MARINE LTD
Editions Hervas-Massin (FR) — D: BOOKS CONTINENTAL
Editions Juridiques Associees (FR) — D: EUROPEAN SCHOOLBOOKS
Editions Mayer (Partial) (FR) — D: HILMARTON MANOR
Editions Olizane (Partial) (SZ) — D: CORDEE
Editions Pen Duick (FR) — D: BOOKS CONTINENTAL
Editions Renyi Inc (CA) — D: ACCENT EDUCATIONAL
Editions Rivage (FR) — D: ROGER LASCELLES
Editions Van Wilder (Partial) (FR) — D: HILMARTON MANOR
Editora Ulisseia (PG) — D: EUROPEAN SCHOOLBOOKS
Editoria Alpina (Partial) (SP) — D: CORDEE
Editorial Peregrino — I: EVANGELICAL PRESS
Editorial Verbo (PG) — D: EUROPEAN SCHOOLBOOKS
Editrice Militaire (Partial) (IT) — D: S HENEAGE DIST
EDS
Education Resource Centre — D: LATIN AMERICA BUREAU
Educational Bookshelf — D: BIBLIOS PUB DIST
EDUCATIONAL COMPANY OF IRELAND
EDUCATIONAL EXPLORERS
Edwards, A — D: DALENNAU
Eerdmans Publishing Co (Ltd) (Partial) (US) — D: T & T CLARK LTD
Eerdmans, Wm B (Partial) — D: SEND THE LIGHT
Eerdmans, Wm B (US) — D: GRACEWING/FOWLER
EF Communications (US) — D: EVENLODE BOOK DIST
EFFECTIVE PUBLISHING
Efstathiadis (GR) — D: MCCARTA LTD
Efstathiadis Group (GR) — D: ZENO
Efstathiadis Group (GR) — D: GAZELLE BOOK SERVICE
Efstathiadis Maps — A: WORLD LEISURE MKTG
EGMONT PUBLISHING LTD
Egypt Exploration Society — D: TURPIN DISTRIBUTION

EIA (US) — A: AMERICAN TECH PUB
Eiffel Editions (Partial) (BG) — D: S HENEAGE DIST
Eighth Mountain Press (US) — D: AIRLIFT BOOK CO
Eilers & Schunemann (GE) — D: EUROPEAN SCHOOLBOOKS
Einaudi (IT) — D: EUROPEAN SCHOOLBOOKS
Einaudi (IT) — D: S HENEAGE DIST
EITB Publishing — ENTRA PRESS
Ejlers, Christian (English Language Books Only) (DN) — D: SPA BOOKS LTD
Ekdotike Athenon Ltd (Partial) (GR) — D: OLD VICARAGE PUB
Elanagan, Mel (IR) — D: ASHFORD BUCHAN
Eland — D: CONSTABLE & CO LTD
ELAND
Eland (Ireland only) — A: BLACKSTAFF PRESS LTD
Elbrooke (AU) — D: LAVIS MARKETING
ELC PUBLISHING
Elcott Books — I: MARLBOROUGH BOOKS
Electa (IT) — D: S HENEAGE DIST
ELECTRONICA BOOKS
Elefanten Press (GE) — D: ART DATA
Elektor Electronics Electuur BV (NT) — D: GAZELLE BOOK SERVICE
ELEMENT BOOKS LTD
Element Books (Partial) — D: ALIF INTERNATIONAL
Elephant Editions — D: AK DISTRIBUTION
Elfen — D: WELSH BOOKS COUNCIL
Elgar, Edward — I: ASHGATE PUB GROUP
ELI (IT) — D: ACCENT EDUCATIONAL
Elias Modern Publishing House Egypt (Partial) (EG) — D: P M LLEWELLYN CO
Elite Words & Image — D: BOOKPOINT LIMITED
ELITE WORDS & IMAGE
Elkin — I: NOVELLO & CO LTD
Ellenbank Press — D: BOOKSPEED
ELLIOT RIGHT WAY BOOKS
Ellis Horwood — D: INT BOOK DIST
ELLIS HORWOOD
Ellis Publishing, Aidan — D: CASSELL PLC
ELLIS PUBLISHING, AIDAN
ELM PUBLICATIONS
ELMDON PUBLICATIONS
El-Sayed Publications (US) — D: GAZELLE BOOK SERVICE
El-Sayed Publications (US) — D: GAZELLE BOOK SERVICE
ELSEVIER SCIENCE PUBLISHERS
ELSTEAD MAPS — W
ELT Press (US) — D: COLIN SMYTHE LTD
Elvendon Press — WILLIAM REED DIRECTORIES
Elysium Growth Press (US) — D: GAZELLE BOOK SERVICE
EMAP BUSINESS PUBLISHING
Emblem Books — No reply 92/93
EMC Publishing (US) — D: ACCENT EDUCATIONAL
EMERY, GORDON
EMI Music Publishing — D: INT MUSIC PUB
Empire Features — A: ACADEMY BOOKS LTD
Emporer Publishing — D: BOOKPOINT LIMITED
ENCYCLOPAEDIA BRITANNICA INTERNATIONAL LTD
Encyclopaedia Univerdis (FR) — D: ENCYC BRITANNICA LTD
ENERGY CONSULTANCY
Energy Medicine Press — I: ASHGROVE PRESS
ENERGY PUBLICATIONS
Engineering Training Authority — ENTRA PUBNS
England, David — A: NEWS PRODUCTIONS
ENGLANG BOOKS
English Heritage (Partial List) — D: HMSO BOOKS
ENGLISH LIFE PUBLICATIONS
Enitharmon Press — D: PASSWORD (BOOKS) LTD
ENITHARMON PRESS
ENSIGN PUBLICATIONS
ENTRA PUBLICATIONS
Entsian — I: KNIGHTSCROSS LTD
Envirobook — D: JON CARPENTER PUB
Environmental & Development Agency (SA) — D: LEISHMAN & TAUSSIG
ENVOI POETS PUBLICATIONS
EOTHEN PRESS
EP Publishing — I: A & C BLACK LTD
EPA PRESS
EPB Publishers Pte Ltd (SI) — D: GAZELLE BOOK SERVICE
EPS PLC
Epworth Press — D: SCM PRESS LTD
EQUESTRIAN MANAGEMENT CONSULTANTS
Era Publications (Partial) (AU) — D: RAGGED BEARS LTD
ERA TECHNOLOGY LTD
ERD PUBLICATIONS LTD
Erdmann, Robert Publishing (US) — D: GAZELLE BOOK SERVICE
ERLBAUM ASSOCIATES, LAWRENCE

Ermor Enterprises (US) — D: GAZELLE BOOK SERVICE
Ernest Press, The — D: CORDEE
Ernst & John — I: ACADEMY GROUP LTD
Erskine Press — I: ARCHIVAL FACSIMILES
ESC Publishing — I: SWEET & MAXWELL LTD
Escreet Publications — D: CENTRAL BOOKS
ESM (Educational Software for Microcomputers) — I: LEARNING DEV AIDS
Espasa Calpe (SP) — D: EUROPEAN SCHOOLBOOKS
ESRC — I: ESRC
Essex Co-operative Publishing — I: FREEDOM GRAPHICS GP
ESSEX CO-OPERATIVE PUBLISHING
Estamp — D: AN PUBLICATIONS
Estamp — D: CENTRAL BOOKS
ESTAMP
ESTATE PUBLICATIONS
ESTATES GAZETTE LTD
Ethics & Public Policy Center (US) — D: EDS
Eurail Guide (US) (Travel Books) — D: KUPERARD LTD
Eureka Publishing Ltd — D: GAZELLE BOOK SERVICE
EUROBOOK LTD
Euromoney Publications — A: WOODHEAD-FAULKNER
Euromoney Publications — D: PLYMBRIDGE DIST LTD
EUROMONITOR PLC
EUROPA PUBLICATIONS LTD
European Action for Racial Equality & Social Justice — D: NEW BEACON BOOKS LTD
European Business Publications — I: CLEMENT PUBS LTD
EUROPEAN BUSINESS PUBLISHING
European Communities (LX) — D: HMSO BOOKS
European Entrepreneurs Association (Partial) — D: THOMAS LYSTER LTD
European Inst for the Media (English Titles Only) — D: JOHN LIBBEY & CO LTD
European Labour Forum — I: SPOKESMAN BOOKS
European Law Centre — I: SWEET & MAXWELL LTD
European Leisure Maps — I: ESTATE PUBLICATIONS
European Library Publishers (NT) — D: BIBLIOS PUB DIST
European Photography (GE) — D: CENTRAL BOOKS
European Plastics Directory — I: WATERLOW INFO SERV
EUROPEAN PRESS SERVICE
EUROPEAN SCHOOLBOOKS
European Schoolbooks Publishing Ltd — D: EUROPEAN SCHOOLBOOKS
Europhone Language Institute — D: BAY FOREIGN BOOKS
EUROSPAN GROUP, THE
Eurospan Ltd — A: ACADEMIC BOOK ASSOC
Eurostudy — I: IBC PUBLISHING LTD
Eurostudy — D: PROBUS EUROPE
Evan Moor (US) — D: SCHOLASTIC PUB LTD
Evangel Publishing House (KY) — D: LEISHMAN & TAUSSIG
Evangelical Library (London) — D: EVANGELICAL PR WALES
Evangelical Library of Wales — I: EVANGELICAL PR WALES
Evangelical Movement of Wales — I: EVANGELICAL PR WALES
EVANGELICAL PRESS ENGLAND
Evangelical Press (UK) — A: INTERVARSITY PRESS
EVANGELICAL PRESS WALES
EVANGELICAL PRESS WALES — A
Evans Brothers Ltd — D: BOOKPOINT LIMITED
EVANS BROTHERS LTD
EVENLODE BOOK DISTRIBUTION
Everest (SP) — D: EUROPEAN SCHOOLBOOKS
Everyday Publications — A: JOHN RITCHIE LTD
Everyman's Library — I: RANDOM HOUSE UK LTD
Everyman's Library — D: TIPTREE BOOK SERV
Everywoman — D: CENTRAL BOOKS
Evidan (Partial) (FR) — D: CORDEE
EX LIBRIS PRESS
Exact Change (US) — D: TURNAROUND
EXCALIBUR PRESS OF LONDON
Executive Grapevine — A: MERCURY BOOKS
EXECUTIVE GRAPEVINE INTERNATIONAL
EXEL LOGISTICS DMS
EXLEY PUBLICATIONS
Exley Publications (Ireland Only) — D: ISLAND PUBLICATIONS
Exley Publications (UK only) — A: JARROLD PUBLISHING
Exmoor Books — D: WEST COUNTRY BOOKS
Exmoor Press — D: WEST COUNTRY BOOKS
EXPERT BOOKS
Exploramaps — I: JARROLD PUBLISHING
Express Books — I: EXPRESS NEWSPAPERS
Express Books — D: BOOKPOINT LIMITED
EXPRESS NEWSPAPERS PLC
Exton Publishing Company (US) — D: CHARTWELL-BRATT
Eyebright Publications — D: EVENLODE BOOK DIST
Eyre & Spottiswoode — CAMBRIDGE UNIVERSITY PRESS
Eyre & Spottiswoode Bibles — D: B MCCALL BARBOUR

Fabbri-Bompiani (IT) — D: EUROPEAN SCHOOLBOOKS
Faber & Faber — D: IMRAY LAURIE & NORIE
FABER & FABER
FABER & FABER — A
FABIAN SOCIETY
Facsimile Reprints — I: CHIVERS PRESS LTD
Factfinders — I: EUROMONITOR PLC
Faction Books — I: MANOR HOUSE PUB
FACTORY SHOP GUIDE
Facts on File — D: ROUNDHOUSE PUB LTD
FACTS ON FILE
Facts on File Ltd — D: BOOKPOINT LIMITED
Facts on File Ltd — D: BOOKPOINT LIMITED
Facts on File (US) — D: ROUNDHOUSE PUB LTD
Facts on File (US) (Jewish Interest) — D: KUPERARD LTD
Failsafe — I: EUROPEAN BUS PUB
Fairacres Publications — I: SLG PRESS
Faircape Books (SA) — D: LAKESIDE PUBNS
Fairfax — I: MEREHURST FAIRFAX
Fairfax Ltd, J B — D: BOOKPOINT LIMITED
Fairfax Press, J B — MEREHURST FAIRFAX
Fairleigh Dickinson U P — I: GOLDEN COCKEREL
Fairmount Press — I: SIMON & SCHUSTER INT
FAIRPLAY PUBLICATIONS LTD
Faith & Bardi Books — No reply 92/93
Faith in Print — I: CHRISTIAN BOOK PROMO
Faithful Words — I: HUGHES & COLEMAN LTD
Falco — I: HAWK BOOKS LTD
Falcon Press (Partial) (US) — D: VERULAM PUB LTD
Falcon Press (Partial) (US) — D: CORDEE
Falcon Press Publishing Co Inc (US) — D: GAZELLE BOOK SERVICE
Falk (Ltd) (GE) — D: SPRINGFIELD BOOKS
Falling Wall Press — A: LOXWOOD STONELEIGH
Falling Wall Press — D: TURNAROUND
Falmer Press Ltd — I: TAYLOR & FRANCIS LTD
FAMEDRAM PUBLISHERS LTD
Family Fun — I: KINGSCLERE PUB LTD
Family Law — I: JORDAN & SONS LTD
FAMILY PLANNING ASSOCIATION
FAMILY POLICY STUDIES CENTRE
FAMILY PUBLICATIONS
Family Walks — I: SCARTHIN BOOKS
FAMILY WELFARE ENTERPRISES
Fanny — I: KNOCKABOUT COMICS
Fantail — I: PENGUIN BOOKS LTD
Fanz-Millers Fan Clubs — D: XYLOPRESS LTD
Far Eastern Economic Review (HK) — D: ROGER LASCELLES
Farm Holiday Guides — D: GRANTHAM BOOK SERV
Farm Holiday Guides — A: WORLD LEISURE MKTG
FARMING PRESS BOOKS
Farragut Publishing Company (US) — D: GAZELLE BOOK SERVICE
Farrand Press — D: PORTLAND PRESS LTD
Farrand Press — A: ROGER BAYLISS
FARRAND PRESS
Farrar, Straus & Giroux (Partial) (US) — D: CASSELL PLC
Farrar, Straus & Giroux (US) — D: EUROPEAN PRESS SERV
FASA Books (US) — D: GAZELLE BOOK SERVICE
FASTLANE DISTRIBUTION LTD — W
Fat Man Press — D: KNOCKABOUT COMICS
FAULKNER PUBLISHING LTD, IAN
FAWCETT, R T & A — W
Fearon Education — I: SIMON & SCHUSTER INT
FEATHER BOOKS
FEDERATION OF FAMILY HISTORY SOCIETIES
Federation Press (Partial List) (AU) — D: BLACKSTONE PRESS LTD
Feedback Theatrebooks (US) — D: GAZELLE BOOK SERVICE
Feeds & Feeding — I: HGM PUBLICATIONS
Fell & Rock Climbing Club — D: CORDEE
Feltrinelli (IT) — D: EUROPEAN SCHOOLBOOKS
Feminist Press (US) — D: AIRLIFT BOOK CO
Feral House (US) — D: TEMPLE PRESS LTD
Feral House (US) — D: TURNAROUND
Ferendune — I: E W CLASSEY LTD
Fernand Nathan Editeur SA (FR) — D: ROY YATES BOOKS
FERNHURST BOOKS
Fernwood Press — D: BAY FOREIGN BOOKS
Ferrari, Marianne (US) — D: GMP PUBLISHERS LTD
FERRY PRESS
Festerman (Partial) — D: S HENEAGE DIST
Ffynnon Press — I: PENINSULA BOOKS
FHG PUBLICATIONS LTD
Ficedula Books — D: A & C BLACK LTD

Fielding Guides — D: HODDER & STOUGHTON
Fielding Guides — A: WORLD LEISURE MKTG
Financial Times Business Information — A: ROGER BAYLISS
FINANCIAL TIMES, THE
Financial Times/Pitman — I: PITMAN PUBLISHING
Financial Training (Partial List) — D: MARY GLASGOW PUB
Financial Training (Study Packs) — D: STANLEY THORNES PUB
Findex (US) — D: EUROMONITOR PLC
FINDHORN PRESS
Findhorn Press (Diaries/Calendars/Cards Only) — D: WORLDLY GOODS
Findhorn Press (Not Scotland & Europe) — D: ASHGROVE PRESS
Fine Arts Museum of San Francisco — I: SIMON & SCHUSTER INT
Fine Line Books — D: ELEMENT BOOKS LTD
Fingerpost Publications — D: CHAPMAN
Finishing Publications Ltd (Partial) — D: WOODHEAD PUBLISHING
Fire Engineering Books (Penwell Publishing) (US) — A: FMJ BOOKS
Firebird Books — D: CHRIS LLOYD SALES
FIREBIRD BOOKS LTD
Firebrand Books (US) — D: AIRLIFT BOOK CO
Firecrest Books — I: CHIVERS PRESS LTD
Firefly Ltd — D: WAYLAND (PUB) LTD
Fireside — I: SIMON & SCHUSTER LTD
Firestone Hispania (SP) — D: ROGER LASCELLES
Firestone (SP) — D: ROGER LASCELLES
FIRST (1ST) WORLD PUBLISHING LTD
FIRST IMPRESSIONS PUBLICATIONS
FIRST TIME PUBLICATIONS
FIS PUBLICATIONS LTD
Fischer, Carl (HG) — D: BOOSEY & HAWKES LTD
Fischer (GE) — D: EUROPEAN SCHOOLBOOKS
Fisher Books — D: FOUNTAIN PRESS LTD
Fishing News Books — I: BLACKWELL SCIENTIFIC
Fitzhouse — I: B T BATSFORD LTD
Fitzjames Press — I: MOTOR RACING PUB LTD
FITZWILLIAM MUSEUM ENTERPRISES LTD
Fiuedit (FR) — D: SPRINGFIELD BOOKS
Five Mile Press (AU) — D: CHRIS LLOYD SALES
FLAME BOOKS LTD
Flamingo — I: HARPERCOLLINS TRADE
Flammarion (Children's only) (FR) — D: ROY YATES BOOKS
Flammarion (FR) — D: EUROPEAN SCHOOLBOOKS
Flammarion (FR) — D: THAMES & HUDSON LTD
FLATMAN LTD, DAVID — R
FLEET BOOKS
Fleetfoot Books — D: GAZELLE BOOK SERVICE
FLEGON PRESS
FLICKS BOOKS
FLIGHT DIRECTORIES
Flint River Press — I: PHILIP WILSON PUB
Flint River (Travel Books) — D: KUPERARD LTD
Floodlight — D: CENTRAL BOOKS
Floppyback Books — I: BLACK FROG PRESS
Flora Zambesiaca — A: NATURAL HIST MUSEUM
Floraprint — I: BURALL FLORAPRINT
Floraprint Books — D: BIBLIOS PUB DIST
FLORIS BOOKS
Flower Remedy Programme — D: ELEMENT BOOKS LTD
Flowers East (Partial) — D: S HENEAGE DIST
FMJ BOOKS
Focal Press — I: BUTTERWORTH-HEINEMAN
Focal Press — D: REED BOOK SERVICES
Focus Christian Ministries — D: EVANGELICAL PRESS
Focus (NT) — D: ART DATA
Focus Publications — D: CORDEE
FOCUS PUBLICATIONS
Fodor's — I: RANDOM HOUSE UK LTD
Fodor's — D: GRANTHAM BOOK SERV
Foghorn Press — A: WORLD LEISURE MKTG
Foghorn Press (Partial) — D: GRANTHAM BOOK SERV
Folding Landscapes — D: CORDEE
FOLENS PUBLISHERS
Folger Shakespeare Library — I: GOLDEN COCKEREL
Folklore Society — D: SHEFFIELD ACD PRESS
Follow Your Finger Books — D: MINIMAX BOOKS LTD
FOLLOW YOUR FINGER BOOKS
Fontana — I: HARPERCOLLINS TRADE
Fontana Press — I: HARPERCOLLINS TRADE
Food & Agriculture Organisation (IT) — D: HMSO BOOKS
Food & Nutrition Press (US) — D: FOOD TRADE PRESS LTD
Food Hygiene Bureau — D: HOTEL & CATERING CO
Food Processors Institute (US) — D: FOOD TRADE PRESS LTD
Food Products Press (US) — D: EDS

FOOD TRADE PRESS LTD
Football Directories — D: LITTLE RED WITCH
Footprint — D: CORDEE
Footslogger — I: TRAIL CREST PUB
Forbes Publications — D: PLYMBRIDGE DIST LTD
FORBES PUBLICATIONS LTD
Ford, Mary — A: REED CONSUMER ILLUS
Ford, Mary — D: REED BOOK SERVICES
Fordham University Press (US) — D: EDS
Foreign Policy Perspectives — I: LIBERTARIAN ALLIANCE
FOREST
FOREST BOOKS
Forest Press — I: OCLC EUROPE
Format Books — D: GRANTHAM BOOK SERV
Format Books — A: WORLD LEISURE MKTG
Forte — D: HOTEL & CATERING CO
Fortean Tomes — No reply 93
Fortress Books — D: CENTRAL BOOKS
FORTRESS BOOKS
Fortress Press (US) — D: SCM PRESS LTD
Fortune Press — I: CHARLES SKILTON LTD
Forum Books — D: DRAGONS WORLD LTD
Foto Olympic (Partial) (GR) — D: OLD VICARAGE PUB
Foucher (FR) — D: EUROPEAN SCHOOLBOOKS
Foulis & Company, G T — I: J H HAYNES & CO LTD
Foulsham — A: PEGASUS PUB SERV
FOULSHAM & COMPANY LTD, W
Foulsham Educational — I: W FOULSHAM & CO LTD
Foundation Books (Partial) (US) — D: NEW BEACON BOOKS LTD
Foundation for Education with Production — D: AFRICAN BOOKS COLL
FOUNDATIONAL BOOK COMPANY
Foundery Press — I: METHODIST PUBLISHING
Fount — I: HARPERCOLLINS RELIG
FOUNTAIN PRESS LTD
Four Courts Press — D: GILL & MACMILLAN LTD
FOUR COURTS PRESS
Four Dragons — I: BLACKWELL SCIENTIFIC
Four Seasons Publishing — D: SHEPHEARD-WALWYN
Four Walls Eight Windows (US) — D: TURNAROUND
Fourmat Publishing — A: ROGER BAYLISS
FOURMAT PUBLISHING
Fourmat Publishing Ltd — D: SPRINGFIELD BOOKS
Fourth Dimension Pub Co Ltd (NG) — D: AFRICAN BOOKS COLL
Fourth Estate — D: TIPTREE BOOK SERV
FOURTH ESTATE
FOWLER & COMPANY LTD, L N
Fowler Wright — GRACEWING/FOWLER WRIGHT
Foxbury Press — I: ST PAUL'S BIBLIO
Foxline Publishing — D: PLATFORM 5 PUB LTD
FOYLE LTD, W & G
Foyle Ltd, W G — D: BOOKPOINT LIMITED
Foyles Art — A: DEREK SEARLE ASS LTD
Foyles Handbooks — I: W & G FOYLE LTD
Fragment (NT) — D: ART DATA
FRAMEWORK PRESS EDUCATIONAL PUBLISHERS LTD
Frameworks — I: INTERVARSITY PRESS
Frances Publishing, Kevin (Partial) — A: P M LLEWELLYN CO
FRANCIS PUBLISHERS, PETER
Frandsen Publishers Ltd (SA) — D: LAKESIDE PUBNS
Frank Books (FR) — D: CALDER PUB LTD
Frank Books (FR) (Travel Books) — D: KUPERARD LTD
Frank Foundation, Anne (NT) — D: KUPERARD LTD
Frankfort Press (Only title - Through the Cities) (IR) — D: TRANSPORT PUB CO LTD
Franklin Press, Charles (US) — D: NORTHCOTE HOUSE PUB
Free Association Books — D: TIPTREE BOOK SERV
Free Association Books — A: TURNAROUND
Free Association Books — A: TURNAROUND
FREE ASSOCIATION BOOKS
Free Life — I: LIBERTARIAN ALLIANCE
Free Presbyterian Publications — D: EVANGELICAL PRESS
Free Press, The — I: MAXWELL MACMILLAN
Free Press, The (US) — D: MARSTON BOOKS SERV
Freedom Press — D: AK DISTRIBUTION
Freedonia Group, The (US) — D: ROSKILL INFO SERVICE
FREEMAN & CO LTD, W H
Freeman, Cooper & Co — D: OXFORD UNI PRESS DIS
Freemantle Arts Centre Press (Partial) (AU) — D: LIVERPOOL UNIV PRESS
Freer, Frederica — A: NEWS PRODUCTIONS
Freestone Press — I: D J COSTELLO PUB LTD
FRENCH LTD, SAMUEL
French Trade, Samuel (US) — D: GAZELLE BOOK SERVICE
Freytag Berndt Ltd (AS) — D: SPRINGFIELD BOOKS

Friedlander (US) — D: COMBINED BOOK SERV
Friedman, Barry (US) — D: ART DATA
FRIENDLY PRESS, THE
FRIENDS OF THE EARTH
Friends of The Earth (Not Leaflets) — D: WORLDLY GOODS
Friends of the Library — I: THE USSHER PRESS
Friends United Press (US) — D: QUAKER HOME SERVICE
FROGELTS PUBLICATIONS LTD
Frommer's Guide — I: SIMON & SCHUSTER LTD
Front Line Publishing — D: NEW WINE MINISTRIES
Front Page Books — No reply 93
Fudge & Co — I: CHARLES SKILTON LTD
Fulcrum (Partial) (US) — D: CORDEE
Fulcrum Publishing — D: GRANTHAM BOOK SERV
Fulcrum Publishing — A: WORLD LEISURE MKTG
Fuller d'Arch Smith — D: MANDRAKE
Fulton Publishers Ltd, David — D: B T BATSFORD LTD
FULTON PUBLISHERS LTD, DAVID
Fundacion Caja De Pensiones (SP) — D: ART DATA
Funfax — I: HENDERSON PUB LTD
Further Education Staff College, The (To End 1990) — I: THE STAFF COLLEGE
Futura — LITTLE BROWN
Futura Publishing Co (US) — D: MCGRAW HILL BOOK CO
FUTURE PUBLISHING
Futures Publications — D: LAVIS MARKETING
FUTURES PUBLICATIONS LTD
Fyfield Books — I: CARCANET PRESS
Gaba Publications (KY) — D: LEISHMAN & TAUSSIG
Gabelli (FR) — D: MCCARTA LTD
Gaia Books — D: AIRLIFT BOOK CO
GAIA BOOKS LTD
Gaia's Guide International — D: AIRLIFT BOOK CO
Gairfish — D: VENNEL PRESS
GAIRM PUBLICATIONS
Gakken (Partial) (JP) — D: P M LLEWELLYN CO
GALACTIC CENTRAL PUBLICATIONS
Gale Odgers Publications — STANLEY THORNES
Gale Research International — D: INT THOMSON PUB SERV
GALE RESEARCH INTERNATIONAL
Galerie Bruno Bischofberger (SZ) — D: S HENEAGE DIST
Galerie Janssen (GE) — D: GMP PUBLISHERS LTD
Gallaudet University Press (US) — D: GAZELLE BOOK SERVICE
Gallery Books Publishing — I: HARDWICK HOUSE
Gallery Childrens Books — I: EAST WEST PUB LTD
GALLERY PRESS
Gallery Press (IR) — A: PASSWORD (BOOKS) LTD
GALLERY PRESS (IR)
GALLIARD PUBLISHERS
Gallimard (FR) — D: EUROPEAN SCHOOLBOOKS
Gallimard-Jeunesse (FR) — D: ROY YATES BOOKS
Galloping Dog Press — D: AK DISTRIBUTION
GALLOPING DOG PRESS
Garborg (US) — D: NOVA DISTRIBUTION
Garden Art Press — D: ANTIQUE COLLECTORS
Gardner Books, Juliet — I: COLLINS & BROWN
GARDNER LTD, WALTER H — R
Gardner Press (US) — D: EDS
GARDNERS BOOKS LTD — W
Garland (US) — D: EUROPEAN PRESS SERV
Garnet — I: GARNET PUB LTD
GARNET PUBLISHING LTD
Garzanti (IT) — D: EUROPEAN SCHOOLBOOKS
Gateway Books — D: ASHGROVE PRESS
GATEWAY BOOKS
Gateways Books & Tapes (US) — D: ELEMENT BOOKS LTD
Gault Millau (FR) — D: EUROPEAN SCHOOLBOOKS
Gautier-Languereau (FR) — D: ROY YATES BOOKS
Gautier-Languereau (FR) — D: EUROPEAN SCHOOLBOOKS
Gay Liberation Front — I: GAY LIBERATION FRONT
GAY LIBERATION FRONT
Gay Men's Press — I: GMP PUBLISHERS LTD
Gay Men's Press — A: TURNAROUND
GAZELLE BOOK SERVICE
Gebr Konig (GE) — D: NEWS PRODUCTIONS
Geddes & Grosset — D: GRANTHAM BOOK SERV
GEE & SON LTD
Geigy Scientific Tables — D: FARRAND PRESS
GEISER PRODUCTIONS
GELOFER PRESS
GEMINI BOOK DISTRIBUTION LTD
GEMINI BOOK DISTRIBUTION LTD — W
Gemini Books — D: MULTILINGUAL MATTERS

General Agreement on Tariffs & Trade (SZ) — D: HMSO BOOKS
General (CA) — D: DUNDURN DISTRIBUTION
GENERAL GRAMOPHONE PUBLICATIONS LTD
Generations Ltd (Partial) — D: S HENEAGE DIST
GENESIS PUBLICATIONS
Genesis Trading Company — D: ELEMENT BOOKS LTD
Geocart Ltd (BG) — D: SPRINGFIELD BOOKS
Geocenter International — A: WORLD LEISURE MKTG
Geocenter Verlagsvertrieb (GE) — D: EUROPEAN SCHOOLBOOKS
Geocentre International — D: GRANTHAM BOOK SERV
GEOGRAPHERS A-Z MAP CO LTD
Geographia — I: HARPERCOLLINS BARTH
GEOGRAPHICAL ASSOCIATION
GEOGRAPHICAL PUBLICATIONS LTD
GEOLOGICAL SOCIETY
Geoprojects — D: ROGER LASCELLES
GEOPROJECTS (UK) LTD
Gerber — D: HAWK BOOKS LTD
Gerber Verlag, Carl — D: BAY FOREIGN BOOKS
GERBIL BOOKS
German Historical Institute London — D: OXFORD UNI PRESS DIS
German Standards Institute (Beuth) (GE) (Eng Lang only) — D: WOODHEAD PUBLISHING
German Welding Society (DVS) (Eng Lang) (GE) — D: WOODHEAD PUBLISHING
Germany Iron & Steel Institute (Stalheisen) (Eng Lang) (GE) — D: WOODHEAD PUBLISHING
Ghana Publishing Corporation (GH) — D: AFRICAN BOOKS COLL
Ghana Universities Press (GH) — D: AFRICAN BOOKS COLL
Gian Press (IN) — I: MOTILAL BOOKS
Gibb Memorial Trust — A: ARIS & PHILLIPS LTD
Gibb Memorial Trust — D: LA HAULE BOOKS LTD
GIBBONS PUBLICATIONS, STANLEY
Gibraltar Books — D: ASHFORD BUCHAN
GIBSON & SONS, ROBERT
Gifford, John — I: W & G FOYLE LTD
Gill & MacMillan (GB only) (IR) — A: OLDCASTLE BOOKS LTD
Gill & MacMillan (IR) — A: TURNAROUND
GILL & MACMILLAN LTD
GINN & CO LTD
Ginn Press — I: SIMON & SCHUSTER INT
GIRL GUIDES ASSOCIATION
Glamorgan County History Trust Ltd — D: UNI OF WALES PRESS
Glasgow Publications, Mary — I: STANLEY THORNES PUB
GLASGOW PUBLICATIONS, MARY
Glasgow Publishing — D: VINE HOUSE DIST
Glazier, Michael (US) — D: COLUMBA BOOK SERVICE
GLB (US) — D: TURNAROUND
GLENNIFER PRESS, THE
GLIDDON BOOKS
Global Press (US) — D: VACATION WORK
Globe Book Company — I: SIMON & SCHUSTER INT
Globe Book Services — MACMILLAN DISTRIBUTION
Globe Pequot Press, The (Partial) (US) — D: CORDEE
Globe Press Books (US) — D: ELEMENT BOOKS LTD
Globe Travel (US) — D: SPRINGFIELD BOOKS
Gloss & Co, R (Partial) (GE) — D: MICELLE PRESS
Gloucester Archaeological Reports — D: OXBOW BOOKS
Gloucester Press — I: THE WATTS GROUP
Glynn, Sean (Irish Orders Direct) (IR) — D: GAZELLE BOOK SERVICE
GMP — D: COMBINED BOOK SERV
GMP PUBLISHERS LTD
GO TEACH PUBLICATIONS
GODFREY MAPS, ALAN
Godine Publisher Inc, David R (US) — D: GAZELLE BOOK SERVICE
GOLD & SON LTD, DAVID
Gold Arrow Publications — I: MERCURY BOOKS
Gold Arrow Publications — D: BIBLIOS PUB DIST
Gold Eagle — I: MILLS & BOON LTD
Golden — I: WESTERN PUB CO INC
Golden Acorn — I: XYLOPRESS LTD
GOLDEN AGE BOOKS
GOLDEN COCKEREL PRESS
Golden Cockerel Publications — D: BIBLIOS PUB DIST
Golden Dawn — I: MANDRAKE
Golden Handshake — I: JAY LANDESMAN
Golden Point (US) — D: EVENLODE BOOK DIST
Golden Press (Partial) (AU) — D: MILLBANK BOOKS LTD
Golden Stone Trust Press (GE) — D: ELEMENT BOOKS LTD
GOLDENEYE MAPS
Goldmann (GE) — D: EUROPEAN SCHOOLBOOKS
Golf Digest (US) — D: GAZELLE BOOK SERVICE
Golf Partners Press (US) — D: GAZELLE BOOK SERVICE
Golgonooza Press — D: ELEMENT BOOKS LTD
Gollancz Ltd, Victor — I: CASSELL PLC

Gomer Press — I: J D LEWIS & SONS LTD
Gomer Press — D: WELSH BOOKS COUNCIL
GOOCH LTD, BRIAN
Good Books (US) — D: ART DATA
Good Books (US) — D: CHARLES LETTS & CO
GOOD NEWS CRUSADE PUBLICATIONS
Good News Trailer — No reply 93
GOODALL PUBLICATIONS LTD
Gooday Publishers — I: GOODAY STUDIOS LTD
GOODAY STUDIOS LTD
GOODLIFFE LTD, NEALE C
Goodyer Associates — D: VINE HOUSE DIST
Gordon & Breach Science Publishers — D: SCI & TECH BOOK SVCE
Gordon, George — D: ANTIQUE COLLECTORS
Gordon Transport Books, Adam — D: BREWIN BOOK DIST
Gorilla Books — A: JOHN WILSON BOOKS
Gorilla (MJM) — D: BOOKPOINT LIMITED
Gorse Publications — D: GAZELLE BOOK SERVICE
Gospel Cards — D: EVANGELICAL PR WALES
Gospel Folio Press — D: CHAPTER TWO
Gospel Light — I: THE OFFICE LONDON
Gospel Standard Trust — D: EVANGELICAL PRESS
Gospel Standard Trust Publications — D: EVANGELICAL PR WALES
Go-Teach Sunday School Teaching Aids — D: EVANGELICAL PRESS
Gothic Image Publications — D: ASHGROVE PRESS
GOTHIC IMAGE PUBLICATIONS
Gousha (US) — D: ROGER LASCELLES
Gouvoussis Ltd, Nick (Partial) (GR) — D: OLD VICARAGE PUB
Gower Medical Publishing (US) — D: PLYMBRIDGE DIST LTD
GOWER MEDICAL PUBLISHING
Gower Press — I: ASHGATE PUB GROUP
GP Publications Ltd (NZ) — D: PACKARD PUB LTD
GPC Books — I: UNI OF WALES PRESS
Grabert Verlag (GE) — D: S HENEAGE DIST
Grace Publications — D: EVANGELICAL PRESS
Grace Publications Inc (US) — D: OPEN BIBLE TRUST
GRACEWING/FOWLER WRIGHT
GRACEWING/FOWLER WRIGHT — W
Grafic Comense (IT) — D: ROGER LASCELLES
Grafocarte (FR) — D: MCCARTA LTD
Grafton Paperbacks — I: HARPERCOLLINS TRADE
Graham & Trotman — D: KLUWER ACADEMIC PUB
GRAHAM & TROTMAN LTD
GRAHAM LTD, W F
GRAHAM-DIXON GALLERY, FRANCIS
Grail — D: GRACEWING/FOWLER
GRANDREAMS LTD
GRANT & CUTLER LTD
GRANT BOOKS
Granta Books — D: PENGUIN BOOKS LTD
Granta Editions — D: VINE HOUSE DIST
GRANTA EDITIONS
Grantham Book Centre — I: MALLORY INT
GRANTHAM BOOK SERVICES
GRANVILLE PUBLISHING
Grapevine Publications (US) — D: COMPUTER STEP LTD
Graphic Books Int — CREATIVE BOOKS INT
Graphis Press (SZ) — D: INTERNOS BOOKS
Graphis (US) — D: EUROPEAN PRESS SERV
Grassfield Press (US) — D: ART DATA
Gray, H W (US) — D: INT MUSIC PUB
Graywolf Press (US) — D: AIRLIFT BOOK CO
Great Impressions (US) — D: GAZELLE BOOK SERVICE
Great Wen Publications — D: BIBLIOS PUB DIST
Green Books — D: CENTRAL BOOKS
GREEN BOOKS
Green Inc, Warren H (US) — D: GAZELLE BOOK SERVICE
Green Library — D: ELEMENT BOOKS LTD
Green Press — D: VINE HOUSE DIST
Green Print — I: MERLIN PRESS
Green Print — D: CENTRAL BOOKS
Green Tiger Press Inc (Partial) (US) — D: RAGGED BEARS LTD
Green, W — D: INT THOMSON PUB SERV
GREEN, W
GREENCROFT BOOKS
Greenhill Books — D: BOOKPOINT LIMITED
GREENHILL BOOKS
Greenpeace (Diaries/Calendars Only) — D: WORLDLY GOODS
GREENWICH EXCHANGE
Greenwood, Henry — No reply 93
Greenwood Press (US) — A: WOODHEAD-FAULKNER
Greenwood Press (US) — D: EDS

Greenwood Publishing (UK ISBN 0 946824) — D: WINDSOR BOOKS INT
Gregg Revivals — I: ASHGATE PUB GROUP
Gremese International — D: BOOKPOINT LIMITED
GRESHAM BOOKS
GREVATT & GREVATT
GREVILLE PRESS
GREY EDITIONS
Grey Seal — D: CENTRAL BOOKS
GREY SEAL PUBLICATIONS LTD
Greystone Books — D: CORDEE
GRIFFIN, BRIAN
Griffith Institute — A: ARIS & PHILLIPS LTD
Griffith Institute — D: LA HAULE BOOKS LTD
Grijalbo (SP) — D: EUROPEAN SCHOOLBOOKS
GRISEWOOD & DEMPSEY
Grisewood & Dempsey Ltd — D: EXEL LOGISTICS
GROCs Candid Guides — I: WILLOWBRIDGE PUB
Grondahl Dreyers AS (NW) — D: GAZELLE BOOK SERVICE
Groninger Museum (NT) — D: ART DATA
Groot, D E (NT) — D: MICELLE PRESS
GROSSOHAUS WEGNER & CO GMBH (GE) — W
GROSVENOR BOOKS
GROTIUS PUBLICATIONS LTD
Groundwood (CA) — D: ROY YATES BOOKS
Group Books — D: ALLIANCE BOOK SERV
Groupement pour les Droits des Minorites (FR) — D: MINORITY RIGHTS GRP
GROVE BOOKS LTD
Grove Press (US) — D: COMBINED BOOK SERV
GROWER BOOKS
Grub Street — D: CHRIS LLOYD SALES
GRUB STREET
Grund (FR) — D: ROY YATES BOOKS
Grund (FR) — D: EUROPEAN SCHOOLBOOKS
Grune Stratton — I: HARCOURT BRACE JOVAN
Grunwald Center for Graphic Arts (US) — A: UNI PRESSES MARKETNG
Gruppo Ensieme Italia (IT) — D: BAHAI PUBLISHING
GT International (US) — D: EVENLODE BOOK DIST
Guardian Books — I: FOURTH ESTATE
GUARDIAN COMMUNICATIONS LTD
Guernica Editions Inc (CA) — D: GAZELLE BOOK SERVICE
GUERNSEY PRESS, THE
Guerra (IT) — D: EUROPEAN SCHOOLBOOKS
Guggenheim Museum Publications (US) — D: RIZZOLI INT PUBNS
Guggenheim Museum (US) — D: ART DATA
Guides Vagnon (FR) — D: IMRAY LAURIE & NORIE
Guild Large Print Books — D: VINE HOUSE DIST
Guild of Master Craftsmen Publications — D: CHRIS LLOYD SALES
GUILD OF MASTER CRAFTSMEN PUBLICATIONS
GUILD OF ONE NAME STUDIES
GUILD OF PASTORAL PSYCHOLOGY
Guilford Publications (US) — D: LAWRENCE ERLBAUM ASS
GUINNESS PUBLISHING
Gulbenkian Foundation, Calouste — D: TURNAROUND
Gulf Publishing Company (US) — D: KOGAN PAGE LTD
Gungarden Books — D: RAGGED BEARS LTD
Gunsmoke Westerns — I: CHIVERS PRESS LTD
Gunter Books — D: VINE HOUSE DIST
Gustavo Gili (SP) — D: ART DATA
Gwasg Aeron — D: WELSH BOOKS COUNCIL
Gwasg Cambria — D: WELSH BOOKS COUNCIL
Gwasg Carreg Gwalch — D: WELSH BOOKS COUNCIL
Gwasg Dwyfor — D: WELSH BOOKS COUNCIL
Gwasg Efengylaidd Cymru — I: EVANGELICAL PR WALES
Gwasg Ffrancon — D: WELSH BOOKS COUNCIL
Gwasg Gee — D: WELSH BOOKS COUNCIL
Gwasg Gomer — D: WELSH BOOKS COUNCIL
GWASG GREGYNOG LTD
Gwasg Gwalia — D: WELSH BOOKS COUNCIL
GWASG GWENFFRWD
Gwasg Gwynedd — D: WELSH BOOKS COUNCIL
Gwasg Pantycelyn — D: WELSH BOOKS COUNCIL
Gwasg Prifysgol Cymru — I: UNI OF WALES PRESS
Gwasg Taf — D: WELSH BOOKS COUNCIL
GWASG Y DREF WEN
Gwasg Y Ffynnon — I: PENINSULA BOOKS
Gwenffrwd — I: GWASG GWENFFRWD
Gwuaghwa Co (Partial) — A: P M LLEWELLYN CO
Gwynedd Archives — D: WELSH BOOKS COUNCIL
Gyosei (JP) — D: HAN SHAN TANG LTD
H I MARKETING
Haag Ltd, Michael — I: IMMEL PUBLISHING LTD
Haags Gemeentemuseum (NT) — D: ART DATA

HAAN ASSOCIATES
Hachette (Children's Only) (FR) — D: ROY YATES BOOKS
Hachette Classiques (FR) — D: EUROPEAN SCHOOLBOOKS
Hachette Edition et Diffusion (FR) — D: EUROPEAN SCHOOLBOOKS
Hachette Jeunesse (FR) — D: EUROPEAN SCHOOLBOOKS
Hachette (Partial) (FR) — D: ACCENT EDUCATIONAL
Hacker Art Books Inc (US) — D: ART BOOK DIST CO
Hackett Publishing Co Inc (US) — D: GAZELLE BOOK SERVICE
HADDOCK LTD, PETER
Hakluyt Society — D: TURPIN DISTRIBUTION
HAKLUYT SOCIETY
Halban, Peter — I: ORION PUBLISHING
Halban, Peter Ltd — D: LITTLEHAMPTON BK SVC
Halban, Peter Ltd (Jewish Interest) — D: KUPERARD LTD
HALBAN PUBLISHERS, PETER
Hale & Iremonger (Partial) (AU) — D: TURNAROUND
HALE LTD, ROBERT
Half Halt Press Inc (US) — D: KENILWORTH PRESS LTD
HALFSHIRE BOOKS
HALI PUBLICATIONS
Halil, Lola — I: PROSPERITY PUB
HALL & SONS LTD, J H
HALL LTD, C E — R
Hallewell Publishing, John — D: ROADMASTER PUB
Hall-Twayne, G K — I: MAXWELL MACMILLAN
Hall-Twayne, G K (US) — D: MARSTON BOOKS SERV
Hallwalls (US) — D: CENTRAL BOOKS
Ham Publishing — D: VINE HOUSE DIST
HAMBLEDON PRESS
Hamilton Childrens, Hamish — I: PENGUIN BOOKS LTD
Hamilton, Hamish — I: PENGUIN BOOKS LTD
HAMILTON HOUSE PUBLISHING
Hamilton Press — No reply 92/93
Hamlyn — I: REED CONSUMER ILLUS
Hamlyn — D: REED BOOK SERVICES
Hamlyn Children's Books — I: REED CONSUMER TRADE
HAMMICK'S MAIL ORDER SERVICE
Hammick's Wholesale — TOTAL BOOK DISTRIBUTION
Hampshire County Council - Recreation Dept — D: COUNTRYSIDE BOOKS
HAN SHAN TANG LTD
HANBURY PLAYS
Handbooks for Teachers — I: INST OF EDUCATION
Handsel Press — I: SCOTTISH ACAD PRESS
Hanes Gweithwyr Cymru — I: GWASG GWENFFRWD
Hanover Gallery — D: ART DATA
Hanser Verlag (GE) — D: VCH PUB (UK) LTD
HANSIB — D: TURNAROUND
HANSIB PUBLISHING
Hanuman (US) — D: TURNAROUND
Harare Publishing House (ZB) — D: LEISHMAN & TAUSSIG
Harbinger House Inc (US) — D: GAZELLE BOOK SERVICE
Harbinger International — D: BIBLIOS PUB DIST
Harbour Publishing (CA) — D: DUNDURN DISTRIBUTION
HARCOURT BRACE JOVANOVICH
HARDWICK HOUSE
Hardy, Patrick — I: LUTTERWORTH PRESS
Hardy Society, Thomas — A: PATTEN PRESS
Hardy Society, Thomas — No reply 93
Harenberg Kommunikation (GE) — D: EUROPEAN SCHOOLBOOKS
Harewood House — D: LAVIS MARKETING
Haringey Multicultural Resource — D: ROY YATES BOOKS
Harlan Davidson (US) — D: EDS
Harlem River Press (US) — D: AIRLIFT BOOK CO
Harlequin Books Ltd — D: BOOKPOINT LIMITED
HARLEY BOOKS
HARLEY PRESS, THE
Harmony — D: TURNAROUND
Harmony Books — D: COMBINED BOOK SERV
Harmony Guides — D: HODDER & STOUGHTON
Harmony House (US) — D: AIRLIFE PUBLISHING
Harmsworth Ltd — D: BMS LTD
HARMSWORTH PUBLISHING CO, THOMAS
HARNSER PRESS
HarperBusiness — I: HARPERCOLLINS INTER
HarperCollege — I: HARPERCOLLINS HARCOL
HarperCollins (Bibles & Testaments) — D: BIBLE SOCIETY
HARPERCOLLINS DISTRIBUTION
HarperCollins Publishers — I: HARPERCOLLINS GENREF
HarperCollins Publishers — D: HARPERCOLLINS DIST
HARPERCOLLINS PUBLISHERS
HARPERCOLLINS PUBLISHERS — A
HarperCollins Religious — I: HARPERCOLLINS RELIG

HarperCollins Trade USA — I: HARPERCOLLINS INTER
HarperPerennial — I: HARPERCOLLINS INTER
HarperReference — I: HARPERCOLLINS INTER
HarperSanFrancisco — I: HARPERCOLLINS INTER
HarperSanFrancisco — I: HARPERCOLLINS RELIG
HarperSanFrancisco — I: HARPERCOLLINS THORS
HarperSanFrancisco Ltd (Partial) (US) — D: T & T CLARK LTD
Harpswell Press, The (Partial) (US) — D: CORDEE
Harrap — D: TIPTREE BOOK SERV
Harrap Books — I: W & R CHAMBERS LTD
Harrington Park Press — D: TURNAROUND
Hart Press, The Thomas — I: FUTURES PUB LTD
Harvard Business School Press (US) — D: MCGRAW HILL BOOK CO
Harvard Common Press (US) — D: GAZELLE BOOK SERVICE
Harvard University Press — D: JOHN WILEY & SONS
HARVARD UNIVERSITY PRESS
Harvest House (US) — D: NOVA DISTRIBUTION
Harvester Wheatsheaf — I: SIMON & SCHUSTER INT
Harvester Wheatsheaf — D: INT BOOK DIST
Harvestime — D: SEND THE LIGHT
HARVESTIME PUBLISHING
HARVEY MAP SERVICES
Harveys — I: HARVEY MAP SERVICES
HARVEYS BOOKS LTD
HARVEYS BOOKS LTD — R
Harvill — I: HARPERCOLLINS TRADE
Harwel — I: WILLIAMS & WILKINS
Harwood Academic Publishers — D: SCI & TECH BOOK SVCE
Hassle Free Press — I: KNOCKABOUT COMICS
Hatier (FR) — D: EUROPEAN SCHOOLBOOKS
Hatje, Gerd (GE) — D: ART DATA
Haug Verlag, Karl F (Eng Lang Books only) (GE) — D: C W DANIEL CO LTD
HAUNTED LIBRARY
Haupt, Paul (SZ) — D: NORTHCOTE HOUSE PUB
HAWGOOD, DAVID
HAWK BOOKS LTD
Hawker Publications — D: BOOKPOINT LIMITED
HAWKER PUBLICATIONS
Hawksmere Ltd — D: BOOKPOINT LIMITED
Haworth Medical (US) — D: EDS
Haworth Press (US) — D: EDS
Hawthorn Midi Cookery Collection — I: AUSTRALIAN CON PRESS
Hawthorn Mini Series — I: AUSTRALIAN CON PRESS
HAWTHORN PRESS
HAWTHORNS PUBLICATIONS LTD
Hay House Inc (US) — D: AIRLIFT BOOK CO
Hayden Books — I: SIMON & SCHUSTER INT
Hayit Publishing GB — D: BOOKPOINT LIMITED
Haymarket — I: SIMON & SCHUSTER INT
HAYNES & COMPANY LTD, J H
HAYWARD PROMOTIONS — W
Hazan Editions (FR) — D: ART DATA
Hazar Publishing — A: DEREK SEARLE ASS LTD
HAZAR PUBLISHING
Hazelden (US) — D: AIRLIFT BOOK CO
Hazelton — A: REED CONSUMER ILLUS
Hazleton — D: REED BOOK SERVICES
Hazleton Publishing — D: BOOKPOINT LIMITED
Headland Publications — D: PASSWORD (BOOKS) LTD
HEADLAND PUBLICATIONS
HEADLEY BROTHERS LTD
Headline Book Publishing PLC — D: BOOKPOINT LIMITED
HEADLINE BOOK PUBLISHING
Headline Feature — I: HEADLINE BOOK PUB
Headlions — I: PACKARD PUB LTD
HEADQUARTERS PUBLISHING COMPANY
HEADSTART HISTORY
Headstock Publications — D: PLATFORM 5 PUB LTD
Headway — I: HODDER & STOUGHTON
Headway Home & Law — D: COMBINED BOOK SERV
Healing Arts Press (US) — D: AIRLIFT BOOK CO
Healing Tao Books (US) — D: AIRLIFT BOOK CO
Healing Workshops Press — D: AIRLIFT BOOK CO
Health Communications (US) — D: AIRLIFT BOOK CO
HEALTH EDUCATION AUTHORITY
Health Press (US) — D: GAZELLE BOOK SERVICE
Health Professions Press (US) — D: KOGAN PAGE LTD
HEALTH PROMOTION AUTHORITY FOR WALES
Health Service Press — I: L N FOWLER & CO LTD
Healthbooks — I: CHILTON DESIGNS
Hearst Books International (US) — D: INTERNOS BOOKS
Hearst Ltd (US) — D: SPRINGFIELD BOOKS

Hearst (US) — D: EUROPEAN PRESS SERV
HEART OF ALBION PRESS
Heart of America Press (US) — D: LISTER ART BOOKS
Heart Talk/Tampa Tracing (US) — D: GAZELLE BOOK SERVICE
Heath & Co, D & C (US) — D: PLYMBRIDGE DIST LTD
Heath, D C (US) — D: W C BROWN PUBLISHING
HEATHCOTE BOOKS — W
HEBDON ROYD PUBLICATIONS
Heian International (US) — A: PREMIER BOOK MKTNG
Heibonsha (JP) — D: ART DATA
Heineman, James H (US) — D: DAWSON UK LTD
HEINEMANN CHILDRENS REFERENCE
Heinemann (CM) — A: EVANS BROTHERS LTD
Heinemann Drama Inc (US) — D: CENTRAL BOOKS
HEINEMANN EDUCATIONAL
Heinemann Educational Books Ltd (NG) — D: AFRICAN BOOKS COLL
Heinemann Inc (Partial) (US) — D: ABSOLUTE PRESS
Heinemann Kenya Ltd (KY) — D: AFRICAN BOOKS COLL
Heinemann Professional — I: BUTTERWORTH-HEINEMAN
Heinemann Professional — D: REED BOOK SERVICES
Heinemann, William — I: REED CONSUMER TRADE
Heinemann, William — D: REED BOOK SERVICES
Heinemann Young Books — I: REED CONSUMER TRADE
Heinle & Heinle (US) — D: THOMAS NELSON & SONS
Helicon — I: EDUC CO OF IRELAND
Helicon Press — TOBIN MUSIC
Helicon Publishing — D: TIPTREE BOOK SERV
Helm, Christopher — I: A & C BLACK LTD
Helm, Christopher (Ireland only) — A: BLACKSTAFF PRESS LTD
Helm, Christopher (Natural History Series) — I: HARCOURT BRACE JOVAN
HELM INFORMATION LTD
Helmers & Howard (Partial) (US) — D: GROSVENOR BOOKS
Helmsman — I: THE CROWOOD PRESS
Hemisphere Publishing Corporation — I: TAYLOR & FRANCIS LTD
HENDERSON PUBLISHING LTD
HENDON PUBLISHING COMPANY LTD
Hendrickson Publishers (US) — D: EVANGELICAL PRESS
HENEAGE DISTRIBUTION, SHAUNAGH
Heneage, Thomas — I: S HENEAGE DIST
Henle, G — D: NOVELLO & CO LTD
HENRY PUBLICATIONS LTD, IAN
Henston Ltd — D: GAZELLE BOOK SERVICE
HERALDRY TODAY
HERB SOCIETY, THE
Herbert Press (Ireland only) — A: BLACKSTAFF PRESS LTD
Herbert Press Ltd, The — D: A & C BLACK LTD
HERBERT PRESS, THE
Here's Life — D: SCRIPTURE PRESS
Heretic Books — D: GMP PUBLISHERS LTD
HERIOT & CO LTD, ALEXANDER
Heritage House — D: ROGER LASCELLES
HERITAGE PRESS
Hermetician Press (US) — D: EVENLODE BOOK DIST
Hermetika (GE) — D: ELEMENT BOOKS LTD
Hermitage (RU) — D: NEWS PRODUCTIONS
Hern Books, Nick — D: TIPTREE BOOK SERV
Hern, Nick — I: RANDOM HOUSE UK LTD
Hero Books (US) — D: GREENHILL BOOKS
Herzl Press — I: GOLDEN COCKEREL
Hestair Hope — HOPE EDUCATION
Heterodox — D: VINE HOUSE DIST
HETERODOX PUBLISHERS
Heyne (GE) — D: EUROPEAN SCHOOLBOOKS
HFL — I: BUTTERWORTH & CO LTD
HFL — D: BUTTERWORTH & CO LTD
HGM PUBLICATIONS
HI Marketing — D: TIPTREE BOOK SERV
Hidden Places Series — I: M & M PUBLISHING LTD
High Adventure — I: HARVESTIME PUB LTD
High Noon — I: ANN ARBOR PUBLISHERS
High Noon Books (US) — D: ANN ARBOR PUBLISHERS
High Pines Press — D: ROGER LASCELLES
Higher Consciousness (US) — D: EVENLODE BOOK DIST
Highland Books — I: INTER PUB SERVICE
Highland Books — D: SEND THE LIGHT
Hildebrand (GE) — D: SPRINGFIELD BOOKS
Hilger, Adam — I: IOP PUBLISHING LTD
HILLER AIRGUNS
HILLS WHOLESALE — W
Hillside Publications — D: CORDEE
Hillside Publishing — I: NAT CHRIST EDUC COUN
HILMARTON MANOR PRESS

Himalayan Club, The (IN) — D: CORDEE
Himalayan Publishers (US) — D: AIRLIFT BOOK CO
Hind Pocket Books Delhi (IN) — D: BOOKS FROM INDIA
Hinde Productions, Gerald (SA) — D: LAKESIDE PUBNS
Hingston Associates — A: P M LLEWELLYN CO
Hippo — I: SCHOLASTIC PUB LTD
Hippocrene Books Inc (US) — D: GAZELLE BOOK SERVICE
HIPPOPOTAMUS PRESS
Hirmer (GE) — D: S HENEAGE DIST
Hirshberg Publishing, Ron (US) — D: GAZELLE BOOK SERVICE
Hisarlik Press — D: VINE HOUSE DIST
HISTORICAL ASSOCIATION
Historical Publications Ltd — D: PHILLIMORE & CO LTD
HISTORICAL PUBLICATIONS LTD
History of Boston Project — I: RICHARD KAY PUB
History Today Books — I: COLLINS & BROWN
HLT PUBLICATIONS
HMSO BOOKS
HMSO (Nautical) — D: IMRAY LAURIE & NORIE
Hobby House Press (US) — D: GAZELLE BOOK SERVICE
Hobsons Publishing — D: BIBLIOS PUB DIST
HOBSONS PUBLISHING
HODDER & STOUGHTON
Hodder & Stoughton (Bibles & Testaments) — D: BIBLE SOCIETY
HODGE PUBLISHERS, ALISON
Hodgson Wholesale — No reply 93
Hoepli (IT) — D: EUROPEAN SCHOOLBOOKS
HOGAR DEL LIBRO SA (SP) — W
Hogarth Press — D: TIPTREE BOOK SERV
Hogarth Press, The — I: RANDOM HOUSE UK LTD
Hogrefe & Huber (CA) — A: MOMENTA PUB CO LTD
Hoikusha (JP) — A: PREMIER BOOK MKTNG
Hokuseido Press (JP) — A: PREMIER BOOK MKTNG
HOLLAND ENTERPRISES — R
Holland Press — I: NEW HOLLAND PUB LTD
HOLLIS DIRECTORIES
Holloway, Clive — D: AIRLIFE PUBLISHING
Holman (Bibles & Testaments) (US) — D: BIBLE SOCIETY
Holmes & Meier Publishers — I: BOOK REP & DIST LTD
Holt & Co Inc, Henry (US) — D: GAZELLE BOOK SERVICE
Holt, Reinhart & Winston — I: HARCOURT BRACE JOVAN
Holyoake Books — I: CO-OPERATIVE UNION
HOME & SCHOOL COUNCIL
Home Health Education Service — D: STANBOROUGH PRESS
HOME OFFICE
Home Planners Inc — D: FOUNTAIN PRESS LTD
Homes & Meier Inc (US) — D: BOOK REP & DIST LTD
Homespun (US) — D: INT MUSIC PUB
Homoeopathic Book Service — I: BOOKS FROM INDIA
Honey Publications — No reply 93
Honeyglen Publishing — D: BIBLIOS PUB DIST
HONEYGLEN PUBLISHING LTD
Honno (Export) — D: DALENNAU
HONNO LTD
Hooligan Press — D: AK DISTRIBUTION
Hoover Institute (US) — D: CLIO PRESS LTD
HOPE EDUCATION LTD
HOPE IN ACTION
Hopefulmonster (IT) — D: S HENEAGE DIST
Hopkins University Press, Johns (US) — D: PLYMBRIDGE DIST LTD
Hopkins University Press, Johns (US) — A: UNI PRESSES MARKETNG
Horizon Books — D: GRANTHAM BOOK SERV
Horizon Books — A: WORLD LEISURE MKTG
Horizon Books Ltd — I: NORTHCOTE HOUSE PUB
Horizon Publishers & Distributors Inc (US) — D: GAZELLE BOOK SERVICE
Horn Book of Boston (US) — A: IMAGES
Horne, Jonathan — D: ANTIQUE COLLECTORS
HORTON PUBLISHING LTD
Hospital Research & Education Trust — I: SIMON & SCHUSTER INT
Hostaction Ltd — D: BOOKPOINT LIMITED
HOTEL & CATERING TRAINING CO
Houghton Mifflin (Partial) (US) — D: CASSELL PLC — ACADEMIC FROM LITTLEHAMPTON
Housetop Ltd — D: MCCRIMMON PUBLISHING
Housmans — D: AK DISTRIBUTION
HOUSMANS BOOKSHOP
Houston Fine Art Press (US) — D: ART DATA
Hove Collectors Books — D: FOUNTAIN PRESS LTD
Hove Foto Books — D: FOUNTAIN PRESS LTD
Hove Foto Books — D: NEWPRO UK LTD
Hove-Fountain Books — I: FOUNTAIN PRESS LTD
How to Books — D: PLYMBRIDGE DIST LTD
HOW TO BOOKS LTD

How to Books (Partial) — A: P M LLEWELLYN CO
Howell Book House — I: MAXWELL MACMILLAN
Howell (US) — D: MARSTON BOOKS SERV
Howkins, Christopher — D: COUNTRYSIDE BOOKS
Hoxton Books — GERALD DUCKWORTH
HP Books — D: FOUNTAIN PRESS LTD
HRD Press (US) — D: KOGAN PAGE LTD
HT (BOOK DISTRIBUTION) LTD
Hudson Hills Press (US) — D: S HENEAGE DIST
Hudson, Norman — D: BIBLIOS PUB DIST
Hueber, Max (GE) — D: EUROPEAN SCHOOLBOOKS
Hughes a'i Fab — D: WELSH BOOKS COUNCIL
HUGHES & COLEMAN LTD
HUGHES BOOK SERVICES — W
Hughes Ltd, A & Z — I: GWASG GWENFFRWD
HUGO'S LANGUAGE BOOKS LTD
Human Horizon — I: SOUVENIR PRESS LTD
HUMAN KINETICS PUBLISHERS
Human Sciences Press (US) — D: EDS
Humana Press (US) — A: JOHN WILEY & SONS
Humanics New Age (US) — D: AIRLIFT BOOK CO
Humanities Press International (US) — D: EDS
HUME INSTITUTE, DAVID
HUNKYDORY DESIGNS — W
Hunt & Thorpe — D: SEND THE LIGHT
Hunter House Inc (US) — D: GAZELLE BOOK SERVICE
Huntington House (US) — D: NOVA DISTRIBUTION
Huntington Library (US) — D: DAWSON UK LTD
Hurst & Co — D: CENTRAL BOOKS
HURST & CO PUBLISHERS LTD, C
HURTWOOD PRESS LTD
Hutchinson — I: RANDOM HOUSE UK LTD
Hutchinson — D: TIPTREE BOOK SERV
Hutchinson Children's Books — I: RANDOM HOUSE UK LTD
Hutchinson Children's Books — D: TIPTREE BOOK SERV
HUTTON PRESS LTD
HYDATUM
Hyddgen — I: GWASG GWENFFRWD
Hyde Park Group — A: WORLD LEISURE MKTG
Hyde Park Publishing — D: GRANTHAM BOOK SERV
Hyden House — D: WORLDLY GOODS
HYDEN HOUSE LTD
Hyland House Publishers Pty (AU) — D: GAZELLE BOOK SERVICE
Hymns Ancient & Modern — A: SPCK
HYMNS ANCIENT & MODERN
Hypergraphics (CA) — D: COMPUTER STEP LTD
Hyperion (Free Market & Europe) — D: LITTLE BROWN & CO
Hyphen Press — D: CENTRAL BOOKS
HYPHEN PRESS
I Libri del Bargello (IT) — D: GAZELLE BOOK SERVICE
IANMEAD LTD
Ibadan University Press (NG) — D: AFRICAN BOOKS COLL
IBC Financial Publishing — I: IBC PUBLISHING LTD
IBC PUBLISHING
IC Guides — D: ROGER LASCELLES
IC Publications Ltd — D: LEISHMAN & TAUSSIG
IC PUBLICATIONS LTD
ICA PUBLISHING
ICC Recordings — A: NOVA DISTRIBUTION
ICC UNITED KINGDOM
Iceland Information Centre — D: CORDEE
ICOM — D: TURNAROUND
Icon Books Ltd — D: BOOKPOINT LIMITED
Icrisat (IN) — D: INTERMEDIATE TEC PUB
ICS Books Inc (US) — D: CORDEE
ICSA Publishing — A: WOODHEAD-FAULKNER
ICSU (FR) — D: PORTLAND PRESS LTD
Idea Books Edizioni (IT) — D: ART DATA
Idea Group Publishing (US) — D: EDS
IDEAS UNLIMITED
IDG Books Worldwide (US) — D: COMPUTER BOOKSHOPS
IDRC (CA) — D: INTERMEDIATE TEC PUB
Idylwild Books (US) — D: EVENLODE BOOK DIST
IEEE Computer Society (US) — D: ELECTRONICA BOOKS
IES (US) — A: AMERICAN TECH PUB
IFI/Plenum — I: PLENUM PUBLISHING CO
IFS Ltd — D: MERCURY BOOKS
IFS LTD
IFS Publishing — I: IFS LTD
Igaku Shoin — I: WILLIAMS & WILKINS
IGN Blue & Red Series — A: WORLD LEISURE MKTG
IGN Blue Series — D: GRANTHAM BOOK SERV

IGN Blue Series (FR) — A: MCCARTA LTD
Ignatius Press (US) — D: VERITAS PUBLICATIONS
IHRDC — I: SIMON & SCHUSTER INT
III Publishing — D: COUNTER PRODUCTIONS
III Publishing (US) — D: AK DISTRIBUTION
Ikeda & Locker (Partial) — D: S HENEAGE DIST
Iliffe — I: BUTTERWORTH-HEINEMAN
Iliffe — D: REED BOOK SERVICES
Illuminet Press — D: COUNTER PRODUCTIONS
Imagenes Press — I: SIMON & SCHUSTER INT
IMAGES
IMAGES DISTRIBUTION
Images Press — D: NEWPRO UK LTD
Images Publishing (AU) — D: BIBLIOS PUB DIST
Imam Sahe-Bu-Zaman Association (US) — D: ALIF INTERNATIONAL
Imamia Center Inc (US) — D: ALIF INTERNATIONAL
IMG Publishing (US) — D: GAZELLE BOOK SERVICE
Immel Publishing — D: BIBLIOS PUB DIST
IMMEL PUBLISHING LTD
IMP — D: D SERVICES
IMP Music Publications — I: INT MUSIC PUB
Impact Books — A: VERULAM PUB LTD
Impact Books — D: NEW WINE MINISTRIES
IMPACT BOOKS
Impact Publications (US) — D: GAZELLE BOOK SERVICE
Impact Publishers (US) — D: AIRLIFT BOOK CO
Impala Books — D: GAZELLE BOOK SERVICE
Imperial War Museum — D: PEN & SWORD BOOKS
Imray — D: CORDEE
IMRAY LAURIE NORIE & WILSON
In Camera — I: QUOTES LTD
IN PRINT PUBLISHING
In Print Publishing Ltd — D: BAILEY DIST LTD
Inaugural & Special Lectures — I: INST OF EDUCATION
Inbal Travel Information (IS) (Travel Books) — D: KUPERARD LTD
Incorporated Council of Law Reporting for Ireland, The — D: BUTTERWORTH IRELAND
Indelible Inc — D: COUNTER PRODUCTIONS
Indelible Inc — D: AK DISTRIBUTION
Index Books — I: INDEXREACH LTD
Index Books — D: BOOKMARKS
Index on Censorship — I: WRITERS & SCHOLARS
INDEXREACH LTD
Indiana University Press (US) — D: OPEN UNIV PRESS
Indiana University Press (US) — A: TREVOR BROWN ASSOC
Indispensable (FR) — D: ROGER LASCELLES
Industrial Press Inc (US) — D: GAZELLE BOOK SERVICE
INDUSTRIAL PRODUCT EVALUATION
Industrial Society — A: JOHN WILSON BOOKS
Industrial Society Press (Backlist) — I: NICHOLAS BREALEY PUB
INDUSTRIAL SOCIETY PRESS
Ines May - Publicity (KY) — D: LEISHMAN & TAUSSIG
Information Gatekeepers Inc (US) — D: GAZELLE BOOK SERVICE
Infotech — I: TECHNICAL INFO SVCS
Ingham Associates Ltd, Jennie — D: ROY YATES BOOKS
Ingham Yates — I: ROY YATES BOOKS
Ingram International Inc — D: ROUNDHOUSE PUB LTD
Ingram International Inc (US) — D: ROUNDHOUSE PUB LTD
INGRAM INTERNATIONAL INC (US) — W
Inner Circle Books — I: PIATKUS BOOKS
Inner City Books (CA) — D: AIRLIFT BOOK CO
Inner Traditions (US) — D: REAL BOOKS
Inprint Publishing — D: ROGER LASCELLES
INPUT-OUTPUT PUBLISHING COMPANY
Inroads (US) — D: CORDEE
Insight Books — I: PLENUM PUBLISHING CO
Insight Guides — D: GRANTHAM BOOK SERV
Insight Guides — A: WORLD LEISURE MKTG
INSPEC — I: INST OF ELEC ENGINE
Institut De Soudure (FR) (Eng Lang only) — D: WOODHEAD PUBLISHING
Institut Geographiqe National (FR) — D: MCCARTA LTD
Institut Geographique National (Partial) (FR) — D: CORDEE
Institute for African Alternatives — D: CENTRAL BOOKS
Institute for Archaeo-Metallurgical Studies — D: THAMES & HUDSON LTD
Institute for Cultural Research — D: OCTAGON PRESS
Institute for International Economics — D: LONGMAN GROUP UK LTD
Institute for Public Policy Research — D: CENTRAL BOOKS
INSTITUTE FOR THE STUDY OF DRUG DEPENDENCE
INSTITUTE OF ADMINISTRATIVE MANAGEMENT
INSTITUTE OF BIOLOGY
Institute of Business Planning — I: SIMON & SCHUSTER INT
INSTITUTE OF CHARTERED ACCOUNTANTS OF SCOTLAND
Institute of Chartered Accountants — ACCOUNTANCY BOOKS

Institute of Chemical Engineers — A: MOMENTA PUB CO LTD
Institute of Contemporary Art — D: ART DATA
INSTITUTE OF DEVELOPMENT STUDIES
INSTITUTE OF ECONOMIC AFFAIRS
INSTITUTE OF EDUCATION - HULL
INSTITUTE OF EDUCATION - LONDON
Institute of Education, University of London — D: KOGAN PAGE LTD
Institute of Electrical & Electronic Engineers (US) — D: ELECTRONICA BOOKS
INSTITUTE OF EMPLOYMENT RIGHTS
Institute of Energy — D: ENERGY PUBLICATIONS
Institute of Ethiopian Studies (ET) — D: ELM PUBLICATIONS
INSTITUTE OF HEALTH SERVICES MANAGEMENT
Institute of Historical Research — D: DAWSON UK LTD
Institute of Historical Research — D: OXFORD UNI PRESS DIS
Institute of Management Foundation — D: BURSTON DIST SERV
INSTITUTE OF MANAGEMENT FOUNDATION
INSTITUTE OF MANPOWER STUDIES
INSTITUTE OF MATERIALS
Institute of Personnel Management — D: PLYMBRIDGE DIST LTD
INSTITUTE OF PERSONNEL MANAGEMENT
Institute of Physics Publishing — D: IOP PUBLISHING LTD
Institute of Psychiatry (Maudsley Monographs only) — D: OXFORD UNI PRESS DIS
Institute of Psychophysical Research — D: ELEMENT BOOKS LTD
Institute of Race Relations — D: TURNAROUND
INSTITUTE OF RACE RELATIONS
Institute of Real Estate Management (Partial) (US)   D: RICS BOOKS
Institute of Social & Economic Research (CA) — D: DUNDURN DISTRIBUTION
Institute of Terrestrial Ecology (Partial list) — D: HMSO BOOKS
INSTITUTE OF TRADING STANDARDS ADMINISTRATION
Institution of Chemical Engineers, The — D: TAYLOR & FRANCIS LTD
INSTITUTION OF ELECTRICAL ENGINEERS
INSTITUTION OF MINING & METALLURGY
INSURANCE INSTITUTE OF LONDON
Insurance Learners — I: WITHERBY & CO LTD
Int Council Bird Preservation — No reply 93
Integral Yoga Publications (US) — D: ELEMENT BOOKS LTD
Integrated Publishing Services — D: BREWIN BOOK DIST
Intellect — D: LAVIS MARKETING
INTELLECT
Intellect Books — I: INTELLECT
Inter Hemispheric (US) — D: LATIN AMERICA BUREAU
INTER PUBLISHING SERVICE
Interbook International Holland (Partial) (NT) — D: HILMARTON MANOR
INTERCEPT LTD
Interchange Books — Ceased publishing 92
Interfisc Publishing — D: SHEED & WARD LTD
Interlink Inc (US) — D: EVENLODE BOOK DIST
INTERLIST
Intermediate Technology Development Group — D: WORLDLY GOODS
INTERMEDIATE TECHNOLOGY PUBLICATIONS
International Academic Pub (CH) — D: WILLIAM SNYDER PUB
International African Institute — D: OXFORD UNI PRESS DIS
International Agency for Research on Cancer Scientific Pub — D: OXFORD UNI PRESS DIS
International Atomic Energy Agency (AS) — D: HMSO BOOKS
INTERNATIONAL BEE RESEARCH ASSOCIATION
International Bible Reading Association (IBRA) — I: NAT CHRIST EDUC COUN
International Biographical Centre — I: MELROSE PRESS LTD
International Book Distributors (IN) — D: STOBART DAVIES LTD
INTERNATIONAL BOOK DISTRIBUTORS
International Business Press (US) — D: EDS
INTERNATIONAL CARGO HANDLING CO-ORDINATION ASSOCIATION
International Centre for Public Enterprise (ICPE) (YG) — D: LAVIS MARKETING
International Chamber of Shipping — D: WITHERBY & CO LTD
International Chamber of Commerce — I: ICC UNITED KINGDOM
International Editions — I: MAXWELL MACMILLAN
International Exhibitions Foundations — I: SIMON & SCHUSTER INT
International Food Information Service — D: FOOD TRADE PRESS LTD
International Foundation for Educ with Production (BO) — D: LEISHMAN & TAUSSIG
International General (NT) — D: CENTRAL BOOKS
International Graphics (GE) — D: NEWS PRODUCTIONS
International Inform Assoc Inc (US) — D: GAZELLE BOOK SERVICE
International Institute of Welding (Partial) — D: WOODHEAD PUBLISHING
International Institute for Strategic Studies — I: BRASSEY'S (UK) LTD
International Institute for Strategic Studies — D: MARSTON BOOKS SERV
International Jewelry Publications (US) — D: GAZELLE BOOK SERVICE
INTERNATIONAL LABOUR OFFICE
International Log Book (NW) — D: VINE HOUSE DIST
International Marine (US) — D: AIRLIFE PUBLISHING
International Monetary Fund (US) — D: HMSO BOOKS
International Monographs in Prehistory (US) — D: OXBOW BOOKS
INTERNATIONAL MUSIC PUBLICATIONS
INTERNATIONAL NGO TRAINING & RESEARCH CENTRE

International Orienteering Federation (SW) — A: HARVEY MAP SERVICES
INTERNATIONAL PLANNED PARENTHOOD FEDERATION
International Publishers (US) — D: CENTRAL BOOKS
International Socialism Journal — I: BOOKMARKS
International Society for Individual Liberty — D: LIBERTARIAN ALLIANCE
International Textbook Company — I: BLACKIE ACAD & PROF
International Theatre Bookshop (NT) — D: GAZELLE BOOK SERVICE
INTERNATIONAL THOMSON PUBLISHING SERVICES
International Youth Hostels — D: GRANTHAM BOOK SERV
International Youth Hostels — A: WORLD LEISURE MKTG
INTERNOS BOOKS
Intertec Publishing Corp (Part) (US) — D: BARNACLE MARINE LTD
Intertek — D: COUNTER PRODUCTIONS
INTERVARSITY PRESS
Interweave Press Inc (US) — D: GAZELLE BOOK SERVICE
Interworld Publications — D: GAZELLE BOOK SERVICE
INTERWORLD PUBLICATIONS
INTRAC — I: INTRAC
In-Tune Books (AU) — D: ASHGROVE PRESS
INVADER LTD
Invincible — I: HARPERCOLLINS BARTH
I/O PRESS
IOM — I: INST OF MATERIALS
Ion Press — D: BOOKPOINT LIMITED
IOP PUBLISHING LTD
IOS Press (NT) — D: LAVIS MARKETING
Iowa University Press (US) — D: HARCOURT BRACE JOVAN
IPA (Partial) (IR) — D: EUROMONITOR PLC
IPC Magazines Ltd (Nautical only) — D: BARNACLE MARINE LTD
IPC (Shoot! Annual) — A: JOHN WILSON BOOKS
IPC/Marketforce — D: BOOKPOINT LIMITED
Ipelegeng Publishers (BO) — D: LEISHMAN & TAUSSIG
Iris Publications (US) — D: GAZELLE BOOK SERVICE
Irish Academic Press — D: GILL & MACMILLAN LTD
IRISH ACADEMIC PRESS
Irish Book Sales — POOLBEG PRESS
Irish Cruising Club (IR) — D: IMRAY LAURIE & NORIE
Irish Heritage Series — I: EASON & SON LTD
IRL Press at Oxford University Press — I: OXFORD UNIV PRESS
Iron Press — D: PASSWORD (BOOKS) LTD
IRON PRESS
Ironbark — I: RONALDSON PUB
IRWELL PRESS
Irwin, Richard (US) — A: ADDISON-WESLEY PUB
Irwin, Richard (US) — D: SOUTHPORT BOOK DIST
ISA (US) — A: AMERICAN TECH PUB
ISHI (US) — D: CLIO PRESS LTD
ISHI (US) — D: CLIO PRESS LTD
Ishiyaku EuroAmerica Inc (US) — D: GAZELLE BOOK SERVICE
ISIS — D: BOOKPOINT LIMITED
Isis Audio Books — I: CLIO PRESS LTD
ISIS Audio Books — A: DEREK SEARLE ASS LTD
Isis Large Print — I: CLIO PRESS LTD
Isis School Guide — A: DEREK SEARLE ASS LTD
Islamic Art Foundation (US) — D: OXFORD UNI PRESS DIS
Islamic Center of Detroit (US) — D: ALIF INTERNATIONAL
Islamic Circle Organisation — D: ALIF INTERNATIONAL
Islamic Civilization Books — D: ALIF INTERNATIONAL
Islamic Classical Library — I: MADINAH PRESS
Islamic Education Center (US) — D: ALIF INTERNATIONAL
Islamic Educational Publications — VOLCANO PRESS
Islamic Foundation, The (Partial) — A: P M LLEWELLYN CO
Islamic Seminary (PK) — D: ALIF INTERNATIONAL
ISLAMIC TEXTS SOCIETY
Islamic Texts Society (Partial) — A: P M LLEWELLYN CO
ISLAND PUBLICATIONS
Island Records (Books) — A: TURNAROUND
ISM (US) — D: TURNAROUND
I-Spy — I: MICHELIN TYRE PLC
Israel Physical Society Conference Proceedings (IS) — D: IOP PUBLISHING LTD
Istituto Geografico Centrale (Partial) (IT) — D: CORDEE
Istituto Geografico Di Agostini Ltd (Partial) (IT) — D: OLD VICARAGE PUB
Istituto Poligrafico E Zecca Dello Stato Ltd (Partial) (IT) — D: OLD VICARAGE PUB
Italica Press (US) — D: EVENLODE BOOK DIST
ITEM GROUP LTD
Ithaca Press — I: GARNET PUB LTD
ITMA
ITRC — D: CORDEE
ITSA — I: INST TRADING STAND
IUCN - THE WORLD CONSERVATION UNION
Ivanhoe Press — I: CHARLES LETTS & CO
IVP (US) — D: INTERVARSITY PRESS

Ivy Publications — D: LAKESIDE PUBNS
J & J Verlag — D: LAVIS MARKETING
JA Marketing — A: HEADSTART HISTORY
Jachin Publications — D: CHAPTER TWO
Jacobson Gallery, Bernard — D: S HENEAGE DIST
Jacques Damase (FR) — D: S HENEAGE DIST
Jade Publishers — D: BOOKPOINT LIMITED
JAEGGI & SONS, LEON
Jahn Galerie, Fred (GE) — D: ART DATA
JAI Press — D: INT BOOK DIST
JAI PRESS LTD
Jalmar Press (US) — D: AIRLIFT BOOK CO
Jam Books — D: BOOKPOINT LIMITED
JAMES & JAMES SCIENCE PUBLISHERS LTD
James, Arthur — D: VERITAS PUBLICATIONS
James, Arthur — A: SPCK
JAMES LTD, ARTHUR
Jamieson Library — I: PATTEN PRESS
J&S Antiquarian Networking (US) — D: EVENLODE BOOK DIST
JANE'S INFORMATION GROUP
Janus Publishing — D: DISTRIBUTION BOOK CO
JANUS PUBLISHING
Japan Library — I: CURZON PRESS LTD
Japan Library — D: BIBLIOS PUB DIST
Japan Publication Trading Co (JPT) (JP) — D: BIBLIOS PUB DIST
Japan Publications (JP) — A: PREMIER BOOK MKTNG
Japan Publications (Partial) (JP) — D: P M LLEWELLYN CO
Japan Times (JP) — A: PREMIER BOOK MKTNG
JARROLD PUBLISHING
JAY BOOKS
Jefferson University Press, The Thomas (US) — D: EDS
Jemisik Cultural Books Ltd (KY) — D: LEISHMAN & TAUSSIG
Jensen, E A — I: AMCD (PUB) LTD
JERSEY ARTISTS LTD
Jerusalem Publishing House (IS) — D: KUPERARD LTD
Jester Books — I: KNOCKABOUT COMICS
Jets — I: HARPERCOLLINS CHILD
Jettisoundz Video — D: MANDRAKE
Jeux Nathan (FR) — D: EUROPEAN SCHOOLBOOKS
Jewish Chronicle Publications — D: SPA BOOKS LTD
Jewish Chronicle Publications — D: KUPERARD LTD
JEWISH CHRONICLE PUBLICATIONS
Jewish Quarterly — D: KUPERARD LTD
Jews College — D: KUPERARD LTD
JNCC — D: NATURAL HIST BOOK SV
JNM Publications — TRAIL CREST PUBLICATIONS
Johansens — I: HOBSONS PUBLISHING
Johansens — D: BIBLIOS PUB DIST
Johnson Associates — I: JAI PRESS LTD
Johnson Reprint — I: HARCOURT BRACE JOVAN
JOHNSTON & BACON BOOKS LTD
Joint Nature Conservation Committee — D: NATURAL HIST BOOK SV
Jolla Museum of Contemporary Art, La (US) — D: ART DATA
JONATHAN PRESS
Jones & Bartlett Publishers Inc (US) — D: PLYMBRIDGE DIST LTD
JONES & BARTLETT PUBLISHERS INTERNATIONAL
Jones, John — D: WELSH BOOKS COUNCIL
JONES PUBLICATIONS, BRIAN
Jones University Press, Bob (US) — D: B MCCALL BARBOUR
Jonquil Publishing — No reply 93
Jordan & Sons — A: ROGER BAYLISS
JORDAN & SONS LTD
JORDANHILL COLLEGE
Joseph, Michael — I: PENGUIN BOOKS LTD
JOSEPH PUBLISHERS, RICHARD
Jossey-Bass Inc — I: MAXWELL MACMILLAN
Jossey-Bass Inc (US) — D: MARSTON BOOKS SERV
Journal of Biological Chemistry (Partial) (US) — D: PORTLAND PRESS LTD
Journal of Biosocial Science — D: PORTLAND PRESS LTD
Journal of Commerce (Partial) (US) — D: WILLIAM SNYDER PUB
Journal of Philosophy & The Visual Arts — I: ACADEMY GROUP LTD
Journal of Reproduction & Fertility — D: PORTLAND PRESS LTD
Journeyman Press — I: PLUTO PUBLISHING
JPL Fine Art — D: ART DATA
JPS (US) (Jewish Interest) — D: KUPERARD LTD
JSOT Press — I: SHEFFIELD ACD PRESS
Judah Anbesa (US) — D: CENTRAL BOOKS
Jude Publications — D: EVANGELICAL PRESS
Judge, Edward E (US) — D: FOOD TRADE PRESS LTD
Judson Press — D: ALLIANCE BOOK SERV
Judy/Instructor — I: SIMON & SCHUSTER INT
Jungle Doctor — I: THE OFFICE LONDON

Junior Funfax — I: HENDERSON PUB LTD
Junk, Dr W — I: KLUWER ACADEMIC PUB
Just Us Books (US) — D: AIRLIFT BOOK CO
Juta (Partial) — D: BAY FOREIGN BOOKS
Juta (SA) — A: HAMMICKS MAIL ORDER
Juventud (SP) — D: EUROPEAN SCHOOLBOOKS
Kabet Press — D: IAN HENRY PUB LTD
Kahn & Averill — D: BAILEY DIST LTD
KAHN & AVERILL
Kaleidoscope (FR) — D: ROY YATES BOOKS
Kalimat Press (US) — D: BAHAI PUBLISHING
Kalmus (US) — D: INT MUSIC PUB
KAM Publicity — AEROSPACE PROFILES
Kane-Miller (US) — D: ROY YATES BOOKS
Kangaroo Press Pty Ltd (AU) — D: GAZELLE BOOK SERVICE
KARGER AG, S
KARNAC BOOKS LTD, H
KARNAK HOUSE
Katabasis — D: CENTRAL BOOKS
KAY PUBLICATIONS, RICHARD
Kaye Corporation — D: VINE HOUSE DIST
Keats Publishing Inc (US) — D: REAL BOOKS
KEAY'S PUBLICATIONS
Kedros Publishing (Partial) — D: ROUNDHOUSE PUB LTD
Kegan Paul International Ltd — D: JOHN WILEY & SONS
KEGAN PAUL INTERNATIONAL
Kelley, Augustus M (US) — D: MERLIN PRESS
Kelly's Directories — I: REED INFO SERVICES
Kelpies — I: CANONGATE PRESS PLC
Kelsey Publishing — D: VINE HOUSE DIST
Kelsey Publishing (US) — D: CORDEE
KEMPS PUBLISHING LTD
KENILWORTH PRESS LTD
Kensal Press — D: LAVIS MARKETING
KENSAL PRESS, THE
KENSINGTON PUBLICATIONS LTD
KENSINGTON WEST PRODUCTIONS LTD
Kent State University Press (US) — D: EDS
Kenway Publications Ltd (KY) — D: LEISHMAN & TAUSSIG
Kenya Literature Bureau (inc EALB)(KY) — D: LEISHMAN & TAUSSIG
Kenyon-Deane — I: CRESSRELLES PUB LTD
Kerr, Charles H (US) — D: AK DISTRIBUTION
Kesho Publications (KY) — D: LEISHMAN & TAUSSIG
Kestrel — I: PENGUIN BOOKS LTD
Kesva An Tavas Kernewek — D: DYLLANSOW TRURAN
Keter (IS) — D: KUPERARD LTD
Kettle's Yard — D: ART DATA
Kettle's Yard — D: CENTRAL BOOKS
Key Curriculum Press — D: JONATHAN PRESS
Key Porter Books Ltd (Partial) (CA) — D: VERULAM PUB LTD
KEYDEX PUBLISHERS
Keyfacts — I: BPP PUBLISHING LTD
Khalili Family Trust — D: OXFORD UNI PRESS DIS
Khaniqahi-Nimatullahi Publications — D: ELEMENT BOOKS LTD
Kidston Mill Press — D: ASHFORD BUCHAN
Kiepenheuer & Witsch (GE) — D: EUROPEAN SCHOOLBOOKS
Killingley, S Y — I: GREVATT & GREVATT
KIME PUBLISHING
KIMPTON MEDICAL PUBLICATIONS
Kincaid House (US) — D: EVENLODE BOOK DIST
KING EDUCATIONAL SERVICES, HILDA
KING EDUCATIONAL SERVICES, HILDA — A
King, Laurence — D: THAMES & HUDSON LTD
KING PUBLISHING, LAURENCE
Kingfisher Books — I: GRISEWOOD & DEMPSEY
Kingfisher Books - UK Retail Trade Only — A: W & R CHAMBERS LTD
King's Fund — D: BEBC DISTRIBUTION
Kingsclere Contract Publishing — I: KINGSCLERE PUB LTD
KINGSCLERE PUBLICATIONS LTD
Kingsfleet — No reply 93
Kingsley Publishers, Jessica — D: KOGAN PAGE LTD
KINGSLEY PUBLISHERS, JESSICA
KINGSMEAD PRESS
Kingsmead Reprints — I: KINGSMEAD PRESS
Kingston Publishers Ltd (JM) — D: GAZELLE BOOK SERVICE
Kingsway (Bibles & Testaments) — D: BIBLE SOCIETY
Kingsway Publications — D: SEND THE LIGHT
KINGSWAY PUBLICATIONS
Kingswood — I: REED CONSUMER TRADE
Kingswood — D: REED BOOK SERVICES
Kinnell Publications — D: VINE HOUSE DIST
KIRKLEES CULTURAL SERVICES

Kiryat Sefer (IS) — D: KUPERARD LTD
Kiscadale Publications — D: ELEMENT BOOKS LTD
Kit Press (NT) — D: INTERMEDIATE TEC PUB
Kitchen Sink (US) — D: COMBINED BOOK SERV
Kite Books — No reply 92/93
Kittiwake Press (Scottish Titles) — D: CLAN BOOKS
Klett Edition Deutsch (GE) — D: EUROPEAN SCHOOLBOOKS
Klett, Ernst (GE) — D: EUROPEAN SCHOOLBOOKS
Klinkhardt & Biermann (GE) — D: S HENEAGE DIST
Kluwer — I: CRONER PUBLICATIONS
KLUWER ACADEMIC PUBLISHERS GROUP
Kluwer Algemene Uitgeverijen (BG) — D: GAZELLE BOOK SERVICE
Kluwer Technical Books (NT) — D: GAZELLE BOOK SERVICE
Knight Books — I: HODDER & STOUGHTON
Knight Publishing, Charles — I: TOLLEY PUBLISHING CO
Knights Templar of Aquarius — D: L N FOWLER & CO LTD
KNIGHTSCROSS LTD
Knockabout Comics — D: BOOKPOINT LIMITED
KNOCKABOUT COMICS
Knowledge Industry Publications Inc (US) — D: GAZELLE BOOK SERVICE
KNOWLES PUBLICATIONS
Knox Press — D: EVANGELICAL PRESS
Knox Press, John (US) — D: GRACEWING/FOWLER
KOCH NEFF & OETINGER & CO GMBH (GE) — W
Kodak — D: NEWPRO UK LTD
Kodansha Europe (JP) — D: BIBLIOS PUB DIST
KODANSHA EUROPE LTD
Kodansha International — I: KODANSHA EUROPE LTD
Kodansha International (JP) — A: PREMIER BOOK MKTNG
Kodansha International (Partial) (JP) — D: P M LLEWELLYN CO
Kodansha (Partial) (JP) — D: WISDOM BOOKS
KOGAN PAGE LTD
KOGAN PAGE LTD — A
Kompass Publishers — I: REED INFO SERVICES
Konark Publishers (IN) — D: SANGAM BOOKS LTD
Konig, Walther (GE) — D: ART DATA
Kosei (JP) — A: PREMIER BOOK MKTNG
Kosei (Partial) (JP) — D: WISDOM BOOKS
Kosmos Book Distributors — FASTLANE DISTRIBUTION
Kount Kisco (US) — D: MCGRAW HILL BOOK CO
Kozmik Press — D: VINE HOUSE DIST
KOZMIK PRESS
KQBX PRESS, THE
Kramer, H J (US) — D: AIRLIFT BOOK CO
Kraus International Publications (US) — D: EDS
Krause Publications (US) — D: GAZELLE BOOK SERVICE
Kregel Publications — A: JOHN RITCHIE LTD
KROPOTKIN'S LIGHTHOUSE PUBLICATIONS
KSL — D: AK DISTRIBUTION
Kuma Computers — D: COMPUTER STEP LTD
KUMA COMPUTERS LTD
Kummerley & Frey Maps — A: WORLD LEISURE MKTG
Kummerly & Frey (SZ) — D: MCCARTA LTD
Kunsthaus Zurich (SZ) — D: ART DATA
KUPERARD LTD
Kuraz Publishing Agency (ET) — D: LEISHMAN & TAUSSIG
KW Publications (US) — D: GAZELLE BOOK SERVICE
Kyoto Shoin (JP) — D: ART DATA
L M International — LAKESIDE PUBLICATIONS
LA HAULE BOOKS LTD
La Rose Tribute Committee, John — D: NEW BEACON BOOKS LTD
LAAS AVIATION LTD
LABOUR PARTY
LAC (IT) — D: ROGER LASCELLES
Lace Publications (US) — D: GMP PUBLISHERS LTD
LADYBIRD BOOKS LTD
Laffont (FR) — D: EUROPEAN SCHOOLBOOKS
LAING & BUISSON PUBLICATIONS
Lake District National Park — D: CORDEE
Lake Publishers & Enterprises (KY) — D: LEISHMAN & TAUSSIG
LAKESIDE PUBLICATIONS
Lale Yayineui (NT) — D: ROY YATES BOOKS
Lamb Books, Fiona — D: JOHN DONALD PUB LTD
LAMBENT BOOKS
Lambourn — D: MARLBOROUGH BOOKS
LAME DUCK PUBLISHING
LANCASHIRE BIBLIOGRAPHY
Lancashire County Books — D: CARNEGIE PUB LTD
Lancer International (IN) — D: GREENHILL BOOKS
LANDESMAN, JAY
Landfall Productions — D: COMBINED BOOK SERV
Landmark Publications (US) — D: RICS BOOKS

Landscape Institute — D: RIBA PUBLICATIONS
LANDSCAPE PRESS
LANDY PUBLISHING
Lanes Publishing — D: ROADMASTER PUB
LANG SYNE PUBLISHERS
Lange Medical Publications — I: SIMON & SCHUSTER INT
Langenscheidt Dictionaries — A: REED CONSUMER ILLUS
Langenscheidt Dictionaries — D: REED BOOK SERVICES
Langenscheidt (GE) — D: EUROPEAN SCHOOLBOOKS
LANGUAGE INFORMATION CENTRE
Language Survival Kit Phrase Books — I: LONELY PLANET PUB
LANGUAGE TEACHING PUBLICATIONS
Lannoo Publications (BG) — D: BIBLIOS PUB DIST
Lapis Press (US) — D: ART DATA
Large Print Books — I: CHIVERS PRESS LTD
Large Print Swift Books — I: CHIVERS PRESS LTD
Lark (Partial) (US) — D: CASSELL PLC
Larousse (FR) — D: EUROPEAN SCHOOLBOOKS
Larson Publications (US) — D: ELEMENT BOOKS LTD
LASCELLES, ROGER
Laser Institute of America (US) — D: WOODHEAD PUBLISHING
Last Gasp (US) — D: KNOCKABOUT COMICS
Last Gasp (US) — D: AK DISTRIBUTION
LATIN AMERICA BUREAU
Latin American & Caribbean Contemporary Record — I: BOOK REP & DIST LTD
Latin American Bureau — D: CENTRAL BOOKS
Laurel House Publishing Co Inc (US) — D: GAZELLE BOOK SERVICE
Laurier University Press, Wilfrid (CA) — A: TREVOR BROWN ASSOC
Lavender (US) — D: TURNAROUND
LAVIS MARKETING
Lavoisier (FR) — D: FOOD TRADE PRESS LTD
Law Book Company (AU) — A: HAMMICKS MAIL ORDER
Law Society — A: ROGER BAYLISS
Lawrence & Wishart — D: CENTRAL BOOKS
LAWRENCE & WISHART
Lawrence Hill (US) — D: TURNAROUND
LDA - Learning Development Aids — D: CHRIS LLOYD SALES
Lea & Febiger — I: WILLIAMS & WILKINS
LEACH & CO, R J
Leadership Education & Development Inc (US) — D: GAZELLE BOOK SERVICE
Leading Edge — D: GRANTHAM BOOK SERV
Leading Edge — A: WORLD LEISURE MKTG
LEADING EDGE PRESS & PUBLISHING LTD
LEARNING DEVELOPMENT AIDS
LEARNING MATERIALS
Leatherhead Food — D: FOOD TRADE PRESS LTD
Leaves of Grass (Selected titles) (US) — D: PAUPERS' PRESS
L'Ecole des Loisirs (FR) — D: ROY YATES BOOKS
L'Ecole (FR) — D: EUROPEAN SCHOOLBOOKS
Lecon Arts — I: SUSSEX PUBLICATIONS
LEESON, BILL
Lefebvre et Gillet (Partial) (BG) — D: HILMARTON MANOR
Left Bank (US) — D: AK DISTRIBUTION
Legal Action Group — A: ROGER BAYLISS
LEGAL ACTION GROUP
Legal Studies Publishing — I: IBC PUBLISHING LTD
LEGALEASE
Legend — I: RANDOM HOUSE UK LTD
Legend — I: RANDOM HOUSE (ARROW)
Legend — D: TIPTREE BOOK SERV
Lehigh U P — I: GOLDEN COCKEREL
Leicester University Press — I: PINTER PUBLISHERS
Leicester University Press — A: BOOK REP & DIST LTD
Leicester University Press — PINTER PUBLISHERS
LEISHMAN & TAUSSIG
Leisure Books (US) — D: BIBLIOS PUB DIST
Leisure Press — I: HUMAN KINETICS PUB
Leisuretime Publications (UK) Ltd — D: BOOKPOINT LIMITED
Lelong Galerie (FR) — D: ART DATA
Lemma (Higher Educ titles) (NT) — A: JESSICA KINGSLEY PUB
Lemma (Higher Educ titles) (NT) — D: KOGAN PAGE LTD
Lemon Book Co (Partial) — D: THOMAS LYSTER LTD
Lenart (Partial) (SU) — D: S HENEAGE DIST
LENNARD ASSOCIATES
Lennard Publishing — I: LENNARD ASSOCIATES
Lennard Publishing — D: CHRIS LLOYD SALES
Leonard, Hal (US) — D: INT MUSIC PUB
Leopard's Head Press (Partial) — D: OXBOW BOOKS
Lerner Publications — D: TURNAROUND
Lesome Press (CA) — D: MILLBANK BOOKS LTD
Lesotho Printing & Publishing Co (LE) — D: LEISHMAN & TAUSSIG
Letts & Co, Charles — D: BOOKPOINT LIMITED

LETTS & CO, CHARLES
Letts Educational — I: BPP PUBLISHING LTD
Leventis Foundation, A G — I: TRIGRAPH LTD
Levin Associates Inc, Hugh Lauter (US) — D: GAZELLE BOOK SERVICE
LEWIS & SONS LTD, J D
Lewis, H K — I: CHAPMAN & HALL
Lewis, H K — D: INT THOMSON PUB SERV
Lewis Publishers — D: TURPIN DISTRIBUTION
Lewis Publishers Inc (US) — D: MOSBY-YEARBOOK EUR
Lexington Books — I: MAXWELL MACMILLAN
Lexington Books — D: MARSTON BOOKS SERV
Lexington Books (US) — D: MARSTON BOOKS SERV
LF Publishing (US) — D: VINE HOUSE DIST
Liam Dale — D: VINE HOUSE DIST
Libbey & Co, John — D: FABER BOOK SERVICES
LIBBEY & CO LTD, JOHN
Libbey Publishing Ltd, John — A: BOOK REP & DIST LTD
Libel Books — D: MARLBOROUGH BOOKS
Liber Press — D: BOOKPOINT LIMITED
Liber Press — A: WINDSOR BOOKS INT
LIBER PRESS
Liberal Democrat Publications — I: HEBDON ROYD PUB
LIBERTARIAN ALLIANCE
Liberty Fund (US) — D: TURPIN DISTRIBUTION
Librairie du Commerce International (FR) — D: CEDAR TREE HOUSE
Librairie Du Liban (Children's) (LB) — D: ROY YATES BOOKS
Librairie Du Liban (LB) — D: PACKARD PUB LTD
Librairie Du Liban (Partial) (LB) — D: P M LLEWELLYN CO
Libraries Unlimited (US) — D: EDS
LIBRARY & INFORMATION STATISTICS UNIT
Library Association Publishing Ltd — D: BOOKPOINT LIMITED
LIBRARY ASSOCIATION PUBLISHING
Libreria Editrice Vaticana (Selected titles) (Vatican City) — D: ST PAUL'S PUB
LIBRO (GR) — W
Libro Port (JP) — D: ART DATA
LICOSA LIBRERIA COMISSIONARIA (IT) — W
Lidel, Edicoes Tecnicas (PG) — D: EUROPEAN SCHOOLBOOKS
Life Action (US) — D: AIRLIFT BOOK CO
Life Choices — I: HARVESTIME PUB LTD
Life Concerns — I: HARVESTIME PUB LTD
LIFE EDUCATION CENTRES UK FOUNDATION
LIFESPACE PUBLISHING
Lifetime Books Inc (US) — D: GAZELLE BOOK SERVICE
Lighthouse Press (US) — D: VINE HOUSE DIST
Lilliput Press — D: GILL & MACMILLAN LTD
Lilliput Press (IR) — D: CENTRAL BOOKS
Lilmur Publishing (CA) — D: ROY YATES BOOKS
Lime Tree — I: REED CONSUMER TRADE
Lime Tree — D: REED BOOK SERVICES
Lime Tree Calendars — D: TIPTREE BOOK SERV
Limelight Editions (Partial) — D: IANMEAD LTD
Limelight Editions (US) — D: GAZELLE BOOK SERVICE
Limitcode Ltd — D: EUROPEAN SCHOOLBOOKS
Lincoln, Frances — D: HODDER & STOUGHTON
LINCOLN PUBLISHERS, FRANCES
Lincoln Records Society — D: BOYDELL & BREWER LTD
Lincolnshire & Humberside Arts — D: RICHARD KAY PUB
Linden Hall — D: GROSVENOR BOOKS
Linden Press — I: CENTAUR PRESS LTD
Linden Press — I: SIMON & SCHUSTER LTD
Lindisfarne Press (US) — D: FLORIS BOOKS
Lines Review Editions — I: SALTIRE SOCIETY
LINEWRIGHTS LTD
Lingore Press — I: SIMON & SCHUSTER INT
Link House — D: GRANTHAM BOOK SERV
Link House — A: WORLD LEISURE MKTG
Link Press — D: CENTRAL BOOKS
Lion — D: ALLIANCE BOOK SERV
Lion Paperbacks — I: LION PUBLISHING PLC
LION PUBLISHING PLC
Lions — I: HARPERCOLLINS CHILD
Lion's Den Publications Inc (US) — D: GAZELLE BOOK SERVICE
Lippincott Company, J B (US) — D: PLYMBRIDGE DIST LTD
Lipsmackers Inc (US) — D: GAZELLE BOOK SERVICE
LISTEN FOR PLEASURE — A
Listen Productions — No reply 92/93
LISTER ART BOOKS
LISU — I: LIBRARY & INFO UNIT
LITTLE BROWN & CO
Little Brown Medical — D: CHURCHILL LIVINGSTON
Little Brown (UK) — D: TIPTREE BOOK SERV
Little Lions — I: LION PUBLISHING PLC

Little Mammoth — I: REED CONS MANDARIN
Little Owl — I: EGMONT PUB LTD
LITTLE RED WITCH BOOK DISTRIBUTION CO
LITTLEHAMPTON BOOK SERVICES
Littlewood Arc — D: PASSWORD (BOOKS) LTD
LITTLEWOOD ARC
Littlewood Press — I: LITTLEWOOD ARC
Littman Library of Jewish Civilization — D: BURSTON DIST SERV
LITTMAN LIBRARY OF JEWISH CIVILIZATION
Liturgical Press (US) — D: COLUMBA BOOK SERVICE
Liturgy Training Publications (US) — D: MCCRIMMON PUBLISHING
Live Food Products (US) — D: REAL BOOKS
Liver Press — I: COUNTYVISE LTD
Liveright — I: W W NORTON & CO LTD
Liverpool University Press — A: BOOK REP & DIST LTD
Liverpool University Press — D: BURSTON DIST SERV
LIVERPOOL UNIVERSITY PRESS
Livewire Books for Teenagers — I: WOMEN'S PRESS
Living & Learning Ltd — I: LEARNING DEV AIDS
Living Batch Books (US) — A: UNI PRESSES MARKETNG
Living Media India Ltd (IN) — A: NILE & MACKENZIE LTD
Living Options in Practice — D: BEBC DISTRIBUTION
Living Quest (US) — D: GAZELLE BOOK SERVICE
Living Stories Inc (US) — D: B MCCALL BARBOUR
Livre de Poche, Le (FR) — D: EUROPEAN SCHOOLBOOKS
LLANERCH PUBLISHERS
LLEWELLYN COMPANY, P M
Llewellyn Publications (US) — D: W FOULSHAM & CO LTD
Lloyd, Chris — A: PEGASUS PUB SERV
Lloyd Sales & Marketing Services, Chris — D: BAILEY DIST LTD
LLOYD SALES, CHRIS
Lloyd's of London Press — A: ROGER BAYLISS
Lloyd's of London Press — D: BIBLIOS PUB DIST
LLOYD'S OF LONDON PRESS LTD
Llyfragell Genedlaethol Cymru (Partial) — D: WELSH BOOKS COUNCIL
Llyfrau'r Faner (Partial) — D: WELSH BOOKS COUNCIL
Llyfrgell Efengylaidd Cymru — I: EVANGELICAL PR WALES
Lochar Publishing — Ceased trading 92
Lochar Publishing (Six Titles Only) — I: NEIL WILSON PUB LTD
LOCHEE PUBLICATIONS LTD
Lochee Soft — I: LOCHEE PUB LTD
Locker Verlag (AS) — D: ART DATA
Lodenek Press — D: DYLLANSOW TRURAN
LOGASTON PRESS
Login Enterprises — D: COMBINED BOOK SERV
Loizeaux Brothers — A: JOHN RITCHIE LTD
Loizeaux Brothers Inc (US) — D: B MCCALL BARBOUR
LOMOND BOOKS — W
Lomond Music — D: BOOSEY & HAWKES LTD
LONDON & SE REGION ADVISORY COUNCIL FOR EDUC & TRAINING
London Architectural — No reply 93
London Educational Studies — I: INST OF EDUCATION
London File — I: INST OF EDUCATION
London Gay Teenage Group — D: CENTRAL BOOKS
London Initiative — D: BEBC DISTRIBUTION
LONDON LIMITED EDITIONS
London Review of Books — D: CENTRAL BOOKS
LONDON SCHOOL OF ECONOMICS
London Stamp Exchange — A: GREENHILL BOOKS
LONDON STAMP EXCHANGE
LONDON TOPOGRAPHICAL SOCIETY
London Tourism Manpower Project — D: HOTEL & CATERING CO
London Transport — A: WORLD LEISURE MKTG
LONDON TRANSPORT
London Transport Publications — D: GRANTA EDITIONS
London Voluntary Service Committee — D: TURNAROUND
London Yearly Meeting — I: QUAKER HOME SERVICE
Lone Eagle Publishing Co (US) — D: GAZELLE BOOK SERVICE
Lone Pine Publishing (US) — D: CORDEE
Lonely Planet — A: WORLD LEISURE MKTG
Lonely Planet (AU) — D: GRANTHAM BOOK SERV
Lonely Planet (AU) — D: ROGER LASCELLES
LONELY PLANET PUBLICATIONS PTY LTD
Long Books, Barry — I: BARRY LONG FOUND
LONG FOUNDATION, BARRY
Long Island Music Co Ltd — D: BOOKPOINT LIMITED
Longman Botswana (BO) — D: LEISHMAN & TAUSSIG
Longman Dictionaries — A: H I MARKETING
Longman Education - School Books (Ireland Only) — D: EDUC CO OF IRELAND
LONGMAN GROUP UK LTD
Longman Kenya (KY) — D: LEISHMAN & TAUSSIG
LONGMAN LAW TAX & FINANCE

Longman Namibia (NA) — D: LEISHMAN & TAUSSIG
Longman Zimbabwe (ZB) — D: LEISHMAN & TAUSSIG
Longsight Press — D: NEW BEACON BOOKS LTD
Longstone Press — D: ELEMENT BOOKS LTD
Longwood — I: SIMON & SCHUSTER INT
Lookout (Partial) (SP) — D: IANMEAD LTD
Loompanics Unlimited (Partial) — D: COUNTER PRODUCTIONS
Loony Balloonies — I: HENDERSON PUB LTD
Lorenz Publishing Company (US) — D: BOOSEY & HAWKES LTD
Lorimer, James (CA) — D: DUNDURN DISTRIBUTION
Los Arboles Publications (US) — D: EVENLODE BOOK DIST
Losada (AT) — D: DOLPHIN BOOK CO LTD
Lothian Books (Partial) (AU) — D: SPA BOOKS LTD
Lotsawa (US) — D: ELEMENT BOOKS LTD
Louisiana State University Press (US) — A: ACADEMIC & UNIV PUB
Love Child Publishing (US) — D: GAZELLE BOOK SERVICE
Love Line Books (US) — D: AIRLIFT BOOK CO
Lovell, Percy — D: GREVATT & GREVATT
LOW PAY UNIT
Lowe, Peter — I: EUROBOOK LTD
LOXWOOD STONELEIGH
Loyola University Press (Partial) (US) — D: ANTHONY CLARKE PUB
LRTA — D: TRANSPORT PUB CO LTD
LST — No reply 92/93
LTWA (IN) — D: WISDOM BOOKS
Luath Press — D: AK DISTRIBUTION
LUATH PRESS LTD
Lucas Publications — I: PENINSULA BOOKS
Luce Inc, Robert B (Partial List) (US) — D: KAHN & AVERILL
Luchterhand (GE) — D: EUROPEAN SCHOOLBOOKS
LUCIS PRESS LTD
Lucky Tree Books — I: THE O'BRIEN PRESS
Lumen (SP) — D: EUROPEAN SCHOOLBOOKS
Lund Humphries Publishers Ltd — D: BOOKPOINT LIMITED
LUND HUMPHRIES PUBLISHERS
Lund University Press — I: CHARTWELL-BRATT
Lunwerg (SP) — D: EUROPEAN SCHOOLBOOKS
Lustre Press (IN) — D: BOOKS FROM INDIA
Lutheran Publishing (AU) — D: NOVA DISTRIBUTION
Lutheran Publishing House (US) — D: GRACEWING/FOWLER
Lutterworth Press — A: H I MARKETING
LUTTERWORTH PRESS
Luxor Press — I: CHARLES SKILTON LTD
Luzac — D: ROY YATES BOOKS
LW Book Sales (Partial) (US) — D: LISTER ART BOOKS
LYLE PUBLICATIONS
Lynx Communications — D: LION PUBLISHING PLC
Lyon Books, Richard — No reply 93
Lyons & Burford Publications (US) — D: GAZELLE BOOK SERVICE
Lyons, Stanley — D: JOHN DAWES PUB
LYONS, STANLEY
LYSTER LTD, THOMAS
Lythway — I: CHIVERS PRESS LTD
M & A Verlag (GE) — D: CEDAR TREE HOUSE
M & J Publications — D: CHRIS LLOYD SALES
M & J PUBLICATIONS
M & M PUBLISHING LTD
M & T Publishers — D: SIMON & SCHUSTER INT
McBooks (US) — D: EVENLODE BOOK DIST
MCCALL BARBOUR, B
MCCARTA LTD
McCarta — D: GRANTHAM BOOK SERV
McCarta — A: WORLD LEISURE MKTG
McClanahan Books (US) — D: XYLOPRESS LTD
McClelland & Stewart (CA) — D: UCL PRESS LTD
MCCRIMMON PUBLISHING
McCrimmon — D: VERITAS PUBLICATIONS
Macdonald & Co — LITTLE BROWN
MacDonald & Evans — I: PITMAN PUBLISHING
McDonald Books, Deirdre — I: BELLEW PUBLISHING
McFarland & Company Inc (US) — D: SHELWING LTD
McGibbon, Robin — D: VINE HOUSE DIST
McGill-Queen's University Press (CA) — A: ACADEMIC & UNIV PUB
MCGRAW HILL BOOK COMPANY
McIndoe (Partial) (NZ) — D: CORDEE
Mackay Publishing — D: ALLOWAY PUB LTD
McLachlan — D: GAZELLE BOOK SERVICE
Maclean Press — D: CLAN BOOKS
MacLennan & Petty (AU) — A: JESSICA KINGSLEY PUB
MacLennan & Petty (AU) — D: KOGAN PAGE LTD
Macmillan Boleswa Publishers (3X) — D: LEISHMAN & TAUSSIG
Macmillan Childrens Books — I: MACMILLAN DIST LTD

MACMILLAN DISTRIBUTION LTD
Macmillan Education Schoolbooks — D: THOMAS NELSON & SONS
Macmillan Kenya (Publishers) (KY) — D: LEISHMAN & TAUSSIG
Macmillan London — D: MACMILLAN DIST LTD
Macmillan Press — A: GILL & MACMILLAN LTD
Macmillan Press — D: MACMILLAN DIST LTD
Macmillan Reference (US) — I: MAXWELL MACMILLAN
Macmillan Reference (US) — D: MARSTON BOOKS SERV
Macmillan (US) — I: MAXWELL MACMILLAN
Macmillan (US) — D: MARSTON BOOKS SERV
McPherson & Company (US) — D: ART DATA
MacQuarie University (AU) — D: LA HAULE BOOKS LTD
MacQuarrie Univ Ancient Hist Doc Res Centre (Partial) (AU) — D: LIVERPOOL UNIV PRESS
MacRae, Julia — I: RANDOM HOUSE UK LTD
MacRae, Julia — D: TIPTREE BOOK SERV
Mad Hatter Books (US) — D: GAZELLE BOOK SERVICE
Mad River Press (US) — D: RICHMOND PUB CO LTD
Made Simple — I: BUTTERWORTH-HEINEMAN
Made Simple — D: REED BOOK SERVICES
MADINAH PRESS
Maeght (FR) — D: S HENEAGE DIST
Magi Publications — D: A & C BLACK LTD
Magi Publications (Ireland only) — A: BLACKSTAFF PRESS LTD
MAGI PUBLIOCATIONS
Magic Image Filmbooks (US) — D: GAZELLE BOOK SERVICE
Magical Child — D: MANDRAKE
Magickal Childe (US) — D: TEMPLE PRESS LTD
Magna Books — I: HARVEYS BOOKS LTD
Magna Graecia's Books — I: AAB BRIT BOOK SEARCH
MAGNA LARGE PRINT BOOKS
Magna Sources — C E HALL
Magpie — I: ROBINSON PUBLISHING
Magwood Press — D: STRIDE PUBLICATIONS
Mahayana Sutra & Tantra Press (US) — D: WISDOM BOOKS
Mainstream — D: SEND THE LIGHT
Mainstream - Baptists for Life and Growth — I: MOORLEY'S PRINT PUB
MAINSTREAM PUBLISHING COMPANY
Mainstream Publishing (Ireland only) — A: BLACKSTAFF PRESS LTD
Maison D'Editions Bahai (BG) — D: BAHAI PUBLISHING
Majority Press, The (US) — D: KARNAK HOUSE
Majority Press (US) — D: TURNAROUND
Malayan Law Journal (Partial List) (SI) — D: BUTTERWORTH & CO LTD
Malaysian Rubber Association (ML) — D: TURPIN DISTRIBUTION
Malibran, La (FR) — D: NEWS PRODUCTIONS
Malice Aforethought Press — D: CENTRAL BOOKS
Mallard Reprints — I: TERENCE DALTON LTD
MALLORY INTERNATIONAL
Malone Society — D: OXFORD UNI PRESS DIS
Malstead, Roger — D: SEND THE LIGHT
Malthouse Press Ltd (NG) — D: AFRICAN BOOKS COLL
Malthouse Publishing — D: LAVIS MARKETING
Malvern Publishing — D: IMAGES DISTRIBUTION
Mambo Press (ZB) — D: LEISHMAN & TAUSSIG
Mammoth — I: REED CONS MANDARIN
Management Publications — D: FOOD TRADE PRESS LTD
MANAGEMENT UPDATE
MANCHESTER STATISTICAL SOCIETY
Manchester U P (Nonlinear Science List) — I: JOHN WILEY & SONS
MANCHESTER UNIVERSITY PRESS
Mandagora (FN) — D: HEART OF ALBION
Mandala — I: HARPERCOLLINS THORS
Mandarin — I: REED CONS MANDARIN
Mandarin — D: REED BOOK SERVICES
Mandarin Humour — I: REED CONS MANDARIN
Manderino Books (US) — D: GAZELLE BOOK SERVICE
MANDEVILLE PRESS
Mandira (IN) — D: ROY YATES BOOKS
Mandrake — D: TEMPLE PRESS LTD
MANDRAKE
MANN BOOKS, GEORGE
Manor Books — I: DAVID GOLD & SON LTD
MANOR HOUSE PUBLISHING
Manor Place Press — D: AUSTICKS PUBLICATION
Mansell Publishing — I: CASSELL PLC
MANSK-SVENSKA PUBLISHING CO
MANUTIUS PRESS
MAO Management Group Ltd (Partial) (HK) — D: HILMARTON MANOR
MAP COLLECTOR PUBLICATIONS
Mapbooks — D: VINE HOUSE DIST
Mapin Publishing Pvt Ltd (IN) — D: GAZELLE BOOK SERVICE
Marboro Books Inc (partial) (US) — D: VERULAM PUB LTD
Marc — I: MONARCH PUB

MARC Europe — D: SEND THE LIGHT
MARC EUROPE
MARCAN PUBLICATIONS, PETER
Marcham Books — I: APPLEFORD PUB GROUP
Ma'rifat Publishing House (AU) — D: ALIF INTERNATIONAL
MARINE MANAGEMENT
MARITIME BOOKS
Mark One Publications (Partial) — D: BARNACLE MARINE LTD
Mark-Age Inc (US) — D: EVENLODE BOOK DIST
Market Direction — I: EUROMONITOR PLC
MARKET RESEARCH ASSOCIATION
Marketing Media Associates — D: BAY FOREIGN BOOKS
Marks Music Corporation, E B (US) — D: BOOSEY & HAWKES LTD
Marlboro Press (US) — D: TURNAROUND
Marlborough Books — D: VINE HOUSE DIST
MARLBOROUGH BOOKS
Marlborough Fine Art — D: ART DATA
Marlor Press (US) — D: GAZELLE BOOK SERVICE
Marshall Cavendish — No longer book publishing
Marshall Pickering — D: VERITAS PUBLICATIONS
Marshall Pickering — I: HARPERCOLLINS RELIG
Marshall Pickering — D: B MCCALL BARBOUR
MARSHALLE PUBLICATIONS
Marsland Press — I: VOLTURNA PRESS
MARSTON BOOK SERVICES
Marston House — A: CHRIS LLOYD SALES
Martech Publications — I: METRA MARTECH LTD
Martin Books — I: SIMON & SCHUSTER LTD
MARUZEN CO LTD (JP) — W
Marval (FR) — D: S HENEAGE DIST
Marvel — D: D SERVICES
Marvell Press (Philip Larkin only) — D: PETERLOO POETS
Marwain Publishing — D: SPRINGFIELD BOOKS
Mask Noir — I: SERPENT'S TAIL
Maskew Miller Longman (SA) — D: LEISHMAN & TAUSSIG
Masks — I: SERPENT'S TAIL
Mason Publications, Kenneth — D: BIBLIOS PUB DIST
MASON PUBLICATIONS, KENNETH
Mason University Press, George (US) — D: EDS
Masquerade Publications — D: VINE HOUSE DIST
Masters Publications (CA) — D: PAUL H CROMPTON LTD
Matchbox Toys — D: MILLBANK BOOKS LTD
Materials Research Society (US) — D: CLARKE ASSOCIATES
Math Ware (US) — D: CHARTWELL-BRATT
Mathaids (AU) — D: QED
Mathaids (US) — D: QED
Mathematical Association of America (US) — D: QED
Mathematical Association of America (US) — D: CLARKE ASSOCIATES
MATTHEW PUBLICATIONS, ADAM
Maurizio Martino (US) — D: DAWSON UK LTD
Mavibulut Yayinlari (TK) — D: ROY YATES BOOKS
MAXWELL MACMILLAN
Maxwell Macmillan Int (Europe) Ltd — D: MARSTON BOOKS SERV
Maxwell Macmillan International Editions — D: MARSTON BOOKS SERV
Mayfield Publishing Co (US) — D: W C BROWN PUBLISHING
Mayflower Publications — D: EVANGELICAL PRESS
MAYHEW LTD, KEVIN
Maypop Books (US) — D: EVENLODE BOOK DIST
Mazda (US) — D: ROY YATES BOOKS
Mazzotta Editore (IT) — D: ART DATA
MBC Info Services — WATERLOW INFO SERVICES
MBI (US) — D: J H HAYNES & CO LTD
MCA (US) — D: INT MUSIC PUB
MCB UNIVERSITY PRESS
Meadowbrook Press (US) — D: CHRIS LLOYD SALES
Meadowfield Press Ltd — I: MERROW PUBLISHING CO
MECHANICAL ENGINEERING PUBLICATIONS
Meckler — D: BIBLIOS PUB DIST
MECKLER LTD
Media Marketing Communications (BG) — D: D SERVICES
Media Masters Pty Ltd — D: BOOKPOINT LIMITED
Media Masters (SI) — A: JOHN WILSON BOOKS
MEDIA MEDICA PUBLICATIONS
MEDIAN BOOKS LTD
Medical Economics Data (US) — D: LAVIS MARKETING
Medical Physics Publishing (US) — D: VINE HOUSE DIST
MEDICI SOCIETY LTD
Medieval & Renaissance Texts & Studies (NB One Title) (US) — D: UNI OF WALES PRESS
Medilaw — I: BARRY ROSE LAW PUB
Medin Comments — I: MOZAMBIQUE INSTITUTE
Medmaster Inc (US) — D: QUEST MERIDIEN LTD
Meeramma Publications (US) — D: ELEMENT BOOKS LTD

Megiddo Press — No reply 92
Mei — D: DALENNAU
Mel-Bay Publications Inc (US) — D: CELEBRATION SERV LTD
Melbourne University Press (AU) — D: UCL PRESS LTD
Melia Publishing Services — A: PEGASUS PUB SERV
MELIA PUBLISHING SERVICES
MELLEN PRESS, EDWIN
MELROSE PRESS LTD
Melrose Square (US) — D: ROY YATES BOOKS
Melven Press — I: MERCAT PRESS
Menard Press — D: CENTRAL BOOKS
MENARD PRESS, THE
Menasha Ridge Press (US) — D: CORDEE
MENCAP
MENOSHIRE LTD — W
Mercantila Publishers (DN) — D: FOOD TRADE PRESS LTD
MERCAT PRESS
Mercier (IR) — A: TURNAROUND
Mercier Press — D: COLUMBA BOOK SERVICE
Mercier Press (GB only) (IR) — A: OLDCASTLE BOOKS LTD
Mercier Press (IR) — D: CENTRAL BOOKS
MERCIER PRESS LTD
Merck Publishing (US) — D: HARCOURT BRACE JOVAN
Mercury Arts Publications — D: RUDOLF STEINER PRESS
MERCURY BOOKS
Mercury House (US) — D: GAZELLE BOOK SERVICE
Merehurst — A: PEGASUS PUB SERV
MEREHURST FAIRFAX
Merehurst Ltd — D: BOOKPOINT LIMITED
Merehurst (Partial) — A: P M LLEWELLYN CO
MERESBOROUGH BOOKS
MERESBOROUGH BOOKS — W
Meridian Books — D: CORDEE
MERIDIAN BOOKS
Meriwether Publishing Ltd (US) — D: GAZELLE BOOK SERVICE
MERLIN BOOKS LTD
Merlin Press — D: CENTRAL BOOKS
MERLIN PRESS
Merlin Publications — D: VINE HOUSE DIST
Merlion Publishing — A: DEREK SEARLE ASS LTD
MERLION PUBLISHING
Merlion Publishing Ltd — D: BOOKPOINT LIMITED
Merrill, Charles — I: MAXWELL MACMILLAN
Merrill, Charles (US) — D: MARSTON BOOKS SERV
MERROW PUBLISHING COMPANY
Merry Walk Antiques (US) — D: LISTER ART BOOKS
Mersey Port Folios — I: COUNTYVISE LTD
MESSAGGERIE LIBRI SPA (IT) — W
MESSANGER PUBLICATIONS
Meta Publications — D: DEEP BOOKS LTD
Metal Bulletin Books — I: METAL BULLETIN PLC
METAL BULLETIN PLC
Metamorphic Press (US) — D: WORLDLY GOODS
Metaphysical Research Group — I: SOC OF METAPHYSICIAN
METCALFE PUBLISHING TRUST, JOHN
METHODIST PUBLISHING HOUSE
Methuen — I: REED CONSUMER TRADE
Methuen & Co — I: ROUTLEDGE
Methuen (CA) — D: DUNDURN DISTRIBUTION
Methuen Children's Books — I: REED CONSUMER TRADE
Metra Consultants — I: METRA MARTECH LTD
METRA MARTECH LTD
METRASTOCK LTD — W
Meulenhoff Educatief (NT) — D: EUROPEAN SCHOOLBOOKS
Meyerstone (US) — D: GRACEWING/FOWLER
Mho & Mho (US) — D: EVENLODE BOOK DIST
MICELLE PRESS
Micelle Press Inc (US) — D: MICELLE PRESS
Michaels Guides (IS) (Travel Books) — D: KUPERARD LTD
Michelin (Motoring & Road Atlases) — A: REED CONS MANDARIN
MICHELIN TYRE PLC
Michelle — I: MICELLE PRESS
Micropatent (US) — D: CHADWYCK-HEALEY LTD
Microsoft Press (US) — D: PENGUIN BOOKS LTD
Microtrend (US) — D: PITMAN PUBLISHING
MID NORTHUMBERLAND ARTS GROUP
MID-BORDER BOOKS
Middle East Economic Digest (Partial) — A: P M LLEWELLYN CO
Middle East Editorial Associates (US) — D: ROGER LASCELLES
Middle East Media — D: SEND THE LIGHT
MIDDLETON PRESS
MIDLAND COUNTIES LTD

Midland Publishing — D: MIDLAND COUNTIES LTD
Midnight Press — D: BURSTON DIST SERV
Milepost Publications — D: PLATFORM 5 PUB LTD
MILESTONE PUBLICATIONS
Military Press Ltd, The — I: TAYLOR & FRANCIS LTD
Millbank Books — D: COMBINED BOOK SERV
Millbank Books (Ireland Only) — D: ISLAND PUBLICATIONS
MILLBANK BOOKS LTD
Millbank Pub — No reply 93
Millenium — I: ORION PUBLISHING
Millenium — D: LITTLEHAMPTON BK SVC
Miller Art Books, Harvey (RubenianumLudwig Burchard Series) — D: ART BOOK DIST CO
Miller Gallery, Robert — D: ART DATA
Miller, Harvey — D: BIBLIOS PUB DIST
Miller, Harvey (Medical books only) — D: OXFORD UNI PRESS DIS
Miller, J Garnet — I: CRESSRELLES PUB LTD
MILLER PUBLISHERS, HARVEY
Millers — I: REED CONSUMER ILLUS
Millivres — D: TURNAROUND
Mills & Boon Large Print — D: MAGNA LARGE PRINT
Mills & Boon Ltd — D: EXEL LOGISTICS
MILLS & BOON LTD
Millstream Books — D: ASHGROVE PRESS
Millstream Publishing — D: IAN ALLAN PUBLISHING
Millwood Press (NZ) — D: PETER MOORE BOOKS
Milner (Partial) (AU) — D: CASSELL PLC
Milner Publishing, Sally (AU) — D: GAZELLE BOOK SERVICE
Milton — D: MARLBOROUGH BOOKS
Mind — No reply 93
Minerva — I: REED CONS MANDARIN
MINIFLASHCARD LANGUAGE GAMES
MINIMAX BOOKS LTD
MINING JOURNAL BOOKS
Ministero De Cultura (SP) — D: ART DATA
Minneapolis Institute of Art (US) — D: ART DATA
Minority Rights Group — D: CENTRAL BOOKS
MINORITY RIGHTS GROUP
Minority Rights Publications — I: MINORITY RIGHTS GRP
Minstrel — I: KINGSWAY PUB
MINTON & MINTON
Minuit (FR) — D: EUROPEAN SCHOOLBOOKS
MIR (SU) — D: CENTRAL BOOKS
Mirror Books (Partial) — A: JOHN WILSON BOOKS
MIS Press (US) — D: PITMAN PUBLISHING
Mission Press (ZM) — D: LEISHMAN & TAUSSIG
Mississippi Museum of Art (US) — D: ART DATA
Mistral Publishing — D: VINE HOUSE DIST
MIT Press & Loeb, The — D: JOHN WILEY & SONS
MIT PRESS LTD
Mitchell Beazley — I: REED CONSUMER ILLUS
Mitchell Beazley — D: REED BOOK SERVICES
Mitchell, Valentine (Jewish Interest) — D: KUPERARD LTD
Mitchell's Building Series — I: LONGMAN GROUP UK LTD
Mitre — I: MONARCH PUB
Mitre House Pub — No reply 93
Mizan Press (US) — D: ALIF INTERNATIONAL
Mizen Books — D: AIRLIFT BOOK CO
Mkuki na Nyota Publishers (TZ) — D: AFRICAN BOOKS COLL
Modern Bu-Jutsu (US) — D: GAZELLE BOOK SERVICE
Modern Curriculum Press — I: SIMON & SCHUSTER INT
Modern Welsh Publications — D: WELSH BOOKS COUNCIL
Moksha Foundation (US) — D: CENTRAL BOOKS
Molino (SP) — D: EUROPEAN SCHOOLBOOKS
Molloy Publishing — D: DALENNAU
MOMENTA PUBLISHING COMPANY LTD
Moments With The Book — D: CHAPTER TWO
Monad Press — I: PATHFINDER PRESS
Monarch — I: WOLFHOUND PRESS
MONARCH PUBLICATIONS LTD
Mondadori Arte (IT) — D: S HENEAGE DIST
Mondadori Espana (SP) — D: EUROPEAN SCHOOLBOOKS
Mondadori, Giorgio (IT) — D: BOOKS CONTINENTAL
Mondadori (IT) — D: EUROPEAN SCHOOLBOOKS
Monnier, Le (IT) — D: EUROPEAN SCHOOLBOOKS
Montagud Editores SA (SP) — D: FOOD TRADE PRESS LTD
Monthly Review (US) — D: CENTRAL BOOKS
Montrose Music & Book Sales — No reply 92/93
Monument — I: WITHERBY & CO LTD
Moon Travel Handbooks (US) — A: HODDER & STOUGHTON
Moonfox (US) — D: EVENLODE BOOK DIST
Moonlight Publishing Ltd — D: RAGGED BEARS LTD
Moonstone Books — D: AIDAN ELLIS PUB

Moonstone Press Inc (US) — D: APOLLO PRESS LTD
MOORE BOOKSELLER, PETER
Moorland Publishing — D: GRANTHAM BOOK SERV
Moorland Publishing — A: WORLD LEISURE MKTG
MOORLAND PUBLISHING COMPANY LTD
Moorley's Bible & Bookshop Ltd — I: MOORLEY'S PRINT PUB
MOORLEY'S PRINT & PUBLISHING
Moral Re-Armament — D: GROSVENOR BOOKS
Moravian Music Foundation Press — I: GOLDEN COCKEREL
Morgan & Morgan Inc (US) — D: GAZELLE BOOK SERVICE
MORGAN BOOKSELLERS, CALVIN — W
Morgan Grampian — I: BENN BUSINESS INFO
Morgan Kaufmann Publishers (US) — D: LAWRENCE ERLBAUM ASS
Morgan Technical Books Ltd — D: BARNACLE MARINE LTD
Morija Sesuto Book Depot (LE) — D: LEISHMAN & TAUSSIG
Morris, Joshua — D: DAVID & CHARLES PLC
Morris Publishing Inc, Joshua — I: VICTORIA HOUSE PUB
Morrisson Leahy — D: INT MUSIC PUB
Morrow Fielding Guides, Wm — D: GRANTHAM BOOK SERV
MORTEN PUBLISHERS, E J
Mosaic Press (Partial) (CA) — D: CALDER PUB LTD
Mosby-Yearbook Europe — D: EXEL LOGISTICS
MOSBY-YEARBOOK EUROPE
Moscovitch & Co — D: CENTRAL BOOKS
MOTHERS' UNION
MOTILAL BOOKS
Motilal Books (UK) Ltd — D: LAVIS MARKETING
Motivate Publishing (AR) — D: ROGER LASCELLES
Motor Racing Publications — D: BIBLIOS PUB DIST
MOTOR RACING PUBLICATIONS LTD
Motorbooks International (US) — D: J H HAYNES & CO LTD
MOTOROLA LTD
Mount Kenya Sundries (KY) — D: LEISHMAN & TAUSSIG
Mountain Club of Kenya (KY) — D: CORDEE
Mountain Press Publishing Co (US) — D: GAZELLE BOOK SERVICE
Mountain Shadows (US) — D: EVENLODE BOOK DIST
Mountaineers Books (US) — D: CORDEE
Mouse That Spins — D: MANDRAKE
Mouse That Spins — D: TEMPLE PRESS LTD
Mowbray — I: CASSELL PLC
Mowbray (Ireland Only) — D: COLUMBA BOOK SERVICE
Moyer Bell Ltd (US) — D: GAZELLE BOOK SERVICE
Moytura Press — I: CORK PUBLISHING LTD
Moytura Press (IR) — D: PROFESSIONAL BK SALE
MOZAMBIQUE INSTITUTE
Mr Bridge — I: MILESTONE PUB
MRG Reports — I: MINORITY RIGHTS GRP
Msprint Publishing — D: CENTRAL BOOKS
MTMS — D: TRANSPORT PUB CO LTD
MTP Press — I: KLUWER ACADEMIC PUB
MTP Press Ltd — I: KLUWER ACADEMIC PUB
Mudiad Efengylaidd Cymru — I: EVANGELICAL PR WALES
Mudiad Ysgolion Meithrin (Partial) — D: WELSH BOOKS COUNCIL
Muhammadi Trust — D: ELEMENT BOOKS LTD
Muhammadi Trust — D: ALIF INTERNATIONAL
Muhyiddin Ibn Arabi Society — D: ALIF INTERNATIONAL
Muir Publications, John (US) — D: EVENLODE BOOK DIST
Mulberry Editions — PARRAGON BOOK SERVICE
Muller — I: RANDOM HOUSE UK LTD
MULTILINGUAL MATTERS
Multilingual Matters Ltd — D: PLYMBRIDGE DIST LTD
Multimedia Books Ltd — D: BOOKPOINT LIMITED
MULTIMEDIA BOOKS LTD
Multimedia Zambia Publications (ZM) — D: LEISHMAN & TAUSSIG
Multimedia Zambia (ZM) — D: AFRICAN BOOKS COLL
MULTISCOPE BOOKS
Municipal Journal — I: NEWMAN BOOKS LTD
Munksgaard International Publishers Ltd (Partial) (DN) — D: BLACKWELL SCIENTIFIC
Munro & Co, James — I: BROWN SON & FERGUSON
Murach & Associates Inc, Mike (US) — D: GAZELLE BOOK SERVICE
Murdoch Books — D: AUSTRALIAN CON PRESS
MURRAY EDINBURGH, GRAEME
Murray, John — D: GRANTHAM BOOK SERV
Murray (Publishers) Ltd, John (KY) — A: EVANS BROTHERS LTD
MURRAY PUBLISHERS LTD, JOHN
Mursia (IT) — D: EUROPEAN SCHOOLBOOKS
Musee De Marseille (FR) — D: ART DATA
Musees Et Monuments De France (FR) — D: S HENEAGE DIST
Museum Boymans - Van Beuningen Publications (NT) — D: EVENLODE BOOK DIST
Museum of Modern Art (New York) Publications (US) — D: THAMES & HUDSON LTD
Museum of Modern Art Oxford — D: ART DATA
Museum of New Mexico Press (US) — D: ART DATA

MUSEUMS ASSOCIATION
MUSIC BOOK DISTRIBUTORS LTD — W
MUSIC COLLECTION INTERNATIONAL — A
Music Master — I: WATERLOW INFO SERV
MUSIC PRESS
Music Sales — OMNIBUS PRESS
Muslim Education & Literary Services (MELS) — D: ALIF INTERNATIONAL
Mustang Publishing (Partial List) (US) — D: VACATION WORK
Mustang Publishing (US) — D: GAZELLE BOOK SERVICE
Mystic Fire Audio (US) — D: AIRLIFT BOOK CO
NACE (US) — A: AMERICAN TECH PUB
Nadder — I: ELEMENT BOOKS LTD
NAG Press — D: TIPTREE BOOK SERV
NAG PRESS
Nahanni (CA) — D: DUNDURN DISTRIBUTION
NAHUM, PETER
Nahum, Peter (Partial) — D: S HENEAGE DIST
Naiad Press (US) — D: AIRLIFT BOOK CO
Nairobi University Press (KY) — D: LEISHMAN & TAUSSIG
Nalta Publishing (US) — D: EVENLODE BOOK DIST
N&P Publishing — D: BOOKPOINT LIMITED
Nanholme Press — I: LITTLEWOOD ARC
Nara Verlag — D: PHOTOBOOK INFO SERV
Nascimanere (AU) — D: WORLDLY GOODS
Nash Publishing, Steven J (US) — D: EVENLODE BOOK DIST
Nasou (Partial) — D: BAY FOREIGN BOOKS
Nathan (FR) — D: EUROPEAN SCHOOLBOOKS
Nathanael Literature Distributors — D: CHAPTER TWO
National Academy Press (US) — A: BOOK REP & DIST LTD
National Academy Press (US) — D: PLYMBRIDGE DIST LTD
National Army Museum — D: BOOKPOINT LIMITED
National Association for Asian Youth — I: SHAKTI COMMUNICATION
NATIONAL ASSOCIATION FOR THE TEACHING OF ENGLISH
NATIONAL CHILDBIRTH TRUST
National Childrens Bureau — A: BOOK REP & DIST LTD
NATIONAL CHILDRENS' BUREAU
NATIONAL CHRISTIAN EDUCATION COUNCIL
National Council for Civil Liberties — D: CENTRAL BOOKS
National Council of Teachers of Mathematics — D: JONATHAN PRESS
National Council of Teachers of Mathematics — D: QED
NATIONAL CURRICULUM COUNCIL
NATIONAL EXTENSION COLLEGE
NATIONAL FOSTER CARE ASSOCIATION
National Galleries of Scotland (For Eng & Wales) — A: LUND HUMPHRIES PUB
National Gallery of Art (Partial) (US) — D: ALPINE FINE ARTS
National Gallery of Art (US) — A: UNI PRESSES MARKETNG
National Gallery of Ireland (IR) — D: CENTRAL BOOKS
National Gallery Publications London — D: OXFORD UNI PRESS DIS
NATIONAL GALLERY PUBLICATIONS LTD
NATIONAL GARDENS CHARITABLE TRUST
National Geographic Society — A: WORLD LEISURE MKTG
National Geographic Society (US) — D: PLYMBRIDGE DIST LTD
NATIONAL INSTITUTE FOR SOCIAL WORK
National Institute of Adult Continuing Education — D: CENTRAL BOOKS
NATIONAL INSTITUTE OF CONTINUING ADULT EDUCATION
National Joint Consultative Computer for Building — D: RIBA PUBLICATIONS
National League for Nursing (US) — D: GAZELLE BOOK SERVICE
NATIONAL LIBRARY OF SCOTLAND
National Library of Wales (Partial) — D: WELSH BOOKS COUNCIL
National Money Advice Training Unit — I: BIRMINGHAM SETTLEMNT
National Museum of Scotland (Dept of Museum Services) — D: GAZELLE BOOK SERVICE
National Museum of Wales — D: WELSH BOOKS COUNCIL
NATIONAL POETRY FOUNDATION
National Portrait Gallery (Partial) — D: HMSO BOOKS
National Portrait Gallery — D: PLYMBRIDGE DIST LTD
NATIONAL PORTRAIT GALLERY PUBLICATIONS
National Press Books (US) — D: GAZELLE BOOK SERVICE
National Radiological Protection Board — D: HMSO BOOKS
National Series of Waterway, Railway & Tramway Atlases — I: G L CROWTHER
National Society, The — I: CHURCH HOUSE PUB
National Sound Archive — I: BRITISH LIB MK & PUB
National Speleological Society (US) — D: CORDEE
National Textbook Company (Partial) (US) — D: ACCENT EDUCATIONAL
National Trust — D: HODDER & STOUGHTON
NATIONAL TRUST
National Trust for Scotland — D: CLAN BOOKS
NATIONAL TRUST (IR)
NATIONAL YOUTH AGENCY
Natural Health Publications — D: ASHGROVE PRESS
NATURAL HISTORY BOOK SERVICE
NATURAL HISTORY MUSEUM PUBLICATIONS
Naturegraph (US) — D: BAHAI PUBLISHING

NATURETREK EDUCATIONAL
Naturist Society (US) — D: GAZELLE BOOK SERVICE
Naval Institute Press (US) — D: AIRLIFE PUBLISHING
Naval, Military & Air Force Bible Society — I: SCRIPTURE GIFT MISS
NAVPRESS
Naya Prokash Calcutta (IN) — D: BOOKS FROM INDIA
Nazraeli Press (GE) — D: CENTRAL BOOKS
NBM (US) — D: COMBINED BOOK SERV
NC Press (CA) — D: DUNDURN DISTRIBUTION
NCC Blackwell — A: BLACKWELL PUB LTD
NCC Blackwell — D: MARSTON BOOKS SERV
NCLC Publishing Society Ltd — I: FABIAN SOCIETY
NCVO PUBLICATIONS
Neal-Schuman Publishers (US) — D: EDS
Nehanda Publishers (ZB) — D: LEISHMAN & TAUSSIG
Nelles Verlag — D: MCCARTA LTD
NELSON & SONS, THOMAS
Nelson Bibles, Thomas (US) — D: B MCCALL BARBOUR
NELSON LTD, ANTHONY
Nelson Publications Ltd, Don — D: METAL BULLETIN PLC
Nelson, Thomas — D: INT THOMSON PUB SERV
Nelson, Thomas — A: JOHN RITCHIE LTD
Nelson, Thomas (Bibles & Testamants) (US) — D: BIBLE SOCIETY
Nelson-Hall Inc (US) — D: GAZELLE BOOK SERVICE
NEMA (US) — A: AMERICAN TECH PUB
Nene Valley Publishing — I: CHALKSOFT LTD
Nentori (Partial) — D: PARFITTS BOOK SERV
Neruda Press — D: AK DISTRIBUTION
Netherlands Hydrographic Dept (NT) — D: IMRAY LAURIE & NORIE
Netherwood Ltd, Richard (Military Titles only) — A: SPELLMOUNT LTD
Netherwood, Richard — D: SPRINGFIELD BOOKS
NETHERWOOD, RICHARD
Network Books — I: BBC BOOKS
NETWORK EDUCATIONAL PRESS
NETWORK PUBLISHING
Neugebauer Press Ltd — D: RAGGED BEARS LTD
New Abbey Publications — I: FOURTH ESTATE
New Amsterdam Books (US) — D: GAZELLE BOOK SERVICE
NEW BEACON BOOKS LTD
New Cavendish Books — D: LITTLEHAMPTON BK SVC
NEW CAVENDISH BOOKS
New Century Press — D: GAZELLE BOOK SERVICE
New Cherwell Press — D: GROSVENOR BOOKS
NEW CITY
New City Press Ltd (Partial) (US) — D: T & T CLARK LTD
NEW CLARION PRESS
New Consumer — D: JON CARPENTER PUB
New Directions — D: W W NORTON & CO LTD
New English Library — I: HODDER & STOUGHTON
NEW ERA PUBLICATIONS LTD
New Falcon Publications (US) — D: AIRLIFT BOOK CO
NEW FOREST LEAVES
New Harbinger (US) — D: AIRLIFT BOOK CO
New Holland (Publishers) Ltd — D: BOOKPOINT LIMITED
NEW HOLLAND PUBLISHERS LTD
New Horizon (Partial) (US) — D: NEW BEACON BOOKS LTD
New Horizons — I: THAMES & HUDSON LTD
New Horn Press Ltd (NG) — D: AFRICAN BOOKS COLL
New Humanity Books (AU) — D: ELEMENT BOOKS LTD
New Internationalist — D: CENTRAL BOOKS
New Knowledge Books — D: RUDOLF STEINER PRESS
New Leaf Publishers (US) — D: LISTER ART BOOKS
New Mexico - Central America Country Guide Series — D: LATIN AMERICA BUREAU
New Namibia Books (NA) — D: AFRICAN BOOKS COLL
New Orchard Editions — I: CASSELL PLC
New Park — D: AK DISTRIBUTION
New Park Publications — D: INDEXREACH LTD
New Park Publications — D: BOOKMARKS
New Park (US) — A: TURNAROUND
NEW PLAYWRIGHTS' NETWORK
New Riders Publishing — I: SIMON & SCHUSTER INT
New Riders Publishing (US) — D: COMPUTER BOOKSHOPS
New Seed Press (US) — D: ROY YATES BOOKS
New Society Publishers (US) — D: TURNAROUND
New Victoria (US) — D: AIRLIFT BOOK CO
NEW WINE MINISTRIES
New World Library (US) — D: AIRLIFT BOOK CO
New World Press — I: KNIGHTSCROSS LTD
New World Publishing (US) — D: GAZELLE BOOK SERVICE
New York Academy of Sciences (US) — D: EDS
New York Institute of Finance — A: WOODHEAD-FAULKNER
New York University Press (US) — D: EDS

New York Zoetrope Inc (US) — D: GAZELLE BOOK SERVICE
New Zealand National Bibliography — D: DAWSON UK LTD
Newbury House (US) — D: THOMAS NELSON & SONS
NEWBY BOOKS
Newcastle Publishing (US) — D: AIRLIFT BOOK CO
Newest Press (CA) — D: DUNDURN DISTRIBUTION
NEWMAN BOOKS LTD
NEWMAN PUBLICATIONS LTD, OWEN
Newnes — I: BUTTERWORTH-HEINEMAN
Newnes — D: REED BOOK SERVICES
Newpoint — D: BUTTERWORTH-HEINEMAN
Newpoint — D: REED BOOK SERVICES
Newpoint Publishing Co — I: REED INFO SERVICES
NEWPRO UK LTD
News Brothers — EASON & SONS
NEWS PRODUCTIONS
News Productions (SZ) — D: NEWS PRODUCTIONS
Newtech — I: BUTTERWORTH-HEINEMAN
Newtech — D: REED BOOK SERVICES
Newton Books — I: NEWTON PUBLISHERS
NEWTON PUBLISHERS
Nexus — I: VIRGIN PUBLISHING
NFER/Routledge — I: ROUTLEDGE
Niche Publications — D: MIDLAND COUNTIES LTD
Nicholson/Ordnance Survey — I: HARPERCOLLINS BARTH
Nicolas - Hays (US) — D: AIRLIFT BOOK CO
Nieswand Verlag (GE) — D: ART DATA
Nigerian Institute of International Affairs (NG) — D: AFRICAN BOOKS COLL
NIGH & SONS LTD, W J — W
Nightingale Books — I: BAHAI PUBLISHING
Nijhoff Publishers, Martinus (NT) — D: KLUWER ACADEMIC PUB
NILE & MACKENZIE LTD
Nimbus Publishing Ltd (CA) — D: GAZELLE BOOK SERVICE
Nimrod Press — I: BEECH PUBLISHING
Nineties (90's) — I: SERPENT'S TAIL
Nippon Shuppan Hanbai (JP) — D: BIBLIOS PUB DIST
NISBET & CO, JAMES
Nishen Publishing, Dirk — No reply 92/93
No Exit Press — I: OLDCASTLE BOOKS LTD
No Exit Press — A: TURNAROUND
Noddy — I: BBC BOOKS
Nonesuch Press, The — I: REINHARDT BOOKS LTD
Non-League Publications — D: LITTLE RED WITCH
NORBURY PUBLICATIONS LTD, PAUL
Norbury Publications, Paul — I: CURZON PRESS LTD
Norbury Publications, Paul — D: BIBLIOS PUB DIST
NORHEIMSUND BOOKS & CARDS
North Atlantic Books (US) — D: AIRLIFT BOOK CO
North East Publishing — I: NORTH EAST WORSHIP
NORTH EAST WORSHIP RESOURCE
North Light Books (US) — A: H I MARKETING
North Light Books (US) — D: TIPTREE BOOK SERV
North Star Publications — D: W FOULSHAM & CO LTD
North West Video — D: IAN ALLAN PUBLISHING
NORTH YORK MOORS NATIONAL PARK
Northcote House — D: PLYMBRIDGE DIST LTD
Northcote House (Partial) — A: P M LLEWELLYN CO
NORTHCOTE HOUSE PUBLISHERS
Northeastern University Press (US) — A: ACADEMIC & UNIV PUB
Northern Bee Books — D: SPRINGFIELD BOOKS
Northern Books — I: FAMEDRAM PUB LTD
NORTHERN IRELAND CENTRE FOR LEARNING RESOURCES
Northland Publishing (Partial) (US) — D: MILLBANK BOOKS LTD
North-South Books — D: RAGGED BEARS LTD
Northumberland Mountaineering Club — D: CORDEE
Northwestern Publishing House (US) — D: CONCORDIA PUB LTD
Northwestern University Press (US) — A: TREVOR BROWN ASSOC
NORTHWICK PUBLISHERS
Norton — I: W W NORTON & CO LTD
Norton & Co, W W (Nautical only) — D: BARNACLE MARINE LTD
NORTON & COMPANY LTD, W W
Norton Medical Books — I: W W NORTON & CO LTD
Norton Professional Books — I: W W NORTON & CO LTD
Norton, W W — D: JOHN WILEY & SONS
Norton, W W (US) — D: IMRAY LAURIE & NORIE
Norwalk Press (US) — D: REAL BOOKS
Norwegian Hydrographic Dept (NW) — D: IMRAY LAURIE & NORIE
NORWOOD PUBLISHERS
Nottingham Wayfarers — D: CORDEE
NOVA DISTRIBUTION
Nova Publishing — I: NOVA DISTRIBUTION
NOVELLO & COMPANY LTD

NOVEMBER BOOKS
NOVIB — I: INTRAC
Novox Inc (US) — D: MICELLE PRESS
NTC Publishing Group - Trade Division (US) — D: VERULAM PUB LTD
NUCLEAR TECHNOLOGY PUBLISHING
Nucleus (US) — D: EVENLODE BOOK DIST
Nuit Isis — I: MANDRAKE
Nuova Alfa (IT) — D: S HENEAGE DIST
Nuprint — D: SEND THE LIGHT
Nur Corporation (US) — D: ALIF INTERNATIONAL
NUTMEG PRESS
Nutshell Press — I: PICTON PUBLISHING
Nutshell Publishing Co — SPELLMOUNT
Nutshell Publishing Co Ltd — I: SPELLMOUNT LTD
Oak Publications — I: OMNIBUS PRESS
Oak Tree Press — I: CORK PUBLISHING LTD
Oak Tree Press (IR) — D: PROFESSIONAL BK SALE
OAKWOOD PRESS
Oakwood Publications (US) — D: ANTHONY CLARKE PUB
Obafemi Awolowo University Press (NG) — D: AFRICAN BOOKS COLL
OBERON BOOKS LTD
O'Brien Educational — I: THE O'BRIEN PRESS
O'Brien Press — D: GILL & MACMILLAN LTD
O'Brien Press (GB only) (IR) — A: OLDCASTLE BOOKS LTD
O'Brien Press (IR) — D: CENTRAL BOOKS
O'Brien Press (IR) — A: TURNAROUND
O'BRIEN PRESS, THE
Ocean Press (AU) — D: CENTRAL BOOKS
OCLC EUROPE
OCTAGON PRESS
Octopus Publishing — REED CONSUMER BOOKS
Odyssey Guides — D: HODDER & STOUGHTON
OFFICE LONDON, THE
OFFICE OF HEALTH ECONOMICS
Office of the Data Protection Registrar — I: HOME OFFICE
Official Tourist Maps — I: ESTATE PUBLICATIONS
Offroad Cycling — D: CORDEE
Ohara Publications (US) — D: PAUL H CROMPTON LTD
Ohio State University Press (US) — D: EDS
Ohio University Press (US) — A: ACADEMIC & UNIV PUB
Oil Companies International Marine Forum — D: WITHERBY & CO LTD
Oilfields Workers Trade Union (Partial) (TT) — D: NEW BEACON BOOKS LTD
Old Bailey Press — I: HLT PUBLICATIONS
Old House Books — D: BOOKPOINT LIMITED
Old House Books — A: JOHN WILSON BOOKS
OLD STILE PRESS, THE
OLD VICARAGE PUBLICATIONS
Oldcastle Books — D: BOOKPOINT LIMITED
OLDCASTLE BOOKS LTD
OLDROYD BOOKS, JIM — R
OLEANDER PRESS, THE
Oleander Press, The (Partial) — A: P M LLEWELLYN CO
Olive Press — I: IMPACT BOOKS
Olive Press — A: VERULAM PUB LTD
Oliver & Boyd — I: LONGMAN GROUP UK LTD
Oliver & Boyd - School Books (Ireland Only) — D: EDUC CO OF IRELAND
Olivia & Hill (US) — D: ACCENT EDUCATIONAL
Olms, Georg (Partial) (GE) — D: ST PAUL'S BIBLIO
OM Publishing — D: SEND THE LIGHT
O'Mara Books — A: MACMILLAN DIST LTD
O'MARA BOOKS, MICHAEL
Omega Books — GODFREY CAVE ASSOCIATES
OMF BOOKS
OMNIBUS PRESS
On Line Video — D: IAN ALLAN PUBLISHING
Ondorisha (JP) — A: PREMIER BOOK MKTNG
ONEWORLD PUBLICATIONS
Oneworld Publications Ltd — D: ELEMENT BOOKS LTD
Online Press (US) — D: COMPUTER BOOKSHOPS
Only Women Press — D: AIRLIFT BOOK CO
Onslow Books — D: EPA PRESS
ONT — D: VINE HOUSE DIST
Ontario Economic Council (CA) — A: TREVOR BROWN ASSOC
OPC Ltd — I: J H HAYNES & CO LTD
OPEN BIBLE TRUST
OPEN BOOKS PUBLISHERS LTD
Open Books Publishing Ltd — D: CLIPPER DIST SERVICE
Open Chain Publishing Inc (US) — D: GAZELLE BOOK SERVICE
Open Court Publishing Company (US) — D: EDS
Open Gate Press — A: BOOK REP & DIST LTD
Open Gate Press — D: TBC DISTRIBUTION
OPEN GATE PRESS

Open House — I: NEWS PRODUCTIONS
Open Letters — Ceased trading 92
Open Magazine Pamphlet Series (US) — D: AK DISTRIBUTION
Open Pamphlets Series — D: COUNTER PRODUCTIONS
Open University — I: OPEN UNIV EDUC ENT
OPEN UNIVERSITY EDUCATIONAL ENTERPRISES
OPEN UNIVERSITY PRESS
Open University Press (Life & Earth Sciences list) — I: JOHN WILEY & SONS
Optima — I: LITTLE BROWN & CO
Optima — D: TIPTREE BOOK SERV
Orafa Publishing Company (US) — D: NORTHCOTE HOUSE PUB
ORBACH & CHAMBERS
Orbis — Macdonald imprint no longer used
ORBIS BOOKS LTD
Orbis Books (US) — D: GRACEWING/FOWLER
Orbit — I: LITTLE BROWN & CO
Orbit — D: TIPTREE BOOK SERV
Orchard Books — I: THE WATTS GROUP
Ordnance Survey — A: ESTATE PUBLICATIONS
ORDNANCE SURVEY
Ordnance Survey Landranger Guides — I: JARROLD PUBLISHING
Ordnance Survey (Motoring & Road Atlases) — A: REED CONS MANDARIN
Ordnance Survey of the Republic of Ireland (IR) — D: ESTATE PUBLICATIONS
Ordnance Survey of the Republic of Ireland (IR) — D: ORDNANCE SURVEY
Ordnance Survey Pathfinder Guides — I: JARROLD PUBLISHING
Oregon Catholic Press (US) — D: MCCRIMMON PUBLISHING
O'Reilly & Associates (US) — A: ADDISON-WESLEY PUB
O'Reilly & Associates (US) — D: SOUTHPORT BOOK DIST
Organisation for Economic Co-operation & Development (FR) — D: HMSO BOOKS
ORIEL/WELSH ARTS COUNCIL
Orient Longman Ltd (IN) — D: SANGAM BOOKS LTD
Orient Paperbacks Delhi (IN) — D: BOOKS FROM INDIA
ORIFLAMME PUBLISHING
Orion Books — I: ATTIC BOOKS
Orion Books (US) — D: AIRLIFE PUBLISHING
Orion Publishing Group — D: LITTLEHAMPTON BK SVC
ORION PUBLISHING LTD
ORKNEY PRESS LTD
Orpheus (Partial) — D: PC PUBLISHING
Oryx Press, The (US) — D: EDS
Osborne — I: MCGRAW HILL BOOK CO
OSBORNE BOOKS LTD
Oscars — D: TURNAROUND
Osmiroid — A: DEREK SEARLE ASS LTD
Osprey — I: REED CONSUMER ILLUS
Osterreichischer Bundesverlag (AS) — D: ROY YATES BOOKS
Other People Publications (AU) — D: ROGER LASCELLES
Otherway — D: TURNAROUND
Ouest Editions (Partial) (FR) — D: INTERCEPT LTD
Our Sunday Visitor (US) — D: GRACEWING/FOWLER
Outline Press — D: FOUNTAIN PRESS LTD
Outposts Publications — Ceased trading 92
Oval Projects — I: CLASS PUBLISHING
Overlook Press (Partial) (US) — D: ELEMENT BOOKS LTD
OVERSEAS DEVELOPMENT INSTITUTE
OVUM LTD
Owen Ltd, Peter — D: LITTLEHAMPTON BK SVC
OWEN LTD, PETER
Owen, Peter — D: AK DISTRIBUTION
Owens, Tuppy — D: MANDRAKE
Owens, Tuppy — D: BIBLIOS PUB DIST
Owen's World Trade — No reply 92/93
OWL BOOKS
OWL PRESS
OXBOW BOOKS
Oxbow Monographs in Archaeology — I: OXBOW BOOKS
Oxbridge Communications (US) — D: CEDAR TREE HOUSE
OXFAM
Oxfam Audio-Visual Resources — I: OXFAM
Oxfam Education — I: OXFAM
Oxfam Publications — I: OXFAM
Oxfam Publications — D: CENTRAL BOOKS
Oxford & IBH Pub Co (IN) — D: BOOKS FROM INDIA
Oxford & IBH Publishers (IN) — D: INTERCEPT LTD
OXFORD BUSINESS PUBLISHING
Oxford Computer Training — D: COMPUTER BOOKSHOPS
Oxford Group, The — D: GROSVENOR BOOKS
Oxford Illustrated Press — I: J H HAYNES & CO LTD
Oxford Institute for Energy Studies — D: OXFORD UNI PRESS DIS
Oxford Paperbacks — I: OXFORD UNIV PRESS
Oxford Polytechnic Press (Partial)   D: ST PAUL'S BIBLIO
Oxford Publishing Company — I: J H HAYNES & CO LTD

Oxford University Committee for Archaeology — D: OXBOW BOOKS
Oxford University Press (Bibles & Testaments) — D: BIBLE SOCIETY
Oxford University Press (Partial) — A: P M LLEWELLYN CO
Oxford University Press - Southern Africa (SA) — D: LEISHMAN & TAUSSIG
Oxford University Press - Eastern Africa (KY) — D: LEISHMAN & TAUSSIG
OXFORD UNIVERSITY PRESS
OXFORD UNIVERSITY PRESS DIST
Oxmoor House — D: LITTLE BROWN & CO
Oxon Distribution — Ceased trading 92
P4 Spares — A: ACADEMY BOOKS LTD
P4 SPARES
Pace Gallery (US) — D: ART DATA
Pace University Press (US) — D: EDS
Pacific Press Publishing Assoc — D: STANBOROUGH PRESS
Packard Publishing Company (US) — D: GAZELLE BOOK SERVICE
PACKARD PUBLISHING LTD
Paganiniana — I: TFH PUBLICATIONS
Pakua Journal (US) — D: PAUL H CROMPTON LTD
Palace Books (Partial) — D: WELSH BOOKS COUNCIL
Palace Publications (US) — D: ELEMENT BOOKS LTD
Paladin Press (US) — D: AAB BRIT BOOK SEARCH
Palamalandos — D: MARITIME BOOKS
Palatine Books — I: CARNEGIE PUB LTD
Palau (SP) — D: DOLPHIN BOOK CO LTD
Pali Text Society — D: LAVIS MARKETING
PALLADIO PRESS
PALLAS ATHENE
Pallas Guides — I: PALLAS ATHENE
Palm Tree — I: KEVIN MAYHEW LTD
Pamplemouse — D: VINE HOUSE DIST
Pan Macmillan Ltd — D: MACMILLAN DIST LTD
PAN MACMILLAN LTD
Panaf Books — I: ZED BOOKS LTD
Panda Books — I: HENDERSON PUB LTD
PANDEMIC LTD
PANDIT
Pandon Press Ltd — I: BLOODAXE BOOKS
Pandora Press — I: HARPERCOLLINS THORS
PANGBOURNE ENGLISH CENTRE
Panos Institute — D: CENTRAL BOOKS
Papaloizos Publications (US) — D: ZENO
Paper Mac — I: MACMILLAN DIST LTD
Paper Tiger Books — I: DRAGONS WORLD LTD
Paperbird — I: LADYBIRD BOOKS LTD
Paperfronts — I: ELLIOT RIGHT WAY
Papers Inc (NZ) — D: TURNAROUND
Paperweight Press (US) — D: VOLO EDITION
Para Publishing (Partial) (US) — D: CORDEE
Parabola (US) — D: AIRLIFT BOOK CO
Paragon House (US) — D: GAZELLE BOOK SERVICE
Paragon Publishing — I: ALFRED WALLER LTD
Paragon Publishing — D: COMPUTER BOOKSHOPS
Parallax Press (US) — D: ELEMENT BOOKS LTD
Parallax (US) — D: WISDOM BOOKS
Paraninfo (SP) — D: EUROPEAN SCHOOLBOOKS
Parco View (JP) — D: ART DATA
Pardoe Blacker Publishing — D: WINDSOR BOOKS INT
Parent & Child — I: REED CONS MANDARIN
PARFITTS BOOK SERVICES
Paris Audiovisuel (FR) — D: ART DATA
Paris-Musees (FR) — D: S HENEAGE DIST
Park Publications (HG) — D: ROGER LASCELLES
Parke Sutton — A: JARROLD PUBLISHING
PARKE SUTTON PUBLISHING LTD
Parker Pen — D: EXEL LOGISTICS
Parkett Verlag (SZ) — D: CENTRAL BOOKS
PARLIAMENTARY PROFILE SERVICES
Parragon — D: D SERVICES
PARRAGON BOOK SERVICE
Parramon (SP) — D: EUROPEAN SCHOOLBOOKS
PARTHENON PUBLISHING GROUP
Partridge Press — I: TRANSWORLD PUB
Party World — I: EGMONT PUB LTD
Parvis Books — D: GREVATT & GREVATT
PAS Publications (Partial) (US) — D: IANMEAD LTD
Pasold Research Fund — D: OXFORD UNI PRESS DIS
PASS Publications — I: PASS PUBLICATIONS
Passport Books — D: VERULAM PUB LTD
Passport Books (US) (Travel Books) — D: KUPERARD LTD
Passport Press (US) — D: CORDEE
Password — I: BPP PUBLISHING LTD
PASSWORD (BOOKS) LTD

PASTEST SERVICE
PASTEST SERVICE — A
PASTIME PUBLICATIONS
Pastoral Press (US) — D: COLUMBA BOOK SERVICE
Patakis (GR) — D: ROY YATES BOOKS
PATEMAN'S WHOLESALE BOOK SERVICE — W
Paternoster (Partial) — D: BIBLE SOCIETY
Paternoster Press — D: SEND THE LIGHT
Paterson's — I: NOVELLO & CO LTD
Pathfinder Press — D: PLYMBRIDGE DIST LTD
PATHFINDER PRESS
Pathfinder Publishing (US) — D: ELEMENT BOOKS LTD
PATTEN PRESS
Patten-Hardy Library — I: PATTEN PRESS
Patterson Publishers, Neil (Partial) (US) — D: PORTLAND PRESS LTD
PATTON PUBLICATIONS
Paul, Louis F — No reply 92/93
Paul, Stanley — I: RANDOM HOUSE UK LTD
Paul, Stanley — D: TIPTREE BOOK SERV
Pauli Publishing (NT) — D: LAVIS MARKETING
Paulinus Press — No reply 92/93
Paulist Press (US) — D: VERITAS PUBLICATIONS
Paulist Press (US) — D: GRACEWING/FOWLER
Pauper Press, Peter (US) — D: CHRIS LLOYD SALES
PAUPERS' PRESS
PAVIC PUBLICATIONS
Pavilion — D: EXEL LOGISTICS
Pavilion Books — D: BLOOMSBURY PUB LTD
PAVILION BOOKS LTD
Pavilion Productions — I: PAVILION BOOKS LTD
PAVILION PUBLISHING (BRIGHTON)
PAWSEY & SONS, F W — W
Paxton — I: NOVELLO & CO LTD
Payame Anian (US) — D: ALIF INTERNATIONAL
PB Publications — D: AK DISTRIBUTION
PBI PUBLICATIONS
PBI Publications Press — D: BIBLIOS PUB DIST
PBN PUBLICATIONS
PC PUBLISHING
Peace News — D: HOUSMANS BOOKSHOP
Peachpit Press (US) — D: COMPUTER STEP LTD
Peachpit Press (US) — D: LONGMAN GROUP UK LTD
Peachtree Publishers (Partial) (US) — D: WILLIAM SNYDER PUB
Peacock Publishers Inc, F E (US) — D: GAZELLE BOOK SERVICE
PEACOCK VANE PUBLISHING
Peak Skill Publishing (US) — D: EVENLODE BOOK DIST
Pearson & Co, J M — D: IMRAY LAURIE & NORIE
PEARSON & SON, J M
Pearson, J M & Son — D: CORDEE
PEARSON PUBLISHING
Peartree Books — D: BIBLIOS PUB DIST
PEARTREE PUBLICATIONS
PEEPAL TREE BOOKS
Peepal Tree Press — D: PASSWORD (BOOKS) LTD
Peerage Books — I: REED CONS BOUNTY
Peerage Publications — D: FOUNTAIN PRESS LTD
Peermahomed Ebrahim Trust (PK) — D: ALIF INTERNATIONAL
Pegasus Publishing Ltd — D: BOOKPOINT LIMITED
PEGASUS PUBLISHING SERVICES
Pelham — I: PENGUIN BOOKS LTD
Pelican (Partial) (US) — D: SPA BOOKS LTD
Pelican Publishing Co (US) — D: NORTHCOTE HOUSE PUB
Pelican Publishing (US) — D: ROGER LASCELLES
PEMBERTON & SONS, G R & J — W
PEN & SWORD BOOKS
Pencil Press — I: ROUNDHOUSE PUB LTD
Pendle Hill Publication (US) — D: QUAKER HOME SERVICE
Pendulum Gallery Press — D: BIBLIOS PUB DIST
PENDULUM GALLERY PRESS
Penfield Press (US) — D: GAZELLE BOOK SERVICE
PENGUIN BOOKS LTD
PENINSULA BOOKS
Peninsula Publishing (US) — A: PREMIER BOOK MKTNG
Peninsular Publishing — I: IMMEL PUBLISHING LTD
Penn Cottage Books — No reply 93
Penny Dreadful Publishers (US) — D: GAZELLE BOOK SERVICE
PENNY PRESS
Penn-Yale Expedition (US) — D: LA HAULE BOOKS LTD
Pentacle (US) — D: EVENLODE BOOK DIST
Pentech Press — A: JOHN WILEY & SONS
PENTLAND PRESS LTD
Penton Overseas Inc (US) — D: GAZELLE BOOK SERVICE

Penton Press — I: JESSICA KINGSLEY PUB
Penton Press — D: KOGAN PAGE LTD
Peppercanister — I: THE DEDALUS PR (IR)
Peregrinus Ltd, Peter — I: INST OF ELEC ENGINE
PERGAMON PRESS
Perineum Press (US) — D: GMP PUBLISHERS LTD
Periplus - Indonesia Travel Library (ID) — D: MCCARTA LTD
Permanent Publications — I: HYDEN HOUSE LTD
PERRY LTD, COLIN A
Persona (US) — D: TURNAROUND
PERVAIZ PUBLICATIONS
Peter Projection World Map — A: WORLD LEISURE MKTG
PETERHOUSE PRESS, THE
Peterloo Poets — A: PASSWORD (BOOKS) LTD
PETERLOO POETS
PETERLOO POETS — A
Peters, Frank — D: CORDEE
Petersburg — No reply 92/93
Petersen, Duncan — D: GRANTHAM BOOK SERV
Petersen, Duncan — A: WORLD LEISURE MKTG
Peterson Music, John W (US) — D: B MCCALL BARBOUR
Petersons Guides (Partial List) (US) — D: VACATION WORK
Pevensey Press — I: DAVID & CHARLES PLC
PEVENSEY PRESS
Pfalzische Ver (Gemalde der Rembrandt Schuler Series) (GE) — D: ART BOOK DIST CO
Pfeiffer & Co (US) — D: MERCURY BOOKS
Phaidon Press Ltd — D: BOOKPOINT LIMITED
PHAIDON PRESS LTD
Phalanx Publlishing Co (Partial) (US) — D: IAN ALLAN PUBLISHING
Phanes Press (US) — D: ASHGROVE PRESS
PHARMACEUTICAL PRESS
Pharmaceutical Products Press (US) — D: EDS
Philadelphia Art Alliance — I: GOLDEN COCKEREL
Philadelphia Museum of Art (US) — D: ART DATA
Philip, George — I: REED CONSUMER ILLUS
Philip, George — D: REED BOOK SERVICES
Philip Publishers, David (SA) — D: LEISHMAN & TAUSSIG
Philippe Daverio (IT) — D: S HENEAGE DIST
PHILLIMORE & CO LTD
PHILOGRAPH PUBLICATIONS LTD
Philosophia Verlag (GE) — D: UNI PRESSES MARKETNG
Philosophical Research Society — D: DEEP BOOKS LTD
Phoenix — I: ORION PUBLISHING
Phoenix — I: KINGSWAY PUB
Phoenix Books — D: PRINTWISE PUB LTD
PHOENIX BOOKS — R
Phoenix House — D: LITTLEHAMPTON BK SVC
Phoenix Press — D: AK DISTRIBUTION
Phoenix Publishers (KY) — D: LEISHMAN & TAUSSIG
Phoenix Publishing — D: DEEP BOOKS LTD
Photo Data Research (US) — D: GAZELLE BOOK SERVICE
PHOTOBOOK INFORMATION SERVICES
Photographers Gallery — D: ART DATA
Photographers Gallery — D: CENTRAL BOOKS
Photovision (SP) — D: ART DATA
Piacere, A — D: BOOSEY & HAWKES LTD
Piatkus Books — D: GRANTHAM BOOK SERV
PIATKUS BOOKS
Pic — D: CORDEE
Picadilly Press — A: BOXTREE LTD
Picador — I: PAN MACMILLAN LTD
Piccadilly Press — D: TIPTREE BOOK SERV
Piccadilly Press (Ireland only) — A: BLACKSTAFF PRESS LTD
PICCADILLY PRESS LTD
Piccin Editore (IT) — D: GAZELLE BOOK SERVICE
Piccolo — I: PAN MACMILLAN LTD
Pickering & Chatto (Publishers) Ltd — D: TURPIN DISTRIBUTION
Pickwick Group — No reply 93
Pickwick Papers — A: VERULAM PUB LTD
Picton Press — I: COUNTYVISE LTD
PICTON PUBLISHING
Picture Corgi — I: TRANSWORLD PUB
Picture Lions — I: HARPERCOLLINS CHILD
Picture Palace — A: NEWS PRODUCTIONS
Picture Press — D: CENTRAL BOOKS
Pidgeon Audio Visual — I: SUSSEX PUBLICATIONS
PIG PRESS
Pilgrim Book Services — D: L N FOWLER & CO LTD
PILGRIM PRESS LTD
Pilgrim Publications (US) — D: EVANGELICAL PRESS
Pilgrims — D: BEBC DISTRIBUTION
PILLAR PUBLICATIONS

Pimlico — I: RANDOM HOUSE UK LTD
Pimlico — D: TIPTREE BOOK SERV
Pindar Press — No reply 92/93
Pindari Publications (Partial) (AU) — D: CORDEE
Pineapple Press Inc (US) — D: GAZELLE BOOK SERVICE
PINES PRESS
PINHORNS
Pinnacle Club — D: CORDEE
PINTER PUBLISHERS
Pinter Publishers Ltd — A: BOOK REP & DIST LTD
Pinter Publishers Ltd — D: MARSTON BOOKS SERV
PION LTD
Pion Publishers — D: TURPIN DISTRIBUTION
Pioneer Drama (US) — D: HANBURY PLAYS
PIPELINE BOOKS — W
Piper — I: PAN MACMILLAN LTD
Pirate Press — D: AK DISTRIBUTION
Pisces Angling Publications — D: HUGO'S LANGUAGE BOOK
PISCES ANGLING PUBLICATIONS
PITKIN PICTORIALS
Pitman Publishing — D: SOUTHPORT BOOK DIST
PITMAN PUBLISHING
Pixel Press (US) — D: GAZELLE BOOK SERVICE
Planeta (SP) — D: EUROPEAN SCHOOLBOOKS
PLATFORM 5 PUBLISHING LTD
Players Press (US) — D: IAN HENRY PUB LTD
Playful Wisdom (US) — D: EVENLODE BOOK DIST
PLAYWRIGHTS PUBLISHING CO
Plaza & Janes (SP) — D: EUROPEAN SCHOOLBOOKS
Plenum Medical — I: PLENUM PUBLISHING CO
Plenum Press — I: PLENUM PUBLISHING CO
PLENUM PUBLISHING COMPANY
PLEXUS PUBLISHING
Plexus Publishing Ltd — D: BOOKPOINT LIMITED
PLOUGH PUBLISHING
PLRG — I: EUROPEAN BUS PUB
PLUME PRESS
PLUNKETT FOUNDATION
Pluribus Press Inc (US) — D: GAZELLE BOOK SERVICE
Pluto Press — A: TURNAROUND
PLUTO PUBLISHING
PLYMBRIDGE DISTRIBUTORS LTD
Plymouth (US) — D: INT MUSIC PUB
PM & E (US) — D: TEMPLE PRESS LTD
PMA (US) — D: EDS
PN Review — A: CARCANET PRESS
PNL Press — I: UNI NORTH LONDON
Pocket Books — I: SIMON & SCHUSTER LTD
Pocket Books — D: GAZELLE BOOK SERVICE
Poetical Histories — I: PETER RILEY (BOOKS)
Poetry Business, The — D: PASSWORD (BOOKS) LTD
POETRY BUSINESS, THE
POETRY BUSINESS, THE — A
POETRY WALES PRESS
Polebridge Press (US) — D: SCM PRESS LTD
Polecat Press — D: CORDEE
POLECAT PRESS LTD
POLICE REVIEW PUBLISHING
Policy Studies Instititue — A: BOOK REP & DIST LTD
Policy Studies Institute — D: BEBC DISTRIBUTION
POLICY STUDIES INSTITUTE
Poligrafa (SP) — D: S HENEAGE DIST
Politi Editore, Giancarlo (IT) — D: CENTRAL BOOKS
Polity Press — A: BLACKWELL PUB LTD
Polity Press — D: MARSTON BOOKS SERV
Polygon — I: EDINBURGH UNIV PRESS
Polygon — D: AK DISTRIBUTION
Polymath Publishing — D: SPA BOOKS LTD
Polytantric Press — I: JAY LANDESMAN
Polytech — I: PITMAN PUBLISHING
Pomegranate Calendars & Books (US) — D: POMEGRANATE EUROPE
POMEGRANATE EUROPE
Pomp, Peter (Partial) (GE) — D: MICELLE PRESS
Pond View — I: HAWTHORNS PUB LTD
Pont — I: J D LEWIS & SONS LTD
Pontifical Inst of Mediaeval Studies (CA) — A: ACADEMIC & UNIV PUB
Pony Club, The — D: KENILWORTH PRESS LTD
Pookie Productions — D: AMAISING PUB HOUSE
Pookie Productions — D: VINE HOUSE DIST
Poolbeg Press (GB only) (IR) — A: OLDCASTLE BOOKS LTD
Poolbeg Press (IR) — D: CENTRAL BOOKS
Poolbeg Press (IR) — A: TURNAROUND

POOLBEG PRESS LTD
POPPYLAND PUBLISHING
Popular Culture, Ink (US) — D: EDS
Popular Dogs — I: RANDOM HOUSE UK LTD
Popular Dogs — D: TIPTREE BOOK SERV
Popular Prakashan (IN) — D: SANGAM BOOKS LTD
Popular Publications (MA) — D: LEISHMAN & TAUSSIG
PORDES LTD, H — R
Portcullis Press Ltd — I: FMJ BOOKS
Porteous Associates, David — D: BOOKPOINT LIMITED
Porteous Associates, David — A: DEREK SEARLE ASS LTD
PORTEOUS EDITIONS, DAVID
Porter Publishing Videos — D: J H HAYNES & CO LTD
Porter Sargeant Ltd (US) — D: HOUSMANS BOOKSHOP
Porthill Publishers — D: ASHFORD BUCHAN
PORTHILL PUBLISHERS
Portikus (GE) — D: ART DATA
Portland Press — A: ROGER BAYLISS
Portland Press Inc (US) — D: PORTLAND PRESS LTD
PORTLAND PRESS LTD
Portmanteau Press (US) — D: MIT PRESS LTD
Porto Editora (PG) — D: ROY YATES BOOKS
Porto Editora (PG) — D: EUROPEAN SCHOOLBOOKS
Poseidon Press — I: SIMON & SCHUSTER LTD
POSITIVE PRODUCTS
Postal History Society, The — D: CBD RESEARCH LTD
Post-Apollo Press (US) — D: ELEMENT BOOKS LTD
Potala (US) — D: WISDOM BOOKS
Potton, Craig (NZ) — D: CENTRAL BOOKS
POUND HOUSE, THE
Power Institute of Fine Arts (AU) — D: TURNAROUND
Power Point — D: SEND THE LIGHT
Power Publications — D: COUNTRYSIDE BOOKS
POWER PUBLICATIONS
POWERFRESH LTD
Poyser, T & A D — I: HARCOURT BRACE JOVAN
Praeger Publishers (US) — D: EDS
Prakash (PK) — D: VERITAS PUBLICATIONS
Prancing Tortoise Publications — D: VINE HOUSE DIST
Praxis Institute Press — I: AGORA BOOKS
PRC — I: PROMOTIONAL REPRINT
Precinct Press, The — I: ENSIGN PUBLICATIONS
PRECISE EDUCATIONAL
Prehistory Press (US) — D: OXBOW BOOKS
Premier Book Marketing — D: BIBLIOS PUB DIST
PREMIER BOOK MARKETING
Premier Editions — I: MEREHURST FAIRFAX
Prentice Hall — I: SIMON & SCHUSTER INT
Prentice Hall — D: INT BOOK DIST
Prentice Hall Press — I: SIMON & SCHUSTER LTD
Prentice Hall Regents — I: SIMON & SCHUSTER INT
Presbyterian & Reported Publishing (US) — D: EVANGELICAL PRESS
Preservation Press (US) — D: S HENEAGE DIST
Presidio Press (US) — D: GREENHILL BOOKS
Press Gang (US) — D: TURNAROUND
Presses de la Cite (FR) — D: EUROPEAN SCHOOLBOOKS
Presses Universitaires de France (FR) — D: EUROPEAN SCHOOLBOOKS
Presses Universitaires de Grenoble (FR) — D: EUROPEAN SCHOOLBOOKS
Pressure Drop Press (US) — D: AK DISTRIBUTION
Pressure Points — I: HARVESTIME PUB LTD
Prestel Verlag (GE) — D: THAMES & HUDSON LTD
Prestige Sales & Marketing — D: BOOKSPEED
Pride Publications — I: E J MORTEN PUB
Prima Publishing (US) — D: COMPUTER BOOKSHOPS
Primal (US) — D: AK DISTRIBUTION
Primary House Publications — I: THE FRIENDLY PRESS
Primary Point (US) — D: EVENLODE BOOK DIST
Primrose Educ Research — No reply 93
Princeton Architectural Press (US) — D: BIBLIOS PUB DIST
Princeton Book Company (US) — D: DANCE BOOKS LTD
Princeton University Press (US) — A: UNI PRESS CALIFORNIA
Princeton University Press (US) — D: JOHN WILEY & SONS
Principio Press (US) — D: EVENLODE BOOK DIST
PRINT ORGANISATION
PRINTFORCE UNITED
PRINTWISE PUBLICATIONS LTD
Prion — I: MULTIMEDIA BOOKS LTD
Prion (Bird Watchers Guides) — D: NATURAL HIST BOOK SV
Prion (Jewish Interest) — D: KUPERARD LTD
Prion (Multimedia) — A: CHARLES LETTS & CO
Priory Press Ltd — D: WAYLAND (PUB) LTD
Priory Publications — D: VINE HOUSE DIST

Priory Publications — D: ROGER LASCELLES
Prism Press — D: BOOKPOINT LIMITED
PRISM PRESS
Prism Unity — I: PRISM PRESS
Prison Source — I: HOME OFFICE
PRITAM BOOKS
PRIVATE ACADEMIC & SCIENTIFIC STUDIES
Private Consultations — I: CHILTON DESIGNS
Private Eye Books — D: TRANSWORLD PUB
Probation Monographs — I: SOCIAL WORK MONO
Probus Books (Partial) — D: METAL BULLETIN PLC
PROBUS EUROPE
Probus Publishing (US) — D: BIBLIOS PUB DIST
Product Liability Briefing — I: EUROPEAN BUS PUB
PROFESSIONAL BOOK SALES
Professional Books — I: BUTTERWORTH & CO LTD
Professional Books — D: BUTTERWORTH & CO LTD
Professional Books (US) — D: REAL BOOKS
Professional Business Communications (US) — D: EVENLODE BOOK DIST
Professional Publishers (Partial List) (SA) — D: BUTTERWORTH & CO LTD
Professor Playtime Audio — D: SULLIVAN ASSOCIATES
Professors World Peace Academy (ZM) — D: LEISHMAN & TAUSSIG
Progress Books (SU) — D: CENTRAL BOOKS
Prolog (IS) — D: KUPERARD LTD
Prometheus Books — D: LAVIS MARKETING
PROMETHEUS BOOKS UK
PROMIS LTD
Promises — I: HARVESTIME PUB LTD
PROMOTIONAL REPRINT CO
Proscenium Publishers Inc (US) — D: GAZELLE BOOK SERVICE
Prospect Publishing — D: BOOKPOINT LIMITED
PROSPERITY PUBLICATIONS
Proteus Books — I: OMNIBUS PRESS
PROTON PUBLISHING HOUSE LTD
PROVIDENCE BOOKS
PRS LTD
PRU — D: AVANTI BOOKS
Pruett Publishing Co (US) — D: CORDEE
Pruett Publishing (US) — D: GAZELLE BOOK SERVICE
PRYOR PUBLICATIONS
PSDS — I: WATERLOW INFO SERV
PSI Publishing — I: POLICY STUDIES INST
PSSRV — D: WHITING & BIRCH LTD
Psychic Press — No reply 93
Psychological Corp, The — I: HARCOURT BRACE JOVAN
PSYCHOLOGY NEWS
PUBLIC FINANCE FOUNDATION
Publications for Companies — No reply 93
Publications India (Partial) — D: BAY FOREIGN BOOKS
Publishers Distribution Service (US) — D: GAZELLE BOOK SERVICE
Publishing Pathways — I: ST PAUL'S BIBLIO
Pudoc (NT) — D: EUROPEAN PRESS SERV
Pudoc (UK orders only) (NT) — D: CAB INTERNATIONAL
Pueblo Publishing Company (US) — D: COLUMBA BOOK SERVICE
Puffin — I: PENGUIN BOOKS LTD
Punches Productions (US) — D: GAZELLE BOOK SERVICE
PUNCHESTOWN BOOKS
Punchestown Books (IR) — D: PROFESSIONAL BK SALE
Purnell Distribution — Ceased trading 92
Putnam Aeronautical Books — I: CONWAY MARITIME
PWS Kent (US) — D: INT THOMSON PUB SERV
Pyramid — I: REED CONSUMER ILLUS
Pythagaorean Press — D: JONATHAN PRESS
QED
QED Information Sciences (US) — D: ELECTRONICA BOOKS
Quail Map Company — D: PLATFORM 5 PUB LTD
Quaker Council for European Affairs (BG) — D: QUAKER HOME SERVICE
QUAKER HOME SERVICE
Quaker Peace & Service — I: QUAKER HOME SERVICE
Quakers Social Responsibility & Education — I: QUAKER HOME SERVICE
Quality Medical Publishing — I: WILLIAMS & WILKINS
Quantum — I: W FOULSHAM & CO LTD
Quartermaine House — I: DICKSON PRICE PUB
Quartet Books — D: PLYMBRIDGE DIST LTD
QUARTET BOOKS LTD
Quarto Publishing — D: BIBLIOS PUB DIST
Quay Publishing — D: LAVIS MARKETING
QUAY PUBLISHING
Que Corporation — I: SIMON & SCHUSTER INT
Que Publishing (US) — D: COMPUTER BOOKSHOPS
Queen Anne Press — I: LENNARD ASSOCIATES
Queensland Department of Primary Industries (AU) — D: BOOKS EXPRESS

Quellen Verlag (SZ) — D: SEARCH PRESS LIMITED
Quercus — I: SIMON & SCHUSTER INT
Quest Books — I: THEOSOPHICAL PUB LTD
Quest Books — D: VINE HOUSE DIST
QUEST BOOKS (NI)
QUEST MERIDIEN LTD
Quest Wheaton (US) — D: THEOSOPHICAL PUB LTD
Questron — D: CHILD'S PLAY
Quill Hedgehog Books — D: EVENLODE BOOK DIST
Quiller Press — D: COMBINED BOOK SERV
QUILLER PRESS LTD
Quilliam Press — D: ELEMENT BOOKS LTD
Quince Tree Press — I: J L CARR
Quinlan Press (US) — D: GAZELLE BOOK SERVICE
Quinta Essentia — I: ISLAMIC TEXTS SOC
Quinta Essentia — ISLAMIC TEXTS SOCIETY
Quintessence Publishing Co Ltd — D: SHEED & WARD LTD
QUINTESSENCE PUBLISHING COMPANY
Quintessenz (GE) — D: EUROPEAN SCHOOLBOOKS
Quorum Books (US) — D: EDS
QUOTES LTD
R & B Publishing — D: VINE HOUSE DIST
R & B PUBLISHING
R & R PUBLICATIONS
R & S Books (SW) — D: RAGGED BEARS LTD
RAC Motoring Services Ltd — D: BOOKPOINT LIMITED
RAC Publishing — A: DEREK SEARLE ASS LTD
RAC PUBLISHING
RAC Travel Guides — I: JARROLD PUBLISHING
Race Today — D: TURNAROUND
Raceform — D: COMBINED BOOK SERV
RADCLIFFE MEDICAL PRESS
Radcliffe Professional Press — I: RADCLIFFE MEDICAL
Radiant Publishers (IN) — D: SANGAM BOOKS LTD
Radiation — D: MANDRAKE
Radical Quarterly — D: CARNEGIE PUB LTD
Radio Amateur Call Books (US) — D: WINDSOR BOOKS INT
Radio France (FR) — D: EUROPEAN SCHOOLBOOKS
RADIO SOCIETY OF GB
Radius — I: RANDOM HOUSE UK LTD
Raduga Press (SU) — D: CENTRAL BOOKS
RAGGED BEARS LTD
Ragweed (US) — D: TURNAROUND
Rahenajat (PK) — D: ALIF INTERNATIONAL
Rail Photoprints — D: TRANSPORT PUB CO LTD
Rail Photoprints — D: PLATFORM 5 PUB LTD
Rail Scene — D: IAN ALLAN PUBLISHING
RAILWAY CORRESPONDANCE & TRAVEL SOCIETY
Rainbow Books — I: ARTHUR JAMES LTD
Rainbow Publishers — I: THE OFFICE LONDON
Ramblers' Association — D: W FOULSHAM & CO LTD
RAMBORO BOOKS
RAMBORO BOOKS — R
Ramira Publications — D: ELEMENT BOOKS LTD
RAMSAY HEAD PRESS
Rand McNally Ltd (US) — D: SPRINGFIELD BOOKS
Random Century Audio Books — D: GRANTHAM BOOK SERV
Random Century Children's Books — D: GRANTHAM BOOK SERV
Random Century (one title) (AU) — D: MILLBANK BOOKS LTD
Random House — D: TIPTREE BOOK SERV
Random House Children's Books — I: RANDOM HOUSE UK LTD
Random House Electronic Publishing — I: RANDOM HOUSE UK LTD
RANDOM HOUSE GROUP
RANDOM HOUSE GROUP — A
Random House (Jewish Interest) (US) — D: KUPERARD LTD
Random House (US) — D: EUROPEAN PRESS SERV
RANDOM THOUGHTS LTD
Randonnees Pyreneenes (FR) — D: MCCARTA LTD
Randonnees Pyreneennes Maps — A: WORLD LEISURE MKTG
Rands Video — D: IAN ALLAN PUBLISHING
Ranjung Yeshe (NP) — D: WISDOM BOOKS
Rapid Communication of Oxford — D: INT THOMSON PUB SERV
Rapid Eye Publishing — D: TEMPLE PRESS LTD
Rato Publications (US) — D: WISDOM BOOKS
Ravan Press (SA) — D: CENTRAL BOOKS
Raven Arts Press (IR) — D: PASSWORD (BOOKS) LTD
Raven Press (US) — D: EUROPEAN PRESS SERV
Ravensburger Buchuerlag (GE) — D: ROY YATES BOOKS
Ravenstein (GE) — D: ROGER LASCELLES
RAVENSWOOD PUBLICATIONS LTD
Ravette Books — I: EGMONT PUB LTD
RAVETTE BOOKS LTD

Raw Vision — D: TURNAROUND
Rawson Associates — I: MAXWELL MACMILLAN
Rawson Associates (US) — D: MARSTON BOOKS SERV
Ray Society — A: NATURAL HIST MUSEUM
RCTS Publications — I: RAILWAY CORR SOCIETY
Readers Digest — A: DAVID & CHARLES PLC
Readers Digest — D: EXEL LOGISTICS
Readers International — D: SERPENT'S TAIL
READERS INTERNATIONAL
Reaktion Books Ltd — D: LITTLEHAMPTON BK SVC
REAKTION BOOKS LTD
REAL BOOKS
Rebec Press — D: DALENNAU
Rebel Press — D: AK DISTRIBUTION
Rebel Publishing House (GE) — D: GAZELLE BOOK SERVICE
Reclam (GE) — D: EUROPEAN SCHOOLBOOKS
RECO-PRESS PUBLISHERS
Record Books (Partial) (US) — D: CLIO PRESS LTD
Recta Foldex (FR) — D: ROGER LASCELLES
Red Balloon — D: IMAGES DISTRIBUTION
Red Books — I: ESTATE PUBLICATIONS
Red Fox — I: RANDOM HOUSE (ARROW)
Red House — I: NEWS PRODUCTIONS
Red Man — No reply 92/93
Red Notes — D: AK DISTRIBUTION
Redan — D: D SERVICES
REDCLIFFE PRESS LTD
Reddy & Reddy (US) — D: GAZELLE BOOK SERVICE
REDEMPTORIST PUBLICATIONS
Redhouse Yayinevi (TK) — D: ROY YATES BOOKS
Redstone Press — D: CENTRAL BOOKS
Redwords — D: BOOKMARKS
REED BOOK SERVICES
REED CONSUMER BOOKS
REED DIRECTORIES, WILLIAM
REED INFORMATION SERVICES
REED PUBLICATIONS LTD, THOMAS
Reed Publications, Thomas — D: BARNACLE MARINE LTD
Reed Travel Group — D: ASHFORD BUCHAN
Reed's Nautical Books — I: THOMAS REED PUB LTD
REEVES LTD, WILLIAM
Reference Press, The (US) — D: WILLIAM SNYDER PUB
REFLECTIONS OF A BYGONE AGE
Reflex Publishers (NT) — D: ART DATA
Refract — D: AK DISTRIBUTION
REFUGEE ACTION
Regal Books — I: THE OFFICE LONDON
Reidel Publishing Co, D — I: KLUWER ACADEMIC PUB
Reinhard Ryborsch Verlag (GE) — D: CORDEE
Reinhardt Books — D: PENGUIN BOOKS LTD
REINHARDT BOOKS LTD
Relate — No reply 93
Relaxation Centre of Queensland (AU) — D: L N FOWLER & CO LTD
Religious & Moral Education Press (RMEP) — I: HYMNS ANCIENT & MOD
Renaissance House Publishers (US) — D: GAZELLE BOOK SERVICE
Renaissance Ltd — D: BAILEY DIST LTD
Renaissance du Livre (Partial) (BG) — D: HILMARTON MANOR
Renditions (HK) — D: TURNAROUND
Research & Education Association (US) — D: INT BOOK DIST
RESEARCH INSTITUTE FOR CONFLICT & TERRORISM
Research Publishing — I: CHARLES SKILTON LTD
RESEARCH STUDIES LTD
Research Study Press — A: JOHN WILEY & SONS
RE/Search (US) — D: AIRLIFT BOOK CO
Re/Search (US) — D: AK DISTRIBUTION
Resource Masters — I: PEARSON PUBLISHING
Resource Publications (US) — D: COLUMBA BOOK SERVICE
Resources Occasional Papers — I: ASR RESOURCES LTD
Reston — I: SIMON & SCHUSTER INT
Resurgence Books — I: GREEN BOOKS
Reunion Des Musees Nationaux (FR) — D: ART DATA
Revelations 23 Press — D: TEMPLE PRESS LTD
Review & Herald Publishing Assoc — D: STANBOROUGH PRESS
Revue Noire (FR) — D: CENTRAL BOOKS
Rex Collings — No reply 93
RHINEGOLD PUBLISHING LTD
Rhode Island School of Design (US) — D: ART DATA
Rhodos International (Craft Books only) (US) — D: ALISON HODGE PUB
RHS (Wisley Handbooks only) — D: CASSELL PLC
Riad El Rayyes Books — A: P M LLEWELLYN CO
RIAD EL-RAYYES BOOKSELLERS LTD
RIBA PUBLICATIONS

Ribeiro Francisco (PG) — D: SUNFLOWER BOOKS
Richards, Ray (NZ) — D: PICTON PUBLISHING
Richardson, J — No reply 92/93
RICHMOND PUBLISHING COMPANY LTD
RICS BOOKS
Rider — D: WISDOM BOOKS
Rider — I: RANDOM HOUSE UK LTD
Rider — D: TIPTREE BOOK SERV
Rienner Publishers, Lynne (US) — D: EDS
Ries & Erler (GE) — D: BOOSEY & HAWKES LTD
Rietveld Academie, Gerrit (NT) — D: ART DATA
Right Now Books — D: LAVIS MARKETING
RIGHT NOW BOOKS
Right Way — I: ELLIOT RIGHT WAY
Rightangle — I: INTERCEPT LTD
RILEY BOOKS, PETER
RILKO (Research Into Lost Knowledge Organisation) — D: SHEPHEARD-WALWYN
Rinchen Editions (SI) — D: WISDOM BOOKS
Ring O'Bells Publishing — I: BARN DANCE PUB LTD
Ringpress Books — A: DEREK SEARLE ASS LTD
Ringpress Books Ltd — D: BOOKPOINT LIMITED
Rinsen (JP) — D: WISDOM BOOKS
Rip Off Press (US) — D: KNOCKABOUT COMICS
RIPON HISTORICAL SOCIETY
RITCHIE LTD, JOHN
Ritter Verlag (AS) — D: ART DATA
RIVELIN GRAPHEME PRESS
RIVERS ORAM PRESS
Rivers Publishing — D: CORDEE
Riverside Bibles (US) — D: B MCCALL BARBOUR
Riverside World (Bibles & Testaments) (US) — D: BIBLE SOCIETY
Rizzoli International Publications (US) — D: BIBLIOS PUB DIST
RIZZOLI INTERNATIONAL PUBLICATIONS
Rizzoli (IT) — D: EUROPEAN SCHOOLBOOKS
RKP — I: ROUTLEDGE
RMEP — A: SPCK
Road Books (IR) — D: CENTRAL BOOKS
ROADMASTER PUBLISHING
Roberts, Don (IR) — A: WORDSWORTH EDITIONS
ROBERTS PUBLICATIONS
Roberts Rinehart (US) — D: AIRLIFT BOOK CO
Robertson McCarta — D: GRANTHAM BOOK SERV
Robertson Scientific Publications (US) — D: JAMES & JAMES LTD
Robinson Publishing — D: CONSTABLE & CO LTD
ROBINSON PUBLISHING
Robinson Publishing (Ireland only) — A: BLACKSTAFF PRESS LTD
Roblaw Publishers (ZB) — D: LEISHMAN & TAUSSIG
ROBSON BOOKS
Robson Books (Export) — D: BIBLIOS PUB DIST
Rochester Press — D: ROADMASTER PUB
Rockport Publishers (US) — D: WINDSOR BOOKS INT
Rocky Mountain Books (CA) — D: CORDEE
Roeder Publications (SI) — D: GAZELLE BOOK SERVICE
Rollo Publishing Co — D: GAZELLE BOOK SERVICE
Romance of, The — I: CHRIS ANDREWS PHOTO
RONALD PUBLISHER, GEORGE
RONALDSON PUBLICATIONS
Rongwrong Foundation (NT) — D: CENTRAL BOOKS
Ronin Publishing Inc — D: COUNTER PRODUCTIONS
Roof Publications — D: CENTRAL BOOKS
Roof Top Art — A: NEWS PRODUCTIONS
Rookledge International Publication — I: SAREMA PRESS LTD
Root, A I (US) — D: BEE BOOKS NEW & OLD
Ropac Galerie, Thaddeus (AS) — D: ART DATA
ROSE LAW PUBLISHERS, BARRY
ROSEDENE PUBLISHERS
Rosendale Press — A: BOXTREE LTD
Rosendale Press — D: BIBLIOS PUB DIST
ROSENDALE PRESS
Rosendale Press (Partial) — A: P M LLEWELLYN CO
ROSENHEATH SCIENTIFIC PUBLICATIONS
ROSKILL INFORMATION SERVICES
Rosmini House — D: BREWIN BOOK DIST
ROSSLYN PUBLISHING
ROSTERS LTD
ROTOGRAPHIC PUBLICATIONS
Rotovision SA (SZ) — D: WINDSOR BOOKS INT
Rough Guides — D: PENGUIN BOOKS LTD
Round Hall Press — D: GILL & MACMILLAN LTD
ROUND HALL PRESS, THE
Roundhouse Publishing Ltd — D: BOOKPOINT LIMITED
ROUNDHOUSE PUBLISHING LTD

ROUNDOAK PUBLISHING
Routiers Guides — I: ALAN SUTTON PUB LTD
Routledge — D: INT THOMSON PUB SERV
ROUTLEDGE
Routledge Chapman & Hall Inc (US) — D: ROUTLEDGE
Routledge/Thoemmes Press — I: ROUTLEDGE
Routledge/Thoemmes Press — I: THOEMMES PRESS
Rowan — I: RANDOM HOUSE (ARROW)
Rowman & Littlefield Publishers (US) — D: EDS
ROWNTREE FOUNDATION, JOSEPH
Rowohlt (GE) — D: EUROPEAN SCHOOLBOOKS
ROXIMILLION PUBLICATIONS CO
ROYAL AERONAUTICAL SOCIETY
Royal Armouries — A: GREENHILL BOOKS
Royal Asiatic Society — D: LAVIS MARKETING
ROYAL ASSOCIATION FOR DISABILITY & REHABILITATION
Royal College of Nursing (Partial) — D: SCUTARI PRESS
ROYAL COLLEGE OF PHYSICIANS OF EDINBURGH
ROYAL COMMISSION ON THE HISTORICAL MONUMENTS OF ENGLAND
Royal Entomological Society — A: NATURAL HIST MUSEUM
Royal Genealogies — I: STACEY INTERNATIONAL
Royal Historical Society — D: BOYDELL & BREWER LTD
Royal Horticultural Society — D: B T BATSFORD LTD
Royal Institute of Chartered Surveyors — A: MOMENTA PUB CO LTD
Royal Institute of International Affairs — A: BOOK REP & DIST LTD
ROYAL INSTITUTE OF INTERNATIONAL AFFAIRS
ROYAL IRISH ACADEMY
Royal Microscopical Society — D: OXFORD UNI PRESS DIS
ROYAL SCHOOL OF CHURCH MUSIC
ROYAL SOCIETY
Royal Society Chemistry — No reply 93
Royal Society of Chemistry — D: TURPIN DISTRIBUTION
ROYAL SOCIETY OF MEDICINE SERVICES
ROYAL TOWN PLANNING INSTITUTE
ROYAL UNITED SERVICES INSTITUTE FOR DEFENCE STUDIES
Royal Yachting Association — D: BARNACLE MARINE LTD
ROYSTON
RSCM — I: RSCM
RSPB (Partial) — D: A & C BLACK LTD
RSPTS (Ireland only) — A: BLACKSTAFF PRESS LTD
Rubank — D: NOVELLO & CO LTD
RUBICON PRESS, THE
Rudall Carte — I: BOOSEY & HAWKES LTD
Rudin, BO (SW) — D: CENTRAL BOOKS
Rugby Press (NZ) — D: VINE HOUSE DIST
Runneymede — D: TURNAROUND
RUNNING ANGEL
Runpast — D: IAN ALLAN PUBLISHING
Rupa Books (IN) — D: BOOKS FROM INDIA
RUSHWORTH LITERATURE LTD
RUSI — I: RUSI
RUSSELL LTD, MICHAEL
Russell, Michael — D: BIBLIOS PUB DIST
Russian Information Centre Ltd — D: BOOKPOINT LIMITED
Ruston-Bradlow — D: FOOD TRADE PRESS LTD
Rutgers University Press (Partial) (US) — D: ROUNDHOUSE PUB LTD
Rutledge Hill Press (Partial) (US) — D: VERULAM PUB LTD
Rux (IT) — D: EUROPEAN SCHOOLBOOKS
RV Maps — A: WORLD LEISURE MKTG
RYBURN DISTRIBUTION
Ryburn Publishing — I: RYBURN DISTRIBUTION
S A Writers (GE) — D: CENTRAL BOOKS
Sabotage Editions — D: AK DISTRIBUTION
Sacks Fine Art (Partial) (SA) — D: S HENEAGE DIST
Sackville Books — D: SPRINGFIELD BOOKS
SAE International (US) — A: AMERICAN TECH PUB
SAF Publishing — D: AIRLIFT BOOK CO
Safari — I: DELAMARE PUBLISHING
Safari Press (US) — D: ASHFORD BUCHAN
Saga — I: QUOTES LTD
Saga — QUOTES
Sagamore Publishing Inc (US) — D: GAZELLE BOOK SERVICE
SAGE PUBLICATIONS
Sage Publications Ltd — A: BOOK REP & DIST LTD
Sagep (IT) — D: S HENEAGE DIST
Sain Recordings — D: DALENNAU
SAINSBURY PUBLISHING LTD
St Andrews Press — A: SPCK
ST ANDREW PRESS
St Anne's Music Society — D: BIBLIOS PUB DIST
St Bede's Publications (US) — D: GRACEWING/FOWLER
St George & Dragon Press — I: BIBLIAGORA

St James Press — I: GALE RESEARCH INT
St James Press — D: INT THOMSON PUB SERV
St John Thomas, David — D: BOOKPOINT LIMITED
ST JOHN THOMAS, DAVID
St Martins Press (US) — D: EUROPEAN PRESS SERV
St Mary's Press (US) — D: COLUMBA BOOK SERVICE
St Paul Publications (Partial List) (IR) — D: ST PAUL'S PUB
St Paul Publications (KY) — D: LEISHMAN & TAUSSIG
ST PAUL PUBLICATIONS
ST PAUL'S BIBLIOGRAPHIES
ST Publishing — D: BOOKPOINT LIMITED
St Vladimir's Seminary Press (Partial) (US) — D: CASSELL PLC
Salamander — A: IAN ALLAN PUBLISHING
Salamander — D: HODDER & STOUGHTON
Salamander Books Ltd — D: BOOKPOINT LIMITED
Salem Press (US) — D: CLIO PRESS LTD
Salmon Publishing — No reply 93
Salmon Publishing (IR) — D: PASSWORD (BOOKS) LTD
Saltire Society — D: JOHN DONALD PUB LTD
SALTIRE SOCIETY
Salvat (SP) — D: EUROPEAN SCHOOLBOOKS
Sams, Howard — I: SIMON & SCHUSTER INT
SAMSON BOOKS LTD
Samuel French Inc (US) — D: SAMUEL FRENCH LTD
San Diego State University Press (US) — D: EDS
San Francisco Museum of Art (US) — D: ART DATA
Sanders Publishing, Nick (Red Bus) — D: ASHFORD BUCHAN
SANDPIPER BOOKS — R
Sang Kyu Shim — I: SIMON & SCHUSTER INT
Sangam Book India Ltd (IN) — D: SANGAM BOOKS LTD
SANGAM BOOKS LTD
Sankore Publishers (NG) — D: AFRICAN BOOKS COLL
Santillana (SP) — D: EUROPEAN SCHOOLBOOKS
Sapes Trust (ZB) — D: LEISHMAN & TAUSSIG
SAQI BOOKS
SAREMA PRESS LTD
Saros International Publishers (NG) — D: AFRICAN BOOKS COLL
SARSEN PUBLISHING
Saunders College — I: HARCOURT BRACE JOVAN
Saunders Company, W B — I: HARCOURT BRACE JOVAN
Saur (Allgemeines Kunstlerlexicon Series) (GE) — D: ART BOOK DIST CO
Saur, K G — I: BOWKER-SAUR LTD
Saur, K G (Partial list) (GE) — D: BUTTERWORTH & CO LTD
SAUS PUBLICATIONS
Savacou (Partial) (JM) — D: NEW BEACON BOOKS LTD
Sawbridge Enterprises — D: ELEMENT BOOKS LTD
SAWD BOOKS
Sawd Publications — D: BOOKPOINT LIMITED
Sawers Publishing, Robert G — No reply 92/93
SAYCE PUBLISHING
SB Publications — D: BIBLIOS PUB DIST
SB PUBLICATIONS
SCA Education — I: WHITING & BIRCH LTD
Scala Publications — I: PHILIP WILSON PUB
SCALA PUBLICATIONS LTD
Scandinavian University Press (NW) — D: OXFORD UNI PRESS DIS
Scarab Publications — D: GAZELLE BOOK SERVICE
Scarecrow Press Inc (US) — D: SHELWING LTD
Scarlet Dagger Large Print Books — I: CHIVERS PRESS LTD
Scarlet Press — D: PLUTO PUBLISHING
Scarlet Press — A: TURNAROUND
SCARLET PRESS
SCARTHIN BOOKS
Sceptre Books — I: HODDER & STOUGHTON
SCEPTRE PRESS LTD
Schellman Edition (GE) — D: ART DATA
Schiffer Publishing (US) — D: MILLBANK BOOKS LTD
Schirmer Art Books (GE) — D: PANDEMIC LTD
Schirmer Books — I: MAXWELL MACMILLAN
Schirmer Books (US) — D: MARSTON BOOKS SERV
Schirmer-Mosel Verlag (GE) — D: ART DATA
Schirn Kunsthalle Frankfurt (GE) — D: ART DATA
Schneider, Franz (GE) — D: EUROPEAN SCHOOLBOOKS
Schocken (US) — D: KUPERARD LTD
Schoettle Publishing Co (US) — D: B MCCALL BARBOUR
SCHOFIELD & SIMS LTD
Scholarly Resources (US) — D: EDS
Scholastic Childrens' Books — I: SCHOLASTIC PUB LTD
Scholastic Inc (US) — D: SCHOLASTIC PUB LTD
SCHOLASTIC PUBLICATIONS LTD
Scholastic Tab (CA) — D: SCHOLASTIC PUB LTD
School Action Packs — I: HAMILTON HOUSE PUB

School Garden Company — I: CHALKSOFT LTD
School of Oriental and African Studies(University of London) — D: OXFORD UNI PRESS DIS
SCHOOL OF ORIENTAL & AFRICAN STUDIES
School of the Word — I: HARVESTIME PUB LTD
Schroders Ord & Bildbyra (SW) — D: CORDEE
Schwinn (GE) — D: CENTRAL BOOKS
Science & Behaviour Books — D: DEEP BOOKS LTD
Science & Technology Letters — I: SCIENCE REVIEWS LTD
SCIENCE MUSEUM
Science of Mind Publications (US) — D: L N FOWLER & CO LTD
Science Press — D: NOVELLO & CO LTD
Science Press Beijing (CH) — D: WILLIAM SNYDER PUB
Science Press New York (US) — D: WILLIAM SNYDER PUB
SCIENCE REVIEWS LTD
Sciences Nat (FR) — D: E W CLASSEY LTD
Scientific American Books — I: W H FREEMAN & CO LTD
Scientific American Library — I: W H FREEMAN & CO LTD
SCIENTIFIC & TECHNICAL BOOK SERVICE
Scientific Educational Systems — D: GAZELLE BOOK SERVICE
SCIPTURE PRESS FOUNDATION
SCIPTURE UNION PUBLISHING
Sci-Tech Publications Ltd (LI) — D: GAZELLE BOOK SERVICE
SCM PRESS LTD
Scolar — I: ASHGATE PUB GROUP
Scope International — MILESTONE PUBLICATIONS
Scopus Films Ltd (Jewish Interest) — D: KUPERARD LTD
SCORPION PUBLISHING
Scorpion Publishing (Partial) — A: P M LLEWELLYN CO
Scots Law Times — I: W GREEN
Scott Foresman (US) — D: HARPERCOLLINS DIST
Scottish Academic Press — A: BOOK REP & DIST LTD
SCOTTISH ACADEMIC PRESS
Scottish Child — D: BOOKSPEED
SCOTTISH COUNCIL FOR VOLUNTARY ORGANISATIONS
Scottish Examination Board — I: ROBERT GIBSON & SONS
Scottish Falcon — I: ORKNEY PRESS LTD
SCOTTISH GENEALOGY SOCIETY
SCOTTISH LIBRARY ASSOCIAYTION
Scottish Mountaineering Club/Trust — D: CORDEE
SCOTTISH TOURIST BOARD
Scottish Universities Summer Schools in Physics, Edinburgh — D: IOP PUBLISHING LTD
SCOTTISH YOUTH HOSTELS ASSOCIATION
SCOUT ASSOCIATION
Scribner Reference — I: MAXWELL MACMILLAN
Scribner Reference — D: MARSTON BOOKS SERV
Scribners — Macdonald imprint no longer used
Scribner's Sons, Charles — I: MAXWELL MACMILLAN
Scribner's Sons, Charles — I: MAXWELL MACMILLAN
Scribner's Sons, Charles Ltd (Partial) (US) — D: T & T CLARK LTD
Scribner's Sons, Charles (US) — D: MARSTON BOOKS SERV
Scriptographic — D: HOTEL & CATERING CO
SCRIPTURE GIFT MISSION
SCUTARI PRESS
Scutari Press (RCN) — D: GAZELLE BOOK SERVICE
SCVO — D: BOOKSPEED
SDU Publishers (NT) — D: ART DATA
Sea Challengers Inc — D: STEVEN SIMPSON BOOKS
SEABY LTD, B A
Seafarer Books — D: BARNACLE MARINE LTD
Seafarer Books — I: MERLIN PRESS
Seaflower Books — I: EX LIBRIS PRESS
Seagull Books — I: BOOK GUILD LTD
Seagull (IN) — D: CENTRAL BOOKS
SEAGULL SA
Seal Press (US) — D: AIRLIFT BOOK CO
Search Press — D: SPRINGFIELD BOOKS
SEARCH PRESS
SEARLE ASSOCIATES LTD, DEREK
Seatrade Publications — I: CITY PRESS LTD
Secker & Warburg, Martin — I: REED CONSUMER TRADE
Secker & Warburg, Martin — D: REED BOOK SERVICES
Second Story Press (CA) — D: AIRLIFT BOOK CO
See Sharp Press (US) — D: AK DISTRIBUTION
Seibu Museum (JP) — D: ART DATA
SELDEN SOCIETY
SELECT BOOKS LTD
SELECTABOOK LTD — R
Self Publishing Association — D: IMAGES DISTRIBUTION
Self Realization Fellowship (US) — D: ELEMENT BOOKS LTD
Self-Counsel Press (Partial) — D: ROUNDHOUSE PUB LTD
Sells Publications — I: BENN BUSINESS INFO
SEMICON INDEXES

Semiotext (US) — D: CENTRAL BOOKS
Semiotext (US) — D: AK DISTRIBUTION
SEND THE LIGHT
SEND THE LIGHT — A
SEND THE LIGHT — W
Senior Publications — I: TRANSPORT PUB CO LTD
Senior Scribe Publications (US) — D: LAVIS MARKETING
Sensible Supplies (AU) — D: POSITIVE PRODUCTS
Seren Books — I: POETRY WALES PRESS
Serif — D: CENTRAL BOOKS
Serindia Publications — D: ELEMENT BOOKS LTD
Serpentine Gallery — D: ART DATA
SERPENT'S TAIL
Serpent's Tail Publishing — D: PLYMBRIDGE DIST LTD
Sessions Book Trust — I: WILLIAM SESSIONS LTD
SESSIONS LTD, WILLIAM
Settle Press — D: BIBLIOS PUB DIST
SETTLE PRESS
Seuil (FR) — D: EUROPEAN SCHOOLBOOKS
SEVEN MIRRORS PUBLISHING HOUSE
Seven Points Publications Ltd — D: BOOKPOINT LIMITED
Severn House — D: TIPTREE BOOK SERV
Severn House Paperbacks — I: SEVERN HOUSE PUB LTD
SEVERN HOUSE PUBLISHERS LTD
SEWELLS INTERNATIONAL
SEYMOUR
SFIA EDUCATIONAL TRUST
SFS — I: SPECTRUM TRAINING
SGC Books — I: CHALKSOFT LTD
SGEL (SP) — D: EUROPEAN SCHOOLBOOKS
SGM Publishing — SCRIPTURE GIFT MISSION
SHAC — D: TURNAROUND
Shadow & Light (US) — D: EVENLODE BOOK DIST
Shakespeare Head Press — I: BLACKWELL PUB LTD
SHAKTI COMMUNICATION
Shambhala — I: RANDOM HOUSE UK LTD
Shambhala — D: TIPTREE BOOK SERV
Shambhala (US) — D: WISDOM BOOKS
SHANTI SADAN
Shapolsky (Jewish Interest) (US) — D: KUPERARD LTD
SHARE INTERNATIONAL
SHARON PUBLICATIONS
Sharpe Publisher, M E (US) — D: EDS
Shaw & Sons — A: ROGER BAYLISS
Shaw & Sons Ltd — D: BOOKPOINT LIMITED
SHAW & SONS LTD
Shaw Publishers, Harold (Partial) — D: SEND THE LIGHT
SHEAF PUBLISHING LTD
SHEARWATER PRESS LTD
Sheba Feminist Publishers — D: AIRLIFT BOOK CO
SHEED & WARD LTD
SHEFFIELD ACADEMIC PRESS
Sheldon Press — I: SPCK
Sheldrake Press — D: AURUM PRESS LTD
SHELF PUBLISHING
Shelter — D: TURNAROUND
SHELWING LTD
SHEPHEARD-WALWYN
Shepheard-Walwyn (Publishers) Ltd — D: BAILEY DIST LTD
Sheppard — I: RICHARD JOSEPH PUB
Sher Enterprises (CA) — D: ALIF INTERNATIONAL
Sher Music (US) — D: INT MUSIC PUB
SHERBOURNE PUBLICATIONS
Sheridan Square (US) — D: AK DISTRIBUTION
SHERRATT & SON, JOHN
SHERWOOD FOREST PUBLISHERS
Sherwood Press — D: SHEPHEARD-WALWYN
SHETLAND TIMES LTD
Shikosha (JP) — D: ART DATA
Ship Pictorial Publications — A: SB PUBLICATIONS
SHIP PICTORIAL PUBLICATIONS
SHIPMAN, HILARY
SHIRE PUBLICATIONS
Shiva Books — I: VOLTURNA PRESS
Shoestring Guides — I: LONELY PLANET PUB
Shoestring Press (US) — D: CLIO PRESS LTD
Shola — D: CENTRAL BOOKS
Shom-French Hydrographic Service (Partial) (FR) — D: BARNACLE MARINE LTD
Shoreline Books — A: LOXWOOD STONELEIGH
SHROPSHIRE BOOKS
Shufunotomo (JP) — A: PREMIER BOOK MKTNG
Shuter & Shooter (SA) — D: LEISHMAN & TAUSSIG

Shutter Press — I: NEWS PRODUCTIONS
Siam Society (TH) — D: LAVIS MARKETING
Side By Side — D: ROY YATES BOOKS
Sidgwick & Jackson — D: MACMILLAN DIST LTD
SIDGWICK & JACKSON
Siemens — I: VCH PUB (UK) LTD
Sierra Club (Partial) (US) — D: CORDEE
Sierra Press (US) — D: EVENLODE BOOK DIST
Sight & Sound (US) — D: INT MUSIC PUB
Sigloch Edition (GE) — D: GAZELLE BOOK SERVICE
Sigma Forlag (Eng Lang titles) (NW) — A: JESSICA KINGSLEY PUB
Sigma Forlag (Eng Lang titles) (NW) — D: KOGAN PAGE LTD
SIGMA LEISURE
Sigma Leisure Press — D: BREWIN BOOK DIST
Sigma Press — A: JOHN WILEY & SONS
SIGMA PRESS
Sign Publications Ltd (FR) — D: MCCRIMMON PUBLISHING
Signet — I: PENGUIN BOOKS LTD
Signpost Books — D: EVENLODE BOOK DIST
Signpost Ltd — D: W FOULSHAM & CO LTD
SILCO BOOKS LTD
SILENT BOOKS
Silhouette — I: MILLS & BOON LTD
Silicon Press — I: SIMON & SCHUSTER INT
Silman James Press (US) — D: GAZELLE BOOK SERVICE
Silver Burdett & Ginn — I: SIMON & SCHUSTER INT
Silver Fox Publishing (Exc railway titles in UK) — D: GAZELLE BOOK SERVICE
Silver Link Publications — D: IAN ALLAN PUBLISHING
SILVER LINK PUBLISHERS LTD
Silver Moon Books — D: AIRLIFT BOOK CO
Silver Moon Books — D: THOMAS LYSTER LTD
SILVER MOON BOOKS
Silver Trumpet Publications — D: EVANGELICAL PRESS
SILVEY-JEX PUBLICATIONS LTD
Simon & Pierre (CA) — D: DUNDURN DISTRIBUTION
Simon & Schuster International Group — D: INT BOOK DIST
SIMON & SCHUSTER INTERNATIONAL GROUP
Simon & Schuster (Jewish Interest) (US) — D: KUPERARD LTD
SIMON & SCHUSTER LTD
SIMON & SCHUSTER LTD — A
Simon & Schuster (Partial) — A: P M LLEWELLYN CO
Simon & Schuster (Trade Books) — D: INT BOOK DIST
Simon & Schuster Young Books — I: SIMON & SCHUSTER INT
Simon & Schuster Young Books — D: INT BOOK DIST
Simple Books — I: PAUL NORBURY PUB LTD
Simply Classics — D: VINE HOUSE DIST
SIMPSON NATURAL HISTORY BOOKS, STEVEN
Sinauer Associates (US) — D: W H FREEMAN & CO LTD
Sinclair-Stevenson — I: REED CONSUMER TRADE
Sinclair-Stevenson — D: REED BOOK SERVICES
Singapore University Press (SI) — A: ACADEMIC & UNIV PUB
Singspiration Inc (US) — D: B MCCALL BARBOUR
Singular Publishing Group Inc (US) — D: CHAPMAN & HALL
SIR Publishing (US) — D: EDS
Sistervision (US) — D: TURNAROUND
Sita (UK) — A: FMJ BOOKS
Skandinavia Publishing House — D: STANBOROUGH PRESS
Skarv Hoest (Partial) (DN) — D: CORDEE
SKELLIG PRESS
Skellig Press (IR) — D: COLIN SMYTHE LTD
Skennerton, Ian (AU) — D: GREENHILL BOOKS
Skidmore-Roth Publishing (US) — D: GAZELLE BOOK SERVICE
Skilton Aquarist, C J — No reply 92/93
SKILTON LTD, CHARLES
Skira Art Books — I: RIZZOLI INT PUBNS
Skira (SZ) — D: BIBLIOS PUB DIST
Skoob Books Publishing — D: GAZELLE BOOK SERVICE
Skotaville Publishers (SA) — D: AFRICAN BOOKS COLL
Skotaville Publishers (SA) — D: LEISHMAN & TAUSSIG
Slack Inc (US) — D: MCGRAW HILL BOOK CO
Sladden, C — D: CORDEE
Slavica (stockists) (US) — A: THORNTON'S OF OXFORD
Slawson (Potential List) (US) — D: PITMAN PUBLISHING
Slawsons Communications Inc (US) — D: GAZELLE BOOK SERVICE
SLG PRESS
SME (US) — A: AMERICAN TECH PUB
Smith Books, Bruce — D: COMPUTER BOOKSHOPS
SMITH BOOKS, BRUCE
Smith Club, Adam — D: LIBERTARIAN ALLIANCE
Smith, Gibbs M (US) — D: AIRLIFT BOOK CO
SMITH GRYPHON LTD
SMITH HEALTH CASSETTES, ALBERT — A

SMITH LTD, OWEN
Smith, Monica (IT) — D: S HENEAGE DIST
SMITH SETTLE LTD
Smith/Doorstop Books — I: THE POETRY BUSINESS
Smith/Doorstop Books — D: PASSWORD (BOOKS) LTD
Smithsonian Institution Press, The (US) — D: INT BOOK DIST
Smithsonian Institution Press, The (US) — A: UNI PRESSES MARKETNG
SMYTHE LTD, COLIN
Snow Lion (US) — D: WISDOM BOOKS
Snow Lion (US) — D: ELEMENT BOOKS LTD
SNYDER PUBLISHING ASSOCIATES, WILLIAM
SOCIAL CARE ASSOCIATION LTD
SOCIAL WORK MONOGRAPHS
Socialist Health Association — D: CENTRAL BOOKS
Socialist Workers Party — I: BOOKMARKS
Society for Experimental Biology — D: PORTLAND PRESS LTD
SOCIETY FOR PROMOTING CHRISTIAN KNOWLEDGE
Society for Research into Higher Education — I: OPEN UNIV PRESS
SOCIETY FOR THE PROMOTION OF ROMAN STUDIES
SOCIETY FOR THE PROTECTION OF ANCIENT BUILDINGS
SOCIETY FOR THEATRE RESEARCH
Society of Antiquaries of Scotland, The — D: OXBOW BOOKS
Society of Antiquaries (Partial) — D: HERLADRY TODAY
Society of Dairy Technology — D: FOOD TRADE PRESS LTD
SOCIETY OF GENEALOGISTS
Society of German Electrical Engineers (vde)(Eng Lang) (GE) — D: WOODHEAD PUBLISHING
Society of International Gas Tanker and Terminal Operators — D: WITHERBY & CO LTD
SOCIETY OF METAPHYSICIANS
SOCIETY OF MOTOR MANUFACTURERS & TRADERS
SODANEY PUBLISHERS
Soho Book Co Ltd — D: GAZELLE BOOK SERVICE
Soho Press (US) — D: BELLEW PUBLISHING
Solidarity — D: AK DISTRIBUTION
SOLO BOOKS LTD
SOLOMON INTERNATIONAL PUBLISHING COMPANY
Solos Press — D: ASHGROVE PRESS
Solum Forlag (SW) — D: LAVIS MARKETING
Somerset Books — D: WEST COUNTRY BOOKS
Sopena (SP) — D: EUROPEAN SCHOOLBOOKS
Sorbier (FR) — D: ROY YATES BOOKS
Sotheby's Publications — A: ANTIQUE COLLECTORS
Sotheby's Publications — I: PHILIP WILSON PUB
Soulsource Publishing (US) — D: EVENLODE BOOK DIST
Sound View Press (Partial) (US) — D: HILMARTON MANOR
Sounds True Audio (US) — D: AIRLIFT BOOK CO
Source Books (Partial) (US) — D: ANTHONY CLARKE PUB
South Coast Transport Publishing — D: PLATFORM 5 PUB LTD
South End Press (US) — D: TURNAROUND
South End Press (US) — D: AK DISTRIBUTION
South London Business Initiative — D: FUTURES PUB LTD
South Western (US) — D: INT THOMSON PUB SERV
Southern Africa Printing & Publishing House — D: AFRICAN BOOKS COLL
Southern Africa Research & Documentation Centre — D: AFRICAN BOOKS COLL
Southern Book Publishers (SA) — D: CORDEE
Southern Book Publishers Ltd (SA) — D: LAKESIDE PUBNS
SOUTHERN COLLECTORS
Southern Counties — D: BIBLIOS PUB DIST
Southgate Publishing — D: BIBLIOS PUB DIST
Southover Press — D: VINE HOUSE DIST
SOUTHPORT BOOK DISTRIBUTORS
Souvenir Press Ltd — D: BOOKPOINT LIMITED
SOUVENIR PRESS LTD
Sovereign Book Ltd — D: WAYLAND (PUB) LTD
Sovereign Grace — No reply 93
Sovereign Publications — D: EVANGELICAL PRESS
Sovereign World — D: NEW WINE MINISTRIES
Soyfood Center (US) — D: FOOD TRADE PRESS LTD
SPA BOOKS LTD
Sparrow Hawk — D: DEEP BOOKS LTD
Sparrowhawk — I: HAWK BOOKS LTD
SPARTACUS EDUCATIONAL
Spath Dene — I: E J MORTEN PUB
SPCC (UK) Ltd — D: INTERCEPT LTD
SPCK — D: VERITAS PUBLICATIONS
SPCK — I: SPCK
Spearman, Neville — I: L N FOWLER & CO LTD
Spectrum — I: SIMON & SCHUSTER INT
Spectrum Books Ltd (NG) — D: AFRICAN BOOKS COLL
SPECTRUM TRAINING SERVICES
Spellbound (IR) — D: DALENNAU
SPELLMOUNT LTD
Spenser Books — D: CENTRAL BOOKS

Sphere — LITTLE BROWN
Sphinx — D: ELEMENT BOOKS LTD
SPI Books — D: BOOKPOINT LIMITED
Spike Press — D: AVANTI BOOKS
Spinal Publications — Ceased trading 92
SPINDLEWOOD
SPINK & SON LTD
Spinsters Book Co (US) — D: AIRLIFT BOOK CO
Spoken Language Services (Partial) (US) — D: P M LLEWELLYN CO
Spokesman — I: SPOKESMAN BOOKS
SPOKESMAN BOOKS
Spon, E & F N — I: CHAPMAN & HALL
Spon, E & F N — D: INT THOMSON PUB SERV
Sport Aviation Publications (US) — D: CORDEE
Sporting & Leisure Press — I: QUOTES LTD
Sporting & Leisure Press — QUOTES
SPORTING LIFE, THE
Sports Support Syndicate Inc (US) — D: GAZELLE BOOK SERVICE
Sportsman's Press — D: TIPTREE BOOK SERV
SPORTSMAN'S PRESS
Sportsprint — I: JOHN DONALD PUB LTD
SPREAD EAGLE PUBLICATIONS
SPREDDEN PRESS, THE
Spring Audio (US) — D: AIRLIFT BOOK CO
Spring Publications (US) — D: AIRLIFT BOOK CO
SPRINGER-VERLAG
SPRINGFIELD BOOKS
Springhouse Publishing (US) — D: HARCOURT BRACE JOVAN
Sprinkle Publications (US) — D: EVANGELICAL PRESS
Sprogforlaget (Partial) (DN) — D: ACCENT EDUCATIONAL
Squadron Signal — I: REED CONSUMER ILLUS
Square Dance Partners — I: BARN DANCE PUB LTD
Square Mile Books — I: METAL BULLETIN PLC
Square Mile Books Ltd (London Business Finder only) — D: WOODHEAD PUBLISHING
Square Mile Publications — I: METAL BULLETIN PLC
Square One Books — D: BEBC DISTRIBUTION
SQUARE ONE PUBLICATIONS
Stabur Corporation (US) — D: GAZELLE BOOK SERVICE
Stacey International — D: BIBLIOS PUB DIST
STACEY INTERNATIONAL
Stackpole Books (Partial) (US) — D: CORDEE
Stackpole Books (US) — D: GREENHILL BOOKS
STAFF COLLEGE, THE
STAGECOACH
STAINER & BELL LTD
Stamps Baxter Music (US) — D: B MCCALL BARBOUR
STANBOROUGH PRESS
Stanford Tutors Video Tapes — D: COMPUTER STEP LTD
Stanfords — I: BARNACLE MARINE LTD
Starmont House (Selected titles) (US) — D: PAUPERS' PRESS
Starnite — D: INT MUSIC PUB
State University of New York Press (US) — A: TREVOR BROWN ASSOC
Statens Kartverk (Partial) — D: CORDEE
Station Hill Press (US) — D: ELEMENT BOOKS LTD
STEEL CONSTRUCTION INSTITUTE
Steiner Press, Rudolf — D: BIBLIOS PUB DIST
STEINER PRESS, RUDOLF
Stemmer House Publishers Inc (US) — D: GAZELLE BOOK SERVICE
STENLAKE PUBLISHING, RICHARD
Stephens Ltd, Patrick — I: J H HAYNES & CO LTD
Sterling Publishing (Partial) (US) — D: CASSELL PLC
Stevens & Sons — I: SWEET & MAXWELL LTD
Stevens & Sons — D: INT THOMSON PUB SERV
Stevens, Jose (US) — D: EVENLODE BOOK DIST
STEWART BOOKS, MALCOLM
Stewart Tabori & Chang (US) — D: GRANTHAM BOOK SERV
Stewart Tabori & Chang (US) — D: MELIA PUB SERVICES
Stillpoint (US) — D: AIRLIFT BOOK CO
Stills Gallery — D: ART DATA
Stipes Publishing Co (US) — D: PACKARD PUB LTD
STM Distribution — Ceased trading 93
Stobart & Son Ltd — I: STOBART DAVIES LTD
STOBART DAVIES LTD
Stockham, Peter — I: IMAGES
STOCKWELL LTD, A H
Stoddart (CA) — D: DUNDURN DISTRIBUTION
STOKESBY HOUSE PUBLICATIONS
Stone Bridge Press (US) — A: PREMIER BOOK MKTNG
STONE FLOWER LTD
Storm Group — No reply 93
Storm Group Video — D: GRANTHAM BOOK SERV
Storm Group Video — A: WORLD LEISURE MKTG

Story Sound Audio — I: MAGNA LARGE PRINT
STORYTELLER AUDIO — A
STORYVILLE PUBLICATIONS & CO LTD
Stott's Correspondance College — I: SUSSEX PUBLICATIONS
STOURTON PRESS, THE
Stows Classics — D: VINE HOUSE DIST
Strategy 2000 — I: EUROMONITOR PLC
Strawberry Hill Press — D: COMBINED BOOK SERV
Streamline (BZ) — D: ROGER LASCELLES
Streetwise Maps Inc (US) — D: GAZELLE BOOK SERVICE
STRIDE PUBLICATIONS
Stride/Taxus — A: PASSWORD (BOOKS) LTD
STRINGER, ORIEL
STROKE ASSOCIATION, THE
Strong Oak Press — I: SPA BOOKS LTD
Struik Publishers (SA) — D: NEW HOLLAND PUB LTD
Studentlitteratur — I: CHARTWELL-BRATT
Studies in Insular Art & Archaeology (US) — D: OXBOW BOOKS
Studio Designs — I: STUDIO EDITIONS LTD
Studio Editions — D: SEND THE LIGHT
STUDIO EDITIONS LTD
Studio Publications — I: WATERMARK PUB LTD
Studio Vista — I: CASSELL PLC
SUBJECT PUBLICATIONS
Success Study Books — I: JOHN MURRAY PUB LTD
Suffolk Records Society — D: BOYDELL & BREWER LTD
Suhada Press — D: THORNHILL PRESS LTD
Suhrkamp (GE) — D: EUROPEAN SCHOOLBOOKS
SULLIVAN ASSOCIATES
Sumach Press — I: RANDOM HOUSE UK LTD
Sumach Press — D: TIPTREE BOOK SERV
Summerhill Press (CA) — D: DUNDURN DISTRIBUTION
SUMMERS LTD, GLYN — W
Summersdale Press — D: CENTRAL BOOKS
SUMMERSDALE PRESS
Sun Publishing — D: DEEP BOOKS LTD
Sun Tavern Fields — D: TURNAROUND
Sun Tree Publishing (SI) — D: RIGHT NOW BOOKS
Sun Ya Publications (HK) — D: ROY YATES BOOKS
Sunbird — I: LADYBIRD BOOKS LTD
Sunburst — I: PROMOTIONAL REPRINT
Sunburst — D: COMBINED BOOK SERV
Sundeep Prakashan (IN) — I: MOTILAL BOOKS
Sunflower Books — D: A & C BLACK LTD
SUNFLOWER BOOKS
Sunflower Books (Ireland only) — A: BLACKSTAFF PRESS LTD
Sunset Books — D: LITTLE BROWN & CO
Supha Publications (Partial) (US) — D: HILMARTON MANOR
Surrey Beatty & Sons (AU) — D: PACKARD PUB LTD
Surrey University Press — I: BLACKIE ACAD & PROF
Survey & Land Information (Partial) (NZ) — D: CORDEE
Survey of Persian Art — D: SCORPION PUBLISHING
Survival Books — D: EVENLODE BOOK DIST
Susquehanna U P — I: GOLDEN COCKEREL
SUSSEX PUBLICATIONS
Sussex Tapes & Video — I: SUSSEX PUBLICATIONS
Sussex University Press — I: SCOTTISH ACAD PRESS
Sussex Videos — D: BIBLIOS PUB DIST
SUT ANUBIS
Sutton Courtenay Press (Isle of Man) — I: APPLEFORD PUB GROUP
SUTTON PUBLISHING LTD, ALAN
Suzuki (US) — D: INT MUSIC PUB
Swallow Press — D: SPRINGFIELD BOOKS
Swan Hill Press — I: AIRLIFE PUBLISHING
Swayne Publications — D: ELEMENT BOOKS LTD
SWEDENBORG SOCIETY
Sweet & Maxwell — D: INT THOMSON PUB SERV
SWEET & MAXWELL LTD
Sweet Ch'i Press (US) — D: PAUL H CROMPTON LTD
Sweet Dreams — I: TRANSWORLD PUB
Sweet Valley — I: TRANSWORLD PUB
SWEETHAWS PRESS
Swift Publishers — D: BOOKPOINT LIMITED
Swimming Times — ASA SWIMMING ENTERPRISES
Swiss Alpine Club (SZ) — D: CORDEE
Swiss Foundation Alpine Research (SZ) — D: CORDEE
Swiss Pharmaceutical Society (SZ) — D: PHARMACEUTICAL PRESS
Sword of the Lord Publishers (US) — D: B MCCALL BARBOUR
Sybex (US) — D: PITMAN PUBLISHING
Sybylla Co-operative Press (AU) — D: CENTRAL BOOKS
Sydney University Press (AU) — D: OXFORD UNI PRESS DIS
Symposia Press — I: SCIENCE REVIEWS LTD

Synergy Press (US) — D: VINE HOUSE DIST
SYNTHESIS PUBLISHING
System Pub House — No reply 93
TA HA PUBLISHERS LTD
Ta Ha Publishers (Partial) — A: P M LLEWELLYN CO
TAB — I: MCGRAW HILL BOOK CO
TAB Aero (US) — D: AIRLIFE PUBLISHING
Tabacco (IT) — D: ROGER LASCELLES
Tabb House — D: COUNTYVISE LTD
TABB HOUSE
Tabor (US) — D: VERITAS PUBLICATIONS
Tackmark Publications — D: ELEMENT BOOKS LTD
Tafelberg — D: BAY FOREIGN BOOKS
Tagari (AU) — D: WORLDLY GOODS
Tahrike Tarsile Qur'an (US) — D: ALIF INTERNATIONAL
Tahrike Tarsile (US) — D: EVENLODE BOOK DIST
Take That — D: VINE HOUSE DIST
Talbot Press — I: EDUC CO OF IRELAND
TALKING POINTS PUBLICATIONS
Talking Tape Company — A: DEREK SEARLE ASS LTD
Talking Tape Company Ltd — D: BOOKPOINT LIMITED
TALKTAPES — A
Tallis Press — I: CHARLES SKILTON LTD
TALLIS PRESS
Tamarind — D: CHILD'S PLAY
TAMARIND LTD
Tamesis Books — D: BOYDELL & BREWER LTD
Tan Books (US) — D: AUGUSTINE PUB CO
Tanam Press (US) — D: ART DATA
Tanat Books — I: ANTHONY NELSON LTD
Tango Books — D: DISTRIBUTION BOOK CO
Tango Books — A: DEREK SEARLE ASS LTD
TANTIVY PRESS LTD
Tanzania Commission for Science and Technology (TZ) — D: AFRICAN BOOKS COLL
Tanzania Publishing House (TZ) — D: AFRICAN BOOKS COLL
Tanzania Publishing House (TZ) — D: LEISHMAN & TAUSSIG
TAPEWORM CHILDRENS CASSETTES — A
TAPPI (US) — A: AMERICAN TECH PUB
TAPROBANE LTD
Tara Books — I: IRISH ACADEMIC PRESS
Tara Press — I: SHARE INTERNATIONAL
Taranis — D: AK DISTRIBUTION
Tardy (Partial) (FR) — D: HILMARTON MANOR
Target — I: VIRGIN PUBLISHING
TARQUIN PUBLICATIONS
Tarragon Press — D: LAVIS MARKETING
TARRAGON PRESS
Tasende Gallery (US) — D: S HENEAGE DIST
TATE GALLERY PUBLICATIONS
Taunton Press (US) — D: GAZELLE BOOK SERVICE
TAURIS & COMPANY LTD, I B
Tauris, I B — D: BIBLIOS PUB DIST
Tauris, I B — A: BOOK REP & DIST LTD
Tauris, I B (Jewish Interest) — D: KUPERARD LTD
Tauris, I B (Partial) — A: P M LLEWELLYN CO
Tauris Parke Books — I: I B TAURIS & CO LTD
Tauris Parke Books — D: BIBLIOS PUB DIST
Taurus Publishing — D: CENTRAL BOOKS
Tavistock — I: ROUTLEDGE
TAW VALLEY WHOLESALE — W
Taxus Press — I: STRIDE PUBLICATIONS
TAYLOR & FRANCIS LTD
Taylor Book Ventures, John (DTP Series) — D: SPA BOOKS LTD
TAYLOR BOOK VENTURES, JOHN
Taylor, D J — D: FARMING PRESS BOOKS
TBC DISTRIBUTION
T-Bone Records — D: SEND THE LIGHT
Teach Yourself — I: HODDER & STOUGHTON
Teacher Created Materials (Partial) (US) — D: FOLENS PUBLISHERS
Teacher Ideas Press (US) — D: EDS
Teachers College Press (US) — D: EDS
Teaching Resource Centre — D: JONATHAN PRESS
TeakWood Press Inc (US) — D: GAZELLE BOOK SERVICE
Tearcraft — D: SEND THE LIGHT
Technical & Educational Press — D: PLYMBRIDGE DIST LTD
TECHNICAL INFORMATION SERVICES
TECHNOLOGY APPRAISALS LTD
TEE PUBLISHING
TEECOLL PUBLICATIONS
Teen Search — I: GO TEACH PUB
TEENEY BOOKS LTD
Teens — I: REED CONS MANDARIN

Teitan Press Inc (US) — D: GAZELLE BOOK SERVICE
TELEGRAPH BOOKS
Telegraph Books (Business & Finance Only) — D: KOGAN PAGE LTD
Telford Ltd, Thomas — A: MOMENTA PUB CO LTD
TELFORD LTD, THOMAS
Telos (US) — D: AK DISTRIBUTION
Telynfab — I: GWASG GWENFFRWD
Temenos — D: ELEMENT BOOKS LTD
TEMPLAR PUBLISHING COMPANY PLC
Temple House Books — I: BOOK GUILD LTD
TEMPLE LECTURES LTD
TEMPLE LODGE PUBLISHING
Temple Press — D: MANDRAKE
Temple Press — D: AK DISTRIBUTION
TEMPLE PRESS LTD
Temple Press Traditions — I: TEMPLE PRESS LTD
Temple University Press (NB One Title Only) (US) — D: UNI OF WALES PRESS
Templegate (US) — D: GRACEWING/FOWLER
Tempo Children's Video & Audio — A: DEREK SEARLE ASS LTD
Ten 8 — D: CENTRAL BOOKS
Ten Speed Press (US) — D: AIRLIFT BOOK CO
Terra (Partial) (NT) — D: HILMARTON MANOR
Terrac (Ltd) (GE) — D: SPRINGFIELD BOOKS
TERTIARY PUBLICATIONS
Tessloff (GE) — D: EUROPEAN SCHOOLBOOKS
Tetradon Publications Ltd — D: MERIDIAN BOOKS
TETRAHEDRON BOOKS
TEXTILE INSTITUTE
Textile Musuem (US) — D: ART DATA
TFH PUBLICATIONS
TFH Publications (Ireland Only) — D: ISLAND PUBLICATIONS
TFPL PUBLISHING
Thames & Hudson (Jewish Interest) — D: KUPERARD LTD
THAMES & HUDSON LTD
Thames Publishing — D: NOVELLO & CO LTD
Thames Publishing — D: BAILEY DIST LTD
Thames Publishing — No reply 93
THARPA PUBLICATIONS
THEMETREE LTD
THEOSOPHICAL PUBLISHING HOUSE LTD
Thessaly Press — No reply 92/93
Thieme Verlag, Georg (GE) — A: MOMENTA PUB CO LTD
THIMBLE PRESS
Third Eye Centre — No reply 93
Third Millenium Publications — D: ELEMENT BOOKS LTD
Third World Centre Ltd (Partial List) — D: DARF PUBLISHERS LTD
Thirteen Colonies Press (US) — D: EVENLODE BOOK DIST
Thoemmes Press — I: THOEMMES PRESS
THOEMMES PRESS
Thomas International Publishing Co (US) — D: EDS
Thomas Technical Publications Ltd — D: GAZELLE BOOK SERVICE
Thomson Press (India) Ltd (IN) — A: NILE & MACKENZIE LTD
THORESBY SOCIETY, THE
THORNES PUBLISHERS, STANLEY
THORNHILL PRESS LTD
Thornton Cox — D: ROGER LASCELLES
THORNTON'S OF OXFORD LTD
Thoroughbred Books — I: SILVER LINK PUB LTD
Thorpe, D W — I: BOWKER-SAUR LTD
Thorpe, D W (Partial List) (AU) — D: BUTTERWORTH & CO LTD
Thorsons — I: HARPERCOLLINS THORS
THOTH PUBLICATIONS
Thoth Publishers (NT) — D: BIBLIOS PUB DIST
Thoth Uitgeverij (NT) — D: ART DATA
Three Hills Books — No reply 93
Three Rivers Books — Ceased trading 92
Three Trees (CA) — D: TURNAROUND
Threshold Books (UK, NOT US) — I: KENILWORTH PRESS LTD
Threshold Books (US) — D: ELEMENT BOOKS LTD
Threshold Books (US) — D: EVENLODE BOOK DIST
Thubten Dhargye Ling (US) — D: WISDOM BOOKS
Thule Press — I: FINDHORN PRESS
Thunder's Mouth Press (US) — D: AIRLIFT BOOK CO
TIGER BOOKS INTERNATIONAL PLC — R
Time Life Books — D: BOOKPOINT LIMITED
Time Life Books — A: WINDSOR BOOKS INT
TIME TAPES — A
Timeless Books (US) — D: ELEMENT BOOKS LTD
Times - Chambers (2 titles) (SI) — D: W & R CHAMBERS LTD
Times Bartholomew Guides — I: HARPERCOLLINS BARTH
Times Books — I: HARPERCOLLINS BARTH
Times Change Press (US) — D: AK DISTRIBUTION

Times Editions (SI) — D: MILLBANK BOOKS LTD
Times Editions (SI) (Travel Books) — D: KUPERARD LTD
Timken Publishers (US) — D: RIZZOLI INT PUBNS
Tippet — D: CORDEE
TIPTREE BOOK SERVICES LTD
Tir Eolas (IR) — D: COLIN SMYTHE LTD
Titan Books — D: KNOCKABOUT COMICS
Titan Books — D: BOOKPOINT LIMITED
TITAN DISTRIBUTORS — W
TOAT PRESS, THE
TOBIN MUSIC
Toccata Press — D: FOUNTAIN PRESS LTD
Toccata Press — No reply 93
Tolkien — I: HARPERCOLLINS TRADE
TOLLEY PUBLISHING COMPANY
Tomkinson, Michael — D: ROGER LASCELLES
Tomlinson Book Centre — TBC DISTRIBUTION
Top 25 Maps — D: GRANTHAM BOOK SERV
Top 25 Maps — A: WORLD LEISURE MKTG
Top 25 Maps (FR) — A: MCCARTA LTD
Top of the Mountain Publishers (US) — D: GAZELLE BOOK SERVICE
Tophi — I: RAMBORO BOOKS
TOPY Heart — D: TEMPLE PRESS LTD
Tor Mark Press — D: DYLLANSOW TRURAN
TOTAL BOOK DISTRIBUTION — W
Total Press (AU) — D: AIRLIFT BOOK CO
TOUCAN PRESS
Touch — D: AK DISTRIBUTION
Touchstone — I: SIMON & SCHUSTER LTD
Touchwood Press — I: NEWS PRODUCTIONS
Tough Dove — D: DEEP BOOKS LTD
Toulon Publishers (BG) — A: BARKER & HOWARD LTD
Touring Club Italiano — A: WORLD LEISURE MKTG
Touring Club Italiano (IT) — D: MCCARTA LTD
Town & Country — I: IAN ALLAN PUBLISHING
Town & Country Books — Ceased trading 92
Town House — D: GILL & MACMILLAN LTD
Town House Publishers (partial) (IR) — D: ASHFORD BUCHAN
TPC — I: TRANSPORT PUB CO LTD
Tracks — I: HARPERCOLLINS CHILD
TRADE & TRAVEL PUBLICATIONS
TRADE COUNTER, THE
Trade Media (HK) — D: GAZELLE BOOK SERVICE
TRADE RESEARCH PUBLICATIONS
Trade Winds (SA) — A: WORDSWORTH EDITIONS
Traffic Models — D: BREWIN BOOK DIST
Trafton Publishing — D: SPRINGFIELD BOOKS
Trafton Publishing — No reply 93
TRAIL CREST PUBLICATIONS
Trailblazers — D: ROGER LASCELLES
Trails Illustrated (US) — D: CORDEE
TRAINING INFORMATION NETWORK
Trame — D: PHOTOBOOK INFO SERV
Transaction Publishers — A: ROGER BAYLISS
Transaction Publishers (US) — D: PLYMBRIDGE DIST LTD
Transafrica Press (KY) — D: LEISHMAN & TAUSSIG
Translations (Wales) — I: GWASG GWENFFRWD
Translegal AG (SZ) — D: CHRIS LLOYD SALES
TRANSPORT 2000
TRANSPORT BOOKMAN
TRANSPORT PUBLISHING COMPANY LTD
TRANSWORLD PUBLISHERS
Travel Survival Kit Guides — I: LONELY PLANET PUB
TRAVELLERS' TALES — A
Travellers World Guides — I: TRADE & TRAVEL PUB
Travelling Light — D: CENTRAL BOOKS
Treadwell Publishing — I: TREADWELLS ART MILL
TREADWELLS ART MILL
Treasure Books — No reply 92/93
Treasure Press — I: REED CONS BOUNTY
Treehouse Children's Books — D: RAGGED BEARS LTD
Trefoil Design Library — I: TREFOIL PUB LTD
Trefoil Publications Ltd — D: BOOKPOINT LIMITED
TREFOIL PUBLICATIONS LTD
TREMATON PRESS
TRENT VALLEY PUBLICATIONS
TRENTHAM BOOKS LTD
TRESSELL PUBLICATIONS
Treville (JP) — D: ART DATA
Triangle — I: SPCK
Tricolour Books — I: BOOKS FROM INDIA
TRIGRAPH LTD

TRINDER LTD, VERA — W
Trinity Press International (US) — D: SCM PRESS LTD
TRIPLE CAT PUBLISHING
TRITON PUBLISHING COMPANY LTD
Triumph Books (US) — D: COMBINED BOOK SERV
Trombone Press — I: STRIDE PUBLICATIONS
TROTMAN & COMPANY LTD
Trotman Ltd, Ken — D: SPA BOOKS LTD
True Crime — I: VIRGIN PUBLISHING
Truran — I: DYLLANSOW TRURAN
Trust for Urban Ecology — D: PACKARD PUB LTD
Trustline — D: VINE HOUSE DIST
Truth Consciousness (US) — D: EVENLODE BOOK DIST
TSR Inc (US) — D: RANDOM HOUSE (ARROW)
TT Maps & Publications (IN) — D: BOOKS FROM INDIA
TTG Directory — I: BENN BUSINESS INFO
Tube Walking — D: GRANTHAM BOOK SERV
Tube Walking — A: WORLD LEISURE MKTG
TUFNELL PRESS
Tumi Latin American Crafts (Craft Books only) (US) — D: ALISON HODGE PUB
Tundra Books (Partial) (CA) — D: RAGGED BEARS LTD
Tundra Publishing — D: KNOCKABOUT COMICS
TURNAROUND
TURNAROUND — W
TURPIN DISTRIBUTION
Turtle Point Press (US) — D: TURNAROUND
TURTON & CHAMBERS
Tuttle, Charles E — I: SIMON & SCHUSTER INT
Tuttle, Charles E (JP) — D: BIBLIOS PUB DIST
Tuttle, Charles E (JP) — A: PREMIER BOOK MKTNG
Tuttle, Charles E (Partial) (JP) — D: WISDOM BOOKS
Tuttle Co Inc, Charles E — I: KODANSHA EUROPE LTD
Tuttostoria (IT) — D: PHOTOBOOK INFO SERV
TWELVEHEADS PRESS
Twelvetrees Press (US) — D: GMP PUBLISHERS LTD
Twenty First Century Books (Partial) (US) — D: NEW BEACON BOOKS LTD
Twenty-Third Publications (US) — D: COLUMBA BOOK SERVICE
Twin Palms Publishers (US) — D: GMP PUBLISHERS LTD
TWIST IN THE TALE, A
Two Part Art — A: NEWS PRODUCTIONS
Two(2):Thirteen(13):Sixty One(61) (US) — D: AK DISTRIBUTION
TWO-CAN PUBLISHING
Two-Can Publishing Ltd — D: SCHOLASTIC PUB LTD
Ty ar y Graig — D: WELSH BOOKS COUNCIL
Ty John Penry — D: WELSH BOOKS COUNCIL
Tycooly Publishing — I: CASSELL PLC
Tyndale & Panda — No reply 93
Tyndale Fellowship — D: SEND THE LIGHT
Tynron Press — D: GAZELLE BOOK SERVICE
U Bar Verlag (SZ) — D: TURNAROUND
UBD (AU) — D: MCCARTA LTD
UBD Maps — A: WORLD LEISURE MKTG
UBS PUBLISHERS DISTRIBUTORS
UCL — D: GRANTHAM BOOK SERV
UCL PRESS LTD
UCW Aberystwyth Resource Centre (Partial) — D: WELSH BOOKS COUNCIL
UFAW — I: UFAW
Uffington Books — I: VENTON EDUCATIONAL
Uganda Literature Bureau (incl EALB) (UG) — D: LEISHMAN & TAUSSIG
UIA Journal of Architectural Theory & Criticism — I: ACADEMY GROUP LTD
Uit Het Woord Der Waarheid — D: CHAPTER TWO
Uitgeverij 010 (NT) — D: ART DATA
Uitgeverji Uniepers (NT) — D: CENTRAL BOOKS
UK Atomic Energy Authority — D: HMSO BOOKS
UKHM — D: ROGER LASCELLES
Ullstein (GE) — D: EUROPEAN SCHOOLBOOKS
Ulysses Press — D: GRANTHAM BOOK SERV
Ulysses Press — A: WORLD LEISURE MKTG
Underwater World Pub — No reply 93
Underwater World Publications Ltd — D: BARNACLE MARINE LTD
Unesco (FR) — D: HMSO BOOKS
Uni Books — I: VOLTURNA PRESS
Unicorn Books — D: ROADMASTER PUB
Unicorn Books — No reply 92/93
Unicorn Books (US) — D: ASHFORD BUCHAN
Union of Tao & Man — D: DEEP BOOKS LTD
Unique Publications (US) — D: PAUL H CROMPTON LTD
United Bibles Societies (Bibles & Testaments) — D: BIBLE SOCIETY
UNITED BOOK SUPPLIERS — W
UNITED KINGDOM COUNCIL OF HUMAN RIGHTS
United Nations Music — I: BOOSEY & HAWKES LTD
United Nations University (JP) — D: HMSO BOOKS

United Nations (US) — D: HMSO BOOKS
United Oxford & Cambridge Club (Partial) — D: ALFRED WALLER LTD
UNITED REFORMED CHURCH
United States Government Printing Office (US) — D: BOOKS EXPRESS
United Writers Press — MANUTIUS PRESS
UNITED WRITERS PUBLICATIONS
Universal Books — BOOKS & TOYS
Universal Press (AU) — D: SPRINGFIELD BOOKS
Universal Publications — I: EXCALIBUR PRESS
Universal Publications (HK) — D: ROGER LASCELLES
Universe Publishing (US) — D: BIBLIOS PUB DIST
Universe Publishing (US) — A: WINDSOR BOOKS INT
UNIVERSITIES FEDERATION FOR ANIMAL WELFARE
Universities Press (IN) — D: SANGAM BOOKS LTD
University — I: RAMBORO BOOKS
University Art Musuem Santa Barbara (US) — D: ART DATA
University Book Marketing — D: BIBLIOS PUB DIST
University of Alabama Press (US) — D: EDS
University of Arizona Press (Partial) (US) — D: ROUNDHOUSE PUB LTD
University of Arkansas (US) — A: TREVOR BROWN ASSOC
University of British Columbia Press (CA) — D: UCL PRESS LTD
University of California Press (US) — A: UNI PRESS CALIFORNIA
University of California Press (US) — D: JOHN WILEY & SONS
University of Delaware Press — I: GOLDEN COCKEREL
UNIVERSITY OF EXETER - AGRICULTURAL ECONOMICS UNIT
UNIVERSITY OF EXETER - SCHOOL OF EDUCATION
University of Exeter Press — A: BOOK REP & DIST LTD
University of Exeter Press — D: PLYMBRIDGE DIST LTD
UNIVERSITY OF EXETER PRESS
University of Georgia Press (US) — D: EDS
UNIVERSITY OF GLASGOW
University of Glasgow, Dept of Celtic — D: GAIRM PUBLICATIONS
University of Hawaii Press — A: TREVOR BROWN ASSOC
UNIVERSITY OF HULL & LAMPADA PRESS
University of Illinois Press (US) — A: TREVOR BROWN ASSOC
University of Lagos Press (NG) — D: AFRICAN BOOKS COLL
University of Life Press (Craft Books only) (US) — D: ALISON HODGE PUB
UNIVERSITY OF LONDON
UNIVERSITY OF LONDON - INSTITUTE OF CLASSICAL STUDIES
UNIVERSITY OF LONDON - INSTITUTE OF GERMANIC STUDIES
University of Manitoba Press (CA) — D: DUNDURN DISTRIBUTION
University of Massachusetts Press (US) — D: EDS
University of Michigan Press (US) — A: TREVOR BROWN ASSOC
University of Michigan Press (US) — D: PLYMBRIDGE DIST LTD
University of Minnesota Press (US) — D: UCL PRESS LTD
University of Missouri Press (US) — D: EDS
University of Natal Press (SA) — D: LEISHMAN & TAUSSIG
University of Nebraska Press (US) — A: ACADEMIC & UNIV PUB
University of Nevada Press (US) — D: UCL PRESS LTD
University of Nevada Press (Basque Series) (US) — D: IANMEAD LTD
University of New Mexico Press (Partial) (US) — D: ROUNDHOUSE PUB LTD
UNIVERSITY OF NEWCASTLE UPON TYNE
University of Nigeria Press (NG) — D: AFRICAN BOOKS COLL
University of North Carolina Press (US) — A: TREVOR BROWN ASSOC
UNIVERSITY OF NORTH LONDON PRESS
University of Notre Dame Press (US) — D: EDS
University of Oklahoma Press (US) — D: EDS
University of Ottawa Press (Partial) (CA) — D: INTERCEPT LTD
University of Penn Press (US) — A: ACADEMIC & UNIV PUB
University of Pittsburgh Press (US) — D: EDS
University of Port Harcourt Press (NG) — D: AFRICAN BOOKS COLL
University of Sankore Press (US) — D: KARNAK HOUSE
University of Scranton Press — I: GOLDEN COCKEREL
University of South Carolina (Partial) (US) — D: ROUNDHOUSE PUB LTD
University of South Dakota Press (US) — D: EDS
University of Sydney (History Dept) (AU) — A: HEADSTART HISTORY
University of Texas Press (US) — A: TREVOR BROWN ASSOC
University of the South Pacific (Fiji) — D: PETER MOORE BOOKS
University of Tokyo Press (JA) — A: ACADEMIC & UNIV PUB
University of Toronto Press (CA) — A: TREVOR BROWN ASSOC
University of Toronto Press — D: INT BOOK DIST
University of Wales Press — A: BOOK REP & DIST LTD
UNIVERSITY OF WALES PRESS
UNIVERSITY OF WARWICK
University of Washington Press (Partial) (US) — D: REAKTION BOOKS LTD
University of Washington Press (US) — A: TREVOR BROWN ASSOC
University of Western Australia Press (AU) — D: PETER MOORE BOOKS
University of Wisconsin Press (US) — D: EDS
University of Zimbabwe Publications (ZB) — D: LEISHMAN & TAUSSIG
University Paperbacks — I: ROUTLEDGE
University Press of America (US) — D: EDS
University Press of Florida (US) — D: EDS

University Press of Kansas (US) — D: EDS
University Press of Kentucky (US) — A: TREVOR BROWN ASSOC
University Press of Mississippi (Partial) (US) — D: ROUNDHOUSE PUB LTD
University Press of New England (US) — A: TREVOR BROWN ASSOC
University Press of New England (US) — D: PLYMBRIDGE DIST LTD
University Press of Virginia (US) — D: EDS
University Presses Marketing — D: INT BOOK DIST
UNIVERSITY PRESSES MARKETING
UNIVERSITY PRESSES OF CALIFORNIA, COLUMBIA & PRINCETON
University Science Books (US) — D: W H FREEMAN & CO LTD
Unix Press — I: SIMON & SCHUSTER INT
Unspeakable Tomes — I: COUNTER PRODUCTIONS
Unwin Books, Merlin — D: CHRIS LLOYD SALES
UNWIN BOOKS, MERLIN
Unwin Hyman — I: HARPERCOLLINS TRADE
Unwin Hyman Academic — I: ROUTLEDGE
Update Communications Ltd (NG) — D: AFRICAN BOOKS COLL
Upper Room, The (US) — D: METHODIST PUBLISHING
Upstart (US) — D: KOGAN PAGE LTD
Upstarts — I: VIRAGO PRESS
Urania Verlag AG (Partial) (SZ) — D: ELEMENT BOOKS LTD
Urban & Schwarzenberg — I: WILLIAMS & WILKINS
Urban Fox — D: BOOKSPEED
Urban Institute Press — I: SIMON & SCHUSTER INT
Urban Institute Press (US) — D: EDS
Urdd Gobaith Cymru — D: WELSH BOOKS COUNCIL
US Games Inc (US) — D: AIRLIFT BOOK CO
US Industrial Directory — I: REED INFO SERVICES
US Pharmacopeial Convention (Partial List) (US) — D: PHARMACEUTICAL PRESS
Usborne Books at Home — D: BOOKPOINT LIMITED
Usborne Publishing — D: D SERVICES
USBORNE PUBLISHING LTD
Useable Portable (US) — D: CHARLES LETTS & CO
USPG — A: SPCK
USSHER PRESS, THE
Uzima Press (KY) — D: LEISHMAN & TAUSSIG
V & H COMPUTER SERVICES
VAC Job (FR) — D: VACATION WORK
Vacant Lot — I: NEWS PRODUCTIONS
Vacation Work — D: AN PUBLICATIONS
Vacation Work — D: ROGER LASCELLES
VACATION WORK
Vahid — I: ROYSTON
Valentine Mitchell — I: FRANK CASS & CO LTD
Vallardi (IT) — D: VINE HOUSE DIST
VALLEY BOOKS — W
Valor Foundation (US) — D: L N FOWLER & CO LTD
Van Abbe Museum (NT) — D: ART DATA
Van & Van Publiciteit (NT) — D: VINE HOUSE DIST
Van Arkel, Jan (English Language Titles Only) — D: JON CARPENTER PUB
Van Duren — I: COLIN SMYTHE LTD
Van Gendt bv, A L (Hollstein Series) (NT) — D: ART BOOK DIST CO
Van Nostrand Reinhold (US) — D: INT THOMSON PUB SERV
Van Weenen, John — D: BIBLIOS PUB DIST
Vanguard Books — No reply 92/93
Vanwell Books (CA) — D: AIRLIFE PUBLISHING
Variorum — I: ASHGATE PUB GROUP
VCH PUBLISHERS (UK) LTD
Vector Services Ltd — D: BREWIN BOOK DIST
Vefa Alexiadou Editions (GR) — D: MILLBANK BOOKS LTD
Vegetarian Society — D: BOOKSPEED
Veloce — D: BIBLIOS PUB DIST
VELOCE PUBLISHING
VENNEL PRESS
Ventana Press (US) — D: COMPUTER BOOKSHOPS
Venton, Colin — I: VENTON EDUCATIONAL
VENTON EDUCATIONAL
Ventura Publishing — No reply 93
VENTURE PRESS
Ventus Books — I: PLAYWRIGHTS PUB CO
VERBATIM
Verbo (PG) — D: ROY YATES BOOKS
Vergara, Javier (SP) — D: EUROPEAN SCHOOLBOOKS
VERIFICATION TECHNOLOGY INFORMATION CENTRE
VERITAS FOUNDATION
Veritas Publications — D: COLUMBA BOOK SERVICE
VERITAS PUBLICATIONS
Verlag Constructiv Berlin (GE) — D: CENTRAL BOOKS
Verlag Ellen Ismail-Schmidt (GE) — D: LEISHMAN & TAUSSIG
Verlag Enzyklopadie (GE) — D: EUROPEAN SCHOOLBOOKS
Verlag fur Deutsch (GE) — D: EUROPEAN SCHOOLBOOKS
Verlag Josef Margraf (GE) — D: CAB INTERNATIONAL

Verlag Photographie (Partial) (SZ) — D: HILMARTON MANOR
Verlag Presse Informations Agentur (Partial) (GE) — D: S HENEAGE DIST
Verlag Saverlander (SZ) — D: ROY YATES BOOKS
Verlag Ullstein (Partial) (GE) — D: S HENEAGE DIST
Vermilion — I: RANDOM HOUSE UK LTD
Vermilion — D: TIPTREE BOOK SERV
Vernal Equinox Press (US) — D: EVENLODE BOOK DIST
Verso — D: MARSTON BOOKS SERV
Verso — D: AK DISTRIBUTION
VERSO
Verso (Imprint of New Left Books) — I: VERSO
Vertic — I: VERIFICATION TECH
Verulam Publishing — D: TIPTREE BOOK SERV
Verulam Publishing (Ireland Only) — D: ISLAND PUBLICATIONS
VERULAM PUBLISHING LTD
Vesta Publications — D: VENTON EDUCATIONAL
Vestal Press Ltd (US) — D: GAZELLE BOOK SERVICE
Vezina Editeur (Partial List) (CA) — D: ACCENT EDUCATIONAL
Victoria & Albert Museum Publications — A: CASSELL PLC
Victoria & Albert Museum Publications — D: LITTLEHAMPTON BK SVC
VICTORIA & ALBERT MUSEUM
VICTORIA HOUSE PUBLISHING
Victory Press (US) — D: EVENLODE BOOK DIST
Video 125 — D: IAN ALLAN PUBLISHING
VIDEO ARTS LTD
Video Medica (SP) — D: BOOKS CONTINENTAL
Vie Art Cite (Partial) (SZ) — D: HILMARTON MANOR
Vieueg (GE) — A: JOHN WILEY & SONS
Vikas Publishing House (IN) — D: SANGAM BOOKS LTD
Viking — I: PENGUIN BOOKS LTD
Viking Childrens — I: PENGUIN BOOKS LTD
Village Press — No reply 92/93
Village Publishing — No reply 93
VILLIERS PUBLICATIONS LTD
Vincent Publishing — No reply 92/93
VINE HOUSE DISTRIBUTION
VINE HOUSE REMAINDERS — R
VINE PUBLISHING LTD
Vintage — I: RANDOM HOUSE (ARROW)
Vipasana Dhura (US) — D: WISDOM BOOKS
Virago Modern Classics — I: VIRAGO PRESS
Virago Press — A: RANDOM HOUSE UK LTD
Virago Press — D: GRANTHAM BOOK SERV
VIRAGO PRESS
Virba Publishing — No reply 93
Virgin — A: PEGASUS PUB SERV
Virgin Music Publishing — D: INT MUSIC PUB
Virgin Publishing — D: TIPTREE BOOK SERV
VIRGIN PUBLISHING
VIRTUE & CO LTD
Vision Books New Delhi (IN) — D: BOOKS FROM INDIA
Vision Poster Co — D: CORDEE
Vision Press — D: VINE HOUSE DIST
VISION PRESS LTD
Visionbank — D: CENTRAL BOOKS
Visitor Publications — D: VINE HOUSE DIST
Vista Point Verlag (GE) — D: GAZELLE BOOK SERVICE
VISUAL ARTS PUBLISHING
VITA BOOKS
Vita Books (2 Titles Only) — D: CALDER PUB LTD
Vitessie Press (Ltd) (US) — D: SPRINGFIELD BOOKS
Vitriol (US) — D: TEMPLE PRESS LTD
VNR Int — I: CHAPMAN & HALL
VNU BUSINESS PUBLICATIONS
Volcano Press — D: ALIF INTERNATIONAL
VOLCANO PRESS LTD
Volcano Press (Partial) (US) — D: AIRLIFT BOOK CO
VOLO EDITION
VOLTAIRE FOUNDATION
VOLTURNA PRESS
Volunteers in Asia (US) — D: CORDEE
Vorderman Video, Carol — A: WORLD LEISURE MKTG
Voss Training Services — D: HOTEL & CATERING CO
Voyageur Press — D: AIRLIFE PUBLISHING
Vrakas Publishers (CY) — D: ZENO
W E ASSOCIATES LTD — R
Wadsworth (US) — D: INT THOMSON PUB SERV
Wagtails Pub — No reply 93
Waite Group Press (US) — D: PITMAN PUBLISHING
Wakefield Press (AU) — D: CENTRAL BOOKS
WALDEN PUBLISHING
Wales Tourist Board Accommodation Guide — D: JARROLD PUBLISHING

Walker Books — D: TIPTREE BOOK SERV
WALKER BOOKS LTD
Walker's Map — I: HARVEY MAP SERVICES
Walkers (Partial) (US) — D: WILLIAM SNYDER PUB
Walking Guides — I: LONELY PLANET PUB
Waller Ltd, Alfred — D: PLYMBRIDGE DIST LTD
WALLER LTD, ALFRED
WARBURG INSTITUTE
Ward Lock — I: CASSELL PLC
Ward Lock Educational — D: BOOKPOINT LIMITED
WARD LOCK EDUCATIONAL COMPANY
WARD'S PUBLISHING SERVICES
WAREHAM BEARS PUBLICATIONS
Warne, Frederick — I: PENGUIN BOOKS LTD
Warner Books — D: TIPTREE BOOK SERV
Warner Books (UK) — I: LITTLE BROWN & CO
Warner Bros (US) — D: INT MUSIC PUB
Warner Chappell — D: INT MUSIC PUB
Warner Futura — I: LITTLE BROWN & CO
Warner Futura — D: TIPTREE BOOK SERV
Warner Paperbacks (US) — D: COMBINED BOOK SERV
Warners/ETS (US) — D: PASTEST SERVICE
Warwick Press (US) — D: EVENLODE BOOK DIST
Warwickshire County Council — D: BREWIN BOOK DIST
Watari (JP) — D: NEWS PRODUCTIONS
Watchword Video — I: RANDOM HOUSE UK LTD
Water Environment Association (US) — D: CLARKE ASSOCIATES
Water Press, The — D: S HENEAGE DIST
Waterfront Publications — D: CHRIS LLOYD SALES
Waterline Books — I: AIRLIFE PUBLISHING
Waterlow — I: WATERLOW INFO SERV
Waterlow Directories — I: WATERLOW INFO SERV
WATERLOW INFORMATION SERVICES LTD
Waterlow Law — I: SWEET & MAXWELL LTD
Waterlow Law — D: INT THOMSON PUB SERV
WATERMARK PUBLICATIONS LTD
Waters & Associates — D: VINE HOUSE DIST
WATKINS PUBLISHING, PAUL
Watson & Dwyer (CA) — D: DUNDURN DISTRIBUTION
Watson Guptill (US) — A: PHAIDON PRESS LTD
Watts, Franklin — I: THE WATTS GROUP
Watts Group — D: TIPTREE BOOK SERV
WATTS GROUP, THE
Watts Publishing, Peter — D: TRANSPORT PUB CO LTD
Wayland — A: GILL & MACMILLAN LTD
Wayland (Partial List) — D: MARY GLASGOW PUB
WAYLAND PUBLISHERS LTD
Weatherhill (JP) — D: NEW HOLLAND PUB LTD
Weatherhill (Partial) (JP) — D: WISDOM BOOKS
Weatherhill (Partial) (JP) — A: P M LLEWELLYN CO
WEAVERS PRESS PUBLISHING
Webb & Bower — No longer book publishing
WEBB & SON, S — W
Websters New World Dictionaries — I: SIMON & SCHUSTER LTD
WEBUCATIONAL — A
WEEDON BOOKS, GEOFF — A
Weidenfeld & Nicholson (Jewish Interest) — D: KUPERARD LTD
Weidenfeld & Nicolson — I: ORION PUBLISHING
Weidenfeld & Nicolson — D: LITTLEHAMPTON BK SVC
Weir Books — D: BREWIN BOOK DIST
Weiser, Samuel (US) — D: AIRLIFT BOOK CO
Wellesley College Museum (US) — D: ART DATA
WELLS PUBLISHING COMPANY, OWEN
Wellspring Publications — D: AIRLIFT BOOK CO
WELLSWEEP PRESS
Wellsweep Publications — D: PASSWORD (BOOKS) LTD
Welsh Academy, The — D: WELSH BOOKS COUNCIL
WELSH BOOKS COUNCIL
WELSH BOOKS COUNCIL — W
Welsh Joint Education Committee — D: WELSH BOOKS COUNCIL
Welsh National Centre for Religious Education (Partial) — D: WELSH BOOKS COUNCIL
WELSH OFFICE
Were Press, Gideon S (KY) — D: LEISHMAN & TAUSSIG
WERNER SHAW LTD
Wescott Cove Publishing (US) — D: GAZELLE BOOK SERVICE
Wesleyan University Press (US) — A: TREVOR BROWN ASSOC
WESSEX ELECTRONIC PUBLISHING
West Col — D: CORDEE
WEST COUNTRY BOOKS
West Publishing Company (US) — D: INT BOOK DIST
West (US) — A: HAMMICKS MAIL ORDER
West Wind Press (AU) — D: WORLDLY GOODS

Western Producer (CA) — D: DUNDURN DISTRIBUTION
Western Publishing — D: EGMONT PUB LTD
WESTERN PUBLISHING CO
Western Reserve Historical Society — I: GOLDEN COCKEREL
Western World Publishers (US) — D: LISTER ART BOOKS
Westgate Press (US) — D: MANDRAKE
Westgate Press (US) — D: GAZELLE BOOK SERVICE
Westminster & Overseas Productions Ltd — D: GROSVENOR BOOKS
Westminster Press (Partial) (US) — D: T & T CLARK LTD
Westminster Press (US) — D: GRACEWING/FOWLER
Westminster Productions Ltd — D: GROSVENOR BOOKS
Westminster Properties Owners Association — D: VINE HOUSE DIST
Westmorland Gazette — No reply 93
Westport Publishing Group (US) — D: GAZELLE BOOK SERVICE
Westview Press (US) — D: PLYMBRIDGE DIST LTD
Wexas International — D: TRADE & TRAVEL PUB
Wharncliffe — D: AIRLIFE PUBLISHING
Wharncliffe — I: PEN & SWORD BOOKS
What's On & Where Guides — I: AJK LTD
WHC Publications — D: SEARCH PRESS LIMITED
Wheaton T P H (US) — D: THEOSOPHICAL PUB LTD
WHELDON & WESLEY LTD
Whetstone Direct — D: COMBINED BOOK SERV
WHIGMALEERIE STORY CASSETTES — A
WHITAKER & SONS, J
White & Co — D: DOT PUBLICATIONS
White Cliffs Media (US) — D: AIRLIFT BOOK CO
WHITE COCKADE PUBLISHING
White Crescent Press — D: THE BOOK CASTLE LTD
White Dove (US) — D: AIRLIFT BOOK CO
WHITE EAGLE PUBLISHERS TRUST
White Eagle Publishing Trust — D: L N FOWLER & CO LTD
White Horse — I: JARROLD PUBLISHING
White Horse Library — I: VENTON EDUCATIONAL
White House Editions — I: NEW CAVENDISH BOOKS
White Lion — D: DEEP BOOKS LTD
White Lion Books — I: COLT BOOKS
White Pine Press (US) — D: WISDOM BOOKS
White Pine Press (US) — D: GAZELLE BOOK SERVICE
White Tree Books — I: REDCLIFFE PRESS LTD
Whitecap Books Ltd (CA) — D: GAZELLE BOOK SERVICE
Whitechapel Art Gallery — D: ART DATA
Whitford Press (US) — D: AIRLIFT BOOK CO
Whiting & Birch Ltd — A: BOOK REP & DIST LTD
WHITING & BIRCH LTD
Whitney Library (US) — A: PHAIDON PRESS LTD
Whittet Books — D: BIBLIOS PUB DIST
WHITTET BOOKS LTD
WHITTINGTON PRESS
WHITTLES PUBLISHING SERVICES
Who's Who Editions Gmbh (GE) — D: CEDAR TREE HOUSE
Who's Who In Italy (US) — D: EDS
Whurr Publishers Ltd — D: TURPIN DISTRIBUTION
WHURR PUBLISHERS LTD
Wiese Productions, Michael (US) — D: GAZELLE BOOK SERVICE
Wight, Oliver (US) — D: GAZELLE BOOK SERVICE
Wigmore Press — No reply 93
Wild Caret Press — D: CENTRAL BOOKS
Wild Goose Publications — D: HYMNS ANCIENT & MOD
Wild Side, The — D: CORDEE
WILD SWAN PUBLICATIONS LTD
Wilderness Press (US) — D: CORDEE
Wilderwiess Press Ltd (US) — D: SPRINGFIELD BOOKS
WILEY & SONS, JOHN
WILLIAMS & SON, W J — R
WILLIAMS & WILKINS
Williams Publications, Tony — D: LITTLE RED WITCH
Williams Publications, Tony — A: DEREK SEARLE ASS LTD
WILLIAMS PUBLISHING, STEWART
Williams, W — D: DALENNAU
Williams Wallace (CA) — D: TURNAROUND
Williamson Music (US) — D: INT MUSIC PUB
Williamson Publishing Co (US) — D: GAZELLE BOOK SERVICE
WILLINGHAM PRESS
Willis Music (US) — D: INT MUSIC PUB
WILLOW PUBLISHING
WILLOWBRIDGE PUBLISHING
Wilshire (US) — D: REAL BOOKS
WILSON BOOK SALES, JOHN
Wilson Booksales Ltd, John — D: BOOKPOINT LIMITED
WILSON PUBLISHERS, PHILIP
Wilson Publishing Ltd, Neil — D: EXEL LOGISTICS

WILSON PUBLISHING, NEIL
Wincanton Press — I: DORSET PUB CO
Winchester Bibliographies of Twentieth Century Writers — I: ST PAUL'S BIBLIO
Windbell — D: WISDOM BOOKS
Windcrest — I: MCGRAW HILL BOOK CO
WINDHORSE PUBLICATIONS
Windmill Publishing (US) — D: LISTER ART BOOKS
Windrow & Greene — A: IAN ALLAN PUBLISHING
Windrow & Greene — D: BOOKPOINT LIMITED
WINDROW & GREENE
Windrush Press — D: EVENLODE BOOK DIST
WINDSOR BOOKS INTERNATIONAL
Windsor Large Print Books — I: CHIVERS PRESS LTD
Windsor Publications — D: SPA BOOKS LTD
Wine Appreciation Guild (US) — D: D SERVICES
Wine Price File (US) — D: GAZELLE BOOK SERVICE
Wingbow Press (US) — D: AIRLIFT BOOK CO
Winning International — D: GAZELLE BOOK SERVICE
Winning Through — I: HARVESTIME PUB LTD
Winslow Press — D: BEBC DISTRIBUTION
WINSLOW PRESS
Wintergarden Press (AU) — D: ROY YATES BOOKS
WISDEN & COMPANY LTD, JOHN
Wisden, John — A: CASSELL PLC
Wisden, John — D: LITTLEHAMPTON BK SVC
WISDOM BOOKS
Wisdom Works Press (US) — D: ELEMENT BOOKS LTD
Wise Owl Books — I: HLT PUBLICATIONS
Wise Owl Quiz Promotions — I: FIREBIRD BOOKS LTD
Wise Publications — I: OMNIBUS PRESS
WISEBUY PUBLICATIONS
Wiseweighs — D: BOOKPOINT LIMITED
WITHERBY & COMPANY LTD
Witherby, H F & G — I: CASSELL PLC
Witherby (Insurance and Martime) — A: ROGER BAYLISS
Witwatersrand University Press (SA) — D: UCL PRESS LTD
Woburn Press — I: FRANK CASS & CO LTD
Woeli Publishing Services (GH) — D: AFRICAN BOOKS COLL
Wofsy, Alan (Partial) (US) — D: DAWSON UK LTD
Wolff Books, Oswald — I: BERG PUBLISHERS LTD
Wolfhound (IR) — A: TURNAROUND
Wolfhound Press — D: GILL & MACMILLAN LTD
WOLFHOUND PRESS
Wolfhound Press (GB only) (IR) — A: OLDCASTLE BOOKS LTD
Wolfhound Press (IR) — D: CENTRAL BOOKS
Wolley Dale Press — ATLAS
Women Working Worldwide — D: CENTRAL BOOKS
Women's Environmental Network — D: WORLDLY GOODS
WOMEN'S PRESS
Womens Press of Canada (CA) — D: TURNAROUND
Womens Press, The — D: PLYMBRIDGE DIST LTD
Wonder Kids Publications (US) — D: ROY YATES BOOKS
Wonderland Entertainment Ltd — D: BOOKPOINT LIMITED
Wood River Publishing (US) — D: BIBLIOS PUB DIST
Woodbine House (US) — D: GAZELLE BOOK SERVICE
Woodbridge Press Publishers (US) — D: GAZELLE BOOK SERVICE
Woodbridge Press (US) — D: AIRLIFT BOOK CO
Woodenboat Publications Inc (US) — D: BARNACLE MARINE LTD
WOODFIELD PUBLISHING
Woodgate Press — D: CORDEE
Woodhead Publishing — D: COMBINED BOOK SERV
WOODHEAD PUBLISHING
Woodhead-Faulkner — D: INT BOOK DIST
WOODHEAD-FAULKNER
Woodpecker — D: TRANSPORT PUB CO LTD
WOODSTOCK BOOKS
Woodward Publishing, Tim — D: BOOKPOINT LIMITED
Word Is Out — I: GAY LIBERATION FRONT
WORD PUBLISHING
Words of Truth — D: CHAPTER TWO
Wordsearch — D: CENTRAL BOOKS
Wordsmith — D: CENTRAL BOOKS
WORDSWORTH EDITIONS
WORDSWORTH EDITIONS — R
Wordware Publishing (US) — D: COMPUTER STEP LTD
Wordware Publishing (US) — D: GAZELLE BOOK SERVICE
Workbox, Audrey Babington's — D: GAZELLE BOOK SERVICE
Workers International — D: INDEXREACH LTD
Workers Revolutionary Party — D: INDEXREACH LTD
Working Press — D: CENTRAL BOOKS
Working Press — D: AK DISTRIBUTION
Workman (US) — D: EUROPEAN PRESS SERV

WORLD BOOK CHILDCRAFT INTERNATIONAL
World Council of Churches Publications (SZ) — D: CCBI PUBLICATIONS
World Directory of Environmental Organizations (US) — D: EUROPA PUBS LTD
World Economy Research Unit (PL) — D: CENTRAL BOOKS
World Federation of KSIMC — D: ALIF INTERNATIONAL
World Health Organisation (SZ) — D: HMSO BOOKS
World Horizons — I: EGMONT PUB LTD
World International Publishing Ltd — I: EGMONT PUB LTD
WORLD LEISURE MARKETING
World Leisure (US) — D: ROGER LASCELLES
World Microfilms — I: SUSSEX PUBLICATIONS
World of Information — I: WALDEN PUBLISHING
World of Islam Festival Trust — D: SCORPION PUBLISHING
World Organisation For Islamic Services (IA) — D: ALIF INTERNATIONAL
World Radio TV Handbook (US) — D: WINDSOR BOOKS INT
World Relief Network (US) — D: EVENLODE BOOK DIST
WORLD SCIENTIFIC PUBLISHING
WORLD SERVICE PUBLICATIONS
World Stationery — I: EGMONT PUB LTD
World Wide Book Supply — Ceased trading 92
World Wide Fund Nature Field Studies Council — D: RICHMOND PUB CO LTD
World Wide Publications — D: THE OFFICE LONDON
WORLDLY GOODS
Worldwide — I: MILLS & BOON LTD
Worldwide Media (US) — D: BIBLIOS PUB DIST
Worship Workshops — D: SEND THE LIGHT
Worth (US) — D: EUROPEAN PRESS SERV
Wright, John — I: BUTTERWORTH-HEINEMAN
Wright, John — D: REED BOOK SERVICES
Wright Publishing, Gordon — D: JOHN DONALD PUB LTD
WRIGHT PUBLISHING, GORDON
Wright State University Press (US) — D: EDS
Wright, Steve — A: NEWS PRODUCTIONS
Wrightson Biomedical Publishers — D: TURPIN DISTRIBUTION
WRIGHTSON BIOMEDICAL PUBLISHING
Write Stuff Syndicate Inc (US) — D: GAZELLE BOOK SERVICE
Writers & Readers (US) — D: AIRLIFT BOOK CO
WRITERS & SCHOLARS INTERNATIONAL LTD
Writers & Their Work — D: NORTHCOTE HOUSE PUB
Writers Block — D: CORDEE
Writers Digest (US) — A: H I MARKETING
Writers Digest (US) — D: TIPTREE BOOK SERV
Writers News — I: DAVID ST JOHN THOMAS
Wrox Press — D: COMPUTER BOOKSHOPS
Xanadu Blue Murder — I: XANADU PUBLICATIONS
Xanadu Publications — D: COMBINED BOOK SERV
XANADU PUBLICATIONS
Xanadu Publications Ltd — D: BOOKPOINT LIMITED
Xanthyros Foundation (US) — D: ELEMENT BOOKS LTD
XYLOPRESS LTD
Y Lolfa — D: WELSH BOOKS COUNCIL
Y Lolfa — D: DALENNAU
Y LOLFA CYF
Y LOLFA CYF — A
Yale Center for British Art (US) — A: PREMIER BOOK MKTNG
Yale Egyptological Studies — A: ARIS & PHILLIPS LTD
Yale University Press — D: JOHN WILEY & SONS
YALE UNIVERSITY PRESS
YATES BOOKS, ROY
Yearling — I: TRANSWORLD PUB
YELLOW BRICK PUBLISHERS
Yes International (US) — D: AIRLIFT BOOK CO
Yes International (US) — D: EVENLODE BOOK DIST
Yesteryear Books — I: P4 SPARES
Yesteryear Books — A: ACADEMY BOOKS LTD
YHA — D: GRANTHAM BOOK SERV
YMAA Publications Centre (US) — D: PAUL H CROMPTON LTD
Yoga Publication Society (US) — D: L N FOWLER & CO LTD
YORICK BOOKS
York University, Dept of Archaeology — D: OXBOW BOOKS
Yorkshire Arts Circus — D: TURNAROUND
Yorkshire Television — A: BOXTREE LTD
Young Corgi — I: TRANSWORLD PUB
Young Library Ltd — D: CLIPPER DIST SERVICE
YOUNG LIBRARY LTD
Young Lions — I: HARPERCOLLINS CHILD
Young Poolbeg — I: POOLBEG PRESS LTD
Young Wordsworth — I: WORDSWORTH EDITIONS
Yourdon Press — I: SIMON & SCHUSTER INT
Youth Hostel Association — D: GRANTHAM BOOK SERV
Youth Hostel Association — A: WORLD LEISURE MKTG
Youth Specialities — D: ALLIANCE BOOK SERV

Youth With A Mission — D: NEW WINE MINISTRIES
Youth Work Press — I: NAT YOUTH AGENCY
Yr Academi Gymreig — D: WELSH BOOKS COUNCIL
Yr Undeb Cristnogol — D: EVANGELICAL PR WALES
Zahra Publications — D: ALIF INTERNATIONAL
Zahra Trust UK — D: ELEMENT BOOKS LTD
Zambia Educational Publishing House (ZM) — D: LEISHMAN & TAUSSIG
Zambia Publishing Co (ZM) — D: MALLORY INT
Zanichelli (IT) — D: EUROPEAN SCHOOLBOOKS
Zebra Books (US) — D: BIBLIOS PUB DIST
Zed Books — D: PLYMBRIDGE DIST LTD
ZED BOOKS LTD
Zell, Hans — I: BOWKER-SAUR LTD
Zell, Hans — D: BUTTERWORTH & CO LTD
Zen Centre — D: WISDOM BOOKS
Zena Publications (NB One Title Only) — D: UNI OF WALES PRESS
ZENO
Zephyr Press (US) — D: AIRLIFT BOOK CO
Zephyr Press (US) — D: COMBINED BOOK SERV
ZEUS RECORDING COMPANY — A
Ziff-Davis Press (US) — D: COMPUTER BOOKSHOPS
Zimbabwe Educational Books (ZB) — D: LEISHMAN & TAUSSIG
Zimbabwe Publishing House (ZB) — D: AFRICAN BOOKS COLL
Zimbabwe Publishing House (ZB) — D: LEISHMAN & TAUSSIG
Zimmermann (US) — D: ROGER LASCELLES
Ziolkowsky, H (Partial) (GE) — D: MICELLE PRESS
Zomba Books — I: OMNIBUS PRESS
Zon International (US) — D: MILLBANK BOOKS LTD
Zondervan — I: HARPERCOLLINS RELIG
Zondervan Corporation (US) — D: B MCCALL BARBOUR
Zone Books (US) — D: MIT PRESS LTD
Zoological Society of London — D: OXFORD UNI PRESS DIS
Zwemmer — I: PHILIP WILSON PUB

PUBLISHERS & DISTRIBUTORS

AA PUBLISHING
Fanum House, Basing View, Basingstoke, Hampshire
RG21 2EA
ISBN Prefix(es): 0 7495, 0 86145
Tel: 0256 20123
Fax: 0256 22575
Telex: 858538 AA BAS G
Account No: _____ SM 0280·002
Sales Rep: _____
Tel: _____

Orders to
EXEL LOGISTICS - MEDIA SERVICES, 3 Sheldon Way,
Larkfield, Aylesford, Kent ME20 6SF
Tel: 0622 882000
Fax: 0622 718036

Order Information

All Dues Automatically Recorded
Representation Available
Invoice Payments: Exel Logistics

Personnel
Head of Company: John Howard (Managing Director)
Head of Sales (Home): David Vincent (UK Trade Sales Manager)
Head of Sales (Export): Stephen Mesquita (Export Sales Director)
Head of Marketing: John Barrett (Sales & Marketing Director)
Head of Publicity: David Tribe (Publicity & Promotions Manager)
Head of Accounts: Alan Heppell (Accountant)
Other Important Personnel:
David Watchus (Sales Administration Manager)

Number of titles published annually: 100
Percentage of Export Sales: 20%
Number of Staff: 75
PA Member
NBA Signatory
All New Titles are Bar Coded
Book Data Subscriber
WBIP Updating: Jean Fullilove

Parent Company: AA Developments Ltd

Trade Terms
35% on all orders
Credit Cards Accepted: Access/Master, Visa

Returns Procedures
Authority to Return: David Vincent
Address for Returns: Exel Logistics
Imperfect Returns: £15 retail sales price whole book returned, otherwise just return cover or title page, authorisation not required

AAB BRITISH BOOK SEARCH SERVICE - OXFORD

PO Box 342, Oxford, Oxfordshire OX1 1NN
ISBN Prefix(es): 0 86340
Tel: 0865 792610
Tel: 0865 790686
Fax: 0865 792611
VAT No: 533 1206 90

Personnel
Head of Company: L Gigliotti
Head of Sales (Home): L de Sybaris

Number of titles published annually: 1
Percentage of Export Sales: 20%
WBIP Updating: L Gigliotti

Trade Terms
25%

AANS = Marston Book Services

A B ACADEMIC PUBLISHERS

PO Box 42, Bicester, Oxfordshire OX6 7NW
ISBN Prefix(es): 0 907360
Tel: 0869 320949
VAT No: 448 5409 27

Order Information

Order Dept Opening Times
Mon - Fri 9.30am - 5pm
All Dues Automatically Recorded
Representation Available

Personnel
Head of Company: E Adam (Publisher)

Percentage of Export Sales: 60%
WBIP Updating: E Healey

Trade Terms
20% plus post & hdlg (Stock order negotiable)

ABC/THE ALL CHILDRENS CO LTD

33 Museum Street, London WC1A 1LD
ISBN Prefix(es): 0 948149, 1 85406
Tel: 071-436 6300
Fax: 071-240 6923
Telex: 21134
VAT No: 523 2777 49

Account No: _____
Sales Rep: _____
Tel: _____

Orders to
PLYMBRIDGE DISTRIBUTORS LTD, Plymbridge House, Estover Road, Plymouth, Devon PL6 7PZ
Tel: 0752 735251
Fax: 0752 695699

Order Information

All Dues Automatically Recorded
Representation Available
Representation: Derek Searle Associates

Personnel
Head of Company: T J M Chadwick (Chairman)
Head of Accounts: M Raine
Other Important Personnel:
S Tarsky (Managing Director)

Number of titles published annually: 90
Percentage of Export Sales: 75%

ISBN 0 86340 020 5   ISSN 0966-2413

—NEW AND UNIQUE USEFUL PUBLICATION—

AAB'S
REGISTER OF WANTED PUBLICATIONS UPDATED DAILY
ISSUED DAILY

- YOU ONLY PAY ONCE — YOU SAVE MONEY IN SEARCH FEES AND REPEATING ADVERTISING WEEKLY OR MONTHLY.
- YOU WILL HAVE PEACE OF MIND IN HAVING EXPERIENCED RESEARCH EDITORS HELPING YOU UNTIL THE BOOK IS FOUND.
- WE ARE UNIQUE — CHEAP AND THE BEST WORLD-WIDE.

NEW ADDITIONS ARE WELCOME. APPLY IN WRITING TO:
The Editor, AAB-REGISTER-ADDITIONS
AAB'S **EDITORIAL RESEARCH CENTRE** — OXFORD
- *ESTABLISHED IN* 1975
P.O. BOX 342 — OXFORD OX1 1NN
Tel: (0865) 790686 — Fax: 792611 — Night Line: 792610

COST OF THE REGISTER PER ISSUE
UK £10.95
OVERSEAS £19.95. P&P *INCLUDED*

Please order to: **The Publications' Officer**
AAB-BBSS — EDITORIAL RESEARCH CENTRE — OXFORD
P.O. BOX 342 (Paradise Street Business Centre)
OXFORD OX1 1NN, *U.K.*
Tel: (0865) 790686 — Fax: 792611 — Night Line: 792610

All New Titles are Bar Coded
WBIP Updating: T J M Chadwick

Trade Terms
35%

Returns Procedures
Authority to Return: All returns must be authorised by T Chadwick or M Raine

ABCO DESIGN LTD
Unit 11, Stirling Ind Centre, Stirling Way, Borehamwood, Hertfordshire WD6 2BT
ISBN Prefix(es): 0 907792, 1 85181
Tel: 081-953 9292
Fax: 081-953 6777
VAT No: 544 7894 00

Order Information

All Dues Automatically Recorded

Personnel
Head of Company: Joachim Holmes

Number of titles published annually: 6
Number of Staff: 2
All New Titles are Bar Coded

Trade Terms
25% small orders, otherwise 35%
Credit Cards Accepted: Access/Master, Visa, Diners

[handwritten: ABLEX - Direct Distribution]

ABERDEEN & NE SCOTLAND FAMILY HISTORY SOCIETY
152 King Street, Aberdeen, Grampian AB2 3BD
Tel: 0224 646323

[handwritten: Aberdeen University Press = James Thin (Mercat Press)]

HARRY N ABRAMS INC
100 Fifth Avenue, New York, 10011
Tel: 212 2067715
Fax: 212 6458437
Telex: 175975
Cables: ABRAMBOOK

Account No: _____
Sales Rep: _____
Tel: _____

Orders to
Harry N Abrams BV, PO Box 34, 21100 AA Aerdenhout, The Netherlands
Tel: 23 249031
Fax: 23 244709

Order Information

Order Dept Opening Times
Mon - Fri 8am - 4pm (UK Time)
All Dues Automatically Recorded
Representation Available
Invoice Payments: Harry N Abrams BV, The Netherlands

Other Important Locations
Publicity:Harry N Abrams Inc, 24 Litchfield Street, London WC2H 9NJ
Tel: 071-240 1311 Fax:071-836 7049

Personnel
Head of Company: Wim Kramers (Managing Director) Aerdenhout

Head of Sales (Home): Karin de Graaf (European Trade Sales) Aerdenhout
Head of Publicity: Ms Hazel Hutchison (Publicity & Promotions Manager) London 071-240 1311
Head of Accounts: Theo Koelemeijer (Bookkeeper) Aerdenhout

Number of titles published annually: 100
Number of Staff: 10
All New Titles are Bar Coded
WBIP Updating: Annemieke v d Meij

Trade Terms
35%

Returns Procedures
Authority to Return: Harry N Abrams BV, The Netherlands
Address for Returns: Compumail, Osloweg 21, 9723 BG Groningen, The Netherlands
Imperfect Returns: Title pages can always be returned

ABSOLUTE PRESS

14 Widcombe Crescent, Bath, Avon BA2 6AH
ISBN Prefix(es): 0 948230
Tel: 0225 316013
Fax: 0225 445836
VAT No: 328 3964 31

Orders to
CENTRAL BOOKS, 99 Wallis Road, London E9 5LN
Tel: 081-986 4854
Fax: 081-533 5821

Order Information

All Dues Automatically Recorded
Representation Available
Invoice Payments: Central Books

Personnel
Head of Company: Jon Croft
Head of Sales (Home): Aidan Lunn
Head of Publicity: Nicki Morris
Head of Accounts: Linda Sorisi

Number of titles published annually: 15
Number of Staff: 5
IPG Member
All New Titles are Bar Coded
WBIP Updating: Nicki Morris

Returns Procedures
Authority to Return: Central Books
Address for Returns: Central Books

ABSON BOOKS

Abson, Wick, Bristol, Avon BS15 5TT
ISBN Prefix(es): 0 902920
Tel: 0272 372446 Tel/Fax
VAT No: 138 7484 34

Order Information

Order Dept Opening Times
Sun - Mon 9am - 6pm
All Dues Automatically Recorded
Representation Available

Personnel
Head of Company: A Bickerton/P McCormack (Partners)

Number of titles published annually: 5
PA Member
All New Titles are Bar Coded

Trade Terms
35% Single Copy 25%
Girobank Number: 23 043 4002

Returns Procedures
Authority to Return: A Bickerton
Stock Returns: Produce evidence of damage

ACADEMIC AND UNIVERSITY PUBLISHERS GROUP

1 Gower Street, London WC1E 6HA
Tel: 071-580 3994
Fax: 071-580 3995
VAT No: 371 2758 46

Account No: _____

Sales Rep: _____

Tel: _____

Orders to
BIBLIOS PUBLISHERS DISTRIBUTION SERVICE LTD,
Star Road, Partridge Green, West Sussex RH13 8LD
Tel: 0403 710971
Fax: 0403 711143

Order Information

All Dues Automatically Recorded
Representation Available
Invoice Payments: Biblios

Personnel
Head of Company: Donald Deeks (Director)
Head of Sales (Home): Haydn Jenkins (Director)
Head of Marketing: Julia Monk

Number of titles published annually: 500
Percentage of Export Sales: 30%
Number of Staff: 4
WBIP Updating: D Deeks

Trade Terms
From 20% negotiable

Returns Procedures
Address for Returns: Biblios
Stock Returns: Prior authorisation required except for incorrectly supplied items
Imperfect Returns: No prior authorisation.

ACADEMIC BOOK ASSOCIATES

173 Marine Drive, Rhos On Sea, Colwyn Bay, Clwyd
LL28 4LA
Tel: 0492 543603
Tel: 0492 540328

Personnel
Head of Company: John Walter

ACADEMY BOOKS LTD

35 Pretoria Avenue, London E17 7DR
ISBN Prefix(es): 1 873361
Tel: 081-521 7647
Fax: 081-503 6655

Orders to
24 Hour Ansafone Number: 081-424 9868 ext4303

Order Information

Order Dept Opening Times
Mon - Sat 9am - 6pm

Orders for more than one publisher can be bulked
All Dues Automatically Recorded

Personnel
Head of Company: Tony Freeman

Number of titles published annually: 12
PA Member
IPG Member
NBA Signatory
All New Titles are Bar Coded
Book Data Subscriber

Trade Terms
35%
Credit Cards Accepted: Access/Master, Amex, Visa

Returns Procedures
Stock Returns: Incorrectly supplied or damaged books are replaced FOC, overstocks are dealt with on a case by case basis
Imperfect Returns: £20 price limit, title & cover to be returned

ACADEMY GROUP LIMITED

42 Leinster Gardens, Bayswater, London W2 3AN
ISBN Prefix(es): 0 85458, 0 85670, 0 90262, 1 85490
Tel: 071-402 2141
Fax: 071-723 9540
VAT No: 599 3179 76

Account No: _____

Sales Rep: _____

Tel: _____

Orders to
VCH PUBLISHERS (UK) LTD, 8 Wellington Court, Cambridge, Cambridgeshire CB1 1HZ
Tel: 0223 321111
Fax: 0223 313321

Order Information

All Dues Automatically Recorded
Representation Available
Invoice Payments: VCH Publishers (UK) Ltd
Trade Counter:Trade Counter Ltd, The Airfield, Norwich Rd, Mendlesham, Suffolk IP4 5NA Tel:0449 766629 Fax:0449 767122

Personnel
Head of Company: Dr Andreas C Papdakis (Managing Director)
Head of Sales (Home): Richard Ross
Head of Sales (Export): Paul Kwaiatkowskyj VCH Weinheim (Germany) Tel: 010 49 6201 606402
Head of Marketing: Sheila De Vallee
Head of Accounts: John Stoddart

Number of titles published annually: 30
Percentage of Export Sales: 20%
Number of Staff: 20
PA Member
NBA Signatory
All New Titles are Bar Coded
Book Data Subscriber
WBIP Updating: Mira Joka

Trade Terms
35% on all orders
Credit Cards Accepted: Access/Master, Amex, Diners, Visa

Returns Procedures
Authority to Return: VCH Cambridge (Returns)

ACAIR LTD
Unit 7, 7 James Street, Stornoway, Isle of Lewis PA87 2QP
Tel: 0851 703020
Fax: 0851 703294

Order Information

Order Dept Opening Times
Mon- Fri 9am - 5.30pm

Personnel
Head of Company: Joan M Morrison (Manager)
Head of Customer Services: Donalda Macleod

Number of titles published annually: 35
Number of Staff: 6
PA Member

Trade Terms
35%, 30 Days

Returns Procedures
Authority to Return: Prior permission required
Stock Returns: Returns with retail value under £20 will be subject to a handling charge of 10% of retail value
Imperfect Returns: Complete book and explanation required

ACCENT EDUCATIONAL PUBLISHERS LTD
17 Isbourne Way, Winchcombe, Gloucestershire GL54 5NS
ISBN Prefix(es): 1 85693
Tel: 0242 604466
Fax: 0242 604480
VAT No: 576 0048 41

Order Information

Order Dept Opening Times
Mon - Fri 9am - 5.30pm
All Dues Automatically Recorded
Representation Available

Personnel
Head of Company: Ron Gellert-Binnie (Managing Director)
Head of Accounts: Susan Blackett (Administrator)

Number of titles published annually: 15
Number of Staff: 3
All New Titles are Bar Coded
WBIP Updating: Susan Blackett

Trade Terms
30% (special orders variable), 15% cassette tapes
Non-Net: 17.5% (subscription, stock and special orders variable)
Other Terms: P&P charged on invoice value below £10

Returns Procedures
Authority to Return: Ron Gellert-Binnie

ACCOUNTANCY BOOKS
40 Bernard Street, London WC1N 1LD
ISBN Prefix(es): 0 85291, 1 85355
Tel: 071-833 3291
Fax: 071-833 9034
VAT No: 245 7889 11

Account No: _____
Sales Rep: _____
Tel: _____

Orders to
Accountancy Books, PO Box 620, Milton Keynes, Buckinghamshire MK9 2JX

Tel: 0908 668833
Fax: 0908 691165

Order Information

Order Dept Opening Times
Mon - Fri 9.15am - 5.15pm
Cyclical Ordering Policy
All Dues Automatically Recorded
Representation Available
Invoice Payments: Milton Keynes

Personnel
Head of Company: Nick del Rio
Head of Marketing: Judy Hubbard
Head of Distribution: Richard Mather 0908 225122
Head of Customer Services: Julia Wood 0908 668833

Number of titles published annually: 50
All New Titles are Bar Coded
Book Data Subscriber
WBIP Updating: John Fraser

Parent Company: Institute of Chartered Accountants in England & Wales

Trade Terms
35% to registered stockists 15% to other bookshops
Credit Cards Accepted: Access/Master, Visa

Returns Procedures
Authority to Return: Mrs D Roberts
Address for Returns: Milton Keynes

ACE BOOKS (AGE CONCERN ENGLAND)

1268 London Road, London SW16 4ER
ISBN Prefix(es): 0 86242
Tel: 081-679 8000
Fax: 081-679 6069

Orders to
BOOKPOINT LIMITED, 39 Milton Park, Abingdon, Oxfordshire OX14 4TD
Tel: 0235 835001
Fax: 0235 861038

Order Information

All Dues Automatically Recorded
Representation Available
Invoice Payments: Bookpoint Ltd
Representation:Amalgamated Book Services

Personnel
Head of Company: David Moncrieff (Publishing Manager)
Head of Marketing: Gill Cronin (Marketing Officer)
Head of Publicity: Katrina Webster (Media Unit Manager)

Number of titles published annually: 10
Number of Staff: 12
PA Member
NBA Signatory
All New Titles are Bar Coded
Book Data Subscriber
WBIP Updating: Gill Cronin

Returns Procedures
Address for Returns: Bookpoint Ltd

ACT 3 PUBLISHING

67 Upper Berkeley Street, London W1H 7DH
Tel: 071-402 2231

IPG Member

ADAMSON BOOKS

Akeman House, High Street, Stretham, Ely, Cambridgeshire CB6 3JQ
ISBN Prefix(es): 0 948543
Tel: 0353 649238
Fax: 0353 648184
VAT No: 407 6067 58

Personnel
Head of Company: Stephen Adamson
Head of Sales (Home): Nicky Adamson

Number of titles published annually: 1
Number of Staff: 2
All New Titles are Bar Coded

Trade Terms
35% no surcharges

ADDISON-WESLEY PUBLISHERS LTD

Finchampstead Road, Wokingham, Berkshire RG11 2NZ
ISBN Prefix(es): 0 201, 8 053
Tel: 0734 794000
Fax: 0734 794035
VAT No: 238 6027 59
Account No: 006/1697/001
Sales Rep:
Tel: Nicola Lyons calls here

Order Information
Teleordering: ADWES

All Dues Automatically Recorded
Representation Available

Personnel
Head of Company: Derek Hall (Managing Director)
Head of Sales (Home): James Green (Academic Sales Manager)
Head of Marketing: Jane Moody (Marketing Manager)
Head of Accounts: Kelvin Tunley
Head of Distribution: Pat Symes

Number of titles published annually: 400
PA Member
NBA Signatory
All New Titles are Bar Coded
Open University Publications
WBIP Updating: Jane Moody

Parent Company: Addison-Wesley Publishing Co Inc (Owned by Pearson PLC)

Trade Terms
20-30% no surcharges
Credit Cards Accepted: Access/Master, Visa, Amex, Diners, Other

Returns Procedures
Address for Returns: Southport Book Distributors Ltd, 12-14 Slaidburn Crescent, Southport, Merseyside PR9 9YF
Stock Returns: Permission from Head of Sales, Addison-Wesley

ADULT LITERACY & BASIC SKILLS UNIT (ALBSU)

Kingsbourne House, 229-231 High Holborn, London WC1V 7DA
Tel: 071-405 4017
Fax: 071-404 5038
VAT No: 523 4776 41

Orders to
AVANTI BOOKS, 8 Parsons Green, Boulton Road,
Stevenage, Hertfordshire SG1 4QG
Tel: 0483 350155
Fax: 0483 741131

ADVISORY CENTRE FOR EDUCATION (ACE)
1B Aberdeen Studios, 22 Highbury Grove, London N5 2EA
Tel: 071-354 8318
Fax: 071-359 1962
VAT No: 213 3815 93

ADVISORY UNIT FOR MICROTECHNOLOGY IN EDUCATION
Education Centre, Butterfield Road, Wheathampstead, Hertfordshire AL4 8PY
Tel: 0582 830274
Fax: 0582 830273
Fax: 0582 830312
VAT No: 214 5278 77

AEDIFICAMUS PRESS
113 The Ridgeway, Northaw, Hertfordshire EN6 4BG
ISBN Prefix(es): 0 9511701
Tel: 0707 872720
Fax: 0707 873444
VAT No: 473 0120 85

Order Information

All Dues Automatically Recorded
Representation Available

Personnel
Head of Company: Sam Morley

Number of titles published annually: 1
Number of Staff: 1
IPG Member
All New Titles are Bar Coded

Trade Terms
35% (+ p&p for single copies)
Other Terms: Small order surcharge £1.60
Credit Cards Accepted: Access/Master, Visa

AEROSPACE PROFILES
11 Southbank Road, Kenilworth, Warwickshire CV8 1LA
Tel: 0926 511524
Fax: 0926 56930

Order Information

Order Dept Opening Times
Mon - Fri 9am - 5.30pm

Personnel
Head of Company: Andrew Mobbs (Managing Director)
Head of Sales (Home): Mrs Pat Doxey (Sales Manager)

Number of titles published annually: 1
Percentage of Export Sales: 60%
Number of Staff: 6

Parent Company: KAM Publicity Ltd

Trade Terms
Credit Cards Accepted: Access/Master, Visa, Other

Returns Procedures
Authority to Return: Mrs P A Doxey

AESCULUS PRESS

PO Box 10, Oswestry, Shropshire SY10 7QR
ISBN Prefix(es): 1 871093
Tel: 0691 70426
Fax: 0691 70315
VAT No: 394 5726 12

Order Information

Order Dept Opening Times
Mon - Sat 9.30am - 6pm
All Dues Automatically Recorded

Personnel
Head of Company: David Ikerrin
Head of Sales (Home): Phillipa Ikerrin

Number of titles published annually: 10
Number of Staff: 3
All New Titles are Bar Coded
WBIP Updating: Phillipa Ikerrin

Trade Terms
35%
Other Terms: Postage charged on any orders with total value of less than £20
Credit Cards Accepted: Access/Master, Visa

Returns Procedures
Stock Returns: Paperbacks - covers only, hardbacks - full book
Imperfect Returns: As above

AFRICA CHRISTIAN PRESS

50 Loxwood Avenue, Worthing, West Sussex BN14 7RA
ISBN Prefix(es): 0 85352, 0 996487
Tel: 0903 232208

Order Information

Order Dept Opening Times
Mon - Fri 9am - 5pm

Personnel
Head of Sales (Home): Mrs Ruth Banks

Number of titles published annually: 5
Percentage of Export Sales: 95%
WBIP Updating: Donald Banks

Trade Terms
35%, postage charged

Returns Procedures
Imperfect Returns: All imperfect books replaced

AFRICAN BOOKS COLLECTIVE LTD

The Jam Factory, 27 Park End Street, Oxford, Oxfordshire OX1 1HU
Tel: 0865 726686 24 Hours
Fax: 0865 793298
Fax: 0865 311534
Telex: 94012872 ZELL G
VAT No: 537 1619 41

Account No: _____

Sales Rep: _____

Tel: _____

Order Information

Order Dept Opening Times
Mon - Fri 9am - 1pm, 2pm - 5pm
All Dues Automatically Recorded
Representation Available
Showroom on premises

Personnel
Head of Company: Hans Zell/Mary Jay (Consultants)
Head of Accounts: Ray Bannister
Head of Customer Services: Tracey Piper (Administrator)

Number of titles published annually: 150
Number of Staff: 7
WBIP Updating: Fiona Scarff

Trade Terms
Single copy 20% (CWO below £10), 2-5 copies 33%, 6+ 35% Credit Terms (30 days UK)(60 days Europe)(90 days USA etc)
Other Terms: Orders net invoice value £40+ carriage free, under £40 carriage charged, all Oxford deliveries carriage free
Girobank Number: 210 3109
Credit Cards Accepted: Access/Master, Visa

Returns Procedures
Authority to Return: Prior permission required from Head Office
Address for Returns: African Books Collective Ltd, Unit 3, off Pytts Lane, Burford, Oxon OX18 4SJ
Stock Returns: All books supplied on firm account. Some returns, but only with authorisation.
Imperfect Returns: May be returned without authorisation

AGE CONCERN SCOTLAND

54A Fountainbridge, Edinburgh, Lothian EH3 9PT
Tel: 031-228 5656
Fax: 031-228 5416

Book Data Subscriber

AGENDA & EDITIONS CHARITABLE TRUST

5 Cranbourne Court, Albert Bridge Road, London SW11 4PE
ISBN Prefix(es): 0 902400
Tel: 071-228 0700

Order Information

Order Dept Opening Times
Mon - Fri 10am -12.30pm
Representation Available

Personnel
Head of Company: William Cookson (Editor)
Other Important Personnel:
Mrs M R Corbett-Singleton (Assistant Editor & Hon Treasurer), Peter Dale (Co-Editor)

Number of titles published annually: 2
Number of Staff: 3

Trade Terms
33.3%

Returns Procedures
Authority to Return: Firm order only

AGORA BOOKS

China Hill, Brightling Road, Robertsbridge, East Sussex
TN32 5EH
ISBN Prefix(es): 1 872292
Tel: 0580 881137 24 Hours
Fax: 0580 881703

Order Information

Order Dept Opening Times
9am - 5pm
All Dues Automatically Recorded

Personnel

Head of Company: Martin Gordon (Partner)
Other Important Personnel:
Robin Amis (Partner (US)) +1 508 462 0563

Number of titles published annually: 3
Percentage of Export Sales: 80%
Number of Staff: 2
All New Titles are Bar Coded

Trade Terms

Single copy 25% plus carriage otherwise 35% carriage paid

Returns Procedures

Imperfect Returns: £25 price limit for annotated pages

AGRICOLA TRAINING LTD

Riseholme Hall, Riseholme, Lincoln, Lincolnshire LN2 2LG
Tel: 0522 544756 Tel/Fax
Fax: 0522 787026
VAT No: 497 7735 72

AGS PUBLICATIONS LTD

AGS Centre, Avon Bank, Pershore, Worcestershire
WR10 1JP
Tel: 0386 554790
Fax: 0386 554801
VAT No: 347 2065 62

ALEX AIKEN

48 Merrycrest Avenue, Glasgow, Strathclyde G46 6BJ
ISBN Prefix(es): 0 8502134
Tel: 041-637 2430

Trade Terms

33.3%

AIR-BRITAIN (HISTORIANS) LTD

1 East Street, Tonbridge, Kent TN9 1HP
VAT No: 119 2551 78

Orders to

Air-Britain Sales, Stone Cottage, Great Sampford, Saffron Walden, Essex CB10 2RS
Tel: 079 986 323

AIRLIFE PUBLISHING LTD

101 Longden Road, Shrewsbury, Shropshire SY3 9EB
ISBN Prefix(es): 0 906393, 0 950454, 1 85310
Tel: 0743 235651
Fax: 0743 232944

Cables: AIRLIFE, SHREWSBURY
VAT No: 163 1252 94

Account No: _____ BLRE01 _____

Sales Rep: _____

Tel: _____

Order Information
Teleordering: AIRLIFE

Order Dept Opening Times
Mon - Fri 9am - 5pm
All Dues Automatically Recorded
Representation Available

Personnel
Head of Company: Alastair Simpson
Head of Sales (Home): Andrew Johnston
Head of Publicity: Judith Sale
Head of Accounts: Peter Holmes
Head of Distribution: Paul Rice
Head of Customer Services: Christine Felton
Other Important Personnel:
Barry Richards (UK Sales Manager)

Number of titles published annually: 80
Percentage of Export Sales: 20%
Number of Staff: 18
All New Titles are Bar Coded
Book Data Subscriber
WBIP Updating: Judith Sale

Trade Terms
35%
General Net: Single Copy 25%
Girobank Number: 4821718
Credit Cards Accepted: Access/Master, Visa

Returns Procedures
Stock Returns: All returns must be authorized with special labels provided. Must be used or books will be returned at senders cost.
Imperfect Returns: Complete books must be returned

AIRLIFT BOOK COMPANY
26/28 Eden Grove, London N7 8EF
Tel: 071-607 5792 24 Hours
Fax: 071-607 6714
VAT No: 350 7630 67

Account No: _____ BLACRE _____

Sales Rep: _____

Tel: _____

Order Information
Teleordering: ABC

Order Dept Opening Times
Mon - Thur 9am - 5.30pm, Fri 9am - 5pm
Orders for more than one publisher can be bulked
All Dues Automatically Recorded
Representation Available

Personnel
Head of Company: Beth Grossman (Director)
Head of Sales (Home): Stuart Binns (Sales Director)
Head of Publicity: Carolyn Clarke (Promotion & Publicity Manager)
Head of Accounts: Nabela Ishtiaq (Accounts Manager)
Head of Distribution: William Ingram (Distribution Director)
Head of Customer Services: Sarah Hills (Trade Manager)

Number of titles published annually: 500
Percentage of Export Sales: 20%

Number of Staff: 25
WBIP Updating: Eamon James

Trade Terms
35% on orders over £25 retail 25% prepaid orders under £25 retail
Girobank Number: 57 273 4204
Credit Cards Accepted: Access/Master, Visa

Returns Procedures
Authority to Return: Sarah Hills
Stock Returns: Errors must be notified within 7 days of receipt. Returns must be authorized. Accepted after 90 days & up to 6 months
Imperfect Returns: Damaged overstock returns credited at 60% Annotated titles page accepted for imperfect books up to £20

AJK (BUSINESS MANAGEMENT) LTD
61 Wick Street, Wick, Littlehampton, West Sussex BN17 7JN
Tel: 0903 732590
Fax: 0903 732592
VAT No: 390 0385 61

AK DISTRIBUTION
3 Balmoral Place, Stirling, Central FK8 2RD
ISBN Prefix(es): 1 873176
Tel: 031-667 1507 24 Hr&Fax
VAT No: 592 9826 81

Account No: _____
Sales Rep: _____
Tel: _____

Orders to
AK Distribution, 22 Lutton Place, Edinburgh, Lothian EH8 9PE

Order Information
Order Dept Opening Times
Mon - Sat 9am - 6pm
All Dues Automatically Recorded
Representation Available

Personnel
Head of Sales (Home): Ramsey Kanaan
Head of Accounts: Bob Goupillot
Head of Distribution: Alexis McKay

Number of titles published annually: 500
Percentage of Export Sales: 40%
Number of Staff: 3
WBIP Updating: Ramsey Kanaan

Parent Company: AKA Books Co-operative Ltd

Trade Terms
35% no surcharges, 25% single copy

Returns Procedures
Address for Returns: 22 Lutton Place, Edinburgh EH8 9PE
Stock Returns: Whole copy only, authorised returns only
Imperfect Returns: Whole copy only

ALADDIN BOOKS LTD
28 Percy Street, London W1P 9FF
Tel: 071-323 3319
Fax: 071-323 4029
Telex: 21115 ALADIN

Cables: ARCHON, LONDON
VAT No: 340 0943 88

Personnel
Head of Company: Charles Nicholas (Managing Director)
Other Important Personnel:
Lynn Lockett (Director)

Number of titles published annually: 90
Percentage of Export Sales: 70%
Number of Staff: 16
All New Titles are Bar Coded

THE ALASTAIR PRESS

2 Hatter Street, Bury St Edmunds, Suffolk IP33 1LZ
ISBN Prefix(es): 1 870567
Tel: 0284 750963

Order Information

Order Dept Opening Times
Mon -Sat 9am - 5.30pm
Representation Available

Personnel
Head of Company: Stephen & Alison Du Sautoy

Number of titles published annually: 5
Number of Staff: 2

Trade Terms
General Net: Single copy/single line 20%, 2 books or more 35%, CWO 35%

Returns Procedures
Imperfect Returns: Title pages on all titles

ALECTO HISTORICAL EDITIONS

46 Kelso Place, London W8 5QG
Tel: 071-937 6611
Fax: 071-937 5795

THE ALEMBIC PRESS

139 Upper Road, Kennington, Oxford, Oxfordshire
OX1 5LR
Tel: 0865 730381
Fax: 0865 327368

THE ALEXIUS PRESS LTD

50 South Parade, Edgware, Middlesex HA8 5QL
Tel: 081-951 0888
Fax: 081-951 3524

Orders to
L W Hudson, 22 Oldfield Road, Bexleyheath, Kent
DA7 4DX
Tel: 081-304 6957

IPG Member

ALIF INTERNATIONAL

37 Princes Avenue, Watford, Hertfordshire WD1 7RR
ISBN Prefix(es): 1 85408
Tel: 0923 240844
Fax: 0923 237722

Account No: _____
Sales Rep: _____
Tel: _____

Order Information

Order Dept Opening Times
Mon - Sat 9am - 6pm
Orders for more than one publisher can be bulked
All Dues Automatically Recorded

Personnel
Head of Company: Murtaza Bandali

Number of Staff: 3

Trade Terms
Credit Cards Accepted: Access/Master, Visa

ALKIN BOOKS LTD

28 Phillimore Walk, Kensington, London W8 7SA
Tel: 071-937 2351 Tel/Fax

Orders to
CLIPPER DISTRIBUTION SERVICES LTD, Windmill Grove, Porchester, Hampshire PO16 9HT
Tel: 0705 200080
Fax: 0705 200090

IAN ALLAN PUBLISHING

Terminal House, Station Approach, Shepperton, Middlesex TW17 8AS
ISBN Prefix(es): 0 7110
Tel: 0932 228950
Fax: 0932 247520
VAT No: 207 5323 87

Account No: _____
Sales Rep: _____
Tel: _____

Orders to
BOOKPOINT LIMITED, 39 Milton Park, Abingdon, Oxfordshire OX14 4TD
Tel: 0235 835001
Fax: 0235 861038

Order Information

All Dues Automatically Recorded
Representation Available
Invoice Payments: Bookpoint Ltd

Personnel
Head of Company: Martin Kenny (Chief Executive)
Head of Sales (Home): Bill Lucas (Director Sales)
Head of Marketing: John Gammons (Marketing Manager)
Head of Accounts: Richard Spark
Other Important Personnel:
Nick Moore (Sales Manager)

Number of titles published annually: 55
Number of Staff: 22
All New Titles are Bar Coded
WBIP Updating: John Gammons

Trade Terms
35%, reduced discount for orders under £40
Girobank Number: 302 4156
Credit Cards Accepted: Access/Master, Visa

Returns Procedures
Authority to Return: Ian Allan Ltd

Address for Returns: Bookpoint Ltd, 39 Milton Park, Abingdon, Oxon OX14 4TD
Stock Returns: Contact Bookpoint Ltd
Imperfect Returns: All imperfect copies should be notified to Bookpoint Ltd who will issue instructions

[handwritten: Allan (Philip) = Simon + Schuster]

ALLARDYCE, BARNETT PUBLISHERS

14 Mount Street, Lewes, East Sussex BN7 1HL
ISBN Prefix(es): 0 907954
Tel: 0273 479393

Order Information

All Dues Automatically Recorded

Personnel

Head of Company: Anthony Barnett (Publisher & Managing Director)
Other Important Personnel:
Fiona Allardyce (Publisher)

Number of titles published annually: 2
All New Titles are Bar Coded

Trade Terms

Single copy - 0-20% dependent on title, 2 books or more 35%
Other Terms: Carriage charged on some small orders.

Returns Procedures

Stock Returns: Incorrect supply or damaged in transit - no request for authority to return required.
Imperfect Returns: No request required

[handwritten: Allen & Unwin (Australia) = Marston.]

J A ALLEN LTD

1 Lower Grosvenor Place, London SW1W 0EL
ISBN Prefix(es): 0 85131
Tel: 071-834 0090
Fax: 071-976 5816
Cables: AllenBooks-London
VAT No: 240 1754 94

Orders to

SHEED & WARD LTD, 14 Coopers Row, London EC3N 2BH
Tel: 071-702 9799
Fax: 071-702 3583

Order Information

All Dues Automatically Recorded
Representation Available
Invoice Payments: Sheed & Ward Ltd

Personnel

Head of Company: Mr J A Allen (Managing Director)
Head of Sales (Home): Caroline Burt

Number of titles published annually: 20
Percentage of Export Sales: 35%
Number of Staff: 3
IPG Member
NBA Signatory
All New Titles are Bar Coded
WBIP Updating: Jane Lake

Parent Company: J A Allen & Co Ltd

Trade Terms

General Net: Single copy/single line 25%, 2 or more single titles 35%, 2 books or more 35%, 10 or more of single title 40%

Other Terms: Under list price of £20 £1.50 surcharge.
Carriage free in UK
Girobank Number: 549 3455

Returns Procedures
Authority to Return: Mrs C Burt
Address for Returns: Trade Counter Ltd, The Airfield, Norwich Road, Mendlesham, Suffolk IP14 5NA Tel:0449 766629 Fax:0449 767122
Imperfect Returns: Title page up to £5

ALLEN PUBLISHING CO LTD

Unit B, 6 Citadel Park, Garrison Road, Hull, Humberside HU9 1TQ
Tel: 0482 26625
Fax: 0482 20908
VAT No: 475 4396 12

PA Member
IPG Member

ALLENHOLME PRESS

10 Woodcroft Road, Wylam, Northumberland NE41 8DJ
Tel: 0661 853174

IPG Member

ALLIANCE BOOK SERVICES

Wesley Hall, Palalwyf Avenue, Pontyclun, Mid Glamorgan CF7 9EG
Tel: 0443 226915 Tel/Fax
Tel: 0443 224834

Account No: _____
Sales Rep: _____
Tel: _____

ALLOWAY PUBLISHING LTD

Hastings Square, Darvel, Ayrshire KA17 0DS
ISBN Prefix(es): 0 907526
Tel: 0560 20237
Fax: 0560 22209
VAT No: 356 9099 09

Order Information

Order Dept Opening Times
Mon - Fri 9am - 5pm
All Dues Automatically Recorded
Representation Available

Personnel
Head of Company: R McBride
Head of Sales (Home): J Hyslop, B.Sc

Number of titles published annually: 6
All New Titles are Bar Coded
WBIP Updating: Mrs A Ross

Trade Terms
35%
Other Terms: £2 small order surcharge on orders having a retail value of under £24

[handwritten at top: ALMQUIST + WICKSELL International AB, ALSNOGATAN 7, P.O. Box 4627, S-116 91 STOCKHOLM - SWEDEN. FAX 010 468 641 1180]

ALPINE FINE ARTS COLLECTION (UK) LTD
43 Manchester Street, London W1M 5PE
Tel: 071-935 0797
Fax: 071-935 0656
VAT No: 444 0523 78

ALSTON BOOKS
Bridge House, Stratton Strawless, Norwich, Norfolk
NR10 5LP
ISBN Prefix(es): 0 900049
Tel: 0603 279305

Order Information

All Dues Automatically Recorded

Personnel
Head of Company: A W Edgar

Number of titles published annually: 1

Trade Terms
A third on all orders
Other Terms: Carriage charges for overseas

THE AMAISING PUBLISHING HOUSE LTD
PO Box, Musselburgh, Lothian EH21 7UJ
ISBN Prefix(es): 1 871512
Tel: 031-665 8237
Fax: 031-665 2582
VAT No: 502 3560 89

Order Information

All Dues Automatically Recorded
Representation Available

Personnel
Head of Company: Katrena Allen
Head of Sales (Home): Norma Rutherford
Head of Marketing: Charles Watt
Head of Publicity: Aileen Paterson
Head of Accounts: Janet Wilson

Number of titles published annually: 10
All New Titles are Bar Coded
WBIP Updating: Katrena Allan

Trade Terms
Single Copy/Two or more single titles 20% Two Books or more 35% Special orders 20%-45%
Credit Cards Accepted: Access/Master, Visa

Returns Procedures
Authority to Return: Norma Rutherford, Lochar Publishing Ltd, Moffat, Scotland
Stock Returns: Authorisation must be agreed no credit for damaged books or books damaged in transit
Imperfect Returns: Return with reason

AMALGAMATED BOOK SERVICES
Suite One, Royal Star Arcade, High Street, Maidstone, Kent
ME14 1SL
Tel: 0622 764555
Fax: 0622 763197

Account No: _____
Sales Rep: _____
Tel: _____

Order Information
Teleordering: ABS

All Dues Automatically Recorded
Representation Available

Personnel
Head of Company: John Masters
Head of Sales (Home): Neill French

Number of Staff: 14
All New Titles are Bar Coded

Trade Terms
25% single, 35% multiple

Returns Procedures
Authority to Return: Amalgamated Book Services
Address for Returns: To relevant distributor returns sent to sales office will not be accepted or credited.

THE AMATE PRESS

St John's Lodge, 14A Magdalen Road, Oxford, Oxfordshire OX4 1RW
Tel: 0865 722091

Order Information

Invoice Payments: R E Waterfield

Personnel
Head of Company: R E Waterfield

Number of titles published annually: 7
NBA Signatory

Trade Terms
1-3 - 25%, 4-50 - 33.3%
Other Terms: Small order surcharges 10%. Carriage always charged.

Returns Procedures
Authority to Return: Firm sale only unless ordered as 'see safe'

AMBASSADOR PRODUCTIONS LTD

Providence House, 16 Hillview Avenue, Belfast, County Antrim BT5 6JT
ISBN Prefix(es): 0 907927
Tel: 0232 658462
Fax: 0232 659518
VAT No: 331 7347 70

AMBER LANE PRESS LTD   A/C No. 142

Cheorl House, Church Street, Charlbury, Oxfordshire OX7 3PR
ISBN Prefix(es): 0 906399, 1 872868
Tel: 0608 810024
Fax: 0608 810024
VAT No: 345 9412 44

Order Information

Order Dept Opening Times
Mon - Fri 9am - 5.30 Sat 9am - 12.30pm
All Dues Automatically Recorded
Representation Available

Personnel
Head of Company: Judith Scott

Number of titles published annually: 10
All New Titles are Bar Coded

Trade Terms
General Net: 30%(pb)35%(hb) - single copy, 25+ copies 35%
Other Terms: Carriage Charges: Single copy order & all overseas orders

Returns Procedures
Imperfect Returns: No Limit

AMCD (PUBLISHERS) LTD
PO Box 102, Purley, Surrey CR8 3YX
ISBN Prefix(es): 0 9515066, 1 897762
Tel: 081-668 4535 24 Hours
Fax: 081-668 4535

Order Information

Cyclical Ordering Policy
Representation Available

Personnel
Head of Company: J S Adams

Number of titles published annually: 3
WBIP Updating: J S Adams

Trade Terms
On request

[Handwritten: American Inst of Physics = Oxford University Press]

[Handwritten: American Maths Soc = Oxford University Press]

[Handwritten: American Society of Agronomy, 677 S. Segoe Road. Madison, WI 53711-1086. USA FAX 0101 608 273 2021]

AMERICAN PSYCHIATRIC PRESS
3 Henrietta Street, London WC2E 8LU
Tel: 071-240 0856
Fax: 071-379 0609

Orders to
PLYMBRIDGE DISTRIBUTORS LTD, Plymbridge House, Estover Road, Plymouth, Devon PL6 7PZ
Tel: 0752 735251
Fax: 0752 695699

Order Information

All Dues Automatically Recorded
Representation Available

Personnel
Head of Company: Michael Geelan
Head of Marketing: Andrew Hartley
Head of Accounts: James Mealings
Head of Distribution: Danny Maher
Head of Customer Services: Patrick Geelan

Number of titles published annually: 50
Percentage of Export Sales: 45%
Book Data Subscriber
WBIP Updating: Patrick Geelan

Trade Terms
As Plymbridge

Returns Procedures
Authority to Return: As Plymbridge

[Handwritten: American Society for Microbiology (ASM) c/o Blackwell Sci (MARSTON)]

[Handwritten: AMERICAN ACADEMY OF ORTHOPAEDIC SURGEONS (AAOS) c/o LIPPINCOTT]

AMERICAN TECHNICAL PUBLISHERS LTD
27-29 Knowl Piece, Wilbury Way, Hitchin, Hertfordshire SG4 0SX
Tel: 0462 437933
Fax: 0462 433678
Telex: 825684 ATPG
VAT No: 335 2230 92

Order Information
Teleordering: AMERTEC

All Dues Automatically Recorded
Representation Available

Personnel
Head of Company: J C Shipley
Head of Marketing: P J Furr
Head of Customer Services: J F Leeson

Number of titles published annually: 400
Percentage of Export Sales: 60%
Number of Staff: 18

Trade Terms
15% no surcharges 30 days
Other Terms: Carriage charges: if order not prepaid (except trade)
Girobank Number: 305 7550
Credit Cards Accepted: Access/Master, Visa, Amex

AMNESTY INTERNATIONAL PUBLICATIONS
99-119 Rosebery Avenue, London EC1R 4RE
ISBN Prefix(es): 0 86210, 1 87332
Tel: 071-814 6200
Fax: 071-833 1510
Telex: 917621 AIBS

Orders to
CENTRAL BOOKS, 99 Wallis Road, London E9 5LN
Tel: 081-986 4854
Fax: 081-533 5821

Order Information

Representation Available

Number of titles published annually: 10
All New Titles are Bar Coded
WBIP Updating: David Cameron

Trade Terms
See Central Books

Returns Procedures
Authority to Return: Central Books

THE AMPERSAND PRESS (CI) LTD
39 Victoria Street, Alderney, Channel Islands
ISBN Prefix(es): 0 946346
Tel: 0481 823462

PA Member
NBA Signatory
All New Titles are Bar Coded
WBIP Updating: Paul Davies

Trade Terms
General Net: Single copy 25% + carriage charges, other orders 35%

AMRA IMPRINT
c/o B Griffiths, 21 Alfred Street, Seaham, County Durham
SR7 7LH
Tel: 091-581 6738

AN PUBLICATIONS
PO Box 23, Sunderland, Tyne & Wear SR4 6DG
Tel: 091-567 3589
Tel: 091-514 3600
Fax: 091-564 1600

Analytic Press c/o Karnac Books.

ANAYA PUBLISHERS
3rd Floor, Strode House, 44-50 Osnaburgh Street, London NW1 3ND
ISBN Prefix(es): 1 85470
Tel: 071-383 2997
Fax: 071-383 3076
VAT No: 503 2056 02

Account No: _____

Sales Rep: _____

Tel: _____

Orders to
FABER BOOK SERVICES, 16 Burnt Mill, Elizabeth Way, Harlow, Essex CM20 2HX
Tel: 0279 417134
Fax: 0279 417366

Order Information

All Dues Automatically Recorded
Representation Available

Personnel
Head of Company: Colin Ancliffe (Managing Director)
Head of Sales (Home): Colin Gower (Sales & Marketing Director)
Head of Accounts: Martin Ware
Head of Customer Services: Bridget Latimer-Jones

Number of titles published annually: 30
Number of Staff: 12
All New Titles are Bar Coded
WBIP Updating: Bridget Latimer Jones

Parent Company: Anaya Spain

Trade Terms
35%, 30 days credit
Credit Cards Accepted: Access/Master, Visa, Amex, Diners

Returns Procedures
Authority to Return: Required in all cases
Address for Returns: Faber Book Services
Stock Returns: All returns must be authorised by rep
Imperfect Returns: Books under £10 retail price: title pages may be returned All others must be authorised by rep on sight of book

PETER ANDREW PUBLISHING CO LTD
4 Charlecot Road, Droitwich, Worcestershire WR9 7RP
ISBN Prefix(es): 0 946796
Tel: 0905 778543
Fax: 0905 795077
VAT No: 551 3486 46

Personnel
Head of Company: Philip Checkley (Managing Director)

Book Data Subscriber

CHRIS ANDREWS PHOTOGRAPHIC ART
1 North Hinksey Village, Oxford, Oxfordshire OX2 0NA
Tel: 0865 723404

Fax: 0865 725294
VAT No: 348 6995 88

IPG Member

ANGLO-GERMAN FOUNDATION FOR THE STUDY OF INDUSTRIAL SOCIETY
17 Bloomsbury Square, London WC1A 2LP
ISBN Prefix(es): 0 905492
Tel: 071-404 3137
Fax: 071-405 2071

Orders to
BEBC DISTRIBUTION, PO Box 1496, Poole, Dorset BH12 3YD
Tel: 0202 715555
Fax: 0202 715556

Order Information

Invoice Payments: BEBC Ltd

Personnel
Head of Company: Dr Connie Martin (Secretary General)
Other Important Personnel:
Clare Haworth-Maden (Publications Officer)

Number of titles published annually: 6
All New Titles are Bar Coded
WBIP Updating: Clare Haworth-Maden

ANGLO ISRAEL ASSOCIATION
9 Bentinck Street, London W1M 5RP
Tel: 071-486 2300
Fax: 071-224 3908

ANNESS PUBLISHING
Boundary Row Studios, 1/7 Boundary Row, London SE1 8HP
ISBN Prefix(es): 1 85238
Tel: 071-401 2077
Fax: 071-633 9499
VAT No: 510 4832 82

Orders to
CHARLES LETTS & CO LTD, Letts of London House, Parkgate Road, London SW11 4NQ
Tel: 071-407 8891
Fax: 071-403 6729

Order Information

All Dues Automatically Recorded

Personnel
Head of Company: Paul Anness

Number of titles published annually: 30
Percentage of Export Sales: 60%
Number of Staff: 6
All New Titles are Bar Coded
WBIP Updating: Charles Moxham

Trade Terms
As Charles Letts

Returns Procedures
Authority to Return: As Charles Letts

ANNUAL CONCEPTS LTD

1 High Street, Princes Risborough, Buckinghamshire
HP27 0AG
ISBN Prefix(es): 1 874507
Tel: 0844 275927
Fax: 0844 274402
VAT No: 585 7288 82

Orders to
JOHN WILSON (BOOKSALES) LTD, 1 High Street,
Princes Risborough, Buckinghamshire HP27 0AG
Tel: 0844 275927
Fax: 0844 274402

Order Information

All Dues Automatically Recorded
Representation Available
Invoice Payments: Bookpoint Ltd

Personnel
Head of Company: Michael Thomas/John Wilson
Head of Customer Services: Pat Wilson

Number of titles published annually: 12
Number of Staff: 5
All New Titles are Bar Coded
WBIP Updating: Mrs P E Wilson

Trade Terms
35% orders over £50, single copy 20%

Returns Procedures
Authority to Return: John Wilson (Booksales) Ltd
Address for Returns: Bookpoint Ltd
Imperfect Returns: £5 price limit for annotated pages

ANTIQUE COLLECTORS' CLUB LTD

5 Church Street, Woodbridge, Suffolk IP12 1DS
ISBN Prefix(es): 0 902028, 0 907462, 1 85149
Tel: 0394 385501
Fax: 0394 384434
Telex: 987271 ANTBOK G
VAT No: 285 4413 47

Account No: _____ 1345 _____
Sales Rep: _____
Tel: _____

Order Information
Teleordering: ANTCC

Order Dept Opening Times
Mon - Fri 8.30am - 5.30pm
All Dues Automatically Recorded
Representation Available

Personnel
Head of Company: Diana Steel
Head of Sales (Export): Sarah Smye
Head of Marketing: John Andrews
Head of Publicity: Jean Johnson
Head of Accounts: Robert Woolnough
Head of Distribution: Ray Hallett
Other Important Personnel:
Jenny Gosling (Field Sales Manager)

Number of titles published annually: 10
Percentage of Export Sales: 40%
Number of Staff: 58
NBA Signatory
All New Titles are Bar Coded
Book Data Subscriber
WBIP Updating: Susan Ryall

Trade Terms
25% single copy 33.3% two or more

Returns Procedures
Authority to Return: Sarah Smye
Address for Returns: Antique Collectors' Club, The Old Maltings, Crown Place, Off Quay Street, Woodbridge, Suffolk IP12 1BU

ANVIL BOOKS (CHILDRENS PRESS) LTD
48 Palmerston Road, Dublin 6, County Dublin
ISBN Prefix(es): 0 900068, 0 947962
Tel: 01 973 628 24 Hours
VAT No: 9F 92459V

Order Information

Order Dept Opening Times
Mon - Fri 9am - 5pm
All Dues Automatically Recorded

Personnel
Head of Company: Rena Dardis

Number of titles published annually: 10
Number of Staff: 2
IPG Member
All New Titles are Bar Coded

Trade Terms
General Net: Single copy/single line 25%, all other orders 35%
Other Terms: Carriage charges on single orders

Returns Procedures
Stock Returns: Make application to return. Full copies/mint condition.

ANVIL PRESS POETRY
69 King George Street, London SE10 8PX
ISBN Prefix(es): 0 85646, 0 900977
Tel: 081-858 2946
VAT No: 335 9176 37

Orders to
PASSWORD (BOOKS) LTD, 23 New Mount Street, Manchester, Greater Manchester M4 4DE
Tel: 061-953 4009
Fax: 061-953 4001

Order Information

All Dues Automatically Recorded
Representation Available
Invoice Payments: Password (Books) Ltd

Personnel
Head of Company: Peter Jay
Other Important Personnel:
Julia Sterland, Alison Smith

Number of titles published annually: 12
Number of Staff: 3
All New Titles are Bar Coded
WBIP Updating: Alison Smith

Trade Terms
35%, £1.50 surcharge on orders below £25 invoice value
Girobank Number: 6134599

Returns Procedures
Authority to Return: Password Representative
Address for Returns: Clipper Distribution Service
Imperfect Returns: Return complete book

APA Publications (Hong Kong) Ltd c/o Grantham.

AP INFORMATION SERVICES
33 Ashbourne Avenue, London NW11 0DU
ISBN Prefix(es): 0 906247, 0 906288
Tel: 081-458 1607
Fax: 081-455 6381
VAT No: 231 8073 84

Order Information
Order Dept Opening Times
Mon - Fri 8am - 6pm
All Dues Automatically Recorded
Representation:Mercury Books

Personnel
Head of Company: Alan Philipp
Head of Sales (Home): Anthony Margolis
Head of Accounts: Gail Philipp
Head of Customer Services: Estelle Freedman

Number of titles published annually: 12
Percentage of Export Sales: 20%
Number of Staff: 12
IPG Member
Book Data Subscriber
WBIP Updating: Alan Philipp

Trade Terms
General Net: 20% - 33%
Other Terms: Carriage charged
Credit Cards Accepted: Access/Master, Visa

Returns Procedures
Authority to Return: On request from Estelle Freedman or Sales Dept

APEX BOOKS CONCERN
Darus Salaam, 13 Trimley Close, Luton, Bedfordshire
LU4 9HJ
Tel: 0582 572216 Tel/Fax
Telex: 825562 CHACOM APEX

APOLLO PRESS LTD
11 Baptist Gardens, London NW5 4ET
Tel: 071-267 3951
Fax: 071-431 0311
VAT No: 421 3145 04

Orders to
BIBLIOS PUBLISHERS DISTRIBUTION SERVICE LTD,
Star Road, Partridge Green, West Sussex RH13 8LD
Tel: 0403 710971
Fax: 0403 711143

IPG Member

THE APPLE PRESS
6 Blundell Street, London N7 9BH
ISBN Prefix(es): 1 85076
Tel: 071-700 6700
Fax: 071-700 4191
VAT No: 341 1282 95

Orders to
D SERVICES, 6 Euston Street, Freemen's Common,
Leicester, Leicestershire LE2 7SS
Tel: 0533 547671
Fax: 0533 544670

Order Information

All Dues Automatically Recorded
Representation Available
Invoice Payments: D Services

Personnel
Head of Company: Stephen Paul (Publishing Director)
Head of Sales (Home): John Timmis (Sales Director) D Services

Number of titles published annually: 80
PA Member
All New Titles are Bar Coded
WBIP Updating: Andy Vaughn - D Services

Returns Procedures
Authority to Return: D Services
Address for Returns: D Services

APPLEFORD PUBLISHING GROUP

Appleford, Abingdon, Oxfordshire OX14 4PB
Tel: 0235 848319

Order Information

Order Dept Opening Times
Mon - Fri 9am - 6pm
All Dues Automatically Recorded

Percentage of Export Sales: 80%

Trade Terms
Variable, but do not want small orders

Returns Procedures
Stock Returns: Must be agreed in writing previously
Imperfect Returns: Whole book must be returned for hardbacks over £10

APPLETREE PRESS LTD

19-21 Alfred Street, Belfast, County Antrim BT2 8DL
ISBN Prefix(es): 0 86281, 0 904651
Tel: 0232 243074
Fax: 0232 246756
Telex: 9312 100435 (AT) G
VAT No: 252 8140 75

Orders to
BOOKPOINT LIMITED, 39 Milton Park, Abingdon, Oxfordshire OX14 4TD
Tel: 0235 835001
Fax: 0235 861038

Order Information
Teleordering: APLTRE

All Dues Automatically Recorded
Invoice Payments: Bookpoint
Representation:Charles Letts & Co

Other Important Locations
London Office:10 Barley Mow Passage, Chiswick, London W4 4PH
Tel: 081-994 6477
Fax: 081-994 1533

Personnel
Head of Company: John Murphy (Managing Director)
Head of Sales (Home): David Ross (Marketing Director) London
Head of Accounts: John McClelland

Number of titles published annually: 80
Number of Staff: 20
All New Titles are Bar Coded
Open University Publications

Book Data Subscriber
WBIP Updating: Claire Skillen

Trade Terms
35%

Returns Procedures
Authority to Return: Charles Letts & Co, Parkgate Rd, London SW11 4NQ

APPLIED MARKET INFORMATION LTD
AMI House, 45-47 Stokes Croft, Bristol, Avon BS1 3QP
Tel: 0272 249442
Fax: 0272 241598
VAT No: 449 1071 52

ANN ARBOR PUBLISHERS
PO Box 1, Belford, Northumberland NE70 7JX
Tel: 06684 460
Fax: 06684 484
VAT No: 358 6827 05

Order Information

Order Dept Opening Times
Mon - Sat 9am - 5pm
All Dues Automatically Recorded

Personnel
Head of Company: P Laverack

Number of titles published annually: 20
Number of Staff: 2
PA Member
NBA Signatory

Trade Terms
17.5%
Other Terms: Carriage charges £2.72
BA/Girobank Small Order Scheme: Cheque with order
Credit Cards Accepted: Access/Master, Visa

Returns Procedures
Imperfect Returns: Return book

[handwritten: AQUA GROUP = Marston Book Service]

ARCHITECTURAL ASSOCIATION PUBLICATIONS
34-36 Bedford Square, London WC1B 3ES
Tel: 071-636 0974
Fax: 071-414 0782
VAT No: 524 3144 77

Book Data Subscriber

[handwritten: Arcade Publishing = Tiptree.]

[handwritten: Architectural Design + Tech Press. 128 Long Acre, LONDON. WC2E 9AN]

ARCHIVAL FACSIMILES LTD
The Old Bakery, 52 Crown Street, Banham, Norwich, Norfolk NR16 2HW
ISBN Prefix(es): 0 948285, 0 9506104, 1 85297
Tel: 0603 667021
Fax: 0603 760284
VAT No: 427 9628 15

Personnel
Head of Company: Stephen Easton
Head of Marketing: Chris De Boos

Number of titles published annually: 4
Number of Staff: 2
WBIP Updating: C De Boos

Trade Terms
25% on all orders
Credit Cards Accepted: Access/Master, Visa, Amex

ARCHIVE RESEARCH LTD
The Broadway, Farnham Common, Slough, Berkshire
SL2 3PQ
ISBN Prefix(es): 1 85207
Tel: 0753 636633
Fax: 0753 636746
VAT No: 527 1798 22

Orders to
Archive Int Group, CP 719, 2001 Neuchatel, Switzerland
Tel: 010-41 38 252131
Fax: 010-41 38 247927

Order Information
Order Dept Opening Times
Mon - Fri 9am - 5pm
All Dues Automatically Recorded
Invoice Payments: Archive International Group

Personnel
Head of Company: J M Dening/W R Buchanan
Head of Sales (Home): D C Tennant

Number of titles published annually: 10
Percentage of Export Sales: 80%
WBIP Updating: J M Dening

Trade Terms
25% + 30 days. Extra discount negotiable
Credit Cards Accepted: Amex

Returns Procedures
Stock Returns: Advance consultation essential. Returns only if supplied in error or defective.

ARCTURUS PRESS
The Manse, Fleet Hargate, Spalding, Lincolnshire PE12 8LL
Tel: 0406 23971

ARGUS PUBLICATIONS
Argus House, Boundary Way, Hemel Hempstead, Hertfordshire HP2 7ST
Tel: 0442 66551
Fax: 0442 66998
VAT No: 492 4008 51

Orders to
BAILEY DISTRIBUTION LTD, Unit 1, Learoyd Road, Mountfield Rd Ind Est, New Romney, Kent TN28 8XU
Tel: 0679 66905
Fax: 0679 66638

Order Information
Teleordering: ARGUSPR
Representation:Chris Lloyd

Personnel
Head of Company: Terry Pattisson/Beverly Laughlin

Number of titles published annually: 12
Percentage of Export Sales: 20%
IPG Member
Book Data Subscriber

Trade Terms
35% Extra discount negotiable

Returns Procedures
Stock Returns: Advance consultation essential

ARIAN PUBLICATIONS
Sunbury, Eastcote Lane, Hampton-in-Arden, Solihull, West Midlands B92 0AS
ISBN Prefix(es): 0 9519288
Tel: 0675 442175
VAT No: 585 0344 36

Order Information

Invoice Payments: To: J Hashemi

Personnel
Head of Company: Arian Hashemi
Head of Sales (Home): J Hashemi

Number of Staff: 2

Trade Terms
35%
Minimum Order: 200
Other Terms: Small order surcharge 50p per copy, carriage charges 10% of the order cost
Credit Cards Accepted: Access/Master, Visa

Returns Procedures
Stock Returns: Only damaged items in transit

ARIS & PHILLIPS LTD
Teddington House, Church Street, Warminster, Wiltshire BA12 8PQ
ISBN Prefix(es): 0 85668
Tel: 0985 213409
Fax: 0985 212910
VAT No: 137 6801 59

Orders to   PROFORMA
LA HAULE BOOKS LTD, West Lodge, La Haule, Jersey, Channel Islands
Tel: 0534 44957
Fax: 0534 47414

Order Information

All Dues Automatically Recorded
Representation Available
Invoice Payments: La Haule Books

Personnel
Head of Company: Adrian Phillips
Head of Publicity: Janet Davis
Other Important Personnel:
Mrs Lucinda Phillips (Director)

Number of Staff: 6
Book Data Subscriber
WBIP Updating: Mrs J M Davis

Trade Terms
25%, single copy 20%, negotiable
Credit Cards Accepted: Access/Master, Visa

Returns Procedures
Address for Returns: La Haule Books
Stock Returns: Only imperfect or wrong titles accepted

THE ARKLETON TRUST
Enstone, Chipping Norton, Oxfordshire OX7 4HH
Tel: 0608 677255
Fax: 0608 677276

EDWARD ARNOLD = Hodder Bookpoint
E. J. ARNOLD = Thomas Nelson.

THE ART BOOK DISTRIBUTION CO

Old Castle Laundry, Abbotsbury, Dorset DT3 4LA
Tel: 0305 871731 Tel/Fax

Account No: _____

Sales Rep: _____

Tel: _____

Order Information
Teleordering: ART

Orders for more than one publisher can be bulked

Personnel
Head of Company: Priscilla Pilkington
Head of Sales (Home): Mrs P Graham

Trade Terms
10% Educational, 25% Single Copy Orders, 30% Multiple
Other Terms: Carriage Charges Variable
Credit Cards Accepted: Access/Master, Amex, Diners, Visa

ART DATA

Unit U03, Acton Bus Centre, School Road, London NW10 6TD
ISBN Prefix(es): 0 948835
Tel: 081-961 3643
Fax: 081-965 3092
VAT No: 225 1188 85

Account No: _____

Sales Rep: _____

Tel: _____

Order Information
Teleordering: ARTDATA

All Dues Automatically Recorded
Representation Available

Personnel
Head of Company: T G Borton
Head of Sales (Home): Veronique Truffant
Head of Accounts: Martin Duignan

Number of titles published annually: 4
Percentage of Export Sales: 30%
WBIP Updating: T G Borton

Trade Terms
Non-Net: On application

Returns Procedures
Authority to Return: By arrangement only

ART SALES INDEX LTD

1 Thames Street, Weybridge, Surrey KT13 8JG
ISBN Prefix(es): 0 903872
Tel: 0932 856426
Fax: 0932 842482
VAT No: 212 2413 27

Order Information

Order Dept Opening Times
Mon - Fri 9am - 5pm
Cyclical Ordering Policy

Personnel
Head of Company: Duncan Hislop (Technical Director)

Number of titles published annually: 3
Percentage of Export Sales: 50%
Book Data Subscriber

Trade Terms
10%
Credit Cards Accepted: Access/Master, Visa, Amex

ART TRADE PRESS LTD

9 Brockhampton Road, Havant, Hampshire PO9 1NU
Tel: 0705 484943

ARTECH HOUSE

6 Buckingham Gate, London SW1E 6JP
ISBN Prefix(es): 0 89006
Tel: 071-973 8077
Fax: 071-630 0166
VAT No: 224 1980 75   A/C No 100234

Order Information
Teleordering: ADTECH

Order Dept Opening Times
Mon - Fri 9am - 5.30pm
Cyclical Ordering Policy
All Dues Automatically Recorded

Personnel
Head of Company: Mr William Waller
Head of Sales (Home): Ms Anne Diamant
Head of Publicity: Ms Lisa Adcock
Head of Customer Services: Ms Yolanta Struzik

Number of titles published annually: 48
Percentage of Export Sales: 70%
Number of Staff: 5
Book Data Subscriber
WBIP Updating: Lisa Adcock

Parent Company: Horizon House

Trade Terms
Basic discount 20%
Girobank Number: 541 5667
Credit Cards Accepted: Access/Master, Visa, Amex

Returns Procedures
Authority to Return: Anne Diamant
Address for Returns: Vale Packaging, 420 Vale Road, Tonbridge, Kent TN9 1TD

ASA SWIMMING ENTERPRISES LTD

Harold Fern House, Derby Square, Loughborough, Leicestershire LE11 0AL
Tel: 0509 234408
Fax: 0509 211982

Personnel
Head of Company: Mrs M J Avery (Publications Manager)

WBIP Updating: Mrs M J Avery

ASHFORD, BUCHAN, & ENRIGHT

31 Bridge Street, Leatherhead, Surrey KT22 8BN
ISBN Prefix(es): 0 90706, 0 907675, 1 85253
Tel: 0372 373355
Fax: 0372 363550
VAT No: 424 9026 61

Orders to
TBC DISTRIBUTION, Unit 10, Bunting Close, Mitcham, Surrey CR4 4ND

Tel: 081-687 1744
Fax: 081-687 1747

Order Information
Teleordering: ABE

All Dues Automatically Recorded
Representation Available
Invoice Payments: TBC Distribution

Personnel
Head of Company: Mr J Mole (Managing Director)
Head of Sales (Home): Michael Jull (Sales & Marketing Manager)
Head of Publicity: Mrs Lynn Halliday (Publicity Officer) 5 Hall Court, Row Ash, Shedfield, Hants

Number of titles published annually: 12
Number of Staff: 3
IPG Member
All New Titles are Bar Coded
WBIP Updating: Mr J Mole

Subsidiary Companies: Mole Books

Trade Terms
General Net: Single copy/single line 25%, otherwise 35%
Other Terms: All export orders under £20 net, pro-forma only
Credit Cards Accepted: Access/Master, Visa

Returns Procedures
Authority to Return: Mr J Mole
Address for Returns: TBC Distribution
Stock Returns: Refer to TBC
Imperfect Returns: Title page only up to £20

ASHGATE PUBLISHING GROUP
Gower House, Croft Road, Aldershot, Hampshire GU11 3HR
ISBN Prefix(es): 0 566, 0 7045, 0 7512, 0 85967, 0 86078, 1 85278, 1 85521, 1 85628, 1 85742
Tel: 0252 331551
Fax: 0252 344405
Telex: 858001 GOWER G
VAT No: 413 8038 72
Account No: _____ H005041.000
Sales Rep: _____
Tel: _____

Orders to
Ashgate Dist Service, Unit 3, Lower Farnham Road, Aldershot, Hampshire GU12 4PY
Tel: 0252 317707 (24 Hr)
Fax: 0252 317446

Order Information
Teleordering: GOWER

Order Dept Opening Times
Mon - Fri 9am - 5pm
All Dues Automatically Recorded
Representation Available

Personnel
Head of Company: N A E Farrow (Chairman)
Head of Marketing: Michelle Hughes (Head of Sales & Marketing)
Head of Accounts: N R Young (Financial Director)
Head of Distribution: Margaret Mold (Distribution Manager)

PA Member
Open University Publications
Book Data Subscriber
WBIP Updating: Elaine Winter

ASHGROVE PRESS

4 Brassmill Centre, Brassmill Lane, Bath, Avon BA1 3JN
ISBN Prefix(es): 0 906798, 1 85398
Tel: 0225 425539 24 Hours
Fax: 0225 319137
VAT No: 324 7567 45
Account No: _____00856002_____
Sales Rep: _____
Tel: _____

Order Information
Teleordering: ASH

Order Dept Opening Times
Mon - Fri 9am - 5.15pm
Cyclical Ordering Policy
Orders for more than one publisher can be bulked
All Dues Automatically Recorded
Representation Available

Personnel
Head of Company: Robin Campbell
Head of Sales (Home): Adrian Gilbert
Head of Marketing: Tina Ryan
Head of Accounts: Jeanette Woods
Head of Distribution: Norma Pitman

Number of titles published annually: 10
Number of Staff: 6
All New Titles are Bar Coded
WBIP Updating: Tina Ryan

Parent Company: Ashgrove Press Ltd

Trade Terms
General Net: Single copy 20% (cwo 25%), 2 or more under £20 25% (cwo 35%) Two books or more over £20 35%
Girobank Number: 344 3353
Credit Cards Accepted: Access/Master, Visa

Returns Procedures
Authority to Return: Jeanette Woods
Stock Returns: If its our error, return in good condition for full credit. Other returns reps perm or head office written perm
Imperfect Returns: Title page only under £12

ASHMOLEAN MUSEUM PUBLICATIONS

Ashmolean Museum, Beaumont Street, Oxford, Oxfordshire OX1 2PH
ISBN Prefix(es): 0 90009, 0 907849, 1 85444
Tel: 0865 278010
Fax: 0865 278018
VAT No: 195 2753 34

Orders to
GAZELLE BOOK SERVICES LTD, Falcon House, Queen Square, Lancaster, Lancashire LA1 1RN
Tel: 0524 68765
Fax: 0524 63232

Order Information

All Dues Automatically Recorded
Representation Available
Invoice Payments: Gazelle

Personnel
Head of Company: R I H Charlton (Publications Officer) Pubns Dept 0865 278009
Head of Customer Services: Declan McCarthy Pubns Dept 0865 278010

Number of titles published annually: 12
Percentage of Export Sales: 20%
Number of Staff: 5
All New Titles are Bar Coded
Book Data Subscriber
WBIP Updating: Susan Moss

Parent Company: University of Oxford

Trade Terms
35%
Credit Cards Accepted: Access/Master, Visa, Amex

Returns Procedures
Authority to Return: Gazelle Book Services Ltd
Address for Returns: Gazelle Book Services Ltd

ASLIB, THE ASSOCIATION FOR INFORMATION MANAGEMENT

Information House, 20-24 Old Street, London EC1V 9AP
ISBN Prefix(es): 0 85142
Tel: 071-253 4488
Fax: 071-430 0514
VAT No: 417 8857 12

Order Information
Representation:Mercury Books

Book Data Subscriber

ASM - American Soc. for Microbiology c/o Blackwell (Marston)

ASR RESOURCES LTD
465 Twickenham Road, Isleworth, Middlesex TW7 7DZ
Tel: 081-892 1933

Book Data Subscriber

ASSOCIATION OF COMMONWEALTH UNIVERSITIES
John Foster House, 36 Gordon Square, London WC1H 0PF
Tel: 071-387 8572
Fax: 071-387 2655
Cables: ACUMEN LONDON WC1
VAT No: 233 9567 42

ASSOCIATION OF CRICKET STATISTICIANS
3 Radcliffe Road, West Bridgford, Nottingham,
Nottinghamshire NG2 5FF
Tel: 0602 455407
VAT No: 353 5853 39

ASSOCIATION OF METROPOLITAN AUTHORITIES
35 Great Smith Street, London SW1P 3BJ
Tel: 071-222 8100
Fax: 071-222 0878
VAT No: 240 9200 00

ATC (PUBLICATIONS) LTD
Unit C7, New Yatt Bus Centre, New Yatt, Witney,
Oxfordshire OX8 6TQ
Tel: 0993 868185
Fax: 0993 868386
VAT No: 243 2360 92

Orders to
ATC Foulks Lynch, (FAO Julie Murphy), 28 Farringdon Street, London EC4A 4EU
Tel: 071-634 1000
Fax: 071-250 0786

ATHLONE PRESS LTD
1 Park Drive, London NW11 7SG
ISBN Prefix(es): 0 485
Tel: 081-458 0888
Fax: 081-201 8115
VAT No: 362 3116 82

Orders to
BMS LTD, Merlin Way, North Weald Industrial Estate, Epping, Essex CM16 6HR
Tel: 0992 524343
Fax: 0992 524552

Order Information
All Dues Automatically Recorded
Representation Available

Personnel
Head of Company: Brian Southam
Head of Sales (Home): Doris Southam
Head of Publicity: Helen Drake

Number of titles published annually: 30
Percentage of Export Sales: 40%
IPG Member
NBA Signatory
All New Titles are Bar Coded
Book Data Subscriber
WBIP Updating: Helen Drake

Trade Terms
30%
Academic Net: Commissioned Series: 25%
Non-Net: Single Copy 17.5%
Credit Cards Accepted: Access/Master, Visa, Amex

Returns Procedures
Address for Returns: Hoddle, Doyle, Meadows Ltd
Stock Returns: Contact Athlone c/o BMS
Imperfect Returns: Contact Athlone Head Office Limit £45

ATLANTIC EUROPE PUBLISHING CO LTD
86 Peppard Road, Sonning Common, Reading, Berkshire RG4 9RP
ISBN Prefix(es): 1 869860
Tel: 0734 723751
Fax: 0734 724488
VAT No: 537 7545 13

Account No: _____
Sales Rep: _____
Tel: _____

Order Information
Order Dept Opening Times
Mon - Fri 8am - 6pm
All Dues Automatically Recorded

Personnel
Head of Company: Dr B J Knapp
Head of Sales (Home): Mr D L R McCrae
Head of Accounts: Mr D Cooper
Head of Distribution: Mrs G Gatehouse

Number of titles published annually: 30
IPG Member
All New Titles are Bar Coded
WBIP Updating: Dr B J Knapp

ATLAS

16 Talfourd Road, London SE15 5NY
ISBN Prefix(es): 0 907508
Tel: 071-701 3689

All New Titles are Bar Coded

Trade Terms
Upon request

ATTIC BOOKS

The Folly, Rhosgoch, Painscastle, Builth Wells, Powys LD2 3JY
ISBN Prefix(es): 0 946400, 0 948083
Tel: 0497 851205

Order Information

Order Dept Opening Times
Mon/Wed/Fri 2pm - 5pm
Representation Available

Personnel
Head of Company: Jack Bowyer (Managing Director)
Head of Sales (Home): Audrey Bowyer

Number of titles published annually: 4
IPG Member
NBA Signatory
WBIP Updating: Jack Bowyer

Trade Terms
General Net: Two single titles or less 25%, 3 books or more 35% Special orders by agreement
Other Terms: Small order surcharges 50p single copy Carriage Charges export only

Returns Procedures
Imperfect Returns: Advise in writing first stating defect or damage

AUGUSTINE PUBLISHING CO

Chulmleigh, Devon EX18 7HL
Tel: 0769 80540 Tel/Fax
VAT No: 142 9530 72

AUKANA TRUST

9 Masons Lane, Bradford-on-Avon, Wiltshire BA15 1QN
ISBN Prefix(es): 0 9511769
Tel: 0225 866821
VAT No: 452 7471 41

Order Information

Representation Available

Personnel
Head of Company: Robert Mann

Number of titles published annually: 1
All New Titles are Bar Coded

Trade Terms
35% on all orders, no surcharges

AURUM PRESS LTD
10 Museum Street, London WC1A 1JS
ISBN Prefix(es): 0 906053, 1 85410, 1 873329
Tel: 071-379 1252
Fax: 071-580 2469
VAT No: 242 2076 95

Account No: _____
Sales Rep: _____
Tel: _____

Orders to
EXEL LOGISTICS - MEDIA SERVICES, 3 Sheldon Way,
Larkfield, Aylesford, Kent ME20 6SF
Tel: 0622 882000
Fax: 0622 718036

Order Information

All Dues Automatically Recorded
Representation Available

Personnel
Head of Company: Bill McCreadle
Head of Marketing: Sheilla Murphy
Head of Accounts: Piers Burnett
Head of Customer Services: Suzanne Collier

Number of titles published annually: 30
Number of Staff: 9
All New Titles are Bar Coded
WBIP Updating: Mandy Greenfield

Trade Terms
35%

Returns Procedures
Authority to Return: Prior permission required from Aurum Press
Address for Returns: Exel Logistics
Imperfect Returns: No authorisation necessary

AUSTICKS PUBLICATIONS
21 Blenheim Terrace, Leeds, West Yorkshire LS2 9HJ
ISBN Prefix(es): 0 900116
Tel: 0532 432446
Fax: 0532 430661
VAT No: 169 7961 96

Orders to
24 Hour Ansafone Number: 0532 455879

Personnel
Head of Company: David Austick (Managing Director)
Head of Sales (Home): John Lauder (General Manager)
Head of Accounts: Alan Kilburn (Group Accountant)

NBA Signatory

Trade Terms
35%
Other Terms: Carriage charges: Post free cwo
Girobank Number: 60 410 0000
Credit Cards Accepted: Access/Master, Visa

Returns Procedures
Imperfect Returns: Title page up to £20

AUSTRALIAN CONSOLIDATED PRESS (UK) LTD
20 Galowhill Road, Brackmills, Northampton,
Northamptonshire NN4 0EE
Tel: 0604 760456
Fax: 0604 702272

Order Information

Order Dept Opening Times
Mon - Thur 9am - 5pm Fri 9am - 4.30pm
All Dues Automatically Recorded
Representation Available

Personnel
Head of Company: G M Porter (Managing Director)
Head of Sales (Home): E Pajak (Sales Manager)
Head of Accounts: June Porter
Head of Distribution: Nicola Elvey
Head of Customer Services: Janette Gray
Other Important Personnel:
A Cullis (National Account Controller)

Number of titles published annually: 15
Number of Staff: 29
All New Titles are Bar Coded
WBIP Updating: Janette Gray

Trade Terms
General Net: 25%
Minimum Order: 12 books
Credit Cards Accepted: Access/Master, Visa

Returns Procedures
Stock Returns: Full copies for credit
Imperfect Returns: Only full copies allowable for full credit

AUTODATA LTD
Priors Way, Maidenhead, Berkshire SL6 2HP
ISBN Prefix(es): 0 85666
Tel: 0628 34321
Fax: 0628 770385
VAT No: 208 4782 54

Order Information

Order Dept Opening Times
Mon - Tue 9am - 5pm Fri 9am - 4pm

Personnel
Head of Company: R J Atherton (Managing Director)
Head of Sales (Home): B P Quinlan (Sales Director)
Head of Accounts: P Hillier (Accountant)
Head of Distribution: G Willett (Sales Office Manager)

Number of titles published annually: 50
Percentage of Export Sales: 50%
Number of Staff: 60
All New Titles are Bar Coded
WBIP Updating: R Brewer

Trade Terms
Academic Net: 25% trade titles
Non-Net: single copy 25%, Two or more 35%
Credit Cards Accepted: Access/Master, Visa

Returns Procedures
Authority to Return: G Willett

AVGQY c/o BIBLIOS

AVANTI BOOKS
8 Parsons Green, Boulton Road, Stevenage, Hertfordshire
SG1 4QG
Tel: 0483 350155
Tel: 0483 745876
Fax: 0483 741131
VAT No: 440 7623 63

AWARD PUBLICATIONS LTD

Spring House, Spring Place, Kentish Town, London
NW5 3BH
ISBN Prefix(es): 0 86163
Tel: 071-485 7747
Fax: 071-267 2140
VAT No: 229 3737 44

Account No: _____

Sales Rep: _____

Tel: _____

Orders to
Award Pub Ltd, The Old Riding School, Welbeck Estate, Nr Worksop, Nottinghamshire S80 3LR
Tel: 0909 478170
Fax: 0909 484632

Order Information

Order Dept Opening Times
Mon-Thur 8am-4.30pm, Fri 8am-4pm, Lunch 12.45-1.15
All Dues Automatically Recorded
Representation Available

Personnel
Head of Company: Ron Wilkinson (Managing Director)
Head of Sales (Home): Anna Wilkinson
Head of Accounts: Maggie Smyth
Head of Distribution: John Crookes

Number of titles published annually: 50
Percentage of Export Sales: 40%
Number of Staff: 20
All New Titles are Bar Coded
WBIP Updating: Miss Shirley Murrell

Trade Terms
35% on all orders
Other Terms: Carriage Charges part carriage payable if nett order value below £500

Returns Procedures
Imperfect Returns: Tel: 0909 478 170 for authority to return & authorisation no Complete books(no title pages) return to Old Riding School

THE AYLESFORD PRESS

158 Moreton Road, Upton, Wirral, Merseyside L49 4NZ
Tel: 051-678 7749

AZIMUTH EDITIONS LTD

33 Ladbroke Grove, London W11 3AY
Tel: 071-727 6254
Fax: 071-792 3094
VAT No: 577 0539 16

BERNARD BABANI (PUBLISHING) LTD

The Grampians, Shepherds Bush Road, London W6 7NF
ISBN Prefix(es): 0 85934, 0 900162
Tel: 071-603 2581
Tel: 071-603 7296
Fax: 071-603 8203
Cables: RadioBooksLondonW6
VAT No: 226 5110 96

Order Information

All Dues Automatically Recorded
Representation Available

Personnel
Head of Company: M H Babani
Other Important Personnel:
Miss P Pragnall (PA to MD)

Number of titles published annually: 50
IPG Member
NBA Signatory
All New Titles are Bar Coded
WBIP Updating: P Pragnall

Trade Terms
General Net: Single copy 20%, 2 or more single titles/2 books or more 25% Stock/Special orders 35%
Minimum Order: 6 books
Other Terms: Small order surcharge 50p, carriage charge 50p

Returns Procedures
Stock Returns: Write to head office for permission
Imperfect Returns: The whole book must be returned

[handwritten: BACIE - 35 Harbour Exchange Square off Marsh Wall, LONDON E14 9GE - Tel:- 071 987 8989 A/C NO BAC013 FAX - 071 987 9898]

BACSA (BRITISH ASSOCIATION FOR CEMETRIES IN SOUTH ASIA)

76 Chartfield Avenue, Putney, London SW15 6HQ
ISBN Prefix(es): 0 907799
Tel: 081-788 6953

Order Information

Order Dept Opening Times
Mon - Fri 9am - 10am, 4pm - 6pm

Personnel
Head of Company: T C Wilkinson (Hon Secretary)
Head of Publicity: J Wall (Press & Publicity Officer) 071-270 2444
Head of Accounts: J Quick (Hon Treasurer)

Number of titles published annually: 8
WBIP Updating: T C Wilkinson

Trade Terms
33.3% on all orders plus postage

Returns Procedures
Stock Returns: Return to Hon. Secretary
Imperfect Returns: £10 a copy, return to Hon. Secretary

BADGER PUBLISHING LTD

Unit 1, Parsons Green Estate, Stevenage, Hertfordshire SG1 4QG
Tel: 0438 356907
Fax: 0438 747015
VAT No: 563 3352 48

IPG Member

BAHAI PUBLISHING

6 Mount Pleasant, Oakham, Leicestershire LE15 6HU
ISBN Prefix(es): 0 900125, 1 870989
Tel: 0572 722780 24 Hours
Fax: 0572 724280
VAT No: 121 2613 26

Order Information

Order Dept Opening Times
Mon - Fri 9am - 5.30pm
Representation Available

Personnel
Head of Company: Gordon J Kerr
Head of Accounts: Miss Simin Yousefi
Head of Customer Services: George M Ballentyne

Number of titles published annually: 25
Percentage of Export Sales: 60%
Number of Staff: 10
NBA Signatory
WBIP Updating: George M Ballentyne

Trade Terms
35% on all orders
Other Terms: 10% postage on orders less than £20 net
Credit Cards Accepted: Access/Master, Visa

Returns Procedures
Authority to Return: Required in writing

BAILEY DISTRIBUTION LTD
Unit 1, Learoyd Road, Mountfield Rd Ind Est, New Romney, Kent TN28 8XU
Tel: 0679 66905
Tel: 0679 64777 Accounts
Fax: 0679 66638
Fax: 0679 67373 Accounts
VAT No: 201 1386 22

Account No: _____
Sales Rep: _____
Tel: _____

Order Information
Teleordering: BAIDIST

Order Dept Opening Times
Mon - Fri 9am - 4.30pm
Invoice Payments: Bailey Distribution Ltd

Personnel
Head of Company: Robin Mortimore (Managing Director)
Head of Accounts: Darran Quinn (Accounts Manager)
Head of Distribution: Alan Crabb (Distribution Director)
Other Important Personnel:
Tony Lamberton (Warehouse Manager), David Addison (Office/DP Manager)

IPG Member
NBA Signatory

Parent Company: Bailey Bros & Swinfen Ltd

Trade Terms
Refer to publisher
Girobank Number: 317 5154

Returns Procedures
Authority to Return: Refer to Publisher

MARTIN BAIRSTOW
Fountain Chambers, Fountain Street, Halifax, West Yorkshire HX1 1LR
ISBN Prefix(es): 0 9510302, 1 871944
Tel: 0422 352267
Tel: 0532 562711
VAT No: 399 3233 15

All New Titles are Bar Coded

[Handwritten at top: Baker + Taylor - 1114 Avenue of the Americas, NY 10036-7794 A/C No E71833-8 USA]

M & M BALDWIN

24 High Street, Cleobury Mortimer, Kidderminster, Worcestershire DY14 8BY
ISBN Prefix(es): 0 947712
Tel: 0299 270110
VAT No: 547 6638 05

[Handwritten: Baker + Taylor ENGLAND Northdale House, North Circular LONDON NW10 7UH 081-453 3627]

Order Information
Representation Available

Personnel
Head of Company: M Baldwin

Number of titles published annually: 3

Trade Terms
General Net: Single Copy 25%, Two or more 33.3%
Girobank Number: 43 737 3703
Credit Cards Accepted: Access/Master, Visa

Returns Procedures
Authority to Return: Prior permission required

JOHN BALL PRESS

Sheepcot, Folly Lane, May Hill, Gloucester, Gloucestershire GL17 0NP
ISBN Prefix(es): 1 871240
Tel: 0452 830098

Personnel
Head of Company: K R Smith (Managing Director)

Number of titles published annually: 1

Trade Terms
35% no surcharges, quantity discounts

BALNAIN BOOKS

Druim House, Lochloy Road, Nairn, Highland IV12 5LF
ISBN Prefix(es): 0 9509792, 1 872557
Tel: 0667 52940 24 Hour
Fax: 0667 55099
VAT No: 552 8096 28

Order Information
Order Dept Opening Times
Mon - Fri 9am - 1pm, 2pm - 5.30pm
All Dues Automatically Recorded
Representation Available

Personnel
Head of Company: Simon Fraser
Head of Marketing: Hugh Andrew 031-228 6189
Head of Publicity: Sarah Fraser
Other Important Personnel:
Stewart Joseph (Business Management) 081-968 8775

Number of titles published annually: 7
Number of Staff: 5
All New Titles are Bar Coded
Book Data Subscriber
WBIP Updating: Sarah Fraser

Trade Terms
Single copy 20% Up to £30 invoice value 25% Above £30 35%
Credit Cards Accepted: Access/Master, Visa

Returns Procedures
Authority to Return: Authorisation required from Head Office or Representative

BANKERS BOOKS LTD
17 St Swithins Lane, London EC4N 8AL
ISBN Prefix(es): 0 85297
Tel: 071-623 3531
Fax: 071-929 4301
VAT No: 447 2632 45

Orders to
Bankers Books Ltd, C/O Chart Ins of Bankers, Emmanuel Hse, Burgate Ln, Canterbury, Kent CT1 2XJ
Tel: 0227 762600
Fax: 0227 763788

Order Information

Order Dept Opening Times
Mon - Fri 9am - 5pm
All Dues Automatically Recorded
Representation Available
Invoice Payments: Canterbury

Personnel
Head of Company: Mr Justyn Young
Head of Sales (Home): Mr A R Moffatt
Head of Accounts: Mr Brian Sheehan
Head of Distribution: Mrs G Hurley
Other Important Personnel:
Mr Jeremy Benson (Bankers Bookshop Manager)

Number of titles published annually: 10
Percentage of Export Sales: 25%
Number of Staff: 10
IPG Member
All New Titles are Bar Coded
WBIP Updating: Uschi Gubser

Parent Company: The Chartered Institute of Bankers

Trade Terms
Single Copy 25%, Two or more 35%, 50 or over 40%
Non-Net: CIB members' discount 15-20%
Credit Cards Accepted: Access/Master, Visa

Returns Procedures
Authority to Return: Mrs Gaye Hurley, Canterbury (by negotiation)
Address for Returns: Bankers Books Ltd, Canterbury

THE BANNER OF TRUTH TRUST
The Grey House, 3 Murrayfield Road, Edinburgh, Lothian EH12 6EL
ISBN Prefix(es): 0 85151
Tel: 031-337 7310
Fax: 031-346 7484
VAT No: 232 3732 89

Order Information

Order Dept Opening Times
Mon - Fri 9am - 5pm
All Dues Automatically Recorded
Representation Available

Personnel
Head of Company: Mervyn T Barter
Head of Marketing: Murdo MacLeod
Head of Distribution: Frank Eunson
Head of Customer Services: William Lyall

Number of titles published annually: 20
Percentage of Export Sales: 65%
Number of Staff: 13
All New Titles are Bar Coded
WBIP Updating: Katrina Ironside

Trade Terms
35% on orders above £25, 25% on orders below £25
Girobank Number: 16 614 4002

Returns Procedures
Authority to Return: William Lyall
Imperfect Returns: Title page up to £35

THE BANTON PRESS
75 Nelson Street, Largs, Strathclyde KA30 9AB
Tel: 0475 674513

BARKER & HOWARD LTD
Barker House, 106-110 Watney Street, London E1 2QE
ISBN Prefix(es): 0 900133
Tel: 071-790 5081
Tel: 071-790 5082
Fax: 071-790 1622
VAT No: 244 0091 00

Order Information

Order Dept Opening Times
Mon - Fri 9am - 4.30pm
All Dues Automatically Recorded

Personnel
Head of Company: Mr Quentin J B Phillips
Head of Sales (Export): Mr Moti Surujnarain
Head of Accounts: Mr Babu Majithia
Head of Customer Services: Mrs Karen Cheyne

Number of titles published annually: 1
Percentage of Export Sales: 40%
Number of Staff: 23
WBIP Updating: Quentin Phillips

Trade Terms
25%
Other Terms: Carriage Charge at cost

Returns Procedures
Imperfect Returns: Return whole book for replacement

BARMARICK PUBLICATIONS
Enholmes Hall, Patrington, Hull, Humberside HU12 0PR
Tel: 0964 630033
VAT No: 390 3775 33

Personnel
Head of Company: Prof B O Pettman (Partner)

Number of titles published annually: 20
Percentage of Export Sales: 50%
Number of Staff: 4

Trade Terms
10%

BARN DANCE PUBLICATIONS LTD
62 Beechwood Road, South Croydon, Surrey CR2 0AA
ISBN Prefix(es): 0 9514285
Tel: 081-651 6080
Tel: 081-657 2813
Tel: 081 657 8788
Fax: 081-651 6080

Personnel
Head of Company: Derek Jones

Number of titles published annually: 2
Number of Staff: 2
IPG Member

Allied Companies: Time Tapes

Trade Terms
35%

BARNACLE MARINE LTD
PO Box 1539, Hazelbury Manor, Corsham, Wiltshire SN13 9ZZ
ISBN Prefix(es): 0 948788
Tel: 0225 812024
Fax: 0225 812025
VAT No: 386 7279 93

Order Information
Teleordering: MARINE

Order Dept Opening Times
Mon - Fri 8.30am - 5pm
All Dues Automatically Recorded
Representation Available

Personnel
Head of Company: Roger N Hunter
Head of Sales (Home): Colin Michell (Sales Manager)
Head of Accounts: Diana M Hunter FCA

Number of titles published annually: 6
Percentage of Export Sales: 20%
Number of Staff: 6
All New Titles are Bar Coded
WBIP Updating: Roger N Hunter

Trade Terms
General Net: Single Copy 35% plus £2 unless prepaid Two or more 35%
Other Terms: Carriage Charges: at cost for orders under £40 retail
Girobank Number: 312 4488 05
Credit Cards Accepted: Access/Master, Visa

BARNY BOOKS
Hough on the Hill, Grantham, Lincolnshire NG32 2BB
ISBN Prefix(es): 0 948204
Tel: 0400 50246 24 Hours
Fax: 0522 790009

Order Information

Order Dept Opening Times
Mon - Fri 9am - 12pm

Personnel
Head of Company: Molly Burkett
Head of Sales (Home): Ben Cann
Head of Accounts: E Hair
Head of Distribution: J H Burkett
Other Important Personnel:
Tom Cann (Artistic & Printing)

Number of titles published annually: 6
Number of Staff: 4
NBA Signatory
WBIP Updating: Molly Burkett

Trade Terms
40% + p&p

Returns Procedures
Authority to Return: Molly Burkett, Barny Books

BARTON HOUSE PUBLISHING
51 Audley Park Road, Bath, Avon BA1 2XF
ISBN Prefix(es): 1 855885
Tel: 0225 317675
Fax: 0225 465612

Orders to
ASHGROVE PRESS, 4 Brassmill Centre, Brassmill Lane, Bath, Avon BA1 3JN
Tel: 0225 425539
Fax: 0225 319137

Order Information

Representation Available

Personnel
Head of Company: Jane Chrzaudwska
Head of Marketing: David Bowles

Number of titles published annually: 15
All New Titles are Bar Coded
WBIP Updating: David Bowles

Trade Terms
35% (orders over £15, 25% cwo, 20% credit)
Credit Cards Accepted: Access/Master, Visa

BARTON PUBLISHERS LTD
Unit 7, Oakland Court, Martock Business Park, Martock, Somerset TA12 6HP
ISBN Prefix(es): 0 900417
Tel: 0935 822542
Fax: 0935 822258
VAT No: 515 7791 25

Orders to
B T BATSFORD LTD, PO Box 4, Springwood Ind Est, Rayne Rd, Braintree, Essex CM7 7QY
Tel: 0376 321276
Fax: 0376 552854

Personnel
Head of Company: M Reyland (Manager)

Number of titles published annually: 1

Trade Terms
General Net: 25% 1-5 copies

Returns Procedures
Authority to Return: B T Batsford Ltd
Address for Returns: B T Batsford Ltd

B T BATSFORD LTD
4 Fitzhardinge Street, London W1H 0AH
ISBN Prefix(es): 0 7099, 0 7134, 0 7470, 0 8521, 0 8819
Tel: 071-486 8484
Fax: 071-487 4296
Telex: 943763 CROCUM G BAT
VAT No: 362 3991 36

Account No: _____ 114510 _____
Sales Rep: _____
Tel: _____

Orders to
B T BATSFORD LTD, PO Box 4, Springwood Ind Est,
Rayne Rd, Braintree, Essex CM7 7QY
Tel: 0376 321276
Fax: 0376 552854

Order Information
Teleordering: BAT

All Dues Automatically Recorded
Representation Available
Invoice Payments: Braintree, Essex

Personnel
Head of Company: Mr P A J Kemmis Betty (Managing Director)
Head of Sales (Home): Mr R Beard (Sales Director)
Head of Sales (Export): Miss K Ensink (Export Sales Manager)
Head of Publicity: Mr A L Lea (Publicity Manager)
Other Important Personnel:
Miss P Daniels (UK Sales Administrator)

Number of titles published annually: 170
Percentage of Export Sales: 30%
Number of Staff: 65
PA Member
NBA Signatory
All New Titles are Bar Coded
Open University Publications
Book Data Subscriber
WBIP Updating: A L Lea

Parent Company: Batsford Holdings Ltd

Trade Terms
35%
Academic Net: 30%
Other Terms: Small Order surcharge: £1 on orders less than £25 net
Girobank Number: 513 3254
Credit Cards Accepted: Access/Master, Amex, Visa

Returns Procedures
Authority to Return: Requests to reps who may issue authorised returns labels.
Address for Returns: Braintree, Essex

B T BATSFORD LTD

PO Box 4, Springwood Ind Est, Rayne Rd, Braintree, Essex CM7 7QY
Tel: 0376 321276 24 Hours
Fax: 0376 552854

Account No: _____ 114510 _____

Sales Rep: _____

Tel: _____

Order Information
Teleordering: BAT

Order Dept Opening Times
Mon - Fri 8am - 4.45pm
Cyclical Ordering Policy
Orders for more than one publisher can be bulked
All Dues Automatically Recorded

Personnel
Head of Accounts: Mr A N Finlay
Head of Distribution: Mr I Frost
Head of Customer Services: Mrs J Gladen

Trade Terms
35%
Academic Net: 30%

Other Terms: Small order surcharge: £1 on orders less than £25 net
Girobank Number: 513 3254
Credit Cards Accepted: Access/Master, Visa, Amex, Diners

Returns Procedures
Authority to Return: All requests to rep who may issue authorised address labels Incorrect or damaged books must bear BA Error Address Label
Imperfect Returns: Annotated title pages may be returned for all replacements

BATTLE OF BRITAIN PRINTS INTERNATIONAL LIMITED

Church House, Church Street, Stratford, London E15 3JA
ISBN Prefix(es): 0 900913
Tel: 081-534 8833 24 Hours
Fax: 081-555 7567
VAT No: 248 8439 19

Order Information

Order Dept Opening Times
8.15am - 4.30pm

Personnel
Head of Company: W G Ramsey

Number of titles published annually: 2

Trade Terms
1-99 copies 35%, 100+ 40%
Other Terms: £1 on orders under £25
Girobank Number: 597 2450
Credit Cards Accepted: Access/Master, Visa

Returns Procedures
Stock Returns: Firm sale only - no sale or return terms
Imperfect Returns: Defective book to be returned to us before credit or replacement can be issued

COLIN BAXTER PHOTOGRAPHY LTD

Unit 2/3, Block 6,, Caldwellside Industrial Estate, Lanark, Strathclyde ML11 6SR
Tel: 0555 665022
Fax: 0555 664775
VAT No: 376 5963 00

Orders to
BOOKPOINT LIMITED, 39 Milton Park, Abingdon, Oxfordshire OX14 4TD
Tel: 0235 835001
Fax: 0235 861038

Order Information
Representation:Derek Searle Associates (England & Ireland)

PA Member

BAY FOREIGN LANGUAGE BOOKS

19 Dymchurch Road, St Mary's Bay, Romney Marsh, Kent TN29 0ET
Tel: 0679 64417 Tel/Fax
Account No: _____
Sales Rep: _____
Tel: _____

Order Information
Teleordering: BAY

Trade Terms
Girobank Number: 312 0368

BAY VIEW BOOKS LTD
13A Bridgeland Street, Bideford, Devon EX39 2QE
ISBN Prefix(es): 1 870979
Tel: 0237 479225
Tel: 0237 421285
Fax: 0237 421286
VAT No: 430 4879 50

Orders to
CHRIS LLOYD SALES AND MARKETING SERVICES,
463 Ashley Road, Parkstone, Poole, Dorset BH14 0AX
Tel: 0202 715349
Fax: 0202 736191

Order Information

All Dues Automatically Recorded
Representation Available
Invoice Payments: Chris Lloyd

Personnel
Head of Company: Charles Herridge

All New Titles are Bar Coded
WBIP Updating: Chris Lloyd

Trade Terms
35%
Other Terms: Small order surcharge 50p under £5 Carriage charged £1 on invoice value under £15

Returns Procedures
Authority to Return: Chris Lloyd Sales & Marketing
Address for Returns: Bailey Distribution Ltd, Learoyd Road, Mountfield Rd Ind Est
Imperfect Returns: Books over £10 returned whole

ROGER BAYLISS PROFESSIONAL REPRESENTATION
81 Milehouse Road, Plymouth, Devon PL3 4AE
Tel: 0752 563281
VAT No: 434 3858 39

Account No: _____
Sales Rep: _____
Tel: _____

Personnel
Head of Company: Roger Bayliss
Head of Customer Services: Kathleen Bayliss

BBC BOOKS (A DIVISION OF BBC ENTERPRISES LTD)
Woodlands, 80 Wood Lane, London W12 0TT
ISBN Prefix(es): 0 563
Tel: 081-576 2000
Fax: 081-749 8766
Telex: 265781
Cables: Broadcast London
VAT No: 232 3276 89

Account No: _____
Sales Rep: _____
Tel: _____

Orders to
EXEL LOGISTICS - MEDIA SERVICES, 3 Sheldon Way, Larkfield, Aylesford, Kent ME20 6SF
Tel: 0622 882000
Fax: 0622 718036

Order Information

All Dues Automatically Recorded
Representation Available
Invoice Payments: Exel Logistics

Personnel
Head of Company: Chris Weller (Director of BBC Books)
Head of Sales (Home): Barry Fletcher (UK Sales Manager)
Head of Sales (Export): Richard Gay (Export Sales Manager)
Head of Marketing: John Allgrove (Head of Sales & Marketing)
Head of Publicity: Suzanna Zsohar (Publicity Manager)

Number of titles published annually: 130
Number of Staff: 65
PA Member
All New Titles are Bar Coded
Open University Publications
Book Data Subscriber
WBIP Updating: Fernando Benito

Parent Company: BBC Enterprises Ltd

Trade Terms
36%, no surcharges all BBC books product. 30% for Radio Collection
BA/Girobank Small Order Scheme: Yes
Girobank Number: 545 1450
Credit Cards Accepted: Access/Master, Visa, Amex

Returns Procedures
Authority to Return: Sales Representative or Sales Manager
Address for Returns: Exel Logistics
Stock Returns: Overstocks must be accompanied by authorization to return, incorrectly supp/damaged in transit return direct to Exel
Imperfect Returns: Imperfect books must be returned stating imperfection to Exel Logistics

BBC TELEVISION TRAINING

BBC Elstree Centre, Borehamwood, Hertfordshire WD6 1JF
Tel: 081-953 6100
Fax: 081-207 8168
Telex: 265781
VAT No: 333 2894 54

Book Data Subscriber

BEACONSFIELD PUBLISHERS LTD

20 Chiltern Hills Road, Beaconsfield, Buckinghamshire HP9 1PL
ISBN Prefix(es): 0 906584
Tel: 0494 672118
Fax: 0494 672118
VAT No: 321 2561 03

Orders to
Haigh & Hochland Ltd, Precinct Centre, Oxford Road, Manchester, M13 9QA
Tel: 061-273 4156
Fax: 061-273 4340

Order Information

All Dues Automatically Recorded
Representation Available
Invoice Payments: Haigh & Hochland

Personnel
Head of Company: John Churchill

Number of titles published annually: 4
Percentage of Export Sales: 20%
Number of Staff: 1
IPG Member
NBA Signatory
All New Titles are Bar Coded
Book Data Subscriber

Trade Terms
General Net: Single Copy 25% Two or more 35% plus post
Other Terms: Carriage free on prepayment
Girobank Number: 20 309 1604
Credit Cards Accepted: Access/Master, Visa, Amex, Diners

RUTH BEAN PUBLISHERS

Victoria Farmhouse, Carlton, Bedford, Bedfordshire
MK43 7LP
ISBN Prefix(es): 0 903585
Tel: 0234 720356 24 Hours
Fax: 0234 720590
VAT No: 335 3597 43

Order Information

Order Dept Opening Times
Mon - Sat 9am - 9pm
All Dues Automatically Recorded
Representation Available

Personnel
Head of Company: Mrs R Bean/Mr N W Bean

Number of titles published annually: 2
Percentage of Export Sales: 20%
IPG Member
All New Titles are Bar Coded
WBIP Updating: N W Bean

Trade Terms
25% up to £20 retail, 35% over £20 retail
Academic Net: 25%
Other Terms: Carriage charges for overseas
Girobank Number: 30 397 4508

DEREK BEATTIE PUBLISHING

PO Box 29, Twickenham, Middlesex TW1 3BN
ISBN Prefix(es): 0 907591
Tel: 081-891 3513
VAT No: 318 0034 01

Order Information

Order Dept Opening Times
Mon - Fri 9am - 5pm
All Dues Automatically Recorded
Representation Available

Personnel
Head of Company: Derek Beattie

Percentage of Export Sales: 20%
IPG Member
NBA Signatory
WBIP Updating: Derek Beattie

Trade Terms
30% all orders, no surcharges
Other Terms: Carriage charges, outside London

BEBC DISTRIBUTION

PO Box 1496, Poole, Dorset BH12 3YD
Tel: 0202 715555
Fax: 0202 715556
Telex: 418350
VAT No: 187 3139 42
Account No: _____ O13SM01 _____
Sales Rep:_____
Tel: _____

Order Information
Teleordering: BEBC

Order Dept Opening Times
Mon - Fri 9am - 5pm
All Dues Automatically Recorded

Personnel
Head of Company: John H Walsh
Head of Accounts: Philip Radwanski
Head of Distribution: Philippa Monks

WBIP Updating: John Walsh

Parent Company: The Bournemouth English Book Centre

Trade Terms
Refer to publisher
Girobank Number: 271 7050
Credit Cards Accepted: Access/Master, Visa, Amex

Returns Procedures
Authority to Return: Unauthorised returns not accepted
Address for Returns: BEBC Distribution, 15 Albion Close, Parkstone, Poole, Dorset BH12 3LL
Stock Returns: Refer to publisher
Imperfect Returns: Title page only

BEE BOOKS NEW & OLD

Tapping Wall Farm, Burrowbridge, Bridgwater, Somerset TA7 0RY
ISBN Prefix(es): 0 905652
Tel: 0823 69781

Order Information

All Dues Automatically Recorded
Representation Available

Personnel
Head of Company: J S Kinross
Head of Distribution: Mrs J S N Kinross

Number of Staff: 2
All New Titles are Bar Coded
WBIP Updating: J S Kinross

Trade Terms
General Net: Single copy/2 or more single titles/2 books or more 33.3%, Sub orders 35%, stock orders 33.3%, special orders variable
Girobank Number: 279 7151
Credit Cards Accepted: Access/Master, Visa

Returns Procedures
Imperfect Returns: Send complete book

BEECH PUBLISHING
15 The Maltings, Turk Street, Alton, Hampshire GU34 1DL
Tel: 0420 87040
Fax: 0420 89129

BELAIR - P.O. Box 12, Twickenham, TW1 1NR

THE GEORGE BELDAM COLLECTION
46 Knowsley Road, London SW11 5BL
Tel: 071-228 7515 Tel/Fax
Tel: 0483 232609

Orders to
VINE HOUSE DISTRIBUTION, Waldenbury, North Chailey, East Sussex BN8 4DR
Tel: 082-572 3398
Fax: 082-572 4188

BELHAVEN = Marston Book Service

BELLEVUE BOOKS
Unit E4, Sunbury International, Business Cen, Brooklands Close, Sunbury-on-Thames, Middlesex TW16 1DX
ISBN Prefix(es): 1 873335
Tel: 0932 765119
Fax: 0932 765429

Order Information

All Dues Automatically Recorded
Representation Available

Personnel
Head of Company: Howard Barkway
Head of Accounts: Anthony Head

Number of titles published annually: 3
Percentage of Export Sales: 55%
All New Titles are Bar Coded
WBIP Updating: Howard Barkway

Trade Terms
35%
Credit Cards Accepted: Access/Master, Visa, Amex, Diners

BELLEW PUBLISHING CO LTD
Nightingale Centre, 8 Balham Hill, London SW12 9EA
ISBN Prefix(es): 0 947792, 1 85725
Tel: 081-675 2142
Tel: 081-673 5611
Fax: 081-675 3542
Telex: 8951182 GECOMS G
VAT No: 372 7915 25

Orders to
PLYMBRIDGE DISTRIBUTORS LTD, Plymbridge House, Estover Road, Plymouth, Devon PL6 7PZ
Tel: 0752 735251
Fax: 0752 695699

Order Information

All Dues Automatically Recorded
Representation Available
Invoice Payments: Plymbridge

Personnel
Head of Company: I B Bellew (Managing Director)
Other Important Personnel:
Suzie Burt (Customer Services), Mandi Gomez (Customer Services)

Number of titles published annually: 30
Percentage of Export Sales: 50%

Number of Staff: 3
All New Titles are Bar Coded
WBIP Updating: Suzie Burt

Trade Terms
Single Copy 10%, Multiple Copies 35%
Girobank Number: 221 2951
Credit Cards Accepted: Access/Master, Amex, Diners, Visa

Returns Procedures
Authority to Return: Prior permission required
Address for Returns: Plymbridge
Stock Returns: Damaged books may only be returned for credit
Imperfect Returns: Return complete book

RAYMOND BENARDOUT

18 Grosvenor Street, Mayfair, London W1X 9FD
ISBN Prefix(es): 0 9503968
Tel: 071-355 4531
Fax: 071-491 9710
VAT No: 238 9055 39

Trade Terms
35%

BENEDICT BOOKS

30 Topsfield Parade, Crouch End, London N8 8PT
Tel: 081-341 4223
Fax: 081-341 0495
VAT No: 396 6331 18

BENN BUSINESS INFORMATION SERVICES LTD

PO Box 20, Sovereign Way, Tonbridge, Kent TN9 1RQ
ISBN Prefix(es): 0 86382
Tel: 0732 362666 24 Hours
Fax: 0732 770483
Telex: 95162 BENTON G
VAT No: 205 5180 95

Account No: _____

Sales Rep: _____

Tel: _____

Order Information
Teleordering: BENTEC

Order Dept Opening Times
Mon - Fri 9am - 5pm
All Dues Automatically Recorded
Invoice Payments: Morgan Grampian PLC, 30 Calderwood Street, Woolwich, London SE18 6HQ

Personnel
Head of Company: Mark Simpson (Managing Director)
Head of Accounts: Stuart Miskimmin
Other Important Personnel:
Glen Wilders (Publishing Director), Leslie G Kelly (Publishing Director), Ms Jean Neville (Publishing Director)

Number of titles published annually: 35
Number of Staff: 120
PA Member
NBA Signatory
Book Data Subscriber

Parent Company: Morgan Grampian

Trade Terms
20%
Credit Cards Accepted: Access/Master, Visa, Amex

DAVID BENNETT BOOKS LTD
94 Victoria Street, St Albans, Hertfordshire AL1 3TG
Tel: 0727 55878
Fax: 0727 864085
VAT No: 539 9950 80

JIM BENNETT TRAINING SYSTEMS
50 Princesway, Wallasey, Merseyside L45 4PR
Tel: 051-691 1111

THE BEREAN PUBLISHING TRUST
10 Dukes Close, Cranleigh, Surrey GU6 7JU
Tel: 0483 272016
VAT No: 358 8721 11

BERG PUBLISHERS LTD
150 Cowley Road, Oxford, Oxfordshire OX4 1JJ
ISBN Prefix(es): 0 85496, 0 907582
Tel: 0865 245104
Fax: 0865 791165
VAT No: 398 3460 10

Order Information
Order Dept Opening Times
9am - 1pm, 2pm - 6pm
All Dues Automatically Recorded
Representation Available

Personnel
Head of Company: Marion Berghahn
Head of Sales (Home): Sarah Miles
Head of Marketing: Vanessa Doughty
Head of Publicity: Joanne Harris

Number of titles published annually: 50
Percentage of Export Sales: 75%
Number of Staff: 4
Book Data Subscriber
WBIP Updating: Nigel Hope

Trade Terms
All Orders - Major Accounts : 35% (Home) 30% (Export)
Others : 20% (Home) 25% (Export)
Minimum Order: £1.50 surcharge on orders below £25 invoice value
Credit Cards Accepted: Access/Master, Visa

Returns Procedures
Authority to Return: Contact Sarah Miles at Head Office
Address for Returns: Clipper Distribution Services, Windmill Grove, Porchester, Hants PO16 9HT
Imperfect Returns: Return complete book

BERLITZ PUBLISHING CO LTD
Berlitz House, Peterley Road, Horspath, Oxford, Oxfordshire OX4 2TX
Tel: 0865 747033
Fax: 0865 779700
VAT No: 596 1055 25

Account No: _____
Sales Rep: _____
Tel: _____

Orders to
Charles Letts & Co, Thornybank Ind Estate, Dalkeith, Midlothian EH22 2NE
Tel: 031 663 1971
Fax: 031 660 5435

Order Information

Representation Available
Invoice Payments: Charles Letts & Co

Personnel
Head of Company: Charles Halpin
Head of Sales (Home): Jacki Heppard
Head of Publicity: Sue Whittaker
Head of Accounts: William Findlay
Head of Distribution: Ann-Marie Harty
Other Important Personnel:
Julian Parish (International Sales Manager)

Number of Staff: 50
All New Titles are Bar Coded
Book Data Subscriber
WBIP Updating: Jacqui Pugh (Letts)

Returns Procedures
Authority to Return: Charles Letts & Co

BERTIE RAMIFICATIONS LTD

125 Abingdon Road, Standlake, Oxfordshire OX8 7QN
ISBN Prefix(es): 0 712610, 0 950833
Tel: 0865 300259
Fax: 0865 300022

Order Information

Order Dept Opening Times
Mon - Fri 9am - 5pm

Personnel
Head of Company: Mr Ralph Windle
Head of Customer Services: Mrs Ariana Windle

Number of titles published annually: 2
WBIP Updating: Ms Ariana Windle

BESHARA PUBLICATIONS

24 Sidney Street, Oxford, Oxfordshire OX4 3AG
ISBN Prefix(es): 0 904975
Tel: 0865 243406
Fax: 0865 52154

Orders to
ELEMENT BOOKS LTD, Unit 25, Longmead, Shaftesbury, Dorset SP7 8PL
Tel: 0747 51339
Fax: 0747 51394

Order Information

Invoice Payments: Element

Number of titles published annually: 2
Percentage of Export Sales: 50%
WBIP Updating: R Clark

BETTER BOOKS

3 Paganel Drive, Dudley, West Midlands DY1 4AZ
Tel: 0384 253276
Fax: 0384 457979
VAT No: 610 8640 63

Account No: _____

Sales Rep: _____

Tel: _____

BFI PUBLISHING

British Film Institute, 21 Stephen Street, London WLP 1PL
ISBN Prefix(es): 0 85170
Tel: 071-255 1444
Fax: 071-436 7950
Telex: 27624 BFILDN G
VAT No: 238 6152 56

M/C No S-452

Orders to
PLYMBRIDGE DISTRIBUTORS LTD, Plymbridge House, Estover Road, Plymouth, Devon PL6 7PZ
Tel: 0752 735251
Fax: 0752 695699

Order Information

Invoice Payments: Plymbridge

PA Member
IPG Member
NBA Signatory

Returns Procedures
Address for Returns: Plymbridge

BFP BOOKS

Focus House, 497 Green Lanes, London N13 4BP
ISBN Prefix(es): 0 907297
Tel: 081-882 3315
Fax: 081-886 5174

Orders to
B T BATSFORD LTD, PO Box 4, Springwood Ind Est, Rayne Rd, Braintree, Essex CM7 7QY
Tel: 0376 321276
Fax: 0376 552854

Order Information

Invoice Payments: B T Batsford

Personnel
Head of Company: John Tracy (Managing Director)

Number of titles published annually: 5
All New Titles are Bar Coded

Trade Terms
Batsford Terms Apply

Returns Procedures
Authority to Return: B T Batsford

THE BIBLE READING FELLOWSHIP

Peter's Way, Sandy Lane West, Oxford, Oxfordshire OX4 5HG
ISBN Prefix(es): 0 7459
Tel: 0865 748227
Fax: 0865 773150
VAT No: 238 5574 35

Orders to
LION PUBLISHING PLC, Peter's Law, Sandy Lane West, Oxford, Oxfordshire OX4 5HG
Tel: 0865 747550
Fax: 0865 747568

Order Information

All Dues Automatically Recorded
Representation Available
Invoice Payments: Lion Publishing

Personnel
Head of Company: Richard Fisher
Other Important Personnel:
Karen Teal (Office Administrator)

Number of titles published annually: 10
Number of Staff: 1
All New Titles are Bar Coded
WBIP Updating: Miss Leanne Little

Trade Terms
35% on books, £2 surcharge on orders below £25 retail value
Girobank Number: 309 9458

Returns Procedures
Authority to Return: Lion Publishing
Address for Returns: Lion Publishing
Stock Returns: Contact customer service manager or Lion area manager for authorisation
Imperfect Returns: Return title page. Book will be replaced or credit given according to customers' wishes. Price limit £20

BIBLE SOCIETY (THE BRITISH AND FOREIGN BIBLE SOCIETY)

Stone Hill Green, Westlea, Swindon, Wiltshire SN5 7DG
ISBN Prefix(es): 0 564
Tel: 0793 513713
Tel: 0800 521229 Order/Free   A/C NO 00176109
Fax: 0793 512539
Telex: 44283
Cables: CABLES TESTAMENTS SWINDON
VAT No: 243 1364 89

Order Information
Teleordering: BFBS

Order Dept Opening Times
8.45am - 5pm
All Dues Automatically Recorded
Representation Available
Invoice Payments: Finance Dept
Orders To: Sales Dept

Personnel
Head of Company: Neil Crosbie (Executive Director)
Head of Sales (Home): Peter Duke (Sales Manager)
Head of Marketing: Brian Lincoln (Marketing Manager)
Head of Accounts: Paul Clark (Finance Manager)
Head of Distribution: Veronica Pagett (Distribution Manager)

Number of titles published annually: 30
Percentage of Export Sales: 40%
Number of Staff: 135
All New Titles are Bar Coded
WBIP Updating: Joyce Longney

Allied Companies: National Bible Society of Ireland, National Bible Society of Scotland

Trade Terms
35% on all books (except some educational materials)

Returns Procedures
Authority to Return: Sales Dept

Imperfect Returns: Complete books £14 retail price and over otherwise title page only

BIBLIAGORA
PO Box 77, Feltham, Middlesex TW14 8JF
ISBN Prefix(es): 0 906031
Tel: 081-898 1234
Fax: 081-844 1777
Telex: 935918 BRIDGE G
VAT No: 224 0440 15

PA Member
NBA Signatory
All New Titles are Bar Coded

Trade Terms
Girobank Number: 35 193 4006

BIBLIOS PUBLISHERS DISTRIBUTION SERVICE LTD
Star Road, Partridge Green, West Sussex RH13 8LD
Tel: 0403 710971
Tel: 0403 710851 orders
Fax: 0403 711143
VAT No: 193 9421 36

Account No: _261289/001_
Sales Rep: _____
Tel: _____

Hotline No 0403 711415

Order Information
Teleordering: BIBLIOS

Personnel
Head of Company: Anthony Wagstaff (Managing Director)
Head of Sales (Home): Louise Mallard (Sales Manager)
Head of Accounts: Ian Dumbleton (Financial Controller)
Head of Customer Services: Helen Negus (Administration Manager)
Other Important Personnel:
David Mansfield (Client Services), Mike Purdy (Warehouse), David Brown (Accounts), Julian Heathcock (Data Processing)

Number of Staff: 73
IPG Member

Trade Terms
Credit Cards Accepted: Access/Master, Visa

Returns Procedures
Address for Returns: Biblios 2, Old London Road, Washington, W Sussex RH20 3BN

BIOS SCIENTIFIC PUBLISHERS LTD
St Thomas House, Becket Street, Oxford, Oxfordshire OX1 1SJ
Tel: 0865 726286
Fax: 0865 246823

A/c 200718/004.

Returns Procedures
Authority to Return: Prior permission required
Address for Returns: Clipper Distribution Services

BIRKHAUSER = Springer

BIRMINGHAM SETTLEMENT
318 Summer Lane, Birmingham, West Midlands B19 3RL
Tel: 021-359 3562

Fax: 021-359 6357
VAT No: 461 9820 31

BISHOPGATE PRESS LTD
Bartholomew House, 15 Tonbridge Road, Hildenborough, Kent TN11 9BH
Tel: 0732 933778
Fax: 0732 933090

Order Information

Order Dept Opening Times
Mon - Fri 9am - 5pm

Personnel
Head of Company: Mr Ian Straker (Managing Director)

A & C BLACK (PUBLISHERS) LTD
35 Bedford Row, London WC1R 4JH
ISBN Prefix(es): 0 22911, 0 510, 0 54007, 0 7136, 0 7158, 0 7470, 0 85177, 0 906670
Tel: 071-242 0946
Fax: 071-831 8478
Telex: 32524
VAT No: 215 0391 03
Account No: __0053430__
Sales Rep:_____
Tel: _____

Orders to
A & C BLACK (PUBLISHERS) LTD, PO Box 19, Huntingdon, Cambridgeshire PE19 3SF
Tel: 0480 212666
Fax: 0480 405014

Order Information
Teleordering: ACBL

All Dues Automatically Recorded
Representation Available
Invoice Payments: A & C Black, Huntingdon

Personnel
Head of Company: Charles Black (Chairman & Managing Director)
Head of Publicity: Jane Thorne
Other Important Personnel:
David Gadsby (Joint Managing Director)

Number of titles published annually: 180
Percentage of Export Sales: 25%
PA Member
NBA Signatory
All New Titles are Bar Coded
Book Data Subscriber
WBIP Updating: Ronald Joyce (Head Office)

Parent Company: A & C Black plc
Subsidiary Companies: Adlard Coles Ltd, Helm (Christopher) Publishers Ltd

Trade Terms
35% (except yearbooks and non-net) no surcharge

Returns Procedures
Address for Returns: A & C Black, PO Box 19, Huntingdon, Cambs, PE19 3SF

A & C BLACK (PUBLISHERS) LTD
PO Box 19, Huntingdon, Cambridgeshire PE19 3SF
Tel: 0480 212666 24 Hours
Fax: 0480 405014
Telex: 32524

Account No: _____

Sales Rep: _____

Tel: _____

Order Information
Teleordering: ACBL

Order Dept Opening Times
Mon - Fri 8.45am - 4.45pm
All Dues Automatically Recorded
Representation Available

Personnel
Head of Sales (Home): Susan Kodicek
Head of Accounts: William Still
Head of Distribution: Terry Rouelett
Head of Customer Services: Valerie Chamberlain

All New Titles are Bar Coded
Book Data Subscriber

Trade Terms
Girobank Number: 2569159
Credit Cards Accepted: Access/Master, Visa

Returns Procedures
Authority to Return: Sales Manager
Imperfect Returns: Price limit for annotated title page £5

THE BLACK FROG PRESS
53 Heronscroft, Putnoe, Bedford, Bedfordshire MK41 9LS
ISBN Prefix(es): 1 872444
Tel: 0234 360164 24 Hours

Order Information

All Dues Automatically Recorded
Representation Available

Personnel
Head of Company: Graham Couch/Clare Jamieson

Number of titles published annually: 4
All New Titles are Bar Coded
WBIP Updating: Clare Jamieson

Trade Terms
1 copy 20%, 2-29 copies 35%, 30-49 copies 37.5%, 50+ 40%

BLACK SPRING PRESS LTD
63 Harlescott Road, Nunhead, London SE15 3DA
ISBN Prefix(es): 0 948238
Tel: 071-639 2492
Fax: 071-639 2508
VAT No: 238 2888 27

Orders to
AIRLIFT BOOK COMPANY, 26/28 Eden Grove, London N7 8EF
Tel: 071-607 5792
Fax: 071-607 6714

Order Information

All Dues Automatically Recorded
Representation Available

Personnel
Head of Company: Simon Pettifar (Managing Director)

Number of titles published annually: 6
Number of Staff: 2
NBA Signatory
All New Titles are Bar Coded

Trade Terms
35% on orders over £25 retail. 25% + prepayment on orders less than £25 retail.
Girobank Number: 57 273 4204
Credit Cards Accepted: Access/Master, Visa

Returns Procedures
Authority to Return: Airlift Book Company
Imperfect Returns: £20 price limit

THE BLACK SWAN PRESS

28 Bosley's Orchard, Grove, Wantage, Oxfordshire OX12 7JP
ISBN Prefix(es): 0 905475
Tel: 02357 4517
VAT No: 348 4839 15

Order Information

Order Dept Opening Times
Mon - Fri 9am - 5.30pm
All Dues Automatically Recorded
Representation Available

Personnel
Head of Company: Peter Lord
Head of Sales (Home): Margaret Lord
Head of Sales (Export): Patrick Lord

Number of titles published annually: 4
Percentage of Export Sales: 40%
Number of Staff: 3
WBIP Updating: Margaret Lord

Trade Terms
General Net: Single copy/single line 25%, all other orders 35%
Other Terms: Carriage charges on single copy orders

Returns Procedures
Stock Returns: Return books to head office address
Imperfect Returns: Return book, title page not accepted

Blackie - CHILDRENS - %o Penguin

BLACKIE ACADEMIC & PROFESSIONAL (IMPRINT OF CHAPMAN & HALL)

Wester Cleddens Road, Bishopbriggs, Glasgow, Strathclyde G64 2NZ
ISBN Prefix(es): 0 216
Tel: 041-762 2332
Fax: 041-772 7524
Cables: Blackie, Glasgow

Account No: _____ *00 61697-001* _____
Sales Rep: _____
Tel: _____

Orders to
INTERNATIONAL THOMSON PUBLISHING SERVICES LTD, Cheriton House, North Way, Andover, Hampshire SP10 5BE
Tel: 0264 332424
Fax: 0264 364418

Personnel
Other Important Personnel:
Dr Graeme Mackintosh (Publishing Director)

Book Data Subscriber

Parent Company: The Thomson Corporation

BLACKSTAFF PRESS LTD
3 Galway Park, Dundonald, Belfast, County Antrim
BT16 0AN
ISBN Prefix(es): 0 85640
Tel: 0232 487161
Fax: 0232 489552
VAT No: 252 0302 18

[Handwritten: From 1/6/94 distribution will be Gill & Macmillan]

Account No: _____
Sales Rep: _____
Tel: _____

Orders to
BIBLIOS PUBLISHERS DISTRIBUTION SERVICE LTD,
Star Road, Partridge Green, West Sussex RH13 8LD
Tel: 0403 710971
Fax: 0403 711143

Order Information

All Dues Automatically Recorded
Representation Available
Invoice Payments: Blackstaff Press

Personnel
Head of Company: Anne Tanahill (Managing Director)
Head of Sales (Home): Lawrence Greer
Head of Marketing: Liam Carson
Head of Accounts: Rhoda Cassidy (Bookkeeper)
Head of Distribution: Ron Watson (Store Manager)
Head of Customer Services: Rhoda Cassidy (Administrator)

Number of titles published annually: 25
Percentage of Export Sales: 35%
Number of Staff: 9
All New Titles are Bar Coded
WBIP Updating: Rhoda Cassidy

Trade Terms
35% on all orders. Small order surcharge
Credit Cards Accepted: Access/Master, Visa

BLACKSTONE PRESS LTD
9-15 Aldine Street, London W12 8AW
ISBN Prefix(es): 1 85431
Tel: 081-740 1173/1111
Fax: 081-743 2292
Telex: 265871 MONREF G
VAT No: 466 4516 29

Account No: _____ OSM13 _____
Sales Rep: _____
Tel: _____

Order Information

Order Dept Opening Times
Mon - Fri 9.30am - 5.30pm
All Dues Automatically Recorded
Representation Available

Personnel
Head of Company: Alistair MacQueen (Managing Director)
Head of Marketing: Jonathan Harris (Marketing Director)

Number of titles published annually: 30
Number of Staff: 9
All New Titles are Bar Coded
WBIP Updating: Sarah Tigwell

Trade Terms
Single copy 20%, Two or more books 30%
Credit Cards Accepted: Access/Master, Visa

Returns Procedures
Authority to Return: Prior permission is required from Head Office.
Address for Returns: Livesey Airlife Ltd: FAO: Paul Rice, 101 Longden Road, Shrewsbury, Shropshire SY3 9EB
Stock Returns: Title pages may be returned for old editions which must be returned within three months of publication of new edition.
Imperfect Returns: After permission is obtained whole book to be returned.

BLACKWATER PRESS

8 Airton Road, Tallagat, Dublin 24, County Dublin
Tel: 01 515 311
Tel: 01 515 519
Fax: 01 515 306

BLACKWELL PUBLISHERS LTD

108 Cowley Road, Oxford, Oxfordshire OX4 1JF
ISBN Prefix(es): 0 631, 1 55786
Tel: 0865 791100
Fax: 0865 791347
Telex: 837022 OXBOOK G
VAT No: 195 7258 19
Account No: _____1614|001_____
Sales Rep: _____
Tel: _____

Orders to
MARSTON BOOK SERVICES LTD, PO Box 87, Osney Mead, Oxford, Oxfordshire OX2 0DT
Tel: 0865 791155
Fax: 0865 791927

Order Information
All Dues Automatically Recorded
Representation Available
Invoice Payments: Marston

Personnel
Head of Company: Rene Oliveri
Head of Sales (Home): Philip Blackwell (International Sales Manager)
Head of Marketing: Janet Joyce (International Marketing Manager)
Head of Publicity: Philippa Scoones (Senior Marketing Manager)
Head of Accounts: Mark Houlton (Finance Director)
Other Important Personnel:
Clare Moulam (Bibliographic & Information Systems Manager), Rebecca Harkin (Marketing - Polity Press)

Number of titles published annually: 230
Number of Staff: 100
PA Member
NBA Signatory
All New Titles are Bar Coded
Open University Publications
Book Data Subscriber
WBIP Updating: Mrs Helen Steele

Parent Company: Basil Blackwell Ltd
Allied Companies: NCC Blackwell, Polity Press

Trade Terms
20-35% depending on turnover
Girobank Number: 236 6053
Credit Cards Accepted: Access/Master, Amex, Diners, Visa, Other

Returns Procedures
Authority to Return: Susan Knowles 0865 240201
Address for Returns: Marston
Stock Returns: No returns accepted unless authorised

BLACKWELL SCIENTIFIC PUBLICATIONS

Osney Mead, Oxford, Oxfordshire OX2 0EL
ISBN Prefix(es): 0 632, 0 85238, 0 86542, 0 86793, 0 8716
Tel: 0865 240201
Fax: 0865 721205
Telex: 83355 MEDBOX G
Cables: RESEARCH, OXFORD
Account No: 1614/001
Sales Rep: _____
Tel: _____

Orders to
MARSTON BOOK SERVICES LTD, PO Box 87, Osney Mead, Oxford, Oxfordshire OX2 0DT
Tel: 0865 791155
Fax: 0865 791927

Order Information
All Dues Automatically Recorded
Representation Available
Invoice Payments: Marston Book Services Ltd

Personnel
Head of Company: Robert Campbell (Managing Director)
Head of Sales (Home): Susan Knowles
Head of Sales (Export): Christoph Cheshire
Head of Marketing: Edward Crutchley

Number of titles published annually: 200
Percentage of Export Sales: 50%
Number of Staff: 147
All New Titles are Bar Coded
Open University Publications
Book Data Subscriber
WBIP Updating: Annie Copeland

Parent Company: Blackwell Scientific Publications Ltd

Trade Terms
25-30% no surcharges

Returns Procedures
Authority to Return: Prior permission required from Susan Knowles
Address for Returns: Marston

BLAKE PUBLISHING LIMITED

158 Fulham Palace Road, London W6 9ER
ISBN Prefix(es): 0 905846
Tel: 081-748 7606
Fax: 081-748 7613
VAT No: 587 0120 46

Orders to
BOOKPOINT LIMITED, 39 Milton Park, Abingdon, Oxfordshire OX14 4TD
Tel: 0235 835001
Fax: 0235 861038

Order Information

All Dues Automatically Recorded
Representation Available
Invoice Payments: Bookpoint

Personnel
Head of Company: John Blake (Managing Director)
Head of Sales (Home): Rosie Ries
Head of Accounts: Paul Blake (Accounts Director)
Head of Customer Services: Lorna Russell

Number of titles published annually: 15
Number of Staff: 3
All New Titles are Bar Coded
WBIP Updating: Rosie Ries

Trade Terms
35%, 30 days
Credit Cards Accepted: Access/Master, Visa

Returns Procedures
Authority to Return: ABS, Suite 1, Royal Star Arcade, High Street, Maidstone, Kent ME14 1JL
Address for Returns: Bookpoint
Stock Returns: Prior authorisation required
Imperfect Returns: Prior authorisation required

BLAKETON HALL LTD

1 Devon Units, Budlake Road, Marsh Barton Industrial Estate, Exeter, Devon EX2 8PY
ISBN Prefix(es): 0 907854
Tel: 0392 210602
Fax: 0392 421165

Order Information

Representation Available

Personnel
Head of Company: John Shillingford
Head of Sales (Home): Pat Shillingford
Head of Distribution: Robert Heath

Number of titles published annually: 4
Percentage of Export Sales: 40%
All New Titles are Bar Coded
WBIP Updating: J Shillingford

Trade Terms
40%
General Net: Single copy/single line 35%
Academic Net: Single copy/single line 35%
Other Terms: Carriage charges £3.50 for invoice under £40

BLENHEIM ONLINE

630 Chiswick High Road, London W4 5BG
ISBN Prefix(es): 0 86353
Tel: 081-742 2828
Fax: 081-747 3856

BLEWBURY PRESS

Pound House, Church Road, Blewbury, Oxfordshire OX11 9PY
Tel: 0235 850110
Fax: 0235 843336
VAT No: 570 0567 53

IPG Member

BLOODAXE BOOKS
PO Box 1SN, Newcastle upon Tyne, Tyne & Wear
NE99 1SN
ISBN Prefix(es): 0 906427, 1 85224, 1 85557
Tel: 091-232 5988
Fax: 091-222 0020
VAT No: 414 4062 89

Order Information
Teleordering: BLOOD

Order Dept Opening Times
Mon - Fri 9am - 5.30pm
All Dues Automatically Recorded
Representation Available

Personnel
Head of Company: Neil Astley (Managing Director)
Head of Publicity: Andrew McAllister (Publicity Manager)
Head of Accounts: Karen Buchan (Finance Manager)
Head of Distribution: Margaret Akuamoah (Distribution Manager)
Head of Customer Services: Linda Healy (Customer Services)

Number of titles published annually: 50
Number of Staff: 8
All New Titles are Bar Coded
WBIP Updating: Val Hannan

Trade Terms
Multiples 35% (UK) 30% (Eire), Single Copy 25%
Other Terms: Small order surcharge of £1.25 on orders under £25
Credit Cards Accepted: Access/Master, Visa, Other

Returns Procedures
Authority to Return: Neil Astley
Address for Returns: Bloodaxe Books, Hawthorn House, Forth Banks, Newcastle upon Tyne NE1 3SG
Stock Returns: Authorized returns only, damaged & shop soiled books will not be credited
Imperfect Returns: Title page under £6, whole book over £6

BLOOMSBURY PUBLISHING LTD
2 Soho Square, London W1V 5DE
ISBN Prefix(es): 0 7475
Tel: 071-494 2111
Fax: 071-434 0151
Telex: 21323 BLOOMS
VAT No: 440 6562 62

Account No: _____

Sales Rep: _____

Tel: _____

Orders to
EXEL LOGISTICS - MEDIA SERVICES, 3 Sheldon Way, Larkfield, Aylesford, Kent ME20 6SF
Tel: 0622 882000
Fax: 0622 718036

Order Information

All Dues Automatically Recorded
Representation Available

Personnel
Head of Company: Nigel Newton (Managing Director)
Head of Sales (Home): Lucy Juckes (Sales Director)
Head of Sales (Export): Lucy Broke (Export Sales Manager)
Head of Marketing: Alan Wherry (Marketing Director)
Head of Publicity: Sarah Beal (Publicity Director)
Head of Accounts: Nigel Batt (Finance Director)

Number of titles published annually: 160
Number of Staff: 45
PA Member
NBA Signatory
All New Titles are Bar Coded
Book Data Subscriber
WBIP Updating: Kay Marshall

Trade Terms
Credit Cards Accepted: Access/Master, Visa

Returns Procedures
Authority to Return: Prior authorisation required from Lucy Juckes
Address for Returns: Exel Logistics

BMJ PUBLISHING GROUP

BMA House, Tavistock Square, London WC1H 9JR
ISBN Prefix(es): 0 7279
Tel: 071-387 4499
Fax: 071-383 6662
Telex: 265929
VAT No: 232 1432 14

Order Information

Order Dept Opening Times
Mon - Fri 9am - 5pm
All Dues Automatically Recorded
Representation Available

Personnel
Head of Company: Geoffrey Burn (Executive Director)
Head of Sales (Home): Jane Youens (Home Sales & Europe)
Head of Sales (Export): Neil Poppmacher (Export Sales (Excluding Europe))
Head of Marketing: Neil Poppmacher (Books Marketing Manager)
Head of Customer Services: Joanne Willis

All New Titles are Bar Coded
Book Data Subscriber
WBIP Updating: Jane Youens

Parent Company: BMJ Publishing Group
Subsidiary Companies: Professional and Scientific Publications

Trade Terms
Details on application
Credit Cards Accepted: Access/Master, Visa, Amex

Returns Procedures
Authority to Return: Joanne Willis

BMS LTD

Merlin Way, North Weald Industrial Estate, Epping, Essex CM16 6HR
Tel: 0992 524343
Fax: 0992 524552
VAT No: 424 8304 64

Account No: _____
Sales Rep: _____
Tel: _____

Order Information
Teleordering: BMS

Order Dept Opening Times
Mon - Fri 9am - 5.30pm
All Dues Automatically Recorded

Representation Available
Invoice Payments: Publishers Name

Personnel
Head of Company: Lyn Reed
Head of Sales (Home): G Bullock
Head of Distribution: Glen Mercer

Number of Staff: 23

Trade Terms
(see publisher)
Other Terms: Carriage Charges for overseas only
Credit Cards Accepted: Access/Master, Visa, Amex, Other

Returns Procedures
Authority to Return: See publisher
Address for Returns: see invoice for details

BNA INTERNATIONAL INC
17 Dartmouth Street, London SW1H 9BL
Tel: 071-222 8831
Fax: 071-222 0294

BOBS-MERRILL = IBD.

BODLEIAN LIBRARY
Oxford, Oxfordshire OX1 3BG
ISBN Prefix(es): 0 900177, 1 85124
Tel: 0865 277000
Fax: 0865 277182
Telex: 83656
VAT No: 195 2753 34

Order Information

Order Dept Opening Times
Mon - Fri 8.30am - 4.30pm, Sat 9am - 12pm

Personnel
Head of Sales (Home): Joanna Dodsworth (Publications Officer) 0865 277213/277091

Number of titles published annually: 4
Percentage of Export Sales: 50%
Number of Staff: 2

Trade Terms
35% plus postage at cost
Credit Cards Accepted: Access/Master, Amex, Diners, Visa

Returns Procedures
Authority to Return: Prior permission required from Joanna Dodsworth
Address for Returns: Publications Stores
Imperfect Returns: Return complete book

BODMIN BOOKS
4 Turf Street, Bodmin, Cornwall PL31 2DH
ISBN Prefix(es): 0 904534, 0 9501732

Personnel
Head of Company: Mrs P I Munn

Trade Terms
33.3% plus P&P

Returns Procedures
Imperfect Returns: New book sent in replacement upon receipt of imperfect/ damaged book.

BOOK BARGAINS LTD

Liston Court, High Street, Marlow, Buckinghamshire
SL7 1ER
Tel: 0628 890022
Tel: 0628 890007
Fax: 0628 477774
VAT No: 314 1929 74

Other Important Locations
Book Bargains Ltd, 43 Park Street, Bristol, Avon BR1 5NL
Tel/Fax: 0272 265565

Personnel
Head of Company: Philip Weatherburn
Head of Sales (Home): Ian Murphy
Head of Accounts: Sylvia Moore
Head of Customer Services: Jean Clements

Number of titles published annually: 20
Number of Staff: 52
WBIP Updating: Ian Murphy

Trade Terms
35% Firm Sale
Minimum Order: Six books or £15 invoice value

THE BOOK CASTLE (DELTASTAR) LTD

12 Church Street, Dunstable, Bedfordshire LU5 4RU
Tel: 0582 605670
Fax: 0582 662431
VAT No: 336 8911 32

THE BOOK GUILD LTD

Temple House, 25/26 High Street, Lewes, East Sussex
BN7 2LU
ISBN Prefix(es): 0 86332, 1 85776
Tel: 0273 472534
Fax: 0273 476472
VAT No: 509 0151 79

Account No: _____

Sales Rep: _____

Tel: _____

Orders to
BAILEY DISTRIBUTION LTD, Unit 1, Learoyd Road,
Mountfield Rd Ind Est, New Romney, Kent TN28 8XU
Tel: 0679 66905
Fax: 0679 66638

Order Information
All Dues Automatically Recorded
Representation Available

Personnel
Head of Company: Carol Biss
Head of Sales (Home): Karen Ross-Wham
Head of Sales (Export): Jonathan Ingoldby
Head of Publicity: Jonathan Palmer
Head of Accounts: David Wilcock
Head of Customer Services: Amanda Hargie

Number of titles published annually: 80
PA Member
IPG Member
All New Titles are Bar Coded
WBIP Updating: Ann Sobolewski

Trade Terms
35% (20% single order)

Returns Procedures
Address for Returns: Bailey
Stock Returns: Return books to distribution company
Imperfect Returns: Return title page/damaged book to publisher for replacement

BOOK MARKETING ASSOCIATES INTERNATIONAL

15 Roehampton Lane, London SW15 5LS
Tel: 081-876 2340
Fax: 081-392 9845

Account No: _____
Sales Rep: _____
Tel: _____

Personnel
Head of Company: Neville Mendelson (Managing Director)

Book Data Subscriber

Trade Terms
30%

Returns Procedures
Authority to Return: Prior permission required

BOOK REPRESENTATION & DISTRIBUTION (BRAD) LTD

244A London Road, Hadleigh, Essex SS7 2DE
Tel: 0702 552912
Fax: 0702 556095
VAT No: 545 9075 20

Account No: _____
Sales Rep: _____
Tel: _____

Order Information

Order Dept Opening Times
10am - 6pm
All Dues Automatically Recorded
Representation Available

Personnel
Head of Company: Dan Levey
Head of Sales (Home): Celia Stocks
Head of Accounts: John Fielder
Head of Customer Services: Doreen Levey
Other Important Personnel:
Miriam Holmes (Managing Director - Publishing)

All New Titles are Bar Coded
Open University Publications
WBIP Updating: Doreen Levey

Trade Terms
Africana & Holmes & Meier: Single copy 25%, multiples 35%, Titles retail price over £50 10%, other publishers vary

Returns Procedures
Authority to Return: Prior permission required
Stock Returns: Must be in mint condition

BOOKMARKS

265 Seven Sisters Road, London N4 2DE
ISBN Prefix(es): 0 905998, 0 906224, 1 872208
Tel: 081-802 6145
Fax: 081-802 3835
VAT No: 375 5603 36

A/C No 0000527

Order Information
Teleordering: BOOKMKS

Order Dept Opening Times
Mon - Sat 10am - 6pm
All Dues Automatically Recorded
Representation Available

Personnel
Head of Sales (Home): Lindi Gonzalez
Head of Marketing: Duncan Blackie
Head of Accounts: Ersy Contogouris

Number of titles published annually: 10
Number of Staff: 8
All New Titles are Bar Coded
WBIP Updating: Duncan Blackie

Parent Company: I S Books Ltd

Trade Terms
35%, orders below £10 25%
BA/Girobank Small Order Scheme: 35% no surcharges
Girobank Number: 58 512 4000
Credit Cards Accepted: Access/Master, Visa

Returns Procedures
Stock Returns: Return whole book for credit, permission required unless damaged, imperfect etc.

BOOKPOINT LIMITED

39 Milton Park, Abingdon, Oxfordshire OX14 4TD
~~Tel: 0235-835001~~ 24 Hours 0235 400400
Fax: 0235 861038
Fax: 0235 832068
Telex: 837091
VAT No: 532 5829 40

Account No: _____135m24_____
Sales Rep: _____
Tel: _____

Order Information
Teleordering: BOOKP

Order Dept Opening Times
Mon - Fri 9am - 5pm

Personnel
Head of Company: Ken Pickett (Managing Director)
Head of Sales (Home): Val Huxley (Sales Office Manager)
Head of Accounts: John Hunt (Financial Director)
Head of Distribution: Alan Rakes (Warehouse Operations Director)
Head of Customer Services: Rose Loveridge (PA to MD)

Number of Staff: 120

Parent Company: Headline Book Publishing PLC

Trade Terms
See individual publishers
Girobank Number: 200 9455
Credit Cards Accepted: Access/Master, Visa, Amex, Diners

Returns Procedures
Authority to Return: See Individual Publishers

BOOKS CONTINENTAL LTD

4-12 Old Christchurch Road, Bournemouth, Dorset BH1 1LG
Tel: 0202 296102
Tel: 0202 528263
Fax: 0202 537595

Account No: _____
Sales Rep: _____
Tel: _____

BOOKS EXPRESS
PO Box 10, Saffron Walden, Essex CB11 4EW
Tel: 0799 513726
Fax: 0799 513248
VAT No: 532 2532 78

Account No: _____
Sales Rep: _____
Tel: _____

Order Information

Order Dept Opening Times
Mon - Fri 9am - 5pm
Cyclical Ordering Policy
Orders for more than one publisher can be bulked
All Dues Automatically Recorded
Representation Available

Personnel
Head of Company: John Evans
Head of Sales (Export): Duncan Gregory

Number of titles published annually: 3000
Percentage of Export Sales: 30%
Number of Staff: 3

Trade Terms
25% no surcharges
Credit Cards Accepted: Access/Master, Visa

Returns Procedures
Authority to Return: Required in writing
Stock Returns: Written request or fax request
Imperfect Returns: Return up to £30

BOOKS FROM INDIA UK LTD
45 Museum Street, London WC1A 1LR
ISBN Prefix(es): 0 86186, 1 85127
Tel: 071-405 7226
Tel: 071-405 3784
Fax: 071-831 4517
VAT No: 333 2244 93

Account No: _____
Sales Rep: _____
Tel: _____

Order Information

Order Dept Opening Times
Mon - Fri 10am - 5.30pm, Sat 10am - 5pm
Cyclical Ordering Policy
All Dues Automatically Recorded

Personnel
Head of Company: Mrs Vidyarthi (Managing Director)
Head of Sales (Home): Mr S Vidyarthi
Head of Accounts: Mrs K Hammond
Other Important Personnel:
V Nachiketa (Credit Control), Anurag Vidyarthi (Book Design)

Number of titles published annually: 60
Percentage of Export Sales: 40%
Number of Staff: 4

NBA Signatory
WBIP Updating: S Vidyarthi

Allied Companies: Tricolour Books Delhi (IN)

Trade Terms
33.3% own publications, 25% single copies carriage extra.
Non-Net: 25%
Minimum Order: £10 invoice value
Other Terms: Carriaged always charged Payment by credit card 5% less discount
Credit Cards Accepted: Access/Master, Amex, Diners, Visa, Other

Returns Procedures
Stock Returns: not allowed
Imperfect Returns: return the books for credit. Books up to £10 value title page can be returned.

BOOKSELLERS ASSOCIATION OF GREAT BRITAIN AND IRELAND

Minster House, 272 Vauxhall Bridge Road, London SW1V 1BA
ISBN Prefix(es): 0 907972
Tel: 071-834 5477
Fax: 071-834 8812
VAT No: 242 2650 89

Order Information

Order Dept Opening Times
Mon - Fri 9.30am - 5.00pm
All Dues Automatically Recorded
Invoice Payments: Booksellers Association Service House Ltd

Personnel
Head of Company: Tim Godfray (Director)
Head of Sales (Home): Kevin Ramage (Membership Services Executive)
Head of Accounts: Paul Somers (Accounts Manager)
Other Important Personnel:
Anna Diamanti (Orders and Customer Services)

Number of titles published annually: 3
Number of Staff: 20
NBA Signatory
All New Titles are Bar Coded
Book Data Subscriber
WBIP Updating: Kevin Ramage

Trade Terms
Directories for trade use only - no discount
Other Terms: Overseas orders £4 carriage per copy
Girobank Number: 512 9451
Credit Cards Accepted: Access/Master, Visa

Returns Procedures
Authority to Return: Anna Diamanti
Imperfect Returns: Return cover and title page

BOOKSPEED

48 Hamilton Place, Edinburgh, Lothian EH3 5AX
Tel: 031-225 4950
Fax: 031-220 6515

Account No: _____
Sales Rep: _____
Tel: _____

Order Information
Teleordering: BKSPEED

Order Dept Opening Times
Mon - Fri 8am - 6pm
Orders for more than one publisher can be bulked
All Dues Automatically Recorded
Representation Available

Personnel
Head of Company: Annie Rhodes/Kingsley Dawson (Joint Managing Directors)
Head of Sales (Home): Kingsley Dawson
Head of Accounts: Margo Forrest
Head of Distribution: Yvonne Brady
Head of Customer Services: Shona Rowan

Number of titles published annually: 40
Number of Staff: 2
All New Titles are Bar Coded
WBIP Updating: Kingsley Dawson

Parent Company: Rhodawn Ltd

Trade Terms
Single Copy 25%, Two or more 35%
Girobank Number: 147 1961

Returns Procedures
Authority to Return: Fiona Atkinson
Stock Returns: Contact first

BOOSEY & HAWKES MUSIC PUBLISHERS LTD

295 Regent Street, London W1R 8JH
ISBN Prefix(es): 0 85162
Tel: 071-580 2060
Fax: 071-436 5675
VAT No: 229 2853 47

Orders to
Boosey & Hawkes, The Hyde, Edgware Road, London NW9 6JN
Tel: 081-205 3861
Fax: 081-200 3737

Order Information

Order Dept Opening Times
Mon - Fri 9am - 5pm
All Dues Automatically Recorded

Personnel
Head of Company: R A Fell (Managing Director)
Head of Sales (Home): N D King (Sales Manager)
Head of Marketing: S A Richards (Sales & Marketing Director)
Head of Accounts: A J Arnold (Finanace Director)
Head of Distribution: W G Lacey
Head of Customer Services: R Llewellyn
Other Important Personnel:
J K Sillito (Marketing Executive) London, NW9

Number of titles published annually: 60
Percentage of Export Sales: 50%
Book Data Subscriber

Parent Company: Boosey & Hawkes PLC

Trade Terms
Dependent on size of account

BORTHWICK INSTITUTE PUBLICATIONS

St Anthony's Hall, Peasholme Green, York, North Yorkshire YO1 2PW
Tel: 0904 642315
VAT No: 170 9763 40

BOSSINEY BOOKS

Land's End, St Teath, Bodmin, Cornwall PL30 3JH
ISBN Prefix(es): 0 948158
Tel: 0840 213401
VAT No: 281 8734 31

Order Information

Representation Available

Personnel
Head of Company: Michael & Sonia Williams

Number of titles published annually: 8
Number of Staff: 5
WBIP Updating: Angela Larcombe

Returns Procedures
Authority to Return: Prior permission required

[handwritten: Bournmouth English Books - 9 Albion Close Parkstone, Poole BH12 3LL   A/C No 013SM01]

BOWKER-SAUR LTD

59-60 Grosvenor Street, London W1X 9DA
ISBN Prefix(es): 0 86291, 0 905450
Tel: 071-493 5841
Fax: 071-580 4089
Telex: 95678
VAT No: 246 3981 37

Account No: _____

Sales Rep: _____

Tel: _____

Orders to
BUTTERWORTH & CO LTD, Borough Green, Sevenoaks, Kent TN15 8PH
Tel: 0732 884567
Fax: 0732 885996

Order Information

Invoice Payments: Butterworths

Personnel
Head of Company: Dr Shane O'Neill (Managing Director)
Head of Marketing: Carolyn Daugherty (Sales & Marketing Director)
Head of Publicity: Vicky Shipton (Promotions Manager)
Head of Accounts: Tim Hickson (Financial & Administration Manager)
Head of Customer Services: Karen Judge (Special Sales Manager)
Other Important Personnel:
Richard Hollis (Professional Sales Manager), Leslie Lees (Northern European Sales Manager), Sheila McKenna (Southern Europe Area Sales Manager)

Number of Staff: 68
Book Data Subscriber

Parent Company: Reed International Books

Returns Procedures
Address for Returns: Butterworths

BOXTREE LTD

2nd Floor, Broadwall House, 21 Broadwall, London SE1 9PL
ISBN Prefix(es): 1 85283
Tel: 071-928 9696
Fax: 071-928 5632

Account No: _____

Sales Rep: _____

Tel: _____

Orders to
LITTLEHAMPTON BOOK SERVICES, 14 Eldon Way,
Lineside Ind Estate, Littlehampton, West Sussex BN17 7HE
Tel: 0903 721596
Fax: 0903 730914

Order Information

All Dues Automatically Recorded
Representation Available
Invoice Payments: Littlehampton

Personnel
Head of Company: Sarah Mahaffy
Head of Sales (Home): David Inman
Head of Publicity: Nichola Motley
Head of Accounts: Christine Brown
Other Important Personnel:
Chantal Noel (Bookseller Enquiries)

Number of titles published annually: 60
Number of Staff: 24
All New Titles are Bar Coded
Book Data Subscriber
WBIP Updating: Jenni Davies

Trade Terms
35% on all orders
Credit Cards Accepted: Access/Master, Visa

Returns Procedures
Authority to Return: David Inman/Local Representative
Address for Returns: Littlehampton

MARION BOYARS PUBLISHERS LTD

24 Lacy Road, London SW15 1NL
ISBN Prefix(es): 0 7145
Tel: 081-788 9522
Fax: 081-789 8122
VAT No: 241 3635 86

Order Information

Order Dept Opening Times
Mon - Fri 9.30am - 5.30pm
All Dues Automatically Recorded
Representation Available

Personnel
Head of Company: Marion Boyars
Head of Sales (Home): David Lines

Number of titles published annually: 25
PA Member
NBA Signatory
All New Titles are Bar Coded
WBIP Updating: D Lines

Trade Terms
General Net: Single copy 25%, two or more 35%, special orders negotiable low value surcharge of £1.50 on invoice value below £25

Returns Procedures
Authority to Return: D Lines
Address for Returns: Clipper
Imperfect Returns: Title Page up to £10 otherwise return book to Clipper

BOYDELL & BREWER LTD

PO Box 9, Woodbridge, Suffolk IP12 3DF
ISBN Prefix(es): 0 85115, 0 85991
Tel: 0394 411320
Fax: 0394 411477

VAT No: 102 7861 81

Account No: _____
Sales Rep: _____
Tel: _____

Order Information
Teleordering: BOYDELL

Order Dept Opening Times
Mon - Fri 8.30am - 5pm
All Dues Automatically Recorded
Representation Available

Personnel
Head of Company: Richard Barber
Head of Sales (Home): Andrew Cocks
Head of Marketing: Helen Barber
Head of Accounts: Barbara Kevern
Head of Distribution: Joan Jordan

Number of titles published annually: 70
Book Data Subscriber
WBIP Updating: Ms Pam Cope

Subsidiary Companies: University of Rochester Press (US)

Trade Terms
Single Copy 20%, Two or more 35%
Other Terms: Carriage charged on overseas orders at cost
Girobank Number: 237 6156
Credit Cards Accepted: Access/Master, Visa

Returns Procedures
Authority to Return: From Sales Director or Rep
Address for Returns: College Farm, Forward Green, Stowmarket, Suffolk IP14 5EH
Stock Returns: May be returned with appropriate documentation - copy order, copy invoice and authorisation.
Imperfect Returns: Annotated title page up to £25, whole book £25 and over.

BPP PUBLISHING LTD
Aldine House, Aldine Place, 142-144 Uxbridge Road, London W12 8AW
ISBN Prefix(es): 0 86277, 1 871824
Tel: 081-740 1111
Tel: 081-740 6808
Fax: 081-740 1184
VAT No: 466 4516 29
Account No: _____ 05029 _____
Sales Rep: _____
Tel: _____

Order Information

Order Dept Opening Times
Mon - Fri 9am - 5.30pm
All Dues Automatically Recorded
Representation Available

Personnel
Head of Company: Clare Donnelly (Managing Director)
Head of Sales (Home): Justin West (Sales Director)
Head of Marketing: Claire Wright (Marketing Director)
Head of Accounts: Lynn Chandler
Head of Distribution: Alison Harris (Order Processing Director)

Number of titles published annually: 30
Percentage of Export Sales: 25%
Number of Staff: 30
All New Titles are Bar Coded

Book Data Subscriber
WBIP Updating: Alison Harris

Allied Companies: Blackstone Press, BPP (Letts Educational), DP Publications

Trade Terms
Upon request

Returns Procedures
Authority to Return: Alison Harris
Address for Returns: Unit 6, Grand Union Industrial Estate, Twyford Abbey Road, London NW10
Stock Returns: Contact Alison Harris

DR BARRY BRACEWELL-MILNES

26 Lancaster Court, Banstead, Surrey SM7 1RR
Tel: 0737 350736
Fax: 0737 362341

IPG Member

BRADFORD LIBRARIES

Central Library, Bradford, West Yorkshire BD1 1NN
Tel: 0274 753622
Fax: 0274 395108
Telex: 51480
VAT No: 180 8082 62

BRADT PUBLICATIONS

41 Nortoft Road, Chalfont St Peter, Buckinghamshire SL9 0LA
ISBN Prefix(es): 0 946983
Tel: 0494 873478 Tel/Fax
Fax: 0753 646580
VAT No: 301 9694 60

Orders to
SPRINGFIELD BOOKS LTD, Norman Road, Denby Dale, Huddersfield, West Yorkshire HD8 8TH
Tel: 0484 864955
Fax: 0484 865443

Order Information

Invoice Payments: Springfield Books

Personnel
Head of Company: Hilary Bradt
Head of Accounts: Janet Mears
Other Important Personnel:
Dilys Saunders (Accounts)

Number of titles published annually: 15
Percentage of Export Sales: 55%
Number of Staff: 3
IPG Member
NBA Signatory
All New Titles are Bar Coded
WBIP Updating: Hilary Bradt

Trade Terms
See Springfield Books
Girobank Number: 27 393 4007

BRAINIAC BOOKS LTD

42 Heysham Road, London N15 6HL
ISBN Prefix(es): 1 874057
Tel: 081-809 3056 24 Hours

Orders to
TURNAROUND, 27 Horsell Road, London N5 1XL
Tel: 071-609 7836/7
Fax: 071-700 1205

Order Information

All Dues Automatically Recorded
Representation Available
Invoice Payments: Turnaround

Personnel
Head of Company: Pete Tombs
Head of Marketing: Foss Hagman
Head of Accounts: Alison Downie

Number of titles published annually: 3
Number of Staff: 3
All New Titles are Bar Coded
WBIP Updating: Pete Tombs

Trade Terms
35%

Returns Procedures
Authority to Return: Turnaround Representative
Address for Returns: Turnaround
Imperfect Returns: Title page up to £10, then by arrangement

BRAINWAVE

33 Lorn Road, Stockwell, London SW9 0AB
Tel: 071-733 7883
Fax: 071-978 9062
VAT No: 547 8365 04

BRASS WIND PUBLICATIONS

4 St Mary's Road, Manton, Oakham, Leicestershire
LE15 8SU
Tel: 057 285 409 Tel/Fax
VAT No: 283 9202 47

IPG Member

BRASSEY'S (UK) LTD

165 Great Dover Street, London SE1 4YA
ISBN Prefix(es): 0 08, 1 85753
Tel: 071-334 4924
Fax: 071-334 4913
VAT No: 596 0597 91

Account No: _____
Sales Rep: _____
Tel: _____

Orders to
MARSTON BOOK SERVICES LTD, PO Box 87, Osney Mead, Oxford, Oxfordshire OX2 0DT
Tel: 0865 791155
Fax: 0865 791927

Order Information

All Dues Automatically Recorded
Representation Available
Invoice Payments: Marston Book Services

Personnel
Head of Company: Maj-Gen A J Trythall (Executive Deputy Chairman)
Head of Publicity: Marion Jones 071-334 4921

Number of titles published annually: 60
Percentage of Export Sales: 50%
Number of Staff: 13
NBA Signatory
All New Titles are Bar Coded
WBIP Updating: Nikki Sutton

Trade Terms
General Net: Single copy 25%, Two or more single titles 33-35%
Academic Net: Single copy 20%, Multi 25-30%
Credit Cards Accepted: Access/Master, Visa, Amex

Returns Procedures
Authority to Return: Graham Uden, Maxwell Macmillan International
Address for Returns: Marston Book Services

NICHOLAS BREALEY PUBLISHING LTD
14 Stephenson Way, London NW1 2HD
ISBN Prefix(es): 0 85290, 1 85788
Tel: 071-388 0644
Fax: 071-380 0511
VAT No: 577 8255 87

Orders to
BOOKPOINT LIMITED, 39 Milton Park, Abingdon, Oxfordshire OX14 4TD
Tel: 0235 835001
Fax: 0235 861038

Order Information

All Dues Automatically Recorded
Representation Available
Invoice Payments: Bookpoint
Representation: John Wilson (Booksales) Ltd

Other Important Locations
Corporate Address: 156 Cloudesley Road, London N1 0EA
Tel/Fax: 071-713 7455

Personnel
Head of Company: Nicholas Brealey (Managing Director)
Head of Publicity: Pete Daly (Publicity & Promotions Manager)

Number of titles published annually: 30
Percentage of Export Sales: 30%
Number of Staff: 2
IPG Member
All New Titles are Bar Coded

Trade Terms
As Bookpoint/John Wilson

Returns Procedures
Authority to Return: John Wilson
Address for Returns: Bookpoint

BREEDON BOOKS
44 Friar Gate, Derby, Derbyshire DE1 1DA
Tel: 0332 384235
Fax: 0332 292755
VAT No: 395 6461 11

Order Information

Order Dept Opening Times
Mon - Fri 7.30am - 5pm, Sat 7.30am - 12pm
Representation Available

Personnel
Head of Company: Anton Rippon/John Grainger (Managing Editor/Managing Director)
Head of Customer Services: Lucy Green

Number of titles published annually: 25
Number of Staff: 10

Trade Terms
Credit Cards Accepted: Access/Master, Visa

MARTIN BREESE PUBLISHING

164 Kensington Park Road, London W11 2ER
ISBN Prefix(es): 0 947533
Tel: 071-727 9426
Tel: 071-727 6422
Tel: 071-727 9378
Fax: 071-229 3395
VAT No: 446 1919 36

Orders to
CLIPPER DISTRIBUTION SERVICES LTD, Windmill Grove, Porchester, Hampshire PO16 9HT
Tel: 0705 200080
Fax: 0705 200090

IPG Member

Returns Procedures
Address for Returns: Clipper Distribution Services, Eastmead Industrial Estate, Lavant, Chichester, W Sussex PO18 0DB

BREFI PRESS

Plas Y Gorwydd, Llanddewi Brefi, Tregaron, Dyfed SY25 6NY
Tel: 0570 45374
Fax: 0570 45590
VAT No: 359 5804 16

BRENTHAM PRESS

40 Oswald Road, St Albans, Hertfordshire AL1 3AQ
ISBN Prefix(es): 0 905772
Tel: 0727 835731

Order Information

All Dues Automatically Recorded
Representation Available

Personnel
Head of Company: Margaret Tims (Editorial Director)

Number of titles published annually: 4
Number of Staff: 1
All New Titles are Bar Coded

Trade Terms
General Net: Single copy 25%, 2 or more single titles 35%, 2 books or more 35%, special orders 40%

Returns Procedures
Imperfect Returns: Title page accepted for all books

BRESLICH & FOSS

Golden House, 28-31 Great Pulteney Street, London
W1R 3DD
Tel: 071-734 0706
Fax: 071-494 0854

Order Information
Orders To:Cathy Stubbs

Personnel
Head of Company: Paula Breslich (Managing Director)

BREWIN BOOK DISTRIBUTION SERVICES

Doric House, 56 Alcester Road, Studley, Warwickshire
B80 7LG
ISBN Prefix(es): 0 947731, 0 9505510, 1 85858
Tel: 0527 854228 24 Hours
Fax: 0527 852746
VAT No: 378 1070 47

Account No: _____

Sales Rep: _____

Tel: _____

Order Information

Order Dept Opening Times
Mon - Fri 9am - 1pm 2pm - 5pm
*Orders for more than one publisher can be bulked
All Dues Automatically Recorded
Representation Available*

Personnel
Head of Company: K A F Brewin

Number of titles published annually: 20
All New Titles are Bar Coded

Parent Company: Brewin Books

Trade Terms
35% on all orders

Returns Procedures
Address for Returns: Brewin Books, Supaprint Works, Unit 19, Enfield Estate, Redditch, Worcs
Stock Returns: Prior written agreement required for overstocks. Incorrectly supplied or damaged books will be accepted automatically
Imperfect Returns: Request on usual multipart returns form. Title page accepted for imperfect books valued up to £10

MARTIN BRIAN & O'KEEFFE LTD

78 Coleraine Road, London SE3 7PE
ISBN Prefix(es): 0 85616
Tel: 081-858 5164

BRIGHT BOOKS LTD

Carpenters, Moor End, Great Sampford, Saffron Walden, Essex CB10 2RQ
ISBN Prefix(es): 1 873967
Tel: 0799 86576 Tel/Fax
VAT No: 538 2363 39

Order Information

Order Dept Opening Times
Mon - Fri 9am - 5.30pm
Representation Available

Personnel
Head of Company: Camilla Hair (Director)
Head of Accounts: Robin Hair (Company Accounts Director)
Head of Customer Services: Jane Freeman (Administration Services)

Number of titles published annually: 4
IPG Member
All New Titles are Bar Coded
WBIP Updating: Jane Freeman

Trade Terms
35%, 30 days
Minimum Order: 5 copies, orders below this attract low level discount

Returns Procedures
Authority to Return: Prior authority must be obtained and goods must be returned in a saleable condition

> E.J. Brill, PO Box 560. LONDON. N11 2UX — OR
> PLANTIJNSTRAAT 2, PO Box 9000, 2300 PA LEIDEN
> NETHERLANDS
> FAX 010 3171 317532

BRIMAX BOOKS LTD
4/5 Studlands Park, Industrial Estate, Newmarket, Suffolk CB8 7AU
ISBN Prefix(es): 0 86112, 1 85854
Tel: 0638 664611
Fax: 0638 665220
Telex: 817625 BRIMAX

Account No: _____
Sales Rep: _____
Tel: _____

Orders to
REED BOOK SERVICES, Northampton Road, Rushden, Northamptonshire NN10 9PU
Tel: 0933 58521
Fax: 0933 50284

Order Information

Representation Available
Invoice Payments: Reed Book Services

Personnel
Head of Company: Patricia Gillette (Managing Director)
Head of Sales (Home): Keith Baxter (Sales & Marketing Director)
Head of Customer Services: Daphne Coombs (Home Trade Manager)

Number of titles published annually: 50
Percentage of Export Sales: 75%
Number of Staff: 20
All New Titles are Bar Coded
WBIP Updating: Carol Owen/Daphne Coombs

Parent Company: Reed International Books Ltd

Trade Terms
35% firm sale
Minimum Order: £75

Returns Procedures
Imperfect Returns: Title page only all prices

> Bristol Classical Press = DUCKWORTH

THE BRITISH ACADEMY
20-21 Cornwall Terrace, London NW1 4QP
ISBN Prefix(es): 0 19726, 0 85672
Tel: 071-487 5966
Fax: 071-224 3807
Telex: 263194
Cables: BRITACADEMY, LONDON NW1
VAT No: 238 5788 16

Order Information

All Dues Automatically Recorded
Representation Available
Invoice Payments: NEW BOOKS: Oxford University Press
BACKLIST: Oxbow Books Ltd

Personnel
Other Important Personnel:
James Rivington (Publications Officer), Hilary Kent (Publications Assistant)

Number of titles published annually: 15
Percentage of Export Sales: 55%
Number of Staff: 2
All New Titles are Bar Coded
Book Data Subscriber
WBIP Updating: James Rivington

Trade Terms
25%

Returns Procedures
Authority to Return: NEW BOOKS: Oxford University Press
BACKLIST: Oxbow Books Ltd

British Archaeological Reports (BAR)
122 Banbury Road
OXFORD OX2 7BP

BRITISH ASSOCIATION FOR COMMERCIAL & INDUSTRIAL EDUCATION

35 Harbour Exchange Square, Marsh Wall, London E14 9GE
ISBN Prefix(es): 0 85171
Tel: 071-987 8989
Fax: 071-987 9898
VAT No: 233 8378 50

Order Information

All Dues Automatically Recorded

Personnel
Head of Company: B V Murphy (Director)
Head of Accounts: C A Stead (Company Secretary)

Number of titles published annually: 4
Number of Staff: 12
PA Member
All New Titles are Bar Coded
WBIP Updating: Ms G Louch

Trade Terms
25%
Other Terms: Surcharge of 10% up to £100
Credit Cards Accepted: Access/Master, Visa

Returns Procedures
Stock Returns: Returns accepted provided invoiced within 12 months, invoice details required
Imperfect Returns: As above

BRITISH ATHLETICS FEDERATION

3 Duchess Place, Edgbaston House, Hagley Road, Birmingham, West Midlands B16
Tel: 021-456 4050
Fax: 021-456 4061
Telex: 334253 BAAB G

Orders to
BAF Book Centre, 5 Church Road, Great Bookham, Surrey KT23 3PN
Tel: 0372 452804

BRITISH CERAMIC RESEARCH LTD
Queens Road, Penkhull, Stoke-on-Trent, Staffordshire
ST4 7LQ
Tel: 0782 45431
Fax: 0782 412331
Telex: 36228 BCRA G

THE BRITISH COUNCIL
Production & Publishing Dept, 10 Spring Gardens, London
SW1A 2BN
ISBN Prefix(es): 0 86355
Tel: 071-930 8466
Fax: 071-839 6347
Telex: 8952201 BRICON G

Personnel
Other Important Personnel:
Ms Angela Rivett (Sales Assistant)

Trade Terms
General Net: Single Copy 25%, Two Books or more 33.3%

BRITISH ENTOMOLOGICAL & NATURAL HISTORY SOCIETY
c/o 30D Meadowcroft Close, Horley, Surrey RH6 9EL
ISBN Prefix(es): 1 9502891
Tel: 02934 783397

Personnel
Head of Sales (Home): R D Hawkins
Head of Accounts: A J Pickles

Number of titles published annually: 2
Percentage of Export Sales: 20%

Trade Terms
28-33% varying by title, P&P at cost

THE BRITISH HORSE SOCIETY (TRADING CO) LTD
British Equestrian Centre, Stoneleigh Park, Kenilworth,
Warwickshire CV8 2LR
Tel: 0203 696697
Fax: 0203 692351
VAT No: 584 9334 00

BRITISH LIBRARY DOCUMENT SUPPLY CENTRE   c/o TURPIN DISTRIBUTION
Boston Spa, Wetherby, West Yorkshire LS23 7BQ
ISBN Prefix(es): 0 7123
Tel: 0937 546080
Fax: 0937 536333
VAT No: 240 6927 64

A/C No 145

Orders to
The British Library, Publications Sales Unit, Boston Spa,
Wetherby, West Yorkshire LS23 7BQ
Tel: 0937 546077 (24 Hr)
Fax: 0937 546333

Order Information
Teleordering: BRITLIB

Order Dept Opening Times
Mon - Fri 8.30am - 5pm
Cyclical Ordering Policy
All Dues Automatically Recorded

Personnel
Head of Company: Des Seaton
Head of Sales (Home): Andrea Seed
Head of Distribution: Dave Wilkie
Other Important Personnel:
John Lowery (Publishing Executive)

Number of titles published annually: 47
Number of Staff: 16
PA Member
NBA Signatory
WBIP Updating: John M Lowery

Trade Terms
10%
Credit Cards Accepted: Access/Master, Amex, Diners, Visa, Other

BRITISH LIBRARY MARKETING AND PUBLISHING c/o TURPIN DISTRIBUTION
41 Russell Square, London WC1B 3DG
ISBN Prefix(es): 0 7123
Tel: 071-323 7704
Fax: 071-323 7736
Telex: 21462
VAT No: 240 6927 64

A/C No 145

Orders to
The British Library, Publications Sales Unit, Boston Spa, Wetherby, West Yorkshire LS23 7BQ
Tel: 0937 546077
Fax: 0937 546236

Order Information
Teleordering: BRITLIB

Order Dept Opening Times
Mon - Fri 8am - 5pm
Representation Available
Invoice Payments: Publications Sales Unit, Boston Spa

Personnel
Head of Company: Jane Carr
Head of Publicity: Anne Young
Head of Accounts: Alison Masom
Head of Distribution: David Wilkie

Number of titles published annually: 40
Percentage of Export Sales: 35%
Number of Staff: 8
PA Member
NBA Signatory
All New Titles are Bar Coded
Book Data Subscriber
WBIP Updating: Kathleen Houghton

Trade Terms
General Net: 35%
Academic Net: 25%
Credit Cards Accepted: Access/Master, Visa

Returns Procedures
Authority to Return: David Way
Address for Returns: Publications Sales Unit, Boston Spa
Stock Returns: Contact Jez Raynes

THE BRITISH LIBRARY NATIONAL BIBLIOGRAPHIC SERVICE c/o TURPIN DISTR.
Boston Spa, Wetherby, West Yorkshire LS23 7BQ
ISBN Prefix(es): 0 7123, 0 900220
Tel: 0937 546585
Fax: 0937 546586
VAT No: 240 6927 64

A/C No 145

Orders to
Tel: 0937 546251
Fax: 0937 546185

Order Information
Teleordering: BRITLIB

Order Dept Opening Times
Mon - Fri 8.30am - 4pm
Cyclical Ordering Policy

Personnel
Head of Company: Mr Stuart Ede (Director) 0937 546588
Head of Sales (Home): Mr A E Cunningham (Head of Publications) 0937 546610
Head of Publicity: Jonathan Pursday
Head of Accounts: Judy Watkins
Head of Customer Services: Cathy Lott

Number of titles published annually: 5
Percentage of Export Sales: 25%
Number of Staff: 29
PA Member
WBIP Updating: Jean Murdoch

Trade Terms
10% trade discount

Returns Procedures
Imperfect Returns: Return imperfect copies to Sales & Subscriptions

BRITISH MUSEUM PRESS

46 Bloomsbury Street, London WC1B 3QQ
ISBN Prefix(es): 0 7141
Tel: 071-323 1234
Fax: 071-436 7315
Telex: 28592 BM PUBS G
VAT No: 342 0854 75

Orders to
THAMES & HUDSON LTD, 44 Clockhouse Road, Farnborough, Hampshire GU14 7QZ
Tel: 0252 541602
Fax: 0252 377380

Order Information

All Dues Automatically Recorded
Invoice Payments: Thames & Hudson Ltd

Personnel
Head of Company: Hugh Campbell (Managing Director)
Head of Marketing: Alasdair MacLeod
Other Important Personnel:
Celia Clear (Publishing Manager)

Number of titles published annually: 40
PA Member
NBA Signatory
All New Titles are Bar Coded
WBIP Updating: Liz Edwards

Trade Terms
Distributor's terms apply

Returns Procedures
Authority to Return: Refer to Distributor

BRITISH NORTH AMERICAN RESEARCH ASSOCIATION

35-37 Grosvenor Gardens House, Grosvenor Gardens, London SW1W 0BS
ISBN Prefix(es): 0 902594

Tel: 071-828 6644
Fax: 071-828 5830

Order Information
Order Dept Opening Times
9.30am - 5.30pm

Personnel
Head of Company: Simon Webley (Director)

Number of titles published annually: 3
Number of Staff: 2

Allied Companies: National Planning Association (US)

Trade Terms
Minimum Order: 5 or more 33.3%
Other Terms: Carriage charges: P&P on orders under 6

> BRITISH SCHOOL AT ROME
> c/o Research School of
> Archaeology + Archaeological
> Science
> Broomspring Lane Bldg,
> University of Sheffield
> Western Bank
> Sheffield S10 2TN
> Tel/Fax 0742 750986.

BRITISH PSYCHOLOGICAL SOCIETY

St Andrews House, 48 Princess Road East, Leicester,
Leicestershire LE1 7DR
ISBN Prefix(es): 0 901715, 1 85433
Tel: 0533 549568
Fax: 0533 470787

Orders to
PLYMBRIDGE DISTRIBUTORS LTD, Plymbridge House,
Estover Road, Plymouth, Devon PL6 7PZ
Tel: 0752 735251
Fax: 0752 695699

Order Information
All Dues Automatically Recorded
Representation Available
Representation:Book Representation & Distribution (BRAD)

Personnel
Head of Company: Joyce Collins (Publications Manager)

Number of titles published annually: 15
Percentage of Export Sales: 20%
IPG Member
All New Titles are Bar Coded
Book Data Subscriber

Trade Terms
Single copy/single line 25%, Two or more single titles 30%

Returns Procedures
Authority to Return: Joyce Collins
Address for Returns: Plymbridge

> BRITISH STANDARDS
> INST - BSI
> LINFORD WOOD
> MILTON KEYNES
> MK14 6LE
> TEL 0908 220022
> FAX 0908 320856
> WRITTEN ORDERS ONLY
> MARK INV TO KLR
> DELIVER TO UBS.

BROAD OAK PRESS

Ragstones, Broad Oak, Heathfield, East Sussex TN21 8UD
ISBN Prefix(es): 0 906716
Tel: 0435 862012
Fax: 0435 862012
VAT No: 508 6037 53

Personnel
Head of Company: Anthony P Harvey
Other Important Personnel:
Margaret Harvey (Secretary)

Trade Terms
25%

> Broadleys. Burton House, Station Road, Newport
> Saffron Walden. Essex. CB11 3PL   0799-40922

BROADSIDE

68 Limes Road, Tettenhall, Wolverhampton, West Midlands
WV6 8RB

ISBN Prefix(es): 0 9503722
Tel: 0902 753047
Tel: 0902 741536
VAT No: 100 6535 20

Order Information

Order Dept Opening Times
Mon - Sat 9.30am - 5.30pm
Representation Available

Personnel
Head of Company: Jon Raven

Number of titles published annually: 4
Number of Staff: 1

Parent Company: Venturechief Ltd

Trade Terms
33.3% + postage on orders up to £50

BROOKS BOOKS

23 Sylvan Avenue, Bitterne, Southampton, Hampshire
SO2 5JW
Tel: 0703 434131 Tel/Fax

DAVID BROWN

PO Box 9, Heathfield, Sussex TN21 0DN
ISBN Prefix(es): 0 9514641
Tel: 04353 2506
VAT No: 475 6057 24

Order Information

Cyclical Ordering Policy

Personnel
Head of Company: David Brown

Trade Terms
General Net: 25-35%

BROWN, SON & FERGUSON, LTD

4/10 Darnley Street, Glasgow, Strathclyde G41 2SD
ISBN Prefix(es): 0 85174
Tel: 041-429 1234 24hrs
Tel: 041-429 5922
Tel: 041-429 7798
Fax: 041-420 1694
Cables: SKIPPER, GLASGOW
VAT No: 259 5244 36

Order Information

Order Dept Opening Times
Mon - Thu 8.15am - 4.45pm, Fri 8.15am - 1.30pm
All Dues Automatically Recorded
Representation Available

Personnel
Head of Company: T Nigel Brown/L Ingram-Brown (Joint Managing Directors)
Other Important Personnel:
D H Provan (Sales & Advertising Manager)

Number of titles published annually: 500
Percentage of Export Sales: 65%
Number of Staff: 49
All New Titles are Bar Coded
Book Data Subscriber
WBIP Updating: Sales Manager

Subsidiary Companies: Gowans (James) Ltd

Trade Terms
General Net: 30% technical, 37.5% non-technical
Other Terms: Post paid (UK) £100 gross
Credit Cards Accepted: Access/Master, Visa, Other

Returns Procedures
Authority to Return: Written request required
Stock Returns: Request for authorization to return books required before returning
Imperfect Returns: Title page only for credit/replace urgent. Instructions to be included on returns

TREVOR BROWN ASSOCIATES

First Floor, Dilke House, Malet Street, London WC1E 7JA
Tel: 071-436 1874
Fax: 071-436 1868

Account No: _____

Sales Rep: _____

Tel: _____

Order Information
Teleordering: UNIBKS

All Dues Automatically Recorded
Representation Available
Distribution:IBD/Biblios/Plymbridge

Personnel
Head of Company: J Trevor Brown (Director)
Head of Sales (Export): Anna Simpson-Muellner
Head of Customer Services: Carole Crampton

WBIP Updating: Carole Crampton

Trade Terms
Academic Net: Single copy 25%, Two books or more 30%, Sub orders 33.3%, Stock orders & Special orders 35%

W C BROWN PUBLISHING

Holywell House, Osney Mead, Oxford, Oxfordshire OX2 0ES
ISBN Prefix(es): 0 697
Tel: 0865 791378
Fax: 0865 790102

Account No: _____

Sales Rep: _____

Tel: _____

Orders to
INTERNATIONAL BOOK DISTRIBUTORS, Campus 400, Maylands Avenue, Hemel Hempstead, Hertfordshire HP2 7EZ
Tel: 0442 881900
Fax: 0442 882099

Order Information

All Dues Automatically Recorded
Representation Available
Invoice Payments: IBD
D C Heath Orders: Plymbridge Distributors

Personnel
Head of Sales (Home): Miss K Ridge
Head of Sales (Export): Mr M Brightmore

Number of titles published annually: 300
Percentage of Export Sales: 70%
PA Member
All New Titles are Bar Coded

Open University Publications
WBIP Updating: Mrs Kate Finn

Trade Terms
35%
Credit Cards Accepted: Access/Master, Amex, Diners, Visa

Returns Procedures
Authority to Return: Mrs J Cook, W C Brown, Oxford
Address for Returns: IBD/Plymbridge
Stock Returns: Returns requests have to be submitted in writing in the first instance

BROWN WATSON (LEICESTER) LTD
The Old Mill, 76 Fleckney Road, Kibworth, Leicester, Leicestershire LE8 0HG
ISBN Prefix(es): 0 9780709
Tel: 0533 796333
Fax: 0533 796303

Personnel
Head of Company: Michael McDonald (Managing Director)

Number of Staff: 12

Trade Terms
50%, minimum order £300 net

Returns Procedures
Authority to Return: No returns

[handwritten: BRUNNER/MAZEL = Afterhurst Publishers Ltd, 27 Church Road, Hove, E. Sussex BN3 2FA = Direct Distribution]

THE BRYNMILL PRESS
Pockthorpe Cottage, Denton, Nr Harleston, Norfolk
IP20 0AS
Tel: 0986 86419
VAT No: 331 4610 96

[handwritten: BSI - Linford Wood, Milton Keynes MK14 6CE - Written orders only - Marked invoice RR- deliver UBS]

THE BUCKLEBURY PRESS
1 Bucklebury Place, Upper Woolhampton, Reading, Berkshire RG7 5UD
Tel: 0734 712079
VAT No: 491 7210 47

[handwritten: FAX 0908 320856 TEL 0908 220022]

Orders to
INTERNATIONAL BOOK DISTRIBUTORS, Campus 400, Maylands Avenue, Hemel Hempstead, Hertfordshire
HP2 7EZ
Tel: 0442 881900
Fax: 0442 882099

BUDDHIST PUBLISHING GROUP
Sharpham North, Ashprington, Totnes, Devon TQ9 7UT
ISBN Prefix(es): 0946672
Tel: 0803 732542

Orders to
WISDOM BOOKS, 402 Hoe Street, Walthamstow, London
E17 9AA
Tel: 081-520 5588
Fax: 081-520 0932

Order Information

All Dues Automatically Recorded
Representation Available
Invoice Payments: Wisdom

Personnel
Head of Company: Richard St Ruth

Percentage of Export Sales: 60%

Trade Terms
35%

Returns Procedures
Authority to Return: Wisdom Books
Address for Returns: Wisdom Books

BUILDING BLOCKS EDUCATIONAL
Save The Children Fund, 17 Grove Lane, London SE5 8RD
ISBN Prefix(es): 0 951428
Tel: 071-703 5400

Account No: _____

Sales Rep: _____

Tel: _____

Order Information

Order Dept Opening Times
Mon - Fri 10am - 4.30pm
All Dues Automatically Recorded

Personnel
Head of Company: Mr K Simms (Co-ordinator)
Other Important Personnel:
Mrs D Illing (Secretary/Administrator)

Number of titles published annually: 2
Number of Staff: 4
PA Member
WBIP Updating: Mr K Simms

Parent Company: Save The Children Fund

Trade Terms
33.3%

BUILDING SOCIETIES ASSOCIATION
3 Savile Row, London W1X 1AF
Tel: 071-437 0655
Fax: 071-734 6416

Order Information

Order Dept Opening Times
Mon - Fri 9am - 12pm, 2pm - 4.30pm

Personnel
Head of Company: Mark Boleat (Director General)
Head of Sales (Home): John Murray (Under Secretary)

BURALL FLORAPRINT LTD
PO Box 29, Oldfield Lane, Wisbech, Cambridgeshire
PE13 2TH
ISBN Prefix(es): 0 903001
Tel: 0945 61165
Fax: 0945 474396
VAT No: 116 5792 59

Orders to
BIBLIOS PUBLISHERS DISTRIBUTION SERVICE LTD,
Star Road, Partridge Green, West Sussex RH13 8LD
Tel: 0403 710971
Fax: 0403 711143

Order Information

All Dues Automatically Recorded
Representation Available
Invoice Payments: Biblios Publishers Distribution Services Ltd

Personnel
Head of Company: B Pinker (Managing Director)

Number of titles published annually: 1
Percentage of Export Sales: 20%
Number of Staff: 27
All New Titles are Bar Coded
Book Data Subscriber
WBIP Updating: B Pinker

Parent Company: Burall Ltd

Trade Terms
35%
Credit Cards Accepted: Access/Master, Visa

Returns Procedures
Authority to Return: Biblios

JOHN BURGESS PUBLICATIONS
28 Holme Fauld, Scotby, Carlisle, Cumbria CA4 8BL
Tel: 0228 513173

BURKE'S PEERAGE
205 St John's Hill, Battersea, London SW11 1TH
ISBN Prefix(es): 0 8501
Tel: 071-924 5132
Fax: 071-978 5732
VAT No: 461 5039 62

Order Information

Order Dept Opening Times
Mon - Fri 10am - 7pm
All Dues Automatically Recorded
Representation Available
Invoice Payments: Bookpoint Ltd

Personnel
Head of Company: H B Brooks-Baker (Publishing Director) 071-730 2342
Head of Sales (Home): Katy Heywood-Lonsdale (Office Manager)

Number of Staff: 3

Trade Terms
Credit Cards Accepted: Access/Master, Visa, Amex, Diners

GRAHAM BURN PUBLISHERS
9-13 Soulbury Road, Linslade, Leighton Buzzard, Bedfordshire LU7 2RL
ISBN Prefix(es): 0 907721
Tel: 0525 377963
Tel: 0525 376390
Fax: 0525 382498
VAT No: 335 1566 64

Order Information

All Dues Automatically Recorded

Personnel
Head of Company: Graham Burn (Propietor)

Trade Terms
1-5 copies 25%, 6-10 copies 30%, 10+ copies 35%

BURSTON DISTRIBUTION SERVICES

Unit 2A, Newbridge Trading Est, Newbridge Close, Off Whitby Rd, Bristol, Avon BS4 4AX
Tel: 0272 724248
Fax: 0272 711056
VAT No: 501 9957 38

Account No: _____

Sales Rep: _____

Tel: _____

Order Information

Order Dept Opening Times
Mon - Fri 9am - 5pm

Personnel
Head of Company: Mr L Burston (Proprietor)

Number of Staff: 6

Trade Terms
Credit Cards Accepted: Access/Master, Visa

BUSINESS EDUCATION PUBLISHERS LTD

Leighton House, 10 Grange Cres, Stockton Road, Sunderland, Tyne and Wear SR2 7BN
ISBN Prefix(es): 0 907679
Tel: 091-567 4963 Sales Off
Tel: 091-512 0151 Edit Off
Fax: 091-514 3277 Sales Off
Fax: 091-512 0145 Edit Off

Order Information

Order Dept Opening Times
Mon - Fri 9.30am - 5.15pm
All Dues Automatically Recorded
Representation Available

Personnel
Head of Company: Paul Callaghan (Managing Director)
Head of Sales (Export): Tom Harrison (Director)
Head of Customer Services: Lilias Smith

Number of titles published annually: 6
All New Titles are Bar Coded
WBIP Updating: Caroline White

Trade Terms
26%
Credit Cards Accepted: Access/Master, Visa

Returns Procedures
Address for Returns: Printers Express
Stock Returns: Request received at sales office - return books to despatch office - credit raised on appropriate account

BUTTERWORTH & CO LTD

88 Kingsway, London WC2B 6AB
ISBN Prefix(es): 0 406
Tel: 071-405 6900
Fax: 071-405 1332
Telex: 95678

Account No: _____ 00706922 _____

Sales Rep: _____

Tel: _____

Orders to
BUTTERWORTH & CO LTD, Borough Green, Sevenoaks, Kent TN15 8PH

Tel: 0732 884567
Fax: 0732 885996

Order Information
Teleordering: BUTT

Invoice Payments: Butterworths

Personnel
Head of Company: David Summers (Chief Executive)
Head of Marketing: Kevin Cassidy (Marketing Director)
Head of Publicity: Chris Marshall (Promotion Director)
Head of Accounts: Chris Day (Commercial Director)

Book Data Subscriber
WBIP Updating: John Lord

Parent Company: Reed International Books

Trade Terms
Based on performance. Details available on request. No carriage or handling charges

Returns Procedures
Authority to Return: No prior authorisation necessary
Address for Returns: Borough Green

BUTTERWORTH & CO LTD

Borough Green, Sevenoaks, Kent TN15 8PH
Tel: 0732 884567 24 Hours
Fax: 0732 885996
Telex: 95678
VAT No: 340 2429 92
Account No: _____ 00706922 _____
Sales Rep: _____
Tel: _____

Order Information
Teleordering: BUTT

Order Dept Opening Times
Mon - Fri 9am - 5pm

Personnel
Head of Company: Philip Waxman (MD Butterworth (Services) Ltd)
Head of Sales (Home): Roy Heathfield (Sales Director)
Head of Sales (Export): Phillip Woods (International Sales Director)
Head of Customer Services: Ann Morrison (Customer Services Director)
Other Important Personnel:
Jack Brabovskie (Trade Sales Manager) 061-432 6351

Parent Company: Reed International Books

Trade Terms
Variable discount based on title and turnover
Credit Cards Accepted: Access/Master, Amex, Diners, Visa

BUTTERWORTH IRELAND LTD

26 Upper Ormond Quay, Dublin 7, County Dublin
Tel: 01 731 555
Fax: 01 731 876

Account No: _____
Sales Rep: _____
Tel: _____

Orders to
BUTTERWORTH & CO LTD, Borough Green, Sevenoaks, Kent TN15 8PH

Tel: 0732 884567
Fax: 0732 885996

Order Information
Teleordering: BUTT

Book Data Subscriber

Parent Company: Reed International Books

Trade Terms
See Butterworth UK

Returns Procedures
Authority to Return: Finola O'Sullivan, Trade Sales Manager

BUTTERWORTH-HEINEMANN
Linacre House, Jordan Hill, Oxford, Oxfordshire OX2 8DP
ISBN Prefix(es): 0 240, 0 407, 0 408, 0 433, 0 434, 0 7236, 0 7506
Tel: 0865 310366
Fax: 0865 310898
Fax: 0865 314519 Sales
Telex: 83111 BHPOXF G
VAT No: 340 2429 92
Account No: _____ 4679105 _____
Sales Rep: _____
Tel: _____

Orders to
REED BOOK SERVICES, Northampton Road, Rushden, Northamptonshire NN10 9PU
Tel: 0933 58521
Fax: 0933 50284

Order Information

All Dues Automatically Recorded
Representation Available
Invoice Payments: Reed Book Services

Personnel
Head of Company: Douglas Fox (Managing Director)
Head of Sales (Home): Tom McGorry (Sales Director)
Head of Marketing: Tony Llwellyn (Marketing Director)
Head of Publicity: Martin De La Bedoyere (Marketing Manager)
Other Important Personnel:
Caroline Haw (Sales Promotion Manager), Peter Hyde (Credit Control Director)

Number of titles published annually: 300
Percentage of Export Sales: 40%
All New Titles are Bar Coded
Open University Publications
Book Data Subscriber
WBIP Updating: Caroline Haw

Parent Company: Reed International Books
Allied Companies: Future Publishing

Trade Terms
By agreement with Sales Director
Credit Cards Accepted: Access/Master, Amex, Diners, Visa

Returns Procedures
Authority to Return: Requests to local area representative
Address for Returns: Reed Book Services
Stock Returns: Books should only be returned with completed authorisation form and address label

BYRONIC BOOKS

15 Pixies Hill Crescent, Hemel Hempstead, Hertfordshire
HP1 2BU
Tel: 0442 254259

CAB INTERNATIONAL

Wallingford, Oxfordshire OX10 8DE
ISBN Prefix(es): 0 85198
Tel: 0491 32111
Fax: 0491 33508
Telex: 847964 (COMAGG G)
VAT No: 208 8646 42

A/C No 60000939

Order Information

Order Dept Opening Times
Mon - Fri 9am - 1pm, 2pm - 5.30pm
All Dues Automatically Recorded
Representation Available

Personnel

Head of Company: Mr D Laing (Director General)
Head of Sales (Home): Dr C Cunliffe (Marketing Manager - Printed Products)
Head of Marketing: Mr J H Gilmore
Head of Publicity: John D Allen
Head of Accounts: John Wason
Head of Distribution: Peter Slater
Head of Customer Services: Maureen Legg

Number of titles published annually: 45
Percentage of Export Sales: 70%
Number of Staff: 500
PA Member
Book Data Subscriber
WBIP Updating: Fiona Davison

Trade Terms

Annual turnover 0 - £500 25%, £500 - £1000 30%, £1000 + 35%
Credit Cards Accepted: Access/Master, Visa, Amex

Returns Procedures

Authority to Return: Maureen Legg
Stock Returns: Returns only accepted if still in saleable condition
Imperfect Returns: If damaged in transit or faulty goods supplied, will accept returns.

CADOGAN BOOKS

Mercury House, 195 Knightsbridge, London SW7 1RE
ISBN Prefix(es): 0 946313, 0 947754
Tel: 071-225 2050
Fax: 071-225 3008
VAT No: 493 4044 41

Orders to

GRANTHAM BOOK SERVICES LTD, Isaac Newton Way, Alma Park Industrial Estate, Grantham, Lincolnshire NG31 9SD
Tel: 0476 67421
Fax: 0476 590223

Order Information

All Dues Automatically Recorded
Representation Available
Invoice Payments: Grantham Book Services
Representation: World Leisure Marketing

Other Important Locations

Cadogan Chess & Bridge, 369 Euston Road, London NW1

Tel: 071-388 2404
Fax: 071-388 2407

Personnel
Head of Company: Bill Colegrave (Chairman & Managing Director)
Head of Marketing: James Johnson (Marketing Director)
Head of Accounts: Diana Whyte (Office Administrator)
Head of Customer Services: Jackie O'Sullivan

Number of titles published annually: 25
Percentage of Export Sales: 50%
Number of Staff: 5
All New Titles are Bar Coded
Book Data Subscriber
WBIP Updating: Diana Whyte

Trade Terms
35% (Subject to negotiation)
Credit Cards Accepted: Access/Master, Visa, Amex

Returns Procedures
Authority to Return: World Leisure Marketing Services Ltd
Address for Returns: Grantham Book Services
Imperfect Returns: Return title pages of any imperfect guide to Cadogan Books

CADW:WELSH HISTORIC MONUMENTS

Brunel House, Fitzalan Road, Cardiff, South Glamorgan CF2 1UY
Tel: 0222 465511
Fax: 0222 450859

CALDER PUBLICATIONS LTD

9-15 Neal Street, London WC2H 9TU
ISBN Prefix(es): 0 7145
Tel: 071-497 1741
VAT No: 577 3413 23

Orders to
COMBINED BOOK SERVICES, 406 Vale Road, Tonbridge, Kent TN9 1SW
Tel: 0732 357755
Fax: 0732 770219

Order Information
All Dues Automatically Recorded
Representation Available
Invoice Payments: Combined Book Services

Personnel
Head of Company: John Calder (Chairman & Managing Director)

PA Member
NBA Signatory
All New Titles are Bar Coded
WBIP Updating: Susan Herbert

Subsidiary Companies: Riverrun Press (US)

Trade Terms
General Net: Single copy/single line 20%, otherwise 35%
Other Terms: Carriage charged on overseas orders
BA/Girobank Small Order Scheme: Yes
Girobank Number: 304 3177
Credit Cards Accepted: Access/Master, Visa

Returns Procedures
Authority to Return: Calder Publications
Address for Returns: Combined Book Services
Stock Returns: Advise Combined Book Services prior to return

CALIBAN BOOKS: 193 BLAEN-CWMIAR LLANLLWNI, LLANYBYDDER, DYFED SA40 9SJ

Imperfect Returns: Price limit for title pages £15. Return title page with details of fault to Calder Publications Ltd

CALEDONIAN BOOKS
Slains House, Collieston, Ellon, Grampian AB41 8RT
Tel: 035 887 275
Tel: 035 887 288 Tel/Fax
VAT No: 297 2352 32

CALOUSTE GULBENKIAN FOUNDATION
98 Portland Place, London W1N 4ET
ISBN Prefix(es): 0 903319
Tel: 071-636 5313
Fax: 071-636 2948

Orders to
TURNAROUND, 27 Horsell Road, London N5 1XL
Tel: 071-609 7836/7
Fax: 071-700 1205

Order Information

Representation Available
Invoice Payments: Turnaround Distribution Ltd

Number of titles published annually: 5
Number of Staff: 2
All New Titles are Bar Coded
WBIP Updating: Millicent Bowerman

Trade Terms
Refer to Turnaround

CAMBRIDGE UNIVERSITY PRESS
The Edinburgh Building, Shaftesbury Road, Cambridge, Cambridgeshire CB2 2RU
ISBN Prefix(es): 0 521
Tel: 0223 312393
Fax: 0223 315052
Telex: 817256 CUPCAM G
VAT No: 214 1416 14
Account No: _0274081011_
Sales Rep: _____
Tel: _____

Rep:-
Ben Newbold
Rose Cottage
Barrack Common
Newnham
Hants
RG27 9NW.

Orders to
Tel: 0223 325970
Fax: 0223 325959

Order Information
Teleordering: CAMB

Order Dept Opening Times
Mon - Fri 9am - 5pm
Representation Available

Personnel
Head of Company: Jeremy Mynott (Managing Director)
Head of Sales (Home): Nigel Atkinson (UK Sales Director)
Head of Sales (Export): Nicholas Reckert (International Sales Director)
Head of Accounts: James Berry (Press Financial Director)
Head of Distribution: Ian Bradie (Distribution Director)
Head of Customer Services: Paul Driver (Trade Manager)
Other Important Personnel:
Michael Holdsworth (Sales & Publishing Operations Director), Charly Nobbs (Warehouse Director)

PA Member
NBA Signatory
All New Titles are Bar Coded
Book Data Subscriber
WBIP Updating: Mary Chaplin

Trade Terms
General Net: 35%
Academic Net: 35% on all paperbacks, 30% on hardbacks, 25% on hardback academic monographs
Non-Net: 17.5%
Girobank Number: 571 6055
Credit Cards Accepted: Access/Master, Amex, Diners, Visa, Other

Returns Procedures
Authority to Return: Must be obtained from Representative or the Sales Office
Address for Returns: Mark 'Returns Department'
Stock Returns: Any items supplied see-safe may be returned only if in mint condition & within 6 months (12 overseas) of invoice date
Imperfect Returns: Return items well packed quoting invoice no. For damaged pb return t/page only or damaged hb up to £25, t/page + cover

CAMDEN PRESS

46 Colebrooke Row, London N1 8AF
ISBN Prefix(es): 0 9488491
Tel: 071-226 2061
Fax: 071-226 2418

Personnel
Head of Company: Bob Borzello

Number of titles published annually: 10
Number of Staff: 2
All New Titles are Bar Coded

Parent Company: Camden Press Ltd

Trade Terms
35%
General Net: Single copy 20%, Pro forma under £25 trade order (after dis)
Minimum Order: For credit £25 trade net

Returns Procedures
Stock Returns: No SOR for proforma orders. No returns after 6 months

CAMPBELL BOOKS

12 Half Moon Court, London EC1A 7HE
ISBN Prefix(es): 1 85292
Tel: 071-600 1693
Fax: 071-600 2043
VAT No: 456 5503 40

Orders to
GRANTHAM BOOK SERVICES LTD, Isaac Newton Way, Alma Park Industrial Estate, Grantham, Lincolnshire NG31 9SD
Tel: 0476 67421
Fax: 0476 590223

Order Information

All Dues Automatically Recorded
Representation Available

Number of titles published annually: 20
All New Titles are Bar Coded
WBIP Updating: Mark Dicken

CAMPBELL MATTHEWS & CO LTD
30 Burghill Road, Sydenham, London SE26 4HN
Tel: 081-778 2091

Campion Press, 354 Lanark Road, Edinburgh, EH13 OLX
Tel:- 031 441 2006   A/C No 0149322

CAMPUS PUBLISHING
26 Tirellan Heights, Galway, County Galway
Tel: 091 24662
Tel: 091 67408

Canada Law Books, 240 Edward St, Aurora ONTARIO. L4S 359 CANADA

CANAL PUBLISHING CO LTD
23 Golden Square, London W1R 3PA
ISBN Prefix(es): 0 907237
Tel: 071-439 8639
Fax: 071-437 0696
Telex: 295929
VAT No: 242 5314 90

Order Information
Order Dept Opening Times
10am - 4pm
All Dues Automatically Recorded
Representation Available

Personnel
Head of Company: Mr Austen S Kark CBE (Chairman)
Head of Sales (Home): Mr Peter Bertolotti
Head of Accounts: Peter Betts
Head of Distribution: M Simon

Number of titles published annually: 6
Percentage of Export Sales: 40%
All New Titles are Bar Coded
WBIP Updating: M Simon

Trade Terms
General Net: Single copy/single line 20%, otherwise 35%
Minimum Order: 12 copies
Other Terms: Postage & packing, carriage charged

Returns Procedures
Authority to Return: M Simon

CANONGATE PRESS PLC
14 Frederick Street, Edinburgh, Lothian EH2 2HB
ISBN Prefix(es): 0 86241, 0 90002, 0 90393
Tel: 031-220 3800
Fax: 031-220 3888
Telex: 777582 TELRAY G
VAT No: 553 6634 30

Account No: _____
Sales Rep: _____
Tel: _____

Orders to
BOOKPOINT LIMITED, 39 Milton Park, Abingdon,
Oxfordshire OX14 4TD
Tel: 0235 835001
Fax: 0235 861038

Order Information
All Dues Automatically Recorded
Representation Available
Invoice Payments: Bookpoint

Personnel
Head of Company: Stephanie Wolfe Murray (Managing Director)

Head of Sales (Home): Joanne Rutherford (Sales & Publicity Manager)
Head of Accounts: Sheila McAinsh
Head of Customer Services: Sheila McAinsh

Number of titles published annually: 50
Number of Staff: 8
PA Member
All New Titles are Bar Coded
Open University Publications
WBIP Updating: Sarah Merrill Mowat

Trade Terms
35% on all orders except small orders
Other Terms: Carriage charges on orders under £30
Credit Cards Accepted: Access/Master, Visa, Amex

Returns Procedures
Authority to Return: Prior permission must be obtained from Canongate
Address for Returns: All returns must go to Bookpoint

CAPABILITY PUBLISHING

Sarah Greenwood Associates, 10/11 Lower John Street, London W1R 3PE
Tel: 071-734 0985
Fax: 071-287 5488
VAT No: 503 3410 05

CAPE (Jonathan) - Random Century

CAPITAL PLANNING INFORMATION LTD

52 High Street, St Martin's, Stamford, Lincolnshire PE9 2LG
ISBN Prefix(es): 0 906011
Tel: 0780 57300
Fax: 0780 54333
VAT No: 293 7880 06

Personnel
Head of Company: Don Kennington
Head of Sales (Home): Mrs Margaret Ashcroft

Number of titles published annually: 10
Number of Staff: 3
WBIP Updating: Mrs Margaret Ashcroft

Trade Terms
General Net: Two or more single titles 10-30% Two books or more 10%

Returns Procedures
Stock Returns: Agreement to be sought before returns sent
Imperfect Returns: Agreement to be sought before returns made

CAPITAL TRANSPORT PUBLISHING

38 Long Elmes, Harrow Weald, Middlesex HA3 5JL
ISBN Prefix(es): 0 904711, 1 85414
Tel: 081-427 4707
VAT No: 225 5774 52

Order Information

Order Dept Opening Times
Mon - Fri 9am - 5pm

Personnel
Head of Company: James Whiting (Managing Director)

Number of titles published annually: 15

Trade Terms
Single copy/single line 25%, otherwise 35%. Cash with order required for total net value below £15
BA/Girobank Small Order Scheme: Yes
Girobank Number: 318 5559

Returns Procedures
Imperfect Returns: Title page up to £10

CARCANET PRESS
208 Corn Exchange Buildings, Manchester, Greater Manchester M4 3BQ
ISBN Prefix(es): 0 85635, 0 902145, 1 85754
Tel: 061-834 8730
Fax: 061-832 0084

Account No: _____

Sales Rep: _____

Tel: _____

Orders to
LITTLEHAMPTON BOOK SERVICES, 14 Eldon Way, Lineside Ind Estate, Littlehampton, West Sussex BN17 7HE
Tel: 0903 721596
Fax: 0903 730914

Order Information

All Dues Automatically Recorded
Representation Available
Invoice Payments: Littlehampton
Representation: Cassell

Personnel
Head of Company: Michael Schmidt
Head of Sales (Home): Janette Walls
Head of Accounts: Barbara Welsh
Other Important Personnel:
Lucy Watkinson (Marketing & Sales Assistant)

Number of titles published annually: 40
Number of Staff: 5
All New Titles are Bar Coded
WBIP Updating: Janette Walls

Parent Company: Folio Holdings

Trade Terms
35% on all trade orders, no small order surcharge
Other Terms: Carriage charges on export only
Credit Cards Accepted: Access/Master, Visa

Returns Procedures
Authority to Return: Janette Walls
Address for Returns: Littlehampton
Imperfect Returns: Return the title page to Carcanet Press

CARGATE PRESS
25 Marylebone Road, London NW1 5JR
Tel: 071-486 5502
Fax: 071-935 1507

Parent Company: Methodist Church Overseas Division

CARLTON BOOKS
20 St Anne's Court, Wardour Street, London W1V 3AW
ISBN Prefix(es): 1 85868
Tel: 071-734 7338
Fax: 071-434 1196
VAT No: 605 8174 43

Account No: _____
Sales Rep: _____
Tel: _____

Personnel
Head of Company: Jonathan Goodman (Managing Director)
Head of Accounts: Lynn Mawdsley 071-499 8050
Head of Customer Services: Hilary Cohen (Sales Administrator)
Other Important Personnel:
John Maynard (Operations Director)

WBIP Updating: Hilary Cohen

Parent Company: Carlton Communications

CARNEGIE PUBLISHING LTD

18 Maynard Street, Preston, Lancashire PR2 2AL
ISBN Prefix(es): 0 948789, 1 874181
Tel: 0772 881246 24 Hours
Fax: 0772 881442
VAT No: 416 5244 66

IPG Member
NBA Signatory
All New Titles are Bar Coded
Book Data Subscriber

JON CARPENTER PUBLISHING

PO Box 129, 33 Newton Road, Oxford, Oxfordshire
OX1 4PH
Tel: 0865 790715 Tel/Fax
VAT No: 596 3374 96

Orders to
CENTRAL BOOKS, 99 Wallis Road, London E9 5LN
Tel: 081-986 4854
Fax: 081-533 5821

J L CARR

27 Milldale Road, Kettering, Northamptonshire NN15 6QD
ISBN Prefix(es): 0 900847
Tel: 0536 514995
VAT No: 121 5181 14

Order Information

All Dues Automatically Recorded

Personnel
Head of Company: J L Carr

Trade Terms
General Net: Single Copy 30%, 2 or more single titles 35%, 2 books or more 35-40%, Subscription orders 40%, stock orders 40%
Girobank Number: 49 014 4004

RD & JM CARR

17 Home Farm Lane, Bury St Edmunds, Suffolk IP33 2QJ
Tel: 0284 753228

CARRICK MEDIA
2/7 Galt House, 31 Bank Street, Irvine, Ayrshire KA12 0LL
ISBN Prefix(es): 0 946724
Tel: 0294 311322 Tel/Fax
VAT No: 383 5246 39

Order Information

Order Dept Opening Times
Mon - Fri 9am - 5pm
All Dues Automatically Recorded

Personnel
Head of Company: Kenneth Roy (Managing Editor)
Head of Customer Services: Fiona MacDonald

Number of titles published annually: 6
WBIP Updating: Fiona MacDonald

Trade Terms
40%

[Handwritten: CARSWELL - Corporate Plaza, 2075 Kennedy Road Scarborough - ONTARIO. M1T 3V4 - CANADA]

CASDEC LTD
Casdec House, 22 Harraton Terrace, Birtley, Chester-le-Street, County Durham DH3 2QG
Tel: 091-410 5556
Fax: 091-410 0229
VAT No: 353 9034 55

[Handwritten: CASCADE UNIT, LEICESTER COUNTY COUNCIL, COUNTY HALL, GLENFIELD, LEICS. LE3 8RF 0533 656688]

FRANK CASS & CO LTD
Gainsborough House, 11 Gainsborough Road, London
E11 1RS
ISBN Prefix(es): 0 7130, 0 7146, 0 85303
Tel: 081-530 4226
Fax: 081-530 7795
VAT No: 232 7273 75

Orders to
BIBLIOS PUBLISHERS DISTRIBUTION SERVICE LTD,
Star Road, Partridge Green, West Sussex RH13 8LD
Tel: 0403 710971
Fax: 0403 711143

Order Information

All Dues Automatically Recorded
Representation Available

Personnel
Head of Company: Frank Cass
Head of Sales (Home): Richard Norris
Head of Marketing: Hayley Osen
Head of Publicity: Fraser Lovatt (Marketing Manager - Books)
Head of Accounts: Mr M P Zaidner
Other Important Personnel:
Anne Kidson (Marketing - Journals)

Number of titles published annually: 35
WBIP Updating: Fraser Lovatt

Trade Terms
25% singles, 35% orders of 2 or more

Returns Procedures
Authority to Return: Richard Norris

CASSELL PLC
Villiers House, 41/47 Strand, London WC2N 5JE
ISBN Prefix(es): 0 225, 0 264, 0 289, 0 304, 0 7063, 0 7137, 0 7201, 0 8069, 0 85368, 0 910676, 1 85079, 1 85148, 1 85409

Tel: 071-839 4900
Fax: 071-839 1804
Cables: Cassell Pub
VAT No: 444 0594 55

Account No: ___928518___

Sales Rep: _____

Tel: _____

Orders to
CASSELL PLC, Stanley House, 3 Fleets Lane, Poole, Dorset BH15 3AJ
Tel: 0202 670581
Fax: 0202 666219

Order Information
Teleordering: CASS

Representation Available

Personnel
Head of Company: Philip Sturrock (Chairman & Managing Director)
Head of Sales (Home): Stephen Butcher (Sales & Marketing Director)
Head of Sales (Export): Jo Gill
Head of Marketing: Adrienne Maguire (Publicity & Promotion Director)
Head of Publicity: Jo Gill (General Publicity)
Other Important Personnel:
Alan Badger (Cassell Sales), Michael Goff (Gollancz Sales)

Number of titles published annually: 500
Percentage of Export Sales: 35%
Number of Staff: 140
PA Member
NBA Signatory
All New Titles are Bar Coded
Book Data Subscriber
WBIP Updating: Alan Smith

Trade Terms
From 35% (General) From 20% (Academic)
BA/Girobank Small Order Scheme: Contact Cassell plc for details
Credit Cards Accepted: Access/Master, Visa

Returns Procedures
Authority to Return: Prior permission required from Alan Badger or Michael Goff.
Address for Returns: Poole Warehouse
Stock Returns: No credit for o/p titles. Overstocks must be mint condition, otherwise credited at 65%. Unauthorised returns credit 65%.
Imperfect Returns: Return annotated title pages up to £13.99 cover price within 12 months of supply date, over £13.99 complete book.

CASSELL PLC
Stanley House, 3 Fleets Lane, Poole, Dorset BH15 3AJ
Tel: 0202 670581
Fax: 0202 666219

Account No: ___928518___

Sales Rep: _____

Tel: _____

Order Information
Teleordering: CASS

Order Dept Opening Times
Mon - Fri 8.30am - 5.30pm
Cyclical Ordering Policy
All Dues Automatically Recorded

Personnel
Head of Accounts: Norren Monga (Credit Control Manager)
Head of Distribution: Martyn Chapman
Head of Customer Services: Pat Brown

Trade Terms
BA/Girobank Small Order Scheme: Contact Cassell Plc for details
Girobank Number: 249 0250

Returns Procedures
Stock Returns: No credit for o/p titles, overstocks must be mint condition, otherwise credited at 65%. Unauthorised returns credit 65%.
Imperfect Returns: Return annotated title page up to £13.99 cover price within 12 months of supply date, over £13.99 complete book.

CASTEBERG

18 Yealand Avenue, Giggleswick, Settle, North Yorkshire BD24 0AY
Tel: 0729 822371

CASTLE BOOKS

Blackdown, Leamington Spa, Warwickshire CV32 6RA
ISBN Prefix(es): 0 95
Tel: 0926 428370

Order Information

Representation Available

Personnel
Head of Company: Margaret Bradshaw
Head of Sales (Home): O R Tring

IPG Member
All New Titles are Bar Coded
WBIP Updating: O R Tring

Trade Terms
Non-Net: Single copy /two or more single titles 10% Two books or more 35%
Credit Cards Accepted: Access/Master, Visa

Returns Procedures
Stock Returns: Return them with explanatory note
Imperfect Returns: Return them stating reason

KYLE CATHIE LTD

3 Vincent Square, London SW1P 2LX
ISBN Prefix(es): 1 85626
Tel: 071-834 8027
Tel: 071-233 6674
Fax: 071-821 9258
VAT No: 503 5737 60

Orders to
LITTLEHAMPTON BOOK SERVICES, 14 Eldon Way, Lineside Ind Estate, Littlehampton, West Sussex BN17 7HE
Tel: 0903 721596
Fax: 0903 730914

Order Information

All Dues Automatically Recorded
Representation Available
Invoice Payments: Littlehampton
Representation: Cassell

Personnel
Head of Company: Kyle Cathie
Head of Sales (Home): Laura Beckwith
Head of Accounts: Peter Cox

Number of titles published annually: 25
Percentage of Export Sales: 25%
Number of Staff: 2
All New Titles are Bar Coded
Book Data Subscriber
WBIP Updating: Sue Collins

Trade Terms
35% on all orders, no surcharges

Returns Procedures
Authority to Return: Kyle Cathie Ltd
Address for Returns: Littlehampton

CATHOLIC INSTITUTE FOR INTERNATIONAL RELATIONS (CIIR)
Unit 3, Canonbury Yard, 190A New North Road, London N1 7BJ
ISBN Prefix(es): 0 946848, 1 85287
Tel: 071-354 0883
Fax: 071-359 0017

Orders to
CENTRAL BOOKS, 99 Wallis Road, London E9 5LN
Tel: 081-986 4854
Fax: 081-533 5821

Order Information

All Dues Automatically Recorded
Representation Available
Invoice Payments: Central Books

Personnel
Head of Company: Ian Linden
Head of Sales (Export): Angela Warren
Head of Accounts: James Collins

Number of titles published annually: 10
All New Titles are Bar Coded
WBIP Updating: Angela Warren

Trade Terms
Enquiries to Central Books

Returns Procedures
Authority to Return: Central Books
Address for Returns: Central Books
Stock Returns: Enquiries to Central Books
Imperfect Returns: Enquiries to Central Books

CATHOLIC TRUTH SOCIETY
38/40 Eccleston Square, London SW1V 1PD
Tel: 071-834 4392
Tel: 071-834 1363
Fax: 071-630 5166
Telex: 29942 PAVIS G
Cables: APOSTOLIC LONDON SW1
VAT No: 238 9048 36

JOHN CATT EDUCATIONAL LTD
Great Glemham, Saxmundham, Suffolk IP17 2DH
ISBN Prefix(es): 1 869863
Tel: 0728 78666

Fax: 0728 78415
VAT No: 390 6161 53

Orders to
HUGO'S LANGUAGE BOOKS LTD, Old Station Yard, Marlesford, Woodbridge, Suffolk IP13 0AG
Tel: 0728 746546
Fax: 0728 746236

Order Information

Representation Available
Invoice Payments: Hugos Language Books Ltd

Personnel
Head of Company: J Evans (Managing Director)
Head of Marketing: J Wilding
Head of Publicity: S Downing
Head of Accounts: M Boast
Head of Distribution: C Evans

Number of titles published annually: 14
Number of Staff: 10
All New Titles are Bar Coded
WBIP Updating: C Evans

Trade Terms
Under £15 - 25%, Over £15 - 35%

Returns Procedures
Authority to Return: Hugo's Language Books Ltd
Address for Returns: Hugo's Language Books Ltd
Imperfect Returns: Send Title Page

CAUSEWAY PRESS LTD 129 New Court Way
PO Box 13, ~~48 Southport Road~~, Ormskirk, Lancashire L39 5HP
ISBN Prefix(es): 0 946183, 1 873929
Tel: 0695 576048
Tel: 0695 577360
Fax: 0695 570714
VAT No: 325 3357 70

A/C No 20107

Order Information

All Dues Automatically Recorded

Personnel
Head of Company: Michael Haralambos (Chairman)
Head of Accounts: Ingrid Hamer

Number of titles published annually: 12
Number of Staff: 6
IPG Member
All New Titles are Bar Coded
WBIP Updating: Michael Haralambos

Trade Terms
17.5% home 25% overseas, no surcharges. All titles are non-net.
Girobank Number: 67 383 7602

Returns Procedures
Authority to Return: Permission required from Causeway Press
Address for Returns: Trade Counter, The Airfield, Mendlesham, Suffolk IP14 5NA

PAUL CAVE PUBLICATIONS LTD
74 Bedford Place, Southampton, Hampshire SO1 2DF
ISBN Prefix(es): 0 86146
Tel: 0703 223591
Tel: 0703 333457
Fax: 0703 227190

Order Information

All Dues Automatically Recorded

Personnel
Head of Company: Paul Cave

Number of titles published annually: 10
Number of Staff: 6
All New Titles are Bar Coded

Trade Terms
33.3%, no surcharges
Other Terms: 30 days

CAVENDISH PUBLISHING LTD The Glass House, Wharton Street ~~23A Countess Road, London NW5 2XH~~ London WC1X 9PX
ISBN Prefix(es): 1 874241
Tel: ~~071-485-0303~~ 24 Hours 071 278 8000
Fax: ~~071-485-0304~~ 071 278 8080
VAT No: 544 7494 16

Account No: _____
Sales Rep: _____
Tel: _____

Order Information

Order Dept Opening Times
Mon - Fri 9am - 5.30pm
All Dues Automatically Recorded
Representation Available

Personnel
Head of Company: Jo Reddy (Managing Editor)
Head of Sales (Home): Sonny Leong (Publishing Director)
Head of Accounts: Mrs Kundan Rao
Head of Customer Services: Ms Diana Parry

Number of titles published annually: 55
Percentage of Export Sales: 30%
Number of Staff: 6
IPG Member
NBA Signatory
All New Titles are Bar Coded
WBIP Updating: Ms Jo Reddy

Trade Terms
30%
Academic Net: Single copies 20%
Credit Cards Accepted: Access/Master, Visa

Returns Procedures
Authority to Return: Head Office
Address for Returns: The Trade Counter Ltd, Unit D, Trading Estate Road, London NW10 7LU Tel: 081-963 0322
Stock Returns: Invoice numbers must be quoted, return whole copies
Imperfect Returns: Return annotated title page

CBD RESEARCH LTD

15 Wickham Road, Beckenham, Kent BR3 2JS
ISBN Prefix(es): 0 900246
Tel: 081-650 7745
Fax: 081-650 0768
VAT No: 205 4233 08

Order Information

All Dues Automatically Recorded

Personnel
Head of Company: G P Henderson (Managing Director)

Head of Sales (Home): C A P Henderson (Sales Director)
Head of Accounts: Mrs S F Henderson (Accounts Manager)

Number of titles published annually: 4
Percentage of Export Sales: 20%
Number of Staff: 7
IPG Member
WBIP Updating: G P Henderson

Trade Terms
20%
Credit Cards Accepted: Access/Master, Visa, Other

Returns Procedures
Stock Returns: By negotiation
Imperfect Returns: Imperfect copies replaced on return of complete volume. Any damaged in post must be returned promptly with packing

CCBI PUBLICATIONS

The Bookroom Interchurch House, 35-41 Lower Marsh, London SE1 7RL
ISBN Prefix(es): 0 85169
Tel: 071-620 4444
Fax: 071-928 0010
Telex: 916504 CHRAID G
VAT No: 239 4759 22

Order Information

Order Dept Opening Times
Mon - Fri 9.30am - 4.30pm
All Dues Automatically Recorded
Representation Available

Personnel
Head of Company: Rev John Reardon (General Secretary CCBI)
Head of Sales (Home): Derek A Collins (Sales Manager)
Head of Accounts: Richard Bong

Number of titles published annually: 10
Number of Staff: 3
WBIP Updating: Derek A Collins

Parent Company: Council of Churches for Britain & Ireland

Trade Terms
35% carriage free over £30 invoice value
Other Terms: Small order surcharge on less than £30 invoice

Returns Procedures
Authority to Return: Derek A Collins
Stock Returns: No returns without prior permission. Please apply for terms and conditions
Imperfect Returns: Title page only returned with full details of imperfection.

CCH EDITIONS

Telford Road, Bicester, Oxfordshire OX6 0XD
ISBN Prefix(es): 0 86325
Tel: 0869 253300
Fax: 0869 245814
VAT No: 233 1779 67
Account No: 0770172
Sales Rep: ___
Tel: ___

Order Information

Order Dept Opening Times
Mon - Fri 8.30am - 4.45pm

All Dues Automatically Recorded
Representation Available

Personnel
Head of Company: Barrie McKay (Managing Director)
Head of Sales (Home): Michael Bennett (General Sales Manager)
Head of Sales (Export): Adrian Magson (Regional Manager - Europe)
Head of Marketing: David Broome (Marketing Manager)
Head of Accounts: Christopher Whitehead (Company Secretary)
Head of Distribution: John Flint (Production Manager)
Head of Customer Services: Julie Peterkin (Customer Services Manager)
Other Important Personnel:
Angela Gibbs (Manager - Books Division), David Hammond-Medhurst (Education Sales), Robert Wilson (Product Manager), David McKail (Manager - Bookshop Sales)

Number of titles published annually: 700
Number of Staff: 7180
Book Data Subscriber
WBIP Updating: Angela Gibbs

Parent Company: Commerce Clearing House Inc

Trade Terms
35%
Other Terms: Carriage Charges: 20% p&p outside Europe
Credit Cards Accepted: Access/Master, Amex, Diners, Visa

Returns Procedures
Authority to Return: Returns Note must be requested from Customer Services Dept & returned completed with books in a saleable condition
Imperfect Returns: Return complete copies

CEDAR TREE HOUSE
7-9 Church Hill, Loughton, Essex IG10 1QP
Tel: 081-508 8856 Tel/Fax
VAT No: 466 6561 14

Order Information
Teleordering: CEDARTH

Order Dept Opening Times
Mon - Fri 9am - 1pm, 2pm - 5pm
All Dues Automatically Recorded
Representation Available

Personnel
Head of Company: Roger Barnett
Head of Accounts: M L Barnett

Number of titles published annually: 10
Percentage of Export Sales: 20%
IPG Member
WBIP Updating: R Barnett

Trade Terms
15%
Credit Cards Accepted: Amex

Returns Procedures
Stock Returns: No returns except by prior arrangement

CELEBRATION SERVICES LTD
Berry House, 58 High Street, Bletchingley, Redhill, Surrey RH1 4PA
ISBN Prefix(es): 0 906309
Tel: 0883 743737 24 Hours

Fax: 0883 744721
VAT No: 392 9085 16

Order Information

Order Dept Opening Times
Mon - Fri 9.30am - 4.30pm

Trade Terms
35% some items 25% some items
Other Terms: Carriage Charge: 10% of retail value subject to min of 50p and max of £3

CENTAUR PRESS LTD

Fontwell, Sussex BN18 0TA
ISBN Prefix(es): 0 900000, 0 900001
Tel: 0243 543302
VAT No: 193 4081 59

Order Information

All Dues Automatically Recorded

Personnel
Head of Company: T J L Wynne-Tyson

Number of titles published annually: 4
Number of Staff: 1

Trade Terms
Except for subscription orders, 5% discount for CWO.
General Net: Single copy 20%, 2 or more single titles 25%, 2 books or more 30%, subscription/stock orders 35%.
Other Terms: Full retail price charged, but no postage, if book price £5 or less (singles). Below £50 invoice value postage charged.

Returns Procedures
Stock Returns: If the fault is not the publisher's, prior notification required. Please state what the fault is.
Imperfect Returns: Whole book must be returned.

CENTRAL BOOKS

99 Wallis Road, London E9 5LN
ISBN Prefix(es): 0 7417
Tel: 081-986 4854 24 Hours
Fax: 081-533 5821
Cables: CEN Books London E9
VAT No: 232 2069 02
Account No: _____ 301145 _____
Sales Rep: _____
Tel: _____

Order Information
Teleordering: CEBK

Order Dept Opening Times
Mon/Tue 9am - 5pm Fri 9am - 4pm
Orders for more than one publisher can be bulked
All Dues Automatically Recorded
Representation Available

Personnel
Head of Company: William James Norris
Head of Sales (Home): Mark Chilver
Head of Publicity: Kirstie Kemp
Head of Accounts: Hamid Moheebob
Head of Distribution: David Crystal
Other Important Personnel:
David Cope (Credit Control)

Number of titles published annually: 250
Number of Staff: 15

Open University Publications
WBIP Updating: Mark Chilver

Trade Terms
35% orders under £30 retail, surcharge 15% of invoice value.
Subscribed orders are not surcharged
Girobank Number: 56 510 0009
Credit Cards Accepted: Access/Master, Visa

Returns Procedures
Authority to Return: Mark Chilver
Imperfect Returns: Title page accepted up to £10

CENTRAL BUREAU FOR EDUCATIONAL VISITS & EXCHANGES

Seymour Mews House, Seymour Mews, London W1H 9PE
ISBN Prefix(es): 0 900087
Tel: 071-486 5101
Tel: 071-725 9448 Orders
Fax: 071-935 5741

Order Information

Order Dept Opening Times
Mon- Fri 9.15am - 5.30pm
All Dues Automatically Recorded
Orders To:Print, Marketing & IT Unit

Personnel
Head of Company: Antony H Male

Number of titles published annually: 4
Number of Staff: 5
PA Member
NBA Signatory
All New Titles are Bar Coded

Trade Terms
35%, Single Orders 20%
Credit Cards Accepted: Access/Master, Visa

CENTRAL LAW TRAINING LTD

Centre City Tower, 7 Hill Street, Birmingham, West Midlands B5 4UA
ISBN Prefix(es): 1 85811
Tel: 021-633 4440
Fax: 021-616 1006

Order Information

Order Dept Opening Times
Mon - Fri 9.30am - 5pm
All Dues Automatically Recorded

Personnel
Head of Company: Peter A Turtle

Number of titles published annually: 20
All New Titles are Bar Coded

Trade Terms
20% all orders, or by negotiation
Credit Cards Accepted: Access/Master, Visa

Returns Procedures
Authority to Return: Prior permission required
Address for Returns: The Trade Counter Ltd, Unit D, Trading Estate Road, London NW10 7LU

CENTRE FOR BUSINESS RESEARCH

Manchester Business School, Booth Street West, Manchester, Greater Manchester M15 6PB

Tel: 061-275 6561
Fax: 061-273 7732

*[Handwritten: FAX: 010 331 4347 5943
Centre D'Exportation Du Livre Francais (CELF)
9, Rue de Toul, 75012, Paris. FRANCE   A/C No 084524]*

CENTRE FOR INDEPENDENT TRANSPORT RESEARCH IN LONDON (CILT)

3rd Floor, Universal House, 88-94 Wentworth Street,
London E1 7SA
Tel: 071-247 1302
Fax: 071-247 4725

CENTRE FOR INFORMATION ON LANGUAGE TEACHING & RESEARCH

20 Bedfordbury, London WC2N 4LB
ISBN Prefix(es): 0 903466, 0 948003, 0 9500528, 1 874016
Tel: 071-379 5101
Fax: 071-379 5082

Orders to
CILT Mail Order, PO Box 8, Llandysul, Dyfed SA44 4ZB

Order Information

All Dues Automatically Recorded

Personnel
Head of Company: Dr L King (Director)
Head of Sales (Home): Ute Hitchin (Head of Publications)
Head of Accounts: Tina Thorpe (Head of Finance)

Number of titles published annually: 15
Number of Staff: 18
PA Member
Book Data Subscriber
WBIP Updating: Ute Hitchin

Trade Terms
15%

Returns Procedures
Authority to Return: CILT Mail Order

CENTRE FOR JEWISH EDUCATION

80 East End Road, Finchley, London N3 2SY
Tel: 081-343 4303
Fax: 081-349 0694

CENTRE FOR POLICY ON AGEING

25-31 Ironmonger Row, London EC1V 3QP
Tel: 071-253 1787
Fax: 071-490 4206
VAT No: 524 9245 41

Orders to
BAILEY DISTRIBUTION LTD, Unit 1, Learoyd Road,
Mountfield Rd Ind Est, New Romney, Kent TN28 8XU
Tel: 0679 66905
Fax: 0679 66638

IPG Member

CENTRE FOR URBAN & REGIONAL RESEARCH

University of Sussex, Brighton, East Sussex BN1 9QN
Tel: 0273 678473
Fax: 0273 678466

Order Information
Orders To: Mrs M Wooll, Arts E
Tel: 0273 606755 Ext 2402

CESARA PUBLICATIONS
Clonegal Castle, Enniscorthy, County Wexford
Tel: 054 77552

Personnel
Head of Company: Baron Strathloch
Head of Publicity: Hon Olivia Robertson

Trade Terms
30%

CHADWYCK-HEALEY LTD THE QUORUM, BARNWELL RD
~~Cambridge PLace, Cambridge, Cambridgeshire CB2 1NR~~ CAMBRIDGE CB5 8SW
ISBN Prefix(es): 0 85964
Tel: ~~0223 311479~~ Tel 0223 215512
~~**Fax:** 0223 66440~~ FAX 0223 215513 (All Depts)
~~**Fax:** 0223 301278~~ Sales Dept 0223 215514 (Sales)
Telex: 9312102281 CHG 0223 215515 (Cust. Serv.)
VAT No: 214 2891 76
Account No: _____
Sales Rep: _____
Tel: _____

Order Information

Order Dept Opening Times
Mon - Fri 9am - 5pm
All Dues Automatically Recorded

Personnel
Head of Company: Sir Charles Chadwyck-Healey
Head of Sales (Home): Steven Hall
Head of Publicity: John Russell
Head of Accounts: Don McCrae
Head of Distribution: Nick Laskey

Number of titles published annually: 30
Number of Staff: 50
Book Data Subscriber
WBIP Updating: John Russell

Trade Terms
Please apply to publisher
Girobank Number: 373 4250

Returns Procedures
Imperfect Returns: Return complete book

Chalcombe - Highwoods Drive, Marlow Bottom,
Marlow. Bucks. SL7 3PU
CHALCOMBE PUBLICATIONS
Church Lane, Kingston, Canterbury, Kent CT4 6HX
Tel: 0227 830158
Tel: 0223 813470
Fax: 0233 813320
VAT No: 385 7963 86

CHALKSOFT LTD
PO Box 49, Spalding, Lincolnshire PE11 1NZ
ISBN Prefix(es): 1 85116
Tel: 0775 769518 24 Hours
Fax: 0775 769518 24 Hours
VAT No: 379 4075 16

Order Information

Order Dept Opening Times
Mon - Fri 9am - 4.30pm
All Dues Automatically Recorded
Representation Available

Personnel
Head of Company: David Baldwin
Head of Sales (Home): Gillian Baldwin

Number of titles published annually: 10
Number of Staff: 4
IPG Member
All New Titles are Bar Coded
WBIP Updating: David Baldwin

Trade Terms
35% Orders under £20 retail 25% plus carriage
Credit Cards Accepted: Access/Master, Visa

Returns Procedures
Authority to Return: Contact Gillian Baldwin

W & R CHAMBERS LTD — order to Macmillan
43-45 Annandale Street, Edinburgh, Lothian EH7 4AZ
ISBN Prefix(es): 0 550, 0 86267, 1 85296
Tel: 031-557 4571
Fax: 031-557 2936
Telex: 727967
VAT No: 268 3443 39
Account No: _____0049061_____
Sales Rep: _____
Tel: _____

Order Information
Teleordering: CHAMBER

All Dues Automatically Recorded
Representation Available

Personnel
Head of Company: Mr John Clement (Chairman)
Head of Sales (Home): Mr Chris McLaren (Sales & Marketing Director)
Head of Sales (Export): Mr Richard Drew (Director)
Head of Publicity: Mrs Linda Orton (Marketing Manager)
Head of Accounts: Mrs Marion King (Financial Controller)
Head of Distribution: Mrs Lavinia Drew (Administration Manager)
Other Important Personnel:
Dr T M Shepherd (Managing Director)

Number of titles published annually: 45
Number of Staff: 59
PA Member
NBA Signatory
All New Titles are Bar Coded
Book Data Subscriber
WBIP Updating: Linda Orton

Parent Company: Groupe de la Cite

Trade Terms
35%
Other Terms: Small order surcharge £2 on orders under £30 net value
Girobank Number: 158 3050
Credit Cards Accepted: Access/Master, Visa

CHANGE PUBLICATIONS
49 Mucklestone Wood Lane, Loggerheads, Market Drayton, Shropshire TF9 4ED
ISBN Prefix(es): 0 9511519
Tel: 0630 872370

Order Information

Order Dept Opening Times
Mon - Fri 9am - 5pm

Personnel
Head of Company: Dr J R Hegarty 0630 653912
Head of Sales (Home): Mr R W DeCann

Number of titles published annually: 2
All New Titles are Bar Coded
WBIP Updating: Dr J R Hegarty

Trade Terms
35% no surcharges

Returns Procedures
Imperfect Returns: £15

CHAPMAN
4 Broughton Place, Edinburgh, Lothian EH1 3RX
Tel: 031-557 2207

CHAPMAN & HALL
2-6 Boundary Row, London SE1 8HN
ISBN Prefix(es): 0 412, 0 419, 0 718, 0 948
Tel: 071-865 0066
Fax: 071-522 9623
Telex: 290 164 CHAPMAG
VAT No: 198 9232 09
Account No: 0305(6)1.0001
Sales Rep: _____
Tel: _____

Orders to
INTERNATIONAL THOMSON PUBLISHING SERVICES LTD, Cheriton House, North Way, Andover, Hampshire SP10 5BE
Tel: 0264 332424
Fax: 0264 364418

Order Information

All Dues Automatically Recorded
Representation Available
Invoice Payments: International Thomson Publishing Services

Personnel
Head of Company: David Inglis (Managing Director)
Head of Sales (Home): Nick Perry (Sales Manager)
Head of Sales (Export): Graham Boaler/Mima Birks (Export Sales Managers)
Head of Marketing: John Lavender (Sales & Marketing Director)
Head of Accounts: Aileen Davis (Finance Director)

Number of titles published annually: 400
Percentage of Export Sales: 50%
Number of Staff: 160
PA Member
NBA Signatory
All New Titles are Bar Coded
Open University Publications
Book Data Subscriber
WBIP Updating: Peter Clay

Parent Company: International Thomson
Subsidiary Companies: Routledge

Trade Terms
25%
Girobank Number: 209 6919
Credit Cards Accepted: Access/Master, Amex, Diners, Visa

Returns Procedures
Authority to Return: Prior permission Required
Address for Returns: ITPS
Imperfect Returns: Return whole book

PAUL CHAPMAN PUBLISHING

144 Liverpool Road, London N1 1LA
ISBN Prefix(es): 1 85396
Tel: 071-609 5315
Tel: 071-609 5316
Fax: 071-700 1057
VAT No: 480 6433 45

Orders to
PLYMBRIDGE DISTRIBUTORS LTD, Plymbridge House, Estover Road, Plymouth, Devon PL6 7PZ
Tel: 0752 735251
Fax: 0752 695699

A/C 705771

Order Information

All Dues Automatically Recorded
Invoice Payments: Plymbridge

Personnel
Head of Company: Paul Chapman (Managing Director)
Head of Sales (Home): Joyce Lynch

Number of titles published annually: 25
Percentage of Export Sales: 25%
IPG Member
All New Titles are Bar Coded
Open University Publications
WBIP Updating: Joyce Lynch

Trade Terms
20-30% no surcharges
Credit Cards Accepted: Access/Master, Visa, Amex

Returns Procedures
Address for Returns: Plymbridge
Stock Returns: Permission required: request must be within 6 months of invoice date. no credit for copies not in mint condition.
Imperfect Returns: Cover and title page returned: reason of imperfection to be stated

CHAPMANS PUBLISHERS LTD

141-143 Drury Lane, London WC2B 5TB
Tel: 071-379 9799
Fax: 071-497 2728
VAT No: 523 1919 60

Account No: _____
Sales Rep: _____
Tel: _____

Orders to
MACMILLAN DISTRIBUTION LTD, Brunel Road, Houndmills Industrial Estate, Basingstoke, Hampshire RG21 2XS
Tel: 0256 29242
Fax: 0256 842004

Personnel
Head of Company: Ian Chapman (Chairman & Managing Director)
Head of Sales (Home): David North (Sales Director)
Head of Marketing: Greg Hill (Marketing Director)
Head of Accounts: Graham Brown (Finance Director)

Number of Staff: 24
PA Member
NBA Signatory
Book Data Subscriber

Trade Terms
35%

Returns Procedures
Address for Returns: Macmillan Distribution

CHAPTER TWO

13 Plum Lane, Plumstead Common, London SE18 3AF
Tel: 081-316 5389
Fax: 081-854 5963
VAT No: 527 4079 39

DEBORAH CHARLES PUBLICATIONS

173 Mather Avenue, Liverpool, Merseyside L18 6JZ
ISBN Prefix(es): 0 9513793
Tel: 051-724 2500
VAT No: 453 9495 11

Order Information

Order Dept Opening Times
Mon - Fri 9am - 5pm

Personnel
Head of Company: B S Jackson
Head of Sales (Home): R Jackson

Number of titles published annually: 2
IPG Member
Book Data Subscriber
WBIP Updating: B S Jackson

Trade Terms
25% on all orders
Credit Cards Accepted: Access/Master, Visa

Returns Procedures
Authority to Return: Prior permission required

[handwritten annotation: Chartec Books (Inst of Chartered Accountants) 399 Silbury Road, Central Milton Keynes MK9 2HL A/C No 17307]

THE CHARTERED BUILDING SOCIETIES INSTITUTE

19 Baldock Street, Ware, Hertfordshire SG12 9DH
Tel: 0920 465051
Fax: 0920 460016
VAT No: 215 4968 46

CHARTERED INSTITUTE OF PURCHASING & SUPPLY

Easton House, Easton on the Hill, Stamford, Lincolnshire PE9 3NZ
ISBN Prefix(es): 0 900607
Tel: 0780 56777 24 Hours
Fax: 0780 51610
Telex: 32251
VAT No: 342 6489 42

Order Information

Order Dept Opening Times
Mon - Fri 9am - 5pm
All Dues Automatically Recorded
Representation Available

Personnel
Head of Company: Mr Peter Thomson (Director General)
Head of Sales (Home): Bridget Yardley (Bookshop Manager)
Head of Marketing: Mr Jim McColl (Marketing Manager)
Head of Accounts: Mr Malcolm Croft (Accountant)

Number of titles published annually: 3
Number of Staff: 4
WBIP Updating: Bridget Yardley

Subsidiary Companies: IPS Study Services

Trade Terms
10%
Credit Cards Accepted: Access/Master, Visa

Returns Procedures
Authority to Return: CIPS Bookshop

CHARTWELL-BRATT (PUBLISHING & TRAINING) LTD

Old Orchard, Bickley Road, Bromley, Kent BR1 2NE
ISBN Prefix(es): 0 86238
Tel: 081-467 1956
Fax: 081-467 1754
VAT No: 299 4102 33

A/C No SM18

Order Information

Order Dept Opening Times
9am - 5.30pm
All Dues Automatically Recorded

Personnel
Head of Company: Kevin Munro (Managing Director)
Head of Accounts: Doreen Rossiter
Head of Customer Services: Gloria Jacobs
Other Important Personnel:
Philip Yorke (Director of Publishing)

Number of titles published annually: 30
Percentage of Export Sales: 20%
All New Titles are Bar Coded
WBIP Updating: Philip Yorke

Parent Company: Studentlitteratur ab

Trade Terms
30%, no surcharges
Credit Cards Accepted: Access/Master, Visa

Returns Procedures
Authority to Return: Gloria Jacobs
Address for Returns: "The Trade Counter", The Airfield, Norwich Road, Mendlesham Suffolk, IP14 5NA
Stock Returns: First send returns request to Gloria Jacobs. Upon approval send returns to warehouse

ZELDA CHEATLE PRESS

8 Cecil Court, London WC2N 4HE
ISBN Prefix(es): 0 951837
Tel: 071-836 0507
Fax: 071-497 8911
VAT No: 577 3318 17

Order Information

All Dues Automatically Recorded
Representation Available

Personnel
Head of Company: Zelda Cheatle
Head of Sales (Home): Ronnie Scott Simpson
Head of Accounts: Michael Mack

Number of titles published annually: 1
Percentage of Export Sales: 25%
WBIP Updating: R S Simpson

Trade Terms
35% on all orders
Credit Cards Accepted: Access/Master, Visa

Returns Procedures
Stock Returns: No returns unless authorised

CHECKMATE PUBLICATIONS
PO Box 585, Chester, Cheshire CH3 7TF
ISBN Prefix(es): 0 946973, 1 85313
Tel: 0829 40540 24 Hours

THE CHESS PLAYER
12 Burton Avenue, Carlton, Nottinghamshire NG4 1PT
ISBN Prefix(es): 0 900928, 0 906042
Tel: 0602 871891
VAT No: 385 4563 20

Personnel
Head of Company: A J Gillam

Number of titles published annually: 6
Percentage of Export Sales: 80%

Trade Terms
General Net: Single copies 25%, 2 or more single titles 35%, 2 books or more 35%, stock orders 35%, special orders ask.
Girobank Number: 450 4151
Credit Cards Accepted: Amex

Returns Procedures
Imperfect Returns: No price limit for title pages

THE CHEVERELL PRESS
Manor Studios, Manningford Abbots, Pewsey, Wiltshire SN9 6HS
ISBN Prefix(es): 1 872390
Tel: 0672 63163
Fax: 0672 64301
VAT No: 521 9185 51

Order Information

Order Dept Opening Times
Mon - Fri 9am - 5pm
All Dues Automatically Recorded

Personnel
Head of Company: S De Larrinaga
Other Important Personnel:
Ms Lisa Giles (Orders & Enquiries)

Number of titles published annually: 4
Number of Staff: 2
All New Titles are Bar Coded

Trade Terms
General Net: Single copy 20%, Two or more 35%

Returns Procedures
Imperfect Returns: Please return whole book

FRANCIS CHICHESTER LTD

9 St James's Place, London SW1A 1PE
Tel: 071-493 0931 24 Hours
Tel: 071-493 0932
Fax: 071-409 1830
VAT No: 238 5801 50

Order Information

Order Dept Opening Times
Mon - Fri 9am - 1pm, 2pm - 5.30pm
Representation Available

Personnel
Head of Company: Mr G B Chichester
Head of Sales (Home): Miss M Cooper
Head of Accounts: Mrs V Chichester

Number of titles published annually: 3
Number of Staff: 4

Trade Terms
35% Nett monthly, 40% on orders 50+ copies
Other Terms: Carriage Charges at cost

Returns Procedures
Stock Returns: Return for Credit Note
Imperfect Returns: Guides must be returned for a Credit Note

THE CHILDREN'S SOCIETY

Edward Rudolf House, Margery Street, London WC1X 0JL
ISBN Prefix(es): 0 907324
Tel: 071-837 4299
Fax: 071-837 0211
VAT No: 237 4799 22

Order Information

Order Dept Opening Times
Mon - Fri 9am - 6pm
All Dues Automatically Recorded
Representation Available

Personnel
Head of Company: Annabel Warburg (Publications Editor)

Number of titles published annually: 15
Number of Staff: 3
PA Member
IPG Member
WBIP Updating: Ravi Wickremasinghe

Trade Terms
15% on all non-net titles (negotiable)

Returns Procedures
Imperfect Returns: £2 price limit

CHILD'S PLAY (INTERNATIONAL) LTD

Ashworth Road, Bridgemead, Swindon, Wiltshire SN5 7YD
ISBN Prefix(es): 0 85953
Tel: 0793 616286
Fax: 0793 512795
VAT No: 194 4604 47

Account No: _____
Sales Rep: _____
Tel: _____

Trade Terms
35%
Minimum Order: £50

Other Terms: Small order surcharge 20% P&P Carriage Charges on all orders below £50 net
Girobank Number: 295 9151
Credit Cards Accepted: Access/Master, Visa

Returns Procedures
Authority to Return: Prior permission required

[handwritten: Chiltern Society Footpath Maps = Shire Publications]

CHILTON DESIGNS PUBLISHERS

Preston House, Kentisbury, Barnstaple, Devon EX31 4NH
ISBN Prefix(es): 0 9503527
Tel: 0271 882875
Fax: 0271 882235
VAT No: 307 0922 82

Order Information

All Dues Automatically Recorded

Personnel
Head of Company: V Coleman
Head of Sales (Home): S Ward

Number of titles published annually: 2
Number of Staff: 3
All New Titles are Bar Coded
WBIP Updating: Sue Ward

Trade Terms
35% Single copy & overseas orders 25%

Returns Procedures
Authority to Return: Contact Sue Ward
Stock Returns: Replace or credit

CHIVERS PRESS LTD

Windsor Bridge Road, Bath, Avon BA2 3AX
ISBN Prefix(es): 0 7451, 0 85594, 0 85997, 0 86220
Tel: 0225 335336
Fax: 0225 310771
Telex: 444633
VAT No: 318 7863 24
Account No: _____ *[handwritten: 003SM02]* _____
Sales Rep: _____
Tel: _____

Order Information
Teleordering: CHIV

Order Dept Opening Times
Mon - Fri 9am - 12.30pm 1pm - 5pm
Representation Available

Personnel
Head of Company: Roger Lewis (Managing Director)
Head of Sales (Home): Chris Fernie (Sales Manager)
Head of Publicity: Lesley Barnes (Production Manager)
Head of Accounts: Alastair Prescott (Chief Accountant)
Head of Customer Services: Terry Dove (Customer Services Manager)
Other Important Personnel:
Julian Batson (Publishing Director)

Number of titles published annually: 1000
Number of Staff: 70
NBA Signatory
WBIP Updating: Christine Graham

Allied Companies: Curley Publishing Inc (US)

Trade Terms
Single copy 25%, Two or more 35%

Returns Procedures
Stock Returns: Quote invoice and order number
Imperfect Returns: Quote invoice and order number

THE CHRISTADELPHIAN MAGAZINE & PUBLISHING ASSOCIATION LTD
404 Shaftmoor Lane, Hall Green, Birmingham, West Midlands B28 8SZ
Tel: 021-777 6328
Tel: 021-777 6324
Fax: 021-778 5024
VAT No: 109 7692 42

CHRISTCHURCH PUBLISHERS LTD
2 Caversham Street, London SW3
ISBN Prefix(es): 0 284
Tel: 071-351 4995 Tel/Fax
Tel: 071-351 5932
VAT No: 497 6045 05

Order Information

All Dues Automatically Recorded
Representation Available

Personnel
Head of Company: Leonard Holdsworth
Head of Sales (Home): Jane Hughes
Head of Sales (Export): James Hughes
Head of Publicity: Jessica Allen
Head of Accounts: Joan Holdsworth

Number of titles published annually: 20
Percentage of Export Sales: 50%
Number of Staff: 7
All New Titles are Bar Coded
WBIP Updating: J Holdsworth

Subsidiary Companies: Caversham, Communications Ltd

Trade Terms
Single Copy 25%, Two or more 35%
Other Terms: Postage & Package charged on small orders
Credit Cards Accepted: Access/Master, Visa, Amex, Diners

Returns Procedures
Authority to Return: J Holdsworth
Stock Returns: Only by prior agreement

CHRISTIAN BOOK PROMOTION TRUST
The Market House, Cantelupe Road, East Grinstead, West Sussex RH19 3BH
ISBN Prefix(es): 1 873367
Tel: 0342 312750 24 Hours
Tel: 0342 715889

Order Information

Order Dept Opening Times
Mon - Fri 9am - 5pm
All Dues Automatically Recorded
Representation Available

Personnel
Head of Company: Eric Thorn
Head of Accounts: Dick Martin

Number of titles published annually: 2
WRIP Updating: Eric Thorn

Trade Terms
35%, no surcharges, no pro-forma invoices

Returns Procedures
Imperfect Returns: Return title page (no price limit)

CHRISTIAN BOOKSTALL MANAGERS' ASSOCIATION
c/o 277 Ewell Road, Surbiton, Surrey KT6 7AB
ISBN Prefix(es): 0 95115
Tel: 0342 715889 Cust Serv

Orders to
17 Rowan Walk, Crawley Down, West Sussex RH10 4JP

Order Information

Order Dept Opening Times
Mon - Fri 9am - 5pm
All Dues Automatically Recorded

Personnel
Head of Company: Harry Hunter (Chairman)
Head of Sales (Home): Eric Thorn (Vice Chairman)

Number of titles published annually: 1
WBIP Updating: Eric Thorn

Trade Terms
35%, under £10 retail value - postage charged extra at cost

Returns Procedures
Authority to Return: Eric Thorn
Imperfect Returns: Return Title Page

CHRISTIAN FOCUS PUBLICATIONS LTD
Geanies House, Fearn, Tain, Highland IV20 1TW
Tel: 0862 87541
Fax: 0862 87532
VAT No: 268 1092 52

CHRISTIAN LITERATURE CRUSADE
51 The Dean, Alresford, Hampshire SO24 9BJ
ISBN Prefix(es): 0 900284
Tel: 0962 733142
Tel: 0800 373755 Orders
Fax: 0962 733141
VAT No: 208 0352 02

Orders to
24 Hour Ansafone Number: 0800 373755

Order Information

Order Dept Opening Times
Mon - Fri 9am - 5.30pm
Representation Available

Personnel
Head of Sales (Home): P M Hayward (Wholesale Director)
0962 732402
Head of Accounts: Mrs G Scott (Cashier)

All New Titles are Bar Coded
WBIP Updating: P M Hayward

Trade Terms
35%
Credit Cards Accepted: Access/Master, Visa

Returns Procedures
Stock Returns: Approved returns in mint condition only
Imperfect Returns: Title page only

CHRISTIAN MUSIC MINISTRIES
325 Bromford Road, Hodge Hill, Birmingham, West Midlands B36 8ET
Tel: 021-783 3291 Tel/Fax
VAT No: 377 3900 28

THE CHRISTIAN SCIENCE PUBLISHING SOCIETY
Monitor House, 20 Beulah Road, London SW19 3SU
Tel: 081-543 9393
Fax: 081-545 0392
VAT No: 444 0445 72

CHRISTIE'S WINE PUBLICATIONS
8 King Street, St James's, London SW1Y 6QT
ISBN Prefix(es): 0 903432
Tel: 071-839 9060
Fax: 071-839 7869
Telex: 916429 INTART G
VAT No: 503 3060 06

Personnel
Head of Company: J M Broadbent
Head of Sales (Home): Mrs R Ward

Number of titles published annually: 2
WBIP Updating: R Ward

Parent Company: Christie, Manson & Woods Ltd

Trade Terms
33.3% + postage on more than 1 copy
Credit Cards Accepted: Access/Master, Visa, Amex, Diners

CHTHONIOS BOOKS
7 Tamarisk Steps, Hastings, East Sussex TN34 3DN
Tel: 0424 433302
VAT No: 530 7954 39

CHURCH HOUSE PUBLISHING
Great Smith Street, London SW1P 3NZ
ISBN Prefix(es): 0 7151, 0 901819
Tel: 071-222 9011
Fax: 071-799 2714
VAT No: 491 5547 22

Orders to
The Canterbury Press, St Mary's Works, St Mary's Plain, Norwich, Norfolkshire NR3 3BH
Tel: 0603 612914
Fax: 0603 624483

Order Information

Order Dept Opening Times
Mon - Fri 9.30am - 5.00pm
All Dues Automatically Recorded
Representation Available

Personnel
Head of Company: Robin Brookes
Head of Marketing: Nigel Sustins
Head of Accounts: Jane Fone
Head of Distribution: Brenda Nixson
Head of Customer Services: Judy Speed

Number of titles published annually: 20
Number of Staff: 4

PA Member
All New Titles are Bar Coded
WBIP Updating: Nigel Sustins

Trade Terms
35%, some titles 30%
Minimum Order: £20 invoice value
Other Terms: Carriage charges as post

Returns Procedures
Authority to Return: Nigel Sustins
Address for Returns: Canterbury Press
Imperfect Returns: No Limit

CHURCH LITERATURE ASSOCIATION

7 Tufton Street, Westminster, London SW1P 3QN
ISBN Prefix(es): 0 85191
Tel: 071-222 6952
Fax: 071-976 7180
VAT No: 227 4828 48

Order Information

Order Dept Opening Times
Mon - Fri 9.30am - 5pm

Personnel
Head of Company: Arthur Leggatt (General Secretary)
Other Important Personnel:
David Chapman (Bookshop Manager)

Number of Staff: 8
NBA Signatory

Parent Company: Church Union

Trade Terms
33% on net books
Credit Cards Accepted: Access/Master, Amex, Visa

CHURCH PASTORAL AID SOCIETY

Athena Drive, Tachbrook Park, Leamington Spa, Warwickshire CV34 6NG
Tel: 0926 334242
Fax: 0926 337613
VAT No: 243 2271 91

CHURCH SOCIETY

Dean Wace House, 16 Rosslyn Road, Watford, Hertfordshire WD1 7EY
ISBN Prefix(es): 0 85190
Tel: 0923 235111

Order Information

Order Dept Opening Times
Mon - Fri 9am - 5pm

Personnel
Head of Company: Revd D A Streater
Head of Marketing: M J W Barker

Number of titles published annually: 4
Number of Staff: 3
WBIP Updating: M J W Barker

Trade Terms
35% trade discount p&p extra

CHURCHILL LIVINGSTONE

Robert Stevenson House, 1-3 Baxter's Place, Leith Walk, Edinburgh, Lothian EH1 3AF
ISBN Prefix(es): 0 443
Tel: 031-556 2424
Fax: 031-558 1278
Telex: 727511
Cables: CHURCHLIV EDINBURGH

Account No: _____
Sales Rep: _____
Tel: _____

Orders to
LONGMAN GROUP UK LTD, Fourth Avenue, Pinnacles, Harlow, Essex CM19 5AA
Tel: 0279 429655
Fax: 0279 431067

Order Information

All Dues Automatically Recorded
Representation Available
Invoice Payments: Pinnacles

Personnel
Head of Company: A T Stevenson (Managing Director)
Head of Sales (Home): Timothy Wright (UK & European Sales Manager) Harlow 0279 426721
Head of Sales (Export): Gerard Dummett (International Sales & Marketing Manager)
Head of Marketing: Peter Shepherd (Sales & Marketing Director)
Head of Publicity: J Grounsell (Sales Promotion Manager)

Number of titles published annually: 200
Percentage of Export Sales: 65%
Number of Staff: 100
PA Member
NBA Signatory
All New Titles are Bar Coded
Book Data Subscriber
WBIP Updating: David Newland Pinns

Parent Company: Longman Group UK

Trade Terms
25%

Returns Procedures
Address for Returns: Pinnacles
Stock Returns: Incorrect supplies and overstocks see representative for authorisation.

CICERONE PRESS

2 Police Square, Milnthorpe, Cumbria LA7 7PY
ISBN Prefix(es): 0 902363, 1 85284
Tel: 05395 62069 24 Hours
Fax: 05395 63417
VAT No: 305 1165 06

Order Information

Order Dept Opening Times
Mon - Fri 9am - 5.30pm
All Dues Automatically Recorded
Representation Available

Personnel
Head of Company: Dorothy Unsworth
Head of Publicity: Walt Unsworth

Number of titles published annually: 24
Number of Staff: 6
IPG Member

All New Titles are Bar Coded
WBIP Updating: Dorothy Unsworth

Trade Terms
General Net: Single copy 25%, 2 or more single titles/ 2 books or more/ subscription orders/ stock orders/ special orders 35%
Other Terms: Carriage charges for overseas
Girobank Number: 67 464 7106

Returns Procedures
Stock Returns: All returned books must be in mint condition
Imperfect Returns: Title page accepted up to £14

CIMTECH LTD
University of Hertfordshire, College Lane, Hatfield, Hertfordshire AL10 9AD
Tel: 0707 284691
Fax: 0707 272121
VAT No: 539 9596 72

[handwritten: C10B, Kings Ride, Ascot, Berks. SL5 88J.]

[handwritten: CITADEL Press (Film Titles only) = Tiptree. ALL OTHER CITADEL = BIBLIOS.]

CITY MUSEUM & ART GALLERY
Museum Shop, Bethseda Street, Hanley, Stoke-on-Trent, Staffordshire ST1 3DW
ISBN Prefix(es): 0 905080
Tel: 0782 202173
Fax: 0782 205033
VAT No: 280 0653 77

[handwritten: C10C, PO Box 348, Bristol BS99 7FE, Tel 0272 777199, 0272 724509]

CITY PRESS LTD
Seatrade House, 42-48 North Station Road, Colchester, Essex CO1 1RB
ISBN Prefix(es): 0 901129
Tel: 0206 45121
Fax: 0206 45190
Telex: 98517 DISOP G
VAT No: 289 6124 20

Personnel
Head of Company: P M Hetherington (Publisher)

Number of titles published annually: 1

Trade Terms
15% no surcharges

CIVIC TRUST
17 Carlton House Terrace, London SW1Y 5AW
Tel: 071-930 0914
Fax: 071-930 0180
VAT No: 239 8681 13

CLAN BOOKS
Clandon House, The Cross, Doune, Perthshire FK16 6BE
Tel: 0786 841330
Fax: 0786 841326
VAT No: 369 1426 35

Account No: _____
Sales Rep: _____
Tel: _____

Order Information

Order Dept Opening Times
Mon - Fri 8.45am - 5.15pm
All Dues Automatically Recorded
Representation Available

Personnel
Head of Company: David Warburton/Jean Warburton (Partners)
Head of Sales (Home): Jonathan Hildrey (Sales Manager)

Number of Staff: 16

Trade Terms
25%-35%, 30 Days

CLARIDGE PRESS
27 Windridge Close, St Albans, Hertfordshire AL3 4JP
ISBN Prefix(es): 1 870626
Tel: 0727 869486
Fax: 0727 835227

Orders to
BAILEY DISTRIBUTION LTD, Unit 1, Learoyd Road, Mountfield Rd Ind Est, New Romney, Kent TN28 8XU
Tel: 0679 66905
Fax: 0679 66638

Order Information

All Dues Automatically Recorded
Representation Available
Invoice Payments: Head Office or Bailey Distribution
Orders can also be placed with Head Office

Personnel
Head of Company: Prof R V Scruton
Head of Sales (Home): Mrs A C Downing
Head of Accounts: Mrs J Price

Number of titles published annually: 8
Number of Staff: 3
All New Titles are Bar Coded
WBIP Updating: Mrs A C Downing

Trade Terms
35%
Other Terms: P&P charged on all orders under £30

Returns Procedures
Authority to Return: If ordered direct apply direct to company, if ordered through Bailey apply to them
Address for Returns: Claridge Press

T & T CLARK LTD
59 George Street, Edinburgh, Lothian EH2 2LQ
ISBN Prefix(es): 0 567
Tel: 031-225 4703
Fax: 031-220 4260
VAT No: 271 1696 55

Account No: _____
Sales Rep: _____
Tel: _____

Order Information

Order Dept Opening Times
Mon - Fri 9am - 5pm
All Dues Automatically Recorded
Representation Available

Personnel
Head of Company: Geoffrey Green

Head of Marketing: Callum Fisken
Head of Accounts: Karen Watt

Number of titles published annually: 40
Percentage of Export Sales: 40%
Number of Staff: 12
PA Member
NBA Signatory
WBIP Updating: Callum Fisken

Trade Terms
32.5% freight free
Other Terms: 25% on net invoice value below £38
Girobank Number: 1845055

Returns Procedures
Stock Returns: No returns except by prior arrangement
Imperfect Returns: Title page up to retail £25, with imperfection marked. Above £25 complete book to be returned (postage credited)

ANTHONY CLARKE PUBLISHERS

16 Garden Court, Wheathampstead, Hertfordshire AL4 8RF
ISBN Prefix(es): 0 85650
Tel: 058 283 2460
VAT No: 196 2579 18

Order Information

Order Dept Opening Times
Mon - Fri 8am - 9.30pm
All Dues Automatically Recorded
Representation Available

Personnel
Head of Company: Anthony Clarke
Head of Customer Services: Elaine Clarke

Number of titles published annually: 5
Percentage of Export Sales: 30%
Number of Staff: 3
NBA Signatory
All New Titles are Bar Coded
Open University Publications
WBIP Updating: A S Clarke

Trade Terms
General Net: Single copy 25%, Two or more 35%
Other Terms: Small order surcharges £1.95 to £10 invoice value Carriage charges: export only.

Returns Procedures
Stock Returns: Incorrect titles accept for credit including cost of return. Damaged books: title page only up to £10 value - full credit
Imperfect Returns: Title pages only required

CLARKE ASSOCIATES - EUROPE LTD

13A Small Street, Bristol, Avon BS1 1DE
Tel: 0272 268864 24 Hours
Tel: 0272 225864 Orders
Fax: 0272 226437
Telex: 445591 CALORB G
VAT No: 464 7815 16

Account No: _____
Sales Rep: _____
Tel: _____

Order Information

Order Dept Opening Times
Mon - Fri 8am - 12.30pm, 2pm - 4.15pm

Orders for more than one publisher can be bulked
All Dues Automatically Recorded
Representation Available

Personnel
Head of Company: Malcolm Clarke (Managing Director)
Head of Accounts: Sue Phillips (Director)
Other Important Personnel:
Tricia Jones (Sales Order Processing)

Number of titles published annually: 150
Percentage of Export Sales: 70%
Number of Staff: 3
WBIP Updating: Malcolm Clarke

Trade Terms
1-4 copies 20%, 5+ 35%
Other Terms: Carriage charges £2.50 UK orders, £5 overseas
Girobank Number: 277 8524
Credit Cards Accepted: Access/Master, Visa

Returns Procedures
Stock Returns: Books to be returned, unmarked prior authorisation required except in case of damaged or incorrect supply.
Imperfect Returns: Book must be returned. Title pages not accepted

JAMES CLARKE & CO LTD

PO Box 60, Cambridge, Cambridgeshire CB1 2NT
ISBN Prefix(es): 0 227, 0 906554
Tel: 0223 350865
Fax: 0223 66951
VAT No: 213 3349 96

A/CNO   UNIREAD

Order Information
Teleordering: CLAJAS

All Dues Automatically Recorded
Representation Available
Represenation:H I Marketing

Personnel
Head of Company: Adrian Brink
Head of Sales (Home): Patricia Shelton
Head of Publicity: Emma Rintoul
Head of Accounts: David Baker
Head of Customer Services: Mike Kimberley

Number of titles published annually: 5
PA Member
IPG Member
NBA Signatory
All New Titles are Bar Coded
Book Data Subscriber
WBIP Updating: Emma Rintoul

Trade Terms
33.3%, Single Copy 25%
Academic Net: Single copy 20% Two or more 25%
Non-Net: 17.5%
Minimum Order: £10 invoice value
Other Terms: Small order surcharge £3 up to £30 invoice value £1 only cwo Carriage charges on exports only
Girobank Number: 20 898 1608

Returns Procedures
Stock Returns: Sold on firm basis only. Unauthorised returns sent back. Authorisation given for pub errors request within one week
Imperfect Returns: Return title page marked to show imperfection

CLASS PUBLISHING

PO Box 1498, London W6 7RS
ISBN Prefix(es): 1 872362
Tel: 071-371 2119 Tel/Fax
Fax: 071-371 2119
VAT No: 503 5208 87

Orders to
PLYMBRIDGE DISTRIBUTORS LTD, Plymbridge House, Estover Road, Plymouth, Devon PL6 7PZ
Tel: 0752 735251
Fax: 0752 695699

Order Information

All Dues Automatically Recorded
Representation Available
Invoice Payments: Plymbridge Distributors

Personnel
Head of Company: Richard Warner

Number of titles published annually: 6
IPG Member
All New Titles are Bar Coded

Trade Terms
General Net: Single copy/single line 25%, 2 or more single titles 35%, 2 books or more 35%
Academic Net: Single copy/single line 10%, 2 or more single titles 20%, 2 books or more 20%
Credit Cards Accepted: Access/Master, Visa, Amex

Returns Procedures
Authority to Return: Prior authorisation required from Richard Warner
Address for Returns: Plymbridge Distributors
Imperfect Returns: Title page up to £20 retail

E W CLASSEY LTD

PO Box 93, Faringdon, Oxfordshire SN7 7DR
ISBN Prefix(es): 0 86096
Tel: 0367 820399
Tel: 0367 820390
Fax: 0367 820429
Cables: BUGBOOKS FARINGDON OXON ENG
VAT No: 222 2766 84

A/C No 09507

Order Information

All Dues Automatically Recorded

Personnel
Head of Company: P Classey

Number of titles published annually: 10
Percentage of Export Sales: 70%
Number of Staff: 5
PA Member
IPG Member

Trade Terms
25% - 35%
Girobank Number: 313 3125
Credit Cards Accepted: Access/Master, Visa

CLB PUBLISHING

Godalming Business Centre, Woolsack Way, Godalming, Surrey GU7 1XW
Tel: 0483 426277
Fax: 0483 426947

CLEMATIS PRESS

18 Old Church Street, London SW3 5DQ
ISBN Prefix(es): 0 568
Tel: 071-352 8755
Cables: CLEMATIS SW3
VAT No: 239 4872 26

Order Information

Representation Available
Trade Counter:Amor Way, Dunhams Lane, Letchworth, Herts SG6 1UG Tel:0462 673470

Personnel
Head of Company: Clara Waters

PA Member
NBA Signatory
All New Titles are Bar Coded

Trade Terms
35% on two copies or more - assorted titles
Other Terms: Small order surcharges under £20 in value
Girobank Number: 0598 9353

Returns Procedures
Address for Returns: Letchworth
Imperfect Returns: Title page only required

CLEMENT PUBLISHERS LTD

Omega Cottage, 14 The Forty, Cholsey, Oxfordshire OX10 9LH
ISBN Prefix(es): 0 907027, 0 946262
Tel: 0491 651142
VAT No: 342 5093 72

[handwritten: CLIFF Notes = Littlehampton Book Services.]

CLIO PRESS LTD

55 St Thomas' Street, Oxford, Oxfordshire OX1 1JG [handwritten: Old Clarendon Ironworks]
ISBN Prefix(es): 1 85089 [handwritten: 35A Great Clarendon Street, Oxford OX2 6]
Tel: 0865 250333
Fax: 0865 790358
VAT No: 196 1148 50 [handwritten: Now c/o PLYMBRIDGE]
Account No: _____ [handwritten: 705771]
Sales Rep: _____
Tel: _____

Order Information
Teleordering: CLIO

All Dues Automatically Recorded

Personnel
Head of Company: John Durrant (Managing Director)
Head of Sales (Home): David Meggs (Sales Manager)
Head of Marketing: Rob Poulton (Promotions Manager)
Head of Accounts: Betty Smith (Financial Manager)
Head of Distribution: Lesley Chaundy (Distribution & Warehouse Manager)
Head of Customer Services: Janet Randle (Office Manager)

Number of titles published annually: 150
Number of Staff: 30
NBA Signatory
WBIP Updating: Louise Collins

Parent Company: ABC Clio

Trade Terms
Credit Cards Accepted: Access/Master, Visa, Amex

Returns Procedures
Stock Returns: Permission required from Sales Manager
Imperfect Returns: Title page required - no price limit

CLIPPER DISTRIBUTION SERVICES LTD
Windmill Grove, Porchester, Hampshire PO16 9HT
Tel: 0705 200080
Fax: 0705 200090

Account No: _____

Sales Rep: _____

Tel: _____

Order Information
Teleordering: CLIPPER

Order Dept Opening Times
Mon - Fri 9am - 5pm

Personnel
Head of Company: J P C Delieu (Managing Director)
Head of Accounts: M Walters
Head of Distribution: A Wood (Distribution Manager)
Head of Customer Services: P Delieu

CLOVER PUBLICATIONS
32 Ickwell Road, Northill, Biggleswade, Bedfordshire
SG18 9AB
Tel: 0767 627363

Personnel
Head of Company: Martin Woodrow

Trade Terms
5% on indexes 20% on books

Returns Procedures
Stock Returns: Not accepted
Imperfect Returns: Title page and page 12 of item to be returned

[handwritten: COCHRANES OF OXFORD, Fairspear House, Leafield, Witney, Oxford, OX8 5NY - Tel:- 0993 87531 Fax 0993 878416]

COLD TONNAGE BOOKS
136 New Road, Bedfont, Middlesex TW14 8HT
Tel: 081-751 3162
Fax: 081-751 6200
VAT No: 530 1816 81

Personnel
Head of Company: Andy Richards

Percentage of Export Sales: 60%

Trade Terms
Credit Cards Accepted: Access/Master, Amex, Diners, Visa

[handwritten: COLD SPRING HARBOUR LABS P.O. Box 100 Cold Spring Harbour, NY 11724 A/C No 03095400]

LLOYD COLE
37 College Avenue, Maidenhead, Berkshire SL6 6AZ
Tel: 0628 20809

Order Information

Representation Available

Personnel
Head of Company: Lloyd Cole

Number of titles published annually: 12
All New Titles are Bar Coded
WBIP Updating: Ray Addicott

Trade Terms
35% or negotiable

FRANK COLEMAN PUBLISHING LTD

Maulden Road, Flitwick, Bedfordshire MK45 5BW
ISBN Prefix(es): 0 948103
Tel: 0525 712261
Fax: 0525 718205
Telex: 825115

Personnel
Head of Company: Neil Goldman
Head of Customer Services: Debbie Smith

All New Titles are Bar Coded

THE COLLEGE OF ESTATE MANAGEMENT

Whiteknights, Reading, Berkshire RG6 2AW
Tel: 0734 861101
Fax: 0734 755344
VAT No: 533 3507 66

COLLETS

Denington Road, Wellingborough, Northamptonshire NN8 2QT
ISBN Prefix(es): 0 569
Tel: 0933 224351
Fax: 0933 276402
Telex: 317320 COLLET G
VAT No: 576 6940 88

Account No: _____ 6043 _____
Sales Rep: _____
Tel: _____

Order Information
Teleordering: COLLET

Order Dept Opening Times
Mon - Fri 9am - 5pm
Orders for more than one publisher can be bulked
All Dues Automatically Recorded
Representation Available

Personnel
Head of Company: Harry Moore
Head of Sales (Home): Jonathan Waring
Head of Accounts: Chris Seamarks

Number of titles published annually: 6
PA Member
NBA Signatory
All New Titles are Bar Coded
Open University Publications
Book Data Subscriber
WBIP Updating: Carol Sherwood

Trade Terms
General Net: Single copy 25% Two books or more 35%
Academic Net: 20%
Non-Net: 15%
Other Terms: Small order surcharge £1.50
Credit Cards Accepted: Access/Master, Visa

Returns Procedures
Authority to Return: Prior permission required

PETER COLLIN PUBLISHING LTD

8 The Causeway, Teddington, Middlesex TW11 0HE
ISBN Prefix(es): 0 948549
Tel: 081-943 3386

Fax: 081-943 3386
VAT No: 391 6455 30

Orders to
BEBC DISTRIBUTION, PO Box 1496, Poole, Dorset
BH12 3YD
Tel: 0202 715555
Fax: 0202 715556

Order Information

All Dues Automatically Recorded
Representation Available
Invoice Payments: BEBC Distribution Ltd

Personnel
Head of Company: Peter Collin

Number of titles published annually: 6
Percentage of Export Sales: 60%
IPG Member
All New Titles are Bar Coded
Book Data Subscriber

Trade Terms
Academic Net: Single Copy 25%, Two or more 35%

Returns Procedures
Authority to Return: Peter Collin
Address for Returns: BEBC Distribution

[handwritten: J.R. Collis Pubs (Dept of Arch + Prehistory Univ of Sheffield — now merged with Sheffield Academic Press Ltd.]

PETER COLLIN PUBLISHING LTD
PUBLISHERS OF SPECIALIST DICTIONARIES

English-French
Dictionary of Business
ISBN: 0-948549-10-6 £19.95
Paperback –28-9 £12.50

Dictionary of Computing
ISBN: 0-948549-24-6 £19.95

Dictionary of Ecology/Environment
ISBN: 0-948549-29-7 £19.95

English-German
Dictionary of Agriculture
ISBN: 0-948549-25-4 £25.00

Dictionary of Banking & Finance (April 1993)
ISBN: 0-948549-35-1 £30.00

Dictionary of Business
ISBN: 0-948549-17-3 £25.00

Dictionary of Computing/IT
ISBN: 0-948549-20-3 £25.00

Dictionary of Ecology
ISBN: 0-948549-21-1 £25.00

Dictionary of Law
ISBN: 0-948549-18-1 £25.00

Sales and Editorial
8 The Causeway, Teddington,
Middlesex TW11 0HE
Tel & Fax: (081) 943 3386

UK Representation:
Book Representation
& Distribution,
224A London Road, Hadleigh,
Essex, SS7 2DE

Distribution:
BEBC Distribution, PO Box 1496,
Poole, Dorset, BH12 3YD

Dictionary of Marketing
ISBN: 0-948549-22-X £25.00

Dictionary of Medicine
ISBN: 0-948549-26-2 £30.00

Dictionary of Printing & Publishing
ISBN: 0-948549-19-X £25.00

English-Greek
Glossary of Business Terms (April 1993)
ISBN: 0-948549-34-3 abt. £9.95

English-Spanish
Dictionary of Business (March 1993)
ISBN: 0-948549-30-0 £19.95

English-Swedish
Dictionary of Business
ISBN: 0-948549-14-9 £30.00

Dictionary of Law
ISBN: 0-948549-15-7 £30.00

Dictionary of Computing/IT
ISBN: 0-948549-16-5 £30.00

Dictionary of Medicine (March 1993)
ISBN: 0-948549-23-8 £30.00

[handwritten: COLLINS — Harper Collins.]

COLLINS & BROWN
Mercury House, 195 Knightsbridge, London SW7 1RE
ISBN Prefix(es): 1 85585
Tel: 071-584 2002
Fax: 071-584 0138
VAT No: 503 4369 68

Account No: _____
Sales Rep: _____
Tel: _____

Orders to
BIBLIOS PUBLISHERS DISTRIBUTION SERVICE LTD,
Star Road, Partridge Green, West Sussex RH13 8LD
Tel: 0403 710971
Fax: 0403 711143

Order Information

All Dues Automatically Recorded
Representation Available
Invoice Payments: Biblios

Personnel
Head of Company: Mark Collins/Cameron Brown
Head of Sales (Home): Gillian Hawkins
Head of Publicity: Rochelle Levy
Head of Accounts: Sharon D'Souza

Number of titles published annually: 50
Number of Staff: 22
NBA Signatory
All New Titles are Bar Coded
Book Data Subscriber
WBIP Updating: Marian Silvester

Trade Terms
35%

Returns Procedures
Authority to Return: Gillian Hawkins
Address for Returns: Biblios Publishers Distribution Services
Stock Returns: Apply to local representative or Gillian Hawkins
Imperfect Returns: £12.99 plus send book back to Biblios with covering letter, under £12.99 send title page

COLT BOOKS

9 Clarendon Road, Cambridge, Cambridgeshire CB2 2BH
Tel: 0223 357047
Fax: 0223 65866
VAT No: 285 5629 19

THE COLUMBA BOOK SERVICE

93 The Rise, Mount Merrion, Blackrock, County Dublin
ISBN Prefix(es): 0 948183, 1 85607
Tel: 01 283 2954
Tel: 01 283 6236 Orders
Fax: 01 288 3770
VAT No: 4805 799B

Order Information

Order Dept Opening Times
Mon - Fri 9am - 5.30pm
All Dues Automatically Recorded
Representation Available

Personnel
Head of Company: Sean O'Boyle
Head of Sales (Home): Cecilia West
Head of Accounts: Monica O'Boyle
Head of Customer Services: Patricia Lowth
Other Important Personnel:
Michael Brennan (Irish Sales Representative), Ken Lyon (UK Sales Representative) 0604 412951

Number of titles published annually: 200
Percentage of Export Sales: 65%

Number of Staff: 6
WBIP Updating: Cecilia West

Trade Terms
35%, carriage charged on orders under £50 invoice
Credit Cards Accepted: Access/Master, Visa

Returns Procedures
Authority to Return: Head Office or Sales Rep
Stock Returns: Overstocks accepted only with permission of sales office or representative
Imperfect Returns: Title pages only for all imperfect returns

[handwritten: Columbia University Press - 136 South Broadway Irvington, NY 10533 A/C SMITUNIRE]

COMBINED BOOK SERVICES
406 Vale Road, Tonbridge, Kent TN9 1SW
Tel: 0732 357755
Fax: 0732 770219
VAT No: 522 6088 58

Account No: _____

Sales Rep: _____

Tel: _____

Order Information
Teleordering: EDDING

Order Dept Opening Times
Mon - Fri 9am - 5pm
Orders for more than one publisher can be bulked
All Dues Automatically Recorded

Personnel
Head of Company: David Turner (Managing Director)
Head of Distribution: Owen Hazell (Distribution Manager)

All New Titles are Bar Coded
Open University Publications

Trade Terms
General Net: Publishers terms apply
Girobank Number: 304 3177
Credit Cards Accepted: Access/Master, Visa

Returns Procedures
Authority to Return: Refer to individual publishers for all returns information

COMMERCE BUSINESS COMMUNICATIONS
Station House, Station Road, Newport Pagnell, Milton Keynes, Buckinghamshire MK16 0AG
Tel: 0908 614477
Fax: 0908 616441

PA Member

COMMISSION FOR RACIAL EQUALITY
Elliot House, 10-12 Allington Street, London SW1E 5EH
ISBN Prefix(es): 0 907920, 0 95150, 1 85442
Tel: 071-828 7022

Orders to
LAVIS MARKETING, 73 Lime Walk, Headington, Oxfordshire OX3 7AD
Tel: 0865 67575
Fax: 0865 750079

Personnel
Head of Sales (Home): Desrie Thomson

Trade Terms
General Net: Single copy/single line 25%, 2 or more single titles, 2 bks or more 30%, subscription/stock orders 35%, special o's 25%

Returns Procedures
Authority to Return: Lavis Marketing
Address for Returns: Lavis Marketing

COMMONWEALTH SECRETARIAT

Publications Section, Marlborough House, Pall Mall, London SW1Y 5HX
Tel: 071-839 3411
Fax: 071-930 0827
Telex: 27678
Cables: COMSECGEN LONDON SW1

COMMUNITY DEVELOPMENT FOUNDATION

60 Highbury Grove, London N5 2AG
Tel: 071-226 5375
Fax: 071-704 0313
VAT No: 589 9290 61

COMPUTATIONAL MECHANICS PUBLICATIONS

Ashurst Lodge, Ashurst, Southampton, Hampshire SO4 2AA
ISBN Prefix(es): 0 905451, 1 85312
Tel: 0703 293223
Fax: 0703 292853
Telex: 47388 Attn COMPMECH
VAT No: 329 9443 23

Order Information

All Dues Automatically Recorded

Personnel
Head of Company: Lance Sucharov
Head of Marketing: Catherine Short
Head of Accounts: Mary Johnston
Head of Customer Services: Myra Mouland

Number of titles published annually: 30
Percentage of Export Sales: 35%
Number of Staff: 10
PA Member
WBIP Updating: Lance Sucharov

Trade Terms
15%

COMPUTER BOOKSHOPS LTD

50 James Road, Tyseley, Birmingham, West Midlands B11 2BA
Tel: 021-706 1250 Field Sale
Tel: 021-706 1188 CB Express
Fax: 021-706 3301
VAT No: 378 2479 08
Account No: _O11310_
Sales Rep: _____
Tel: _____

Order Information
Teleordering: COMBIR

Order Dept Opening Times
Mon - Fri 8.30am - 5.30pm

Orders for more than one publisher can be bulked
All Dues Automatically Recorded
Representation Available

Personnel
Head of Company: Mr Ian MacLean
Head of Sales (Home): Ms Delia Tracey
Head of Sales (Export): Mr Ian Wooley
Head of Marketing: Mr Tim Beaumont
Head of Accounts: Mr Nick Frost
Head of Distribution: Ms Pauline Reader
Head of Customer Services: Mrs Dena Thornton
Other Important Personnel:
Miss Liz Recci (CBL Express Sales)

Trade Terms
Basic trade terms
Minimum Order: £100 trade
Other Terms: Carriage charged
Credit Cards Accepted: Access/Master, Visa, Amex

Returns Procedures
Authority to Return: Authorization required
Imperfect Returns: Return with imperfections listed

COMPUTER STEP LTD

14 Boleyn Close, Warwick, Warwickshire CV34 6LP
ISBN Prefix(es): 1 874029
Tel: 0926 887366
Fax: 0926 887363
VAT No: 545 1531 60

Account No: _____
Sales Rep: _____
Tel: _____

Order Information

Order Dept Opening Times
Mon - Fri 9am - 5.30pm
Orders for more than one publisher can be bulked
All Dues Automatically Recorded
Representation Available

Personnel
Head of Company: Sevanti Kotecha/Harshad Kotecha

Number of titles published annually: 6
Number of Staff: 12
PA Member
All New Titles are Bar Coded
WBIP Updating: Sevanti Thakrar

Trade Terms
General Net: 30%, Stock orders - depending on quantity,
Spec orders 20%
Other Terms: Carriage charges £2.95
Credit Cards Accepted: Access/Master, Visa

Returns Procedures
Stock Returns: Request authorisation by mail or through reps
Imperfect Returns: As for stock returns

CONCORDIA PUBLISHING HOUSE LTD

28 Huntingdon Road, Cambridge, Cambridgeshire CB3 0HH
ISBN Prefix(es): 0 570, 0 8066, 0 8100
Tel: 0223 65113
Fax: 0223 355265
VAT No: 243 2762 72

Order Information

All Dues Automatically Recorded
Representation Available

Personnel
Head of Customer Services: Bernard Anton

Number of Staff: 5

Trade Terms
35%, no carriage for orders of £10+

ALLAN T CONDIE PUBLICATIONS
40 Main Street, Carlton, Nuneaton, Warwickshire CV13 0RG
ISBN Prefix(es): 0 907742, 1 85638
Tel: 0455 290389
VAT No: 485 6437 07

Orders to
Midland Counties Ltd, Unit 3 Maizefield, Hinckley Fields, Hinckley, Leicestershire LE10 1YF
Tel: 0455 233747
Fax: 0455 841805

Order Information

Order Dept Opening Times
Mon - Fri 9.00am - 5.30pm, Sat 9am - 12pm
All Dues Automatically Recorded
Representation Available

Number of titles published annually: 15
Percentage of Export Sales: 20%
NBA Signatory
All New Titles are Bar Coded
WBIP Updating: A T Condie

Trade Terms
General Net: Single copy/single line, 2 or more single titles, 2 books or more 25%, subscription/stock orders 30%, special orders 35%
Minimum Order: Pro-forma on orders under £25
Credit Cards Accepted: Access/Master, Visa

Returns Procedures
Stock Returns: Authority must be obtained on all returns
Imperfect Returns: Return whole volume

CONFEDERATION OF BRITISH INDUSTRY
Centre Point, 103 New Oxford Street, London WC1A 1DU
ISBN Prefix(es): 0 8520130
Tel: 071-379 7400
Fax: 071-240 2826
Fax: 071-497 2597

CONSERVATIVE CENTRAL OFFICE
32 Smith Square, London SW1P 3HH
ISBN Prefix(es): 0 85070, 0 85071
Tel: 071-222 9000
Fax: 071-222 1135
Telex: 8814563
VAT No: 240 2057 14

Order Information

Order Dept Opening Times
Mon - Fri 9.30am - 5pm
All Dues Automatically Recorded

Number of titles published annually: 50
WBIP Updating: Alistair B Cooke

Trade Terms
No trade discount normally
Credit Cards Accepted: Access/Master, Amex, Diners, Visa, Other

CONSTABLE & CO LTD
3 The Lanchesters, 162 Fulham Palace Road, London W6 9ER
ISBN Prefix(es): 0 09, 0 486
Tel: 081-741 3663
Fax: 081-748 7562
Telex: 27950 REF 830
VAT No: 238 4540 57

Account No: _____

Sales Rep: _____

Tel: _____

Orders to
TIPTREE BOOK SERVICES LTD, Church Road, Tiptree, Colchester, Essex CO5 0SR
Tel: 0621 819600
Fax: 0621 819011

Order Information

All Dues Automatically Recorded
Representation Available
Invoice Payments: Tiptree

Personnel
Head of Company: Mr B K Glazebrook (Chairman & Managing Director)
Head of Sales (Home): Mr R A Dodman (Sales Director)
Head of Publicity: Ms Y Evans-Foster (Publicity Director)
Head of Accounts: Adrian Andrews
Other Important Personnel:
Mr E Shedd (UK & Dover Sales Manager)

Number of titles published annually: 570
Percentage of Export Sales: 20%
Number of Staff: 19
PA Member
NBA Signatory
All New Titles are Bar Coded
Open University Publications
WBIP Updating: P Freeman

Trade Terms
35% all orders
Credit Cards Accepted: Access/Master, Visa, Amex

Returns Procedures
Authority to Return: R A Dodman, Constable
Address for Returns: Tiptree
Stock Returns: Returns only authorised for titles published within one year of returns authorisation. All Dover titles firm sale only

CONWAY MARITIME PRESS LTD
101 Fleet Street, London EC4Y 1DE
ISBN Prefix(es): 0 85177
Tel: 071-583 2412
Fax: 071-936 2153
VAT No: 524 2948 42

Account No: _____

Sales Rep: _____

Tel: _____

Orders to
MARSTON BOOK SERVICES LTD, PO Box 87, Osney Mead, Oxford, Oxfordshire OX2 0DT
Tel: 0865 791155
Fax: 0865 791927

Order Information

All Dues Automatically Recorded
Representation Available
Invoice Payments: Marston Book Services Ltd

Personnel
Head of Company: W R Blackmore
Head of Accounts: D C Greening

Number of titles published annually: 25
Percentage of Export Sales: 50%
Number of Staff: 7
NBA Signatory
All New Titles are Bar Coded
WBIP Updating: Oliver Colman

Trade Terms
General Net: Single copy/single line 25%, 2 or more single titles, 2 books or more 35%
BA/Girobank Small Order Scheme: Yes
Girobank Number: 236 6053
Credit Cards Accepted: Access/Master, Visa, Amex

Returns Procedures
Authority to Return: Martson Book Services Ltd
Address for Returns: Marston Book Services Ltd
Imperfect Returns: Title page up to £20, thereafter return whole book

THOMAS COOK PUBLISHING

PO Box 227, Peterborough, Cambridgeshire PE3 6SB
ISBN Prefix(es): 0 906273
Tel: 0733 268937
Fax: 0733 505792
VAT No: 239 3841 42

Orders to
ALAN SUTTON PUBLISHING LTD, Phoenix Mill, Far Tarupp, Stroud, Gloucestershire GL5 2BU
Tel: 0453 731114
Fax: 0453 731117

Order Information

Invoice Payments: Alan Sutton Publishing Ltd

Personnel
Head of Company: Jennifer Rigby 0733 269300
Head of Sales (Home): David J Laud (Business Development Manager)
Head of Accounts: Richard Dearing

Number of titles published annually: 20
Number of Staff: 14
All New Titles are Bar Coded
Book Data Subscriber
WBIP Updating: S G York

Parent Company: Thomas Cook Group Ltd

Trade Terms
Refer to Alan Sutton Publishing

CO-OPERATIVE UNION LTD

Holyoake House, Hanover Street, Manchester, Greater Manchester M60 0AS
ISBN Prefix(es): 0 85195

Tel: 061-832 4300
Fax: 061-831 7684
VAT No: 147 8611 47

Order Information

Order Dept Opening Times
Mon - Fri 9am - 5pm
All Dues Automatically Recorded

Personnel
Head of Company: D L Wilkinson (Chief Executive)

Number of titles published annually: 5
IPG Member
NBA Signatory
All New Titles are Bar Coded
WBIP Updating: Joyce Darlington

Trade Terms
35% no surcharges
Credit Cards Accepted: Visa

COPPER BEECH PUBLISHING LTD

11 Martyns Place, East Grinstead, Sussex RH19 4HF
ISBN Prefix(es): 0 9516295
Tel: 0342 314734 24 Hours
Fax: 0342 822586
VAT No: 528 4463 32

Order Information

Order Dept Opening Times
Mon - Fri 8.30am - 6pm
All Dues Automatically Recorded
Representation Available

Personnel
Head of Company: J Barnes
Head of Accounts: A A Barnes

Number of titles published annually: 4
IPG Member
All New Titles are Bar Coded
WBIP Updating: J Barnes

Trade Terms
General Net: 35%, Single copy/single line 25%

Returns Procedures
Imperfect Returns: Complete book required and prior permission from publisher

CORDEE

3a DeMontfont Street, Leicester, Leicestershire LE1 7HO
Tel: 0533 543579
Fax: 0533 471176
VAT No: 115 8575 58
Account No: ISB009
Sales Rep: _____
Tel: _____

Order Information
Teleordering: CORDEE

Order Dept Opening Times
Mon - Fri 8.30am - 5.30pm
Orders for more than one publisher can be bulked
All Dues Automatically Recorded
Representation Available

Personnel
Head of Company: Ken Vickers

Head of Accounts: June Vickers
Head of Distribution: Mike Johnson

Number of titles published annually: 30
Number of Staff: 10
All New Titles are Bar Coded
WBIP Updating: Ken Vickers

Trade Terms
General Net: Single copy 25%, Two or more 35%
Non-Net: Single copy 25%
Girobank Number: 480 4058

Returns Procedures
Authority to Return: Mike Johnson
Imperfect Returns: £25

CORK PUBLISHING LTD
Granary House, 19 Rutland Street, Cork, County Cork
ISBN Prefix(es): 1 871305, 1 872853
Tel: 021 313 855
Fax: 021 313 496

Orders to
PROFESSIONAL BOOK SALES, 4 Arran Quay, Dublin 7, County Dublin
Tel: 01 722 373
Fax: 01 723 902

Order Information

Representation Available

Personnel
Head of Company: Brian O'Kane
Head of Accounts: Anne O'Mahoney
Other Important Personnel:
David Givens

Number of titles published annually: 20
Percentage of Export Sales: 20%
Number of Staff: 5
WBIP Updating: David Givens

Trade Terms
On application

Returns Procedures
Authority to Return: Professional Book Sales

CORK UNIVERSITY PRESS
University College, Cork, County Cork
ISBN Prefix(es): 0 902561
Tel: 021 276 871
Fax: 021 275 948
VAT No: 488 1343 J

Order Information

Order Dept Opening Times
Mon - Fri 9am - 5pm
Cyclical Ordering Policy
All Dues Automatically Recorded
Representation Available

Personnel
Head of Company: Sara Wilbourne
Head of Sales (Home): Anne Lee
Head of Accounts: Donal Counihan
Head of Distribution: Fouad Alaaragi
Head of Customer Services: Eileen O'Carroll

Number of titles published annually: 6
Percentage of Export Sales: 60%
Number of Staff: 5

NBA Signatory
All New Titles are Bar Coded
WBIP Updating: Anne Lee

Trade Terms
30% single copies, 35% multiple orders
Credit Cards Accepted: Access/Master, Visa

Returns Procedures
Authority to Return: Anne Lee

[handwritten: Cornell University Press, = CUP Services]

[handwritten: ORDERS TO: NEVILLE GOSLING, UNIV. PRESSES MARKETING, THE OLD MILL, MILL STREET, WANTAGE, OXON OX12 9AB. Phone: 02357-66662 FAX: 02357-66545 ↓ orders will be supplied by Plymbridge]

CORNERHOUSE PUBLICATIONS

70 Oxford Street, Manchester, Greater Manchester M1 5NH
ISBN Prefix(es): 0 948797
Tel: 061-228 7621
Fax: 061-236 7323
VAT No: 451 4551 64

Order Information
Order Dept Opening Times
Mon - Fri 9.30am - 5.30pm
All Dues Automatically Recorded
Representation Available

Personnel
Head of Company: Dewi Lewis
Head of Sales (Home): Alison Buchan

Number of titles published annually: 12
Percentage of Export Sales: 30%
Number of Staff: 4
PA Member
NBA Signatory
All New Titles are Bar Coded
Book Data Subscriber
WBIP Updating: Alison Buchan

Parent Company: Greater Manchester Arts Centre Ltd

Trade Terms
General Net: Single copy/single line 25%, 2 or more single titles 35%
Other Terms: Carriage charges for overseas only
Credit Cards Accepted: Access/Master, Visa

Returns Procedures
Stock Returns: Permission required except in cases of damage, defect or dispatch error
Imperfect Returns: Return of book required

CORTNEY PUBLICATIONS

57 Ashwell Street, Ashwell, Baldock, Hertfordshire SG7 5QT
Tel: 0462 742185
VAT No: 491 3382 38

D J COSTELLO (PUBLISHERS) LTD

134 Upper Grosvenor Road, Tunbridge Wells, Kent TN1 2EX
ISBN Prefix(es): 0 7104
Tel: 0892 513278
Fax: 0892 528263
VAT No: 356 6777 06

Order Information
Order Dept Opening Times
9am - 5.30pm Mon - Fri. Ansafone in lunch hour
Invoice Payments: Weald UK Ltd

WBIP Updating: R Costello

Trade Terms
25% special education titles, 35% all other titles
Returns Procedures
Address for Returns: Weald UK Ltd, same address

COUNCIL FOR BRITISH ARCHAEOLOGY
~~112 Kennington Road, London SE11 6RE~~
~~Tel: 071-582 0494~~
~~Fax: 071-587 5152~~

[handwritten:] Bowes Morrell House, 111 Walmgate, York. YO1 2UA. 0904 671417 FAX 0904 671384.

Personnel
Head of Company: Mrs Christine Pietrowski (Managing Editor)

COUNTER PRODUCTIONS
PO Box 556, London SE5 0RW
Tel: 071-274 9009

Account No: _____
Sales Rep: _____
Tel: _____

COUNTRYSIDE BOOKS
6 Pound Street, Newbury, Berkshire RG14 6AB
ISBN Prefix(es): 0 905392, 1 85306
Tel: 0635 43816 24 Hours
Fax: 0635 551004
VAT No: 314 8550 64

Order Information

Order Dept Opening Times
Mon - Fri 9am - 5.30pm
All Dues Automatically Recorded
Representation Available
Invoice Payments: Local Heritage Books
Orders To: Local Heritage Books

Personnel
Head of Company: Mr Nicholas Battle/Mrs Suzanne Battle (Partners)
Head of Sales (Home): Wendy Smith (Sales Co-ordinator)
Head of Accounts: Mrs Valerie Sowden

Number of titles published annually: 60
All New Titles are Bar Coded
WBIP Updating: Mrs Amanada Smith

Trade Terms
35%, 20% on single copy orders. 5% discount on all invoices if paid within 7 days.
Other Terms: Invoices may be paid via Booksellers Clearing House using Local Heritage Books name.

Returns Procedures
Stock Returns: Write for permission
Imperfect Returns: Return title page for credit or replacement

COUNTYVISE LTD
1-3 Grove Road, Rock Ferry, Birkenhead, Merseyside L42 3XS
ISBN Prefix(es): 0 907768, 0 9516129, 1 871201, 1 873245
Tel: 051-645 2872
Tel: 051-645 2311
Fax: 051-645 8999
VAT No: 320 1341 28

Order Information

Order Dept Opening Times
Mon - Fri 8.45am - 5pm
All Dues Automatically Recorded
Representation Available

Personnel

Head of Company: John Emmerson
Head of Sales (Home): Jim O'Neil
Head of Accounts: Angela McKay

Number of titles published annually: 10
PA Member
IPG Member
NBA Signatory
All New Titles are Bar Coded
WBIP Updating: John Emmerson

Allied Companies: Birkenhead Books, Birkenhead Press Ltd

Trade Terms

35% on all titles
Other Terms: Carriage charges on orders under £10 invoice value
Credit Cards Accepted: Access/Master, Visa, Amex

Returns Procedures

Authority to Return: John Emmerson
Stock Returns: Overstocks by arrangement with rep. Other contact Angela McKay
Imperfect Returns: Title page under £10, otherwise whole book

COVENANT PUBLISHING CO LTD

8 Blades Court, Deodar Road, Putney, London SW15 2NU
ISBN Prefix(es): 0 85205
Tel: 081-877 9010
Fax: 081-871 4770
VAT No: 503 4376 71

Personnel

Head of Company: R B H Hall (General Manager)

PA Member
NBA Signatory
All New Titles are Bar Coded

Trade Terms

25% up to £25, 35% thereafter

RICHARD & ERIKA COWARD PARTNERSHIP

16 Sturgess Avenue, London NW4 3TS
ISBN Prefix(es): 0 9515019
Tel: 081-202 9592
VAT No: 420 4361 96

Order Information

Order Dept Opening Times
Mon - Thu 10am - 6pm, Fri 10am - 12pm

Personnel

Head of Company: Erika Coward/Richard Coward

Number of titles published annually: 1
IPG Member
All New Titles are Bar Coded
WBIP Updating: Erika Coward

Trade Terms

All orders are firm unless otherwise agreed in writing by the publisher
Non-Net: Single copy 15%, 2 or more single titles 35%.
Increased discounts by negotiation for large order sizes.

Returns Procedures
Imperfect Returns: Books with printer's errors must be returned to the head office. Damages must be immediately reported to the pub

CPL SCIENTIFIC LTD
Science House, Winchcombe Road, Newbury, Berkshire RG14 5QX
Tel: 0635 524064
Fax: 0635 529322
VAT No: 450 2737 66

CRABTREE PUBLISHING
73 Lime Walk, Headington, Oxford, Oxfordshire OX3 7AD
ISBN Prefix(es): 0 86505
Tel: 0865 67575
Fax: 0865 750079
Telex: 83147 LAVMARK

Orders to
LAVIS MARKETING, 73 Lime Walk, Headington, Oxfordshire OX3 7AD
Tel: 0865 67575
Fax: 0865 750079

Order Information
Invoice Payments: Lavis Marketing

Trade Terms
General Net: Single copy/single line 25%, 2 or more single titles, 2 bks or more 30%, subscription/stock/ orders 35%, special o's 25%
Girobank Number: 442 4913
Credit Cards Accepted: Access/Master, Visa

Returns Procedures
Authority to Return: Lavis Marketing
Address for Returns: Lavis Marketing

CRAFTS COUNCIL
44A Pentonville Road, London N1 9BY
ISBN Prefix(es): 0 903798, 1 870145
Tel: 071-278 7700
Fax: 071-837 6891
VAT No: 239 0141 85

Order Information
Order Dept Opening Times
Tues - Sat 11am - 6pm, Sun 2pm - 6pm

Number of titles published annually: 3
WBIP Updating: Sam Yates

Trade Terms
Credit Cards Accepted: Access/Master, Visa, Amex

CRANE PRESS
30 South Street, Ashby-de-la-Zouch, Leicestershire LE6 5BT
ISBN Prefix(es): 0 9517074
Tel: 0530 414111
Fax: 0530 417022

Order Information
All Dues Automatically Recorded

Personnel
Head of Company: Edwin Arthur Crane

Number of titles published annually: 1
All New Titles are Bar Coded

Trade Terms
33.3% on all orders, no surcharges

CRANSWICK PRESS
97 Victor Road, Teddington, Middlesex TW11 8SS
ISBN Prefix(es): 0 9509399
Tel: 081-977 2635

Personnel
Head of Company: Robin Waterfield

Number of titles published annually: 1

Trade Terms
35%

CREATION PRESS
83 Clerkenwell Road, London EC1M 5RJ
ISBN Prefix(es): 1 871592
Tel: 071-430 9878
Fax: 071-430 9878
VAT No: 577 7579 66

Orders to
COMBINED BOOK SERVICES, 406 Vale Road,
Tonbridge, Kent TN9 1SW
Tel: 0732 357755
Fax: 0732 770219

Order Information

Invoice Payments: Combined Book Services

Personnel
Head of Company: James Williamson
Head of Sales (Home): Simon Ashton
Head of Marketing: Adele Gladwell
Head of Publicity: Jack Hunter
Head of Accounts: Mike Philbin

Number of titles published annually: 12
Percentage of Export Sales: 20%
All New Titles are Bar Coded
WBIP Updating: James Williamson

Trade Terms
35% on all orders

Returns Procedures
Authority to Return: Combined Book Services

CREATIVE BOOKS INTERNATIONAL LTD
PO Box 349, Lowlands Ind Est, Vale, Guernsey
ISBN Prefix(es): 0 86250
Tel: 0481 48181
Fax: 0481 48989

Personnel
Head of Company: David Le Tissier

Number of titles published annually: 5
Number of Staff: 4
WBIP Updating: D LeTissier

Trade Terms
30%

Other Terms: Carriage charged £2.50 first book, 50p per additional
Credit Cards Accepted: Access/Master, Visa

Returns Procedures
Stock Returns: Telephone or write for authorisation and instructions

CREATIVE MONOCHROME

20 St Peters Road, Croydon, Surrey CR0 1HD
Tel: 081-686 4436
VAT No: 574 2856 12

Orders to
VINE HOUSE DISTRIBUTION, Waldenbury, North Chailey, East Sussex BN8 4DR
Tel: 082-572 3398
Fax: 082-572 4188

IPG Member

CRESCENT MOON PUBLISHING

18 Chaddesley Road, Kidderminster, Worcestershire DY10 3AD

CRESSRELLES PUBLISHING CO LTD

311 Worcester Road, Malvern, Worcestershire WR14 1AN
ISBN Prefix(es): 0 85343, 0 85956, 0 900024
Tel: 0684 565045
VAT No: 199 4015 36

Order Information

Order Dept Opening Times
Mon - Fri 9am - 5pm

Personnel
Head of Company: Leslie Smith
Head of Marketing: Simon Smith
Head of Accounts: Audrey Smith

Number of titles published annually: 18
Number of Staff: 3
IPG Member
NBA Signatory
WBIP Updating: Simon Smith

Trade Terms
25% - 35%
Other Terms: Carriage Charges: invoice value under £20
Girobank Number: 294 91 56

Returns Procedures
Stock Returns: Request to return first
Imperfect Returns: Annotated title page

CRESTA PUBLISHING CO

14 Beechfield Road, Liverpool, Merseyside L18 3EH
ISBN Prefix(es): 0 408486, 0 947567, o 40870
Tel: 051-722 7400

Order Information

All Dues Automatically Recorded

Personnel
Head of Company: J K P Edwards/A M Edwards (Partners)

Number of titles published annually: 1
Number of Staff: ?
WBIP Updating: J K P Edwards

Trade Terms
20% all orders, no surcharges

Returns Procedures
Stock Returns: Permission required before returning books

PAUL H CROMPTON LTD

102 Felsham Road, London SW15 1DQ
ISBN Prefix(es): 0 901764
Tel: 081-780 1063
Tel: 081-788 9130
Fax: 081-318 1439
VAT No: 226 9918 28

Orders to
AIRLIFT BOOK COMPANY, 26/28 Eden Grove, London N7 8EF
Tel: 071-607 5792
Fax: 071-607 6714

Order Information

All Dues Automatically Recorded
Representation Available
Invoice Payments: Airlift Book Co

Personnel
Head of Company: Paul Crompton
Other Important Personnel:
Rose Brookhouse (General Secretary)

Trade Terms
See Airlift terms

Returns Procedures
Authority to Return: Paul Crompton
Address for Returns: Airlift Book Co

CRONER PUBLICATIONS LTD

Croner House, London Road, Kingston-upon-Thames, Surrey KT2 6SR
Tel: 081-547 3333
Fax: 081-547 2637
Telex: 267778
VAT No: 318 3288 52

Account No: _____

Sales Rep: _____

Tel: _____

Order Information

Order Dept Opening Times
Mon - Fri 9am - 5pm
All Dues Automatically Recorded
Representation Available

Personnel
Head of Company: Hans Staal (Managing Director)
Head of Marketing: Yvonne Baxter (Marketing Services Manager)
Head of Accounts: Chris Hilton-Childs (Financial Director)
Head of Customer Services: Susan Grizzelle (Teleservices Supervisor)

Number of titles published annually: 40
Number of Staff: 220
Book Data Subscriber

Parent Company: Wolters-Kluwer, The Netherlands
Subsidiary Companies: Financial Training, Glasgow, Mary, Parks, Shaws Linton, Thornes, Stanley, Trident, Wayland
Allied Companies: C E D Samson (BG)

Trade Terms
20% single orders of bound books, 30% multiple orders, Special orders: 20% 1st year of loose leaf book (10% after)
Other Terms: P&P charged on first class or express delivery of books and on all loose-leaf products
Credit Cards Accepted: Access/Master, Amex, Diners, Visa, Other

Returns Procedures
Authority to Return: All returns must be requested in writing
Imperfect Returns: Enclose copy of invoice & title page, replacement or credit will be given

THE CROWOOD PRESS

The Stable Block, Crowood Lane, Ramsbury, Marlborough, Wiltshire SN8 2HR
ISBN Prefix(es): 0 946284, 1 85223
Tel: 0672 20320
Fax: 0672 20280
VAT No: 348 6934 11

Account No: _____135M24_____
Sales Rep: _____
Tel: _____

Orders to
BOOKPOINT LIMITED, 39 Milton Park, Abingdon, Oxfordshire OX14 4TD
Tel: 0235 835001
Fax: 0235 861038

Order Information

All Dues Automatically Recorded
Representation Available
Invoice Payments: Bookpoint Ltd

Personnel
Head of Company: J F Dennis (Chairman)
Head of Sales (Home): Stephen Lambe
Head of Publicity: Julie Sankey
Head of Accounts: Pat Dyson
Head of Distribution: Ken Hathaway

Number of titles published annually: 30
Number of Staff: 8
IPG Member
NBA Signatory
All New Titles are Bar Coded
Book Data Subscriber
WBIP Updating: Julie Sankey

Trade Terms
General Net: Single copy/single line 25%, 2 or more single titles 35%

Returns Procedures
Address for Returns: Bookpoint Ltd
Stock Returns: Report to Bookpoint Ltd within 3 days of receipt
Imperfect Returns: Up to £20 retail title pages to Crowood detailing the fault and retail price. Above £20 whole book to Bookpoint

G L CROWTHER

224 South Meadow Lane, Preston, Lancashire PR1 8JP
Tel: 0772 257126

CRYSTAL PALACE FOUNDATION

84 Anerley Road, London SE19 2AH
ISBN Prefix(es): 0 9508334, 1 897754
Tel: 081-778 2173

Orders to
24 Hour Ansafone Number: 2173 until 23.00 hrs

Order Information

Order Dept Opening Times
Mon - Tue/Thur - Sat 9am - 5pm
All Dues Automatically Recorded
Representation Available
Invoice Payments: Mr M Harrison, 58 Laurier Road, Addiscombe, Croydon, Surrey CR0 6JQ
Collection by appointment only

Personnel
Head of Company: Ian Bevan (Chairman)
Head of Sales (Home): Melvyn Harrison (Sales Manager) 081-654 9684
Head of Accounts: David Robinson (Treasurer)

Number of titles published annually: 1
WBIP Updating: Mr M Harrison

Trade Terms
35% on all orders
Other Terms: Postage at cost
Credit Cards Accepted: Access/Master, Visa

Returns Procedures
Authority to Return: Mr M Harrison
Stock Returns: Overstocks non-returnable, others write first
Imperfect Returns: Write first

C.S.O. = c/o HMSO.

CSV EDUCATION

237 Pentonville Road, London N1 9NJ
Tel: 071-278 6601
Fax: 071-833 0149
Telex: 937 400 ONECOM G

CT PROJECTS

109 Depot Road, Horsham, West Sussex RH13 5HN
Tel: 0403 261903 Tel/Fax
VAT No: 475 6881 92

CUP Services Po Box 6525 Ithaca NY 14851
A/c No. ~~EUREUNIM~~
ENREUNIWI

CURLEW PUBLISHING CO

56 Sutherland Street, London SW1V 4JZ
ISBN Prefix(es): 0 9512539
Tel: 071-828 1683
Fax: 071-828 7907

Orders to
IMAGES DISTRIBUTION, Unit 7-10, Hanley Workshops, Hanley Road, Hanley Swan, Worcestershire WR8 0DX
Tel: 0684 310897
Fax: 0684 310281

Order Information

Invoice Payments: Images

Personnel
Head of Company: Mrs J A L Phibbs

All New Titles are Bar Coded
WBIP Updating: Images

Returns Procedures
Authority to Return: Images
Address for Returns: Images

CURRENT SCIENCE LTD
Middlesex House, 24-42 Cleveland Street, London W1P 2FB
Tel: 071-323 0323
Fax: 071-580 1938
VAT No: 466 2477 23

CURZON PRESS LTD
St John's Studios, Church Road, Richmond, Surrey
TW9 2QA
Tel: 081-948 5322/6
Fax: 081-332 6735

Orders to
BIBLIOS PUBLISHERS DISTRIBUTION SERVICE LTD,
Star Road, Partridge Green, West Sussex RH13 8LD
Tel: 0403 710971
Fax: 0403 711143

Order Information
Representation: Africa Book Centre

Personnel
Head of Company: Malcolm Campbell/Martina Seifert
(Directors)

Book Data Subscriber

CWR
Waverley Abbey House, Waverley Lane, Farnham, Surrey
GU9 8EP
Tel: 02518 3761
Fax: 02518 3847
VAT No: 212 9828 60

CYPRESS BOOK COMPANY (UK) LTD
10 Swinton Street, London WC1X 9NX
Tel: 071-833 0220
Fax: 071-837 7768
VAT No: 417 8913 28

Order Information

Order Dept Opening Times
Mon - Fri 9am - 5pm

Personnel
Head of Company: Qian Min
Head of Sales (Home): Du Wei
Other Important Personnel:
Bai Jinmao (Head of Purchase)

Number of Staff: 3
WBIP Updating: Qian Min

Parent Company: China International Book Trading Corporation

Trade Terms
30-35%

D SERVICES

6 Euston Street, Freemen's Common, Leicester, Leicestershire
LE2 7SS
Tel: 0533 547671
Fax: 0533 544670

Account No: 0294756
Sales Rep: _____
Tel: _____

Order Information
Teleordering: DSVCS

Order Dept Opening Times
Mon - Fri 9am - 5pm
Orders for more than one publisher can be bulked
All Dues Automatically Recorded
Representation Available

Personnel
Head of Company: Trevor Martin (General Manager)
Head of Sales (Home): John Timmis (Sales Manager)
Head of Marketing: Richard Curry (Marketing Manager)
Head of Accounts: Brian Ruston (Financial Controller)
Head of Distribution: Steve While (Operations Manager)
Head of Customer Services: David Marr (Customer Services Manager)

Number of titles published annually: 250
Number of Staff: 48
All New Titles are Bar Coded
WBIP Updating: Andy Vaughan

Parent Company: W H Smith Ltd

Trade Terms
35%
Minimum Order: Small order surcharge may be levied on orders under £50
Other Terms: Carriage charged only overnight when requested
Credit Cards Accepted: Access/Master, Visa

Returns Procedures
Authority to Return: Only returns authorised by Head Office or Representative will be accepted
Imperfect Returns: Title pages should carry name and address of customer, ISBN retail price and full details of imperfection

DAISY BOOKS

PO Box 123, Peterborough, Cambridgeshire PE1 5EX
ISBN Prefix(es): 1 8708510
Tel: 0733 62490

Order Information

Order Dept Opening Times
Mon - Fri 9am - 5pm

Personnel
Head of Company: James Auty

Number of titles published annually: 1

Parent Company: Monitor House

Trade Terms
35% on all orders, no surcharges, no sale or return (UK)
30% Europe, 25% elsewhere, payment with order overseas

Returns Procedures
Address for Returns: No sale or return
Stock Returns: Return covers
Imperfect Returns: Return covers

DALENNAU

12 Parc-yr-Afon, Caerfyrddin, Dyfed SA31 1RL
Tel: 0267 232338 24 Hours
Fax: 0267 235985
VAT No: 431 8721 59

Account No: _____

Sales Rep: _____

Tel: _____

Order Information

Order Dept Opening Times
Mon - Sat 9.30am - 3pm
All Dues Automatically Recorded

Personnel
Head of Company: Leigh Verrill-Rhys

Number of titles published annually: 30
Percentage of Export Sales: 25%
Number of Staff: 2
Book Data Subscriber

Trade Terms
General Net: Single copy 25%, Two books or more 33.3-35%
Non-Net: Single copy 10%
Other Terms: Small order surcharge £2.50 on orders under £30 + 20% P&P. Pro-forma or trade account established.

Returns Procedures
Stock Returns: Returns request to head office with explanation, when book is returned, credit note or refund is issued.
Imperfect Returns: Title pages returned for credit on invoice value.

DALESMAN PUBLISHING COMPANY LTD

Clapham, Via Lancaster, Lancaster, Lancashire LA2 8EB
ISBN Prefix(es): 0 85206, 1 85568
Tel: 05242 51225
Fax: 05242 51708
VAT No: 494 6590 95

Order Information

Order Dept Opening Times
Mon - Fri 9am - 5pm
All Dues Automatically Recorded
Representation Available
Representation (exc North):Ken Dickson Marketing

Personnel
Head of Company: Robert Flanagan (General Manager)
Head of Sales (Home): Barry Cox (Sales & Marketing Manager)
Other Important Personnel:
Roger Arnold (Book Sales Executive (North))

Number of titles published annually: 25
PA Member
NBA Signatory
All New Titles are Bar Coded
WBIP Updating: Barry Cox

Trade Terms
33.3%
Other Terms: Sos on orders under £20 net invoice value. Exact postage (books delivered direct by reps in North of England)

Returns Procedures
Authority to Return: Barry Cox

TERENCE DALTON LTD
47 Water Street, Lavenham, Sudbury, Suffolk CO10 9RN
ISBN Prefix(es): 0 86138, 0 900963, 0 904623
Tel: 0787 247572 24 Hours
Fax: 0787 248267
VAT No: 102 7212 27

Order Information

Order Dept Opening Times
Mon - Fri 9am - 1pm 2pm - 5.30pm
All Dues Automatically Recorded
Representation Available

Personnel
Head of Company: Mrs E H Whitehair (Director)

Number of titles published annually: 5
Number of Staff: 2
All New Titles are Bar Coded
WBIP Updating: Mrs E H Whitehair

Parent Company: Lavenham Holdings PLC
Allied Companies: Dalton Origination Ltd (UK), Lavenham Press Ltd (UK)

Trade Terms
Payment within 30 days. 35% on all orders. Postage charged on 1 or 2 books unless cwo. Export despatch charged
Girobank Number: 200 5050
Credit Cards Accepted: Access/Master, Visa

Returns Procedures
Stock Returns: Overstocks permission first. Credit given if title in print Incorrect/damaged credited or resupplied. Post credited
Imperfect Returns: Title page not accepted at any price, return whole book and postage will be credited.

DALTON WATSON FINE BOOKS
14 Highfield Road, Edgbaston, Birmingham, West Midlands B15 3DU
ISBN Prefix(es): 0 901564, 1 85443
VAT No: 558 5193 09

Orders to
Dalton Watson Books, Sales Dept, PO Box 2, Belton, Loughborough, Leicestershire LE12 9UW
Tel: 0530 223569 Tel/Fax

Order Information

All Dues Automatically Recorded

Number of titles published annually: 10
Percentage of Export Sales: 20%
All New Titles are Bar Coded

Parent Company: Autostyle Publishing Ltd

Trade Terms
1-4 books 25%, 5-9 30%, 10-20 35%, 21 + 40%, bulk stock by arrangement, carriage extra unless otherwise agreed
Other Terms: CWO unless credit terms agreed, small orders CWO, carriage extra

Returns Procedures
Authority to Return: No returns policy, unless imperfect
Imperfect Returns: Return insured carriage with full report & submit claim

DANCE BOOKS LTD
9 Cecil Court, St Martin's Lane, London WC2N 4EZ
ISBN Prefix(es): 0 903102, 0 903102, 1 85273, 1 85273

Tel: 071-836 2314
Fax: 071-497 0473
VAT No: 238 6405 53

Order Information

All Dues Automatically Recorded

Personnel
Head of Company: David Leonard
Head of Sales (Home): Sanjoy Roy
Head of Sales (Export): Richard Holland

Number of titles published annually: 10
Number of Staff: 4
NBA Signatory
WBIP Updating: David Leonard

Trade Terms
General Net: Single copy/single line 25%, otherwise 35% own - 30% distributed
BA/Girobank Small Order Scheme: Yes
Credit Cards Accepted: Access/Master, Visa

Returns Procedures
Authority to Return: David Leonard
Stock Returns: Authorization required
Imperfect Returns: Title page up to £12.50, otherwise whole book

THE C W DANIEL CO LTD

1 Church Path, Saffron Walden, Essex CB10 1JP
ISBN Prefix(es): 0 85032, 0 85207, 0 85435, 0 85978
Tel: 0799 521909
Fax: 0799 513462
VAT No: 250 4003 20

Order Information

Order Dept Opening Times
Mon - Fri 8.30am - 6.30pm
All Dues Automatically Recorded
Representation Available

Personnel
Head of Company: Ian Miller (Managing Director)
Head of Sales (Home): Genevieve Miller
Head of Publicity: Genevieve Miller
Head of Accounts: Sarah Freeborn

Number of titles published annually: 12
Percentage of Export Sales: 40%
Number of Staff: 7
All New Titles are Bar Coded
WBIP Updating: Genevieve Miller

Subsidiary Companies: Health Science Press, Spearman Publishers, Neville

Trade Terms
25% + Surcharge (P&P) single copy Two or more 33.3% + Surcharge (P&P)
Girobank Number: 308 8359
Credit Cards Accepted: Access/Master, Visa, Diners

Returns Procedures
Stock Returns: Return books to HO after authority has been granted. If books are damaged credit will not be given
Imperfect Returns: Return title page of imperfect book stating reason

DANIELS PUBLISHING

38 Cambridge Place, Cambridge, Cambridgeshire CB2 1NS
ISBN Prefix(es): 0 948920, 1 85467

Tel: 0223 467144 24 Hours
Fax: 0223 467145
VAT No: 386 0479 23

Order Information

Order Dept Opening Times
Mon - Fri 9am - 1pm 1.30pm - 5pm
Cyclical Ordering Policy

Personnel
Head of Company: Dr Victor G Daniels
Head of Sales (Home): Dr Lisa MacGregor
Head of Distribution: Cath McKee

Number of titles published annually: 8
Number of Staff: 5
IPG Member
WBIP Updating: Lisa MacGregor

Trade Terms
By negotiation with Publisher

Returns Procedures
Authority to Return: Lisa MacGregor
Stock Returns: By negotiation with the Publisher

DARF PUBLISHERS LTD

277 West End Lane, London NW6 1QS
ISBN Prefix(es): 1 85077
Tel: 081-965 4339
Fax: 081-961 8660
VAT No: 394 5672 09

Order Information

Order Dept Opening Times
Mon - Fri 10am - 4pm
All Dues Automatically Recorded
Representation Available

Personnel
Head of Company: M B Fergiani (Managing Director)
Head of Sales (Home): A Bentaleb
Head of Distribution: Miss Peta Dawdry

Number of titles published annually: 12
Percentage of Export Sales: 35%
Number of Staff: 3
All New Titles are Bar Coded
WBIP Updating: Miss Peta Dawdry

Trade Terms
Single copy, two or more single titles 20%, two books or more 35%, special orders negotiable

Returns Procedures
Stock Returns: Sign request to return forms, issue credits on receipt of books in good condition
Imperfect Returns: Return book which will be replaced

Dartmouth = Ashgate

DARTON, LONGMAN AND TODD LTD

1 Spencer Court, 140/142 Wandsworth High Street, London SW18 4JJ
ISBN Prefix(es): 0 232
Tel: 081-875 0155
Tel: 081-875 0134 24 Hours
Fax: 081-875 0133
VAT No: 238 6999 95

Account No: _____
Sales Rep: _____
Tel: _____

Order Information

All Dues Automatically Recorded
Representation Available

Personnel
Head of Sales (Home): Martin Sheppard (Marketing Manager)
Head of Publicity: Fleur Dorrell (Publicity Officer)
Head of Accounts: Colleen Goddard (Accounts Manager)
Head of Distribution: Trevor Price (Warehouse Manager) 0462 673470
Head of Customer Services: Mary Chapman (Trade Manager)

Number of titles published annually: 50
Percentage of Export Sales: 20%
Number of Staff: 12
PA Member
NBA Signatory
All New Titles are Bar Coded
WBIP Updating: Helen Milne

Trade Terms
35%
Minimum Order: £20
Other Terms: Small order surcharge £2
Girobank Number: 522 3458

Returns Procedures
Authority to Return: Martin Sheppard, Marketing Manager
Address for Returns: Unit 9, Amor Way, Letchworth, Herts, SG6 1VG
Stock Returns: Authorised returns only in mint condition, carriage paid
Imperfect Returns: Title page up to £15 except bibles

DATA CONSULTANCY

7 Southern Court, South Street, Reading, Berkshire RG1 4QS
Tel: 0734 588181
Fax: 0734 597637

DATA NETWORK PUBLISHING LTD

5 The Edge Business Centre, Humber Road, London NW2 6EW
Tel: 081-208 2046
Fax: 081-208 2058

DAVID & CHARLES PLC

Brunel House, Forde Close, Newton Abbot, Devon TQ12 4PU
ISBN Prefix(es): 0 276, 0 7153, 0 907115, 1 85724
Tel: 0626 61121
Fax: 0626 64463
Fax: 0626 331367
Telex: 42904
VAT No: 365 8070 37
Account No: ___152146___
Sales Rep: _____
Tel: _____

Orders to
EXEL LOGISTICS - MEDIA SERVICES, 3 Sheldon Way, Larkfield, Aylesford, Kent ME20 6SF
Tel: 0622 882000
Fax: 0622 718036

Order Information
Teleordering: DCHL

All Dues Automatically Recorded
Representation Available
Invoice Payments: Exel Logistics

Personnel
Head of Company: Terry Stubbs
Head of Sales (Home): Matthew Clarke
Head of Marketing: Jacqueline Thomas
Head of Accounts: Neil Page
Head of Customer Services: Veronica Lyons
Other Important Personnel:
Phil McCallion (UK Sales Manager), Linda Mitchell (Export Sales Manager)

Number of titles published annually: 90
Number of Staff: 64
PA Member
NBA Signatory
All New Titles are Bar Coded
Book Data Subscriber
WBIP Updating: Veronica Lyons

Parent Company: The Readers Digest Association Ltd

Trade Terms
35%
Girobank Number: 289 1158
Credit Cards Accepted: Access/Master, Visa

Returns Procedures
Address for Returns: Exel
Stock Returns: As overstocks
Imperfect Returns: Up to £9.99 title pages accepted

CHRISTOPHER DAVIES (PUBLISHERS) LTD
PO Box 403, Swansea, West Glamorgan SA2 9BE
ISBN Prefix(es): 0 7154, 0 904652
Tel: 0792 648825 24 Tel/Fax
VAT No: 123 3832 94

Order Information

All Dues Automatically Recorded

Personnel
Head of Company: Christopher Davies
Head of Customer Services: Morwenna Davies

Number of titles published annually: 5
Number of Staff: 2
All New Titles are Bar Coded
WBIP Updating: Christopher Davies

Trade Terms
General Net: single copy 25%, 2 or more single titles/2 books or more/ subscription orders/stock orders/special orders 35%
Other Terms: Carriage charges on all orders under £30 net

Returns Procedures
Imperfect Returns: Return the title page, signed by the returning bookseller, and the imperfect pages

F.A. Davis Co = Waverley Europe

JOHN DAWES PUBLICATIONS
12 Mercers, Hawkhurst, Kent TN18 4LH
Tel: 0580 753346
VAT No: 373 8438 22

DAWSON UK LTD
Cannon House, Park Farm Road, Folkestone, Kent CT19 5EE
ISBN Prefix(es): 0 7129

Tel: 0303 850101
Fax: 0303 850440

Personnel
Head of Company: Bryan Ingleby
Head of Sales (Home): Gerald Dorman (Sales (Dawson Publishing only))
Head of Accounts: Phillip Moore
Head of Distribution: Tom Hickey
Head of Customer Services: Mike Lennie/Fred Cunningham/Shane Cleary

Number of titles published annually: 4
PA Member
NBA Signatory
WBIP Updating: Gerald Dorman

Allied Companies: Dawson Book Division (UK), Quality Books (US)

Trade Terms
On application

Returns Procedures
Stock Returns: Please write quoting invoice number and reason for return
Imperfect Returns: As above please telephone if urgent replacement required (Extension 150)

DEBRETTS PEERAGE LTD
73/77 Britannia Road, London SW6 2JY
ISBN Prefix(es): 1 87052
Tel: 071-736 6524
Fax: 071-731 7768
VAT No: 241 6554 71

DEDALUS LTD
Langford Lodge, St Judith's Lane, Sawtry, Cambridgeshire PE17 5XE
ISBN Prefix(es): 0 946626, 0 946626, 1 873982, 1 873982
Tel: 0487 832382
Fax: 0487 832 382
VAT No: 437 3295 39

Orders to
CENTRAL BOOKS, 99 Wallis Road, London E9 5LN
Tel: 081-986 4854
Fax: 081-533 5821

Order Information

All Dues Automatically Recorded
Representation Available
Invoice Payments: Central Books
Representation:Troika/Central

Personnel
Head of Company: George Barrington/Juri Gabriel
Head of Sales (Home): Eric Lane
Head of Sales (Export): George Barrington
Head of Publicity: Robert Irwin

Number of titles published annually: 14
Percentage of Export Sales: 40%
Number of Staff: 5
All New Titles are Bar Coded
WBIP Updating: Eric Lane

Trade Terms
See Centrals terms

Returns Procedures
Authority to Return: George Barrington, Dedalus
Address for Returns: Central Books

THE DEDALUS PRESS
24 The Heath, Cypress Downs, Dublin 6, County Dublin
ISBN Prefix(es): 0948268, 1873790
Tel: 01 902 582

Orders to
PASSWORD (BOOKS) LTD, 23 New Mount Street, Manchester, Greater Manchester M4 4DE
Tel: 061-953 4009
Fax: 061-953 4001

Order Information

All Dues Automatically Recorded
Representation Available

Personnel
Head of Company: John F Deane

Number of titles published annually: 10

Trade Terms
35% on all orders

Returns Procedures
Authority to Return: Apply to Password

DEEP BOOKS LTD
Unit 33, Cannon Wharf Bus Cent, 35 Evelyn Street, London SE8 4RT
Tel: 071-232 2747 Tel/Fax
VAT No: 607 9641 21

Account No: _____
Sales Rep: _____
Tel: _____

Order Information
Teleordering: DEEP

[handwritten: DEKKER (Marcel) % IBS Book Services, Mutgasse 4 CH-4001, Basel, Switzerland. A/C No 12279 FAX 010 41 61 261 8896]

DELAMARE PUBLISHING
4A Dunkeld Road, Bournemouth, Dorset BH3 7EN
ISBN Prefix(es): 0 9508203
Tel: 0202 290125

Personnel
Head of Company: Edward Konigsberger

Trade Terms
Trade Discount 30% on invoiced prices

[handwritten: De Gruyter. W., P.O. Box 30 3421, 10728 Berlin GERMANY. FAX 010 49 30 26005251]

DELECTUS BOOKS
27 Old Gloucester Street, London WC1N 3XX
ISBN Prefix(es): 1 897767
Tel: 081-963 0979
Fax: 081-963 0502
VAT No: 532 3080 82

Orders to
TURNAROUND, 27 Horsell Road, London N5 1XL
Tel: 071-609 7836/7
Fax: 071-700 1205

Order Information

All Dues Automatically Recorded
Representation Available

Personnel
Head of Company: Michael R Goss

Number of titles published annually: 6
Percentage of Export Sales: 25%
Number of Staff: 4
All New Titles are Bar Coded
WBIP Updating: Michael R Goss

Trade Terms
35%, 40% cwo, Single Copy 25%
Other Terms: Carriage charged on export only.
Credit Cards Accepted: Access/Master, Visa

Returns Procedures
Authority to Return: Prior permission required
Stock Returns: Phone first
Imperfect Returns: Phone first

DELTA PRESS LTD
Unit 5, Riverpark Estate, Berkhamsted, Hertfordshire
HP4 1HL
Tel: 0442 877794
Fax: 0442 877828
VAT No: 443 7682 29

PA Member

[Handwritten: DENT % Littlehampton Book Services]

THE DESIGN COUNCIL
28 Haymarket, London SW1Y 4SU
ISBN Prefix(es): 0 85072
Tel: 071-839 8000
Fax: 071-925 2130

[Handwritten: DES – (Dept of Education Science) Elizabeth House York Road, LONDON SE1 7PH.]

Orders to
SHEED & WARD LTD, 14 Coopers Row, London
EC3N 2BH
Tel: 071-702 9799
Fax: 071-702 3583

Order Information
All Dues Automatically Recorded
Representation Available

Personnel
Head of Company: Anthony Land (Publisher)
Head of Sales (Home): Tracey Robins
Head of Accounts: Chris Jones

Number of titles published annually: 15
Percentage of Export Sales: 30%
All New Titles are Bar Coded
Book Data Subscriber
WBIP Updating: Tracey Robins

Trade Terms
35%

Returns Procedures
Authority to Return: Sheed & Ward

[Handwritten: DEPT OF TRADE & INDUSTRY PUBS, PO BOX 30 ALTON, HANTS GU34 4PX]

ANDRE DEUTSCH LTD
106 - 106 Great Russell Street, London WC1B 3LJ
ISBN Prefix(es): 0 233
Tel: 071-580 2746
Fax: 071-631 3253
VAT No: 232 116021

Account No: _____
Sales Rep: _____
Tel: _____

[Handwritten: DEPT OF AGRICULTURE, WESTERN AUSTRALIA, 3 BARON-HAY COURT, SOUTH PERTH 6151, W. AUSTRALIA]

Orders to
LITTLEHAMPTON BOOK SERVICES, 14 Eldon Way,
Lineside Ind Estate, Littlehampton, West Sussex BN17 7HE
Tel: 0903 721596
Fax: 0903 730914

Order Information
All Dues Automatically Recorded
Representation Available
Invoice Payments: Littlehampton
Representation: Cassell

Personnel
Head of Company: Tom Rosenthal
Head of Sales (Home): Lois Edwards
Head of Publicity: Christobel Kent
Head of Accounts: K Patel

Number of titles published annually: 50
Percentage of Export Sales: 40%
PA Member
All New Titles are Bar Coded
WBIP Updating: Pauline Allen

Trade Terms
35%

Returns Procedures
Address for Returns: Littlehampton, only when authorized
Stock Returns: Prior authorization is required
Imperfect Returns: Title page to be returned once authorized, limit £20

[handwritten: Dept of Environment, Room 1, Spur 2, Block 3, Government Building, Lime Grove, Eastcote, Ruislip, Middx HA4 8SE]

DEVELOPMENT EDUCATION PROJECT

801 Wilmslow Road, Didsbury, Manchester, Greater Manchester M20 8RG
Tel: 061-445 2495

Orders to
DEDU, 153 Cardigan Road, Leeds, West Yorkshire LS6 1LJ
Tel: 0532 784030

[handwritten: D.H.S.S. P.O Box 21, Stanmore, Middx HA7 1AY]

KEN DICKSON (MARKETING) LTD

14 Crossways, Silwood Road, Sunninghill, Ascot, Berkshire SL5 0PY
Tel: 0344 25421
VAT No: 285 2112 71

Account No: _____

Sales Rep: _____

Tel: _____

Order Information
Teleordering: DICKSON

Order Dept Opening Times
9am - 5pm

Personnel
Head of Company: K A Dickson

Number of Staff: 6

DICKSON PRICE PUBLISHERS LTD

Hawthorn House, Bowdell Lane, Brookland, Romney Marsh, Kent TN29 9RW
ISBN Prefix(es): 0 85380, 0 905898, 0 907827
Tel: 0797 344626
Fax: 0797 344668
VAT No: 370 8477 30

Order Information
Teleordering: DPRICE

All Dues Automatically Recorded

Personnel
Head of Company: K Dickson/D Wanstall

Number of titles published annually: 4
Number of Staff: 2
NBA Signatory
WBIP Updating: D Wanstall

Trade Terms
General Net: Single copy 25%, Two or more 35% stock orders 35%
Academic Net: Single copy 25%, Stock orders 30%
Other Terms: Carriage charged on overseas, inc Eire
Credit Cards Accepted: Access/Master, Visa

Returns Procedures
Authority to Return: Prior permission required
Address for Returns: Dickson Price Publishers, c/o Vale Packaging, 420 Vale Road, Tonbridge, Kent TN9 1TD
Imperfect Returns: Limit £30, return pages to head office

THE DISTRIBUTION BOOK CO
4-5 Colwell Drive, Abingdon, Oxfordshire OX14 1AU
Tel: 0235 527544
Fax: 0235 530435
VAT No: 524 3201 91

Account No: _____

Sales Rep: _____

Tel: _____

DLF PUBLICATIONS
Haigh & Hochland, The Precinct Centre, Oxford Rd, Manchester, Greater Manchester M13 9QA
Tel: 061-273 4156
Fax: 061-273 4340

Order Information
Invoice Payments: Haigh & Hochland

Other Important Locations
Info & Catalogues:DLF, 380-384 Harrow Road, London W9 2HU
Tel: 071-289 6111

DOBSON BOOKS LTD
Brancepeth Castle, Durham, Durham DH7 8DF
ISBN Prefix(es): 0 234 72, 0 234 77
Tel: 091 3780628

DOD'S PARLIAMENTARY COMPANION LTD
Hurst Green, Etchingham, East Sussex TN19 7PX
ISBN Prefix(es): 0 9057022
Tel: 0580 87264
VAT No: 192 2849 39

Order Information
Cyclical Ordering Policy

Personnel
Head of Company: Andrew Cox (Publisher)

Head of Accounts: Mrs J Wass
Other Important Personnel:
Michael Bedford (Editor) 0932 860288

Number of titles published annually: 1
WBIP Updating: Michael Bedford

Trade Terms
15%
Credit Cards Accepted: Access/Master, Visa

Returns Procedures
Authority to Return: Written permission essential

DOLPHIN BOOK CO LTD
Tredwr, Llangrannog, Llandysul, Dyfed SA44 6BA
ISBN Prefix(es): 0 85215
Tel: 0239 654404
VAT No: 124 4784 68

Order Information

Order Dept Opening Times
Mon - Fri 9am - 1pm, 2pm - 5pm
All Dues Automatically Recorded

Personnel
Head of Company: Mr M L Gili

Number of titles published annually: 1
Percentage of Export Sales: 20%
Number of Staff: 2
All New Titles are Bar Coded
WBIP Updating: Mr M L Gili

Trade Terms
Single copy single line 20%, 2 books or more 25%

Returns Procedures
Stock Returns: Prior authority required
Imperfect Returns: Return whole book

JOHN DONALD PUBLISHERS LTD
138 St Stephen Street, Edinburgh, Lothian EH3 5AA
ISBN Prefix(es): 0 85976
Tel: 031-225 1146
Fax: 031-220 0567
VAT No: 270 8848 29

Account No: _____

Sales Rep: _____

Tel: _____

Order Information
Teleordering: DONALD

Order Dept Opening Times
Mon - Fri 9am - 5pm
All Dues Automatically Recorded
Representation Available

Personnel
Head of Company: Donald Morrison
Head of Sales (Home): Gordon Angus
Head of Accounts: Jack Elder

Number of titles published annually: 30
Percentage of Export Sales: 20%
Number of Staff: 8
NBA Signatory
All New Titles are Bar Coded
WBIP Updating: Gordon Angus

Trade Terms
Single Copy 20%, Two plus 35%
Credit Cards Accepted: Access/Master, Visa, Amex

Returns Procedures
Authority to Return: Apply to Jack Elder
Address for Returns: John Donald Pub Ltd, 2/12 Marionville Rd, Edinburgh EH7 5TX Tel: 031-652 0823
Imperfect Returns: Title pages only up to retail value £20

DONHEAD PUBLISHING LTD

28 Southdean Gardens, Wimbledon, London SW19 6NU
Tel: 081-789 0138 Tel/Fax
VAT No: 603 0257 91

IPG Member

DORLING KINDERSLEY HOLDINGS PLC

9 Henrietta Street, Covent Garden, London WC2E 8PS
ISBN Prefix(es): 0 7513, 0 86318, 1 87185
Tel: 071-836 5411
Fax: 071-836 7570
Fax: 071-753 3564 UK Sales
Telex: 8954527 DEEKAY G
VAT No: 429 5337 34

Account No: _____
Sales Rep: _____
Tel: _____

Orders to
TIPTREE BOOK SERVICES LTD, Church Road, Tiptree, Colchester, Essex CO5 0SR
Tel: 0621 819600
Fax: 0621 819011

Order Information

All Dues Automatically Recorded
Representation Available
Invoice Payments: Tiptree Book Services

Personnel
Head of Company: Peter Kindersley (Chairman & Chief Executive)
Head of Sales (Home): David Hight (UK Sales Director)
Head of Sales (Export): Nettie Brooke (Head of English Language Export)
Head of Marketing: David Holmes (Marketing Director)
Head of Accounts: Edward Slack (Commercial Director)
Head of Customer Services: Peter Williams (Trade Manager) 071-753 3586
Other Important Personnel:
Tim Moyler (UK Sales Manager), Fiona Collins (Export Sales Manager), Ros Wesson (Adult Marketing Manager), Gavin Thomas (Childrens Marketing Manager), Katie White (Head of Adult List Publicity), Jacqui Morley-Brown (Head of Children's List Publicity), Denise Yates (Telesales)

Number of titles published annually: 155
Number of Staff: 479
NBA Signatory
All New Titles are Bar Coded
Book Data Subscriber
WBIP Updating: Helen Taylor

Trade Terms
35% discount 30 days settlement
Non-Net: Some titles
Credit Cards Accepted: Access/Master, Visa

Returns Procedures
Authority to Return: See Local Rep
Address for Returns: Tiptree
Imperfect Returns: Title page to be returned stating reason for imperfection to limit of £20

DORSET PUBLISHING CO
National School, North Street, Wincanton, Somerset BA9 9AT
ISBN Prefix(es): 0 902129, 0 948699
Tel: 0963 32583
VAT No: 185 3398 30

Order Information

Order Dept Opening Times
Mon - Fri 9.30am - 12.45pm 2pm - 5.30pm
Cyclical Ordering Policy
All Dues Automatically Recorded
Representation Available
Dorset Area Rep: Maurice Hann, 36 Langdon Road, Parkstone, Poole, Dorset BH14 9EH
Tel: 0202 738248

Personnel
Head of Company: Rodney Legg
Head of Marketing: Maurice Hann

Number of titles published annually: 12
Number of Staff: 2
All New Titles are Bar Coded
WBIP Updating: Rodney Legg

Trade Terms
General Net: Single Titles 25%, Two books or more 33.3%, Special Orders 25%, Subscription orders 25%
Other Terms: Payment with order required from non-account customers

Returns Procedures
Authority to Return: Rodney Legg
Stock Returns: Return wrongly supplied books by parcel post, ditto agreed overstocks allowable for credit.
Imperfect Returns: Title pages only may be returned from imperfect books valued below £15 retail

DOT PUBLICATIONS
54A Haig Avenue, Whitley Bay, Tyne & Wear NE25 8JD
ISBN Prefix(es): 1 871086
Tel: 091-252 1239

Order Information

All Dues Automatically Recorded
Representation Available

Personnel
Head of Company: Dorothy Thomas
Other Important Personnel:
David Thomas (General Administration)

Number of titles published annually: 2
IPG Member
NBA Signatory
All New Titles are Bar Coded
WBIP Updating: David Thomas

Trade Terms
35% all orders of 5 or more books
General Net: Single copy/single line 25%, 2 books or more 25% up to 4

Returns Procedures
Authority to Return: From Rep or Head Office

THE DOVECOTE PRESS LTD

Stanbridge, Wimborne, Dorset BH21 4JD
ISBN Prefix(es): 0 946159, 1 874336
Tel: 0258 840549
Fax: 0258 840958
VAT No: 187 4058 37

Order Information

All Dues Automatically Recorded
Representation Available

Personnel

Head of Company: David Burnett
Head of Accounts: Elizabeth Dean

Number of titles published annually: 12
Number of Staff: 2
All New Titles are Bar Coded
WBIP Updating: David Burnett

Trade Terms

General Net: Single copy/single line 20%, 2 books or more 35%, no surcharges

Returns Procedures

Imperfect Returns: Return title page, marked with bookseller's stamp and details of fault

DOWNLANDER PUBLISHING

Downlander, 88 Oxendean Grdns, Lower Willingdon, Eastbourne, East Sussex BN22 0RS
ISBN Prefix(es): 0 906369
Tel: 0323 505814 24 Hours

Order Information

Order Dept Opening Times
8.30am - 6pm
All Dues Automatically Recorded

Personnel

Head of Company: Derek Bourne-Jones (Directing Editor)
Head of Sales (Home): Hilary Clare (Deputy Editor)

Number of titles published annually: 8
NBA Signatory
WBIP Updating: Derek Bourne-Jones

Trade Terms

40%, 45% over ten copies

Returns Procedures

Imperfect Returns: No limit

DP PUBLICATIONS LTD

Aldine House, Aldine Place, 142-144 Uxbridge Road, London W12 8AW
ISBN Prefix(es): 0 905435, 1 870941, 1 873981
Tel: 081-746 0044 4 Lines
Fax: 081-743 8692
Telex: 265871 (MONREF G)
VAT No: 466 4516 29

Order Information

Order Dept Opening Times
Mon - Fri 9am - 5.30pm
Cyclical Ordering Policy
All Dues Automatically Recorded
Representation Available

Personnel

Head of Company: Mr R J Chapman
Head of Sales (Home): Pippa Banner

Head of Marketing: Catherine Tilley
Other Important Personnel:
Joanne Kemp (Marketing Assistant)

Number of titles published annually: 20
Number of Staff: 7
All New Titles are Bar Coded
Book Data Subscriber
WBIP Updating: Joanne Kemp

Trade Terms
Non-Net: 25% Account, 33.3% CWO
Other Terms: Small order surcharge: £1.25 for orders of less than 4 books
Credit Cards Accepted: Access/Master, Visa

Returns Procedures
Authority to Return: Pippa Banner, DP Publications
Address for Returns: Trade Counter Ltd, The Airfield, Norwich Road, Mendlesham, Suffolk IP14 5NA Tel:0449 76629 Fax:0449 767122
Stock Returns: Accounts will be credited for returns that arrive in saleable condition at the warehouse
Imperfect Returns: Return for credit

DRAGONS WORLD LTD
26 Warwick Way, London SW1V 1RX
ISBN Prefix(es): 1 85028
Tel: 071-976 5477
Fax: 071-976 5429
VAT No: 293 8029 33

Account No: _____
Sales Rep: _____
Tel: _____

Orders to
GRANTHAM BOOK SERVICES LTD, Isaac Newton Way, Alma Park Industrial Estate, Grantham, Lincolnshire NG31 9SD
Tel: 0476 67421
Fax: 0476 590223

Order Information

All Dues Automatically Recorded
Representation Available
Invoice Payments: Grantham Books Services Ltd

Personnel
Head of Company: Mr Hubert Schaafsma
Head of Sales (Home): Mr Leslie Cramphorn
Head of Publicity: Mr Peter Daly
Head of Accounts: Mr Graham Turner

Number of titles published annually: 25
Percentage of Export Sales: 40%
Number of Staff: 14
All New Titles are Bar Coded
WBIP Updating: Sales Office

Trade Terms
35% on all orders
BA/Girobank Small Order Scheme: Through Distributors - Grantham Book Services Ltd
Girobank Number: 508 7457
Credit Cards Accepted: Access/Master, Visa, Amex

Returns Procedures
Authority to Return: Sales Office, Dragons World Ltd
Address for Returns: Grantham Book Services Ltd

DRAKE PUBLISHING SERVICES LTD

St Fagans Road, Fairwater, Cardiff, South Glamorgan
CF5 3AE
Tel: 0222 560333
Fax: 0222 554909

Orders to
BAILEY DISTRIBUTION LTD, Unit 1, Learoyd Road, Mountfield Rd Ind Est, New Romney, Kent TN28 8XU
Tel: 0679 66905
Fax: 0679 66638

Order Information

All Dues Automatically Recorded
Representation Available
Invoice Payments: Bailey Distribution

Personnel
Head of Company: Mr R G Drake (Managing Director)
Head of Marketing: Norman Drake (Director)
Head of Publicity: Mrs Moya Hassan
Head of Accounts: Mrs Joan Smith
Head of Customer Services: Mrs Joy Drake
Other Important Personnel:
Mrs Maureen Forsyth (Rights & Permissions Manager)

Number of titles published annually: 200
Number of Staff: 50
PA Member
IPG Member
All New Titles are Bar Coded
WBIP Updating: Norman Drake

Parent Company: Drake Group

Trade Terms
General Net: 35%
Academic Net: 30%
Non-Net: 17%

Returns Procedures
Authority to Return: Norman Drake
Address for Returns: Bailey Distribution

GERALD DUCKWORTH & CO LTD

48 Hoxton Square, London N1 6PB
ISBN Prefix(es): 0 7156
Tel: 071-729 5986
Fax: 071-729 0015
VAT No: 232 5658 65
Account No: 1045
Sales Rep:
Tel:

Order Information

Order Dept Opening Times
9.30am - 5.30pm
All Dues Automatically Recorded
Representation Available

Personnel
Head of Company: Colin Haycraft
Head of Sales (Home): Jonathan Earl
Head of Accounts: Christine Halsey
Head of Customer Services: Vicky Blake

Number of titles published annually: 40
Percentage of Export Sales: 20%
Number of Staff: 12
NBA Signatory
All New Titles are Bar Coded

Trade Terms
General Titles 35%, surcharge if invoice value under £10
General Net: Single copy 25%, two or more 35%
Academic Net: Single copy 20%, 2 or more single titles 25%, Two books or more 35%
Non-Net: 17.5%
Girobank Number: 506 7952
Credit Cards Accepted: Access/Master, Visa

Returns Procedures
Authority to Return: Jonathan Earl
Imperfect Returns: £25

DUN & BRADSTREET LTD

Business Reference Division, Holmers Farm Way, High Wycombe, Buckinghamshire HP12 4UL
ISBN Prefix(es): 0 900625, 0 901491
Tel: 0494 423690
Fax: 0494 422260
VAT No: 505 1891 58

Account No: _____
Sales Rep: _____
Tel: _____

Order Information

Order Dept Opening Times
Mon - Fri 9am - 5pm
Cyclical Ordering Policy
All Dues Automatically Recorded
Representation Available

Personnel
Head of Company: Andrew Dick (Managing Director)
Head of Marketing: Nigel Dickinson (Marketing Manager)
Other Important Personnel:
Sheila Liddell (General Manager), Iris Willsher (Sales Administration Supervisor)

Number of titles published annually: 100
Book Data Subscriber
WBIP Updating: Jane Bingham

Parent Company: The Dun & Bradstreet Corporation

Trade Terms
20% discount on list price + carriage charges
Credit Cards Accepted: Access/Master, Visa, Amex

Returns Procedures
Stock Returns: Request permission from the Sales Administration Supervisor Business Reference Division
Imperfect Returns: As above

DUNDURN DISTRIBUTION

73 Lime Walk, Headington, Oxford, Oxfordshire OX3 7AD
Tel: 0865 67575
Fax: 0865 742024
Telex: 83147 LAVMARK

Account No: _____
Sales Rep: _____
Tel: _____

Order Information

All Dues Automatically Recorded
Representation Available
Invoice Payments: Lavis Marketing

Personnel
Head of Company: Jim Lavis

Parent Company: Dundurn Press

Trade Terms
General Net: Single copy/single line 25%, 2 or more single titles, 2 bks or more 30%, subscription/stock orders 35%, special o's 25%
BA/Girobank Small Order Scheme: Yes
Credit Cards Accepted: Access/Master, Visa, Other

Returns Procedures
Authority to Return: Lavis Marketing
Address for Returns: Lavis Marketing

MARTIN DUNITZ LTD

The Livery House, 7-9 Pratt Street, London NW1 0AE
ISBN Prefix(es): 0 906348, 0 948269, 1 853170, 1 853171
Tel: 071-482 2202
Fax: 071-267 0159
Telex: 296307
VAT No: 242 4714 79

Account No: _____

Sales Rep: _____

Tel: _____

Orders to
BOOKPOINT LIMITED, 39 Milton Park, Abingdon, Oxfordshire OX14 4TD
Tel: 0235 835001
Fax: 0235 861038

Order Information

All Dues Automatically Recorded
Representation Available
Invoice Payments: Bookpoint Ltd

Personnel
Head of Company: Martin Dunitz (Chairman)
Head of Publicity: Wendy Blood (Publicity Manager)
Head of Accounts: John Slaytor (Finance Director)
Head of Customer Services: Theresa Davey (Customer Services Manager)

Number of titles published annually: 15
Percentage of Export Sales: 80%
Number of Staff: 19
All New Titles are Bar Coded
Book Data Subscriber
WBIP Updating: Wendy Blood

Trade Terms
25% - 60 days
Credit Cards Accepted: Access/Master, Visa

Returns Procedures
Address for Returns: Bookpoint Ltd

DUNROD PRESS

8 Brown's Road, Antrim Road, Newtownabbey, County Antrim BT36 8RN
ISBN Prefix(es): 0 86202
Tel: 0232 832362
Fax: 0232 848780
VAT No: 331 7301 94

Order Information

Order Dept Opening Times
Mon - Fri 9am - 5pm
All Dues Automatically Recorded
Representation Available

Personnel
Head of Company: Ken Lindsay (General Manager)
Head of Sales (Home): Hugh Hall
Head of Publicity: John Graham

Number of titles published annually: 5
Number of Staff: 6
NBA Signatory
WBIP Updating: Ken Lindsay

Allied Companies: Dunrod Press (Ireland)

Trade Terms
General Net: Single Copy 25%, Two or more 35%
Minimum Order: No minimum order requirement
Girobank Number: 69 314 4009
Credit Cards Accepted: Access/Master, Visa, Amex, Diners

Returns Procedures
Authority to Return: Sales Manager
Imperfect Returns: Return annotated title page up to 5 copies. Request permission if more than 5 copies

DYLLANSOW TRURAN

'Trewolsta', Trewirgie, Redruth, Cornwall TR15 2TB
ISBN Prefix(es): 0 907566, 0 9506431, 1 850220
Tel: 0209 216796
VAT No: 383 7786 94

Order Information

Order Dept Opening Times
7 days a week 9.30am - 6.30pm
Cyclical Ordering Policy
All Dues Automatically Recorded

Personnel
Head of Company: Len Truran
Head of Sales (Home): Joan Truran
Head of Customer Services: Sharon Langley

Number of titles published annually: 10
Number of Staff: 3
NBA Signatory
WBIP Updating: Sharon Langley

Trade Terms
33.3% post free over £25 net
Other Terms: Carriage charges on orders under £25 net

EAGLE BOOKS

Third Floor, 4 Brandon Road, London N7 9TR
ISBN Prefix(es): 1 85511
Tel: 071-607 3322
Fax: 071-700 2951
VAT No: 341 1282 95

PA Member
All New Titles are Bar Coded
Book Data Subscriber

EARTH RESOURCES RESEARCH LTD

258 Pentonville Road, London N1 9JY
Tel: 071-278 3833
Fax: 071-278 0955

EARLSGATE PRESS
THE PLANTATION
ROWDYKE LANE
WYBERTON
BOSTON, LINCS
PE21 7AQ

Tel 0205 350764
Fx 0205 359459

EARTHSCAN = Kogan Page

EASON & SON LTD

66 Middle Abbey Street, Dublin, County Dublin
ISBN Prefix(es): 0 900346, 1 873430
Tel: 01 733 811
Fax: 01 733 545
Fax: 01 730 620
Telex: 32566
VAT No: IE8T49114D

Order Information
Teleordering: EASON

Order Dept Opening Times
Mon - Fri 8.30am - 5pm
Trade Counter:Brickfield Drive, Crumlin, Dublin 12
Tel: 01 536 211
Fax: 01 539 400

Personnel
Head of Company: W H Clarke (Chairman)
Head of Sales (Home): Timothy Carpenter
Head of Publicity: Marcus McQuiston
Other Important Personnel:
G Bolton (Director)

Allied Companies: Irish Representations Ltd Dublin

Trade Terms
General Net: 25% - Single Copy/Two or more single titles/ Special Orders 33.3% Two Books or more 35% subscription orders/stock orders
Credit Cards Accepted: Visa

Returns Procedures
Stock Returns: Non returnable
Imperfect Returns: Whole imperfect copy

EAST WEST PUBLICATIONS (UK) LTD

8 Caledonia Street, London N1 9DZ
ISBN Prefix(es): 0 85692
Tel: 071-837 5061
Fax: 071-278 4429
VAT No: 235 3811 75

Personnel
Head of Company: L W Carp (Chairman)
Head of Sales (Home): B G Thompson (Managing Director)

Number of titles published annually: 10
Percentage of Export Sales: 60%
PA Member
All New Titles are Bar Coded
WBIP Updating: B G Thompson

ECONOMIC & SOCIAL RESEARCH COUNCIL

Polaris House, North Star Avenue, Swindon, Wiltshire SN2 1UJ
Tel: 0793 413000
Fax: 0793 413001
VAT No: 233 2193 92

THE ECONOMIST BOOKS

25 St James's Street, London SW1A 1HG
ISBN Prefix(es): 0 85058
Tel: 071-839 7000
Fax: 071-403 9485
VAT No: 340 4368 76

Orders to
MARSTON BOOK SERVICES LTD, PO Box 87, Osney
Mead, Oxford, Oxfordshire OX2 0DT
Tel: 0865 791155
Fax: 0865 791927

Order Information

All Dues Automatically Recorded
Invoice Payments: Marston Book Services

Personnel
Head of Company: Johanna Collett (Business Manager)
Head of Marketing: Paul Irwin (Marketing Manager)
Head of Accounts: James Munro

Number of titles published annually: 1
WBIP Updating: Adria Kinloch

Parent Company: The Economist Newspaper Ltd

Trade Terms
25%
Credit Cards Accepted: Access/Master, Visa, Amex, Diners

Returns Procedures
Authority to Return: Johanna Collett
Address for Returns: Marston Book Services
Stock Returns: Overstocks only returned if prior agreement in place, otherwise orders are on a firm sale basis

[handwritten: EDDINGTON HOOK = Combined Book Services]

EDINBURGH UNIVERSITY PRESS
22 George Square, Edinburgh, Lothian EH8 9LF
ISBN Prefix(es): 0 7486, 0 85224, 0 904919, 0 948275
Tel: 031-650 4218 Enquiries
Tel: 031-650 6207 Trade
Tel: 031-662 0553 24 Hour
Fax: 031-662 0053
Telex: 727442 UNIVED G

[handwritten: From 4/4/94 via Marston Book Services. TROIKA.]

Account No: _____ *[handwritten: IENB142]* _____
Sales Rep: _____
Tel: _____

Order Information

Order Dept Opening Times
Mon - Fri 9am - 5pm
All Dues Automatically Recorded
Representation Available

Personnel
Head of Company: Ms Vivian Bone
Head of Publicity: Ms Alison Munro 4220
Head of Distribution: Mr Allan Woods 6207
Head of Customer Services: Mrs Hazel Spalding 6207

Number of titles published annually: 100
Percentage of Export Sales: 33%
Number of Staff: 19
All New Titles are Bar Coded
Book Data Subscriber
WBIP Updating: Alison Munro

Trade Terms
General Net: Single copy/single line 25%, HB 30%, PB 35% (Home) 30% (Ex) 30 days from end of invoice
Other Terms: Order surcharge of £2 on invoice value under £20
Girobank Number: 150 1054
Credit Cards Accepted: Access/Master, Visa

Returns Procedures
Authority to Return: Written authorisation required from EUP or rep

Stock Returns: Must be in mint condition and not more than one year old. Credit may be held on titles returned without permission
Imperfect Returns: Damaged books must be reported within two weeks of receipt

EDS
3 Henrietta Street, Covent Garden, London WC2E 2LU
Tel: 071-240 0856
Fax: 071-379 0609
VAT No: 241 7937 46
Account No: ENG-01360
Sales Rep:
Tel:

Order Information
Teleordering: EDS

Order Dept Opening Times
Mon - Thur 8.30am - 5.30pm, Fri 8.30am - 4pm
All Dues Automatically Recorded
Representation Available

Personnel
Head of Company: Danny Maher
Head of Accounts: James Mealings
Head of Customer Services: Pam Mullan

Number of titles published annually: 1500
Percentage of Export Sales: 45%
WBIP Updating: Gillian Brookes

Parent Company: Eurospan Ltd

Trade Terms
Terms available on request Standing order plan
Girobank Number: 530 1459
Credit Cards Accepted: Access/Master, Visa

Returns Procedures
Authority to Return: A Reid
Stock Returns: Within 12 mths of inv date prior authorisation to be sought Surcharges for returns rec without prior authorisation
Imperfect Returns: Request to return within 1 week of receipt quoting inv no & reason. Title page only for defective supply.

THE EDUCATIONAL COMPANY OF IRELAND
PO Box 43A, Ballymount Rd, Walkinstown, Dublin 12
Tel: 01 500 611
Fax: 01 500 993
VAT No: IE66 07678B
Account No:
Sales Rep:
Tel:

PA Member

EDUCATIONAL EXPLORERS (PUBLISHERS)
11 Crown Street, Reading, Berkshire RG1 2TQ
ISBN Prefix(es): 0 85225
Tel: 0734 873103 Tel/Fax
VAT No: 199 0191 36

Subsidiary Companies: The Cuisenaire Company
Allied Companies: Educational Solutions Inc (US)

EFFECTIVE PUBLISHING

58 St Wulstan Way, Southam, Warwickshire CV33 0TQ
ISBN Prefix(es): 0 9518558
Tel: 0926 812110

Orders to
Effective Publishing, 17 Rowan Walk, Crawley Down, West Sussex RH10 4JP
Tel: 0342 715889

Order Information

Order Dept Opening Times
Mon - Fri 9am - 5pm
All Dues Automatically Recorded

Personnel
Head of Sales (Home): Eric Thorn
Head of Accounts: Chris Pratt

WBIP Updating: Eric Thorn

Trade Terms
35% all orders over £10 retail value
Minimum Order: £10 retail value (under £10 - discount is 25%)

Returns Procedures
Authority to Return: Eric Thorn
Imperfect Returns: Title page - limit £12.50, title page & all prelims over £12.50

EGMONT PUBLISHING LTD

Egmont House, PO Box 111, Great Ducie St, Manchester, Greater Manchester M60 3BL
ISBN Prefix(es): 0 7235, 0 7498
Tel: 061-834 3110
Fax: 061-834 0059
Fax: 061-832 5825
Telex: 668609
Cables: World Manchester

Account No: _____
Sales Rep: _____
Tel: _____

Order Information
Teleordering: WINT

Order Dept Opening Times
Mon - Fri 9am - 5.30pm
All Dues Automatically Recorded
Representation Available

Personnel
Head of Company: Tony Palmer
Head of Sales (Home): Steve Travis
Head of Sales (Export): Pat McGuire
Head of Marketing: Tony Pickup
Head of Publicity: Peter Hey
Head of Accounts: Tony Paulaskas
Head of Distribution: Robert Rough
Head of Customer Services: Jackie Locke

Number of titles published annually: 300
Percentage of Export Sales: 20%
Number of Staff: 90
All New Titles are Bar Coded
WBIP Updating: John Molam

Trade Terms
35% normally
Minimum Order: £50

Returns Procedures
Authority to Return: Mr Tony Paulaskas, Childrens Best Sellers, Egmont Ltd
Address for Returns: Childrens Best Sellers

ELAND

53 Eland Road, London SW11 5JX
ISBN Prefix(es): 0 907871
Tel: 071-228 5450
Fax: 071-924 2229
VAT No: 237 6147 55

Orders to
TIPTREE BOOK SERVICES LTD, Church Road, Tiptree, Colchester, Essex CO5 0SR
Tel: 0621 819600
Fax: 0621 819011

Order Information

All Dues Automatically Recorded
Representation Available

Personnel
Head of Company: John Hatt
Other Important Personnel:
Patricia Rudland (Assistant to John Hatt)

Number of titles published annually: 2
All New Titles are Bar Coded
WBIP Updating: P Rudland

Trade Terms
Distributor's terms

ELC PUBLISHING LTD

109 Uxbridge Road, Ealing, London W5 5TL
Tel: 081-566 2288
Fax: 081-566 4931
VAT No: 538 8388 90

Order Information

Order Dept Opening Times
Mon - Fri 9am - 5pm

Personnel
Head of Company: J Clarke
Head of Accounts: L Pitcher
Head of Customer Services: F Lawler
Other Important Personnel:
J Cameron (Lists Manager)

WBIP Updating: J Clarke

Parent Company: CAS (UK) Ltd

Trade Terms
15%
Other Terms: Carriage charges: £7.50 per book
Credit Cards Accepted: Amex, Diners

Returns Procedures
Authority to Return: Contact L Pitcher

ELECTRONICA BOOKS LTD

Unit E4, Sunbury Int Bus Cent, Brooklands Close, Sunbury-on-Thames, Middlesex TW16 1DX
Tel: 0932 765119
Fax: 0932 765429
VAT No: 529 9730 04

Account No: UNBORE
Sales Rep:
Tel:

Order Information

Order Dept Opening Times
Mon - Fri 9am - 6pm
Orders for more than one publisher can be bulked
All Dues Automatically Recorded
Representation Available

Personnel
Head of Company: Howard Barkway
Head of Sales (Home): Jan Kimber
Head of Accounts: Anthony Head
Other Important Personnel:
Sarah Hewson (Accounts)

Number of titles published annually: 200
Percentage of Export Sales: 45%
Number of Staff: 4
Book Data Subscriber
WBIP Updating: Howard Barkway

Trade Terms
10-35%
Girobank Number: 376 9569
Credit Cards Accepted: Access/Master, Visa, Amex, Diners

Returns Procedures
Authority to Return: Jan Kimber

ELEMENT BOOKS LTD

The Old School House, The Courtyard, Bell Street,
Shaftesbury, Dorset SP7 8BP
ISBN Prefix(es): 1 85230
Tel: 0747 51448
Fax: 0747 55721
VAT No: 320 5363 95

Account No:
Sales Rep:
Tel:

Orders to
ELEMENT BOOKS LTD, Unit 25, Longmead, Shaftesbury,
Dorset SP7 8PL
Tel: 0747 51339
Fax: 0747 51394

Order Information
Teleordering: ELEMENT

All Dues Automatically Recorded
Representation Available

Personnel
Head of Company: Michael Mann (Chairman)
Head of Sales (Home): Martin Drake (Sales Administration Manager)
Head of Marketing: David Alexander (Managing Director)
Head of Publicity: Jenny Carradice (Press & Promotions Officer)

Number of titles published annually: 100
Percentage of Export Sales: 33%
Number of Staff: 33
IPG Member
All New Titles are Bar Coded
WBIP Updating: Martin Drake

Trade Terms
35% - 30 days credit

General Net: Single Copy 25% + £1 p&p Special orders - variable
Girobank Number: 275 4258
Credit Cards Accepted: Access/Master, Visa, Amex, Diners

Returns Procedures
Authority to Return: Martin Drake
Stock Returns: Overstock & general returns by prior arrangement only. Books damaged in transit must be reported within 7 days
Imperfect Returns: £10. Damaged or faulty books may be returned for credit (title page only up to £10 trade value)

ELEMENT BOOKS LTD

Unit 25, Longmead, Shaftesbury, Dorset SP7 8PL
Tel: 0747 51339
Fax: 0747 51394
VAT No: 320 5363 95
Account No: _____ UNIV 72 _____
Sales Rep: _____
Tel: _____

Order Information
Teleordering: ELEMENT

Order Dept Opening Times
Mon - Fri 8.30am - 5pm
Cyclical Ordering Policy
Orders for more than one publisher can be bulked
All Dues Automatically Recorded
Representation Available

Personnel
Head of Accounts: Malvern Carvell
Head of Distribution: Andy Robertson (Distribution Manager)
Head of Customer Services: Sue Foot (Operations Manager)

All New Titles are Bar Coded
WBIP Updating: Martin Drake

Trade Terms
35% 30 days
General Net: Single copy 25% + £1 p&p Special orders variable
Girobank Number: 275 4258
Credit Cards Accepted: Access/Master, Visa, Amex, Diners

Returns Procedures
Authority to Return: Martin Drake
Address for Returns: The Old School House, The Courtyard, Bell St, Shaftesbury, Dorset SP7 8BP
Stock Returns: Overstock & general returns by prior arrangement only. Books damaged in transit must be reported within 7 days.
Imperfect Returns: Damaged or faulty books may be returned for credit (title page only up to £10 trade value)

ELITE WORDS & IMAGE

PO Box 24, Sherborne, Dorset DT9 3SN
ISBN Prefix(es): 0 9516677, 0 9518992
Tel: 0935 816410
Fax: 0935 816409
VAT No: 585 9704 84

Orders to
BOOKPOINT LIMITED, 39 Milton Park, Abingdon, Oxfordshire OX14 4TD
Tel: 0235 835001
Fax: 0235 861038

Order Information

All Dues Automatically Recorded
Representation Available

Personnel
Head of Company: A J Burns-Hill
Head of Accounts: G S Hill

Number of titles published annually: 5
IPG Member
All New Titles are Bar Coded
Book Data Subscriber
WBIP Updating: A J Burns-Hill

Trade Terms
35%
Minimum Order: Three books
Credit Cards Accepted: Access/Master, Visa

Returns Procedures
Authority to Return: Prior permission required
Address for Returns: Bookpoint
Imperfect Returns: Return to Bookpoint with reason for return

ELLIOT RIGHT WAY BOOKS

Brighton Road, Lower Kingswood, Tadworth, Surrey
KT20 6TD
ISBN Prefix(es): 0 7160
Tel: 0737 832202
Fax: 0737 830311
VAT No: 209 5188 55

Order Information

All Dues Automatically Recorded
Representation Available

Personnel
Head of Company: Clive Elliot (Home Sales)
Head of Sales (Export): Malcolm Elliot (Export Sales & Marketing)
Head of Accounts: Chris Maynard (Accounts & Distribution)

Number of titles published annually: 15
All New Titles are Bar Coded
WBIP Updating: Clive Elliot

Parent Company: Andrew Elliot & Sons Ltd

Trade Terms
1-3 books 10%, 4-29 books 25%, 30+ 37.5%, nett monthly.
Any quantity cash with order 37.5%
BA/Girobank Small Order Scheme: 37.5% discount any quantity
Girobank Number: 390 6256

Returns Procedures
Authority to Return: No authority required, all books returnable for credit
Imperfect Returns: Title page on all prices

AIDAN ELLIS PUBLISHING

Cobb House, Nuffield, Henley-on-Thames, Oxfordshire
RG9 5RT
ISBN Prefix(es): 0 85628
Tel: 0491 641496
Fax: 0491 641678
VAT No: 199 2743 13

Orders to
CASSELL PLC, Stanley House, 3 Fleets Lane, Poole, Dorset
BH15 3AJ

Tel: 0202 670581
Fax: 0202 666219

Order Information

All Dues Automatically Recorded
Representation Available
Invoice Payments: Cassell Plc

Personnel

Head of Company: Aidan Ellis

Number of titles published annually: 20
Percentage of Export Sales: 20%
Number of Staff: 2
NBA Signatory

Trade Terms
35% on all orders, postage paid

Returns Procedures
Authority to Return: Prior permission in writing from Aidan Ellis
Address for Returns: Cassell
Imperfect Returns: To Aidan Ellis enclosing title page

ELLIS HORWOOD

Simon & Schuster Int Group, Market Cross Ho, Cooper Street, Chichester, West Sussex PO19 1EB
ISBN Prefix(es): 0 13, 0 7458, 0 85312, 0 87077
Tel: 0243 789942
Fax: 0243 778855
Telex: 86516 ELWOOD G
Cables: Horwood Chichester
VAT No: 193 3949 24
Account No: _____ 1111734002 _____
Sales Rep: _____
Tel: _____

Orders to
INTERNATIONAL BOOK DISTRIBUTORS, Campus 400, Maylands Avenue, Hemel Hempstead, Hertfordshire HP2 7EZ
Tel: 0442 881900
Fax: 0442 882099

Order Information

Invoice Payments: IBD
Sales & Marketing: Simon & Schuster International Group

Personnel

Head of Company: Clive Horwood (Managing Director)

Book Data Subscriber

Parent Company: Paramount Communications Inc

ELM PUBLICATIONS

Seaton House, Kings Ripton, Huntingdon, Cambridgeshire PE17 2NJ
ISBN Prefix(es): 0 946139, 1 85450
Tel: 04873 254
Tel: 04873 238
Fax: 04873 359 24 Hours

Order Information

Order Dept Opening Times
Mon - Fri 9am - 5pm

Personnel

Head of Company: Sheila Ritchie
Head of Sales (Home): Sheila Hillyer

Head of Publicity: Jacqueline Wieczorek
Head of Accounts: Trudy Arnold
Head of Distribution: Lesley Taylor

Number of titles published annually: 30
Percentage of Export Sales: 20%
Number of Staff: 11
All New Titles are Bar Coded
WBIP Updating: Jacqueline Wieczorek

Trade Terms
25% - 40%
Non-Net: 10%
Other Terms: Postage & Packing charged if invoice value is under £25

Returns Procedures
Authority to Return: Prior permission required. Must be in mint condition
Stock Returns: Damaged copies return title page. Incorrect whole book

ELMDON PUBLICATIONS
Elmdon, Saffron Walden, Essex CB11 4NH
Tel: 0763 838359

[handwritten: Elsevier Science Pubs, P.O. Box 211, 1000 AE Amsterdam Holland. A/C No. 0000625309 FAX. 010 31 20 5803705]

ELSEVIER SCIENCE PUBLISHERS LTD
Crown House, Linton Road, Barking, Essex IG11 8JU
ISBN Prefix(es): 0 85334, 0 946395, 1 85166
Tel: 081-594 7272
Fax: 081-594 5942
Fax: 081-594 5094
Telex: 896950
VAT No: 311 8226 91

[handwritten: 38932001]

Account No: [handwritten: 136082]
Sales Rep:
Tel:

[handwritten: ELSEVIER SCIENCE LTD
THE BOULEVARD
LANGFORD LANE
KIDLINGTON
OXFORD OX5 1GB
Tel 0865 843000
Fax 0865 843010]

Order Information
Order Dept Opening Times
Mon - Fri 9am - 5pm
Representation Available

Personnel
Head of Company: Brian D Scanlan (Managing Director)
Head of Sales (Home): J Kumar Patel (General Manager - Marketing)
Head of Accounts: Peter van Woerden (General Manager - Finance)
Head of Distribution: Richard Wood (General Manager - Distribution)
Other Important Personnel:
Mr Ron Potter (Book Orders Manager), Mr Keith Jarmen (Head of Accounts Receivable)

Number of titles published annually: 120
Percentage of Export Sales: 80%
Number of Staff: 270
PA Member
NBA Signatory
WBIP Updating: Claire Coakley

Trade Terms
25% Basic terms negotiable on turnover
Other Terms: UK post free
Girobank Number: 316 704 504
Credit Cards Accepted: Access/Master, Visa, Amex

Returns Procedures
Authority to Return: Book Orders Department

Address for Returns: Elsevier Science Pubs Ltd, Units 30-32 Eastbury Road, The London Ind Park, Beckton, London E6 4LP
Imperfect Returns: Returns permission must always be obtained from book orders manager.

EMAP BUSINESS PUBLISHING LTD
Wentworth House, Wentworth Street, Peterborough, Cambridgeshire PE1 1DS
ISBN Prefix(es): 1 85438
Tel: 0733 63100
Fax: 0733 61313

GORDON EMERY
27 Gladstone Road, Chester, Cheshire CH1 4BZ
Tel: 0244 377955

ENCYCLOPAEDIA BRITANNICA INTERNATIONAL LTD
Carew House, Station Approach, Wallington, Surrey SM6 0DA
ISBN Prefix(es): 0 85229
Tel: 081-669 4355
Fax: 081-773 3631
Telex: 23866
VAT No: 232 8328 71

Order Information

Order Dept Opening Times
Mon - Fri 9.15am - 5.15pm

Personnel
Head of Company: Joe D Adams
Head of Sales (Home): Carol Seale (Head of Trade Sales)
Head of Sales (Export): Dennis Dare (Head of Educational Sales)
Head of Accounts: John Williams

Number of titles published annually: 10
PA Member
NBA Signatory
Book Data Subscriber
WBIP Updating: Carol Seale

Trade Terms
35%. When invoice includes a multi-volume work, there is a 5% cash discount for 14-day settlement.
Girobank Number: 59 517 4058
Credit Cards Accepted: Access/Master, Visa, Amex, Diners

Returns Procedures
Authority to Return: Carol Seale
Address for Returns: Enclyclopaedia Britannica, c/o Hammond Transport Group Salbrook Road, Salfords, Redhill RH1 5HB
Imperfect Returns: Notify Carol Seale

THE ENERGY CONSULTANCY
24 Elm Close, Bedford, Bedfordshire MK41 8BZ
Tel: 0234 262677

ENERGY PUBLICATIONS

1st Floor Suite, 6 Angel Pavement, Royston, Hertfordshire SG8 9AF
Tel: 0763 245322
Fax: 0763 246130
VAT No: 599 5390 70

ENGLANG BOOKS

PO Box 240, Southampton, Hampshire SO9 7RJ
Tel: 0703 582606
Fax: 0703 237646

IPG Member

ENGLISH LIFE PUBLICATIONS LTD

Lodge Lane, Derby, Derbyshire DE1 3HE
ISBN Prefix(es): 0 85101
Tel: 0332 47087
Fax: 0332 290688
VAT No: 125 4976 53

Order Information

Order Dept Opening Times
Mon - Fri 9am - 5pm

Personnel
Head of Company: B C Wood (Managing Director)

Number of titles published annually: 8

Trade Terms
Single copy 25%, Two books or more 35%
Other Terms: Carriage charged on orders under £20

Returns Procedures
Authority to Return: Returns not accepted

ENITHARMON PRESS

36 St George's Avenue, London N7 0HD
ISBN Prefix(es): 0 905289, 1 870612
Tel: 071-607 7194
Fax: 071-607 8694
VAT No: 544 0049 72

Orders to
PASSWORD (BOOKS) LTD, 23 New Mount Street, Manchester, Greater Manchester M4 4DE
Tel: 061-953 4009
Fax: 061-953 4001

Order Information

All Dues Automatically Recorded
Representation Available
Invoice Payments: Password (Books) Ltd

Personnel
Head of Company: Stephen Stuart-Smith (Director)

Number of titles published annually: 12
Number of Staff: 1
All New Titles are Bar Coded

Allied Companies: Dufour Editions Inc (US)

Trade Terms
35% no surcharges
Girobank Number: 6134599

Returns Procedures
Authority to Return: Representative

Address for Returns: Clipper Distribution Service
Stock Returns: Return to Clipper

ENSIGN PUBLICATIONS

2 Redcar Street, Southampton, Hampshire SO1 5LL
ISBN Prefix(es): 1 85455
Tel: 0703 702639 24 Hours
Fax: 0703 785251
VAT No: 522 0325 03

Order Information

Order Dept Opening Times
Mon - Fri 9am - 12pm, 2 - 5.30pm
Cyclical Ordering Policy
All Dues Automatically Recorded
Representation Available

Personnel
Head of Company: David Graves (Managing Director)
Head of Sales (Home): Barry Miles (Sales Manager)
Head of Customer Services: Debbie Campion (Sales Office Supervisor)

Number of titles published annually: 15
Number of Staff: 4
WBIP Updating: David Graves

Parent Company: Hampshire Books Ltd

Trade Terms
General Net: Single copy/single line 20% CWO, otherwise 35%
Credit Cards Accepted: Access/Master, Visa

Returns Procedures
Address for Returns: Ensign Books, 226 Portswood Road, Portswood, Southampton S09 4XS
Stock Returns: Authorized returns only to Portswood address
Imperfect Returns: Title pages for books below £6 retail price

ENTRA PUBLICATIONS

Vector House, 41 Clarendon Road, Watford, Hertfordshire WD1 1HS
Tel: 0923 238441
Fax: 0923 213144
VAT No: 579 1544 06

Orders to
EnTra Publications, PO Box 75, Stockport, Cheshire SK4 1PH
Tel: 061-480 5285
Fax: 061-474 7502

Order Information

Order Dept Opening Times
Mon - Fri 8.30am - 5pm
Invoice Payments: EnTra Publications, Stockport

Personnel
Head of Company: P M Farrer (General Manager)
Head of Publicity: Miss S Deane (Editorial & Publicity)
Head of Distribution: Mr J Atkinson (Warehouse & Distribution) 061-480 5285
Other Important Personnel:
Mrs B M Bowsher (Rights & Permissions)

Number of Staff: 20
WBIP Updating: Mrs B M Bowsher

Parent Company: Engineering Training Authority

Trade Terms
Non-Net Negotiable

Returns Procedures
Authority to Return: Prior permission required
Address for Returns: Stockport

[handwritten: ENVIRONMENT PRESS - 26 BROCK ST, BATH BA1 2LN
Tel 0225 330312
Fax 0225 330305]

ENVOI POETS PUBLICATIONS
Pen Ffordd, Mill Lane, Newport, Dyfed SA42 0QT
Tel: 0239 820285

EOTHEN PRESS
10 Manor Road, Hemingford Grey, Huntingdon,
Cambridgeshire PE18 9BX
ISBN Prefix(es): 0 906719
Tel: 0480 66106
VAT No: 317 0664 71

Order Information

Order Dept Opening Times
Mon - Fri 9am - 5pm
All Dues Automatically Recorded
Representation Available

Personnel
Head of Company: Clement H Dodd
Head of Sales (Home): Nesta Dodd

Number of titles published annually: 5
Percentage of Export Sales: 30%
Number of Staff: 2
WBIP Updating: Nesta Dodd

Trade Terms
33.3%, Single Order Lines 25%
Academic Net: 25%

Returns Procedures
Stock Returns: Incorrectly supp or damaged books - Replacement or refund Overstocks - Accept returns only in special cases
Imperfect Returns: No limit

EPA PRESS
Blythburgh House, Duck Street, Wendens Ambo, Saffron Walden, Essex CB11 4JU
ISBN Prefix(es): 0 9517362
Tel: 0799 41207 24 Hours
Fax: 0799 41166 24 Hours
VAT No: 573 0207 65

Order Information

Order Dept Opening Times
Mon - Fri 8am - 5pm
All Dues Automatically Recorded
Representation Available

Personnel
Head of Company: Dr K M Petty Saphon

Number of titles published annually: 2
Number of Staff: 2
All New Titles are Bar Coded

Trade Terms
Academic Net: Single copy/single line 10%, 2-9 books 20%, 10+ 30%, stock orders 35%
Credit Cards Accepted: Access/Master, Visa

EPS PLC

Banbury Logistics Centre, Appletree Rd Ind Est, Banbury, Oxfordshire OX17 1LL
Tel: 0295 86621
Fax: 0295 86629

Account No: _____

Sales Rep: _____

Tel: _____

Order Information

Order Dept Opening Times
Mon - Fri 8am - 6pm

Personnel
Head of Company: John Hillidge (Director of Logistics)
Head of Sales (Home): Richard Pineo
Head of Publicity: Sue Wintersgill
Head of Accounts: Sandra Williams

Trade Terms
Refer to Publisher

Returns Procedures
Authority to Return: Refer to Publisher

EQUESTRIAN MANAGEMENT CONSULTANTS LTD

Wothersome Grange, Bramham, Wetherby, West Yorkshire LS23 6LY
ISBN Prefix(es): 0 907029
Tel: 0532 892267
Fax: 0532 893352
VAT No: 313 4019 07

Order Information

Cyclical Ordering Policy

Personnel
Head of Company: A C Wakeham
Head of Sales (Home): P Quinn-Pelletier
Head of Distribution: Mrs R Jones

Number of titles published annually: 1
Percentage of Export Sales: 25%
Number of Staff: 6
WBIP Updating: A C Wakeham

Trade Terms
30% sale or return, 40% firm sale
Other Terms: Carriage charged
Credit Cards Accepted: Access/Master, Visa

Returns Procedures
Stock Returns: Covers acceptable on some unsold sale or return orders
Imperfect Returns: Return book for full replacement

ERA TECHNOLOGY LTD

Cleeve Road, Leatherhead, Surrey KT22 7SA
Tel: 0372 374151
Fax: 0372 374496
Telex: 264045
VAT No: 209 7152 66

Book Data Subscriber

ERD PUBLICATIONS LTD

51 Ashleigh Road, Exmouth, Devon EX8 2JY
ISBN Prefix(es): 0 7153, 0 900343

Tel: 0395 272769
VAT No: 140 8269 74

Order Information

Order Dept Opening Times
Mon - Sat 9am - 1pm

Personnel
Head of Company: E R Delderfield (Director)

Number of Staff: 3

Trade Terms
33.3%
Other Terms: Carriage free for orders over £40

LAWRENCE ERLBAUM ASSOCIATES LTD
27 Church Road, Hove, East Sussex BN3 2FA
ISBN Prefix(es): 0 8058, 0 86377, 0 89859
Tel: 0273 207411 748427
Tel: 0273 748427 Orders
Fax: 0273 205612
Fax: 0273 722180 Orders   UNO 1
VAT No: 355 0360 75
Account No: ___013 BLO1_____
Sales Rep: _____
Tel: _____

Order Information

Order Dept Opening Times
Mon - Thu 9am - 5pm, Fri 9am - 4pm
All Dues Automatically Recorded
Representation Available

Personnel
Head of Company: Michael Forster
Head of Publicity: Rachel Windwood
Head of Accounts: Jan Green 0273 748427
Head of Distribution: Meryl Stanton 0273 748427

Number of titles published annually: 200
Number of Staff: 18
Open University Publications
Book Data Subscriber
WBIP Updating: Sonia Sharma

Trade Terms
Variable
Credit Cards Accepted: Access/Master, Visa, Amex

Returns Procedures
Address for Returns: C/O Vale Packaging, 420 Vale Road,
Tonbridge, Kent TN9 1TD

ESCOM Science Pubs, BV, P.O. Box 214, 2300 AE LEIDEN Netherlands. FAX. 31-71-12-17-72

ESTAMP
204 St Albans Avenue, London W4 5JU
Tel: 081-994 2379 Tel/Fax
VAT No: 578 6179 81

Orders to
CENTRAL BOOKS, 99 Wallis Road, London E9 5LN
Tel: 081-986 4854
Fax: 081-533 5821

IPG Member
Book Data Subscriber

ESTATE PUBLICATIONS

Bridewell House, Bridewell Lane, Tenterden, Kent TN30 6JB
ISBN Prefix(es): 0 86084
Tel: 0580 764225
Fax: 0580 763720
VAT No: 201 2961 09

Order Information

Order Dept Opening Times
Mon - Fri 9am - 5pm
All Dues Automatically Recorded
Representation Available

Personnel

Head of Company: R J E Taylor (Managing Partner)
Head of Accounts: Mrs A M Wilson

Number of titles published annually: 150
All New Titles are Bar Coded
WBIP Updating: Mrs D Bugden

Trade Terms

General Net: 3 copies or less 25% + P&P, 4-20 maps 25% carriage paid, 35% 20+ maps
Credit Cards Accepted: Access/Master, Visa

Returns Procedures

Authority to Return: Firm sale only

THE ESTATES GAZETTE LTD

151 Wardour Street, London W1V 4BN
Tel: 071-437 0141
Fax: 071-437 2432

[handwritten: A/C No UN10026]
[handwritten: Closed for lunch 1-2pm.]

EUROBOOK LIMITED

PO Box 52, Wallingford, Oxfordshire OX10 0XU
ISBN Prefix(es): 0 85654
Tel: 0867 328 333 24 Hours
Fax: 0867 328 263
VAT No: 226 7346 57

Order Information

Order Dept Opening Times
Mon - Fri 9am - 5.30pm
All Dues Automatically Recorded

Personnel

Head of Company: P S Lowe

All New Titles are Bar Coded
Book Data Subscriber
WBIP Updating: R McFarlane

Trade Terms

All orders are firm
General Net: Orders with retail value of £35 upwards - 35% discount. Low value orders - sliding scale reduced discount or surcharge
Girobank Number: 588 6457

Returns Procedures

Authority to Return: All orders are firm - any enquiries to Head Office
Stock Returns: As advised when notified by bookseller
Imperfect Returns: Sample of imperfection plus title page, for books up to £10. Contact Sales Admin for all other cases.

EUROMONITOR PLC

87-88 Turnmill Street, London EC1M 5QU
ISBN Prefix(es): 0 86338
Tel: 071-251 8024
Fax: 071-608 3149
Telex: 262433 MONREF G
VAT No: 239 2559 40

Account No: _____

Sales Rep: _____

Tel: _____

Order Information

Order Dept Opening Times
9.30am - 6pm
All Dues Automatically Recorded
Representation Available
Trade Counter:Trade Counter Ltd, Unit D, Trading Estate Road London NW10 7LU Tel:081-963 0322 Fax:081-965 9765

Personnel

Head of Company: Trevor Fenwick
Head of Sales (Home): David Gudgin
Head of Marketing: Andy Maslen
Head of Accounts: Ian Sismey

Number of titles published annually: 150
Percentage of Export Sales: 50%
Number of Staff: 52
All New Titles are Bar Coded
Book Data Subscriber
WBIP Updating: Mr David Gudgin

Trade Terms

10%, Subscription/Stock/Special orders by agreement
Credit Cards Accepted: Access/Master, Visa, Amex, Diners

Returns Procedures

Authority to Return: Customer Services Manager

EUROPA PUBLICATIONS LTD

18 Bedford Square, London WC1B 3JN
ISBN Prefix(es): 0 946658
Tel: 071-580 8236
Tel: 071-631 3361
Fax: 071-636 1664
Fax: 071-637 0922
Telex: 21540 EUROPA G
VAT No: 232 3624 92

Account No: _____

Sales Rep: _____

Tel: _____

Order Information

Order Dept Opening Times
Mon - Fri 9.30am - 5.30pm
All Dues Automatically Recorded
Representation Available

Personnel

Head of Company: Patrick McGinley
Head of Sales (Home): Peter Jackson
Head of Marketing: Sue Whitehead
Head of Publicity: Mary Sweny
Head of Accounts: Philip Desmond
Other Important Personnel:
Marie Manning (Sales Enquiries)

Number of titles published annually: 8
Percentage of Export Sales: 75%

Number of Staff: 50
IPG Member
NBA Signatory
Book Data Subscriber
WBIP Updating: Mary Sweny

Parent Company: Martins Printing Group

Trade Terms
20% UK, 25% Export
BA/Girobank Small Order Scheme: Yes
Girobank Number: 540 6358
Credit Cards Accepted: Amex, Diners

Returns Procedures
Authority to Return: Peter Jackson
Stock Returns: Request permission from Sales Dept
Imperfect Returns: Request permission for all returns

EUROPEAN BUSINESS PUBLISHING LTD

Sampford Lodge, Oxenden Square, Herne Bay, Kent
CT6 8TW
Tel: 0227 362233
VAT No: 466 5990 93

EUROPEAN PRESS SERVICE (EPS)

[handwritten: was European Book Services, UK office now closed]

Dyna House, Lympne Ind Park, Hythe, Kent CT21 4LR
Tel: 0303 263031
Fax: 0303 263029
VAT No: 573 5185 24

[handwritten: EUROPEAN PRESS SERVICE BV, PO BOX 182, 3417 ZK, 14 TASVELD, 3417 XS, MONTFOORT, NETHERLANDS. TEL. 010 31 3484 75155 FAX 010 31 3484 75111]

Account No: 013184
Sales Rep: 26132
Tel: _____

Order Information
Teleordering: EBS

Order Dept Opening Times
Mon - Thu 9am - 4pm
Orders for more than one publisher can be bulked

Personnel
Head of Company: Esther Matthews (UK Manager)
Other Important Personnel:
Sandy Ward-Lewis (Office Manager)

WBIP Updating: Esther Matthews

Parent Company: European Press Service, The Netherlands
Subsidiary Companies: European Press Service GmbH (GE), PBD America Inc (US)

Trade Terms
Vary from Publisher to Publisher

Returns Procedures
Authority to Return: Esther Matthews

EUROPEAN SCHOOLBOOKS LTD

Ashville Trading Estate, The Runnings, Cheltenham,
Gloucestershire GL51 9PQ
ISBN Prefix(es): 0 85048
Tel: 0242 245252
Fax: 0242 224137
VAT No: 274 4347 47

Account No: 51879 (51868)
Sales Rep: _____
Tel: _____

Order Information
Teleordering: ESB

Order Dept Opening Times
Mon - Fri 8.30am - 5pm
All Dues Automatically Recorded
Representation Available

Personnel
Head of Company: Frank Preiss (Managing Director)
Head of Sales (Home): David Young (Sales & Marketing Director)

Number of Staff: 24
All New Titles are Bar Coded

Trade Terms
Non-Net: 17.5-25%
Other Terms: Carriage charged at cost on all initial invoices
Girobank Number: 512 6150
Credit Cards Accepted: Access/Master, Visa

Returns Procedures
Stock Returns: For overstocks with prior permission only. For incorrect supply or damaged in transit prior permission not required
Imperfect Returns: Return complete book

THE EUROSPAN GROUP

3 Henrietta Street, Covent Garden, London WC2E 8LU
Tel: 071-240 0856
Fax: 071-379 0609
VAT No: 241 7937 46

Account No: ENGO1360

Sales Rep:

Tel:

Orders to
EDS, 3 Henrietta Street, Covent Garden, London WC2E 2LU
Tel: 071-240 0856
Fax: 071-379 0609

Order Information
Teleordering: EUR

All Dues Automatically Recorded
Representation Available
Invoice Payments: Eurospan/EDS

Personnel
Head of Company: Michael Geelan
Head of Sales (Home): Andrew Hartley
Head of Publicity: Kate Symonds
Head of Accounts: James Mealings
Head of Distribution: Danny Maher
Head of Customer Services: Pam Mullan

Number of titles published annually: 2500
Percentage of Export Sales: 45%
Number of Staff: 30
Book Data Subscriber

Trade Terms
See EDS

Returns Procedures
Authority to Return: A Reid

EVANGELICAL PRESS

12 Wooler Street, Darlington, County Durham DL1 1RQ
ISBN Prefix(es): 0 85234

Tel: 0325 380232 24 Hours
Fax: 0325 466153
VAT No: 197 9450 05

Order Information
Teleordering: EVANPR

Order Dept Opening Times
Mon Fri 8.30am - 5.15pm
All Dues Automatically Recorded
Representation Available

Personnel
Head of Company: J H Rubens (General Manager)
Head of Publicity: Peter Cooper
Head of Accounts: Brenda Hodginson
Head of Distribution: Roger Hodgkinson

Number of titles published annually: 15
Percentage of Export Sales: 50%
Number of Staff: 13
All New Titles are Bar Coded
WBIP Updating: Peter Cooper

Subsidiary Companies: Europresse SARL (FR)
Allied Companies: Europresse Afrique (Ivory Coast)

Trade Terms
35% on all orders above £40 retail, 25% on all orders under £40 retail
Girobank Number: 39 690 8004

Returns Procedures
Address for Returns: Evangelical Press, Blossomgate, Ripon, North Yorkshire
Stock Returns: Please contact head office for approval
Imperfect Returns: Title page up to £10

EVANGELICAL PRESS OF WALES

Bryntirion, Bridgend, Mid Glamorgan CF31 4DX
ISBN Prefix(es): 0 900898, 0 9502686, 1 85049
Tel: 0656 656095 Tel/Fax
VAT No: 136 1308 96

Order Information

Order Dept Opening Times
Mon - Fri 9am - 1pm, 2pm - 5pm
All Dues Automatically Recorded

Personnel
Head of Company: E Wyn James
Head of Sales (Home): Matthew Evans
Head of Accounts: Patricia Layton
Head of Distribution: Jill Richards

Number of titles published annually: 12
Number of Staff: 5
All New Titles are Bar Coded
WBIP Updating: E W James

Parent Company: Evangelical Movement of Wales

Trade Terms
33.3%, carriage on orders under £15 retail

Returns Procedures
Stock Returns: By negotiation
Imperfect Returns: By negotiation

EVANS BROTHERS LTD

2A Portman Mansions, Chiltern Street, London W1M 1LF
ISBN Prefix(es): 0 237
Tel: 071-935 7160
Fax: 071 487 5034

Telex: 8811713 Evbook G
Cables: Byronitic London W1
VAT No: 440 6864 46

Account No: _____
Sales Rep: _____
Tel: _____

Orders to
BOOKPOINT LIMITED, 39 Milton Park, Abingdon,
Oxfordshire OX14 4TD
Tel: 0235 835001
Fax: 0235 861038

Order Information

All Dues Automatically Recorded
Representation Available
Invoice Payments: Bookpoint

Personnel
Head of Company: Mr S T Pawley (Managing Director)
Head of Sales (Home): Jill Sharpe (UK Sales Manager)
Head Office or Mobile 0831 139956
Head of Sales (Export): Mr Brian Jones (International Publishing Director)
Head of Marketing: Mrs Christine James (UK Publicity)
Head of Accounts: Mr D Winstone (Accountant)

Number of titles published annually: 30
Percentage of Export Sales: 90%
Number of Staff: 11
PA Member
NBA Signatory
All New Titles are Bar Coded
Book Data Subscriber
WBIP Updating: Christine James

Parent Company: Imperial Securities Ltd

Trade Terms
35% 30 days credit on net books
Non-Net: Single copy 17.5%
Girobank Number: 501 4158
Credit Cards Accepted: Access/Master, Visa

Returns Procedures
Authority to Return: Christine James, Evans Brothers
Address for Returns: Bookpoint
Stock Returns: Apply for credit or replacement whichever is required
Imperfect Returns: £2.95

EVENLODE BOOK DISTRIBUTION

Windrush House, Adlestrop, Moreton-in-Marsh,
Gloucestershire GL56 0YN
ISBN Prefix(es): 0 900075
Tel: 0608 ~~658075~~ 652012
Tel: 0608 658018
Tel: 0451 870159 Accounts
Fax: 0608 658860
VAT No: 437 4445 41

Account No: _____
Sales Rep: _____
Tel: _____

Order Information

Order Dept Opening Times
Mon - Fri 9am - 6pm
All Dues Automatically Recorded
Representation Available

Personnel
Head of Company: Geoffrey Smith
Head of Publicity: Victoria Huxley
Head of Accounts: Jane Moore

Number of titles published annually: 12
All New Titles are Bar Coded
WBIP Updating: Victoria Huxley

Trade Terms
35%, Single copy 25%, Special orders negotiable
Other Terms: Carriage charges of £1.20 on single copy orders

Returns Procedures
Authority to Return: Prior permission required from Geoffrey Smith
Address for Returns: TBC Distribution
Imperfect Returns: Title page only under £12

EX LIBRIS PRESS
1 The Shambles, Bradford-on-Avon, Wiltshire BA15 1JS
ISBN Prefix(es): 0 948578
Tel: 0225 863595 Fax/Tel

Order Information

All Dues Automatically Recorded
Representation Available

Personnel
Head of Company: Roger Jones

Number of titles published annually: 8
Number of Staff: 1
IPG Member
All New Titles are Bar Coded

Trade Terms
General Net: Single copy 25% (30% CWO) Two books or more 35% (40% CWO)
Credit Cards Accepted: Access/Master, Visa, Amex

Returns Procedures
Authority to Return: Roger Jones
Stock Returns: Discuss with above

EXCALIBUR PRESS OF LONDON
13 Knightsbridge Green, London SW1X 7QL
Tel: 071-371 9044
Fax: 071-371 9851

EXECUTIVE GRAPEVINE INTERNATIONAL
79 Manor Way, Blackheath, London SE3 9XG
ISBN Prefix(es): 1 870441
Tel: 081-318 4462 24 Hours
Fax: 081-318 9456

Order Information

Order Dept Opening Times
9am - 6pm
Representation Available

Personnel
Head of Company: Robert B Baird
Head of Marketing: Helen L Barrett

Number of titles published annually: 6
All New Titles are Bar Coded
Book Data Subscriber

Trade Terms
20%, (Blackheath Court Press titles 35%, single copies 20%)
Credit Cards Accepted: Access/Master, Visa

Returns Procedures
Stock Returns: Returns not accepted for single orders unless damaged
Imperfect Returns: Book must be returned in full

EXEL LOGISTICS - MEDIA SERVICES
3 Sheldon Way, Larkfield, Aylesford, Kent ME20 6SF
Tel: 0622 882000 24 Hours
Fax: 0622 718036 Cust Serv
Telex: 965514
VAT No: 230 1130 42
Account No: BL 0100.041

Handwritten: INVICTA HOUSE Sir Thomas hengley Rd Medway City estate Rochester, Kent ME2 4DJ 0634 297123 FAX 0634 298000

Sales Rep:
Tel:

Order Information
Teleordering: DMS

Order Dept Opening Times
Mon - Fri 9am - 5pm
Cyclical Ordering Policy
Orders for more than one publisher can be bulked
All Dues Automatically Recorded

Personnel
Head of Company: Ian Rogers
Head of Marketing: Graham Read
Head of Publicity: David Buck
Head of Accounts: Neville Crane
Head of Distribution: Tony Hartley
Head of Customer Services: Bridget Radnedge

Percentage of Export Sales: 30%
Number of Staff: 220

Parent Company: National Freight Consortium

Trade Terms
All terms set by Individual Publishers
Credit Cards Accepted: Access/Master, Visa, Amex, Diners

Returns Procedures
Authority to Return: Authority required from individual publishers

EXLEY PUBLICATIONS LTD
16 Chalk Hill, Oxhey, Watford, Hertfordshire WD1 4BN
ISBN Prefix(es): 1 85015
Tel: 0923 250505
Tel: 0923 248328
Fax: 0923 818733
VAT No: 288 0408 42

Order Information

All Dues Automatically Recorded
Representation Available
Representation: Jarrold Publishing

Personnel
Head of Company: Helen Exley
Head of Sales (Home): Lincoln Exley
Head of Accounts: Alan Byrant
Head of Customer Services: Julie Eames
Other Important Personnel:
David Haste (UK Sales Manager)

Number of titles published annually: 40
IPG Member
All New Titles are Bar Coded
Book Data Subscriber
WBIP Updating: Heather O'Connell

Trade Terms
35% firm sale 30 days
Minimum Order: £50 at invoice
Other Terms: Small order surcharge: £3 under £50 invoice unless order accompanied by cash.
Credit Cards Accepted: Access/Master, Visa

Returns Procedures
Authority to Return: Firm Sale
Imperfect Returns: Faulty books only to: The Trade Counter, The Airfield, Norwich Road, Mendlesham, Suffolk

EXPERT BOOKS

18 Rawlins Close, Woodhouse Eaves, Nr Loughborough, Leicestershire LE12 8SD
ISBN Prefix(es): 0 9515787
Tel: 0509 890607
VAT No: 395 5598 86

Personnel
Head of Company: Dr H McArthur

Number of titles published annually: 1
IPG Member

Trade Terms
General Net: Single copy/single line 25%, 2 or more single titles 33%
Minimum Order: 1 payment with order
Other Terms: Post & packing on invoiced orders

Returns Procedures
Authority to Return: Prior permission required
Stock Returns: Confirm date of delivery and condition of return prior to postage
Imperfect Returns: Return with covering note

EXPORTLIVRE - CP 305 - St Lambert, Canada. J4P 3P8 · A/C No ANGL0038

EXPRESS NEWSPAPERS PLC

Ludgate House, 245 Blackfriars Road, London SE1 9UX
ISBN Prefix(es): 0 85079
Tel: 071-928 8000
Fax: 071-922 7966

Order Information

All Dues Automatically Recorded
Representation Available

Personnel
Other Important Personnel:
Sue Baily (Manager, Books Department)

Number of titles published annually: 30
Percentage of Export Sales: 30%
Number of Staff: 4
All New Titles are Bar Coded
Book Data Subscriber
WBIP Updating: Sue Bailey

Parent Company: United Newspapers

FABER & FABER

3 Queen Square, London WC1N 3AU
ISBN Prefix(es): 0 571
Tel: 071-465 0045

Fax: 071-465 0034
Fax: 071 465 0043
Telex: 299633 FABER G
VAT No: 572 9170 23

Out to lunch between 1pm + 2pm !!

Account No: _23079001_
Sales Rep: _____
Tel: _____

Orders to
FABER BOOK SERVICES, 16 Burnt Mill, Elizabeth Way,
Harlow, Essex CM20 2HX
Tel: 0279 417134
Fax: 0279 417366

Order Information
Teleordering: FABER

All Dues Automatically Recorded
Representation Available
Invoice Payments: Burnt Mill

Personnel
Head of Company: Matthew Evans
Head of Sales (Home): Tim Davies (UK Sales Manager)
Head of Sales (Export): Nick Kenney (Export Sales Manager)
Head of Publicity: Joanna Mackle (Director)
Head of Accounts: Peter Simpson (Finance Director)
Other Important Personnel:
Brigid Macleod (Sales Director)

Number of titles published annually: 250
Percentage of Export Sales: 25%
Number of Staff: 100
PA Member
NBA Signatory
All New Titles are Bar Coded
Book Data Subscriber
WBIP Updating: Sarah Fitzpatrick

Trade Terms
On application
Minimum Order: £35 order value

Returns Procedures
Authority to Return: UK Sales Reps or UK Sales Manager
Address for Returns: Faber Book Services, Burnt Mill
Stock Returns: See Faber Book Services

FABER BOOK SERVICES

16 Burnt Mill, Elizabeth Way, Harlow, Essex CM20 2HX
Tel: 0279 417134
Fax: 0279 417366
VAT No: 572 9170 23

Account No: _23079001_
Sales Rep: _____
Tel: _____

Orders to
24 Hour Ansafone Number: 0279 444040

Order Information
Teleordering: FABER

Order Dept Opening Times
Mon - Fri 8.30am - 6pm
All Dues Automatically Recorded

Personnel
Head of Distribution: Patrick Curran (Distribution Director)
Head of Customer Services: Jean Simpkins (Distribution Manager)

Trade Terms
See publishers
Minimum Order: £35 order value
Girobank Number: 557 6059 GB
Credit Cards Accepted: Access/Master, Amex, Diners, Visa

Returns Procedures
Authority to Return: UK Sales Reps or UK Sales Manager
Stock Returns: Authorised labels must be obtained from rep or sales admin

FABIAN SOCIETY
11 Dartmouth Street, London SW1H 9BN
ISBN Prefix(es): 0 7163
Tel: 071-222 8877
Fax: 071-976 7153
VAT No: 239 0832 58

Order Information

Order Dept Opening Times
Mon - Fri 9.30am - 5.30pm

Personnel
Head of Company: Simon Crine (General Secretary)
Head of Sales (Home): Tim Upton (Finance Officer)
Head of Publicity: Stephen Tindale (Research & Publications Officer)
Other Important Personnel:
Giles Wright (Book Sales Assistant)

Number of titles published annually: 20
Number of Staff: 6
Book Data Subscriber
WBIP Updating: Stephen Tindale

Parent Company: Fabian Society

Trade Terms
25%, 35% on standing orders
Other Terms: Carriage Charge on orders up to £5
Girobank Number: 55 571 0009
Credit Cards Accepted: Access/Master, Visa

Returns Procedures
Authority to Return: Tim Upton

THE FACTORY SHOP GUIDE
34 Park Hill, London SW4 9PB
Tel: 071-622 3722
Fax: 071-498 2823
VAT No: 437 2426 55

IPG Member

FACTS ON FILE
c/o Roundhouse Publishing Ltd, PO Box 140, Oxford, Oxfordshire OX2 7SF
ISBN Prefix(es): 0 8160, 0 87196, 0 948894
Tel: 0865 512682
Fax: 0865 59594
Telex: 83147 via or by attn
Telex: FACTS
VAT No: 394 5462 20

Account No: _____
Sales Rep: _____
Tel: _____

Orders to
BOOKPOINT LIMITED, 39 Milton Park, Abingdon,
Oxfordshire OX14 4TD
Tel: 0235 835001
Fax: 0235 861038

Order Information

All Dues Automatically Recorded
Representation Available
Invoice Payments: Bookpoint Ltd

Personnel
Head of Company: Alan Goodworth

Number of titles published annually: 80
Percentage of Export Sales: 30%
IPG Member
NBA Signatory
Book Data Subscriber
WBIP Updating: Alan Goodworth

Parent Company: CCH Editions Inc
Allied Companies: CCH Editions Ltd

Trade Terms
Single copy 25%, two or more 35%
Credit Cards Accepted: Access/Master, Visa, Amex

Returns Procedures
Authority to Return: Write to Alan Goodworth
Address for Returns: Bookpoint Ltd
Imperfect Returns: Price limit £20

FAIRPLAY PUBLICATIONS LTD

20 Ullswater Crescent, Ullswater Business Park, Coulsdon,
Surrey CR5 2HR
Tel: 081-660 2811
Fax: 081-660 2824

FAMEDRAM PUBLISHERS LTD

Mill Business Centre, PO Box 3, Ellon, Aberdeen, Grampian
AB41 9EA
ISBN Prefix(es): 0 142558, 0 905489, 0 9501944, 8 526110
Tel: 06513 2429
Tel: 06513 2428
Fax: 06513 2180
VAT No: 264 0020 09

Order Information

Order Dept Opening Times
Mon - Fri 9am - 5pm
Representation Available

Personnel
Head of Company: Mr J F Williams
Head of Sales (Home): Mrs Eleanor Stewart

Number of titles published annually: 8
All New Titles are Bar Coded
WBIP Updating: Mrs Eleanor Stewart

Trade Terms
33.3%

FAMILY PLANNING ASSOCIATION

27-35 Mortimer Street, London W1N 7RJ
Tel: 071-436 3288
Fax: 071-436 5723

IPG Member

FAMILY POLICY STUDIES CENTRE

231 Baker Street, London NW1 6XE
ISBN Prefix(es): 0 907051
Tel: 071-486 8211 24 Hours
Tel: 071-486 7680
Tel: 071-486 8179
Fax: 071-224 3510

Order Information

Order Dept Opening Times
Mon - Fri 9.30am - 5pm

Personnel

Head of Company: Ms Ceridwen Roberts (Director)
Head of Sales (Home): Lucy Auty (Publications Officer)
Other Important Personnel:
Chris Butcher (Information Officer), Lucy Auty (Publications Secretary)

Number of titles published annually: 10
Number of Staff: 9
WBIP Updating: Lucy Auty

Trade Terms
30%

Returns Procedures
Authority to Return: Contact Lucy Auty
Imperfect Returns: At our discretion

FAMILY PUBLICATIONS

Wicken, Milton Keynes, Buckinghamshire MK19 6BU
ISBN Prefix(es): 0 906229, 1 871217
Tel: 0908 57234
Fax: 0908 57331

Personnel
Head of Company: P D Riches

Number of titles published annually: 6
Percentage of Export Sales: 25%

Allied Companies: Family & Youth Concern, Family Education Trust

Trade Terms
35%, carriage free for orders over £50 retail value
Credit Cards Accepted: Access/Master, Visa

FAMILY WELFARE ENTERPRISES

501-505 Kingsland Road, London E8 4AU
Tel: 071-254 6251
Fax: 071-249 5443
VAT No: 221 4103 31

FARMING PRESS BOOKS

Wharfedale Road, Ipswich, Suffolk IP1 4LG
ISBN Prefix(es): 0 85236
Tel: 0473 241122
Fax: 0473 240501

Order Information

Order Dept Opening Times
Mon - Fri 9am - 1pm, 1.45pm - 5pm
All Dues Automatically Recorded
Representation Available

Personnel
Head of Company: Roger Smith (General Manager)

Head of Accounts: Anne Shead
Head of Customer Services: Samantha Blain

Number of titles published annually: 10
Number of Staff: 8
All New Titles are Bar Coded
Book Data Subscriber
WBIP Updating: Samantha Blain

Parent Company: United Newspapers Plc

Trade Terms
Single Copy 25%, Two or more 35%
Credit Cards Accepted: Access/Master, Visa

Returns Procedures
Authority to Return: Prior permission required from Samantha Blain
Stock Returns: Only perfect copies accepted

FARRAND PRESS

50 Ferry Street, Isle of Dogs, London E14 3DT
ISBN Prefix(es): 1 85083
Tel: 071-515 7322
Fax: 071-537 3559
VAT No: 410 1778 85

Orders to
Portland Press Ltd, PO Box 32, Commerce Way, Colchester, Essex CO2 8HP
Tel: 0206 46351
Fax: 0206 549331

Order Information

Order Dept Opening Times
Mon - Thur 9am - 5pm Fri 9am - 4pm
Cyclical Ordering Policy
All Dues Automatically Recorded

Personnel
Head of Company: R A Farrand (Factotum)

Number of titles published annually: 8
Percentage of Export Sales: 20%
Open University Publications
Book Data Subscriber

Parent Company: Portland Press

Trade Terms
General Net: Single Copy 25%, Two or more single titles 30%, Six books or more 33.3%
Credit Cards Accepted: Access/Master, Amex, Diners, Visa

Returns Procedures
Authority to Return: Prior permission required
Address for Returns: Portland Press, Colchester
Stock Returns: Books must be between 6 and 18 months of invoice date

[Handwritten: Farrar, Strauss + Giroux = Littlehampton Book Service]

IAN FAULKNER PUBLISHING LTD

Lincoln House, 347 Cherry Hinton Road, Cambridge, Cambridgeshire CB1 4DJ
ISBN Prefix(es): 1 85763
Tel: 0223 416865
Tel: 0223 416601 Tel/Fax
VAT No: 599 4384 70

Order Information

Order Dept Opening Times
9am - 5pm
All Dues Automatically Recorded
Representation Available

Personnel
Head of Company: Ian Faulkner

Number of titles published annually: 20
Number of Staff: 2
All New Titles are Bar Coded
WBIP Updating: Jonathan Sansom

Trade Terms
35%

Returns Procedures
Authority to Return: Jonathan Sansom

FEATHER BOOKS

Fairview, Old Coppice Lyth Bank, Shrewsbury, Shropshire SY3 0BW
Tel: 0743 872177

FEDERATION OF FAMILY HISTORY SOCIETIES

Benson Room, Birmingham Inst, Margaret Street, Birmingham, West Midlands B3 3BS
VAT No: 408 1276 68

FERNHURST BOOKS

33 Grand Parade, Brighton, East Sussex BN2 2QA
ISBN Prefix(es): 0 906754
Tel: 0273 623174
Fax: 0273 623175
VAT No: 340 7573 60

Order Information

Order Dept Opening Times
Mon - Fri 9am - 1pm, 2pm - 5.30pm or Ansaphone
All Dues Automatically Recorded
Representation Available

Personnel
Head of Company: T J Davison (Managing Director)
Head of Sales (Home): Jon Hutchings (UK Sales Manager)
Head of Marketing: Murray Kenneth (Commercial Manager)
Head of Accounts: Jackie Phillips (Operations Manager)

Number of titles published annually: 10
Percentage of Export Sales: 25%
Number of Staff: 6
IPG Member
All New Titles are Bar Coded
Book Data Subscriber
WBIP Updating: Murray Kenneth

Trade Terms
35%. Surcharge of £1.50 on orders under £25. Single copy orders 25% plus £1.50 surcharge.

Returns Procedures
Authority to Return: Prior permission required.
Address for Returns: Clipper Distribution Services, Windmill Grove, Portchester, Hants PO16 9HT Tel:0705 200080

FERRY PRESS

Bridges Farmhouse, Laughton, Lewes, East Sussex BN8 6BS

FHG PUBLICATIONS LTD
Abbey Mill Business Centre, Seedhill, Paisley, Renfrewshire
PA1 1JN
ISBN Prefix(es): 1 85055
Tel: 041-887 0428
Fax: 041-889 7204
VAT No: 573 9420 20

Orders to
WORLD LEISURE MARKETING, 117 The Hollow,
Littleover, Derby, Derbyshire DE23 7BS
Tel: 0332 272020
Fax: 0332 774287

Order Information

All Dues Automatically Recorded
Representation Available
Invoice Payments: Grantham Book Services Ltd

Personnel
Head of Company: P M Clark

Number of titles published annually: 15
All New Titles are Bar Coded
WBIP Updating: P M Clark

Parent Company: United Newspapers plc

Trade Terms
35%

Returns Procedures
Authority to Return: World Leisure Marketing
Address for Returns: Grantham Book Services Ltd

THE FINANCIAL TIMES
FT Business Information, 102 Clerkenwell Road, London
EC1M 5SA
Tel: 071-251 9321
VAT No: 278 5371 21

Order Information
Orders To:Books Marketing

Book Data Subscriber

Financial Training = % Blackstone

FINDHORN PRESS
The Park, Findhorn, Forres, Morayshire IV36 0TZ
ISBN Prefix(es): 0 905249, 0 906191
Tel: 0309 690582
Tel: 0309 690036
Fax: 0309 690933
VAT No: 297 2612 32

Orders to
ASHGROVE PRESS, 4 Brassmill Centre, Brassmill Lane,
Bath, Avon BA1 3JN
Tel: 0225 425539
Fax: 0225 319137

Order Information

Order Dept Opening Times
Mon - Thur 9am - 12.30, 2pm - 4pm, Fri 2pm - 4pm
Representation Available
Scottish & European Orders To Head Office

Personnel
Head of Company: Karin Aubrey (Manager)
Head of Customer Services: Mary Carrol
Other Important Personnel:
Sandra Kramer (Editor)

Number of titles published annually: 5
Percentage of Export Sales: 50%
Number of Staff: 7
IPG Member
All New Titles are Bar Coded
Book Data Subscriber
WBIP Updating: Karin Aubrey

Parent Company: New Findhord Directions Ltd

Trade Terms
35%
Credit Cards Accepted: Access/Master, Visa

FIREBIRD BOOKS LTD

PO Box 327, Poole, Dorset BH15 2RG
ISBN Prefix(es): 1 85314
Tel: 0202 715349 Sales
Tel: 0258 454675 Editorial
Fax: 0202 736191
VAT No: 504 1236 96

Orders to
CHRIS LLOYD SALES AND MARKETING SERVICES,
463 Ashley Road, Parkstone, Poole, Dorset BH14 0AX
Tel: 0202 715349
Fax: 0202 736191

Order Information

All Dues Automatically Recorded
Representation Available

Personnel
Head of Sales (Home): Chris Lloyd

Number of titles published annually: 6
Percentage of Export Sales: 50%
All New Titles are Bar Coded
Book Data Subscriber
WBIP Updating: Chris Lloyd

Trade Terms
35%
Minimum Order: £1 surcharge on invoices under £15

Returns Procedures
Authority to Return: Chris LLoyd Sales & Marketing
Address for Returns: Bailey Distribution Ltd, Learoyd Road, Mountfield Road Ind Estate, New Romney, Kent, TN28 8XU
Imperfect Returns: Title pages up to £10

FIRST IMPRESSIONS PUBLICATIONS

185 Dock Road, Tilbury, Essex RM18 7BT
ISBN Prefix(es): 1 8701300
Tel: 0375 859103 24 Hours
Tel: 0375 859500
Tel: 0375 842052
Fax: 0375 856108
VAT No: 545 8341 30

All New Titles are Bar Coded

FIRST TIME PUBLICATIONS

Burdett Cottage, 4 Burdett Place, George Street, Hastings, East Sussex TN34 3ED
ISBN Prefix(es): 0 2660520, 0 951285
Tel: 0424 428855 Tel/Fax

Order Information

Order Dept Opening Times
Mon - Fri 9am - 5pm
All Dues Automatically Recorded

Personnel
Head of Company: Josephine Austin
Head of Customer Services: Pat Wootton

Number of titles published annually: 2

Trade Terms
35% on all orders

Returns Procedures
Imperfect Returns: Book will be replaced

1ST WORLD PUBLISHING LTD

The Plough at Cadsden, Cadsden, Princes Risborough, Buckinghamshire HP17 0NB
ISBN Prefix(es): 1 8728210
Tel: 0844 43302
VAT No: 524 2987 32

Order Information

Order Dept Opening Times
Mon - Fri 10am - 1pm, 2pm - 6pm
Cyclical Ordering Policy
All Dues Automatically Recorded
Representation Available

Personnel
Head of Company: P G Hatter
Head of Sales (Home): N Hatter

Number of titles published annually: 5
Number of Staff: 2
All New Titles are Bar Coded
WBIP Updating: N Hatter

Trade Terms
35% all orders

Returns Procedures
Authority to Return: N Hatter
Stock Returns: Authority to return first

FIS PUBLICATIONS LTD

30 Hoghton Street, Southport, Merseyside PR9 0NZ
Tel: 0704 538515
Tel: 0704 539395
Fax: 0704 535133
VAT No: 163 6466 50

FITZWILLIAM MUSEUM ENTERPRISES LTD

Trumpington Street, Cambridge, Cambridgeshire CB2 1RB
ISBN Prefix(es): 0 904454
Tel: 0223 332900
Fax: 0223 332923
VAT No: 215 4106 08

Order Information

Order Dept Opening Times
Mon - Fri 9.30am - 5pm

Personnel
Head of Company: Richard Maddicott (General Manager)
Head of Marketing: Judith Sanders (Marketing Manager)
Head of Accounts: Anne Newman (Accounts)

Number of titles published annually: 5
Number of Staff: 8
Book Data Subscriber
WBIP Updating: Richard Maddicott

Trade Terms
35% + carriage charges

Returns Procedures
Imperfect Returns: Imperfect copies or books damaged in transit must be returned complete for credit

FLAME BOOKS LTD

9 Kensington Park Gardens, London W11 3HB
ISBN Prefix(es): 0 905340
Tel: 071-727 6941

Personnel
Head of Company: M I H Becket

Trade Terms
Single Copy 25%, 2 or more single copies 25%, 4 or more 33%

Returns Procedures
Authority to Return: No returns

FLEET BOOKS

10 Belvedere Road, Oxford, Oxfordshire OX4 2AZ
VAT No: 150 7880 60

FLEGON PRESS

37B New Cavendish Street, London W1M 8JR
Tel: 081-752 1296
Fax: 071-486 2094

IPG Member

FLICKS BOOKS

29 Bradford Road, Trowbridge, Wiltshire BA14 9AN
ISBN Prefix(es): 0 948911
Tel: 0225 767728 24 Hours
Fax: 0225 760418

Order Information

Order Dept Opening Times
Mon - Fri 9am - 6pm
All Dues Automatically Recorded
Representation Available

Personnel
Head of Company: Matthew Stevens/Aletta Stevens

Number of titles published annually: 6
Percentage of Export Sales: 75%
WBIP Updating: Matthew Stevens

Trade Terms
30%
Other Terms: Carriage Charge - outside UK 15% of invoice value (unless client has UK shipper - then no charge)
Credit Cards Accepted: Amex, Diners

Returns Procedures
Stock Returns: Overstocks - client request return on usual form/letter Damaged/Incorrectly supplied - return books with note
Imperfect Returns: Return whole book with reason

FLIGHT DIRECTORIES LTD

PO Box 1315, Potters Bar, Hertfordshire EN6 1PU
ISBN Prefix(es): 0 9514185
Tel: 0707 46952 24 Hours
Fax: 0707 46936
Telex: 94019508 MALC G
VAT No: 233 6950 58

Order Information

Order Dept Opening Times
Mon - Fri 9am - 7pm

Personnel

Head of Company: Malcolm Ginsberg
Head of Sales (Home): Linda Ginsberg

Number of titles published annually: 2
Number of Staff: 10
WBIP Updating: Linda Ginsberg

Trade Terms

33%, prepayment required
Other Terms: Carriage charges: inclusive to UK & Ireland, £6 to mainland Europe, £12 to rest of the world
Credit Cards Accepted: Access/Master, Visa, Amex

FLORIS BOOKS

15 Harrison Gardens, Edinburgh, Lothian EH11 1SH
ISBN Prefix(es): 0 86315, 0 903540
Tel: 031-337 2372 24 Hours
Fax: 031-346 7516

Order Information

Order Dept Opening Times
Mon - Fri 9am - 5pm
All Dues Automatically Recorded
Representation Available

Personnel

Head of Company: Christian MacLean
Head of Sales (Home): Alan Smart
Head of Accounts: Christine McPhillips

Number of titles published annually: 25
Number of Staff: 4
PA Member
NBA Signatory
All New Titles are Bar Coded
Book Data Subscriber
WBIP Updating: Alan Smart

Trade Terms

General Net: Single copy/single line 25%, otherwise 35%
Non-Net: 20%
Other Terms: Surcharge of £1 for orders below £10 invoice value
Girobank Number: 15 2004009
Credit Cards Accepted: Access/Master, Visa, Other

Returns Procedures

Authority to Return: Christine McPhillips
Address for Returns: Clipper Distribution
Stock Returns: Return damaged or wrongly supplied book to Clipper Dist with note stating reason for return
Imperfect Returns: Up to price limit of £25 send annotated title page only to the Edinburgh office

FMJ BOOKS (FMJ INTERNATIONAL PUBLICATIONS LTD)

Queensway House, 2 Queensway, Redhill, Surrey RH1 1QS
ISBN Prefix(es): 0 86108

Tel: 0737 768611
Fax: 0737 761685
Cables: 948669 TOPJNL G

Order Information

Order Dept Opening Times
Mon - Fri 9am - 1pm, 2 - 5pm

Personnel

Head of Company: John Clarke (Managing Director)
Head of Sales (Home): Colin C Dann
Head of Publicity: Pam Gudge
Head of Accounts: Ian Cuthbertson
Head of Customer Services: Majorie Booth

Number of titles published annually: 1
Percentage of Export Sales: 40%
Number of Staff: 350
PA Member
WBIP Updating: Pam Gudge

Parent Company: Argus Business Publications Ltd
Subsidiary Companies: FMJ International Publications Ltd, International Trade Publications Ltd

Trade Terms

30%, no surcharges
Credit Cards Accepted: Access/Master, Visa, Amex

Returns Procedures

Stock Returns: Returns will be accepted if books returned are in mint condition
Imperfect Returns: Contact Mrs Booth

FOCUS PUBLICATIONS LTD

9 Priors Road, Windsor, Berkshire SL4 4PD
ISBN Prefix(es): 0 9505053, 1 852050
Tel: 0753 831522
VAT No: 370 2848 51

Order Information

All Dues Automatically Recorded
Representation Available
Mountain Walking Titles Dist:Cordee Tel:0533 543579 Home Learning Titles Dist:Book Systems Tel:0279 814228

Personnel

Head of Company: R D Maddern

All New Titles are Bar Coded
Book Data Subscriber

Trade Terms

35% on all orders

FOLENS PUBLISHERS

Albert House, Apex Bus Centre, Boscombe Road, Dunstable, Bedfordshire LU5 4RL
ISBN Prefix(es): 1 85276
Tel: 0582 472788
Fax: 0582 472575
VAT No: 446 2002 84

Order Information

Order Dept Opening Times
Mon - Fri 8.30am - 5pm
All Dues Automatically Recorded
Representation Available

Personnel

Head of Company: Malcolm Watson (Managing Director)

Head of Sales (Home): Shona Tweddle (Sales & Marketing Manager)
Head of Distribution: Lee Cooper
Head of Customer Services: Angela Winward

Number of titles published annually: 90
PA Member
All New Titles are Bar Coded
WBIP Updating: Shona Tweddle

Parent Company: Folens Publishers (Dublin)

Trade Terms
Non-Net: 17.5% Subscription/Stock orders negotiable
Credit Cards Accepted: Access/Master, Visa

Returns Procedures
Authority to Return: Contact Shona Tweddle

FOLLOW YOUR FINGER BOOKS
42 The Ridgeway, Radlett, Hertfordshire WD7 8PS
ISBN Prefix(es): 0 907581
Tel: 0923 857696

Order Information
All Dues Automatically Recorded
Representation Available

Personnel
Head of Company: J P Hurst

Number of titles published annually: 1

Trade Terms
35%

[handwritten: Fontana = Harper Collins.]

FOOD TRADE PRESS LTD
Station House, Hortons Way, Westerham, Kent TN16 1BZ
ISBN Prefix(es): 0 900379, 0 903962
Tel: 0959 563944
Fax: 0959 561285
VAT No: 205 4078 91

Order Information
Order Dept Opening Times
Mon - Fri 9am - 6.30pm
All Dues Automatically Recorded

Personnel
Head of Company: Mr Adrian Binsted
Head of Accounts: Mrs P A Howard

Number of titles published annually: 6
Percentage of Export Sales: 40%
Number of Staff: 5
WBIP Updating: Adrian Binsted

Allied Companies: Attwood & Binsted, Chiriotti Editori (IT), Regies Et Actions Publicitaire (FR)

Trade Terms
20%
Girobank Number: 589 3151
Credit Cards Accepted: Access/Master, Visa

Returns Procedures
Imperfect Returns: Up to £12 title page

FORBES PUBLICATIONS LTD
2 Drayson Mews, London W8 4LY
ISBN Prefix(es): 0 901762

Tel: 071-938 1035
Fax: 071-938 4425
VAT No: 239 0467 55

Orders to
PLYMBRIDGE DISTRIBUTORS LTD, Plymbridge House, Estover Road, Plymouth, Devon PL6 7PZ
Tel: 0752 735251
Fax: 0752 695699

Order Information

All Dues Automatically Recorded
Invoice Payments: Plymbridge Distributors

Personnel
Head of Company: Mrs Joan Forbes/Mrs Crellin
Head of Sales (Home): Colin Forbes

Number of titles published annually: 8
Number of Staff: 8
WBIP Updating: Colin Forbes

Trade Terms
17.5% non net
Girobank Number: 221 2951
Credit Cards Accepted: Access/Master, Amex, Diners, Visa

Returns Procedures
Authority to Return: Prior permission required
Address for Returns: Plymbridge Distributors
Stock Returns: Return clearly stating reason

FOREST (FREEDOM ORG FOR RIGHT ENJOY SMOKING TOBACCO)

2 Grosvenor Gardens, London SW1W 0DH
ISBN Prefix(es): 1 871833
Tel: 071-823 6550
Fax: 071-823 4534

Order Information

All Dues Automatically Recorded

Personnel
Head of Company: Chris R Tame (Director)

Number of Staff: 3

Trade Terms
33.3% on all orders: no surcharge: no postage

FOREST BOOKS

20 Forest View, London E4 7AY
ISBN Prefix(es): 0 948259, 0 950487, 1 85610
Tel: 081-529 8470 24 Hours
Fax: 081-524 7890
Telex: 891182 GECOMS G
VAT No: 406 4042 90

Order Information

Order Dept Opening Times
Mon - Sat 9am - 6pm
All Dues Automatically Recorded
Representation Available

Personnel
Head of Company: Brenda Walker
Head of Marketing: Judith Palmer
Head of Accounts: Hazel Aldridge

Number of titles published annually: 20
Percentage of Export Sales: 20%
Number of Staff: 5
IPG Member

NBA Signatory
All New Titles are Bar Coded
WBIP Updating: Judith Palmer

Trade Terms
General Net: Single copy 25%, 2 or more single titles/2 books or more/ subscription orders/stock orders 35%, special orders 40%
Other Terms: Postage charged on single copy orders
Credit Cards Accepted: Access/Master, Visa, Amex

Returns Procedures
Stock Returns: Through representative or request to head office

FORIS Pubs = De Gruyter.

FORTRESS BOOKS
PO Box 141, London E2 0RL
ISBN Prefix(es): 1 870958
Tel: 081-985 7394
VAT No: 506 9284 33

W FOULSHAM & CO LTD
837 Yeovil Road, Slough, Berkshire SL1 4JH
ISBN Prefix(es): 0 572
Tel: 0753 526769
Tel: 0753 530596
Tel: 0753 538637 24 Hours
Fax: 0753 811409
Telex: 41671 TCS G
VAT No: 207 8239 61

Account No: _____
Sales Rep: _____
Tel: _____

Order Information
Teleordering: FLAM

Order Dept Opening Times
Mon - Fri 9am - 5pm
Representation Available

Personnel
Head of Company: Ronald S Belasco (Chairman)
Head of Sales (Home): Robin Cortie
Head of Publicity: Margaret Lashbrook
Head of Accounts: Mrs A Twyman
Head of Distribution: M Hiron
Head of Customer Services: Pat Vance
Other Important Personnel:
B A R Belasco (Managing Director), G M Kitchen (Finance Director), Wendy Tearle (Trade Manager)

NBA Signatory
All New Titles are Bar Coded
WBIP Updating: Pat Vance

Trade Terms
35%
Other Terms: 20% postage & packing for orders under £5 invoice value
Girobank Number: 246 6058

Returns Procedures
Authority to Return: Local representative or Wendy Tearle at H/O
Stock Returns: Covers for Check Your Tax and Raphael's Almanac for last yr to current Ed only. O'stocks in mint condition by neg
Imperfect Returns: Title page required for copies up to £5 retail value, over which full copies required

THE FOUNDATIONAL BOOK CO LTD
PO Box 659, London SW3 6SJ
Tel: 071-584 1053

FOUNTAIN PRESS LTD
Queensborough House, 2 Claremont Road, Surbiton, Surrey KT6 4QU
Tel: 081-390 7768
Fax: 081-390 8062
VAT No: 370 1341 90

Account No: _____
Sales Rep: _____
Tel: _____

FOUR COURTS PRESS LTD
Kill Lane, Blackrock, County Dublin
ISBN Prefix(es): 1 85182
Tel: 01 289 2922
Fax: 01 289 3072
VAT No: 083 8224 U

Orders to
GILL & MACMILLAN LTD, Goldenbridge, Inchicore, Dublin 8, County Dublin
Tel: 01 531 005
Fax: 01 541 688

Order Information

All Dues Automatically Recorded
Representation Available
Invoice Payments: Gill & Macmillan

Personnel
Head of Company: Michael Adams
Head of Accounts: Claire Kenna

Number of titles published annually: 5
Percentage of Export Sales: 50%
Number of Staff: 1
WBIP Updating: M Adams

Allied Companies: Irish Academic Press

Trade Terms
Single copy 25%, 2 or more single titles 35%
Credit Cards Accepted: Access/Master, Visa, Amex

Returns Procedures
Address for Returns: Gill & Macmillan

FOURMAT PUBLISHING
133 Upper Street, London N1 1QP
ISBN Prefix(es): 1 85190
Tel: 071-226 7497 24 Hours
Fax: 071-359 3031

Order Information

All Dues Automatically Recorded
Representation Available

Personnel
Head of Company: Pauline Callow

Number of titles published annually: 30
IPG Member
Book Data Subscriber

Trade Terms
33.3% multiples, 25% single copy/single line, no carriage charges

Returns Procedures
Address for Returns: Returns Dept, 27&28 St Albans Place, London, N1 0NX

FOURTH ESTATE
289 Westbourne Grove, London W11
ISBN Prefix(es): 0 947795, 1 857020, 1 872180
Tel: 071-727 8993
Fax: 071-792 3176

Account No: _____

Sales Rep: _____

Tel: _____

Orders to
TIPTREE BOOK SERVICES LTD, Church Road, Tiptree, Colchester, Essex CO5 0SR
Tel: 0621 819600
Fax: 0621 819011

Order Information

All Dues Automatically Recorded
Representation Available
Invoice Payments: Tiptree

Personnel
Head of Company: Victoria Barnsley (Managing Director)
Head of Sales (Home): Michael Halden (Sales Director)
Head of Marketing: Joanna Prior (Marketing Director)
Head of Publicity: Camilla Barker (Press Officer)
Head of Accounts: Patric Duffy (Finance Director)

Number of titles published annually: 50
Percentage of Export Sales: 20%
Number of Staff: 12
NBA Signatory
All New Titles are Bar Coded
Book Data Subscriber
WBIP Updating: Clive Priddle

Trade Terms
35%

Returns Procedures
Authority to Return: Michael Halden
Address for Returns: Tiptree
Imperfect Returns: £10 price limit for annotated pages

L N FOWLER & CO LTD
1201-3 High Road, Chadwell Heath, Romford, Essex RM6 4DH
ISBN Prefix(es): 0 85243
Tel: 081-597 2491
Fax: 081-598 2428
VAT No: 243 5118 84

Order Information

Order Dept Opening Times
9am - 6pm
Orders for more than one publisher can be bulked
All Dues Automatically Recorded
Representation Available

Personnel
Head of Company: Christopher Nagle
Head of Sales (Home): Pauline Martin

Number of Staff: 5
NBA Signatory
All New Titles are Bar Coded
WBIP Updating: C J Nagle

Trade Terms
Over £30.00 retail value 35%
Minimum Order: Retail value of under £10-10%, £20-20%, £30-30%, over £30-35% Cheque or credit card no sent with order under £30-5% extra
Credit Cards Accepted: Access/Master, Visa

Returns Procedures
Authority to Return: Mrs Pauline Martin
Stock Returns: Authorisation required from Returns Dept or Representative
Imperfect Returns: Return title page only on imperfectly bound/printed books No price limit

W & G FOYLE LTD

113-119 Charing Cross Road, London WC2H 0EB
ISBN Prefix(es): 0 7071
Tel: 071-437 5660
Tel: 071-437 0216
VAT No: 238 7867 10

Order Information

Order Dept Opening Times
Mon - Fri 9am - 5pm
All Dues Automatically Recorded
Representation Available

Personnel
Head of Company: Christina Foyle
Head of Sales (Home): John Cruickshanks

Trade Terms
35%; 50p surcharge on any orders under £10. Invoice value except subscription orders.
Girobank Number: 519 1254
Credit Cards Accepted: Access/Master, Visa, Amex

FRAMEWORK PRESS EDUCATIONAL PUBLISHERS LTD

St Leonard's House, St Leonardgate, Lancaster, Lancashire LA1 1NN
ISBN Prefix(es): 1 85008
Tel: 0524 39602
Tel: 0524 841520
VAT No: 378 5167 12

Order Information

All Dues Automatically Recorded

Personnel
Head of Company: Brenda Abercrombie (Editorial Director)
Head of Sales (Home): Pamela Kitching (Sales Manager)
Head of Marketing: Nicholas Abercrombie (Marketing Director)
Head of Publicity: Mary Ayres (Publicity Generator)
Head of Accounts: Pamela Ebdon (Financial Controller) 0524 841520

Number of titles published annually: 12
Number of Staff: 6
IPG Member
WBIP Updating: Chris Needham

Trade Terms
17.5% no surcharges

PETER FRANCIS PUBLISHERS

The Old School House, Little Fransham, Dereham, Norfolk
NR19 2JP
ISBN Prefix(es): 1 870167
Tel: 036 287 455
VAT No: 532 8473 38

Order Information

All Dues Automatically Recorded

Personnel
Head of Company: Dr P J Hills

Trade Terms
Terms available on request

FREE ASSOCIATION BOOKS

26 Freegrove Road, London N7 9RQ
Tel: 071-609 5646
Tel: 071-609 0507
Fax: 071-700 0330
VAT No: 396 6559 85

A/C No 0061697-001

FREEDOM GRAPHICS GROUP

Unit 11, Blackwall Industrial Estate, Chelmsford, Essex
CM3 5UW
ISBN Prefix(es): 1 897780
Tel: 0860 445342
Fax: 0245 323211

W H FREEMAN & CO LTD

20 Beaumont Street, Oxford, Oxfordshire OX1 2NQ
ISBN Prefix(es): 0 7167, 0 74840, 0 75070, 0 85066, 1 85000
Tel: 0865 726975
Fax: 0865 790391
VAT No: 199 1094 29

Account No: 01614001

Sales Rep:

Tel:

Orders to
MARSTON BOOK SERVICES LTD, PO Box 87, Osney
Mead, Oxford, Oxfordshire OX2 0DT
Tel: 0865 791155
Fax: 0865 791927

Order Information

All Dues Automatically Recorded
Representation Available
Invoice Payments: Martson Book Services

Personnel
Head of Company: Judy Botherway (Managing Director)
Head of Marketing: Ms Jana Bek
Head of Accounts: Mr H Morgan

Number of titles published annually: 60
Percentage of Export Sales: 55%
Number of Staff: 10
NBA Signatory
WBIP Updating: Via Martson Book Services

Parent Company: W H Freeman & Co New York

Trade Terms
General Net: 25% base
Academic Net: 25% base

Returns Procedures
Authority to Return: Marston Book Services
Address for Returns: Marston Book Services

SAMUEL FRENCH LTD
52 Fitzroy Street, London W1P 6JR
ISBN Prefix(es): 0 573
Tel: 071-387 9373 24 Hours
Fax: 071-387 2161
VAT No: 241 1290 07

Order Information

Order Dept Opening Times
Mon - Fri 9.30am - 5.30pm
All Dues Automatically Recorded
Representation Available

Personnel
Head of Company: John Bedding (Managing Director)
Head of Sales (Home): Paul Barlow
Head of Marketing: Amanda Smith (Director)
Head of Accounts: P J Stalworth (Company Secretary)

Number of titles published annually: 50
Number of Staff: 50
PA Member
All New Titles are Bar Coded
WBIP Updating: Amanda Smith

Parent Company: Samuel French Inc

Trade Terms
30%
Other Terms: Small order surcharge of £1.50 if under £10
Girobank Number: 5977355
Credit Cards Accepted: Access/Master, Amex, Diners, Visa, Other

Returns Procedures
Authority to Return: Prior permission required from Paul Barlow
Stock Returns: 15% Handling Charge

THE FRIENDLY PRESS
300 Gloucester Road, Horfield, Bristol, Avon BS7 8PD
Tel: 0272 429142 Tel/Fax
VAT No: 567 4006 38

IPG Member

FRIENDS OF THE EARTH
26-28 Underwood Street, London N1 7JQ
Tel: 071-490 1555
Fax: 071-490 0881
Fax: 071-251 0818
VAT No: 242 3265 87

Orders to
WORLDLY GOODS, 10-12 Picton Street, Montpelier, Bristol, Avon BS6 5QA
Tel: 0272 420164
Fax: 0272 420164

Order Information
Orders To:FoE for Non-Book Items inc Reports

Personnel
Head of Sales (Home): Athena Lamnisos
Head of Accounts: Sarah Welsh
Head of Distribution: Christina Hansford

Number of titles published annually: 40
Number of Staff: 140
WBIP Updating: Athena Caminisos

Trade Terms
35%

Returns Procedures
Authority to Return: Tim Bartlett - Worldly Goods (For Books)
Imperfect Returns: Return book with returns notes. Annotated title page for publications £1 or under

FROGLETS PUBLICATIONS

Brasted Chart, Westerham, Kent TN16 1LY
ISBN Prefix(es): 0 9513019, 1 872337
Tel: 0959 562972 24 Hours
Fax: 0959 565365
VAT No: 479 6903 84

Order Information

Order Dept Opening Times
Mon - Fri 9am - 5.30pm
Representation Available

Personnel
Head of Company: Fern Flynn
Head of Customer Services: Jane Wilkinson
Other Important Personnel:
Bob Ogley (Partner)

Number of titles published annually: 3
Number of Staff: 4
IPG Member
All New Titles are Bar Coded
Book Data Subscriber
WBIP Updating: Jill Goldsworthy

Trade Terms
35%
Other Terms: Carriage charge £1.75 on orders under three copies
Credit Cards Accepted: Access/Master, Visa

DAVID FULTON PUBLISHER LTD

2 Barbon Close, London WC1N 3JX
ISBN Prefix(es): 0 921217, 1 85346
Tel: 071-405 5606
Fax: 071-831 4840
VAT No: 454 2572 48

Orders to
B T BATSFORD LTD, PO Box 4, Springwood Ind Est, Rayne Rd, Braintree, Essex CM7 7QY
Tel: 0376 321276
Fax: 0376 552854

Order Information

All Dues Automatically Recorded
Invoice Payments: B T Batsford Ltd

Personnel
Head of Company: David Fulton
Head of Sales (Home): Patrick Bruce-Gardyne

Number of titles published annually: 35
Number of Staff: 2
IPG Member
NBA Signatory
All New Titles are Bar Coded
WBIP Updating: Patrick Bruce-Gardyne

Trade Terms
35% computing
Academic Net: 30%
Credit Cards Accepted: Access/Master, Visa

Returns Procedures
Authority to Return: Prior permission required from Head Office
Address for Returns: B T Batsford

FUTURA = Marston

FUTURE PUBLISHING LTD
30 Monmouth Street, Bath, Avon BA1 2BW
Tel: 0225 442244
Fax: 0225 446019

FUTURES PUBLICATIONS LTD
8 Nursery Road, London SW9 8BP
Tel: 071-738 7707
Fax: 071-737 7814
VAT No: 542 1681 59

Orders to
LAVIS MARKETING, 73 Lime Walk, Headington, Oxfordshire OX3 7AD
Tel: 0865 67575
Fax: 0865 750079

Book Data Subscriber

GAIA BOOKS LTD
66 Charlotte Street, London W1P 1LR
ISBN Prefix(es): 1 85675
Tel: 071-323 4010
Fax: 071-323 0435
VAT No: 237 8351 46

Orders to
AIRLIFT BOOK COMPANY, 26/28 Eden Grove, London N7 8EF
Tel: 071-607 5792
Fax: 071-607 6714

Personnel
Head of Company: Joss Pearson (Managing Director)
Head of Sales (Home): Imogen Bright (Sales Director)
Head of Accounts: Robin Hayfield (Financial Director)

Book Data Subscriber

GAIRM PUBLICATIONS
29 Waterloo Street, Glasgow, Strathclyde G2 6BZ
ISBN Prefix(es): 0 901771, 1 871901
Tel: 041-221 1971 Tel/Fax

Order Information

All Dues Automatically Recorded

Personnel
Head of Company: Derick S Thomson 041-638 0957
Head of Marketing: Ranald Thomson
Head of Accounts: Mrs Margaret Macleod

Number of titles published annually: 10
Percentage of Export Sales: 20%
Number of Staff: 3
Book Data Subscriber
WBIP Updating: Ranald Thomson

Trade Terms
Single Copy 25%, Multiples 35%

GALACTIC CENTRAL PUBLICATIONS

Imladris, 25A Copgrove Road, Leeds, West Yorkshire
LS8 2SP

GALE RESEARCH INTERNATIONAL LTD
2-6 Boundary Row, London SE1 8HP
ISBN Prefix(es): 1 55862, 1 873477
Tel: 071-865 0190
Fax: 071-865 0192
VAT No: 393 8306 25

Account No: _____
Sales Rep: _____
Tel: _____

Orders to
Gale Research Int, PO Box 699, Cheriton Hse, North Way, Andover, Hampshire SP10 5YE
Tel: 0264 334446
Fax: 0264 334158

Order Information

Order Dept Opening Times
Mon - Thurs 9am - 5pm, Fri 9am - 4pm
All Dues Automatically Recorded
Invoice Payments: Andover

Personnel
Head of Company: Ian Savage (Managing Director) 0264 334446
Head of Accounts: Mrs J Lancaster (Credit Controller)
Head of Customer Services: Mrs V Louden (Customer Services Supervisor)

Number of titles published annually: 20
Percentage of Export Sales: 50%
IPG Member
All New Titles are Bar Coded
Book Data Subscriber
WBIP Updating: I Savage

Parent Company: The Thomson Corporation

Trade Terms
15% on all orders
Credit Cards Accepted: Access/Master, Visa, Amex, Diners

Returns Procedures
Authority to Return: Mrs V Louden, Andover
Address for Returns: Andover

GALLERY PRESS

Devonshire House, Devon Street, Liverpool, Merseyside
L3 8HA
ISBN Prefix(es): 0 900389
Tel: 051-427 6266

Personnel
Head of Company: James Parkinson

Number of titles published annually: 3
Number of Staff: 1

Trade Terms
33.3% postage on invoice value under £10
Credit Cards Accepted: Access/Master, Visa

Returns Procedures
Stock Returns: Preliminary letter required
Imperfect Returns: Return title page

THE GALLERY PRESS

Loughcrew, Oldcastle, County Meath
Tel: 049 41779 Tel/Fax

Order Information

All Dues Automatically Recorded
Representation Available
UK Representation: Password (Books) Ltd

Personnel
Head of Company: Peter Fallon
Head of Marketing: Jean Barry
Head of Accounts: Patricia Nicol
Other Important Personnel:
Fergus Corcoran (Irish Representative)

Number of titles published annually: 12
Number of Staff: 3
All New Titles are Bar Coded
WBIP Updating: Jean Barry

Trade Terms
35%
Other Terms: Carriage charged on one line orders

Returns Procedures
Authority to Return: Patricia Nicol
Stock Returns: Overstocks: Request to return necessary.
Books must be in mint condition. Credit only given - no cash returned

GALLIARD PUBLISHERS

45 Pentland Terrace, Edinburgh, Lothian EH9 1EF
Tel: 031-229 3680

GALLOPING DOG PRESS

29 Hartside Gardens, Newcastle-upon-Tyne, Tyne & Wear
NE2 2JR
ISBN Prefix(es): 0 984837, 1 871537
Tel: 091-281 7838

Order Information

All Dues Automatically Recorded
Representation Available

Personnel
Head of Company: Peter Hodgkiss

Trade Terms
40%
General Net: Single copy 20%, two or more 40%

GARNET PUBLISHING LTD

8 Southern Court, South Street, Reading, Berkshire RG1 4QS
ISBN Prefix(es): 0 86372, 0 903729, 1 873938
Tel: 0734 597847
Fax: 0734 597356
VAT No: 569 9240 90

Order Information

All Dues Automatically Recorded

Personnel
Head of Company: Ken Banerji (Managing Director)
Head of Sales (Home): Beverley Charlton (Administrator)
Head of Marketing: Alison Gridley
Other Important Personnel:
Anthony J Hobbs (Manager EFL Division)

Number of titles published annually: 20
Percentage of Export Sales: 50%
Number of Staff: 6
All New Titles are Bar Coded
WBIP Updating: Mrs Beverley Charlton

Allied Companies: Geoprojects UK Ltd

Trade Terms
Single Copy 25%, Two or more 35%

Returns Procedures
Authority to Return: Prior written authorisation required
Address for Returns: Clipper Distribution Ltd, Portchester
Stock Returns: Return copy in all cases for full refund or substitution
Imperfect Returns: Return imperfects to Reading

GATEWAY BOOKS
The Hollies, Wellow, Bath, Avon BA2 8QJ
ISBN Prefix(es): 0 946551, 1 85860
Tel: 0225 835127
Fax: 0225 840012
VAT No: 341 2262 96

Orders to
ASHGROVE PRESS, 4 Brassmill Centre, Brassmill Lane, Bath, Avon BA1 3JN
Tel: 0225 425539
Fax: 0225 319137

Order Information

All Dues Automatically Recorded
Representation Available

Personnel
Head of Company: Alick Bartholomew
Head of Sales (Home): Chris Nalder
Head of Sales (Export): Rosie Abbey
Head of Publicity: Tina Currie
Head of Distribution: Robin Campbell

Number of titles published annually: 12
Percentage of Export Sales: 25%
Number of Staff: 2
IPG Member
All New Titles are Bar Coded
Book Data Subscriber
WBIP Updating: C Nalder

Trade Terms
As Ashgrove Distribution
Girobank Number: 50 406 1402
Credit Cards Accepted: Access/Master, Visa

Returns Procedures
Authority to Return: Christine Nalder, Gateway Books
Address for Returns: Ashgrove Distribution
Stock Returns: No authority required to return incorrect or damages

GAY LIBERATION FRONT INFORMATION SERVICE
Box G, 5 Caledonian Road, London N1 9DX
ISBN Prefix(es): 0 9502854
Tel: 081-392 9476

Order Information
All Dues Automatically Recorded

Personnel
Head of Company: David McLellan
Other Important Personnel:
Peter Madders (Secretary)

Trade Terms
33.3% + postage
Girobank Number: 57 977 1903

GAZELLE BOOK SERVICES LTD
Falcon House, Queen Square, Lancaster, Lancashire
LA1 1RN
Tel: 0524 68765
Fax: 0524 63232
VAT No: 483 0015 75

Account No: _____ 2499 _____
Sales Rep: _____
Tel: _____

Order Information
Teleordering: GAZELLE

Order Dept Opening Times
Mon - Fri 9am - 5.30pm
Orders for more than one publisher can be bulked
All Dues Automatically Recorded
Representation Available

Personnel
Head of Company: Christopher Timms (Managing Director)
Head of Sales (Home): Trevor Witcher (Sales Director)
Head of Marketing: Barbara Wood
Head of Publicity: Pat Fawley
Head of Accounts: Brian Haywood
Head of Distribution: Graham Chamberlain
Head of Customer Services: Mark Trotter

Number of titles published annually: 750
Percentage of Export Sales: 20%
WBIP Updating: Maurice Simmel

Trade Terms
General Net: 35%
Academic Net: 30%
Girobank Number: 15 9286 905
Credit Cards Accepted: Access/Master, Visa, Amex

Returns Procedures
Stock Returns: Books may be returned after obtaining permission in writing.
Imperfect Returns: Return book/s or title page (price limit £15)

[Handwritten: GCSE Publications = Secondary Examinations Council, Newcombe House, 45 Notting Hill Gate, London W11 3JB]

GEE & SON (DENBIGH) LTD
Chapel Street, Denbigh, Clwyd LL16 3SW
Tel: 0745 812020
VAT No: 310 0586 10

GEISER PRODUCTIONS
7 The Corner, Grange Road, London W5 3PQ
Tel: 081-579 4653
Fax: 081-567 6593
VAT No: 228 7866 19

IPG Member

GELOFER PRESS
29 Chalcot Square, London NW1 8YA
ISBN Prefix(es): 0 9506529
Tel: 071-586 1209

Personnel
Head of Company: G Goodwin

Trade Terms
33.3% off single copy plus postage & packing

GEMINI BOOK DISTRIBUTION LTD
Vale Road, Tonbridge, Kent TN9 1TD
Tel: 0732 359387
Fax: 0732 770620
Telex: 957144 Gemini G
VAT No: 210 8037 11

Order Information

All Dues Automatically Recorded

Personnel
Head of Company: Brian A Austin
Head of Sales (Export): Mrs Angela Mitchell

Percentage of Export Sales: 100%

GENERAL GRAMOPHONE PUBLICATIONS LTD
177-179 Kenton Road, Harrow, Middlesex HA3 0HA
Tel: 081-907 4476
Fax: 081-907 0073

GENESIS PUBLICATIONS LTD
51 Lynwood, Guildford, Surrey GU2 5NY
Tel: 0483 37431
Fax: 0483 304709
VAT No: 212 8362 85

GEO ABSTRACTS = Chapman & Hall = Int. Thomson

GEOGRAPHERS' A-Z MAP CO LTD
Fairfield Road, Borough Green, Sevenoaks, Kent TN15 8PP
ISBN Prefix(es): 0 85039
Tel: 0732 781000
Fax: 0732 780677
VAT No: 209 6060 76

Order Information

Order Dept Opening Times
Mon - Fri 9am - 5pm
Representation Available

Other Important Locations
Showroom:44 Gray's Inn Road, London WC1X 8LR
Tel: 071-242 9246
Fax: 071-430 2081

Personnel
Head of Company: J N Syrett (Managing Director)
Head of Sales (Home): P Stevens (Sales Director)

Number of titles published annually: 10
NBA Signatory
All New Titles are Bar Coded
Book Data Subscriber
WBIP Updating: Mrs H Rolan

Parent Company: Geographers Map Trustees Ltd

Trade Terms
35%
Other Terms: Carriage charged for under 4 copies.
Girobank Number: 344 4155

Returns Procedures
Imperfect Returns: Complete book must be returned.

THE GEOGRAPHICAL ASSOCIATION
343 Fulwood Road, Sheffield, South Yorkshire S10 3BP
Tel: 0742 670666
Fax: 0742 670688
VAT No: 172 9919 23

GEOGRAPHICAL PUBLICATIONS LTD
The Keep, Berkhamsted Place, Berkhamsted, Hertfordshire HP4 1HQ
ISBN Prefix(es): 0 900394
Tel: 0442 862981
VAT No: 207 9594 36

Order Information

All Dues Automatically Recorded

Personnel
Head of Company: Audrey N Clark

Number of Staff: 1

Trade Terms
Academic Net: 1-4 copies 20%, 5-9 copies 25%, 10+ 33.3%
Other Terms: Carriage charges on all orders

GEOLOGICAL SOCIETY PUBLISHING HOUSE
Unit 7, Brassmill Ent Centre, Brassmill Lane, Bath, Avon BA1 3JN
ISBN Prefix(es): 0 903917
Tel: 0225 445046
Fax: 0225 442836
VAT No: 446 2593 35

Order Information

All Dues Automatically Recorded

Personnel
Head of Company: Mike Collins

Number of titles published annually: 10
Percentage of Export Sales: 40%
Number of Staff: 7
All New Titles are Bar Coded
WBIP Updating: David Ogden

Trade Terms
Single Copy 10%, Multiples 20%
Credit Cards Accepted: Access/Master, Amex, Diners, Visa

Returns Procedures
Authority to Return: Frances Bond

GEOPROJECTS (UK) LTD
9/10 Southern Court, South Street, Reading, Berkshire RG1 4QS
ISBN Prefix(es): 0 86351
Tel: 0734 393567
Fax: 0734 598283
VAT No: 199 2239 24

Order Information

All Dues Automatically Recorded

Personnel
Head of Company: Ken Banerji (General Manager)
Head of Sales (Home): Robert Hawkins
Head of Accounts: Maie Knight (Accounts Clerk)

Number of titles published annually: 6
Percentage of Export Sales: 20%
Number of Staff: 20
WBIP Updating: Robert J Hawkins

Allied Companies: Garnet Publishing Ltd

Trade Terms
35% plus postage

Returns Procedures
Authority to Return: Written authority only
Stock Returns: Copy to be returned for full refund or exchange
Imperfect Returns: Copy to be returned for credit or exchange

GERBIL BOOKS

12 Blind Lane, Leeds, West Yorkshire LS17 8HE
ISBN Prefix(es): 1 871331
Tel: 0532 736984

Personnel
Head of Company: Sheila Guy

Trade Terms
35%
Other Terms: Small order surcharges £1.75

STANLEY GIBBONS PUBLICATIONS LTD

399 Strand, London WC2R OLX
Tel: 071-836 8444
Fax: 071-836 7342

Orders to
Stanley Gibbons Ltd, Sales Department, 517 Parkside, Ringwood, Hampshire BH24 3SH
Tel: 0425 472363 (24 Hrs)
Fax: 0425 470247

Order Information

Order Dept Opening Times
Mon - Fri 8.30am - 5.30pm
Representation Available
Invoice Payments: Ringwood

Personnel
Head of Company: Mr P Fraser (Chairman) Ringwood
Head of Sales (Home): Ms P Westcott (Sales Manager)
Head of Publicity: Mrs S Baltishire
Head of Accounts: Mr A Pandit (Finance Director)

Number of titles published annually: 20
Number of Staff: 55
All New Titles are Bar Coded

Trade Terms
30 days net for credit accounts otherwise CWO
Non-Net: 35%
Minimum Order: £50
Credit Cards Accepted: Access/Master, Visa

Returns Procedures
Authority to Return: Sales Manager

ROBERT GIBSON & SONS, GLASGOW, LTD

17 Fitzroy PLace, Glasgow, Strathclyde G3 7SF
Tel: 041-248 5674
Fax: 041-221 8219
VAT No: 260 1857 70

Order Information

Order Dept Opening Times
Mon - Fri 9am - 5pm
All Dues Automatically Recorded

Personnel

Head of Company: Mr R D C Gibson
Head of Sales (Home): Mr N J Crawford
Head of Accounts: Mrs M Pinkerton

Number of titles published annually: 12
Percentage of Export Sales: 70%
PA Member
NBA Signatory
All New Titles are Bar Coded
WBIP Updating: Mr N J Crawford

Trade Terms
35%, Non-net 20%

Returns Procedures
Authority to Return: Mrs Pinkerton

GILL & MACMILLAN LTD

Goldenbridge, Inchicore, Dublin 8, County Dublin
ISBN Prefix(es): 0 7171
Tel: 01 531 005
Fax: 01 541 688
VAT No: IE9T4 7502D
Account No: _____ 9835 _____
Sales Rep: _____
Tel: _____

Order Information
Teleordering: GILL

Order Dept Opening Times
Mon - Fri 9am - 5pm
Orders for more than one publisher can be bulked
All Dues Automatically Recorded
Representation Available

Other Important Locations
Publicity:Eveleen Coyle, 27 Lr Camden Street, Dublin 8
Tel: 01-534 440

Personnel
Head of Company: Michael Gill (Managing Director)
Head of Sales (Home): Peter Thew (Sales & Marketing Director)
Head of Marketing: Pamela Coyle (Marketing Manager)
Head of Publicity: Eveleen Coyle
Head of Accounts: Dermot O'Dwyer (Financial Director)
Head of Distribution: Dermot O'Brien (Distribution Manager)
Head of Customer Services: Karen Gallagher (Customer Services Manager)

Number of titles published annually: 75
Number of Staff: 35
PA Member
All New Titles are Bar Coded
Book Data Subscriber
WBIP Updating: Eveleen Coyle

Allied Companies: Macmillan Publishers Ltd

Trade Terms
General Net: Single copy 25%, Two or more 35%
Academic Net: Single copy 25%, Two or more 30%
Non-Net: 20%
Other Terms: Small order surcharge £1 under £15 net invoice value Carriage charge nil within UK & Ireland
Credit Cards Accepted: Access/Master, Visa, Amex

Returns Procedures
Authority to Return: From Client Publishers - Head Office
Stock Returns: Advise Gill & MacMillan Distribution
Imperfect Returns: Full copies back to Gill-Macmillan Distribution for credit/ replacement. No title pages

GINN & CO LTD
Prebendal House, Parson's Fee, Aylesbury, Buckinghamshire HP20 2QZ
ISBN Prefix(es): 0 602
Tel: 0296 88411/6
Fax: 0296 25487
Telex: 83535 GINN G
VAT No: 194 4274 42

Account No: _____
Sales Rep: _____
Tel: _____

Order Information

All Dues Automatically Recorded

Personnel
Head of Company: William Shepherd (Managing Director)
Head of Sales (Home): Valerie Fry (UK Sales Manager)
Head of Sales (Export): David Johns (International Manager)
Head of Marketing: Nigel Hall (Sales & Marketing Director)
Head of Publicity: Emma Randall (Marketing Manager)
Head of Accounts: Roger Spittles (Finance Manager)
Head of Distribution: David Miller (Operations Director)
Head of Customer Services: Margaret Woods (Customer Services Manager)
Other Important Personnel:
Ann Foster (Editorial Director)

WBIP Updating: Mrs Eileen Goodyer

Parent Company: Reed International Books

Trade Terms
17.5%
Other Terms: Small order surcharge £3 for £40 or under
Credit Cards Accepted: Access/Master, Visa

Returns Procedures
Authority to Return: Margaret Woods
Address for Returns: Unit 1, Block H, Long Eaton Ind Est, Acton Grove, Long Eaton Nottinghamshire NG10 1GG

THE GIRL GUIDES ASSOCIATION
Trading Service, Atlantic Street, Broadheath, Altrincham, Cheshire WA14 5EQ
Tel: 061-941 2237
Fax: 061-941 6326
VAT No: 238 7469 22

MARY GLASGOW PUBLICATIONS
Avenue House, 131-133 Holland Park Avenue, London W11 4UT

ISBN Prefix(es): 0 86158, 0 900400, 0 905999, 1 85234
Tel: 071-603 4688
Fax: 071-602 5197
Telex: 311890 MGPUBS
VAT No: 273 4959 22

Account No: _____

Sales Rep: _____

Tel: _____

Orders to
Mary Glasgow Pubs, Brookhampton Lane, Kineton, Warwick, Warwickshire CV35 0JB
Tel: 0926 640606
Fax: 0926 641016

OR//
Stanley Thornes

Order Information
Teleordering: GLASGOW

Order Dept Opening Times
Mon - Fri 9am - 5pm
All Dues Automatically Recorded

Personnel
Head of Company: Chris Blake
Head of Sales (Export): Esther Heasman
Head of Publicity: Ian Bartley
Head of Accounts: Norman Lott
Head of Distribution: Bob Horne
Head of Customer Services: Mora Angus

Number of titles published annually: 50
Number of Staff: 100
PA Member

Parent Company: Wolters Kluwer (UK) PLC
Allied Companies: Sound Communication (Publishers)

Trade Terms
35% on all orders no surcharges
Credit Cards Accepted: Access/Master, Visa, Amex, Diners

Returns Procedures
Authority to Return: Mary Glasgow Publications, Kineton
Address for Returns: Mary Glasgow Publications, Kineton

THE GLENIFFER PRESS

11 Low Road, Castlehead, Paisley, Renfrewshire PA2 6AQ
ISBN Prefix(es): 0 906005, 0 9502177
Tel: 041-889 9579

Personnel
Head of Company: Ian Macdonald
Head of Marketing: Helen R Macdonald

Number of titles published annually: 3
Percentage of Export Sales: 90%
WBIP Updating: Ian Macdonald

Trade Terms
33.3% all orders, no surcharges
Credit Cards Accepted: Access/Master, Visa, Other

GLIDDON BOOKS

The Reading Room, 79 The Street, Brooke, Norwich, Norfolk NR15 1JT
ISBN Prefix(es): 0 947893
Tel: 0508 58050
VAT No: 283 2167 58

Personnel
Head of Company: Gerald Gliddon

Trade Terms
General Net: Single copy 20%, 2 or more single titles/ 2 books or more/ subscription orders 35%
Credit Cards Accepted: Access/Master, Visa

Returns Procedures
Stock Returns: Standard returns form to be sent.

GMP PUBLISHERS LTD

Millmead Business Centre, Millmead Road, London N17 9QU
Tel: 081-365 1545
Fax: 081-365 1252
VAT No: 330 7641 76

Orders to
GMP Publishers Ltd, PO Box 247, London N17 9QR
Tel: 081-365 1545
Fax: 081-365 1252

Order Information
Teleordering: GMP

Order Dept Opening Times
Mon - Fri 10am - 6pm
All Dues Automatically Recorded
Representation Available

Personnel
Head of Company: Aubrey Walter
Head of Sales (Home): Jim Sprague
Head of Publicity: Alistair Clarke
Head of Accounts: Mark Watkins

Number of titles published annually: 25
Number of Staff: 7
IPG Member
All New Titles are Bar Coded
Book Data Subscriber
WBIP Updating: Ron Eddy

Trade Terms
Minimum Order: £30 invoice value for full trade terms
BA/Girobank Small Order Scheme: 25% cwo/credit card
Credit Cards Accepted: Access/Master, Visa, Amex

Returns Procedures
Stock Returns: Authorised returns only cancelled customer orders mint only o/p titles up to 6 months from o/p date old editions
Imperfect Returns: Title page only up to £15. Full book £15 upwards

GO TEACH PUBLICATIONS

2 Radford Road, Leamington Spa, Warwickshire CV31 1LX
ISBN Prefix(es): 0 95118
Tel: 0926 426573
Fax: 0926 426573
VAT No: 307 0160 09

ALAN GODFREY MAPS

57 Spoor Street, Dunston, Gateshead, Tyne & Wear NE11 9BD
Tel: 091-276 1155
Fax: 091-224 0080
VAT No: 499 7265 71

Orders to
Alan Godfrey Maps, 12 The Off Quay Building, Foundry Lane, Newcastle, Tyne & Wear NE6 1LH

DAVID GOLD & SON (HOLDINGS) LTD

Units 15-17A, Rich Ind Est, Crimscott Street, London
SE1 5TE
Tel: 071-237 4334
Tel: 071-237 3037
Fax: 071-237 6379
VAT No: 494 2642 25

Account No: _____

Sales Rep: _____

Tel: _____

Order Information

Order Dept Opening Times
Mon - Fri 9am - 5.30pm
Representation Available

Personnel
Head of Company: David Gold (Chairman)
Head of Sales (Home): Ian Gold (Sales Director)
Head of Accounts: Placy Gunawardine (Company Accountant)
Head of Distribution: Stephen Lowe (Managing Director)
Head of Customer Services: Robin Fleming (Director)
Other Important Personnel:
Mike Meakins (Display Manager)

Number of Staff: 72

Allied Companies: APB UK Group of Companies

Trade Terms
Negotiable

Returns Procedures
Stock Returns: Details on application
Imperfect Returns: Details on application

GOLDEN AGE BOOKS

25 Cowleigh Bank, Malvern, Worcestershire WR14 1QP
ISBN Prefix(es): 0 9506212

Order Information

Order Dept Opening Times
Mon - Fri 9am - 12.30pm, 2pm - 5.30pm

Personnel
Head of Company: Anthony & Joyce Byatt (Proprietors)

Number of titles published annually: 1
Percentage of Export Sales: 20%

Trade Terms
General Net: Single copy/single line 35%, 5 books or more 40%
Academic Net: Single copy/single line 25% (Ltd ed)
Other Terms: P&P for under 20 copies

Returns Procedures
Imperfect Returns: By agreement

GOLDEN COCKEREL PRESS

25 Sicilian Avenue, London WC1A 2QH
ISBN Prefix(es): 0 08386, 0 8387, 0 8453, 0 87413, 0 87982, 0 897290, 0 911704, 0 918016, 0 934223, 0 940866, 0 941642, 0 941664, 0 944190, 0 945636
Tel: 071-405 7979 Fax also
Telex: 23365
VAT No: 237 3793 39

Orders to
BIBLIOS PUBLISHERS DISTRIBUTION SERVICE LTD,
Star Road, Partridge Green, West Sussex RH13 8LD
Tel: 0403 710971
Fax: 0403 711143

Order Information

All Dues Automatically Recorded
Representation Available
Invoice Payments: Biblios

Personnel
Head of Company: Tamar Yoseloff
Head of Publicity: Thomas Buhler

Number of titles published annually: 75
Number of Staff: 2
WBIP Updating: Thomas Butler

Parent Company: Associated University Presses
Subsidiary Companies: Brown Watson Ltd (UK), Children's Leisure Products Ltd (UK)

Trade Terms
30%, 35% Cornwall Books
Credit Cards Accepted: Access/Master, Visa, Amex

Returns Procedures
Authority to Return: Tamar Yoseloff at Golden Cockerel Press
Address for Returns: Biblios

GOLDENEYE MAPS

The Cottage, Mill Street, Prestbury, Cheltenham, Gloucestershire GL52 3BS
Tel: 0242 244889 Tel/Fax
VAT No: 366 1951 34

GOLLANCZ = Littlehampton Book Services.

BRIAN GOOCH LTD

Myrtle Cottages, Deane Road, Stoke in Teignhead, Newton Abbot, Devon TQ12 4QQ
Tel: 0626 872435 24 Hours
Tel: 0626 872548 24 Hours
VAT No: 568 8252 94

Order Information

Order Dept Opening Times
Mon - Sat 8am - 6pm
All Dues Automatically Recorded
The Computer Guides must be stated on all orders

Personnel
Head of Company: Brian Gooch
Head of Accounts: Kate Templeton

Number of titles published annually: 6
Number of Staff: 5
IPG Member
All New Titles are Bar Coded
WBIP Updating: Kate Templeton

Trade Terms
Single copy 25%, 2-5 copies 35%, 6 plus copies 45% All orders carriage paid & CWO only
Credit Cards Accepted: Access/Master, Visa

Returns Procedures
Authority to Return: Prior permission is required
Imperfect Returns: Notification required in writing within 7 days of receipt

GOOD NEWS CRUSADE PUBLICATIONS
15-17 High Cross Street, St Austell, Cornwall PO25 4AN
Tel: 0726 63945
Fax: 0726 69853
VAT No: 132 0334 27

GOODALL PUBLICATIONS LTD
Larchwood House, 274 London Road, St Albans,
Hertfordshire AL1 1HY
ISBN Prefix(es): 0 907579
Tel: 0727 861611
VAT No: 540 0715 85

Order Information

Order Dept Opening Times
9am - 8pm
All Dues Automatically Recorded
Representation Available

Personnel
Head of Company: G R Goodall
Head of Distribution: Mrs J Goodall

Number of titles published annually: 2
Number of Staff: 2
All New Titles are Bar Coded
WBIP Updating: G R Goodall

Trade Terms
Multiples 35% no surcharges, Singles 25% cheque with order
BA/Girobank Small Order Scheme: Normal trade terms as above single copy orders: extra 5% discount cash with order

Returns Procedures
Authority to Return: Prior permission required
Stock Returns: Normal returns procedure
Imperfect Returns: Normal returns procedure

GOODAY STUDIOS (UK) LTD
31 St Martins Way, Thetford, Norfolk IP24 3PY
ISBN Prefix(es): 0 947785, 1 870568
VAT No: 397 6796 65

Order Information

All Dues Automatically Recorded

Personnel
Head of Company: Mr M E Aldridge
Head of Sales (Home): Mr T Aldridge
Head of Publicity: Mrs E Aldridge

Number of titles published annually: 6
Number of Staff: 2
NBA Signatory
All New Titles are Bar Coded

Trade Terms
35% plus carriage at cost. Cheque with order for customer order. Pro-forma invoice sent

NEALE C GOODLIFFE LTD
Arden Forest Industrial Estate, Alcester, Warwickshire
B49 6ER
Tel: 0789 763261
Fax: 0789 764343
VAT No: 274 6821 35

GOTHIC IMAGE PUBLICATIONS

7 High Street, Glastonbury, Somerset BA6 9DP
ISBN Prefix(es): 0 906362
Tel: 0458 831453
Fax: 0458 831666
VAT No: 131 3939 81

Orders to
ASHGROVE PRESS, 4 Brassmill Centre, Brassmill Lane, Bath, Avon BA1 3JN
Tel: 0225 425539
Fax: 0225 319137

Order Information

Invoice Payments: Ashgrove Distribution

All New Titles are Bar Coded

Gower = Ashgate Distribution.

GOWER MEDICAL PUBLISHING

Middlesex House, 34-42 Cleveland Street, London W1P 5FB
ISBN Prefix(es): 0 39744, 0 39746, 0 906923, 1 56375
Tel: 071-636 8300
Fax: 071-631 3594
Telex: 21736
VAT No: 524 2180 78

Account No: _____

Sales Rep: _____

Tel: _____

Orders to
PLYMBRIDGE DISTRIBUTORS LTD, Plymbridge House, Estover Road, Plymouth, Devon PL6 7PZ
Tel: 0752 735251
Fax: 0752 695699

Order Information

All Dues Automatically Recorded
Representation Available
Invoice Payments: Gower Medical Publishing, c/o Plymbridge

Personnel
Head of Company: Fiona Foley (Managing Director)
Head of Marketing: Elly Myers
Head of Accounts: Elizabeth Johnston

Number of titles published annually: 40
Percentage of Export Sales: 70%
Number of Staff: 40
All New Titles are Bar Coded
Book Data Subscriber
WBIP Updating: Beth Wise Hayes

Parent Company: J B Lippincott

Trade Terms
Credit Cards Accepted: Access/Master, Amex, Visa

Returns Procedures
Address for Returns: Plymbridge

GRACEWING/FOWLER WRIGHT BOOKS

Gracewing House, 2 Southern Avenue, Leominster, Herefordshire HR6 0QF
ISBN Prefix(es): 0 85244
Tel: 0568 616835 3 lines
Fax: 0568 613289

Account No: _____

Sales Rep: _____

Tel: _____

Order Information
Teleordering: FWLW

Orders for more than one publisher can be bulked
All Dues Automatically Recorded
Representation Available

Personnel
Head of Company: Thomas W Longford (Managing Director)
Head of Marketing: Sheridan Swinson (Publishing Manager)
Head of Accounts: Harry Gardner
Head of Customer Services: Sue Morgan
Other Important Personnel:
Julia Haslam (Trade & Academic Representative)

Number of titles published annually: 20
Percentage of Export Sales: 30%
Number of Staff: 14
IPG Member
WBIP Updating: Julia Haslam

Parent Company: Fowler Wright Books

Trade Terms
33%
General Net: Single copy 25%
Academic Net: Single copy 20% Two or more 33% - 20%
Non-Net: 33%
Other Terms: Carriage charged on orders under £50

Returns Procedures
Authority to Return: Thomas Longford or Sheridan Swinson
Stock Returns: All returns need to be authorised by the managing director or publishing manager
Imperfect Returns: Return whole book with reason for return clearly marked.

Grafton = Harper Collins

GRAHAM & TROTMAN LTD

Sterling House, 66 Wilton Road, London SW1V 1DE
ISBN Prefix(es): 0 86010, 1 85333
Tel: 071-821 1123
Fax: 071-630 5229
Telex: 298878 GRAMCO G
VAT No: 240 8945 52

Orders to
KLUWER ACADEMIC PUBLISHERS GROUP,
Distribution Centre, PO Box 322, AH Dordrecht, The Netherlands
Tel: 010-31-78 524400
Fax: 010-31-78 524474

Order Information

All Dues Automatically Recorded
Representation Available
Invoice Payments: Kluwer Distribution, The Netherlands

Personnel
Head of Company: A M W Graham (Managing Director)
Head of Sales (Home): R H Utley (Sales Manager (UK & Ireland))
Head of Sales (Export): A Harris (Sales Director)
Head of Marketing: S J Willcox (Marketing Director)
Head of Accounts: W Fortuin
Head of Distribution: S van Geuns

Number of titles published annually: 50
All New Titles are Bar Coded
Book Data Subscriber
WBIP Updating: Ms Diane Butler

Parent Company: Wolters-Kluwer, The Netherlands

Trade Terms
20% plus postage & handling

Returns Procedures
Authority to Return: Returns Dept, Kluwer Distribution, The Netherlands
Address for Returns: See Kluwer Distribution Centre, The Netherlands
Stock Returns: Request permission quoting invoice number & date
Imperfect Returns: Please contact Returns Dept

W F GRAHAM (NORTHAMPTON) LTD

2 Pondwood Close, Moulton Park Industrial Estate, Northampton, Northamptonshire NN3 1RT
ISBN Prefix(es): 1 85128
Tel: 0604 645537
Fax: 0604 648414
Cables: TOYBOOK
VAT No: 119 9513 51

Personnel
Head of Company: R F Graham
Head of Sales (Export): C Graham
Head of Marketing: L Craddock
Head of Publicity: T Graham
Head of Distribution: I Wilson

Number of titles published annually: 20
Percentage of Export Sales: 20%
Number of Staff: 15
PA Member
All New Titles are Bar Coded

Trade Terms
50% to Wholesalers

FRANCIS GRAHAM-DIXON GALLERY LTD

17-18 Great Sutton Street, London EC1V 0DN
Tel: 071-250 1962
Fax: 071-490 1069

GRANDREAMS LTD

Jadwin House, 205/211 Kentish Town Road, London NW5 2JU
Tel: 071-485 0648
Fax: 071-482 4947
Fax: 071-267 2819
Cables: BOOKSTOCKS LONDON
VAT No: 242 4925 66

Order Information

All Dues Automatically Recorded
Representation Available

Personnel
Head of Company: Peter Babani/Brian Babani
Head of Sales (Home): David Taylor
Head of Publicity: Andrew Harley Rabin
Head of Accounts: Maurice Ferguson
Head of Distribution: Ronald Williams
Head of Customer Services: Henry Daniel Glass

Number of titles published annually: 100
Percentage of Export Sales: 45%
All New Titles are Bar Coded
WBIP Updating: Henry Daniel Glass

Trade Terms
35%
Minimum Order: £500 carriage paid

GRANT & CUTLER LTD
55-57 Great Marlborough Street, London W1V 2AY
ISBN Prefix(es): 0 7293
~~Tel: 071-734 2012~~
~~Fax: 071-734 2013~~
VAT No: 238 9687 02

TEL: 071 734 2012
FAX: 071 734 9272

Order Information

All Dues Automatically Recorded

Number of Staff: 40
NBA Signatory

Trade Terms
25% or 33.3% according to series
Other Terms: Carriage charged on small orders
Girobank Number: 519 9050
Credit Cards Accepted: Access/Master, Visa

GRANT BOOKS
Victoria Square, Droitwich, Worcestershire WR9 8DE
Tel: 0905 778155
Fax: 0905 794507
VAT No: 275 8638 10

GRANTA EDITIONS
47 Norfolk Street, Cambridge, Cambridgeshire CB1 2LE
ISBN Prefix(es): 0 906782
Tel: 0223 352790
Fax: 0223 460718
VAT No: 386 0315 53

Account No: _____
Sales Rep: _____
Tel: _____

Personnel
Head of Company: Tony Littlechild/Colin Walsh
Head of Sales (Home): Stephanie Zarach
Head of Publicity: Hilary Hulford
Head of Accounts: Thora Dix
Head of Customer Services: Franca Holden

Number of titles published annually: 17
Number of Staff: 20
IPG Member
Book Data Subscriber
WBIP Updating: Franca Holden

Parent Company: Book Production Consultants

Trade Terms
Single Copy, Stock Orders & Special Orders 25% All other 35%
Other Terms: Carriage charged
Credit Cards Accepted: Access/Master, Visa

Returns Procedures
Imperfect Returns: Title page returned up to £15

GRANTHAM BOOK SERVICES LTD

Isaac Newton Way, Alma Park Industrial Estate, Grantham, Lincolnshire NG31 9SD
Tel: 0476 67421 *Customer Services*
Fax: 0476 590223
VAT No: 102 8389 80 0274075·027

Account No: _____
Sales Rep: _____
Tel: _____

Orders to
24 Hour Ansafone Number: 0476 67314

Order Information
Teleordering: GBS

Order Dept Opening Times
Mon - Thurs 8.30am - 5pm, Fri 8.30am - 4.30pm
Orders for more than one publisher can be bulked

Personnel
Head of Company: Alan Bingley (Managing Director)
Head of Accounts: John Furnish (Financial Director) Tiptree Book Services
Head of Distribution: Bob Anderson (Operations Director)
Head of Customer Services: Julie Nix (Trade Manager)
Other Important Personnel:
David Goodere (Sales Ledger), Jeff Chambers (Warehouse Manager)

WBIP Updating: Penny Cornwall (Tiptree)

Parent Company: Random House Group

Trade Terms
Refer to Publisher
Girobank Number: 508 7457
Credit Cards Accepted: Access/Master, Visa

Returns Procedures
Authority to Return: To Individual Publisher

GRANVILLE PUBLISHING

102 Islington High Street, London N1 8EG
ISBN Prefix(es): 0 948214
Tel: 071-226 2904

Order Information

All Dues Automatically Recorded

Personnel
Head of Company: Paul Duguid

All New Titles are Bar Coded
WBIP Updating: W J M Murray-Browne

Parent Company: Angel Bookshop

Trade Terms
General Net: Single copy 25%, 2 or more single titles 35%
Credit Cards Accepted: Access/Master, Visa

Returns Procedures
Stock Returns: Authorized returns only.

GREEN BOOKS

Ford House, Hartland, Bideford, Devon EX39 6EE
ISBN Prefix(es): 1 870098
Tel: 0237 441621
Fax: 0237 441203
VAT No: 472 3860 36

Orders to
CENTRAL BOOKS, 99 Wallis Road, London E9 5LN
Tel: 081-986 4854
Fax: 081-533 5821

Order Information

All Dues Automatically Recorded
Representation Available
Invoice Payments: Central Books

Personnel
Head of Company: John Elford (Managing Director)

Number of titles published annually: 5
Number of Staff: 2
IPG Member
All New Titles are Bar Coded
Book Data Subscriber
WBIP Updating: John Elford

Trade Terms
35% except orders below £5 retail value 10%, £5-£30 20%, single copy orders 20%

Returns Procedures
Address for Returns: Central Books
Stock Returns: Contact Central Books
Imperfect Returns: Title page below £10

W GREEN
21 Alva Street, Edinburgh, Lothian EH2 4PS
ISBN Prefix(es): 0 414
Tel: 031-225 4879
Fax: 031-225 2104

Account No: _____
Sales Rep: _____
Tel: _____

Orders to
INTERNATIONAL THOMSON PUBLISHING SERVICES LTD, Cheriton House, North Way, Andover, Hampshire SP10 5BE
Tel: 0264 332424
Fax: 0264 364418

Order Information

All Dues Automatically Recorded
Representation Available

Personnel
Head of Company: Steven Mair (Managing Director)
Head of Marketing: Gilly Michie

Number of titles published annually: 30
Number of Staff: 20
PA Member
NBA Signatory
All New Titles are Bar Coded
WBIP Updating: Dionnie Herelle, Sweet & Maxwell

Parent Company: Thomson Corporation

Trade Terms
General Net: 20%
Academic Net: 20%

Returns Procedures
Address for Returns: W Green, Cheriton House
Stock Returns: By prior arrangement with W Green, Cheriton House

GREENCROFT BOOKS

Trefelin, Cilgwyn, Newport, Pembroke, Dyfed SA42 0QN
ISBN Prefix(es): 0 905559, 0 9504014, 0 9505014
Tel: 0239 820470
Fax: 0239 820470

Personnel
Head of Company: Dr Brian John (Sole Proprietor)

Number of titles published annually: 4
Number of Staff: 1
IPG Member

Trade Terms
33.3%

GREENHILL BOOKS

Park House, 1 Russell Gardens, London NW11 9NN
ISBN Prefix(es): 0 947898, 1 85367
Tel: 081-458 6314 24 Hours
Fax: 081-905 5245
VAT No: 386 4613 25

Order Information

All Dues Automatically Recorded
Representation Available
Invoice Payments: Bookpoint

Personnel
Head of Company: Lionel Leventhal
Head of Sales (Home): David Farnsworth

Number of titles published annually: 25
All New Titles are Bar Coded
WBIP Updating: Antonia Sharpe

Parent Company: Lionel Leventhal Ltd

Trade Terms
Single Copy 20%, Two or more single titles 20% Two books or more & subscription orders 35%

Returns Procedures
Address for Returns: Bookpoint

[handwritten: GREGG REVIVALS C/O Wildwood]

GREENWICH EXCHANGE

161 Charlton Church Lane, London SE7 7AA
Tel: 081-858 6004 Tel/Fax
VAT No: 474 6676 02

IPG Member

[handwritten: Greenwood = Distropa, 3 Henrietta St. London WC2E 8LU A/C No 830]

GRESHAM BOOKS LTD

PO Box 61, Henley-on-Thames, Oxfordshire RG9 3LQ
ISBN Prefix(es): 0 905418, 0 946095, 0 9502121
Tel: 0734 403789 24 Hours
Fax: 0734 403789
VAT No: 347 2223 70

Order Information

All Dues Automatically Recorded

Personnel
Head of Company: Mary Green

Number of titles published annually: 10
Number of Staff: 3

Trade Terms
Single copy 25%, 2 or more single titles 25%, 2 books or more 35%, stocks orders 35%, special orders 35%

Non-Net: 15%
Other Terms: Small order surcharge 50p

Returns Procedures
Stock Returns: Invoice number and reason for return required.
Imperfect Returns: Return title page and give reason

GREVATT & GREVATT
9 Rectory Drive, Newcastle-upon-Tyne, Tyne & Wear
NE3 1XT
ISBN Prefix(es): 0 947722, 0 9507918

Personnel
Head of Company: Dr S Y Killingley

Number of titles published annually: 3
Number of Staff: 1

Trade Terms
33.3% + 15% p&p on single copies, Two books or more
33.3% + 10% p&p, Subscription/Special orders - various discounts
Other Terms: Service charge: Handling for overseas £1
Girobank Number: 62 630 2609

Returns Procedures
Stock Returns: Send back to address with reason. No returns accepted unless fault of publisher.
Imperfect Returns: No price limit

GREVILLE PRESS
Emscote Lawn, Emscote Road, Warwick, Warwickshire
CV34 5QD
Tel: 0926 492086
Tel: 071-580 0767 Orders

GREY EDITIONS
14 Northwick House, 1 St Johns Wood Road, London
NW8 8RD
ISBN Prefix(es): 0 9508703
Tel: 071-289 3684 24 Hours
Fax: 071-289 3684
VAT No: 302 9981 51

Order Information

Order Dept Opening Times
9.30am - 6pm
All Dues Automatically Recorded

Personnel
Head of Company: Paul Graham

Number of titles published annually: 3
Percentage of Export Sales: 25%

Trade Terms
General Net: Single copy/single line 20%, otherwise 35%
Other Terms: Carriage charges for overseas orders

Returns Procedures
Authority to Return: Prior permission required, telephone for authorisation

GREY SEAL (PUBLICATIONS) LTD
28 Burgoyne Road, London N4 1AD
Tel: 081-340 6061
VAT No: 554 2883 23

IPG Member

BRIAN GRIFFIN
Storey House, White Cross, South Road, Lancaster, Lancashire LA1 4XQ
Tel: 0524 846446
Fax: 0524 846395
VAT No: 416 6067 57

GRISEWOOD AND DEMPSEY
4th Floor, Elsley House, 24-30 Great Titchfield Street, London W1P 7AD
ISBN Prefix(es): 0 86272, 1 85697
Tel: 071-631 0878
Fax: 071-323 4694
Fax: 071-323 2753 Sales Off

Account No: _____
Sales Rep: _____
Tel: _____

Orders to
EXEL LOGISTICS - MEDIA SERVICES, 3 Sheldon Way, Larkfield, Aylesford, Kent ME20 6SF
Tel: 0622 882000
Fax: 0622 718036

Order Information

All Dues Automatically Recorded
Representation Available
Invoice Payments: Exel Logistics

Personnel
Head of Company: Dan Grisewood (Chairman)
Head of Sales (Home): Henryk Wesolowski (Sales & Marketing Director)
Head of Publicity: Sasha Udell (Publicity Manager)
Head of Accounts: Margaret Barret (Financial Director)
Other Important Personnel:
Rupert Harbour (Sales Manager), Robin Shields (Key Accounts Manager)

Number of titles published annually: 150
Number of Staff: 68
NBA Signatory
All New Titles are Bar Coded
Book Data Subscriber
WBIP Updating: Muriel Adamson

Parent Company: Group de la Cite

Trade Terms
35% on all orders
Credit Cards Accepted: Access/Master, Visa

Returns Procedures
Authority to Return: Prior authorisation required from Rupert Harbour
Stock Returns: Return book with details to Exel Logistics
Imperfect Returns: Title page up to £15

[Handwritten at top: GROSSOHAUS WEGNER - PO BOX 102540 20017 HAMBURG GERMANY - AG No 00388 FAY 01049 40 25 10 42 50 FROM 1/5/94 KOCH, NEFF + OETINGER (KNO) Postfach 800569 D70505 Stuttgart Germany. Customer No 8654 FAX 01049 711 789220]

GROSVENOR BOOKS

54 Lyford Road, Wandsworth, London SW18 3JJ
ISBN Prefix(es): 0 901269, 1 85239
Tel: 081-870 2124
Fax: 081-871 9239
VAT No: 238 8830 28

Order Information

Order Dept Opening Times
Mon/Tues/Thur/Fri 10am - 5pm
All Dues Automatically Recorded

Personnel

Head of Company: David Locke (Managing Director)
Head of Accounts: Catherine Hutchinson (Chief Accountant) 071-828 6591
Head of Distribution: Robert Normington (Distribution Manager)
Head of Customer Services: Elizabeth Locke (Director Customer Services)

Number of Staff: 8
PA Member
NBA Signatory
Book Data Subscriber
WBIP Updating: David Locke

Parent Company: Grosvenor Productions Ltd

Trade Terms

Single copy 20%, Two or more 35%, Sub. orders negotiable
Minimum Order: C.W.O. under £20 net invoice value except for established credit accounts
Girobank Number: 571 7353

Returns Procedures

Authority to Return: Robert Normington
Imperfect Returns: Title page accepted under £10 retail price

GROTIUS PUBLICATIONS LTD

PO Box 115, Cambridge, Cambridgeshire CB3 9BP
ISBN Prefix(es): 0 906496, 0 949009, 1 85701
Tel: 0223 323410
Fax: 0223 311032
VAT No: 215 3543 88

Order Information

Order Dept Opening Times
Mon - Fri 9am - 1pm, 2pm - 5pm
All Dues Automatically Recorded
Representation Available

Personnel

Head of Company: Ms C J Daly (Managing Director)
Head of Sales (Home): Mr S R Pirrie (Director)

Number of titles published annually: 15
Percentage of Export Sales: 60%
WBIP Updating: S R Pirrie

Trade Terms

Other Terms: All books remain the property of the publisher until payment is received
Credit Cards Accepted: Access/Master, Visa

Returns Procedures

Imperfect Returns: All requests for returns should be sent to our head office address

GROVE BOOKS LTD

Bramcote, Nottinghamshire NG9 3DS
ISBN Prefix(es): 0 901710, 0 905422, 0 907536, 1 85174

Tel: 0602 430786 24 Hours
Fax: 0602 220134
VAT No: 416 2899 32

Order Information

Order Dept Opening Times
Mon - Fri 9am - 5pm
Representation Available

Personnel

Head of Company: Rt Rev C O Buchanan (Editor & Company Secretary) 0634 851818
Head of Sales (Home): Mike Clark (Sales Manager)
Head of Accounts: Liz Toms
Head of Distribution: Sharon Edwards
Other Important Personnel:
Susanne Thompson (Subscriptions)

Number of titles published annually: 24
Percentage of Export Sales: 20%
Number of Staff: 5
PA Member
NBA Signatory
WBIP Updating: Rt Rev C O Buchanan

Trade Terms

Apply to company for terms
Girobank Number: 48 821 4009

Returns Procedures

Authority to Return: Prior permission required
Imperfect Returns: See invoice

GROWER BOOKS

50 Doughty Street, London WC1N 2LS
Tel: 071-405 7135
Fax: 071-831 2230
VAT No: 577 8868 54

PA Member

GRUB STREET

The Basement, 10 Chivalry Road, London SW11 1HT
ISBN Prefix(es): 0 948817
Tel: 071-924 3966
Tel: 071-738 1008
Fax: 071-738 1009
VAT No: 340 5527 77

Orders to

CHRIS LLOYD SALES AND MARKETING SERVICES,
463 Ashley Road, Parkstone, Poole, Dorset BH14 0AX
Tel: 0202 715349
Fax: 0202 736191

Order Information

All Dues Automatically Recorded
Representation Available
Invoice Payments: Bailey Distribution

Personnel

Head of Company: John Davies (Managing Director)
Head of Marketing: Anne Dolamore

Number of titles published annually: 10
Percentage of Export Sales: 25%
Number of Staff: 3
IPG Member
All New Titles are Bar Coded
WBIP Updating: Chris Lloyd

Trade Terms
Standard
Returns Procedures
Authority to Return: Chris Lloyd

GUARDIAN COMMUNICATIONS LTD

Queensway House, 2 Queensway, Redhill, Surrey RH1 1QS
Tel: 07377 68611
Fax: 07377 60510
VAT No: 492 4008 51

PA Member

THE GUERNSEY PRESS CO LTD

The Press Wholesale, PO Box 57, Braye Road, Vale, Guernsey, Channel Islands
Tel: 0481 45866
Fax: 0481 48650

GUILD OF MASTER CRAFTSMAN PUBLICATIONS

166 High Street, Lewes, East Sussex BN7 1XU
ISBN Prefix(es): 0 946819
Tel: 0273 486034
Fax: 0273 478606
VAT No: 242 1775 74

Orders to
CHRIS LLOYD SALES AND MARKETING SERVICES, 463 Ashley Road, Parkstone, Poole, Dorset BH14 0AX
Tel: 0202 715349
Fax: 0202 736191

Order Information

All Dues Automatically Recorded
Representation Available
Invoice Payments: Chris Lloyd Sales & Marketing

Personnel
Head of Company: Alan Phillips
Head of Publicity: John Kilroy

Number of titles published annually: 12
All New Titles are Bar Coded
WBIP Updating: Elizabeth Inman

Trade Terms
35%
Other Terms: £1 surcharge on invoices up to £15 retail

Returns Procedures
Authority to Return: Chris Lloyd Sales & Marketing
Address for Returns: Bailey Distribution Ltd
Imperfect Returns: Title pages up to £10 retail

GUILD OF ONE NAME STUDIES

Box G, 14 Charterhouse Bdgs, Goswell Road, London EC1M 7BA

GUILD OF PASTORAL PSYCHOLOGY

c/o Hon Secretary, 5 Kilmeny, 36 Arterberry Road, London SW20 8AQ
Tel: 081-946 3172

Orders to
Ms Linnea Johnson, 56 Whitehall Park Road, Gunnersbury,
London W4 3NB
Tel: 081-747 8697

[handwritten: GUILDFORD PRESS - Direct Distribution]

GUINNESS PUBLISHING

33 London Road, Enfield, Middlesex EN2 6DJ
ISBN Prefix(es): 0 85112
Tel: 081-367 4567
Fax: 081-367 5912
Telex: 23573 GBRLDN
Cables: MOSTEST ENFIELD

[handwritten: GULF PUBLISHING = Plymbridge]

Account No: _____
Sales Rep: _____
Tel: _____

Order Information

Order Dept Opening Times
Mon - Fri 9am - 5pm
All Dues Automatically Recorded
Representation Available
Teleordering

Personnel
Head of Company: Mark Cohen (Managing Director)
Head of Sales (Home): Fred Buxton (Sales & Marketing Director)
Head of Marketing: Sarah Duncan (Marketing Manager)
Head of Publicity: Cathy Brooks (Press Officer)
Head of Accounts: Adrian Morris (Finance Director)
Head of Customer Services: Joyce Lee (Customer Services Supervisor)

Number of titles published annually: 55
Percentage of Export Sales: 20%
Number of Staff: 55
PA Member
NBA Signatory
All New Titles are Bar Coded
Book Data Subscriber
WBIP Updating: F Buxton

Parent Company: Guinness PLC

Trade Terms
35% on all orders no surcharges

Returns Procedures
Authority to Return: Prior permission required from Customer Service Supervisor
Address for Returns: Macmillan Distribution Ltd, Lyle Industrial Estate, Pontardulais, Swansea SA4 1QD
Imperfect Returns: Title page up to £10 retail price.

GWASG GREGYNOG LTD

Gregynog, Newtown, Powys SY16 3PW
Tel: 0686 650625
Tel: 0686 650224
Fax: 0686 650656
VAT No: 326 5195 54

GWASG GWENFFRWD

Talwrn Glas, Afonwen, Mold, Clwyd CH7 5UB
ISBN Prefix(es): 0 9501861, 1 85651
Tel: 0352 720413

Order Information

Order Dept Opening Times
Mon - Fri 8am - 4pm
All Dues Automatically Recorded

Personnel
Head of Company: Dr H G A Hughes

Number of titles published annually: 20
Percentage of Export Sales: 95%

Trade Terms
35% on all net books. No service/carriage charges
Non-Net: 20% on all orders

GWASG Y DREF WEN

28 Church Road, Yr Eglwys Newydd, Cardiff, South Glamorgan CF4 2EA
ISBN Prefix(es): 0 904910, 0 946962, 1 85596
Tel: 0222 617860 Tel/Fax
VAT No: 135 2517 88

Order Information

All Dues Automatically Recorded

Personnel
Head of Company: Roger Boore/Anne Boore

Number of titles published annually: 30
WBIP Updating: Anne Boore

Trade Terms
33.3%
Other Terms: Carriage charged on orders less than £20 net

H I MARKETING

38 Carver Road, London SE24 9LT
Tel: 071-738 7751
Fax: 071-274 9160
VAT No: 607 9369 11

Account No: _____
Sales Rep: _____
Tel: _____

Orders to
TIPTREE BOOK SERVICES LTD, Church Road, Tiptree, Colchester, Essex CO5 0SR
Tel: 0621 819600
Fax: 0621 819011

Order Information

All Dues Automatically Recorded
Representation Available
Invoice Payments: Tiptree Book Services

Personnel
Head of Company: Medwyn Hughes/Cathy Parson
Head of Sales (Export): Claire Lavedan

Number of titles published annually: 200
Number of Staff: 5
All New Titles are Bar Coded
WBIP Updating: Medwyn Hughes

Trade Terms
35% on all orders, no surcharges
BA/Girobank Small Order Scheme: Yes
Credit Cards Accepted: Access/Master, Visa, Amex, Diners

Returns Procedures
Authority to Return: Head Office
Address for Returns: Tiptree

Stock Returns: Obtain authorisation form
Imperfect Returns: £10

HAAN ASSOCIATES

195 Streatham High Road, London SW16 6EG
Tel: 081-677 5568
Fax: 081-769 8921

Orders to
Haan Associates, PO Box 607, Streatham, London SW16 1EB
Tel: 081-677 5568 Tel/Fax

PETER HADDOCK LTD

Pinfold Lane Industrial Est, Bridlington, East Yorkshire YO16 5BT
ISBN Prefix(es): 0 7105
Tel: 0262 678121
Fax: 0262 400043
Telex: 52180
VAT No: 167 1844 45

Order Information

Order Dept Opening Times
Mon - Fri 9am - 5pm
All Dues Automatically Recorded

Number of titles published annually: 50
Percentage of Export Sales: 50%
Number of Staff: 50
All New Titles are Bar Coded
WBIP Updating: P H Hornby

Trade Terms
35%
Minimum Order: £200

Returns Procedures
Authority to Return: No returns - firm sale only

HAKLUYT SOCIETY

C/O Map Library, British Library, Gt Russel St, London WC1B 3DG
ISBN Prefix(es): 0 904180
Tel: 0986 86359
Fax: 0986 868181
VAT No: 233 4481 77

Order Information

Order Dept Opening Times
Mon - Fri 9am - 5pm

Personnel
Head of Company: Sir Harold Shedley KCMG MBE
Head of Sales (Home): Fiona Easton (Administrative Assistant)

Number of titles published annually: 2
Percentage of Export Sales: 60%
Number of Staff: 1
IPG Member
WBIP Updating: Fiona Easton

Trade Terms
20% on all orders, no surcharges, 35% CWO
Credit Cards Accepted: Access/Master, Visa

Returns Procedures
Authority to Return: Prior permission required

Address for Returns: Box 3, Harleston, Norfolk IP20 0AH
Stock Returns: The complete book must be returned

PETER HALBAN PUBLISHERS

42 South Molton Street, London W1Y 1HB
ISBN Prefix(es): 1 870015
Tel: 071-491 1582
Fax: 071-629 5381
VAT No: 446 0799 25

Orders to
LITTLEHAMPTON BOOK SERVICES, 14 Eldon Way, Lineside Ind Estate, Littlehampton, West Sussex BN17 7HE
Tel: 0903 721596
Fax: 0903 730914

Order Information

All Dues Automatically Recorded
Representation Available
Invoice Payments: Littlehampton
Sales & Marketing:Orion Publishing Group

Personnel
Head of Company: Peter Halban (Director)

Number of titles published annually: 10
Number of Staff: 3
IPG Member
NBA Signatory
All New Titles are Bar Coded
Open University Publications
Book Data Subscriber
WBIP Updating: Daniel Jaffe

Trade Terms
35%, no surcharges
Girobank Number: 516 6152
Credit Cards Accepted: Access/Master, Visa

Returns Procedures
Authority to Return: Andrew Macmillan - Orion Pub Group
Address for Returns: Littlehampton

ROBERT HALE LTD

Clerkenwell House, 45-47 Clerkenwell Green, London EC1R 0HT
ISBN Prefix(es): 0 7090, 0 7091
Tel: 071-251 2661
Fax: 071-490 4958
Cables: Barabbas London EC1

Account No: _____

Sales Rep: _____

Tel: _____

Order Information
Teleordering: HALE

Order Dept Opening Times
9am - 5pm
All Dues Automatically Recorded
Representation Available

Personnel
Head of Company: John Hale
Head of Sales (Home): Martin Kendall
Head of Publicity: Jo Burgess
Head of Accounts: Iris Kynaston
Head of Distribution: Robert Kynaston

Number of titles published annually: 200
Number of Staff: 30

NBA Signatory
All New Titles are Bar Coded
Book Data Subscriber
WBIP Updating: Jo Burgess

Trade Terms
General Net: Single copy/single line 20%, otherwise 35%
BA/Girobank Small Order Scheme: Yes
Girobank Number: 309 5495
Credit Cards Accepted: Access/Master, Visa

Returns Procedures
Authority to Return: Martin Kendall
Address for Returns: 4 Vestry Road, Nr Otford, Sevenoaks, Kent TN14 5EL
Stock Returns: Books to be returned with adequate paperwork to the ware-house
Imperfect Returns: Title pages may be returned for books up to £10. Above this price it is essential the books themselves are returned

HALFSHIRE BOOKS

6 High Street, Bromsgrove, Worcestershire B61 8HQ
ISBN Prefix(es): 0 9513525
Tel: 0527 76625
VAT No: 113 4883 79

Order Information

Order Dept Opening Times
Mon/Tues/Wed/Fri 9am - 5pm, Thur 9.30am - 12.30pm
All Dues Automatically Recorded
Representation Available

Personnel
Head of Company: Margaret Cooper
Head of Accounts: Michael H Cooper

Number of titles published annually: 2
Number of Staff: 1
IPG Member
All New Titles are Bar Coded
WBIP Updating: Margaret Cooper

Parent Company: Bromsgrove Books

Trade Terms
35% on orders £25 and above retail value, below £25 25% CWO No carriage charges

HALI PUBLICATIONS LTD

Kingsgate House, Kingsgate Place, Kilburn, London NW6 4TA
Tel: 071-328 9341 24 Hours
Fax: 071-372 5924

Order Information

Order Dept Opening Times
Mon - Fri 9.30am - 5.30pm
6-8 weeks delivery

Personnel
Head of Company: A H Marcuson (Managing Director)
Head of Sales (Home): S Ghandchi (Associate Publisher)
Other Important Personnel:
Ashley Spinks (Order Processing)

Number of Staff: 18

Parent Company: Centaur Communications Ltd

Trade Terms
Pre-payment on all orders, 30 days net on some bulk orders
Credit Cards Accepted: Access/Master, Visa

J H HALL & SONS LTD

Siddals Road, Derby, Derbyshire DE1 2PZ
ISBN Prefix(es): 0 946
Tel: 0332 45218
Fax: 0332 296146

Order Information

All Dues Automatically Recorded
Representation Available

Personnel

Head of Company: Michael G Morris
Head of Accounts: Hazel Street

Number of titles published annually: 5
Number of Staff: 10
WBIP Updating: Hazel Street

Trade Terms

33.3%
Other Terms: Carriage Charges: Plus postage & Packing

Returns Procedures

Authority to Return: Prior permission required

HAMBLEDON PRESS

102 Gloucester Avenue, London NW1 8HX
ISBN Prefix(es): 0 907628, 0 9506882, 1 85285
Tel: 071-586 0817
Fax: 071-586 9970
VAT No: 354 2798 30

Order Information

Order Dept Opening Times
Mon - Fri 9am - 6pm
All Dues Automatically Recorded

Personnel

Head of Company: Martin Sheppard
Head of Sales (Home): Eva Osborne

Number of titles published annually: 25
Percentage of Export Sales: 40%
Number of Staff: 2
IPG Member

Trade Terms

20%
Other Terms: Carriage charges at cost.

Returns Procedures

Stock Returns: Permission required.

HAMILTON HOUSE PUBLISHING

17 Staveley Way, Brixworth, Northamptonshire NN6 9EL
Tel: 0604 881889
Fax: 0604 880735
VAT No: 354 9075 35

HAMMICKS MAIL ORDER DEPARTMENT

Hounslow House, 730 London Road, Hounslow, Middlesex TW3 1PD
Tel: 081-899 5070
Fax: 081-899 5075
VAT No: 592 5056 27

Account No: _____
Sales Rep: _____
Tel: _____

Order Information

Order Dept Opening Times
Mon - Fri 9am - 5pm
Orders for more than one publisher can be bulked
All Dues Automatically Recorded
Representation Available

Personnel
Head of Company: Vincent Campbell (Managing Director)
081-899 5060
Head of Accounts: Stephen Wilder (Finance Director)

Allied Companies: Hammicks Bookshops

Trade Terms
10-20%, carriage charged if order value less than £100
Credit Cards Accepted: Access/Master, Visa, Amex

Returns Procedures
Stock Returns: Requests for return must be accompanied by invoice numbers. Returns will not be accepted without prior authorisation.

HAN SHAN TANG LTD

8 Duke Street, St James's, London SW1Y 6BN
ISBN Prefix(es): 0 906610, 1 870076
Tel: 071-839 6599
Fax: 071-976 1832
VAT No: 242 5086 77

Order Information

Order Dept Opening Times
Mon - Fri 10am - 5.30pm
Orders for more than one publisher can be bulked
All Dues Automatically Recorded
Representation Available

Personnel
Head of Company: Mr Christer von der Burg
Head of Marketing: Mr John Cayley
Head of Accounts: Miss Myrna Chua
Head of Distribution: Mrs Maya Donelan

Percentage of Export Sales: 30%
Number of Staff: 4
All New Titles are Bar Coded
WBIP Updating: John Cayley

Trade Terms
35% No surcharges (UK)
Girobank Number: 587 4459
Credit Cards Accepted: Access/Master, Visa, Amex

HANBURY PLAYS

Keeper's Lodge, Broughton Green, Droitwich, Worcestershire WR9 7EE
ISBN Prefix(es): 0 85197, 0 907926, 1 85205
Tel: 0905 23132

Order Information

Order Dept Opening Times
Mon - Fri 9.30am - 1pm 2pm - 5.30pm
Orders for more than one publisher can be bulked
All Dues Automatically Recorded

Personnel
Head of Company: Brian Burton

Number of titles published annually: 20

Trade Terms
33.3%

General Net: Single Copy 20%
Other Terms: Carriage Charged at cost

Returns Procedures
Authority to Return: Prior permission required
Imperfect Returns: Return title page only for replacement or credit

HANSIB PUBLISHING
Tower House, 3rd Floor, 139/149 Fonthill Road, London N4 3HF
Tel: 071-281 1191
Fax: 071-263 9656

PA Member

HARCOURT BRACE ~~JOVANOVICH~~
24-28 Oval Road, London NW1 7DX
ISBN Prefix(es): 0 03, 0 12, 0 15, 0 7020, 0 7216, 0 8089, 0 85661, 4 8367
Tel: 071-267 4466
Fax: 071-482 2293
Fax: 071-485 4752
Telex: 25775 ACPRES G
Cables: Acadinc London
VAT No: 494 6272 12
Account No: _20780005_
Sales Rep: _____
Tel: _____

Orders to
Harcourt Brace Jovan, Foots Cray High Street, Sidcup, Kent DA14 5HP
Tel: 081-300 3322 (24 Hr)
Fax: 081-309 0807

Order Information
Teleordering: HBJ
First Edition Subscriber

Order Dept Opening Times
Mon - Fri 9am - 5pm
All Dues Automatically Recorded
Representation Available

Personnel
Head of Company: Joan M Fujimoto
Head of Sales (Home): Des Brennan
Head of Marketing: Peter McKay
Head of Publicity: Jane Lawrence
Head of Accounts: C J Sehmer
Head of Customer Services: Sheila O'Reilly (Books)

Number of titles published annually: 700
Number of Staff: 250
PA Member
NBA Signatory
All New Titles are Bar Coded
Open University Publications
Book Data Subscriber
WBIP Updating: Jane Lawrence

Parent Company: Harcourt Brace Jovanovich Inc

Trade Terms
On application
Non-Net: 17.5%
BA/Girobank Small Order Scheme: Yes
Girobank Number: 504 3158
Credit Cards Accepted: Access/Master, Visa, Amex, Diners

Returns Procedures
Authority to Return: Sales Correspondent
Address for Returns: Harcourt Brace Jovanovich, 23 Edison Road, Hampden Park, Eastbourne, East Sussex BN23 6PY
Stock Returns: Notify within 7 days of receipt
Imperfect Returns: No pre-set limits, all by negotiation

HARDWICK HOUSE

Hardwick House, Hardwick, Ellesmere, Shropshire SY12 9HF
ISBN Prefix(es): 0 9512955
Tel: 0691 622503
VAT No: 163 1131 09

Orders to
WELSH BOOKS COUNCIL DISTRIBUTION CENTRE, Glan Yr Afon Industrial Estate, Llanbadarn, Aberystwyth, Dyfed SY23 3AQ
Tel: 0970 624455
Fax: 0970 625506

HARLEY BOOKS

Martins, Great Horkesley, Colchester, Essex CO6 4AH
ISBN Prefix(es): 0 946589
Tel: 0206 271216
Fax: 0206 271182
VAT No: 386 7650 04

Order Information

Order Dept Opening Times
Mon - Fri 8.30am - 6pm, Sat 8.30am - 5pm
All Dues Automatically Recorded

Personnel
Head of Company: Basil H Harley
Head of Sales (Home): Annette Harley

Number of titles published annually: 3
Number of Staff: 2
IPG Member
All New Titles are Bar Coded
Book Data Subscriber
WBIP Updating: Annette Harley

Parent Company: B H & A Harley Ltd

Trade Terms
General Net: £20 & under 25%, Single Titles CWO 30%, Multiple Stock 35% Over £20 - Single copy 20%, Single titles CWO 25%
Other Terms: Carriage Charges under £5 net and overseas
Girobank Number: 365 2661
Credit Cards Accepted: Access/Master, Visa, Amex

Returns Procedures
Stock Returns: Firm orders only - no returns
Imperfect Returns: Please return whole book. Postage refunded on faulty or publishers error returns.

THE HARLEY PRESS

11a Beehive Lane, Ferring, West Sussex BN12 5NN
ISBN Prefix(es): 0 951646
Tel: 0903 506302

Personnel
Head of Company: Mary Harley

Number of titles published annually: 1

Trade Terms
33%
Other Terms: £2 postage & packing charged

THOMAS HARMSWORTH PUBLISHING COMPANY

Old Rectory Offices, Stoke Abbott, Beaminster, Dorset DT8 3JT
ISBN Prefix(es): 0 948807, 0 9506012
Tel: 0308 68118 24 Hours
Fax: 0308 68995
VAT No: 318 0165 83

Order Information

Order Dept Opening Times
Mon - Fri 9am - 1pm, 2pm - 5pm
All Dues Automatically Recorded
Representation Available

Number of titles published annually: 5
All New Titles are Bar Coded
WBIP Updating: Thomas Harmsworth

Trade Terms
General Net: Single copy/single line 25% + £1.50 carriage, 2 or more books, subscription/stock/special (unless single) 35%
Credit Cards Accepted: Access/Master, Visa

Returns Procedures
Authority to Return: From Head Office or Rep
Address for Returns: Clipper Distribution Services
Imperfect Returns: Title pages only (to publisher)

HARNSER PRESS

Manor House, Itteringham, Norwich, Norfolk NR11 7AF
ISBN Prefix(es): 0 04, 0 12, 0 907665
Tel: 0263 87 4219 24 Hours

Personnel
Head of Company: Martin MacKeown
Other Important Personnel:
Mrs Ann F MacKeown

Trade Terms
35% on all orders, but 20% on orders less than £10

HARPERCOLLINS PUBLISHERS

77-85 Fulham Palace Road, Hammersmith, London W6 8JB
ISBN Prefix(es): 0 00
Tel: 081-741 7070
Fax: 081-307 4440
Telex: 25611 COLINS G
VAT No: 259 6397 06

Account No: _____130038300_____
Sales Rep: _____
Tel: _____

Orders to
HARPERCOLLINS PUBLISHERS DISTRIBUTION CENTRE, PO Box, Glasgow, Strathclyde G4 0NB
Tel: 041-772 3200
Fax: 041-306 3119

Order Information
Teleordering: HARCOL
First Edition Subscriber

Personnel
Head of Company: Eddie Bell (Executive Chairman & Publisher)
Head of Sales (Home): Iain Ogston (UK & Ireland Sales MD)
Head of Sales (Export): Adrian Bourne (International Sales MD)
Head of Accounts: David Houston (Chief Financial Officer)
Head of Customer Services: John Sexton (Director of Customer Development)
Other Important Personnel:
David Singer (Group Product Director), Peter Winslow (Chief Executive Officer - Publishing), Andy Jones (Publishing Finance Director), Peter Carroll (Personnel Director), Juliet Annan (Group Rights & Contracts Director)

Number of Staff: 850
PA Member
NBA Signatory
Book Data Subscriber

HARPERCOLLINS PUBLISHERS (BARTHOLOMEW/ TIMES DIVISION)

also Newbury House

77-85 Fulham Palace Road, Hammersmith, London W6 8JB
ISBN Prefix(es): 0 00, 0 09, 0 7028, 0 7230, 0 85152, 0 85543, 0 900568, 0 905522, 0 906329, 0 948576, 1 85456
Tel: 081-741 7070
Fax: 081-307 4813
Telex: 25611 COLINS G
VAT No: 259 6397 06

Account No: _____ 130038300
Sales Rep: _____
Tel: _____

Orders to
HARPERCOLLINS PUBLISHERS DISTRIBUTION CENTRE, PO Box, Glasgow, Strathclyde G4 0NB
Tel: 041-772 3200
Fax: 041-306 3119

Order Information
Teleordering: HARCOL
First Edition Subscriber

All Dues Automatically Recorded
Representation Available

Personnel
Head of Company: Barry Winkleman (Managing Director)
Head of Sales (Home): Iain Ogston (UK & Ireland Sales MD)
Head of Sales (Export): Adrian Bourne (International Sales MD)
Head of Marketing: Julie Clarke (Marketing Director)
Other Important Personnel:
Jeremy Westwood (Director of Rights), Peter Hornby (UK Sales Director)

Number of titles published annually: 40
PA Member
NBA Signatory
All New Titles are Bar Coded
Book Data Subscriber
WBIP Updating: Alan Hunter

Parent Company: HarperCollins Publishers

HARPERCOLLINS PUBLISHERS (CHILDRENS DIVISION)

77-85 Fulham Palace Road, Hammersmith, London W6 8JB
ISBN Prefix(es): 0 00, 0 411, 0 851

Tel: 081-741 7070
Fax: 081-307 4440
Telex: 25611 COLINS G
Account No: _____ 130038300 _____
Sales Rep: _____
Tel: _____

Orders to
HARPERCOLLINS PUBLISHERS DISTRIBUTION CENTRE, PO Box, Glasgow, Strathclyde G4 0NB
Tel: 041-772 3200
Fax: 041-306 3119

Order Information
Teleordering: HARCOL
First Edition Subscriber

Representation Available

Personnel
Head of Company: Roy Davey (Managing Director)
Head of Sales (Home): Iain Ogston (UK Sales MD)
Head of Sales (Export): Adrian Bourne (International Sales MD)
Head of Publicity: Rosanna Nissen (Publicity Manager)
Other Important Personnel:
Peter Hornby (UK Sales Director), Paul Litherland (Product Manager - Key Accounts)

Number of titles published annually: 250
All New Titles are Bar Coded
Book Data Subscriber
WBIP Updating: Jane Frost

HARPERCOLLINS PUBLISHERS (COLLINS EDUCATIONAL)

77-85 Fulham Palace Road, Hammersmith, London W6 8JB
ISBN Prefix(es): 0 00, 0 04
Tel: 081-741 7070
Fax: 081-307 4440
Telex: 25611 COLINS G
Account No: _____ 130038300 _____
Sales Rep: _____
Tel: _____

Orders to
HARPERCOLLINS PUBLISHERS DISTRIBUTION CENTRE, PO Box, Glasgow, Strathclyde G4 0NB
Tel: 041-772 3200
Fax: 041-306 3119

Order Information
Teleordering: HARCOL
First Edition Subscriber

Representation Available

Personnel
Head of Company: Roy Davey (Managing Director)
Head of Sales (Home): Mike Taylor (UK Sales & Marketing Director)
Head of Publicity: Helen McManners (Publicity Manager)
Other Important Personnel:
Jean Fenton (Product Manager - Key Accounts) 041-306 3358

Number of titles published annually: 150
All New Titles are Bar Coded
Book Data Subscriber
WBIP Updating: Jean Fenton

HARPERCOLLINS PUBLISHERS (GENERAL REFERENCE DIVISION)

77-85 Fulham Palace Road, Hammersmith, London W6 8JB
ISBN Prefix(es): 0 00, 0 01, 0 06, 0 261
Tel: 081-741 7070
Fax: 081-307 4440
Telex: 25611 COLINS G
Account No: 130038300
Sales Rep:
Tel:

Orders to
HARPERCOLLINS PUBLISHERS DISTRIBUTION CENTRE, PO Box, Glasgow, Strathclyde G4 0NB
Tel: 041-772 3200
Fax: 041-306 3119

Order Information
Teleordering: HARCOL
First Edition Subscriber

Representation Available

Personnel
Head of Company: Robin Wood (Managing Director)
Head of Sales (Home): Iain Ogston (UK & Ireland Sales MD)
Head of Sales (Export): Adrian Bourne (International Sales MD)
Head of Marketing: Nick Wells (Marketing Director)
Other Important Personnel:
Peter Hornby (UK Sales Director), Nick Ford (Product Manager)

All New Titles are Bar Coded
Book Data Subscriber
WBIP Updating: Jane Frost

HARPERCOLLINS PUBLISHERS (HARPER COLLEGE DIVISION)

77-85 Fulham Palace Road, Hammersmith, London W6 8JB
ISBN Prefix(es): 0 06, 0 465, 0 673, 0 88410, 0 88730
Tel: 081-741 7070
Fax: 081-307 4440
Telex: 25611 COLINS G
Account No: 130038300
Sales Rep:
Tel:

Orders to
HARPERCOLLINS PUBLISHERS DISTRIBUTION CENTRE, PO Box, Glasgow, Strathclyde G4 0NB
Tel: 041-772 3200
Fax: 041-306 3119

Order Information
Teleordering: HARCOL
First Edition Subscriber

Representation Available

Personnel
Head of Company: Peter Winslow (Managing Director)
Head of Marketing: John Parsons (Sales & Marketing Manager)
Head of Publicity: Sarah Mackey (Marketing Co-Ordinator)

Number of titles published annually: 100
All New Titles are Bar Coded
Book Data Subscriber
WBIP Updating: Jean Fenton

HARPERCOLLINS PUBLISHERS (INTERNATIONAL DIVISION)

77-85 Fulham Palace Road, Hammersmith, London W6 8JB
ISBN Prefix(es): 0 06, 0 465, 0 88410, 0 88730
Tel: 081-741 7070
Fax: 081-307 4440
Telex: 25611 COLINS G
Account No: 13 00 38300
Sales Rep: _____
Tel: _____

Orders to
HARPERCOLLINS PUBLISHERS DISTRIBUTION CENTRE, PO Box, Glasgow, Strathclyde G4 0NB
Tel: 041-772 3200
Fax: 041-306 3119

Order Information
Teleordering: HARCOL
First Edition Subscriber

Representation Available

Personnel
Head of Company: Adrian Bourne (Managing Director)
Head of Sales (Home): Iain Ogston (UK & Ireland Sales MD)
Head of Marketing: Mike Cheyne (Marketing Director)
Head of Publicity: Helen Ellis (Publicity Director)
Other Important Personnel:
Sue Page (Product Manager - Key Accounts)

Number of titles published annually: 50
All New Titles are Bar Coded
Book Data Subscriber
WBIP Updating: Sue Page

HARPERCOLLINS PUBLISHERS (RELIGIOUS DIVISION)

77-85 Fulham Palace Road, Hammersmith, London W6 8JB
ISBN Prefix(es): 0 00, 0 06, 0 310, 0 551, 0 85924
Tel: 081-741 7070
Fax: 081-307 4440
Telex: 25611 COLINS G
Account No: 130038300
Sales Rep: _____
Tel: _____

Orders to
HARPERCOLLINS PUBLISHERS DISTRIBUTION CENTRE, PO Box, Glasgow, Strathclyde G4 0NB
Tel: 041-772 3200
Fax: 041-306 3119

Order Information
Teleordering: HARCOL
First Edition Subscriber

Representation Available

Personnel
Head of Company: Ron Chopping (Managing Director)
Head of Sales (Home): Iain Ogston (UK & Ireland Sales MD)
Head of Sales (Export): Adrian Bourne (International Sales MD)
Head of Marketing: Jeremy Yates-Round (Sales & Marketing Director)
Head of Publicity: Zarina Parmiter (Publicity & Promotions Controller)
Other Important Personnel:

Sylvia Graham (Product Manager), Peter Hornby (UK Sales Director)

Number of titles published annually: 120
All New Titles are Bar Coded
Book Data Subscriber
WBIP Updating: Leslie Walmsley

HARPERCOLLINS PUBLISHERS (THORSONS DIVISION)

77-85 Fulham Palace Road, Hammersmith, London W6 8JB
ISBN Prefix(es): 0 04, 0 06, 0 7135, 0 7225, 0 85030, 0 85269, 0 86358, 1 85274, 1 85538
Tel: 081-741 7070
Fax: 081-307 4440
Telex: 25611 COLINS G

Account No: 130038300

Sales Rep:

Tel:

Orders to
HARPERCOLLINS PUBLISHERS DISTRIBUTION CENTRE, PO Box, Glasgow, Strathclyde G4 0NB
Tel: 041-772 3200
Fax: 041-306 3119

Order Information
Teleordering: HARCOL
First Edition Subscriber

Representation Available

Personnel
Head of Company: Eileen Campbell (Managing Director)
Head of Sales (Home): Iain Ogston (UK & Ireland Sales MD)
Head of Sales (Export): Adrian Bourne (International Sales MD)
Head of Marketing: Geoff Duffield (Marketing Director)
Other Important Personnel:
Peter Hornby (UK Sales Director), Sheila Crowley (Product Manager - Key Accounts)

Number of titles published annually: 150
All New Titles are Bar Coded
Book Data Subscriber
WBIP Updating: David Brawn

HARPERCOLLINS PUBLISHERS (TRADE DIVISION)

77-85 Fulham Palace Road, Hammersmith, London W6 8JB
ISBN Prefix(es): 0 00, 0 04, 0 207, 0 261, 0 583, 0 586, 0 86358
Tel: 081-741 7070
Fax: 081-407 4440
Telex: 25611 COLINS G

Account No: 130038300

Sales Rep:

Tel:

Orders to
HARPERCOLLINS PUBLISHERS DISTRIBUTION CENTRE, PO Box, Glasgow, Strathclyde G4 0NB
Tel: 041-772 3200
Fax: 041-306 3119

Order Information
Teleordering: HARCOL
First Edition Subscriber

Representation Available

Personnel
Head of Company: Jonathan Lloyd (Managing Director)
Head of Sales (Home): Iain Ogston (UK & Ireland Sales MD)
Head of Sales (Export): Adrian Bourne (International Sales MD)
Head of Marketing: Mike Cheyne (Marketing Director)
Head of Publicity: Helen Ellis (Publicity Director)
Other Important Personnel:
David Young (Deputy Managing Director), Steven Williams (Publicity - Harvill), Peter Hornby (UK Sales Director - Trade Paperbacks), Sylvia Graham (Product Manager - Key Accounts (Hardback)), Alistair Giles (Product Manager - Key Accounts (Paperback))

All New Titles are Bar Coded
Book Data Subscriber
WBIP Updating: Barbara Westmore

HARPERCOLLINS PUBLISHERS DISTRIBUTION CENTRE

PO Box, Glasgow, Strathclyde G4 0NB
Tel: 041-772 3200
Tel: 041-762 0999 24 Hours
Tel: 041-306 3100 Orders
Fax: 041-306 3119
Fax: 041-762 0584 Orders
Telex: 778107
VAT No: 259 6397 06
Account No: _____ 130038300
Sales Rep: _____
Tel: _____

Order Information
Teleordering: HARCOL
First Edition Subscriber

Order Dept Opening Times
Mon - Fri 8.30am - 4.45pm
Cyclical Ordering Policy
Orders for more than one publisher can be bulked
All Dues Automatically Recorded
Representation Available

Personnel
Head of Accounts: Ian Callan (Group Credit Manager) 041-306 3352
Head of Distribution: Tom Davison (Managing Director) 041-306 3250
Head of Customer Services: Jim Neilson (UK Customer Services) 041-306 3240
Other Important Personnel:
Gordon McLelland (Export Customer Services), Billy Burns (Assistant Credit Manager)

All New Titles are Bar Coded

Trade Terms
All net hardbacks & paperbacks 35%: 17.5% non net
Other Terms: Small order surcharge: £2.50 orders net value less than £50
Girobank Number: 116 0311
Credit Cards Accepted: Access/Master, Visa, Amex

Returns Procedures
Authority to Return: Local Representative
Address for Returns: HarperCollins Publishers, Returns Dept, Westerhill Road, Bishopbriggs, Glasgow G64 2QT
Imperfect Returns: Return title page only for books up to £20. Return whole book if over £20.

HART-DAVIS = Grafton

Harvard Business School = McGraw Hill

HARVARD UNIVERSITY PRESS
14 Bloomsbury Square, London WC1A 2LP
ISBN Prefix(es): 0 674
Tel: 071-404 0712
Fax: 071-404 0601
VAT No: 241 0229 15

Account No: _____

Sales Rep: _____

Tel: _____

Orders to
JOHN WILEY & SONS LTD, Southern Cross Trading Estate, 1 Oldlands Way, Bognor Regis, West Sussex PO22 9SA
Tel: 0243 829121
Fax: 0243 820250

Order Information

All Dues Automatically Recorded
Representation Available
Invoice Payments: John Wiley & Sons Ltd

Personnel
Head of Company: Ann Sexsmith
Head of Publicity: Clare Williams

Number of titles published annually: 120
Percentage of Export Sales: 60%
NBA Signatory
All New Titles are Bar Coded
Book Data Subscriber
WBIP Updating: Clare Williams

Trade Terms
Depends on turnover, arrangements with reps or publisher direct
Credit Cards Accepted: Access/Master, Visa, Amex, Diners

Returns Procedures
Authority to Return: Manager, Harvard University Press
Address for Returns: Reurns Dept, John Wiley & Sons, 1 Oldlands Way, Bognor Regis, Sussex, PO22
Stock Returns: As above

HARVESTIME PUBLISHING LTD
Nettle Hill, Brinklow Road, Anstey, Coventry, West Midlands CV7 9JL
ISBN Prefix(es): 0 947714, 1 87877
Tel: 0203 602717
Fax: 0203 602732
VAT No: 381 2710 67

HARVEY MAP SERVICES LTD
12-16 Main Street, Doune, Perthshire FK16 6BJ
Tel: 0786 841202
Fax: 0786 841098
VAT No: 309 0358 73

Order Information

Order Dept Opening Times
Mon - Fri 8.30am - 4.30pm
All Dues Automatically Recorded

Personnel
Head of Company: Robin Harvey/Susan Harvey
Head of Sales (Home): Peta Jeffrey
Head of Marketing: Catherine Nelson (Marketing Co-ordinator)

Head of Accounts: Helen Craig
Head of Distribution: Vivien Shannon

Number of titles published annually: 5
Number of Staff: 9
All New Titles are Bar Coded
WBIP Updating: Peta Jeffrey

Trade Terms
35%
Minimum Order: Orders under £45 retail value £5 surcharge unless c.w.o.
Girobank Number: 16 030 4008

Returns Procedures
Stock Returns: Overstocks: request in writing within 12 months Damaged/Incorrectly supplied:notify in writing within 7 days
Imperfect Returns: Title page accepted under £5 retail

HARVEYS BOOKS LTD

Magna Road, Wigston, Leicester, Leicestershire LE18 4ZH
ISBN Prefix(es): 1 85422
Tel: 0533 785154 24 Hours
Fax: 0533 782534
VAT No: 115 7309 84

Account No: _____

Sales Rep: _____

Tel: _____

Order Information

Order Dept Opening Times
Mon - Fri 9am - 5.30pm
All Dues Automatically Recorded
Representation Available

Personnel
Head of Company: Vance Harvey (Managing Director)
Head of Sales (Home): Andrew Tindall (Sales Director)
Head of Marketing: Nicola Hayes
Head of Accounts: Stephen Taylor (Financial Controller)
Head of Distribution: Paul Bennett (Operations Manager)
Head of Customer Services: Maragaret Walker
Other Important Personnel:
Mike Edwards (European Sales Manager), Robert Guy (Export Sales Manager (Australia/S Africa/Far East))

Number of titles published annually: 100
Percentage of Export Sales: 40%
Number of Staff: 40
PA Member
All New Titles are Bar Coded
WBIP Updating: Mrs Jane Scott

Trade Terms
35% NEGOTIABLE
Minimum Order: £50
Other Terms: Carriage charged £3 under £50

Returns Procedures
Authority to Return: firm sale only

[handwritten: HARWAL- Waverley Europe Ltd]

HAUNTED LIBRARY

Flat One, 36 Hamilton Street, Hoole, Chester, Cheshire
CH2 3JQ
Tel: 0244 313685

DAVID HAWGOOD

26 Cloister Road, Acton, London W3 0DE
ISBN Prefix(es): 0 948151
Tel: 081-993 2897
VAT No: 346 7442 39

Order Information

All Dues Automatically Recorded

Personnel
Head of Company: David Hawgood

Number of titles published annually: 1
Number of Staff: 1
IPG Member

Trade Terms
35% except single copy not prepaid 30%
Girobank Number: 46 461 2004

Returns Procedures
Stock Returns: Overstock returns not allowed

HAWK BOOKS LTD

Suite 309, Canalot Studios, 222 Kensal Road, London W10 5BN
ISBN Prefix(es): 0 948 248
Tel: 081-969 8091
Fax: 081-968 9012
VAT No: 494 6992 75

Orders to
BOOKPOINT LIMITED, 39 Milton Park, Abingdon, Oxfordshire OX14 4TD
Tel: 0235 835001
Fax: 0235 861038

Order Information

All Dues Automatically Recorded
Representation Available
Invoice Payments: Bookpoint

Personnel
Head of Company: Patrick Hawkey
Head of Sales (Home): John Masters
Head of Publicity: Alex Giri

Number of titles published annually: 15
Number of Staff: 2
All New Titles are Bar Coded
WBIP Updating: Alex Giri

Trade Terms
35%
Credit Cards Accepted: Access/Master, Visa, Amex

Returns Procedures
Authority to Return: ABS, Queen Ann Court, 19-21 Albion Place, Maidstone ME14 5EG
Address for Returns: Bookpoint

HAWKER PUBLICATIONS LTD

140 Battersea Park Road, London SW11 4NB
ISBN Prefix(es): 0 9514649, 1 874790
Tel: 071-720 2108
Fax: 071-498 3023

Orders to
BOOKPOINT LIMITED, 39 Milton Park, Abingdon, Oxfordshire OX14 4TD
Tel: 0235 835001
Fax: 0235 861038

Order Information

All Dues Automatically Recorded
Invoice Payments: Bookpoint

Personnel
Head of Company: Dr R Hawkins
Head of Sales (Home): Mr P Petker
Head of Accounts: Ms A Sheppard

Number of titles published annually: 10
Number of Staff: 13
IPG Member
All New Titles are Bar Coded
WBIP Updating: Dr R Hawkins

Trade Terms
40%

Returns Procedures
Authority to Return: Dr Hawkins or Bookpoint
Address for Returns: Bookpoint
Stock Returns: See Bookpoint
Imperfect Returns: Return to head office, title page only up to £10

HAWTHORN PRESS

Bankfield House, 13 Wallbridge, Stroud, Gloucestershire GL5 3JA
ISBN Prefix(es): 1 869890
Tel: 0453 757040 Tel/Fax
VAT No: 408 4399 37

Order Information

Order Dept Opening Times
Tue/Wed/Fri 9am - 5pm
All Dues Automatically Recorded

Personnel
Head of Company: Martin Large
Head of Customer Services: Joyce Ballinger

Number of titles published annually: 7
Percentage of Export Sales: 60%
Book Data Subscriber
WBIP Updating: M Rickard, Book Data

Trade Terms
Single copy 25% CWO, Multiples 35%
Other Terms: Surcharge of £1.25 on orders under £25

Returns Procedures
Authority to Return: Joyce Ballinger
Address for Returns: Clipper Distribution, Windmill Grove, Portchester, Hants PO16 9BT

HAWTHORNS PUBLICATIONS LTD

Pond View House, 6A High Street, Otford, Sevenoaks, Kent TN14 5PQ
ISBN Prefix(es): 1 871044
Tel: 0959 522325 24 Hours
Tel: 0959 522368 Tel/Fax
VAT No: 492 3451 39

Order Information

Order Dept Opening Times
Mon - Fri 9am - 5.30pm

Personnel
Head of Company: D G Cracknell
Head of Sales (Home): Gillian Black

Number of titles published annually: 2
PA Member
NBA Signatory
WBIP Updating: D G Cracknell

Trade Terms
33.3% (generally), no surcharges except for orders under £15

J H HAYNES & CO LTD

Sparkford, Nr Yeovil, Somerset BA22 7JJ
ISBN Prefix(es): 0 75080, 0 85059, 0 85429, 0 85614, 0 85696, 0 86093, 0 900550, 0 902280, 0 902888, 0 908081, 0 946137, 0 946609, 1 85010, 1 85260, 1 85509
Tel: 0963 40635 440635
Tel: 0963 40614 440614
Fax: 0963 40001 440001
Fax: 0963 40835
Telex: 46212
VAT No: 323 6351 79

Account No: _____

Sales Rep: _____

Tel: _____

Order Information
Teleordering: HAYNES

Order Dept Opening Times
8.30am - 5pm
Cyclical Ordering Policy
All Dues Automatically Recorded
Representation Available

Personnel
Head of Company: J H Haynes (Chairman)
Head of Sales (Home): Richard Henwood (Book Trade Sales Director)
Head of Sales (Export): Chris Wilding (Export Sales Manager)
Head of Publicity: Karen Ley (Promotions Manager)
Head of Accounts: Les Purcell (Financial Accounting Manager)
Head of Customer Services: Sian Brammer (Sales Office Manager)
Other Important Personnel:
Tony Kemp (Key Accounts Manager), Helen Lazenby (Book Trade Liaison), Barry Squance (Motor Trade Sales Director)

Number of titles published annually: 60
Number of Staff: 256
NBA Signatory
All New Titles are Bar Coded
Book Data Subscriber
WBIP Updating: Alison Roelich/Corinne Elliston

Allied Companies: Haynes Publications, Inc (US)

Trade Terms
Variable
General Net: Single Copy 10%, Two books 25%, Three books or more 35% Carriage Paid
Minimum Order: £50 retail
Other Terms: Carriage Charges: on special orders only
Girobank Number: 282 5058
Credit Cards Accepted: Access/Master, Visa

Returns Procedures
Authority to Return: Via Area Sales Representatives Address obtainable from sales dept at head office
Stock Returns: Obtain authorisation from Head Office within three working days of receipt of books. Contact Sales Office Manager.
Imperfect Returns: As above (but only title page and three other pages to be returned).

HAZAR PUBLISHING

147 Chiswick High Road, Chiswick, London W4 2DT
Tel: 081-994 9296
Fax: 081-994 1407
Telex: 9419879

Orders to
BOOKPOINT LIMITED, 39 Milton Park, Abingdon, Oxfordshire OX14 4TD
Tel: 0235 835001
Fax: 0235 861038

HEADLAND PUBLICATIONS

38 York Avenue, West Kirby, Wirral, Merseyside L48 3JF
ISBN Prefix(es): 0 903074
Tel: 051-625 9128

Orders to
PASSWORD (BOOKS) LTD, 23 New Mount Street, Manchester, Greater Manchester M4 4DE
Tel: 061-953 4009
Fax: 061-953 4001

Order Information

Invoice Payments: Password Books

Trade Terms
Girobank Number: 613 4599

HEADLEY BROTHERS LTD

The Invicta Press, Queens Road, Ashford, Kent TN24 8HH
Tel: 0233 623131
Fax: 0233 612345 Office
Fax: 0233 641471 Works
Fax: 0233 622704 Works
VAT No: 201 1754 19

Order Information

Cyclical Ordering Policy

Personnel
Head of Company: H Christopher Pitt (Managing Director)
Head of Sales (Home): Derek J Rigden (Sales Director)
Head of Marketing: Stephen H Pitt (Marketing Director)

Number of titles published annually: 3
Percentage of Export Sales: 25%
Number of Staff: 3

Trade Terms
Academic Net: Subscription orders: cwo

HEADLINE BOOK PUBLISHING PLC

Headline House, 79 Great Titchfield Street, London W1P 7FN
ISBN Prefix(es): 0 7472
Tel: 071-631 1687
Fax: 071-631 1958
VAT No: 443 9953 14

Account No: _____
Sales Rep: _____
Tel: _____

Orders to
BOOKPOINT LIMITED, 39 Milton Park, Abingdon, Oxfordshire OX14 4TD

Tel: 0235 835001
Fax: 0235 861038

Order Information

All Dues Automatically Recorded
Representation Available
Invoice Payments: Bookpoint

Personnel
Head of Company: Tim Hely-Hutchinson (Managing Director)
Head of Sales (Home): Paul Maycock (Home Sales Manager)
Head of Sales (Export): Peter Newsom (Export Sales Manager)
Head of Marketing: Wendy Suffield (Marketing Manager)
Head of Publicity: Louise Page (Publicity Manager)
Head of Accounts: Paul Coley (Financial Director)
Head of Customer Services: Jenny Gray
Other Important Personnel:
Sian Thomas (Joint Deputy MD/Sales & Publicity)

Number of titles published annually: 400
Percentage of Export Sales: 25%
Number of Staff: 50
IPG Member
NBA Signatory
All New Titles are Bar Coded
WBIP Updating: Jill Collard

Trade Terms
35%

Returns Procedures
Authority to Return: Representative or Sales Manager
Address for Returns: Bookpoint

THE HEADQUARTERS PUBLISHING COMPANY LTD

5 Alexandria Road, West Ealing, London W13 0NP
ISBN Prefix(es): 0 947823
Tel: 081-579 7011
Fax: 081-579 0991

PA Member
NBA Signatory
All New Titles are Bar Coded

Subsidiary Companies: Two Worlds Publishing (1986) Ltd

HEADSTART HISTORY

PO Box 41, Bangor, Gwynedd LL57 1SB
Tel: 0248 351816
Fax: 0248 362115
VAT No: 559 8957 57

IPG Member
All New Titles are Bar Coded
Book Data Subscriber

HEALTH EDUCATION AUTHORITY

Hamilton House, Mabledon PLace, London WC1H 9TX
ISBN Prefix(es): 0 903652, 1 85448
Tel: 071-383 3833
Fax: 071-413 0339
VAT No: HA 988

Order Information

Order Dept Opening Times
Mon - Fri 9am - 5pm

Promoting a healthier future

For health professionals, teachers and trainers, social workers, employers and the general public

The Health Education Authority

- is the UK's leading health publisher
- develops and distributes over 50 million printed items annually
- publishes information leaflets for the public, books and packs for students and teachers at all levels plus training resources for professionals and practitioners
- publishes materials for use in schools, youth centres, hospitals and clinics, factories and offices – the whole spectrum of organisations for whom health is an issue

For FREE catalogue and information on trade terms, please contact:

**Assistant Sales Manager
Health Education Authority
Hamilton House
Mabledom Place
London WC1H 9TX
FAX 071 433 0339**

*Cyclical Ordering Policy
All Dues Automatically Recorded*
Orders To:Distribution Dept

Personnel
Head of Company: Irene Fekete (Publisher)
Head of Sales (Home): Paul Kane
Head of Accounts: Peter Trowell (Director of Finanace)
Head of Customer Services: Lynn Tomlinson
Other Important Personnel:
Mark McDonagh, Tim Jennings

Number of titles published annually: 300
PA Member
*Open University Publications
Book Data Subscriber*

Trade Terms
35%, no surcharges, except postage & packing

Returns Procedures
Imperfect Returns: No limit

HEALTH PROMOTION AUTHORITY FOR WALES

Brunel House, 2 Fitzalan Road, Cardiff, South Glamorgan CF2 1EB
Tel: 0222 472472
Fax: 0222 480851

IPG Member

HEART OF ALBION PRESS

2 Cross Hill Close, Wymeswold, Loughborough, Leicestershire LE12 6UJ
Tel: 0509 880725 Tel/Fax

HEBDON ROYD PUBLICATIONS
8 Fordington Green, Dorchester, Dorset DT1 1GB
Tel: 0305 264646
Fax: 0305 250150
VAT No: 427 3161 67

HEINEMANN CHILDRENS REFERENCE
Halley Court, Jordan Hill, Oxford, Oxfordshire OX2 8EJ
ISBN Prefix(es): 0 431
Tel: 0865 311366
Fax: 0865 310043
Telex: 837292 HEBOXF G
VAT No: 340 2429 92
Account No: 101736E
Sales Rep:
Tel:

Orders to
Heinemann Pub Ltd, PO Box 382, Halley Court, Jordan Hill, Oxford, Oxfordshire OX2 8RU
Tel: 0865 311366
Fax: 0865 310029
24 Hour Ansafone Number: 0865 511480

Order Information
Teleordering: HEB

Order Dept Opening Times
Mon - Fri 8.30am - 5.00pm
Cyclical Ordering Policy
All Dues Automatically Recorded
Representation Available
Invoice Payments: Heinemann Pub Ltd, PO Box 384, Halley Court, Jordan Hill Oxford, Oxon OX2 8RY

Personnel
Head of Company: Bob Osborne
Head of Sales (Home): David Hall
Head of Sales (Export): Wendy Greenberg
Head of Accounts: David Evered
Head of Distribution: Peter Pounds

Number of titles published annually: 50
Percentage of Export Sales: 35%
NBA Signatory
All New Titles are Bar Coded
Book Data Subscriber
WBIP Updating: Wendy Greenberg

Parent Company: Reed International Books

Trade Terms
General Net: 25%
Academic Net: 25%
Non-Net: 17.5%
Credit Cards Accepted: Access/Master, Visa, Amex, Diners

Returns Procedures
Authority to Return: Returns Authorization Dept, H/O
Address for Returns: Heinemann Childrens Reference, Warehouse 2, Sanders Lodge Est, Rushden, Northants NN10 9BR
Stock Returns: Contact publisher for authorization, applications in writing only
Imperfect Returns: Title page up to cover price of £10. Prior authorization for all others

HEINEMANN EDUCATIONAL
Halley Court, Jordan Hill, Oxford, Oxfordshire OX2 8EJ
ISBN Prefix(es): 0 435

Tel: 0865 311366
Fax: 0865 310043
Telex: 837292 HEBOXF G
VAT No: 340 2429 92
Account No: 101736E
Sales Rep:
Tel:

Orders to
Heinemann Pub Ltd, PO Box 382, Halley Court, Jordan Hill, Oxford, Oxfordshire OX2 8RU
Tel: 0865 311366
Fax: 0865 310029
24 Hour Ansafone Number: 0865 511480

Order Information
Teleordering: HEB

Order Dept Opening Times
Mon - Fri 8.30am - 5pm
Cyclical Ordering Policy
All Dues Automatically Recorded
Representation Available
Invoice Payments: Heinemann Publishers (Oxford) Ltd, PO Box 384, Halley Court Jordan Hill, Oxford, Oxon OX2 8RY

Personnel
Head of Company: Bob Osborne (Managing Director)
Head of Sales (Home): Simon Watts (Sales & Marketing Director)
Head of Publicity: Rod Smith (Marketing Manager)
Head of Accounts: David Evered (Credit Control Manager)
Head of Distribution: Peter Pounds (Customer Services Manager)

Number of titles published annually: 200
NBA Signatory
All New Titles are Bar Coded
Open University Publications
Book Data Subscriber
WBIP Updating: Alison Price

Parent Company: Reed International Books

Trade Terms
General Net: 25%
Academic Net: 25%
Non-Net: 17.5%
Credit Cards Accepted: Access/Master, Amex, Diners, Visa

Returns Procedures
Authority to Return: Returns Authorisation Dept, Heinemann Educ, Halley Court, Jordan Hill, Oxford OX2 8EJ
Address for Returns: Heinemann Educational, Warehouse 2, Sanders Lodge Estate Rushden
Stock Returns: For all returns contact publisher for authorisation. Application should be made in writing.
Imperfect Returns: Return title pages to publisher up to maximum cover price value of £10. Prior authorisation required for all orders.

HELM INFORMATION LTD
The Banks, Mountfield, Robertsbridge, East Sussex
TN32 5JY
Tel: 0580 880561
Fax: 0580 880541
VAT No: 583 5218 28

IPG Member
Book Data Subscriber

HENDERSON PUBLISHING LTD

Tide Mill Way, Woodbridge, Suffolk IP12 1BY
ISBN Prefix(es): 1 85597
Tel: 0394 380622
Fax: 0394 380618
VAT No: 521 3673 68

Order Information

All Dues Automatically Recorded
Representation Available

Personnel
Head of Company: Barrie Henderson
Head of Publicity: Hazel Jones
Head of Accounts: Elizabeth Henderson

Number of titles published annually: 50
Percentage of Export Sales: 30%
All New Titles are Bar Coded
WBIP Updating: B Henderson

Trade Terms
35%
Other Terms: Orders under £25 will be charged small order surcharges and carriage charges

Returns Procedures
Authority to Return: Prior permission required
Address for Returns: Trade Counter Ltd, The Airfield, Norwich Road Mendlesham, Suffolk IP14 5NA
Imperfect Returns: Books only returned

HENDON PUBLISHING CO LTD

Hendon Mill, Nelson, Lancashire BB9 8AD
ISBN Prefix(es): 0 86067, 902907
Tel: 0282 613129 24 Hours
Tel: 0282 697725
Fax: 0282 870215
VAT No: 174 7473 35

Order Information

Cyclical Ordering Policy
All Dues Automatically Recorded
Representation Available

Personnel
Head of Company: H J H Nelson
Head of Marketing: James Nelson
Head of Accounts: Jean Marden

Number of titles published annually: 3
Number of Staff: 3
PA Member
NBA Signatory
WBIP Updating: Jean Marsden

Parent Company: Hendon Mill Company Ltd

Trade Terms
33.3%
General Net: Two books or less 25%
Academic Net: Two books or less 25%

Returns Procedures
Stock Returns: Pack well - telephone for details
Imperfect Returns: Title page to be returned

SHAUNAGH HENEAGE DISTRIBUTION

1 Stewart's Court, 220 Stewart's Road, London SW8 4UD
ISBN Prefix(es): 0 946708, 1 874044
Tel: 071-720 1503
Fax: 071-720 3158

VAT No: 548 1215 52
Account No: _____
Sales Rep: _____
Tel: _____

Order Information

Order Dept Opening Times
Mon - Fri 9am - 5pm
Orders for more than one publisher can be bulked
All Dues Automatically Recorded
Representation Available

Personnel
Head of Company: Shaunagh Hencage
Head of Accounts: Grace Fisher
Head of Distribution: Judith Gray
Other Important Personnel:
Jean-Marc Evans (Sales Rep (London & South)), James Attlee (Sales Rep (North England & Scotland))

Number of titles published annually: 4
Percentage of Export Sales: 25%
Number of Staff: 6
All New Titles are Bar Coded
WBIP Updating: Judith Gray

Parent Company: Art Books International Ltd

Trade Terms
Non-Net: Single copy 20/25%, Two or more 35%, Special orders variable
Girobank Number: 302 7368
Credit Cards Accepted: Access/Master, Visa

Returns Procedures
Authority to Return: Judith Gray
Imperfect Returns: Whole book must be returned

IAN HENRY PUBLICATIONS LTD

20 Park Drive, Romford, Essex RM1 4LH
ISBN Prefix(es): 0 86025
Tel: 0708 749119
VAT No: 247 6695 17

Order Information

Order Dept Opening Times
Mon - Sat 8.30am - 6pm
All Dues Automatically Recorded
Representation Available
Trade Counter:8 Galliford Road, Maldon, Essex CM9 7XU
Tel:0621 850269 Fax:0621 850862

Personnel
Head of Company: Ian Wilkes

Number of titles published annually: 12
IPG Member
NBA Signatory
Book Data Subscriber

Trade Terms
Two or more 35%, Single Copies 20% (Pro-forma)

Returns Procedures
Address for Returns: PO Box 300, Maldon Essex CM9 7XU

HERALDRY TODAY

Parliament Piece, Ramsbury, Nr Marlborough, Wiltshire
SN8 2QH
Tel: 0672 20617

Fax: 0672 20183
VAT No: 238 8244 41

PA Member

THE HERB SOCIETY

PO Box 599, London SW11 4RW
ISBN Prefix(es): 0961-5873
Tel: 071-350 2703
VAT No: 243 0813 91

THE HERBERT PRESS

46 Northchurch Road, London N1 4EJ
ISBN Prefix(es): 0 906969, 1 871569
Tel: 071-254 4379
Fax: 071-254 4332
VAT No: 231 1932 00

Orders to
A & C BLACK (PUBLISHERS) LTD, PO Box 19, Huntingdon, Cambridgeshire PE19 3SF
Tel: 0480 212666
Fax: 0480 405014

Order Information

All Dues Automatically Recorded
Representation Available

Personnel
Head of Company: David Herbert (Managing Director)
Head of Accounts: Brenda Herbert (Director & Co Secretary)

Number of titles published annually: 12
Percentage of Export Sales: 30%
Number of Staff: 4
PA Member
NBA Signatory
All New Titles are Bar Coded
Book Data Subscriber
WBIP Updating: Clare Foster

Trade Terms
Refer to A&C Black

Returns Procedures
Authority to Return: Refer to A&C Black

ALEXANDER HERIOT & CO LTD

PO Box 1, Northleach, Cheltenham, Gloucestershire GL54 3JB
ISBN Prefix(es): 0 906382
Tel: 0451 860530
Fax: 0451 860084
VAT No: 241 2429 94

Order Information

All Dues Automatically Recorded

Personnel
Head of Company: J R Fleming

Number of titles published annually: 2
Percentage of Export Sales: 75%
Number of Staff: 1

Trade Terms
Single copy 25%, Two books or more 35%
General Net: Single copy 25%, 2 books or more 35%
Girobank Number: 5319358

Returns Procedures
Stock Returns: Return to Publisher

HERITAGE PRESS
1 St James's Drive, Malvern, Worcestershire WR14 2UD
Tel: 0684 561755

IPG Member

HETERODOX PUBLISHERS
Suite 20, 3 Abbey Orchard Street, London SW1P 2JJ
Tel: 071-222 1339 Tel/Fax

Orders to
VINE HOUSE DISTRIBUTION, Waldenbury, North Chailey, East Sussex BN8 4DR
Tel: 082-572 3398
Fax: 082-572 4188

[handwritten: HEXAGON PUBS - 5, Dickerage Lane, New Malden Surrey KT3 3RZ]

HGM PUBLICATIONS
Abney House, Baslow, Bakewell, Derbyshire DE45 1RZ
ISBN Prefix(es): 1 872246
Tel: 0246 582470
Tel: 0246 582329
Fax: 0246 582425
VAT No: 314 6310 94

Personnel
Head of Company: Howard G Mounsey
Head of Sales (Home): Simon P Mounsey
Head of Accounts: Howard G Mounsey

Number of titles published annually: 5
Percentage of Export Sales: 33%
Number of Staff: 3
WBIP Updating: Simon Mounsey

Trade Terms
No Trade Terms
Credit Cards Accepted: Access/Master, Visa

[handwritten: Hilgar (Adam) C/o IOP Publishing]

HILLER AIRGUNS
56 Princess Way, Euxton, Chorley, Lancashire PR7 6PJ
ISBN Prefix(es): 0 9507046
Tel: 0257 265489 Tel/Fax

Number of titles published annually: 1
Percentage of Export Sales: 20%
All New Titles are Bar Coded
WBIP Updating: D E Hiller

[handwritten: HILL + Wang Direct USA]

Trade Terms
35% + postage
Credit Cards Accepted: Access/Master, Visa

HILMARTON MANOR PRESS
Hilmarton Manor Press, Calne, Wiltshire SN11 8SB
ISBN Prefix(es): 0 904722, 9 500508
Tel: 0249 76208
Fax: 0249 76379
VAT No: 139 1010 06

Order Information

Order Dept Opening Times
Mon - Fri 9am - 5pm
All Dues Automatically Recorded
Representation Available

Personnel
Head of Company: Charles Baile de Laperriere
Other Important Personnel:
Sarah Baile de Laperriere

Number of titles published annually: 4
Number of Staff: 3
Book Data Subscriber
WBIP Updating: Charles Baile de Laperriere

Trade Terms
up to 35%

HIPPOPOTAMUS PRESS

22 Whitewell Road, Frome, Somerset BA11 4EL
ISBN Prefix(es): 0 904179
Tel: 0373 466653
VAT No: 425 0436 81

Order Information

Order Dept Opening Times
Mon - Fri 9am - 5pm
All Dues Automatically Recorded
Representation Available

Personnel
Head of Company: R W John
Head of Sales (Export): B A Martin
Head of Marketing: M Pargitter

Number of titles published annually: 4
Number of Staff: 3
All New Titles are Bar Coded
WBIP Updating: R W John

Trade Terms
35% no surcharges
Credit Cards Accepted: Access/Master, Visa

Returns Procedures
Authority to Return: Prior permission required

THE HISTORICAL ASSOCIATION

59A Kennington Park Road, London SE11 4JH
ISBN Prefix(es): 0 85278
Tel: 071-735 3901
Fax: 071-582 4989
VAT No: 235 6778 32

HISTORICAL PUBLICATIONS LTD

32 Ellington Street, London N7 8PL
ISBN Prefix(es): 0 948667, 0 9503656
Tel: 071-607 1628
Fax: 071-609 6451
VAT No: 231 4465 87

Orders to
PHILLIMORE & CO LTD, Shopwyke Hall, Chichester,
West Sussex PO20 6BQ
Tel: 0243 787636
Fax: 0243 787639

Personnel
Head of Company: John Richardson
Head of Marketing: Helen English

[Handwritten annotation: Historical Geography Research Group (HGRG), c/o Prof CWJ Withers, Dept of Geography, Cheltenham & Gloucester, College of Education, The Park, Cheltenham, Glos GL50 3PP]

Number of titles published annually: 5
Number of Staff: 2
All New Titles are Bar Coded
WBIP Updating: J Richardson

Trade Terms
As per distributor

Returns Procedures
Authority to Return: As per Distributor

HLT PUBLICATIONS

200 Greyhound Road, London W14 9RY
ISBN Prefix(es): 0 7510, 1 85352
Tel: 071-385 3377
Fax: 071-381 3377
Telex: 266386 HLT
VAT No: 244 5782 45
Account No: _____ 9BSRUB _____
Sales Rep: _____
Tel: _____

Order Information

Order Dept Opening Times
Mon - Fri 9am - 5.30pm
All Dues Automatically Recorded
Representation Available

Personnel
Head of Company: Mr John Grenier (Chairman)
Head of Sales (Home): Mr Steve Turner (Sales Manager)
Head of Publicity: Ms Tonie Derwent (Managing Editor)
Head of Accounts: Mr M Kumar (Chief Accountant)
Head of Distribution: Mr Rajiv Gupta (Operations Director)
Head of Customer Services: Mr Robert Mayhall

Number of titles published annually: 350
Percentage of Export Sales: 40%
Number of Staff: 100
PA Member
IPG Member
NBA Signatory
All New Titles are Bar Coded
Book Data Subscriber
WBIP Updating: Ms Tonie Derwent

Parent Company: The HLT Group
Subsidiary Companies: Holborn Law Tutors SND BHD (ML)

Trade Terms
30%
Academic Net: Single copy 20%, Stock orders 30%
Credit Cards Accepted: Access/Master, Visa, Amex

Returns Procedures
Authority to Return: Steve Turner at Head Office
Address for Returns: Unit 5, 92-104 Carnwath Road, London SW6 3HW
Stock Returns: By agreement prior to return
Imperfect Returns: Within 14 days of receipt permission required.

HMSO BOOKS

St Crispins, Duke Street, Norwich, Norfolk NR3 1PD
ISBN Prefix(es): 0 10, 0 11, 0 337
Tel: 0603 622211
Fax: 0603 695582
VAT No: GD 245

Account No: 44 1212 *(handwritten)*
Sales Rep: _____
Tel: _____

Orders to
HMSO Books, PO Box 276, London SW8 5DT
Tel: 071-873 9090
Fax: 071-873 8200

Enquiries 071 873 0011 *(handwritten)*

Order Information
Teleordering: HMSO

Order Dept Opening Times
Mon - Fri 9am - 5pm
All Dues Automatically Recorded
Representation Available
Invoice Payments: To London Address
Trade Counter:HMSO Books, 49 High Holborn, London WC1V 6HB
Tel: 071-873 0011
Fax: 071-831 1326

Other Important Locations
Sales Office:51 Nine Elms Lane, London SW8 5DR
Tel: 071-873 0011
Fax: 071-873 8203

Personnel
Head of Company: Chris Southgate (Director of Publications) 0603 695457
Head of Sales (Home): John Hudson (Sales Director) 071-873 8404
Head of Sales (Export): Julie McNair (Export Manager) 071-873 8211
Head of Publicity: Andrew Cullum (Publicity Director) 0603 695745
Head of Accounts: Michael Eaton (Accounts Director) 071-873 8464
Head of Distribution: Brian Minett (Distribution Director) 071-873 8293
Other Important Personnel:
Phil Garrood (Subscriptions Manager) 071-873 8456,
Malcolm Wilson (Credit Control Manager) 071-873 8289,
John Hosford (Warehouse Manager) 071-873 8410, Robin Henry (International Publications Manager) 071-873 8400

Number of titles published annually: 11000
Number of Staff: 475
PA Member
All New Titles are Bar Coded
Book Data Subscriber
WBIP Updating: John Wreford

Trade Terms
General Net: 35%
Academic Net: 33.3%
Other Terms: 'Send to' discount 10%
Girobank Number: 582 1002
Credit Cards Accepted: Access/Master, Visa, Amex

Returns Procedures
Authority to Return: Sales Office
Address for Returns: 51 Nine Elms Lane
Stock Returns: Wrong Supply: Enquiry Section Peter Raggett in London Office Overstocks: Contact Sales Office or HMSO Representative
Imperfect Returns: Contact enquiry section (Peter Raggett) at London Office

HOBSONS PUBLISHING PLC
Bateman Street, Cambridge, Cambridgeshire CB2 1LZ
ISBN Prefix(es): 1 85324
Tel: 0223 354551

Tel: 0223 464334
Fax: 0223 323154
Telex: 81546 HOBCAM G

Orders to
BIBLIOS PUBLISHERS DISTRIBUTION SERVICE LTD,
Star Road, Partridge Green, West Sussex RH13 8LD
Tel: 0403 710971
Fax: 0403 711143

Order Information

Invoice Payments: Biblios Publishers Distribution Services Ltd

Personnel
Head of Company: Martin Morgan (Managing Director)
Head of Sales (Home): Annie Van Heerden (Sales Manager)
Head of Sales (Export): Julie Bushell (Sales Development Manager)
Head of Marketing: Gillian Moore (Publishing Director)
Head of Publicity: Amanda Norman (Promotions Manager)
Head of Accounts: Stuart Mott (Company Accountant)
Head of Distribution: David Hepburn (Operations Director)
Head of Customer Services: Rachel Emerson (Customer Services)

Number of titles published annually: 50
All New Titles are Bar Coded
WBIP Updating: Gillian Moore

Parent Company: Daily Mail General Trust

Trade Terms
35% standard (more than one copy), 25% single copy orders
Non-Net: Category A titles as above, Category B titles 10%
Credit Cards Accepted: Access/Master, Visa, Amex, Diners

Returns Procedures
Authority to Return: Rachel Emerson, Customer Services Co-ordinator
Address for Returns: Biblios 2, Old London Road, Washington, West Sussex
Stock Returns: Damaged/missing - claims within 3 days of receipt
Imperfect Returns: Request for authorization as above

HODDER & STOUGHTON LTD
Mill Road, Dunton Green, Sevenoaks, Kent TN13 2YA   NOW BOOKPOINT
ISBN Prefix(es): 0 340, 0 450, 0 7131
Tel: 0732 450111 24 Hours
Fax: 0732 460134
Telex: 95122
Cables: EXPOSITOR SEVENOAKS
VAT No: 205 5053 05
Account No: 101 11425
Sales Rep: _____
Tel: _____

Order Information
Teleordering: HODD
First Edition Subscriber

Order Dept Opening Times
Mon - Thur 8.45am - 5pm, Fri 9am - 4pm
Cyclical Ordering Policy
All Dues Automatically Recorded
Representation Available

Other Important Locations
47 Bedford Square, London WC1B 3DP (Trade Edi/Pub/Sales)
Tel: 071-636-9851 071 873 6000
Fax: 071-631 5248

Personnel
Head of Company: Philip Attenborough (Chairman)
Head of Sales (Home): Charles Nettleton
Head of Sales (Export): Paul Sheldon
Head of Marketing: Anthony Hammond
Head of Accounts: Stuart Hughes
Head of Distribution: Anthony Brown
Head of Customer Services: Peter Stockman
Other Important Personnel:
Patrick Wright (Chief Executive), Philip Walters (Academic & Educational Home Sales), Richard Tucker (UK Sales Manager - Trade), Philip Saunderson (UK Sales Manager - Academic), Michael Ambler (Credit Manager), Beth MacDougall (Publicity Director)

Number of titles published annually: 1000
Percentage of Export Sales: 20%
Number of Staff: 480
PA Member
NBA Signatory
All New Titles are Bar Coded
Open University Publications
Book Data Subscriber

Trade Terms
General Net: 35%
Academic Net: 30%
Non-Net: 17.5%
Girobank Number: 517 1156
Credit Cards Accepted: Access/Master, Visa

Returns Procedures
Authority to Return: Sales Office
Stock Returns: Via customer services department
Imperfect Returns: Title pages for titles with published price less than £25 (Fault to be clearly stated) otherwise complete book.

ALISON HODGE PUBLISHERS & BOOK DISTRIBUTORS

Bosulval, Newmill, Penzance, Cornwall TR20 8XA
ISBN Prefix(es): 0 906720
Tel: 0736 68093
VAT No: 464 8950 05

Orders to
J BARNICOAT LTD, Parkengue, Penryn, Cornwall TR10 9EN
Tel: 0326 372628
Fax: 0326 378151

Order Information

All Dues Automatically Recorded
Representation Available
Invoice Payments: J Barnicoat Ltd

Personnel
Head of Company: Alison Hodge
Head of Distribution: Paul Ingram
Other Important Personnel:
Jan Chivers (Publishing Assistant)

Number of titles published annually: 2
Number of Staff: 2
All New Titles are Bar Coded
WBIP Updating: Alison Hodge

Trade Terms
35% on all orders
Other Terms: Small order surcharge of £1.50 on orders under £15 invoice
Credit Cards Accepted: Access/Master, Visa

Returns Procedures
Authority to Return: Paul Ingram
Address for Returns: Barnicoats
Stock Returns: Overstocks not accepted. Incorrectly supplied or damaged in transit - details in writing to Barnicoats
Imperfect Returns: No price limit - just return title page to Barnicoats with details of imperfections.

HOLLIS DIRECTORIES LTD

Contact House, Lower Hampton Road, Sunbury-on-Thames, Middlesex TW16 5HG
ISBN Prefix(es): 0 900967
Tel: 0932 784781
Fax: 0932 787844
VAT No: 321 5992 58

Order Information

Order Dept Opening Times
Mon - Fri 9am - 5.30pm
All Dues Automatically Recorded
Representation Available

Personnel
Head of Company: Gary Zabel (Chief Executive)
Head of Distribution: Christine Dewey (Subscriptions Executive)

Number of titles published annually: 3
Number of Staff: 15
PA Member
WBIP Updating: Gary Zabel

Parent Company: Threadneedle Publishing Group PLC

Trade Terms
20% or 30% on 6+ orders
Other Terms: Carriage charges £4.00
Credit Cards Accepted: Access/Master, Visa, Amex

[handwritten: Holmes + Meier - BRAD, P.O. Box 17, Canvey Island Essex SS8 8HZ]

HOME & SCHOOL COUNCIL

40 Sunningdale Mount, Sheffield, South Yorkshire S11 9HA
ISBN Prefix(es): 0 901181
Tel: 0742 364181 24 Hours

Order Information

All Dues Automatically Recorded

Personnel
Head of Company: Mrs B Bullivant (Honorary Secretary)

Number of titles published annually: 3

Trade Terms
Minimum Order: 1 copy basic price, includes P&P. 25+ copies (singles or mixed) small reduction in price - 20%

Returns Procedures
Stock Returns: Return stating reason
Imperfect Returns: Return the book

HOME OFFICE

Queen Anne's Gate, London SW1H 9AT
Tel: 071-273 3000
Fax: 071-273 2190
Telex: 24986

Orders to
Home Office Library, Pubns Sales, Room 1001, Queen Anne's Gate, London SW1H 9AT

Tel: 071-273 3327
Fax: 071-273 3957

[handwritten: HOMEGROWN CEREALS AUTHORITY, Hamlyn House, Highgate Hill, London N19 5PR 071 263 3391]

HONEYGLEN PUBLISHING LTD
56 Durrels House, Warwick Gardens, London W14 8QB
ISBN Prefix(es): 0 907855
Tel: 071-602 2876
VAT No: 341 0451 06

Orders to
BIBLIOS PUBLISHERS DISTRIBUTION SERVICE LTD,
Star Road, Partridge Green, West Sussex RH13 8LD
Tel: 0403 710971
Fax: 0403 711143

Order Information

Representation Available
Invoice Payments: Biblios

Personnel
Head of Company: N S Poderegin/Jelena Poderegin

Number of titles published annually: 2
IPG Member
All New Titles are Bar Coded
Book Data Subscriber
WBIP Updating: Nadja Poderegin

Trade Terms
Variable in line with the bookshops requests

Returns Procedures
Stock Returns: Request for authority to return
Imperfect Returns: Request for authority to return

HONNO LTD
Ailsa Craig, Heol Y Cawl, Dinas Powys, South Glamorgan CF6 4AH
ISBN Prefix(es): 1 870206
Tel: 0222 515014
Tel: 0267 232338
VAT No: 433 4692 48

Orders to
TURNAROUND, 27 Horsell Road, London N5 1XL
Tel: 071-609 7836/7
Fax: 071-700 1205

Order Information
Orders in Wales: Canolfan Llyfrau Cymraeg, Stad Glanyrafon, Llanbadarn, Aberystwyth, Dyfed, Wales

Personnel
Head of Company: Rosanne Reeves/Ailsa Craig

Number of titles published annually: 4
Number of Staff: 10
All New Titles are Bar Coded
Book Data Subscriber
WBIP Updating: Rosanne Reeves

Trade Terms
33.3%
Other Terms: Carriage charges: 10-15% of invoice total

HOPE EDUCATION LTD
Orb Mill, Huddersfield Road, Oldham, Lancashire OL4 2ST
Tel: 061-633 6611
Fax: 061-633 3431

HOPE IN ACTION

25(F) Copperfield Street, London SE1 0EN
Tel: 071-928 0848
VAT No: 340 8730 65

HORTON PUBLISHING LTD

6 Southbrook Terrace, Great Horton, Bradford, West Yorkshire BD7 1AB
ISBN Prefix(es): 1 871099
Tel: 0274 306245 24 Hours
VAT No: 447 8090 25

Account No: _____
Sales Rep: _____
Tel: _____

Order Information

Order Dept Opening Times
Mon - Fri 9am - 3.30pm

Personnel
Head of Sales (Home): P Thomas
Head of Marketing: G Wright
Head of Distribution: D Woodward

Number of titles published annually: 15
Number of Staff: 4
WBIP Updating: Paul Thomas

Trade Terms
20%

Returns Procedures
Authority to Return: Prior permission required from P Thomas
Imperfect Returns: Replacement with prior agreement

HOTEL & CATERING TRAINING COMPANY

International House, High Street, Ealing, London W5 5DB
ISBN Prefix(es): 0 7033
Tel: 081-579 2400
Fax: 081-840 6217
VAT No: 532 3299 53

Order Information

Order Dept Opening Times
Mon - Fri 9am - 5pm
All Dues Automatically Recorded

Personnel
Head of Company: Duncan Rutter (Chief Executive)
Head of Marketing: Mike Fellows (Marketing Director)
Head of Publicity: Nicci Heslop (Promotions Manager)
Head of Accounts: David Churchill (Finance Director)
Other Important Personnel:
Roy Hayter (Publications Manager), Marie Learie (Publications Orders)

Number of titles published annually: 10
Number of Staff: 2
WBIP Updating: Roy Hayter

Trade Terms
Single Copy 25%, Stock Orders 30-45%
Credit Cards Accepted: Access/Master, Visa

Returns Procedures
Authority to Return: Marie Leary

[Handwritten at top: HOUGHTON MIFFLIN = CASSELL BUT ACADEMIC TITLES FROM LITTLEHAMPTON BOOK SERVICES]

HOUSMANS BOOKSHOP LTD

5 Caledonian Road, London N1 9DX
ISBN Prefix(es): 0 85283
Tel: 071-837 4473
VAT No: 233 1909 80

WBIP Updating: Craig Liddle

Parent Company: Peace News Trustees

Trade Terms
General Net: Single Copy 20%, Two Books 25%, Over £10
Retail 33%
Girobank Number: 564 5565
Credit Cards Accepted: Access/Master, Visa

Returns Procedures
Imperfect Returns: Phone for details

HOW TO BOOKS LTD

Plymbridge House, Estover Road, Plymouth, Devon PL6 7PZ
ISBN Prefix(es): 1 85703
Tel: 0752 695745 Cust Serv
Tel: 0752 735251 Enquiries
Fax: 0752 695699
Telex: 45635 HARDIS G
VAT No: 557 5074 23

Orders to
PLYMBRIDGE DISTRIBUTORS LTD, Plymbridge House, Estover Road, Plymouth, Devon PL6 7PZ
Tel: 0752 735251
Fax: 0752 695699

Order Information

All Dues Automatically Recorded
Representation Available
Invoice Payments: Plymbridge Distributors Ltd

Personnel
Head of Company: Roger Ferneyhough (Managing Director)

Number of titles published annually: 25
IPG Member
All New Titles are Bar Coded

Trade Terms
25% on single copies, 35% on more than one copy. Carriage free (UK), no surcharges.

Returns Procedures
Address for Returns: Plymbridge Distributors Ltd
Stock Returns: Must be authorised by publisher

[Handwritten: HSE BOOKS A/C 0062330 Dept B, PO Box 1999, Sudbury, Suffolk CO10 6FS]

HT (BOOK DISTRIBUTION) LTD

Bolholt, Walshaw Road, Bury, Lancashire BL8 1RP
Tel: 061-764 2296
Fax: 061-764 8213

Account No: _____
Sales Rep: _____
Tel: _____

HUGHES & COLEMAN LTD

Delta Close, Norwich, Norfolk NR6 6BG
ISBN Prefix(es): 0 9481650, 0 9506352
Tel: 0603 426159 24 Hours
Tel: 0603 404301

Fax: 0603 486853
VAT No: 104 8711 89

Order Information
Teleordering: HGHC

HUGO'S LANGUAGE BOOKS LTD

Old Station Yard, Marlesford, Woodbridge, Suffolk
IP13 0AG
ISBN Prefix(es): 0 85285
Tel: 0728 746546
Fax: 0728 746236
Telex: 8951182
VAT No: 232 6425 83

Account No: _____

Sales Rep: _____

Tel: _____

Order Information
Teleordering: HUGO

Order Dept Opening Times
Mon - Fri 9am - 5pm
All Dues Automatically Recorded
Representation Available

Other Important Locations
Hugos Language Books Ltd, Redvers House, 13 Fairmile,
Henley-on-Thames RG9 2JR
Tel: 0491 572656
Fax: 0491 573590

Personnel
Head of Company: Peter G Lock (Managing Director)
Head of Publicity: Jackie Brooker
Other Important Personnel:
Robin Batchelor-Smith (Editorial Director)
Henley-on-Thames

Number of titles published annually: 12
Percentage of Export Sales: 33%
Number of Staff: 9
NBA Signatory
All New Titles are Bar Coded
WBIP Updating: Jackie Brooker

Trade Terms
35%
General Net: 25% orders under £15 invoice value
Girobank Number: 558 9355

Returns Procedures
Authority to Return: Wendy Watson, Hugos Language Books, Old Station Yard
Stock Returns: Returns to be complete current editions to qualify for full credit.
Imperfect Returns: Title pages only (specify fault) no limit.

HUMAN KINETICS PUBLISHERS (EUROPE) LTD

PO Box IW 14, Leeds, West Yorkshire LS16 6TR
ISBN Prefix(es): 0 87322, 0 88011, 0 918438, 0 931250
Tel: 0532 781708 24 Hours
Fax: 0532 781709
VAT No: 500 5423 04

Order Information

Order Dept Opening Times
Mon - Fri 9am - 6.30pm
All Dues Automatically Recorded
Representation Available

Personnel
Head of Company: Mr G R McKinney (Managing Director)
Head of Marketing: Ms K Llewellyn (Marketing Manager)
Head of Accounts: Mr Colin Oldmeadow (Financial Manager)
Head of Distribution: Mr M Harrison (Distribution Manager)
Head of Customer Services: Ms K Ingram
Other Important Personnel:
Ms F Royle (Trade Title Editor & Trade Liaison)

Number of titles published annually: 80
Number of Staff: 6
All New Titles are Bar Coded
WBIP Updating: Karen Llewellyn

Parent Company: Human Kinetic Publishers Inc

Trade Terms
General Net: 35% on all trade list titles, no surcharges
Academic Net: 20% on all non-trade titles, no surcharges
BA/Girobank Small Order Scheme: Payable to HKP (Europe)
Girobank Number: 607 3174
Credit Cards Accepted: Access/Master, Visa, Amex

Returns Procedures
Authority to Return: Contact for details
Address for Returns: HKP (Europe) Ltd, Clayton Wood Bank, Leeds, LS16 6QZ

THE DAVID HUME INSTITUTE
21 George Square, Edinburgh, Lothian EH8 9LD
Tel: 031-650 4633
Fax: 031-667 9111

C HURST & CO PUBLISHERS LTD
38 King Street, London WC2E 8JT
ISBN Prefix(es): 0 903983, 0 905838, 1 850650
Tel: 071-240 2666
Fax: 071-240 2667
VAT No: 206 3276 86

Orders to
CENTRAL BOOKS, 99 Wallis Road, London E9 5LN
Tel: 081-986 4854
Fax: 081-533 5821

Order Information

All Dues Automatically Recorded
Representation Available
Invoice Payments: Central Books

Personnel
Head of Company: Christopher Hurst
Head of Sales (Home): Michael Dwyer

Number of titles published annually: 20
Percentage of Export Sales: 60%
Number of Staff: 2
PA Member
IPG Member
NBA Signatory
All New Titles are Bar Coded
Book Data Subscriber
WBIP Updating: Michael Dwyer

Trade Terms
35%, No surcharges

Returns Procedures
Authority to Return: C Hurst
Address for Returns: Central Books

Stock Returns: Write to Michael Dwyer
Imperfect Returns: Send title page to H/O

HURTWOOD PRESS LTD
Silversted Lane, Westerham Hill, Westerham, Kent
TN16 2HY
Tel: 0959 574248
Fax: 0959 540593
VAT No: 356 6154 42

HUTTON PRESS LTD
130 Canada Drive, Cherry Burton, Beverley, North Humberside HU17 7SB
Tel: 0964 550573 24 Hours
VAT No: 317 2943 57

Order Information
Order Dept Opening Times
Mon - Sat 9am - 6pm
All Dues Automatically Recorded
Representation Available
For German Academic Titles:The Old Manse, Queen St, Tayport, Fife DD6 9NS

Personnel
Head of Company: Charles F Brook (Managing Director)
Head of Sales (Home): Mrs D C Brook (Sales & Publicity Director)
Head of Marketing: Michael E Ulyatt (Marketing Director)

Number of titles published annually: 20
Number of Staff: 3
All New Titles are Bar Coded
WBIP Updating: Charles Brook

Trade Terms
35%
Academic Net: 25%
Other Terms: Small order surcharge on single copies - part carriage cost

Returns Procedures
Authority to Return: Prior permission required from Mrs D C Brook
Imperfect Returns: Title page only for single copy, full book for multiples, postage refunded

HYDATUM
PO Box 4, Ross-on-Wye, Herefordshire HR9 6EB
ISBN Prefix(es): 0 904682
Tel: 0600 890 599
Fax: 0600 714 514
Telex: 497737 AAAAAAG
VAT No: 484 1206 57

Order Information
All Dues Automatically Recorded
Representation Available
Invoice Payments: Hydatum, Monmouth
Trade Counter:Hydatum, 1 Worcester Street, Monmouth, Gwent NP5 3DF Tel:0600 714511 Fax:0600 714514

Personnel
Head of Company: Dr Phil Holmes
Head of Sales (Home): Miss J Smith

Number of titles published annually: 6
Percentage of Export Sales: 30%
WBIP Updating: Miss J Smith

Trade Terms
30%
Minimum Order: £1
Girobank Number: 40 502 4002

HYDEN HOUSE LTD

Little Hyden Lane, Clanfield, Hampshire PO8 0RU
ISBN Prefix(es): 1 85623
Tel: 0705 596500 24 Hours
Fax: 0705 595834
VAT No: 544 1333 70

Order Information

Order Dept Opening Times
Mon - Fri 9am - 6pm
All Dues Automatically Recorded

Personnel
Head of Company: Tim Harland
Head of Sales (Home): Glen Finn
Head of Marketing: Madeleine Harland
Head of Publicity: Tiffany Robinson

Number of titles published annually: 2
Number of Staff: 4
IPG Member
All New Titles are Bar Coded
WBIP Updating: Tim Harland

Parent Company: Hyden House Ltd

Trade Terms
30 days see safe
General Net: Single Copy 25%, Two or more 30%, 10 or more 35%
Credit Cards Accepted: Access/Master, Visa, Amex

Returns Procedures
Authority to Return: Glen Finn
Stock Returns: Requests to return in writing
Imperfect Returns: Return whole book direct for replacement or credit

HYMNS ANCIENT & MODERN LTD

St Mary's Works, St Mary's Plain, Norwich, Norfolk NR3 3BH
ISBN Prefix(es): 0 900274, 0 907547, 1 85175, 1 85371
Tel: 0603 612914 Hymns A&M
Tel: 0603 616563 Cant Press
Tel: 0603 615995 Chansitor
Fax: 0603 624483
VAT No: 283 2968 24

Order Information
Teleordering: HYMNS

Order Dept Opening Times
Mon - Thu 9am - 5.30pm, Fri 9am - 5pm
All Dues Automatically Recorded
Representation Available

Other Important Locations
Marketing: Mr Stuart Ager, 4 Silwood, Woodenhill, Bracknell Berkshire Tel/
Fax: 0344 422131

Personnel
Head of Company: Gordon Knights (Chief Executive) 0603 612914

Head of Sales (Home): Miss Judy Speed (Sales & Customer Service (Canterbury Press)) 0603 616563
Head of Marketing: Stuart Ager 0344 422131
Head of Accounts: Mrs Brenda Nixson (Accountant) 0603 612914
Head of Distribution: Mr Cyril Moore (Warehouse Manager) 0603 612914
Head of Customer Services: Gordon Knights 0603 612914
Other Important Personnel:
Mrs Susan Fletcher (Sales & Customer Service (RMEP/Chansitor)) 0603 615995

Number of titles published annually: 20
Number of Staff: 36
IPG Member
All New Titles are Bar Coded
Book Data Subscriber
WBIP Updating: Gordon Knights/Ken Baker

Subsidiary Companies: Palmer & Sons (G J) Ltd

Trade Terms
35%
Non-Net: Canterbury Press 25%, Chansitor Publications 17.5%
Other Terms: Carriage or surcharge for orders under £20 net value, except on subscription orders

Returns Procedures
Authority to Return: Miss J Speed (Canterbury Press)/Mrs R Fletcher (RMEP)
Stock Returns: Request permission
Imperfect Returns: Up to £20 please return title page only and write on it nature of imperfection

HYPHEN PRESS

51 Grafton Road, London NW5 3DX
ISBN Prefix(es): 0 907259
Tel: 071-485 9726
Fax: 071-485 9726

Orders to
CENTRAL BOOKS, 99 Wallis Road, London E9 5LN
Tel: 081-986 4854
Fax: 081-533 5821

Order Information

Invoice Payments: Central Books

Personnel
Head of Company: Mr Robin Kinross

Number of titles published annually: 1
All New Titles are Bar Coded

Trade Terms
As per Central Books

Returns Procedures
Authority to Return: Central Books
Address for Returns: Central Books

I/O PRESS

Oak Tree House, St Matthews Terrace, Leyburn, North Yorkshire DL8 5SE
Tel: 0969 24402
Fax: 0969 24375
VAT No: 422 5536 70

Book Data Subscriber

IANMEAD LTD
15 Stanley Rise, Haslemere, Surrey GU27 1AF
Tel: 0428 644846

Order Information
Teleordering: IANMEAD

IBC PUBLISHING LTD
First Floor, 9-13 St Andrew Street, London EC4A 3AE
ISBN Prefix(es): 1 85271
Tel: 071-936 2016
Fax: 071-936 2303
VAT No: 429 7678 95

Account No: _____

Sales Rep: _____

Tel: _____

Personnel
Head of Company: Sue Kerry (Publisher)

Number of Staff: 1

Parent Company: International Business Communications (Holdings) Ltd

Trade Terms
Credit Cards Accepted: Access/Master, Visa, Amex, Diners, Other

IC PUBLICATIONS LTD
7 Coldbath Square, London EC1R 4LQ
ISBN Prefix(es): 0 905268
Tel: 071-713 7711
Fax: 071-713 7898
Telex: 8811757
VAT No: 242 3863 67

Order Information

All Dues Automatically Recorded
Invoice Payments: Yearbooks:Leishman & Taussig Guides:Roger Lascelles
Orders for Yearbooks:Leishman & Taussig Orders for Guides:Roger Lascelles

Personnel
Head of Company: Afif Ben Yedder
Head of Sales (Home): M Cooper
Head of Publicity: Jean Tomlinson
Head of Accounts: D Rawlings

Number of titles published annually: 5
Percentage of Export Sales: 40%
Number of Staff: 20
WBIP Updating: M Cooper

Trade Terms
35%

Returns Procedures
Authority to Return: Yearbooks:Leishman & Taussig Guides:Roger Lascelles

ICA PUBLISHING (INSTITUTE OF CONTEMPORARY ARTS)
12 Carlton House Terrace, London SW1Y 5AH
ISBN Prefix(es): 0 905263
Tel: 071-930 0493

Fax: 071-873 0051
VAT No: 239 9610 31

Orders to
ART DATA, Unit U03, Acton Bus Centre, School Road, London NW10 6TD
Tel: 081-961 3643
Fax: 081-965 3092

Order Information

All Dues Automatically Recorded
Representation Available
Orders can be placed direct to Head Office address (Attn ICA Publishing)

Personnel
Head of Sales (Home): Mr Ragnar Farr

Number of titles published annually: 10
Percentage of Export Sales: 50%
WBIP Updating: Mr Ragnar Farr

Trade Terms
General Net: 10% single copy, Two or more 33.3%
Other Terms: Postage charged on order direct from ICA
Credit Cards Accepted: Access/Master, Visa, Amex

Returns Procedures
Authority to Return: Ragnar Farr, ICA
Stock Returns: Overstock returns only accepted if see-safe terms agreed in advance of supply.
Imperfect Returns: Title pages not accepted. Entire book must be returned for replacement or credit

ICC UNITED KINGDOM

14/15 Belgrave Square, London SW1X 8PS
ISBN Prefix(es): 92 842
Tel: 071-823 2811
Fax: 071-235 5447

Account No: _____
Sales Rep: _____
Tel: _____

Order Information

Order Dept Opening Times
Mon - Fri 9.30am - 3.30pm
All Dues Automatically Recorded
Representation Available

Personnel
Head of Company: Richard Bate
Head of Sales (Home): Caroline T Jobson
Head of Accounts: Margaret Hewitt
Head of Distribution: Renee Cohen

Number of titles published annually: 20
Number of Staff: 6
Book Data Subscriber
WBIP Updating: Caroline T Jobson

Parent Company: ICC Publishing S A

Trade Terms
Mail Order, CWO

IDEAS UNLIMITED (PUBLISHING)

Unit 202, Victory House, Somers Road North, Portsmouth, Hampshire PO1 1PJ
ISBN Prefix(es): 1 871964
Tel: 0705 819162

Fax: 0705 734814
VAT No: 543 9673 12

Order Information

Order Dept Opening Times
Mon - Fri 9am - 6pm
Representation Available

Personnel
Head of Company: H R Samiy (Managing Director)
Head of Publicity: Lucy Williams

Number of titles published annually: 5
Number of Staff: 3
IPG Member
All New Titles are Bar Coded
WBIP Updating: H R Samiy

Trade Terms
35% on all orders (no surcharges) up to 200 copies. 200 copies or more 40% - see safe basis.

Returns Procedures
Stock Returns: Notify publisher, get authorisation, return books, publisher will issue credit

[handwritten: I.E.E.E c/o Electronica]

IFS LTD

Wolseley Business Park, Kempston, Bedfordshire MK42 7PW
ISBN Prefix(es): 0 903608, 0 948507, 1 85423
Tel: 0234 853605
Fax: 0234 854499
VAT No: 196 8750 04

Book Data Subscriber

IMAGES

4/6 Dam Street, Lichfield, Staffordshire WS13 6AA
Tel: 0543 264093
VAT No: 241 9052 80

Order Information

Order Dept Opening Times
Mon - Sat 9.30am - 5pm
All Dues Automatically Recorded
Invoice Payments: Peter Stockham Ltd

Personnel
Head of Company: Peter Stockham

Number of titles published annually: 2
Percentage of Export Sales: 20%
Number of Staff: 2
NBA Signatory
Book Data Subscriber

Parent Company: Peter Stockham Ltd

Trade Terms
30% three or more titles, 25% singles & limited editions

Returns Procedures
Authority to Return: Prior permission required
Stock Returns: Whole book
Imperfect Returns: Whole book

IMAGES DISTRIBUTION

Unit 7-10, Hanley Workshops, Hanley Road, Hanley Swan, Worcestershire WR8 0DX
ISBN Prefix(es): 0 947554, 0 947993, 1 85421
Tel: 0684 310897

Fax: 0684 310281
VAT No: 589 1667 80

Account No: _____
Sales Rep: _____
Tel: _____

Order Information

Order Dept Opening Times
Mon - Fri 9am - 5pm
Orders for more than one publisher can be bulked
All Dues Automatically Recorded
Representation Available

Personnel

Head of Company: Sandra Hill (Manageress)
Head of Marketing: Vanessa Bradock
Head of Accounts: Sandra Hill
Head of Customer Services: Tony Harold

Number of titles published annually: 120
Number of Staff: 6
All New Titles are Bar Coded
WBIP Updating: Pauline Mason

Trade Terms

General Net: Any title: Single copy 20%, 2 - 4 copies 25%, 5+ - 35% Special orders 45%
Credit Cards Accepted: Access/Master, Visa

IMMEL PUBLISHING LTD

20 Berkeley Street, Berkeley Square, London W1X 5AE
ISBN Prefix(es): 0 900891, 0 902675, 0 902743, 0 907151
Tel: 071-491 1799
Fax: 071-493 5524
VAT No: 429 5823 25

Orders to

BIBLIOS PUBLISHERS DISTRIBUTION SERVICE LTD,
Star Road, Partridge Green, West Sussex RH13 8LD
Tel: 0403 710971
Fax: 0403 711143

Order Information

All Dues Automatically Recorded
Representation Available

Personnel

Head of Company: Peter Vine (Production Director)
Head of Sales (Home): Ann Johnson
Head of Accounts: Fionnuala MacNeill (Financial Controller)

Number of titles published annually: 10
Percentage of Export Sales: 75%
Number of Staff: 4
IPG Member
All New Titles are Bar Coded
WBIP Updating: Ann Johnson

Trade Terms

25 - 35%
Other Terms: Carriage charges - overseas only
Credit Cards Accepted: Access/Master, Amex, Visa

IMPACT BOOKS

112 Bolingbroke Grove, London SW11 1DA
ISBN Prefix(es): 0 245, 0 946889, 1 874687
Tel: 081-673 6858 Tel/Fax
VAT No: 238 1139 73

Orders to
TIPTREE BOOK SERVICES LTD, Church Road, Tiptree, Colchester, Essex CO5 0SR
Tel: 0621 819600
Fax: 0621 819011

Order Information

All Dues Automatically Recorded
Representation Available
Invoice Payments: Tiptree
Representation: Verulam Publishing

Personnel
Head of Company: Jean-Luc Barbanneau
Head of Sales (Home): David Collins 0727 873866

Number of titles published annually: 7
Percentage of Export Sales: 20%
Number of Staff: 2
IPG Member
All New Titles are Bar Coded
Book Data Subscriber
WBIP Updating: J L Barbanneau

Trade Terms
See Verulam Publishing

Returns Procedures
Authority to Return: Verulam Publishing
Address for Returns: Tiptree

IMRAY, LAURIE, NORIE & WILSON

Wych House, The Broadway, St Ives, Huntingdon, Cambridgeshire PE17 4BT
ISBN Prefix(es): 0 85288
Tel: 0480 62114 24 Hours
Fax: 0480 496109
Telex: 329195 IMRAYS G
VAT No: 213 5442 96

Order Information

Order Dept Opening Times
Mon - Fri 9am - 5pm
All Dues Automatically Recorded
Representation Available

Personnel
Head of Company: William Wilson
Head of Accounts: M Barnes

Number of titles published annually: 8
Percentage of Export Sales: 55%
Number of Staff: 16
All New Titles are Bar Coded
WBIP Updating: W G Wilson

Trade Terms
35%, Carriage charged on single copy orders
Girobank Number: 245 0259
Credit Cards Accepted: Access/Master, Visa, Amex

Returns Procedures
Authority to Return: J McCabe
Stock Returns: Return within 7 days

IN PRINT PUBLISHING

9 Beaufort Terrace, Brighton, East Sussex BN2 2SU
Tel: 0273 682836
Fax: 0273 620958
VAT No: 550 4738 46

Orders to
BAILEY DISTRIBUTION LTD, Unit 1, Learoyd Road, Mountfield Rd Ind Est, New Romney, Kent TN28 8XU
Tel: 0679 66905
Fax: 0679 66638

INDEXREACH LTD

28 Charlotte Street, London W1P 1HJ
ISBN Prefix(es): 1 871518
Tel: 071-636 3532
VAT No: 494 8032 22

Order Information

Order Dept Opening Times
Mon - Fri 9am - 7pm, Sat 10am - 5pm
All Dues Automatically Recorded

Personnel
Head of Marketing: M P Daly
Head of Accounts: G Thurley
Head of Distribution: B E Leach

Number of titles published annually: 3
Number of Staff: 3
All New Titles are Bar Coded
WBIP Updating: G Thurley

Trade Terms
General Net: Single Copy 20%, Two Books or More 33.33%
Credit Cards Accepted: Access/Master, Visa

Returns Procedures
Stock Returns: Application in writing required - no unauthorized returns
Imperfect Returns: Title page only up to £15 - only return authorized books If unauthorized no credit or carriage paid

INDIANA UNIV PRESS - Go Open University Press.

INDUSTRIAL PRODUCT EVALUATION LTD

22B High Street, Witney, Oxfordshire OX8 6HB
Tel: 0993 776958
Fax: 0993 778052
VAT No: 439 4828 13

INDUSTRIAL SOCIETY PRESS

48 Bryanston Square, London W1H 7LN
ISBN Prefix(es): 0 85290, 1 85835
Tel: 071-262 2401
Fax: 071-706 1096
VAT No: 233 0768 77

Orders to
Industrial Society, 49 Calthorpe Road, Birmingham, West Midlands B15 1TH
Tel: 021-454 6769
Fax: 021-456 2715

Order Information

Order Dept Opening Times
Mon - Fri 9.15am - 5pm
All Dues Automatically Recorded
Representation Available

Personnel
Head of Company: Sheridan Maguire
Head of Distribution: Jim Fraser
Head of Customer Services: Valerie Durrant

Number of titles published annually: 20
Number of Staff: 10

IPG Member
All New Titles are Bar Coded
WBIP Updating: Anne Townley

Trade Terms
35% free UK delivery
Minimum Order: £10
Credit Cards Accepted: Access/Master, Visa

Returns Procedures
Address for Returns: Calthorpe Road

Informedia - 5 High St, Beckenham Kent BR3 1AZ

INPUT-OUTPUT PUBLISHING CO

Roy Field & Co, 30 Alexandra Road, Lowestoft, Suffolk
NR32 1PJ
Tel: 0502 512240
Fax: 0502 583848

INRA - Inst National de la Recherche Agronomique c/o DRAKE PUBLISHING = BAILEY DISTR.

INSTITUTE FOR THE STUDY OF DRUG DEPENDENCE

1 Hatton Place, London EC1N 8ND
Tel: 071-430 1991
Fax: 071-404 4415

IPG Member

INSTITUTE OF ADMINISTRATIVE MANAGEMENT

40 Chatsworth Parade, Petts Wood, Orpington, Kent
BR5 1RW
Tel: 0689 875555
Fax: 0689 870891
Telex: 8952569

INSTITUTE OF BIOLOGY

20 Queensberry Place, London SW7 2DZ
Tel: 071-581 8333
Fax: 071-823 9409

Personnel
Head of Company: Jonathan Cowie

THE INSTITUTE OF CHARTERED ACCOUNTANTS OF SCOTLAND

27 Queen Street, Edinburgh, Lothian EH2 1LA
Tel: 031-225 5673
Fax: 031-225 3813
VAT No: 270 7760 48

INSTITUTE OF DEVELOPMENT STUDIES

Publications Office, The University of Sussex, Brighton, East Sussex BN1 9RE
ISBN Prefix(es): 0 903354, 0 903715, 1 85864
Tel: 0273 606261
Tel: 0273 678269
Fax: 0273 621202
Fax: 0273 678420

Order Information

Order Dept Opening Times
Mon - Fri 9am - 5.15pm

Personnel
Head of Company: John Toye (Director)
Head of Publicity: Katherine Orme (Head of Publications Services & Publicity)
Head of Accounts: John Sanders

Number of titles published annually: 35
Percentage of Export Sales: 65%
WBIP Updating: Katherine Orme

INSTITUTE OF ECONOMIC AFFAIRS
2 Lord North Street, London SW1P 3LB
Tel: 071-799 3745
Fax: 071-799 2137

INSTITUTE OF EDUCATION
University of Hull, Cottingham Road, Hull, Humberside HU10 6JU
Tel: 0482 465406
Fax: 0482 466205

INSTITUTE OF EDUCATION
University of London, 20 Bedford Way, London WC1H 0AL
ISBN Prefix(es): 0 85473
Tel: 071-580 1122
Tel: 071-612 6142
Fax: 071-612 6126

Orders to
KOGAN PAGE LTD, 120 Pentonville Road, London N1 9JN
Tel: 071-278 0433
Fax: 071-837 6348

Order Information

All Dues Automatically Recorded
Representation Available
London File Orders To: The Tufnell Press, 47 Dalmeny Road, London N7 0DY

Personnel
Other Important Personnel:
Denis Baylis (Publications Officer), Mary Cottingham (Information Manager)

Number of titles published annually: 10
All New Titles are Bar Coded
Book Data Subscriber

Trade Terms
Distributor's terms apply

Returns Procedures
Authority to Return: Kogan Page Ltd

INSTITUTE OF EMPLOYMENT RIGHTS
112 Greyhound Lane, Streatham, London SW16 5RN
Tel: 081-677 9644
Fax: 081-664 6022
VAT No: 523 2046 88

THE INSTITUTE OF HEALTH SERVICES MANAGEMENT

75 Portland Place, London W1N 4AN
Tel: 071-580 5041
Fax: 071-255 1289

Personnel
Head of Company: Ms Pamela Charlwood
Head of Marketing: Ms Hazel Coad
Head of Accounts: Ms Joan Grover

Number of Staff: 35
WBIP Updating: Hazel Coad

Trade Terms
16.5%
Credit Cards Accepted: Access/Master, Visa, Other

Returns Procedures
Authority to Return: Prior permission required from Hazel Coad

INSTITUTE OF MANAGEMENT FOUNDATION

Management House, Cottingham Road, Corby, Northamptonshire NN17 1TT
ISBN Prefix(es): 0 85946
Tel: 0536 204222
Fax: 0536 201651
VAT No: 232 6844 63

Account No: _____
Sales Rep: _____
Tel: _____

Orders to
BURSTON DISTRIBUTION SERVICES, Unit 2A, Newbridge Trading Est, Newbridge Close, Off Whitby Rd, Bristol, Avon BS4 4AX
Tel: 0272 724248
Fax: 0272 711056

Order Information

All Dues Automatically Recorded
Invoice Payments: Burston Distribution Services

Personnel
Head of Company: Jonathan Glasspool

Number of titles published annually: 40
Percentage of Export Sales: 20%
PA Member
NBA Signatory
WBIP Updating: Publications Secretary

Trade Terms
10 - 25%
Credit Cards Accepted: Access/Master, Visa

Returns Procedures
Address for Returns: Burston Distribution Services
Stock Returns: Return complete item for full refund.

INSTITUTE OF MANPOWER STUDIES

Mantell Building, University of Sussex, Falmer, Brighton, East Sussex BN1 9RF
Tel: 0273 686751
Fax: 0273 690430
VAT No: 449 5535 16

THE INSTITUTE OF MATERIALS
1 Carlton House Terrace, London SW1Y 5DB
Tel: 071-976 1338
Fax: 071-839 2078
Telex: 8814813
VAT No: 232 0589 83

PA Member

INSTITUTE OF PERSONNEL MANAGEMENT
IPM House, 35 Camp Road, Wimbledon, London
SW19 4UX
ISBN Prefix(es): 0 85292
Tel: 081-946 9100
Fax: 081-947 2570
VAT No: 318 5014 79

Orders to
PLYMBRIDGE DISTRIBUTORS LTD, Plymbridge House, Estover Road, Plymouth, Devon PL6 7PZ
Tel: 0752 735251
Fax: 0752 695699

Order Information
All Dues Automatically Recorded
Representation Available
Invoice Payments: Plymbridge

Personnel
Head of Company: Judith Tabern
Head of Sales (Home): Cathy Doyle
Head of Distribution: Michael Beevers
Head of Customer Services: Carol Downing

Number of titles published annually: 15
Number of Staff: 5
IPG Member
All New Titles are Bar Coded
WBIP Updating: Finn Jensen

Trade Terms
20% on 1 book, 30% 2 or more
Credit Cards Accepted: Access/Master, Visa, Amex

Returns Procedures
Authority to Return: Cathy Doyle, Institute of Personnel Management
Address for Returns: Plymbridge Distributors
Imperfect Returns: Return books to Plymbridge

INSTITUTE OF RACE RELATIONS
2-6 Leeke Street, London WC1X 9HS
Tel: 071-837 0041
Fax: 071-278 0623
VAT No: 238 8869 01

INSTITUTE OF TRADING STANDARDS ADMINISTRATION
4/5 Hadleigh Business Centre, 351 London Road, Hadleigh, Essex SS7 2BT
Tel: 0702 559922
Fax: 0702 559902

INSTITUTION OF ELECTRICAL ENGINEERS
Michael Faraday House, Six Hills Way, Stevenage, Hertfordshire SG1 2AY

ISBN Prefix(es): 0 85296, 0 86341
Tel: 0438 313311
Fax: 0438 360079
Fax: 0438 313465
Telex: 825578 IEESTV G
VAT No: 240 3420 16

A/C No 833819

Orders to
Pubns Sales Dept, PO Box 96, Stevenage, Hertfordshire
SG1 2SD
Tel: 0438 313311
Fax: 0438 742792

Order Information

Order Dept Opening Times
Mon - Fri 9am - 5pm
All Dues Automatically Recorded
Representation Available

Personnel
Head of Company: B Clifton (Director of Publishing)
Head of Marketing: G Mears
Head of Publicity: J Porter
Head of Accounts: S Riding
Head of Customer Services: M C Bass
Other Important Personnel:
R Mellors (Publisher)

Number of titles published annually: 70
Percentage of Export Sales: 50%
Number of Staff: 100
NBA Signatory
Book Data Subscriber
WBIP Updating: R Mellors

Trade Terms
20%, 30% if +10 books/order. Carriage free to trade in UK
Credit Cards Accepted: Access/Master, Visa

Returns Procedures
Authority to Return: Publication Sales Department
Address for Returns: A Jacques, IEE, Park View House,
Nightingale Road, Hitchin Herts
Stock Returns: Stock returns accepted if resaleable and within 4 months of receipt
Imperfect Returns: Not applicable

Institute of Mental Handicap = Plymbridge

THE INSTITUTION OF MINING & METALLURGY

44 Portland Place, London W1N 4BR
Tel: 071-580 3802
Fax: 071-436 5388
Telex: 261410
VAT No: 232 6711 82

THE INSURANCE INSTITUTE OF LONDON

20 Aldermanbury, London EC2V 7HY
Tel: 071-600 1343 Tel/Fax

INTELLECT

Suite 2, 108-110 London Road, Oxford, Oxfordshire
OX3 9AW
ISBN Prefix(es): 1 871516
Tel: 0865 67575
Fax: 0865 742024
VAT No: 533 1867 46

Orders to
LAVIS MARKETING, 73 Lime Walk, Headington,
Oxfordshire OX3 7AD
Tel: 0865 67575
Fax: 0865 750079

Order Information

All Dues Automatically Recorded
Representation Available
Invoice Payments: Lavis Marketing

Personnel
Head of Company: Mr M Yazdani
Head of Sales (Home): Mr D Grant
Head of Marketing: Mr M Lewis

Number of titles published annually: 12
Percentage of Export Sales: 60%
WBIP Updating: Mr Mark Lewis

Trade Terms
Single Copy 25%, Two or more 30%, Sub/Stock orders 35%
Special orders 25%
Girobank Number: 442 9413
Credit Cards Accepted: Access/Master, Visa

Returns Procedures
Authority to Return: Prior permission required
Address for Returns: Lavis Marketing
Stock Returns: Granted on 10% of turnover
Imperfect Returns: Return whole book

[handwritten: Inst of Mental Handicap = Plymbridge]

INTER PUBLISHING SERVICE (IPS) LTD

59 Woodbridge Road, Guildford, Surrey GU1 4RF
Tel: 0483 306309
Fax: 0483 579196
VAT No: 572 6168 25

Orders to
SEND THE LIGHT, PO Box 300, Kingstown Broadway,
Carlisle, Cumbria CA3 0QS
Tel: 0228 512512
Fax: 0228 514949

PA Member

INTERCEPT LTD

PO Box 716, Andover, Hampshire SP10 1YG
ISBN Prefix(es): 0 946707
Tel: 0264 334748
Fax: 0264 334058
VAT No: 579 8965 44

Personnel
Head of Company: Mr A N Russell
Head of Marketing: Mrs I Hindley
Head of Customer Services: Mrs G Parker

Number of titles published annually: 20
Percentage of Export Sales: 60%
Book Data Subscriber
WBIP Updating: Mrs G Parker

Parent Company: Lavoisier Publishers Paris, France

Trade Terms
Variable
Other Terms: Carriage charge - extra
Credit Cards Accepted: Access/Master, Amex, Visa

Returns Procedures
Authority to Return: Prior permission required

INTERLIST

4th Floor, 6 Cavendish Square, London W1M 9HA
Tel: 071-323 4464
Fax: 071-323 5258
Telex: 22357

Orders to
Order Processing Mgr, J P Kenny Intershelf Ltd, Waltham House, Mill Lane, Guildford, Surrey GU1 3TZ
Tel: 0483 303303
Fax: 0483 37252

Book Data Subscriber

INTERMEDIATE TECHNOLOGY PUBLICATIONS LTD

103-105 Southampton Row, London WC1B 4HH
ISBN Prefix(es): 0 946688, 1 85339
Tel: 071-436 9761
Fax: 071-436 2013
Telex: 268312 WESCOM G
Telex: Attn Intec
Cables: Itdev, LondonWC1
VAT No: 240 9203 91

[handwritten: Warehouse 0747 851339. Fax 0747 851394 A/C NO SMITO4 ITUNIU41]

Order Information

Order Dept Opening Times
Mon - Fri 9.30am - 5.30pm
All Dues Automatically Recorded
Representation Available

Personnel

Head of Company: Neal Burton (Managing Editor)
Head of Sales (Home): Guy Bentham (Sales & Marketing Manager)

Number of titles published annually: 25
Percentage of Export Sales: 40%
Number of Staff: 11
NBA Signatory
All New Titles are Bar Coded
Book Data Subscriber
WBIP Updating: Emma Greengrass

Parent Company: ITDG, Rugby

Trade Terms

UK & Europe - 30% (25% on single copy/single line orders)
Outside Europe - 35%
Other Terms: Carriage charges at cost for orders outside the UK
BA/Girobank Small Order Scheme: Yes
Girobank Number: 549 0456
Credit Cards Accepted: Access/Master, Visa, Amex, Other

Returns Procedures

Authority to Return: Guy Bentham, Head Office
Address for Returns: IT Publications Ltd, Unit 25, Longmead, Shaftesbury, Dorset SP7 8PL

INTERNATIONAL BEE RESEARCH ASSOCIATION

18 North Road, Cardiff, South Glamorgan CF1 3DY
ISBN Prefix(es): 0 86098
Tel: 0222 372409 24 Hours
Fax: 0222 665522
Telex: 262433 MONREF G
VAT No: 208 1348 85

Order Information

Order Dept Opening Times
Mon - Fri 9am - 4pm

Personnel
Head of Company: Mr A G Matheson (Director)
Head of Sales (Home): Mrs J Gibson
Head of Publicity: Dr P A Munn
Head of Accounts: Mr P F Gillam

Number of titles published annually: 5
Percentage of Export Sales: 75%
Number of Staff: 11
WBIP Updating: Dr Pamela A Munn

Trade Terms
20% basic on most orders
Minimum Order: £3 Minimum Order No discount on orders under £5
Credit Cards Accepted: Access/Master, Visa

Returns Procedures
Stock Returns: return goods with reasons for their return

INTERNATIONAL BOOK DISTRIBUTORS
Campus 400, Maylands Avenue, Hemel Hempstead, Hertfordshire HP2 7EZ
Tel: 0442 881900 Switch
Tel: 0442 882222 UK Orders   0442 882016 - orders
Tel: 0442 882233/44 Eur/Int
Fax: 0442 882099 General
Fax: 0442 882288 UK Orders
Fax: 0442 882277 Eur/Int
Telex: 82445
VAT No: 490 5885 08
Account No: 150033
Sales Rep: Chris Bunting
Tel: 20 Jay Close, Southwater, Nr Horsham RH13 7TT.

Order Information
Teleordering: IBD
First Edition Subscriber

Jane - Customer Services
Fax 0442 882288

Order Dept Opening Times
Mon - Fri 8.30am - 5pm
Orders for more than one publisher can be bulked
All Dues Automatically Recorded
S&S Young Books Orders:
Tel: 0442 882211
Fax: 0442 882299 Cash Sale Orders:
Tel: 0442 882255

Other Important Locations
IBD Distribution Centre, Coventry Road, Magna Park, Lutterworth, Leics LE17 4XH Tel:0442 881900 Fax:0442 882177

Personnel
Head of Company: Jeremy Moss (Director)
Head of Accounts: Alan Martin (Finance Director)
Head of Distribution: Arthur Cotton (Distribution Director)
Head of Customer Services: Michael Walford (Customer Services Manager)
Other Important Personnel:
Ian Turner (Distribution Manager), Eunice Ford (Credit Control Manager), Michael Forster (MIS Director)

Number of Staff: 150
PA Member
All New Titles are Bar Coded
WBIP Updating: Michael Forster

Parent Company: Simon & Schuster

Trade Terms
Variable by Publisher
Girobank Number: 34 7724 000

Returns Procedures
Authority to Return: IBD, Hemel Hempstead
Address for Returns: IBD, Lutterworth
Stock Returns: All return requests to be sent to Head Office address
Imperfect Returns: Apply to IBD, Hemel Hempstead

INTERNATIONAL CARGO HANDLING CO-ORDINATION ASSOCIATION

71 Bondway, London SW8 1SH
Tel: 071-793 1022
Fax: 071-820 1703

INTERNATIONAL LABOUR OFFICE

CH 1211, Geneva 22, Switzerland
Tel: 0104122 7996111
Fax: 0104122 7988685
Telex: 415647 ilo ch

Orders to
ILO, London Branch, Vincent Ho, Vincent Sq, London SW1P 2NB
Tel: 071-828 6401
Fax: 071-233 5925

A/C No 20349

Order Information
Teleordering: ILO

Order Dept Opening Times
9am - 1pm, 2pm - 5pm
All Dues Automatically Recorded
Invoice Payments: London Office

Personnel
Head of Sales (Home): Marion Motts (Publications Manager/Librarian)
Other Important Personnel:
Mrs Graciella Carrill (Information Officer)

All New Titles are Bar Coded
Book Data Subscriber
WBIP Updating: Marion Motts

Trade Terms
25% 1 book, 30% 2 or more books
Credit Cards Accepted: Access/Master, Visa

Returns Procedures
Authority to Return: London Office
Address for Returns: London Office

INTERNATIONAL MUSIC PUBLICATIONS

Unit 15-16, Woodford Trdg Est, Southend Road, Woodford Green, Essex IG8 8HN
ISBN Prefix(es): 0 86175, 0 86359
Tel: 081-551 6131
Fax: 081-551 3919
Fax: 081-551 9121 Sales Dept

Order Information
Teleordering: IMP

Order Dept Opening Times
Mon - Fri 9am - 5.30pm
All Dues Automatically Recorded
Representation Available

Other Important Locations
Park Street, London

Tel: 071-629 7600
Fax: 071-499 9718

Personnel
Head of Company: Mr Ron Fry
Head of Sales (Home): David Kenton (Sales Manager Bookshop Sales Division)
Head of Marketing: Mr Ian Bishop
Head of Accounts: Mr Trevor Callaghan
Head of Distribution: Mr David Taylor
Head of Customer Services: Miss Linda Tierney (Bookshop Sales Co-ordinator)

Number of titles published annually: 426
Percentage of Export Sales: 50%
Number of Staff: 40
PA Member
NBA Signatory
All New Titles are Bar Coded
WBIP Updating: David Kenton

Parent Company: Warner Chappell
Subsidiary Companies: Express Music, Express Prints
Allied Companies: Carisch SRL (IT), Warner Chappell Music (GE)

Trade Terms
35%
Credit Cards Accepted: Access/Master, Amex, Diners, Visa, Other

Returns Procedures
Authority to Return: Prior permission required
Stock Returns: Returns authorisation number must be obtained before sending

INTERNATIONAL NGO TRAINING & RESEARCH CENTRE

PO Box 563, Oxford, Oxfordshire OX2 6RZ
Tel: 0865 53062
Fax: 0865 514523

INTERNATIONAL PLANNED PARENTHOOD FEDERATION

Regent's College, Inner Circle, Regent's Park, London NW1 4NS
Tel: 071-486 0741
Fax: 071-487 7950
Telex: 919573 IPEPEE G
VAT No: 242 6693 51

INTERNATIONAL THOMSON PUBLISHING SERVICES LTD

Cheriton House, North Way, Andover, Hampshire SP10 5BE
Tel: 0264 332424 Switchbd
Tel: 0264 342832 UK Orders
Tel: 0264 342908 OS Orders
Fax: 0264 364418 UK Orders
Fax: 0264 333471 OS Orders
Telex: 47214 ITP AND G
Cables: APT ANDOVER
VAT No: 198 9232 09
Account No: ____032030 0009____
Sales Rep: _____
Tel: _____

Order Information
Teleordering: ITPS

Order Dept Opening Times
9am - 4.45pm
Orders for more than one publisher can be bulked
All Dues Automatically Recorded
Invoice Payments: See Invoice or Statement

Personnel
Head of Company: Desmond Clarke (Managing Director) 0264 342893
Head of Sales (Home): Wendy Edge (Home Customer Service Manager) 0264 342910
Head of Sales (Export): John Perrett (Export Customer Service Manager) 0264 342838
Head of Marketing: Peter Clay (Marketing Services Manager) 0264 342935
Head of Accounts: David Langridge (Credit Control Manager) 0264 342867
Head of Distribution: David Silk (Operations Director) 0264 342834
Head of Customer Services: Rodney Peake (Customer Services Director) 0264 342927

PA Member
NBA Signatory
All New Titles are Bar Coded

Parent Company: The Thomson Corporation

Trade Terms
See individual publishers
Girobank Number: 209 6919
Credit Cards Accepted: Access/Master, Visa, Amex, Diners

Returns Procedures
Authority to Return: See individual publishers
Stock Returns: See individual publishers

[Handwritten: Returns: Fergus Hall, Berkshire House, 168-173 High Holborn, LONDON WC1V 7AA. 071-497 1422]

INTERNOS BOOKS

18 Colville Road, London W3 8BL
ISBN Prefix(es): 0 904866, 1 873968
Tel: 071-992 0008
Fax: 071-752 1474
VAT No: 241 0255 14

Account No: _____
Sales Rep: _____
Tel: _____

Order Information
Teleordering: INTENOS

Order Dept Opening Times
Mon - Fri 9.00am - 5.30pm
All Dues Automatically Recorded
Representation Available

Personnel
Head of Company: Ann Tandy (Managing Director)
Head of Sales (Home): James Booth Clibborn (Sales Director)
Head of Distribution: Diana Smith (Distribution Manager)
Other Important Personnel:
Edward Booth Clibborn (President), Toby Waller (Sales Manager)

Number of titles published annually: 10
Percentage of Export Sales: 80%
Number of Staff: 8
All New Titles are Bar Coded

Parent Company: Booth-Clibborn Editions

Trade Terms
General Net: Single copy/single line 25%, 2 or more 35%
Credit Cards Accepted: Access/Master, Visa, Amex, Diners

Returns Procedures
Authority to Return: Prior arrangement required

INTERVARSITY PRESS

38 De Montfort Street, Leicester, Leicestershire LE1 7GP
ISBN Prefix(es): 0 85110, 0 85111, 0 9464
Tel: 0553 551700
VAT No: 233 7652 61

Account No: _____

Sales Rep: _____

Tel: _____

Orders to
IVP, Norton Street, Nottingham, Nottinghamshire NG7 3HR
Tel: 0602 781054
Fax: 0602 422694
24 Hour Ansafone Number: 0800 622968

Order Information

Order Dept Opening Times
Mon - Fri 9am - 5pm
All Dues Automatically Recorded
Representation Available

Personnel
Head of Company: Frank Entwistle (Publishing Director)
Head of Sales (Home): Paul Rusted (Commercial Director)
Head of Sales (Export): Janet Wileman (Export Administrator)
Head of Marketing: Mark Finnie (Sales & Marketing Executive)
Head of Publicity: Robin Croxon (Reading Development Officer)
Head of Accounts: Audrey Pegler (Accounts Controller)
Head of Distribution: Vanda Powell (Warehouse Supervisor)
Head of Customer Services: Shelagh Robinson (Customer Services Officer)

Number of titles published annually: 50
Percentage of Export Sales: 40%
Number of Staff: 27
PA Member
All New Titles are Bar Coded
WBIP Updating: Jo Bramwell

Parent Company: UCCF, Leicester

Trade Terms
35%, 30 days, 5% prompt payment discount
Other Terms: £1 if under £10
Girobank Number: 494 7053
Credit Cards Accepted: Access/Master, Visa

Returns Procedures
Authority to Return: Shelagh Robinson
Address for Returns: IVP
Stock Returns: Books must be invoiced by IVP within last 12 months. Invoice no must be quoted
Imperfect Returns: Return title page or book if more than £10

INTERWORLD PUBLICATIONS

12 The Fairway, New Barnet, Hertfordshire EN5 1HN
ISBN Prefix(es): 0 948853
Tel: 081-449 5938
Fax: 081-447 0599

Orders to
GAZELLE BOOK SERVICES LTD, Falcon House, Queen Square, Lancaster, Lancashire LA1 1RN
Tel: 0524 68765
Fax: 0524 63232

Order Information

Invoice Payments: Gazelle

Personnel
Head of Company: R G Lavithis

Number of Staff: 2
All New Titles are Bar Coded

Parent Company: Tophill Advertising & Iromotions Ltd

Trade Terms
35% on all order, no surcharges

Returns Procedures
Authority to Return: Gazelle
Address for Returns: Gazelle

INVADER LTD

North Barn, Appledram Barns, Birdham Road, Appledram, Chichester, West Sussex PO20 7EQ
ISBN Prefix(es): 1 85129
Tel: 0243 783587
Fax: 0243 531880
VAT No: 415 1985 50

Order Information

Order Dept Opening Times
Mon - Fri
Representation Available

Personnel
Head of Company: Campbell L Goldsmid (Managing Director)
Head of Sales (Home): Richard House (Sales Director)

Number of titles published annually: 150
Number of Staff: 11
All New Titles are Bar Coded
WBIP Updating: Rosemary Harris

Parent Company: Znu, Belguim

Trade Terms
35%
Minimum Order: £100
Other Terms: Surcharge of £2.57 P&P for very small orders

Returns Procedures
Authority to Return: Prior permission required from Head Office

IOP PUBLISHING LTD

Techno House, Redcliffe Way, Bristol, Avon BS1 6NX
Tel: 0272 297481
Fax: 0272 294318
Telex: 449149 INSTP G

Account No: _____

Sales Rep: _____

Tel: _____

Orders to
24 Hour Ansafone Number: 0800 373921

Order Information
Teleordering: IOP

Order Dept Opening Times
Mon - Fri 8.30am - 1pm, 2pm - 5pm
All Dues Automatically Recorded
Representation Available

Personnel
Head of Company: Mr Anthony Pearce
Head of Sales (Home): Ms Anne Davenport
Head of Marketing: Mr Kurt Paulus
Head of Publicity: Pamela Whichard
Head of Accounts: Mr S Prendiville
Head of Distribution: Ms A Pomroy

Number of titles published annually: 70
Percentage of Export Sales: 80%
Number of Staff: 100
PA Member
NBA Signatory
All New Titles are Bar Coded
Book Data Subscriber
WBIP Updating: Ms A Pomroy

Parent Company: Institute of Physics

Trade Terms
25-30% on all orders
Credit Cards Accepted: Access/Master, Visa, Amex

Returns Procedures
Authority to Return: Ms Anne Davenport
Address for Returns: Burston Distribution Services, Unit 2A, Newbridge Trading Estate, Newbridge Close, Off Whitby Rd, Bristol BS4 4AX
Stock Returns: Notification needed within 30 days of receipt
Imperfect Returns: Notify publisher within 30 days of receipt. Title page only up to £15

IRISH ACADEMIC PRESS
Kill Lane, Blackrock, County Dublin
ISBN Prefix(es): 0 7165
Tel: 01 289 2922
Fax: 01 289 3072
VAT No: 9Y5 9494 N

Orders to
GILL & MACMILLAN LTD, Goldenbridge, Inchicore, Dublin 8, County Dublin
Tel: 01 531 005
Fax: 01 541 688

Order Information

All Dues Automatically Recorded
Representation Available
Invoice Payments: Gill & Macmillan

Personnel
Head of Company: Michael Adams
Head of Sales (Home): Martin Healy
Head of Accounts: Claire Kenna

Number of titles published annually: 20
Percentage of Export Sales: 75%
Number of Staff: 4
WBIP Updating: M Adams

Subsidiary Companies: Round Hall Press, The
Allied Companies: Four Courts Press Ltd

Trade Terms
25% for single copies, 35% for 2 or more single titles
Credit Cards Accepted: Access/Master, Visa, Amex

Returns Procedures
Address for Returns: Gill & Macmillan

IRON PRESS
5 Marden Terrace, Cullercoats, North Shields, Tyne & Wear
NE30 4PD
ISBN Prefix(es): 0 906228
Tel: 091-253 1901

Orders to
PASSWORD (BOOKS) LTD, 23 New Mount Street,
Manchester, Greater Manchester M4 4DE
Tel: 061-953 4009
Fax: 061-953 4001

Order Information

All Dues Automatically Recorded
Representation Available

Personnel
Head of Company: Peter Mortimer (Editor)

Number of titles published annually: 3
Number of Staff: 3

Trade Terms
35%

Returns Procedures
Authority to Return: Password Books
Address for Returns: Password Books

IRWELL PRESS
15 Lover's Lane, Grascroft, Oldham, Greater Manchester
OL4 4DP
Tel: 0457 820288
Fax: 081-866 6915

[handwritten: ISBN AGENCY (UBA) 121 Charlton Road New Providence, NJ 07974 - USA]

THE ISLAMIC TEXTS SOCIETY
5 Green Street, Cambridge, Cambridgeshire CB2 3JU
ISBN Prefix(es): 0 946621, 1 870196
Tel: 0223 314387
Fax: 0223 324342
VAT No: 385 9402 19

Order Information
Teleordering: ITS

Order Dept Opening Times
9.30am - 5.30pm
All Dues Automatically Recorded
Representation Available

Personnel
Head of Company: Abdul Rahman Azzam/Batul Salazar
(Directors)
Head of Accounts: Sue Nicholson

Number of titles published annually: 7
Number of Staff: 6
PA Member
All New Titles are Bar Coded
Book Data Subscriber
WBIP Updating: B Salazar

Trade Terms
35%, single copy 25%
Credit Cards Accepted: Access/Master, Visa

Returns Procedures
Authority to Return: Via Reps

Handwritten at top: ITALIAN BOOKSHOP: 7 CECIL COURT, LONDON WC2N 4E?
Tel 071 2401634   FAX 071 240 1635 * NOT OPEN MON[D]

ISLAND PUBLICATIONS LTD
3 Cookstown Enterprise Park, Tallaght, Dublin 24, County Dublin
Tel: 01 512 610
Tel: 01 512 354
Fax: 01 512 636
VAT No: 480 0788 R

Handwritten: I.T. Pubs - Unit 25, Long Mead - Shaftesbury Dorset. SP7 8PL (0747) 57339

ITEM GROUP LTD
Burnham House, High Street, Burnham, Buckinghamshire SL1 7JZ
Tel: 0628 662517
Fax: 0628 667155

ITMA
93c Venner Road, Sydenham, London SE26 5HY
Tel: 081-659 7713

Order Information
Pre-paid only please

IUCN - THE WORLD CONSERVATION UNION
Publications Services Unit, 181a Huntingdon Road, Cambridge, Cambridgeshire CB3 0DJ
Tel: 0223 277894
Fax: 0223 277175
Telex: 817036 SCMU G

Order Information
Teleordering: IUCN

LEON JAEGGI AND SONS LTD
231 London Road, Staines, Middlesex TW18 4HR
Tel: 0784 463663
Fax: 0784 460871

Trade Terms
2-10 books 30% (Pro-forma Only), 11-49 35% plus 5% for cash, 40+ 40%

Returns Procedures
Authority to Return: Firm sale only
Imperfect Returns: Return whole book for replacement

Handwritten: 378 0171 8834

JAI PRESS LTD
The Courtyard, 28 High Street, Hampton Hill, Middlesex TW12 1PD
ISBN Prefix(es): 0 89232, 1 55938
Tel: 081-943 9296
Fax: 081-943 9317
VAT No: 524 8625 36

Account No: _____
Sales Rep: _____
Tel: _____

Orders to
~~INTERNATIONAL BOOK DISTRIBUTORS, Campus 400,~~
Maylands Avenue, Hemel Hempstead, Hertfordshire HP2 7EZ
Tel: 0442 881900
Fax: 0442 882099

Handwritten: FROM 1/3/95 Marston

Order Information

All Dues Automatically Recorded
Representation Available
Invoice Payments: IBD
Continuation orders serials/journal subs:JAI Press, not IBD

Personnel

Head of Company: Piers R Allen (Managing Director)
Head of Customer Services: Nell McCreadie
Other Important Personnel:
George Sainsbury (UK Rep)

Number of titles published annually: 150
Percentage of Export Sales: 60%
Number of Staff: 4
IPG Member
Book Data Subscriber
WBIP Updating: Miss Nell McCreadie

Parent Company: JAI Press Inc (US)

Trade Terms
20% on all orders, no surcharges

Returns Procedures
Authority to Return: JAI Press
Address for Returns: IBD
Stock Returns: Contact Returns Dept at IBD
Imperfect Returns: Return all imperfect books to IBD

JAMES & JAMES SCIENCE PUBLISHERS LTD

5 Castle Road, London NW1 8PR
ISBN Prefix(es): 1 873936
Tel: 071-284 3833
Fax: 071-284 3737
VAT No: 554 0747 41

Order Information

All Dues Automatically Recorded

Personnel
Head of Company: Edward Milford

Number of titles published annually: 10
Percentage of Export Sales: 65%
Number of Staff: 4
IPG Member
Book Data Subscriber
WBIP Updating: John Pacione

Trade Terms
25% Postage charged
Credit Cards Accepted: Access/Master, Amex, Visa

ARTHUR JAMES LTD

1 Cranbourne Road, London N10 2BT
ISBN Prefix(es): 0 85305
Tel: 081-883 1831
Tel: 0386 446566 Tel/Fax
Tel: 081-883 8307 Tel/Fax
VAT No: 274 1074 71

Order Information

Order Dept Opening Times
Mon - Fri 8.30am - 4pm
All Dues Automatically Recorded
Representation Available

Personnel
Head of Company: D Duncan
Head of Sales (Home): Beryl Coles
Head of Marketing: Jillian Tallon

Head of Distribution: Margaret Bayliss
Head of Customer Services: Susan Cummings

Number of titles published annually: 10
Number of Staff: 5
All New Titles are Bar Coded
WBIP Updating: D M Duncan

Trade Terms
35%
Other Terms: Carriage charged under £25 orders

Returns Procedures
Address for Returns: 4 Broadway Road, Evesham, Worcs WR11 6BH Tel/Fax: 0386 446566
Stock Returns: Returns must not be under six months or over one year from publication and must be in mint condition

JANE'S INFORMATION GROUP

Sentinel House, 163 Brighton Road, Coulsdon, Surrey CR5 2NH
ISBN Prefix(es): 0 7106
Tel: 081-763 1030
Fax: 081-763 1005/6
Fax: 081-763 0276
Telex: 916907 JANES G
VAT No: 492 4056 40

Account No: _____

Sales Rep: _____

Tel: _____

Order Information
Teleordering: JANES

Order Dept Opening Times
Mon - Fri 9am - 5pm
All Dues Automatically Recorded
Representation Available

Personnel
Head of Company: Michael Goldsmith (Managing Director)
Head of Sales (Home): Rupert Webb (UK Trade Sales Manager)
Head of Sales (Export): George Rainey (Export Trade Sales Manager)
Head of Marketing: Ruth Jowett (Marketing Manager)
Head of Accounts: Martyn Atkins (Credit Control Manager)
Head of Distribution: Beth Neilsen (Customer Service Manager)

Number of titles published annually: 30
Book Data Subscriber
WBIP Updating: Rupert Webb

Trade Terms
Non-Net: 15% single copy, 20% two or more
Girobank Number: 533 3563
Credit Cards Accepted: Access/Master, Visa, Amex

Returns Procedures
Authority to Return: Books are supplied on a firm sale basis only
Imperfect Returns: Title page only accepted up to £25 list price. Permission to be obtained prior to return for £25+

JANUS PUBLISHING

Duke House, 37 Duke Street, London W1M 5DF
ISBN Prefix(es): 1 85756
Tel: 071-486 8591
Tel: 071-486 2373

Fax: 071-487 3837
VAT No: 564 4056 41

Orders to
THE DISTRIBUTION BOOK CO, 4-5 Colwell Drive,
Abingdon, Oxfordshire OX14 1AU
Tel: 0235 527544
Fax: 0235 530435

Order Information

All Dues Automatically Recorded
Representation Available
Invoice Payments: The Distribution Book Co Ltd

Personnel
Head of Company: Ronald Ross Stanton
Head of Accounts: Bob Tyminski

Number of titles published annually: 50
Number of Staff: 5
IPG Member
All New Titles are Bar Coded
WBIP Updating: Mrs Lesley Astier

Trade Terms
35%

Returns Procedures
Authority to Return: The Distribution Book Co Ltd
Address for Returns: Distribution Book Co Ltd
Imperfect Returns: No price limit. Complete book should be returned.

JARROLD PUBLISHING

Whitefriars, Norwich, Norfolk NR3 1TR
ISBN Prefix(es): 0 7117, 0 85306
Tel: 0603 763300 24 Hours
Fax: 0603 662748
VAT No: 104 6067 03
Account No: _____ A223 _____
Sales Rep: _____
Tel: _____

Order Information

Order Dept Opening Times
Mon - Fri 8.30am - 5pm
All Dues Automatically Recorded
Representation Available

Personnel
Head of Company: Antony Jarrold
Head of Sales (Home): Tony Thompson
Head of Marketing: Joy Hodge
Head of Accounts: David Loombe
Head of Distribution: Bryan Wilde
Head of Customer Services: Roberta Sharpe
Other Important Personnel:
Caroline Jarrold (Publishing Director)

Number of titles published annually: 20
Number of Staff: 48
IPG Member
All New Titles are Bar Coded
WBIP Updating: Mrs R Sharpe

Trade Terms
35% on all orders
Other Terms: Under £30 pro forma or open cheque with order Carriage charges: 20% under £30, £3 £30-£60 orders
Credit Cards Accepted: Access/Master, Visa

JAY BOOKS

30 The Boundary, Langton Green, Tunbridge Wells, Kent
TN3 0YB
ISBN Prefix(es): 0 9510086, 1 870404
Tel: 0892 545198
VAT No: 395 4026 39

Order Information

Order Dept Opening Times
Mon - Sat 9am - 5pm
All Dues Automatically Recorded
Representation Available

Personnel
Head of Company: Ken Jackson

Number of titles published annually: 6
All New Titles are Bar Coded

Trade Terms
35%
Minimum Order: £10 published price for full discount, otherwise 25%
Other Terms: Carriage charged on overseas orders

Returns Procedures
Stock Returns: Request permission
Imperfect Returns: Request permission

JERSEY ARTISTS LTD

23 Pier Road, St Helier, Jersey, Channel Islands JE2 4UW
ISBN Prefix(es): 0 901845
Tel: 0534 52816
Tel: 0542 32621 April 93
Fax: 0534 50855

Orders to
G Behrend, c/o 9 Station Road, Findochty, Buckie
AB56 2PN
Tel: 0542 32621 (24 Hr)
Fax: 0542 34307

Order Information

Order Dept Opening Times
Sun - Sat 9am - 7pm
Representation Available

Personnel
Head of Company: G Behrend (Chairman & Secretary)

Number of titles published annually: 1
Percentage of Export Sales: 20%
NBA Signatory
All New Titles are Bar Coded
Book Data Subscriber
WBIP Updating: G Behrend

Trade Terms
General Net: Single copy/single line 25%, 2 or more single titles 35%, Subscription orders 35-50%, stock/special orders negotiable
Minimum Order: 100 copies of a title for 50%, less by negotiation
Other Terms: Carriage charges on small orders 2.5% on overdue accounts monthly
Girobank Number: 02599252
Credit Cards Accepted: Access/Master, Visa, Amex, Other

Returns Procedures
Authority to Return: G Behrend
Address for Returns: G Behrend, Findochty
Stock Returns: Contact first
Imperfect Returns: Return whole book

JEWISH CHRONICLE PUBLICATIONS
25 Furnival Street, London EC4A 1JT
Tel: 071-405 9252
Fax: 071-405 9040

Orders to
SPA BOOKS LTD, PO Box 47, Stevenage, Hertfordshire
SG2 8UH
Tel: 0462 482812
Fax: 0438 310104

Order Information
Teleordering: JEWISH

Invoice Payments: Spa Books Ltd

Personnel
Head of Marketing: Mr M Weinberg (Executive Director/Marketing)

Trade Terms
Contact Spa Books

[Handwritten: JOHNS HOPKINS c/o Phymbridge - any queries with their titles phone Mrs Calloway on 0604 604384]

JOHNSTON & BACON BOOKS LTD
PO Box 1, Stirling, Central FK7 0BH
ISBN Prefix(es): 0 7179
Tel: 0786 841867
Fax: 0786 841326
VAT No: 353 7022 72

Order Information

Order Dept Opening Times
Mon - Fri 9am - 5.15pm
All Dues Automatically Recorded
Representation Available

Personnel
Head of Sales (Home): D Warburton
Head of Accounts: L Bennie

Number of titles published annually: 10
Percentage of Export Sales: 25%
NBA Signatory
All New Titles are Bar Coded
WBIP Updating: D Warburton

Trade Terms
General Net: Single copy/single line 25%, 2 or more single titles, 2 books or more 33.3%
Other Terms: Pro-forma

Returns Procedures
Address for Returns: Returns C/O Clan Books
Imperfect Returns: Title page only up to £9.99

JONATHAN PRESS
Tey Brook Craft Centre, Brook Road, Great Tey, Colchester,
Essex CO6 2EB
Tel: 0206 212755 Tel/Fax
Tel: 0206 211020
VAT No: 387 0044 52

IPG Member

JONES & BARTLETT PUBLISHERS INTERNATIONAL
PO Box 1498, London W6 7RS
ISBN Prefix(es): 0 86720
Tel: 071-371 2119 Tel/Fax
VAT No: 591 1375 37

Orders to
PLYMBRIDGE DISTRIBUTORS LTD, Plymbridge House, Estover Road, Plymouth, Devon PL6 7PZ
Tel: 0752 735251
Fax: 0752 695699

Order Information

All Dues Automatically Recorded
Representation Available
Invoice Payments: Plymbridge Distributors

Personnel
Head of Company: Donald Jones (Chairman) Boston, USA
Head of Sales (Home): Richard Warner

Number of titles published annually: 50
Number of Staff: 1
All New Titles are Bar Coded
WBIP Updating: Richard Warner

Trade Terms
Academic Net: 20%
Credit Cards Accepted: Access/Master, Visa

Returns Procedures
Authority to Return: Prior authorisation required from Richard Warner
Address for Returns: Plymbridge Distributors
Imperfect Returns: Title page only up to £20 retail

BRIAN JONES PUBLICATIONS

2 Chatsworth Close, Market Deeping, Lincolnshire PE6 8AZ
Tel: 0778 380755 Tel/Fax
VAT No: 493 2502 47

IPG Member

JORDAN & SONS LTD

21 St Thomas Street, Bristol, Avon BS1 6JS
ISBN Prefix(es): 0 85308
Tel: 0272 230600
Fax: 0272 250486
Telex: 449119
VAT No: 137 4442 71

Order Information

All Dues Automatically Recorded
Representation Available

Personnel
Head of Company: Richard Hudson
Head of Marketing: Mark McDonnell
Head of Customer Services: Shirley Pullen

Number of titles published annually: 20
NBA Signatory
All New Titles are Bar Coded
Book Data Subscriber
WBIP Updating: Tim Hine

Trade Terms
1-2 copies 20%, Three plus 33.3% Subscription orders 20%
Credit Cards Accepted: Access/Master, Visa, Amex, Diners

JORDANHILL COLLEGE

Sales & Publications Dept, 76 Southbrae Drive, Glasgow, Strathclyde G13 1PP
Tel: 041-950 3170/1

Fax: 041-950 3268
VAT No: 261 5733 62

RICHARD JOSEPH PUBLISHERS LTD
Unit 2, Monks Walk, Farnham, Surrey GU9 8HT
ISBN Prefix(es): 1 872699
Tel: 0252 734347
Fax: 0252 734307
VAT No: 529 2107 58

Order Information
Order Dept Opening Times
Mon - Fri 9am - 5pm
All Dues Automatically Recorded

Personnel
Head of Company: Richard Joseph
Head of Customer Services: C Underdown

Number of titles published annually: 8
Percentage of Export Sales: 20%
Number of Staff: 6
IPG Member

Trade Terms
20%
Credit Cards Accepted: Visa

Returns Procedures
Authority to Return: All books sold on firm sale only
Imperfect Returns: Return whole book

JOSSEY-BASS c/o Marston

KAHN & AVERILL
9 Harrington Road, London SW7 3ES
ISBN Prefix(es): 0 900707, 1 871082
Tel: 081-743 3278
VAT No: 240 4836 77

Orders to
BAILEY DISTRIBUTION LTD, Unit 1, Learoyd Road,
Mountfield Rd Ind Est, New Romney, Kent TN28 8XU
Tel: 0679 66905
Fax: 0679 66638

Order Information
All Dues Automatically Recorded
Representation Available

Personnel
Head of Company: M Kahn

Number of titles published annually: 8
Percentage of Export Sales: 25%
Number of Staff: 2
IPG Member
NBA Signatory
All New Titles are Bar Coded

Trade Terms
General Net: Single Copy 25%, Two or More Single Titles 35%

Returns Procedures
Authority to Return: Bailey Distribution Ltd
Stock Returns: Write to distribution for permission to return

S KARGER AG
Allschwilerstr 10, PO Box, CH 4009 Basel, Switzerland
Tel: 010-41-61 3061111

Fax: 010-41-61-3061234
Telex: CH 962 652

Orders to
S Karger AG, 11 Ravenscroft Road, Beckenham, Kent
BR3 4TP
Tel: 081-659 1198 (24 Hr)
Fax: 081-659 7207

Order Information

Cyclical Ordering Policy
All Dues Automatically Recorded
Representation Available

Personnel
Head of Company: Dr Thomas Karger
Head of Sales (Home): Andrew Fernandes
Head of Sales (Export): Peter Lawson
Head of Marketing: Bettina Wackwitz
Head of Accounts: Rolf Zurlinden
Head of Distribution: Esther Coscino

Number of titles published annually: 110
Number of Staff: 250
Book Data Subscriber
WBIP Updating: Gertrud Maeder

Subsidiary Companies: Katakura Libri Inc (JP), Librairie Luginbuhl (FR)
Allied Companies: DA Books & Journals (AU)

Trade Terms
25%

Returns Procedures
Stock Returns: Any title may be returned within one year from invoice date quoting invoice number & date, if in mint condition.
Imperfect Returns: Imperfectly bound or printed books may be returned for 100% credit or replacement.

H KARNAC BOOKS LTD

58 Gloucester Road, London SW7 4QY
Tel: 071-584 3303
Fax: 071-823 7743
VAT No: 238 7579 15

Order Information

Order Dept Opening Times
Mon - Sat 9am - 6pm
All Dues Automatically Recorded

Personnel
Head of Company: Cesare D S Sacerdoti
Head of Accounts: Navin Patel
Head of Customer Services: Larry Fisher

Number of titles published annually: 25
Percentage of Export Sales: 50%
WBIP Updating: Mark Chaloner

Trade Terms
1-5 books 25% plus £2.85 surcharge, 6+ books 30%
Other Terms: Pre-payment required
Credit Cards Accepted: Access/Master, Amex, Visa

KAROMA Publishers Inc 2509 N. Campbell Ave Suite 45, Tucson AZ 85719 USA

KARNAK HOUSE
300 Westbourne Park Road, London W11 1EH
Tel: 071-221 6490 Tel/Fax

Phone/Fax
602 795 6465

Kaufmann (Morgan) = Direct Distribution

RICHARD KAY PUBLICATIONS

80 Sleaford Road, Boston, Lincolnshire PE21 8EU
ISBN Prefix(es): 0 902662
Tel: 0205 353231 24 Hours
VAT No: 129 8076 45

Order Information
Teleordering: RKAY

Order Dept Opening Times
Mon - Sat 9am - 6pm
All Dues Automatically Recorded

Personnel
Head of Company: R K Allday

Number of titles published annually: 6
Number of Staff: 1

Trade Terms
Single copy 25%, otherwise 33.3%, stockholding 3+ titles 35% 40+ books of 2 or more titles 40%

Returns Procedures
Authority to Return: Prior permission required
Imperfect Returns: Title page up to £10

KEAY'S PUBLICATIONS

PO Box 350, Burwell, Cambridge, Cambridgeshire CB5 0AX
ISBN Prefix(es): 1 873310
Tel: 0638 741303
Fax: 0638 743551

Personnel
Head of Company: John Foulkes
Head of Accounts: Sue Taylor

Number of titles published annually: 2
Number of Staff: 3
All New Titles are Bar Coded
WBIP Updating: John Foulkes

Trade Terms
33.3% no surcharges
BA/Girobank Small Order Scheme: Invoice on 30 days
Credit Cards Accepted: Access/Master, Visa

KEGAN PAUL INTERNATIONAL

PO Box 256, 118 Bedford Court Mansions, London WC1B 3SW
ISBN Prefix(es): 0 7103
Tel: 071-580 5511
Fax: 071-436 0899
VAT No: 404 6017 91

Account No: _____

Sales Rep:_____

Tel: _____

Orders to
JOHN WILEY & SONS LTD, Southern Cross Trading Estate, 1 Oldlands Way, Bognor Regis, West Sussex PO22 9SA
Tel: 0243 829121
Fax: 0243 820250

Personnel
Head of Company: Peter Hopkins
Head of Marketing: Kaori O'Connor

KEMPS PUBLISHING LTD
11 The Swan Courtyard, Charles Edward Road, Yardley, Birmingham, West Midlands B26 1BU
Tel: 021-765 4144
Fax: 021-706 5941
VAT No: 580 3725 39

THE KENILWORTH PRESS LTD
Addington, Buckingham, Buckinghamshire MK18 2JR
ISBN Prefix(es): 0 900226, 0 901366, 1 872082
Tel: 0296 715101 24 Hours
Fax: 0296 715148
VAT No: 476 0290 42

Order Information

Order Dept Opening Times
Mon - Fri 9am - 5.30pm
All Dues Automatically Recorded

Personnel
Head of Company: David Blunt (Managing Director)
Head of Sales (Home): Mrs Deirdre Blunt (Director)
Head of Customer Services: Linda McIlwraith

Number of titles published annually: 10
Percentage of Export Sales: 30%
Number of Staff: 5
IPG Member
All New Titles are Bar Coded
WBIP Updating: Mrs Deirdre Blunt

Trade Terms
35% no surcharges
Credit Cards Accepted: Access/Master

Returns Procedures
Authority to Return: Prior permission required
Stock Returns: Request permission - A returns note & label will be issued
Imperfect Returns: Return title page only

THE KENSAL PRESS
Riverview, Headington Hill, Oxford, Oxfordshire OX3 0BT
ISBN Prefix(es): 0 946041
Tel: 0865 750302
Fax: 0865 62922
Telex: 849462 TELFAC
VAT No: 341 2602 01

Orders to
LAVIS MARKETING, 73 Lime Walk, Headington, Oxfordshire OX3 7AD
Tel: 0865 67575
Fax: 0865 750079

Order Information

All Dues Automatically Recorded

Personnel
Head of Company: B Millan

Number of titles published annually: 6
NBA Signatory
WBIP Updating: G E A Shomroni

Returns Procedures
Address for Returns: Lavis Marketing

KENSINGTON PUBLICATIONS LTD
1 Great Cumberland Place, London W1H 7AL
Tel: 071-630 5596
Fax: 071-872 0197
Telex: 936012 KENPUB G
VAT No: 420 4434 95

IPG Member

KENSINGTON WEST PRODUCTIONS LTD
338 Old York Road, Wandsworth, London SW18 1SS
ISBN Prefix(es): 8 71349
Tel: 081-877 9394
Fax: 081-870 4270
VAT No: 420 3058 05

Order Information

All Dues Automatically Recorded
Representation Available

Personnel
Head of Company: Julian West
Head of Sales (Home): Giles Appleton
Head of Publicity: Jacqui Hawthorn
Head of Accounts: Nova Jayne Heath
Other Important Personnel:
Sally Conner (Sales)

Number of titles published annually: 5
Number of Staff: 10
All New Titles are Bar Coded
WBIP Updating: Nova Jayne Heath

Trade Terms
Up to 35%, less on small orders
Credit Cards Accepted: Access/Master, Visa, Amex, Diners

KEYDEX PUBLISHERS
10 Meads Gate, Darley Road, Eastbourne, East Sussex BN20 7PG
ISBN Prefix(es): 0 905720
Tel: 0323 410208

Order Information

Representation Available

Personnel
Head of Company: Hilbert Hardy

Trade Terms
Less than 5 single copies 25%, 5+ 35% + postage

KIME PUBLISHING
PO Box 1, Hunstanton, Norfolk PE36 5JY
ISBN Prefix(es): 0 9513406
Tel: 048525 347

Personnel
Head of Company: Dr C Layton

Number of titles published annually: 1

Trade Terms
1 copy 33%, 2-5 copies 35%, 6-9 copies 37%, 10-20 copies 40% % for orders over 20 upon application. Postage paid

KIMPTON MEDICAL PUBLICATIONS

82 Great King Street, Edinburgh, Lothian EH3 6QY
Tel: 031-332 8764
Fax: 031-343 2633
VAT No: 300 8123 17

HILDA KING EDUCATIONAL SERVICES

Ash Cottage, Ashwells Manor Drive, Penn, High Wycombe, Buckinghamshire HP10 8EU
Tel: 0494 813947 Tel/Fax

PA Member

LAURENCE KING PUBLISHING

71 Great Russell Street, London WC1B 3BN
Tel: 071-831 6351
Fax: 071-831 8356
VAT No: 241 7495 56

Orders to
THAMES & HUDSON LTD, 44 Clockhouse Road, Farnborough, Hampshire GU14 7QZ
Tel: 0252 541602
Fax: 0252 377380

PA Member
Book Data Subscriber

KINGSCLERE PUBLICATIONS LTD

Highfield House, 2 Highfield Avenue, Newbury, Berkshire RG14 5DS
ISBN Prefix(es): 0 86204
Tel: 0635 38888
Fax: 0635 528638
VAT No: 200 7866 81

Personnel
Head of Company: Julian Armfield (Managing Director)
Head of Sales (Home): Charles Bishop (Sales Director)
Head of Accounts: Roger Dunford (Financial Co-ordinator)

Number of titles published annually: 30
Number of Staff: 7
All New Titles are Bar Coded
Book Data Subscriber
WBIP Updating: Diana Breadmore

Trade Terms
45%

Returns Procedures
Stock Returns: Return to publishers
Imperfect Returns: Return to publishers

JESSICA KINGSLEY PUBLISHERS

116 Pentonville Road, London N1 9JB
ISBN Prefix(es): 1 85302, 1 85718
Tel: 071-833 2307
Fax: 071-837 2917
VAT No: 455 2134 66

Orders to
KOGAN PAGE LTD, 120 Pentonville Road, London N1 9JN
Tel: 071-278 0433
Fax: 071-837 6348

Order Information

All Dues Automatically Recorded
Representation Available
Invoice Payments: Kogan Page

Personnel
Head of Company: Jessica Kingsley
Head of Publicity: Charlotte Burrows

Number of titles published annually: 40
Number of Staff: 5
IPG Member
NBA Signatory
All New Titles are Bar Coded
Book Data Subscriber
WBIP Updating: Helen Skelton

Trade Terms
Kogan Pages' terms

Returns Procedures
Authority to Return: Jessica Kingsley
Address for Returns: Kogan Page

KINGSMEAD PRESS

4 Woodspring Avenue, Worlebury, Weston-super-Mare, Avon BS22 9RJ
ISBN Prefix(es): 0 901571, 0 905466, 0 906230, 1 85026
Tel: 0934 631616
VAT No: 302 9211 03

Personnel
Head of Company: Geoffrey Body MCIT

KINGSWAY PUBLICATIONS

Nottbridge Drove, Eastbourne, East Sussex BN23 6NT
Tel: 0323 410930
Fax: 0323 411970
VAT No: 403 2455 93

Account No: _____

Sales Rep: _____

Tel: _____

Orders to
SEND THE LIGHT, PO Box 300, Kingstown Broadway, Carlisle, Cumbria CA3 0QS
Tel: 0228 512512
Fax: 0228 514949

Order Information

All Dues Automatically Recorded
Representation Available
Invoice Payments: STL

Personnel
Head of Company: John Paculabo (Managing Director)
Head of Sales (Home): Bob Clark (Sales Director)
Head of Sales (Export): Richard Martin (Export Sales Manager)
Head of Marketing: Phil Bacon (Marketing Director)
Head of Publicity: Jane Harding (Publicity Manager)
Head of Accounts: Bill Owen (Accounts Manager)

Number of titles published annually: 50
Number of Staff: 40
PA Member
NBA Signatory
All New Titles are Bar Coded
WBIP Updating: Carolyn Owen

Parent Company: The Kingsway Trust Group Ltd

Trade Terms
35% on all books, 33% on all music. Carriage free on orders over £60 retail.

Returns Procedures
Address for Returns: STL
Stock Returns: Apply in writing for permission

KIRKLEES CULTURAL SERVICES

Red Doles Lane, Huddersfield, West Yorkshire HD2 1YF
Tel: 0484 513808
Fax: 0484 531901
Telex: 94013537
VAT No: 184 3524 57

Order Information
Orders To: Technical & Commercial Unit

[handwritten: KLUTZ % Mr Goolnik, 20 Denewood Road, Highgate, N6 4AJ]

KLUWER ACADEMIC PUBLISHERS GROUP

Distribution Centre, PO Box 322, AH Dordrecht, The Netherlands
ISBN Prefix(es): 0 7462, 0 7923, 0 85200, 0 86010, 0 89838, 1 55608, 1 85333, 90 247, 90 277, 90 6193
Tel: 010-31-78 524400
Fax: 010-31-78 524474 Orders
Fax: 010-31-78-183273 Marketing
Telex: 20083

Account No: _5502020_
Sales Rep: _____
Tel: _____

Order Information
Teleordering: KAP

[handwritten: KLUWER LAW + TAXATION, PO Box 23, 7400 GA Deventer, The Netherlands (ISBN'S 906544 + 90268)]

Order Dept Opening Times
Mon - Fri 8.30am - 5pm (UK Plus One Hour)
All Dues Automatically Recorded
Representation Available

Personnel
Head of Company: F W B van Eysinga (President)
Head of Sales (Export): S D Dissel (Sales Director)
Head of Accounts: W Fortuin (Credit Controller)
Head of Distribution: H Pabbruwe (Group Services Director)
Head of Customer Services: S P van Geuns (General Manager - Distribution Centre)
Other Important Personnel:
A M Harris (Sales Manager)

Number of titles published annually: 600
Book Data Subscriber
WBIP Updating: Ms Els Rens

Parent Company: Wolters-Kluwer NV, The Netherlands

Trade Terms
20% plus postage & handling

Returns Procedures
Authority to Return: Returns Dept
Address for Returns: Maxwellstraat 4-10, 3316 GP Dordrecht, The Netherlands
Stock Returns: Request permission, quote invoice number & date
Imperfect Returns: Request permission, quote invoice number & date

KLUWER ACADEMIC PUBLISHERS

UK Medical Division, PO Box 55, Lancaster, Lancashire
LA1 1PE
ISBN Prefix(es): 0 7462, 0 7923, 0 85200
Tel: 0524 34996
Fax: 0524 32144
Telex: 6517 LEL WXG
VAT No: 531 6192 62

Account No: _____ 55 02020 _____
Sales Rep: _____
Tel: _____

Orders to
KLUWER ACADEMIC PUBLISHERS GROUP,
Distribution Centre, PO Box 322, AH Dordrecht, The
Netherlands
Tel: 010-31-78 524400
Fax: 010-31-78 524474

Order Information
Teleordering: KLUW

All Dues Automatically Recorded
Representation Available
Invoice Payments: Kluwer Distribution, The Netherlands

Personnel
Head of Company: Dr P L Clarke (Publisher)
Head of Sales (Home): R H Utley (Sales Manager (UK & Ireland))
Head of Sales (Export): A Harris (Sales Director)
Head of Accounts: W Fortuin
Head of Distribution: S van Geuns

Number of titles published annually: 30
All New Titles are Bar Coded
WBIP Updating: Miss L Thomas

Parent Company: Wolters-Kluwer, The Netherlands

Trade Terms
20% plus postage & handling

Returns Procedures
Authority to Return: Returns Dept, Kluwer Distribution, The Netherlands
Address for Returns: See Kluwer Distribution Centre, The Netherlands
Stock Returns: Request permission quoting invoice number & date
Imperfect Returns: Please contact Returns Dept

KNIGHTSCROSS LTD

21 Gaywood Road, Ashtead, Surrey KT21 1BL
ISBN Prefix(es): 0 854, 1 874373
Tel: 0372 274059
Fax: 0372 271544
Telex: 934755

Order Information

Order Dept Opening Times
Mon - Fri 8.30am - 5.30pm
Representation Available

Personnel
Head of Company: Dr B Adefope

Number of titles published annually: 12
Percentage of Export Sales: 35%
Number of Staff: 5
All New Titles are Bar Coded

Trade Terms
30% on all orders
Credit Cards Accepted: Access/Master, Visa

Returns Procedures
Stock Returns: No unauthorised returns
Imperfect Returns: Title pages up to £5, otherwise return book

KNOCKABOUT COMICS

10 Acklam Road, London W10 5QZ
ISBN Prefix(es): 0 86166
Tel: 081-969 2945
Fax: 081-968 7614
VAT No: 242 5636 68

Orders to
BOOKPOINT LIMITED, 39 Milton Park, Abingdon, Oxfordshire OX14 4TD
Tel: 0235 835001
Fax: 0235 861038

Order Information

All Dues Automatically Recorded
Representation Available

Personnel
Head of Company: Tony Bennett/Carol Bennett
Head of Sales (Home): Christopher Andrew
Head of Sales (Export): Joe Toussaint
Head of Publicity: David Brown

Number of titles published annually: 20
Number of Staff: 5
NBA Signatory
All New Titles are Bar Coded
WBIP Updating: Tony Bennett

Parent Company: Toskanex Ltd

Trade Terms
35%
General Net: Single Copy 20%, Subscriptions Orders 40%
Other Terms: Carriage charged up to £150 invoice
Credit Cards Accepted: Access/Master, Visa

Returns Procedures
Authority to Return: Head Office
Address for Returns: Bookpoint
Imperfect Returns: Return title page at any value

KNOWLES PUBLICATIONS

Wardle House, King Street, Knutsford, Cheshire WA16 6PD
Tel: 0565 755439 Tel/Fax
VAT No: 527 5357 32

PA Member

KODANSHA EUROPE LTD

38-44 Gillingham Street, London SW1V 1HU
Tel: 071-630 0588
Fax: 071-233 5717
VAT No: 524 2864 48

Orders to
BIBLIOS PUBLISHERS DISTRIBUTION SERVICE LTD, Star Road, Partridge Green, West Sussex RH13 8LD
Tel: 0403 710971
Fax: 0403 711143

Book Data Subscriber
<ins>KOELTZ SCIENTIFIC BOOKS.
P.O. Box 1360 - D6240 - KOENIGSTEIN
GERMANY</ins>

KOGAN PAGE LTD

120 Pentonville Road, London N1 9JN
ISBN Prefix(es): 0 7494, 0 85038, 1 85091, 1 85302
Tel: 071-278 0433
Fax: 071-837 6348
Telex: 263088 KOGAN G
VAT No: 417 8457 28

Account No: <ins>BLA 010</ins>

Sales Rep: _____

Tel: _____

Order Information
Teleordering: KOGAN

Order Dept Opening Times
Mon - Fri 9.30am - 5.30 pm
Orders for more than one publisher can be bulked
All Dues Automatically Recorded
Representation Available

Personnel
Head of Company: Philip Kogan (Managing Director)
Head of Sales (Home): Kate Griffin (Sales Director)
Head of Marketing: Caroline Hird (Marketing Director)
Head of Accounts: Praba Kan (Finance Director)
Other Important Personnel:
Adrian Grey (UK Sales Manager)

Number of titles published annually: 200
Percentage of Export Sales: 25%
Number of Staff: 60
PA Member
IPG Member
NBA Signatory
All New Titles are Bar Coded
Book Data Subscriber
WBIP Updating: Liz Farrant

Trade Terms
33.3% trade titles 30% professional/reference titles
General Net: single copy 25%
Girobank Number: 55 6061 403
Credit Cards Accepted: Access/Master, Visa, Amex, Diners

Returns Procedures
Authority to Return: Sales Department
Address for Returns: Hoddle Doyle Meadows Ltd, Old Mead Lane Elsenham, Herts CM22 6JN
Stock Returns: Authorised returns only
Imperfect Returns: Title pages for titles priced up to £25 accepted for credit

<ins>KOLB Pub. Co, 7175 SW. 47th St - Suite 210
Miami, Florida 33155
A/C UNIUBOOKSH</ins>

KOZMIK PRESS

134 Elsenham Street, London SW18 5NP
ISBN Prefix(es): 0 905116
Tel: 081-874 8218
Fax: 071-935 5913
VAT No: 318 4374 54

Order Information

All Dues Automatically Recorded
Representation Available

Personnel
Head of Company: David Ryan

Number of titles published annually: 3
Percentage of Export Sales: 50%

IPG Member
All New Titles are Bar Coded

Trade Terms
General Net: Single copy/single line 25%, 2 or more single titles 35%

Returns Procedures
Authority to Return: David Ryan
Stock Returns: Require prior request for authorization
Imperfect Returns: Return books

THE KQBX PRESS

16 Scotter Road, Bournemouth, Dorset BH7 6LY
Tel: 0202 426155

[handwritten: Krieger - Box 9542 - Melbourne - FL 32902-9542 USA]

KROPOTKIN'S LIGHTHOUSE PUBLICATIONS

Box KLP, Housemans Bookshop, 5 Caledonian Roadp, London N1 9DX
ISBN Prefix(es): 0 906317, 0 9501816

Order Information

Order Dept Opening Times
Mail Order only
All Dues Automatically Recorded
Representation Available
Invoice Payments: J Huggon, 59 Leiston Road, Knodishall, Suffolk IP17 1UQ

Personnel
Head of Company: J Huggon

Number of Staff: 1

Trade Terms
35% + postage

Returns Procedures
Imperfect Returns: No price limit

KUMA COMPUTERS LTD

12 Horseshoe Park, Pangbourne, Berkshire RG8 7JW
ISBN Prefix(es): 0 7457
Tel: 0734 844335 24 Hours
Fax: 0734 844339

Order Information

Order Dept Opening Times
Mon - Fri 8.30am - 6.30pm
All Dues Automatically Recorded
Representation Available

Personnel
Head of Company: T W Moore
Head of Sales (Home): Jon Day
Head of Accounts: Di Williams
Head of Distribution: June Weller

Number of titles published annually: 100
Percentage of Export Sales: 30%
NBA Signatory
All New Titles are Bar Coded
Book Data Subscriber
WBIP Updating: Jon Day

Trade Terms
35%
Credit Cards Accepted: Access/Master, Visa

Returns Procedures
Stock Returns: Returns authorisation number must be applied for and quoted on outside of package

KUPERARD (LONDON) LTD
9 Hampstead West, 224 Iverson Road, W Hampstead, London NW6 2HL
ISBN Prefix(es): 1 857330, 1 870668
Tel: 071-372 4722
Fax: 071-372 4599
VAT No: 446 0865 38

Account No: _____
Sales Rep: _____
Tel: _____

Order Information
Teleordering: KUPER

Order Dept Opening Times
Mon - Fri 9.30am - 5.30pm
Orders for more than one publisher can be bulked
All Dues Automatically Recorded
Representation Available

Personnel
Head of Company: Joshua Kuperard
Head of Sales (Home): Peter Roberts
Head of Accounts: Vicky Halperin
Head of Distribution: Desmond Spencer
Head of Customer Services: Tanya Babel

All New Titles are Bar Coded
WBIP Updating: Peter Roberts

Trade Terms
35% net Under £30 retail 20%
Girobank Number: 509 7347
Credit Cards Accepted: Access/Master, Visa

Returns Procedures
Authority to Return: Peter Roberts
Stock Returns: Permission from head office must be received. Unauthorised returns not accepted. Shortages/damages notified 7days rec.
Imperfect Returns: Return complete books via post

LA HAULE BOOKS LTD
West Lodge, La Haule, Jersey, Channel Islands
ISBN Prefix(es): 0 861200
Tel: 0534 44957
Fax: 0534 47414

Order Information
Teleordering: LAHAULE

PROFORMA

Order Dept Opening Times
9am - 5pm
Orders for more than one publisher can be bulked
All Dues Automatically Recorded
Representation Available

Personnel
Head of Company: S Marett-Crosby
Head of Accounts: Isabel De Celis

All New Titles are Bar Coded
WBIP Updating: Lucinda Phillips

Trade Terms
20% UK 25% Foreign

Other Terms: Small order surcharge £1 single order. Carriage charged on all foreign orders.
Credit Cards Accepted: Access/Master, Visa, Amex

LAAS AVIATION LTD

Mikalian, Blackmore Road, Kelvedon Hatch, Brentwood, Essex CM15 0AP
VAT No: 311 7147 92

Orders to
Aviation Hobby Shop, 4 Horton Parade, Horton Road, West Drayton, Middlesex UB7 8EA
Tel: 0895 442123

LABOUR PARTY

150 Walworth Road, London E6 2BD
Tel: 071-234 3410/1
Tel: 071-234 3339
Fax: 071-234 3416
Telex: 8811237 Labour G
VAT No: 240 2927 84

LADYBIRD BOOKS LTD

Beeches Road, Loughborough, Leicestershire LE11 2NQ
ISBN Prefix(es): 0 7214, 0 86215, 1 85543
Tel: 0509 268021 24 Hours
Fax: 0509 234672 General
Fax: 0509 219158 Sales
Telex: 341347
Cables: LADYBIRD, LOUGHBOROUGH
VAT No: 114 0688 91

Account No: _____

Sales Rep: _____

Tel: _____

Order Information

Order Dept Opening Times
Mon - Fri 8.45am - 5pm
Representation Available
Teleordering

Personnel
Head of Company: Anthony Forbes Watson (Managing Director)
Head of Sales (Home): Brian Cotton (Sales & Marketing Director)
Head of Sales (Export): Muriel Dahan (Export Sales Manager)
Head of Marketing: Janet Riley (Marketing Manager)
Head of Publicity: Mary Hagger (Publicity Manager)
Head of Accounts: Phil Tapp (Head of Accounts)
Head of Distribution: Jerry Dwyer (Distribution Manager)
Head of Customer Services: Pat Lewin (Head of Trade)
Other Important Personnel:
John Mackay (Field Sales Manager), Charles Sanderson (National Accounts Sales Manager), Mike Gabb (Publishing Director), Philippa Wood (Rights & Co-Editions Manager)

Number of titles published annually: 120
Percentage of Export Sales: 40%
Number of Staff: 280
PA Member
NBA Signatory
All New Titles are Bar Coded
Book Data Subscriber
WBIP Updating: Mrs Pat Ross

Parent Company: Longman Group UK

Trade Terms
33.3%
Other Terms: P&P charged on small orders

Returns Procedures
Authority to Return: John Mackay, Field Sales Manager
Imperfect Returns: Return title page plus details of defect

LAING & BUISSON PUBLICATIONS LTD

Lymehouse Studios, Block B, 38 Georgiana Street, London NW1 0EB
Tel: 071-284 1268
Fax: 071-267 8269
VAT No: 523 3088 67

LAKESIDE PUBLICATIONS

Longdene House, Haslemere, Surrey GU27 2PH
Tel: 0428 645309
Fax: 0428 645312
VAT No: 413 9737 41

Account No: _____

Sales Rep: _____

Tel: _____

Order Information
Teleordering: LMI

Order Dept Opening Times
Mon - Fri 9am - 5.30pm
Cyclical Ordering Policy
All Dues Automatically Recorded
Representation Available

Personnel
Head of Company: Malcolm Thomas (Director)
Head of Sales (Home): Lynne Thomas (Director)
Head of Customer Services: Brian Bloomfield

All New Titles are Bar Coded
WBIP Updating: Lynne Thomas

Trade Terms
Single Copy 25%, Two or more 35%
Other Terms: Carriage charges: using discounted parcel service

Returns Procedures
Stock Returns: By permission only, except in cases of defect, damaged stock to be returned within 10 days.

LAMBENT BOOKS

4 Coombe Gardens, New Malden, Surrey KT3 4AA
ISBN Prefix(es): 0 9512155
Tel: 081-715 2559
Fax: 081-715 2560

Order Information

All Dues Automatically Recorded
Representation Available

Personnel
Head of Company: Joseph O'Connor

Number of titles published annually: 1
All New Titles are Bar Coded

Trade Terms
35% on all orders

LAME DUCK PUBLISHING

71 South Road, Portishead, Avon BS20 9DY
Tel: 0836 389702

LANCASHIRE BIBLIOGRAPHY

Central Library, St Peter's Square, Manchester, Greater Manchester M2 5PD
Tel: 061-234 1946
Fax: 061-234 1963
Telex: 667149
VAT No: 305 8362 66

IPG Member

JAY LANDESMAN

8 Duncan Terrace, London N1 8BZ
ISBN Prefix(es): 0 905150
Tel: 071-837 7290 Tel/Fax

Personnel
Head of Company: Jay Landesman

Number of titles published annually: 10
Percentage of Export Sales: 20%

Trade Terms
Single copy 25%, 2 or more single titles 35%

LANDSCAPE PRESS

420 Crewe Road, Wistaston, Crewe, Cheshire CW2 6QN
ISBN Prefix(es): 0 947849
Tel: 0270 68397

Personnel
Head of Company: Bridget Pellow

Number of titles published annually: 2

Trade Terms
33.3% on 10 or more
General Net: Single copy/single line 25% plus postage & packing

LANDY PUBLISHING

3 Staining Rise, Staining, Blackpool, Lancashire FY3 0BU
ISBN Prefix(es): 1 8728950
Tel: 0253 886103 24 Hours
VAT No: 534 3982 30

Order Information

Representation Available

Personnel
Head of Company: Bob Dobson (Owner)

Number of titles published annually: 6
IPG Member
NBA Signatory
WBIP Updating: Bob Dobson

Trade Terms
Cash with order 35%
General Net: 25% Post Free 4 or more 35% Post Free

Returns Procedures
Stock Returns: Advise before sending for instructions
Imperfect Returns: Return title page any copy

LANG (Peter) Jupiterstrasse 15 CH-3015 - Berne Switzerland

LANG SYNE PUBLISHERS LTD
Unit 2F, Clydeway Ind Centre, 45 Finnieston Street,
Glasgow, Strathclyde G3 8JU
Tel: 041-204 3104
Fax: 041-204 3101
VAT No: 272 1505 82

LANGUAGE INFORMATION CENTRE
32 Stryd Ebeneser, Pontypridd, Mid Glamorgan CF37 5PB
ISBN Prefix(es): 0 948565
Tel: 0443 492243

Order Information
Post Orders Only

Personnel
Head of Company: Joseph Biddulph

Number of titles published annually: 10

Trade Terms
20%

LANGUAGE TEACHING PUBLICATIONS
35 Church Road, Hove, East Sussex BN3 2BE
ISBN Prefix(es): 0 906717
Tel: 0273 736344
Fax: 0273 720898
Telex: 87250 ELC
VAT No: 390 0950 56

Order Information

Order Dept Opening Times
Mon - Fri 9.30am - 1pm, 2 - 5.30pm
All Dues Automatically Recorded
Representation Available

Personnel
Head of Company: Michael Lewis/James Hill
Head of Sales (Home): Stuart Tipping

Number of titles published annually: 6
Percentage of Export Sales: 80%
Number of Staff: 3
All New Titles are Bar Coded
WBIP Updating: Jimmie Hill

Trade Terms
25% UK, 30% abroad
Other Terms: £1 surcharge for orders under £20 gross value
Girobank Number: 30 435 4007
Credit Cards Accepted: Access/Master, Visa

Returns Procedures
Stock Returns: Please check first with head office
Imperfect Returns: Return only title page of imperfect book

ROGER LASCELLES
47 York Road, Brentford, Middlesex TW8 0QP
ISBN Prefix(es): 0 903909, 1 872815
Tel: 081-847 0935 Two Lines
Tel: 081-568 6169 Private
Fax: 081-568 3886
VAT No: 227 8218 55

Account No: _____

Sales Rep: _____

Tel: _____

Order Information
Teleordering: RLAS

All Dues Automatically Recorded
Representation Available

Personnel
Head of Company: Roger Lascelles (Publisher)
Head of Accounts: Tom Towler

Number of titles published annually: 20
Percentage of Export Sales: 20%
Number of Staff: 21
All New Titles are Bar Coded
WBIP Updating: Helen Cyster

Trade Terms
35%
General Net: Single copy 10%, two or more 20%, 3 or more 35%

Returns Procedures
Authority to Return: Must be authorised
Imperfect Returns: Return whole book

LATIN AMERICA BUREAU

1 Amwell Street, London EC1R 1UL
ISBN Prefix(es): 0 911213
Tel: 071-278 2829
Fax: 071-278 0165
VAT No: 404 6300 96

Orders to
CENTRAL BOOKS, 99 Wallis Road, London E9 5LN
Tel: 081-986 4854
Fax: 081-533 5821

Order Information

All Dues Automatically Recorded
Representation Available
Invoice Payments: Central Books

Personnel
Head of Sales (Home): Chris Lee
Head of Accounts: Liz Morrell

Number of titles published annually: 6
Percentage of Export Sales: 40%
Number of Staff: 5
All New Titles are Bar Coded
Book Data Subscriber
WBIP Updating: Chris Lee

Trade Terms
Enquiries to Central Books

Returns Procedures
Authority to Return: Central Books
Address for Returns: Central Books

LAVIS MARKETING

73 Lime Walk, Headington, Oxfordshire OX3 7AD
Tel: 0865 67575
Fax: 0865 750079
Telex: 83147 LAVMARK
VAT No: 348 7025 43

Account No: _____
Sales Rep: _____
Tel: _____

Order Information
Teleordering: LAVIS

Orders for more than one publisher can be bulked
All Dues Automatically Recorded
Representation Available

Personnel
Head of Company: Jim Lavis
Head of Accounts: Fay Lavis

IPG Member
WBIP Updating: Jim Lavis

Trade Terms
Single Copy 25%, Two Books or more 30%, Subscription/Stock orders 35% Special Orders 25%
Girobank Number: 442 4913
Credit Cards Accepted: Access/Master, Visa

Returns Procedures
Imperfect Returns: Title pages only on all titles

[handwritten: Law Book Co (Australia) 90 Hammicks]

LAWRENCE & WISHART
144A Old South Lambeth Road, London SW8 1XX
ISBN Prefix(es): 0 85315
Tel: 071-820 9281
Fax: 071-587 0469

Orders to
CENTRAL BOOKS, 99 Wallis Road, London E9 5LN
Tel: 081-986 4854
Fax: 081-533 5821

Order Information

All Dues Automatically Recorded
Representation Available
Invoice Payments: Central Books Ltd

Personnel
Head of Company: Sally Davison (Managing Director)
Head of Sales (Home): Lindsay Thomas
Head of Accounts: Vicky Grut

Number of titles published annually: 22
Number of Staff: 4
IPG Member
NBA Signatory
All New Titles are Bar Coded
Book Data Subscriber
WBIP Updating: Lindsay Thomas

Trade Terms
35%, 30 days, orders under £30 - 15% surcharge
BA/Girobank Small Order Scheme: Yes

Returns Procedures
Authority to Return: Central Books
Address for Returns: Central Books
Stock Returns: Request permission to return on all books
Imperfect Returns: Title page for £10 and under

[handwritten: Lea + Febiger = Waverley Europe Ltd]

R J LEACH & CO
38 Inglemere Road, Forest Hill, London SE23 2BE
Tel: 081-699 4946

LEADING EDGE PRESS & PUBLISHING LTD
Old Chapel Burtersett, Hawes, North Yorkshire DL8 3PB
ISBN Prefix(es): 0 948135
Tel: 0969 667566
Fax: 0969 667788
VAT No: 409 2691 45

Orders to
GRANTHAM BOOK SERVICES LTD, Isaac Newton Way,
Alma Park Industrial Estate, Grantham, Lincolnshire
NG31 9SD
Tel: 0476 67421
Fax: 0476 590223

Order Information

All Dues Automatically Recorded
Representation Available
Invoice Payments: Grantham
Representation:World Leisure Marketing

Number of titles published annually: 10
Number of Staff: 6
IPG Member
All New Titles are Bar Coded
Book Data Subscriber
WBIP Updating: Bridget Swann

Trade Terms
35%
Credit Cards Accepted: Access/Master, Visa

Returns Procedures
Authority to Return: World Leisure Marketing
Address for Returns: Grantham
Stock Returns: Refer to Distributor
Imperfect Returns: Return Book(s)

LEARNING DEVELOPMENT AIDS
Duke Street, Wisbech, Cambridgeshire PE13 2AE
ISBN Prefix(es): 0 905114, 1 85503
Tel: 0945 63441
Fax: 0945 587361
VAT No: 330 2206 22

Orders to
CHRIS LLOYD SALES AND MARKETING SERVICES,
463 Ashley Road, Parkstone, Poole, Dorset BH14 0AX
Tel: 0202 715349
Fax: 0202 736191

Order Information

All Dues Automatically Recorded
Representation Available
Invoice Payments: Chris Lloyd Sales & Marketing

Other Important Locations
Publicity Dept:Abbey Gate House, East Rd, Cambridge CB1 1DB
Tel: 0223 357744
Fax: 0223 460557

Personnel
Head of Company: Dennis Blackmore (Head of Publishing Division) Abbey Gate House
Head of Publicity: Amanda Clarke Abbey Gate House

IPG Member
All New Titles are Bar Coded
WBIP Updating: Chris Lloyd

Trade Terms
35%
Other Terms: £1 surcharge on invoices under £15

Returns Procedures
Authority to Return: Chris Lloyd Sales & Marketing
Address for Returns: Bailey Distribution Ltd
Imperfect Returns: Title pages up to £10 retail

LEARNING MATERIALS LTD

Dixon Street, Wolverhampton, West Midlands WV2 2BX
Tel: 0902 454026
Fax: 0902 457596
VAT No: 101 6814 10

Personnel
Head of Company: R H Mellor (Managing Director)
Head of Marketing: B Mitchel Hill

Number of Staff: 8

Trade Terms
Other Terms: Carriage charges on all orders

BILL LEESON

5 St Agnells Lane Cottages, Hemel Hempstead, Hertfordshire HP2 7HJ
ISBN Prefix(es): 0 095089, 1 870341
Tel: 0442 241051

Order Information

Order Dept Opening Times
Mon - Fri 9am - 12pm, 1pm - 5pm
All Dues Automatically Recorded

Number of titles published annually: 3
Number of Staff: 1

Trade Terms
33.3%, 30 days

Returns Procedures
Authority to Return: Only imperfect returns accepted

LEGAL ACTION GROUP

242 Pentonville Road, London N1 9UN
ISBN Prefix(es): 0 905099
Tel: 071-833 2931
Fax: 071-837 6094
VAT No: 480 8458 19

Order Information

Order Dept Opening Times
Mon - Fri 9.30am - 1pm, 2pm - 5pm
All Dues Automatically Recorded
Representation Available

Personnel
Head of Company: Roger Smith
Head of Sales (Home): Paul Crane
Head of Accounts: Stephen Davies
Head of Distribution: Maggie Warner

Number of titles published annually: 6
Number of Staff: 4
IPG Member
All New Titles are Bar Coded
Book Data Subscriber
WBIP Updating: James Lamb

Trade Terms
33.3% on all orders

Returns Procedures
Authority to Return: Stephen Davies

LEGALEASE

28-33 Cato Street, London W1H 5HS
ISBN Prefix(es): 1 870854

Tel: 071-396 9292
Fax: 071-396 9300
VAT No: 446 0273 63

Order Information

Order Dept Opening Times
Mon - Fri 9.30am - 5.30pm
All Dues Automatically Recorded

Personnel
Head of Company: John Pritchard (Managing Director)
Other Important Personnel:
Carol Barnes (Book Sales)

Number of titles published annually: 6
WBIP Updating: John Harris

Trade Terms
33% plus P&P

Returns Procedures
Authority to Return: Firm Sale Only

LEISHMAN & TAUSSIG: AFRICAN BOOKS
2B Westgate, Southwell, Nottinghamshire NG25 0JH
Tel: 0636 813774
Fax: 0636 813774

Account No: _____

Sales Rep: _____

Tel: _____

Order Information
Teleordering: LEITAU

Order Dept Opening Times
8.30am - 6.30pm (or Ansafone/Fax)
Orders for more than one publisher can be bulked
All Dues Automatically Recorded
Representation Available

Personnel
Head of Company: A D H Leishman (Proprietor)

Number of Staff: 4

Trade Terms
33.3% (35% if specified) no surcharges except single copy order postage to irregular customers
Girobank Number: 41 637 6606

Returns Procedures
Stock Returns: Request in advance (if overstocks) - return, if agreed, credit note issued
Imperfect Returns: Always return whole book

LENNARD ASSOCIATES LTD
Windmill Cottage, Mackerye End, Harpenden, Hertfordshire AL5 5DR
ISBN Prefix(es): 1 85291
Tel: 0582 715866
Fax: 0582 715121
VAT No: 540 2547 70

Orders to
CHRIS LLOYD SALES AND MARKETING SERVICES,
463 Ashley Road, Parkstone, Poole, Dorset BH14 0AX
Tel: 0202 715349
Fax: 0202 736191

Order Information

All Dues Automatically Recorded
Representation Available
Invoice Payments: Bailey Distribution

Personnel
Head of Company: Adrian Stephenson
Head of Accounts: Rosemary Stephenson

Number of titles published annually: 10
Number of Staff: 2
All New Titles are Bar Coded
WBIP Updating: Chris Lloyd

Trade Terms
See Chris Lloyd

Returns Procedures
Authority to Return: Chris Lloyd
Address for Returns: Bailey Distribution

CHARLES LETTS & CO LTD
Letts of London House, Parkgate Road, London SW11 4NQ
ISBN Prefix(es): 0 934672, 1 85238, 2 83150
Tel: 071-407 8891
Fax: 071-403 6729
Telex: 884498 LETTS G
VAT No: 235 5393 57

Account No: _____
Sales Rep: _____
Tel: _____

Orders to
Charles Letts, Thornybank Ind Estate, Dalkeith, Midlothian
EH22 2NE
Tel: 031-663 1971
Fax: 031-660 5435

Order Information
Teleordering: LETTS

All Dues Automatically Recorded
Representation Available

Personnel
Head of Company: Carole Saunders (Managing Director)
Head of Sales (Home): Murray Mahon (Sales & Marketing Director)
Head of Sales (Export): Nigel Browning
Head of Publicity: Gary Chapman (Publicity Manager)
Head of Accounts: Jacqui Pugh (Commercial Manager)
Other Important Personnel:
Jenny David (Marketing Manager - Berlitz), Colin Edwards (UK Sales Manager)

Number of titles published annually: 60
Percentage of Export Sales: 25%
Number of Staff: 25
PA Member
All New Titles are Bar Coded
Book Data Subscriber
WBIP Updating: Jacqui Pugh

Trade Terms
35% - 30 days

Returns Procedures
Authority to Return: Local Representative

[handwritten: Letts Educational, Aldine House, Aldine Place, LONDON, WC128AW, T. 0817437514, F 0817438451]

[handwritten: Lewis Publishers = Exel Logistics]

J D LEWIS & SONS LTD
Gomer Press, Wind Street, Llandysul, Dyfed SA44 4BQ
Tel: 0559 362371/2

Fax: 0559 363758
VAT No: 122 0971 04

JOHN LIBBEY & CO LTD

13 Smiths Yard, Summerley Street, London SW18 4HR
ISBN Prefix(es): 0 86196
Tel: 081-947 2777
Fax: 081-947 2664
Telex: 94013503 JOHN G
VAT No: 242 7479 48

Account No: _____

Sales Rep: _____

Tel: _____

Orders to
FABER BOOK SERVICES, 16 Burnt Mill, Elizabeth Way, Harlow, Essex CM20 2HX
Tel: 0279 417134
Fax: 0279 417366

Order Information

All Dues Automatically Recorded
Invoice Payments: Faber & Faber
Representation:Book Representation & Distribution (BRAD)

Personnel
Head of Company: Mr J Libbey
Head of Marketing: Mrs A Needs
Head of Accounts: Mrs A Needs

Number of titles published annually: 50
Percentage of Export Sales: 70%
Number of Staff: 20
Book Data Subscriber
WBIP Updating: Mrs A Needs

Trade Terms
25%
Other Terms: Trade Export 10% P&P
Credit Cards Accepted: Access/Master, Visa, Amex, Diners

Returns Procedures
Authority to Return: From Head Office
Address for Returns: Faber & Faber
Stock Returns: Authorisation for return first from Head Office

LIBER PRESS

4 Kirklea Farm, Badgworth, Axbridge, Somerset BS26 2QH
ISBN Prefix(es): 1 85734
Tel: 0934 733424
Tel: 0934 732150
Fax: 0934 733442
VAT No: 569 9318 79

Orders to
BOOKPOINT LIMITED, 39 Milton Park, Abingdon, Oxfordshire OX14 4TD
Tel: 0235 835001
Fax: 0235 861038

Order Information

All Dues Automatically Recorded
Representation Available
Invoice Payments: Bookpoint

Personnel
Head of Company: John Skinner (Chief Executive & Publisher)
Head of Customer Services: Judith Skinner 0823 400080

Number of titles published annually: 35
Percentage of Export Sales: 30%
Number of Staff: 6
PA Member
IPG Member
NBA Signatory
All New Titles are Bar Coded
WBIP Updating: Judith Skinner

Trade Terms
35% on all orders
General Net: 25% single copy, two or more 30%, Sub/stock orders 40%
Girobank Number: 702 11079
Credit Cards Accepted: Access/Master, Visa

Returns Procedures
Authority to Return: See Bookpoint

LIBERTARIAN ALLIANCE

25 Chapter Chambers, Esterbrooke Street, London SW1P 4NN
ISBN Prefix(es): 1 856370, 1 870614
Tel: 071-821 5502
Fax: 071-834 2031

Order Information

All Dues Automatically Recorded

Number of titles published annually: 50
WBIP Updating: Chris R Tame

Trade Terms
33.3% on all orders, no postage, no surcharge

[handwritten: Liberty Fund Inc - 8335 Allison Pointe Trail - Suite 300, Indianapolis: IN 46250-1687. USA FAX. 317-577-9067]

LIBRARY & INFORMATION STATISTICS UNIT

Loughborough University, Loughborough, Leicestershire LE11 3TU
ISBN Prefix(es): 0 94884
Tel: 0509 223071
Fax: 0509 223053

Order Information

Cyclical Ordering Policy

Personnel
Head of Company: John Sumison

Number of titles published annually: 8
WBIP Updating: Mary Ashworth

Trade Terms
Direct Sale

LIBRARY ASSOCIATION PUBLISHING LTD

7 Ridgmount Street, London WC1E 7AE
ISBN Prefix(es): 0 85157, 0 85365, 1 85604
Tel: 071-636 7543
Fax: 071-636 3627
Telex: 9312134504 LAG
VAT No: 354 3237 65

Orders to
BOOKPOINT LIMITED, 39 Milton Park, Abingdon, Oxfordshire OX14 4TD
Tel: 0235 835001
Fax: 0235 861038

Order Information

All Dues Automatically Recorded
Representation Available
Invoice Payments: Bookpoint Ltd

Personnel
Head of Company: Gill Davies (Managing Director)
Head of Sales (Home): Ray Attwood (Sales Director)
Head of Publicity: Heather Leary (Promotions Executive)
Head of Accounts: Martin Wright (Financial Director)
Head of Customer Services: Rohini Ranachandran

Number of titles published annually: 30
Percentage of Export Sales: 50%
Number of Staff: 6
PA Member
NBA Signatory
Book Data Subscriber
WBIP Updating: Heather Leary

Trade Terms
20%

Returns Procedures
Authority to Return: Permission reuired from publisher
Address for Returns: Bookpoint Ltd
Stock Returns: See Bookpoint

LIFE EDUCATION CENTRES UK FOUNDATION

115-123 Bayham Street, Camden Town, London NW1 0AG
ISBN Prefix(es): 1 874277
Tel: 071-267 2516
Tel: 071-911 0458
Tel: 071-911 0460
Fax: 071-267 2044

Orders to
Vince Hatton, PO Box 137, London N10 3JJ
Tel: 071-267 2516 (24 Hr)
Fax: 071-267 2044

Order Information

Order Dept Opening Times
Mon - Fri 9am - 5pm
All Dues Automatically Recorded

Personnel
Head of Company: Jill Pearman
Head of Sales (Home): Vince Hatton

Number of titles published annually: 5
Number of Staff: 2
IPG Member
All New Titles are Bar Coded
WBIP Updating: Vince Hatton

Trade Terms
33%
Credit Cards Accepted: Access/Master, Visa, Amex

LIFESPACE PUBLISHING

The Old School House, Kingston on Soar, Nottingham, Nottinghamshire NG11 0DE
ISBN Prefix(es): 1 870244
Tel: 0509 673569
Fax: 0509 673569

Personnel
Head of Company: I Stewart
Head of Distribution: K Norman

Number of titles published annually: 1
Number of Staff: 2

All New Titles are Bar Coded
WRIP Updating: I Stewart

Trade Terms
Single 10% proforma only, 2-9 10% 30 days, 10+ 35% 30 days

Returns Procedures
Stock Returns: Return books in orig cond for refund (incorrectly supplied) Return book in damaged cond not front page for refund
Imperfect Returns: Return title page for refund of cost.

FRANCES LINCOLN PUBLISHERS LTD

Apollo Works, 5 Charlton Kings Road, London NW5 2SB
Tel: 071-482 3302
Fax: 071-485 0490

Orders to
HODDER & STOUGHTON LTD, Mill Road, Dunton Green, Sevenoaks, Kent TN13 2YA
Tel: 0732 450111
Fax: 0732 460134

Personnel
Head of Company: Frances Lincoln (Managing Director)
Head of Sales (Home): Paula Saunders (Sales & Marketing Director)
Head of Sales (Export): Charlotte Francis (US Sales Manager)
Head of Accounts: Sara Borthwick (Business Manager)
Other Important Personnel:
Dorine Louwerens (Translation Rights Manager)

Number of Staff: 31
Book Data Subscriber

<ins>LINCOLN INST OF LAND POLICY, 113 BRATTLE ST, CAMBRIDGE, MA 02138-3400, USA</ins>

LINEWRIGHTS LTD <ins>FAX 617-661-7235</ins>

PO Box 832, Ongar, Essex CM5 0NH
ISBN Prefix(es): 0 946958
VAT No: 370 2794 48

Personnel
Head of Company: R D Chesneau

Number of titles published annually: 4
Percentage of Export Sales: 25%
All New Titles are Bar Coded

Trade Terms
35% but 25% on orders £10 and below carriage free (UK only) Discounts on bulk orders are negotiable

Returns Procedures
Stock Returns: No returns from stock accepted except by prior written arrangement.
Imperfect Returns: Return title page & proof of damage

LION PUBLISHING PLC

Peter's Law, Sandy Lane West, Oxford, Oxfordshire OX4 5HG
ISBN Prefix(es): 0 7459, 0 85648
Tel: 0865 747550
Fax: 0865 747568
Telex: 837161 LION G
VAT No: 285 2317 53

Account No: <ins>32403</ins>
Sales Rep: _____
Tel: _____

Order Information

Order Dept Opening Times
Mon - Fri 9am - 5pm
All Dues Automatically Recorded
Representation Available

Personnel

Head of Company: David Alexander (Chairman)
Head of Sales (Home): Colin Nutt
Head of Sales (Export): Peter Young
Head of Marketing: Philip Henderson
Head of Accounts: Diana Leyland
Head of Distribution: Bill Reynolds

Number of titles published annually: 80
Percentage of Export Sales: 60%
Number of Staff: 67
PA Member
NBA Signatory
All New Titles are Bar Coded
Book Data Subscriber
WBIP Updating: Leanne Little

Trade Terms

35%. Bonus discount: Lion Stockist Scheme. Details from Area Managers.
Non-Net: 17.5-35%
Other Terms: £2 on orders with retail value of less than £25.
Carriage charges on export orders
Girobank Number: 309 9458

Returns Procedures

Authority to Return: Paul Knight
Address for Returns: Lion Publishing Warehouse, 2-5 Ashville Way, Cowley, Oxford OX4 5TU
Stock Returns: Authorization is required for all returns, irrespective of reason. Full details available on application.
Imperfect Returns: Title pages may be returned with cover price up to £20. Above £20 book needs to be returned.

[Handwritten: Lippincott = Plymbridge]

LISTER ART BOOKS (OF SOUTHPORT)

22 Station Road, Banks, Nr Southport, Lancashire PR9 8BB
Tel: 0704 232033 24 Hours
Fax: 0704 505926
VAT No: 483 6290 23

Order Information

Order Dept Opening Times
Mon - Sat 9am - 5pm
Orders for more than one publisher can be bulked
Representation Available

Personnel

Head of Company: Graham Lister
Head of Sales (Home): Joanne Proctor
Head of Marketing: James Lister
Head of Customer Services: Karen Stevenson

All New Titles are Bar Coded
WBIP Updating: Graham Lister

Trade Terms

30 - 33.3 - 35% varies with imprint, 2 or more titles
Minimum Order: £25
Credit Cards Accepted: Access/Master, Visa

Returns Procedures

Stock Returns: No unauthorised returns. Copy authorization note with goods to be returned.
Imperfect Returns: No authorisation required for faulty or damaged goods. Whole book to be returned.

LITTLE BROWN & CO LTD

165 Great Dover Street, London SE1 4YA
Tel: 071-334 4800
Fax: 071-334 4905
Fax: 071-334 4906
Fax: 071-334 4861 Export
Telex: 885233 LB G
VAT No: 512 5549 60

Account No: _____

Sales Rep: _____

Tel: _____

Orders to
TIPTREE BOOK SERVICES LTD, Church Road, Tiptree, Colchester, Essex CO5 0SR
Tel: 0621 819600
Fax: 0621 819011

Order Information

All Dues Automatically Recorded
Representation Available
Invoice Payments: Tiptree

Personnel
Head of Company: Philippa Harrison (Managing Director)
Head of Sales (Home): David Kent (Home Sales Director)
Head of Sales (Export): Charlie Viney (Export Sales Director)
Head of Marketing: Jane Warren
Head of Publicity: Rosalie McFarlane
Head of Accounts: David Owen
Head of Customer Services: Kathy Law
Other Important Personnel:
John O'Connor (Group Sales & Marketing Director), Don Hughes (Home Sales Manager), Christina McPhail (Asia Sales Manager)

Number of titles published annually: 400
Percentage of Export Sales: 40%
Number of Staff: 85
NBA Signatory
All New Titles are Bar Coded
Book Data Subscriber
WBIP Updating: Liz Mammett

Parent Company: Little Brown Inc

Trade Terms
35%
Credit Cards Accepted: Access/Master, Visa, Diners, Other

Returns Procedures
Authority to Return: Requests must be made to Representative or Head Office
Address for Returns: Tiptree Book Services
Imperfect Returns: Title page/annotation to Tiptree

LITTLE RED WITCH BOOK DISTRIBUTION COMPANY

24 Queens Square, North Curry, Taunton, Somerset TA3 6LE
Tel: 0823 490080
Tel: 0823 490469
Fax: 0823-490281
VAT No: 453 7482 30

Order Information

All Dues Automatically Recorded
Representation Available

Personnel
Head of Company: Tony Williams

Head of Sales (Home): Keith Rye
Head of Publicity: Greg Tesser

Number of titles published annually: 11
Number of Staff: 8
All New Titles are Bar Coded
WBIP Updating: K Rye

Trade Terms
35% No surcharges, Single book 25%
Credit Cards Accepted: Access/Master, Visa

Returns Procedures
Stock Returns: Written agreement to be received before return
Imperfect Returns: Agreement needed before return

LITTLEHAMPTON BOOK SERVICES   *was Gollancz*

14 Eldon Way, Lineside Ind Estate, Littlehampton, West Sussex BN17 7HE
Tel: 0903 721596 General
Tel: 0903 726410 Trade – *orders*
Tel: 0903 722756 Cred.Cont.
Fax: 0903 730914
Telex: 877398 GSBOOKG
VAT No: 241 3415 03

Account No: _____ 642701
Sales Rep: _____
Tel: _____

Order Information
Teleordering: GOLL

Orders for more than one publisher can be bulked

Personnel
Head of Company: Mr Ian D Smith (Managing Director)
Head of Distribution: Mr Richard Fernley (Distribution Director)
Other Important Personnel:
Mr Terry Giles (Trade Director), Mrs Rose Mellish (Trade Manager), Mrs Mary Phillips (Credit Manager), Mr Tim Lane (Warehouse Manager)

Number of Staff: 70
PA Member

Parent Company: Houghton Mifflin

Trade Terms
Girobank Number: 516 6152
Credit Cards Accepted: Access/Master, Visa

Returns Procedures
Authority to Return: Apply to publishers direct

LITTLEWOOD ARC

Nanholme Centre, Shaw Wood Road, Todmorden, Lancashire OL14 6DA
Tel: 0706 812338
Fax: 0706 818948

Orders to
PASSWORD (BOOKS) LTD, 23 New Mount Street, Manchester, Greater Manchester M4 4DE
Tel: 061-953 4009
Fax: 061-953 4001

Order Information

Order Dept Opening Times
Mon - Fri 9am - 5pm

All Dues Automatically Recorded
Representation Available

Personnel
Head of Company: R Jones/T Ward/A Jarman (Partners)
Other Important Personnel:
M Hulse/D Morley (Associate Editors)

Number of titles published annually: 11
Number of Staff: 2
All New Titles are Bar Coded
WBIP Updating: Rosemary Jones

Trade Terms
35% no surcharges
Other Terms: Small order surcharge - see Password
Girobank Number: 6134599

Returns Procedures
Authority to Return: Password Representative
Address for Returns: Clipper Distribution Service

LITTMAN LIBRARY OF JEWISH CIVILIZATION

64 Great Clarendon Street, Oxford, Oxfordshire OX2 6AX
Tel: 0865 311749 Editorial
Tel: 0865 722964 Marketing
Fax: 0865 311949 Editorial
Fax: 0865 722964 Marketing

Orders to
BURSTON DISTRIBUTION SERVICES, Unit 2A,
Newbridge Trading Est, Newbridge Close, Off Whitby Rd,
Bristol, Avon BS4 4AX
Tel: 0272 724248
Fax: 0272 711056

Personnel
Head of Company: Colette Littman
Head of Marketing: Ludo Craddock
Other Important Personnel:
Connie Wilsack (Head of Editorial)

Number of titles published annually: 4
All New Titles are Bar Coded
Book Data Subscriber
WBIP Updating: Ludo Craddock

Trade Terms
Details on application
Credit Cards Accepted: Access/Master, Visa

Returns Procedures
Authority to Return: Ludo Craddock
Address for Returns: Burston Distribution Services
Imperfect Returns: Return complete book

LIVERPOOL UNIVERSITY PRESS

PO Box 147, Liverpool, Merseyside L69 3BX
ISBN Prefix(es): 0 85323
Tel: 051-794 2231-2237
Fax: 051-708 6502
Telex: 627095 UNILPL G
VAT No: 165 1927 53

Orders to
BURSTON DISTRIBUTION SERVICES, Unit 2A,
Newbridge Trading Est, Newbridge Close, Off Whitby Rd,
Bristol, Avon BS4 4AX
Tel: 0272 724248
Fax: 0272 711056

Order Information

All Dues Automatically Recorded
Representation Available
Invoice Payments: Burston Distribution Services

Personnel
Head of Company: Mr Robin Bloxsidge

Number of titles published annually: 18
Percentage of Export Sales: 50%
Number of Staff: 4
PA Member
NBA Signatory
All New Titles are Bar Coded
Book Data Subscriber
WBIP Updating: Sandra Burns/Robin Bloxsidge

Trade Terms
Single Copy 25%, Multiple Copies 30%, Export 30% (ELBS 45%) Special Terms Negotiable
Credit Cards Accepted: Access/Master, Visa

Returns Procedures
Authority to Return: Prior permission must be obtained from Liverpool University Press or Burston
Address for Returns: Burston Distribution Services

LLANERCH (PUBLISHERS)

Felinfach, Lampeter, Dyfed SA48 8PJ
ISBN Prefix(es): 0 947992
Tel: 0570 470567
VAT No: 366 6899 82

Order Information

All Dues Automatically Recorded

Personnel
Head of Company: Dr D Bryce

Number of titles published annually: 22

Trade Terms
1 book 30%, 2 or more 35%, 10 or more 40%, no surcharges & no postage within the UK

P M LLEWELLYN (TRADING) COMPANY

27 Edison Road, Rabans Lane, Aylesbury, Buckinghamshire HP19 3TE
ISBN Prefix(es): 0 9509541
Tel: 0296 433379 24 Hours
Fax: 0296 398522
VAT No: 349 0656 37

Account No:	
Sales Rep:	
Tel:	

Order Information
Teleordering: PML

Order Dept Opening Times
Mon - Fri 10am - 5pm
Orders for more than one publisher can be bulked
Representation Available

Personnel
Head of Company: P M & K E Llewellyn

Trade Terms
33.3% to a min invoice value of £30 (25% cassettes), 25% below £30 (20% cassettes), single copies 20%
Other Terms: Books and tapes supplied on firm sale only and remain the property of P M Llewellyn until paid for in full

Returns Procedures
Authority to Return: Prior permission required within 14 days of delivery, Invoice queries must be notified within 30 days of inv date

CHRIS LLOYD SALES AND MARKETING SERVICES
463 Ashley Road, Parkstone, Poole, Dorset BH14 0AX
Tel: 0202 715349 24 Hours
Fax: 0202 736191
VAT No: 423 8720 56

Account No: _____

Sales Rep: _____

Tel: _____

Order Information
Teleordering: LLOYD

Order Dept Opening Times
Mon - Fri 9am - 5.30pm, Sat 9am - 12pm
All Dues Automatically Recorded
Representation Available

Personnel
Head of Company: Chris Lloyd

Number of titles published annually: 100
Percentage of Export Sales: 25%
IPG Member
All New Titles are Bar Coded
Book Data Subscriber

Trade Terms
35%
Other Terms: Orders under £15 net surcharged.

Returns Procedures
Address for Returns: Bailey Distribution Ltd (New Romney)
Imperfect Returns: Title pages up to £10 retail

LLOYD'S OF LONDON PRESS LTD
Sheepen Place, Colchester, Essex CO3 3LP
ISBN Prefix(es): 0 907432, 1 85044
Tel: 0206 772277
Tel: 0206 772113/4 Orders
Fax: 0206 772880
Fax: 0206 772118 Orders
Telex: 987321 (LLOYDS G)
VAT No: 472 8119 36

Account No: _____

Sales Rep: _____

Tel: _____

Order Information

Order Dept Opening Times
Mon - Fri 9am - 5pm
All Dues Automatically Recorded
Representation Available

Personnel
Head of Company: Ian Lindsay-Smith
Head of Marketing: James Smith
Head of Accounts: Richard Lawson

Number of titles published annually: 40
NBA Signatory
Book Data Subscriber
WBIP Updating: June Nash

Trade Terms
General Net: Single copy 25%, two books plus 35%, Subscription orders 10%
Credit Cards Accepted: Access/Master, Visa, Amex, Diners

Returns Procedures
Stock Returns: Returns requests first to James Smith

LOCHEE PUBLICATIONS LTD

Oak Villa, New Alyth, Blairgowrie, Perthshire PH11 8NN
ISBN Prefix(es): 0 947584, 1 870139
Tel: 082 83 2154
Fax: 082 83 3308
VAT No: 398 1212 39

Order Information

Order Dept Opening Times
Mon - Fri 9am - 12pm, 2 - 5pm
All Dues Automatically Recorded

Personnel
Head of Company: Professor Rex W Last (Managing Director)
Head of Sales (Home): Mrs O S Last

Number of Staff: 2
NBA Signatory
WBIP Updating: Mrs O S Last

Trade Terms
30% (1-5), 35% (6-20), 40% (21+)
Other Terms: Carriage charged

LOGASTON PRESS

Little Logaston, Woonton, Almeley, Herefordshire HR3 6QH
Tel: 0544 327344
VAT No: 359 1426 42

IPG Member

LONDON & SE REGION ADVISORY COUNCIL FOR EDUCATION & TRAINING

232 Vauxhall Bridge Road, London SW1V 1AU
Tel: 071-233 6191
Fax: 071-233 6121

LONDON LIMITED EDITIONS

31 Long Acre, Covent Gardens, London WC2E 9LT
Tel: 071-836 0723
Fax: 071-497 9058
VAT No: 239 5177 39

Personnel
Head of Company: George Lawson
Head of Sales (Home): Mrs Penny Swannell
Head of Marketing: Alec Morrison

Number of titles published annually: 10

Trade Terms
20%
Credit Cards Accepted: Access/Master, Visa

LONDON SCHOOL OF ECONOMICS AND POLITICAL SCIENCE
Houghton Street, Aldwych, London WC2A 2AE
Tel: 071-405 7686
Fax: 071-242 0392

LONDON STAMP EXCHANGE LTD
5 Buckingham Street, Strand, London WC2N 6BS
Tel: 071-839 4684
Fax: 071-839 3478

LONDON TOPOGRAPHICAL SOCIETY
Bishopsgate Institute, 230 Bishopsgate, London EC2M 4QH
Tel: 071-247 6844

Order Information

Order Dept Opening Times
Mon - Fri 9.30am - 5.30pm

Number of titles published annually: 2
WBIP Updating: Simon Morris

Trade Terms
25% plus postage & packing

LONDON TRANSPORT
55 Broadway, London SW1H 0BD
Tel: 071-222 5600
Fax: 071-222 5719
Telex: 893633 LRT BDY
VAT No: 238 7244 46

LONELY PLANET PUBLICATIONS PTY LTD
Devonshire House, 12 Barley Mow Pssge, Chiswick, London W4 4PH
ISBN Prefix(es): 0 86442, 0 908086
Tel: 081-742 3161
Fax: 081-742 3161

Orders to
GRANTHAM BOOK SERVICES LTD, Isaac Newton Way, Alma Park Industrial Estate, Grantham, Lincolnshire NG31 9SD
Tel: 0476 67421
Fax: 0476 590223

Order Information

All Dues Automatically Recorded
Representation Available
Representation: World Leisure Marketing

Personnel
Head of Company: Charlotte Hindle

Number of titles published annually: 25
Percentage of Export Sales: 75%
Number of Staff: 4
All New Titles are Bar Coded
WBIP Updating: Charlotte Hindle

Parent Company: Lonely Plant Pub Pty Ltd (Australia)

Trade Terms
Refer to Grantham Book Services

THE BARRY LONG FOUNDATION

Whistlands, Langley Marsh, Wiveliscombe, Taunton, Somerset TA4 2UJ
ISBN Prefix(es): 0 9508050
Tel: 0984 23426 24 Hours
Fax: 0984 24446
VAT No: 396 5318 15

Personnel
Head of Company: Clive Tempest
Head of Sales (Home): Howard Lidiard
Head of Marketing: Paul Crosse
Head of Accounts: Diana Tempest

Number of titles published annually: 3
Number of Staff: 4
IPG Member
All New Titles are Bar Coded
WBIP Updating: Clive Tempest

Trade Terms
35%
Other Terms: Carriage charges for overseas
Girobank Number: 330 0757
Credit Cards Accepted: Access/Master, Visa

Returns Procedures
Stock Returns: By prior agreement
Imperfect Returns: All returns to be full bound copies

LONGMAN GROUP UK LTD

Fourth Avenue, Pinnacles, Harlow, Essex CM19 5AA
ISBN Prefix(es): 0 05, 0 582
Tel: 0279 429655
Tel: 0279 623928
Fax: 0279 431067
Telex: 817484
Cables: Longman, Harlow
VAT No: 213 6785 61
Account No: _____ 01752626 _____
Sales Rep: _____
Tel: _____

Orders to
Longman Group UK Ltd, PO Box 88, Fourth Avenue, Harlow, Essex CM19 5AA
Tel: 0279 623928/623923
Fax: 0279 414130
24 Hour Ansafone Number: 0279 623658

Order Information
Teleordering: LONG

Order Dept Opening Times
Mon - Fri 8.15am - 5.30pm
All Dues Automatically Recorded
Representation Available

Other Important Locations
Longman House, Burnt Mill, Harlow, Essex CM20 2JE
Tel: 0279 426721
Fax: 0279 431059
Longman Industry & Public Service Management, Westgate House The High, Harlow, Essex CM20 1YR Tel:0279 442601 Fax:444501

Personnel
Head of Company: Paul Kahn (Chairman & Chief Executive)
Head of Sales (Home): Terry Shaughnessy (UK Sales - Longman Higher Education)
Head of Sales (Export): Bob Stock Export Sales - Longman Higher Education

Head of Marketing: Lesley Wilson Marketing - Longman Higher Education
Head of Publicity: Caroline Maskell (PR & Corporate Communications Manager)
Head of Distribution: David Pemberton (Director, Longman Distribution)
Head of Customer Services: Elizabeth H Shearn (Director, Customer Services)
Other Important Personnel:
Michael Wymer (Operations Director), Patrick Mahony Export Sales & Marketing - Longman International Education, Roger Cauthery UK & Export Sales - Longman ELT, Shirley Greenall Marketing - Longman ELT, Sheila Devereux UK Sales - Longman Industry & Public Service Management, Iain Pulley Marketing - Longman Industry & Public Service Management, Julian Emslie UK Sales - Longman Education, David Barnes Export Sales - Longman Education, Paul Uttley Marketing - Longman Education

Number of titles published annually: 1300
Percentage of Export Sales: 60%
Number of Staff: 1200
PA Member
NBA Signatory
All New Titles are Bar Coded
Book Data Subscriber
WBIP Updating: Irene Duffy

Parent Company: Pearson
Subsidiary Companies: Cartermill Ltd, Logotron Ltd

Trade Terms
Variable according to category
Other Terms: Carriage charge of 5% if publisher is asked to supply the booksellers customer direct. No liability loss in transit.
Girobank Number: 315 0259
Credit Cards Accepted: Access/Master, Amex, Diners, Diners

Returns Procedures
Authority to Return: Prior authorisation required from Rep, Senior Member of Sales Dept or by contacting Customer Services
Address for Returns: Returns Department
Imperfect Returns: Price limit for title page £20. All imperfect returns (books or title page) must state nature of imperfection.

LONGMAN LAW TAX & FINANCE

21-27 Lamb's Conduit Street, London WC1N 3NJ
ISBN Prefix(es): 0 582, 0 8512
Tel: 071-242 2548
Fax: 071-831 8119

Account No: _____
Sales Rep: _____
Tel: _____

Orders to
LONGMAN GROUP UK LTD, Fourth Avenue, Pinnacles, Harlow, Essex CM19 5AA
Tel: 0279 429655
Fax: 0279 431067

Order Information

All Dues Automatically Recorded
Representation Available

Other Important Locations
Showroom:5 Bentinck Street, London W1M 5RN
Tel: 071-935 0121

Personnel
Head of Marketing: Mike Smith

Number of titles published annually: 60
All New Titles are Bar Coded
Book Data Subscriber
WBIP Updating: Laura Goodwin-Harlow

Parent Company: Longman Group UK Ltd

Trade Terms
25%
General Net: 25%, Subscription Orders 20%
Academic Net: 25%, Subscription Orders 20%
Non-Net: 30%, Subscription Orders 20%
Credit Cards Accepted: Access/Master, Visa, Amex, Diners

Returns Procedures
Authority to Return: Caroline Bull, London
Address for Returns: Pinnacles
Stock Returns: Return to the Returns Dept stating the reason
Imperfect Returns: Title page only stating the reason

[Handwritten note: Louisiana State U.P. ℅ AUP Group, 1 Gower St, LONDON. WC1E]

LOW PAY UNIT

27-29 Amwell Street, London EC1R 1UN
Tel: 071-713 7616
Fax: 071-713 7581

LOXWOOD STONELEIGH

11 Colston Yard, Colston Street, Bristol, Avon BS1 5BD
Tel: 0272 225719

Orders to
TURNAROUND, 27 Horsell Road, London N5 1XL
Tel: 071-609 7836/7
Fax: 071-700 1205

LUATH PRESS LTD

Forest Bank, Barr, Ayrshire KA26 9TN
ISBN Prefix(es): 0 946487
Tel: 046 586636 24 Hours
VAT No: 366 7569 01

Order Information

Order Dept Opening Times
Mon - Sat 9am - 5pm
All Dues Automatically Recorded
Representation Available

Personnel
Head of Company: T W Atkisnon
Head of Sales (Home): R A Atkinson

Number of titles published annually: 6
Number of Staff: 4
All New Titles are Bar Coded
WBIP Updating: T W Atkinson

Trade Terms
33.3%, no surcharges
Other Terms: Orders over £10 carriage free

Returns Procedures
Imperfect Returns: Return title page in all cases

LUCIS PRESS LTD

Suite 54, 3 Whitehall Court, London SW1A 2EF
Tel: 071-839 4512
Fax: 071-839 5575
VAT No: 229 7417 42

Order Information

Order Dept Opening Times
Mon - Fri 9am - 5pm
All Dues Automatically Recorded

Personnel

Head of Company: Simon Marlow (Managing Director)
Head of Accounts: Mrs Joan Gifford

Number of titles published annually: 3
Number of Staff: 3
IPG Member
All New Titles are Bar Coded

Trade Terms

1-2 books 25%, 3-19 books 35%, 20+ books 40%

Returns Procedures

Authority to Return: Prior permission required

LUND HUMPHRIES PUBLISHERS LTD

Park House, 1 Russell Gardens, London NW11 9NN
ISBN Prefix(es): 0 85331
Tel: 081-458 6314 24 Hours
Fax: 081-905 5245
VAT No: 429 7964 94

Order Information

All Dues Automatically Recorded
Representation Available
Invoice Payments: Bookpoint Ltd

Personnel

Head of Company: Lionel Leventhal
Head of Sales (Home): David Farnsworth

Number of titles published annually: 20
All New Titles are Bar Coded
WBIP Updating: Antonia Sharpe

Trade Terms

Single copy/2 or more single titles 20%, 2 books + 35%

Returns Procedures

Address for Returns: Bookpoint Ltd

THE LUTTERWORTH PRESS

PO Box 60, Cambridge, Cambridgeshire CB1 2NT
ISBN Prefix(es): 0 7188, 0 7444
Tel: 0223 350865
Fax: 0223 66951
VAT No: 213 3349 96

Account No: _____
Sales Rep: _____
Tel: _____

Order Information

Teleordering: CLAJAS

All Dues Automatically Recorded
Representation Available
Invoice Payments: James Clarke & Co Ltd, PO Box 60, Cambridge CB1 2NT
Representation:H I Marketing

Personnel
Head of Company: Adrian Brink
Head of Sales (Home): Patricia Shelton
Head of Publicity: Emma Rintoul
Head of Accounts: David Baker
Head of Customer Services: Mike Kimberley

Number of titles published annually: 25
PA Member
IPG Member
NBA Signatory
All New Titles are Bar Coded
Book Data Subscriber
WBIP Updating: Emma Rintoul

Parent Company: James Clarke & Co

Trade Terms
35%, Single Copy 25%
Non-Net: 17.5%
Minimum Order: £10 invoice value
Other Terms: Small Order surcharge £3 - £30 invoice value (£1 only cwo) Carriage charges on exports only
Girobank Number: 20 898 1608

Returns Procedures
Stock Returns: Sold on firm basis only. Unauthorised returns sent back. Authorisation automatic for publishers errors(within a week)
Imperfect Returns: Return title page marked to show imperfection

LYLE PUBLICATIONS
Glenmayne, Galashiels TD1 3NR
ISBN Prefix(es): 0 86248
Tel: 0896 2005
Tel: 0896 4125
Fax: 0896 4696
VAT No: 193 1354 65

Order Information

Order Dept Opening Times
Mon - Fri 9am - 5pm
Representation Available

Personnel
Head of Company: Tony Curtis
Head of Sales (Home): John Masters
Head of Marketing: Annette Curtis
Head of Publicity: Eelin McIvor
Head of Accounts: Donna Rutherford
Head of Distribution: James Brown
Head of Customer Services: Jacqueline Leddy

Number of titles published annually: 5
PA Member
NBA Signatory
All New Titles are Bar Coded
Book Data Subscriber
WBIP Updating: Tony Curtis

Trade Terms
35%
Credit Cards Accepted: Access/Master, Amex, Diners, Other

Returns Procedures
Stock Returns: Overstocks need authorisation Damaged books no authorisation required
Imperfect Returns: Return title page

STANLEY LYONS

4 The Rise, Shipton Oliffe, Cheltenham, Gloucestershire GL54 4JQ
Tel: 0242 820023
Fax: 0242 820022

Orders to
JOHN DAWES PUBLICATIONS, 12 Mercers, Hawkhurst, Kent TN18 4LH
Tel: 0580 753346

THOMAS LYSTER LTD

Unit 9, Ormskirk Ind Park, Old Boundary Way, Burscough Rd, Ormskirk, Lancashire L39 2YW
Tel: 0695 575112
Fax: 0695 570120
VAT No: 482 7026 41

Account No: _____
Sales Rep: _____
Tel: _____

IPG Member

M & J PUBLICATIONS

The Hollies, Cattlegate Road, Crews Hill, Enfield, Middlesex EN7 9DW
ISBN Prefix(es): 0 9509748
Tel: 0992 461895
Fax: 0992 451482

Orders to
CHRIS LLOYD SALES AND MARKETING SERVICES, 463 Ashley Road, Parkstone, Poole, Dorset BH14 0AX
Tel: 0202 715349
Fax: 0202 736191

Order Information

Invoice Payments: Chris Lloyd

Personnel
Head of Company: John Clowes

All New Titles are Bar Coded
Book Data Subscriber

Returns Procedures
Authority to Return: Chris Lloyd
Address for Returns: Chris Lloyd

M & M PUBLISHING LTD

Tryfan House, Warwick Drive, Hale, Altrincham, Cheshire WA15 9EA
Tel: 061-926 9963
Fax: 061-926 9965
VAT No: 527 0166 64

B MCCALL BARBOUR

28 George IV Bridge, Edinburgh, Lothian EH1 1ES
ISBN Prefix(es): 0 7132
Tel: 031-225 4816
Fax: 031-225 4816
Cables: 031-225 4816
VAT No: 268 6632 21

Order Information

Order Dept Opening Times
Mon - Fri 9am-1pm & 2.15pm-5.30pm, Sat 9am-1pm
Orders for more than one publisher can be bulked
All Dues Automatically Recorded
Representation Available

Personnel
Head of Company: Dr T C Danson Smith
Head of Accounts: Miss G A Danson-Smith

Number of titles published annually: 1
WBIP Updating: Dr T C Danson-Smith

Trade Terms
33.3% (25% on singles)
Other Terms: Small order surcharges - postage only

Returns Procedures
Stock Returns: Faulty books only accepted, phone for instructions
Imperfect Returns: Return complete books

MCCARTA LTD

15 Highbury Place, London N5 1QP
ISBN Prefix(es): 1 85365
Tel: 071-354 1616
Fax: 071-354 9905

Orders to
GRANTHAM BOOK SERVICES LTD, Isaac Newton Way, Alma Park Industrial Estate, Grantham, Lincolnshire NG31 9SD
Tel: 0476 67421
Fax: 0476 590223

Order Information
Teleordering: RMC

All Dues Automatically Recorded
Representation Available
Invoice Payments: Grantham Book Services
Representation: World Leisure Marketing

Personnel
Head of Company: Joost Bloemsma
Head of Sales (Home): Anna Perring

Number of titles published annually: 20
Number of Staff: 4
All New Titles are Bar Coded
WBIP Updating: Jan Choudhury

Parent Company: HET Spectrum/Nelles Verlag

Trade Terms
35% Distributors terms apply

Returns Procedures
Authority to Return: McCarta
Address for Returns: Grantham

MCCRIMMON PUBLISHING COMPANY LIMITED

10-12 High Street, Great Wakering, Essex SS3 0EQ
ISBN Prefix(es): 0 85597
Tel: 0702 218956
Tel: 0702 218906
Fax: 0702 216082
VAT No: 250 4975 56

Order Information

Order Dept Opening Times
Mon - Thur 9am - 5pm, Fri 9am - 3.45pm
Cyclical Ordering Policy

All Dues Automatically Recorded
Representation Available

Personnel
Head of Company: Mrs Joan McCrimmon (Managing Director)
Head of Sales (Home): Don McCrimmon
Head of Marketing: Michael Shaw
Head of Accounts: Miss V Rudge

Number of titles published annually: 20
Percentage of Export Sales: 20%
Number of Staff: 10
All New Titles are Bar Coded
WBIP Updating: David Rooke

Trade Terms
10-35%
Non-Net: Single copy/sing;e line 25%, 2 or more single titles up to £10 - 25%
Other Terms: Under £10 £1.50 surcharge
BA/Girobank Small Order Scheme: Yes
Credit Cards Accepted: Access/Master, Visa

Returns Procedures
Stock Returns: Prior notice required and return postage label supplied

McGraw-Hill Medical + Healthcare % Marston

MCGRAW HILL BOOK COMPANY EUROPE
McGraw Hill House, Shoppenhangers Road, Maidenhead, Berkshire SL6 2QL
ISBN Prefix(es): 0 023, 0 024, 0 026, 0 029, 0 070, 0 071, 0 074, 0 075, 0 077, 0 078, 0 079, 0 080, 0 830, 0 875, 0 962, 1 556, 3 890
Tel: 0628 23431/2
Fax: 0628 770224 Sales/Mark
Fax: 0628 35895 Cust Serv
Fax: 0628 777342 Export
Telex: 848484
VAT No: 208 0341 07
Account No: _____ 01906101 _____

Customer Service 01628 502509

Sales Rep: _____
Tel: _____

Orders to
24 Hour Ansafone Number: 0628 28134

Order Information
Teleordering: MCGR

Order Dept Opening Times
Mon - Fri 9am - 5pm
All Dues Automatically Recorded
Representation Available
Credit Control
Fax: 0628 777891

Personnel
Head of Company: Steve White (Managing Director)
Head of Sales (Home): Carolyn Brice (European Sales & Marketing Director)
Head of Sales (Export): Andrew Phillips (Sales & Marketing Director (Middle East/Africa/E Europe))
Head of Accounts: Peter Kitley (Financial Controller)
Head of Distribution: Dan Jennings (Operations & Administration Director)
Head of Customer Services: Ann Moore (European Customer Services Manager)
Other Important Personnel:
Hans David (Director Medical Publishing)

Number of titles published annually: 800
Percentage of Export Sales: 50%

Number of Staff: 120
PA Member
NBA Signatory
All New Titles are Bar Coded
Open University Publications
Book Data Subscriber
WBIP Updating: Pam Roberts

Parent Company: McGraw Hill Inc
Subsidiary Companies: Makron Books Ltd (BZ)

Trade Terms
Girobank Number: 212 9515
Credit Cards Accepted: Access/Master, Visa, Amex, Diners

Returns Procedures
Authority to Return: Local Representative or apply in writing to Customer Service Department
Imperfect Returns: Return Title Page and Spine

MACMILLAN DISTRIBUTION LTD
Brunel Road, Houndmills Industrial Estate, Basingstoke, Hampshire RG21 2XS
ISBN Prefix(es): 0 283, 0 330, 0 333, 1 855, 1 954
Tel: 0256 29242
Fax: 0256 842084
Telex: 858493
Cables: PUBLISH BASINGSTOKE
VAT No: 199 4406 21
Account No: _01494 0426_   Rep: J. Connelly
Sales Rep: _____
Tel: _____

Order Information
Teleordering: MAC
First Edition Subscriber

Order Dept Opening Times
Mon - Thurs 8.30am - 4.45pm, Fri 8.30am - 3.30pm
Cyclical Ordering Policy
Orders for more than one publisher can be bulked
All Dues Automatically Recorded
Representation Available

Personnel
Head of Company: Michael Barnard (Managing Director)
Head of Sales (Home): Christopher Paterson (Macmillan Press Sales)
Head of Marketing: Vivienne Wordley London 071-373 6070
Head of Accounts: Robin Garner (Credit Control Director)
Other Important Personnel:
Brian Davies (Pan Macmillan Sales), David Smith (Warehouse Director), David Bleasdale (Export & Shipping Director), Jane Campbell (Manager Home Customer Services)

Number of titles published annually: 2000
Percentage of Export Sales: 50%
Number of Staff: 150
PA Member
NBA Signatory
All New Titles are Bar Coded
Book Data Subscriber

Parent Company: Macmillan Ltd
Allied Companies: Gill & Macmillan Ltd (IR), Groves Dictionary of Music Inc (US), St Martins Press Inc (US)

Trade Terms
Available on request
Credit Cards Accepted: Access/Master, Amex, Diners, Visa

Returns Procedures
Stock Returns: Authorisation required from Company Representative. Return labels provided. Alternative is to telephone sales dept.

MADINAH PRESS
586 Harrow Road, London W10 4NJ
Tel: 071-286 8982
Fax: 071-266 1993

MAFF - Pubs Dept - LONDON SE99 7TP

MAGI PUBLICATIONS
55 Crowland Avenue, Hayes, Middlesex UB3 4JP
Tel: 071-387 0610
Tel: 071-388 9832
Fax: 071-383 5003
VAT No: 460 7976 16

Orders to
A & C BLACK (PUBLISHERS) LTD, PO Box 19, Huntingdon, Cambridgeshire PE19 3SF
Tel: 0480 212666
Fax: 0480 405014

MAGNA LARGE PRINT BOOKS
Magna House, Long Preston, Nr Skipton, North Yorkshire BD23 4ND
ISBN Prefix(es): 0 75050, 1 85389, 1 86009, 1 87267
Tel: 0729 840225
Tel: 0729 840526
Tel: 0729 840251
Fax: 0729 840683
VAT No: 180 8719 41

Order Information
Teleordering: MAGNA

Order Dept Opening Times
Mon-Thu 8.30am-12.30pm, 1.30-5pm, Fri 8.30-12.30
All Dues Automatically Recorded
Representation Available

Personnel
Head of Company: John Cressey/Ron Moody (Joint Managing Director)
Head of Sales (Home): Alan Fletcher (Sales & Marketing Manager)
Head of Accounts: David Mellin

Number of titles published annually: 264
Number of Staff: 20
NBA Signatory
WBIP Updating: Marie Mitton

Parent Company: Ulverscroft Group Ltd

Trade Terms
20%, all orders firm, no returns except faulty copies

MAINSTREAM PUBLISHING CO (EDINBURGH) LTD
7 Albany Street, Edinburgh, Lothian EH1 3UG
ISBN Prefix(es): 1 85158
Tel: 031-557 2959
Fax: 031-556 8720
VAT No: 300 8319 00

Account No: _____
Sales Rep: _____
Tel: _____

Order Information
Teleordering: MAINPUB

Order Dept Opening Times
Mon - Thur 9am - 5.30pm Fri 9am - 5pm
Orders for more than one publisher can be bulked
All Dues Automatically Recorded
Representation Available

Personnel
Head of Company: Bill Campbell/Peter Mackenzie
Head of Publicity: Andrew Young (Publicity Manager)
Head of Accounts: Douglas Nicoll (Financial Controller)
Head of Customer Services: Lorraine Ford (Office Administrator)
Other Important Personnel:
Raymond Cowie (Sales Manager - Scotland)

Number of titles published annually: 60
Number of Staff: 25
PA Member
All New Titles are Bar Coded
Book Data Subscriber
WBIP Updating: Lorraine Ford

Trade Terms
General Net: 20% cash with order Two books or more 35%
Other Terms: Small order surcharge of £1.50 if nett value of invoice under £35
Girobank Number: 11 55 156
Credit Cards Accepted: Access/Master, Visa

Returns Procedures
Authority to Return: Peter MacKenzie
Address for Returns: Unit 8, Phoenix Ind Est, Phoenix Lane, Dunfermline KY12
Imperfect Returns: No credit will be allowed for title page returns - complete book only accepted

MALLORY INTERNATIONAL

Potter's Market, West Hill, Ottery St Mary, Devon
EX11 1TY
Tel: 0404 815310
Fax: 0404 812245
Telex: 42618
VAT No: 416 3493 55

MANAGEMENT UPDATE

99a Underdale Road, Shrewsbury, Shropshire SY2 5EE
ISBN Prefix(es): 0 946679
Tel: 0743 232556

Orders to
Powney's, 4-5 St Alkmund's Place, Shrewsbury, Shropshire
SY1 1UJ
Tel: 0743 369165
Fax: 0743 357568

Order Information

Order Dept Opening Times
Mon - Fri 9am - 5pm
All Dues Automatically Recorded

Personnel
Head of Company: Mr H Johannsen 0743 369165
Head of Customer Services: Mrs C Howard 0743 369165

Number of titles published annually: 4
Number of Staff: 5
NBA Signatory
All New Titles are Bar Coded
WBIP Updating: H Johannsen

Trade Terms
General Net: Single copy 20%, 2 copies or titles 25%, 3 books or more, subscription/stock orders 35%
Credit Cards Accepted: Access/Master, Visa

MANCHESTER STATISTICAL SOCIETY

CIS Building, Miller Street, Manchester, Greater Manchester M60 0AL
Tel: 061-837 4011
Fax: 061-837 4048
Telex: 668621 CIS G

MANCHESTER UNIVERSITY PRESS

Oxford Road, Manchester, Greater Manchester M13 9PL
ISBN Prefix(es): 0 7190
Tel: 061-273 5539
Fax: 061-274 3346
VAT No: 149 3169 49

Account No: _____ ISM TWMU _____
Sales Rep: _____
Tel: _____

Order Information
All Dues Automatically Recorded
Representation Available

Personnel
Head of Company: Francis C Brooke
Head of Sales (Home): John Murray
Head of Accounts: Norma Ashton
Head of Distribution: Michael Gott

Number of titles published annually: 100
Percentage of Export Sales: 40%
Number of Staff: 25
PA Member
IPG Member
All New Titles are Bar Coded
Open University Publications
Book Data Subscriber
WBIP Updating: John Murray

Trade Terms
Academic Net: Terms available upon request
BA/Girobank Small Order Scheme: Yes
Credit Cards Accepted: Access/Master, Visa

Returns Procedures
Authority to Return: Returns Section
Imperfect Returns: Title page up to £15. Over this amount return complete book

MANDEVILLE PRESS

2 Taylor's Hill, Hitchin, Hertfordshire SG4 9AD
ISBN Prefix(es): 0 904533, 1 870410
Tel: 0493 450796

Personnel
Head of Company: Peter Scupham

Number of titles published annually: 5
Number of Staff: 1

Trade Terms
33.3% on all orders

MANDRAKE

PO Box 250, Oxford, Oxfordshire OX1 1AP
ISBN Prefix(es): 1 869928
Tel: 0865 243671 24 Hours
Fax: 0865 59298 Order only
VAT No: 537 2500 61

Orders to
TURNAROUND, 27 Horsell Road, London N5 1XL
Tel: 071-609 7836/7
Fax: 071-700 1205

Order Information

All Dues Automatically Recorded
Representation Available

Personnel
Head of Company: Chris Morgan/Shantidevi Nath

Number of titles published annually: 10
Percentage of Export Sales: 50%
All New Titles are Bar Coded
WBIP Updating: Chris Morgan

Parent Company: Moggruth Ltd

Trade Terms
25% less than £25, above £25 35-40%
Minimum Order: On some pamphlets
Credit Cards Accepted: Access/Master, Visa

Returns Procedures
Authority to Return: Chris Morgan
Address for Returns: 15 Parsons Place, Oxford, OX4 1NL
Stock Returns: By negotiation
Imperfect Returns: For Mandrake titles only, below £10 send title page and back page

GEORGE MANN BOOKS

PO Box 22, Maidstone, Kent ME14 1AH
ISBN Prefix(es): 0 7041
Tel: 0622 759591

Order Information

Order Dept Opening Times
Mon - Fri 9.30am - 6pm
Invoice Payments: Arnefold

Personnel
Head of Company: George Mann
Head of Sales (Home): John Arne

Subsidiary Companies: Arnefold

Trade Terms
Single copy/single line 25%, 2 or more single titles/ 2 books or more 35%, special orders negotiable
BA/Girobank Small Order Scheme: 45% and carriage paid, even on single copy/single line
Girobank Number: 350 8250

Returns Procedures
Stock Returns: Contact head office
Imperfect Returns: Complete book must be returned

MANOR HOUSE PUBLISHING LTD
57 Manor Way, Beckenham, Kent BR3 3LN
ISBN Prefix(es): 1 872345, 1 873056
Tel: 081-658 2801
Fax: 081-658 2801
VAT No: 574 1128 50

Order Information

All Dues Automatically Recorded

Personnel
Head of Company: Rob Cooper
Head of Accounts: Bill Burchell 081-428 1768

Number of titles published annually: 5
All New Titles are Bar Coded

Trade Terms
35%

MANSK-SVENSKA PUBLISHING CO LTD
17 North View, Peel, Isle of Man
Tel: 0624 842855
Fax: 0624 844241
VAT No: 000 4617 36

MANUTIUS PRESS
506 Allerton Road, Liverpool, Merseyside L18 9UY
ISBN Prefix(es): 1 873534
Tel: 051-427 6838

Orders to
Manutius Press, Orders Dept, 24 Heathcote Street, Kingston Upon Hull, Humberside HU6 7LP
Tel: 0482 472549

Order Information

Order Dept Opening Times
Mon - Sat 9am - 6pm
All Dues Automatically Recorded
Invoice Payments: Manutius Press, Kingston Upon Hull

Personnel
Head of Company: Mr K A Spencer
Head of Sales (Home): Mr A Macintosh
Head of Marketing: Ms I Wright
Head of Distribution: Mr D Driver
Head of Customer Services: Ms J Spencer

Number of titles published annually: 5
Number of Staff: 5
All New Titles are Bar Coded
WBIP Updating: Mr A Macintosh

Trade Terms
General Net: Single copy/single line 25%, 2 books or more 30%
Academic Net: Single copy/single line 20%, special orders 30-35%
Other Terms: 1-3 books £1 carriage charged
Credit Cards Accepted: Access/Master, Visa

Returns Procedures
Authority to Return: 24 Heathcote Street, Kingston Upon Hull, HU6 7LP
Address for Returns: As above
Stock Returns: Contact Mr A Macintosh at above address
Imperfect Returns: No limit

MAP COLLECTOR PUBLICATIONS

48 High Street, Tring, Hertfordshire HP23 5BH
ISBN Prefix(es): 0 906430
Tel: 0442 824977
Tel: 0442 891004
Fax: 0296 623398
VAT No: 367 0156 55

Order Information

Order Dept Opening Times
Mon - Fri 9am - 5pm

Personnel

Head of Company: Mrs V Scott (Managing Director)
Head of Sales (Home): Mrs J Robens
Other Important Personnel:
Ben Lane (Advertising Manager)

Number of titles published annually: 5
Percentage of Export Sales: 50%
Number of Staff: 3
WBIP Updating: Mrs V Scott

Trade Terms

Single book 25% 2-4 books 30% 5 or more books 35%
Credit Cards Accepted: Access/Master, Visa, Amex

Returns Procedures

Authority to Return: Ben Lane

MARC EUROPE

Vision Building, 4 Footscray Road, Eltham, London
SE9 2TZ
ISBN Prefix(es): 0 947697, 1 85321
Tel: 081-294 1989
Fax: 081-294 0014
VAT No: 396 9851 74

Order Information

Order Dept Opening Times
Mon - Fri 9.15am - 5pm
All Dues Automatically Recorded

Personnel

Head of Company: P W Brierley (European Director)
Head of Publicity: D R Longley (Commercial Director)
Head of Accounts: S Wardall (Director of Administration)

Number of titles published annually: 5
Number of Staff: 10
All New Titles are Bar Coded
WBIP Updating: P W Brierley

Trade Terms

35%
Credit Cards Accepted: Access/Master, Visa

Returns Procedures

Stock Returns: Notify Mr Longley in advance, who will authorize credit.
Imperfect Returns: £10

PETER MARCAN PUBLICATIONS

31 Rowliff Road, High Wycombe, Buckinghamshire
HP12 3LD

Order Information

All Dues Automatically Recorded

Number of titles published annually: 3
Number of Staff: 1

Trade Terms
General Net: Single Copy 25%, Two books or more 35%

MARINE MANAGEMENT (HOLDINGS) LTD
76 Mark Lane, London EC3R 7JN
Tel: 071-481 8493
Fax: 071-488 1854
Telex: 886841
VAT No: 244 3343 81

MARITIME BOOKS
Penmilder, Lodge Hill, Liskeard, Cornwall PL14 4EL
ISBN Prefix(es): 0 907771
Tel: 0579 343663
Fax: 0579 346747
VAT No: 326 7291 48

Order Information

Order Dept Opening Times
Mon - Fri 8.30am - 9pm, Sat 9am - 12pm
Cyclical Ordering Policy
All Dues Automatically Recorded

Personnel
Head of Company: Mr M A Critchley
Head of Sales (Home): Mr R A May

Number of titles published annually: 4
Number of Staff: 5
All New Titles are Bar Coded
WBIP Updating: Mr R A May

Trade Terms
35% on all orders
Other Terms: Small order surcharges on orders under £40 retail. Carriage charges up to £2
Girobank Number: 298 3257
Credit Cards Accepted: Access/Master, Visa

Returns Procedures
Stock Returns: Only with company office approval.
Imperfect Returns: Return to company office after approval is sought.

THE MARKET RESEARCH SOCIETY
15 Northburgh Street, London EC1V 0AH
Tel: 071-490 4911
Fax: 071-490 0608

MARLBOROUGH BOOKS
6 Milton Road, Swindon, Wiltshire SN1 5JG
ISBN Prefix(es): 1 873919
Tel: 0793 421320
Fax: 0793 421640

Order Information

Order Dept Opening Times
Mon - Fri 8.30am - 5.30pm Sat Nov, Sat/Sun Dec
All Dues Automatically Recorded

Personnel
Head of Company: A White
Head of Sales (Home): Rupert Mackeson
Head of Accounts: Pat Turner

Number of titles published annually: 10
Number of Staff: 8
NBA Signatory
All New Titles are Bar Coded
WBIP Updating: Eamonn Mullane

Trade Terms
30-40%
Minimum Order: 1 Book

Returns Procedures
Authority to Return: Sales Director
Imperfect Returns: Return book

MARSHALLE PUBLICATIONS
1 Saltburn Road, St Budeaux, Plymouth, Devon PL5 1PB
Tel: 0752 361832

MARSTON BOOK SERVICES LTD
PO Box 87, Osney Mead, Oxford, Oxfordshire OX2 0DT
Tel: 0865 791155 24 Hours
Fax: 0865 791927
Telex: 837515 OXBOOK G
VAT No: 532 5222 78
Account No: _____
Sales Rep: _____
Tel: _____

Order Information
Teleordering: MARS

Order Dept Opening Times
Mon - Thur 8.30am - 5pm, Fri 8.30am - 4.30pm
Cyclical Ordering Policy

Personnel
Head of Company: Charles Ashford (Managing Director)
Head of Accounts: Mark Oliver (Finance Director)
Head of Distribution: Wayne Ellis (Operations Director)
Head of Customer Services: Micheline Jebb (Customer Services Director)

Trade Terms
Refer to Publishers
Girobank Number: 236 6053

Returns Procedures
Authority to Return: Refer to Publishers

KENNETH MASON PUBLICATIONS LTD
Dudley House, 12 North Street, Emsworth, Hampshire PO10 7DQ
ISBN Prefix(es): 0 85937
Tel: 0243 377977
Fax: 0243 379136
VAT No: 107 5975 52

Orders to
BIBLIOS PUBLISHERS DISTRIBUTION SERVICE LTD,
Star Road, Partridge Green, West Sussex RH13 8LD
Tel: 0403 710971
Fax: 0403 711143

Order Information

All Dues Automatically Recorded
Invoice Payments: Biblios Publishers' Distribution Services Ltd

Personnel
Head of Company: Piers Mason

PA Member
NBA Signatory
All New Titles are Bar Coded
WBIP Updating: Mrs Jane Jeffree

ADAM MATTHEW PUBLICATIONS

8 Oxford Street, Marlborough, Wiltshire SN8 1AP
Tel: 0672 511921
Fax: 0672 511663
VAT No: 569 7870 67

MAXWELL MACMILLAN INTERNATIONAL (EUROPE) LTD

Little Baldon House, Nuneham Courtenay, Oxford, Oxfordshire OX44 9PU
Tel: 086738 491
Fax: 086738 530
VAT No: 596 0247 21
Account No: 150033
Sales Rep:
Tel:

Orders to
MARSTON BOOK SERVICES LTD, PO Box 87, Osney Mead, Oxford, Oxfordshire OX2 0DT
Tel: 0865 791155
Fax: 0865 791927

Order Information

All Dues Automatically Recorded
Representation Available
Invoice Payments: Marston Book Services

Personnel
Head of Company: Kenneth B Collins (Managing Director)
Head of Sales (Home): Graham Uden (Home Trade Manager)
Head of Sales (Export): Uli Bruno (Export Sales Manager) +44 837 6698
Head of Marketing: Mary Seddon (Manager of Marketing)
Head of Publicity: Harriet Johansson (Marketing Co-ordinator)
Head of Accounts: Ian Henson (Fiancial Director)

Number of titles published annually: 1500
Percentage of Export Sales: 50%
Number of Staff: 38
All New Titles are Bar Coded
Book Data Subscriber
WBIP Updating: Alan Steel

Parent Company: Macmillan Inc (US)

Trade Terms
Depending on turnover, Trade 25%-35%, College 25%-30%, Reference 10%-20%.
Credit Cards Accepted: Access/Master, Amex, Diners, Visa

Returns Procedures
Authority to Return: Customer Service, Returns Section, Marston Book Services
Address for Returns: Marston Book Services

KEVIN MAYHEW LTD

Rattlesden, Bury St Edmunds, Suffolk IP30 0SZ
Tel: 0449 747978
Fax: 0449 737834 Fax/24 Tel
VAT No: 128 3009

Order Information
Teleordering: KEVMAY

Order Dept Opening Times
Mon - Fri 9am - 5pm
All Dues Automatically Recorded
Representation Available
Trade Counter:Pie Hatch Farm, Buxhall, Stowmarket, Suffolk

Personnel
Head of Company: Kevin Mayhew
Head of Publicity: Anne Haskell
Head of Distribution: Bunny Harvey
Head of Customer Services: Alison Hubbard
Other Important Personnel:
Gordon Carter (Managing Director)

Number of titles published annually: 200
Number of Staff: 30
All New Titles are Bar Coded
WBIP Updating: Jane Rayson

Trade Terms
Generally 35%, Specific titles 17%/20%
Other Terms: Carriage charges: min £2/10% up to £50/Free over £80
Credit Cards Accepted: Access/Master, Visa, Amex

Returns Procedures
Imperfect Returns: Return to head office books or title pages full refund given

MCB UNIVERSITY PRESS LTD

60/62 Toller Lane, Bradford, West Yorkshire BD8 9BY
ISBN Prefix(es): 0 86176
Tel: 0274 499821
Fax: 0274 547143
Fax: 0274 543576
Telex: 51317 MCBUNI G
VAT No: 303 4687 70

Personnel
Head of Customer Services: Mike Driver

MECHANICAL ENGINEERING PUBLICATIONS

Northgate Avenue, Bury St Edmunds, Suffolk IP32 6BW
ISBN Prefix(es): 0 85298
Tel: 0284 763277
Tel: 0284 724384 24Hr Sales
Fax: 0284 704006
Telex: 817376
Cables: IMEBSE
VAT No: 299 9304 93

Order Information

Order Dept Opening Times
Mon - Fri 9am - 5pm
Cyclical Ordering Policy
All Dues Automatically Recorded
Representation Available

Other Important Locations
Registered Head Office: Mechanical Eng Pub, 1 Birdcage Walk London SW14 9JJ

Mechanical Engineering Publications Limited

★ **MEP are the publishers to the Institution of Mechanical Engineers, one of the most senior engineering societies in the world. MEP publish the Conference, Seminar and Journal material of the IMechE.**

★ **MEP have an extensive list of reference and R & D books for mechanical engineers.**

★ **MEP are publishers to many other learned societies and organisations.**

★ **MEP are exclusive European agents for the Book, Conference and Symposia publications of The American Society of Mechanical Engineers.**

For a comprehensive catalogue listing all available titles please contact:

Sales Department, Mechanical Engineering Publications Limited, Northgate Avenue, Bury St Edmunds, Suffolk, IP32 6BW, England. Tel: Sales Department direct line: 0284 724384 (24hr service) Telephone: 0284 763277 Fax: 0284 704006 Telex: 817376

Tel: 071-222 7899
Fax: 071-222 4557

Personnel
Head of Company: Mr Patrick Caird-Daley (Director - Publications)
Head of Sales (Home): Mr Peter Williams (Sales & Marketing Manager)
Head of Accounts: Mr Esmond Hamilton (Director of Finance)

Number of titles published annually: 40
Percentage of Export Sales: 60%
Number of Staff: 32
Book Data Subscriber
WBIP Updating: Peter Williams

Parent Company: Institution of Mechanical Engineers

Trade Terms
General Net: Mech Eng Pub: Single copy 20%, two books or more 30% Amer Soc Mech Eng: Single copy 10% two books or more 15%
Other Terms: 10% delivery charge for orders outside UK
Credit Cards Accepted: Access/Master, Visa

Returns Procedures
Stock Returns: Prior permission required. Quote invoice details. Full credit given on perfect copies within 12mths of invoice date

MECKLER LTD

4th Floor, Artillery House, Artillery Row, London SW1P 1RT
ISBN Prefix(es): 0 88736
Tel: 071-976 0405
Fax: 071-976 0506
VAT No: 461 5917 36

Orders to
BIBLIOS PUBLISHERS DISTRIBUTION SERVICE LTD, Star Road, Partridge Green, West Sussex RH13 8LD
Tel: 0403 710971
Fax: 0403 711143

Order Information

All Dues Automatically Recorded
Representation Available
Invoice Payments: Biblios

Personnel
Head of Company: Andrew Parker (General Manager - Publishing & Marketing)
Head of Accounts: Raj Sharma
Other Important Personnel:
Alice Taylor (General Manager - Conferences & Exhibitions)

Number of titles published annually: 65
Percentage of Export Sales: 50%
Number of Staff: 7
Book Data Subscriber
WBIP Updating: Stella Filmer

Trade Terms
20%
Credit Cards Accepted: Access/Master, Visa, Amex

Returns Procedures
Stock Returns: Contact Biblios
Imperfect Returns: Contact Biblios

MEDIA MEDICA PUBLICATIONS LTD
51 West Street, Chichester, West Sussex PO19 1RP
Tel: 0243 532542
Fax: 0243 528547
VAT No: 582 9703 07

MEDIAN BOOKS LTD
Ty Derw, Dinas Mawddwy, Machynlleth, Powys SY20 9LR
Tel: 0650 531444
Fax: 0650 531337
Telex: 94012236 MEDI G

Medical Economics Data - Waverley Europe Ltd

MEDICI SOCIETY LTD
34-42 Pentonville Road, London N1 9HG
Tel: 071-837 7099
Tel: 071-837 9002 Orders
Fax: 071-837 9152
VAT No: 342 0169 90

Order Information

Order Dept Opening Times
Mon - Fri 9am - 5pm

Personnel
Head of Sales (Home): Sebastian Watt (Sales Manager)
Head of Sales (Export): Catriona Mitchell (Export Manager)

Number of titles published annually: 6
Number of Staff: 200

Trade Terms
35% on books published at over £2, books under £2 minimum order of 3 per title

Returns Procedures
Authority to Return: Sales Manager

Melbourne University Press - Marston

MELIA PUBLISHING SERVICES LTD
192 Courthouse Road, Maidenhead, Berkshire SL6 6HY
Tel: 0628 70597
Fax: 0628 789758
VAT No: 581 4185 34

Account No: _____
Sales Rep: _____
Tel: _____

Orders to
GRANTHAM BOOK SERVICES LTD, Isaac Newton Way, Alma Park Industrial Estate, Grantham, Lincolnshire NG31 9SD
Tel: 0476 67421
Fax: 0476 590223

Order Information

All Dues Automatically Recorded
Representation Available
Invoice Payments: Grantham Book Services

Personnel
Head of Company: Terry Melia
Head of Accounts: David Owen

Number of titles published annually: 100
Percentage of Export Sales: 30%
All New Titles are Bar Coded
Book Data Subscriber

Trade Terms
35%, 30 Days
Girobank Number: 508 7457
Credit Cards Accepted: Access/Master, Visa

Returns Procedures
Authority to Return: Signed authorisation required from representative
Address for Returns: Grantham Book Services
Imperfect Returns: No limit but must have authorisation in advance

THE EDWIN MELLEN PRESS LTD
Mellen House, Lampeter, Dyfed SA48 7DY
Tel: 0570 423356
Fax: 0570 423775
VAT No: 485 0213 59

A/C NO SMIT05

MELROSE PRESS LTD
3 Regal Lane, Soham, Ely, Cambridgeshire CB7 5BA
ISBN Prefix(es): 0 948875
Tel: 0353 721091
Fax: 0353 721839
VAT No: 215 5140 03

Order Information

All Dues Automatically Recorded
Representation Available

Personnel
Head of Company: Nicholas Law
Head of Sales (Home): Jean Pearson
Head of Distribution: Cicely Watson
Head of Customer Services: Jeremy Kay

Number of titles published annually: 6
Percentage of Export Sales: 90%
Number of Staff: 28
Book Data Subscriber
WBIP Updating: Jean Pearson

Trade Terms
25% on all orders + 5% standing orders + carriage charges
Credit Cards Accepted: Access/Master, Visa, Amex

Returns Procedures
Authority to Return: Jean Pearson
Stock Returns: Written permission required
Imperfect Returns: £75

THE MENARD PRESS
8 The Oaks, Woodside Avenue, London N12 8AR
ISBN Prefix(es): 0 903400, 0 9513753, 1 874320
Tel: 081-446 5571

Orders to
CENTRAL BOOKS, 99 Wallis Road, London E9 5LN
Tel: 081-986 4854
Fax: 081-533 5821

Order Information

All Dues Automatically Recorded
Representation Available
Invoice Payments: Central Books (Troika)

Personnel
Head of Company: Tony Rudolf

Number of titles published annually: 5
Number of Staff: 1
All New Titles are Bar Coded

Trade Terms
Single copy 25%, all other orders 35%

Returns Procedures
Authority to Return: Central Books (Troika)

MENCAP

123 Golden Lane, London EC1Y 0RT
ISBN Prefix(es): 0 855
Tel: 071-454 0454
Fax: 071-608 3254

Order Information

Order Dept Opening Times
Mon - Fri 9.30am - 5pm

Personnel
Head of Marketing: Steve Billington
Head of Accounts: Daniel Ross
Head of Customer Services: Jo Hardy (Customer Services & Sales)
Other Important Personnel:
Graham Simpson (Print Manager)

Parent Company: Royal Society for Mentally Handicapped Children and Adults

Trade Terms
General Net: Single copy/single line no discount, 2 or more single titles 25%
Academic Net: As above
Non-Net: As above
Other Terms: Pre-payment on orders under £25 retail
Credit Cards Accepted: Access/Master, Visa

Returns Procedures
Authority to Return: Jo Hardy

MERCAT PRESS

James Thin, 53 South Bridge, Edinburgh, Lothian EH1 1YS
ISBN Prefix(es): 0 901824, 1 873644
Tel: 031-556 6743
Fax: 031-557 8149
VAT No: 271 4114 88

Order Information

Order Dept Opening Times
Mon - Fri 9am - 5pm
All Dues Automatically Recorded
Representation Available

Personnel
Head of Company: Ainslie Thin (Managing Director)
Head of Sales (Home): Tom Johnstone/Sean Costello
Head of Accounts: Muriel Veitch
Head of Distribution: Kerry Lomas

Number of titles published annually: 15
Number of Staff: 2
PA Member
NBA Signatory
All New Titles are Bar Coded
WBIP Updating: Tom Johnstone/Sean Costello

Parent Company: James Thin Ltd

Trade Terms
Single copy 25% plus postage, 2-5 copies 35% post free, 6 or more copies 40% post free
Credit Cards Accepted: Access/Master, Visa, Amex

Returns Procedures
Authority to Return: Permission must be given in writing by Mercat
Imperfect Returns: Send with description of fault, stating whether credit or replacement is required

MERCIER PRESS LTD
PO Box No 5, 5 French Church Street, Cork, County Cork
ISBN Prefix(es): 0 85342, 1 85635
Tel: 021 275 040
Fax: 021 274 969
Telex: 75463 MRCREI
VAT No: 8T 05826 T

Orders to
CENTRAL BOOKS, 99 Wallis Road, London E9 5LN
Tel: 081-986 4854
Fax: 081-533 5821

Order Information

All Dues Automatically Recorded
Representation Available
Invoice Payments: Central Books
UK Sales: Ion Mills, Oldcastle Books 0508 761264

Personnel
Head of Company: J Spillane

Number of titles published annually: 30
Percentage of Export Sales: 25%
All New Titles are Bar Coded
WBIP Updating: Marian Murphy

Parent Company: Mercier Press St
Subsidiary Companies: C K Distributors Ltd (IR), Mercier Bookshops Ltd

Trade Terms
35%

Returns Procedures
Authority to Return: Central Books Ltd
Address for Returns: Central Books Ltd
Stock Returns: As per Central Books
Imperfect Returns: As per Central Books

MERCURY BOOKS
862 Garratt Lane, London SW17 0NB
ISBN Prefix(es): 1 85251, 1 85252
Tel: 081-682 3858
Fax: 081-682 3859
VAT No: 562 0002 96

[handwritten note: Now MANAGEMENT BOOKS 2000 LTD, 125A THE BROADWAY, DIDCOT, OXON OX11 8AW, 0235 815544, FAX 0235 817188]

Orders to
BIBLIOS PUBLISHERS DISTRIBUTION SERVICE LTD,
Star Road, Partridge Green, West Sussex RH13 8LD
Tel: 0403 710971
Fax: 0403 711143

Order Information

All Dues Automatically Recorded
Representation Available
Invoice Payments: Biblios

Personnel
Head of Company: Nicholas Dale-Harris (Managing Director)

Head of Sales (Home): Roger Kirkpatrick (Marketing Director)
Head of Customer Services: Ruth Rimell (Administration Manager)

Number of titles published annually: 80
All New Titles are Bar Coded
WBIP Updating: Roger Kirkpatrick

Trade Terms
35%
General Net: Single copy 25%, Two or more 35%
Academic Net: 25%
Girobank Number: 37 97044 04
Credit Cards Accepted: Access/Master, Visa

Returns Procedures
Address for Returns: Biblios
Stock Returns: All returns to be authorised by rep or marketing director
Imperfect Returns: Return complete title to Mercury Books

MEREHURST FAIRFAX

Ferry House, 51-57 Lacy Road, Putney, London SW15 1PR
ISBN Prefix(es): 0 948075, 1 85391, 1 86343, 1 874567, 1 897730
Tel: 081-780 1177
Tel: 0933 402330 Wellingb'
Fax: 081-780 1714
Fax: 0933 402234 Wellingb'
Telex: 296616 (London)
VAT No: 466 3164 39

Account No:_____

Sales Rep:_____

Tel: _____

Orders to
BOOKPOINT LIMITED, 39 Milton Park, Abingdon, Oxfordshire OX14 4TD
Tel: 0235 835001
Fax: 0235 861038

Order Information

All Dues Automatically Recorded
Representation Available
Invoice Payments: Bookpoint
Fairfax Paperback Orders:J B Fairfax Press Ltd, 9 Trinity Centre, Park Farm, Wellingborough, Northants NN8 6ZB

Personnel
Head of Company: Nicolas Wright (Managing Director)
Head of Sales (Home): Debbie Kent (Sales Director)
Head of Marketing: Kirsten Schlesinger (Marketing Director)
Head of Publicity: Eliza Dunlop
Head of Accounts: Roger Potter (Finance Director)
Other Important Personnel:
Paul Mockett (Sales Director (Fairfax)) Wellingborough

Number of titles published annually: 50
Percentage of Export Sales: 40%
Number of Staff: 17
All New Titles are Bar Coded
Book Data Subscriber
WBIP Updating: Sandie Phillips

Parent Company: J B Fairfax International PTY Ltd
Allied Companies: Michael Friedman Publishing Group Inc (US), T B Clarke (Overseas) PTY Ltd (AU)

Trade Terms
35% on all orders, no surcharges

Returns Procedures
Authority to Return: Prior permission required from Debbie Kent at Head Office
Address for Returns: Bookpoint
Imperfect Returns: In all cases return the complete book

MERESBOROUGH BOOKS

17 Station Road, Rainham, Gillingham, Kent ME8 7RS
ISBN Prefix(es): 0 905270, 0 948193
Tel: 0634 388812
Fax: 0634 378501
VAT No: 205 1050 31

Account No: _____

Sales Rep: _____

Tel: _____

Order Information
Teleordering: MERE

Order Dept Opening Times
Mon - Sat 9am - 1pm 2pm - 5.30pm
Orders for more than one publisher can be bulked
All Dues Automatically Recorded
Representation Available

Personnel
Head of Company: Hamish & Barbara Mackay Miller (Partners)

Number of titles published annually: 12
Number of Staff: 14
All New Titles are Bar Coded
WBIP Updating: H B Mackay Miller

Trade Terms
33.3% Orders under £30 retail 25%
Girobank Number: 39 771 8004
Credit Cards Accepted: Access/Master, Visa

Returns Procedures
Stock Returns: By prior permission except on errors and imperfects
Imperfect Returns: No price limit for title pages on own publications. Title pages not accepted on distributed titles.

MERIDIAN BOOKS

40 Hadzor Road, Oldbury, Warley, West Midlands B68 9LA
ISBN Prefix(es): 0 906070, 1 869922
Tel: 021-429 4397 24 Hours
VAT No: 488 4226 12

Order Information

Order Dept Opening Times
Mon - Fri 8.30am - 6pm, Sat 10am - 5pm
All Dues Automatically Recorded
Representation Available

Personnel
Head of Company: Peter Groves

Number of titles published annually: 6
Number of Staff: 2
IPG Member
All New Titles are Bar Coded

Trade Terms
35%
Other Terms: Postage & packing on orders less than £7.50 net value

Returns Procedures
Stock Returns: Request permission from Peter Groves
Imperfect Returns: No limit if permission obtained from Peter Groves

MERLIN BOOKS LTD
Stonycroft, East Hill, Braunton, Devon EX33 2LD
ISBN Prefix(es): 0 86303
Tel: 0271 812117 Tel/Fax
VAT No: 365 7229 31

Orders to
Merlin Books, 40 East Street, Braunton, Devon EX33 2EA
Tel: 0271 816430
Fax: 0271 812117

Order Information

Cyclical Ordering Policy
All Dues Automatically Recorded

Personnel
Head of Company: D A Stockwell (Managing Director)
Head of Sales (Home): Pam Stevens (Manager) 0271 816430
Head of Marketing: Christine Evenden (Manager) 0271 816430
Head of Publicity: Janice Oberg-Thorn
Head of Accounts: Elaine Suttie (Accounts Manager) 0271 816430
Head of Distribution: Keith Chapman (Manager) 0271 816430
Head of Customer Services: Pat Williams (Manager) 0271 816430

Number of titles published annually: 30
Number of Staff: 10
All New Titles are Bar Coded
WBIP Updating: Christine Evenden

Trade Terms
35%

Returns Procedures
Authority to Return: Elaine Suttie
Address for Returns: East Street

MERLIN PRESS
10 Malden Road, London NW5 3HR
ISBN Prefix(es): 0 85036, 1 85425
Tel: 071-267 3399
Fax: 071-284 3092
VAT No: 232 7215 89

Orders to
CENTRAL BOOKS, 99 Wallis Road, London E9 5LN
Tel: 081-986 4854
Fax: 081-533 5821

Order Information

All Dues Automatically Recorded
Representation Available
Invoice Payments: Central Books

Personnel
Head of Company: Martin Eve
Head of Publicity: Judith Alpe

Number of titles published annually: 10
IPG Member
All New Titles are Bar Coded

Trade Terms
35%, orders below £30 retail 25%, orders below £5 10%

Returns Procedures
Address for Returns: Central Books
Stock Returns: Return the book if incorrectly supplied
Imperfect Returns: Title pages up to £20

MERLION PUBLISHING LTD

2 Belinger Close, Greenways Business Park, Chippenham, Wiltshire SN15 1BN
ISBN Prefix(es): 1 85737
Tel: 0249 447444
Fax: 0249 447222
VAT No: 543 5276 42

Orders to
DEREK SEARLE ASSOCIATES LTD, Burlington House, 14 High Street, Slough, Berkshire SL1 1EE
Tel: 0753 539295
Fax: 0753 551863

Personnel
Head of Company: Felicia K Law (Publishing Director)
Head of Sales (Home): Roy Fisher
Head of Marketing: Maria Fairchild
Head of Accounts: Roy Fisher (Finance Director)

Number of titles published annually: 50
Percentage of Export Sales: 100%
Number of Staff: 20
All New Titles are Bar Coded
WBIP Updating: Julie Hitchens

Returns Procedures
Authority to Return: Roy Fisher
Address for Returns: Bookpoint Ltd
Imperfect Returns: Defective books only

MERROW PUBLISHING CO LTD

Isa Building, Hackworth Industrial Park, Shildon, Durham DL3 8LR
ISBN Prefix(es): 0 900541, 0 904095
Tel: 0388 773065
Fax: 774888
Telex: 587188
VAT No: 422 5394 64

Order Information
Teleordering: MEADOW

All Dues Automatically Recorded

Personnel
Head of Company: Dr J Gordon Cook

Trade Terms
25%
Girobank Number: 399 0257

MESSANGER PUBLICATIONS

37 Lower Leeson Street, Dublin 2, County Dublin
Tel: 01 767 491/2
Fax: 01 611 606
VAT No: 9T 4240 3R

METAL BULLETIN PLC

Park House, Park Terrace, Worcester Park, Surrey KT4 7HY
ISBN Prefix(es): 0 900542, 0 947671
Tel: 081-330 4311

Fax: 081-337 8943
Telex: 21383 METBUL G
VAT No: 232 4922 79

Order Information

All Dues Automatically Recorded
Trade Counter:16 Lower Marsh Street, London SE1 7RJ
Tel: 071-633 0525
Fax: 071-928 6539

Personnel

Head of Company: Tom Hempenstall (Chief Executive)
Head of Marketing: Diana Little (Marketing Resources)
Head of Accounts: Paul Vincent (Finance Director)
Head of Distribution: John Fea (Fulfilment Manager)

Number of titles published annually: 12
Percentage of Export Sales: 75%
Number of Staff: 150
Book Data Subscriber
WBIP Updating: Diana Little

Trade Terms

20% on all orders
Other Terms: Carriage charges dependent on destination
Credit Cards Accepted: Access/Master, Visa, Amex

JOHN METCALFE PUBLISHING TRUST

Church Road, Tylers Green, Penn, Buckinghamshire
HP10 8LN
ISBN Prefix(es): 0 9502515, 0 9506366, 1 870039
Tel: 0494 813174
VAT No: 209 1346 83

Order Information

Order Dept Opening Times
Mon - Fri 9.00am - 5.00pm
Representation Available

Personnel

Head of Company: John Metcalfe
Head of Sales (Home): John D Nichol
Head of Sales (Export): Paul F Kendall
Head of Publicity: Audrey H Simpson
Head of Accounts: Graham Young
Head of Distribution: Katharine J Munday
Head of Customer Services: John Darroch

WBIP Updating: John Darroch

Trade Terms

33.3% on all orders
Other Terms: Carriage charges for orders under £10 retail

Returns Procedures

Stock Returns: All undamaged books refunded at 33.3% or credit note
Imperfect Returns: Replaced, reduced or refunded

METHODIST PUBLISHING HOUSE

20 Ivatt Way, Peterborough, Cambridgeshire PE3 7PG
ISBN Prefix(es): 0 946550
Tel: 0733 332202
Fax: 0733 331201
VAT No: 229 5495 32

Order Information

Order Dept Opening Times
Mon - Thur 8.30am - 5pm Fri 8.30am - 4.30pm
All Dues Automatically Recorded

Personnel
Head of Company: Brian Thornton (General Manager)
Head of Sales (Home): Mrs Maureen Patchett
Head of Accounts: Derek Harris (Administration & Accounts)
Head of Distribution: Nigel Lightfoot (Warehouse Manager)
Head of Customer Services: Jan Kew

Number of titles published annually: 12
Number of Staff: 18
PA Member
NBA Signatory

Parent Company: The Methodist Church

Trade Terms
25% account; 30% cwo
Other Terms: Small order surcharge of £1.50 on orders below £10
Girobank Number: 531 3252
Credit Cards Accepted: Access/Master, Visa

Returns Procedures
Imperfect Returns: Up to £10 title page accepted, over this figure whole book

METRA MARTECH LTD

Glenthorne House, Hammersmith Grove, London W6 0LG
Tel: 081-563 0666
Fax: 081-563 0040
VAT No: 503 3063 00

MICELLE PRESS

12 Ullswater Crescent, Weymouth, Dorset DT3 5HE
ISBN Prefix(es): 1 870228
Tel: 0305 781574 Tel/Fax

Order Information

All Dues Automatically Recorded

Personnel
Head of Company: Tony Hunting

Number of titles published annually: 2
Percentage of Export Sales: 50%
Number of Staff: 2
IPG Member
All New Titles are Bar Coded
Book Data Subscriber

Trade Terms
Single copy 20%(17.5% Imports), Two or more 25%(20% Imports) Extra 2.5% for cash with order
Other Terms: Small order surcharge of £1 for orders less than £20
Girobank Number: 510 8071

Returns Procedures
Stock Returns: Request permission
Imperfect Returns: Request permission

MICHELIN TYRE PLC

Davy House, Lyon Road, Harrow, Essex HA1 2DQ
ISBN Prefix(es): 2 06
Tel: 081-861 2121
Fax: 081-863 0680

Account No: _____
Sales Rep: _____
Tel: _____

Order Information
Teleordering: MICH

All Dues Automatically Recorded
Representation Available

Personnel
Head of Sales (Home): J Lewis
Head of Sales (Export): D C Brown
Head of Marketing: P Snelling
Head of Accounts: D Dooley
Head of Distribution: G Sinclair

Number of titles published annually: 350
All New Titles are Bar Coded
Book Data Subscriber
WBIP Updating: K L Nicholls

Parent Company: Manufacture Francaise des Pneumatiques Michelin

Trade Terms
35%

Returns Procedures
Authority to Return: C Pluck
Address for Returns: Michelin Tyre PLC, Bramston Link, Southfields Industrial Area, Basildon, Essex SS15 6TX
Stock Returns: Firm sale. Contact C Pluck to discuss return of incorrectly supplied books or books damaged in transit.
Imperfect Returns: Whole book should be returned

[handwritten: MICROINFO LTD. P.O. Box 3 - Omega Park - Alton - Hants. GU34 2PG Tel:- 0420 86848 FAX 0420 89889]

MID NORTHUMBERLAND ARTS GROUP

Wansbeck Square, Ashington, Northumberland NE63 9XL
ISBN Prefix(es): 0 904790
Tel: 0670 814444
Fax: 0670 520136
VAT No: 177 8460 31

Order Information

Order Dept Opening Times
Mon - Fri 9am - 4.30pm

Personnel
Head of Company: Mr G R Stephenson

Number of titles published annually: 3
Number of Staff: 2

Trade Terms
35% on all orders, except single copies 20%

MID-BORDER BOOKS

Castle Hill House, Kington, Herefordshire HR5 3AG
ISBN Prefix(es): 0 9518644
Tel: 0544 231161
Tel: 0544 231195
VAT No: 489 2054 19

Personnel
Head of Company: Peter Newman

Number of titles published annually: 2

Trade Terms
33%
Other Terms: Postage extra under 10 books

MIDDLETON PRESS

Easebourne Lane, Midhurst, Kent GU29 9AZ
ISBN Prefix(es): 0 906520, 1 873973
Tel: 0730 813169
Fax: 0730 812601
VAT No: 397 5435 05

Order Information

All Dues Automatically Recorded
Representation Available

Personnel
Head of Company: J C V Mitchell

Number of titles published annually: 12
Number of Staff: 3
All New Titles are Bar Coded

Trade Terms
35%
Other Terms: Small order surcharges £1 p&p on one book

Returns Procedures
Stock Returns: Return
Imperfect Returns: Return annotated title pages

MIDLAND COUNTIES PUBLICATIONS (AEROPHILE) LTD

24 The Hollow, Earl Shilton, Leicester, Leicestershire LE9 7NA
ISBN Prefix(es): 0904597
Tel: 0455 847256
Fax: 0455 841805
VAT No: 290 2261 77

Orders to
Midland Counties Pub, Unit 3, Maizefield, Hinckley Fields, Hinckley, Leicester, Leicestershire LE10 1YF
Tel: 0455 233747 (24 Hr)
Fax: 0455 841805

Order Information

Order Dept Opening Times
Mon - Fri 9am - 5.30pm Sat 9am - 1.00pm
All Dues Automatically Recorded
Representation Available

Personnel
Head of Sales (Home): Tom Ferris
Head of Customer Services: Mike Everton

Number of titles published annually: 4
Percentage of Export Sales: 40%
Number of Staff: 20
All New Titles are Bar Coded
WBIP Updating: N P Lewis

Trade Terms
Girobank Number: 450 6154
Credit Cards Accepted: Access/Master, Visa

Returns Procedures
Stock Returns: Obtain permission first

MILESTONE PUBLICATIONS

62 Murray Road, Horndean, Waterlooville, Hampshire PO8 9JL
ISBN Prefix(es): 0 903852, 1 85265
Tel: 0705 592255
Tel: 0705 597440
Fax: 0705 591975
VAT No: 193 7217 45

Order Information

Order Dept Opening Times
Mon - Fri 8am - 5.30pm
Cyclical Ordering Policy
All Dues Automatically Recorded
Representation Available

Personnel
Head of Company: Nicholas J Pine
Head of Marketing: Philip Robinson
Head of Accounts: Sarah Hughes
Head of Distribution: Andrew Swainbank
Head of Customer Services: Sally Milligan

Number of titles published annually: 10
Number of Staff: 17
IPG Member
NBA Signatory
All New Titles are Bar Coded
Book Data Subscriber
WBIP Updating: N J Pine

Parent Company: Goss & Crested China Ltd

Trade Terms
Single copies 25%, 2 books or more 35%, subscription 35%,
no surcharges, CWO 25%
Girobank Number: 244 3252
Credit Cards Accepted: Access/Master, Visa, Amex, Diners

Returns Procedures
Stock Returns: Inform of damaged books before returning.
Imperfect Returns: Title pages not accepted. Inform by letter and substitute will be sent.

[Handwritten: Millionaires in Motion = MLM International, 5 Cornwall Cres, London W11 1PP, Tel 071 221 5611]

MILLBANK BOOKS LTD
Victorian Wing, Rawdon House, High Street, Hoddesdon,
Hertfordshire EN11 8TE
Tel: 0992 470177
Fax: 0992 470178
VAT No: 473 0010 92

Account No: _____
Sales Rep: _____
Tel: _____

Orders to
COMBINED BOOK SERVICES, 406 Vale Road,
Tonbridge, Kent TN9 1SW
Tel: 0732 357755
Fax: 0732 770219

Order Information

Orders for more than one publisher can be bulked
All Dues Automatically Recorded
Representation Available
Invoice Payments: Combined Book Services

Personnel
Head of Company: Diana Walsh/Christine Walsh
Head of Customer Services: Barbara Robinson

Percentage of Export Sales: 40%
WBIP Updating: Barbara Robinson

Trade Terms
General Net: Single copy 25%, Two or more 35%
Other Terms: Carriage charged on overseas orders only
Credit Cards Accepted: Access/Master, Visa

Returns Procedures
Address for Returns: Combined Book Services

Stock Returns: Authorised returns in mint cond. with inv no & not over 1yr Credit 50% overstocks. Damaged/incorrect suppl full credit.
Imperfect Returns: Title page up to £35 retail price. Above that contact H/O for authorization to return whole book.

HARVEY MILLER PUBLISHERS

20 Marryat Road, Wimbledon, London SW19 5BD
ISBN Prefix(es): 0 199210, 0 905203, 1 872501
Tel: 081-946 4426
Fax: 081-944 6082
VAT No: 350 5745 60

Orders to
BIBLIOS PUBLISHERS DISTRIBUTION SERVICE LTD, Star Road, Partridge Green, West Sussex RH13 8LD
Tel: 0403 710971
Fax: 0403 711143

Order Information

All Dues Automatically Recorded
Representation Available
Invoice Payments: Biblios Distribution Services

Personnel
Head of Company: Mr H I Miller (Managing Director)
Head of Marketing: Ms Kate Glasgow (Marketing Manager)

Number of titles published annually: 4
Number of Staff: 3
PA Member
NBA Signatory
All New Titles are Bar Coded
WBIP Updating: Ms K Glasgow

Trade Terms
General Net: Single copy/single line 25%, 2 books or more 35%

Returns Procedures
Authority to Return: Harvey Miller
Address for Returns: Biblios Distribution Services

MILLS & BOON LTD

Eton House, 18-24 Paradise Road, Richmond, Surrey TW9 1SR
ISBN Prefix(es): 0 263, 0 373
Tel: 081-948 0444
Fax: 081-940 5899
Telex: 24420 MILBON G
Cables: MILLSATOR, RICHMOND, SURREY
VAT No: 232 4334 96

Account No: _____
Sales Rep: _____
Tel: _____

Orders to
EXEL LOGISTICS - MEDIA SERVICES, 3 Sheldon Way, Larkfield, Aylesford, Kent ME20 6SF
Tel: 0622 882000
Fax: 0622 718036

Order Information

Cyclical Ordering Policy
Representation Available
Invoice Payments: Exel Logistics

Personnel
Head of Company: Mr Robert Williams (Managing Director)

Head of Sales (Home): Mr Gerry Howe (Home Paperback Sales Director)
Head of Sales (Export): Ron Hedley (Export & Hardback Sales Director)
Head of Marketing: Ms Heather Walton (Marketing Director, Retail)
Head of Publicity: Ms Carol Cherry (PR Manager)
Head of Accounts: Mr M J Westwell (Finance Director)
Head of Distribution: Mr Chris Stevens (Sales Operation Manager)
Head of Customer Services: Mr C Stevens
Other Important Personnel:
Ms S Critchlow (Export Sales Manager), Mr J T Boon (Chairman)

Number of titles published annually: 500
Number of Staff: 200
PA Member
NBA Signatory
All New Titles are Bar Coded
WBIP Updating: C Cherry

Parent Company: Harlequin Enterprises Ltd (Canada)
Subsidiary Companies: Allman & Son Ltd, Marshall Editions Ltd

Trade Terms
General Net: Subscription Orders & Stock Orders 30%
Special Orders 25%
Minimum Order: £20 net invoice value
Other Terms: Small order surcharges/Carriage: sliding scale up to £5

Returns Procedures
Authority to Return: Essential - From M&B Representative
Address for Returns: Exel Logistics
Imperfect Returns: All imperfects to be returned as whole book

MINIFLASHCARD LANGUAGE GAMES

PO Box 1526, London W7 1ND
Tel: 081-567 1076
Tel: 081-566 3930 Tel/Fax
VAT No: 579 3347 95

MINIMAX BOOKS LTD

Broadgate House, Langtoft Fen, Peterborough, Cambridgeshire PE69 Q13
ISBN Prefix(es): 0 906791, 0 907581, 1 871173
Tel: 0778 347609
Fax: 0778 341198

Trade Terms
General Net: Single copy/single line 10%, 2 books or more 35%
Non-Net: 2 or more single titles 17.5%, 6 or more 35%, less 25% (for AYB titles)

MINING JOURNAL BOOKS LTD

60 Worship Street, London EC2A 2HD
Tel: 071-377 2020
Fax: 071-247 4100
Telex: 8952809 Mining G
VAT No: 425 2341 82

Orders to
Mining Journal Books, PO Box 10, Edenbridge, Kent TN8 5NE

Tel: 0732 864333
Fax: 0732 865747

MINORITY RIGHTS GROUP
379 Brixton Road, London SW9 7DE
ISBN Prefix(es): 0 903114, 0 946690, 1 873194
Tel: 071-978 9498
Fax: 071-738 6265

Orders to
CENTRAL BOOKS, 99 Wallis Road, London E9 5LN
Tel: 081-986 4854
Fax: 081-533 5821

Order Information

All Dues Automatically Recorded
Representation Available
Invoice Payments: Central Books

Personnel
Head of Company: Alan Phillips (Executive Director)
Head of Sales (Home): Robert Webb (Publications Officer (Marketing))
Head of Accounts: Pat Pons

Number of titles published annually: 12
Percentage of Export Sales: 30%
Number of Staff: 10
All New Titles are Bar Coded
Book Data Subscriber
WBIP Updating: Robert Webb

Trade Terms
35%

Returns Procedures
Authority to Return: Central Books
Address for Returns: Central Books

MINTON & MINTON
Greylands, Bicton Pool, Kingsland, Nr Leominster, Herefordshire HR6 9PR
Tel: 0568 85338

MIT PRESS LTD
14 Bloomsbury Square, London WC1A 2LP
ISBN Prefix(es): 0 262, 0 942299
Tel: 071-404 0712
Fax: 071-404 0601
VAT No: 239 9164 28

Account No: _____
Sales Rep: _____
Tel: _____

Orders to
JOHN WILEY & SONS LTD, Southern Cross Trading Estate, 1 Oldlands Way, Bognor Regis, West Sussex PO22 9SA
Tel: 0243 829121
Fax: 0243 820250

Order Information

All Dues Automatically Recorded
Representation Available
Invoice Payments: John Wiley & Sons Ltd

Personnel
Head of Company: Ann Sexsmith

Head of Publicity: Ann Twisclton
Other Important Personnel:
Judith Bullent (Exhibitions/Texts)

Number of titles published annually: 150
Percentage of Export Sales: 60%
NBA Signatory
All New Titles are Bar Coded
Open University Publications
Book Data Subscriber
WBIP Updating: Ann Twiselton

Trade Terms
Depends on turnover, arrangements via reps and with publisher direct
Credit Cards Accepted: Access/Master, Visa, Amex, Diners

Returns Procedures
Authority to Return: Manager
Address for Returns: Returns Dept, John Wiley & Sons, 1 Oldlands Way, Bognor Regis, Sussex PO22

MOMENTA PUBLISHING COMPANY LTD

40 Barrow Road, Streatham, London SW16 5PF
Tel: 081-542 2465 Tel/Fax
VAT No: 451 0662 75

Account No: _____

Sales Rep: _____

Tel: _____

Orders to
Momenta Pub Co Ltd, Broadway House, The Broadway, London SW19 1RH

Order Information
Teleordering: MPC

Order Dept Opening Times
Mon - Fri 9.30am - 5.30pm
All Dues Automatically Recorded
Representation Available

Personnel
Head of Company: Robert J Leech
Head of Sales (Home): Marie-Louise Scott

WBIP Updating: Robert Leech

Trade Terms
25%

MONARCH PUBLICATIONS

Owl Lodge, Langton Road, Speldhurst, Kent TN3 0NP
Tel: 0892 863129 Tel/Fax
VAT No: 583 7802 09

Orders to
SEND THE LIGHT, PO Box 300, Kingstown Broadway, Carlisle, Cumbria CA3 0QS
Tel: 0228 512512
Fax: 0228 514949

Order Information

All Dues Automatically Recorded
Representation Available
Invoice Payments: STL
Representation:Kingsway Publications

Personnel
Head of Company: Tony Collins

Number of titles published annually: 30
Percentage of Export Sales: 20%
Number of Staff: 2
All New Titles are Bar Coded
WBIP Updating: Jane P Collins

Trade Terms
35%
Minimum Order: £60 retail
Other Terms: Small order surcharge £2 or 5% of retail under £60

Returns Procedures
Authority to Return: Kingsway Publications
Address for Returns: STL

PETER MOORE BOOKSELLER

PO Box 66, Cambridge, Cambridgeshire CB1 3PD
Tel: 0223 411177
Cables: ANTIPODES CAMBRIDGE
VAT No: 215 3610 02

Account No: _____

Sales Rep: _____

Tel: _____

Trade Terms
1 or 2 copies 25%, 3+ copies 35%, pro-forma only
Girobank Number: 22 695 4005
Credit Cards Accepted: Access/Master, Visa, Other

Returns Procedures
Authority to Return: Firm sale only

MOORLAND PUBLISHING CO LTD

Moorfarm Road West, Ashbourne, Derbyshire DE6 1HD
ISBN Prefix(es): 0 86190, 0 873775
Tel: 0335 44486
Fax: 0335 46397
VAT No: 318 8086 39

Account No: _____

Sales Rep: _____

Tel: _____

Orders to
GRANTHAM BOOK SERVICES LTD, Isaac Newton Way, Alma Park Industrial Estate, Grantham, Lincolnshire NG31 9SD
Tel: 0476 67421
Fax: 0476 590223

Order Information

All Dues Automatically Recorded
Representation Available
Invoice Payments: Grantham Book Services

Personnel
Head of Company: Mr C L M Porter (Managing Director)
Head of Publicity: Mrs P A Robey
Head of Accounts: Mr P Tomlinson
Head of Customer Services: Miss K Oldknow

Number of titles published annually: 24
Percentage of Export Sales: 20%
Number of Staff: 9
All New Titles are Bar Coded
Book Data Subscriber
WBIP Updating: Mrs P A Robey

Trade Terms
35%

Returns Procedures
Address for Returns: Grantham Book Services
Imperfect Returns: £10

MOORLEY'S PRINT & PUBLISHING

23 Park Road, Ilkeston, Derbyshire DE7 5DA
ISBN Prefix(es): 0 86071, 0 901495
Tel: 0602 320643 24 Tel/Fax
VAT No: 116 7436 71

Order Information

Order Dept Opening Times
Mon - Fri 9am - 5pm
All Dues Automatically Recorded
Representation Available

Personnel
Head of Company: John R Moorley
Head of Sales (Home): Jean E Moorley

Number of titles published annually: 20
Number of Staff: 7
WBIP Updating: Mrs S Stones

Parent Company: Moorley's Bible & Bookshop Ltd

Trade Terms
35%, except Mainstream & Cliff College 25%
Minimum Order: Orders for less than 5 books should be accompanied by limited open cheque.
Other Terms: Carriage charges sliding scale.
BA/Girobank Small Order Scheme: Limited cheque with order limits carriage to half.

Returns Procedures
Stock Returns: Overstocks must be previously authorized before return. Incorrect or damaged items to be returned with returns form.
Imperfect Returns: Titles retailing at less than £3 annotated title page. More than £3 complete book.

Morgan Kaufmann = Direct Distribution

E J MORTEN PUBLISHERS

6 Warburton Street, Didsbury, Manchester, Greater Manchester M20 0RA
ISBN Prefix(es): 0 85972, 0 907592
Tel: 061-445 7629 Tel/Fax
VAT No: 437 6243 43

Order Information

All Dues Automatically Recorded
Representation Available

Personnel
Head of Company: John A Morten
Head of Marketing: M J G Pardoe
Head of Accounts: Trevor Whitehurst

Number of titles published annually: 5
Number of Staff: 4
All New Titles are Bar Coded
WBIP Updating: Administration Manager

Trade Terms
33.3%, £2.50 small order surcharge on orders under £25

Returns Procedures
Authority to Return: The Administration Manager

MOSBY-YEARBOOK EUROPE LTD

Brook House, 2-16 Torrington Place, London WC1E 7LT
ISBN Prefix(es): 0 7234, 0 8016, 0 8151, 1 5605
Tel: 071-636 4622 24 Hours
Fax: 071-637 3021
Fax: 071-436 3706 Marketing
Telex: 8814230
Cables: WOLFEBOOKS LONDON
VAT No: 234 9354 53
Account No: SM0280'002
Sales Rep:
Tel:

Orders to
EXEL LOGISTICS - MEDIA SERVICES, 3 Sheldon Way, Larkfield, Aylesford, Kent ME20 6SF
Tel: ~~0622 882000~~ 0634 297123
Fax: 0622 718036

Order Information

All Dues Automatically Recorded
Representation Available

Personnel
Head of Company: Tim Hailstone (Chairman & Senior Vice President)
Head of Sales (Home): P Chrystal (UK Sales Manager) Tel/Fax: 0904 750050
Head of Sales (Export): Graham Crossley (Export Sales Manager)
Head of Marketing: R Maund (Marketing Manager)
Head of Publicity: A Walker (Promotion Manager)
Head of Accounts: Peter Heilbrunn (Chief Financial Officer)
Head of Distribution: Barrie Harvey (Operations Director)
Other Important Personnel:
S Sidaway (MD Sales & Marketing Division), Richard Furn (European Sales Manager), J Bartley (Sales Office Administrator)

Number of titles published annually: 600
Percentage of Export Sales: 80%
Number of Staff: 86
PA Member
NBA Signatory
All New Titles are Bar Coded
Book Data Subscriber
WBIP Updating: Susan Little

Parent Company: Mosby Inc

Trade Terms
30% no surcharges

Returns Procedures
Authority to Return: Prior permission required
Address for Returns: Exel Logistics
Imperfect Returns: Title Pages only should be returned to Wolfe Publishing at its head office address

THE MOTHERS' UNION

Mary Sumner House, 24 Tufton Street, London SW1P 3RB
Tel: 071-222 5533 Tel/Fax

MOTILAL BOOKS

52 Crown Road, Wheatley, Oxford, Oxfordshire OX9 1UL
Tel: 0865 67575
Fax: 0865 750079
VAT No: 596 0573 08

Orders to
LAVIS MARKETING, 73 Lime Walk, Headington,
Oxfordshire OX3 7AD
Tel: 0865 67575
Fax: 0865 750079

Order Information
All Dues Automatically Recorded
Invoice Payments: Lavis Marketing

Personnel
Head of Company: Ron Hilsdon
Head of Distribution: A Lavis
Head of Customer Services: P M Hilsdon

Number of titles published annually: 120
Percentage of Export Sales: 30%
Number of Staff: 4
WBIP Updating: Ron Hilsdon

Trade Terms
General Net: Single copy/single line, 2 or more single titles 25%, subscription orders 35%
Credit Cards Accepted: Access/Master, Visa

Returns Procedures
Authority to Return: Written authority must be obtained
Address for Returns: Lavis Marketing

MOTOR RACING PUBLICATIONS LTD

Unit 6, The Pilton Estate, 46 Pitlake, Croydon, Surrey
CR0 3RY
Tel: 081-681 3363
Fax: 081-760 5117
VAT No: 223 0882 86

Orders to
BIBLIOS PUBLISHERS DISTRIBUTION SERVICE LTD,
Star Road, Partridge Green, West Sussex RH13 8LD
Tel: 0403 710971
Fax: 0403 711143

MOTOROLA LTD

88 Tanners Drive, Blakelands, Milton Keynes,
Buckinghamshire MK14 5BP
Tel: 0908 614614
Fax: 0908 618650
Telex: 826366

MOZAMBIQUE INSTITUTE

31 Bedford Square, London WC1B 3SG
ISBN Prefix(es): 1 874162
Tel: 071-323 2722
Fax: 071-631 4659

Personnel
Head of Company: David Hoile

Number of titles published annually: 20

Trade Terms
33.3% post free, no surcharge

MULTILINGUAL MATTERS LTD

Frankfurt Lodge, Clevedon Hall, Victoria Road, Clevedon,
Avon BS21 7SJ
ISBN Prefix(es): 0 905028, 0 906054, 1 85359, 1 85658

Tel: 0275 876519
Fax: 0275 343096
VAT No: 357 9091 19

Orders to
PLYMBRIDGE DISTRIBUTORS LTD, Plymbridge House, Estover Road, Plymouth, Devon PL6 7PZ
Tel: 0752 735251
Fax: 0752 695699

Order Information

All Dues Automatically Recorded
Representation Available
Invoice Payments: Plymbridge Distribution

Personnel
Head of Company: Mike Grover
Head of Customer Services: Kathy King

Number of titles published annually: 25
Percentage of Export Sales: 70%
Number of Staff: 6
All New Titles are Bar Coded
Open University Publications
Book Data Subscriber
WBIP Updating: Marjukta Grover

Trade Terms
General Net: Single Copy 25%, Two or more 35%
Credit Cards Accepted: Access/Master, Amex, Visa, Other

Returns Procedures
Authority to Return: Mike Grover
Address for Returns: Plymbridge

MULTIMEDIA BOOKS LTD

Unit L, 32/34 Gordon House, London NW5 1LP
ISBN Prefix(es): 1 85375
Tel: 071-482 4248
Fax: 071-482 4203
Telex: 295941 ATID G
VAT No: 421 6893 47

Orders to
BOOKPOINT LIMITED, 39 Milton Park, Abingdon, Oxfordshire OX14 4TD
Tel: 0235 835001
Fax: 0235 861038

Order Information

All Dues Automatically Recorded
Representation Available
Invoice Payments: Bookpoint
Representation:Charles Letts & Co

Personnel
Head of Company: Arnon Orbach (Managing Director)
Head of Sales (Export): Maggie Black
Head of Publicity: Anna Kirby
Head of Accounts: Laurence Cohen

Number of titles published annually: 26
Percentage of Export Sales: 60%
Number of Staff: 6
All New Titles are Bar Coded
WBIP Updating: Maggie Black

Trade Terms
35%

Returns Procedures
Stock Returns: To be authorised by Maggie Black and returned to Bookpoint

MULTISCOPE BOOKS

2 Mead Road, Torquay, Devon TQ2 6TE
ISBN Prefix(es): 0 9510106
Tel: 0803 607455

Order Information

Invoice Payments: I Barrada

Personnel
Head of Company: I Barrada

Number of titles published annually: 1

Trade Terms
General Net: Single Copy 10%, Two Books or more 30%

GRAEME MURRAY EDINBURGH

15 Scotland Street, Edinburgh, Lothian EH3 6PU
Tel: 031-556 6020
Fax: 031-557 3214
VAT No: 502 3604 95

JOHN MURRAY (PUBLISHERS) LTD

50 Albemarle Street, London W1X 4BD
ISBN Prefix(es): 0 719 5
Tel: 071-493 4361
Fax: 071-499 1792
Telex: 21312 MURRAY G
VAT No: 238 9662 18

Account No: _____ 00199-002 _____
Sales Rep: _____
Tel: _____

Orders to
GRANTHAM BOOK SERVICES LTD, Isaac Newton Way,
Alma Park Industrial Estate, Grantham, Lincolnshire
NG31 9SD
Tel: 0476 67421
Fax: 0476 590223

Order Information

All Dues Automatically Recorded
Representation Available
Invoice Payments: Grantham Book Services

Personnel
Head of Company: Nicholas Perren (Managing Director)
Head of Sales (Home): John R Murray (General Sales)
Head of Publicity: Victoria Raikes
Head of Accounts: John Roberts
Other Important Personnel:
Judith Reinhold (Educational Sales)

Number of titles published annually: 60
Percentage of Export Sales: 30%
Number of Staff: 36
PA Member
NBA Signatory
All New Titles are Bar Coded
Book Data Subscriber
WBIP Updating: Ed Books Deborah Sanderson/Gen Books
John R Murray

Trade Terms
General Net: Variable, dependent on customer
Academic Net: 30%
Non-Net: 17.5%
BA/Girobank Small Order Scheme: Yes
Girobank Number: 508 7457
Credit Cards Accepted: Access/Master, Visa

Returns Procedures
Stock Returns: No books will be accepted back unless permission has been received from John Murray
Imperfect Returns: £15

MUSEUMS ASSOCIATION
42 Clerkenwell Close, London EC1R 0PA
Tel: 071-608 2933
Fax: 071-250 1929
VAT No: 523 0407 92

MUSIC PRESS
Suite 11, Robins Court, Kings Avenue, London SW4 8EE
ISBN Prefix(es): 1 873260
Tel: 081-674 9226
VAT No: 561 9838 04

Order Information

All Dues Automatically Recorded

Personnel
Head of Company: Ann Harrold

Number of titles published annually: 10
Percentage of Export Sales: 20%

Trade Terms
20% on all orders no surchages

Returns Procedures
Imperfect Returns: Return title page only to a limit of £25

NAG PRESS
Pond House, Great Bentley, Colchester, Essex CO7 8QG
ISBN Prefix(es): 0 7198
Tel: 0206 250343

Orders to
TIPTREE BOOK SERVICES LTD, Church Road, Tiptree, Colchester, Essex CO5 0SR
Tel: 0621 819600
Fax: 0621 819011

Order Information

All Dues Automatically Recorded
Representation Available
Invoice Payments: Tiptree Book Services

Personnel
Head of Company: Eric Bruton
Head of Customer Services: Douglas Westland (0371 850705)

Number of titles published annually: 4
Percentage of Export Sales: 40%
NBA Signatory
WBIP Updating: Douglas Westland

Trade Terms
35% on all orders

PETER NAHUM
5 Ryder Street, London SW1Y 6PY
ISBN Prefix(es): 1 872508
Tel: 071-930 6059
Fax: 071-930 4678
VAT No: 461 5279 42

Personnel
Head of Company: Peter Nahum (Director)
Head of Sales (Home): Renate Nahum (Company Secretary)

Trade Terms
35%, payable 28 days

NATIONAL ASSOCIATION FOR THE TEACHING OF ENGLISH
Birley School Annexe, Fox Lane, Frecheville, Sheffield, South Yorkshire S12 4WY
Tel: 0742 390081
Fax: 0742 648821

NATIONAL CHILDBIRTH TRUST
Alexandra House, Oldham Terrace, Acton, London W3 6NH
Tel: 081-992 8637
Fax: 081-992 5929

Orders to
NCT Sales Ltd, Burnfield Avenue, Glasgow, Strathclyde G46 7TL
Tel: 041-633 5552
Fax: 041-633 5677

Book Data Subscriber

NATIONAL CHILDREN'S BUREAU
8 Wakley Street, London EC1V 7QE
ISBN Prefix(es): 0 902817, 1 874579
Tel: 071-278 9441
Fax: 071-278 9512

Order Information
Order Dept Opening Times
Mon - Fri 9am - 5pm
Representation Available
Representation:Book Representation & Distribution (BRAD)

Personnel
Head of Company: John Rea Price (Director)
Head of Marketing: Fiona Blakemore (Publications Manager)
Head of Accounts: David Pearce (Finance Officer)
Head of Distribution: Denise Hollingbery (Administration Manager)

Number of titles published annually: 20
Number of Staff: 75
All New Titles are Bar Coded
Book Data Subscriber
WBIP Updating: Fiona Blakemore

Trade Terms
Single copy 25%, Two books or more 35%
Credit Cards Accepted: Access/Master, Visa

Returns Procedures
Address for Returns: Book Sales, Wakeley Street
Imperfect Returns: All books fully replaced if imperfect.

NATIONAL CHRISTIAN EDUCATION COUNCIL
Robert Denholm House, Nutfield, Redhill, Surrey RH1 4HW
ISBN Prefix(es): 0 7197
Tel: 0737 822411 24 Hours
Fax: 0737 822116 24 Hours
VAT No: 209 5032 86

Order Information
Teleordering: NCEC

Order Dept Opening Times
Mon - Thur 9am - 5pm Fri 9am - 3.45pm
All Dues Automatically Recorded
Representation Available

Personnel
Head of Sales (Home): Mr Doug Fletcher (Sales & Marketing Manager)
Head of Accounts: Mrs Sheila Sharman
Other Important Personnel:
Mr David Trenaman (Head of Publishing)

Number of titles published annually: 10
Number of Staff: 25
PA Member
NBA Signatory
All New Titles are Bar Coded
WBIP Updating: Mr David Clark

Trade Terms
35%
General Net: Subscription orders 40% no surcharge
Non-Net: Subscription orders 40% no surcharge
Other Terms: Small order surcharge £2 on orders below £15
Credit Cards Accepted: Access/Master, Visa

Returns Procedures
Stock Returns: Advise details of proposed returns & await authorisation

NATIONAL CONSUMER COUNCIL

20 Grosvenor Gardens, London SW1W 0DH
Tel: 071-730 3469
Fax: 071-730 0191
VAT No: 563 1251 64

Book Data Subscriber

NATIONAL CURRICULUM COUNCIL

Albion Wharf, 25 Skeldergate, York, North Yorkshire YO1 2XL
Tel: 0904 622533
Fax: 0904 622921

PA Member

NATIONAL ECONOMIC DEVELOPMENT OFFICE (NEDO) = HMSO

NATIONAL EXTENSION COLLEGE

18 Brooklands Avenue, Cambridge, Cambridgeshire CB2 2HN
ISBN Prefix(es): 0 86082, 1 85356
Tel: 0223 316644
Fax: 0223 313586
VAT No: 215 7137 79

Order Information

Order Dept Opening Times
Mon - Fri 9.15am - 5pm

Personnel
Head of Company: Ros Morpeth
Head of Sales (Home): Roger Merritt
Head of Publicity: Alison Cornell
Head of Accounts: Imre Goller
Head of Distribution: Pat Gouldstone

Number of titles published annually: 35
Book Data Subscriber
WBIP Updating: Glynn Clark

Trade Terms
30 days net. Orders under £250 17%, £250-£1000 20%, over £1000 25%
Other Terms: Minimum order £20
Girobank Number: 278 3258
Credit Cards Accepted: Access/Master, Visa, Amex

Returns Procedures
Authority to Return: Andrea Sayer, Accounts Dept
Stock Returns: Must return invoice with goods returned

NATIONAL FOSTER CARE ASSOCIATION
Leonard House, 5-7 Marshalsea Road, London SE1 1EP
Tel: 071-828 6266
Fax: 071-357 6668

NATIONAL GALLERY PUBLICATIONS LIMITED
5/6 Pall Mall East, London SW1Y 5BA
ISBN Prefix(es): 0 901791, 0 947645, 1 85709
Tel: 071-839 8544
Fax: 071-930 0108

Order Information

Order Dept Opening Times
Mon - Fri 9am - 5.30pm

Personnel
Head of Company: William Silver (Managing Director)
Head of Sales (Home): James Faichnie (Sales & Marketing Manager)
Head of Publicity: Jane West
Head of Accounts: Hugh Armstrong
Head of Distribution: Murtagh Devlin
Head of Customer Services: Simon Thompson

Book Data Subscriber

Trade Terms
35%
Credit Cards Accepted: Access/Master, Visa

NATIONAL GARDENS CHARITABLE TRUST
Hatchlands Park, East Clandon, Guildford, Surrey GU4 7RT
ISBN Prefix(es): 0 9005582
Tel: 0483 211535
Fax: 0483 211537
VAT No: 381 8214 49

Order Information

All Dues Automatically Recorded
Representation Available
Invoice Payments: Seymour
Supplies only available through book wholesalers

Personnel
Head of Company: Lt Col D G Carpenter (Administrator)

Number of titles published annually: 1
Number of Staff: 5
All New Titles are Bar Coded
Book Data Subscriber

Trade Terms
Increasing percentage discount on quantity
BA/Girobank Small Order Scheme: 30 days

Returns Procedures
Authority to Return: Returns via book wholesalers

NATIONAL INSTITUTE FOR SOCIAL WORK
5 Tavistock Place, London WC1H 9SS
Tel: 071-387 9681
Fax: 071-387 7968
VAT No: 417 6759 22

Book Data Subscriber

NATIONAL INSTITUTE OF ADULT CONTINUING EDUCATION
19B De Montfort Street, Leicester, Leicestershire LE1 7GE
ISBN Prefix(es): 0 900559, 1 872941
Tel: 0533 551451
Fax: 0533 854514

Orders to
CENTRAL BOOKS, 99 Wallis Road, London E9 5LN
Tel: 081-986 4854
Fax: 081-533 5821

Order Information

All Dues Automatically Recorded
Representation Available

Personnel
Head of Company: Christopher Feeney

Number of titles published annually: 10

Trade Terms
35%

NATIONAL LIBRARY OF SCOTLAND
George IV Bridge, Edinburgh, Lothian EH1 1EW
Tel: 031-226 4531
Fax: 031-220 6662
Telex: 72638 NLSEDI G

Book Data Subscriber

NATIONAL POETRY FOUNDATION
27 Mill Road, Fareham, Hampshire PO16 0TH
ISBN Prefix(es): 1 870556
Tel: 0329 822218

Order Information

Order Dept Opening Times
7.00am - 10pm 7 days a week

Personnel
Head of Company: Johnathon Clifford (Founder & Trustee)
Other Important Personnel:
Helen Robinson (Trustee), Dr Althea Lord (Trustee), Toni Joyce (Trustee)

Number of titles published annually: 27
All New Titles are Bar Coded

Trade Terms
50% Postage charged on orders of less than five books. Prepayment against pro-forma invoice for all orders.

Returns Procedures
Stock Returns: Firm sale only
Imperfect Returns: Whole book must be returned

NATIONAL PORTRAIT GALLERY PUBLICATIONS

2 St Martin's Place, London WC2H 0HE
ISBN Prefix(es): 0 904017, 1 85514
Tel: 071-306 0055
Fax: 071-306 0056
VAT No: 240 1362 14

Order Information

Order Dept Opening Times
Mon - Fri 9am - 5.30pm
All Dues Automatically Recorded
Representation Available

Personnel

Head of Marketing: Louisa Hearnden
Head of Accounts: Nico Nicholas
Head of Customer Services: Pallavi Vadhia

Number of titles published annually: 6
Number of Staff: 6
PA Member
NBA Signatory
All New Titles are Bar Coded
Book Data Subscriber
WBIP Updating: Louisa Hearnden

Trade Terms

General Net: Single copy/single line, 2 or more single titles 25%, 2 books or more 35%
Girobank Number: 530 8003
Credit Cards Accepted: Access/Master, Visa, Amex

Returns Procedures

Authority to Return: Louisa Hearnden
Stock Returns: Write or telephone for authority to return all books stating the reason for returns. Ostocks credited only in mint cond
Imperfect Returns: Title pages up to £15

THE NATIONAL TRUST

36 Queen Anne's Gate, London SW1H 9AS
ISBN Prefix(es): 0 7078
Tel: 071-222 9251
Fax: 071-222 5097
VAT No: 239 5031 67

Orders to

HODDER & STOUGHTON LTD, Mill Road, Dunton Green, Sevenoaks, Kent TN13 2YA
Tel: 0732 450111
Fax: 0732 460134

Order Information

All Dues Automatically Recorded
Representation Available
Invoice Payments: Hodder & Stoughton

Personnel

Head of Company: Margaret Willes (Publisher)
Head of Publicity: Kate Crookenden
Other Important Personnel:
Sheila Mortimer (Publishing Administration)

Number of titles published annually: 10
Number of Staff: 12
All New Titles are Bar Coded
WBIP Updating: Sheila Mortimer

Trade Terms
See Hodder & Stoughton

Returns Procedures
Authority to Return: Hodder & Stoughton

THE NATIONAL TRUST FOR IRELAND (AN TAISCE)

The Tailors' Hall, Back Lane, Dublin 8, County Dublin
Tel: 01 541786
Fax: 01 533255

Order Information

Order Dept Opening Times
Mon - Fri 9.30am - 5pm
All Enquires:The Secretary

Personnel
Head of Company: Patricia Oliver (Chairwoman)

Number of titles published annually: 4
Number of Staff: 5
Book Data Subscriber
WBIP Updating: Valerie Bond

Trade Terms
33.3% plus post & packing
Credit Cards Accepted: Access/Master, Amex, Visa

Returns Procedures
Stock Returns: Contact first
Imperfect Returns: Contact first

NATIONAL YOUTH AGENCY

17-23 Albion Street, Leicester, Leicestershire LE1 6GD
ISBN Prefix(es): 0 86155
Tel: 0533 471200
Fax: 0533 471043
VAT No: 114 9983 44

Order Information

Order Dept Opening Times
Mon - Fri 9am - 5.30pm
All Dues Automatically Recorded
Orders To:Sales Department

Personnel
Head of Company: Ms J Paraskeva
Head of Sales (Export): Ms G Wilkinson
Head of Marketing: Ms J Scott

Number of titles published annually: 4
Number of Staff: 12

Trade Terms
Min 35% on all orders, no surcharges
Credit Cards Accepted: Access/Master, Visa

Returns Procedures
Authority to Return: Sales Department

NATURAL HISTORY BOOK SERVICE LTD

2 Wills Road, Totnes, Devon TQ9 5XN
Tel: 0803 865913 4 lines
Fax: 0803 865280
VAT No: 407 4846 44

Account No: _____
Sales Rep: _____
Tel: _____

Order Information

Order Dept Opening Times
Mon - Fri 8.30am - 5.30pm
All Dues Automatically Recorded

Personnel
Head of Company: Bernard Mercer

Head of Marketing: Peter Exley
Head of Accounts: Isabel Seward

Number of Staff: 12
WBIP Updating: Peter Exley

Trade Terms
25%/35% depending on publisher
Other Terms: Carriage charges: overseas only

Returns Procedures
Authority to Return: Sue Groom
Stock Returns: Incorrectly supplied/damaged stock must be notified within 7 days. Overstocks can be returned up to 6 mths from inv date

NATURAL HISTORY MUSEUM PUBLICATIONS

Cromwell Road, London SW7 5BD
ISBN Prefix(es): 0 565
Tel: 071-938 9386
Fax: 071-938 9212

Orders to
Nat Hist Mus Pubs, Sales Office, Cromwell Road, London SW7 5BD
Tel: 071-938 9386
Fax: 071-938 9212

Order Information
Teleordering: BMNH

Order Dept Opening Times
Mon - Fri 9am - 5pm
All Dues Automatically Recorded
Invoice Payments: Accounts Office

Personnel
Head of Company: Rachel Laughton-Scott (Head of Commerce & Marketing) 071-938 8963
Head of Publicity: Wendy Ladd 071 938 8769
Head of Customer Services: Pauline Thomas 071-938 8723

Number of titles published annually: 16
Number of Staff: 3
IPG Member
All New Titles are Bar Coded

Trade Terms
General Net: 35%
Academic Net: 25%
Other Terms: 15% carriage charge personal mail order
Girobank Number: 514 7026
Credit Cards Accepted: Access/Master, Visa, Amex

Returns Procedures
Authority to Return: Sales Office
Address for Returns: Nat Hist Mus Pubs, Building 18, Dept of Environment Complex, Stonefield Way, South Ruislip, Middlesex HA4 0NZ
Stock Returns: Notify sales office

NATURETREK EDUCATIONAL

5 Llys Llannerch, St Asaph, Clwyd LL17 0AZ
Tel: 0745 730395 Fax/Tel
VAT No: 372 4379 38

NAVPRESS

The Navigators, Adyar House, 32 Carlton Cres, Southampton, Hampshire SO1 2EW

Tel: 0703 223743
Fax: 0703 237548

[handwritten: NCc = School Curriculum + Assessment Authority, Newcombe House, 35 Notting Hill Gate, London W11 3JB.]

NCVO PUBLICATIONS

Regent's Wharf, 8 All Saints Street, London N1 9RL
ISBN Prefix(es): 0 7199
Tel: 071-713 6161
Fax: 071-713 6300
VAT No: 232 7690 59

Account No: _____

Sales Rep: _____

Tel: _____

Orders to
PLYMBRIDGE DISTRIBUTORS LTD, Plymbridge House, Estover Road, Plymouth, Devon PL6 7PZ
Tel: 0752 735251
Fax: 0752 695699

Order Information

All Dues Automatically Recorded
Representation Available
Invoice Payments: Plymbridge

Personnel
Head of Company: Samantha Hellawell (Head of Communications)
Head of Sales (Home): Marianne Harper (Marketing & Promotions Manager)
Head of Publicity: Veronica Thompson (Press Officer)
Head of Distribution: Simon Cope (Publications Distribution Officer)

Number of titles published annually: 20
PA Member
IPG Member
NBA Signatory
All New Titles are Bar Coded
WBIP Updating: Marianne Harper

Trade Terms
Single copy 25%, Two books or more 35%
Girobank Number: 221 2951
Credit Cards Accepted: Access/Master, Amex, Diners, Visa, Other

Returns Procedures
Authority to Return: Marianne Harper, NCVO Publications
Address for Returns: Plymbridge

ANTHONY NELSON LTD

PO Box 9, Oswestry, Shropshire SY11 1BY
ISBN Prefix(es): 0 904614
Tel: 0691 828447 24 Hours
Fax: 0691 828898
VAT No: 377 8131 24

Order Information

All Dues Automatically Recorded
Representation Available

Personnel
Head of Company: Anthony Nelson

Number of titles published annually: 8
Percentage of Export Sales: 40%
All New Titles are Bar Coded

Trade Terms
35%

Other Terms: Small order surcharges, carriage charges, service charges £3

Returns Procedures
Authority to Return: Prior permission required

THOMAS NELSON & SONS LTD

Nelson House, Mayfield Road, Walton-on-Thames, Surrey KT12 5PL
ISBN Prefix(es): 0 0444, 0 080, 0 17, 0 17444, 0 2375, 0 245, 0 2455, 0 333, 0 560
Tel: 0932 246133
Fax: 0932 246109
Telex: 929365 NELSON G
Cables: THONELSON WALTON-ON-THAMES
VAT No: 358 9005 01
Account No: _____ 032030 0009
Sales Rep: _____
Tel: _____

Orders to
T Nelson & Sons Ltd, PO Box 1487, Andover, Hampshire SP10 1YN
Tel: 0264 342992
Fax: 0264 335977

Order Information
Teleordering: ITPS

Order Dept Opening Times
Mon - Fri 8.30am - 5.30pm
All Dues Automatically Recorded
Representation Available
Invoice Payments: Thomas Nelson & Sons Ltd - Andover

Personnel
Head of Company: Michael Thompson (Managing Director)
Head of Sales (Home): Des Higgins (Director of School Book Sales)
Head of Sales (Export): Noel Jones (International Sales Development Manager)
Head of Marketing: John Tuttle (Sales & Marketing Director)
Head of Publicity: Gary Beahan (Director of Schoolbook Marketing)
Head of Accounts: Brian Snaith (Finance Director)
Head of Distribution: Barry Hinchmore (Marketing Services Director)
Head of Customer Services: Sandi Forte (Director of Marketing Services)
Other Important Personnel:
Pamela Hutchinson (Publishing Director), Malcolm Givans (Production Director)

PA Member
All New Titles are Bar Coded
WBIP Updating: Helen Barnes

Parent Company: The Thomson Corporation

Trade Terms
30 days
General Net: 35%
Non-Net: 17.5%
Girobank Number: 300 6220

Returns Procedures
Authority to Return: Paula Massey, Thomas Nelson, Customer Service Dept, PO Box 1487, Andover, Hants SP10 1YN
Address for Returns: Thomas Nelson, Returns Dept, ITPS, North Way, Andover, Hants SP10 5BE

RICHARD NETHERWOOD LTD
Fulstone Barn, New Mill, Huddersfield, West Yorkshire
HD7 7DL
Tel: 0484 681592
Fax: 0484 682602
VAT No: 516 4743 45

IPG Member
Book Data Subscriber

NETWORK EDUCATIONAL PRESS
Castlefields, Newport Road, Stafford, Staffordshire ST17 0JR
Tel: 0785 225515 Tel/Fax
VAT No: 501 8930 63

Orders to
Network Educ Press, PO Box 635, Stafford, Staffordshire
ST17 0JR

NETWORK PUBLISHING LTD
Palmer House, Palmer Lane, Coventry, West Midlands
CV1 1FW
Tel: 0203 630204
Fax: 0203 630205
VAT No: 478 4076 12

NEW BEACON BOOKS LTD
76 Stoud Green Road, London N4 3EN
ISBN Prefix(es): 0 901241, 1 873201
Tel: 071-272 4889
Fax: 071-281 4662

Order Information

Order Dept Opening Times
Mon - Sat 10.30am - 6pm
Orders for more than one publisher can be bulked
All Dues Automatically Recorded
Representation Available

Personnel
Other Important Personnel:
John La Rose, Sarah White, Michael La Rose, Janice Durham

Number of titles published annually: 4
Number of Staff: 4
NBA Signatory
All New Titles are Bar Coded
Open University Publications
WBIP Updating: Sarah White

Trade Terms
33.3%, 25% on orders up to £20 value
Credit Cards Accepted: Access/Master, Visa

NEW CAVENDISH BOOKS
3 Denbigh Road, London W11 2SJ
ISBN Prefix(es): 0 904568, 1 872727
Tel: 071-229 6765
Tel: 071-792 9984
Fax: 071-792 0027
Telex: 8951182 GECOMS G
VAT No: 340 2601 09

Orders to
LITTLEHAMPTON BOOK SERVICES, 14 Eldon Way,
Lineside Ind Estate, Littlehampton, West Sussex BN17 7HE
Tel: 0903 721596
Fax: 0903 730914

Personnel
Head of Company: Allen Levy/Narisa Chakra
Head of Sales (Home): Christopher Shelley

WBIP Updating: Catrin J Evans

Subsidiary Companies: Golden Age Bookshop

Trade Terms
General Net: Single Copy 25%, Two or more 35%, Special Orders 45-55%
Other Terms: Carriage charges at a percentage of cost

Returns Procedures
Address for Returns: Littlehampton
Stock Returns: Only authorised returns accepted at above address within 7 days of receipt

NEW CITY

57 Twyford Avenue, London W3 9PZ
Tel: 081-993 6944 Tel/Fax
VAT No: 228 2342 78

NEW CLARION PRESS

8 Evesham Road, Cheltenham, Gloucestershire GL52 2AB
ISBN Prefix(es): 1 873797
Tel: 0242 571388 24 Hours
Tel: 0242 529381 24 Hours
VAT No: 575 9671 80

Order Information

Order Dept Opening Times
9am - 5pm
All Dues Automatically Recorded
Representation Available

Personnel
Head of Company: Chris Bessant/Fiona Sewell

Number of titles published annually: 2
Number of Staff: 2

Trade Terms
35% Surcharge of £1.25 on orders under £25. 30 days credit.
Other Terms: The title to goods supplied shall not pass to booksellers until the full price in respect thereof has been paid.

Returns Procedures
Authority to Return: Prior permission required
Address for Returns: Clipper Distribution Services, Windmill Grove, Portchester, Hants PO16 9HT
Stock Returns: Claims for shortage &/or damage must be made within 48 hours of receipt, non-delivery claims within 45 days of invoice.

NEW ERA PUBLICATIONS (UK) LTD

78 Holmethorpe Avenue, Redhill, Surrey RH1 2NL
ISBN Prefix(es): 1 870451
Tel: 0737 766760
Fax: 0737 765942
Telex: 262200 NEWERAG
VAT No: 426 7482 33

Order Information

Order Dept Opening Times
Mon - Fri 9am - 5pm
All Dues Automatically Recorded
Representation Available

Personnel
Head of Company: Gill Bustamante
Head of Sales (Home): Nic Webb
Head of Marketing: Rob Black
Head of Distribution: Tim Porter

Number of titles published annually: 10
Percentage of Export Sales: 20%
Number of Staff: 10
All New Titles are Bar Coded
WBIP Updating: Tim Porter

Parent Company: New Era International

Trade Terms
35%
General Net: Single Copy 25%

Returns Procedures
Authority to Return: Tim Porter
Address for Returns: The Trade Counter, The Airfield, Norwich Road, Mendlesham, Suffolk
Stock Returns: List Quantities by title and ISBN

NEW FOREST LEAVES

Bisterne Close, Burley, Ringwood, Hampshire BH24 4BA
ISBN Prefix(es): 0 907956
Tel: 0425 403315

Order Information

All Dues Automatically Recorded

Personnel
Head of Company: James Mays

Number of titles published annually: 4
Percentage of Export Sales: 20%
All New Titles are Bar Coded

Trade Terms
35%, except single copy/single line, which is 25%

Returns Procedures
Authority to Return: Prior permission required
Imperfect Returns: No limit

NEW HOLLAND PUBLISHERS LTD

37 Connaught Street, London W2 2AZ
ISBN Prefix(es): 1 85368
Tel: 071-258 0204
Fax: 071-262 6184
VAT No: 232 3375 87

Orders to
BOOKPOINT LIMITED, 39 Milton Park, Abingdon, Oxfordshire OX14 4TD
Tel: 0235 835001
Fax: 0235 861038

Order Information

All Dues Automatically Recorded
Representation Available

Personnel
Head of Company: John Beaufoy
Head of Sales (Export): Elena Mannion

Head of Marketing: John Beaufoy
Head of Accounts: David Wood
Head of Customer Services: Joanna Sharland

Number of titles published annually: 50
Number of Staff: 7
PA Member
NBA Signatory
All New Titles are Bar Coded
Book Data Subscriber
WBIP Updating: Joanna Sharland

Parent Company: Macquarie Corp SA

Trade Terms
35%
Credit Cards Accepted: Access/Master, Visa, Amex, Diners

Returns Procedures
Authority to Return: Representatives or Head Office
Address for Returns: Bookpoint Ltd

NEW PLAYWRIGHTS' NETWORK

35 Sandringham Road, Macclesfield, Cheshire SK10 1QB
ISBN Prefix(es): 0 86319, 0 903653, 0 906660
Tel: 0625 425312
Fax: 0625 425312
VAT No: 285 9119 22

Order Information

Order Dept Opening Times
Mon - Fri 9am - 4.30pm

Personnel
Head of Company: Mr J C F Gray (Managing Proprietor)

Number of titles published annually: 60
Number of Staff: 1
WBIP Updating: Mr D B Cartwright

Trade Terms
25% - no surcharges

NEW WINE MINISTRIES

Unit 22, Arun Business Park, Bognor Regis, West Sussex
PO22 9SX
Tel: 0243 867227
Fax: 0243 867292
VAT No: 397 5939 74

NEWBY BOOKS

PO Box 40, Scarborough, North Yorkshire YO12 5TW

NEWMAN BOOKS LTD

32 Vauxhall Bridge Road, London SW1V 2SS
Tel: 071-973 6402
Fax: 071-233 5057

OWEN NEWMAN (PUBLICATIONS) LTD

Langton Green, Tunbridge Wells, Kent TN3 0EG
Tel: 0892 863766
Fax: 0892 863503
VAT No: 565 4552 23

NEWPRO UK LTD

Old Sawmills Road, Faringdon, Oxfordshire SN7 7DS
Tel: 0367 242411
Fax: 0367 241124
VAT No: 417 7939 15

Account No: _____
Sales Rep: _____
Tel: _____

NEWS PRODUCTIONS

Fromehall Mill, Lodgemore Lane, Stroud, Gloucestershire GL5 3EH
ISBN Prefix(es): 1 871110
Tel: 0453 767222 24 Hours
Fax: 0453 767333

Orders to
24 Hour Ansafone Number: 0452 862616

Order Information

Order Dept Opening Times
Mon - Fri 9am - 6pm
Cyclical Ordering Policy
All Dues Automatically Recorded
Representation Available

Personnel
Head of Company: Armond Deriaz
Head of Sales (Home): Peter Ledeboer
Head of Publicity: Charlie Ryrie
Head of Accounts: Sarah Harvey

Number of Staff: 2
All New Titles are Bar Coded
WBIP Updating: Sarah Harvey

Parent Company: News Productions (UK) Ltd

Trade Terms
General Net: Single Copy 25%, Two or more 35%, Orders over £500 retail 40%
Other Terms: Postage at cost up to £50 nett order value

Returns Procedures
Stock Returns: Carriage paid on receipt of return authorization. Carriage forward on incorrect or damaged supplies.

NEWTON PUBLISHERS

PO Box 236, Swindon, Wiltshire SN3 6QZ
ISBN Prefix(es): 1 872308
Tel: 0793 641796
Tel: 0793 641793 24 Hours
Fax: 0793 641793
VAT No: 528 3992 10

Personnel
Head of Company: A J Roberts
Head of Marketing: James Fortune
Head of Publicity: Claudette Hall
Head of Accounts: N Probin
Head of Distribution: Cleo Thomas
Head of Customer Services: Sheila Bedfellow

Number of titles published annually: 6
Number of Staff: 6
IPG Member
WBIP Updating: A J Roberts

NEW YORK STATE 512 UNIV PRESS = CUP SERVICES (USA)

Trade Terms
General Net: Less than five books cash with order at 20%.
Stock orders 30 days 33.3%
Minimum Order: 5 assorted titles 35% dis

Returns Procedures
Stock Returns: Returns not accepted
Imperfect Returns: Return cover and title page and details of damage or defect

[handwritten: NFER - Nelson Pubs. Darville House, 2 Oxford Rd East, Windsor Berks. SL4 1DF - A/C No 30902-001]

NILE & MACKENZIE LTD

13 John Prince's Street, London W1M 9HB
ISBN Prefix(es): 0 86301
Tel: 071-493 0351
Fax: 071-495 0128
Telex: 24168
VAT No: 241 1067 10

Order Information

Order Dept Opening Times
9am - 5pm
Representation Available

Personnel
Head of Company: Mr Daljit Sehbai (Managing Director)

NBA Signatory
WBIP Updating: Mrs Donna Stewart

Trade Terms
35% on all orders, surcharge £2.50 on orders under £50

JAMES NISBET & CO LTD

78 Tilehouse Street, Hitchin, Hertfordshire SG5 2DY
ISBN Prefix(es): 0 7202
Tel: 0462 438331
Fax: 0462 431528
VAT No: 196 9018 23

Order Information

Order Dept Opening Times
Mon - Thur 9am - 5.30pm, Fri 9am - 5pm

Personnel
Head of Company: Miss E M MacKenzie-Wood
Head of Marketing: Mrs A Bierrum
Head of Accounts: Mrs G Wright

NBA Signatory

Trade Terms
17.5%

PAUL NORBURY PUBLICATIONS LTD

Knoll House, 35 The Crescent, Sandgate, Folkestone, Kent CT20 3EE
Tel: 0303 220277
Fax: 0303 243087

Orders to
BIBLIOS PUBLISHERS DISTRIBUTION SERVICE LTD,
Star Road, Partridge Green, West Sussex RH13 8LD
Tel: 0403 710971
Fax: 0403 711143

Order Information
Representation: Africa Book Centre

Book Data Subscriber

NORHEIMSUND BOOKS AND CARDS

1 Whitney Road, Burton Latimer, Kettering, Northamptonshire NN15 5SL
ISBN Prefix(es): 0 948852
Tel: 0536 723004

Order Information

All Dues Automatically Recorded
Representation Available

Personnel
Head of Company: Philip J Mason
Head of Accounts: Mary Mason

Number of titles published annually: 6
WBIP Updating: Mary Mason

Trade Terms
33.3/35%
Other Terms: Postage charged under £25

NORTH EAST WORSHIP RESOURCE

14 Mayfields, Great North Road, Scawthorpe, Doncaster, South Yorkshire DN5 7UA
Tel: 0302 780276
Fax: 0302 784296

NORTH YORK MOORS NATIONAL PARK

The Old Vicarage, Bondgate, Helmsley, North Yorkshire YO6 5BP
Tel: 0439 70657
Fax: 0439 70691
VAT No: 259 1077 49

NORTHCOTE HOUSE PUBLISHERS LTD

Plymbridge House, Estover Road, Estover, Plymouth, Devon PL6 7PZ
ISBN Prefix(es): 0 7463, 1 85461
Tel: 0752 735251
Fax: 0752 695699
VAT No: 434 3061 82

Account No: _____

Sales Rep: _____

Tel: _____

Orders to
PLYMBRIDGE DISTRIBUTORS LTD, Plymbridge House, Estover Road, Plymouth, Devon PL6 7PZ
Tel: 0752 735251
Fax: 0752 695699

Order Information

All Dues Automatically Recorded
Representation Available
Orders for Horizon Books:Grantham Book Services

Personnel
Head of Company: Brian Hulme (Managing Director)
Head of Accounts: Michael Beevers FCA
Head of Distribution: Ken Wasley
Head of Customer Services: Ian Wordsworth 0752 695745

Number of titles published annually: 20
IPG Member
All New Titles are Bar Coded
Open University Publications
WBIP Updating: Brian Hulme

Trade Terms
General Net: Single copy/single line, 2 or more single titles 25%, 2 bks or more, Sub/stock orders 35%, special orders by agreement
Academic Net: 25%
Non-Net: 17.5%
BA/Girobank Small Order Scheme: Yes
Girobank Number: 211 2951
Credit Cards Accepted: Access/Master, Visa, Amex, Diners

Returns Procedures
Authority to Return: Northcote House Publishers, Sales Department. Requests for Horizon Books to: World Leisure Marketing
Address for Returns: Plymbridge Distributors Ltd, except Horizon Books to: Grantham Book Services
Stock Returns: Must be authorized by publisher. There is a 10% handling charge on returns not accompanied by compensatory order
Imperfect Returns: Title page to £10

NORTHERN IRELAND CENTRE FOR LEARNING RESOURCES

Orchard Building, Stranmillis College, Belfast, County Antrim BT9 5DY
Tel: 0232 664525
Fax: 0232 681579
VAT No: 517 4518 46

NORTHWICK PUBLISHERS

14 Bevere Close, Worcester, Worcestershire WR3 7QH
ISBN Prefix(es): 0 907135
Tel: 0905 56876
Tel: 0905 56529
Fax: 0905 54907
VAT No: 327 1974 44

Account No: _____
Sales Rep: _____
Tel: _____

Order Information

Cyclical Ordering Policy
Representation Available

Personnel
Head of Company: William Harrison
Head of Marketing: Philip Harrison
Head of Publicity: David B Cox

Number of titles published annually: 15
Percentage of Export Sales: 20%
IPG Member
All New Titles are Bar Coded
WBIP Updating: William Harrison

Trade Terms
Single Copy 15/20%, Multiple Copies 30/40%

W W NORTON & COMPANY LTD

10 Coptic Street, London WC1A 1PU
ISBN Prefix(es): 0 393, 0 8112, 0 87140
Tel: 071-323 1579
Fax: 071-436 4553
Cables: GAVIA LONDON WC1

Account No: _____
Sales Rep: _____
Tel: _____

Orders to
JOHN WILEY & SONS LTD, Southern Cross Trading Estate, 1 Oldlands Way, Bognor Regis, West Sussex PO22 9SA
Tel: 0243 829121
Fax: 0243 820250

Order Information

Invoice Payments: John Wiley & Sons

Personnel
Head of Company: R A Cameron (Managing Director)
Head of Sales (Home): Judith Pamplin (Sales Manager)
Head of Publicity: Carey Galletti (Publicity Manager)
Other Important Personnel:
Victoria Keown-Boyd (Manager Special Sales)

Book Data Subscriber

Trade Terms
General Net: 35%
Academic Net: 30%
Credit Cards Accepted: Access/Master, Visa, Amex, Diners, Other

Returns Procedures
Authority to Return: John Wiley
Address for Returns: John Wiley
Stock Returns: All returns must be authorised

NORWOOD PUBLISHERS

3 Chapel Street, Norwood Green, Halifax, West Yorkshire HX3 8QU
Tel: 0274 602454
VAT No: 526 0292 65

NOVA DISTRIBUTION LTD

29 Milber Trading Estate, Newton Abbot, Devon TQ12 4SG
ISBN Prefix(es): 0 906
Tel: 0626 333636
Fax: 0626 331465
VAT No: 402 2092 12

Account No: _____
Sales Rep: _____
Tel: _____

Order Information

Order Dept Opening Times
Mon - Fri 9am - 5pm
Orders for more than one publisher can be bulked
All Dues Automatically Recorded
Representation Available

Personnel
Head of Company: John Robertson (Managing Director)
Head of Publicity: Mary Hutchison
Head of Accounts: Jim Beech
Head of Distribution: Kevin Shaw
Head of Customer Services: Pauline Wilson

Number of titles published annually: 10
Number of Staff: 14
All New Titles are Bar Coded
WBIP Updating: Mary Hutchison

Trade Terms
35%
Other Terms: Carriage charges on under £25 orders
BA/Girobank Small Order Scheme: cwo & carriage if under £25 for non account holders
Credit Cards Accepted: Access/Master, Visa

Returns Procedures
Imperfect Returns: Title page up to £15 retail

NOVELLO & CO LTD

3 Primrose Mews, 1A Sharples Hall Street, London NW1 8YL
ISBN Prefix(es): 0 85360
Tel: 071-483 2161
Fax: 071-586 6841

Account No: _____

Sales Rep: _____

Tel: _____

Orders to
Novello & Co Ltd, Block 7, Vestry Estate, Sevenoaks, Kent TN14 5EL
Tel: 0732 464999
Fax: 0732 459779

Order Information

Order Dept Opening Times
Mon - Fri 9am - 5pm
All Dues Automatically Recorded
Representation Available

Personnel
Head of Company: M R Smith
Head of Sales (Home): K Whiteley
Head of Marketing: C Butler
Head of Accounts: G Fry
Head of Distribution: C Chapman

Number of titles published annually: 80
Percentage of Export Sales: 30%
Number of Staff: 45

Parent Company: Classix Investments Ltd

Trade Terms
35%
Other Terms: Carriage charged: £3.25
Credit Cards Accepted: Access/Master, Visa

NOVEMBER BOOKS

46 The Gallop, Sutton, Surrey SM2 5RY
Tel: 081-770 2141
Fax: 081-642 6556

Order Information

Order Dept Opening Times
Use Fax

Personnel
Head of Company: C Cutler

Number of titles published annually: 1
Percentage of Export Sales: 30%
Number of Staff: 1

Parent Company: R E R Megacorp

Trade Terms
35%

NUCLEAR TECHNOLOGY PUBLISHING

PO Box 7, Ashford, Kent TN23 1YW
Tel: 0233 641683
Fax: 0233 610021
Telex: 966119 NTP UK G
VAT No: 378 0235 40

NUFFIELD PROVINCIAL HOSPITALS TRUST - 59 New Cavendish Street, London W1M 7RD. 071-485-6632/3 FAX 071-485-8215

NUTMEG PRESS

9 Southgate, Heaton Chapel, Southport, Greater Manchester SK4 4QL
ISBN Prefix(es): 0 946816
Tel: 061-431 0974 24 Hours

Order Information

Cyclical Ordering Policy
All Dues Automatically Recorded
Representation Available

Personnel
Head of Company: Roy Shipperbottom

Number of titles published annually: 15
Number of Staff: 2
All New Titles are Bar Coded

Trade Terms
35%
General Net: Single copy 35%, Two or more 40%

OAKWOOD PRESS

PO Box 122, Headington, Oxford, Oxfordshire OX3 8LU
ISBN Prefix(es): 0 85361
Tel: 086587 4080 24 Hours
Fax: 086587 5322
VAT No: 410 8480 75

Order Information

All Dues Automatically Recorded

Personnel
Head of Company: Jane Kennedy
Head of Publicity: C Judge

Number of titles published annually: 12
Number of Staff: 1
NBA Signatory
All New Titles are Bar Coded
WBIP Updating: C Judge

Trade Terms
35% post free over £30 orders
Minimum Order: £30 to obtain 35%
Other Terms: Small order surcharge 25% plus 93p (min)
Carriage charged under £30
Girobank Number: 27 578 6900
Credit Cards Accepted: Access/Master, Visa

Returns Procedures
Authority to Return: Jane Kennedy
Stock Returns: Does not apply (firm sale only)
Imperfect Returns: Whole book up to £10 value. Title page under £10.

OBERON BOOKS LTD

521 Caledonian Road, London N7 9RH
ISBN Prefix(es): 1 870259
Tel: 071-607 3637
Fax: 071-607 3629

Order Information

All Dues Automatically Recorded
Representation Available

Personnel
Head of Company: Charles Glanville (Managing Director)
Head of Publicity: James Hogan (Publishing Director)
Head of Distribution: James Haywood

Number of titles published annually: 6
Number of Staff: 3
All New Titles are Bar Coded
WBIP Updating: Charles Glanville

Trade Terms
35% all orders; Carriage and packing charge on orders under 10 books; 60 day terms
Academic Net: 10%

Returns Procedures
Authority to Return: Prior permission required

THE O'BRIEN PRESS

20 Victoria Road, Rathgar, Dublin 6, County Dublin
ISBN Prefix(es): 0 86278
Tel: 01 979 598
Fax: 01 979 274
VAT No: 9F6 8582

Orders to
CENTRAL BOOKS, 99 Wallis Road, London E9 5LN
Tel: 081-986 4854
Fax: 081-533 5821

Order Information

All Dues Automatically Recorded
Representation Available
Invoice Payments: Central Books (Britain) Gill & Macmillan (Ireland)
Distributors in Ireland:Gill & Macmillan

Personnel
Head of Company: Michael O'Brien
Head of Publicity: Mary Webb
Head of Accounts: Charlotte Stevens
Other Important Personnel:
Ide O'Leary (Editoral Director)

Number of titles published annually: 25
Percentage of Export Sales: 30%
Number of Staff: 7
IPG Member
All New Titles are Bar Coded
WBIP Updating: Charlie Bateman

Trade Terms
Usual trade terms 35%
Credit Cards Accepted: Visa

Returns Procedures
Authority to Return: UK: I Mills, 18 Coleswood Rd, Harpenden Tel/Fax 05827 61264 Ireland: The O'Brien Press, Dublin
Address for Returns: UK: Central Books, London Ireland: Gill & Macmillon, Dublin

OCLC EUROPE

7th Floor, Tricorn House, 51-53 Hagley Road, Edgbaston, Birmingham, West Midlands B16 8TP
Tel: 021-456 4656
Fax: 021-456 4680
Telex: 335176 OCLC TFSTRS G

Telex: 336520 OCLC TFSTRS G
VAT No: 346 2374 55

OCTAGON PRESS

PO Box 227, London N6 4EW
ISBN Prefix(es): 0 863040, 0 900860
Tel: 081-348 9392
Fax: 081-341 5971
VAT No: 239 0346 67

Order Information
Teleordering: OCTAGON

All Dues Automatically Recorded

Personnel
Head of Company: G R Schrager
Head of Sales (Home): Mrs P Schneider
Head of Accounts: Mrs V L Sizer

Number of titles published annually: 5
Percentage of Export Sales: 60%
All New Titles are Bar Coded
WBIP Updating: G R Schrager

Trade Terms
Sold firm, payment 30 days, no sale or return, see-safe by arrangement
General Net: Single copy/single line 25%, 2 or more books 35% Order value over £500 retail 40%, over £750 45%
Credit Cards Accepted: Access/Master, Visa

Returns Procedures
Address for Returns: Address supplied with authorization, unauthorized returns are sent back.
Stock Returns: Return of overstocks is only accepted if see-safe and arrangements noted on original invoice
Imperfect Returns: Title page up to £30

THE OFFICE LONDON LTD

Unit C, 41 Dace Road, London E3 2NG
Tel: 081-986 7114
Fax: 081-986 1531
VAT No: 404 4160 96

Order Information

All Dues Automatically Recorded
Representation Available

Personnel
Head of Company: Miss Jean Wilson (Director)

Number of Staff: 7

Trade Terms
35%
Other Terms: Small order surcharge if order under £25

OFFICE OF HEALTH ECONOMICS

12 Whitehall, London SW1A 2DY
Tel: 071-930 9203
Fax: 071-976 1962

THE OLD STILE PRESS

Catchmays Court, Llandogo, Monmouth, Gwent NP5 4TN
Tel: 0291 689226
VAT No: 426 9738 14

OLD VICARAGE PUBLICATIONS

The Old Vicarage, Reades Lane, Dane In Shaw, Congleton, Cheshire CW12 3LL
ISBN Prefix(es): 0 900269, 0 947818, 0 9508635
Tel: 0260 279276
Fax: 0260 298913

Order Information

All Dues Automatically Recorded

Personnel
Head of Company: William Ball

Number of titles published annually: 3
Number of Staff: 1
NBA Signatory
All New Titles are Bar Coded

Trade Terms
General Net: 1-5 copies 20%, 6+ 33%
Other Terms: Cheque with order - extra 5%
Girobank Number: 304 8691
Credit Cards Accepted: Access/Master, Visa

OLDCASTLE BOOKS LTD

18 Coleswood Road, Harpenden, Hertfordshire AL5 1EQ
ISBN Prefix(es): 0 948353, 1 874061
Tel: 0582 761264
VAT No: 404 0990 75

Orders to
BOOKPOINT LIMITED, 39 Milton Park, Abingdon, Oxfordshire OX14 4TD
Tel: 0235 835001
Fax: 0235 861038

Order Information

Representation Available

Personnel
Head of Company: Ion Mills

All New Titles are Bar Coded

Trade Terms
Single Copy 25%, Two or more 35%
Credit Cards Accepted: Access/Master, Visa

THE OLEANDER PRESS

17 Stansgate Avenue, Cambridge, Cambridgeshire CB2 2QZ
ISBN Prefix(es): 0 900891, 0 902675, 0 906672
Tel: 0223 244688

Order Information

Order Dept Opening Times
9am - 9pm 7 days a week
Cyclical Ordering Policy
All Dues Automatically Recorded
Representation Available

Personnel
Head of Company: Philip Ward
Head of Sales (Home): Will Marston
Head of Accounts: Audrey Ward

Number of titles published annually: 6
Number of Staff: 2
WBIP Updating: Philip Ward

Trade Terms
25% discount below £20 retail value 33.33% discount above £20 retail value

Minimum Order: £20 retail value
Other Terms: Post & Packing charged inland unless over £20 retail value

Returns Procedures
Stock Returns: In no case do we supply on sale or return. No overstocks are returnable.
Imperfect Returns: Return whole book

MICHAEL O'MARA BOOKS LTD

9 Lion Yard, Tremadoc Road, Clapham, London SW4 7NQ
ISBN Prefix(es): 1 85479
Tel: 071-720 8643
Fax: 071-627 8953
VAT No: 238 2349 57

Account No: _____

Sales Rep: _____

Tel: _____

Orders to
MACMILLAN DISTRIBUTION LTD, Brunel Road, Houndmills Industrial Estate, Basingstoke, Hampshire RG21 2XS
Tel: 0256 29242
Fax: 0256 842084

Order Information

All Dues Automatically Recorded

Personnel
Head of Company: Michael O'Mara (Chairman)
Head of Sales (Home): Lesley O'Mara (Managing Director)
Head of Marketing: Tracey Greenwood (Publicity Manager)
Head of Accounts: Maureen Daley (Accoutant)

Number of titles published annually: 35
Percentage of Export Sales: 40%
Number of Staff: 14
IPG Member
All New Titles are Bar Coded
WBIP Updating: Catherine Taylor

Trade Terms
As Pan MacMillan

Returns Procedures
Authority to Return: As Pan Macmillan

OMF BOOKS

44 Bethel Road, Sevenoaks, Kent TN13 3UE
Tel: 0732 452334 24 Hour
Fax: 0732 456164
VAT No: 221 2635 08

Order Information

Order Dept Opening Times
Mon - Fri 9.30am - 4.30pm
All Dues Automatically Recorded
Representation Available

Personnel
Head of Marketing: John Caisley

Number of titles published annually: 4
Number of Staff: 3
WBIP Updating: Mrs D Woodman

Trade Terms
35% under £10 £1 surcharge
Other Terms: Small order surcharge £1
Girobank Number: 54 612 008

Returns Procedures
Authority to Return: John Caisley

OMNIBUS PRESS

8/9 Frith Street, London W1V 5TZ
ISBN Prefix(es): 0 7119, 0 86001
Tel: 071-434 0066
Fax: 071-439 2848
Fax: 071-734 2246
Telex: 21892

Account No: _____

Sales Rep: _____

Tel: _____

Orders to
Booksales Ltd, Newmarket Road, Bury St Edmunds, Suffolk
IP33 3YB
Tel: 0284 702600 (24 Hrs)
Fax: 0284 768301

Order Information
Teleordering: BSL

Order Dept Opening Times
Mon - Fri 9am - 5pm
Representation Available

Personnel
Head of Company: Robert Wise (Managing Director)
Head of Sales (Home): Richard Carman (Sales Manager)
0284 702600
Head of Marketing: Hilary Donlon (Sales Administrator)
Head of Accounts: Malcolm Grabham (Financial Director)
Head of Distribution: Frank Johnson (General Manager)
0284 702600

Number of titles published annually: 50
Number of Staff: 10
PA Member
NBA Signatory
All New Titles are Bar Coded
Book Data Subscriber
WBIP Updating: Hilary Donlon

Subsidiary Companies: Music Sales Corp (US), Music Sales Pty Ltd (AU)

Trade Terms
35% no surcharges

Returns Procedures
Authority to Return: Hilary Donlon
Address for Returns: Frith St, London

ONEWORLD PUBLICATIONS

185 Banbury Road, Oxford, Oxfordshire OX2 7AR
ISBN Prefix(es): 1 85168
Tel: 0865 310597
Fax: 0865 310598
VAT No: 440 8514 63

Orders to
ELEMENT BOOKS LTD, Unit 25, Longmead, Shaftesbury, Dorset SP7 8PL
Tel: 0747 51339
Fax: 0747 51394

Personnel
Head of Company: Juliet Mabey
Head of Sales (Home): Novin Doostdar

Book Data Subscriber

Trade Terms
As per distributor

OPEN BIBLE TRUST

36 St Laurence Avenue, Brundall, Norwich, Norfolk
NR13 5QH
ISBN Prefix(es): 0 947778
Tel: 0603 716916 Tel/Fax
VAT No: 363 0310 95

Personnel
Head of Sales (Home): Mrs E Hughes

Number of titles published annually: 6

Trade Terms
35% dis plus postage

Returns Procedures
Stock Returns: Whole book
Imperfect Returns: Whole book

OPEN BOOKS PUBLISHING LTD

Beaumont House, Wells, Somerset BA5 2LD
ISBN Prefix(es): 0 749
Tel: 0749 677276
Fax: 0749 670760

Orders to
CLIPPER DISTRIBUTION SERVICES LTD, Windmill Grove, Portchester, Hampshire PO16 9HT
Tel: 0705 200080
Fax: 0705 200090

Personnel
Head of Company: P Taylor

Trade Terms
General Net: Single copy/single line 25%, 2 or more single titles 35%
Academic Net: As above

OPEN GATE PRESS

51 Achilles Road, London NW6 1DZ
ISBN Prefix(es): 1 871871
Tel: 071-431 4391
Fax: 071-431 5088
VAT No: 527 7187 21

Orders to
TBC DISTRIBUTION, Unit 10, Bunting Close, Mitcham, Surrey CR4 4ND
Tel: 081-687 1744
Fax: 081-687 1747

Order Information

All Dues Automatically Recorded
Representation Available
Invoice Payments: TBC Distribution

Personnel
Head of Company: Jeannie Cohen

Number of titles published annually: 3
Number of Staff: 5
IPG Member
All New Titles are Bar Coded

Trade Terms
Distributor's terms apply

Returns Procedures
Authority to Return: Open Gate Press
Address for Returns: TBC Distribution
Stock Returns: Distributor's procedures apply
Imperfect Returns: Distributor's procedures apply

OPEN UNIVERSITY EDUCATIONAL ENTERPRISES LTD

12 Cofferidge Close, Stony Stratford, Milton Keynes, Buckinghamshire MK11 1BY
ISBN Prefix(es): 0 7492
Tel: 0908 261662
Tel: 0908 262612
Fax: 0908 261001
Telex: 826147
VAT No: 396 8767 68

Account No: _____

Sales Rep: _____

Tel: _____

Order Information
Teleordering: OUEE

Personnel
Head of Company: Paul Bowen (Managing Director)
Head of Sales (Home): Philip Rathkey (General Manager)
Head of Sales (Export): Alan Clarke (Deputy Managing Director)
Head of Marketing: Angela Lewis (Promotion Manager/Publicity)
Head of Accounts: Jackie Thrush (Accounts & Customer Services)

Number of titles published annually: 1200
Percentage of Export Sales: 50%
Number of Staff: 20
PA Member
IPG Member
NBA Signatory
All New Titles are Bar Coded
Open University Publications
WBIP Updating: Mrs Maggie Graham

Trade Terms
Variable
Girobank Number: 235 9154
Credit Cards Accepted: Access/Master, Visa, Amex

Returns Procedures
Address for Returns: 21 Dennington Industrial Estate, Wellingborough, Northants, NN8 2PF
Stock Returns: Contact Warehouse

OPEN UNIVERSITY PRESS

Celtic Court, 22 Ballmoor, Buckingham, Buckinghamshire MK18 1XW
ISBN Prefix(es): 0 335
Tel: 0280 823388
Tel: 0280 822211 Orders
Fax: 0280 823233
Fax: 0280 823681 Orders
VAT No: 485 9975 81

Account No: _____ 1192892 _____

Sales Rep: _____

Tel: _____

Order Information
Teleordering: OPENUP

Order Dept Opening Times
Mon - Fri 8.30am - 5.30pm
All Dues Automatically Recorded
Representation Available

Personnel
Head of Company: John Skelton (Managing Director)
Head of Sales (Home): Barbara Martin (Sales & Rights Manager)
Head of Marketing: Gary Hall (Promotions Manager)
Head of Accounts: Barry Clarke (Financial Director)
Head of Customer Services: Anne Haynes (Customer Services Manager)
Other Important Personnel:
Andrew Hopgood (Northern & Irish Sales Manager), Alison Pearce (Southern Representative)

Number of titles published annually: 100
Percentage of Export Sales: 30%
Number of Staff: 24
IPG Member
NBA Signatory
All New Titles are Bar Coded
Open University Publications
Book Data Subscriber
WBIP Updating: Gary Hall

Parent Company: Clarke, Skelton and Wright Ltd

Trade Terms
25%
Girobank Number: 230 0109
Credit Cards Accepted: Access/Master, Visa, Amex

Returns Procedures
Authority to Return: Prior authorisation from Barbara Martin. Labels issued. Claim errors within 14 days, damaged books within 7 days.
Address for Returns: 21 Denington Road, Denington Estate, Wellingborough Northants, NN8 2RF
Stock Returns: Invoiced less than 12 month prior to return date. Books must be in resaleable condition not price labelled.
Imperfect Returns: Books under £25 credited on return on title page. Books over £25 return whole book with a letter of explaining

ORBACH & CHAMBERS LTD

74 Long Lane, London EC1A 9ET
ISBN Prefix(es): 0 85514
Tel: 071-606 9371
Fax: 071-600 1793

Orders to
BIBLIOS PUBLISHERS DISTRIBUTION SERVICE LTD,
Star Road, Partridge Green, West Sussex RH13 8LD
Tel: 0403 710971
Fax: 0403 711143

Personnel
Head of Company: Michael Chambers

All New Titles are Bar Coded

Trade Terms
Biblios' standard terms

Returns Procedures
Authority to Return: Biblios Publishers Distribution Services Ltd

ORBIS BOOKS (LONDON) LTD
66 Kenway Road, London SW5 0RD
ISBN Prefix(es): 0 901149, 0 920862
Tel: 071-370 2210
Fax: 071-602 5541 6-9pm
Fax: 081-994 5911
VAT No: 239 1481 56

Number of Staff: 6

Trade Terms
Other Terms: Carriage extra
Credit Cards Accepted: Access/Master, Visa, Amex

Returns Procedures
Stock Returns: Sold on firm sale basis only
Imperfect Returns: Book to be returned

ORDNANCE SURVEY
Romsey Road, Maybush, Southampton, Hampshire SO9 4DH
ISBN Prefix(es): 0 319
Tel: 0703 792000
Fax: 0703 792602
Account No: ~~720226 0001~~ *Problems with orders (0703 792810)*
Sales Rep: _____
Tel: _____ 0611100001 A/c No.

Order Information

Order Dept Opening Times
Mon - Fri 8.30am - 4.30pm
Representation Available

Personnel
Head of Company: Prof David Rhind (Director General)
Head of Sales (Home): Mike Cranidge (Sales Manager) 0703 792412
Head of Marketing: Peter Wesley

Number of Staff: 2200
PA Member
All New Titles are Bar Coded

Trade Terms
35%
Minimum Order: £110 retail for 35%

ORIEL/THE WELSH ARTS COUNCIL
Museum Place, Cardiff, South Glamorgan CF1 4AA
ISBN Prefix(es): 0 946329
Tel: 0222 394711
VAT No: 135 0261 10

Orders to
Oriel, The Friary, Cardiff, South Glamorgan CF1 2AA
Tel: 0222 395548

Order Information

Order Dept Opening Times
Mon - Sat 9am - 5.30pm
All Dues Automatically Recorded

Personnel
Head of Company: T A Owen
Head of Sales (Home): Mari Gordon
Head of Marketing: P Finch
Head of Accounts: A Malin

Number of titles published annually: 10
WBIP Updating: P Finch/V Ward

Allied Companies: Arts Council of Great Britain

Trade Terms
General Net: Single Copy 25% + surcharge, Two or more 35%
Credit Cards Accepted: Access/Master, Visa

ORIFLAMME PUBLISHING

60 Charteris Road, London N4 3AB
ISBN Prefix(es): 0 948093
Tel: 071-263 2195
Tel: 0332 510230

Orders to
Oriflamme Publishing, 125 Station Road, Mickleover, Derby DE3 5FN
Tel: 0332 510230

Order Information

Order Dept Opening Times
Mon - Fri 10am - 6pm
All Dues Automatically Recorded
Representation Available
Invoice Payments: Station Road, Derby

Personnel
Head of Company: D A Slade
Head of Sales (Home): Tony Allen Derby 0332 510230
Head of Sales (Export): Edward Marsh
Head of Accounts: D A Sawyer

Number of titles published annually: 6
Number of Staff: 7
All New Titles are Bar Coded
WBIP Updating: Tony Allen

Trade Terms
30% all orders plus p&p, terms on large orders negotiable

Returns Procedures
Authority to Return: Station Road
Address for Returns: Station Road
Imperfect Returns: All imperfect/damaged copies replaced/credited: no other returns

ORION PUBLISHING GROUP

Orion House, 5 Upper St Martins Lane, London WC2H 9EA
ISBN Prefix(es): 0 297, 0 460, 1 85797, 1 85798, 1 85799, 1 87001 5
Tel: 071-240 3444
Fax: 071-240 4822

Account No: _____
Sales Rep: _____
Tel: _____

Orders to
LITTLEHAMPTON BOOK SERVICES, 14 Eldon Way, Lineside Ind Estate, Littlehampton, West Sussex BN17 7HE
Tel: 0903 721596
Fax: 0903 730914

Order Information

All Dues Automatically Recorded
Representation Available
Invoice Payments: Littlehampton

Personnel
Head of Company: Anthony Cheetham (Chairman & Chief Executive)
Head of Sales (Home): Mark Streatfeild (Sales Director)

Head of Marketing: Caroline Michel (Marketing Director)
Head of Publicity: Diane Rowley (Publicity Director)
Head of Accounts: Karl Stott (Financial Controller)
Other Important Personnel:
Andrew MacMillan (Home Sales), Charlotte Syms (Export Sales), Lord Weidenfeld (Chairman - Weidenfeld & Nicolson), David Swarbrick (Marketing Director - Dent)

Number of titles published annually: 350
Percentage of Export Sales: 30%
Number of Staff: 78
NBA Signatory
All New Titles are Bar Coded
Open University Publications
Book Data Subscriber
WBIP Updating: Paula Foote

Trade Terms
35%
Academic Net: 30%
Girobank Number: 516 6152
Credit Cards Accepted: Access/Master, Visa

Returns Procedures
Authority to Return: Andrew Macmillan
Stock Returns: Check with Sales Office
Imperfect Returns: Return title page if book under £20

THE ORKNEY PRESS LTD

12 Craigiefield Park, St Ola, Kirkney, Orkney KW15 1NX
ISBN Prefix(es): 0 907618
Tel: 0856 874058
Fax: 0856 876284

Order Information

Orders for more than one publisher can be bulked
All Dues Automatically Recorded
Representation Available

Personnel
Head of Company: H N Firth
Head of Sales (Home): Mrs S Firth
Head of Accounts: G C Linklater (Credit Control Manager)

Number of titles published annually: 5
NBA Signatory
All New Titles are Bar Coded
WBIP Updating: H N Firth

Trade Terms
35%
General Net: Single Copy 25%
Academic Net: Single Copy 25%
Other Terms: Carriage Charges on order below £20 net

Orwell Press. 5 Pinkneys Lane, Southwold, Suffolk, IP18 6EW
(0502) 723249

OSBORNE BOOKS LTD

Gwernant, The Common, Lower Broadheath, Worcester, Hereford & Worcestershire WR2 6RP
ISBN Prefix(es): 0 9510650, 1 872962
Tel: 0905 333691
Fax: 0905 333693
VAT No: 454 7106 52

Order Information

Order Dept Opening Times
Mon - Fri 9am - 5pm
All Dues Automatically Recorded
Representation Available

Personnel
Head of Company: M P Fardon (Director)

Number of titles published annually: 4
Number of Staff: 5
IPG Member
All New Titles are Bar Coded

Trade Terms
1-2 copies 20%, 3 or more 30%, no surcharges
Credit Cards Accepted: Access/Master, Visa

Returns Procedures
Authority to Return: Prior permission required

OVERSEAS DEVELOPMENT INSTITUTE

Regent's College, Regent's Park, London NW1 4NS
ISBN Prefix(es): 0 85003
Tel: 071-487 7413 24 Hours
Fax: 071-487 7590
Telex: 94082191 ODIUK

Order Information

Order Dept Opening Times
Mon - Fri 9.30am - 5.30pm
All Dues Automatically Recorded
Orders To:Publications Sales

Personnel
Head of Company: Professor John Howell (Director)
Head of Sales (Home): Karen Maxted (Sales Administrator)
Head of Marketing: Dr P J Gee (Publications & IT Officer)

Number of titles published annually: 40
Percentage of Export Sales: 25%
WBIP Updating: Dr P J Gee

Trade Terms
35% on all orders

Returns Procedures
Stock Returns: Return book with invoice

OVUM LTD

1 Mortimer Street, London W1N 7RH
Tel: 071-255 2670
Fax: 071-255 1995
VAT No: 232 7860 60

PETER OWEN LTD

73 Kenway Road, London SW5 0RE
ISBN Prefix(es): 0 7206
Tel: 071-373 5628
Tel: 071-370 6093
Fax: 071-373 6760
VAT No: 239 9526 20

Orders to
LITTLEHAMPTON BOOK SERVICES, 14 Eldon Way,
Lineside Ind Estate, Littlehampton, West Sussex BN17 7HE
Tel: 0903 721596
Fax: 0903 730914

Order Information

All Dues Automatically Recorded
Representation Available
Invoice Payments: Littlehampton

Personnel
Head of Company: Peter Owen
Head of Sales (Home): Richard Bailey
Head of Publicity: Gary Pulsifer

Number of titles published annually: 40
Percentage of Export Sales: 30%
Number of Staff: 5
PA Member
NBA Signatory
All New Titles are Bar Coded
WBIP Updating: Richard Bailey

Trade Terms
35%, but singles 25%

Returns Procedures
Authority to Return: Credit given only for returns authorised by head office
Address for Returns: Littlehampton
Imperfect Returns: Title page up to £20

OWL BOOKS

27 Queensway, Wigan, Lancashire WN1 2JA
ISBN Prefix(es): 0 9514333, 1 873888
Tel: 0942 821831
Tel: 0942 30893 Ansafone
Fax: 0942 821819
VAT No: 483 6146 30

Order Information

Order Dept Opening Times
Mon - Fri 9am - 5pm
Representation Available

Personnel
Head of Company: Mr J A Roby (Proprietor)
Head of Accounts: Mrs J E Roby

Number of titles published annually: 10
Number of Staff: 2
IPG Member
All New Titles are Bar Coded
WBIP Updating: Mrs J E Roby

Trade Terms
General Net: Single copy/single line 25%, 2 books or more 35%

Returns Procedures
Imperfect Returns: Return Title Page

OWL PRESS

PO Box 315, Downtown, Salisbury, Wiltshire SP5 3YE
ISBN Prefix(es): 0 9515917
Tel: 0725 22553 Tel/Fax
VAT No: 579 9982 39

Order Information

Order Dept Opening Times
Mon - Fri 8.30am - 6pm Sat 9am - 1pm
All Dues Automatically Recorded
Representation Available

Personnel
Head of Company: Annie Musgrove/Catherine Jones

Number of titles published annually: 5
Number of Staff: 2
IPG Member
All New Titles are Bar Coded

Trade Terms
35% multiples, 25% singles no surcharges

Returns Procedures
Stock Returns: Write to request authority
Imperfect Returns: Write to request authority

OXBOW BOOKS A|C 008527
Park End Place, Oxford, Oxfordshire OX1 1HN
ISBN Prefix(es): 0 946897
Tel: 0865 241249
Fax: 0865 794449
VAT No: 332 7954 43

Order Information
Teleordering: OXBOW

All Dues Automatically Recorded

Personnel
Head of Company: David Brown

Number of titles published annually: 25
Percentage of Export Sales: 35%
Number of Staff: 9
Book Data Subscriber

Subsidiary Companies: Brown Book Co, The David

Trade Terms
20% - single copy, 25% up to £60, over £60 - 30% Special orders by negotiation
Girobank Number: 25 606 4008
Credit Cards Accepted: Access/Master, Visa, Amex

OXFAM
274 Banbury Road, Oxford, Oxfordshire OX2 7DZ
ISBN Prefix(es): 0 85598
Tel: 0865 311311
Tel: 0865 312415
Tel: 0865 312453
Fax: 0865 312600
Fax: 0865 312380
Telex: 83610 OXFAM G
VAT No: 348 4542 38

Orders to
CENTRAL BOOKS, 99 Wallis Road, London E9 5LN
Tel: 081-986 4854
Fax: 081-533 5821

Order Information

All Dues Automatically Recorded
Representation Available
Invoice Payments: Central Books

Personnel
Head of Company: David Bryer
Head of Sales (Home): Toby Milner

Number of titles published annually: 20
Number of Staff: 5
All New Titles are Bar Coded
Book Data Subscriber
WBIP Updating: Toby Milner

Trade Terms
See Central Books

Returns Procedures
Authority to Return: Central Books
Address for Returns: Central Books

[Handwritten at top: OXFORD BROOKES UNIV. Wheatley Campus, Wheatley Oxford OX33 1HX]

OXFORD BUSINESS PUBLISHING
15 King Edward Street, Oxford, Oxfordshire OX1 4HT
Tel: 0865 791908
Fax: 0865 247393
VAT No: 479 2857 85

OXFORD UNIVERSITY PRESS
Walton Street, Oxford, Oxfordshire OX2 6DP
ISBN Prefix(es): 0 19
Tel: 0865 56767
Fax: 0865 56646
Telex: 837330 OXPRES G
Cables: CLARENDON PRESS OXFORD
VAT No: 227 1983 51

[Handwritten: Journals from:- Walton Street.]

Account No: _____ *[handwritten: 1021 / 20300·023]*
Sales Rep: _____
Tel: _____

Orders to
OXFORD UNIVERSITY PRESS, Distribution Services,
Saxon Way West, Corby, Northamptonshire NN18 9ES
Tel: 0536 741519
Fax: 0536 746337

Order Information
Teleordering: OUP
First Edition Subscriber

Orders for more than one publisher can be bulked
All Dues Automatically Recorded
Representation Available
Invoice Payments: OUP Distribution Services

Personnel
Head of Company: Sir Roger Elliott (Secretary to the Delegates)
Head of Sales (Home): Mike Ward (UK Sales Manager)
Head of Sales (Export): Teresa Armstrong (International Sales Manager)
Head of Publicity: Juliet New (Publicity Manager)
Other Important Personnel:
Simon Wratten (Sales & Marketing Director), Jim Smith (Credit Manager)

Number of titles published annually: 2000
Percentage of Export Sales: 50%
Number of Staff: 2200
PA Member
NBA Signatory
All New Titles are Bar Coded
Open University Publications
Book Data Subscriber
WBIP Updating: Richard Taberner Ext 4277

Allied Companies: Cornelsen/Oxford University Press

Trade Terms
General Net: 35%
Academic Net: 25%
Non-Net: 17.5%
Girobank Number: 500 1056
Credit Cards Accepted: Access/Master, Amex, Diners, Visa

Returns Procedures
Authority to Return: Local Representative or ~~Mike Ward~~ *[handwritten: Head of Sales.]*
Address for Returns: Corby
Imperfect Returns: Return full copies of all books over £50 pub price and all fine bindings

OXFORD UNIVERSITY PRESS

Distribution Services, Saxon Way West, Corby,
Northamptonshire NN18 9ES
Tel: 0536 741519 24 Hours
Fax: 0536 746337

Account No: _____

Sales Rep: _____

Tel: _____

Order Information
Teleordering: OUP
First Edition Subscriber

Order Dept Opening Times
Mon - Fri 8.30am - 5pm
Cyclical Ordering Policy
Invoice Payments: Oxford University Press, Walton St, Oxford

Personnel
Head of Distribution: Neil Killip (Distribution Director)
Head of Customer Services: Valerie Johnston

Trade Terms
Girobank Number: 500 1056
Credit Cards Accepted: Access/Master, Amex, Diners, Visa

Returns Procedures
Authority to Return: Mike Ward
Stock Returns: As Standard
Imperfect Returns: Return full copies of all books over £50 pub price and all fine bindings

[Handwritten: OXON Distribution - P.O. Box 171 - Deddington, Banbury, OXON. OX16 8YG. Tel 0869 38087 FAX 0869 37123 A/C BLA103]

P4 SPARES
60 Woodville Road, London NW11 9TN
Tel: 081-455 6992
VAT No: 227 6721 44

PA Member

PACKARD PUBLISHING LTD

Forum House, Stirling Road, Chichester, West Sussex
PO19 2EN
ISBN Prefix(es): 0 906527, 0 948690, 1 85341
Tel: 0243 537977 24 Hours
Fax: 0243 537977
VAT No: 321 6611 91

Order Information
Teleordering: PACK

Order Dept Opening Times
Mon - Fri 8am - 6.30pm
All Dues Automatically Recorded
Representation Available

Personnel
Head of Company: Michael Packard

Number of titles published annually: 8
Number of Staff: 2
IPG Member
All New Titles are Bar Coded
Book Data Subscriber

Trade Terms
All orders are firm.
General Net: Single copy 25%, 30% at publisher's discretion. Subscription & stock orders 35%.
Other Terms: Non-account or non-stockholders orders must be prepaid. Carriage charged per weight on all orders, unless prepaid.

Returns Procedures
Authority to Return: Michael Packard
Address for Returns: Clipper Distribution Services, Windmill Grove, Portchester, Hants PO16 9HT.
Stock Returns: Request to head office, unauthorised returns will be sent back.
Imperfect Returns: Request to head office, faulty pages usually requested.

PALLADIO PRESS

77 University Road, Aberdeen, Grampian AB2 3DR
ISBN Prefix(es): 0 905292
Tel: 0224 481810

Personnel
Head of Company: Anthony F Schmitz

Trade Terms
35%

PALLAS ATHENE

59 Linden Gardens, London W2 4HJ
ISBN Prefix(es): 1 873429
Tel: 071-229 2798
VAT No: 577 0217 38

Order Information

Representation Available

Personnel
Head of Company: Alexander Fyjis-Walker

Number of titles published annually: 4
All New Titles are Bar Coded

Trade Terms
35%
General Net: Single copy/single line 31%
Credit Cards Accepted: Access/Master, Visa

PAN MACMILLAN LTD

18/21 Cavaye Place, Fulham Road, London SW10 9PG
ISBN Prefix(es): 0 330, 0 333
Tel: 071-373 6070
Fax: 071-370 0746
Account No: _____ 230770088 _____
Sales Rep: _____
Tel: _____

Orders to
MACMILLAN DISTRIBUTION LTD, Brunel Road, Houndmills Industrial Estate, Basingstoke, Hampshire RG21 2XS
Tel: 0256 29242
Fax: 0256 842084

Order Information
Teleordering: PAN

Representation Available

Personnel
Head of Company: Alan Gordon Walker (Managing Director)
Head of Sales (Home): Billy Adair (UK Sales Director) 0256 464481
Head of Sales (Export): David Macmillan (Export Sales Director) 0256 464481
Head of Marketing: Vivienne Wordley (Marketing Director)

Head of Publicity: Martin Nield (Publicity Director)
Head of Accounts: Ian Metcalf (Financial Director) 0256 464481
Other Important Personnel:
Brian Davies (Sales & Marketing Director), Alison Muirden (Sales Department)

All New Titles are Bar Coded
Book Data Subscriber
WBIP Updating: Alison Muirden

Trade Terms
35%
Minimum Order: Paperbacks 12 books £20 retail value. Hardbacks no minimum.
Other Terms: Carriage 10%, unless over £75
Credit Cards Accepted: Access/Master, Visa

Returns Procedures
Authority to Return: Sales Department or Rep
Address for Returns: Basingstoke
Stock Returns: Contact Customer Services in Basingstoke

PANDEMIC LTD

112 Sydney Road, Muswell Hill, London N10 2RN
Tel: 081-442 1783 Tel/Fax

Account No: _____

Sales Rep: _____

Tel: _____

Order Information
Teleordering: PAND

Orders for more than one publisher can be bulked
All Dues Automatically Recorded
Representation Available

Personnel
Head of Company: Jack Stacey
Other Important Personnel:
Mrs Suzanne Stacey

Trade Terms
35% on all orders

PANDIT

9 Ellerslie Road, London W12 7BN
Tel: 081-749 2975
Fax: 081-749 5591

PANGBOURNE ENGLISH CENTRE

Shooters Hill, Pangbourne, Berkshire RG8 7DZ
ISBN Prefix(es): 1 870938
Tel: 0734 842462
Fax: 0734 843777
VAT No: 314 5129 86

Personnel
Head of Company: Peter Collier
Head of Accounts: Eva Collier

IPG Member

PARFITTS BOOK SERVICES

50 Imber Road, Warminster, Wiltshire BA12 0BN
Tel: 0985 216371

Fax: 0985 212982
VAT No: 600 8542 70

PARKE SUTTON PUBLISHING LTD
Hi-Tech House, 10 Blackfriars Street, Norwich, Norfolk
NR3 1SF
ISBN Prefix(es): 1 870337
Tel: 0603 667021
Fax: 0603 760284
VAT No: 595 0360 31

Order Information

Representation Available

Personnel
Head of Company: I S McIntyre
Head of Accounts: C De Boos
Head of Customer Services: Mrs C Cook

Number of titles published annually: 3
Number of Staff: 5
All New Titles are Bar Coded
WBIP Updating: C De Boos

Trade Terms
35% no surcharge
Credit Cards Accepted: Access/Master, Visa, Amex

PARLIAMENTARY PROFILE SERVICES LTD
2 Queen Anne's Gate Buildings, Dartmouth Street, London
SW1H 9BP
Tel: 071-222 5884
Fax: 071-222 5889
VAT No: 240 5474 80

PARTHENON PUBLISHING GROUP LTD
Casterton Hall, Kirkby Lonsdale, Carnforth, Lancashire
LA6 2LA
ISBN Prefix(es): 1 85070
Tel: 05242 72084
Fax: 05242 71587
VAT No: 378 5550 13

Order Information

All Dues Automatically Recorded
Representation Available

Personnel
Head of Company: D G T Bloomer
Head of Publicity: J Tissington
Head of Accounts: P F Bloomer
Head of Distribution: A Bailey
Head of Customer Services: Y Baillie

Number of titles published annually: 70
Percentage of Export Sales: 70%
Book Data Subscriber
WBIP Updating: Mrs Y Baillie

Trade Terms
30%
Girobank Number: 697 1652
Credit Cards Accepted: Access/Master, Visa, Amex

PASSWORD (BOOKS) LTD

23 New Mount Street, Manchester, Greater Manchester
M4 4DE
Tel: 061-953 4009
Fax: 061-953 4001
VAT No: 396 6974 73

Account No: _____

Sales Rep: _____

Tel: _____

Order Information
Teleordering: PASS

Order Dept Opening Times
Mon - Fri 9am - 5pm
All Dues Automatically Recorded
Representation Available

Personnel
Head of Company: David Parrish (Managing Director)
Head of Publicity: Sarah Craig (Publicity Manager)
Head of Distribution: Susan Doogan (Distribution Manager)
Other Important Personnel:
Alice Caswell (Sales Manager (South)), Rosie Ilett (Sales Manager (North))

Number of titles published annually: 50
All New Titles are Bar Coded
WBIP Updating: Sarah Craig

Trade Terms
35%
Other Terms: Low value surcharge of £1.50 on orders below £25 invoice excluding reps orders, subscriptions & dues released
Girobank Number: 613 4599

Returns Procedures
Authority to Return: Representative
Address for Returns: Clipper Distribution Services, Windmill Grove, Portchester, Hampshire PO16 9HT

PASTEST SERVICE

Rankin House, Parkgate Estate, Knutsford, Cheshire
WA16 8DX
ISBN Prefix(es): 0 906896
Tel: 0565 755226
Fax: 0565 650264
VAT No: 349 0358 45

Order Information

Order Dept Opening Times
Mon - Fri 9am - 5pm
All Dues Automatically Recorded
Representation Available

Personnel
Head of Company: Freydis Campbell (Director)

Number of titles published annually: 6
IPG Member
NBA Signatory
All New Titles are Bar Coded
Book Data Subscriber

Trade Terms
30%
Credit Cards Accepted: Access/Master, Visa

PASTIME PUBLICATIONS LTD
32/34 Heriot Hill Terrace, Edinburgh, Lothian EH7 4DY
Tel: 031-556 1105
Tel: 031-557 8092
Tel: 031-556 0057
Fax: 031-556 1129
VAT No: 446 5295 28

PATHFINDER PRESS
47 The Cut, London SE1 8LL
ISBN Prefix(es): 0 87348, 0 913460, 0 937091
Tel: 071-261 1354
Fax: 071-928 7970
VAT No: 548 1616 34

Orders to
PLYMBRIDGE DISTRIBUTORS LTD, Plymbridge House, Estover Road, Plymouth, Devon PL6 7PZ
Tel: 0752 735251
Fax: 0752 695699

Order Information
All Dues Automatically Recorded
Representation Available
Invoice Payments: Plymbridge Distributors Ltd

Personnel
Head of Company: A Harris

Number of titles published annually: 8
Number of Staff: 3
All New Titles are Bar Coded

Parent Company: Pathfinder Press, New York

Trade Terms
Orders for up to 3 books 25%, 4 or more 35%
BA/Girobank Small Order Scheme: Yes
Girobank Number: 221 2951

Returns Procedures
Authority to Return: Pathfinder Press
Address for Returns: Plymbridge Distributors Ltd

PATTEN PRESS
Newmill, The Old Post Office, Penzance, Cornwall TR20 4XN
ISBN Prefix(es): 0 9507689, 1 872229
Tel: 0736 60549
Fax: 0736 330704
VAT No: 317 9939 13

Order Information
Order Dept Opening Times
Mon - Fri 9am - 5pm
All Dues Automatically Recorded

Other Important Locations
Warehousing: 66 Hayle Terrace, Hayle, Cornwall TR27 4BT
Tel: 0736 60549

Personnel
Head of Company: Dr K M Hardie

Number of titles published annually: 5
Number of Staff: 2
NBA Signatory
All New Titles are Bar Coded

Parent Company: Patten Press

Trade Terms
General Net: Single Copy - 33.3%, 3 or more single titles 35% Subscription Orders apply individually
Other Terms: Carriage Charges £1 single copy maximum £3
Credit Cards Accepted: Access/Master, Visa

Returns Procedures
Imperfect Returns: Title Page below £5

PATTON PUBLICATIONS

Orchard House, Swimbridge, Barnstaple, North Devon EX32 0PL
ISBN Prefix(es): 1 872426
Tel: 0271 830229
Tel: 0271 830574
VAT No: 525 1767 45

PAUPERS' PRESS

27 Melbourne Road, West Bridgford, Nottingham, Nottinghamshire NG2 5DJ
ISBN Prefix(es): 0 946650
Tel: 0602 815063

Order Information

All Dues Automatically Recorded

Personnel
Head of Company: Colin Stanley

Number of titles published annually: 6
Number of Staff: 1

Trade Terms
33.3% (20% STARMONT HOUSE TITLES)
Other Terms: Carriage charged on single copy orders

Returns Procedures
Stock Returns: No returns except for imperfect or damaged titles
Imperfect Returns: Whole Book to be returned

PAVIC PUBLICATIONS

Sheffield Hallam University, 36 Collegiate Crescent, Sheffield, South Yorkshire S11 8BZ
Tel: 0742 532380
Fax: 0742 532471

PAVILION BOOKS LTD

196 Shaftesbury Avenue, London WC2H 8JL
ISBN Prefix(es): 1 85145, 1 85793
Tel: 071-836 1306
Fax: 071-240 7684

Account No: _____

Sales Rep: _____

Tel: _____

Orders to
EXEL LOGISTICS - MEDIA SERVICES, 3 Sheldon Way, Larkfield, Aylesford, Kent ME20 6SF
Tel: 0622 882000
Fax: 0622 718036

Order Information

All Dues Automatically Recorded
Representation Available

Personnel
Head of Company: Colin Webb (Managing Director)
Head of Sales (Home): Jonathan Hayden (Marketing Director)
Head of Sales (Export): Anne Timblick (Export Manager)
Head of Marketing: Jonathan Hayden (Marketing Director)
Head of Publicity: Fiona Brownlee (Press Officer)
Head of Accounts: Tim James (Financial Director)

Number of titles published annually: 80
Percentage of Export Sales: 50%
Number of Staff: 30
NBA Signatory
All New Titles are Bar Coded
Book Data Subscriber
WBIP Updating: Fran Banks

Trade Terms
35% on all orders, no surcharges
Credit Cards Accepted: Access/Master, Visa

Returns Procedures
Authority to Return: The Sales Manager, Bloomsbury Publishers Ltd, 2 Soho Square, London, W1V 5DE
Address for Returns: Exel Logistics
Stock Returns: Contact Bloomsbury Publishers for details of policy and procedure

PAVILION PUBLISHING (BRIGHTON) LTD

42 Lansdowne Place, Hove, East Sussex BN3 1HH
Tel: 0273 821650
Fax: 0273 722040
VAT No: 475 7296 01

PBI PUBLICATIONS

Britannica House, High Street, Waltham Cross, Hertfordshire EN8 7DY
ISBN Prefix(es): 0 903505
Tel: 0992 23691
Fax: 0992 26452
Telex: 23957

Account No: _____

Sales Rep: _____

Tel: _____

Orders to
BIBLIOS PUBLISHERS DISTRIBUTION SERVICE LTD, Star Road, Partridge Green, West Sussex RH13 8LD
Tel: 0403 710971
Fax: 0403 711143

Order Information

All Dues Automatically Recorded
Representation Available

Personnel
Head of Company: Dr D G Hessayon (Managing Director)
Head of Sales (Home): Mr D Soulsby (National Accounts Manager)
Head of Sales (Export): Mr P S Norris (Sales Manager)

All New Titles are Bar Coded
Book Data Subscriber
WBIP Updating: Mr P S Norris

Trade Terms
35% on all books. No service or carriage charges

Returns Procedures
Authority to Return: No SOR conditions

Imperfect Returns: Title page with details of imperfections to Mr P S Norris

PBN PUBLICATIONS
22 Abbey Road, Eastbourne, East Sussex BN20 8TE
Tel: 0323 31206

PC PUBLISHING
4 Brook Street, Tonbridge, Kent TN9 2PJ
Tel: 0732 770893
Fax: 0732 770268

IPG Member

PEACOCK VANE PUBLISHING
Yaffles, The Pitts, Bonchurch, Ventnor, Isle of Wight
PO38 1NT
ISBN Prefix(es): 0 9506749, 1 871382
Tel: 0983 852193

J M PEARSON & SON (PUBLISHERS) LTD
Park View, Tatenhill Common, Burton-on-Trent, Staffordshire PE13 9RS
ISBN Prefix(es): 0 907864
Tel: 0283 713674
VAT No: 353 5546 48

Orders to
CORDEE, 3a DeMontfont Street, Leicester, Leicestershire LE1 7HO
Tel: 0533 543579
Fax: 0533 471176

Order Information

All Dues Automatically Recorded
Representation Available

Personnel
Head of Company: J M Pearson

Number of titles published annually: 6
All New Titles are Bar Coded

Trade Terms
Single copy 25%, Two or more 35%
Other Terms: Cheque with order qualifies for 35% on single copy orders

Returns Procedures
Authority to Return: Cordee
Address for Returns: Cordee
Stock Returns: Ask Permission
Imperfect Returns: Title Page

PEARSON PUBLISHING
Chesterton Mill, French's Road, Cambridge, Cambridgeshire CB4 3NP
Tel: 0223 350555
Fax: 0223 356484

PEARTREE PUBLICATIONS

61 Peartree Lane, Little Common, Bexhill, East Sussex
TN39 4PE
ISBN Prefix(es): 1 85254
Tel: 04243 4274

Personnel
Head of Company: R M Stepney

Percentage of Export Sales: 5%

Trade Terms
35% on all orders no surcharges

PEEPAL TREE BOOKS

17 King's Avenue, Leeds, Yorkshire LS6 1QS
ISBN Prefix(es): 0 948833
Tel: 0532 451703 Day
Tel: 0532 676580 Evening
Fax: 0532 300345
VAT No: 447 5193 30

Orders to
PASSWORD (BOOKS) LTD, 23 New Mount Street, Manchester, Greater Manchester M4 4DE
Tel: 061-953 4009
Fax: 061-953 4001

Order Information

All Dues Automatically Recorded
Representation Available
Invoice Payments: Password (Books) Ltd

Personnel
Head of Company: Jeremy Poynting
Other Important Personnel:
Ray Kyte (Art Director)

Number of titles published annually: 18
Percentage of Export Sales: 60%
All New Titles are Bar Coded

Trade Terms
35% no surcharges
Girobank Number: 613 4599

Returns Procedures
Authority to Return: Representative/Password (Books) Ltd
Address for Returns: Clipper Distribution Services

PEGASUS PUBLISHING SERVICES

41 Church Street, Coggeshall, Essex CO6 1TX
Tel: 0376 562871
Fax: 0376 563352
VAT No: 463 4701 52

Personnel
Head of Company: Philip Robey
Head of Customer Services: Caty Robey

PEN & SWORD BOOKS LTD

47 Church Street, Barnsley, South Yorkshire S70 2AS
ISBN Prefix(es): 0 436, 0 85052, 0 9507892, 1 871647
Tel: 0226 734222
Tel: 0226 734555 24hrs
Tel: 071-836 3141 editorial
Fax: 0226 734437
Fax: 071-240 9247 editorial
VAT No: 565 6362 18

Orders to
AIRLIFE PUBLISHING LTD, 101 Longden Road, Shrewsbury, Shropshire SY3 9EB
Tel: 0743 235651
Fax: 0743 232944

Order Information

Orders for more than one publisher can be bulked
All Dues Automatically Recorded
Representation Available
Invoice Payments: Airlife Publishing Ltd

Personnel
Head of Company: Leo Cooper (Managing Director) 071 836 3141
Head of Customer Services: Barbara Bramall (Administration Manager)
Other Important Personnel:
Sir Nicholas Hewitt Bt (Chairman)

Number of titles published annually: 40
Number of Staff: 8
NBA Signatory
All New Titles are Bar Coded
Book Data Subscriber
WBIP Updating: Barbara Bramall

Parent Company: Barnsley Chronicle Holdings Ltd

Trade Terms
35%
Girobank Number: 482 1718
Credit Cards Accepted: Access/Master, Visa

Returns Procedures
Authority to Return: Airlife Publishing Ltd
Address for Returns: Airlife Publishing Ltd
Stock Returns: Authorisation and returns. Labels must be obtained from Airlife Publishing Ltd
Imperfect Returns: Complete book must be returned

PENDULUM GALLERY PRESS

The Manse, 56 Ackender Road, Alton, Hampshire GU34 1JS
Tel: 0420 84483 Tel/Fax
VAT No: 522 1830 82

Orders to
BIBLIOS PUBLISHERS DISTRIBUTION SERVICE LTD, Star Road, Partridge Green, West Sussex RH13 8LD
Tel: 0403 710971
Fax: 0403 711143

IPG Member

PENGUIN BOOKS LTD

27 Wright's Lane, London W8 5TZ
ISBN Prefix(es): 0 140, 0 241, 0 370, 0 451, 0 452, 0 453, 0 670, 0 7139, 0 7181, 0 7207, 0 7232, 0 8099, 0 8289, 0 86350, 0 86616, 0 87997, 0 88677, 0 907516, 0 91845, 1 55615, 1 85145
Tel: 071-416 3000
Fax: 071-416 3099
Telex: 917181
VAT No: 222 3251 15
Account No: _____ 01447 _____
Sales Rep: _____
Tel: _____

Orders to
Penguin Books Ltd, Bath Road, Harmondsworth, Middlesex UB7 0DA
Tel: 081 899 4000
Fax: 081-899 4020
24 Hour Ansafone Number: 081-899 4050

Co-ordinator
Diane Lyndon

Order Information
Teleordering: PENGUIN

Order Dept Opening Times
Mon - Fri 9am - 5pm
Orders for more than one publisher can be bulked
All Dues Automatically Recorded
Representation Available

Personnel
Head of Company: Trevor Glover (Managing Director)
Head of Sales (Home): Patrick Hutchinson (UK Sales & Marketing Director)
Head of Sales (Export): Tony Moggach (European Sales & Marketing Director)
Head of Marketing: Andrew Welham (Marketing Director)
Head of Publicity: Susan Sandon (Publicity Director - Paperback)
Head of Accounts: Nigel Williams (Finance Director)
Head of Distribution: John Peck (Distribution Director)
Head of Customer Services: David Edwards (Customer Services Manager)
Other Important Personnel:
Max Adam (Export Sales & Marketing), Sarah Hodgson (Head of Publicity Penguin), Sally Gritten (Childrens Marketing Director), Clare Harrington (Viking Marketing Director), Karen Geary (Hamish Hamilton Marketing Director), Nellie Flexner (Michael Joseph Marketing Director), Deborah Hooper (Warne Head of Marketing), Kevin Bristow (Paperback Sales Director), Bob Kelly (Hardback Sales Director)

Number of titles published annually: 1000
Percentage of Export Sales: 35%
Number of Staff: 650
PA Member
NBA Signatory
All New Titles are Bar Coded
Open University Publications
Book Data Subscriber
WBIP Updating: Andrew Welham

Subsidiary Companies: NAL (US)
Allied Companies: Longman Penguin Japan, Longman Penguin Espana (SP)

Trade Terms
General Net: 35%
Non-Net: 20% p/b, 17.5% h/b

Returns Procedures
Authority to Return: Representative or appropriate sales office
Address for Returns: Penguin Books Ltd, Harmondsworth
Stock Returns: Overstocks must be authorised by rep
Imperfect Returns: Title pages accepted for book value less than £25

PENINSULA BOOKS
PO Box 3, South Wirral, Merseyside L64 6UB
ISBN Prefix(es): 0 902158, 1 85180

Order Information

All Dues Automatically Recorded

Personnel
Head of Company: Elwyn Jones

WBIP Updating: E Jones

Trade Terms
General Net: Single copy/single line 15%, 2 books or more 25%, 3 or more 35%
BA/Girobank Small Order Scheme: Yes
Girobank Number: 44 040 4002

Returns Procedures
Stock Returns: Return for full credit.
Imperfect Returns: Title page only under £15

PENNY PRESS

176 Greendale Road, Coventry, Warwickshire CV5 8AY
ISBN Prefix(es): 1 871281
Tel: 0203 717275 24 Hours

Order Information

All Dues Automatically Recorded
Representation Available

Personnel
Head of Company: Philip J Brown
Head of Marketing: Michael Condev

Number of titles published annually: 2
Number of Staff: 2
All New Titles are Bar Coded
WBIP Updating: Philip J Brown

Trade Terms
35% on all orders, no surcharges
Credit Cards Accepted: Access/Master, Visa

Returns Procedures
Imperfect Returns: Np price limit

THE PENTLAND PRESS LTD

1 Hutton Close, South Church, Bishop Auckland, County Durham DL14 6XB
ISBN Prefix(es): 0 946270, 1 872795
Tel: 0388 776555
Fax: 0388 776766

Orders to
Pentland Press Ltd, 3 Regal Lane, Soham, Ely, Cambridgeshire CB7 5BA
Tel: 0353 723350
Fax: 0353 721839

Order Information

Order Dept Opening Times
Mon - Thu 9am - 5pm, Fri 9am - 1pm
Representation Available

Personnel
Head of Company: A Phillips (Managing Director)
Head of Sales (Home): D Russell
Head of Marketing: Rosemary Rudd
Head of Accounts: Jean Pearson Ely
Head of Distribution: Libby Jenkins Ely

Number of titles published annually: 100
Number of Staff: 6
IPG Member
WBIP Updating: Mr D Russell

Trade Terms
35% plus carriage
Credit Cards Accepted: Access/Master, Amex, Visa

Returns Procedures
Authority to Return: Permission required from Libby Jennings

PERGAMON PRESS LTD
Headington Hill Hall, Oxford, Oxfordshire OX3 0BW
Tel: 0865-743338   0865-794141
Fax: 0865-743950
Telex: 83177
Account No: 38932001
Sales Rep:
Tel:

Order Information
Teleordering: PERG   NOW.

Personnel
Head of Company: Mr Michael Boswood (Managing Director)
Head of Sales (Home): Ms Della Sar (Sales & Marketing Manager)
Head of Accounts: Mr Tim Davies (Finance Director)

Parent Company: Elsevier NV

Handwritten notes:
From 12/10/92.
Returns.
Yeomans Drive
Brickhill St,
Blakelands
Milton Keynes.
MK14 5LY.

Elsevier Science Ltd
The Boulevard
Langford Lane
Kidlington, Oxford
OX5 1GB
Tel 0865 843000
Fax 0865·843010

*PERGAMON = REED BOOK SERVICES (Jan '95)

PERGAMON PRESS
Oxford • New York • Seoul • Tokyo

Leading the world in scientific publishing

Books • Journals • Major Reference Works

PERGAMON PRESS Ltd
Headington Hill Hall, Oxford, OX3 0BW, UK
Telephone: +44-0865-794141   Fax: +44-0865-60285

PERGAMON PRESS Inc.
660 White Plains Road, Tarrytown, New York, NY 10591-5153, USA
Telephone: +1-914-524-9200   Fax: +1-914-333-2444

A member of the Elsevier Science Publishing Group

CO2A42

COLIN A PERRY LIMITED
The Gables, Mawley Road, Quenington, Cirencester,
Gloucestershire GL7 5BH
ISBN Prefix(es): 0 9506594
Tel: 0285 750443

Personnel
Head of Company: C A Perry

Number of titles published annually: 1

Trade Terms
General Net: Single copy/single line 25% + postage, 2-12 copies 40% + postage, 13+ 50%

PERVAIZ PUBLICATIONS

43 Glastonbury Court, Talbot Road, West Ealing, London W13 0SL
Tel: 081-567 8939
VAT No: 538 6245 25

IPG Member

THE PETERHOUSE PRESS

10 Windmill Street, Brill, Aylesbury, Buckinghamshire HP18 9SZ
Tel: 0844 237795
VAT No: 348 7194 20

Orders to
LAVIS MARKETING, 73 Lime Walk, Headington, Oxfordshire OX3 7AD
Tel: 0865 67575
Fax: 0865 750079

IPG Member

PETERLOO POETS

2 Kelly Gardens, Calstock, Cornwall PL18 9SA
ISBN Prefix(es): 0 905291, 1 871471
Tel: 0822 833473
VAT No: 557 6026 29

Order Information

Order Dept Opening Times
Mon - Fri 9am - 5pm
All Dues Automatically Recorded
Representation Available

Personnel
Head of Company: Harry Chambers
Head of Sales (Home): Lynn Chambers

Number of titles published annually: 9
Number of Staff: 3
IPG Member
All New Titles are Bar Coded
WBIP Updating: Lynn Chambers

Parent Company: Peterloo Poets

Trade Terms
35% no surcharges for Peterloo Titles
Other Terms: Marvell Press: 25% on 1-5 copies, 33.3% on 6-15 copies 35% on 151+ copies
BA/Girobank Small Order Scheme: Pre-payment by cheque - no Girobank account
Credit Cards Accepted: Access/Master, Visa, Amex

Returns Procedures
Authority to Return: Head Office or Rep
Stock Returns: On Request

PEVENSEY PRESS

6 De Freville Avenue, Cambridge, Cambridgeshire CB4 1HR
ISBN Prefix(es): 0 907115
Tel: 0223 351156

Orders to
EXEL LOGISTICS - MEDIA SERVICES, 3 Sheldon Way,
Larkfield, Aylesford, Kent ME20 6SF
Tel: 0622 882000
Fax: 0622 718036

Order Information

All Dues Automatically Recorded
Representation Available

Personnel
Head of Company: T V Buttrey (Publisher)
Head of Accounts: E Frankl

Number of titles published annually: 3
All New Titles are Bar Coded

Parent Company: David & Charles PLC

Returns Procedures
Authority to Return: Exel Logistics
Address for Returns: Exel Logistics

PHAIDON PRESS LTD

140 Kensington Church Street, London W8 4BN
ISBN Prefix(es): 0 7148, 0 8174, 0 8230, 1 85454
Tel: 071-221 5656
Fax: 071-221 8474

Account No: _____13SM24_____

Sales Rep: _____

Tel: _____

Orders to
BOOKPOINT LIMITED, 39 Milton Park, Abingdon,
Oxfordshire OX14 4TD
Tel: 0235 835001
Fax: 0235 861038

Order Information

All Dues Automatically Recorded
Representation Available

Personnel
Head of Company: Richard Schlaghan
Head of Sales (Home): David Graham
Head of Sales (Export): Simon Littlewood
Head of Marketing: Jane Morris
Head of Accounts: Andrew Price
Head of Customer Services: Jenny North

Number of titles published annually: 40
Percentage of Export Sales: 50%
Number of Staff: 45
PA Member
All New Titles are Bar Coded
Open University Publications
Book Data Subscriber
WBIP Updating: Jenny North

Trade Terms
General Net: 35%
Academic Net: 30%

Returns Procedures
Authority to Return: Local Phaidon Representative
Address for Returns: Bookpoint

Stock Returns: Obtain local rep approval first. Mint condition only. Only between 4&12 months of pub. Transit damaged ret within 14days
Imperfect Returns: Return whole book with note of problem

PHARMACEUTICAL PRESS
1 Lambeth High Street, London SE1 7JN
ISBN Prefix(es): 0 85369
Tel: 071-735 9141
Fax: 071-735 7629
Telex: 931213152 (PS G)

Order Information

Order Dept Opening Times
Mon - Fri 9am - 5pm
All Dues Automatically Recorded
Representation Available

Personnel
Head of Company: Bernard Yates (Publications Manager)
Head of Sales (Home): Barry Wimbledon (Sales Manager)
Head of Marketing: Kate Rowan (Marketing Manager)

Number of titles published annually: 8
Percentage of Export Sales: 50%
Number of Staff: 45
NBA Signatory
All New Titles are Bar Coded
Book Data Subscriber
WBIP Updating: Kate Rowan

Trade Terms
16.66% under 50 copies, 20% 50 - 100 copies, 25% over 100 copies

[handwritten: Philip (George) = Reed Book Services]

PHILLIMORE & CO LTD
Shopwyke Hall, Chichester, West Sussex PO20 6BQ
ISBN Prefix(es): 0 85033, 0 85208, 0 900592, 0 948140, 0 950365
Tel: 0243 787636
Fax: 0243 787639
Cables: Phillimore Chichester
VAT No: 193 1088 60

Account No: _____
Sales Rep: _____
Tel: _____

Order Information
Teleordering: PHILL

Order Dept Opening Times
Mon - Fri 9am - 5.30pm
Orders for more than one publisher can be bulked
All Dues Automatically Recorded
Representation Available

Personnel
Head of Company: Philip Harris
Head of Sales (Home): Hilary Clifford Brown
Head of Publicity: Mrs Val White
Head of Accounts: Mrs Carol Cockaday
Head of Distribution: Frank White

Number of titles published annually: 50
Number of Staff: 15
NBA Signatory
All New Titles are Bar Coded
WBIP Updating: Mrs Val White

Trade Terms
General Net: Single copies 25%, Two or more 35%
Other Terms: Small order surcharges £2 on orders under £20 invoice value

Returns Procedures
Stock Returns: All returns can be sent direct to our Trade Counter, well-packed and stating reason for return
Imperfect Returns: Imperfect books should be returned whole to Trade Counter

PHILOGRAPH PUBLICATIONS LTD

North Way, Walworth Industrial Estate, Andover, Hampshire SP10 5BA
Tel: 0264 332226
Fax: 0264 332171

PHOTOBOOK INFORMATION SERVICE LTD

7 Colwall Ind Est, Colwall, Malvern, Worcestershire WR13 6RN
ISBN Prefix(es): 0 951575
Tel: 0684 40825 24 Hours
Fax: 0684 40130
VAT No: 238 1048 76

Order Information
Teleordering: PHOTO

Order Dept Opening Times
Mon - Fri 9am - 5.30pm
Representation Available

Personnel
Head of Company: Roy R Knightley (Managing Director)
Head of Sales (Home): Colin Alten
Head of Publicity: Mary Knightley
Head of Distribution: Mervyn Davies

Number of titles published annually: 2
Percentage of Export Sales: 40%
Number of Staff: 4
All New Titles are Bar Coded
WBIP Updating: Colin Alten

Trade Terms
35%, single copy orders 25%
Girobank Number: 52 244 0401
Credit Cards Accepted: Access/Master, Visa

Returns Procedures
Stock Returns: Please contact head office for authorisation
Imperfect Returns: Please contact head office for authorisation

PIATKUS BOOKS

5 Windmill Street, London W1P 1HF
ISBN Prefix(es): 0 7499, 0 86188, 1 85018
Tel: 071-631 0710
Fax: 071-436 7137
VAT No: 311 7966 56

Account No: _____
Sales Rep: _____
Tel: _____

Orders to
GRANTHAM BOOK SERVICES LTD, Isaac Newton Way, Alma Park Industrial Estate, Grantham, Lincolnshire NG31 9SD

Tel: 0476 67421
Fax: 0476 590223

Order Information

All Dues Automatically Recorded
Representation Available
Invoice Payments: Grantham Book Services

Personnel

Head of Company: Judy Piatkus (Managing Director)
Head of Sales (Home): Philip Cotterell (Marketing Director)
Head of Publicity: Jana Sommerlad (Publicity Manager)
Head of Accounts: David Harris (Financial Manager)
Other Important Personnel:
Simon Colverson (Production Manager), Diane Hill (UK Sales Manager)

Number of titles published annually: 105
Percentage of Export Sales: 20%
Number of Staff: 16
IPG Member
NBA Signatory
All New Titles are Bar Coded
Book Data Subscriber
WBIP Updating: Diane Hill

Trade Terms
35%
Credit Cards Accepted: Access/Master, Visa

Returns Procedures
Authority to Return: Philip Cotterell/Diane Hill
Address for Returns: Grantham Book Services
Imperfect Returns: Title page up to £20

PICCADILLY PRESS LTD

5 Castle Road, London NW1 8PR
ISBN Prefix(es): 0 946826, 1 85340
Tel: 071-267 4492
Fax: 071-267 4493
Telex: 295441

Orders to
TIPTREE BOOK SERVICES LTD, Church Road, Tiptree, Colchester, Essex CO5 0SR
Tel: 0621 819600
Fax: 0621 819011

Order Information

All Dues Automatically Recorded
Representation Available
Representation:Boxtree

Personnel
Head of Company: Brenda Gardner (Managing Director)
Head of Sales (Home): David Inman (Sales Director)
Boxtree 071-928 9696
Head of Marketing: Jacqui Gadd (Special Sales & Marketing Director)
Head of Publicity: Ruth Williams (Editor)
Head of Accounts: Patric Duffy (Financial Director)

Number of titles published annually: 34
Number of Staff: 6
NBA Signatory
All New Titles are Bar Coded
WBIP Updating: Ruth Williams

Trade Terms
35%

Returns Procedures
Authority to Return: Brenda Gardner or Boxtree Reps

Address for Returns: Tiptree
Imperfect Returns: Return Title Page

PICKWICK BOOKS - PO BOX 925, LONDON W2 1FA

PICTON PUBLISHING (CHIPPENHAM) LTD

Queensbridge Cottages, Patterdown, Chippenham, Wiltshire
SN15 2NS
ISBN Prefix(es): 0 948251
Tel: 0249 443430
Fax: 0249 443024
VAT No: 437 0868 33

Order Information

Order Dept Opening Times
Mon - Fri 9.30am - 1pm, 2pm - 4.30pm
All Dues Automatically Recorded
Representation Available

Personnel

Head of Company: D B Picton-Phillips
Head of Sales (Home): A V Picton Phillips
Other Important Personnel:
Clem Addenbrooke (London Rep), Bill Laughton (Byway Books) (Scotland & North England Rep)

Number of titles published annually: 12
Number of Staff: 3
IPG Member
NBA Signatory
All New Titles are Bar Coded
WBIP Updating: D B Picton-Phillips

Trade Terms

30 days nett, all orders firm, no see safe or s.o.r.
General Net: Single copy 25%, 2 books or more 35%, 3-20 mixed titles 35% 21 to 40 - 40% over 40 titles by arrangement.
Minimum Order: 1 copy proforma if not recognised account
Other Terms: Carriaged charged. Service charged overseas.
Credit Cards Accepted: Access/Master, Visa

Returns Procedures

Authority to Return: D B Picton Phillips
Stock Returns: Write for permission giving full details of claim. Inv no. Must be within few days of receipt of books. Wrappings kept.
Imperfect Returns: All imperfect books must be kept, but full detail of damage given. When approved book cover must be returned for credit

PIG PRESS

7 Cross View Terrace, Neville's Cross, Durham, County Durham DH1 4JY
Tel: 091-384 6914
VAT No: 459 7869 67

Order Information

All Dues Automatically Recorded
Representation Available

Personnel

Head of Company: Richard Caddel/Ann Caddel (Joint Directors)

Number of titles published annually: 2
Percentage of Export Sales: 25%
Number of Staff: 2

Trade Terms

Single copy 25%, Multiples 35%

Returns Procedures

Authority to Return: Prior permission required

Stock Returns: Authorised returns accepted within 9 months against credit
Imperfect Returns: Imperfects will be replaced by return

THE PILGRIM PRESS LTD

Lodge Lane, Derby, Derbyshire DE1 3HE
ISBN Prefix(es): 0900594
Tel: 0332 47087
Fax: 0332 290668
VAT No: 125 8281 68

Order Information

Order Dept Opening Times
Mon - Fri 9am - 5pm

Personnel
Head of Company: B C Wood (Managing Director)

Number of titles published annually: 2
NBA Signatory

Trade Terms
General Net: Single copy 25%, two or more single titles 25%, two books or more 35%
Other Terms: Carriage charges on orders under £20.00

PILLAR PUBLICATIONS LTD

45 Woodland Grove, Weybridge, Surrey KT13 9EQ
Tel: 0932 820282
Tel: 0932 859727
Fax: 0932 858035
VAT No: 479 7859 56

PINES PRESS

The Pines, Ballelin, Maughold, Isle of Man
ISBN Prefix(es): 1 870970
Tel: 0624 862030 24 Hours

Order Information

Order Dept Opening Times
9am - 6pm

Personnel
Head of Company: Mr B Shannon (Proprietor & Sales Director)
Head of Publicity: B Clynes 0624 861408
Head of Accounts: N Douglas 0624 861408

Trade Terms
Single Orders 33.3%, Multiples 40%

Returns Procedures
Authority to Return: B Shannon

PINHORNS

Normans, Newbridge, Yarmouth, Isle of Wight PO14 0TY
ISBN Prefix(es): 0 901262

Personnel
Head of Company: Malcolm Pinhorn

Trade Terms
On application

PINTER PUBLISHERS LTD

25 Floral Street, London WC2E 9DS
ISBN Prefix(es): 0 7185, 0 86187, 0 903804, 1 85293, 1 85567
Tel: 071-240 9233
Fax: 071-379 5553
VAT No: 230 5839 73

Account No: _____
Sales Rep: _____
Tel: _____

Orders to
MARSTON BOOK SERVICES LTD, PO Box 87, Osney Mead, Oxford, Oxfordshire OX2 0DT
Tel: 0865 791155
Fax: 0865 791927

Order Information

All Dues Automatically Recorded
Representation Available
Invoice Payments: Marston Book Services

Personnel
Head of Company: Frances Porter (Managing Director)
Head of Sales (Home): Catherine Newman (Sales Manager)
Head of Marketing: Pamela Fulton (Marketing Director)

Number of titles published annually: 150
Percentage of Export Sales: 70%
Number of Staff: 15
PA Member
NBA Signatory
All New Titles are Bar Coded
Open University Publications
Book Data Subscriber
WBIP Updating: Sue Wilson

Trade Terms
25%, no surcharge
BA/Girobank Small Order Scheme: Yes
Girobank Number: 2366053

Returns Procedures
Authority to Return: Prior permission required
Address for Returns: Marston Book Services

PION LTD

207 Brondesbury Park, London NW2 5JN
ISBN Prefix(es): 0 85086
Tel: 081-459 0066
Fax: 081-451 6454
VAT No: 226 8689 22

Orders to
TURPIN DISTRIBUTION SERVICES LTD, Blackhorse Road, Letchworth, Hertfordshire SG6 1HN
Tel: 0462 672555
Fax: 0462 480947

Order Information

Representation Available
Invoice Payments: Turpin Distribution Services

Personnel
Head of Company: Adam Gelbtuch/Dr John Ashby
Head of Sales (Home): Diana Mallett

IPG Member
Book Data Subscriber
WBIP Updating: Diana Mallett

Trade Terms
25%

Returns Procedures
Authority to Return: Turpin Distribution Services

PISCES ANGLING PUBLICATIONS
8 Stumperlows Close, Sheffield, South Yorkshire S10 3PP
ISBN Prefix(es): 0 94858
Tel: 0742 304038
Fax: 0742 306640
VAT No: 173 6807 43

Orders to
HUGO'S LANGUAGE BOOKS LTD, Old Station Yard, Marlesford, Woodbridge, Suffolk IP13 0AG
Tel: 0728 746546
Fax: 0728 746236

Order Information

All Dues Automatically Recorded
Representation Available
Invoice Payments: Hugo's Language Books Ltd
Representation:Peter Lock - Hugo's

Personnel
Head of Company: Colin Dyson (Proprietor)

All New Titles are Bar Coded
WBIP Updating: Colin Dyson

Trade Terms
35%, orders under £15 25%
Girobank Number: 5589355

Returns Procedures
Imperfect Returns: Title page for misprinted copies, otherwise complete book

PITKIN PICTORIALS
Healey House, Dene Road, Andover, Hampshire SP10 2AA
ISBN Prefix(es): 0 85372
Tel: 0264 334303
Fax: 0264 334110
VAT No: 340 2429 92

Order Information

Representation Available
Invoice Payments: Reed Book Services

Personnel
Head of Company: Ian Corsie (Managing Director)
Head of Sales (Home): Rosemarie McCabe (Sales & Marketing Manager)
Other Important Personnel:
Alan Daws (Sales Office Manager), Christine Walkom (Sales Secretary)

Number of titles published annually: 25
Number of Staff: 9
NBA Signatory
All New Titles are Bar Coded
Book Data Subscriber
WBIP Updating: Adrienne Long

Parent Company: Reed International Books

Trade Terms
35%, 40% over 100 single titles
Other Terms: Carriage charged on export All sales firm
Credit Cards Accepted: Access/Master, Amex, Diners, Visa

PITMAN PUBLISHING

128 Long Acre, London WC2E 9AN
ISBN Prefix(es): 0 273, 0 7121, 0 8550, 0 89588
Tel: 071-379 7383
Fax: 071-240 5771
Telex: 261367 Pitman G
Cables: Ipandsons London WC2
VAT No: 213 6785 61
Account No: 0175 2626
Sales Rep: _____
Tel: _____

Orders to
SOUTHPORT BOOK DISTRIBUTORS LIMITED, 12/14 Slaidburn Crescent, Southport, Merseyside PR9 9YF
Tel: 0704 24331
Fax: 0704 231970

Order Information
Teleordering: PIT

All Dues Automatically Recorded
Representation Available
Invoice Payments: Southport Book Distributors

Personnel
Head of Company: Dr Henry Reece (Managing Director)
Head of Sales (Home): Mr Peter Marshall (UK Sales Manager)
Head of Sales (Export): Mrs Stephanie Glover (International Sales Manager)
Head of Marketing: Mr Alick Kitchin (Marketing Manager)
Head of Publicity: Kate Salkilld (Marketing Manager (Professional))
Head of Accounts: Mr John Knight (Accountant)
Other Important Personnel:
Mr David Gooding (Trade Product Executive), Rod Bristow (Sales & Marketing Director)

Number of titles published annually: 200
Percentage of Export Sales: 30%
Number of Staff: 70
PA Member
NBA Signatory
All New Titles are Bar Coded
Open University Publications
Book Data Subscriber
WBIP Updating: Ms J Hall

Parent Company: Longman Group UK

Trade Terms
Subject to negotiation
General Net: 35%
Academic Net: 25%
Non-Net: 25%
Other Terms: Small order surcharge: £3 on invoices under £30 net

Returns Procedures
Address for Returns: Southport
Stock Returns: Full see-safe policy from 3-12 months from invoice date. Quote inv no.(Surcharge if not) Credit only current titles

PLATFORM 5 PUBLISHING LTD

Wyvern House, Old Forge Bus Park, Sark Road, Sheffield, South Yorkshire S2 4HG
ISBN Prefix(es): 0 906579, 1 872524
Tel: 0742 552625
Fax: 0742 552471
VAT No: 390 9904 18

All New Titles are Bar Coded

Trade Terms
Girobank Number: 65 930 4007

THE PLAYWRIGHTS PUBLISHING COMPANY

70 Nottingham Road, Burton Joyce, Nottinghamshire NG14 5AL
ISBN Prefix(es): 1 872758, 1 873130
Tel: 0602 313356 24 Hours

Order Information

Order Dept Opening Times
24 Hour

Personnel
Head of Company: Liz Breeze (Proprietor)
Other Important Personnel:
Tony Breeze (Consultant)

Number of titles published annually: 15
Number of Staff: 2
All New Titles are Bar Coded

Trade Terms
33%
Girobank Number: 466 5554

Returns Procedures
Authority to Return: Liz Breeze

PLENUM PUBLISHING COMPANY LTD

88/90 Middlesex Street, London E1 7EZ
ISBN Prefix(es): 0 306
Tel: 071-377 0686
Fax: 071-247 0555
Telex: via 22914 CCCL G
VAT No: 226 9065 55
Account No: _____ 43651 _____
Sales Rep: _____
Tel: _____

Order Information

Order Dept Opening Times
Mon - Fri 9am - 5pm
All Dues Automatically Recorded
Representation Available

Personnel
Head of Company: Dr Ken Derham (Managing Director)
Head of Sales (Home): Marja-Liisa Puolakka
Head of Sales (Export): Theo van de Bilt
Head of Publicity: Julia Capon
Head of Customer Services: E S Eggins

Number of titles published annually: 320
Number of Staff: 10
PA Member
WBIP Updating: Zohara Jalalpuria

Parent Company: Plenum Publishing Corporation

Trade Terms
20 - 33.3% +P&P
Credit Cards Accepted: Access/Master, Visa, Amex, Diners

Returns Procedures
Stock Returns: Return with invoice details

PLEXUS PUBLISHING LTD

26 Dafforne Road, London SW17 8TZ
ISBN Prefix(es): 0 85965
Tel: 081-672 6067
Fax: 081-672 1631
VAT No: 227 6250 69

Orders to
BOOKPOINT LIMITED, 39 Milton Park, Abingdon, Oxfordshire OX14 4TD
Tel: 0235 835001
Fax: 0235 861038

Order Information

Invoice Payments: Bookpoint

Returns Procedures
Address for Returns: Bookpoint

PLOUGH PUBLISHING HOUSE

Hutterian Brethren, Darvell Bruderhof, Robertsbridge, East Sussex TN32 5DR
Tel: 0580 880626
Fax: 0580 881171

PLUME PRESS

West Bowers Hall, Woodham Walter, Maldon, Essex CM9 6RZ
ISBN Prefix(es): 0 947656
Tel: 0245 222562
Fax: 0245 225489

Order Information

Representation Available

Personnel
Head of Company: Frank Herrmann
Head of Sales (Home): Patricia Herrmann

Number of titles published annually: 1
WBIP Updating: Patricia Herrmann

Trade Terms
General Net: Single copy 25%, Two or more 35%

PLUNKETT FOUNDATION

23 Hanborough Business Park, Long Hanborough, Oxford, Oxfordshire OX8 8LH
Tel: 0993 883636
Fax: 0993 883576

PLUTO PUBLISHING

345 Archway Road, London N6 5AA
ISBN Prefix(es): 0 7453, 0 8610, 0 9045, 1 8517, 1 8530
Tel: 081-348 2724
Fax: 081-348 9133
VAT No: 480 8482 22

Order Information
Teleordering: PLUTO

Order Dept Opening Times
9am - 5.30pm
All Dues Automatically Recorded
Representation Available

Personnel
Head of Company: Roger van Zwanenberg
Head of Sales (Home): Sophie Boswell
Head of Publicity: Anne Beech
Head of Accounts: Qwasi Kodua

Number of titles published annually: 35
Percentage of Export Sales: 20%
Number of Staff: 5
IPG Member
NBA Signatory
All New Titles are Bar Coded
Book Data Subscriber
WBIP Updating: Gillian

Trade Terms
Single copy 20%. Two or more 33.3%. Invoice value less than £25, £1.25 low value surcharge.
Credit Cards Accepted: Access/Master, Visa, Amex, Other

Returns Procedures
Authority to Return: Roger van Zwanenberg
Address for Returns: Clipper Distribution Ltd, Windmill Grove, Portchester, Hants PO16 9HT
Stock Returns: Credit raised on authorised returns, no credit for books in unsaleable condition

PLYMBRIDGE DISTRIBUTORS LTD

Plymbridge House, Estover Road, Plymouth, Devon PL6 7PZ
Tel: 0752 735251
Tel: 0752 695745 — customer service no.
Fax: 0752 695699
Telex: 45635
VAT No: 526 9593 06
Account No: 705771
Sales Rep: _____
Tel: _____

Order Information
Teleordering: PLYM

Order Dept Opening Times
Mon - Fri 8.30am - 5pm
Orders for more than one publisher can be bulked
All Dues Automatically Recorded

Personnel
Head of Company: Mr M W Beevers
Head of Customer Services: Mrs Ann Wigzell
Other Important Personnel:
Mr B G Eagle (Computer Systems), Mr K R Wasley (Warehouse), Mr I Wordsworth (Order Processing)

Trade Terms
Girobank Number: 221 2951

Returns Procedures
Authority to Return: Apply to publisher

THE POETRY BUSINESS LTD

51 Byram Arcade, Westgate, Huddersfield, West Yorkshire HD1 1ND
Tel: 0484 434840
Fax: 0484 426566

Orders to
PASSWORD (BOOKS) LTD, 23 New Mount Street, Manchester, Greater Manchester M4 4DE
Tel: 061-953 4009
Fax: 061-953 4001

POETRY WALES PRESS LTD

Andmar House, Tondu Road, Bridgend, Mid Glamorgan
CF31 4LJ
ISBN Prefix(es): 0 907476, 1 85411
Tel: 0656 767834
VAT No: 484 3231 48

Orders to
BAILEY DISTRIBUTION LTD, Unit 1, Learoyd Road,
Mountfield Rd Ind Est, New Romney, Kent TN28 8XU
Tel: 0679 66905
Fax: 0679 66638

Order Information

All Dues Automatically Recorded
Representation Available

Personnel
Head of Company: Mick Felton (Head of Sales)
Head of Marketing: Simon Dancey
Head of Accounts: Allen Jones

Number of titles published annually: 20
Percentage of Export Sales: 20%
Number of Staff: 5
All New Titles are Bar Coded
WBIP Updating: Mick Felton

Trade Terms
35%, no surcharge
Academic Net: Schools Titles 17%

Returns Procedures
Authority to Return: Drake Marketing Services
Address for Returns: Bailey Distribution

POLECAT PRESS LTD

Quaggs House Farm, Cinderbarrow, Levens, Kendal,
Cumbria LA8 8PA
ISBN Prefix(es): 0 947688
Tel: 05395 61090
VAT No: 393 4494 18

Orders to
CORDEE, 3a DeMontfont Street, Leicester, Leicestershire
LE1 7HO
Tel: 0533 543579
Fax: 0533 471176

Order Information

Order Dept Opening Times
Mon - Fri 9am - 5pm
All Dues Automatically Recorded

Personnel
Head of Company: P W Freeman/G M Bleay

Number of titles published annually: 1

Trade Terms
35% on all orders, no surcharge, except single copies

POLICE REVIEW PUBLISHING CO LTD

South Quay Plaza, 183 Marsh Wall, London E14 9FZ
Tel: 071-537 2575
Fax: 071-537 2553
VAT No: 512 5137 83

POLICY STUDIES INSTITUTE (PSI)

100 Park Village East, London NW1 3SR
ISBN Prefix(es): 0 85374
Tel: 071-387 2171
Fax: 071-388 8914
VAT No: 239 1031 87

Orders to
BEBC DISTRIBUTION, PO Box 1496, Poole, Dorset
BH12 3YD
Tel: 0202 715555
Fax: 0202 715556

Order Information

All Dues Automatically Recorded
Representation Available
Invoice Payments: BEBC Distribution Ltd

Personnel
Head of Company: W W Daniel (Director PSI)
Head of Sales (Home): Nicholas Evans (Head of External Relations)
Other Important Personnel:
Jeremy Lewis (Publications Assistant)

Number of titles published annually: 25
Number of Staff: 2
All New Titles are Bar Coded
Open University Publications
WBIP Updating: Nicholas Evans

Trade Terms
35%
Credit Cards Accepted: Access/Master, Amex, Diners, Visa, Other

Returns Procedures
Authority to Return: Nicholas Evans
Address for Returns: BEBC
Stock Returns: Return to BEBC without authorisation
Imperfect Returns: Return title page of all books over £20

POMEGRANATE EUROPE

Unit 8, Galliford Road, The Causeway, Maldon, Essex
CM9 7XD
Tel: 0621 851646
Fax: 0621 850 862

Order Information

Representation Available

Personnel
Head of Company: Colin Campbell (Managing Director)
Head of Sales (Home): Chris Custance (UK Sales Manager)
Head of Sales (Export): Dave Harris (Sales Director)
Head of Publicity: Liz Hill (Publicity & Promotions Manager)
Head of Accounts: Sue Hall (Administrative Director)

Number of titles published annually: 8
Percentage of Export Sales: 25%
PA Member
WBIP Updating: Liz Hill

Trade Terms
Firm 25% single copy, 35% two or more, 6 or more 40%
See safe Two or more 30%, 6 or more 33%
Girobank Number: 35 045 9703
Credit Cards Accepted: Access/Master, Visa, Amex, Diners

Returns Procedures
Stock Returns: Authority must be obtained and permission given. Goods listed and returned only accepted on see safe orders.

Imperfect Returns: Authority obtained, goods listed and returned.

POOLBEG PRESS LTD
Knocksdean House, Forrest Great Swords, Dublin, County Dublin
ISBN Prefix(es): 1 85371
Tel: 01 8407 433
Fax: 01 8403 753

Account No: _____
Sales Rep: _____
Tel: _____

Orders to
CENTRAL BOOKS, 99 Wallis Road, London E9 5LN
Tel: 081-986 4854
Fax: 081-533 5821

Order Information

Representation Available
Invoice Payments: Central Books

Personnel
Head of Company: Philip MacDermott (Managing Director)
Head of Sales (Home): Breda Purdue (Sales & Marketing Director)
Head of Marketing: Michael McLoughlin (Marketing Manager)
Head of Accounts: Kieran Devlin (Finance Director)

Number of titles published annually: 50
Number of Staff: 12
All New Titles are Bar Coded
WBIP Updating: Jo O'Donoghue

Returns Procedures
Authority to Return: UK Agent: Ion Mills, 18 Coleswood Road, Harpenden, Herts AL5 1EQ
Address for Returns: Central Books

[handwritten: I. Poostchi, 97 St Marks Road, Henley-on-Thames RG9 1LP]

POPPYLAND PUBLISHING
13 Kings Arms Street, North Walsham, Norfolk NR28 9JX
Tel: 0692 403300
VAT No: 426 2963 42

DAVID PORTEOUS EDITIONS
PO Box 5, Chudleigh, Newton Abbot, Devon TQ13 0YZ
Tel: 0626 853310
Fax: 0626 853663
VAT No: 441 2746 66

Orders to
BOOKPOINT LIMITED, 39 Milton Park, Abingdon, Oxfordshire OX14 4TD
Tel: 0235 835001
Fax: 0235 861038

IPG Member

PORTHILL PUBLISHERS
36 West Way, Edgware, Middlesex HA8 9LB
ISBN Prefix(es): 1 870732
Tel: 081-958 6783
Fax: 081-905 4516

Order Information

Order Dept Opening Times
10am - 5pm daily

Personnel
Head of Company: Radomir Putnikovich
Head of Distribution: John Mole
Head of Customer Services: Susan Richardson

Trade Terms
35%

PORTLAND PRESS LTD

59 Portland Place, London W1N 3AJ
ISBN Prefix(es): 0 904498, 1 85578
Tel: 071-580 5530
Fax: 071-323 1136
VAT No: 523 2392 69

Orders to
Portland Press Ltd, PO Box 32, Commerce Way, Colchester, Essex CO2 8HP
Tel: 0206 796351
Fax: 0206 799331

Order Information
Teleordering: BIOCHEM

Order Dept Opening Times
Mon - Fri 8.45am - 4.45pm
Orders for more than one publisher can be bulked
All Dues Automatically Recorded
Representation Available
Invoice Payments: Colchester

Personnel
Head of Company: Glyn Jones (Managing Director)
Head of Marketing: Adam Marshall (Marketing Manager)
Head of Accounts: Chris Finch
Head of Customer Services: Shirley Day 0206 796351

Number of titles published annually: 12
Percentage of Export Sales: 35%
Number of Staff: 35
NBA Signatory
All New Titles are Bar Coded
Book Data Subscriber
WBIP Updating: Shirley Day (Colchester)

Parent Company: The Biochemical Society

Trade Terms
General Net: 35%
Academic Net: 25%
Credit Cards Accepted: Access/Master, Visa, Amex

Returns Procedures
Authority to Return: Shirley Day (Colchester)
Address for Returns: Colchester
Imperfect Returns: Return whole book if below £20

POSITIVE PRODUCTS

PO Box 45, Cheltenham, Gloucestershire GL52 3BX
ISBN Prefix(es): 0 948046
Tel: 021-459 6559 24 Hours
VAT No: 487 0650 25

Personnel
Head of Company: Dr Frank Merrett/Dr Kevin Wheldall

Number of titles published annually: 3
Number of Staff: 3
WBIP Updating: Dr Frank Merrett

Trade Terms
30%, Orders under £30 to be accompanied by cheque to cover cost and postage
Other Terms: Small orders - no discount/postal charged

Returns Procedures
Address for Returns: Positive Products, 18 Bosbury Terrace, Off Warren Road, Stirchley, Birmingham B30 2PB

THE POUND HOUSE

Newent, Gloucestershire GL18 1PS
ISBN Prefix(es): 0 906885, 0 9502040
Tel: 0531 820650

Order Information

Representation Available

Personnel
Head of Company: David Bick

Number of titles published annually: 2
Number of Staff: 1

Trade Terms
33.3%
Other Terms: Small order surcharge 60p

POWER PUBLICATIONS

1 Clayford Avenue, Ferndown, Dorset BH22 9PQ
ISBN Prefix(es): 0 9514502
Tel: 0202 875223
VAT No: 187 9255 10

Order Information

Representation Available

Personnel
Head of Company: Mike Power (Sole Proprietor)

Number of titles published annually: 2
All New Titles are Bar Coded

Trade Terms
35% on all orders
Other Terms: Carriage charged on 2 books or less

POWERFRESH LTD

3 Gray Street, Northampton, Northamptonshire NN1 3QQ
Tel: 0604 30996
Fax: 0604 21013
VAT No: 443 7209 55

PRECISE EDUCATIONAL

Willowbank House, Golden Valley, Riddings, Alfreton, Derbyshire DE55 4ES
Tel: 0773 608722
Fax: 0773 609850
VAT No: 543 7099 28

PREMIER BOOK MARKETING LTD

1 Gower Street, London WC1E 6HA
Tel: 071-636 6005
Fax: 071-580 3995
VAT No: 371 2758 46

Account No: _____

Sales Rep: _____

Tel: _____

Orders to
BIBLIOS PUBLISHERS DISTRIBUTION SERVICE LTD,
Star Road, Partridge Green, West Sussex RH13 8LD
Tel: 0403 710971
Fax: 0403 711143

Order Information

All Dues Automatically Recorded
Representation Available
Invoice Payments: Biblios

Personnel
Head of Company: Donald Deeks (Director)
Head of Sales (Home): Haydn Jenkins (Director)
Head of Publicity: Julia Monk

Number of titles published annually: 175
Percentage of Export Sales: 30%
Number of Staff: 4
WBIP Updating: D Deeks

Trade Terms
35% no surcharges

Returns Procedures
Address for Returns: Biblios
Stock Returns: Prior authorisation required except for incorrectly supplied items
Imperfect Returns: No prior authorisation required.

[handwritten: Prentice Hall = International Book Service]

PRINT ORGANISATION (NW) LTD
Formby Business Park, Formby, Merseyside L37 8EG
Tel: 0704 879231
Fax: 0704 831903
VAT No: 414 8343 61

*[handwritten: Prentice Hall (Australia)
P.O. Box 151,
Brookvale
NSW 2100
Australia]*

PRINTFORCE LTD
Westmead House, 123 Westmead Road, Sutton, Surrey
SM1 4JH
ISBN Prefix(es): 0 948834
Tel: 081-770 1100
Fax: 081-770 2090
VAT No: 468 8515 96

Personnel
Head of Company: David Saint
Head of Accounts: Barbara Saint

Number of titles published annually: 6
Number of Staff: 1
All New Titles are Bar Coded
WBIP Updating: David Saint

Trade Terms
01-19 books 10% 20-49 25%, 50-99 30%, 100+ 40%
Other Terms: Carriage Charges: Only Overseas

PRINTWISE PUBLICATIONS LTD
Unit 9, Bradley Trading Estate, Radcliffe Moor Road,
Radcliffe, Greater Manchester BL2 6RT
ISBN Prefix(es): 1 872226
Tel: 0204 370751
Fax: 0204 370752
VAT No: 519 4866 11

Account No: _____
Sales Rep: _____
Tel: _____

Order Information

Order Dept Opening Times
Mon - Fri 10am - 4pm
All Dues Automatically Recorded
Representation Available

Personnel

Head of Company: Mr Andrew Walsh (Company Director)
Head of Sales (Home): Mr Cliff Hayes
Head of Accounts: Ms Dawn Robinson (Accounts Director)
Head of Distribution: Mr Jeff Wright (Warehouse Manager)
Other Important Personnel:
Mrs D Manning (Accounts Queries)

Number of titles published annually: 50
All New Titles are Bar Coded
WBIP Updating: Dawn Robinson

Allied Companies: Aurora Enterprises Ltd, Party Time Book Co, Phoenix Books, White Rose Books

Trade Terms

Pro-forma invoice or CWO for non-account customers Single Copy 17.5%, Two or more 25%, Stock orders 35%
Other Terms: Small order surcharge on single copies

Returns Procedures

Authority to Return: Prior permission required from Dawn Robinson
Imperfect Returns: Whole book must be returned - we will usually collect.

PRISM PRESS BOOK PUBLISHERS LTD

2 South Street, Bridport, Dorset DT6 3NQ
ISBN Prefix(es): 0 904727, 0 907061, 1 85327
Tel: 0308 27022
Fax: 0308 321015
VAT No: 217 8853 36

Orders to
BOOKPOINT LIMITED, 39 Milton Park, Abingdon, Oxfordshire OX14 4TD
Tel: 0235 835001
Fax: 0235 861038

Order Information

All Dues Automatically Recorded
Representation Available
Invoice Payments: Bookpoint

Personnel

Head of Company: Julian King
Head of Sales (Export): Colin Spooner

Number of titles published annually: 15
Percentage of Export Sales: 45%
Number of Staff: 3
All New Titles are Bar Coded
WBIP Updating: Julian King

Trade Terms
35.0%

Returns Procedures

Address for Returns: Bookpoint
Stock Returns: Apply in writing for authorisation from sales director at head office
Imperfect Returns: Send title page to head office up to £8 retail value for replacement.

PRITAM BOOKS

102 Sandwell Road, Handsworth, Birmingham, West Midlands B21 8PS
ISBN Prefix(es): 1 8699890
Tel: 021-523 7429

Order Information

Order Dept Opening Times
Mon - Fri 9am - 5pm

WBIP Updating: D S Bhogal

PRIVATE ACADEMIC & SCIENTIFIC STUDIES LTD

11 Baring Road, London SE12 0JP
Tel: 081-857 4752
Fax: 081-857 9427

PROBUS EUROPE

Sheraton House, Castle Park, Cambridge, Cambridgeshire CB3 0AX
Tel: 0223 462244
Fax: 0223 460178
Telex: 818436

Order Information

Order Dept Opening Times
Mon - Fri 8.30am - 6pm
All Dues Automatically Recorded
Representation Available
Invoice Payments: Biblios

Personnel
Head of Company: G Drummond (Managing Director)

Number of titles published annually: 100
Percentage of Export Sales: 40%
Book Data Subscriber

Parent Company: Probus Publishing Co Chicago

Trade Terms
Single stock orders 25% Multiple orders 35% Up to 45% by negotiation Subscription orders 35% All carriage free
Credit Cards Accepted: Access/Master, Amex, Diners, Visa

Returns Procedures
Authority to Return: Gilmour Drummond, Probus
Address for Returns: Biblios
Stock Returns: Returns accepted for full credit on merit of the case.

PROFESSIONAL BOOK SALES

4 Arran Quay, Dublin 7, County Dublin
ISBN Prefix(es): 1 871305
Tel: 01 722 373
Fax: 01 723 902

Account No: _____
Sales Rep: _____
Tel: _____

Order Information

Order Dept Opening Times
Mon - Fri 9am - 5pm
All Dues Automatically Recorded
Representation Available

Personnel
Head of Company: Gerard O'Connor
Head of Sales (Home): Karen Armstrong
Head of Accounts: Anne O'Mahoney
Head of Distribution: Elizabeth Hutton
Other Important Personnel:
David Givens (General Manager - Oak Tree Press)

Number of titles published annually: 8
WBIP Updating: Gerard O'Connor

Trade Terms
Single copy 25% Two or more copies 35% Academic 25% & 30%
Other Terms: Carriage charges

Returns Procedures
Stock Returns: Return the whole book
Imperfect Returns: Return the whole book

PROMETHEUS BOOKS UK

10 Crescent View, Loughton, Essex IG10 4PZ
ISBN Prefix(es): 0 87975
Tel: 081-508 2989
VAT No: 466 7617 08

Orders to
LAVIS MARKETING, 73 Lime Walk, Headington, Oxfordshire OX3 7AD
Tel: 0865 67575
Fax: 0865 750079

Order Information

All Dues Automatically Recorded
Representation Available

Personnel
Head of Company: Mike Hutchinson (Proprietor)

Number of titles published annually: 50

Trade Terms
Single copy 25% Two or more 35%

Returns Procedures
Authority to Return: Mike Hutchinson
Address for Returns: Lavis Marketing

PROMIS LTD

2a Pelham Street, London SW7 3HU
Tel: 071-584 6511
Fax: 071-225 1147

PROMOTIONAL REPRINT COMPANY

65 Old Church Street, Chelsea, London SW3 5BS
ISBN Prefix(es): 1 85648, 1 85778
Tel: 071-352 7936
Tel: 071-352 7938
Fax: 071-351 3040
VAT No: 562 1205 77

Order Information

All Dues Automatically Recorded

Personnel
Head of Company: Suneel Jaitly (Managing Director)
Head of Marketing: Joanne Messham (Marketing Manager)
Head of Accounts: Marcus Lecky (Administration)
Other Important Personnel:
Timothy Hailstone (Non-Executive Chairman)

Number of titles published annually: 150
Percentage of Export Sales: 35%
Number of Staff: 6
All New Titles are Bar Coded
WBIP Updating: Suneel Jaitly

Trade Terms
Negotiable

PROSPERITY PUBLICATIONS

1A Oval Road, Regents Park, London NW1 7EA
ISBN Prefix(es): 0 90550
Tel: 071-267 3368

Order Information

All Dues Automatically Recorded

Personnel
Head of Company: Lola Halil
Head of Sales (Home): Kiamran Halil

WBIP Updating: M K Hall

Trade Terms
35%

PROTON PUBLISHING HOUSE LTD

6 Colville Road, London W11 2BP
Tel: 071-727 4404
Fax: 071-792 9124

Personnel
Head of Company: Maria Da Graca Zillo

Parent Company: Centre of Integral Psychoanalysis Ltd

PROVIDENCE BOOKS

38B Station Road, Haddenham, Ely, Cambridgeshire PB6 3XD
ISBN Prefix(es): 0 903803
Tel: 0353 741150

Personnel
Head of Company: H J Mason

Number of titles published annually: 2

Trade Terms
33.3%
Minimum Order: £2 on invoice value below £10

PRYOR PUBLICATIONS

75 Dargate Road, Yorkletts, Whitstable, Kent CT5 3AE
ISBN Prefix(es): 0 946014
Tel: 0227 274655 Tel/Fax
VAT No: 397 7693 70

Order Information

All Dues Automatically Recorded
Representation Available

Personnel
Head of Company: Alan Pryor (Owner)

Number of titles published annually: 2
IPG Member
Book Data Subscriber

Trade Terms
37.5% on all orders no surcharges

Returns Procedures
Authority to Return: Prior permission required

PSYCHOLOGY NEWS

17A Great Ormond Street, London WC1
Tel: 071-831 3385
Tel: 071-831 5771

Personnel
Head of Company: David Cohen (Chief Executive)
Head of Customer Services: Pam Opanocha

Number of Staff: 2

Trade Terms
33.3% - 40%
Credit Cards Accepted: Access/Master, Visa

PUBLIC FINANCE FOUNDATION

3 Robert Street, London WC2N 6BH
Tel: 071-895 8823
Fax: 071-895 8825

PURNELL = Marston

QED

1 Straylands Grove, York, North Yorkshire YO3 0EB
Tel: 0904 424381

IPG Member
Book Data Subscriber

QUAKER HOME SERVICE

Friends Book Centre, Friends House, 173 Euston Road, London NW1 2BJ
ISBN Prefix(es): 0 85245, 0 87584, 0 900469, 0 913408
Tel: 071-388 1977
Fax: 071-387 1977
VAT No: 233 7677 45

Order Information

Order Dept Opening Times
Mon - Fri 10am - 5pm

Personnel
Head of Company: Jim Pym
Head of Sales (Home): Graham Garner

Number of titles published annually: 12
Percentage of Export Sales: 30%
Number of Staff: 2
NBA Signatory
WBIP Updating: Jim Pym

Parent Company: Religious Society of Friends (Quakers)

Trade Terms
General Net: Single Copy 33.3% postage at cost below £20 retail
Other Terms: Carriage Charges on small orders
Girobank Number: 57 399 2800
Credit Cards Accepted: Access/Master, Visa

Returns Procedures
Stock Returns: Please write for authorisation to Graham Garner
Imperfect Returns: Return title page up to £10

Quality Medical = Waverley Europe Ltd

QUARTET BOOKS LTD

27-29 Goodge Street, London W1P 1FD
ISBN Prefix(es): 0 7043, 0 86072
Tel: 071-636 3992
Fax: 071-637 1866
VAT No: 241 4235 00

Account No: _____

Sales Rep: _____

Tel: _____

Orders to
PLYMBRIDGE DISTRIBUTORS LTD, Plymbridge House, Estover Road, Plymouth, Devon PL6 7PZ
Tel: 0752 735251
Fax: 0752 695699

Order Information

All Dues Automatically Recorded
Representation Available
Invoice Payments: Plymbridge

Personnel
Head of Company: N Attallah (Chairman)
Head of Sales (Home): Jeremy Beale

Number of titles published annually: 60
NBA Signatory
All New Titles are Bar Coded
WBIP Updating: Celina Sippy

Parent Company: Namara Ltd

Trade Terms
General Net: Single Copy 20%, Two or More 35%
Girobank Number: 221 2951
Credit Cards Accepted: Access/Master, Visa, Amex, Diners

Returns Procedures
Authority to Return: Head Office or Area Rep
Address for Returns: Plymbridge

QUAY PUBLISHING LTD

Cameron House, White Cross, South Road, Lancaster, Lancashire LA1 4XQ
ISBN Prefix(es): 1 85642
Tel: 0524 843038 24 Hours
Fax: 0524 844629

Order Information

Order Dept Opening Times
Mon - Fri 9am - 5pm
All Dues Automatically Recorded
Representation Available

Personnel
Head of Company: Valery Moran

Number of titles published annually: 20
Number of Staff: 2
All New Titles are Bar Coded

Returns Procedures
Authority to Return: Prior authority required

QUEST BOOKS (NI)

2 Slievenabrock Avenue, Newcastle, County Down
BT33 0HZ
Tel: 03967 23359

Orders to
VINE HOUSE DISTRIBUTION, Waldenbury, North Chailey, East Sussex BN8 4DR
Tel: 082-572 3398
Fax: 082-572 4188

Order Information
Irish Orders to Head Office

IPG Member

QUEST MERIDIEN LTD

34 Scarborough Close, Biggin Hill, Kent TN16 3YB
Tel: 09595 76274 Tel/Fax 24
VAT No: 426 9443 33

Order Information
Teleordering: QUEST

Order Dept Opening Times
Mon - Fri 8.30am - 5.30pm
All Dues Automatically Recorded
Representation Available

Personnel
Head of Company: D A Southwood/B M Skippon (Managing Director/Company Secretary)
Head of Sales (Home): T Eaton (Sales Executive)
Head of Accounts: Mrs J Frazer (Cashier)

Percentage of Export Sales: 40%
Number of Staff: 4
WBIP Updating: B M Skippon

Trade Terms
30 days net by negotiation
Credit Cards Accepted: Access/Master, Visa

Returns Procedures
Authority to Return: By request to Mrs B M Skippon
Address for Returns: Quest-Meridien Ltd, c/o Vale Packaging, 420 Vale Road, Tonbridge, Kent TN9 1TD

QUILLER PRESS LTD

46 Lillie Road, London SW6 1TN
ISBN Prefix(es): 0 907621, 1 870948
Tel: 071-499 6529
Fax: 071-381 8941
Telex: 21120
VAT No: 340 6190 81

Orders to
COMBINED BOOK SERVICES, 406 Vale Road, Tonbridge, Kent TN9 1SW
Tel: 0732 357755
Fax: 0732 770219

Order Information

All Dues Automatically Recorded
Representation Available
Invoice Payments: Combined Book Services
Representation:Amalgamated Book Services

Personnel
Head of Company: J J Greenwood
Head of Publicity: S H Greenwood
Head of Accounts: A E Carlile

Number of titles published annually: 15
Number of Staff: 3
All New Titles are Bar Coded
WBIP Updating: J J Greenwood

Returns Procedures
Authority to Return: Sales Dept, Amalgamated Book Services
Address for Returns: Combined Book Service
Stock Returns: Contact ABS

QUINTESSENCE PUBLISHING CO LTD

2 Blagdon Road, New Malden, Surrey KT3 4AD
ISBN Prefix(es): 0 86715, 1 85097, 3 928036, 4 87417
Tel: 081-949 6087
Fax: 081-336 1484
Telex: 24667 IMPEP G
VAT No: 404 4579 59

Orders to
SHEED & WARD LTD, 14 Coopers Row, London EC3N 2BH
Tel: 071-702 9799
Fax: 071-702 3583

Order Information

All Dues Automatically Recorded
Representation Available
Invoice Payments: Sheed & Ward

Personnel
Head of Company: John Brooks
Head of Sales (Home): Joyce Ronald

Number of titles published annually: 15
Percentage of Export Sales: 60%
WBIP Updating: Mrs Joyce Ronald

Trade Terms
Single Copy 20%, Two or more 25%, Subscription orders 30%
Credit Cards Accepted: Access/Master, Visa, Amex

Returns Procedures
Authority to Return: Jim Osgerby
Imperfect Returns: Books required

QUOTES LTD

The Book Barn, Church Way, Whittlebury, Northamptonshire NN12 8SX
ISBN Prefix(es): 0 86023
Tel: 0327 858301
Fax: 0327 858302
VAT No: 443 8525 40

Order Information

Cyclical Ordering Policy
All Dues Automatically Recorded

Personnel
Head of Company: C F W Birch
Head of Sales (Home): Fiona Martin
Head of Accounts: Barbara Hawkins

Number of titles published annually: 30
IPG Member
NBA Signatory
WBIP Updating: C Birch

Trade Terms
33% (35% for 10+ copies), Minimum order value £10 Single copy orders 20%. CWO or less value
Other Terms: 5% interest per month overdue accounts. Cash sales only for accounts over 2 months overdue.

Returns Procedures
Stock Returns: Firm order only. Returns only against wrong or imperfect supply.

Imperfect Returns: Only return complete books. Valid returns replaced/credited by arrangement. Transit loss/damage advise within 10 days.

R & B PUBLISHING

PO Box 200, Harrogate, North Yorkshire HG2 9RB
ISBN Prefix(es): 0 9516461, 1 873668
Tel: 0423 507545
Fax: 0423 507545
VAT No: 482 0481 52

Orders to
VINE HOUSE DISTRIBUTION, Waldenbury, North Chailey, East Sussex BN8 4DR
Tel: 082-572 3398
Fax: 082-572 4188

Order Information

All Dues Automatically Recorded
Representation Available

Personnel
Head of Company: Chris Brown
Head of Customer Services: C Rothwell

Number of titles published annually: 25
Percentage of Export Sales: 50%
Number of Staff: 4
PA Member
All New Titles are Bar Coded
WBIP Updating: C Rothwell

Trade Terms
standard
BA/Girobank Small Order Scheme: 25% on one book

Returns Procedures
Authority to Return: Vine House Distribution
Address for Returns: Vine House Distribution
Stock Returns: Must be authorised and limited to six months from initial order

R & R PUBLICATIONS

23 Warwick Street, Iffley Fields, Oxford, Oxfordshire OX4 1SZ
Tel: 0865 201252 Tel/Fax
VAT No: 537 3883 14

RAC PUBLISHING

RAC House, PO Box 100, South Croydon, Surrey CR2 6XW
Tel: 081-686 0088
Fax: 081-688 2882

Orders to
BOOKPOINT LIMITED, 39 Milton Park, Abingdon, Oxfordshire OX14 4TD
Tel: 0235 835001
Fax: 0235 861038

Order Information

All Dues Automatically Recorded
Invoice Payments: Bookpoint Ltd
Representation:Derek Searle Associates

Personnel
Head of Company: Chris Milsome (Publisher)
Head of Sales (Home): Bob Macdonald
Head of Sales (Export): Jacqui Bruff

All New Titles are Bar Coded
Open University Publications
Parent Company: Royal Automobile Club

Trade Terms
35%

Returns Procedures
Authority to Return: Must be authorised by Derek Searle
Address for Returns: Derek Searle Associates

RADCLIFFE MEDICAL PRESS
15 Kings Meadow, Ferry Hinksey Road, Oxford, Oxfordshire
OX2 0DP
ISBN Prefix(es): 1 85775, 1 870905
Tel: 0865 790696
Fax: 0865 244651
VAT No: 479 2188 05

Order Information

Order Dept Opening Times
Mon - Fri 9am - 5pm
All Dues Automatically Recorded
Representation Available

Personnel
Head of Company: Andrew Bax (Managing Director)
Head of Sales (Home): Margaret McKeown (Financial Director)
Head of Customer Services: Jayne Bibey

Number of titles published annually: 40
All New Titles are Bar Coded
Book Data Subscriber
WBIP Updating: Kate Martin

Trade Terms
30% UK, 25% OVERSEAS
Other Terms: Carriage charged overseas orders
Credit Cards Accepted: Access/Master, Visa

Returns Procedures
Authority to Return: Jayne Bibey

RADIO SOCIETY OF GREAT BRITAIN
Lambda House, Cranborne Road, Potters Bar, Hertfordshire
EN6 3JE
ISBN Prefix(es): 0 900612, 1 872309
Tel: 0707 59015
Fax: 0707 45105
Telex: 9312 130923 RS G
VAT No: 233 3092 93

Order Information

Order Dept Opening Times
9.15am - 5.15pm

Personnel
Head of Company: Peter Kirby (General Manager)
Head of Publicity: Ray Eckersley
Head of Accounts: Janet Cragg (Finance Officer)
Head of Distribution: Derek Lund (Despatch Manager)
Other Important Personnel:
Jane Hanson (Trade/Membership Sales Administrator)

Number of titles published annually: 6
Number of Staff: 25
All New Titles are Bar Coded
WBIP Updating: Ray Eckersley

Trade Terms
All orders in writing by post or fax on official order forms

Non-Net: 1-4 copies 20%, 5-9 22%, 10-49 25%, 50-99 27%, 100+ 30%
Minimum Order: Orders no less than £25 in value (exc postage)
Other Terms: Carriage charged
Credit Cards Accepted: Access/Master, Amex, Diners, Visa, Other

Returns Procedures
Stock Returns: Contact Jane Hanson
Imperfect Returns: Contact Jane Hanson

RAGGED BEARS LTD

The Orchards, Ragged Appleshaw, Andover, Hampshire SP11 9HX
ISBN Prefix(es): 1 85103, 1 85618, 1 85714, 1 870817
Tel: 0264 772269
Fax: 0264 772391
VAT No: 393 0903 47

Account No: _____

Sales Rep: _____

Tel: _____

Order Information
Teleordering: RAGGED

Order Dept Opening Times
Mon - Fri 8.45am - 4.45pm Sat 9.30am - 12.30pm
Orders for more than one publisher can be bulked
All Dues Automatically Recorded
Representation Available

Personnel
Head of Company: Charles Shirley
Head of Publicity: H Stickland
Head of Accounts: Pamela Shirley
Head of Customer Services: Jackie Horrell

Number of titles published annually: 60
Percentage of Export Sales: 30%
All New Titles are Bar Coded
Book Data Subscriber
WBIP Updating: H Stickland

Trade Terms
35% for orders with retail value of +£25. If less then 25%

Returns Procedures
Address for Returns: The Trade Counter Ltd, The Airfield, Norwich Rd, Mendlesham
Stock Returns: Obtain authorisation and returns label from rep.
Imperfect Returns: We prefer imperfect books to be given to local school or hospital

RAILWAY CORRESPONDANCE & TRAVEL SOCIETY

6 Cherry Lane, Hampton Magna, Warwick, Warwickshire CV35 8SL
Tel: 0926 402651
VAT No: 197 3433 35

RAMBORO BOOKS

Unit 5A, 202-208 New North Road, London N1 7BJ
ISBN Prefix(es): 0 86288
Tel: 071-226 7777
Fax: 071-704 6442
Cables: DONS BAR

Order Information

Order Dept Opening Times
Mon - Fri 9am - 5pm
All Dues Automatically Recorded
Representation Available

Personnel
Head of Company: Donald Murray
Head of Sales (Home): Tim Finch
Head of Publicity: George Pentney
Head of Accounts: Rita Hind

Number of titles published annually: 16
Number of Staff: 7
All New Titles are Bar Coded
Open University Publications
WBIP Updating: Donald Murray

Trade Terms
35%
Minimum Order: £50
Credit Cards Accepted: Access/Master, Visa

Returns Procedures
Authority to Return: Tim Finch
Address for Returns: The Trade Counter, The Airfield, Norwich Road, Mendlesham

RAMSAY HEAD PRESS

15 Gloucester Place, Edinburgh, Lothian EH3 6EE
ISBN Prefix(es): 0 902859, 1 873921
Tel: 031-225 5646
VAT No: 592 8032 26

Order Information

Order Dept Opening Times
Mon - Fri 9am - 5pm
Representation Available

Personnel
Head of Company: C K Wilson
Head of Accounts: M K Young
Head of Distribution: R Smith

Number of titles published annually: 6
All New Titles are Bar Coded
WBIP Updating: C K Wilson

Trade Terms
95p surcharge on small orders up to £6, £1 up to £7 £1.10 up to £12, £1.25 up to £15, £1.45 up to £25
General Net: Single copy 25%, Two or more 35%

RANDOM HOUSE UK LTD

Random House, 20 Vauxhall Bridge Road, London SW1V 2SA
ISBN Prefix(es): 0 091, 0 214, 0 2240, 0 2576, 0 370, 0 3947, 0 679, 0 7011, 0 7012, 0 7126, 0 8522, 0 86264, 0 8777, 1 55936, 1 85381, 1 85459, 1 85656, 1 85681, 1 85686, 1 85715, 1 872031
Tel: 071-973 9000
Fax: 071-828 6681
Fax: 071-233 7398
Telex: 299080 RANDOM G
VAT No: 102 8389 80

Account No: _____

Sales Rep: _____

Tel: _____

Orders to
TIPTREE BOOK SERVICES LTD, Church Road, Tiptree, Colchester, Essex CO5 0SR
Tel: 0621 819600
Fax: 0621 819011

Order Information
All Dues Automatically Recorded
Representation Available

Personnel
Head of Company: Gail Rebuck (Chairman)
Head of Sales (Home): Dallas Manderson (Group Trade Sales Director)
Head of Sales (Export): David Parrish (Group Export Sales Director)
Head of Marketing: David Crane (Group Marketing Director)
Head of Publicity: Liz Sich (Group Publicity Director)
Other Important Personnel:
Stuart Biles (Trade Sales Director), Mike Dugdale (Sales Director), Joanna Carpenter (Sales Manager), Jane Walker (Sales Administration Manager), Sue Bloomfield (Sales Administrator)

Number of titles published annually: 1650
PA Member
NBA Signatory
All New Titles are Bar Coded
Open University Publications
Book Data Subscriber
WBIP Updating: Penny Cornwall (Tiptree)

Trade Terms
35%

Returns Procedures
Authority to Return: From Representative
Imperfect Returns: Title page to retail value of £20

RANDOM HOUSE UK (ARROW SALES DIVISION)
Random House, 20 Vauxhall Bridge Road, London SW1V 2SA
ISBN Prefix(es): 0 0099
Tel: 071-973 9700
Fax: 071-233 6127
Telex: 299080 RANDOM G
VAT No: 102 8389 80

Account No: _____
Sales Rep: _____
Tel: _____

Orders to
TIPTREE BOOK SERVICES LTD, Church Road, Tiptree, Colchester, Essex CO5 0SR
Tel: 0621 819600
Fax: 0621 819011

Order Information
Representation Available
Invoice Payments: Tiptree

Personnel
Head of Company: Simon King (Managing Director)
Head of Sales (Home): Mike Broderick (Divisional Sales Director)
Head of Sales (Export): David Parrish (Group Export Sales Director)
Other Important Personnel:
Ron Beard (Home Sales Director), Angela Duke (Sales Administration Manager)

Number of titles published annually: 430
All New Titles are Bar Coded
Book Data Subscriber
WBIP Updating: Penny Cornwall (Tiptree)

Trade Terms
35%

RANDOM THOUGHTS LTD

46 Old Compton Street, London W1V 5PB
Tel: 071-434 3130
Fax: 071-434 2120
VAT No: 241 6651 73

IPG Member

RAVENSWOOD PUBLICATIONS LTD

35 Windsor Road, London N7 6JG
ISBN Prefix(es): 0 263863, 0 901812, 0 9518061
Tel: 071-272 5032 Tel/Fax

Personnel
Head of Company: Mrs D J Naylor

Number of titles published annually: 1
IPG Member
All New Titles are Bar Coded

Parent Company: Ravenswood Publications Ltd

Trade Terms
20% discount on all orders, no surcharges
Other Terms: £1 carriage charges

RAVETTE BOOKS LTD

Egmont House, 8 Clifford Street, London W1X 1RB

Orders to
EGMONT PUBLISHING LTD, Egmont House, PO Box 111, Great Ducie St, Manchester, Greater Manchester M60 3BL
Tel: 061-834 3110
Fax: 061-834 0059

Order Information

Representation Available
Invoice Payments: Egmont Distribution

Personnel
Head of Company: Tony Palmer (Chief Executive Officer) 061-834 3110
Head of Sales (Home): Steve Travis (Sales Director) 061-834 3110
Head of Marketing: Mrs Margaret Lamb (Marketing Director)

Number of titles published annually: 40
Percentage of Export Sales: 25%
Number of Staff: 6
PA Member
Book Data Subscriber

Parent Company: Egmont Holdings

Trade Terms
Minimum Order: £50 net invoice value

Returns Procedures
Authority to Return: Prior permission required
Address for Returns: Egmont, Manchester

READERS INTERNATIONAL
8 Strathray Gardens, London NW3 4NY
ISBN Prefix(es): 0 930523
Tel: 071-435 4363 Tel/Fax
VAT No: 454 2616 54

Order Information

All New Titles are Bar Coded

REAKTION BOOKS LTD
1-5 Midford Place, Tottenham Court Road, London W1P 9HH
ISBN Prefix(es): 0 948462
Tel: 071-388 8128
Fax: 071-383 2563
VAT No: 429 3394 32

Orders to
LITTLEHAMPTON BOOK SERVICES, 14 Eldon Way, Lineside Ind Estate, Littlehampton, West Sussex BN17 7HE
Tel: 0903 721596
Fax: 0903 730914

Order Information

All Dues Automatically Recorded
Representation Available
Invoice Payments: Littlehampton

Personnel
Head of Company: Michael R Leaman
Head of Sales (Home): Catherine Dean
Head of Accounts: Harry Gilonis

Number of titles published annually: 8
NBA Signatory
All New Titles are Bar Coded
WBIP Updating: Catherine Dean

Trade Terms
35%

Returns Procedures
Authority to Return: Write to Catherine Dean with full details
Address for Returns: Littlehampton
Stock Returns: Returns must be authorised by Reaktion Books and returned within six months of invoice date
Imperfect Returns: Return title page (indicating imperfection) if under £20 net if over £20 net please return the entire book

REAL BOOKS
27 Tatton Court, Woolston, Warrington, Cheshire WA1 4RR
Tel: 0925 819222
Fax: 0925 819805
VAT No: 593 6129 15

Account No: _____
Sales Rep: _____
Tel: _____

Order Information

Order Dept Opening Times
9am - 5pm
Orders for more than one publisher can be bulked
All Dues Automatically Recorded
Representation Available

Personnel
Head of Company: Tom Berry
Head of Sales (Home): Helena Groeneveld
Head of Accounts: Harvey Cawley
Head of Customer Services: Denise Lanceley
Other Important Personnel:
Andrew Price (Order Queries)

Number of titles published annually: 120
Number of Staff: 11
WBIP Updating: Denise Lanceley

Parent Company: Alternative Books (UK) Ltd

Trade Terms
35% on orders over £25 Single copy 25%
Credit Cards Accepted: Access/Master, Visa

Returns Procedures
Stock Returns: Errors & omissions must be notified within 7 days Returns must be authorised Damaged overstocks credited at 60%
Imperfect Returns: Return whole book

RECO-PRESS PUBLISHERS

22 Goldstone Crescent, Hove, East Sussex BN3 6BA
Tel: 0273 503718
Fax: 0273 564698

IPG Member

REDCLIFFE PRESS LTD

49 Park Street, Bristol, Avon BS1 5NT
ISBN Prefix(es): 1 872971
Tel: 0272 290158
Fax: 0272 215431
VAT No: 139 6690 30

Order Information

All Dues Automatically Recorded
Representation Available

Personnel
Head of Company: John Sansom (Director)
Head of Sales (Home): Angela Sansom
Head of Marketing: Judy Simmonds
Head of Accounts: Rita Fong

Number of titles published annually: 20
All New Titles are Bar Coded
WBIP Updating: Clara Sansom

Trade Terms
Stock Orders 25%, Subscription Orders 35%

REDEMPTORIST PUBLICATIONS

Alphonsus House, Chawton, Alton, Hampshire GU34 3HQ
Tel: 0420 88222
Fax: 0420 88805
VAT No: 188 7189 01

Order Information
Teleordering: REDEM

REED BOOK SERVICES

Northampton Road, Rushden, Northamptonshire NN10 9PU
Tel: 0933 58521 24 Hours

Fax: 0933 50284
Telex: 312504
VAT No: 340 2429 92
Account No: _____ 4679105 _____
Sales Rep: _____
Tel: _____

Order Information
Teleordering: REED
First Edition Subscriber

Order Dept Opening Times
Mon - Fri 9am - 5pm
Orders for more than one publisher can be bulked
All Dues Automatically Recorded
Representation Available

Personnel
Head of Company: Arthur Philo (Managing Director)
Head of Accounts: Peter Hyde (Credit Control Manager)
Head of Customer Services: Jim Ward (Customer Services Director)
Other Important Personnel:
Martin Cowell (Group Sales Development Director/Deputy MD), Beryl Gibson (Trade Office Manager)

Number of Staff: 300
All New Titles are Bar Coded
Open University Publications

Parent Company: Reed International Books

Trade Terms
Credit Cards Accepted: Access/Master, Visa

Returns Procedures
Authority to Return: Area Representative

REED CONSUMER BOOKS (BOUNTY BOOKS)
Michelin House, 81 Fulham Road, London SW1V 6RB
ISBN Prefix(es): 0 416, 0 603, 1 850, 1 851
Tel: 071-581 9393
Fax: 071-581 8450
Telex: 920191
VAT No: 340 9173 66
Account No: _____ 4679105 _____
Sales Rep: _____
Tel: _____

Orders to
REED BOOK SERVICES, Northampton Road, Rushden, Northamptonshire NN10 9PU
Tel: 0933 58521
Fax: 0933 50284

Order Information
Teleordering: REED
First Edition Subscriber

All Dues Automatically Recorded
Representation Available

Personnel
Head of Company: Richard Charkin
Head of Sales (Home): Peter Shelley (Sales Manager)
Head of Marketing: Andrea Carr
Other Important Personnel:
Robert Snuggs (Group Sales Director), David Tanner (Operations Manager), Mark Baker (Sales Administrator)

Book Data Subscriber

Trade Terms
35%
Minimum Order: £250 retail

Returns Procedures
Authority to Return: Area Representative
Address for Returns: Reed Book Services

REED CONSUMER BOOKS (ILLUSTRATED SALES)

Michelin House, 81 Fulham Road, London SW3 6RB
ISBN Prefix(es): 0 540, 0 600, 0 85045, 0 85533, 0 905128, 0 905879, 0 906754, 0 946429, 1 85532, 1 85732
Tel: 071-581 9393
Fax: 071-584 4318
Telex: 920191
VAT No: 340 9173 66
Account No: 4679105
Sales Rep: _____
Tel: _____

Orders to
REED BOOK SERVICES, Northampton Road, Rushden, Northamptonshire NN10 9PU
Tel: 0933 58521
Fax: 0933 50284

Order Information
Teleordering: REED
First Edition Subscriber

Representation Available

Personnel
Head of Company: Richard Charkin
Head of Sales (Home): David Rivers (Sales & Marketing Director)
Head of Marketing: Andrea Carr
Other Important Personnel:
Roger Fox (Home Sales Southern Area), Bob Ballard (Home Sales Northern Area), Mary Vacher (UK Sales Office Manager)

All New Titles are Bar Coded
Book Data Subscriber

Trade Terms
General Net: 35%
Non-Net: 17.5%

Returns Procedures
Authority to Return: Area Representative
Address for Returns: Reed Book Services

REED CONSUMER BOOKS (MANDARIN SALES)

Michelin House, 81 Fulham Road, London SW3 6RB
ISBN Prefix(es): 0 413, 0 416, 0 600, 0 749
Tel: 071-581 9393
Fax: 071-589 8450
Telex: 920191
VAT No: 340 9173 66
Account No: 4679105
Sales Rep: _____
Tel: _____

Orders to
REED BOOK SERVICES, Northampton Road, Rushden, Northamptonshire NN10 9PU
Tel: 0933 58521
Fax: 0933 50284

Order Information
Teleordering: REED
First Edition Subscriber

All Dues Automatically Recorded
Representation Available

Personnel
Head of Company: Richard Charkin
Head of Sales (Home): Alan Jessop (UK Sales Director)
Head of Marketing: Mary Harpley (Marketing Adult Books)
Head of Publicity: Angela Martin (Publicity Director)
Other Important Personnel:
Clare Somerville (Marketing Children's Books), Robert Snuggs (Group UK Sales Director), Roy Stevenson (UK Sales Manager), Elizabeth Liddiard (UK Sales Administrator)

All New Titles are Bar Coded
Open University Publications
Book Data Subscriber
WBIP Updating: Elizabeth Liddiard

Trade Terms
35%

Returns Procedures
Authority to Return: Area Representative
Address for Returns: Reed Book Services

REED CONSUMER BOOKS (TRADE SALES)   0413 Methuen = Reed.
Michelin House, 81 Fulham Road, London SW3 6RB
ISBN Prefix(es): 0 413, 0 416, 0 434, 0 436, 1 85029, 1 85619
Tel: 071-581 9393
Fax: 071-581 8454
Telex: 920191
VAT No: 340 9173 66
Account No: _____ 4679105 _____
Sales Rep: _____
Tel: _____

Orders to
REED BOOK SERVICES, Northampton Road, Rushden, Northamptonshire NN10 9PU
Tel: 0933 58521
Fax: 0933 50284

Order Information
Teleordering: REED
First Edition Subscriber

All Dues Automatically Recorded
Representation Available

Personnel
Head of Company: Richard Charkin (Chief Executive - Reed Consumer Books)
Head of Sales (Home): Amanda Ridout (UK Sales Director)
Head of Marketing: Mary Harpley (Marketing Adult Books)
Head of Publicity: Angela Martin (Publicity Director)
Other Important Personnel:
Clare Somerville (Marketing Director - Children's Books), Robert Snuggs (Group UK Sales Director), Sue Sturla (UK Sales Administrator)

All New Titles are Bar Coded
Open University Publications
Book Data Subscriber
WBIP Updating: Janet Thompsett

Trade Terms
35% no surcharges

Returns Procedures
Authority to Return: Area Representative

Address for Returns: Reed Book Services
Imperfect Returns: As above up to £20

REED INFORMATION SERVICES LTD

Windsor Court, East Grinstead House, East Grinstead, West Sussex RH19 1XA
ISBN Prefix(es): 0 6100, 0 61100, 0 8626
Tel: 0342 326972
Fax: 0342 315130
Telex: 95127
VAT No: 235 7235 65

Account No: _____

Sales Rep: _____

Tel: _____

Book Data Subscriber

Trade Terms
Credit Cards Accepted: Access/Master, Amex, Diners, Visa

THOMAS REED PUBLICATIONS LTD

Hazelbury Manor, Corsham, Wiltshire SN14 9HX
ISBN Prefix(es): 0 900335, 0 901281, 0 947637
Tel: 0225 812013
Tel: 0225 812024
Fax: 0225 812014
Fax: 0225 812025
VAT No: 577 0802 27

Orders to
BARNACLE MARINE LTD, PO Box 1539, Hazelbury Manor, Corsham, Wiltshire SN13 9ZZ
Tel: 0225 812024
Fax: 0225 812025

Order Information

All Dues Automatically Recorded
Representation Available
Invoice Payments: Barnacle Marine Ltd

Personnel
Head of Company: Mr R Hunter (Managing Director)
Head of Sales (Home): Mr C Michell (Sales Manager) Head Office or 071-359 5365
Head of Marketing: Ms S J Mark (Marketing Manager)
Head of Accounts: Mrs D Hunter (Financial Director)
Head of Customer Services: Mrs N Martin

Number of titles published annually: 30
Percentage of Export Sales: 20%
Number of Staff: 27
All New Titles are Bar Coded
WBIP Updating: Ms S J Mark

Parent Company: TRP Holdings

Trade Terms
Books 35% Periodicals 25% (SOR) Videos 30% Calendars 30% Mark One Guides 30%
Other Terms: Carriage charged on small orders at cost, single copy £2 charge unless prepaid
BA/Girobank Small Order Scheme: Yes
Credit Cards Accepted: Access/Master, Visa

Returns Procedures
Authority to Return: Barnacle Marine Ltd
Address for Returns: Barnacle Marine Ltd
Stock Returns: Prior permission required
Imperfect Returns: Return title page

WILLIAM REED DIRECTORIES
The Old Surgery, High Street, Goring On Thames, Reading, Berkshire RG8 9AW
ISBN Prefix(es): 0 906552
Tel: 0491 873003
Fax: 0491 874233

WILLIAM REEVES BOOKSELLER LTD
1A Norbury Crescent, London SW16 4JR
ISBN Prefix(es): 0 7211
Tel: 081-764 2108

Order Information

All Dues Automatically Recorded

Trade Terms
1-2 copies 25%, 3 copies 33.5% post free
Girobank Number: 559 2151

Returns Procedures
Imperfect Returns: £2

REFLECTIONS OF A BYGONE AGE
15 Debdale Lane, Keyworth, Nottingham, Nottinghamshire NG12 5HT
Tel: 0602 374079
Fax: 0602 372043
VAT No: 352 8103 73

REFUGEE ACTION
The Offices, The Cedars, Oakwood, Derby, Derbyshire DE21 4FY
Tel: 0332 833310
Fax: 0332 834946

REINHARDT BOOKS LTD
27 Wrights Lane, London W8 5TZ
ISBN Prefix(es): 1 871061
Tel: 071-416 3000
Fax: 071-416 3099
Fax: 071-416 3293
Telex: 917181
VAT No: 241 4021 19

Orders to
Penguin Books Ltd, Bath Road, Harmondsworth, Middlesex UB7 0DA
Tel: 081-899 4000
Fax: 081-899 4020
24 Hour Ansafone Number: 081-899 4050

Order Information

Order Dept Opening Times
Mon - Fri 9am - 5pm
Invoice Payments: Penguin, Harmondsworth

Personnel
Head of Company: Max Reinhardt (Chairman)
Other Important Personnel:
Joan Reinhardt (Director), John Hews (Director)

Number of titles published annually: 4
All New Titles are Bar Coded
Book Data Subscriber

Trade Terms
As Penguin

Returns Procedures
Authority to Return: Penguin Books
Address for Returns: Harmondsworth

RESEARCH INSTITUTE FOR THE STUDY OF CONFLICT & TERRORISM

136 Baker Street, London W1M 1FH
ISBN Prefix(es): 0 069, 8769
Tel: 071-224 2659
Fax: 071-486 3064

Orders to
J A Mailing Services, 133 Downhall Road, Rayleigh, Essex SS6 9PB
Tel: 0268 784725

Order Information

Order Dept Opening Times
Mon - Fri 9am - 5pm

Personnel
Head of Company: Professor Paul Wilkinson (Director)
Head of Publicity: Joan Bates
Head of Accounts: Joan Donald
Head of Distribution: Jenny Allen

Number of titles published annually: 10
Number of Staff: 4
WBIP Updating: Joan Bates

Trade Terms
20% on all orders
Credit Cards Accepted: Access/Master, Visa, Amex

RESEARCH STUDIES PRESS LTD

24 Belvedere Road, Taunton, Somerset TA1 1HD
ISBN Prefix(es): 0 86380
Tel: 0823 336197
Fax: 0823 253252
VAT No: 382 2090 65

Orders to
JOHN WILEY & SONS LTD, Southern Cross Trading Estate, 1 Oldlands Way, Bognor Regis, West Sussex PO22 9SA
Tel: 0243 829121
Fax: 0243 820250

Order Information

All Dues Automatically Recorded
Representation Available
Invoice Payments: John Wiley & Sons Ltd

Personnel
Head of Company: Veronica Wallace (Managing Director)
Other Important Personnel:
William Askew (Publisher)

Number of titles published annually: 15
Percentage of Export Sales: 75%
Number of Staff: 3
IPG Member
Book Data Subscriber
WBIP Updating: Nicola King

Trade Terms
As Wiley

Returns Procedures
Authority to Return: John Wiley & Sons Ltd

Address for Returns: John Wiley & Sons Ltd
Stock Returns: As Wiley
Imperfect Returns: As Wiley

RHINEGOLD PUBLISHING LTD

241 Shaftesbury Avenue, London WC2H 8EH
ISBN Prefix(es): 0 946890
Tel: 071-240 5749 Book Sales
Tel: 071-836 2536 Magazines
Tel: 071-836 2383 Editorial
Fax: 071-528 7991 Books/Mags
Fax: 071-528 8786 Adverts
VAT No: 242 3571 80

Order Information

Order Dept Opening Times
Mon - Fri 10am - 5pm

Personnel

Head of Company: Anthony C Gamble (Managing Director)
Head of Sales (Home): Jo Burns (Sales & Subscriptions Manager)
Head of Marketing: Keith Diggle (Marketing Director)
Head of Distribution: Richard Thomas (Distribution Manager)

Number of titles published annually: 4
Number of Staff: 30
WBIP Updating: J Burns

Trade Terms

30%, post free in the UK. Payment with order or pro-forma. Pro-formas also issued for standing orders.
Credit Cards Accepted: Access/Master, Visa, Amex, Diners

Returns Procedures

Stock Returns: Firm sale only
Imperfect Returns: Notify book sales department of imperfect, damaged or wrong title, replacement copy will be sent on receipt of original

RIAD EL-RAYYES BOOKSELLERS LTD

56 Knightsbridge, London SW1X 7NJ
Tel: 071-235 4240
Fax: 071-235 9305
Telex: 266997 RAYYES G

PA Member

RIBA PUBLICATIONS LTD

Finsbury Mission, 39 Moreland Street, London EC1V 8BB
ISBN Prefix(es): 0 900630, 0 947877
Tel: 071-251 0791
Fax: 071-608 2375
VAT No: 232 3518 91
Account No: 4UN104
Sales Rep:
Tel:

Order Information

Order Dept Opening Times
Mon - Fri 9.30am - 5.30pm
Cyclical Ordering Policy
Orders for more than one publisher can be bulked
All Dues Automatically Recorded

Personnel
Head of Company: Nicholas Jones
Head of Marketing: James Neal
Head of Accounts: Francis Cardoso
Other Important Personnel:
Liza Kershaw (General Manager)

Number of titles published annually: 10
Number of Staff: 25
Book Data Subscriber
WBIP Updating: Liza Kershaw

Parent Company: Royal Institute of British Architects

Trade Terms
30% carriage paid, except single copies
Other Terms: Small order surcharges on orders less than £7.50 gross Carriage charges on single copies
Girobank Number: 51 745 0909
Credit Cards Accepted: Access/Master, Visa

Returns Procedures
Authority to Return: Liza Kershaw
Stock Returns: Return whole item postage returned if in saleable condition No postage refunded for overstocks
Imperfect Returns: Return whole item (postage refunded)

THE RICHMOND PUBLISHING COMPANY LTD
PO Box 963, Slough, Berkshire SL2 3RS
ISBN Prefix(es): 0 85546
Tel: 0753 643104
Fax: 0753 646553
VAT No: 538 1194 41

Account No: _____
Sales Rep: _____
Tel: _____

Order Information

Order Dept Opening Times
Mon - Fri 9.30am - 5.30pm
All Dues Automatically Recorded

Personnel
Head of Company: Sue Dobson
Other Important Personnel:
Jonathan Davie (World Wide Fund for Nature Sales)

Number of titles published annually: 4
Percentage of Export Sales: 20%
Number of Staff: 6
Book Data Subscriber
WBIP Updating: Frank Dobson

Parent Company: Kingston Photographic Services

Trade Terms
35% + P&P (25% Distributed Titles)
Minimum Order: CWO under £20 or pro-forma will be sent
Other Terms: Carriage charged at cost
Girobank Number: 337 7253

Returns Procedures
Stock Returns: Telephone permissions accepted
Imperfect Returns: Title page OK on all titles

RICS BOOKS
12 Great George Street, London SW1P 3AD
ISBN Prefix(es): 0 85406
Tel: 071-222 7000
Fax: 071-222 9430 London
Fax: 071-334 3800 Coventry

VAT No: 314 6969 37
Account No: 02 UNI 008
Sales Rep:
Tel:

Orders to
RICS Books, Surveyor Court, Westwood Way, Coventry, West Midlands CV4 8JE

Order Information

Order Dept Opening Times
Mon - Fri 9am - 5pm
All Dues Automatically Recorded
Representation Available
Invoice Payments: RICS Books, Coventry

Personnel
Head of Company: George Davies (Managing Director)
Head of Marketing: Diane Williams (Marketing Manager)
Head of Accounts: Tony Myers (Financial Controller) Coventry
Head of Distribution: Caroline Grey (Distribution Manager) Coventry
Head of Customer Services: Sharon Allbrighton (Order Processing Supervisor) Coventry

Number of titles published annually: 50
Book Data Subscriber
WBIP Updating: Laura Darling

Parent Company: RICS Business Services

Trade Terms
By Agreement
Credit Cards Accepted: Access/Master, Visa

Returns Procedures
Authority to Return: Prior permission required from Customer Service, RICS Books, Coventry, quoting invoice number
Address for Returns: RICS Books, Coventry
Imperfect Returns: Book must be returned in full

RIGHT NOW BOOKS

36c Sisters Avenue, London SW11 5SQ
ISBN Prefix(es): 0 9518491
Tel: 071-223 8987
Fax: 071-223 8987

Orders to
LAVIS MARKETING, 73 Lime Walk, Headington, Oxfordshire OX3 7AD
Tel: 0865 67575
Fax: 0865 750079

Order Information

Representation Available
Invoice Payments: Lavis Marketing

Number of titles published annually: 2
Number of Staff: 2
IPG Member
All New Titles are Bar Coded
WBIP Updating: John Gammons

Returns Procedures
Authority to Return: Lavis Marketing

PETER RILEY (BOOKS)
27 Sturton Street, Cambridge, Cambridgeshire CB1 2QG
Tel: 0223 327455
VAT No: 411 1948 80

RIPON HISTORICAL SOCIETY & FAMILY HISTORY GROUP
c/o Aldergarth, Galphay, Ripon, North Yorkshire HG4 3NJ
Tel: 0765 658602

JOHN RITCHIE LTD
40 Beansburn, Kilmarnock, Ayrshire KA3 1RH
Tel: 0563 36394
Fax: 0563 71191
VAT No: 264 0265 76

Account No: _____
Sales Rep: _____
Tel: _____

RIVELIN GRAPHEME PRESS
The Annexe, Kennet House, 19 High Street, Hungerford, Berkshire RG17 0NL
Tel: 0488 684645
Fax: 0488 683018
VAT No: 386 4492 11

RIVERS ORAM PRESS
144 Hemingford Road, London N1 1DE
ISBN Prefix(es): 1 85489
Tel: 071-607 0823
Fax: 071-609 2776
VAT No: 524 5357 50

Order Information

All Dues Automatically Recorded
Representation Available

Personnel
Head of Company: Elizabeth Fidlon
Head of Publicity: Shirley Dow

Number of titles published annually: 10
Percentage of Export Sales: 30%
Number of Staff: 3
All New Titles are Bar Coded
Book Data Subscriber
WBIP Updating: Elizabeth Fidlon

Trade Terms
30% single copy, 35% two or more copies
Other Terms: £1.25 carriage charge on single copy

RIZZOLI INTERNATIONAL PUBLICATIONS
40 Voltaire Road, London SW4 6DH
Tel: 071-498 0115
Fax: 071-498 2245
VAT No: 550 4723 59

Account No: _____
Sales Rep: _____
Tel: _____

Orders to
BIBLIOS PUBLISHERS DISTRIBUTION SERVICE LTD,
Star Road, Partridge Green, West Sussex RH13 8LD
Tel: 0403 710971
Fax: 0403 711143

Order Information

All Dues Automatically Recorded
Representation Available
Invoice Payments: Biblios

Personnel
Head of Sales (Home): John Rule

Number of titles published annually: 100
Number of Staff: 2
All New Titles are Bar Coded

Parent Company: Rizzoli (US)

Trade Terms
Single Copy 25%, Multiples 35%
Credit Cards Accepted: Access/Master, Visa

Returns Procedures
Address for Returns: Biblios

ROADMASTER PUBLISHING

1 Polhill Drive, Walderslade, Chatham, Kent ME5 9PN
ISBN Prefix(es): 1 871813, 1 871814
Tel: 0634 862843
Fax: 0634 201555

Order Information

All Dues Automatically Recorded
Representation Available

Personnel
Head of Sales (Home): Malcolm Wright
Head of Accounts: Susan Wright

Number of titles published annually: 8
All New Titles are Bar Coded
WBIP Updating: Malcolm Wright

Trade Terms
General Net: 35% Single copy 25%
Academic Net: 25% Single copy 17.5% CWO +5%
Girobank Number: 306 9168
Credit Cards Accepted: Access/Master, Amex, Visa

Returns Procedures
Authority to Return: Malcolm Wright

ROBERTS PUBLICATIONS

6 Titan House, Calleva Park, Aldermaston, Reading,
Berkshire RG7 4QW
Tel: 0734 819973
Fax: 0734 811176
VAT No: 450 2219 88

ROBINSON PUBLISHING

7 Kensington Church Court, London W8 4SP
ISBN Prefix(es): 0 948164, 1 85487
Tel: 071-938 3830

Fax: 071-938 4214
Telex: 262433 MONREF G
VAT No: 404 3400 10

Orders to
TIPTREE BOOK SERVICES LTD, Church Road, Tiptree, Colchester, Essex CO5 0SR
Tel: 0621 819600
Fax: 0621 819011

Order Information

All Dues Automatically Recorded
Representation Available
Invoice Payments: Tiptree Book Services
Representation:Constable & Co

Personnel
Head of Company: Nick Robinson
Head of Marketing: Alex Stitt

Number of titles published annually: 30
All New Titles are Bar Coded
Book Data Subscriber
WBIP Updating: Penny Horton

Trade Terms
35%

Returns Procedures
Authority to Return: Constable & Co
Address for Returns: Tiptree
Stock Returns: Obtain Rep's authorization and return to Tiptree
Imperfect Returns: As above

ROBSON BOOKS

Bolsover House, 5-6 Clipstone Street, London W1P 7EB
ISBN Prefix(es): 0 86051
Tel: 071-323 1223
Tel: 071-637 5937
Fax: 071-636 0798
Cables: ROBSOBOOK LONDON W1
VAT No: 230 5348 92

Account No: _____ B176 _____

Sales Rep: _____

Tel: _____

Order Information
Teleordering: ROBS

All Dues Automatically Recorded
Representation Available

Personnel
Head of Company: Jeremy Robson
Head of Sales (Home): Carole Robson
Head of Publicity: Cheryll Roberts
Head of Accounts: David Pickin
Other Important Personnel:
Louise Dixon (Head of Editorial)

Number of titles published annually: 70
PA Member
NBA Signatory
All New Titles are Bar Coded
WBIP Updating: Carole Robson

Trade Terms
35%

Returns Procedures
Address for Returns: Robson Books Ltd, Unit 3&4 Peacock Estate, 20 White Hart Lane, London N17

GEORGE RONALD PUBLISHER LTD
46 High Street, Kidlington, Oxfordshire OX5 2DN
ISBN Prefix(es): 0 85398
Tel: 0865 841515
Fax: 0865 841230
VAT No: 194 4705 41

Order Information

Order Dept Opening Times
9am - 4.30pm

Personnel
Head of Company: May Ballerio
Head of Sales (Home): Erica Leith
Head of Marketing: Wendi Momen

Number of titles published annually: 8
Percentage of Export Sales: 95%
Number of Staff: 4
PA Member
WBIP Updating: Dr Wendi Momen

Trade Terms
35% on all orders
Other Terms: Small order surcharge: under £50 add 10%
(Minimum £1)
Girobank Number: 25 822 4002

Returns Procedures
Authority to Return: Contact Erica Leith for authorisation

RONALDSON PUBLICATIONS
13A Linkside Avenue, Oxford, Oxfordshire OX2 8HY
ISBN Prefix(es): 9 510251
Tel: 0865 56209

Other Important Locations
Royal Tennis Court, Hampton Court Palace, East Molesey
Surrey
Tel: 081-977 3015

Personnel
Head of Company: M B Ronaldson
Head of Publicity: C J Ronaldson

Number of titles published annually: 1
WBIP Updating: Mr M B Ronaldson

Trade Terms
No trade terms
Other Terms: Carriage charged p&p

BARRY ROSE LAW PUBLISHERS LTD
Little London, Chichester, West Sussex PO19 1PG
ISBN Prefix(es): 1 872328
Tel: 0243 783637
Tel: 0243 787841
Fax: 0243 779278
VAT No: 193 7860 20

Order Information

All Dues Automatically Recorded

Personnel
Head of Company: Barry Rose
Head of Sales (Home): Jean Harbut
Head of Accounts: Martin Vinter

Number of titles published annually: 10
Percentage of Export Sales: 20%
WBIP Updating: Jean Harbut

Trade Terms
1-2 Copies 20%, 3-9 Copies 25%, 10+ Copies 35%

ROSEDENE PUBLISHERS

615 London Road, Westcliffe-on-Sea, Essex SS0 9PE
ISBN Prefix(es): 0 9514382
Tel: 0702 332313

Orders to
Rosedene Publishers, 110 New Road, Hadleigh, Essex
SS7 2RG
Tel: 0702 551569

Order Information

All Dues Automatically Recorded
Representation:Drake Marketing Services

Personnel
Head of Company: Rose Harris
Head of Sales (Home): R Andrews Essex 0702 551569

Number of titles published annually: 1
NBA Signatory
Open University Publications
WBIP Updating: Mrs R Harris

Trade Terms
30%-35%

Returns Procedures
Authority to Return: R Harris
Address for Returns: Rosedene Publishers, 110 New Road, Hadleigh, Essex SS7 2RG
Stock Returns: Must be in mint condition
Imperfect Returns: Full refund or credit note

ROSENDALE PRESS LTD

Premier House, 10 Greycoat Place, London SW1P 1SB
ISBN Prefix(es): 0 9509182, 1 872808
Tel: 071-222 8866
Fax: 071-799 1416
VAT No: 372 7835 23

Orders to
BIBLIOS PUBLISHERS DISTRIBUTION SERVICE LTD,
Star Road, Partridge Green, West Sussex RH13 8LD
Tel: 0403 710971
Fax: 0403 711143

Order Information

All Dues Automatically Recorded
Representation Available
Invoice Payments: Biblios
Representation:Boxtree

Personnel
Head of Company: Timothy S Green (Chairman)
Head of Sales (Home): David Inman Boxtree Ltd
Other Important Personnel:
Maureen Green (Editorial Director), Pamela Burden (Manager)

Number of titles published annually: 10
Percentage of Export Sales: 70%
IPG Member
All New Titles are Bar Coded
Book Data Subscriber
WBIP Updating: Pamela Burden

Trade Terms
35%, Single copy orders 25%
Minimum Order: 3 copies on some paperback titles

Returns Procedures
Authority to Return: Maureen Green, Rosendale Press
Address for Returns: Biblios

ROSENHEATH SCIENTIFIC PUBLICATIONS

Rosenheath House, Brookside Crescent, Worcester Park, Surrey KT4 8AQ
Tel: 081-337 3196

ROSKILL INFORMATION SERVICES LTD

2 Clapham Road, London SW9 0JA
Tel: 071-582 5155
Fax: 071-793 0008
Telex: 917867 ROSKIL G

ROSSLYN PUBLISHING

94 Station Avenue, West Ewell, Epsom, Surrey KT19 9UG
Tel: 081-393 5854

ROSTERS LTD

23 Welbeck Street, London W1M 7PG
ISBN Prefix(es): 0 948032, 1 85631
Tel: 071-935 4550
Fax: 071-224 1062

All New Titles are Bar Coded

BERTRAM ROTA (PUBLISHING) LTD

9-11 Langley Court, Covent Garden, London WC2E 9RX
ISBN Prefix(es): 0 854000
Tel: 071-836 0723
Fax: 071-497 9058
VAT No: 239 5177 39

Order Information

All Dues Automatically Recorded

Personnel
Head of Company: Anthony Rota
Head of Accounts: Martin Gifford

Number of titles published annually: 2
Percentage of Export Sales: 40%
WBIP Updating: A B Rota

Trade Terms
on request by title
Other Terms: Carriage charged
Credit Cards Accepted: Access/Master, Visa

Returns Procedures
Imperfect Returns: £15

ROTOGRAPHIC PUBLICATIONS

37 St Efrides Road, Torre, Torquay, Devon TQ2 5SG
Tel: 0803 211316
Fax: 0803 211316 Ext73
VAT No: 140 7249 85

THE ROUND HALL PRESS LTD
Kill Lane, Blackrock, County Dublin
ISBN Prefix(es): 0 947686
Tel: 01 289 2922
Fax: 01 289 3072
VAT No: 460 7955 1

Orders to
GILL & MACMILLAN LTD, Goldenbridge, Inchicore, Dublin 8, County Dublin
Tel: 01 531 005
Fax: 01 541 688

Order Information

All Dues Automatically Recorded

Personnel
Head of Company: B Daly
Head of Sales (Home): Terri McDonnell
Head of Accounts: Claire Kenna

Number of titles published annually: 10
Number of Staff: 32
WBIP Updating: M Adams

Parent Company: Irish Academic Press

Trade Terms
20%
Credit Cards Accepted: Access/Master, Visa, Amex

Returns Procedures
Authority to Return: Gill & Macmillan

ROUNDHOUSE PUBLISHING LIMITED
PO Box 140, Oxford, Oxfordshire OX2 7SF
ISBN Prefix(es): 1 85710
Tel: 0865 512682
Fax: 0865 59594
VAT No: 545 7006 49

Orders to
Roundhouse Pub, 31 Oakdale Glen, Harrogate, North Yorkshire HG1 2JY
Tel: 0423 568313
Fax: 0423 531292

Order Information
Teleordering: JRM

All Dues Automatically Recorded
Representation Available
Invoice Payments: Bookpoint

Personnel
Head of Sales (Home): William R Gills
Head of Sales (Export): Alan T Goodworth

Number of titles published annually: 200
Number of Staff: 4
All New Titles are Bar Coded
Book Data Subscriber
WBIP Updating: Alan Goodworth

Subsidiary Companies: Ramsay (John) Marketing Ltd

Trade Terms
General Net: Single copy 25%, Two or more 35%
Credit Cards Accepted: Access/Master, Visa, Amex

Returns Procedures
Address for Returns: Bookpoint
Imperfect Returns: Title pages only - clearly marked with imperfection up to limit £20 otherwise return entire book.

ROUNDOAK PUBLISHING

7 Roundoak Gardens, Nynehead, Wellington, Somerset
TA21 0BX
ISBN Prefix(es): 1 871565
Tel: 0823 662860
Fax: 0823 662860
VAT No: 429 0680 46

Order Information

Order Dept Opening Times
Mon - Fri 9am - 12pm, 1pm - 3pm (Phone Only)
All Dues Automatically Recorded

Personnel
Head of Company: R C Pearson
Other Important Personnel:
C C Pearson

Number of titles published annually: 5
Number of Staff: 2
IPG Member
NBA Signatory
All New Titles are Bar Coded

Parent Company: Nynehead Books

Trade Terms
Single copy 25%, two or more copies 35%
Other Terms: Pro-forma to non established accounts

ROUTLEDGE

11 New Fetter Lane, London EC4P 4EE
ISBN Prefix(es): 0 04, 0 415, 0 416, 0 422, 0 7099, 0 7100, 0 7102, 0 7448
Tel: 071-583 9855
Fax: 071-583 0701
Fax: 071-936 2003 (Sales)
Telex: 263398
Cables: ELEGIACS LONDON EC4
Account No: _____ 030561-001 _____
Sales Rep: _____
Tel: _____

Orders to
INTERNATIONAL THOMSON PUBLISHING SERVICES LTD, Cheriton House, North Way, Andover, Hampshire SP10 5BE
Tel: 0264 332424
Fax: 0264 364418

Order Information

All Dues Automatically Recorded
Representation Available

Personnel
Head of Company: David Croom (Managing Director)
Head of Sales (Home): Alan Leitch (UK Sales Manager)
Head of Marketing: Malcolm Campbell (Marketing Director)
Head of Publicity: Benedicte Page (Publicity Manager)
Other Important Personnel:
Barney Allan (Sales Manager Asia/Africa), Sarah Daniels & Barbara Moeller (European Sales Managers)

PA Member
All New Titles are Bar Coded
Open University Publications
Book Data Subscriber
WBIP Updating: Peter Clay ITPS

Parent Company: The Thomson Corporation

Trade Terms
Girobank Number: 209 6919
Credit Cards Accepted: Access/Master, Visa, Amex, Diners

Returns Procedures
Address for Returns: International Thomson
Stock Returns: Prior authorisation from either Sales Office or Local Sales Representative

JOSEPH ROWNTREE FOUNDATION

The Homestead, 40 Water End, York, North Yorkshire YO3 6LP
Tel: 0904 654328 Publns
Tel: 0904 629241 General
Fax: 0904 620072

ROXIMILLION PUBLICATIONS CO

c/o Cherry Red Records Ltd, 25/29 Fulham High Street, London SW6 3JH
Tel: 071-371 5844
Fax: 071-384 1854
VAT No: 340 6032 02

Orders to
L N FOWLER & CO LTD, 1201-3 High Road, Chadwell Heath, Romford, Essex RM6 4DH
Tel: 081-597 2491
Fax: 081-598 2428

IPG Member

ROYAL AERONAUTICAL SOCIETY

4 Hamilton Place, London W1V 0BQ
Tel: 071-499 3515
Fax: 071-499 6230
Telex: 262826 RAESOC
VAT No: 238 5678 23

[handwritten: Royal Botanic Gdns, Kew, Richmond, Surrey TW9 3AB]

THE ROYAL ASSOCIATION FOR DISABILITY & REHABILITATION

25 Mortimer Street, London W1N 8AB
Tel: 071-637 5400
Fax: 071-637 1827

ROYAL COLLEGE OF PHYSICIANS OF EDINBURGH

9 Queen Street, Edinburgh, Lothian EH2 1JQ
Tel: 031-225 7324
Fax: 031-220 3939

ROYAL COMMISSION ON THE HISTORICAL MONUMENTS OF ENGLAND

Fortress House, Savile Row, London W1X 2JQ
Tel: 071-973 3500
Fax: 071-494 3998

Orders to
RCHME Publ Dept, Alexander House, 19 Fleming Way, Swindon, Wiltshire SN1 2NG
Tel: 0793 414100 Ext 232
Fax: 0793 414185

ROYAL INSTITUTE OF INTERNATIONAL AFFAIRS

Chatham House, 10 St James's Square, London SW1Y 4LE
Tel: 071-957 5700
Fax: 071-957 5710
VAT No: 239 8149 29

Book Data Subscriber

ROYAL IRISH ACADEMY

19 Dawson Street, Dublin 2, County Dublin
ISBN Prefix(es): 0 901714, 1 874045
Tel: 01 762 570
Tel: 01 764 222
Tel: 01 761 642
Fax: 01 762 346

Order Information

Order Dept Opening Times
Mon - Fri 9am - 5pm
All Dues Automatically Recorded
Representation Available

Personnel
Head of Company: Aidan Duggan (Executive Secretary)
Head of Sales (Home): Hugh Shiels (Sales Manager)

Number of titles published annually: 8
Percentage of Export Sales: 45%
WBIP Updating: Barbara Young

Trade Terms
33.3% + postage
Credit Cards Accepted: Access/Master, Visa

Returns Procedures
Imperfect Returns: Contact Hugh Shiels

[Handwritten annotation: Royal Society of Chemistry - Turpin Transactions Distribution Centre, Blackhorse Road, Letchworth, Herts SG6 1HN. Tel. 0462 672555. A/C No 0001733. FAX 0462 480947]

ROYAL SCHOOL OF CHURCH MUSIC

Addington Palace, Croydon, Surrey CR9 5AD
Tel: 081-654 7676
Fax: 081-655 2542
VAT No: 218 5137 71

THE ROYAL SOCIETY

Publications Department, 6 Carlton House Terrace, London SW1Y 5AG
ISBN Prefix(es): 0 85403
Tel: 071-839 5561
Fax: 071-930 2170
Fax: 071-976 1837
Telex: 917876

Order Information

Order Dept Opening Times
Mon - Fri 9am - 5pm

Personnel
Head of Company: Dr P T Warren
Head of Sales (Home): Mr P Cooper
Head of Accounts: Miss D O'Marra
Head of Distribution: Mr M Power
Head of Customer Services: Miss J S Knapp

Number of titles published annually: 10
Percentage of Export Sales: 30%
Number of Staff: 2
All New Titles are Bar Coded
WBIP Updating: Deborah Vaughan

Trade Terms
25% Books, 10% Subscriptions
Minimum Order: Minimum invoice value £3
Credit Cards Accepted: Access/Master, Visa

Returns Procedures
Authority to Return: Prior permission required
Stock Returns: Notification of returns must be made within 3 days (Europe) and 2 weeks (Rest of World) of receipt

ROYAL SOCIETY OF MEDICINE SERVICES LTD

1 Wimpole Street, London W1M 8AE
Tel: 071-408 2119
Fax: 071-355 3198
Telex: 298902
VAT No: 524 4136 71

Book Data Subscriber

THE ROYAL TOWN PLANNING INSTITUTE

26 Portland Place, London W1N 4BE
Tel: 071-636 9107
Fax: 071-323 1582
VAT No: 524 3181 71

THE ROYAL UNITED SERVICES INSTITUTE FOR DEFENCE STUDIES

Whitehall, London SW1A 2ET
Tel: 071-930 5854
Fax: 071-321 0943

ROYSTON

10 Crown Road North, Glasgow, Strathclyde G12 9DH
ISBN Prefix(es): 0 946706
Tel: 041-339 1867
VAT No: 552 3564 46

Order Information

All Dues Automatically Recorded

Personnel
Head of Company: A Amin

Number of titles published annually: 7
WBIP Updating: Ms Royston

Trade Terms
General Net: Single copy/single line 20%, 2 or more single titles/ 2 books or more 33.3%

THE RUBICON PRESS

57 Cornwall Gardens, London SW7 4BE
ISBN Prefix(es): 0 948695
Tel: 071-937 6813
VAT No: 461 5078 52

Order Information

All Dues Automatically Recorded
Representation Available

Personnel
Head of Company: Anthea Page (Partner)

Other Important Personnel:
Juanita Homan (Partner)

Number of titles published annually: 3
Number of Staff: 2
IPG Member
NBA Signatory
All New Titles are Bar Coded
Book Data Subscriber

Trade Terms
General Net: Single copy 25%, 2 or more single titles 33-35%, subscrip- tion orders 35%
Other Terms: Postage

Returns Procedures
Authority to Return: Prior permission required
Imperfect Returns: Title page required

RUNNING ANGEL

55 Telegraph Lane East, Norwich, Norfolkshire NR1 4AR
ISBN Prefix(es): 0 946600
Tel: 0603 611795

Personnel
Head of Company: Elizabeth Orna

RUNNING PRESS = BIBLIOS

RUSHWORTH LITERATURE LTD

2 Dimple Lane, Crich, Nr Matlock, Derbyshire DE4 5BQ
ISBN Prefix(es): 0 900329
Tel: 0773 857313 24 Hours
VAT No: 213 6679 60

Order Information

Order Dept Opening Times
Mon - Fri 9am - 5pm
All Dues Automatically Recorded

Personnel
Head of Company: D F Mickelsen
Head of Sales (Home): Miss C S Cheetham
Head of Accounts: Mrs Doreen Smith

Number of titles published annually: 4
Percentage of Export Sales: 50%
Number of Staff: 3
NBA Signatory
All New Titles are Bar Coded
WBIP Updating: Miss C S Cheetham

Trade Terms
40% on all orders, no surcharges
Credit Cards Accepted: Access/Master, Visa, Other

Returns Procedures
Authority to Return: Prior permission required
Imperfect Returns: Title page, no limit

MICHAEL RUSSELL (PUBLISHING) LTD

Wilby Hall, Wilby, Norwich, Norfolk NR16 2JP
ISBN Prefix(es): 0 85955
Tel: 095 387 776
Fax: 095 387 762
VAT No: 293 5595 19

Personnel
Head of Company: Michael Russell

RUSSELL SAGE FOUNDATION - see info on Cornell Univ. Press. = CUP services

Trade Terms
General Net: Single copy 25%, Two or more 35%, Special orders negotiable.

Returns Procedures
Imperfect Returns: Up to £15

RYBURN DISTRIBUTION

Tenterfields, Luddendenfoot, Halifax, West Yorkshire
HX2 6EJ
Tel: 0422 884907
Fax: 0422 884633
VAT No: 373 3340 64

Account No: _____

Sales Rep: _____

Tel: _____

SAFARI BOOKS LTD = African Books Collective, The Jam Factory, 27 Park end street, Oxford OX1 1HU.

SAGE PUBLICATIONS

6 Bonhill Street, London EC2A 4PU
Tel: 071-374 0645
Fax: 071-374 8741
Telex: 296207 SAGE G
Cables: SAGEPUB
VAT No: 232 6001 16

Account No: _____ 0149322 _____

Sales Rep: _____

Tel: _____

Orders to
Fax: 071-374 0645

Order Information

Order Dept Opening Times
Mon - Fri 8.30am - 5.00pm
All Dues Automatically Recorded
Representation Available

Personnel
Head of Company: David Hill (Managing Director)
Head of Sales (Home): John Gavin (Sales Manager)
Head of Marketing: Ian Eastment (Marketing Director)
Head of Accounts: Lynn Adams (Director of Administration)
Head of Customer Services: Mary Benson (Customer Services & Returns Manager)
Other Important Personnel:
Trilok Vyas (Credit Manager)

Number of titles published annually: 300
Number of Staff: 50
PA Member
NBA Signatory
All New Titles are Bar Coded
Open University Publications
Book Data Subscriber
WBIP Updating: Lynn Adams

Parent Company: Sage Publications Inc

Trade Terms
20 - 30% according to turnover. No surcharges.
Girobank Number: 5480353
Credit Cards Accepted: Access/Master, Visa, Amex, Diners, Other

Returns Procedures
Authority to Return: John Gavin
Stock Returns: Policy letter available on request.

SAINSBURY PUBLISHING LTD

Auldcarn House, Main Street, Bleasby, Nottinghamshire
NG14 7GH
ISBN Prefix(es): 1 870655
Tel: 0636 830499
Fax: 0636 830175
VAT No: 450 1623 86

Order Information

All Dues Automatically Recorded
Representation Available

Personnel
Head of Company: George Sainsbury

Number of titles published annually: 10
Number of Staff: 2
All New Titles are Bar Coded

Trade Terms
35% all orders no surcharges

Returns Procedures
Authority to Return: George Sainsbury
Imperfect Returns: Return title page if below £25

THE SAINT ANDREW PRESS

121 George Street, Edinburgh, Lothian EH2 4YN
ISBN Prefix(es): 0 7152, 0 86153
Tel: 031-225 5722
Fax: 031-220 3113
Cables: FREE, EDINBURGH
VAT No: 270 5962 46

Order Information
Teleordering: STANDRW

Personnel
Head of Sales (Home): Derek Auld (Sales & Production Manager)

NBA Signatory
All New Titles are Bar Coded

DAVID ST JOHN THOMAS PUBLISHER

PO Box 4, Nairn, Nairnshire IV12 5HU
ISBN Prefix(es): 0 946537
Tel: 0667 54441
Fax: 0667 54401
VAT No: 553 0273 36

Orders to
BOOKPOINT LIMITED, 39 Milton Park, Abingdon, Oxfordshire OX14 4TD
Tel: 0235 835001
Fax: 0235 861038

Order Information
Representation:HI Marketing Representation in Scotland:Norma Rutherford 0506 890045

Personnel
Head of Company: David St John Thomas (Director)
Head of Marketing: Sharon Compton
Head of Accounts: Elizabeth Innes

Number of titles published annually: 10
Number of Staff: 11
All New Titles are Bar Coded
Book Data Subscriber
WBIP Updating: Grant Shipcott

Trade Terms
35%
Credit Cards Accepted: Access/Master, Visa

Returns Procedures
Authority to Return: Prior permission required from Head Office
Address for Returns: Bookpoint
Imperfect Returns: Contact publisher

ST PAUL'S BIBLIOGRAPHIES

1 Step Terrace, Winchester, Hampshire SO22 5BW
ISBN Prefix(es): 0 906795, 1 873040
Tel: 0962 860524
Fax: 0962 842409
VAT No: 335 4444 63

Orders to
Niche Marketing, 6 Turville Barns, Eastleach, Cirencester, Gloucestershire GL7 3QB
Tel: 0367 85227
Fax: 0367 85448

Order Information

Order Dept Opening Times
Mon - Fri 9am - 5pm
All Dues Automatically Recorded
Invoice Payments: Niche Marketing & Publishing Services

Personnel
Head of Company: R S Cross
Head of Sales (Home): C Reynard
Head of Accounts: Jane Reynard

Number of titles published annually: 3
Percentage of Export Sales: 25%
Number of Staff: 1
IPG Member
WBIP Updating: R S Cross

Trade Terms
25% post free in UK, single copy/single line 20%
BA/Girobank Small Order Scheme: Yes
Girobank Number: 3390357

Returns Procedures
Authority to Return: Niche Marketing & Publishing Services
Address for Returns: Niche
Stock Returns: No returns acceptable unless customer has cancelled order - damaged books are replaced
Imperfect Returns: Title page up to £40. Above this return whole book

ST PAUL'S PUBLICATIONS

St Paul's House, Middlegreen, Slough, Berkshire SL3 6BT
ISBN Prefix(es): 0 85439
Tel: 0753 520621
Tel: 071-828 5582
Fax: 0753 574240
Fax: 071-828 3329
VAT No: 207 8496 41

Order Information

Order Dept Opening Times
Mon - Fri 9am - 5pm
Orders for more than one publisher can be bulked
Representation Available

Personnel
Head of Company: Karamvelil Sebastian
Head of Sales (Home): Priante Eugene

Head of Marketing: Larry Thoms
Head of Publicity: Teresa Rees
Head of Accounts: Siletti Vincent

Number of titles published annually: 45
Percentage of Export Sales: 40%
All New Titles are Bar Coded
WBIP Updating: Terri Rees

Trade Terms
Surcharge for orders up to £20 + 30% discount, £20-£35 35% discount + surcharge, Over £35 carriage free 35% discount
Other Terms: Small order Surcharges £1.25 to £2.50

Returns Procedures
Authority to Return: Prior authorisation required
Stock Returns: No returns on 'non stock' orders, stock orders request permission at time of ordering
Imperfect Returns: Send title page only

[handwritten: Salimbeni, Via Matteo Palmieri 14-16r, P.O. Box 1450, 50122 Firenze, Spain, FAX. 010395523461371]

[handwritten: Salisbury College - Southampton Road, Salisbury Wilts SP1 2LW]

SALTIRE SOCIETY
9 Fountain Close, 22 High Street, Edinburgh, Scotland E1H 1TF
ISBN Prefix(es): 0 854110, 0 863340, 0 904265
Tel: 031-556 1836
Fax: 031-557 1675
VAT No: 592 9841 85

Orders to
JOHN DONALD PUBLISHERS LTD, 138 St Stephen Street, Edinburgh, Lothian EH3 5AA
Tel: 031-225 1146
Fax: 031-220 0567

Order Information
All Dues Automatically Recorded
Representation Available
Invoice Payments: John Donald Distribution Services

Other Important Locations
Publications Officer:Gleniffer Place, 3 Miller Road, Ayr KA7 2AX Tel/Fax 0292 262359

Personnel
Head of Company: Hugh Andrew (Convener of Publication Committee) Tel/Fax 031-228 6189
Other Important Personnel:
T S Campbell (Publications Officer) Tel/Fax 0292 262359

Number of titles published annually: 6
Number of Staff: 1
PA Member
All New Titles are Bar Coded
WBIP Updating: K T S Campbell

Trade Terms
Payment Terms 30 days net
General Net: Single copy/single line 20%, orders under £20 retail 25%, Subscription/stock/special orders 35%

Returns Procedures
Authority to Return: Written authorisation required from Head Office or Rep
Address for Returns: John Donald Distribution Services
Stock Returns: Books must be in mint condition

[handwritten: SAMS - Prentice Hall.]

SAMSON BOOKS LTD
Down House, Redlynch, Salisbury, Wiltshire SP5 2JP
ISBN Prefix(es): 0 906304
Tel: 0725 20347 Tel/Fax

Personnel
Head of Company: G E M Samson
Head of Sales (Home): M J Howorth 071-731 0975

Trade Terms
33.3% single - variable for quantity

SANGAM BOOKS LTD
57 London Fruit Exchange, Brushfield Street, London
E1 6EP
ISBN Prefix(es): 0 86125, 0 86131, 0 86132, 0 86311
Tel: 071-377 6399
Fax: 071-247 1817
Telex: 895 4111 REPLAY G
VAT No: 393 8557 00

Order Information

Order Dept Opening Times
9.30am - 1pm, 2pm - 5.30pm
All Dues Automatically Recorded
Representation Available

Personnel
Head of Company: Mr J R Rao
Head of Sales (Home): Mr E Raghavan
Head of Sales (Export): Mr A A de Souza

Number of titles published annually: 40
PA Member
NBA Signatory
WBIP Updating: Mr A de Souza

Parent Company: Orient Longman Ltd (India)

Trade Terms
25% on single copy, 35% on more than 1 copy of a title

SAQI BOOKS
26 Westbourne Grove, London W2 5RH
ISBN Prefix(es): 0 86356, 1 85516
Tel: 071-221 9347
Fax: 071-229 7492
Telex: 919595 SAQI G
VAT No: 480 7796 04

Orders to
BAILEY DISTRIBUTION LTD, Unit 1, Learoyd Road,
Mountfield Rd Ind Est, New Romney, Kent TN28 8XU
Tel: 0679 66905
Fax: 0679 66638

Order Information

All Dues Automatically Recorded
Representation Available

Personnel
Head of Company: A Gaspard

Number of titles published annually: 25
Percentage of Export Sales: 80%
Number of Staff: 3
PA Member
NBA Signatory
All New Titles are Bar Coded
Book Data Subscriber

Trade Terms
35%

Returns Procedures
Address for Returns: Bailey Distribution

SAREMA PRESS (PUBLISHERS) LTD

15 Beeches Walk, Carshalton, Surrey SM5 4JS
ISBN Prefix(es): 1 870758
Tel: 081-770 1953
Fax: 081-770 1957
VAT No: 574 2622 37

Order Information

Order Dept Opening Times
Mon - Fri 8.30am - 5.30pm Sat 9am - 12.30pm
All Dues Automatically Recorded
Representation Available

Other Important Locations
Warehouse: 107 Westmead Road, Carshalton, Surrey

Personnel
Head of Company: Gordon Charles Rookledge
Head of Accounts: Jennifer Rookledge

Number of titles published annually: 2
Percentage of Export Sales: 80%
Number of Staff: 2
All New Titles are Bar Coded
Open University Publications
WBIP Updating: G C Rookledge

Trade Terms
General Net: Single Copy 25%, Two or more single titles 35% Subscription/Stock/Special orders - negotiable
Other Terms: Carriage charge on all books outside London

Returns Procedures
Authority to Return: Jennifer M Rookledge
Stock Returns: No returns unless damaged and informed within seven days of receipt of books
Imperfect Returns: Title page up to £25

SARSEN PUBLISHING

Sokens, Green Street, Pleshey, Nr Chelmsford, Essex
CM3 1HT
ISBN Prefix(es): 0 9510556
Tel: 0245 31566
VAT No: 386 7938 79

SAS SOFTWARE LTD: Wittington House, Henley Road, Medmenham, Marlow, Bucks SL7 2EB
Tel 0628 486933 FAX 0628 483203

SAUS PUBLICATIONS

School Advanced Urban Studies, Rodney Lodge, Grange Road, Bristol, Avon BS8 4EA
ISBN Prefix(es): 0 86292, 1 873575
Tel: 0272 741117
Fax: 0272 737308
VAT No: 139 0859 46

Order Information

Order Dept Opening Times
Mon - Fri 9am - 5pm
All Dues Automatically Recorded

Personnel
Head of Company: Alison Shaw
Head of Sales (Home): Jane Raistrick
Head of Publicity: Julia Mortimer
Other Important Personnel:
Julie Platt (Journal Business Manager)

Number of titles published annually: 25
Number of Staff: 4
Book Data Subscriber
WBIP Updating: Alison Shaw

Trade Terms
10%, Stock Orders 25%, Special Stockists 33%
Other Terms: Carriage charges overseas
Credit Cards Accepted: Access/Master, Visa

Returns Procedures
Authority to Return: Firm Sale Only
Imperfect Returns: Return for replacement

SAWD BOOKS
Placketts Hole, Bicknor, Sittingbourne, Kent ME9 8BA
ISBN Prefix(es): 1 872489
Tel: 0795 420314
Tel: 0795 472262
Fax: 0795 422633
VAT No: 516 0599 46

Account No: _____

Sales Rep: _____

Tel: _____

Orders to
BOOKPOINT LIMITED, 39 Milton Park, Abingdon, Oxfordshire OX14 4TD
Tel: 0235 835001
Fax: 0235 861038

Order Information

All Dues Automatically Recorded
Representation Available
Invoice Payments: Bookpoint Ltd
Representation:Amalgamated Book Services

Personnel
Head of Company: Susannah Wainman (Partner)
Head of Customer Services: Claudia Warner

Number of titles published annually: 6
Number of Staff: 9
IPG Member
NBA Signatory
All New Titles are Bar Coded
Book Data Subscriber

Trade Terms
35%, 30 days

Returns Procedures
Authority to Return: Amalgamated Book Services
Address for Returns: Bookpoint Ltd
Stock Returns: Refer to Bookpint

SAYCE PUBLISHING
57 Marlborough Road, St Leonards, Exeter, Devon EX2 4LN
Tel: 0392 424786
Fax: 0392 424762
Telex: 42551 EXONIA G
VAT No: 585 4264 14

SB PUBLICATIONS
c/o 19 Grove Road, Seaford, East Sussex BN25 1TP
ISBN Prefix(es): 1 85770, 1 870708
Tel: 0323 893498
VAT No: 533 2594 50

Orders to
BIBLIOS PUBLISHERS DISTRIBUTION SERVICE LTD, Star Road, Partridge Green, West Sussex RH13 8LD

Tel: 0403 710971
Fax: 0403 711143

Order Information

All Dues Automatically Recorded
Representation Available
Invoice Payments: Biblios Ltd

Personnel
Head of Company: Stephen Benz
Head of Distribution: Mrs C Evans

Number of titles published annually: 30
Number of Staff: 3
All New Titles are Bar Coded
WBIP Updating: S A Benz

Trade Terms
35% no surcharges Single copy 25%

Returns Procedures
Authority to Return: Prior permission required from SB Publications
Address for Returns: Biblios
Stock Returns: Send credit request with details first
Imperfect Returns: Send title page and details

SCALA PUBLICATIONS LTD

3 Greek Street, London W1V 6NX
ISBN Prefix(es): 1 85759, 1 870248
Tel: 071-287 4904
Fax: 071-734 0450

Orders to
PHILIP WILSON PUBLISHERS LTD, 26 Litchfield Street, London WC2H 9NJ
Tel: 071-379 7886
Fax: 071-497 3290

Order Information

All Dues Automatically Recorded
Representation Available
Invoice Payments: Philip Wilson Publishers

Personnel
Head of Company: Hugh Merrell (Managing Director)
Head of Publicity: Kevin Childs (Publishing Manager)

Number of titles published annually: 10
Percentage of Export Sales: 75%
Number of Staff: 4
PA Member
All New Titles are Bar Coded
WBIP Updating: Kevin Childs

Parent Company: Philip Wilson Publishers
Allied Companies: Editions Scala (FR)

Returns Procedures
Authority to Return: Juliana Powney
Address for Returns: Philip Wilson Publishers

SCARLET PRESS

5 Montague Road, London E8 2HN
ISBN Prefix(es): 1 8572700, 1 8572799
Tel: 071-241 3702
Fax: 071-753 5100

Orders to
PLUTO PUBLISHING, 345 Archway Road, London N6 5AA
Tel: 081-348 2724
Fax: 081-348 9133

Order Information

All Dues Automatically Recorded
Representation Available
Invoice Payments: Pluto Publishing
Representation: Turnaround Distribution

Personnel

Head of Marketing: Vicky Wilson Tel: 071-607 8618
Head of Publicity: Belinda Budge Tel: 071-607 8618
Head of Accounts: Ann Treneman
Other Important Personnel:
Avis Lewallen (Administrator/Rights), Christine Considine (Editorial Manager)

Number of titles published annually: 8
Number of Staff: 5
PA Member
WBIP Updating: Christine Considine

Trade Terms

33.3%, single copy under £20 - 20% plus £1.25 surcharge
Credit Cards Accepted: Access/Master, Visa

Returns Procedures

Authority to Return: Pluto Publishing
Address for Returns: Clipper Distribution Services, Windmill Grove, Porchester, Hants PO16 9HT

SCARTHIN BOOKS

The Promenade, Scarthin, Cromford, Derbyshire DE4 3QS
ISBN Prefix(es): 0 907758
Tel: 0629 823272
Fax: 0629 825094

Order Information

Order Dept Opening Times
Mon - Sat 9am - 6pm
All Dues Automatically Recorded
Representation Available

Personnel

Head of Sales (Home): D J Mitchell
Head of Customer Services: G N Cooper
Other Important Personnel:
P A Hopkinson (Editorial)

Number of titles published annually: 10
Number of Staff: 3
IPG Member
All New Titles are Bar Coded
WBIP Updating: G N Cooper

Trade Terms

35%, Single copies 20%, 2-5 paperbacks 25%

Returns Procedures

Stock Returns: Contact customer services

SCEPTRE PRESS LTD

7 College Park Drive, Bristol, Avon BS10 7AN
ISBN Prefix(es): 0 7068
Tel: 0272 509175
Fax: 0272 592260

SCHOFIELD & SIMS LTD

Dogley Mill, Fenay Bridge, Huddersfield, West Yorkshire HD8 0NQ
ISBN Prefix(es): 0 7217
Tel: 0484 607080

Fax: 0484 606815
VAT No: 183 5012 80

Account No: _____

Sales Rep: _____

Tel: _____

Order Information

All Dues Automatically Recorded

Personnel
Head of Company: J S Nesbitt (Chairman)
Head of Sales (Home): Jack Brierley
Head of Accounts: Keith Sykes
Other Important Personnel:
J S Platts (Managing Director)

Number of titles published annually: 30
Number of Staff: 30
IPG Member
WBIP Updating: Anne Brummitt

Trade Terms
General Net: 33.3% + 5% settlements (one month)
Non-Net: 16.6% + 5% settlements (one month)
Minimum Order: Order under £10 value (list price) - 10%

Returns Procedures
Authority to Return: Keith Sykes

SCHOLASTIC PUBLICATIONS LTD

Villiers House, Clarendon Avenue, Leamington Spa, Warwickshire CV32 5PR
ISBN Prefix(es): 0 233, 0 590, 1 85434
Tel: 0926 887799
Fax: 0926 883331
VAT No: 241 3593 76

Account No: _____ 950-0413-1-001

Sales Rep: _____

Tel: _____

Orders to
Scholastic Pub Ltd, Westfield Road, Southam, Leamington Spa, Warwickshire CV33 0JW
Tel: 0926 813910
Fax: 0926 817727

Order Information
Teleordering: SCHOL

Order Dept Opening Times
Mon - Fri 9am - 5pm
Cyclical Ordering Policy
All Dues Automatically Recorded
Representation Available
Invoice Payments: Westfield Road, Southam, Leamington Spa, Warks, CV33 0JW

Other Important Locations
Scholastic Children's Books: 7-9 Pratt Street, London NW1 0AE
Tel: 071-283 4474
Fax: 071-284 4234

Personnel
Head of Company: David Kewley (Managing Director)
Head of Sales (Home): Gavin Lang (Sales & Marketing)
Head of Publicity: Sarah Allison (Publicity Manager) 071-284 4474
Head of Accounts: Ian Bloodworth (Finance Director) 0926 813910
Head of Distribution: Alistair Wood (Operations & Distributions Director) 0926 813910

Head of Customer Services: Sheena Bennett (Customer Services Supervisor) 0926 813910
Other Important Personnel:
Shirley Starbuck (Credit Controller)

Number of titles published annually: 200
Number of Staff: 190
PA Member
NBA Signatory
All New Titles are Bar Coded
Book Data Subscriber
WBIP Updating: Sarah Allison

Parent Company: Scholastic Incorporated

Trade Terms
35%

Returns Procedures
Authority to Return: Authorization for returns by rep. only

SCHOOL OF ORIENTAL & AFRICAN STUDIES (UNIV OF LONDON)

Thornhaugh Street, Russell Square, London WC1H 0XG
ISBN Prefix(es): 0 7286, 0 901877
Tel: 071-637 2388
Fax: 071-436 3844
Telex: 262433 W 6876
VAT No: 233 6746 57

Order Information

Order Dept Opening Times
Mon - Fri 9.45am - 1pm 2pm - 5pm
All Dues Automatically Recorded
Representation Available

Personnel
Head of Company: Mr M J Daly (Publications Officer)
Head of Distribution: Cynthia Daugherty (Publications Assistant)

Number of titles published annually: 12
Percentage of Export Sales: 50%
Number of Staff: 4
WBIP Updating: Mr M J Daly

Trade Terms
Academic Net: Single copy 25%, 2 or more single titles 35%, 2 books or more 35%, subscription orders 35%, stock orders 35%
Minimum Order: Pro-forma (at full trade terms) if invoice value less than £20.00

Returns Procedures
Stock Returns: Any Reasonable request will be considered.
Imperfect Returns: As appropriate in circumstances.

SCIENCE MUSEUM

Publications Unit, Exhibition Road, London SW7 2DD
ISBN Prefix(es): 0 901805
Tel: 071-938 8211
Tel: 071-938 8136
Fax: 071-938 8213

Orders to
Dillons, The Science Museum, Exhibition Road, London SW7 2DD
Tel: 071-938 8255
Fax: 071-938 8118

Order Information

Invoice Payments: Dillons In The Science Museum

Personnel
Head of Company: Dr Anthony Wilson (Publications Manager)
Other Important Personnel:
Ms Victoria Smith (Publications Assistant)

Number of titles published annually: 15
Number of Staff: 2
WBIP Updating: Victoria Smith

Trade Terms
Contact Dillons

Returns Procedures
Authority to Return: Dillons

SCIENCE REVIEWS LTD

18 Oaklands Gate, Northwood, Middlesex HA6 3AA
ISBN Prefix(es): 0 905927, 0 946682
Tel: 0923 82386
Fax: 0923 825066
VAT No: 245 1030 09

Order Information

All Dues Automatically Recorded

Personnel
Head of Company: Dr P J Farago
Other Important Personnel:
Mrs E M Broughton (Head of Administration)

Number of titles published annually: 6
Percentage of Export Sales: 90%
Number of Staff: 3

Trade Terms
General Net: Single copy 20%, Two books or more 33%
Academic Net: Single copy 20%, Two books or more 33%

Scientechnica = Reed Book Services

SCIENTIFIC & TECHNICAL BOOK SERVICE LTD

PO Box 90, Reading, Berkshire RG1 8JL
Tel: 0734 560080
Fax: 0734 568211

Account No: _____ 69220 _____
Sales Rep: _____
Tel: _____

SCM PRESS LTD

26-30 Tottenham Road, London N1 4BZ
ISBN Prefix(es): 0 334, 0 7162
Tel: 071-249 7262
Fax: 071-249 3776
VAT No: 232 8603 75

Account No: _____
Sales Rep: _____
Tel: _____

Order Information
Teleordering: SCM

Order Dept Opening Times
Mon - Fri 9am - 5pm
All Dues Automatically Recorded
Representation Available

Personnel
Head of Company: Rev Dr J Bowden

Head of Sales (Home): Simon Clark
Head of Accounts: R Pygram
Head of Customer Services: Jean Barrett

Number of titles published annually: 50
Percentage of Export Sales: 35%
Number of Staff: 16
PA Member
NBA Signatory
All New Titles are Bar Coded
WBIP Updating: Ms Jennifer Ellis

Trade Terms
35%, no surcharges within the UK
Girobank Number: 545 0357

Returns Procedures
Authority to Return: Simon Clark
Stock Returns: Return complete book if incorrectly supplied (postage paid)
Imperfect Returns: Title page up to £15

SCORPION PUBLISHING

Victoria House, Victoria Road, Buckhurst Hill, Essex
IG9 5ES
ISBN Prefix(es): 0 905906
Tel: 081-506 0606
Fax: 081-506 0553
VAT No: 241 9019 78

Order Information
Teleordering: SCORP

Order Dept Opening Times
Mon - Fri 9am - 5pm
All Dues Automatically Recorded
Representation Available

Personnel
Head of Company: Leonard Harrow/Alan Ball (Directors)
Head of Customer Services: Emma Clark
Other Important Personnel:
James Osgerby (Consultant)

Number of titles published annually: 12
Percentage of Export Sales: 60%
All New Titles are Bar Coded
WBIP Updating: Alan Ball

Trade Terms
35%
Other Terms: Post on single copies and on orders less than £15

Returns Procedures
Stock Returns: Permission required for all returns
Imperfect Returns: All books to be returned

SCOTTISH ACADEMIC PRESS

56 Hanover Street, Edinburgh, Lothian EH2 2DX
ISBN Prefix(es): 0 7073, 0 85621, 1 871
Tel: 031-225 7483
Fax: 031-226 7647
VAT No: 592 9898 56

Order Information
Teleordering: SCOTT

Order Dept Opening Times
Mon - Fri 9am - 1pm, 2pm - 5pm
All Dues Automatically Recorded
Representation Available
Representation:Book Representation & Distribution (BRAD)

Personnel
Head of Company: Dr Douglas Grant
Head of Sales (Home): C Calder
Head of Marketing: K Hunston

Number of titles published annually: 20
Number of Staff: 3
WBIP Updating: Jane Darling

Trade Terms
Large booksellers 35%, Others - One copy 25% plus P&P
Two plus copies 35% post free

Returns Procedures
Authority to Return: Prior permission from Carol Calder
Address for Returns: D & K MacNaughton, Book Warehouse, Unit 2/3 Duns Road, Chirnside Industrial Est, Berwickshire
Imperfect Returns: No Price limit, title pages accepted

SCOTTISH COUNCIL FOR VOLUNTARY ORGANISATIONS

18/19 Claremont Crescent, Edinburgh, Lothian EH7 4QD
Tel: 031-556 3882
Fax: 031-556 0279
VAT No: 446 5610 46

SCOTTISH GENEALOGY SOCIETY

15 Victoria Terrace, Edinburgh, Lothian EH1 2JL
Tel: 031-220 3677

SCOTTISH LIBRARY ASSOCIATION

Motherwell Business Centre, 124/126 Coursington Road, Motherwell, Strathclyde ML1 1PW
Tel: 0698 252527
Fax: 0698 252057
VAT No: 233 1573 87

SCOTTISH TOURIST BOARD

23 Ravelston Terrace, Edinburgh, Lothian EH4 3EU
ISBN Prefix(es): 0 854193
Tel: 031-332 2433
Fax: 031-343 1513
Telex: 72272
VAT No: 270 1061 07

Orders to
EXEL LOGISTICS - MEDIA SERVICES, 3 Sheldon Way, Larkfield, Aylesford, Kent ME20 6SF
Tel: 0622 882000
Fax: 0622 718036

Order Information
All Dues Automatically Recorded
Representation Available
Invoice Payments: Exel Logistics
Sales Representation:AA Publishing (UK & Ireland)

Personnel
Head of Marketing: Norman Chumley (Marketing Director)
Other Important Personnel:
George Anderson

Number of titles published annually: 7
Number of Staff: 100

All New Titles are Bar Coded
WBIP Updating: George Anderson

Trade Terms
See Exel Logistics

Returns Procedures
Authority to Return: See Exel Logistics

SCOTTISH YOUTH HOSTELS ASSOCIATION

7 Glebe Crescent, Stirling, Central FK8 2JA
Tel: 0786 51181
Fax: 0786 50198

THE SCOUT ASSOCIATION

Baden Powell House, Queens Gate, London SW7 5JS
Tel: 071-584 7030
Fax: 071-581 9953

Orders to
Scout Shops Ltd, Churchill Ind Estate, Lancing, West Sussex BN15 8UG
Tel: 0903 755352
Fax: 0903 750993

SCRIPTURE GIFT MISSION

Radstock House, 3 Eccleston Street, London SW1W 9LZ
Tel: 071-730 2155
Fax: 071-730 0240
VAT No: 239 6620 43

Account No: _____
Sales Rep: _____
Tel: _____

Order Information

Order Dept Opening Times
Mon - Fri 9am - 4.30pm
All Dues Automatically Recorded

Personnel
Head of Company: Roger Kennedy (General Secretary)
Head of Sales (Home): Sue French
Head of Sales (Export): Will Delves
Head of Marketing: David Whitfield
Head of Accounts: Robert Merriam

Number of titles published annually: 60
Number of Staff: 80

Trade Terms
31-33% (Posters Only)

SCRIPTURE PRESS FOUNDATION

Unit 8, Raans Road, Amersham-on-the-Hill, Buckinghamshire HP6 6JQ
Tel: 0494 722151
Fax: 0494 726607

Order Information
Teleordering: SCRIPR

Representation Available

Personnel
Head of Company: Mr M J White (Managing Director)
Head of Sales (Home): Mr S J Briars (Sales Director)

Head of Accounts: Mr R St John (Finance Director)
Head of Distribution: Mr A Fox (Distribution Manager)
Head of Customer Services: Mr I B Waterfield (Assistant Managing Director)

Number of Staff: 26

Trade Terms
35%, 30 Days

Returns Procedures
Authority to Return: Mr S J Briars

SCRIPTURE UNION PUBLISHING

130 City Road, London EC1V 2NJ
ISBN Prefix(es): 0 85421, 0 86201
Tel: 071-782 0013
Fax: 071-782 0014
VAT No: 233 4731 80

Account No: _____
Sales Rep: _____
Tel: _____

Orders to
SU Distribution Cent, 9/11 Clothier Road, Bristol, Avon BS4 5RL
Tel: 0272 771131 (24 Hr)
Fax: 0272 711472

Order Information
Teleordering: SU

Order Dept Opening Times
Mon - Fri 8am - 5pm
Orders for more than one publisher can be bulked
All Dues Automatically Recorded
Representation Available
Invoice Payments: SU Accounts Dept, Bristol

Personnel
Head of Company: David Rosser (Publishing Director) Ext 207
Head of Sales (Home): Sandra Millar (Sales & Marketing Manager) Ext 232
Head of Accounts: Peter Shapcott 0272 779371
Head of Distribution: Richard Erickson-Hull (Distribution Manager) 0272 771131
Other Important Personnel:
Eric Lightfoot (Field Sales Manager)

Number of titles published annually: 60
PA Member
NBA Signatory
All New Titles are Bar Coded
WBIP Updating: Elaine Lear

Trade Terms
Books 35%, Periodicals 30%, Audio Visuals 30%, Videos 20%
Other Terms: Small order surcharge under £20 retail 25%
Carriage free within the UK
Credit Cards Accepted: Access/Master, Visa

Returns Procedures
Authority to Return: SU Distribution Centre
Address for Returns: Bristol
Stock Returns: Refer back to appropriate representative
Imperfect Returns: Return title page indicating fault for replacement or credit

SCUTARI PRESS

20 Cavendish Square, London W1M 0AB
Tel: 071-409 3333
Fax: 071-355 1379

Orders to
GAZELLE BOOK SERVICES LTD, Falcon House, Queen Square, Lancaster, Lancashire LA1 1RN
Tel: 0524 68765
Fax: 0524 63232

PA Member
Book Data Subscriber

B A SEABY LTD

7 Davies Street, London W1Y 1LL
Tel: 071-495 2590
Fax: 071-491 1595
VAT No: 417 5974 23

Book Data Subscriber

SEAGULL SA

PO Box 122, Mignot Plateau, St Peter Port, Guernsey
ISBN Prefix(es): 0 905353
Tel: 0481 726641
Fax: 0481 726218
Telex: GUERNSEY 419532

Order Information

Order Dept Opening Times
Mon - Thu 9am - 5pm, Fri 9am - 4.30pm
Trade Counter:London Forwarding, PO Box 74, London SW1X 8AX

Personnel
Head of Company: Avril Evans
Head of Sales (Home): P C Nicholls
Head of Publicity: Anne James
Head of Accounts: M A Morton
Head of Distribution: S West
Head of Customer Services: David Rutherford

Trade Terms
35% on all orders, no surcharges

Returns Procedures
Imperfect Returns: As for overstocks, no price limit

SEARCH PRESS LIMITED

Wellwood, North Farm Road, Tunbridge Wells, Kent TN2 3DR
ISBN Prefix(es): 0 85532, 0 86012
Tel: 0892 510850 24 Hours
Fax: 0892 515903
VAT No: 239 5837 23

Order Information
Teleordering: SEARCH

Order Dept Opening Times
9am - 5pm
All Dues Automatically Recorded
Representation Available

Personnel
Head of Company: Charlotte de la Bedoyere (Managing Director)
Head of Sales (Home): Ruth B Saunders (Director)

Head of Accounts: Paul Watkinson
Head of Distribution: Bernard Grandsion
Head of Customer Services: Val Whitall

Number of titles published annually: 30
Percentage of Export Sales: 40%
Number of Staff: 11
IPG Member
All New Titles are Bar Coded
WBIP Updating: Ruth B Saunders

Trade Terms
35% on all orders above £30 retail value. Orders below £30 reduced discount unless CWO
BA/Girobank Small Order Scheme: Yes
Girobank Number: 537 9350
Credit Cards Accepted: Access/Master, Visa

Returns Procedures
Authority to Return: No returns accepted unless authorized, invoice no's must be quoted
Stock Returns: No claim for damage/non del accepted after 30 days, o'seas 90. Incorrectly supp/damaged bks credited. O'stcks only 50%
Imperfect Returns: Annotated title page of imperfect books may be returned for full credit

DEREK SEARLE ASSOCIATES LTD
Burlington House, 14 High Street, Slough, Berkshire
SL1 1EE
Tel: 0753 539295
Fax: 0753 551863
VAT No: 538 1843 30

Account No: _____

Sales Rep: _____

Tel: _____

Personnel
Head of Company: Derek Searle
Head of Customer Services: June Searle
Other Important Personnel:
Bob Cripps (Key Accounts Sales Manager), Robert Moser (Field Sales Manager)

Trade Terms
35%

Returns Procedures
Authority to Return: Head Office or Representative
Address for Returns: To various distributors

SECKER (Martin) + Warburg = Reed Book Services

SELDEN SOCIETY
Faculty of Laws,, Queen Mary College, Mile End, London
E1 4NS
Tel: 071-975 5136
Fax: 081-981 8733
Telex: 893750

SELECT BOOKS LTD
82 Great Eastern Street, London EC2A 3JL
ISBN Prefix(es): 1 85680
Tel: 071-582 9548
Fax: 071-739 8683

Order Information

Order Dept Opening Times
Mon - Fri 9am - 5pm

Personnel
Head of Company: Bruce Anin-Annor (Managing Director)
Head of Sales (Home): George Armstrong (Sales Manager)

IPG Member
All New Titles are Bar Coded

SEMICON INDEXES

PO Box 470, Lee, London SE12 8AF
ISBN Prefix(es): 0 904944
Tel: 081-852 2309
Fax: 081-852 2309
Telex: 8954111
VAT No: 512 7408 68

Order Information

Order Dept Opening Times
Mon - Fri 9am - 6pm
Cyclical Ordering Policy

Personnel
Head of Company: Mr D Rothschild

Number of titles published annually: 3
Book Data Subscriber

Trade Terms
Non-Net: Single copy/single line 15%, other discounts depend on quantity
Other Terms: First item carriage charged at £3.50, subsequent items + £1

Returns Procedures
Stock Returns: Telephone to request
Imperfect Returns: As above

SEND THE LIGHT

PO Box 300, Kingstown Broadway, Carlisle, Cumbria CA3 0QS
ISBN Prefix(es): 0 85364, 0 903843, 1 85078
Tel: 0228 512512
Tel: 0800 282728 Orders
Fax: 0228 514949
Fax: O800 282530 Orders
VAT No: 205 6950 67

Account No: _____

Sales Rep: _____

Tel: _____

Orders to
Tel: 0800 269601-5
Fax: 0800 282530

Order Information
Teleordering: STL

Order Dept Opening Times
Mon - Thur 9am - 5pm, Fri 9am - 4.30pm
Orders for more than one publisher can be bulked
Representation Available

Personnel
Head of Company: Keith Danby (Chief Executive)
Head of Sales (Home): Daan van Belzen (Sales & Marketing Director)
Head of Sales (Export): Pieter Kwant (Senior Sales Manager)
Head of Accounts: Janet Busk (Director of Finance)
Head of Distribution: Bruce Beattie (General Manager)
Head of Customer Services: Mick Goodman (Customer Support Manager)

Other Important Personnel:
Alan Butler (Sales Manager - (Publishers Representation Group)), Jeremy Mudditt (Publishing Manager - Paternoster Press/OM Publications)

Number of Staff: 150
PA Member
NBA Signatory

Trade Terms
35% on orders over £60 retail, otherwise 5% handling charge - minimum £2

Returns Procedures
Authority to Return: Only with permission from STL Customer Service Department
Imperfect Returns: Title pages to be returned if retail value is less than £10

SERPENT'S TAIL

4 Blackstock Mews, London N4 2BT
ISBN Prefix(es): 1 85242
Tel: 071-354 1949
Fax: 071-704 6467
VAT No: 454 1273 63

Orders to
PLYMBRIDGE DISTRIBUTORS LTD, Plymbridge House, Estover Road, Plymouth, Devon PL6 7PZ
Tel: 0752 735251
Fax: 0752 695699

Order Information

All Dues Automatically Recorded
Representation Available
Invoice Payments: Plymbridge Distributors

Personnel
Head of Company: Peter Ayrton
Head of Sales (Home): John Hampson
Head of Publicity: Becky Shaw

Number of titles published annually: 35
Percentage of Export Sales: 50%
Number of Staff: 4
IPG Member
NBA Signatory
All New Titles are Bar Coded
Book Data Subscriber
WBIP Updating: John Hampson

Trade Terms
35%

Returns Procedures
Address for Returns: Plymbridge Distributors

WILLIAM SESSIONS LTD

The Ebor Press, York, Yorkshire YO3 9HS
ISBN Prefix(es): 0 900657, 1 85072
Tel: 0904 659224
Fax: 0904 644888
Telex: 57712
VAT No: 313 5525 84

Order Information

Order Dept Opening Times
Mon - Fri 8.30am - 4.30pm
All Dues Automatically Recorded
Representation Available

Number of titles published annually: 6

Trade Terms
35%. Orders of more than 20 books or £20 retail value carriage paid.

SETTLE PRESS

10 Boyne Terrace Mews, London W11 3LR
ISBN Prefix(es): 0 907070, 1 872876
Tel: 071-243 0695
VAT No: 340 8242 78

Orders to
BIBLIOS PUBLISHERS DISTRIBUTION SERVICE LTD, Star Road, Partridge Green, West Sussex RH13 8LD
Tel: 0403 710971
Fax: 0403 711143

Order Information

All Dues Automatically Recorded
Representation Available
Invoice Payments: Biblios Publishers Distribution Services Ltd

Personnel
Head of Company: David Settle
Head of Publicity: M Carter

Number of titles published annually: 12
Percentage of Export Sales: 25%
IPG Member
All New Titles are Bar Coded
WBIP Updating: D Settle

Trade Terms
35%, no surcharges
Credit Cards Accepted: Access/Master, Visa

Returns Procedures
Address for Returns: Biblios Publishers Distribution Services Ltd
Stock Returns: Telephone head office
Imperfect Returns: Telephone head office

SEVEN MIRRORS PUBLISHING HOUSE LTD

21 Daleside Avenue, Pudsey, West Yorkshire LS28 8HB
Tel: 0274 662195
Fax: 0274 668554

SEVERN HOUSE PUBLISHERS LTD

1st Floor, 9-15 Sutton High Street, Sutton, Surrey SM1 1DF
ISBN Prefix(es): 0 7278
Tel: 081-770 3930
Fax: 081-770 3850
VAT No: 249 2118 63

Account No: _____
Sales Rep: _____
Tel: _____

Orders to
TIPTREE BOOK SERVICES LTD, Church Road, Tiptree, Colchester, Essex CO5 0SR
Tel: 0621 819600
Fax: 0621 819011

Order Information

Orders for more than one publisher can be bulked
All Dues Automatically Recorded

Representation Available
Invoice Payments: Tiptree

Personnel
Head of Company: Edwin Buckhalter (Chairman)
Head of Sales (Home): Rosalind Wright
Head of Marketing: Angela Herron
Head of Accounts: A J Shaw

Number of titles published annually: 100
NBA Signatory
Book Data Subscriber
WBIP Updating: Samantha Brown

Parent Company: Severn House Books Holdings

Trade Terms
35%
Girobank Number: 304 1255
Credit Cards Accepted: Access/Master, Visa

Returns Procedures
Authority to Return: Prior permission required from Head Office
Address for Returns: Tiptree
Imperfect Returns: Published price up to £12 - title page only
Above £12 letter explaining faults, return finished book

SEWELLS INTERNATIONAL

Dart Business Centre, Dartington, Totnes, South Devon
TQ9 6JE
ISBN Prefix(es): 0 86016
Tel: 0803 867070
Fax: 0803 866507
VAT No: 378 7070 17

Order Information

Order Dept Opening Times
Mon - Fri 9am - 5.30pm

Personnel
Head of Company: Ron Sewell (Chairman)
Head of Sales (Home): Brian Taylor (Director)
Head of Publicity: Alison Ryde (Publicity & Promotions Manager)
Head of Accounts: Chris Lathey (Accountant)
Head of Distribution: Jayne McWatt (Administration & Database Manager)
Other Important Personnel:
Brian Gourlay (Managing Director)

Number of titles published annually: 4
Number of Staff: 22
WBIP Updating: Brian Taylor

Trade Terms
30%
Credit Cards Accepted: Access/Master, Visa, Amex

Returns Procedures
Authority to Return: Brian Taylor

SEYMOUR

Windsor House, 1270 London Road, Norbury, London
SW16 4DH
Tel: 081-679 1899
Fax: 081-679 8907
Telex: 8812945

SFIA EDUCATIONAL TRUST LTD

15 Forelease Road, Maidenhead, Berkshire SL6 1JA
ISBN Prefix(es): 0 906695
Tel: 0628 34291
Fax: 0628 770447
VAT No: 442 4024 88

Order Information

Order Dept Opening Times
Mon - Fri 9am - 5pm

Personnel
Head of Company: Claire Tyrrell (Editor - Book Department)

Trade Terms
25%, 10 or more copies 35%

SHAKTI COMMUNICATION LTD

Unit 28a, Pop In Building, South Way, Wembley, Middlesex HA9 0HB
ISBN Prefix(es): 0 7128, 0 9505
Tel: 081-903 5442
Fax: 081-903 4684

Personnel
Head of Company: Mr R K Jain

Number of titles published annually: 5
Open University Publications

Trade Terms
33.5%
General Net: Single copy 25% + Postage, Two or more books 33.3%
Other Terms: Orders £25 or under will be charged for P&P

Returns Procedures
Imperfect Returns: Return the book with note.

SHANTI SADAN

29 Chepstow Villas, London W11 3DR
Tel: 071-727 7846
Fax: 071-792 9817

SHARE INTERNATIONAL

59 Dartmouth Park Road, London NW5 1SL
Fax: 071-482 1113

Order Information

Order Dept Opening Times
Fax & Mail Order only
All Dues Automatically Recorded
Representation Available

Personnel
Head of Company: Benjamin Creme

Trade Terms
30%
Minimum Order: Three copies

SHARON PUBLICATIONS LTD

49 Coxtie Green Road, Brentwood, Essex CM14 5PS
ISBN Prefix(es): 1 871367
Tel: 0277 373436

Fax: 0277 372225
VAT No: 501 2848 42

Order Information

Representation Available

Personnel
Head of Company: Michael Reid
Head of Sales (Home): Sharon Yaroy
Head of Sales (Export): Carolyn Linnecar
Head of Marketing: Norman Yaroy
Head of Publicity: Meidre Cleminson
Head of Accounts: Melvyn Cooper
Head of Distribution: Tommy Johnson
Head of Customer Services: Diane Wilkinson

Number of titles published annually: 3
NBA Signatory
All New Titles are Bar Coded
WBIP Updating: Meidre Cleminson

Trade Terms
Variable
Other Terms: Carriage charges on small orders

Returns Procedures
Authority to Return: Phyllis Crowley

SHAW & SONS LTD

Shaway House, 21 Bourne Park, Bourne Road, Crayford, Kent DA1 4BZ
ISBN Prefix(es): 0 7219
Tel: 0322 550676
Fax: 0322 550 553
VAT No: 220 0983 01

PA Member
NBA Signatory
Book Data Subscriber

SHEAF PUBLISHING LTD

35 Mooroaks Road, Sheffield, South Yorkshire S10 1BX
Tel: 0742 739067
VAT No: 308 4434 69

SHEARWATER PRESS LIMITED

4 Auckland Terrace, Ramsey, Isle of Man
ISBN Prefix(es): 0 904980
Tel: 0624 812114
Fax: 0624 15525

Personnel
Head of Company: P Crellin

Number of titles published annually: 1
Number of Staff: 2
IPG Member
NBA Signatory
All New Titles are Bar Coded

Trade Terms
General Net: Single copy/single line 30%, 2 books or more 35%
Other Terms: Carriage charged at cost

Returns Procedures
Imperfect Returns: Return title page

SHEED & WARD LTD

14 Coopers Row, London EC3N 2BH
ISBN Prefix(es): 0 7220
Tel: 071-702 9799
Fax: 071-702 3583
VAT No: 239 4349 41

Account No: _____

Sales Rep: _____

Tel: _____

Order Information
Teleordering: SHEED

Cyclical Ordering Policy
Orders for more than one publisher can be bulked
All Dues Automatically Recorded

Personnel
Head of Company: Martin T Redfern
Head of Accounts: Les Nunn

Number of titles published annually: 6
Percentage of Export Sales: 50%
Number of Staff: 3
All New Titles are Bar Coded
WBIP Updating: Martin Redfern

Trade Terms
Single copy 25%, Two or more 35%
Other Terms: Small order surcharge of £1.50 on net order value under £15
Girobank Number: 578 9359
Credit Cards Accepted: Access/Master, Visa, Amex

Returns Procedures
Address for Returns: Sheed & Ward, c/o Trade Counter Ltd, The Airfield, Norwich Road, Mendlesham, Suffolk IP13 5NA
Stock Returns: Title page & invoice no to head office address
Imperfect Returns: Title page & invoice no to head office address £15

SHEFFIELD ACADEMIC PRESS

343 Fulwood Road, Sheffield, South Yorkshire S10 3BP
ISBN Prefix(es): 0 90577, 1 85075
Tel: 0742 670043
Tel: 0742 670044 24 Hr Sale
Tel: 0742 668431
Fax: 0742 660291
Telex: 547216 UGSHEF G
VAT No: 308 2693 55

Order Information

Order Dept Opening Times
Mon - Fri 9am - 4.30pm

Personnel
Head of Company: Jean Allen (General Manager)
Head of Sales (Home): Sylvia Sanderson (Sales Office Supervisor)
Head of Marketing: Anne Dolling (Assistant General Manager)
Other Important Personnel:
Dr Andrew Kirk (Senior Editor)

Number of titles published annually: 70
Percentage of Export Sales: 50%
Number of Staff: 16
WBIP Updating: Maureen Allum

Trade Terms
BA/Girobank Small Order Scheme: Yes
Girobank Number: 63 535 0009
Credit Cards Accepted: Access/Master, Visa

SHELF PUBLISHING

6 St Albans Road, Codicote, Hitchin, Hertfordshire
SG4 8UT
Tel: 0438 820059
Fax: 0438 821015
VAT No: 563 3134 58

IPG Member

SHELWING LTD

127 Sandgate Road, Folkestone, Kent CT20 2BL
ISBN Prefix(es): 0 561
Tel: 0303 850501 24 Hours
Fax: 0303 850162
VAT No: 332 9417 59

Account No: _____ 00094-128 _____
Sales Rep: _____
Tel: _____

Order Information
Teleordering: SHELWNG

Order Dept Opening Times
Mon - Fri 8.30am- 1pm 1.45pm - 4.30pm

Personnel
Head of Company: Mr J R Bailey (Managing Director)
Head of Sales (Home): Iris Farrar/Vi Arnold
Head of Marketing: Eileen Marshall (Publicity Manager)
Head of Accounts: John D Poole (General Manager)

Number of Staff: 18
WBIP Updating: Eileen Marshall

Subsidiary Companies: Bailey Management Services, Creative Colour

Trade Terms
Bailey Bros & Swinfen 1/2 copy 25%, 3 or more 35%, McFarland 20%, Scarecrow 20% (1 or more books)
Girobank Number: 309 5592

Returns Procedures
Authority to Return: Prior authorisation required from Sales Dept
Address for Returns: Shelwing Ltd, 4 Pleydell Gardens, Folkestone, Kent CT20 2DN Tel: 0303 850501 Fax: 0303 850162
Imperfect Returns: Complete books must be returned

SHEPHEARD-WALWYN (PUBLISHERS) LTD

Suite 34, 26 Charing Cross Road, London WC2H 0DH
ISBN Prefix(es): 0 85683
Tel: 071-240 5992
Fax: 071-379 5770
VAT No: 233 6738 56

Account No: _____
Sales Rep: _____
Tel: _____

Orders to
BAILEY DISTRIBUTION LTD, Unit 1, Learoyd Road, Mountfield Rd Ind Est, New Romney, Kent TN28 8XU
Tel: 0679 66905
Fax: 0679 66638

Order Information

All Dues Automatically Recorded
Representation Available
Invoice Payments: Bailey Distribution Ltd

Personnel
Head of Company: Anthony Werner
Head of Sales (Home): Georgina Melville
Head of Publicity: Alan Martin
Head of Accounts: Les Nunn
Head of Customer Services: Patricia Thomas

Number of titles published annually: 6
Number of Staff: 3
IPG Member
NBA Signatory
All New Titles are Bar Coded
Book Data Subscriber
WBIP Updating: A Werner

Trade Terms
Single Copy 25%, Two or more 35%, CWO 30%. Special orders negotiable
Girobank Number: 535 7055
Credit Cards Accepted: Access/Master, Visa

Returns Procedures
Authority to Return: Prior permission required from Head Office
Address for Returns: Bailey Distribution
Imperfect Returns: Send title page (up to £20) or book to Head Office

SHERBOURNE PUBLICATIONS

Sherbourne, Sweeney Mountain, Oswestry, Shropshire SY10 9EX
Tel: 0691 657853
VAT No: 549 4123 36

IPG Member

JOHN SHERRATT & SON LTD

Hotspur House, 2 Cambridge Street, Manchester, Greater Manchester M1 5QR
Tel: 061-236 9963
Fax: 061-236 2026
VAT No: 150 2396 90

Orders to
John Sherratt & Son, 78 Park Row, Timperley, Altrincham, Cheshire WA14 5QQ
Tel: 061-973 5711

SHERWOOD FOREST (PUBLISHERS)

PO Box 10, Nottingham, Nottinghamshire NG1 1LZ
Tel: 0602 200010

SHETLAND TIMES LTD

Prince Alfred Street, Lerwick, Shetland ZE1 0EP
ISBN Prefix(es): 0 900662
Tel: 0595 3622
Fax: 0595 4637
VAT No: 266 0706 60

Orders to
Shetland Times Bksp, 71-79 Commercial Street, Lerwick, Shetland ZE1 0AJ

Tel: 0595 5531
Fax: 0595 2897

Order Information

Order Dept Opening Times
Mon - Sat 9am - 5pm
All Dues Automatically Recorded
Representation Available

Personnel

Head of Company: Mr Robert Wishart (Managing Director)
Head of Accounts: Mrs June Wishart (Company Secretary)
Other Important Personnel:
Mrs Beatrice Nisbet (Publications Manager)

Number of titles published annually: 8
PA Member
NBA Signatory
All New Titles are Bar Coded
WBIP Updating: Mrs Beatrice Nisbet

Trade Terms

35%
General Net: Single Copy 25%
Other Terms: Carriage charged for orders under £30 retail value
Credit Cards Accepted: Access/Master, Visa

Returns Procedures

Authority to Return: Authorisation required from Beatrice Nisbet
Address for Returns: Commercial Street
Stock Returns: No single copy returns accepted. Returns under £30 retail value subject to a £2.50 handling charge
Imperfect Returns: Contact for authorisation first

SHIP PICTORIAL PUBLICATIONS

3 College Close, Coltishall, Norfolk NR12 7DT
ISBN Prefix(es): 0 9516038
Tel: 0603 738577

Order Information

Representation Available

Personnel

Head of Company: A S Mallett
Other Important Personnel:
S Benz

Number of titles published annually: 3
Percentage of Export Sales: 20%
All New Titles are Bar Coded
WBIP Updating: A S Mallett

Trade Terms

1-3 copies 25%, 4 or more copies 35%

Returns Procedures

Authority to Return: Prior permission required
Stock Returns: Must be in mint condition
Imperfect Returns: Return immediately

HILARY SHIPMAN

19 Framfield Road, London N5 1UU
ISBN Prefix(es): 0 948096
Tel: 071-226 0246
VAT No: 396 6207 19

Order Information

Order Dept Opening Times
Mon - Fri 9.30am - 5pm

All Dues Automatically Recorded
Representation Available

Personnel
Head of Company: Hilary Macaskill
Head of Sales (Home): Michael Shipman

Number of titles published annually: 3
All New Titles are Bar Coded
WBIP Updating: Hilary Macaskill

Trade Terms
General Net: Single Copy 25% cwo 35% Two Books or more 35%
Other Terms: Carriage charges: Postage & packing on all overseas orders

Returns Procedures
Stock Returns: Accepted by prior arrangement with publisher
Imperfect Returns: Title page & cover up to £10 retail value;full copy over £10

SHIRE PUBLICATIONS LTD

Cromwell House, Church Street, Princes Risborough, Buckinghamshire HP27 9AJ
ISBN Prefix(es): 0 7478, 0 85263
Tel: 08444 4301
Fax: 08444 7080
VAT No: 194 7086 28

Account No: _____

Sales Rep: _____

Tel: _____

Order Information

All Dues Automatically Recorded
Representation Available

Personnel
Head of Company: John Rotheroe
Head of Sales (Home): Sue Ross
Head of Publicity: Patience Dizon

Number of titles published annually: 30
Number of Staff: 14
All New Titles are Bar Coded
WBIP Updating: Nicholas Christelow

Trade Terms
General Net: Single copy/single line 25%, 2 or more single titles 33.3%
Girobank Number: 30 842 0004

Returns Procedures
Authority to Return: No authority required

SHROPSHIRE BOOKS

Winston Churchill Buildings, Radbrook Centre, Radbrook Rd, Shrewsbury, Shropshire SY3 9BJ
ISBN Prefix(es): 0 903802
Tel: 0743 254043
Fax: 0743 254047

Order Information

Order Dept Opening Times
Mon - Fri 9am - 5pm
All Dues Automatically Recorded
Representation Available
Invoice Payments: Shropshire County Council

Personnel
Head of Company: Helen Sample (Managing Editor)

Other Important Personnel:
Judy Richards (Order Department)

Number of titles published annually: 6
WBIP Updating: Helen Sample

Parent Company: Shropshire County Council

Trade Terms
33.3%
Other Terms: Carriage charges 15% of order

Returns Procedures
Stock Returns: Permission must be sought for all returns
Imperfect Returns: Any imperfect copies over £10 retail should be returned. Title page only for under £10

SIDGWICK & JACKSON

18/21 Cavaye Place, Fulham Road, London SW10 9PG
ISBN Prefix(es): 0 283
Tel: 071-373 6070
Fax: 071-370 0746

Account No: _____
Sales Rep: _____
Tel: _____

Orders to
MACMILLAN DISTRIBUTION LTD, Brunel Road, Houndmills Industrial Estate, Basingstoke, Hampshire RG21 2XS
Tel: 0256 29242
Fax: 0256 842084

Order Information

Representation Available
Sales Representation:Macmillan

Personnel
Head of Company: William Armstrong (Managing Director)
Head of Publicity: Philippa McEwan (Publicity Director)

All New Titles are Bar Coded
Book Data Subscriber
WBIP Updating: Alison Muirden

Trade Terms
35%
Other Terms: Carriage 10% unless over £75
Credit Cards Accepted: Access/Master, Visa

Returns Procedures
Authority to Return: Sales Department or Rep
Address for Returns: Basingstoke
Stock Returns: Contact Customer Services Basingstoke

SIGMA LEISURE

1 South Oak Lane, Wilmslow, Cheshire SK9 6AR
ISBN Prefix(es): 0 905104, 1 85058
Tel: 0625 531035 24 Hour
Fax: 0625 536800

Order Information

Order Dept Opening Times
9am - 6pm
All Dues Automatically Recorded
Representation Available

Personnel
Head of Company: Dr Graham Beech
Head of Accounts: Diana Beech

Number of titles published annually: 80
Number of Staff: 4
IPG Member
All New Titles are Bar Coded
WBIP Updating: Annie Eastwood

Parent Company: Sigma Press

Trade Terms
25% + Postage, Two books or more 30%
Credit Cards Accepted: Access/Master, Visa

Returns Procedures
Authority to Return: Requests to Sigma Press
Imperfect Returns: Send cover page

SIGMA PRESS

1 South Oak Lane, Wilmslow, Cheshire SK9 6AR
ISBN Prefix(es): 0 905104, 1 85058
Tel: 0625 531035
Fax: 0625-536800

Orders to
JOHN WILEY & SONS LTD, Southern Cross Trading Estate, 1 Oldlands Way, Bognor Regis, West Sussex PO22 9SA
Tel: 0243 829121
Fax: 0243 820250

Order Information

All Dues Automatically Recorded
Representation Available

Personnel
Head of Company: Dr Graham Beech
Head of Accounts: Diana Beech

Number of titles published annually: 80
IPG Member
All New Titles are Bar Coded
WBIP Updating: Annie Eastwood

Trade Terms
General Net: single copy/single line 25% + postage, 2 books or more 30%

SILCO BOOKS LTD

7 Russell Gardens, London NW11 9NJ
Tel: 081-455 0716
Fax: 081-458 6478
VAT No: 229 6080 56

Account No: _____
Sales Rep: _____
Tel: _____

Order Information
Teleordering: SILCO

SILENT BOOKS

Boxworth End, Swavesey, Cambridge, Cambridgeshire CB4 5RA
ISBN Prefix(es): 1 85183
Tel: 0954 32199
Tel: 0954 31000 24 Hours
Fax: 0954 32199
VAT No: 393 2995 06

Order Information

Order Dept Opening Times
Mon - Fri 9am - 5pm
All Dues Automatically Recorded
Representation Available

Personnel
Head of Company: Carole A Green (Managing Director)
Head of Accounts: Derek Hedges (Bookkeeper)

Number of titles published annually: 10
Percentage of Export Sales: 20%
Number of Staff: 5
PA Member
NBA Signatory
All New Titles are Bar Coded
WBIP Updating: Kate Duncan

Trade Terms
General Net: 35%
Other Terms: P+P on single copy orders in UK and on all overseas orders, including Eire

Returns Procedures
Authority to Return: Authorised returns only, must be in mint condition (subject to inspection)
Imperfect Returns: Title page up to £10 published price

SILVER LINK PUBLISHING LTD

Unit 5, Home Farm Close, Church Street, Wadenhoe, Peterborough PE8 5TE
ISBN Prefix(es): 0 947971, 1 857940
Tel: 08015 440 Tel/Fax
VAT No: 551 0082 85

Orders to
BOOKPOINT LIMITED, 39 Milton Park, Abingdon, Oxfordshire OX14 4TD
Tel: 0235 835001
Fax: 0235 861038

Order Information

All Dues Automatically Recorded
Representation Available
Invoice Payments: Bookpoint Distribution Ltd
Representation:Ian Allan Publishing

Other Important Locations
Reg Office:The Trundle, Ringstead Road, Great Addington, Kettering, Northants NN14 4BN Tel/Fax:053678-648

Personnel
Head of Company: Peter Townsend
Other Important Personnel:
Louise Townsend (Production & Sales Co-ordinator), Michael Sanders (Production Manager)

Number of titles published annually: 35
Number of Staff: 4
NBA Signatory
All New Titles are Bar Coded
WBIP Updating: Louise Townsend

Trade Terms
35% for all orders over £25.

Returns Procedures
Authority to Return: Specialist Book Sales/Ian Allan Ltd, Terminal House Shepperton, Middlesex
Address for Returns: Bookpoint Distribution Ltd
Stock Returns: All returns must be authorized by representative, or Bookpoint Dist in the case of books damaged in transit
Imperfect Returns: Send title page up to £10 retail. Complete book over £10 to Bookpoint Dist

SILVER MOON BOOKS

68 Charing Cross Road, London WC2H 0BB
ISBN Prefix(es): 1 872642
Tel: 071-836 7906
Fax: 071-379 1018
VAT No: 539 2061 49

Orders to
AIRLIFT BOOK COMPANY, 26/28 Eden Grove, London N7 8EF
Tel: 071-607 5792
Fax: 071-607 6714

Order Information

All Dues Automatically Recorded
Representation Available
Invoice Payments: Airlift Book Company

Personnel
Head of Company: Sue Butterworth
Head of Sales (Home): Jane Cholmeley
Head of Distribution: Beth Grossman

Number of titles published annually: 4
All New Titles are Bar Coded
WBIP Updating: Jane Cholmeley

Trade Terms
35% for orders over £25 retail. 25% prepaid orders under £25 retail.
Girobank Number: 57 273 4204
Credit Cards Accepted: Access/Master, Visa

Returns Procedures
Authority to Return: Airlift Book Company
Address for Returns: Airlift Book Company
Stock Returns: Errors to be notified within 7 days and authorized. Accepted after 90 days up to 6 months. 60% credit on damaged o'stocks
Imperfect Returns: Annotated title pages only for £20 retail or under.

SILVEY-JEX PUBLICATIONS LTD

14 Chaldon Road, London SW6 7NJ
ISBN Prefix(es): 0 907280
Tel: 071-385 7194 24 Hours
VAT No: 340 3497 70

Order Information

Order Dept Opening Times
Mon - Fri 9am - 6pm
All Dues Automatically Recorded
Representation Available

Personnel
Head of Company: Sara Geers (Director)
Head of Sales (Home): Robert E Geers (Director)
Head of Publicity: W Jex (Director)

Number of titles published annually: 2
Number of Staff: 4
All New Titles are Bar Coded
WBIP Updating: Sara Geers

Trade Terms
35% except where negotiated

Returns Procedures
Authority to Return: Sara Geers
Stock Returns: Telephone first

SIMON & SCHUSTER INTERNATIONAL GROUP

Campus 400, Maylands Avenue, Hemel Hempstead, Hertfordshire HP2 7EL
ISBN Prefix(es): 0 08, 0 13, 0 671, 0 7108, 0 7450, 0 8077, 0 85527, 0 87766, 0 901759
Tel: 0442 881900 24 Hours
Fax: 0442 882090
Telex: 82445

Account No: _____

Sales Rep: _____

Tel: _____

Orders to
INTERNATIONAL BOOK DISTRIBUTORS, Campus 400, Maylands Avenue, Hemel Hempstead, Hertfordshire HP2 7EZ
Tel: 0442 881900
Fax: 0442 882099

Order Information

All Dues Automatically Recorded
Representation Available

Personnel
Head of Company: Frans Gianotten (President, International Group)
Head of Sales (Home): Jeff Scott (UK Sales Manager)
Head of Sales (Export): Charles Gibbes (Sales Director)
Head of Marketing: John Wilson (Marketing Director)
Head of Accounts: Jeremy Moss (Chief Financial Officer)
Other Important Personnel:
Gerard Kelly (Sales Manager, Simon & Schuster Young Books), Philippa Stewart (Publisher, Simon & Schuster Young Books), Caroline Somerset (Publicity, Simon & Schuster Young Books)

Number of titles published annually: 2000
Percentage of Export Sales: 60%
PA Member
NBA Signatory
All New Titles are Bar Coded
Open University Publications
Book Data Subscriber

Parent Company: Paramount Communications

Trade Terms
Variable
Credit Cards Accepted: Access/Master, Visa, Amex, Diners, Other

Returns Procedures
Authority to Return: IBD
Address for Returns: IBD

SIMON & SCHUSTER LTD

West Garden Place, Kendal Street, London W2 2AQ
ISBN Prefix(es): 0 13, 0 671, 0 85941
Tel: 071-724 7577
Fax: 071-402 0639

Account No: _____

Sales Rep: _____

Tel: _____

Orders to
INTERNATIONAL BOOK DISTRIBUTORS, Campus 400, Maylands Avenue, Hemel Hempstead, Hertfordshire HP2 7EZ
Tel: 0442 881900
Fax: 0442 882099

Order Information

All Dues Automatically Recorded
Representation Available
Invoice Payments: IBD

Personnel

Head of Company: Nick Webb
Head of Sales (Home): Keith Barnes
Head of Sales (Export): Jonathan Atkins
Head of Marketing: Julian Clayton
Head of Publicity: Mark McCallum
Head of Accounts: Stephen Roberts
Head of Customer Services: Mike Walford

Number of titles published annually: 65
Percentage of Export Sales: 30%
Number of Staff: 35
PA Member
NBA Signatory
All New Titles are Bar Coded
Book Data Subscriber
WBIP Updating: Nikki Schuster

Parent Company: Paramount Communications

Trade Terms

35% on all orders no surcharges
Credit Cards Accepted: Access/Master, Visa, Amex, Diners

Returns Procedures

Authority to Return: Keith Barnes, London
Address for Returns: IBD
Stock Returns: Sales office or representative must authorise returns except damaged or incorrectly supplied.

[handwritten: Sinclair-Stevenson = Tiptree]

STEVEN SIMPSON NATURAL HISTORY BOOKS

PO Box 853, Brighton, East Sussex BN1 5DY
Tel: 0273 727328
Fax: 0273 203754

[handwritten: SINAUGE = Marston]

SKELLIG PRESS

2 The Crescent, Monkstown, County Dublin
ISBN Prefix(es): 0 946241
Tel: 01 280 5930
Fax: 01 280 6020

Order Information

All Dues Automatically Recorded
Representation Available

Personnel

Head of Company: Robert Towers

Number of titles published annually: 2

Trade Terms

35%
Other Terms: Carriage charged - single book

Returns Procedures

Stock Returns: Permission needed in advance
Imperfect Returns: Annotated title page

CHARLES SKILTON LTD

2 Caversham Street, London SW3 4AH
Tel: 071-351 4995 Tel/Fax

SLACK Inc = Marston (handwritten)

SLG PRESS
Convent of the Incarnation, Fairacres, Oxford, Oxfordshire OX4 1TB
ISBN Prefix(es): 0 7283
Tel: 0865 721301

Order Information
Order Dept Opening Times
Mon - Sat 10.30am - 5.30pm

Personnel
Head of Company: Sister Christine J South (Sister in Charge of Press)

Number of titles published annually: 3
Number of Staff: 4

Trade Terms
33.3% on orders for resale. Postage on orders (inland) on orders under £40 invoice value.
Other Terms: P&P on invoices under £40

Returns Procedures
Imperfect Returns: Return whole book for replacement

BRUCE SMITH BOOKS LTD
PO Box 382, St Albans, Hertfordshire AL2 3JD
Tel: 0923 894355
Fax: 0923 894366
VAT No: 600 5400 08

Orders to
COMPUTER BOOKSHOPS LTD, 50 James Road, Tyseley, Birmingham, West Midlands B11 2BA
Tel: 021-706 1250
Fax: 021-706 3301

OWEN SMITH LTD
PO Box 38, Bordon, Hampshire GU35 8LQ
Tel: 0428 712892 Tel/Fax
VAT No: 582 6341 30

SMITH GRYPHON LTD
Swallow House, 11-21 Northdown Street, London N1 9BN
ISBN Prefix(es): 1 85685
Tel: 071-278 2444
Fax: 071-278 1677
VAT No: 577 4636 95

Orders to
TIPTREE BOOK SERVICES LTD, Church Road, Tiptree, Colchester, Essex CO5 0SR
Tel: 0621 819600
Fax: 0621 819011

Order Information
All Dues Automatically Recorded
Representation Available
Invoice Payments: Tiptree

Personnel
Head of Company: Robert Smith (Chairman & Managing Director)
Head of Publicity: Colbert MacAlister 081-675 9155
Head of Accounts: Anne Smith

Number of titles published annually: 20
Percentage of Export Sales: 20%

All New Titles are Bar Coded
WBIP Updating: Robert Smith

Trade Terms
35%

Returns Procedures
Authority to Return: Prior permission required
Address for Returns: Tiptree

SMITH SETTLE LTD

Ilkley Road, Otley, West Yorkshire LS21 3JP
ISBN Prefix(es): 1 85825, 1 870071
Tel: 0943 467958 24 Hours
Fax: 0943 850057
VAT No: 447 7506 25

Order Information

Order Dept Opening Times
Mon - Thu 8am - 5pm, Fri 8am - 4pm
Cyclical Ordering Policy
All Dues Automatically Recorded
Representation Available

Personnel
Head of Company: Ken Smith
Head of Sales (Home): Mark Whitley
Head of Accounts: Mrs Linda Ainley
Head of Customer Services: Miss Tracie Havery

Number of titles published annually: 12
Number of Staff: 3
NBA Signatory
All New Titles are Bar Coded
WBIP Updating: Mark Whitley

Trade Terms
25% single copy, 35% multiple copy, carriage charged on orders under £25 retail
Credit Cards Accepted: Access/Master, Visa

Returns Procedures
Authority to Return: Prior permission is required
Stock Returns: Incorrectly supplied books return for credit. Overstocks contact pub perm to return. Damaged in transit contact pub
Imperfect Returns: Return title pages for credit

COLIN SMYTHE LTD

PO Box 6, Gerrards Cross, Buckinghamshire SL9 8XA
ISBN Prefix(es): 0 85105, 0 86140, 0 900675, 0 901072
Tel: 0753 886000
Fax: 0753 886469
VAT No: 285 2792 23

Order Information
Teleordering: COLSMY

Order Dept Opening Times
Weekdays 9.30am - 5.30pm
All Dues Automatically Recorded

Personnel
Head of Company: Colin Smythe

Number of titles published annually: 15
Percentage of Export Sales: 60%
Number of Staff: 2
PA Member
IPG Member
WBIP Updating: Colin Smythe

Trade Terms
Single copy 25% Two or more 35% All pre-paid orders 35%
50p-£1.25 charged according to weight on invoices under £30
Girobank Number: 284 9151
Credit Cards Accepted: Access/Master, Visa

Returns Procedures
Authority to Return: Colin Smythe
Address for Returns: Clipper Distribution Services Ltd
Stock Returns: Incorrectly supplied/damaged books return to Clipper for replacement. Overstocks Authority to be obtained first.
Imperfect Returns: Return title page to Gerrards Cross and a replacement will be sent.

WILLIAM SNYDER PUBLISHING ASSOCIATES

5 Five Mile Drive, Oxford, Oxfordshire OX2 8HT
Tel: 0865 513186 Tel/Fax
VAT No: 596 2424 15

Order Information

Orders for more than one publisher can be bulked
All Dues Automatically Recorded
Representation Available

Personnel
Head of Company: William A Snyder

Book Data Subscriber

Trade Terms
According to companies/product
Credit Cards Accepted: Access/Master, Visa

SOCIAL CARE ASSOCIATION (EDUCATION) LTD

23A Victoria Road, Surbiton, Surrey KT6 4JZ
ISBN Prefix(es): 0 901244
Tel: 081-390 6831 24 Hours
Fax: 081-399 6183

Order Information

Order Dept Opening Times
9.30am - 4.45pm
All Dues Automatically Recorded

Personnel
Head of Company: Richard Clough
Head of Accounts: Nicola Lewis

Number of titles published annually: 4
WBIP Updating: R Clough

Trade Terms
33.3%
Minimum Order: Cheque with order below £50
Credit Cards Accepted: Access/Master, Visa

SOCIAL WORK MONOGRAPHS

University of East Anglia, Norwich, Norfolk NR4 7TJ
Tel: 0603 592087
Fax: 0603 250434

SOCIETY FOR PROMOTING CHRISTIAN KNOWLEDGE (SPCK)

Holy Trinity Church, Marylebone Road, London NW1 4DU
ISBN Prefix(es): 0 281, 0 85969

Tel: 071-387 5282
Fax: 071-388 2352
VAT No: 232 8071 82

Account No: _____
Sales Rep: _____
Tel: _____

Orders to
SPCK Trade Dept, 7 Castle Street, Reading, Berkshire
RG1 7SB
Tel: 0734 599011
Fax: 0734 599240

Order Information
Teleordering: SPCK

Order Dept Opening Times
Mon - Fri 8.45am - 4.45pm
All Dues Automatically Recorded
Representation Available
Invoice Payments: SPCK

Other Important Locations
Warehouse:13 Markham Centre, Station Road, Theale, Berks

Tel: 0734 323667

Personnel
Head of Company: P G Chandler (General Secretary)
Head of Sales (Home): Brian Keen
Head of Publicity: Christopher Child
Head of Accounts: Frances Williams
Head of Distribution: Roger Corner 0734 323667
Head of Customer Services: Mrs P Bennett 0734 599011

Number of titles published annually: 100
Percentage of Export Sales: 20%
Number of Staff: 35
PA Member
NBA Signatory
All New Titles are Bar Coded
WBIP Updating: Miss L Shapiro

Trade Terms
35% post/packing charge below £30 invoice value
Other Terms: Small order surcharge none on cash with order.
Carriage charged on any order under £30 inv value
Girobank Number: 540 1453

Returns Procedures
Authority to Return: Brian Keen, Head Office
Address for Returns: SPCK Distribution Centre
Stock Returns: Prior authorisation from Sales Manager
Imperfect Returns: Up to £20 retail annotated title pages;
over £20 retail complete books.

SOCIETY FOR THE PROMOTION OF ROMAN STUDIES

31-34 Gordon Square, London WC1H 0PP
ISBN Prefix(es): 0 907764
Tel: 071-387 8157 24 Hours
VAT No: 233 4855 62

Order Information

Order Dept Opening Times
Tue - Fri 9.30am - 4.30pm

Personnel
Head of Company: Dr Helen M Cockle (Secretary)

Number of titles published annually: 1
Percentage of Export Sales: 30%
Number of Staff: 1
WBIP Updating: Dr Lynn F Pitts

Trade Terms
33.3% on all orders
Girobank Number: 58 743 4201

SOCIETY FOR THE PROTECTION OF ANCIENT BUILDINGS

(Wind and Watermill Section), 37 Spital Square, London E1 6DY
Tel: 071-377 1644
Fax: 071-247 5296

THE SOCIETY FOR THEATRE RESEARCH

c/o The Theatre Museum, 1E Tavistock Street, London WC2E 7PA

SOCIETY OF GENEALOGISTS

14 Charterhouse Buildings, Goswell Road, London EC1M 7BA
ISBN Prefix(es): 0 901878, 0 946789
Tel: 071-251 8799
VAT No: 240 6070 02

Order Information

Order Dept Opening Times
Tue - Fri 10am - 5.30pm

Personnel
Head of Company: Anthony Camp (Director & Secretary)
Head of Sales (Home): Mrs Mary Gandy (Publications Manager)
Head of Accounts: Michael McEvoy (Finance Officer)
Head of Customer Services: Mrs Barbara Merrall (Publications Assistant)

Number of titles published annually: 7
WBIP Updating: Mrs Mary Gandy

Trade Terms
33.3% on total order value over £10. 10% on other pubs books 25% (+P&P) on order value up to £10.

Returns Procedures
Stock Returns: Return book in saleable condition; refund or replacement will be supplied
Imperfect Returns: Return books; replacement will be supplied

SOCIETY OF METAPHYSICIANS LTD

Archers' Court, Stonestile Lane, The Ridge, Hastings, East Sussex TN35 4PG
Tel: 0424 751577
Fax: 0424 722387
VAT No: 202 0360 39

SOCIETY OF MOTOR MANUFACTURERS & TRADERS LTD

Forbes House, Halkin Street, London SW1X 7DS
Tel: 071-235 7000
Fax: 071-235 7112
Telex: 21628

SODANEY PUBLISHERS

PO Box 282, London SW15 4HJ
Tel: 081-788 8186

Number of titles published annually: 2
Number of Staff: 3

Trade Terms
General Net: 35%
Non-Net: 17.5%

SOLO BOOKS LTD

49-53 Kensington High Street, London W8 5ED
ISBN Prefix(es): 1 873939
Tel: 071-376 2166
Fax: 071-938 3165

Trade Terms
40%

SOLOMON INTERNATIONAL PUBLISHING CO

Donna Dene, Bridge Road, Burlesdon, Southampton, Hampshire SO3 8AH
Tel: 0703 403152
Fax: 0703 642267

Personnel
Head of Company: D J Gannaway (Managing Director)

Trade Terms
35%
Other Terms: Pro-forma on singles

SOUTHERN COLLECTORS PUBLICATIONS

9 Bedford Place, Southampton, Hampshire SO1 2DB
ISBN Prefix(es): 0 905438
Tel: 0703 223255
Fax: 0703 335634
VAT No: 320 5701 04

Order Information

Order Dept Opening Times
Tues - Sat 9am - 5pm

Personnel
Head of Company: A D Chandos-Adams

Number of titles published annually: 1

Trade Terms
20%
Credit Cards Accepted: Access/Master, Visa, Amex, Diners

[handwritten: Southern Illinois UP - FAX 0101 618 453 1221]

SOUTHPORT BOOK DISTRIBUTORS LIMITED

12/14 Slaidburn Crescent, Southport, Merseyside PR9 9YF
Tel: 0704 24331
Tel: 0704 26881
Fax: 0704 231970
Telex: 67457
VAT No: 213 6785 61

Account No: _____

Sales Rep: _____

Tel: _____

Order Information
Teleordering: PIT

Personnel
Head of Company: David Evans (Distribution Director)
Head of Customer Services: Martin Pickford (Customer Services Manager)
Other Important Personnel:
Tom Ball (Warehouse Manager)

Number of Staff: 35
PA Member

Parent Company: Longman Group UK

SOUVENIR PRESS LTD
43 Great Russell Street, London WC1B 3PA
ISBN Prefix(es): 0 285
Tel: 071-580 9307/8
Tel: 071-637 5711/2/3
Fax: 071-580 5064
Telex: 24710

Account No: _____

Sales Rep: _____

Tel: _____

Orders to
BOOKPOINT LIMITED, 39 Milton Park, Abingdon, Oxfordshire OX14 4TD
Tel: 0235 835001
Fax: 0235 861038

Order Information

All Dues Automatically Recorded
Representation Available
Invoice Payments: Bookpoint Ltd

Personnel
Head of Company: Ernest Hecht
Head of Publicity: Debbie Sheldrick
Head of Accounts: J Manchee
Head of Distribution: Val Huxley

Number of titles published annually: 55
PA Member
NBA Signatory
All New Titles are Bar Coded
WBIP Updating: R Dingwall

Subsidiary Companies: Pictorial Presentations Ltd, Pop Universal Ltd

Trade Terms
General Net: Single Copy 25%, Two or more 35%
Girobank Number: 200 9455
Credit Cards Accepted: Access/Master, Visa, Amex, Diners

Returns Procedures
Authority to Return: Representatives or Sales Manager
Address for Returns: Bookpoint
Stock Returns: As per normal returns
Imperfect Returns: As above to £20

SPA BOOKS LTD
PO Box 47, Stevenage, Hertfordshire SG2 8UH
ISBN Prefix(es): 0 907590, 1 871048
Tel: 0462 482812
Fax: 0438 310104
VAT No: 409 6503 52

Order Information
Teleordering: SPA

Order Dept Opening Times
Mon - Fri 9am - 5pm
All Dues Automatically Recorded
Representation Available

Personnel
Head of Company: Steven Apps

Number of titles published annually: 20
Percentage of Export Sales: 20%
All New Titles are Bar Coded
WBIP Updating: Maria Coles

Trade Terms
Single copy 20% Two or more 35%
Credit Cards Accepted: Access/Master, Visa, Other

Returns Procedures
Authority to Return: Sales Dept
Stock Returns: Only authorised returns accepted

SPARTACUS EDUCATIONAL

139 Garden Avenue, Brighton, East Sussex BN1 8NH
Tel: 0273 561464
VAT No: 436 0027 85

SPECTRUM TRAINING SERVICES LTD

PO Box 170, SSO, Bournemouth, Dorset BH1 1NN
Tel: 0202 471236

SPELLMOUNT LTD (PUBLISHERS)

12 Dene Way, Speldhurst, Tunbridge Wells, Kent TN3 0NX
ISBN Prefix(es): 0 85936, 0 946771, 1 871876, 1 873376
Tel: 0892 862860
Fax: 0892 863861
VAT No: 367 6503 30

Order Information

Order Dept Opening Times
Open most hours - work from home
Trade Counter:Vale Packaging Ltd, 420 Vale Road,
Tonbridge, Kent TN9 1TD Tel:0732 359387 Fax:0732 770620

Personnel
Head of Company: Ian Morley-Clarke
Head of Accounts: Robert Hardcastle
Other Important Personnel:
Kathleen Morley-Clarke (Editorial Director & Co Secretary)

Number of Staff: 2

Trade Terms
General Net: Single Copy 25%, Two or more 35%
Other Terms: Carriage Charges: all overseas orders unless using shippers
Girobank Number: 311 6859

Returns Procedures
Authority to Return: Ian Morley-Clarke Spellmount Ltd
Address for Returns: Vale Packaging
Imperfect Returns: All our titles are highly priced and all damaged/imperfect copies must be returned complete

Sphere = Tiptree

SPINDLEWOOD

70 Lynhurst Avenue, Barnstaple, Devon EX31 2HY
ISBN Prefix(es): 0 907349
Tel: 0271 71612

Fax: 0271 25906
VAT No: 320 9909 57

Order Information

All Dues Automatically Recorded

Personnel
Head of Company: Michael Holloway
Other Important Personnel:
Anne Holloway, Jo Cox

Number of titles published annually: 5
Number of Staff: 3
PA Member
IPG Member
NBA Signatory
All New Titles are Bar Coded
Book Data Subscriber
WBIP Updating: Michael Holloway

Trade Terms
General Net: Single copy 25%, 2 or more single titles 35%, 2 books or more 35%
Girobank Number: 27 506 4409

Returns Procedures
Address for Returns: Spindlewood, c/o Maldram & Jones, 27 Bear Street Barnstaple, Devon, EX32 7BX
Imperfect Returns: Book must be returned for credit

SPINK & SON LTD
5,6 & 7 King Street, St James's, London SW1Y 6QS
Tel: 071-930 7888
Fax: 071-839 4853
Telex: SPINK 916711
Cables: SPINK LONDON SW1
VAT No: 238 4488 33

SPOKESMAN BOOKS
Bertrand Russell House, Gamble Street, Nottingham, Nottinghamshire NG7 4ET
ISBN Prefix(es): 0 85124
Tel: 0602 708318
Fax: 0602 420433
VAT No: 117 4388 65

Order Information

All Dues Automatically Recorded
Representation Available
Representation: Troika/Central

Personnel
Head of Company: Anthony Simpson
Other Important Personnel:
Ken Fleet (Business Manager), Ken Coates (Editor)

Number of titles published annually: 10
Number of Staff: 3
All New Titles are Bar Coded
WBIP Updating: Anthony Simpson

Parent Company: Bertrand Russell Pearce Foundation Ltd

Trade Terms
33.3% on trade order. Surcharges on orders under £15 gross add 15% (minimum 50p)
Girobank Number: 400 7689

Returns Procedures
Authority to Return: Julia James

THE SPORTING LIFE

Orbit House, 1 New Fetter Lane, London EC4A 1AR
ISBN Prefix(es): 0 901091
Tel: 071-822 3291
Fax: 071-822 3230
Fax: 071-583 3885/6
Telex: 263403
VAT No: 577 6123 17

Orders to
ASM Ltd, PO Box 54, Desborough, Northamptonshire
NN14 2UH
Tel: 0536 762860 Tel/Fax

THE SPORTSMAN'S PRESS

25 King Charles Walk, London SW19 6JA
ISBN Prefix(es): 0 948253
Tel: 081-789 0229
VAT No: 391 4314 58

Orders to
TIPTREE BOOK SERVICES LTD, Church Road, Tiptree, Colchester, Essex CO5 0SR
Tel: 0621 819600
Fax: 0621 819011

Order Information

All Dues Automatically Recorded
Representation Available
Invoice Payments: Tiptree Book Services

Personnel
Head of Company: Kenneth Kemp

Number of titles published annually: 10
Percentage of Export Sales: 20%
Number of Staff: 2
IPG Member
All New Titles are Bar Coded
WBIP Updating: K Kemp

Trade Terms
35%, no surcharges

Returns Procedures
Authority to Return: Orders are firm unless previously agreed.
Stock Returns: Apply to Tiptree.
Imperfect Returns: Title pages to be sent to Sportsman's Press

SPREAD EAGLE PUBLICATIONS

The Spread Eagle, Ruthin, Clwyd LL15 1HY
ISBN Prefix(es): 0 907207
Tel: 0824 703840

Order Information

Order Dept Opening Times
Mon - Sat 9.30am - 5.30pm
All Dues Automatically Recorded

WBIP Updating: K M & J R Kenyon-Thompson

Trade Terms
25% single copy, 35% two or more

THE SPREDDEN PRESS

Brockbushes Farm, Stocksfield, Northumberland NE43 7UB
Tel: 0434 633100
Fax: 0434 632965
Book Data Subscriber

SPRINGER-VERLAG

8 Alexandra Road, Wimbledon, London SW19 7JZ
ISBN Prefix(es): 0 387, 3 211, 3 540, 3 7985
~~Tel: 081-947 5885~~ TEL 0483 418800
Tel: 081-947 1280
Fax: 081-947 1274
Fax: 081-947 4651
VAT No: 318 5162 64

Account No: _____115446_____

Sales Rep: _____

Tel: _____

German Address
Postfach 31 1340
D-10643 Berlin
Germany
FAX
010 49 30 8214091

Order Information
Teleordering: SPRVER

Order Dept Opening Times
Mon - Fri 9am - 5pm
Cyclical Ordering Policy
All Dues Automatically Recorded
Representation Available

Springer Verlag London Ltd
Sweetapple House
Catteshall Rd
Godalming, Surrey
GU7 3DJ
Tel 0483 418822
Fax 0483 415151

Personnel
Head of Company: Dr G Graham
Head of Sales (Home): Paul Roberts
Head of Customer Services: Muriel Holt

Number of titles published annually: 1200
Number of Staff: 17
PA Member
All New Titles are Bar Coded
Book Data Subscriber
WBIP Updating: P Roberts

Parent Company: Springer-Verlag GMBH, Germany

Trade Terms
On application
Credit Cards Accepted: Access/Master, Visa

Returns Procedures
Authority to Return: Prior authorisation required from Paul Roberts
Address for Returns: Springer-Verlag, c/o Churchill Freight Ltd, London

SPRINGFIELD BOOKS LTD

Norman Road, Denby Dale, Huddersfield, West Yorkshire HD8 8TH
ISBN Prefix(es): 0 947655, 1 85688
Tel: 0484 864955
Fax: 0484 865443
VAT No: 399 2357 02

Account No: _____

Sales Rep: _____

Tel: _____

Order Information
Teleordering: SPRING

Orders for more than one publisher can be bulked
All Dues Automatically Recorded
Representation Available

Personnel
Head of Company: Brian Lewis (Managing Director)
Head of Publicity: Paula Brennon
Head of Accounts: Walter Poszczynski

Number of titles published annually: 120
Percentage of Export Sales: 20%
Number of Staff: 10
All New Titles are Bar Coded
WBIP Updating: Paula Brennon

Trade Terms
35%
Minimum Order: £20 retail value
Girobank Number: 620 4759
Credit Cards Accepted: Access/Master, Visa, Amex

SQUARE ONE PUBLICATIONS
Saga House, Sansome Place, Worcester, Worcestershire WR1 1UA
ISBN Prefix(es): 1 872017
Tel: 0905 25208
Fax: 0905 726651
VAT No: 488 1405 27

Order Information

Order Dept Opening Times
Mon - Fri 9.30 - 5pm
All Dues Automatically Recorded

Personnel
Head of Company: Mary D Wilkinson
Head of Distribution: Mrs D Thompson 0684 592035

Number of titles published annually: 24
IPG Member
All New Titles are Bar Coded
WBIP Updating: Mary D Wilkinson

Trade Terms
35% (Over 5 copies)
General Net: Two or more single titles 25% 2-5

STACEY INTERNATIONAL
128 Kensington Church Street, London W8 4BH
ISBN Prefix(es): 0 905743
Tel: 071-221 7166
Fax: 071-792 9288
Telex: 928768 STACEY G
VAT No: 241 7010 09

Orders to
BIBLIOS PUBLISHERS DISTRIBUTION SERVICE LTD,
Star Road, Partridge Green, West Sussex RH13 8LD
Tel: 0403 710971
Fax: 0403 711143

Order Information

All Dues Automatically Recorded
Representation Available

Personnel
Head of Company: T C G Stacey (Chairman)
Head of Marketing: G I Milne (Managing Director)
Head of Publicity: M A Carruthers (Office Manager)
Head of Accounts: E Innes (Accounts Manager)

Number of titles published annually: 4
Number of Staff: 6
WBIP Updating: M A Carruthers

Parent Company: Stacey Arts Ltd

Trade Terms
General Net: Single copy/single line 25%, 2 books or more 35%

THE STAFF COLLEGE

Publications Department, Coombe Lodge, Blagdon, Bristol,
Avon BS18 6RG
Tel: 0761 462503
Fax: 0761 463140
Fax: 0761 463104

STAGECOACH

Carriers Crossing, Woodford Rd, Stratford-sub-Castle,
Salisbury, Wiltshire SP4 6AE
Tel: 0722 73369
VAT No: 541 7391 44

STAINER & BELL LIMITED

PO Box 110, Victoria House, 23 Gruneisen Road, London
N3 1DZ
ISBN Prefix(es): 0 85249
Tel: 081-343 3303
Fax: 081-343 3024
VAT No: 230 1613 22

Order Information

Order Dept Opening Times
Mon - Fri 9am - 5pm
All Dues Automatically Recorded

Personnel
Head of Company: Carol & Keith Wakefield

Number of titles published annually: 10
Percentage of Export Sales: 35%
Number of Staff: 10
NBA Signatory
WBIP Updating: Carol Wakefield

Trade Terms
Letter of Terms available on request
Girobank Number: 556 7351

[handwritten: STATE UNIV OF NEW YORK PRESS = PLYMBRIDGE]

THE STANBOROUGH PRESS LTD

Alma Park, Grantham, Lincolnshire NG31 9SL
Tel: 0476 591700
Fax: 0476 77144
Cables: STANPRESS GRANTHAM
VAT No: 385 2622 40

PA Member

[handwritten: STANFORD UNIV PRESS c/o CUP.]

THE STEEL CONSTRUCTION INSTITUTE

Silwood Park, Ascot, Berkshire SL5 7QN
Tel: 0344 23345
Fax: 0344 22944
VAT No: 407 7568 31

RUDOLF STEINER PRESS

PO Box 955, Bristol, Avon BS99 5QN
ISBN Prefix(es): 0 85440, 1 85584
Tel: 0272 239229
Fax: 0272 237229
VAT No: 609 4413 47

Orders to
BIBLIOS PUBLISHERS DISTRIBUTION SERVICE LTD,
Star Road, Partridge Green, West Sussex RH13 8LD
Tel: 0403 710971
Fax: 0403 711143

Order Information

All Dues Automatically Recorded
Representation Available

Personnel
Head of Company: Stephen Roberts (Manager)

Number of titles published annually: 12
Percentage of Export Sales: 20%
Number of Staff: 1
IPG Member
All New Titles are Bar Coded

Trade Terms
35%, Single copy 25%
Credit Cards Accepted: Access/Master, Visa

Returns Procedures
Authority to Return: Biblios
Address for Returns: Biblios
Stock Returns: Damaged copy - title page returned Wrong Book - whole book returned
Imperfect Returns: Title page returned

RICHARD STENLAKE PUBLISHING

1 Overdale Street, Langside, Glasgow, Strathclyde G42 9PZ
Tel: 041-632 2304
VAT No: 552 4603 57

PA Member

STERLING PUBS (INDIA) ISBN 81207 = BAILEY DISTR.

MALCOLM STEWART BOOKS

2 Vines Avenue, Finchley, London N3 2QD
ISBN Prefix(es): 0 904132
Tel: 081-349 2045

Order Information

Invoice Payments: To: Malcolm Breckman

Personnel
Head of Company: Malcolm Breckman

Number of titles published annually: 1
All New Titles are Bar Coded

Trade Terms
Single Copy/Single Line 25% Three or more Books 35%

Returns Procedures
Imperfect Returns: Up to £20

STOBART DAVIES LTD

Priory House, Priory Street, Hertford, Hertfordshire
SG14 1RN
ISBN Prefix(es): 0 85442
Tel: 0992 501518 24 Hours
Fax: 0992 501519
VAT No: 524 7160 59

Order Information

Order Dept Opening Times
Mon - Fri 9.30am - 5.30pm
All Dues Automatically Recorded
Representation Available

Personnel
Head of Company: Brian Davies
Head of Publicity: Joanne Wright
Head of Accounts: Joan Parkinson
Head of Distribution: Milton Collier
Head of Customer Services: Claire Davies

Number of titles published annually: 4
Number of Staff: 6
IPG Member
WBIP Updating: Joanne Wright

Parent Company: Stobart Publishing Ltd

Trade Terms
General Net: Single copy 25%, 2 or more single titles 33.3%, 2 books or more 33.3%, subscription orders 33.3%, stock orders 35%
Non-Net: 17.5%
Other Terms: Carriage charge for overseas
Girobank Number: 5131545
Credit Cards Accepted: Access/Master, Visa

Returns Procedures
Stock Returns: Return title page only for retail value up tp £15. Over £15 return whole book and report fault.

A H STOCKWELL LTD

Elms Court, Torrs Park, Ilfracombe, Devon EX34 8BA
ISBN Prefix(es): 0 7223
Tel: 0271 862557
VAT No: 144 3575 68

Account No: _____

Sales Rep: _____

Tel: _____

Order Information

Order Dept Opening Times
Mon - Thur 8am - 1pm, 2pm - 5pm Fri 8am - 1.30pm
All Dues Automatically Recorded
Representation Available

Personnel
Head of Company: R J Stockwell (Director)
Head of Sales (Home): P Nicholas (Director)
Head of Accounts: R J Nicholas
Head of Customer Services: L McGowan
Other Important Personnel:
D P Stockwell (Company Adviser)

Number of titles published annually: 95
Number of Staff: 18
WBIP Updating: P Nicholas

Trade Terms
33.3%, Special Orders 40-45%
Other Terms: Postage free if invoice value over £15

Returns Procedures
Stock Returns: Return to Head Office

STOKESBY HOUSE PUBLICATIONS

Stokesby House, Stokesby, Great Yarmouth, Norfolk NR29 3ET
Tel: 0493 750645
Fax: 0493 750146
VAT No: 511 0625 04

IPG Member

STONE FLOWER LTD

2 Horder Road, London SW6 5EE
Tel: 071-736 0477

IPG Member

STORYVILLE PUBLICATIONS & CO LTD

66 Fairview Drive, Chigwell, Essex IG7 6HS
Tel: 081-500 6098

THE STOURTON PRESS

21 Moreton Place, London SW1V 2NL
Tel: 071-821 1101

Personnel
Head of Company: James Stourton

STRIDE PUBLICATIONS

37 Portland Street, Newtown, Exeter, Devon EX1 2EG
ISBN Prefix(es): 0 946699, 1 85019, 1 873012

Order Information

Order Dept Opening Times
Mon - Fri 10am - 5pm

Personnel
Head of Company: Rupert Loydell

Number of Staff: 1

Trade Terms
35%, 30 days

Returns Procedures
Stock Returns: Write for permission to return, once given return books

ORIEL STRINGER

66 Tivoli Crescent, Brighton, Sussex BN1 5ND
ISBN Prefix(es): 0 948122
Tel: 0273 550795

Order Information

Order Dept Opening Times
Mon - Sat 9am - 5pm

Personnel
Head of Company: O Stringer

Number of titles published annually: 2
Book Data Subscriber

Trade Terms
30% all orders

Returns Procedures
Stock Returns: Write first, return defective book. New copy sent plus your postage cost

THE STROKE ASSOCIATION

CHSA House, Whitecross Street, London EC1 8JJ
Tel: 071-490 7999
Fax: 071-490 2686
VAT No: 233 8066 69

PA Member

STUDIO EDITIONS LTD

Princess House, 50 Eastcastle Street, London W1N 7AP
ISBN Prefix(es): 1 85170, 5 022357
Tel: 071-636 5070
Fax: 071-580 3001
Telex: 22303 WEBB G
VAT No: 370 7261 58

Account No: _____

Sales Rep: _____

Tel: _____

Order Information

Order Dept Opening Times
Mon - Fri 9am - 5.30pm
All Dues Automatically Recorded
Representation Available

Personnel
Head of Company: Kenneth Webb (Managing Director)
Head of Sales (Home): Lionel Foot
Head of Accounts: Andrew Mollett
Head of Customer Services: Francesca Ferguson (Trade Manager)
Other Important Personnel:
Roderick Webb (Chairman)

Number of titles published annually: 40
Percentage of Export Sales: 50%
Number of Staff: 45
All New Titles are Bar Coded
Book Data Subscriber
WBIP Updating: Patrizia Salerno

Trade Terms
35%, small order surcharge applies except to subscription orders or orders placed with representative
Other Terms: £5 surcharge for orders below £50 for Studio Editions, and below £100 for Studio Designs
Credit Cards Accepted: Access/Master, Visa

Returns Procedures
Authority to Return: Representative
Address for Returns: Bartholomews Storage & Dist, Woodside Road, Boyatt Wood Ind Estate, Eastleigh, Hants SO5 4ET
Stock Returns: Books must be in mint condition and by a reputable carrier. Credits will not be raised for books damaged in transit.
Imperfect Returns: Return the complete book.

SUBJECT PUBLICATIONS

Beech House, Broadstone, Dorset BH18 9NJ
Tel: 0202 696907 Tel/Fax
VAT No: 580 1965 29

SULLIVAN ASSOCIATES

7 Hughes Mews, 143 Chatham Road, London SW11 6HJ
Tel: 071-924 4813
Fax: 071-924 4478
VAT No: 318 5269 46

Account No: _____

Sales Rep: _____

Tel: _____

SUMMERSDALE PUBLISHERS

PO Box 49, Chichester, West Sussex PO19 4LF
ISBN Prefix(es): 1 873475
Tel: 0243 779327
VAT No: 582 9396 87

Orders to
CENTRAL BOOKS, 99 Wallis Road, London E9 5LN
Tel: 081-986 4854
Fax: 081-533 5821

Order Information

All Dues Automatically Recorded
Representation Available
Invoice Payments: Central Books Ltd

Personnel
Head of Company: Stewart Ferris (Managing Editor)
Head of Marketing: Alastair Williams (Marketing Manager)

Number of titles published annually: 12
Percentage of Export Sales: 20%
Number of Staff: 2
All New Titles are Bar Coded
Book Data Subscriber
WBIP Updating: Stewart Ferris

Trade Terms
35%

Returns Procedures
Authority to Return: Central Books Ltd
Address for Returns: Central Books Ltd

SUNFLOWER BOOKS

12 Kendrick Mews, London SW7 3HG
ISBN Prefix(es): 0 948513, 1 85691
Tel: 071-589 1862
Fax: 071-225 1033
Telex: 269388 LONHAN G
VAT No: 241 3331 09

Orders to
A & C BLACK (PUBLISHERS) LTD, PO Box 19,
Huntingdon, Cambridgeshire PE19 3SF
Tel: 0480 212666
Fax: 0480 405014

Order Information

All Dues Automatically Recorded
Representation Available
Invoice Payments: A & C Black

Personnel
Head of Company: Patricia A Underwood/John Seccombe

Number of titles published annually: 6
All New Titles are Bar Coded

Parent Company: P A Underwood Ltd

Trade Terms
35% no surcharges

Returns Procedures
Authority to Return: A & C Black
Address for Returns: A & C Black

SUSSEX PUBLICATIONS LTD

Microworld House, 2-6 Foscote Mews, London W9 2HH
Tel: 071-266 2202
Fax: 071-266 2314

Cables: MICROWORLD LONDON W9
VAT No: 577 3709 02

SUT ANUBIS

73 Kettering Road, Northampton, Northamptonshire
NN1 4AW
ISBN Prefix(es): 0 9477620
Tel: 0604 27727
VAT No: 289 8037 05

Order Information

Order Dept Opening Times
Mon - Sat 10am - 5pm

Personnel
Head of Company: M John Lovett

Number of Staff: 1

Trade Terms
Single copy 20%, Two books 25%, Three books or more 33.33% No surcharges or carriage

Returns Procedures
Stock Returns: By arrangement only
Imperfect Returns: Return whole book

ALAN SUTTON PUBLISHING LTD

Phoenix Mill, Far Thrupp, Stroud, Gloucestershire GL5 2BU
ISBN Prefix(es): 0 7509, 0 86299, 0 904387
Tel: 0453 731114
Fax: 0453 731117
Account No: _____ JG 6090 _____
Sales Rep: _____
Tel: _____

Order Information
Teleordering: SUTTON

All Dues Automatically Recorded
Representation Available

Personnel
Head of Company: Alan Sutton (Chairman & Managing Director)
Head of Sales (Home): Nicholas Mills (Sales Director)
Head of Accounts: Dave Hodge (Administration Manager)
Head of Distribution: James Kinnear (Distribution Manager)
Head of Customer Services: Nigel Brown (Sales Office Manager)

Number of titles published annually: 230
Percentage of Export Sales: 20%
Number of Staff: 60
All New Titles are Bar Coded
WBIP Updating: Mrs Joyce Percival

Parent Company: The Guernsey Press Company Ltd

Trade Terms
General Net: Single copy/single line 25%, 2 or more single titles 35%
Girobank Number: 241 6255
Credit Cards Accepted: Access/Master, Visa

Returns Procedures
Stock Returns: All books supplied see-safe, returns accepted up to 9 months after publication
Imperfect Returns: Title page under £10

THE SWEDENBORG SOCIETY
20/21 Bloomsbury Way, London WC1A 2TH

SWEET & MAXWELL LTD
South Quay Plaza, 183 Marsh Wall, London E14 9FT
ISBN Prefix(es): 0 420, 0 421, 0 906214, 0 907451
Tel: 071-538 8686
Fax: 071-538 9508
Telex: 929 879 ITP INF G
VAT No: 512 5137 83

Account No: _____

Sales Rep: _____

Tel: _____

Orders to
INTERNATIONAL THOMSON PUBLISHING SERVICES LTD, Cheriton House, North Way, Andover, Hampshire SP10 5BE
Tel: 0264 332424
Fax: 0264 364418

Order Information

All Dues Automatically Recorded
Representation Available
Invoice Payments: Sweet & Maxwell, Andover

Personnel
Head of Company: David Evans (Managing Director)
Head of Sales (Home): Steven Harris (Sales Director)
Head of Sales (Export): Nigel Thomas (International Sales Manager)
Head of Marketing: Anthony Kinahan (Marketing Director)
Head of Publicity: Eoin MacGillvray (Promotions Manager)
Head of Accounts: David Langridge (Credit Control Manager) Andover
Head of Customer Services: Ted Pashley (Customer Services Manager) Andover

Number of titles published annually: 100
PA Member
NBA Signatory
All New Titles are Bar Coded
Book Data Subscriber
WBIP Updating: Eoin MacGillivray

Subsidiary Companies: W Green - Scotland

Trade Terms
On application
BA/Girobank Small Order Scheme: Yes
Girobank Number: 209 6919
Credit Cards Accepted: Access/Master, Visa, Amex, Diners

Returns Procedures
Address for Returns: International Thomson Publishing Services
Stock Returns: Details on request
Imperfect Returns: Return imperfect book indicating imperfection. Replacement will be sent or book credited

SWEETHAWS PRESS
Owl House, Poundgate, Nr Uckfield, Sussex TN22 4DE
Tel: 0892 653722 24 Hours

Order Information

Order Dept Opening Times
9am - 9pm 7 days a week

Personnel
Head of Company: Rosalind Bowlby
Head of Sales (Home): Nicholas Bowlby

Trade Terms
35% on all orders

SYNTHESIS PUBLISHING

Portelet, Binstead Hall, Quarr Road, Binstead, Isle of Wight
PO33 4EL
Tel: 0983 565744
Fax: 0983 520866

IPG Member

TA HA PUBLISHERS LTD

1 Wynne Road, London SW9 0BB
ISBN Prefix(es): 0 907461
Tel: 071-737 7266 24 Hours
Fax: 071-737 7267
VAT No: 362 3565 53

Order Information

Order Dept Opening Times
Mon - Fri 9am - 5pm
All Dues Automatically Recorded
Representation Available

Personnel
Head of Company: A Siddiqui
Head of Sales (Export): Dr J Rafai

Number of titles published annually: 12
Percentage of Export Sales: 35%

Trade Terms
Single Copy 25% Two or more single titles 35%
Other Terms: Carriage charged
Girobank Number: 57 816 1400

TABB HOUSE

7 Church Street, Padstow, Cornwall PL28 8BG
ISBN Prefix(es): 0 907018, 1 873951
Tel: 0841 532316 Tel/Fax
Fax: 0841 532316
VAT No: 337 2114 82

Order Information

Order Dept Opening Times
Mon - Fri 8.30am - 1pm 2.30pm - 5.30pm
Cyclical Ordering Policy
All Dues Automatically Recorded
Representation Available
Orders are normally despatched weekly, orders marked
URGENT will be dealt with within 24 hours

Personnel
Head of Company: Mrs Caroline White
Head of Sales (Home): David Balme
Head of Accounts: Mrs Sandra Daniels

Number of titles published annually: 5
Number of Staff: 5
IPG Member
NBA Signatory
All New Titles are Bar Coded
WBIP Updating: David Balme

Trade Terms
General Net: Single copy 25%, Two or more 35%, Stock orders 35% Subscription/Special/Wholesale orders negotiable
BA/Girobank Small Order Scheme: 35% single copy order paid by Giro transfer
Girobank Number: 20 268 9905

Returns Procedures
Authority to Return: Prior permission required quoting invoice number
Stock Returns: Credit issued after receipt of stock in saleable condition
Imperfect Returns: Title and imperfect page(s) to be returned

TALKING POINTS PUBLICATIONS

2 Bishops Road, Tewinwood, Welwyn, Hertfordshire AL6 0NS

TALLIS PRESS

2 Caversham Street, London SW3 4AH
Tel: 071-351 4995 Tel/Fax

TAMARIND LTD

PO Box 296, Camberley, Surrey GU15 1QW
ISBN Prefix(es): 1 870516
Tel: 0276 683979
Fax: 0276 685365
VAT No: 492 6786 90

Orders to
CHILD'S PLAY (INTERNATIONAL) LTD, Ashworth Road, Bridgemead, Swindon, Wiltshire SN5 7YD
Tel: 0793 616286
Fax: 0793 512795

Order Information

All Dues Automatically Recorded
Representation Available

Personnel
Head of Company: Verna Wilkins (Director)
Head of Accounts: Penny Skelton (Administrator)

Number of titles published annually: 4
Number of Staff: 2
IPG Member
All New Titles are Bar Coded
WBIP Updating: Penny Skelton

Trade Terms
By negotiation
Other Terms: Carriage charge on small orders

THE TANTIVY PRESS LTD

2 Bedford Gardens, London W8 7EH
ISBN Prefix(es): 0 900730
Tel: 071-581 3289
Fax: 071-823 7996
VAT No: 239 6247 39

Personnel
Head of Company: Peter Cowie

Number of titles published annually: 5
All New Titles are Bar Coded

Trade Terms
20% singles, 35% multiples

TAPROBANE LTD
PO Box 717, London W5 3EY
ISBN Prefix(es): 1 873344
Tel: 081-998 3024 24 Hours
Fax: 081-998 3024

Personnel
Head of Company: Mr Wimal Ediriwira

Number of titles published annually: 2
IPG Member
NBA Signatory
All New Titles are Bar Coded
Open University Publications

Trade Terms
Single copy 15% post payable, two or more 35% post paid

TARQUIN PUBLICATIONS
Stradbroke, Diss, Norfolk IP21 5JP
ISBN Prefix(es): 0 906212
Tel: 0379 384218
Fax: 0379 384289
VAT No: 106 2299 87

Order Information

Order Dept Opening Times
Mon - Fri 9am - 5pm

Personnel
Head of Company: Gerald Jenkins
Head of Sales (Home): Margaret Jenkins
Head of Publicity: Audrey Semple
Head of Accounts: Jean Howlett

Number of titles published annually: 6
Percentage of Export Sales: 25%
Number of Staff: 11
IPG Member
NBA Signatory
All New Titles are Bar Coded
WBIP Updating: J Howlett

Trade Terms
35% up to £100, 40% £100+, 45% £1000+, 50% £2000+ at retail No surcharges
Other Terms: Under £20 retail cash with order or pro-forma
Girobank Number: 21 668 6601
Credit Cards Accepted: Access/Master, Visa

Returns Procedures
Stock Returns: All sales firm. Please notify immediately of any shortages or damage
Imperfect Returns: Contact office for replacements

TARRAGON PRESS
Moss Park, Ravenstone, Whithorn, Dumfries & Galloway DG8 8DR
ISBN Prefix(es): 1 870781
Tel: 098 885 368

Orders to
LAVIS MARKETING, 73 Lime Walk, Headington, Oxfordshire OX3 7AD
Tel: 0865 67575
Fax: 0865 750079

Order Information

Invoice Payments: Lavis Marketing

Personnel
Head of Company: David Sumner

Number of titles published annually: 2
Number of Staff: 1

Trade Terms
25% on 1 copy, 30% on 2 copies, 35% on 3 or more
Credit Cards Accepted: Access/Master, Visa

Returns Procedures
Authority to Return: Lavis Marketing
Address for Returns: Lavis Marketing

TATE GALLERY PUBLICATIONS

Millbank, London SW1P 4RG
ISBN Prefix(es): 1 85437
Tel: 071-834 5651/2
Fax: 071-828 7357
VAT No: 240 1873 86

Account No: _____

Sales Rep: _____

Tel: _____

Order Information

Order Dept Opening Times
Mon - Fri 9.30am - 5.30pm
All Dues Automatically Recorded
Representation Available

Personnel
Head of Company: Iain Bain
Head of Sales (Home): Brian Lawler
Head of Accounts: Brian McGahon
Head of Distribution: Chris Jung

Number of titles published annually: 16
Number of Staff: 40
All New Titles are Bar Coded
WBIP Updating: Brian Lawler

Trade Terms
35%
Minimum Order: £20, otherwise 25% discount
Credit Cards Accepted: Access/Master, Visa

I B TAURIS AND CO LTD

45 Bloomsbury Square, London WC1A 2HY
ISBN Prefix(es): 1 85043
Tel: 071-916 1069
Fax: 071-916 1068
Telex: 262433/3155 TAURIS

Orders to
BIBLIOS PUBLISHERS DISTRIBUTION SERVICE LTD,
Star Road, Partridge Green, West Sussex RH13 8LD
Tel: 0403 710971
Fax: 0403 711143

Order Information

All Dues Automatically Recorded
Representation Available
Invoice Payments: Biblios

Personnel
Head of Company: Iradj Bagherzade (Publisher & Chairman)

Head of Sales (Home): Jonathan McDonnell (Sales & Marketing Director)
Head of Publicity: Helen Donlon (Publicity & Promotions Manager)

Number of titles published annually: 80
Number of Staff: 10
All New Titles are Bar Coded
Book Data Subscriber

Trade Terms
25% single copies, 35% on bulk copies
Credit Cards Accepted: Access/Master, Visa

Returns Procedures
Authority to Return: Nicky Luckie, I B Tauris
Stock Returns: Please contact sales at IB Tauris office dept

TAYLOR & FRANCIS LTD

4 John Street, London WC1N 2ET
Tel: 071-405 2237
Fax: 071-831 2035
Telex: 858540 TANDF
VAT No: 233 4836 66

Account No: 2510782
Sales Rep: _____
Tel: _____

Orders to
Taylor & Francis Ltd, Rankine Road, Basingstoke, Hampshire RG24 0PR
Tel: 0256 840366
Fax: 0256 479438

Order Information
Teleordering: TAYFRN

Order Dept Opening Times
Mon - Fri 9.00am - 1pm, 1.30pm - 4.30pm
All Dues Automatically Recorded
Representation Available
Invoice Payments: Taylor & Francis Ltd, Basingstoke

Personnel
Head of Company: Anthony R Selvey (Group Managing Director)
Head of Sales (Home): Keith R Courtney (Sales & Marketing Director)
Head of Publicity: Di Owen (Marketing Manager)
Head of Accounts: Anthony M Foye (Financial Director)
Head of Distribution: Mary Messer (Sales Administration Manager)
Head of Customer Services: Wendy Long (Customer Services Supervisor - Books)
Other Important Personnel:
Anne Daly (Customer Services Supervisor - Journals)

Number of titles published annually: 200
Percentage of Export Sales: 75%
PA Member
NBA Signatory
All New Titles are Bar Coded
Open University Publications
Book Data Subscriber
WBIP Updating: W Long

Parent Company: Taylor & Francis Group Ltd

Trade Terms
Single copy 25%, 2-10 copies 30%, 11+ copies 35%, 30 days credit
Credit Cards Accepted: Access/Master, Visa, Amex

Returns Procedures
Authority to Return: Taylor & Francis Ltd, Basingstoke
Address for Returns: Taylor & Francis Ltd, Basingstoke
Stock Returns: Obtain prior permission quoting invoice number. Returns only accepted in mint condition, except where received damaged.

JOHN TAYLOR BOOK VENTURES

7 Cranborne Road, Hatfield, Hertfordshire AL10 8AW
Tel: 0707 265908
Fax: 0707 270536
VAT No: 473 0563 51

Orders to
SPA BOOKS LTD, PO Box 47, Stevenage, Hertfordshire SG2 8UH
Tel: 0462 482812
Fax: 0438 310104

TBC DISTRIBUTION

Unit 10, Bunting Close, Mitcham, Surrey CR4 4ND
Tel: 081-687 1744
Fax: 081-687 1747

Account No: _____
Sales Rep: _____
Tel: _____

Order Information
Teleordering: TOMLIN

Order Dept Opening Times
Mon - Fri 8.30am - 1pm, 2pm - 5pm
Representation Available

Personnel
Head of Company: Roger Tomlinson (Managing Director)
Head of Accounts: Derek Elsdon (Financial Controller)
Head of Distribution: Bryan Nothard (Distribution Director)
Head of Customer Services: Susan Sands (Customer Services Manager)

Trade Terms
Publishers Terms
Credit Cards Accepted: Access/Master, Visa

Returns Procedures
Authority to Return: Refer to publisher
Address for Returns: TBC Distribution
Stock Returns: Refer to publisher
Imperfect Returns: Title page only with defect, normally replaced

TECHNICAL INFORMATION SERVICES

76 Church Street, Larkhall, Strathclyde ML9 1HE
Tel: 0698 883334
Fax: 0698 884585
VAT No: 402 8006 01

[handwritten: TECHNOMIC PUBLISHING AG, MISSIONSTRASSE 44 CH 4055 BASEL, SWITZ. FAX 01041 61 43 52 59]

TECHNOLOGY APPRAISALS LTD

82 Hampton Road, Twickenham, Middlesex TW2 5QS
Tel: 081-893 3986
Fax: 081-744 1149
VAT No: 462 7257 36

[handwritten: ↑ (no 'on approval orders)]

TEE PUBLISHING

Edwards Centre, Regent Street, Hinckley, Leicestershire LE10 0BB
ISBN Prefix(es): 1 85761, 9 05100
Tel: 0455 616419
Tel: 0455 637173
Fax: 0455 616419
VAT No: 328 0133 89

Order Information

Order Dept Opening Times
Mon - Fri 9am - 5pm

Personnel
Head of Company: C L Deith
Head of Accounts: Mrs G Birt
Head of Customer Services: Miss C Willis

Number of titles published annually: 20
Percentage of Export Sales: 20%
WBIP Updating: Claire Willis

Trade Terms
33.3%
Minimum Order: £50 trade
Other Terms: 20% discount, pro forma if order falls below minimum level
Credit Cards Accepted: Access/Master, Visa

Returns Procedures
Imperfect Returns: Book to be returned complete

TEECOLL PUBLICATIONS

Sanctuary House, Oulton Road, Oulton, Lowestoft, Suffolk NR32 4QZ
Tel: 0502 583294
Fax: 0502 561397

Trade Terms
25% plus P&P

TEENEY BOOKS LTD

24 Christchurch Street West, Frome, Somerset BA11 1EB
ISBN Prefix(es): 1 873338
Tel: 0373 452565
Fax: 0373 452567
VAT No: 543 3284 53

Personnel
Head of Company: Martyn Lewis/T de Vries
Head of Sales (Export): Donna Webber

Number of Staff: 6

TELEGRAPH BOOKS

One Canada Square, London E14 5DT
Tel: 071-538 6826
Fax: 071-538 6950
VAT No: 243 3441 87

Orders to
Raymar Computer Serv, Units A3-A4, Lanterns Court, London E14 9TU
Tel: 071-537 2207 (24 Hr)
Fax: 071-537 3594

Order Information

Order Dept Opening Times
Mon - Fri 9am - 4pm

Personnel
Head of Company: Marilyn Warwick (Publishing Director)
Head of Sales (Home): Martin Norton (Sales Director) 071-537 2207
Head of Marketing: Lynne Brannan (Marketing Executive) 071-538 6829
Head of Accounts: Brenda Davis 071-538 7411
Head of Customer Services: Sharon Cunningham 071-537 2207

Book Data Subscriber

Parent Company: The Daily Telegraph Plc

Trade Terms
35% - Payment with order Special orders negotiable
Credit Cards Accepted: Access/Master, Visa, Amex

Returns Procedures
Authority to Return: Raymar Computer Services
Address for Returns: Raymar Computer Services
Imperfect Returns: Contact Martin Norton at Raymark Computer Services

THOMAS TELFORD LTD

Thomas Telford House, 1 Heron Quay, London E14 4JD
ISBN Prefix(es): 0 7277
Tel: 071-987 6999
Fax: 071-538 4101
Telex: 298105 CIVILS E
VAT No: 240 8777 47

A/C No 273447

Order Information

Order Dept Opening Times
9.30am - 5.15pm
Cyclical Ordering Policy
All Dues Automatically Recorded
Representation Available

Personnel
Head of Company: Graham James
Head of Sales (Home): P Scarlett
Head of Marketing: Sarah Watson James
Head of Accounts: D Gregory

Number of titles published annually: 60
Percentage of Export Sales: 40%
PA Member
NBA Signatory
All New Titles are Bar Coded
Book Data Subscriber
WBIP Updating: Sarah Watson James

Trade Terms
25%, no surcharges
Minimum Order: Orders under £10 will be on pro-forma
Credit Cards Accepted: Access/Master, Visa, Other

Returns Procedures
Authority to Return: P Y Scarlett

THE TEMPLAR COMPANY PLC

Pippbrook Mill, London Road, Dorking, Surrey RH4 1JE
Tel: 0306 876361
Fax: 0306 889097
VAT No: 356 7192 29

TEMPLE LECTURES LTD
Charter House, St Leonards Road, Bexhill-on-Sea, East Sussex TN40 1JA
ISBN Prefix(es): 1 870800
Tel: 0404 212021
Tel: 0404 225258
Fax: 0424 730074
VAT No: 365 3342 55

Order Information
Representation Available

Personnel
Head of Company: Mr W Ellis

Number of titles published annually: 4
Number of Staff: 4
WBIP Updating: Miss Verity Owen

Trade Terms
30% no surcharges

Returns Procedures
Stock Returns: We will replace defective books

TEMPLE LODGE PUBLISHING
51 Queen Caroline Street, London W6 9QL
Tel: 081-748 8388
Fax: 081-748 5451

TEMPLE UNIV. PRESS (USA) C/O BAKER + TAYLOR, 652 EAST MAIN STREET BRIDGEWATER NJ 08807, USA.

TEMPLE PRESS LTD
PO Box 227, Brighton, Sussex BN2 3GL
ISBN Prefix(es): 1 871744
Tel: 0273 679129 24 Hours
Fax: 0273 621284
VAT No: 506 8226 52

Order Information
Order Dept Opening Times
Mon - Sat 9am - 9pm
Cyclical Ordering Policy
All Dues Automatically Recorded
Representation Available

Personnel
Head of Company: Paul Cecil

Number of titles published annually: 4
Percentage of Export Sales: 35%
Number of Staff: 4
NBA Signatory
All New Titles are Bar Coded

Trade Terms
Single copy 25%, two plus 35%, 30 days credit. First two orders must be pre-paid.

Returns Procedures
Authority to Return: Rep or Head Office
Stock Returns: All returns must include original invoice number
Imperfect Returns: No title pages accepted. Complete books only

TERTIARY PUBLICATIONS
Brook House, Eriswell Crescent, Walton-on-Thames, Surrey KT12 5DS
Tel: 0932 248358
Fax: 0932 245569
PA Member

TETRAHEDRON BOOKS
30 Birch Crescent, Blairgowrie, Tayside PH10 6TS

THE TEXTILE INSTITUTE
10 Blackfriars Street, Manchester, Greater Manchester M3 5DR
ISBN Prefix(es): 0 900739, 1 870812
Tel: 061-834 8457
Fax: 061-835 3087
Telex: 668297 G
VAT No: 146 6379 41

Orders to
AUSTICKS PUBLICATIONS, 21 Blenheim Terrace, Leeds, West Yorkshire LS2 9HJ
Tel: 0532 432446
Fax: 0532 430661

Order Information

All Dues Automatically Recorded

Personnel
Head of Company: Richard Denyer
Head of Sales (Home): Vanessa L Knowles
Head of Accounts: Alan Young
Head of Customer Services: Jane Cullen

Number of titles published annually: 10
WBIP Updating: Vanessa L Knowles

Trade Terms
25% plus carriage charges, multiple copies carriage paid
Girobank Number: 60 410 0000
Credit Cards Accepted: Access/Master, Visa, Amex

Returns Procedures
Authority to Return: Brian Hazell, Austicks
Address for Returns: Austicks
Stock Returns: Prior authorization required
Imperfect Returns: Title page up to £10

TFH PUBLICATIONS
The Spinney, Parklands, Forest Road, Waterlooville, Hampshire PO7 6AR
ISBN Prefix(es): 0 86622, 0 87666, 1 85279
Tel: 0705 268122
Fax: 0705 268801
VAT No: 479 5120 24

Account No: _____

Sales Rep: _____

Tel: _____

Order Information
Teleordering: TFH

Order Dept Opening Times
9am - 5.30pm Mon - Fri
All Dues Automatically Recorded
Representation Available

Personnel
Head of Company: H E Hardy (Director)
Head of Sales (Home): N J Carter
Head of Accounts: R M Rogers (Director)
Head of Distribution: Mrs J E Hardy

Number of titles published annually: 75
All New Titles are Bar Coded
WBIP Updating: Mrs L Bell

Trade Terms
General Net: Single copy/single line 25%, 2 or more single titles, 2 books or more 35%
BA/Girobank Small Order Scheme: Yes
Girobank Number: 240 23 4308

Returns Procedures
Stock Returns: Request authority
Imperfect Returns: As above

TFPL PUBLISHING (TASK FORCE PRO LIBRA LTD)

22 Peter's Lane, London EC1M 6DS
ISBN Prefix(es): 1 870889
Tel: 071-251 5522
Fax: 071-251 8318
VAT No: 466 3985 96

Order Information

Order Dept Opening Times
Mon - Fri 9am - 5.30pm
All Dues Automatically Recorded

Personnel
Head of Company: Nigel Oxbrow (Managing Director)
Head of Customer Services: Kim Jacks

Number of titles published annually: 6
Percentage of Export Sales: 40%
Number of Staff: 10
Book Data Subscriber
WBIP Updating: Kim Jacks

Trade Terms
General Net: Single copy 10%, Two or more negotiable
Credit Cards Accepted: Access/Master, Visa

THAMES & HUDSON LTD

30-34 Bloomsbury Street, London WC1B 3QP
ISBN Prefix(es): 0 500
Tel: 071-636 5488
Fax: 071-636 4799
Fax: 071-636 1695 Sales/Mktg
Telex: 25992
Cables: Thameshuds London WC1
VAT No: 235 1314 02

Account No: 1300342

Sales Rep: _____

Tel: _____

Orders to
THAMES & HUDSON LTD, 44 Clockhouse Road, Farnborough, Hampshire GU14 7QZ
Tel: 0252 541602
Fax: 0252 377380

Order Information
Teleordering: THAMHUD

All Dues Automatically Recorded
Representation Available

Personnel
Head of Company: Thomas Neurath (Managing Director)
Head of Sales (Home): Andrew Lord (Sales Manager)
Head of Sales (Export): Timothy Evans (Export Sales Director)

Head of Marketing: Simon Huntley (Sales & Marketing Director)
Head of Publicity: Helen Scott Lidgett (Publicity Manager)
Head of Accounts: Timothy Flood (Financial Director)
Head of Customer Services: Suzy Sharland (UK Customer Services)
Other Important Personnel:
Rachel Kelly (Export Customer Services)

Number of titles published annually: 190
PA Member
NBA Signatory
All New Titles are Bar Coded
WBIP Updating: Kate Russ

Allied Companies: Interart Sarl (FR)

Trade Terms
General Net: Single copy single line 20%, all other orders 35%
Academic Net: All orders 20%
Girobank Number: 212 9051
Credit Cards Accepted: Access/Master, Amex, Diners, Visa

Returns Procedures
Authority to Return: Representative
Address for Returns: Thames and Hudson Distributors Ltd
Imperfect Returns: £10 price limit for annotated page

THAMES & HUDSON LTD

44 Clockhouse Road, Farnborough, Hampshire GU14 7QZ
Tel: 0252 541602 24 Hours
Fax: 0252 377380

Account No: _____
Sales Rep: _____
Tel: _____

Order Information
Teleordering: THAMHUD

Order Dept Opening Times
Mon - Fri 8am - 5pm
Orders for more than one publisher can be bulked

Personnel
Head of Distribution: Alan Goode (General Manager)

Trade Terms
Girobank Number: 212 9051
Credit Cards Accepted: Access/Master, Amex, Diners, Visa, Other

Returns Procedures
Imperfect Returns: Title page up to £10

THARPA PUBLICATIONS LTD

15 Bendemeer Road, London SW15 1JX
ISBN Prefix(es): 0 948006
Tel: 081-788 7792
Fax: 071-589 9611
Telex: 8813016
VAT No: 410 3920 01

Orders to
Tharpa Publications, Kilnwick Percy Hall, Pocklington, York, Yorkshire YO4 2UF
Tel: 0759 306446 (24 Hrs)
Fax: 0759 306397

Order Information

Order Dept Opening Times
Mon - Fri 10.30am - 1pm, 2pm - 5.30pm
Orders for more than one publisher can be bulked
All Dues Automatically Recorded
Representation Available
Invoice Payments: York

Personnel
Head of Company: Hugh W P Clift (Director)
Head of Sales (Home): Alison Ramsay (Sales Manager) York
Head of Sales (Export): Hugh Clift (Sales Manager) York
Head of Accounts: Steve Lane (Sales Administration Manager) York

Number of titles published annually: 4
Percentage of Export Sales: 65%
Number of Staff: 5
IPG Member
All New Titles are Bar Coded
WBIP Updating: Hugh Clift

Trade Terms
General Net: Single copy 20% (CWO 25%) plus carriage, two or more 35% carriage paid, special orders - by arrangement
Girobank Number: 552 971901
Credit Cards Accepted: Access/Master, Visa

Returns Procedures
Authority to Return: Alison Ramsay, York
Address for Returns: York
Imperfect Returns: Return for replacement

THEMETREE LTD

2 Prebendal Court, Oxford Road, Aylesbury, Buckinghamshire HP19 3EY
Tel: 0296 28585
Fax: 0296 436622
VAT No: 342 6632 63

THEOSOPHICAL PUBLISHING HOUSE

50 Gloucester Place, London W1H 3HJ
ISBN Prefix(es): 0 7229
Tel: 071-935 9261

Order Information

Order Dept Opening Times
Mon - Fri 10am - 6pm, Sat 10am - 4pm
Representation Available

Personnel
Head of Company: Michael Rainger
Head of Sales (Home): Neil Hedges

Number of titles published annually: 2

Trade Terms
33.3%
Credit Cards Accepted: Access/Master, Visa

THIMBLE PRESS

Lockwood, Station Road, South Woodchester, Nr Stroud, Gloucestershire GL5 5EQ
ISBN Prefix(es): 0 903355
Tel: 0453 873716
Fax: 0453 878599
VAT No: 275 8811 22

Order Information

Order Dept Opening Times
Mon - Fri 9am - 5pm
All Dues Automatically Recorded

Personnel
Head of Company: Nancy Chambers (Proprietor)

Number of titles published annually: 4

Trade Terms
Single copy 25%, Multiples 33.3%, CWO 35%

Returns Procedures
Stock Returns: Permission must be obtained, original invoice no supplied books must be in resaleable condition before credit passed
Imperfect Returns: No price limit

THOEMMES PRESS

85 Park Street, Bristol, Avon BS7 5PJ
ISBN Prefix(es): 1 85506
Tel: 0272 291377
Fax: 0272 221918
VAT No: 366 2097 41

Orders to
BIBLIOS PUBLISHERS DISTRIBUTION SERVICE LTD,
Star Road, Partridge Green, West Sussex RH13 8LD
Tel: 0403 710971
Fax: 0403 711143

Order Information

Invoice Payments: Biblios

Personnel
Head of Company: Rudi Thoemmes
Head of Sales (Home): Deborah Mann
Head of Accounts: Linda Keeble
Head of Distribution: Herb Tandree

Number of titles published annually: 50
Percentage of Export Sales: 50%
Number of Staff: 8
IPG Member
Book Data Subscriber
WBIP Updating: D P Broughton

Trade Terms
25%. Multiple copies 35% (new titles and paperbacks only) Large orders negotiable. P&P Free in UK.
Credit Cards Accepted: Access/Master, Visa, Amex

Returns Procedures
Authority to Return: Biblios
Address for Returns: Biblios
Stock Returns: Request permission stating reason for return
Imperfect Returns: Return whole book

THE THORESBY SOCIETY

Claremont, 23 Clarendon Road, Leeds, West Yorkshire
LS2 9NZ

STANLEY THORNES PUBLISHERS LTD

Old Station Drive, Leckhampton, Cheltenham,
Gloucestershire GL53 0DN
ISBN Prefix(es): 0 7175, 0 7487, 0 85950, 0 85973, 1 871402
Tel: 0242 228888 24 Hours
Tel: 0242 577944

Tel: 0242 578585
Fax: 0242 221914
Telex: 43592
VAT No: 302 3194 07
Account No: 1217100
Sales Rep:
Tel:

Order Information
Teleordering: STANTHN

Order Dept Opening Times
Mon - Fri 8.30am - 5.30pm
All Dues Automatically Recorded
Representation Available

Personnel
Head of Company: Mr David J Smith
Head of Sales (Home): Mr George Monck
Head of Sales (Export): Mrs Esther Heasman
Head of Distribution: Ms Margot van de Weijer
Head of Customer Services: Mrs Joan Norris
Other Important Personnel:
Mr Ron Gellert (Head of Sales - Modern Languages/Humanities)

Number of titles published annually: 186
Number of Staff: 160
PA Member
NBA Signatory
All New Titles are Bar Coded
Book Data Subscriber
WBIP Updating: David Taylor

Parent Company: Wolters Kluwer Group

Trade Terms
25% net 17.5% non-net
Other Terms: £1.50 small order surcharge under £50 5% extra discount CWO orders over £50
Girobank Number: 275 9152
Credit Cards Accepted: Access/Master, Visa

Returns Procedures
Stock Returns: Overstocks - prior permission to be requested in writing
Imperfect Returns: Return title page only stating imperfection - also if credit or replacement required

THORNHILL PRESS LTD

3 Fountain Way, Parkend, Nr Lydney, Gloucestershire
GL15 4JD
ISBN Prefix(es): 0 904110, 0 946328
Tel: 0594 564984 Tel/Fax
VAT No: 302 4210 30

Order Information

Order Dept Opening Times
Mon - Fri 10am - 3.30pm
All Dues Automatically Recorded
Representation Available

Personnel
Head of Company: Desmond Badham-Thornhill/John Pemberthy (Joint Heads of Company)

Number of titles published annually: 8
Number of Staff: 4
NBA Signatory
All New Titles are Bar Coded
WBIP Updating: John Pemberthy

Trade Terms
Single Copy 25%, Two or more 35%

Non-Net: 25%
Other Terms: Carriage charges on orders under £15
Girobank Number: 245 9159

Returns Procedures
Imperfect Returns: Return title page only

THORNTON'S OF OXFORD LTD

11 Broad Street, Oxford, Oxfordshire OX1 3AR
ISBN Prefix(es): 0 85455
Tel: 0865 242939
Fax: 0865 204021
Cables: Thornbook
VAT No: 194 4663 31

Order Information
Teleordering: THORN

Order Dept Opening Times
Mon - Sat 9am - 6pm
All Dues Automatically Recorded

Personnel
Head of Company: W A Meeuws
Head of Publicity: J S Meeuws

Number of titles published annually: 2
Percentage of Export Sales: 65%
Number of Staff: 8
WBIP Updating: M Meeuws

Trade Terms
General Net: Single copy/single line 20% + postage, 2 or more single titles 25% + postage
Academic Net: As above
Other Terms: Carriage charged on all orders
Girobank Number: 245 5056
Credit Cards Accepted: Access/Master, Visa, Amex

Returns Procedures
Stock Returns: No stock returns
Imperfect Returns: Books to be returned with indication of invoice number

THOTH PUBLICATIONS

98 Ashby Road, Loughborough, Leicestershire LE11 3AF
Tel: 0509 210626

Account No: _____

Sales Rep: _____

Tel: _____

Order Information

All Dues Automatically Recorded

Personnel
Head of Company: Tom Clarke

Number of titles published annually: 4
Percentage of Export Sales: 50%
Number of Staff: 2

Trade Terms
Single Copy 25%, Multiple Copies 35%

Returns Procedures
Authority to Return: Prior authorisation required

TIPTREE BOOK SERVICES LTD

Church Road, Tiptree, Colchester, Essex CO5 0SR
Tel: 0621 819600 Orders

Tel: 0621 816362 — x2253 for queries
Fax: 0621 819011
Fax: 0621 819717   0621 819600
Telex: Bookco G 99487
Cables: Literarius Tiptree
VAT No: 102 8389 80
Account No: 0274075.027

Sales Rep: _____
Tel: _____

Order Information
Teleordering: TIPT
First Edition Subscriber

Order Dept Opening Times
Mon - Thurs 8.30am - 5pm, Fri 8.30am - 4.30pm
Cyclical Ordering Policy

Personnel
Head of Company: K J Llewellyn (Managing Director)
Head of Distribution: Roger Springall (Distribution Manager)
Head of Customer Services: Geoffrey Travers (Customer Services Manager)
Other Important Personnel:
Ian Farnell (Deputy Managing Director), Ian Moylan (Warehouse Manager), Maralyn Johnson (Computer Operations Director)

PA Member

Parent Company: Random House Group Ltd

Trade Terms
Credit Cards Accepted: Access/Master, Visa

Returns Procedures
Authority to Return: Refer to Publisher

THE TOAT PRESS

Tullens Toat, Pulborough, West Sussex RH20 1DA
ISBN Prefix(es): 0 9511063
Tel: 0798 872664
VAT No: 192 7967 08

Order Information

Order Dept Opening Times
Mon - Fri 9am -5pm

Personnel
Head of Company: D R Atkins

Number of titles published annually: 1
WBIP Updating: D R Atkins

Trade Terms
General Net: Single copy/single line 25%, 2 books or more 30%

TOBIN MUSIC

The Old Malt House, Knight Street, Sawbridgeworth, Hertfordshire CM21 9AX
Tel: 0279 726625 24 Hours
VAT No: 493 0428 43

Personnel
Head of Company: Candida Tobin
Head of Marketing: Chris Dell (Marketing Manager)
Head of Publicity: David Horchover (Publicity Manager)
Head of Distribution: Cynthia Dewberry (Sales Manager)
Head of Customer Services: Catherine Fox (Liaison Officer)

Number of Staff: 5

Trade Terms
33%

Returns Procedures
Authority to Return: Prior permission required
Imperfect Returns: Replaced without question

TOLLEY PUBLISHING CO LTD

Tolley House, 2 Addiscombe Road, Croydon, Surrey
CR9 5AF
ISBN Prefix(es): 0 85314, 0 85459
Tel: 081-686 9141
Fax: 081-686 3155
Fax: 081-760 0588
VAT No: 729 731
Account No: BLAC 0461/00000004
Sales Rep:
Tel:

Orders to
24 Hour Ansafone Number: 081-686 0115

Order Information

Cyclical Ordering Policy
All Dues Automatically Recorded
Representation Available

Personnel
Head of Company: Harry King
Head of Sales (Home): Robin Webb
Head of Publicity: Gary Palmer
Head of Accounts: Peter Diggles
Head of Customer Services: Gina O'Grady
Other Important Personnel:
Peter Collins, William Cardno

Number of titles published annually: 86
Number of Staff: 175
NBA Signatory
Book Data Subscriber
WBIP Updating: Mr G C Palmer

Parent Company: United Newspapers PLC

Trade Terms
General Net: Single copy 25%, 2 or more single titles 35%, 2 books or more 35%, subcription/stock orders 25%, special orders neg.
Other Terms: Carriage charges if goods mailed to customer
Credit Cards Accepted: Access/Master, Amex

Returns Procedures
Imperfect Returns: Title page up to £50

TOUCAN PRESS

Rue Des Monts, Delancey Park, St Sampson, Guernsey
Tel: 0481 45091

Personnel
Head of Company: G Stevens-Cox

Number of titles published annually: 10
Number of Staff: 3

Trade Terms
33.3%

TRADE & TRAVEL PUBLICATIONS LTD
6 Riverside Court, Riverside Rd, Lwr Bristol Rd, Bath, Avon
BA2 3DZ
ISBN Prefix(es): 0 900751, 0 905802
Tel: 0225 469141
Fax: 0225 462921
VAT No: 138 3847 44

Account No: _____

Sales Rep: _____

Tel: _____

Order Information
Order Dept Opening Times
Mon - Fri 9am - 5pm
Orders for more than one publisher can be bulked
All Dues Automatically Recorded
Representation Available

Personnel
Head of Company: James Dawson
Head of Publicity: Rosemary Dawson
Head of Accounts: Patrick Dawson
Other Important Personnel:
D Richard Bowen (Sales (Europe)) Tel: 40 161200 Fax: 40 161208 SWEDEN

Number of titles published annually: 7
Percentage of Export Sales: 75%
NBA Signatory
All New Titles are Bar Coded
Book Data Subscriber
WBIP Updating: James Dawson

Trade Terms
General Net: Single Copy 25%, Two or more single titles 35%
Other Terms: Carriage charges: overseas extra
Girobank Number: 211 7452
Credit Cards Accepted: Access/Master, Visa, Amex, Diners

Returns Procedures
Authority to Return: Only accepted from UK. Telephone for permission first
Stock Returns: Cut off date: 30 days after publication. Whole book in mint condition to be returned
Imperfect Returns: Telephone for permission. Whole book to be returned. Book will be replaced

THE TRADE COUNTER
Unit D, Trading Estate Road, London NW10 7LU
Tel: 081-963 0322

Account No: _____

Sales Rep: _____

Tel: _____

Order Information
Teleordering: TRADE

TRADE RESEARCH PUBLICATIONS
6 Beech Hill Court, Berkhamsted, Hertfordshire HP4 2PR
ISBN Prefix(es): 0 904783
Tel: 0442 863951
Fax: 0442 230772

Personnel
Head of Company: Douglas Tookey
Other Important Personnel:
Miranda Cummins

WBIP Updating: Miranda Cummins

TRAIL CREST PUBLICATIONS LTD
Winster, Matlock, Derbyshire DE4 2DQ
ISBN Prefix(es): 0 907496, 1 874754
Tel: 0629 650454 24 Hours
Fax: 0629 650416
VAT No: 439 5552 23

Order Information

Order Dept Opening Times
Mon - Fri 9am - 5pm
All Dues Automatically Recorded
Representation Available
Trade Counter:Milne House, Speedwell Mill, Millers Green, Wirksworth, Derbyshire DE4 4BL Tel:0629 826354

Personnel
Head of Company: John N Merrill
Head of Accounts: Jennifer A Piggott
Head of Distribution: Stuart M Jones

Number of titles published annually: 50
Number of Staff: 6
NBA Signatory
All New Titles are Bar Coded
WBIP Updating: John N Merrill

Trade Terms
35%
General Net: Single copy/single line 25%
Girobank Number: 46 598 9608
Credit Cards Accepted: Access/Master, Visa

TRAINING INFORMATION NETWORK LTD
51 High Street, Ruislip, Middlesex HA4 7BG
ISBN Prefix(es): 0 947586
Tel: 0895 622112
Fax: 0895 621582

Order Information

Order Dept Opening Times
Mon - Fri 9am - 5pm

Personnel
Head of Company: Colin Steed (Managing Director)
Head of Sales (Home): Karen Ogier (Sales Manager)
Head of Marketing: Philip DeGroot (Marketing Manager)
Head of Accounts: Jean Westwood

Number of titles published annually: 5
Number of Staff: 9
WBIP Updating: Philip DeGroot

Parent Company: Dawson Holdings plc

Trade Terms
10%

[handwritten: Transnational Pubs. One Bridge Street Irvington-on-Hudson- NY 10533 - USA]

TRANSPORT BOOKMAN PUBLICATIONS LTD
8 South Street, Isleworth, Middlesex TW7 7BG
ISBN Prefix(es): 0 85184
Tel: 081-560 2666 24 Hour
Fax: 081-569 8273

Order Information

All Dues Automatically Recorded

Personnel
Head of Company: F P A Stroud (Managing Director)

Number of titles published annually: 2
Percentage of Export Sales: 20%
Number of Staff: 4
NBA Signatory
All New Titles are Bar Coded

Parent Company: Chater & Scott Booksellers

Trade Terms
General Net: Single copy/single line 25%, 2 or more single titles 35%
Other Terms: Carriage charges on overseas orders, at cost

Returns Procedures
Stock Returns: Not without prior permission by telephone
Imperfect Returns: As above

TRANSPORT PUBLISHING COMPANY LTD

128 Pikes Lane, Glossop, Derbyshire SK13 8EH
ISBN Prefix(es): 0 86317, 0 903839
Tel: 0457 861508
Fax: 0457 865588
VAT No: 286 0453 49

Orders to
24 Hour Ansafone Number: 0457 865588

Order Information

Order Dept Opening Times
Mon - Fri 9am - 5.15pm
Orders for more than one publisher can be bulked
All Dues Automatically Recorded
Representation Available

Personnel
Head of Company: John A Senior
Head of Sales (Home): Mark Senior

Number of titles published annually: 10
NBA Signatory
All New Titles are Bar Coded
WBIP Updating: Mark Senior

Trade Terms
General Net: 35%
Academic Net: 35%
Other Terms: £2 carriage charged on orders under £25
Girobank Number: 468 0251
Credit Cards Accepted: Access/Master, Visa

Returns Procedures
Stock Returns: Contact for permission - return with permission
Imperfect Returns: All imperfect book to be returned to after contact to arrange exchange

TRANSPORT 2000

Walkden House, 10 Melton Street, London NW1 2EJ
ISBN Prefix(es): 0 907347
Tel: 071-388 8386
Fax: 071-388 2481

Order Information

Order Dept Opening Times
Mon - Fri 9.30am - 5.30pm

Personnel
Other Important Personnel:
Jane Puzey (Administrator)

Number of titles published annually: 4
Number of Staff: 4

Trade Terms
30%

TRANSWORLD PUBLISHERS
61/63 Uxbridge Road, Ealing, London W5 5SA
ISBN Prefix(es): 0 385, 0 440, 0 552, 0 553, 0 593, 1 852
Tel: 081-579 2652
Fax: 081-579 5479
Fax: 081-566 3730 UK Sales
Fax: 081-579 1227 Int Sales
Telex: 267974
Cables: Transcable - London W5
VAT No: 226 7112 82
Account No: 1906216/023
Sales Rep:
Tel:

Orders to
Fax: 081-579 5951 Orders
24 Hour Ansafone Number: 0800 282112 UK Free

Order Information
Teleordering: TRANS
First Edition Subscriber

Order Dept Opening Times
Mon - Fri 9am - 5pm
Cyclical Ordering Policy
Representation Available

Personnel
Head of Company: Paul Scherer (Managing Director)
Head of Sales (Home): Garry Prior (Sales Director)
Head of Sales (Export): John Blake (International Sales Director)
Head of Marketing: Larry Finlay (Marketing Director)
Head of Publicity: Judy Turner (Publicity Director)
Head of Accounts: Barry Hempstead (Finance Director)
Head of Distribution: Terry Pink (Distribution Director) Wellingborough 0933 225761
Head of Customer Services: Jack Campbell (Trade Manager)
Other Important Personnel:
Mark Barty-King (Deputy Managing Director), Ian Manhire (Sales Operation Director), Mike Webster (Distribution Manager) Wellingborough, John Stachiewicz (Sales Director (Export))

Number of titles published annually: 500
All New Titles are Bar Coded
WBIP Updating: Alfred Willman

Trade Terms
35%
Minimum Order: Books to retail invoice value £50
Girobank Number: 406 2256

Returns Procedures
Authority to Return: Area Representative or Sales Department, Ealing
Address for Returns: Wellingborough Distribution Centre, Sanders Road, Wellingborough, Northants (with labels provided)

TREADWELLS ART MILL
Upper Park Gate, Little Germany, Bradford, West Yorkshire BD1 5DW
ISBN Prefix(es): 0 9079320

Tel: 0274 306065
Tel: 0274 306064
Fax: 0274 394356
VAT No: 233 158 580

Order Information

Order Dept Opening Times
Sun - Sat 10am - 6pm
All Dues Automatically Recorded
Representation Available

Personnel

Head of Company: Nicholas Treadwell (Director/Owner)
Head of Marketing: Catherine Aldred/Emma Sanders (Gallery Administrator)

Number of titles published annually: 2

Trade Terms
40% on all orders

TREFOIL PUBLICATIONS LTD

108 Blackhorse Road, London E17
ISBN Prefix(es): 0 86294
Tel: 081-527 5823
VAT No: 451 1310 04

Orders to
BOOKPOINT LIMITED, 39 Milton Park, Abingdon, Oxfordshire OX14 4TD
Tel: 0235 835001
Fax: 0235 861038

Order Information

All Dues Automatically Recorded
Representation Available

Personnel
Head of Company: Conway Lloyd Morgan

Number of titles published annually: 10
Percentage of Export Sales: 30%
Number of Staff: 1

Trade Terms
35% on all orders

Returns Procedures
Authority to Return: Prior permission required
Address for Returns: Bookpoint
Imperfect Returns: Imperfect under £10 only

TREMATON PRESS

Trematon Hall, Saltash, Cornwall PL12 4RU
ISBN Prefix(es): 0 950966
Tel: 0752 842351
VAT No: 418 1586 46

Order Information

All Dues Automatically Recorded
Representation Available

Personnel
Head of Company: Miss C Elizabeth Turner

Number of titles published annually: 2
Number of Staff: 1
IPG Member

Trade Terms
Single Copy 25% Two or more 35%
Other Terms: Carriage charged on single books

BA/Girobank Small Order Scheme: Payment 30 days after invoice

TRENT VALLEY PUBLICATIONS
PO Box 9, Burton-on-Trent, Staffordshire DE15 9Q
Tel: 0283 517834

TRENTHAM BOOKS LTD
Westview House, 734 London Road, Stoke-on-Trent, Staffordshire ST4 5NP
ISBN Prefix(es): 0 948080, 0 9507735, 1 85856
Tel: 0782 745567
Fax: 0782 745553
VAT No: 536 9801 18

Order Information

Order Dept Opening Times
Mon - Fri 9am - 5pm
All Dues Automatically Recorded
Representation Available

Personnel
Head of Company: John Eggleston
Head of Sales (Home): Barbara Wiggins
Head of Marketing: John Howells
Head of Publicity: John Stipling
Head of Customer Services: Gillian Klein

Number of titles published annually: 30
Percentage of Export Sales: 20%
Number of Staff: 5
PA Member
NBA Signatory
All New Titles are Bar Coded
WBIP Updating: Gillian Klein

Subsidiary Companies: Trentham Print Design Ltd

Trade Terms
33.3% on all orders
Credit Cards Accepted: Access/Master, Visa

Returns Procedures
Authority to Return: Written authority required
Stock Returns: Covering request
Imperfect Returns: Return whole book

TRESSELL PUBLICATIONS
Lower Ground Floor, 70 Grand Parade, Brighton, East Sussex BN2 2JA
Tel: 0273 600186
Fax: 0273 695932
VAT No: 403 1084 10

TRIGRAPH LTD
West Africa House, Hanger Lane, London W5 3QR
ISBN Prefix(es): 0 947961, 0 9508026
Tel: 081-997 6691

Orders to
Trigraph Ltd, POB 186, Haywards Heath, West Sussex RH16 2YD
Tel: 0444 482298
Fax: 0444 482742

Order Information

TRENTHAM BOOKS

The Academic Publishers that High Street Booksellers have discovered!

Our books on bullying have initiated public debate and made schools safer places.

Our brilliant fun books on education, by Ted Wragg, Mike Kivi and Laurie Taylor, have delighted thousands of teachers.

Our books on classroom practice and social policy have guided schooling for our multicultural society.

Our books on technology education have pioneered this crucial new curriculum area.

Our books on early years have given new dimensions to nursery and infant education.

If you want to provide a full service for readers, you need our new catalogue at the ready.

If your customers include teachers, social workers, nurses and parents you need our books on display.

Trade terms: 33⅓% on each and every order.

Member of 'Book Tokens' payment scheme.

tb

TRENTHAM BOOKS LIMITED
Westview House, 734 London Road, Oakhill, Stoke-on-Trent ST4 5NP
Telephone: (0782) 745567

PS: Our books are so beautiful that they have even won a major design award.

Representation Available

Personnel
Head of Company: Lady Hunt

Trade Terms
35%

Returns Procedures
Authority to Return: Lady Hunt, Haywards Heath
Address for Returns: Haywards Heath

TRIPLE CAT PUBLISHING

3 Back Lane Cottages, Bucks Horn Oak, Farnham, Surrey
GU10 4LN
ISBN Prefix(es): 1 871936
Tel: 0420 22352

Order Information

Order Dept Opening Times
Mon - Fri 9am - 6pm
All Dues Automatically Recorded

Personnel
Head of Company: Mr Robert Field/Mr Roderick Grant

Number of titles published annually: 2
All New Titles are Bar Coded
WBIP Updating: Mr R Grant

Trade Terms
General Net: Single copy 33.3%, Two or more 35%, 15-29 - 37.5%, 30-79 - 40%, 80 plus - by negotiation, cwo extra 2.5%

TRITON PUBLISHING CO LTD

1A Montago Mews North, London W1H 1AJ
ISBN Prefix(es): 0 363
Tel: 071-706 0486

Personnel
Head of Company: Mrs C S Whitaker

Number of Staff: 1

Trade Terms
33.3%

TROTMAN & CO LTD

12 Hill Rise, Richmond, Surrey TW10 6UA
ISBN Prefix(es): 0 85660
Tel: 081-940 5668 24 Hours
Tel: 081-332 2132
Fax: 081-948 9267

A/C No UNIV BKR

Order Information

Order Dept Opening Times
Mon - Fri 9am - 5pm
All Dues Automatically Recorded
Representation Available

Personnel
Head of Company: Andrew Trotman
Head of Sales (Home): Morfydd Jones
Head of Accounts: Alistair George
Head of Distribution: Michael Butler
Head of Customer Services: Tracy Deadman

Number of titles published annually: 15
Number of Staff: 4
PA Member

IPG Member
All New Titles are Bar Coded
WBIP Updating: Morfydd Jones

Trade Terms
35%, orders under £20 25% unless pre-paid
Credit Cards Accepted: Access/Master, Visa

Returns Procedures
Authority to Return: Head Office or Ken Dickson (Marketing) Ltd
Address for Returns: Vale Packaging, 420 Vale Road, Tonbridge, Kent TN9 1TD
Imperfect Returns: Cover & title page only returned with explanation of fault

TUFNELL PRESS

47 Dalmeny Road, London N7 0DY
Tel: 071-272 4861
VAT No: 544 4510 59

TURNAROUND

27 Horsell Road, London N5 1XL
Tel: 071-609 7836/7
Tel: 071-700 0247
Fax: 071-700 1205
VAT No: 396 4918 93

Account No: _____

Sales Rep: _____

Tel: _____

Order Information
Teleordering: TURN

Order Dept Opening Times
Mon - Fri 9.30am - 5pm
Orders for more than one publisher can be bulked
All Dues Automatically Recorded
Representation Available

Personnel
Head of Company: Bill Godber (Managing Director)
Head of Marketing: Claire Thompson (Marketing Director)
Head of Accounts: Kiel Shaw (Finance Director)
Head of Distribution: Geddes Thomas
Head of Customer Services: Roger James
Other Important Personnel:
Helen Holmes (Southern Area Rep), Tom Lawton (Northern Area Rep) 051-734 3551

Number of titles published annually: 200
Open University Publications
WBIP Updating: Bill Godber/Claire Thompson

Trade Terms
General Net: 10% -£10 gross, 25% - £10-£30 gross, 35% - £30 + gross
Academic Net: Single copy 10%, Two books or more 33.3%, Subscription orders 35%
Girobank Number: 57 135 0402

Returns Procedures
Authority to Return: By arrangement with rep or Roger James, Head Office
Stock Returns: Returns requests only considered if accompanied with invoice numbers and signature of rep or Roger James
Imperfect Returns: Title page only

TURPIN DISTRIBUTION SERVICES LTD

Blackhorse Road, Letchworth, Hertfordshire SG6 1HN
Tel: 0462 672555
Fax: 0462 480947
Telex: 825 372 TURPIN G
VAT No: 240 0820 15

Account No: _____ 0001733 _____
Sales Rep: _____
Tel: _____

Order Information

Order Dept Opening Times
Mon - Fri 9am - 5pm
Orders for more than one publisher can be bulked
All Dues Automatically Recorded
Representation Available

Personnel

Head of Company: Lorna M Summers (Director & General Manager)
Head of Marketing: Gervase E Muller (Marketing Services & Development Manager)
Head of Distribution: Peter Spragg (Warehouse Manager)
Head of Customer Services: Sharon Latham

Number of Staff: 60
PA Member
All New Titles are Bar Coded

Parent Company: Royal Society of Chemistry

Trade Terms

Credit Cards Accepted: Access/Master, Visa

TURTON & CHAMBERS

Unit 5, Station Rd Ind Est, South Woodchester, Stroud, Gloucestershire GL5 5EQ
ISBN Prefix(es): 1 872148
Tel: 0453 878598
Fax: 0453 878599
VAT No: 484 9968 64

Orders to
Tel: 0453 878598
Fax: 0453 878599

Order Information

Order Dept Opening Times
Mon - Fri 9am - 5pm
All Dues Automatically Recorded

Personnel

Head of Company: David Turton/Aidan Chambers
Head of Customer Services: Lin Cooksley

Number of titles published annually: 6
All New Titles are Bar Coded
Book Data Subscriber
WBIP Updating: Lin Cooksley

Trade Terms

General Net: Single Copy 30%, Two books or more 35%, Cash with order 35% Subscription orders 40% by agreement

Returns Procedures

Imperfect Returns: Please give full details of imperfection to enable us to check remaining stock

T wayne = ~~Macclston~~ IBD

TWELVEHEADS PRESS

Chy Mengleth, Twelveheads, Truro, Cornwall TR4 8SN
ISBN Prefix(es): 0 906294

Tel: 0209 820978
VAT No: 542 6439 41

Order Information

All Dues Automatically Recorded
Representation Available

Personnel
Head of Customer Services: M J Messenger

Number of titles published annually: 5
All New Titles are Bar Coded

Trade Terms
35% on all orders
Other Terms: Carriage charged: for 2 or less books

A TWIST IN THE TALE
PO Box 25, Retford, Nottinghamshire DN22 7ER
Tel: 0777 700248

Two Bad Mice - 95 Horsey Lane, Highgate LONDON. N6 5LW

TWO-CAN PUBLISHING LTD
346 Old Street, London EC1V 9NQ
Tel: 071-613 3376
Fax: 071-613 3371
VAT No: 447 2071 59

Account No: _____
Sales Rep: _____
Tel: _____

Orders to
Scholastic Pub Ltd, Westfield Road, Southam, Leamington Spa, Warwickshire CV33 0JW
Tel: 0926 813910
Fax: 0926 817727

Order Information
Teleordering: SCHOL

Order Dept Opening Times
Mon - Fri 9am - 5pm
Cyclical Ordering Policy
Sales & Marketing: Gavin Lang, Scholastic, Southam

Personnel
Head of Company: Andrew Jarvis (Chairman)

Number of Staff: 51
Book Data Subscriber

UBS PUBLISHERS DISTRIBUTORS LTD
475 North Circular Road, Neasden, London NW2 7QG
Tel: 081-450 8667
Fax: 081-205 9524

Account No: _____
Sales Rep: _____
Tel: _____

UBC Press (Prefix 07748) = UCL Press (Univ British Columbia)

UCL PRESS LTD — *ORDERS TO MARSTON*
University College London, Gower Street, London WC1E 6BT
ISBN Prefix(es): 1 85728
Tel: 071-380 7707
Fax: 071-413 8392
VAT No: 524 4425 61

Orders to
MARSTON BOOK SERVICES LTD, PO Box 87, Osney Mead, Oxford, Oxfordshire OX2 0DT
Tel: 0865 791155
Fax: 0865 791927

Order Information

All Dues Automatically Recorded
Representation Available
Invoice Payments: Marston Book Services Ltd

Personnel
Head of Company: Roger Jones (Publisher & Chief Executive)
Head of Sales (Home): Nicholas Esson (Marketing Director)
Head of Accounts: Anne Crowther (Finance Director)
Head of Customer Services: Marie Alexander (Sales & Marketing Administrator)

Number of titles published annually: 35
Percentage of Export Sales: 25%
Number of Staff: 10
IPG Member
All New Titles are Bar Coded
Book Data Subscriber
WBIP Updating: Ms Wendy Lane

Trade Terms
25% Hardback, 30% Paperback

Returns Procedures
Authority to Return: Returns must be authorised in accordance with UCL Press & Marston Book Services policies
Address for Returns: Marston Book Services

UNITED KINGDOM COUNCIL FOR HUMAN RIGHTS

17 Ravenscroft, Harpenden, Hertfordshire AL5 1ST
ISBN Prefix(es): 0 9513759
Tel: 0582 715070

Order Information

Order Dept Opening Times
Mon - Fri 9am - 5pm

Personnel
Head of Company: Dr Mark Ponnampalam (Co-ordinator)

Trade Terms
35% on all orders, no surcharges

UNITED REFORMED CHURCH

86 Tavistock Place, London WC1H 9RT
Tel: 071-916 2020
Fax: 071-916 2021
VAT No: 233 5694 55

PA Member

UNITED WRITERS PUBLICATIONS LTD

Ailsa, Castle Gate, Penzance, Cornwall TR20 8BG
ISBN Prefix(es): 0 901976, 1 85200
Tel: 0736 65954 Tel/Fax
VAT No: 337 1639 51

Order Information

Order Dept Opening Times
Mon - Fri 9am - 5pm
All Dues Automatically Recorded

Personnel
Head of Company: Malcolm Sheppard
Head of Sales (Home): Peter Keane
Head of Accounts: Tina Sully

Number of titles published annually: 8
NBA Signatory
All New Titles are Bar Coded
WBIP Updating: M Sheppard

Trade Terms
35% on all orders, no surcharges

UNIVERSITIES FEDERATION FOR ANIMAL WELFARE
8 Hamilton Close, South Mimms, Potters Bar, Hertfordshire
EN6 3QD
Tel: 0707 58202
Fax: 0707 49279

UNIVERSITY COLLEGE OF SWANSEA
The Registrar, Singleton Park, Swansea, West Glamorgan
SA2 8PP
Tel: 0792 205678
Fax: 0792 295618

UNIVERSITY OF EXETER PRESS
Reed Hall, Streatham Drive, Exeter, Devon EX4 4QR
ISBN Prefix(es): 0 85989, 0 900771
Tel: 0392 263066
Fax: 0392 264420
Telex: 42894 EXUNIV G
VAT No: 142 0477 95

Orders to
PLYMBRIDGE DISTRIBUTORS LTD, Plymbridge House,
Estover Road, Plymouth, Devon PL6 7PZ
Tel: 0752 735251
Fax: 0752 695699

[handwritten: CUST. SERV: 0752 695745]

Order Information
All Dues Automatically Recorded
Representation Available
Invoice Payments: Plymbridge
Representation:Book Representation Ltd

Personnel
Head of Company: Simon Baker (Secretary to the University Press)
Head of Marketing: Genevieve Davey

Number of titles published annually: 30
Number of Staff: 2
IPG Member
All New Titles are Bar Coded
Book Data Subscriber
WBIP Updating: Genevieve Davey

Trade Terms
35% on most titles, 30% on others, 25% single copy orders
Credit Cards Accepted: Access/Master, Visa

Returns Procedures
Authority to Return: Written requests only to Exeter. Invoice numbers & dates required. Must be less than one year from invoice date.
Address for Returns: Plymbridge
Imperfect Returns: Title page with full annotation up to £15

UNIVERSITY OF EXETER
Agricultural Economics Unit, Lafrowda House, St German's Rd, Exeter, Devon EX4 6TL
Tel: 0392 263836
Tel: 0392 263839
Fax: 0392 263852
Telex: 42894 EXUNIV G
VAT No: 142 0477 95

UNIVERSITY OF EXETER SCHOOL OF EDUCATION
Heavitree Road, Exeter, Devon EX1 2LU
Tel: 0392 264737
Fax: 0392 264736
VAT No: 142 0477 95

UNIVERSITY OF GLASGOW
French & German Publications, Modern Lang Bdg, Uni Gardens, Glasgow, Strathclyde G12 8QL
Tel: 041-339 8855 Ext 4599

UNIVERSITY OF HULL PRESS & LAMPADA PRESS
University of Hull, Hull, Humberside HU6 7RX
Tel: 0482 465322 Office
Tel: 0482 465834 Editor
Fax: 0482 465936
Telex: 592592 KHMAIL G
VAT No: 168 2000 86

Order Information

Order Dept Opening Times
Mon-Thu 8.45am-5.15pm, Fri 4.15pm Lunch 12.30-1.45

Number of Staff: 3

Trade Terms
Single Copy 25%, Multiple Copies 35%
Other Terms: P&P £1.50 minimum on single orders

Returns Procedures
Authority to Return: Publisher

UNIVERSITY OF LONDON
Room 205, Senate House, Malet Street, London WC1E 7HU
Tel: 071-636 8000 Ext 3268
Fax: 071-636 5894

UNIVERSITY OF LONDON
Institute of Classical Studies, 31-34 Gordon Square, London WC1H 0PY
Tel: 071-380 7498
Fax: 071-383 4807

UNIVERSITY OF LONDON
Institute of Germanic Studies, 29 Russell Square, London WC1B 5DP
Tel: 071-580 2711
Fax: 071-580 3480

UNIVERSITY OF NEWCASTLE UPON TYNE

Centre Health Service Research, 21 Claremont Place, Newcastle upon Tyne, Tyne & Wear NE2 4AA
Tel: 091-222 7045
Fax: 091-22 6043

UNIVERSITY OF NORTH LONDON PRESS

166-220 Holloway Road, London N7 8DB
Tel: 071-753 5073
Fax: 071-753 5075

UNIVERSITY OF WALES PRESS

6 Gwennyth Street, Cathays, Cardiff, South Glamorgan CF2 4YD
ISBN Prefix(es): 0 7083, 0 900786
Tel: 0222 231919 24 Hours
Tel: 0222 206035
Fax: 0222 230908

Order Information

Order Dept Opening Times
Mon - Fri 8.45am - 12.45pm, 1.45pm - 4.45pm
All Dues Automatically Recorded
Representation Available
Representation: BRAD Ltd

Personnel
Head of Company: Ned Thomas (Director) Ext 16
Head of Sales (Home): Richard Houdmont (Commercial Manager) Ext 13
Head of Accounts: Mrs Vida Halford (Senior Clerk) Ext 17

Number of titles published annually: 50
Number of Staff: 15
All New Titles are Bar Coded
Book Data Subscriber
WBIP Updating: Richard Houdmont

Trade Terms
Single copy/single line 25%, otherwise 33.3%. Special orders negotiable.
Other Terms: Delivery to bookseller's customer charged at cost.
BA/Girobank Small Order Scheme: Yes
Girobank Number: 494 9056
Credit Cards Accepted: Access/Master, Visa

Returns Procedures
Stock Returns: All titles supplied firm unless prior arrangements have been made, so permission required before return
Imperfect Returns: Please return complete book

UNIVERSITY OF WARWICK

Dept of Continuing Education, University of Warwick, Coventry, West Midlands CV4 7AL
Tel: 0203 524178
Fax: 0203 524223
VAT No: 273 1784 46

UNIVERSITY PRESSES MARKETING

The Old Mill, Mill Street, Wantage, Oxfordshire OX12 9AB
Tel: 02357 66662
Fax: 02357 66545
VAT No: 491 6261 35

Account No: _____
Sales Rep: _____
Tel: _____

Order Information

All Dues Automatically Recorded
Representation Available
Distribution: IBD/Plymbridge

Personnel
Head of Company: N Gosling (Senior Partner)
Other Important Personnel:
A Gillman (Partner) 0272 711296, R Howells (Partner) 0223 871902

Number of titles published annually: 600
WBIP Updating: Helen Relf

Trade Terms
According to annual volume of business per account.

Returns Procedures
Authority to Return: Prior authorisation required from UPM
Address for Returns: IBD/Plymbridge
Stock Returns: Apply to distributor
Imperfect Returns: Copyright page & short explanation up to £40

THE UNIVERSITY PRESSES OF CALIFORNIA, COLUMBIA & PRINCETON

1 Oldlands Way, Bognor Regis, West Sussex PO22 9SA
Tel: 0243 842165
Fax: 0243 842167

Orders to
JOHN WILEY & SONS LTD, Southern Cross Trading Estate, 1 Oldlands Way, Bognor Regis, West Sussex PO22 9SA
Tel: 0243 829121
Fax: 0243 820250

Order Information
Teleordering: UNICAL

Personnel
Head of Company: Wolfgang Wingerter

Book Data Subscriber

Returns Procedures
Address for Returns: Wiley

[Handwritten: UNWIN-HYMAN = International Thomson]

MERLIN UNWIN BOOKS

21 Corve Street, Ludlow, Shropshire SY8 1DA
Tel: 0584 877456
Fax: 0584 877457
VAT No: 586 9282 78

Orders to
CHRIS LLOYD SALES AND MARKETING SERVICES, 463 Ashley Road, Parkstone, Poole, Dorset BH14 0AX
Tel: 0202 715349
Fax: 0202 736191

[Handwritten: Urban + Schwarzenberg = Waverley Europe Ltd]

USBORNE PUBLISHING LTD

83/85 Saffron Hill, London EC1N 8RT
ISBN Prefix(es): 0 7460, 0 86020
Tel: 071-430 2800
Fax: 071-430 1562

Telex: 8953598
VAT No: 240 8215 89

Account No: _____
Sales Rep: _____
Tel: _____

Orders to
D SERVICES, 6 Euston Street, Freemen's Common, Leicester, Leicestershire LE2 7SS
Tel: 0533 547671
Fax: 0533 544670

Order Information

All Dues Automatically Recorded
Representation Available
Invoice Payments: D Services
Sales & Marketing:D Services

Personnel
Head of Company: Peter Usborne (Managing Director)
Head of Publicity: Gill Davie (Publicity Manager)
Head of Accounts: Keith Ball (Company Secretary)

Number of Staff: 100
NBA Signatory
All New Titles are Bar Coded
WBIP Updating: Gill Davie

Trade Terms
35%
Minimum Order: Small order surcharge may be levied on orders under £50
Other Terms: Carriage charged: Only overnight when requested
Credit Cards Accepted: Access/Master, Visa

Returns Procedures
Authority to Return: Prior authorisation must be obtained from D Services, Head Office or Representative
Address for Returns: D Services
Imperfect Returns: Title pages should carry name and address of customer, ISBN, retail price and full details of imperfection

US Naval Inst Operations % Airlift

THE USSHER PRESS

Friends of the Library, Trinity College Library, Dublin 2, County Dublin
Tel: 01 772 941
Fax: 01 719003
Telex: 93782

WBIP Updating: L W C Bryan

Trade Terms
33.3% on all titles plus carriage charge

Returns Procedures
Imperfect Returns: Request Authority

V & H COMPUTER SERVICES

Mayfield House, Spencer Street, Bognor Regis, West Sussex PO21 1AP
ISBN Prefix(es): 0 946008
Tel: 0243 867721

Order Information

All Dues Automatically Recorded
Representation Available

Personnel
Head of Company: R Valentine

Number of titles published annually: 1
Percentage of Export Sales: 25%
All New Titles are Bar Coded

Trade Terms
33% (5 books or more)
Other Terms: Small order surcharge of 10%, unless prepaid
BA/Girobank Small Order Scheme: Yes
Girobank Number: 39 726 6405

Returns Procedures
Stock Returns: Whole book must be returned
Imperfect Returns: As above

VACATION WORK

9 Park End Street, Oxford, Oxfordshire OX1 1HJ
ISBN Prefix(es): 0 907638, 0 911285, 0 914457, 1 56079, 1 56079, 1 85458, 2 950417
Tel: 0865 241978
Tel: 0865 243311
Fax: 0865 790885
VAT No: 194 8934 06

Order Information
Teleordering: VACWORK

Order Dept Opening Times
Mon - Fri 9am - 5.30pm
All Dues Automatically Recorded

Personnel
Head of Company: Charles James
Head of Sales (Home): Ann Wyatt
Head of Publicity: David Woodworth

Number of titles published annually: 12
Number of Staff: 7
All New Titles are Bar Coded
WBIP Updating: David Woodworth

Trade Terms
Firm single copy 10%, 2 copies 20%, See safe 3 or more 35%, Extra 5% for CWO/Giro for firm or see safe
Girobank Number: 286 0252
Credit Cards Accepted: Access/Master, Visa

Returns Procedures
Authority to Return: Ann Wyatt
Stock Returns: Covers for outdated books (up to 6mths after pub of new ed) Whole book in all other cases
Imperfect Returns: Return whole book

VCH PUBLISHERS (UK) LTD

8 Wellington Court, Cambridge, Cambridgeshire CB1 1HZ
ISBN Prefix(es): 0 854, 0 856, 1 854, 1 856
Tel: 0223 321111
Fax: 0223 313321
VAT No: 453 3777 31

Account No: _____
Sales Rep: _____
Tel: _____

Order Information
Teleordering: VCH

Order Dept Opening Times
Mon - Fri 9am - 5.30pm
Orders for more than one publisher can be bulked
All Dues Automatically Recorded
Representation Available

Personnel
Head of Company: Richard Ross
Head of Marketing: Christine White
Head of Accounts: John Stoddart

Number of titles published annually: 500
Number of Staff: 7
PA Member
NBA Signatory
Book Data Subscriber
WBIP Updating: C A White

Parent Company: VCH Verlags Gesellschaft

Trade Terms
General Net: 35%
Academic Net: Single copy 20%, Two or more 25%, Subscription Orders 30%
Credit Cards Accepted: Access/Master, Amex, Visa, Diners

Returns Procedures
Authority to Return: R Ross
Stock Returns: Returns accepted only with prior agreement
Imperfect Returns: Contact first

VELOCE PUBLISHING PLC

Serendipity Barn, Godmanstone, Dorset DT2 7AE
ISBN Prefix(es): 1 874105
Tel: 0300 341602
Fax: 0300 341065
VAT No: 586 1040 45

All New Titles are Bar Coded

VENNEL PRESS

9 Pankhurst Court, Caradon Close, London E11 4TB

VENTON EDUCATIONAL LTD

Unit 3, Stratton's Walk, High Street, Melksham, Wiltshire SN12 6LA
ISBN Prefix(es): 0 85475, 0 85966, 0 85993
Tel: 0225 703424
VAT No: 140 2939 85

NBA Signatory

VENTURE PRESS

16 Kent Street, Birmingham, West Midlands B5 6RD
Tel: 021-622 3911
Fax: 021-622 4860
VAT No: 487 0131 49

VERBATIM

PO Box 199, Aylesbury, Buckinghamshire HP20 2HY
ISBN Prefix(es): 0 930454
Tel: 0296 395880

Order Information
Order Dept Opening Times
Mon - Fri 9.30am - 5.30pm

Personnel
Head of Company: Laurence Urdang (Director/Editor)
Head of Sales (Home): Hazel Hall (Assistant to Director)

WBIP Updating: Hazel Hall
Parent Company: Laurence Urdang Inc
Trade Terms
35% on all orders, no surcharges
Credit Cards Accepted: Access/Master, Amex
Returns Procedures
Imperfect Returns: No returns, except faulty

VERIFICATION TECHNOLOGY INFORMATION CENTRE

8 John Adam Street, London WC2N 6EZ
Tel: 071-925 0867
Fax: 071-925 0861

VERITAS FOUNDATION

Publication Centre, 63 Jeddo Road, London W12 9EE
Tel: 081-749 4957
Tel: 081-749 4965 Tel/Fax
VAT No: 238 4284 49

VERITAS PUBLICATIONS

7&8 Lower Abbey Street, Dublin 1, County Dublin
ISBN Prefix(es): 0 862170, 0 905092, 1 85390
Tel: 01 788 177
Fax: 01 786 507
VAT No: 974 3032 7
Orders to
Veritas Book Dist, (FAO Pat Hobbs), Lower Avenue, Leamington Spa, Warwickshire CV31 3NP
Tel: 0926 451730 (24 Hrs)
Fax: 0926 451733
Order Information
Order Dept Opening Times
Mon - Fri 9am - 5.15pm
All Dues Automatically Recorded
Representation Available
Personnel
Head of Company: Martin Tierney (Director)
Head of Sales (Home): Tom Griffin (Commercial Manager)
Head of Marketing: Myra Delaney (Marketing Manager)
Head of Publicity: Maeve O'Byrne (Public Relations Officer)
Head of Accounts: Charles Duignan (Financial Controller)
Head of Distribution: Pat Hobbs (Manager - Veritas Book & Video Distribution) Leamington Spa
Head of Customer Services: Therese Moylan (Executive Assistant To The Director)
Number of titles published annually: 12
Number of Staff: 60
PA Member
All New Titles are Bar Coded
WBIP Updating: Maeve O'Byrne

Subsidiary Companies: Veritas Book & Video Distribution Ltd, Veritas Family Bookshop
Trade Terms
90 days credit from date of invoice
General Net: 35%
Academic Net: 20%
Non-Net: 20%
Returns Procedures
Authority to Return: Tom Griffin (IRL) Pat Hobbs (UK)

Address for Returns: Ireland:8 Hanover Quay, Dublin 2
UK:Lower Avenue, Leamington Spa, Warwickshire CV31 3NP
Imperfect Returns: Return complete book

VERSO

6 Meard Street, London W1V 3HR
ISBN Prefix(es): 0 86091
Tel: 071-437 3546
Tel: 071-434 1704
Tel: 071-439 8194
Fax: 071-734 0059
VAT No: 239 3166 54

Orders to
MARSTON BOOK SERVICES LTD, PO Box 87, Osney Mead, Oxford, Oxfordshire OX2 0DT
Tel: 0865 791155
Fax: 0865 791927

Order Information

All Dues Automatically Recorded
Representation Available
Invoice Payments: Marston

Personnel
Head of Company: Colin Robinson (Managing Director)
Head of Marketing: Dusty Miller (Marketing & Sales)
Head of Accounts: Paul Westlake (Accountant)

Number of titles published annually: 50
Percentage of Export Sales: 75%
Number of Staff: 8
NBA Signatory
Open University Publications
Book Data Subscriber
WBIP Updating: Dusty Miller

Trade Terms
33%
Credit Cards Accepted: Access/Master, Visa, Amex, Diners

Returns Procedures
Authority to Return: Permission required from Dusty Miller at Head Office
Address for Returns: Marston Book Services
Imperfect Returns: Up to and including £12.95

VERULAM PUBLISHING LTD

152A Park Street Lane, Park Street, St Albans, Hertfordshire AL2 2AU
ISBN Prefix(es): 0 8442, 0 88029, 0 937959, 1 56044, 1 874504
Tel: 0727 873866
Fax: 0727 873866
VAT No: 600 3495 78

Orders to
TIPTREE BOOK SERVICES LTD, Church Road, Tiptree, Colchester, Essex CO5 0SR
Tel: 0621 819600
Fax: 0621 819011

Order Information

All Dues Automatically Recorded
Representation Available
Invoice Payments: Tiptree Book Services Ltd

Personnel
Head of Company: David Collins
Head of Customer Services: Penny Collins

Number of titles published annually: 120
Number of Staff: 3
All New Titles are Bar Coded
WBIP Updating: Penny Collins

Trade Terms
35%, no surcharges
Credit Cards Accepted: Access/Master, Amex, Diners, Visa

Returns Procedures
Authority to Return: Verulam Head Office or Rep
Address for Returns: Tiptree Book Services Ltd
Imperfect Returns: Return whole copies to Tiptree over £15 published price. Cheaper books title page only accepted

VICTORIA & ALBERT MUSEUM

Cromwell Road, London SW7 2RL
ISBN Prefix(es): 0 901486, 0 905209, 0 948107, 1 85177
Tel: 071-938 8522
Fax: 071-938 8651
Telex: 268831 VICART G
VAT No: 444 0850 63

Orders to
LITTLEHAMPTON BOOK SERVICES, 14 Eldon Way, Lineside Ind Estate, Littlehampton, West Sussex BN17 7HE
Tel: 0903 721596
Fax: 0903 730914

Order Information

All Dues Automatically Recorded
Representation Available
Invoice Payments: Littlehampton
Representation: Cassell

Personnel
Head of Company: Jennifer Blain/Lesley Burton

Number of titles published annually: 10
Number of Staff: 2
All New Titles are Bar Coded
WBIP Updating: Jennifer Blain

Returns Procedures
Authority to Return: Jennifer Blain, Victoria & Albert Museum
Address for Returns: Littlehampton

VICTORIA HOUSE PUBLISHING LTD

Victoria House, 4 North Parade, Bath, Avon BA1 1LF
Tel: 0225 463401
Fax: 0225 460942
Telex: 449218 JOSMOR G
VAT No: 543 5692 28

Account No: _____
Sales Rep: _____
Tel: _____

Order Information

All Dues Automatically Recorded
Representation Available
Invoice Payments: David & Charles Ltd

Personnel
Head of Company: Michael J Morris/William G Gaspero
Head of Sales (Home): Gary Mannings
Head of Sales (Export): Martina Challis
Head of Marketing: Patricia Thomas
Head of Accounts: Andrew Hewetson

Number of titles published annually: 100
Percentage of Export Sales: 50%
Number of Staff: 20
PA Member
All New Titles are Bar Coded

Parent Company: Reader's Digest

Trade Terms
Negotiable

VIDEO ARTS LTD
Dumbarton House, 68 Oxford Street, London W1N 9LA
ISBN Prefix(es): 0 906607
Tel: 071-637 7288
Fax: 071-580 8103
Telex: 298838
VAT No: 440 6447 62

Order Information

Order Dept Opening Times
Mon - Fri 8.30am - 6pm

Personnel
Head of Company: Tina Tietjen
Head of Sales (Home): Michael Seriki
Head of Sales (Export): Tina Sunderland
Head of Marketing: Tony Barritt
Head of Accounts: David Ballinger

Number of titles published annually: 5
Percentage of Export Sales: 20%
Number of Staff: 65
WBIP Updating: Tony Barritt

Trade Terms
negotiable
Credit Cards Accepted: Access/Master, Visa

VILLIERS PUBLICATIONS LTD
19 Sylvan Avenue, London N3 2LE
ISBN Prefix(es): 0 900777
Tel: 081-343 3704 Tel/Fax
VAT No: 229 6542 44

Orders to
Kettering Books, 14 Horsemarket, Kettering, Northants NN16 1DQ

Order Information

Invoice Payments: Kettering Books

Trade Terms
Single Copy 25%, Multiple Copies 33.3%

Returns Procedures
Authority to Return: Prior permission required from Head Office
Imperfect Returns: Title page accepted all prices if fault described

VINE HOUSE DISTRIBUTION
Waldenbury, North Chailey, East Sussex BN8 4DR
Tel: 082-572 3398 24 Hours
Fax: 082-572 4188
VAT No: 475 7334 19

Account No: _____
Sales Rep: _____
Tel: _____

Order Information
Teleordering: VINE

Order Dept Opening Times
Mon - Fri 9am - 5.30pm
Orders for more than one publisher can be bulked
All Dues Automatically Recorded
Representation Available

Personnel
Head of Company: Richard Squibb
Head of Customer Services: Sarah Squibb

IPG Member
All New Titles are Bar Coded
WBIP Updating: Richard Squibb

Trade Terms
General Net: Single copy 25%, Two or more 35%
Other Terms: Carriage charges on orders under £20
Girobank Number: 393 3202
Credit Cards Accepted: Access/Master, Visa

Returns Procedures
Authority to Return: Prior permission required from Richard Squibb
Imperfect Returns: Return title page

VINE PUBLISHING LTD

PO Box 44, Aberdeen, Grampian AB9 8WE
Tel: 0224 315333
VAT No: 384 8510 27

Personnel
Head of Company: Dr Roger Baker (Managing Director)
Head of Sales (Home): Mrs Ann Baker (Director/Secretary)

Trade Terms
35% on paperbacks, no discount on REHAB - sold direct only

Returns Procedures
Authority to Return: Prior permission required

VIRAGO PRESS

Centro House, 20-23 Mandela Street, London NW1 0HQ
ISBN Prefix(es): 0 86068, 1 85381
Tel: 071-383 5150
Fax: 071-383 4892
Cables: CATERWAUL LONDON NW1
VAT No: 494 7749 79

Account No: _____
Sales Rep: _____
Tel: _____

Orders to
GRANTHAM BOOK SERVICES LTD, Isaac Newton Way, Alma Park Industrial Estate, Grantham, Lincolnshire NG31 9SD
Tel: 0476 67421
Fax: 0476 590223

Order Information

All Dues Automatically Recorded
Representation Available

Invoice Payments: Grantham Book Services
Sales Representation: Random House

Personnel
Head of Company: Harriet Spicer (Managing Director)
Head of Marketing: Fiona McIntosh (Publicity & Marketing Director)
Head of Accounts: Nicola Alford (Company Accountant)

Number of titles published annually: 65
Number of Staff: 20
All New Titles are Bar Coded
Open University Publications
Book Data Subscriber
WBIP Updating: Fiona McIntosh

Parent Company: Swapequal Ltd

Trade Terms
as per Random House Division & Grantham Book Services terms

Returns Procedures
Authority to Return: Random House Sales Department
Address for Returns: Grantham Book Services

VIRGIN PUBLISHING LTD

338 Ladbroke Grove, London W10 5AH
ISBN Prefix(es): 0 352, 0 426, 0 7490, 0 85031, 0 86369, 1 85227
Tel: 081-968 7554
Fax: 081-968 0929
VAT No: 577 2642 13

Account No: _____

Sales Rep: _____

Tel: _____

Orders to
~~TIPTREE BOOK SERVICES LTD, Church Road, Tiptree, Colchester, Essex CO5 0SR~~ Exel Logistics
Tel: 0621 819600
Fax: 0621 819011

Order Information

All Dues Automatically Recorded
Representation Available
Invoice Payments: Tiptree Book Services

Personnel
Head of Company: Robert Shreeve
Head of Sales (Home): Ray Mudie
Head of Sales (Export): Graham Eames
Head of Marketing: Siobhan Flynn
Head of Accounts: Michael Cohen
Head of Customer Services: Marcia Jennings

Number of titles published annually: 200
Percentage of Export Sales: 25%
Number of Staff: 27
NBA Signatory
All New Titles are Bar Coded
Book Data Subscriber
WBIP Updating: Gill Woolcott

Parent Company: Virgin Communications

Trade Terms
35%
Credit Cards Accepted: Access/Master, Visa

Returns Procedures
Authority to Return: Head Office or Representative
Address for Returns: Tiptree
Imperfect Returns: Return Title Page to Tiptree

VIRTUE BOOKS LTD

Edward House, Tenter Street, Rotherham, South Yorkshire S60 1LB
ISBN Prefix(es): 0 900778
Tel: 0709 365005
Fax: 0709 829982

Order Information

Order Dept Opening Times
Mon - Fri 8.30am - 5.25pm
All Dues Automatically Recorded

Other Important Locations
Southern Sales Office:Grindfield Farm, Furners Green, Uckfield, East Sussex TN22 3RP Tel:0825 740685 Fax:740742

Personnel
Head of Company: P E Russum (Director)
Head of Sales (Home): M Virtue (Sales Director) Uckfield
Head of Accounts: M Andrews
Head of Distribution: J Windle
Head of Customer Services: Mrs S Fisher

Number of titles published annually: 3
Percentage of Export Sales: 50%
Number of Staff: 15
NBA Signatory
WBIP Updating: M Virtue

Parent Company: E Russum & Sons Ltd

Trade Terms
General Net: Single copy/single line 25%, 2 or more single titles 30% stock orders by arrangement

Returns Procedures
Authority to Return: Mrs S Fisher, Head Office

VISION PRESS LTD

28 Phillimore Walk, Kensington, London W8 7SA
ISBN Prefix(es): 0 85478
Tel: 071-937 2351 Tel/Fax
VAT No: 239 7307 42

Order Information

All Dues Automatically Recorded
Representation Available

Personnel
Head of Company: Alan Moore

Percentage of Export Sales: 25%
NBA Signatory

Trade Terms
General Net: Single copy/single line, 2 or more single titles 25%. 2 or more copies of a title 35%
Academic Net: Single copy/single line, 2 or more single titles 25%, 2 or more copies of a title 35%

Returns Procedures
Stock Returns: Only returns that are made with publisher's permission in writing, quoting invoive No will be accepted for credit

VISUAL ARTS PUBLISHING

82 Sinclair Road, London W14 0NJ
ISBN Prefix(es): 0 9514166
Tel: 071-603 7945
Fax: 071-603 7945

Order Information

Order Dept Opening Times
Mon - Sat 10am - 7pm
All Dues Automatically Recorded
Representation Available

Personnel
Head of Company: C A Dars

Number of titles published annually: 1
All New Titles are Bar Coded

Trade Terms
30%
Academic Net: Subscription orders £15 discount
Other Terms: Part postage

VITA BOOKS
26 Chelsea Square, London SW3 6LF
Tel: 071-352 6919

Order Information

Order Dept Opening Times
Mon - Fri 9am - 5pm

Personnel
Head of Company: Branko Bokun (Managing Director)
Head of Sales (Home): Mrs Anne London

Trade Terms
33%-35%
Credit Cards Accepted: Access/Master, Visa

Returns Procedures
Authority to Return: Prior permission required

VNU BUSINESS PUBLICATIONS
VNU House, 32-34 Broadwick Street, London W1A 2HG
ISBN Prefix(es): 0 862711
Tel: 071-439 4242
Fax: 071-437 8985
VAT No: 174 874

Trade Terms
Credit Cards Accepted: Access/Master, Visa

VOLCANO PRESS LTD
121 Devana Road, Leicester, Leicestershire LE2 1PL
ISBN Prefix(es): 1 870127
Tel: 0533 706714 24 Hours
Tel: 0533 736721
Fax: 0533 706714

Orders to
Volcano Press Ltd, Post Box 139, Leicester, Leicestershire LE2 2YH

Personnel
Head of Company: A Hussain
Head of Sales (Home): F Hussain
Head of Marketing: N Hussain

IPG Member

Trade Terms
35% discount

Returns Procedures
Authority to Return: Volcano Press Ltd, PO Box 139, Leicester LE2 2YH

Stock Returns: Telephone first to order dept at 0533 706714 and inform
Imperfect Returns: Telephone first to order dept and inform

VOLO EDITION

66A Ferme Park Road, London N4 4ED
Tel: 081-889 3445
Fax: 081-889 3272
VAT No: 554 2272 52

Orders to
Volo Edition, 10 Vincent Road, London N22 6NA

IPG Member

VOLTAIRE FOUNDATION

~~Taylor Institution, Oxford, Oxfordshire OX1 3NA~~ UNIVERSITY OF OXFORD, 99 BANBURY ROAD, OXFORD OX2 7BB
ISBN Prefix(es): ~~0 7294~~
Tel: ~~0865 270250~~ 0865 284600
Fax: ~~0865 270740~~ 0865 284610
VAT No: 195 2753 34

Order Information
All Dues Automatically Recorded

Personnel
Head of Company: Andrew Brown

Number of titles published annually: 25
Percentage of Export Sales: 90%
Number of Staff: 10

Trade Terms
General Net: Single Copy 25%
Academic Net: Single Copy 10%
Credit Cards Accepted: Access/Master, Visa

Returns Procedures
Authority to Return: Not accepted

VOLTURNA PRESS

52 Ormonde Road, Hythe, Kent CT21 6DW
ISBN Prefix(es): 0 85606
Tel: 0303 269465

Personnel
Head of Company: D M C MacEwan
Other Important Personnel:
Jean MacEwan

Number of titles published annually: 3
Number of Staff: 2

Trade Terms
35% plus postage & packing
Girobank Number: 16 222 0006

Returns Procedures
Stock Returns: Return book
Imperfect Returns: Return title page

WAITE GROUP = Putman

WALDEN PUBLISHING LTD

2 Market Street, Saffron Walden, Essex CB10 1HZ
ISBN Prefix(es): 0 9044398
Tel: 0799 521150
Fax: 0799 524805
VAT No: 599 5011 07

WALKER BOOKS LTD

87 Vauxhall Walk, London SE11 5HJ
ISBN Prefix(es): 0 7445
Tel: 071-793 0909
Fax: 071-587 1123
Fax: 071-735 3584 Sales/Mark
Telex: 8955572
VAT No: 137 8601

Account No: _____

Sales Rep: _____

Tel: _____

Orders to
TIPTREE BOOK SERVICES LTD, Church Road, Tiptree, Colchester, Essex CO5 0SR
Tel: 0621 819600
Fax: 0621 819011

Order Information

All Dues Automatically Recorded
Representation Available
Invoice Payments: Tiptree Book Services

Personnel

Head of Company: David Lloyd (Chairman)
Head of Sales (Home): Janet Wildish (UK Sales Manager)
Head of Sales (Export): Fiona MacDonald (Export Sales Manager)
Head of Marketing: Catherine Fardell (Promotions Manager)
Head of Publicity: Julie Pike (Publicity Manager)
Head of Accounts: David Heatherwick (Managing & Finance Director)

Number of titles published annually: 300
Percentage of Export Sales: 70%
Number of Staff: 90
NBA Signatory
All New Titles are Bar Coded
WBIP Updating: Ruth Evans/Sarah Carroll

Subsidiary Companies: Candlewick Press (US)

Trade Terms
35%, 30 days credit

Returns Procedures
Authority to Return: Tiptree Book Services
Address for Returns: Tiptree Book Services
Stock Returns: Local Sales Representative or Tiptree for overstocks Tiptree if incorrectly supplied or damaged in transit
Imperfect Returns: Send to Tiptree

ALFRED WALLER LTD

Orchards, Fawley, Henley-on-Thames, Oxfordshire RG9 6JF
Tel: 0491 638694
Fax: 0491 638833
VAT No: 527 2275 49

Orders to
PLYMBRIDGE DISTRIBUTORS LTD, Plymbridge House, Estover Road, Plymouth, Devon PL6 7PZ
Tel: 0752 735251
Fax: 0752 695699

IPG Member
Book Data Subscriber

WARBURG INSTITUTE

University of London, Woburn Square, London WC1H 0AB
ISBN Prefix(es): 0 85481
Tel: 071-580 9663
Fax: 071-436 2852

Order Information

Order Dept Opening Times
Mon - Fri 10am - 5.30pm
All Dues Automatically Recorded

Personnel

Head of Company: Prof C N J Mann (Director)
Head of Sales (Home): Ms E A Witchell (Administrative Assistant)

Number of titles published annually: 4
Percentage of Export Sales: 40%
Number of Staff: 6
PA Member
NBA Signatory
WBIP Updating: E A Witchell

Parent Company: University of London

Trade Terms

25%, plus carriage charges

Returns Procedures

Authority to Return: Ms E A Witchell
Stock Returns: Books should be returned plus slip to say why. Overstocks are not accepted
Imperfect Returns: As above

WARD LOCK EDUCATIONAL CO LTD

1 Christopher Road, East Grinstead, West Sussex RH19 3BT
ISBN Prefix(es): 0 7062
Tel: 0342 318980
Fax: 0342 410980
VAT No: 362 3850 54

Account No: 0061697001
Sales Rep: _____
Tel: _____

Order Information

Order Dept Opening Times
Mon - Thurs 9am - 5.30pm, Fri 9am - 5pm
Cyclical Ordering Policy
All Dues Automatically Recorded
Representation Available

Personnel

Head of Sales (Home): Rodney Pollock
Head of Sales (Export): Quentin Hockliffe
Head of Publicity: Lesley Kennett
Head of Accounts: Eileen Parsons
Head of Distribution: Vincent Winter
Head of Customer Services: Kathy Sims

Number of titles published annually: 48
All New Titles are Bar Coded
Open University Publications
Book Data Subscriber
WBIP Updating: Lesley Kennett

Parent Company: Ling Kee (UK) Ltd

Trade Terms

Net 35%, non-net 17.5%
Minimum Order: Cash with order below £40 published price
Girobank Number: 501 3062
Credit Cards Accepted: Access/Master, Visa

Returns Procedures
Authority to Return: Eileen Parsons
Stock Returns: Written authorization clearing stating invoice number and reason for return
Imperfect Returns: Title page up to £10, quoting invoice/order number, above this written authorization.

WARD'S PUBLISHING SERVICES

12 Little Mundells, Welwyn Garden City, Hertfordshire AL7 1EW
Tel: 0707 320220
Fax: 0707 331012
VAT No: 370 4882 41

PA Member
Book Data Subscriber

WAREHAM BEARS PUBLICATIONS

18 Church Street, Wareham, Dorset BH20 4NF
Tel: 0929 556671
VAT No: 423 4451 77

WATERLOW INFORMATION SERVICES LTD

Paulton House, 8 Shepherdess Walk, London N1 7LB
ISBN Prefix(es): 0 080408
Tel: 071-490 0049
Fax: 071-490 2979
VAT No: 242 3067 91

Order Information

All Dues Automatically Recorded
Representation Available

Personnel
Head of Company: Rory A Conwell
Head of Sales (Home): Stephen Cave
Head of Accounts: Su Dutta

Number of titles published annually: 20
WBIP Updating: Stephen Cave

Trade Terms
20%

WATERMARK PUBLICATIONS (UK) LTD

PO Box 18, Chiddingfold, Godalming, Surrey GU8 4PR
ISBN Prefix(es): 1 8732000, 9 6274600
Tel: 0428 683670 24 Hours
Fax: 0428 683069
VAT No: 528 9340 23

Order Information

Representation Available

Personnel
Head of Company: Ian Lambot (Director)
Head of Sales (Home): Christianne Long (Director)

Number of titles published annually: 3
Percentage of Export Sales: 70%
Number of Staff: 2
PA Member
Book Data Subscriber
WBIP Updating: Christianne Long

Trade Terms
35% on all orders
Other Terms: 90 days

Returns Procedures
Imperfect Returns: Return of book - replacement issued & postage refunded

PAUL WATKINS PUBLISHING

18 Adelaide Street, Stamford, Lincolnshire PE9 2EN
Tel: 0780 56793
VAT No: 576 4800 17

THE WATTS GROUP

96 Leonard Street, London EC2A 4RH
ISBN Prefix(es): 0 7496, 0 86313, 1 85213
Tel: 071-739 2929
Fax: 071-739 2318
Telex: 262655 GROLUK G
VAT No: 230 2864 89

Account No: _____

Sales Rep: _____

Tel: _____

Orders to
TIPTREE BOOK SERVICES LTD, Church Road, Tiptree, Colchester, Essex CO5 0SR
Tel: 0621 819600
Fax: 0621 819011

Order Information

All Dues Automatically Recorded
Representation Available
Invoice Payments: Watts Group

Personnel
Head of Company: Marlene Johnson (Managing & Finance Director)
Head of Sales (Home): George Spicer (Sales Manager)
Head of Publicity: Linda Banner (Publicity Manager)
Head of Accounts: Anne Marimuthu (Financial Controller)

Number of titles published annually: 250
Number of Staff: 40
PA Member
All New Titles are Bar Coded
Book Data Subscriber
WBIP Updating: G Spicer

Parent Company: Hachette

Trade Terms
35% all orders, Grolier Reference Sets 20%
Girobank Number: 200 9455

Returns Procedures
Authority to Return: G Spicer Watts Group
Address for Returns: Tiptree
Stock Returns: Authorised returns only are accepted
Imperfect Returns: Title page only up to £10

[Handwritten note: Waverley Europe Ltd, Broadway House, 2-6 Fulham Broadway, LONDON, SW6 1AA. Phone. 071 385 2357 Fax 071 385 2922. See Williams + Wilkins]

WAYLAND (PUBLISHERS) LTD

61 Western Road, Hove, East Sussex BN3 1JD
ISBN Prefix(es): 0 7502, 0 85078, 0 85340, 0 904724, 1 85210, 1 85485
Tel: 0273 722561
Fax: 0273 29314
Fax: 0273 723526

VAT No: 587 5066 01
Account No: W0024000
Sales Rep:
Tel:

Order Information
Teleordering: WAY

Order Dept Opening Times
Mon - Fri 9am - 1pm, 2pm - 5.30pm
Representation Available

Personnel
Head of Company: John Lewis (Managing Director)
Head of Sales (Home): Bernard Nevin
Head of Sales (Export): Keith Lilley
Head of Marketing: Sally Davis
Head of Accounts: Martin Jane
Head of Customer Services: Oonagh Gretton

Number of titles published annually: 200
Percentage of Export Sales: 50%
Number of Staff: 60
PA Member
NBA Signatory
All New Titles are Bar Coded

Parent Company: Wolters Kluwer (UK)

Trade Terms
35% on all orders no surcharges
Credit Cards Accepted: Access/Master, Visa

Returns Procedures
Authority to Return: Representative
Address for Returns: Bailey Distribution
Imperfect Returns: Requests to be referred to representative or head office

WEAVERS PRESS PUBLISHING

Tregeraint House, Zennor, St Ives, Cornwall TR26 3DB
ISBN Prefix(es): 0 946017
Tel: 0736 797061 24 Hours
Fax: 0736 797061
VAT No: 526 9340 35

Order Information

Order Dept Opening Times
Mon - Fri 9.30am - 5.30pm
All Dues Automatically Recorded

Personnel
Head of Company: John T Wilson
Head of Accounts: Susan Edgley-Wilson

Number of titles published annually: 7
Number of Staff: 4
IPG Member
WBIP Updating: John T Wilson

Trade Terms
35% no postage on invoice value £10 + 25% single copy oders + postage
Non-Net: 25% + Postage (Single Copy), 25% + Postage under £10 (Two) 35% + Postage under £10 (Two Books or more)
Other Terms: Carriage Charges on invoiced orders below £10

Returns Procedures
Stock Returns: No returns accepted unless damaged or incorrectly supplied

Weidenfeld + Nicholson = Littlehampton Book Service

OWEN WELLS PUBLISHING COMPANY

23 Eaton Road, Ilkley, West Yorkshire LS29 9PU
ISBN Prefix(es): 0 904553
Tel: 0943 602270
Fax: 0943 816732
VAT No: 231 5129 01

Order Information

All Dues Automatically Recorded

Personnel
Head of Company: Owen Wells (Partner)

Number of titles published annually: 2
Number of Staff: 3

Trade Terms
Net 30% + 5% cash with order
Academic Net: 30% + 5% cash with order
Non-Net: 25%

Returns Procedures
Authority to Return: No prior authorization required
Stock Returns: All returns automatically accepted
Imperfect Returns: No limit

WELLSWEEP PRESS

8 Duke Street, St James's, London SW1Y 6BN
ISBN Prefix(es): 0 948454
Tel: 071-839 6599
Fax: 071-976 1832
Fax: 071-267 9225
VAT No: 562 8390 21

Orders to
PASSWORD (BOOKS) LTD, 23 New Mount Street, Manchester, Greater Manchester M4 4DE
Tel: 061-953 4009
Fax: 061-953 4001

Order Information

All Dues Automatically Recorded
Representation Available
Invoice Payments: Password (Books) Ltd

Personnel
Head of Company: John Cayley (Publisher)
Other Important Personnel:
Harold Wells (Managing Director), Harriet Evans (Associate Editor)

Number of titles published annually: 7
Number of Staff: 3
All New Titles are Bar Coded
WBIP Updating: John Cayley

Trade Terms
35% no surcharges
Girobank Number: 613 4599

Returns Procedures
Authority to Return: Representative
Address for Returns: Clipper Returns Dept, Eastmead Ind Estate, Lavan, Chichester, PO18 0DB

WELSH BOOKS COUNCIL DISTRIBUTION CENTRE

Glan Yr Afon Industrial Estate, Llanbadarn, Aberystwyth, Dyfed SY23 3AQ
Tel: 0970 624455
Fax: 0970 625506
VAT No: 123 0426 23

Account No: _____
Sales Rep: _____
Tel: _____

Order Information
Teleordering: WBC

Order Dept Opening Times
Mon - Thu 8.30am - 5.30pm Fri 8.30am - 5pm
All Dues Automatically Recorded
Representation Available

Other Important Locations
Welsh Books Council, Castell Brychan, Aberystwyth, Dyfed SY23 2JB
Tel: 0970 624151
Fax: 0970 625385

Personnel
Head of Company: Miss Gwerfyl Pierce Jones (Director) 0970 624151
Head of Marketing: Mr D Philip Davies 0970 624151
Head of Accounts: Mr Pedr ap Llwyd
Head of Distribution: Mr Dafydd Charles Jones

Number of Staff: 41

Trade Terms
33.3% + 2.5% prompt settlement discount

Returns Procedures
Authority to Return: Dafydd Charles Jones
Stock Returns: No books to be returned without prior permission
Imperfect Returns: Complete book should be returned when found to be imperfect Permission in these cases not necessary

WELSH OFFICE

Statistical Publications Unit, Cathays Park, Cardiff, South Glamorgan CF1 3NQ
ISBN Prefix(es): 0 7504
Tel: 0222 825054
Fax: 0222 825350

Order Information

Order Dept Opening Times
8.30am - 4.30pm

Personnel
Head of Sales (Home): E Swires-Hennessy
Head of Accounts: Mrs L O'Neill
Head of Customer Services: Mrs C Owen

Number of titles published annually: 24
All New Titles are Bar Coded

Trade Terms
35%

Returns Procedures
Stock Returns: Return book with invoice for reissue

WERNER SHAW LTD

Suite 34, 26 Charing Cross Road, London WC2H 0DH
ISBN Prefix(es): 0 907961
Tel: 071-240 5991
Fax: 071-379 5770
VAT No: 340 4932 73

Order Information

All Dues Automatically Recorded

Personnel
Head of Company: Barry Shaw

Number of titles published annually: 1
Number of Staff: 3
IPG Member

Trade Terms
35%
Other Terms: Carriage charged on one copy only
Girobank Number: 500 1064

Returns Procedures
Imperfect Returns: No price limit. Title pages accepted

WESSEX ELECTRONIC PUBLISHING
6 Park Place, North Road, Poole, Dorset BH14 0LE
Tel: 0202 735332
Fax: 0202 742043
VAT No: 504 1683 71

WEST COUNTRY BOOKS
1 Chinon Court, Lower Moor Way, Tiverton Bus Park,, Tiverton, Devon EX16 6SS
Tel: 0884 243242
Fax: 0884 243325

Order Information

Order Dept Opening Times
Mon - Fri 9am - 5pm

Personnel
Head of Company: Simon Butler/Steven Pugsley (Joint Managing Directors)
Head of Sales (Home): Nick Aves (Sales & Distribution Manager)
Head of Accounts: Kirsty Atkin

Trade Terms
35% firm sale only, payment due net monthly. Singles 20%. Pro-forma for non-account customers.
Credit Cards Accepted: Access/Master, Visa

Returns Procedures
Authority to Return: Prior permission required from Sales Manager
Imperfect Returns: Return with copy of invoice for replacement

WESTERN PUBLISHING COMPANY INC
1 Devonshire Street, London W1N 1FX
ISBN Prefix(es): 0 307
Tel: 071-323 1212
Fax: 071-255 2051
Telex: 27388 WESPUB G
VAT No: 440 5575 58

Account No: _____
Sales Rep: _____
Tel: _____

Orders to
EGMONT PUBLISHING LTD, Egmont House, PO Box 111, Great Ducie St, Manchester, Greater Manchester M60 3BL
Tel: 061-834 3110
Fax: 061-834 0059

Order Information

All Dues Automatically Recorded
Representation Available
Invoice Payments: Egmont Ltd

Personnel
Head of Company: Ken Kemp (Managing Director UK)
Head of Sales (Home): Mike Strul (UK Sales Director)
Head of Accounts: Akber Kirefu (Finance Manager)

Number of titles published annually: 200
Number of Staff: 12
All New Titles are Bar Coded
WBIP Updating: Sigrun Lyne

Trade Terms
Standard trade terms
Minimum Order: £50 retail customers, £100 wholesalers

Returns Procedures
Address for Returns: Egmont Ltd
Stock Returns: Authorised returns only

WESTVIEW = Plymbridge

WHELDON & WESLEY LTD

Lytton Lodge, Codicote, Hitchin, Hertfordshire SG4 8TE
Tel: 0438 820370
Fax: 0438 821478
VAT No: 197 4319 28

J WHITAKER & SONS LTD

12 Dyott Street, London WC1A 1DF
ISBN Prefix(es): 0 85021
Tel: 071-836 8911
Fax: 071-836 2909
Cables: WHITMANACK LONDON WC1
VAT No: 232 1805 01

Account No: _____

Sales Rep: _____

Tel: _____

Order Information
Teleordering: WHIT

Order Dept Opening Times
Mon - Fri 9am - 5pm

Personnel
Head of Company: Sally Whitaker (Managing Director)
Head of Sales (Home): Martin Whitaker (Sales & Marketing Director)
Head of Accounts: John Lycett (Financial Controller)
Head of Distribution: Mary Stevenson (Marketing & Distribution Manager)
Head of Customer Services: Simon Skinner (Sales Manager)
Other Important Personnel:
Rosemary Bell (CD-ROM Manager)

Number of titles published annually: 17
Percentage of Export Sales: 35%
Number of Staff: 110
PA Member
IPG Member
NBA Signatory
WBIP Updating: Mary Stevenson

Subsidiary Companies: SBN Agency Ltd (The), Teleordering Ltd

Trade Terms
25% single copy, two or more 35%
Other Terms: Bibliographic titles 10% discount resale only where full name of customer is supplied

Girobank Number: 535 3351
Credit Cards Accepted: Access/Master, Visa

Returns Procedures
Address for Returns: Sales Dept
Stock Returns: Enquire first. All orders accepted firm only. Phone/write to Edward Heron for return or collection instruction
Imperfect Returns: Up to £20 title pages may be returned. Above £20 books should be returned attention of Edward Heron

WHITE COCKADE PUBLISHING
Wendlebury House, Church Lane, Wendlebury, Oxfordshire OX6 8PN
ISBN Prefix(es): 0 9513124, 1 873487
Tel: 0869 241450 24 Hours
Fax: 0869 248195
VAT No: 485 8507 02

Order Information
Order Dept Opening Times
Mon - Sat 9am - 6.30pm
All Dues Automatically Recorded
Representation Available

Personnel
Head of Company: Perilla Kinchin (Director)
Head of Sales (Home): Linda Pounds (Sales Manager)

Number of titles published annually: 3
Number of Staff: 2
IPG Member
All New Titles are Bar Coded
WBIP Updating: Perilla Kinchin

Trade Terms
General Net: Single Copy 20% Two or more single titles 35%

Returns Procedures
Authority to Return: Prior permission required
Imperfect Returns: Title page limit £20

WHITE EAGLE PUBLISHING TRUST
New Lands, Brewells Lane, Liss, Hampshire GU33 7HY
ISBN Prefix(es): 0 85487
Tel: 0730 893300
Fax: 0730 892235
VAT No: 193 0956 42

Order Information
Order Dept Opening Times
Mon - Fri 9am - 12.15pm 1.30pm - 5pm
All Dues Automatically Recorded

Personnel
Head of Company: Ylana Hayward
Head of Sales (Home): Geoffrey Dent
Head of Publicity: Colum Hayward

Number of titles published annually: 2
Percentage of Export Sales: 55%
Number of Staff: 12
IPG Member
NBA Signatory
All New Titles are Bar Coded
WBIP Updating: G R H Dent

Parent Company: White Eagle Lodge

Trade Terms
33.3%

Other Terms: On order £5 net or less
Girobank Number: 25 072 4006

Returns Procedures
Imperfect Returns: Return title page no price limit

White Horse Press = Bailey Distribution

WHITING & BIRCH LTD

PO Box 872, 90 Dartmouth Road, Forest Hill, London
SE23 3NL
ISBN Prefix(es): 1 871177
Tel: 081-699 0914
Fax: 081-699 3685
VAT No: 445 3868 23

Order Information

Order Dept Opening Times
8.30am - 7pm
All Dues Automatically Recorded
Representation Available
Representation:Book Representation & Distribution (BRAD)

Personnel
Head of Company: Diana Birch/David Whiting
Head of Customer Services: Pam Gray

Number of titles published annually: 30
Percentage of Export Sales: 30%
Number of Staff: 5
IPG Member
NBA Signatory
All New Titles are Bar Coded
WBIP Updating: Dave Whiting

Subsidiary Companies: Whiting Publishing Services, David

Trade Terms
Single Copy 25%, Two or more or CWO 33%
Non-Net: 20%
Credit Cards Accepted: Access/Master, Visa, Amex, Diners

Returns Procedures
Authority to Return: Pam Gray
Stock Returns: Prior consent required for overstock returns
Imperfect Returns: £6.50

WHITTET BOOKS LTD

18 Anley Road, London W14 0BY
ISBN Prefix(es): 0 905483, 1 873580
Tel: 071-603 1139
Fax: 071-603 8154
VAT No: 213 0731 17

Orders to
BIBLIOS PUBLISHERS DISTRIBUTION SERVICE LTD,
Star Road, Partridge Green, West Sussex RH13 8LD
Tel: 0403 710971
Fax: 0403 711143

Order Information

All Dues Automatically Recorded
Representation Available
Invoice Payments: Biblios Publishers Distribution Services Ltd

Personnel
Head of Company: Annabel Whittet

Number of titles published annually: 10
All New Titles are Bar Coded

Trade Terms
General Net: Single copy/single line 20%, 2 or more single titles 35%, subscription orders 35%

Returns Procedures
Address for Returns: Biblios Publishers Distribution Services Ltd
Imperfect Returns: Return title page only

WHITTINGTON PRESS

Lower Marston Farm, Nr Risbury, Leominster, Herefordshire HR6 0NJ
ISBN Prefix(es): 0 904845, 1 85428
Tel: 0885 400250
Tel: 0242 820724
VAT No: 276 0348 53

Order Information

All Dues Automatically Recorded
Representation Available

Personnel
Head of Company: John Randle
Head of Sales (Home): Rosalind Randle

Number of titles published annually: 6
Percentage of Export Sales: 50%
WBIP Updating: J Randle

Trade Terms
Single Copy 25%, Two or more 33%
Other Terms: Carriage charged at cost of p&p
BA/Girobank Small Order Scheme: Post free
Girobank Number: 27 162 4000
Credit Cards Accepted: Access/Master, Visa

Returns Procedures
Authority to Return: We do not accept returns
Imperfect Returns: Return complete book for replacement

WHITTLES PUBLISHING SERVICES

Roseleigh House, Latheronwheel, Highland KW5 6DW
Tel: 05934 240 Tel/Fax
VAT No: 456 3413 51

PA Member

WHURR PUBLISHERS LTD

19B Compton Terrace, London N1 2UN
ISBN Prefix(es): 1 870332, 1 871381
Tel: 071-359 5979
Fax: 071-226 5290
VAT No: 205 0501

Orders to
TURPIN DISTRIBUTION SERVICES LTD, Blackhorse Road, Letchworth, Hertfordshire SG6 1HN
Tel: 0462 672555
Fax: 0462 480947

Order Information

All Dues Automatically Recorded
Representation Available
Invoice Payments: Turpin Transactions Ltd

Personnel
Head of Company: Colin Whurr
Head of Publicity: Sarah Vicary
Head of Accounts: Edward Kisch

Number of titles published annually: 30
Percentage of Export Sales: 20%
Number of Staff: 4

PA Member
IPG Member
NBA Signatory
All New Titles are Bar Coded
Book Data Subscriber
WBIP Updating: Sarah Vicary

Trade Terms
Negotiable
Credit Cards Accepted: Access/Master, Visa

Returns Procedures
Address for Returns: Turpin Transactions Ltd

WILD SWAN PUBLICATIONS LTD

1-3 Hagbourne Road, Didcot, Oxfordshire OX11 8DP
Tel: 0235 816478
VAT No: 314 3179 81

WILDWOOD = Ashgate Distribution

JOHN WILEY & SONS LTD

Baffins Lane, Chichester, West Sussex PO19 1UD
ISBN Prefix(es): 0 471
Tel: 0243 779777
Fax: 0243 775878
Telex: 86290
VAT No: 376 7669 87
Account No: _____ 60135100 _____
Sales Rep: _____
Tel: _____

Orders to
JOHN WILEY & SONS LTD, Southern Cross Trading Estate, 1 Oldlands Way, Bognor Regis, West Sussex PO22 9SA
Tel: 0243 829121
Fax: 0243 820250

Order Information
Teleordering: WLEY
First Edition Subscriber

Representation Available

Personnel
Head of Company: Michael Foyle (Managing Director)
Head of Sales (Home): Stefan Usansky (UK Sales Manager)
Head of Sales (Export): Robert Long (General Sales/Marketing Manager)
Head of Accounts: Jim Dicks (Finance Director)
Other Important Personnel:
Geoffrey Farrell (Trade Marketing Manager), Lyn Udall (Textbook Marketing Manager), Dr John Jarvis (Deputy Managing Director (MD From 1.5.93))

Number of titles published annually: 1000
Percentage of Export Sales: 60%
Number of Staff: 300
PA Member
NBA Signatory
All New Titles are Bar Coded
Open University Publications
Book Data Subscriber
WBIP Updating: Janet Hill, Book Information Department

Parent Company: John Wiley & Sons Inc
Allied Companies: Jacaranda Wiley Ltd (Brisbane) (AU)

Trade Terms
General Net: 40%
Academic Net: Up to £1,000 20%, £1-3,000 25%, £3-6,000 28%, £6,000+ 30%

Returns Procedures
Authority to Return: Customer Services Dept, Distribution Centre, West Sussex.
Address for Returns: Distribution Centre, West Sussex.

JOHN WILEY & SONS LTD
Southern Cross Trading Estate, 1 Oldlands Way, Bognor Regis, West Sussex PO22 9SA
Tel: 0243 829121 24 Hours
Fax: 0243 820250

Account No: _____

Sales Rep: _____

Tel: _____

Order Information
Teleordering: WLEY
First Edition Subscriber

Order Dept Opening Times
Mon - Fri 8.30am - 5.30pm
All Dues Automatically Recorded

Personnel
Head of Distribution: Mike Ridge (Distribution Manager)
Head of Customer Services: Karin Davies (Customer Service Manager)

Trade Terms
BA/Girobank Small Order Scheme: Based on turnover
Girobank Number: 314 0156
Credit Cards Accepted: Access/Master, Amex, Diners, Visa

Returns Procedures
Stock Returns: Obtain written permission from Customer Serv Dept
Imperfect Returns: Return title page & spine - up to value of £30 Over £30 return complete book

WILLIAMS & WILKINS LTD [Now called - Waverley Europe]
Broadway House, 2-6 Fulham Broadway, London SW6 1AA
ISBN Prefix(es): 0 683
Tel: 071-385 2357 24 Hours
Fax: 071-385 2922
Cables: 919891 WAVLEY G

Account No: _____ C0084 _____

Sales Rep: _____

Tel: _____

Order Information
Teleordering: WMSWLKS

Order Dept Opening Times
Mon - Fri 9.30am - 5.30pm
All Dues Automatically Recorded
Representation Available

Personnel
Head of Company: Raymond Pitt
Head of Sales (Home): Guy Simpson
Head of Publicity: Louise Harnby/Simon Wooldridge
Head of Accounts: Simon Fraser (Financial Controller)
Head of Distribution: Maureen Finneran
Head of Customer Services: Terry King
Other Important Personnel:
Anne Lenehan (Head of Special Sales)

Number of titles published annually: 300
Percentage of Export Sales: 50%
Number of Staff: 16

All New Titles are Bar Coded
WBIP Updating: Maureen Finneran

Parent Company: Waverly Inc

Trade Terms
25%, 30 days
Girobank Number: 567 1000
Credit Cards Accepted: Access/Master, Visa, Amex

Returns Procedures
Authority to Return: Prior permission required
Address for Returns: TBC Distribution

STEWART WILLIAMS PUBLISHING
1 Trem-Y-Don, Barry, South Galmorgan CF6 8QJ
Tel: 0446 735667
VAT No: 133 8593 54

WILLINGHAM PRESS
22 Schole Road, Willingham, Cambridge, Cambridgeshire CB4 5JD
Tel: 0954 61010
Fax: 0954 61486
VAT No: 432 2238 86

WILLOW PUBLISHING
Willow Cottage, 36 Moss Lane, Timperley, Altrincham, Cheshire WA15 6SZ
ISBN Prefix(es): 0 946361
Tel: 061-980 2633 24 Hours

Order Information

All Dues Automatically Recorded
Representation Available

Personnel
Head of Company: J Warrender

Trade Terms
33.3%

WILLOWBRIDGE PUBLISHING
Willowbridge, Stoke Road, Bletchley, Milton Keynes, Buckinghamshire MK2 3JZ
ISBN Prefix(es): 0 948762, 0 9509104
Tel: 0908 643242
VAT No: 382 1389 43

Orders to
Willowbridge Pub, Bridge House, Southwick Village, Nr Fareham, Hampshire PO17 6DZ
Tel: 0705 375570
Fax: 0705 201404

Order Information

Order Dept Opening Times
Mon - Fri 9am - 5pm
All Dues Automatically Recorded
Representation Available
Invoice Payments: Willowbridge Publishing, Bridge House

Personnel
Head of Company: G R O'Connell
Head of Accounts: Mrs Chris Aston

Other Important Personnel:
Ms V Hitie

Number of titles published annually: 2
Number of Staff: 3
NBA Signatory
All New Titles are Bar Coded
WBIP Updating: G R O'Connell

Parent Company: Willowbridge Enterprises

Trade Terms
35% on all titles, carriage paid. Orders for less than 2 mixed books 25% unless cwo

Returns Procedures
Address for Returns: Willowbridge Publishing, Bridge House
Stock Returns: Request permission first. Applicable against sale or return and see-safe invoices. Otherwise firm sale.
Imperfect Returns: Advise intention and return complete book

JOHN WILSON (BOOKSALES) LTD

1 High Street, Princes Risborough, Buckinghamshire HP27 0AG
Tel: 0844 275927
Fax: 0844 274402
VAT No: 370 1565 68

Account No: _____

Sales Rep: _____

Tel: _____

Order Information

Order Dept Opening Times
Daily 9am - 1pm, 2pm - 5.30pm
Representation Available
Invoice Payments: Bookpoint

Returns Procedures
Authority to Return: John Wilson
Address for Returns: Bookpoint

NEIL WILSON PUBLISHING LTD

11 West Chapelton Crescent, Glasgow, Strathclyde G61 2DE
Tel: 041-942 0653

Orders to
EXEL LOGISTICS - MEDIA SERVICES, 3 Sheldon Way, Larkfield, Aylesford, Kent ME20 6SF
Tel: 0622 882000
Fax: 0622 718036

PHILIP WILSON PUBLISHERS LTD

26 Litchfield Street, London WC2H 9NJ
ISBN Prefix(es): 0 85667, 1 871489
Tel: 071-379 7886
Fax: 071-497 3290 Sale/Accnt
Fax: 071-836 7049 Editorial
VAT No: 446 2028 66

Account No: _____

Sales Rep: _____

Tel: _____

Order Information
Teleordering: WILSON

All Dues Automatically Recorded
Representation Available

Personnel
Head of Company: Philip Wilson (Chairman)
Head of Sales (Home): Hugh Merrell (Marketing Director)
Head of Publicity: Lisa Shakespeare
Head of Accounts: Miss Joanna Hamblin (Chief Accountant)

Number of titles published annually: 15
All New Titles are Bar Coded
WBIP Updating: Miss Cussandra Boon

Trade Terms
33.3% on all orders no surcharges
Girobank Number: 538 7353
Credit Cards Accepted: Access/Master, Visa, Amex, Diners

Returns Procedures
Authority to Return: Miss C Boon
Stock Returns: All returns must be contained and properly packed

WINDHORSE PUBLICATIONS
Top Floor, 20 Sanda Street, Glasgow, Strathclyde G20 8PU
ISBN Prefix(es): 0 904766
Tel: 041-946 5821
Fax: 041-333 1018
VAT No: 362 4148 64

Order Information

Representation Available

Personnel
Head of Company: Terry Pilchick
Head of Sales (Home): Rachel Lovering
Head of Marketing: Diane Quin

Number of titles published annually: 5
Percentage of Export Sales: 20%
Number of Staff: 10
All New Titles are Bar Coded
WBIP Updating: Rachel Lovering

Trade Terms
35%, under five books 20%
Girobank Number: 104 396 105

Returns Procedures
Imperfect Returns: Anything imperfect will be replaced

WINDROW & GREENE
5 Gerrard Street, London W1V 7LJ
ISBN Prefix(es): 1 872004
Tel: 071-287 4570
Fax: 071-494 3869
VAT No: 440 0239 02

Orders to
BOOKPOINT LIMITED, 39 Milton Park, Abingdon, Oxfordshire OX14 4TD
Tel: 0235 835001
Fax: 0235 861038

Order Information

All Dues Automatically Recorded
Representation Available
Invoice Payments: Bookpoint

Personnel
Head of Company: Alan Greene
Other Important Personnel:
Martin Windrow (Editorial Director)

Number of titles published annually: 28
Percentage of Export Sales: 60%
Number of Staff: 4
All New Titles are Bar Coded
Book Data Subscriber
WBIP Updating: Daryl Joyce

Trade Terms
35%
Credit Cards Accepted: Access/Master, Amex, Visa

Returns Procedures
Authority to Return: Prior permission required

WINDSOR BOOKS INTERNATIONAL

The Old Workshop, East Avenue, Oxford, Oxfordshire OX4 1XW
ISBN Prefix(es): 1 874111
Tel: 0865 792336 24 Hours
Fax: 0865 792336
VAT No: 537 3951 23

Account No: _____

Sales Rep: _____

Tel: _____

Order Information

All Dues Automatically Recorded
Representation Available

Personnel
Head of Company: Geoff Cowen
Head of Customer Services: Christine Mildenhall
Other Important Personnel:
Rod Murchison (Key Accounts Manager)

Number of titles published annually: 10
Percentage of Export Sales: 50%
Number of Staff: 2
IPG Member
All New Titles are Bar Coded
Book Data Subscriber
WBIP Updating: G Cowen

Trade Terms
Two or more 35%, Single copy 25%, £1.25 postage charge if order invoice value is less than £25

Returns Procedures
Address for Returns: Clipper Distribution Services, Eastmead Ind. Est, Lavant Chichester, West Sussex PO18 0DB
Stock Returns: All returns must be authorised by head office in advance
Imperfect Returns: All copies to be returned

WINSLOW PRESS

Telford Road, Bicester, Oxfordshire OX6 0TS
ISBN Prefix(es): 0 86388
Tel: 0869 244644 24 Hours
Tel: 0869 244733
Fax: 0869 320040
VAT No: 415 0763 73

Order Information

Order Dept Opening Times
8.30am - 5.30pm
All Dues Automatically Recorded

Personnel
Head of Company: John Whitton (Managing Director)
Head of Sales (Home): Sarah Wilson (Sales Director)

Head of Marketing: Ian Franklin (Marketing & Production Director)
Head of Accounts: Cathy Maycock
Head of Distribution: Alyson Carr (Customer Services Manager)
Other Important Personnel:
Catherine McAllister (Editorial Director)

Number of titles published annually: 12
Percentage of Export Sales: 25%
Number of Staff: 11
WBIP Updating: Sue Halliday

Parent Company: Buckingham Group Ltd
Subsidiary Companies: Contour School Supplies

Trade Terms
Single copy 25%, Stock orders 40%
Other Terms: No carriage/surcharges if c.w.o.
Credit Cards Accepted: Access/Master, Visa

Returns Procedures
Authority to Return: Telephone first
Stock Returns: Call customer services 0869 244733 first

JOHN WISDEN & CO LTD

25 Down Road, Merrow, Guildford, Surrey GU1 2PY
ISBN Prefix(es): 0 947766
Tel: 0483 570358
Fax: 0483 33153
VAT No: 440 3885 53

Orders to
LITTLEHAMPTON BOOK SERVICES, 14 Eldon Way, Lineside Ind Estate, Littlehampton, West Sussex BN17 7HE
Tel: 0903 721596
Fax: 0903 730914

Order Information

All Dues Automatically Recorded
Representation Available
Invoice Payments: Littlehampton
Representation: Cassell

Personnel
Head of Company: Peter Medley (Chairman & Managing Director)
Head of Publicity: Chris Lane (General Manager)
Head of Accounts: Geoff Dunks (Company Secretary)

Number of titles published annually: 1
Number of Staff: 1
All New Titles are Bar Coded
WBIP Updating: C Lane

Parent Company: Bowater Plc & Grays of Cambridge (International) Ltd

Returns Procedures
Address for Returns: Littlehampton

WISDOM BOOKS

402 Hoe Street, Walthamstow, London E17 9AA
ISBN Prefix(es): 0 14019, 0 7126, 0 85692, 0 86171, 0 901032, 0 90626, 0 948006, 1 870609
Tel: 081-520 5588
Fax: 081-520 0932
VAT No: 549 0303 54

Order Information
Teleordering: WISDOM

Order Dept Opening Times
Mon - Sat 9.30am - 6pm
All Dues Automatically Recorded
Representation Available

Personnel
Head of Company: Dennis Heslop (Managing Director)
Head of Sales (Home): Mike Gilmore
Head of Marketing: Sally Bailey (Marketing & Publicity Manager)
Head of Accounts: Mike Fenny
Head of Customer Services: Philip Bradley

Number of titles published annually: 1
Percentage of Export Sales: 50%
Number of Staff: 5
PA Member
All New Titles are Bar Coded
WBIP Updating: Sally Bailey

Parent Company: Wisdom Books Distribution Ltd

Trade Terms
Net cash 30 days from invoice, discouts between 20-35%
Other Terms: Single copy order charged 17% postage
Girobank Number: 51 208 1905
Credit Cards Accepted: Access/Master, Visa

Returns Procedures
Authority to Return: Prior written permission essential
Stock Returns: Include copy of invoice and written reason for return of book(s)
Imperfect Returns: The book, fully intact, must be returned, with copy invoice and written reason for return

WISEBUY PUBLICATIONS

25 West Cottages, Off West End Lane, London NW6 1RJ
ISBN Prefix(es): 0 9509751, 0 9514595
Tel: 071-433 1121 24 Hours
VAT No: 341 3816 74

Order Information

Order Dept Opening Times
Mon - Fri 10am - 4pm
Orders posted Tuesdays and Fridays

Personnel
Head of Company: Susan Lewis (Partner)
Head of Marketing: David Lewis (Partner)

Number of titles published annually: 5
Number of Staff: 2
All New Titles are Bar Coded
WBIP Updating: D B Lewis

Trade Terms
35% on orders of 3 copies or over (mixed) Smaller orders 25%, post free

Returns Procedures
Stock Returns: Where authorised, eg on year books, front cover (not title page) can be returned, otherwise whole book returned
Imperfect Returns: Will replace or give credit

WITHERBY & COMPANY LTD

32-36 Aylesbury Street, London EC1R 0ET
ISBN Prefix(es): 0 948691, 1 85609
Tel: 071-251 5341
Tel: 071-253 5413
Fax: 071-251 1296

Order Information

Order Dept Opening Times
Mon - Fri 9am - 5pm
All Dues Automatically Recorded
Representation Available

Personnel
Head of Company: A Witherby
Head of Accounts: A Kelly
Head of Distribution: B Dawes
Head of Customer Services: M K Jenkins

Number of titles published annually: 20
Percentage of Export Sales: 70%
Number of Staff: 3
WBIP Updating: C Sherlock

Trade Terms
General Net: Single Copy 25%, Two or more 30%
Credit Cards Accepted: Access/Master, Visa, Amex, Other

Returns Procedures
Stock Returns: Complete books to be returned plus copy of invoice. No overstocks accepted.
Imperfect Returns: Complete books to be returned plus copy of invoice

[handwritten: Wolfe Pubs. Brook House, 2-16 Torrington Place LONDON. WC1E 7LT A/C No 27081001]

WOLFHOUND PRESS

68 Mountjoy Square, Dublin 1, County Dublin
Tel: 01 740 354
Fax: 01 720 207

Account No: _____

Sales Rep: _____

Tel: _____

Orders to
CENTRAL BOOKS, 99 Wallis Road, London E9 5LN
Tel: 081-986 4854
Fax: 081-533 5821

Order Information

All Dues Automatically Recorded
Representation Available
Invoice Payments: Central Books

Personnel
Head of Company: Seamus Cashman
Head of Sales (Home): Siobhan Campbell
Head of Sales (Export): Ian Mills
Other Important Personnel:
Josephine O'Donovan - Editor

Number of titles published annually: 35
Number of Staff: 10
NBA Signatory
All New Titles are Bar Coded
WBIP Updating: Josephine O'Donovan

Trade Terms
25% single copy, 35% trade discount

Returns Procedures
Authority to Return: Ian Mills, 18 Coleswood Road, Harpenden, Herts AL5 1EQ
Address for Returns: Central Books, 99 Wallis Road, London E9 5LN
Stock Returns: On receipt of authorised signature from Ian Mills. Returns sent to Central Books.

THE WOMEN'S PRESS

34 Great Sutton Street, London EC1V 0DX
ISBN Prefix(es): 0 7043

Tel: 071-251 3007
Fax: 071-608 1938
VAT No: 241 4235 00

Account No: _____

Sales Rep: _____

Tel: _____

Orders to
PLYMBRIDGE DISTRIBUTORS LTD, Plymbridge House, Estover Road, Plymouth, Devon PL6 7PZ
Tel: 0752 735251
Fax: 0752 695699

Order Information

All Dues Automatically Recorded
Representation Available
Invoice Payments: Plymbridge

Personnel
Head of Company: Mary Hemming/Kathy Gale
Head of Marketing: Carole Spedding

Number of titles published annually: 55
Percentage of Export Sales: 25%
Number of Staff: 7
NBA Signatory
All New Titles are Bar Coded
Open University Publications
WBIP Updating: Mary Hemming

Parent Company: Namara Group

Trade Terms
Single Copy 20% Two or More 35% Special Orders - Negotiable
Girobank Number: 221 2951
Credit Cards Accepted: Access/Master, Amex, Diners, Visa

Returns Procedures
Authority to Return: Rep or Head Office
Address for Returns: Plymbridge

WOODFIELD PUBLISHING

Woodfield House, Arundel Road, Fontwell, Arundel, West Sussex BN18 0SD
Tel: 0243 542704 Tel/Fax
VAT No: 430 6630 78

WOODHEAD PUBLISHING

Abington Hall, Abington, Cambridge, Cambridgeshire CB1 6AH
ISBN Prefix(es): 1 85573
Tel: 0223 891358
Fax: 0223 893694
VAT No: 538 2109 53

Order Information

All Dues Automatically Recorded
Representation Available
Invoice Payments: Combined Book Services Ltd

Personnel
Head of Company: Martin Woodhead (Managing Director)
Head of Sales (Home): Rosemary Parravani (Marketing Manager)
Head of Accounts: Duncan Leeper (Finance Director)

Number of titles published annually: 50
Percentage of Export Sales: 45%
Number of Staff: 8

IPG Member
WBIP Updating: Elaine Markey

Trade Terms
on application
Credit Cards Accepted: Access/Master, Visa

Returns Procedures
Authority to Return: Martin Woodhead or Duncan Leeper
Address for Returns: Combined Book Services Ltd
Imperfect Returns: Annotated title page up to £20

WOODHEAD-FAULKNER (PUBLISHERS) LTD

Campus 400, Maylands Avenue, Hemel Hempstead, Hertfordshire HP2 7EZ
ISBN Prefix(es): 0 13, 0 85941, 0 902197, 0 903121, 1 85564, 1 870031, 1 870555, 1 872860
Tel: 0442 881900
Fax: 0442 252544
VAT No: 213 7166 84

Account No: _____
Sales Rep: _____
Tel: _____

Orders to
INTERNATIONAL BOOK DISTRIBUTORS, Campus 400, Maylands Avenue, Hemel Hempstead, Hertfordshire HP2 7EZ
Tel: 0442 881900
Fax: 0442 882099

Order Information
Teleordering: WOODH

Invoice Payments: IBD

Personnel
Head of Marketing: Susanna Lob (Marketing Manager) 0442 882156
Other Important Personnel:
Susan E Richards (Publisher) 0442 882230

Book Data Subscriber

Parent Company: Simon & Schuster

WOODSTOCK BOOKS

Spelsbury House, Spelsbury, Oxford, Oxfordshire OX7 3JR
ISBN Prefix(es): 1 85477
Tel: 0608 810635
Fax: 0608 811401
VAT No: 434 6740 47

Account No: _____
Sales Rep: _____
Tel: _____

Order Information

Order Dept Opening Times
Mon - Fri 9am - 6pm
All Dues Automatically Recorded

Personnel
Head of Company: James Price

Number of titles published annually: 25
Percentage of Export Sales: 60%
All New Titles are Bar Coded

Trade Terms
Single copy 25%, multiples 35%, 25 books or more additional 5% list price
Credit Cards Accepted: Access/Master, Visa

Returns Procedures
Authority to Return: Prior permission required
Imperfect Returns: Title page to value £30

WORD PUBLISHING

9 Holdom Avenue, Bletchley, Milton Keynes, Buckinghamshire MK1 1QR
Tel: 0908 648440
Fax: 0908 648592

Account No: _____

Sales Rep: _____

Tel: _____

Order Information

Order Dept Opening Times
Mon - Fri 9am - 4.45pm

Personnel
Head of Company: Ian Hamilton (Managing Director)
Head of Sales (Home): Bill Williams (Sales Manager)
Head of Sales (Export): Noel Halsey (Publishing Director)
Head of Marketing: David Withers (Commercial Director)
Head of Accounts: Brian Taylor (Financial Controller)
Head of Distribution: John Geoghegan (Distribution Manager)
Head of Customer Services: Donna Harris (Customer Services Manager)
Other Important Personnel:
Cheryl Dann (Telesales)

Number of titles published annually: 80
Percentage of Export Sales: 60%
Number of Staff: 65
PA Member
WBIP Updating: Lin Howe

Parent Company: Word Inc (US)

Trade Terms
35%
Credit Cards Accepted: Access/Master, Visa

WORDSWORTH EDITIONS LTD

8B East Street, Ware, Hertfordshire SG12 9HJ
ISBN Prefix(es): 1 85326
Tel: 0920 465167/8/9
Tel: 0920 487825
Fax: 0920 462267
VAT No: 432 2900 83

Order Information

Order Dept Opening Times
Mon - Fri 9.30am - 5pm
Cyclical Ordering Policy
All Dues Automatically Recorded
Representation Available

Other Important Locations
London Showroom: 23 Chilworth Mews, London W2 3RG
Tel: 071-723 9011
Fax: 071-724 7506

Personnel
Head of Company: Michael Trayler
Head of Sales (Home): Helen Trayler

Head of Marketing: Kim Hartley
Head of Accounts: Mrs Lyne
Head of Distribution: Mandy Irons

Number of titles published annually: 30
Percentage of Export Sales: 40%
Number of Staff: 7
All New Titles are Bar Coded
WBIP Updating: Mrs Helen Trayler

Trade Terms
General Net: Single copy/single line 20% + £2.25 p+p, 2 or more single titles 35%, 50 or more titles 40%
Academic Net: As above
Non-Net: As above
Minimum Order: £50 nett after discount

Returns Procedures
Stock Returns: Must contact head office for authorization to return
Imperfect Returns: As above

WORLD BOOK CHILDCRAFT INTERNATIONAL

World Book House, 77 Mount Ephraim, Tunbridge Wells, Kent TN4 8AZ
ISBN Prefix(es): 0 7166
Tel: 0892 547811 24 Hours
Fax: 0892 516197
Fax: 0892 524702
VAT No: 217 9703 50

Order Information

Order Dept Opening Times
Mon - Fri 9am - 5pm
Representation Available

Personnel
Head of Company: P Favaloro
Head of Sales (Home): Michael J Brown
Head of Accounts: Denis B Manning
Other Important Personnel:
Angela Prater (Sales Administration), Susie Webber (Sales Administration)

Number of titles published annually: 5
Number of Staff: 30
WBIP Updating: Mrs S Webber

Parent Company: World Book Inc, Chicago, USA

Trade Terms
Bookshop customers 5%, schools 10%, export orders 25%, no surcharges
Credit Cards Accepted: Access/Master, Visa

Returns Procedures
Stock Returns: Notify head office for collection
Imperfect Returns: As above

WORLD LEISURE MARKETING

117 The Hollow, Littleover, Derby, Derbyshire DE23 7BS
Tel: 0332 272020
Fax: 0332 774287
VAT No: 580 8193 21

Account No: _____
Sales Rep: _____
Tel: _____

Orders to
GRANTHAM BOOK SERVICES LTD, Isaac Newton Way,
Alma Park Industrial Estate, Grantham, Lincolnshire
NG31 9SD
Tel: 0476 67421
Fax: 0476 590223

Order Information

All Dues Automatically Recorded
Representation Available

Personnel
Head of Company: John D Whitby (Managing Director)
Head of Sales (Home): Duncan Smith (Sales Manager) 0742 556636
Head of Publicity: Judy Whitby (Promotions Director)
Head of Accounts: Jan Cundy (Financial Director) 0629 825913

Number of Staff: 11
All New Titles are Bar Coded
WBIP Updating: Judy Whitby

Trade Terms
35%

Returns Procedures
Authority to Return: Prior permission required
Address for Returns: Contact Head Office

WORLD SCIENTIFIC PUBLISHING CO PTE LTD

A/C No UKUBUR/25
57 SHELTON ST,
LONDON WC2H 9HE
Tel 0171 836 0888
Fax 0171 836 2020

Orders to

Order Information
Teleordering: WSPC

Order Dept Opening Times
Mon - Fri 9am - 1pm, 2pm - 5pm
All Dues Automatically Recorded
Representation Available

Personnel
Head of Company: Mrs Faridah Shahab

Number of titles published annually: 250
Percentage of Export Sales: 70%
Number of Staff: 3
Book Data Subscriber

Parent Company: World Scientific Publishing Singapore

Trade Terms
25%
Girobank Number: 514 3705
Credit Cards Accepted: Access/Master, Amex, Diners, Visa

Returns Procedures
Authority to Return: Sales Dept, PO Box 379, London N12 7JS
Address for Returns: Gazelle Book Services, Unit 2/3 Hightown, Lel Ind Est, White Cross Mills, Lancaster LA1 3XQ
Stock Returns: Enclose invoice or copy for incorrectly supplied books Damaged books - send only title page & spine & copy invoice

WORLD SERVICE PUBLICATIONS

4 Cotham Vale, Bristol, Avon BS6 6HR
ISBN Prefix(es): 0 9515629, 1 874092
Tel: 0272 732010

Other Important Locations
BBC World Service, Publicity Dept, Bush House, London WC2
Tel: 071-257 2941

All New Titles are Bar Coded

[handwritten: World Wildlife Fund UK, Education Dist A/C BLACUN P.O. Box 963, Slough. SL2 3RS Tel 0753 643104 Fax 0753 646553]

WORLDLY GOODS

10-12 Picton Street, Montpelier, Bristol, Avon BS6 5QA
Tel: 0272 420164
Fax: 0272 420164
VAT No: 496 6216 10

Account No: _____
Sales Rep: _____
Tel: _____

Order Information

Order Dept Opening Times
Mon - Fri 10am - 5pm
Cyclical Ordering Policy

Personnel
Head of Company: Matthew Dunwell (Proprietor)
Other Important Personnel:
Tim Bartlett

[handwritten: Worth = From 1/3/94 = Marston Book Services.]

GORDON WRIGHT PUBLISHING LTD

25 Mayfield Road, Edinburgh, Lothian EH9 2NQ
ISBN Prefix(es): 0 903065
Tel: 031-667 1300
Fax: 031-667 1459
VAT No: 270 6352 68

Order Information

All Dues Automatically Recorded
Representation Available
Invoice Payments: Gordon Wright

Personnel
Head of Company: Gordon Wright (Managing Director)

Number of titles published annually: 4
Number of Staff: 1
All New Titles are Bar Coded

Trade Terms
General Net: Single copy 20%, Two or more 35%, 250 + 40%, 500 + 45%
Minimum Order: Anything less than £20 retail CWO
Credit Cards Accepted: Access/Master, Visa, Other

Returns Procedures
Authority to Return: Books only supplied firm.
Imperfect Returns: Copies will be replaced on receipt of title page bearing name and address and details of fault. Credit notes not supp

WRIGHTSON BIOMEDICAL PUBLISHING LTD

Ash Barn House, Winchester Road, Stroud, Petersfield, Hampshire GU32 3PN
Tel: 0730 265647

Fax: 0730 260368
VAT No: 503 9147 61

Orders to
TURPIN DISTRIBUTION SERVICES LTD, Blackhorse Road, Letchworth, Hertfordshire SG6 1HN
Tel: 0462 672555
Fax: 0462 480947

WRITERS & SCHOLARS INTERNATIONAL LTD
32 Queen Victoria, London EC4N 4SS
Tel: 071-329 6434 24 Hours
Fax: 071-329 6461
VAT No: 241 0195 06

Order Information

Order Dept Opening Times
Mon - Fri 9am - 5pm

Personnel
Head of Company: Philip Spender (Director)
Head of Sales (Home): Philip Wilding
Head of Marketing: Susan Kenny
Head of Accounts: Nasir Mir
Head of Distribution: Laura Botha

Number of titles published annually: 1
WBIP Updating: Philip Spender

Trade Terms
33.3%
Credit Cards Accepted: Access/Master, Visa, Amex, Diners

Returns Procedures
Authority to Return: Prior permission required
Stock Returns: Return covers or detailed sales/return sheet

XANADU PUBLICATIONS LTD
19 Cornwall Road, Finsbury Park, London N4 4PH
ISBN Prefix(es): 0 947761, 1 85480
Tel: 071-272 4895
Fax: 071-263 7708
VAT No: 416 7744 36

Orders to
BOOKPOINT LIMITED, 39 Milton Park, Abingdon, Oxfordshire OX14 4TD
Tel: 0235 835001
Fax: 0235 861038

Order Information

All Dues Automatically Recorded
Representation Available
Invoice Payments: Bookpoint Ltd
Representation:John Masters, ABS, Maidstone 0622 764555

Personnel
Head of Company: Richard Glyn Jones

Number of titles published annually: 30
Percentage of Export Sales: 60%
Number of Staff: 2
IPG Member
All New Titles are Bar Coded
WBIP Updating: R G Jones

Returns Procedures
Authority to Return: Bookpoint Ltd
Address for Returns: Bookpoint Ltd

XYLOPRESS LTD

Unit 3B, Carver Road, Astonfields Ind Est, Stafford, Staffordshire ST16 3EF
ISBN Prefix(es): 0 948916, 1 85706
Tel: 0785 55202
Fax: 0785 56609
VAT No: 424 7047 63

Order Information

Representation Available

Personnel

Head of Company: Andrew Harper/David Antley (Joint Managing Directors)
Head of Sales (Home): Don Smith (Sales Manager)
Head of Accounts: Terry Tyler (Financial Manager)
Head of Customer Services: Joanne Vanderwyk (Sales Administrator)

Number of titles published annually: 25
Number of Staff: 15
All New Titles are Bar Coded

Trade Terms

35%
Minimum Order: £200

Y LOLFA CYF

Talybont, Aberystwyth, Dyfed SY23 5HE
Tel: 0970 832304
Fax: 0970 832782
VAT No: 326 9756 20

YALE UNIVERSITY PRESS

23 Pond Street, London NW3 2PN
ISBN Prefix(es): 0 300
Tel: 071-431 4422
Fax: 071-431 3755
Telex: 896075 YUPLDN G
VAT No: 233 5258 75

Account No: _____
Sales Rep: _____
Tel: _____

Orders to

JOHN WILEY & SONS LTD, Southern Cross Trading Estate, 1 Oldlands Way, Bognor Regis, West Sussex PO22 9SA
Tel: 0243 829121
Fax: 0243 820250

Order Information

All Dues Automatically Recorded
Representation Available
Invoice Payments: John Wiley & Sons Ltd

Personnel

Head of Company: John Nicoll (Managing Director)
Head of Marketing: Kate Pocock (Head of Marketing)
Head of Publicity: Ann Geneva (Publicity Manager)
Head of Accounts: Donal Burke (Accountant)
Other Important Personnel:
Henrietta Joy (Sales Manager)

Number of titles published annually: 230
Percentage of Export Sales: 35%
Number of Staff: 22
PA Member
NBA Signatory

All New Titles are Bar Coded
Open University Publications
Book Data Subscriber
WBIP Updating: Organized by transfer of disc from J Wiley

Trade Terms
35% off all general net titles, 25% of academic net titles.
Discounts off special orders negotiable
Credit Cards Accepted: Access/Master, Visa, Amex, Diners

Returns Procedures
Address for Returns: John Wiley & Sons Ltd
Stock Returns: Permission from Sales Manager required within 12 months of invoice date; on authorization, books to J Wiley & Sons
Imperfect Returns: Annotated title page accepted up to £10. Return to J Wiley & Sons

ROY YATES BOOKS

Smallfields Cottage, Cox Green, Rudgwick, Horsham, West Sussex RH12 3DE
ISBN Prefix(es): 0 907264, 1 870045
Tel: 0403 822299
Fax: 0403 823012
VAT No: 528 4386 24

Order Information

Order Dept Opening Times
9.30am - 6pm
All Dues Automatically Recorded

Personnel
Head of Company: Roy Yates
Head of Customer Services: Connie Yates

Number of titles published annually: 5
Number of Staff: 2
All New Titles are Bar Coded
Book Data Subscriber

Trade Terms
General Net: Single copy/single line 25%, otherwise 35%. Special orders variable

Returns Procedures
Authority to Return: Roy Yates
Stock Returns: Quote invoice no, mark parcel "returns". Written authoriza- tion req for returns except damaged/faulty/incorrectly supp
Imperfect Returns: Return title page up to £10

YELLOW BRICK PUBLISHERS

2 Lonsdale Road, Queens Park, London NW6 6RD
Tel: 071-372 5456/7/8
Fax: 071-328 3793

YORICK BOOKS

27 Manwood Avenue, St Stephen's, Canterbury, Kent CT2 7AH
ISBN Prefix(es): 0 947710

Personnel
Head of Company: Peter Brown

Number of titles published annually: 2

Trade Terms
33.3% on all orders

YOUNG LIBRARY LTD

3 The Old Brushworks, 56 Pickwick Road, Corsham,
Wiltshire SN13 9BX
ISBN Prefix(es): 0 946003, 1 85429
Tel: 0249 712025
Fax: 0249 715558
VAT No: 365 3158 48

Orders to
CLIPPER DISTRIBUTION SERVICES LTD, Windmill
Grove, Porchester, Hampshire PO16 9HT
Tel: 0705 200080
Fax: 0705 200090

Order Information

All Dues Automatically Recorded
Invoice Payments: Clipper Distribution Services

Personnel
Head of Company: Roger Cleeve (Managing Director)

Number of titles published annually: 20
Number of Staff: 2
All New Titles are Bar Coded

Trade Terms
1-3 copies 20%, 4 or more 35%
Other Terms: Small order surcharge of £1.25 on orders under £25

Returns Procedures
Authority to Return: Apply in writing
Address for Returns: Clipper Distribution Services
Stock Returns: Overstocks granted on subscription orders only
Imperfect Returns: Permission must be sought in writing

ZED BOOKS LTD

57 Caledonian Road, London N1 9BU
ISBN Prefix(es): 0 86232, 0 901787, 0 905762, 1 85649
Tel: 071-837 4014
Tel: 071-834 0384
Tel: 071-834 8466
Fax: 071-833 3960
VAT No: 393 8978 73

Orders to
PLYMBRIDGE DISTRIBUTORS LTD, Plymbridge House,
Estover Road, Plymouth, Devon PL6 7PZ
Tel: 0752 735251
Fax: 0752 695699

Order Information

All Dues Automatically Recorded
Representation Available
Invoice Payments: Plymbridge Distributors

Personnel
Head of Sales (Home): Farouk Sohawon
Head of Marketing: Kathryn Perry
Head of Publicity: Helen Salmon
Head of Accounts: Paul Westlake

Number of titles published annually: 40
Percentage of Export Sales: 55%
Number of Staff: 12
PA Member
NBA Signatory
WBIP Updating: Helen Salmon

Trade Terms
General Net: single copy/single line 25%, 2 or more single titles 33%, subscription/stock orders 33%, special orders negotiable

Academic Net: Single copy/single line 20%, all other orders 33%, special orders negotiable
Girobank Number: 575636106

Returns Procedures
Imperfect Returns: Whole book to be returned

ZENO

6 Denmark Street, London WC2H 8LP
ISBN Prefix(es): 0 7228, 0 900834
Tel: 071-836 2522 24 Hours
VAT No: 605 9507 37

Order Information

Order Dept Opening Times
Mon - Fri 9.30am - 6pm Sat 9.30am - 5pm
All Dues Automatically Recorded

WBIP Updating: Mr M P Zographos

Trade Terms
General Net: Single Copy 20-25%, Two or more single copies 20-25% Subscription orders or Stock orders 20-35%
Other Terms: Carriage charged on some titles
Girobank Number: 58 090 4008
Credit Cards Accepted: Access/Master, Visa

Returns Procedures
Authority to Return: Prior permission required
Imperfect Returns: Whole book must be returned

DISTRIBUTOR, SALES AGENCY & WHOLESALER SPECIALISATIONS

Notes:
This section lists companies who have distribution or sales and marketing rights for a number of publishers. The list indicates whether the company distributes or represents UK, overseas and small publishers. Any specialist subject areas, where known, are also noted.

UK = Yes to Distributor/Agents for UK Publishers
OS = Yes to Distributor/Agents for Overseas Publishers
SP = Yes to Distributor/Agents for Small Publishers

Company	UK	OS	SP	Specialisation
ACADEMIC & UNIV PUB		OS	SP	None
ACADEMY BOOKS LTD	UK		SP	Transport & Motor Sport
ACCENT EDUCATIONAL	UK	OS	SP	Foreign Languages
AFRICAN BOOKS COLL		OS	SP	Africa
AIRLIFE PUBLISHING	UK	OS	SP	None
AIRLIFT BOOK CO	UK	OS	SP	Mind Body & Spirit, Literature, Women's Titles (Inc Fiction)
AK DISTRIBUTION	UK	OS	SP	Small Publishers & Wholesalers of Selected Large Publishers
ALIF INTERNATIONAL	UK	OS		Islamic Studies
IAN ALLAN PUBLISHING	UK	OS	SP	Aviation, Military & Transport
ALLIANCE BOOK SERV			SP	None
AMALGAMATED BOOK SVC	UK	OS		Sales & Marketing
ARGUS PUBLICATIONS	UK			None
ARIS & PHILLIPS LTD	UK	OS		Egyptology & Middle East Literature
ART BOOK DIST CO	UK	OS		Art
ART DATA	UK	OS	SP	Visual Arts
ASHFORD BUCHAN	UK	OS	SP	None
ASHGROVE PRESS	UK	OS	SP	None
AUTODATA LTD		OS		None
BAHAI PUBLISHING	UK	OS	SP	Bahai Issues, eg Comparative Religion, Moral Education
BAILEY DIST LTD	UK		SP	None
BARNACLE MARINE LTD	UK	OS	SP	Nautical
B T BATSFORD LTD	UK	OS	SP	None
BAY FOREIGN BOOKS		OS		Foreign Languages
ROGER BAYLISS	UK			Legal, Financial & Medical
BEBC DISTRIBUTION	UK	OS	SP	English Language Training
BIBLE SOCIETY	UK	OS	SP	Bibles & Testaments
BIBLIOS PUB DIST	UK	OS	SP	None
A & C BLACK LTD	UK		SP	None
BLACKWELL PUB LTD	UK			None
BMS LTD	UK	OS	SP	None
BOOK MARKETING ASSOC	UK	OS	SP	Medical Sciences, Poetry
BOOK REP & DIST LTD	UK	OS	SP	Academic & High Level General Lists
BOOKMARKS	UK	OS	SP	None
BOOKPOINT LIMITED	UK	OS	SP	None
BOOKS CONTINENTAL		OS		None
BOOKS EXPRESS	UK	OS		Australian & Canadian Official & Semi-Official Publications
BOOKS FROM INDIA	UK	OS	SP	India, Pakistan, Bangladesh, Nepal, Sri Lanka, Afghanistan
BOOKSPEED		OS		None
BOOKWORLD WHOLESALE	UK	OS	SP	Transport, Military & Modelling
BOXTREE LTD	UK		SP	None

BREWIN BOOK DIST	UK		SP	British Transport & Local Midlands History
BURSTON DIST SERV	UK			None
CALDER PUB LTD	UK	OS		None
CASSELL PLC	UK	OS		None
CEDAR TREE HOUSE	UK	OS	SP	EC Business Reference
CENTRAL BOOKS	UK	OS	SP	None
CHARTWELL-BRATT	UK	OS	SP	Mathematics & Computer Algebra
CLAN BOOKS	UK		SP	Scottish Interest
CLAN BOOKS	UK		SP	Scottish Interest
T & T CLARK LTD		OS	SP	Religion/Theology & Law
CLARKE ASSOCIATES		OS	SP	Scientific & Technical
E W CLASSEY LTD	UK	OS	SP	Entomology & Natural History
CLIPPER DIST SERVICE			SP	None
COLLETS	UK	OS	SP	Eastern & Central European Books & Journals
COLLINS & BROWN	UK		SP	General Trade, Adult, Non-Fiction & Illustrated
COLUMBA BOOK SERVICE	UK	OS	SP	Religion & Theology
COMBINED BOOK SERV	UK	OS	SP	None
COMPUTER BOOKSHOPS	UK	OS		Computing
COMPUTER STEP LTD	UK	OS	SP	Computing
CONSTABLE & CO LTD	UK	OS	SP	None
CORDEE	UK	OS	SP	Outdoor Recreation, Sports, Travel & Adventure
COUNTER PRODUCTIONS		OS		None
COUNTRY BOOKSTORE	UK		SP	Tourist Trade & Bargain Books
COUNTRYSIDE BOOKS	UK		SP	Regional Interest
CRESSRELLES PUB LTD		OS		Plays & Theatre
PAUL H CROMPTON LTD		OS	SP	Martial Arts
CYPRESS BOOK COMPANY	UK		SP	China
D SERVICES	UK	OS	SP	None
DALENNAU	UK	OS	SP	Welsh, Cornish, Irish & Women's Interest
DALTON WATSON BOOKS		OS		None
DANIELS PUBLISHING	UK	OS	SP	Health/Medical Education & Training
DAWSON UK LTD	UK	OS	SP	Bibliographies & Reference
DEEP BOOKS LTD		OS	SP	None
KEN DICKSON LTD	UK	OS	SP	None
DOLPHIN BOOK CO LTD	UK	OS		Spanish & Catalan Books
JOHN DONALD PUB LTD	UK		SP	None
DRAGONS WORLD LTD	UK		SP	Freelance Sales Representation
DRAKE PUB SERVICES	UK	OS	SP	Academic & Educational Marketing
DUNDURN DISTRIBUTION		OS	SP	Canada
EDS		OS	SP	Acadmic & Scholarly, STM, Library Science, Business & Prof
EDUC CO OF IRELAND	UK			School Books
ELECTRONICA BOOKS		OS		Computing & Electronics
ELEMENT BOOKS LTD	UK	OS	SP	None
LAWRENCE ERLBAUM ASS		OS	SP	Psychology & Computer Science
ESTATE PUBLICATIONS	UK	OS		Ordnance Survey (UK & Ireland)
EUROPEAN PRESS SERV		OS		Import American Publications, Export British Publications
EUROPEAN SCHOOLBOOKS	UK	OS	SP	Language Learning & European Literature
EVENLODE BOOK DIST	UK	OS	SP	New Age, Travel & Children's
EXEL LOGISTICS	UK			None
FABER BOOK SERVICES	UK		SP	None

FOOD TRADE PRESS LTD	UK	OS	SP	Food Research (NB Not Cookery or Catering)
W FOULSHAM & CO LTD	UK	OS		None
FOUNTAIN PRESS LTD	UK			None
L N FOWLER & CO LTD	UK	OS	SP	None
GAZELLE BOOK SERVICE	UK	OS	SP	None
GILL & MACMILLAN LTD	UK	OS		Irish Publications
GMP PUBLISHERS LTD		OS	SP	None
GRACEWING/FOWLER		OS	SP	None
GRANTHAM BOOK SERV	UK	OS		None
GROSVENOR BOOKS	UK	OS		None
H I MARKETING	UK	OS	SP	Art & Design, Popular Culture, Reference, Travel, Crafts
HAMMICKS MAIL ORDER	UK			Law
HAYWARD PROMOTIONS	UK	OS	SP	Children's Books & Audio Cassettes
S HENEAGE DIST	UK	OS	SP	Art & Architecture
HOBSONS PUBLISHING	UK		SP	Careers
HODDER & STOUGHTON	UK	OS	SP	None
ALISON HODGE PUB	UK	OS	SP	Arts & Crafts
HOTEL & CATERING CO	UK		SP	Hotel & Catering
HUGO'S LANGUAGE BOOK	UK			None
HYMNS ANCIENT & MOD	UK	OS	SP	Religion & Theology
IMAGES		OS	SP	Children's Books & Bibliographies
IMAGES DISTRIBUTION	UK		SP	None
INTERCEPT LTD	UK	OS		None
INT BOOK DIST	UK	OS		Academic & STM
INT MUSIC PUB	UK	OS	SP	Music Related Products
INTERNOS BOOKS		OS	SP	None
JARROLD PUBLISHING	UK		SP	Travel, Biography & Art
JESSICA KINGSLEY PUB		OS		None
KOGAN PAGE LTD	UK	OS	SP	None
KUPERARD LTD	UK	OS	SP	Travel Maps & Guides, Jewish Interest & Montessori Education
LA HAULE BOOKS LTD	UK	OS		None
LAKESIDE PUBNS	UK	OS	SP	Military History, Natural History & Travel
ROGER LASCELLES	UK	OS	SP	Maps & Travel
LAVIS MARKETING	UK	OS	SP	Sales Agency
LEISHMAN & TAUSSIG	UK	OS	SP	Africa
CHARLES LETTS & CO	UK	OS	SP	None
LISTER ART BOOKS		OS	SP	Antiques & Collecting, Crafts
LITTLE RED WITCH	UK			None
LITTLEHAMPTON BK SVC	UK	OS	SP	None
LIVERPOOL UNIV PRESS		OS		None
P M LLEWELLYN CO	UK	OS	SP	Arabic, Chinese, Japanese & Persian Languages, Islam
CHRIS LLOYD SALES			SP	Hobby & Leisure
LONGMAN GROUP UK LTD		OS		None
THOMAS LYSTER LTD	UK			None
B MCCALL BARBOUR	UK	OS	SP	Christian Books & Bibles
MCCARTA LTD		OS		Maps, Atlases & Travel
MACMILLAN DIST LTD	UK			None
MAINSTREAM PUB CO	UK		SP	None
MANDRAKE	UK	OS	SP	Occult
MARLBOROUGH BOOKS	UK		SP	None
MARSTON BOOKS SERV	UK	OS		Business, Scientific & Technical
MAXWELL MACMILLAN	UK	OS	SP	None
MEDIAN BOOKS LTD	UK	OS		Middle East
MELIA PUB SERVICES		OS		None
MICELLE PRESS		OS	SP	None
MILLBANK BOOKS LTD		OS	SP	None

Publisher	Country	OS	SP	Subject
MOMENTA PUB CO LTD	UK	OS	SP	Scientific, Techincal, Academic, Art & Architecture
PETER MOORE BOOKS		OS		Australia & The Pacific
MOSBY-YEARBOOK EUR		OS		None
MOTILAL BOOKS		OS	SP	India
NATURAL HIST BOOK SV	UK		SP	Natural History
NEWPRO UK LTD	UK			Photography
NORTHCOTE HOUSE PUB		OS		None
NOVA DISTRIBUTION	UK	OS	SP	None
OLD VICARAGE PUB		OS		None
OLDCASTLE BOOKS LTD		OS		None
OMNIBUS PRESS	UK	OS		Music Related
OXBOW BOOKS	UK	OS	SP	Archaeology, Ancient & Medieval History/Art/Architecture
OXFORD UNI PRESS DIS	UK	OS	SP	None
PACKARD PUB LTD	UK	OS	SP	Environmental/Nature Conservation, Landscape Architecture & Foreign Languages
PASSWORD (BOOKS) LTD	UK	OS	SP	None
PAUPERS' PRESS		OS	SP	None
PEGASUS PUB SERV	UK		SP	None
PENGUIN BOOKS LTD	UK	OS		None
PHILLIMORE & CO LTD	UK			History
PHOTOBOOK INFO SERV	UK	OS	SP	Military, Aviation & Transport
PLYMBRIDGE DIST LTD	UK	OS		None
PORTLAND PRESS LTD	UK	OS	SP	Biology & Zoology, Medical Sciences
PREMIER BOOK MKTNG		OS	SP	None
PROBUS EUROPE	UK			Business, Finance & Investment
QUEST MERIDIEN LTD		OS		Medical Books & Anatomical Charts/Products
RAGGED BEARS LTD	UK	OS	SP	Children's
REAL BOOKS		OS	SP	Mind, Body & Spirit
REED CONSUMER ILLUS	UK	OS		None
THOMAS REED PUB LTD	UK	OS	SP	Nautical Books, Calendars, Charts, Guides, Magazines Etc
ROADMASTER PUB	UK		SP	Transport
ROUNDHOUSE PUB LTD		OS	SP	None
RYBURN DISTRIBUTION	UK			None
SANGAM BOOKS LTD		OS		India
SCHOLASTIC PUB LTD	UK	OS		Children's & Educational
SCI & TECH BOOK SVCE	UK			Scietific & Technical
SCRIPTURE PRESS		OS		Christian Books
DEREK SEARLE ASS LTD	UK		SP	Sales & Marketing
SEND THE LIGHT	UK	OS	SP	Religious Books
SERPENT'S TAIL		OS		Small US Art/Contemporary Fiction
SEWELLS INT	UK	OS	SP	Motor Industry
SHAKTI COMMUNICATION	UK	OS	SP	Indian Sub-Continent
SHEED & WARD LTD	UK	OS	SP	None
SHEFFIELD ACD PRESS	UK	OS	SP	Biblical Studies, Archaeology & Humanities
COLIN SMYTHE LTD		OS	SP	Irish Interest
SPCK	UK	OS	SP	Religion
SPA BOOKS LTD	UK	OS	SP	Military History
SPRINGFIELD BOOKS	UK	OS	SP	None
SULLIVAN ASSOCIATES	UK			Sales Representation To Toy/Gift Trade Only
TBC DISTRIBUTION	UK	OS	SP	None
TEMPLE PRESS LTD	UK	OS	SP	Small Press Occult Titles
THAMES & HUDSON LTD	UK	OS		Art
TIPTREE BOOK SERV	UK	OS		None

TITAN DISTRIBUTORS	UK	OS	SP	Science Fiction/Fantasy, Horror, True Crime Books, Comics, Videos, Posters, Badges, T Shirts, Models etc
THE TRADE COUNTER	UK	OS	SP	None
TRANSPORT PUB CO LTD	UK	OS	SP	None
TURNAROUND	UK	OS	SP	Multi-Cultural Children's Books, Black Literature/Studies
TURPIN DISTRIBUTION	UK	OS		Scientific, Technical & Medical
UNI PRESSES MARKETNG		OS		University Presses
VERITAS PUBLICATIONS	UK	OS	SP	Religion & Theology
VERULAM PUB LTD	UK	OS	SP	None
VIDEO ARTS LTD	UK			Training
VINE HOUSE DIST	UK	OS	SP	None
WELSH BOOKS COUNCIL	UK			Welsh Publications
WEST COUNTRY BOOKS	UK			None
JOHN WILEY & SONS	UK	OS	SP	Scientific, Technical & Medical
JOHN WILSON BOOKS	UK	OS	SP	Management/Business, Annuals/Yearbooks, Humour
WINDHORSE PUB		OS		Buddhism
WINDSOR BOOKS INT	UK	OS		Sales Agency
WISDOM BOOKS	UK	OS	SP	Buddhism
WOODHEAD PUBLISHING		OS		Engineering, Electronics, Finance & Investment
WOODHEAD-FAULKNER	UK	OS		Business
WORLD LEISURE MKTG	UK	OS	SP	Non-Fiction, Travel
WORLDLY GOODS	UK	OS		None
ROY YATES BOOKS	UK	OS	SP	Children's Books in Dual & Foreign Languages

UK & IRISH WHOLESALERS

Notes:

The wholesalers section of the Directory contains information on wholesale booksellers - ie stockholding distributors supplying retail booksellers at trade terms - in Great Britain and Ireland.

The Booksellers Association aims to promote the services of wholesalers and to encourage booksellers to take advantage of the speedy service, the reduction in paperwork and the possibility of avoiding small order surcharges which they offer.

All the information concerning wholesalers has been provided by the companies themselves. Details concerning each company include the main regions they serve. This information is listed beside the company's name, and uses the following geographic divisions:

>Channel Islands   National
>East Anglia   North West
>Export   Rep Ireland
>London   Scotland
>Midlands   South East
>North East   South West
>N Ireland   Wales

If the wholesaler's activities are limited to a specific local geographical area, this is noted in their entry.

ALTERNATIVE BOOKS (UK) LTD
27 Tatton Court, Kingsland Grange, Woolston, Warrington, Cheshire WA1 4RR
Tel: 0925 819222
Fax: O925-819805
VAT No: 593 6129 15

Order Information

Order Dept Opening Times
Mon - Fri 8am - 5pm
All Dues Automatically Recorded
Representation Available

Personnel
Head of Company: Mr J J Berry
Head of Sales (Home): Mr H C Cawley
Head of Customer Services: Denise Lanceley

Number of Staff: 9

Regions Served: National, Rep Ireland
Paperback Titles in Stock: 2400
Complete Stocks Held of: Thorsons
Selected Stock Held of: Aquarian; Arrow; Ashgrove; Avery; Bantam; BBC; Bloomsbury; Bragg; Corgi; Daniel, C W; Dorling Kindersley; Ebury; Eden Grove; Element; Foulsham; HarperCollins; Keats; Pan Macmillan; Penguin; Piatkus; Sheldon; Vermillion; Wilshire
Other Services: New catalogue every 3 months. Promotional dumpbins.
Other Goods Available: Tarot cards

Trade Terms
35% £3.00 surcharge on orders under £30 net
Credit Cards Accepted: Access/Master, Visa, Other

The tried & tested...

ELECTRONIC ORDERING SYSTEM

GARDLINK CAN GIVE YOU THE UNDISPUTED BENEFITS OF ELECTRONIC ORDERING **NOW.**

Specifically produced to make your life easier and your business more efficient and profitable. It has been designed to incorporate any potential developments in electronic ordering, which means your investment is secure. Seeing is believing – contact us today for your colour brochure or personal demonstration.

- SIMPLE TO OPERATE – TRAINING INCLUDED

- THE BOOKSELLER REMAINS IN TOTAL CONTROL OF ALL TRANSACTIONS

- COMPLETE INTEGRATED SYSTEM INCLUDES COMPUTER, MODEM, BARCODE SCANNER, PRINTER, SOFTWARE, INSTALLATION, TRAINING AND MONTHLY STOCKFILE UPDATE

- AVAILABLE NOW – FOR PROMPT INSTALLATION

Gardners Books,
Eastwood Road, Bexhill-on-Sea,
East Sussex TN39 3PT.
Tel:(0424)224777
Fax:(0424)220560

Gardners Books,
Unit 13, Commercial Road,
Goldthorpe, Rotherham,
South Yorkshire S63 9BL.
Tel:(0709)890661
Fax:(0709)890668

Your keyboard to success

Returns Procedures
Stock Returns: Authorisation number to be obtained
Imperfect Returns: Jackets only required

AMALGAMATED PAPERBACKS UK (BIRMINGHAM) LTD
Unit 10, Bordesley Trdg Est, Bordesley Green Road, Birmingham, West Midlands B8 1BZ
Tel: 021-328 5355
Fax: 021-327 3010
VAT No: 494 2642 25

Order Information
Order Dept Opening Times
Mon - Fri 9am - 5.30pm
Representation Available

Personnel
Head of Company: David Gold
Head of Sales (Home): Mike Elkins
Head of Marketing: Robin Fleming
Head of Accounts: Placy Gunawardine
Head of Customer Services: Roy Harfield
Other Important Personnel:
Ian Gold (Group Sales Director)

Number of Staff: 16

Parent Company: David Gold & Son Ltd
Allied Companies: APB UK Group of Companies, Gold (David) & Son (Holdings) Ltd

Regions Served: Midlands
Hardback Titles in Stock: 4000
Paperback Titles in Stock: 12000
Complete Stocks Held of: ACP Harvestime; ACP Kingsway; ACP Marc; Angel Press; Baker Book House; Banner of Truth; BBC; Bible Readers Fellowship; Bible Society; Bridge Publishing; Brimax; Chapel Lane (Cassettes); Christian Focus Publications; Church House Publications; Churchman Publishing; Clarke, James; Collins; Concordia (UK); Darton, Longman & Todd; Diasozo Trust; Ears & Eyes; Editions Trobisch; Eerdmans; Eyre & Spottiswoode; Faber & Faber (Religious); Fount; Hagin Ministries, Kenneth; Haven; Highland; Hodder & Stoughton; Huntington House; Hutchinson; Inter-Varsity Press; James, Arthur; Jubilee Centre; Klock & Klock; Kregal; Ladybird (Religious); Larkin; Lion Publishing; Logos; Lutterworth Press; MacGregor Ministries; Marshall Pickering; Methodist Publisher (Music); Minstrel; Monarch; Mowbray; Muller, P Strong; New Dawn Books; New Wine Press; Norheinsmund; OMP; Open Scroll; Overcomer Publications; Oxford University Press; Pan (Religious); Paternoster Press; Purnell (Religious); Rainfall Cards; Reed (Religious); Riverside; RMEP; St Andrews Press; Scripture Press; Scripture Union; SPCK; TBS; Word; World Dist (Religious)
Hardback Books Not in Stock Can be Obtained
Paperback Books Not in Stock Can be Obtained
Van Service is Available
Other Services: Full merchandising service from basic stock lists, planograms, feature display units, promotions, pos material
Other Goods Available: Periodicals, maps & guides, childrens book, bargain books fun-faxes

Trade Terms
33.3% on paperbacks, 35% on chartered bookshops
Minimum Order: Average £75 nett per visit
Other Terms: 25% magazines
Cash and Carry Terms: negotiable

Returns Procedures

Stock Returns: Uplifted by van sales rep with instant credit on sales inv
Imperfect Returns: Report and hold for van representative

AMALGAMATED PAPERBACKS UK (BRISTOL) LTD
Unit C2 Greensplott Road, Chittening Estate, Bristol, Avon
BS11 0YB
Tel: 0272 822917
Fax: 0272 235529
VAT No: 494 2642 25

Order Information

Order Dept Opening Times
Mon - Fri 9am - 5.30pm
Representation Available

Personnel
Head of Company: David Gold
Head of Sales (Home): Roger Coleman
Head of Marketing: Robin Fleming
Head of Accounts: Placy Gunawardine
Head of Customer Services: Tracy Gilvear
Other Important Personnel:
Ian Gold (Group Sales Director)

Number of Staff: 20

Parent Company: David Gold & Son Ltd
Allied Companies: APB UK Group of Companies, Gold (David) & Son (Holdings) Ltd

Regions Served: South West, Wales
Hardback Titles in Stock: 4000
Paperback Titles in Stock: 12000
Hardback Books Not in Stock Can be Obtained
Paperback Books Not in Stock Can be Obtained
Van Service is Available
Other Services: Full merchandising service from basic stock lists, Planogram Feature display units, promotions, point of sale material.
Other Goods Available: Periodicals, maps & guides, childrens books, bargains books fun-faxes

Trade Terms
33.3% on paperbacks, 35% chartered bookshops
Minimum Order: Average £75 nett per visit
Other Terms: 25% magazines
Cash and Carry Terms: negotiable

Returns Procedures
Stock Returns: Uplifted by van sales rep with instant credit on sales inv
Imperfect Returns: Report and hold for van sales rep

AMALGAMATED PAPERBACKS UK (LONDON) LTD
15-17A Rich Indust Estate, Crimscott Street, London
SE1 5TE
Tel: 071-237 4334
Tel: 071-237 3037
Fax: 071-237 6379
VAT No: 494 2642 25

Order Information

Order Dept Opening Times
Mon - Fri 9am - 5.30pm
Representation Available

Personnel
Head of Company: David Gold
Head of Sales (Home): Bob Nicholls

Head of Marketing: Robin Fleming
Head of Accounts: Placy Gunawardine
Head of Customer Services: Mike Hill
Other Important Personnel:
Ian Gold (Group Sales Director)

Number of Staff: 32

Parent Company: David Gold & Son Ltd
Allied Companies: APB UK Group of Companies, Gold (David) & Son (Holdings) Ltd

Regions Served: London, South East, East Anglia
Hardback Titles in Stock: 4000
Paperback Titles in Stock: 12000
Selected Stock Held of: All Major HB & PB Publishers
Hardback Books Not in Stock Can be Obtained
Paperback Books Not in Stock Can be Obtained
Van Service is Available
Other Services: Full merchandising service from basic stock lists, Planogram feature display units, promotions, point of sale material
Other Goods Available: Periodicals, Maps & Guides, Childrens Books, Bargain Books, Fun-Faxes

Trade Terms
33.3% on p/b, 35% chartered bookshops
Minimum Order: Average £75 nett per visit
Other Terms: 25% magazines
Cash and Carry Terms: negotiable

Returns Procedures
Stock Returns: Uplifted by van sales representative with instant credit on sales invoice
Imperfect Returns: Report and hold for van sales representative

AMALGAMATED PAPERBACKS UK (WARRINGTON) LTD
Unit D2, Taylor Ind Est, Warrington Road, Risley, Cheshire WA3 6BL
Tel: 0925 765123
Fax: 0925 765259
VAT No: 494 2642 25

Order Information

Order Dept Opening Times
Mon - Fri 9am - 5.30pm
Representation Available

Personnel
Head of Company: David Gold
Head of Sales (Home): Jim Robertson
Head of Marketing: Robin Fleming
Head of Accounts: Placy Gunawardine
Other Important Personnel:
Ian Gold (Group Sales Director)

Number of Staff: 15

Parent Company: David Gold & Son Ltd
Subsidiary Companies: APB UK Group of Companies

Regions Served: North East, North West
Hardback Titles in Stock: 4000
Paperback Titles in Stock: 12000
Hardback Books Not in Stock Can be Obtained
Paperback Books Not in Stock Can be Obtained
Van Service is Available
Other Services: Full merchandising service from basic stock lists, planogram feature display units, promotions, pos material

Other Goods Available: Periodicals, Maps & guides, Childrens Books, Bargain Books, Fun Faxes

Trade Terms
33.3% paperbacks, 35% chartered bookshops
Minimum Order: Average £75 nett per visit
Other Terms: 25% magazines
Cash and Carry Terms: negotiable

Returns Procedures
Stock Returns: Uplifted by van, sales rep with instant credit on sale inv
Imperfect Returns: Report and hold for van sales rep

J BARNICOAT LTD
Parkengue, Penryn, Cornwall TR10 9EN
Tel: 0326 372628 Switchbd
Tel: 0326 377995 24 Orders
Fax: 0326 378151 Accounts
Fax: 0326 376423 Marketing
Fax: 0800 378630 Free Order
VAT No: 131 6778 64

Orders to
24 Hour Ansafone Number: BUYLINE 0800 515504

Order Information
Teleordering: BARNI

Order Dept Opening Times
Mon - Fri 8.45am - 5.15pm
Representation Available

Personnel
Head of Company: Jonathan Barnicoat (Managing Director)
Head of Sales (Home): Raymond Dyer (Sales Director)
Head of Sales (Export): Denise Stanford (Export Co-ordinator)
Head of Marketing: Glyn Barnicoat (Marketing Director)
Head of Accounts: Sue Toseland (Accountant)
Head of Distribution: Steve Averiss (Logistics Manager)
Head of Customer Services: Sue Bartlett (Customer Services Manager)
Other Important Personnel:
John Evans (Sales Manager), Mike Wood (Computer Manager), Tim Briggs (Library & Information Manager), Bruce Izard (Warehouse Manager), Glen Morgan (BUYLINE Co-Ordinator), John Howkins (Representative (South Devon & Cornwall)), David Gilbert (Representative (North)), Darrell Tucker (Representative (North Devon & South))

Number of Staff: 165
Open University Publications

Regions Served: National, Export
Hardback Titles in Stock: 500
Paperback Titles in Stock: 52000
Complete Stocks Held of: AA Essential Explorers & Guides; Abacus; Albatross; Alison & Busby; Angus & Robertson; Apple Press (PB); Aquarian; Arden Shakespeare; Arkana; Armada; Arrow; Asterix; Baedker Guides; Bantam; Barrie & Jenkins; BBC; Black Swan; Blackie Children's; Bluffers Guides; Bodley Head; Bounty Books; Brodies Notes; Buzz Books; Carnival Mini (HB); Cedar; Century; Century Travellers; Chapmans (PB); Chatto; Children's Classics; Classic Thrillers; Collins Children's; Collins Gems; Collins Reference Division; Constable (PB); Consumers Association; Corgi; Coronet; David & Charles; Dent; Diadem; Dinosaur; Dorling Kindersley (PB); Dr Who; Ebury Press; Eland; Elliot Rightway; Everyman; Expert Series; Faber (PB); Farmhouse Kitchen (PB); Flamingo; Fodor; Fontana; Gaia; GCSE Guides; Gollancz; Grafton; Granta; Green Print; Hamilton,

Hamish; Hardy New Wessex; Harlequin; Harrap Dictionaries; Headline; Headway; Healthright; Hippo; Hodder & Stoughton; Hodge, Alison; Hogarth Press; Horizons; I Spy; Joseph, Michael; Jotter Series; Kingfisher; Kipling Centenary; Knight; Know The Game (A&C Black); Ladybird; Legend; Let's Go; Letts; Lion (Inc Picture & Young); Lion Publishing; Little Brown (PB); Little Miss; Livewire; Lonely Planet; Lynx Children's; Made Simple; Mammoth; Mandarin; Master Bridge; Master Musicians; Mastercrime; Masterguides; Mermaid; Methuen; Mills & Boon; Minerva; Mott Cornish Library; Mr Men; Mr Men/ Little Miss; NEL; New Grove MUsic; New Horizons; Nexus; Observer Series; Octopus; Odyssey Guides; O'Mara, Michael; Optima; Orion; OS Landranger; Oxford UP; Paladin; Pan; Pandora; Papermac; Parent & Child; Pavilion; PBI; Pelham; Penguin; Piatkus; Picador; Piccolo; Picturemac; Piper; Positive Health Quotes; Postman Pat; Private Eye; Puffin; Quartet; Random House; Ravette; Ravette; Reader's Digest; Red Fox; Rider; Robinson; ROC; Rowan; RSPCA Pet Guides; St Martin's Press; Sceptre; Search Press; Serpent's Tail; Sheldon; Shire; Sidgwick & Jackson; Signet; Silhouette; Simon & Schuster; Sutton Pocket Classics, Alan; Tabb House; Teach Yourself; Thames & Hudson; Thorsons; Times Books; Titan; Tolkein; Topsy & Tim; Tracks; TSR; Two-Can; Upstarts; Usborne; VGSF Classics; Viking; Vintage; Virago; Virgin; Walker Books; Warne; Warner; Webb & Bower; Weidenfeld; Women's Press; World of Art; Worldwide; York Notes

Selected Stock Held of: AA (PB); Anaya (PB); Bantam (HB); BBC; Boxtree; Collins Audio Cassettes; Dorling Kindersley (HB); Doubleday (HB); Element (PB); Exley (PB); Fairfax; Fernhurst; Foulsham; Foulsham (PB); Garfield; Hamlyn; HMSO; Insight Guides; Kogan Page; Kogan Page; Mitchell Beazley; New Era; OS Pathfinder; Phaidon; Phaidon (PB); Philip, George; Rough Guides; World International

Other Services: Bi-Annual Stock Catalogue (Double Indexed Author/Title), ABC New Title Service, POS Material, Pub Cats, Saturday Delivery

Other Goods Available: OS Maps, Audio Tapes, Calendars, West Country Images Postcards

Trade Terms
35%
Minimum Order: £65 Invoice Value (£100 Saturday Delivery)

Returns Procedures
Authority to Return: Sue Bartlett or Rep
Address for Returns: Returns Department
Stock Returns: All stock sold firm sale
Imperfect Returns: Return front and rear jacket plus title page to customer service for credit or replacement

BERTRAM BOOKS LTD

The Nest, Rosary Road, Norwich, Norfolk NR1 1TF
Tel: 0603 663333
Fax: 0603 617999
VAT No: 104 7825 79

Orders to
Tel: 0603 617617
Fax: 0800 585686 UK Free
24 Hour Ansafone Number: Day 632095 Ev 617617

Order Information
Teleordering: BERT
First Edition Subscriber

Order Dept Opening Times
Mon - Fri 9am - 4.30pm,
All Dues Automatically Recorded
Representation Available

Personnel
Head of Company: Kip Bertram
Head of Sales (Home): Graham White
Head of Sales (Export): Emma Rowley
Head of Marketing: Mike Butler
Head of Accounts: Caroline Green
Head of Distribution: Barry Robinson
Head of Customer Services: Paul Ellis

Number of Staff: 150

Regions Served: National, Export
Hardback Titles in Stock: 10000
Paperback Titles in Stock: 30000
Complete Stocks Held of: APA Insight Guides; Arrow; Bantam; Berlitz; Cadogan Guides; Corgi; Coronet; Elliot Right Way; Everymans Library; Faber; Fontana; Grafton; Headline (PB); Hugo's; Ladybird; Letts; Lonely Planet; Mandarin; Michelin; Ordnance Survey; Pan; Penguin; TFH; Usborne; Warner Books; Warner Futura
Selected Stock Held of: AA; Adlard Coles; Age Concern; Airlife; Airlift/Gaia; Allan, Ian; Allen, J&A; Allison & Busby; Anaya; Anderson Press; Apple Press; Appletree Press; Argus; Arlington; Arms and Armour; Artulen; Ashgrove Press; Ashley Courtenay; Aurum Press; Babani; Balliere Tindall; Barker, Arthur; Barnacle Marine; Barrie & Jenkins; Bartholomew; Batsford; Bay View Books; BBC; Bellew; Berol; Bible Society; Bicycle Books; Black, A & C; Blackie; Blackwell Scientific; Blake; Blandford; Bloomsbury; Bodley Head; Bounty; Boxtree; Boydell Press; Brimax; British Crest Int; British Mountaineering Council; British Museum; Brown, John; Burrall Floraprint; Butterfingers; Butterworth Heinemann; Buzz Books; Calmann & King; Cambridge University Press; Campbell Books; Camra; Canongate Publishing; Cape; Cassell; Cathie, Kyle; Century; Chambers; Chapmans; Chatto & Windus; Child's Play; Churchill Livingstone; Collins & Brown; Conran Octopus; Constable; Cooper, Leo; CRAC; Crowood Press; David & Charles; Debretts; Dent; Deutsch, Andre; Diadem; Dorling Kindersley; Doubleday; DP; Dragon's World; Ebury Press; Eland; Element; Exley; Express Books; Facts on File; Fairfax; Farming Press; Fernhurst; FHG 1993 Publications; Flip Cards; Floraprint; Fodor Guides; Ford, Mary; Foulsham; Fourth Estate; Gaia Publishing; Gallery; Geographer's A-Z Maps; Gollancz; Good Books; Granta Books; Grove Weidenfeld; Grub Street; Guild of Master Craftsmen; Guinness; Hale, Robert; Hamilton, Hamish; Hamlyn; HarperCollins; Harrap; Hawk Books; Hawker; Haynes; Hazleton; Headline (HB); Heinemann; Heinemann; Helm, Christopher; Henderson Publishing; Herbert Press; Hern, Nick; Hippo; HMSO; Hodder & Stoughton; Hunt & Thorpe; Hutchinson; Icon; ICTC Magmix; International Music; Invader Childrens; ISIS; ISO; Jade; Jam Books; Jarrold Publishing; Johansens; Joseph, Michael; Kaye & Ward; Kenilworth; King, Laurence; Kingfisher; Kingsfleet; Lennard; Lincoln, Frances; Linguaphone; Lion; Little Brown; Little Brown; Longman; Lowe, Peter; Lyle; Lyric Books; McCarta; McGraw Hill; Macmillan; MacRae, Julia; Mainstream; Marvel; Mason, Kenneth; Media Masters; Melia Pub Services; Merehurst; Methuen; Millenium; Mills & Boon; Mitchell Beazley; Moon Travel; Moonlight; Moorland; Morris, Joshua; Mowbray & Co; Muller, Frederick; Multimedia; Murray, John; Music Master; National Trust; Nelson; New English Library; New Holland; O'Mara, Michael; Omnibus; Orchard Books; Orion; Osprey; Oxford Publishing Co; Oxford University Press; Partridge; Paul, Stanley; Pavilion; PBI; Pegasus; Pelham; Phaidon; Philips; Phoenix; Piatkus; Pic; Piccadilly; Pimlico; Pitman; Plexus; Poolbeg; Prion; Prism Press; Pyramid; Quartet; Quiller; RAC; Ragged Bears; R&B; Random Audio; Random House Childrens; Ravette; Readers Digest; Redan; Reinhardt; Rider; Ringpress; Riverfirst; Robinson Publishing; Robson;

Rosendale; Rough Guides; Routledge; St John Thomas, David; Salamander; Sawd; Scottish Tourist Board; Seaby; Search Press Ltd; Secker & Warburg; Sheldon Press; Sidgwick & Jackson; Simon & Schuster Young Books; Simon & Schuster; Sinclair-Stevenson; Smith Gryphon Ltd; Souvenir Press; SPI; Sportsman's Press; Springfield Book Co; Stephens, Patrick; Sterling; Studio Editions; Studio Vista; Sumach; Sutton, Alan; Swapmeet; Sweet & Maxwell; Tauris; Taxation Advice Bureau; Thames & Hudson; Thorsons; Times Books; Titan; Tolley Publishing; Trade & Travel; Treehouse; Vacation Work; Viking/Kestrel; Virago; Virgin; Walker Books; Ward Lock; Warne; Watts, Franklin; Weidenfeld & Nicolson; Western Publishing; Which? Consumer Guides; Whitakers; Whittet Books; Williams, Tony; Wisley Handbooks; Witherby; Womens Press; Wordsworth; World International; Worldwide Media Services; Xanadu; Yale University Press; Yorkshire TV
Hardback Books Not in Stock Can be Obtained
Paperback Books Not in Stock Can be Obtained
Other Services: Quarterly stock cat, buyers notes, new title cat monthly, weekly bestseller lists, pos material

Trade Terms
35%
Minimum Order: Carriage paid on orders over £60 retail
Girobank Number: 251 2351

Returns Procedures
Authority to Return: Steve Spurgeon - Claims Dept
Stock Returns: Firm sale except subscription orders where auth label issued For incorrect supp/imperfect books contact claims dept
Imperfect Returns: £20 and under, return title page, all Readers Digest/AA Drive titles return whole book. Copies will be replaced.

BOOKSCENE RETAIL LTD

Unit 2, Weedon Rd Ind Estate, Tyne Road, Northampton, Northamptonshire NN5 5AF
Tel: 0604 751521
Fax: 0604 583397

Order Information
Teleordering: BKSCENE

BOOKSPEED

48 Hamilton Place, Edinburgh, Lothian EH3 5AX
Tel: 031-225 4950
Fax: 031-220 6515

Order Information
Teleordering: BKSPEED

Order Dept Opening Times
Mon - Fri 8am - 6pm
All Dues Automatically Recorded
Representation Available

Personnel
Head of Company: Anne Rhodes/Kingsley Dawson
Head of Accounts: Margo Forrest
Head of Distribution: Yvonne Brady
Head of Customer Services: Shona Rowan

Number of Staff: 20

Parent Company: Rhodawn Ltd

Regions Served: National
Hardback Titles in Stock: 1500
Paperback Titles in Stock: 12000

Complete Stocks Held of: Airlift Eden Grove; Alyson; Amaising Publishing House; Arkana; B & W Publishing; Baxter Photography, Colin; Bicycle Books Inc; Canongate; Daniel, C W Co Ltd; Gaia; GMP; Green Print; Heretic; Kelpies; Ladybird; Mainstream; No Exit; Pandora; Prism Press; Rough Guides; St Martins Press (Gay List); Serpent's Tail; Vermilion; Vintage; Virago; White Cockade; Women's Press
Selected Stock Held of: Aberdeen University Press; Alloway; Angus & Robertson; Aquarian; Ark; Arrow; Ashgrove; Bantam; Bartholomew; BBC; Bloomsbury; Cape; Cedar; Century; Chatto & Windus; Child's Play; Collins Childrens; Collins Dictionaries; Corgi; Coronet; Donald, John; Dorling Kindersley; Earthscan; Ebury Press; Element; Faber & Faber; Fontana; Foulsham; Fourth Estate; Gateway; Gollancz; Grafton; Hale; HarperCollins; HarperSanFrancisco; Little Brown; Little Mammoth; Luath; Lyle; Macmillan; Magna; Mammouth; Mandala; Mandarin; Minerva; Ordnance Survey; Orion; OUP; Pan; PBI; Penguin; Piatkus; Picture Lions; Pimlico; Polygon; Quartet; Ragged Bears; Red Fox; Rider; Shambhala; Sheldon; Simon & Schuster; Souvenir; Thames & Hudson; Thorsons; Usborne; Walker; Warner Futura; World International
Van Service is Available
Other Services: Monthly new titles catalogues two months in advance of pub Stocklists by pub & title, Specialist Lists

Trade Terms
35%
Minimum Order: £50 invoice value
Girobank Number: 147 1961

Returns Procedures
Authority to Return: Contact Fiona Atkinson

BOOKWORLD WHOLESALE

7 Welch Gate, Bewdley, Worcestershire DY12 2AT
Tel: 0299 404140 24 Hours
Fax: 0299 404140
VAT No: 441 8717 43

Order Information
Teleordering: BKWORLD

Order Dept Opening Times
Mon - Fri 9.30am - 4.30pm, Sat 9.30am - 5pm
All Dues Automatically Recorded
Representation Available

Personnel
Head of Company: Janet & Les Gainhan
Head of Sales (Home): Justin Gainham
Other Important Personnel:
Lian Gainham (General Office & Enquiries)

Number of Staff: 4

Regions Served: National
Hardback Titles in Stock: 3500
Paperback Titles in Stock: 1500
Selected Stock Held of: Transport, Military & Modelling Publications only
Hardback Books Not in Stock Can be Obtained
Paperback Books Not in Stock Can be Obtained
Other Services: Securicor delivery normally 24 hrs after collection Order lists available (transport,military & modelling books)

Trade Terms
35% on all orders
Minimum Order: Postage is charged on orders under £25 a nominal £1.50
Credit Cards Accepted: Access/Master, Visa

Returns Procedures
Stock Returns: Normal returns, ie write/phone and immediate authorisation given for damaged in transit/faulty or incorrect supp items

CHRISTIAN LITERATURE CRUSADE
51 The Dean, Alresford, Hampshire SO24 9BJ
Tel: 0962 733142
Tel: 0800 373755 Orders
Fax: 0962 733141
VAT No: 208 0352 02

Order Information

Order Dept Opening Times
Mon - Fri 9am - 5.30pm
Representation Available

Personnel
Head of Company: Mr R J Page (UK Director) 0962 735281
Head of Sales (Home): Mr P M Hayward (Wholesale Director) 0962 732402
Head of Accounts: Mrs G Scott (Cashier) 0962 733142

Number of Staff: 20

Regions Served: National, Export
Selected Stock Held of: 11 other US publishers plus; Ambassador Productions; Banner of Truth; Bible Society; Crossway Books; CUP Scripture Press; Eagle Books; HarperCollins; Highland Books; Hodder & Stoughton; Hunt & Thorpe; IUP; Kingsway Group; Lion Publishing; OUP; Scripture Union Word
Paperback Books Not in Stock Can be Obtained
Other Services: Annual Catalogue, 3 times a year updates
Other Goods Available: Cassettes and CD's

Trade Terms
35% books & bibles, 33.3% vat goods - 30% cass & cd's
Credit Cards Accepted: Access/Master, Visa

Returns Procedures
Stock Returns: Returns accepted of stock in mint condition by prior arrangement
Imperfect Returns: Title page only all paperbacks, complete book - hardback & bibles over £15 RRP

CLAN BOOKS

Clandon House, The Cross, Doune, Perthshire FK16 6BE
Tel: 0786 841330
Fax: 0786 841326
VAT No: 369 1426 35

Order Information
Teleordering: CLAN

Order Dept Opening Times
Mon - Fri 8.45am - 5.15pm
All Dues Automatically Recorded
Representation Available

Personnel
Head of Company: David Warburton/Jean Warburton (Partners)
Head of Sales (Home): Jonathan Hildrey (Sales Manager)

Number of Staff: 16

Subsidiary Companies: Clan of Callander Ltd

Regions Served: Scotland
Hardback Titles in Stock: 5000
Paperback Titles in Stock: 10000

Hardback Books Not in Stock Can be Obtained
Paperback Books Not in Stock Can be Obtained
Van Service is Available
Other Goods Available: Maps & Guides

Trade Terms
From 25% min to 35% max, dependent upon volume of business & seasonal factors.
Other Terms: Accounts 30 days from statement date.

JOHN COLLINSON (WHOLESALE)

Otley Mills, Ilkley Road, Otley, West Yorkshire LS21 3JP
Tel: 0943 465721
Fax: 0943 850398
VAT No: 288 8142 14

Order Information

Order Dept Opening Times
Mon - Fri 8.30am - 5pm Sat 9am - 12.30pm
All Dues Automatically Recorded
Representation Available

Other Important Locations
Yorkshire, Lancashire, Cleveland, Co Durham, Cumbria

Personnel
Head of Company: John Collinson/Bill Milner (Partners)
Head of Customer Services: Colin Sutcliffe

Regions Served: Midlands, North East, North West
Area Served: Yorkshire, Lancashire, Cleveland, Co Durham, Cumbria
Hardback Titles in Stock: 450
Paperback Titles in Stock: 250
Complete Stocks Held of: AA; A-Z; Bartholomew; Berlitz; Cicerone; Estate; FHG; Hillside; Michelin; Ordnance Survey; Pastime; Peters, Frank; Philips; RAC; Westmorland Gazette
Selected Stock Held of: BBC Books; Cassell; Century Hutchinson; Collins; Constable; Crowood; David & Charles; Diadem; Farming Press; Hale, Robert; HMSO; Hutton Press; Jarrold; Joseph, Michael; Leading Edge; Moorland; Oxford Illustrated; Pavilion; Pevensey Press; Pic; Pitkin; Sigma Press; SMC; Springfield; Weidenfeld & Nicholson
Hardback Books Not in Stock Can be Obtained
Paperback Books Not in Stock Can be Obtained
Van Service is Available
Other Services: Map, Book, Accommodation Guide, Globe catalogues available, Urgent orders: 1st class post small/overnight carrier large
Other Goods Available: 3000 map titles in stock, globes, map cases, laminated maps, selected calendars

Trade Terms
35% on all orders

CONCORD BOOKS

128 Alfreton Road, Nottingham, Nottinghamshire NG7 3NS
Tel: 0602 790325

Order Information

Order Dept Opening Times
9am - 5.30pm

Personnel
Head of Company: David Lane

Regions Served: National
Paperback Titles in Stock: 200
Complete Stocks Held of: Green Books; Green Print

Trade Terms

35%
Minimum Order: £100
Other Terms: Less on smaller orders

CORDEE
3a De Montfont Street, Leicester, Leicestershire LE1 7HD
Tel: 0533 543579 24 Hours
Fax: 0533 471176
VAT No: 115 8575 58

Order Information
Teleordering: CORDEE

Order Dept Opening Times
Mon - Fri 8.30am - 5.30pm
All Dues Automatically Recorded

Personnel
Head of Company: Ken Vickers
Head of Sales (Home): Mike Johnson
Head of Accounts: June Vickers

Number of Staff: 10

Regions Served: National, Rep Ireland, Export
Hardback Titles in Stock: 1000
Paperback Titles in Stock: 3000
Complete Stocks Held of: 75 UK & Overseas Publishers Distributed plus; Diadem; Harvey Maps; Merrill; Ordnance Survey; Ordnance Survey of Ireland; Scarthin Books
Selected Stock Held of: 10 UK & Overseas Publishers plus; AA/OS; Bartholomew; Bicycle Books; Constable; Crowood; Hodder & Stoughton; IGN Maps France; Jarrold/OS; Kompass Maps; Lonely Planet; Pelham; Penguin; Robertson McCarta; Rough Guides; Springfield; Wainwright Guides
Other Services: Complete stockist three times per year. Monthly news sheet.
Other Goods Available: Ordnance Survey Maps. European/ US large scale mapping. Map Cases.

Trade Terms
35%
Other Terms: Single copy - single line 25%
Girobank Number: 480 4058

Returns Procedures
Authority to Return: Prior permission required
Imperfect Returns: £25

COUNTRY BOOKSTORE WHOLESALE
Hassop Station, Nr Bakewell, Derbyshire DE45 1NN
Tel: 0629 813444 Work 24 Hr
Tel: 0629 640643 Home
Tel: 0860 587143 Mobile
Fax: 0629 814355

Order Information

Order Dept Opening Times
Mon - Fri 9am - 5pm Sat & Sun 1pm - 5pm
Representation Available

Personnel
Head of Company: David McPhie (Maanging Director)

Number of Staff: 12

Regions Served: National
Hardback Titles in Stock: 2000
Paperback Titles in Stock: 2000
Other Goods Available: Maps, Bargain Stationery & Gift Lines

Trade Terms
36-37.5%
Minimum Order: £100 nett
Other Terms: Sale or exchange by arrangement
Credit Cards Accepted: Access/Master, Visa
Cash and Carry Terms: 37.5%

Returns Procedures
Authority to Return: Please notify first
Imperfect Returns: Return whole book

T COX & SON LTD
1 Alder Close, Eastbourne, East Sussex BN23 6QF
Tel: 0323 647444
Fax: 0323 721357
VAT No: 583 6028 28

J DARLOW
22A + 22B Foster Hill Road, Bedford, Bedfordshire
MK40 2EP
Tel: 0234 354400
Tel: 0234 271199
Fax: 0234 266155
VAT No: 196 4294 24

Order Information

Order Dept Opening Times
Mon - Thurs 9am - 5pm, Fri 9am - 4.30pm
Representation Available

Other Important Locations
Approx 30 mile radius of Bedford

Personnel
Head of Company: John Darlow
Head of Accounts: June Blackmore
Head of Distribution: Robert Wharton
Other Important Personnel:
Ann Harris (Hardback Buyer), David Gray (Adult Paperbacks), Jean Lennon (Childrens Paperbacks), Michael Markham (Merchandiser)

Number of Staff: 8

Area Served: Approx 30 mile radius of Bedford
Hardback Titles in Stock: 5000
Paperback Titles in Stock: 15000
Complete Stocks Held of: Usborne
Selected Stock Held of: AA; Angus & Robertson; Apple Press; Arrow (PB); Aurum Press; Bantam; Barrie & Jenkins; Bartholomew; Batsford; BBC; Blackie; Bodley Head; Bookcastle; Boxtree; Brimax; Cape; Cassell; Century; Chambers; Chapmans; Chatto & Windus; Child's Play; Collins; Conran Octopus; Corgi (PB); Coronet (PB); David & Charles; Deans; Dent; Deutsch, Andre; Dinosaur; Dorling Kindersly; Ebury Press; Faber & Faber; Fontana (PB); Foulsham; Fourth Estate; Gollancz; Grafton; Guinness; Hamilton, Hamish; Hamlyn; Harrap; Headline; Headline (PB); Heinemann; HMSO; Hodder & Stoughton; Hutchinson; Joseph, Michael; Kestrel Viking; Kingfisher; Ladybird; Letts; Lion; Little Brown; Longman; Lyle; Macmillan; Mainstream; Merehurst Press; Mermaid; Methuen; Michelin; Millers; Mills & Boon (PB); Mitchell Beazley; New English Library; Oxford University Press; Pan (PB); Paul, Stanley; Pavilion; PBI; Pelham; Penguin; Philip, George; Piatkus; Picador (PB); Puffin (PB); Purnell; Pyramid Hamlyn; Random House; Readers Digest; Reinhardt; Robson; Salamander; Secker & Warburg; Sidwick & Jackson; Simon & Schuster; Sinclair-Stevenson; Souvenir Press; Star (PB); Telegraph; Thames &

Hudson; Thorsons; Times Books; Unwin (PB); Viking; Virgin Publishing; Walker Books; Ward Lock; Warne; Warner Futura; Weindenfeld & Nicolson; Willow
Hardback Books Not in Stock Can be Obtained
Paperback Books Not in Stock Can be Obtained
Van Service is Available

Trade Terms
35%
Other Terms: Negotiable
Cash and Carry Terms: 37.5% for £750 net

DEE BOOKS
Unit 3G, Brymau Three Ind Est, River Lane, Saltney, Chester, Cheshire CH4 8RQ
Tel: 0244 671177 24 Hours
VAT No: 158 9360 28

Order Information
Teleordering: BKL

Order Dept Opening Times
Mon - Fri 9am - 5.30pm
All Dues Automatically Recorded
Representation Available

Other Important Locations
North Wales & Cheshire

Personnel
Head of Company: E Wakley
Head of Sales (Home): Mr L Gornall

Regions Served: Midlands, North West
Area Served: North Wales & Cheshire
Hardback Titles in Stock: 10000
Paperback Titles in Stock: 5000
Complete Stocks Held of: BBC; Berlitz; Dorling Kindersley; Guinness Superlatives; Hamlyn; Ladybird; Letts; Pan Britannica; Readers Digest; Usborne
Selected Stock Held of: 100 other publishers inc; AA; Century Hutchinson; David & Charles; HarperCollins; Heinemann; Hodder & Stoughton; Little Brown; Macmillan; Penguin Group (HB); Walker
Hardback Books Not in Stock Can be Obtained
Paperback Books Not in Stock Can be Obtained
Van Service is Available
Other Goods Available: Maps, BBC Cassettes

Trade Terms
35% (over £150 retail), strictly monthly credit accounts
Other Terms: Up to £75 retail 25%, £75 - £150 retail 33.3%
Girobank Number: 67 414 0508
Cash and Carry Terms: 36%

DELTA (DISTRIBUTION OF ENGLISH LANGUAGE TEACHING AIDS) LTD
39 Alexandra Road, Addlestone, Surrey KT15 2PQ
Tel: 0932 854776
Fax: 0932 849528

Order Information
Teleordering: DELTA

Order Dept Opening Times
Mon - Fri 9am - 5pm
All Dues Automatically Recorded

Personnel
Head of Company: Mr N J Boisseau
Head of Marketing: Ms E Fryer
Head of Accounts: Mr K G Castle

Percentage of Export Sales: 100%
Number of Staff: 35

Subsidiary Companies: Crofthouse, Keltic Bookshop, Keltic Paris Bookshop

Regions Served: Export
Selected Stock Held of: ELT Publishers
Hardback Books Not in Stock Can be Obtained
Paperback Books Not in Stock Can be Obtained
Other Services: English Language Teaching, Catalogue available, Stock of ELT titles held

Trade Terms
20% on ELT orders

DMS DISTRIBUTION LTD
70 Colindale Avenue, London NW9 5ER
Tel: 081-200 7171
Fax: 081-200 9866

EASON & SON LTD
Brickfield Drive, Crumlin, Dublin 12, County Dublin
Tel: 01 536 211
Fax: 01 539 400
VAT No: IE8T 49114D

Order Information
Teleordering: EASON

Order Dept Opening Times
Mon - Fri 8.30am - 4.45pm
Representation Available

Personnel
Head of Company: W H Clarke (Chairman)
Other Important Personnel:
K Brabazon (Managing Director), C Bolton (Director), T Carpenter (Trade Manager), T Owens (Marketing Manager), D Heeney (Buyer)

Subsidiary Companies: Eason & Son (NI) Ltd, News Bros

Regions Served: Rep Ireland, Export
Hardback Titles in Stock: 1500
Paperback Titles in Stock: 7500
Complete Stocks Held of: Eason Publications; Readers Digest
Selected Stock Held of: All Main UK & Irish Publishers
Van Service is Available
Other Services: General catalogues Seasonal catalogues
Other Goods Available: Greeting cards, stationery, toys, magazines & newspapers

Trade Terms
35% carriage paid
Credit Cards Accepted: Visa

EASON & SON (NI) LTD
21-25 Boucher Road, Belfast, Antrim BT12 6QU
Tel: 0232 381200
Fax: 0232 682979
VAT No: 251 8248 61

Order Information
Teleordering: EASON

Personnel
Other Important Personnel:
J R McKelvey (Director)

Regions Served: N Ireland
Complete Stocks Held of: Eason Publications
Selected Stock Held of: All Main UK & Irish Publishers

ELSTEAD MAPS
Badgery, Hookley Lane, Elstead, Godalming, Surrey GU8 6JE
Tel: 0252 702707 24 Hours
Fax: 0252 703971
Fax: 0800 525621 Free (UK)
VAT No: 335 4441 69

Order Information
Teleordering: SCMS

Order Dept Opening Times
Mon - Fri 9am - 1pm
All Dues Automatically Recorded

Personnel
Head of Company: Stephen Colebrooke (Proprietor)
Head of Accounts: Margaret Stokes

Number of Staff: 6

Regions Served: National, South East, Export
Complete Stocks Held of: AA; A-Z Map Co; Baedeker; Berlitz; Best Bed & Breakfast; Cade's Guides; Estate; Farm Holiday Guides; Geocenter International Maps; Geoproject Arab Maps; I-Spy; Johansens; Lonely Planet; Michelin; National Gardens; Nelles Guides; Odyssey Guides; Off The Beaten Track; Ordnance Survey Landranger; Penguin Maps; RAC; Rand McNally; Rogers Guides; Rough Guides; Touring Club Italiano; Vacation Work
Selected Stock Held of: Appletree Press; Barnett Street Plans; Bartholomew; Collins Dictionaries; Consumers Association; Fodor; Hallwag Maps; Hamlyn; Hildebrand; IGN Maps of France; Insight Guides; Kummerley & Frey Maps; McCarta; Moorland Guides; Ordnance Survey; Philip, George; Service Street Plans; Springfield; Times Books
Other Services: Full catalogue avail arranged in geographical area Stock cards can be supplied
Other Goods Available: Laminated Maps, Globes

Trade Terms
35%
Minimum Order: £75 retail average within delivery area
Other Terms: £75 retail outside area for next-day service
Girobank Number: 302 4989

FASTLANE DISTRIBUTION LTD
3-11 Pensbury Place, London SW8 4TP
Tel: 071-622 5709
Fax: 071-498 0418
VAT No: 607 9814 16

Personnel
Head of Company: S E Reiter (Managing Director)

Percentage of Export Sales: 98%
Number of Staff: 3

Regions Served: Export
Paperback Titles in Stock: 100
Hardback Books Not in Stock Can be Obtained
Paperback Books Not in Stock Can be Obtained
Other Services: Book Data Service Available
Other Goods Available: Periodicals Maps

Trade Terms
35% on paperbacks excl Penguin
Minimum Order: £5000 per annum

Returns Procedures
Stock Returns: Contact customer services for authorisation

R T & A FAWCETT
White Quarry, Tadcaster, North Yorkshire LS24 9NQ
Tel: 0937 833153
Fax: 0937 530327
VAT No: 181 6198

Order Information
Teleordering: FAWCT

Order Dept Opening Times
7 days a week 8.30am - 6pm

Other Important Locations
Yorkshire, Cleveland, North Humberside

Personnel
Head of Company: R T Fawcett
Other Important Personnel:
Angela Fawcett, Jo Parish

Number of Staff: 3

Regions Served: North East
Area Served: Yorkshire, Cleveland, North Humberside
Hardback Titles in Stock: 1500
Paperback Titles in Stock: 8000
Selected Stock Held of: BBC Books; Bloomsbury; Brimax; Cassell; David & Charles; Dent; Dorling Kindersley; Faber; Gollancz; Hale; HarperCollins; Headline; Hodder & Stoughton; Ladybird; Little Brown; Longman; Macmillan; Oxford UP; Pan; Penguin Group; Random House Group; Reed Consumer Books; Robson; Routledge; Transworld
Hardback Books Not in Stock Can be Obtained
Paperback Books Not in Stock Can be Obtained
Other Services: All orders serviced for books in BBIP includ single copies Terms variable according to publisher but normally 35% max

Trade Terms
35%
Other Terms: 25%, 20%, 15% for special orders from Publishers that we do not maintain an account with
Cash and Carry Terms: 35%

Returns Procedures
Authority to Return: R T Fawcett
Address for Returns: Will be collected
Imperfect Returns: Book only accepted

GARDNERS BOOKS LTD
Providence Way, Eastwood Road, Bexhill-on-Sea, East Sussex TN39 3PT
Tel: 0424 224777 24 Hours
Tel: 0709 890661
VAT No: 444 9504 37

Orders to
24 Hour Ansafone Number: 0424 220560

Order Information
Teleordering: GARD

Order Dept Opening Times
Mon - Fri 9am - 4.30pm
Representation Available

Personnel
Head of Company: Alan Little (Chairman)
Head of Sales (Home): Bob Jackson (Sales Manager)

Head of Sales (Export): Warwick Bailey (Export Sales Manager)
Head of Accounts: Mrs C A Little
Head of Distribution: Brian O'Reilly (Warehouse Manager)
Head of Customer Services: John Talbot (Customer Care Manager)
Other Important Personnel:
Jonathan Little (Managing Director), Mrs N Godfrey (Credit Controller), Chris Haslett (Buying Manager)

Open University Publications

Regions Served: National, Export
Hardback Titles in Stock: 15000
Paperback Titles in Stock: 30000
Complete Stocks Held of: Arrow; BBC Radio Collection; Berlitz (English Lang); Blue Moon (Masquerade); Buzz Books; Collins Childrens; Elliot Right Way; Essential Guides; Fantail; Farm Holiday Guides; Fontana; Gardners Books; Grafton PB; Guernsey Press; Headline PB; Hippo; Hodder Childrens; Hodder (PB); Kingfisher; Know the Game; Kyriakou Publications; Ladybird; Letts Educational BPP (Keyfacts); Longman (York Notes); Made Simple; Mammouth; Mandarin; Michelin (I Spy); National Gardens Scheme; New Era; Off the Beaten Track; Ordnance Survey; Pan; PBI; Penguin; Puffin; RAC Publishing; Ravette (Bluffers Guides); Ravette Childrens; Red Fox; Rough Guides; Signet; Swop Meet Toys & Models; Target PB; Teach Yourself; Thrift Editions; Transworld Childrens; Transworld PB; Two-Can; Usborne; Walker PB; Warner Futura; Whitakers
Selected Stock Held of: Lonely Planet
Hardback Books Not in Stock Can be Obtained
Paperback Books Not in Stock Can be Obtained
Other Services: Free UK delivery next day on all orders. Saturday service, Stock catalogues & lists. Monthly new titles buyers notes.
Other Goods Available: Maps, Selected Calendars & Videos, Story tapes

Trade Terms
35% - 30 days from statement date
Minimum Order: £50 net (£77 retail) - orders for less will be processed but a surcharge may be added.
Other Terms: Export terms available on request

Returns Procedures
Authority to Return: Customer care staff in our sales offices
Stock Returns: Apply to your customer care representative for details. Gardlink users may process returns electronically.
Imperfect Returns: For books over £15 apply to your customer care reps. Below £5 state price and reason for return on title page.

GEMINI BOOK DISTRIBUTION LTD

Vale Road, Tonbridge, Kent TN9 1TD
Tel: 0732 359387
Fax: 0732 770620
Telex: 957144 GEMINI G

Order Information

Order Dept Opening Times
Mon - Fri 9am - 5pm
All Dues Automatically Recorded

Personnel
Head of Company: Brian A Austin
Head of Sales (Export): Angela Mitchell
Head of Accounts: Mrs M E Lillie

Percentage of Export Sales: 100%

Regions Served: Export

Hardback Books Not in Stock Can be Obtained
Paperback Books Not in Stock Can be Obtained
Other Services: Buying, Continuation orders, Catalogues and info

GRACEWING/FOWLER WRIGHT BOOKS
Gracewing House, 2 South Avenue, Leominster, Hereford HR6 0QF
Tel: 0568 616835 24 Hours
Fax: 0568 613289
VAT No: 467 8208 14

Order Information
Teleordering: FWLW

Order Dept Opening Times
Mon - Fri 9am - 5pm
All Dues Automatically Recorded
Representation Available

Personnel
Head of Company: Thomas W Longford
Head of Marketing: A C Sheridan Swinson
Head of Accounts: Harold Gardner
Head of Customer Services: Sue Morgan

Percentage of Export Sales: 30%
Number of Staff: 14

Parent Company: Fowler Wright Books Ltd

Regions Served: National, Export
Hardback Titles in Stock: 5000
Paperback Titles in Stock: 25000
Complete Stocks Held of: Burns & Oates; Chapmans, G/ Mowbrays; Darton, Longman & Todd; Lion; McCrimmon Publishing; Sheed & Ward; Sheldon; SPCK; Triangle
Selected Stock Held of: 5 other publishers plus; Argus; Hamlyn; HarperCollins; Hodder & Stoughton; OUP; Pan; Penguin
Other Services: Catalogues, Price Lists, Standing orders
Other Goods Available: Greetings Cards, Posters

Trade Terms
33% on all UK titles except some liturgical works & educational titles
Other Terms: Discounts on US titles 20-33%

Returns Procedures
Authority to Return: Thomas Longford, Managing Director
Stock Returns: All returns need to be authorised by the MD or Publishing Manager
Imperfect Returns: Return whole book with reason for return marked clearly

HAYWARD PROMOTIONS LTD
101 Bashley Road, Park Royal, London NW10 6TH
Tel: 081-961 9990
Fax: 081-961 9911
VAT No: 336 1755 55

Order Information
Teleordering: HAY

Order Dept Opening Times
Mon - Fri 8.30am - 6pm
All Dues Automatically Recorded
Representation Available

Personnel
Head of Company: Caroline Hayward (Chairman)

Head of Sales (Home): Colin MacMillan (Managing & Sales Director)
Head of Accounts: R M Loates (Financial Director)
Head of Distribution: B Elliott (Warehouse & Distribution Manager)
Number of Staff: 15

Regions Served: National, N Ireland, Rep Ireland, Export
Selected Stock Held of: Selected Titles From All Major Children's Publishers
Hardback Books Not in Stock Can be Obtained
Paperback Books Not in Stock Can be Obtained

Trade Terms
35% net 30 days
Minimum Order: £175 carriage paid

Returns Procedures
Stock Returns: Authorised overstocks returnable only
Imperfect Returns: Return with reason for faulty claim

HEATHCOTE BOOKS
Hawkes Drive, Heathcote Estate, Warwick, Warwickshire CV34 6LX
Tel: 0926 451555
Tel: 0926 450180 Orders
Tel: 0926 451697 Orders
Fax: 0926 450256
VAT No: 238 5548 36

Orders to
Fax: 0800 626428 UK Free
24 Hour Ansafone Number: 0926 450180/451697

Order Information
Teleordering: HECOTE

Order Dept Opening Times
Mon - Fri 8.30am - 5.30pm
All Dues Automatically Recorded
Representation Available

Personnel
Head of Company: Graham Nelson (General Manager)
Head of Sales (Home): Roddy O'Halloran (Sales Manager)
Head of Sales (Export): Ann Boyes (Export Sales Administrator)
Head of Accounts: Ian Richards (Finance Manager)
Head of Distribution: David Johnson (Operations Manager)
Head of Customer Services: Hilary Harding (Customer Services Manager)
Other Important Personnel:
John Carr (Sales Executive Scotland & N E England), Terry Collins (Sales Executive Midlands & S Wales), Bob Fairbrother (Sales Executive S East), Bob Hopkins (Sales Executive S West), Nigel Parr (Key Accounts Manager (& N W England/N Wales))

Number of Staff: 125

Parent Company: W H Smith Ltd

Regions Served: National, Rep Ireland, Export
Hardback Titles in Stock: 10000
Paperback Titles in Stock: 50000
Complete Stocks Held of: AA (PB); Absolute Press (PB); Adlib Books (PB); Amalgamated Book Services (PB); Arrow Books (PB); Bartholomew; BBC Books; BBC Radio Collection; Berlitz Books & Cassettes; Blewbury Press; Bloomsbury (PB); BPP Educational; Chambers Dictionaries; Collins Audio; Collins Childrens Books (PB); Collins Children's (PB); Collins Dictionaries; Collins Reference (PB); Dent (PB); Disney; Dorling Kindersley; Faber & Faber (PB);

Fairfax (PB); Fontana (PB); Fourth Estate; Gollancz (PB); Grafton (PB); Green Print (PB); Guinness Books; Harvill (PB); Headline (PB); Henderson; Hippo Books (PB); Hodder & Stoughton (PB); I Spy; Kingfisher; Ladybird; Macmillan Cassettes; Macmillan Educational (PB); Mason, Kenneth; Mermaid (PB); Mills & Boon; O'Mara, Michael; Ordnance Survey; Oxford University Press (PB); Oxford UP Dictionaries; Pan Macmillan Children's; Pan (PB); Papermac; PBI; Penguin Group (PB); Piatkus (PB); Ragged Bears (PB); Random House (PB); Reed Publishing Group (PB); Robson (PB); Salamander; Search Press; Serpent's Tail (PB); Shire; Sidgwick & Jackson (PB); Thames & Hudson (PB); Times Books; Titan (PB); Transworld (PB); Usborne; Virgin Publishing (PB); Walker Books (PB); Warne; Warner Futura; Womens Press (PB); World International; World Leisure Marketing
Selected Stock Held of: AA (HB); ABC; Airlife; Anaya; Apple Press; Associated Christian Publishers (PB); Aurum Press; Babani, Bernard (PB); Black, A&C (KTG Series); Bloomsbury (HB); Boxtree; Cambridge University Press; Campbell Books; Cassell; Century; Chambers (PB); Chapmans; Child's Play; Collins Reference (HB); David & Charles; Debretts; Deutsch, Andre (HB); Dragon's World (Paper Tiger); Drew, Richard; Element Books; Elm Tree; Evans Brothers; Exley; Faber & Faber (HB); Foulsham (PB); Gold Arrow; Gollancz (HB); Grafton (HB); Hamilton, Hamish; HarperCollins General (HB); Headline (HB); Heinemann Professional; HMSO (Driving PB); Hodder & Stoughton (HB); Jarrold; Johansens; Joseph, Michael; Kogan Page; Letts General; Lion; Little Brown; Longman; Lyle (HB); Macmillan (HB); Marlborough; Merehurst; Michelin (Maps & Guides); Murray, John; Omnibus Press; Orchard; Oxford UP (HB); Pan (HB); Pavilion; Pelham; Penguin (HB); Phaidon Press; Piatkus; Pitman; Poolbeg Press (PB); RAC; Ragged Bears (HB); Random House (HB); Ravette (PB); Reader's Digest; Reed Publishing Group (HB); Reinhardt Books; Robson (HB); Routledge (Arden Shakespeare); Sheldon Press (PB); Sidgwick & Jackson (HB); Simon & Schuster; Sinclair-Stevenson; Souvenir Press; Studio Editions; Sutton, Alan; Thames & Hudson (HB); Thorsons; Transworld (HB); Viking; Virgin Publishing (HB); Walker Books (HB); Watts, Franklin; Webb & Bower (Country Diary); Weidenfeld & Nicolson; Western Publications (PB); World International (PB & Cassettes)
Hardback Books Not in Stock Can be Obtained
Paperback Books Not in Stock Can be Obtained
Other Services: BUYline Electronic Ordering/Subscription Service/Sales Team/ Same Day Despatch before 4pm/Euro Agent/Quarterly Directory
Other Goods Available: Maps & Books on tape are supplied on wholesale terms

Trade Terms
35%, 30 days from statement
Minimum Order: £75 (RSV)
Credit Cards Accepted: Access/Master, Visa

Returns Procedures
Authority to Return: Hilary Harding
Stock Returns: Stock is sold firm. For incorrectly supplied lines contact customer services and quote the relevant sales order number
Imperfect Returns: Contact customer services and quote the relevant sales order number

HILLS WHOLESALE BOOKS
Clay Flatts Industrial Estate, Workington, Cumbria
CA14 2DR
Tel: 0900 603031
Tel: 0900 602781

Fax: 0900 61072
VAT No: 256 2712 62

Order Information

Order Dept Opening Times
Mon - Fri 8am - 5pm
All Dues Automatically Recorded
Representation Available

Other Important Locations
Cumbria

Personnel
Head of Company: Ron Hill/John Hill
Head of Accounts: Helen McGuirk
Other Important Personnel:
Susan Pugh (Manageress), Alison Cattanach (Education Dept), Brenda Lloyd (Special Orders)

Regions Served: North West
Area Served: Cumbria
Complete Stocks Held of: Lake District Titles
Selected Stock Held of: Puffin
Hardback Books Not in Stock Can be Obtained
Paperback Books Not in Stock Can be Obtained
Van Service is Available
Other Services: Educational stockist & suppliers. Large showroom. Specialist ordering system
Other Goods Available: Maps

HUGHES BOOK SERVICES LTD

26 Hyndford Street, Belfast, Antrim BT5 5EN
Tel: 0232 456556 24 Hours
Fax: 0232 457696

Order Information

Order Dept Opening Times
Mon - Fri 8.30am - 5.30pm
All Dues Automatically Recorded
Representation Available

Personnel
Head of Company: R Anderson (Sales Director)
Head of Customer Services: H Killen

Allied Companies: Aurora Enterprises Ltd, Phoenix Books, White Rose Books

Regions Served: N Ireland
Hardback Titles in Stock: 200
Paperback Titles in Stock: 1200
Selected Stock Held of: Most main publishers, plus local publishers
Hardback Books Not in Stock Can be Obtained
Paperback Books Not in Stock Can be Obtained
Van Service is Available
Other Services: Master Stock List, Special Orders

Trade Terms
35%

HUGHES BOOK SERVICES LTD

21/22 Lee Road, Dublin Ind Estate, Glasnevin, Dublin 11, County Dublin
Tel: 01 301 166 24 Hours
Tel: 01 800 418 418 Free Order
Fax: 01 307 306
Fax: 01 800 591 591 Free Fax
VAT No: 8T 52531K

Order Information

Order Dept Opening Times
Mon - Fri 8.30am - 5.30pm
Representation Available

Personnel
Head of Company: Derek Hughes (Managing Director)
Head of Sales (Home): Brain Fagen (Sales Manager)
Head of Sales (Export): Aideen Woods
Head of Marketing: Danny Reid (Marketing Manager)
Head of Accounts: Pat Hoey (Financial Director)
Head of Distribution: Robert Hughes (Warehouse Manager)
Head of Customer Services: S Doyle/A Daley
Other Important Personnel:
H R Hughes (Group Chairman)

Number of Staff: 35

Parent Company: Hughes Book Services Ltd
Subsidiary Companies: Hughes & Hughes Booksellers,
Hughes & Hughes Booksellers

Regions Served: National, N Ireland, Rep Ireland
Hardback Titles in Stock: 3000
Paperback Titles in Stock: 10000
Complete Stocks Held of: Australian Consolidated Press; Australian Womans Weekly; Berlitz; Bounty; Fairfax, J B
Selected Stock Held of: All Irish Publishers plus; Appletree Press; Arrow; Berlitz; Blackstaff; Cambridge University Press; Century; Collins; Corgi; Coronet; Coronet; Faber & Faber; Fontana; Fontana; Grafton; Little Brown; Mandarin; Ordnance Survey; Oxford University Press; Pan; Penguin; Thames & Hudson
Hardback Books Not in Stock Can be Obtained
Paperback Books Not in Stock Can be Obtained
Other Services: Catalogues, Promotional Material, Telesales, 'Buzz a Book'
Other Goods Available: Maps, Bargain Books

Trade Terms
33.3% - 35%
Minimum Order: 50 books
Credit Cards Accepted: Access/Master, Visa
Cash and Carry Terms: available on request

Returns Procedures
Stock Returns: Authorisation number given on receipt of goods. Credit given

HUNKYDORY DESIGNS LTD

Millboard Road, Bourne End, Buckinghamshire SL8 5XD
Tel: 0628 529621
Fax: 0628 529488
VAT No: 538 0011 80

Order Information

Order Dept Opening Times
Mon - Fri 9am - 5.30pm
All Dues Automatically Recorded
Representation Available

Personnel
Head of Company: Brian Shawcross
Head of Sales (Home): Christine Moule (Sales Office Manager)

Number of Staff: 50

Regions Served: National
Hardback Titles in Stock: 600
Paperback Titles in Stock: 100
Selected Stock Held of: Abbeville; ABC; Absolute Press; Angus & Robertson; Appletree; Aurum; BBC Books; Blake; Bloomsbury; Books & Toys; Brown Publishing, John; Brown

Watson; Brown Wells & Jacob; Campbell Books; Cassell; Cathie, Kyle; Chapmans; Collins & Brown; David & Charles; Deutsch, Andre; Dorling Kindersley; East West; Educational Insights; Elite Words & Image; Fourth Estate; Gollancz; Grub Street; Hale, Robert; HarperCollins; Headline; Hodder & Stoughton; Ideas Unlimited; Letts; Liber; Lincoln, Frances; Lion; Little Brown; Martin Books; Meadowbrook; Merehurst; Mistral; Murray, John; O'Mara, Michael; Orchard; Overlook Press; Pan Macmillan; Pauper, Peter; Pavilion; Penguin; Piatkus Books; Price, Matthew; Private Eye; Pryor Publications; R & B Publishing; Ragged Bears; Random House; Ravette; Reed International; Salamander; Scholastic; Silent Books; Silver Link Publishing; Simon & Schuster; Souvenir Press; Studio Editions; Templar & Gallery; Transworld; Trodd, Brian; Walker Books; Ward Lock; Warner; Weidenfeld & Nicolson; Windrush Press; Workman; World International; Wright, Gordon; Xylopress
Other Services: Biannual illustrated stock catalogues
Other Goods Available: Wide range of stationery products:cards/gift wrap/diaries & calenders, tins. Merchandise:Liberty/Pooh/Potter/Old Bear

Trade Terms
35% plus 3.75% settlement discount on payment within 14 days
Minimum Order: £200

LOMOND BOOKS

36 West Shore Road, Granton, Edinburgh, Lothian
EH5 1QD
Tel: 031-551 2261 24 Hours
Fax: 031-552 1703

Order Information
Teleordering: LOMOND

Order Dept Opening Times
Mon - Fri 9am - 5pm
All Dues Automatically Recorded
Representation Available

Personnel
Head of Company: David Flatman (Managing Director)
Head of Sales (Home): Trevor Maher (Sales Director)
Head of Accounts: Christine Addison (Financial Director)
Head of Distribution: Jim Craig (Distribution Manager)
Head of Customer Services: Hazel Flatman
Other Important Personnel:
Duncan Baxter (Field Sales Manager)

Number of Staff: 15

Parent Company: David Flatman Ltd

Regions Served: North East, North West, Scotland, Export
Hardback Titles in Stock: 2000
Paperback Titles in Stock: 5000
Complete Stocks Held of: Baxter Photography, Colin; Canongate Publishing; Cascade Publishing; Tachen Art Books
Selected Stock Held of: Ordnance Survey (Scottish Maps)
Van Service is Available
Other Services: Monthly updated catalogue, standing order sub service
Other Goods Available: Maps, Scottish calendars & diaries

Trade Terms
Minimum Order: £50 retail
Other Terms: 33.3% SOR, Firm 35%, CWO 38.25%
Cash and Carry Terms: 40%

Returns Procedures

Authority to Return: From Sales Representative or Field Sales Manager
Stock Returns: Sale or return, accounts should notify sales rep or sales man of details of titles.SOR accounts return at their cost
Imperfect Returns: Imperfect titles can be returned without prior advice and credit will include cost of carriage

MENOSHIRE LTD

Unit 13, 21 Wadsworth Road, Perivale, Greenford, Middlesex UB6 7LQ
Tel: 081-566 7343
Tel: 081-566 7344
Fax: 081-991 2439
VAT No: 228 4512 69

Order Information

Order Dept Opening Times
Mon - Fri 9am - 5.30pm
All Dues Automatically Recorded
Representation Available

Personnel
Head of Company: Mr J M Treacy

Percentage of Export Sales: 40%
Number of Staff: 6

Regions Served: National, London, Export
Hardback Titles in Stock: 1584
Paperback Titles in Stock: 2376
Hardback Books Not in Stock Can be Obtained
Paperback Books Not in Stock Can be Obtained
Van Service is Available
Other Services: Back Orders & Monthly Newsletter
Other Goods Available: Videos (Car & Motorcycle)

Trade Terms
Minimum Order: Single copy 25% + postage, multiples 35% + carriage up to £100
Cash and Carry Terms: yes - 2.5% cash settlement

Returns Procedures
Authority to Return: By permission only

MERESBOROUGH BOOKS

17 Station Road, Rainham, Gillingham, Kent ME8 7RS
Tel: 0634 388812
Fax: 0634 378501
VAT No: 205 1050 31

Order Information
Teleordering: MERE

Order Dept Opening Times
Mon - Sat 9am - 5.30pm
All Dues Automatically Recorded
Representation Available

Personnel
Head of Company: Hamish Mackay Miller
Head of Customer Services: Judith Leunig

Number of Staff: 14
Open University Publications

Regions Served: National
Hardback Titles in Stock: 10000
Paperback Titles in Stock: 25000
Complete Stocks Held of: Bartholomew; Berlitz; Bounty; Elliot Right Way; Estate; FHG; Geographer's A-Z Maps;

Ladybird; Michelin; Middleton; Ordnance Survey (small scale series); PBI; Shire
Selected Stock Held of: Over 200 Publishers
Hardback Books Not in Stock Can be Obtained
Paperback Books Not in Stock Can be Obtained
Other Services: Single copy order service from over 300 publishers, includ many educational and academic.
Other Goods Available: Comprehensive range of British and Foreign maps

Trade Terms
33.3% (Larger customers 35%)
Other Terms: Orders under £30:25%, under £10:10%
Girobank Number: 39 771 8004
Credit Cards Accepted: Access/Master, Visa

Returns Procedures
Stock Returns: Prior permission required for all returns except errors and imperfects
Imperfect Returns: Whole books required except for own publications

METRASTOCK LTD

Unit 7, Cedar Trade Park, Ferndown Industrial Est, Wimborne, Dorset BH21 7PE
Tel: 0202 891992
Fax: 0202 892109
VAT No: 423 7270 66

Order Information

Order Dept Opening Times
Mon - Fri 9am - 4.30pm

Personnel
Head of Company: Norman Green

Regions Served: National
Hardback Books Not in Stock Can be Obtained
Paperback Books Not in Stock Can be Obtained

CALVIN MORGAN BOOKSELLERS

51 York Road, Brentford, Middlesex TW8 0QP
Tel: 081-560 3404
Tel: 081-560 3405
Tel: 081-847 0511 24 Hour
Fax: 081-560 0595
VAT No: 545 7227 33

Order Information
Teleordering: ALBS

Order Dept Opening Times
Mon - Fri 9am - 5.30pm Sat 9.30am - 4pm
Representation Available

Personnel
Head of Company: Calvin Morgan
Head of Accounts: Sue Franklin
Head of Distribution: Simon Honey
Head of Customer Services: Rory Chalmers
Other Important Personnel:
Malcolm Essex (Trade Manager)

Percentage of Export Sales: 60%
Number of Staff: 8

Parent Company: Rewardcare Ltd
Subsidiary Companies: Connoisseur Books

Regions Served: National, Export
Hardback Titles in Stock: 3000
Paperback Titles in Stock: 4000

Selected Stock Held of: Adlard Coles; Aero; Aerofax; Airlife; Albertelli; Allen, Ian; Alloway; Allt Om Hobby; Apple; Argus; Arms & Armour; Ashford; Aston; Athena; Autocitica; Autodata; Automobile Quarterly; Automobilia; Barreira; Batsford; Bayview; Becker; Beekman House; Bellis; Bender; Bentley; Bernard & Graefe; Blandford; Bleicher; Blue & Grey Press; Bonanza; Bookmarque; Boston Mills; Boudriot; Brooklands; Brown Son & Ferguson; Car Styling; Carbonell; Cassell; Cavallino; Century; Chartwell; Chevron; Chilton; Chronicle; Clanford; Collectakit; Collins; Condie; Constable; Consumer Guides; Conway Maritime; Cooper, Leo; Copernic; Cortney; Cosentino; Court; Cranbourn; Crecy; Crescent; Crestline; Crown; Crowood; Dalton, Terence; Dalton Watson; David & Charles; De Krijer; Donald, John; Dorset; Dover; Dupouy; Evergreen; Facts on File; Fairfax; Fairplay; Fasal; Fedorowicz; Ferry; Field; Firebird; Floating Drydock; Foulis; Foulsham; Fountain; Franckh; Frei Korps; Galago; Gallery; Ginter; Gollancz; Gondrom; Grancher; Greenhill; Gregory's; Grub Street; Guinness; Hale; Hallwag; Hamlyn; Haymarket; Haynes; Hazleton; Heaton; Heimdal; Heinemann; Hero; Hippocrene; HMSO; Hodder & Stoughton; Howell Press; HP Books; Hutchinson; Hutton; Hyde Park; Imperial; ISO; Johnson; Johnston; Kimber; Kimberley; Kingfisher; Koehler; Kogan Page; Lavauzelle; LDA; McGraw-Hill; Macmillan; Magna; Main Smith; Mallett Bell; Maranello; Marboro; Maritime Books; Marque; Maru; Massin; Maximilian; MBV; MEP; Merlin; Mid Counties; Mil Heritage; Mil Press; Mittler; Model Art; Modelaid; Moorland; MRP; Natraj; Naval Inst; New Cavendish; Newnes; Nishen; Nutshell; Orbis; Orion; Osprey; Outlet; P4 Spares; Patzwall; Pengel; Penguin; Pentech; PHPC; Picton; Plaistow; Plenk; Podszun; PodzunPallas; Portland Hse; Presidio; Prion; Promontory; PRS; PSL; Putnam; Pygmalion; Quiller; RAFM; Rebecchi; Riku-Kai; Rivista; Rizzoli; Routledge; RRHT; S-A Design; St Martin's; Salamander; San Martin; Schiffer; Schild; Schuetz; Schwend; Shire; Silex; Smith; Spa; Speedsport; Spellmount; Springfield; Sqdn Signal; Sterling; Suedwest; Sutton, Alan; Swapmeet; Tab; TCL; Tee; Thames & Hudson; Tiger; Trodd; Tudor; Urbes; Weishaupt; Wessex; Westlake; Wiley; Willow; Windr Greene; Wordsworth; Worley
Van Service is Available
Other Services: Annual Motoring & Military Catalogues & Updates
Other Goods Available: Videos, Posters, Key Fobs

Trade Terms
35% 30 days credit with references
Credit Cards Accepted: Access/Master, Visa

Returns Procedures
Stock Returns: Contact Head Office for written authorisation
Imperfect Returns: Entire book to be returned

MUSIC BOOK DISTRIBUTORS LTD

44 Station Way, Buckhurst Hill, Essex IG9 6LN
Tel: 081-559 1522
VAT No: 493 2386 23

Order Information

Order Dept Opening Times
Mon - Fri 9.30am - 5pm
All Dues Automatically Recorded
Representation Available

Personnel
Head of Company: Neil Taylor

Percentage of Export Sales: 20%

Regions Served: National, Rep Ireland, Export
Hardback Titles in Stock: 200

Paperback Titles in Stock: 1500
Selected Stock Held of: 60 other publishers plus; Arrow; Bodley Head; Boxtree; Cassell; Century Hutchinson; Chambers; Deutsch, Andre; Dorling Kindersley; Fourth Estate; Guinness; HarperCollins; Hodder & Stoughton; Longman; Making Music; Pan Macmillan; PC Publishing; Penguin Group; Plexus; Ravette; Reed; Sidgwick & Jackson; Transworld; Usborne; Virgin; Weidenfeld/Dent
Hardback Books Not in Stock Can be Obtained
Paperback Books Not in Stock Can be Obtained
Other Goods Available: Sheet Music

Trade Terms
33% with a few exceptions
Other Terms: Firm sale only
Girobank Number: 317 7491

Returns Procedures
Stock Returns: Returns permission must be sought in advance.

W J NIGH & SONS LTD
62 Landguard Road, Shanklin, Isle of Wight PO37 7HX
Tel: 0983 863291
Tel: 0983 863403
Fax: 0983 866283
VAT No: 107 6002 13

Order Information

Order Dept Opening Times
Mon - Fri 9am - 5pm
All Dues Automatically Recorded
Representation Available

Other Important Locations
Isle of Wight

Personnel
Head of Company: Terry Nigh (Managing Director) Ext 25
Head of Sales (Home): Russell Nigh (Sales Manager) Ext 26
Head of Accounts: Adrian Nigh (Director) Ext 24

Number of Staff: 7

Area Served: Isle of Wight
Paperback Titles in Stock: 400
Complete Stocks Held of: Exley; IW County Press; Jarrold; Transworld
Paperback Books Not in Stock Can be Obtained
Other Services: Fill in paperback service, weekly reps call, twice weekly van delivery
Other Goods Available: Greeting cards - postcards - stationery - toys - gifts - beach goods - pottery - confectionery

Trade Terms
35%
Minimum Order: £10

PATEMAN'S WHOLESALE BOOK SERVICE
2A Newington Road, Kingsthorpe, Northampton, Northamptonshire NN2 7TF
Tel: 0604 721233
Fax: 0604 720677

F W PAWSEY & SONS
Dales Road, Ipswich, Suffolk IP1 4JT
Tel: 0473 742311

Fax: 0473 240105
VAT No: 103 5285 04

Order Information

Representation Available

Personnel
Head of Company: Bob Pawsey
Head of Accounts: Ralph Thurston

Regions Served: East Anglia
Complete Stocks Held of: Ladybird
Selected Stock Held of: Collins; Various Other Publishers
Hardback Books Not in Stock Can be Obtained
Paperback Books Not in Stock Can be Obtained
Other Goods Available: Stationery, Greetings Cards, Toys

Trade Terms
33.3%
Minimum Order: £50

G R & J PEMBERTON & SONS

Croft Street (off Marsh Lane), Preston, Lancashire PR1 8SU
Tel: 0772 555110
Fax: 0772 53684

PIPELINE BOOKS

32 Paul Street, London EC2A 4LB
Tel: 071-729 3491
Fax: 071-729 6149
VAT No: 241 4235 00

Order Information
Teleordering: PIPE

Order Dept Opening Times
Mon - Thur 9.30am - 6pm, Fri 9.30am - 5.30pm
All Dues Automatically Recorded
Representation Available

Personnel
Head of Company: Michael Goodwin
Head of Accounts: Tony Silcox

Number of Staff: 16

Parent Company: Namara Ltd

Regions Served: London
Hardback Titles in Stock: 1000
Paperback Titles in Stock: 30000
Complete Stocks Held of: Abacus; Allison & Busby; Aquarian; Ark; Arkana; Bantam; Black Swan; Cadogan; Cardinal; Collins Harvill Paperbacks; Eden Grove; Eland; Flamingo; Gaia; Gay Men's Press; Hogarth; Let's Go Guides; Lonely Planet; Mandala; Minerva; Odyssey Guides; Optima; Pandora; PBI Publications; Penguin; Picador; Pimlico; Puffin; Quartet; Rider; Rough Guides; Sceptre; Serpent's Tail; Shambhala; Thorsons; Vintage; Virago; Women's Press
Selected Stock Held of: AA; Armada Lion; Arrow; Ashgrove; BBC; Bloomsbury; Blossom (HC); Boyars, Marion; Calder, John; Carcanet; Chambers; Corgi; Coronet; Daniel, C W; Dent; Dorling Kindersley; Duckworth; Element; Faber; Fontana; Fourth Estate; Grafton; Granta; HarperCollins; Headline; Hippo; Mammoth; Mandarin; Michelin; Omnibus; Oxford UP; Pan; Papermac; Piatkus; Pluto; Red Fox; Routledge; Sheldon; Usborne; Vermilion; Virgin; Warner Futura
Hardback Books Not in Stock Can be Obtained
Paperback Books Not in Stock Can be Obtained

Van Service is Available
Other Services: Backlist ordering if not stocked. Selected publishers lists. Monthly list new HB & PB and core subject stock lists.

Trade Terms
35% - except certain academic titles which may be subject to lower disc.
Other Terms: Carriage applicable to consignments sent outside our normal delivery area
Cash and Carry Terms: 35%

SEND THE LIGHT
PO Box 300, Kingstown Broadway, Carlisle, Cumbria CA3 0QS
Tel: 0228 512512
Tel: 0800 282728 Orders
Fax: 0228 514949
Fax: 0800 282530 Orders
VAT No: 205 6950 67

Order Information
Teleordering: STL

Order Dept Opening Times
Mon - Thurs 9am - 5pm, Fri 9am - 4.30pm
Representation Available

Personnel
Head of Company: Keith Danby (Chief Executive)
Head of Sales (Home): Daan van Belzen (Sales & Marketing Director)
Head of Sales (Export): Pieter Kwant (Senior Sales Manager)
Head of Accounts: Janet Busk (Director of Finance)
Head of Distribution: Bruce Beattie (General Manager)
Head of Customer Services: Mick Goodman (Customer Support Manager)
Other Important Personnel:
Alan Butler (Sales Manager - Publisher Representation Group), John Lewis (Business Development Manager)

Percentage of Export Sales: 10%
Number of Staff: 150

Parent Company: Operation Mobilisation

Regions Served: National, Export
Selected Stock Held of: 75 other publishers plus; Bible Society; Cassell; DLT; HarperCollins Religious; Hodder & Stoughton Religious; IVP; Lion Publishing; Scripture Union; SPCK; Word
Hardback Books Not in Stock Can be Obtained
Paperback Books Not in Stock Can be Obtained
Other Services: Stock Control Slips, Initial Stock Order Package & Directory Marketing, Handheld Re-Order Terminal, BUYLINE Subscriber

Trade Terms
35% on orders over £60 retail otherwise 5% handling charge - Min £2
Other Terms: 30% on Ladybird (any quantity) short discounts on some hymn books & recorded product

Returns Procedures
Authority to Return: Customer Service Dept - UK Customers Contact Service Line 0345 056568
Imperfect Returns: Title pages to be returned if retail value is less than £10

GLYN SUMMERS LTD
Stanley Mills, Britannia Rd, Milnsbridge, Huddersfield, West Yorkshire HD3 4QW
Tel: 0484 642220
Fax: 0484 645695

Order Information
Teleordering: GLYN

Order Dept Opening Times
Mon - Fri 9am - 5.30pm
All Dues Automatically Recorded
Representation Available

Other Important Locations
North Wales

Personnel
Head of Company: Richard Woodhead (Operations Director)
Head of Sales (Home): Mike Manning (Home Sales Head & Lancashire/West Midlands)
Head of Accounts: Malcolm Hardy
Head of Distribution: Len Field
Head of Customer Services: Sally Walker
Other Important Personnel:
Graeme Hall (North East/North West Rep), David Yates (East Mids, Yorkshire & Humberside Rep)

Number of Staff: 16

Parent Company: Greenhead Books Ltd

Regions Served: Midlands, North East, North West
Area Served: North Wales
Hardback Titles in Stock: 7500
Paperback Titles in Stock: 4000
Complete Stocks Held of: Dorling Kindersley; Ladybird; Usborne
Hardback Books Not in Stock Can be Obtained
Paperback Books Not in Stock Can be Obtained
Other Services: Complete stock catalogue, Regular promotions with bookshops Point of sale material, Xmas highlights stock control books
Other Goods Available: We stock an excellent range of manufactured bargain books and publishers remainders

Trade Terms
35%
Minimum Order: £75 retail carriage paid
Other Terms: Credit and carry 36%
Cash and Carry Terms: 37.5%

Returns Procedures
Authority to Return: Via the representative
Stock Returns: Notification within 7 days with note of income number.
Imperfect Returns: Complete book should be returned

TAW VALLEY WHOLESALE CO
32 High Street, Ilfracombe, Devon EX34 9DD
Tel: 0271 863514
Fax: 0271 862217
VAT No: 143 4487 66

Order Information
Order Dept Opening Times
8.30am - 5.30pm

Personnel
Head of Company: Mr N N Vince (Managing Director)
Head of Sales (Home): Mr D G Vince (Sales Director)
Head of Accounts: Mr D Porter (Office Manager)

Number of Staff: 10

Regions Served: South West
Other Services: Seasonal Stock Only

TITAN DISTRIBUTORS

PO Box 250, London E3 3LT
Tel: 071-538 8300
Fax: 071-987 6744

Orders to
24 Hour Ansafone Number: 071-987 6804

Order Information
Order Dept Opening Times
Mon - Fri 9.30am - 5.30pm
Representation Available

Personnel
Head of Company: Michael Lake (Managing Director)
Head of Sales (Home): Michael Phillips (Sales Manager)
Head of Accounts: Gilbert Labadie
Head of Distribution: Wilf Wood (Distribution Manager)
Other Important Personnel:
Nick Watson (Book Department Manager), Nick Parry Jones (Comic Department Manager), John Nicholls (Imports/Merchandise Manager), Dave Tamlyn (Book Buyer), Pat Sullivan (Catalogue)

Number of Staff: 50

Regions Served: National
Selected Stock Held of: Science Fiction & Fantasy titles
Hardback Books Not in Stock Can be Obtained
Paperback Books Not in Stock Can be Obtained
Van Service is Available
Other Services: Freight To & From Europe/US
Other Goods Available: Comics, Posters, Badges, T Shirts, Model Kits, Videos

Trade Terms
35%, 30 days
Other Terms: Free shipping on consignments exceeding £200 invoice value

Returns Procedures
Authority to Return: Normall firm sale
Address for Returns: Titan Distributors, Unit One, Empson Street, London E3 3LT

TOTAL BOOK DISTRIBUTION

Unit 18-20, Rosevale Road, Parkhouse Industrial Est, Newcastle-under-Lyme, Staffordshire ST5 7QT
Tel: 0782 561000
Tel: 0782 562572
Fax: 0782 564484 Sales Dept
Fax: 0782 566908 Buyer Dept
Fax: 0782 564494 Orders
VAT No: 270 3484 66

Orders to
Total Book Dist, Customer Service, Unit 1, Rosevale Business Park, Newcastle-under-Lyme, Staffordshire ST5 7QT
Tel: 0782 564455
Fax: 0800 626625 Free UK

Order Information
Teleordering: HMCK

Order Dept Opening Times
Mon - Fri 9am - 6pm
All Dues Automatically Recorded
Representation Available

THE COMPLETE BOOKSHOP SERVICE

UK's No 1 Selection Of Hardbacks & Paperbacks

▶ **Unrivalled Monthly** New Titles Information Service

▶ Special Promotions With **Free** Point Of Sale Material

▶ Specialists In **Children's** Books

▶ The **Widest** Range Of Maps

Same Day Despatch By **Securicor** Of All Orders Received By **4.00 P.M.**

No Charge For Saturday Deliveries

For Further Information On: **The Only Complete Bookshop Service** Telephone: **0782 561000**

Tel No: 0782 **564455**
Fax No: 0782 **564494**

Total Book Distribution
Unit One, Rosevale Business Park
Newcastle-under-Lyme
Staffordshire ST5 7QT

FREE FAX
0800 626625

Personnel
Head of Company: Norman Smith (Managing Director) 0782 562572
Head of Sales (Home): Dawn Hunter-Ellis (Sales Manager) 0782 561000
Head of Marketing: Barbara Buckley (Marketing Manager) 0782 561000
Head of Accounts: Phil Ray (Financial Director) 0782 562572
Head of Distribution: Rowland Evans (Operations Director) 0782 562572
Head of Customer Services: Elaine Mandley (Customer Services Manager) 0782 562572
Other Important Personnel:
Phil Richards (National & Key Accounts Manager), Jim Sheehan (Sales Rep (North)), Jill Rose (Sales Rep (Midlands)), Roy Jones (Sales Rep (South))

Number of Staff: 250
Open University Publications

Parent Company: John Menzies (UK) Ltd

Regions Served: National, Export
Hardback Titles in Stock: 15000
Paperback Titles in Stock: 35000
Complete Stocks Held of: Abacus (B-format); Arena; Arena (B-format); Argo; Armada; Arrow; Bantam (A-format only); BBC Radio Collection; Black Swan; Cardinal (B-format); Carousel; Comet; Corgi; Coronet; Dinosaur; Elliot Rightway; Fantail; Flamingo (B-format); Fontana; Fontana Lions (Picture Lions); Fount (Religious); Grafton (A-format); Headline; Knight; Ladybird; Legend; Listen for Pleasure; Magnet; Mammouth; Mandarin; Methuen; Michelin; Minerva (B-format); New English Library (A-format); Optima; Orbit; Ordnance Survey; Paladin (B-format); Pan; PBI; Penguin; Picador (B-format); Piccolo; Piper; Puffin; Reader's Digest; Red Fox; Sceptre (B-format); Target; Teach Yourself; Usborne (PB); Vintage; Virgin; Warner
Selected Stock Held of: Pickwick; Tellastory
Hardback Books Not in Stock Can be Obtained
Paperback Books Not in Stock Can be Obtained
Other Services: Stock Cat 3pa; Monthly Stock Fiche; Recommend Opening Stock; Monthly Buyers Notes/New Titles; Subject Cats; Subs Key Acct
Other Goods Available: Maps, Talking Books

Trade Terms
35% on all orders, no surcharges except £2.50 carriage on orders less than £70 retail.
Other Terms: A few titles at higher or lower discounts depending on publishers discounts.

Returns Procedures
Authority to Return: 1. Overstocks: Anne Bartlett 2. Damaged/Imperfect/Sent in Error: Trevor Bootherstone
Address for Returns: Total Book Dist, Returns Dept, Unit 1, Rosevale Bus Park, Newcastle-under-Lyme ST5 7QT
Imperfect Returns: Complete book must be returned with full details of imperfection

VERA TRINDER LTD

38 Bedford Street, London WC2E 9EU
Tel: 071-836 2365
Tel: 071-836 2366
Tel: 071-836 8332
Fax: 071-83 0873
VAT No: 239 5174 45

Order Information

Order Dept Opening Times
Mon - Fri 8.30am - 5.30pm

Personnel
Head of Company: Mrs V Webster
Other Important Personnel:
Mrs Tracey McKay

Percentage of Export Sales: 30%

Regions Served: National
Other Goods Available: Everything relating to stamps - coins - postcards except the goods themselves

Trade Terms
Girobank Number: 597 0105
Credit Cards Accepted: Access/Master, Visa

TURNAROUND

27 Horsell Road, London N5 1XL
Tel: 071-609 7836/7
Fax: 071-700 1205
VAT No: 396 4918 93

Order Information
Teleordering: TURN

Order Dept Opening Times
Mon - Fri 9.30am - 6pm
All Dues Automatically Recorded
Representation Available

Personnel
Head of Company: Bill Godber (Managing Director)
Head of Marketing: Claire Thompson (Marketing Director)
Head of Accounts: Kiel Shaw (Finance Director)
Head of Distribution: Geddes Thomas
Head of Customer Services: Roger James

Number of Staff: 10
Open University Publications

Regions Served: National, Export
Hardback Titles in Stock: 5
Paperback Titles in Stock: 95
Selected Stock Held of: Bad Boy; Gay Mens Press; Harvester Wheatsheaf; Holloway House; Mantra; Melrose Square; Minerva; Plume; St Martins Press; Verso; Virago
Other Services: Catalogues & Promotional material available. Please discuss with representative

Trade Terms
Minimum Order: 10% on all orders under £10 gross, 25% between £10-£30 gross 35% over £30 gross, 35% on subscription orders.
Girobank Number: 57 135 040

Returns Procedures
Authority to Return: Representatives or Roger James, Customer Services
Imperfect Returns: Whole copy to be returned unless otherwise authorised on phone

UNITED BOOK SUPPLIERS

689 Antrim Road, Newtownabbey, Antrim BT36 8RN
Tel: 0232 832362
Fax: 0232 848780
Telex: 9312132234 UN G
VAT No: 331 7301 94

Order Information

Order Dept Opening Times
Mon - Fri 9am - 5pm
All Dues Automatically Recorded
Representation Available

Personnel
Head of Company: John Lindsay
Head of Sales (Export): Debbie Laird
Head of Customer Services: Sarah Laird

Percentage of Export Sales: 100%

Regions Served: Export
Selected Stock Held of: Main UK/US/German/French/Dutch Academic & General Publishers
Hardback Books Not in Stock Can be Obtained
Paperback Books Not in Stock Can be Obtained
Van Service is Available

Trade Terms
Geared to publishers' terms
Other Terms: Details on application
Girobank Number: 68 674 4004
Credit Cards Accepted: Access/Master, Visa, Amex, Diners

Returns Procedures
Stock Returns: Request permission
Imperfect Returns: Return whole book

VALLEY BOOKS
Hadnock Road, Monmouth, Gwent NP5 3NQ
Tel: 0600 712402 24 Hours
Tel: 0800 7373216
Fax: 0600 716075
VAT No: 298 5485 89

Order Information

Order Dept Opening Times
Mon - Fri 8am - 5.30pm
Representation Available

Personnel
Head of Company: W R Stanbury
Head of Accounts: Lois Merolla
Head of Customer Services: Pauline Stanbury

Subsidiary Companies: Bridge Publishing Inc, USA

Regions Served: National
Hardback Titles in Stock: 4000
Paperback Titles in Stock: 14000
Hardback Books Not in Stock Can be Obtained
Paperback Books Not in Stock Can be Obtained
Other Services: Catalogue of full publishers range by title and author. 24hr service, warehouse visitors welcomed.
Other Goods Available: Greetings cards, stationery videos, games audio cassettes, leather goods, bookmarks, key rings etc.

Trade Terms
35%
Minimum Order: £50 invoice value

Returns Procedures
Stock Returns: Books to be returned in full
Imperfect Returns: Books to be returned in full

S WEBB & SON
Telford Place, Menai Bridge, Anglesey, Gwynedd LL59 5RW
Tel: 0248 712761
Fax: 0248 714619
VAT No: 159 6141 49

Order Information

Order Dept Opening Times
Mon - Fri 8.30am - 5pm, Sun 10am - 4pm

Representation Available
Personnel
Head of Company: Frank Dubberley
Head of Accounts: Chris Jackson
Head of Distribution: Howard Smith
Head of Customer Services: Diana Owens
Other Important Personnel:
Roger Stanley (Northern England), John Turner (South West), Richard Pennington (South East), John Phillips (East Midlands), Mike McDonnell (Southern)

Number of Staff: 50

Regions Served: London, South East, South West, Midlands, East Anglia, North West, Wales
Hardback Titles in Stock: 5000
Paperback Titles in Stock: 2000
Hardback Books Not in Stock Can be Obtained
Paperback Books Not in Stock Can be Obtained
Other Services: Promotional Stickers, Custom made promotions, Computer Listings, Bestseller selection
Other Goods Available: Staionery, Toys, Gifts, 2000 Bargain Books

Trade Terms
35-40%
Minimum Order: £100 cost

WELSH BOOKS COUNCIL DISTRIBUTION CENTRE
Glan Yr Afon Ind Est, Llanbadarn, Aberystwyth, Dyfed SY23 3AQ
Tel: 0970 624455
Fax: 0970 625506
VAT No: 123 0426 23

Order Information
Teleordering: WBC

Order Dept Opening Times
Mon - Thur 8.30am - 5.30pm Fri 8.30am - 5pm
All Dues Automatically Recorded
Representation Available

Personnel
Head of Company: Miss Gwerfyl Pierce Jones (Director) 0970 624151
Head of Marketing: Mr D Philip Davies 0970 624151
Head of Accounts: Mr Pedr ap Llwyd
Head of Distribution: Mr Dafydd Charles Jones (Distribution Centre Manager)

Number of Staff: 41

Regions Served: Wales
Complete Stocks Held of: 30 Welsh Publishers Distributed plus; Davies, Christopher; GPC Books; Gwasg Efengylaidd Cymru/Evangelical Press of Wales; Gwasg Prifysgol Cymru/University of Wales Press; Gwasg y Dref Wen; Honno; Llanerch Enterprises; Seren Books
Selected Stock Held of: 10 Welsh Publishers plus; AA; Bible Society; Bridge Books; Brown, D & Sons; Castle Publications; Child's Play; Collins; Corgi; David & Charles; Dent; Estate; Focus Publications; Grafton; HMSO; Hodder & Stoughton; Jarrold; Ordnance Survey; Oxford University Press; Penguin; Sutton, Alan; Thames & Hudson; Warner Futura
Van Service is Available
Other Services: Monthly book lists, Quarterly mag (Book News from Wales) Ann catalogue of Welsh Lang Books, Twice yearly stock lists
Other Goods Available: Maps, Periodicals

Trade Terms

33.3% + 2.5% prompt settlement discount

Returns Procedures
Authority to Return: Dafydd Charles Jones
Stock Returns: No books to be returned without prior consent
Imperfect Returns: Complete book should be returned when found to be imperfect Permission in these cases not necessary

FOREIGN WHOLESALERS

Notes:

This section lists the names and addresses of foreign wholesalers who may be able to supply UK and Irish booksellers. The list is not comprehensive and inclusion does not constitute an endorsement by the Booksellers Association. For details of stockholding and terms of supply, booksellers are asked to contact the wholesalers direct.

See also the Distributor, Sales Agency and Wholesaler Specialisations section for UK importers of foreign books and the Companies and Imprints Index for specific publishers.

CANADA
Assn for the Export of Canadian Books
1 Nicholas, Suite 504
Ottawa
Ontario K1N 78B7
Tel: 1 613 562 2324
Fax: 1 613 562 2329

FRANCE
Centre d'Exportation
du Livre Francais
9 rue de Toul
75012 Paris
Tel: 33 4347 3003
Fax: 33 4347 5943

GERMANY
Grossohaus Wegner & Co GmbH
Conventstrasse 14
2000 Hamburg 76
Tel: 49 40 251040
Fax: 49 40 25104250
Teleordering: GW

Koch Neff & Oetinger & Co GmbH
Schockenriedstrasse 37
Postfach 800569
D-7000 Stuttgart 80
Tel: 49 711 78600
Fax: 49 711 7892200
Teleordering: KNO

GREECE
Libro
8 Patr. loakim
Athens 10674
Tel: 30 1 724 7116
Fax: 30 1 723 2066

ITALY
Licosa Libreria Comissionaria Sansoni SpA
via Duca di, Calabria 1/1
50125 Florence, Italy
Tel: 39 55 645415
Fax: 39 55 641257

Messaggerie Libri Spa
via Giulio Carcano 32
I-20141 Milano
Tel: 39 2 895231
Fax: 39 2 8463169

JAPAN
Maruzen Co Ltd
International Division
Export Department
PO Box 5050
Tokyo International 100-31
Tel: 81 3 3278 9223/4
Fax: 81 3 3274 2270

THE NETHERLANDS
Centraal Boekhuis BV
Erasmusweg 10
4104 AK Culemborg
Tel: 31 3450 75911
Fax: 31 3450 75343

SPAIN
Hogar Del Libro SA
Ramelleres 17
08001 Barcelona
Tel: 34 3 318 2700
Fax: 34 3 301 0399

CELESA (Centro de exportacion de Libros Espanoles)
Calle Justiniano 9
28004 Madrid
Tel: 34 1 310 1736
Fax: 34 1 319 5308

USA
Baker & Taylor International Ltd
Northdale House
North Circular Road
London NW10 7UH
Tel: 081 453 3627
Fax: 081 965 4974
Teleordering: BTBOOKS

Ingram International Inc
1125 Heil Quaker Blvd
La Vergne
Tennessee 37086-1986
Tel: 1 615 793 5000
Fax: 1 615 793 3810

AUDIO BOOK SUPPLIERS

Notes:

This section lists companies who supply audio books, also known as spoken word cassettes. The term 'supplier' has been used to cover both producers and wholesalers of cassettes. Wholesalers are those who have listed the names of the companies they stock under the heading 'Complete/Selected Stocks Held Of'.

As with the publisher entries, the trade terms given are only intended as a guide, and booksellers are therefore advised to negotiate individually.

ACADEMY SOUND AND VISION LTD
179-181 North End Road, London W14 9NL
Tel: 071-381 8747
Fax: 071-385 2653
Telex: 295441 BUSY BG
VAT No: 1 4995 97

Order Information

Order Dept Opening Times
Mon - Fri 9.30am - 5.30pm
Representation Available

Personnel
Head of Company: Hywel H Davies (Managing Director)
Head of Sales (Home): Ray Crick (Marketing & Sales Manager)
Head of Sales (Export): Richard Harrison (Export Sales & Distribution Manager)
Head of Accounts: Richard Partington (Chief Accountant)

Number of titles published annually: 2
Number of Staff: 12
All New Titles are Bar Coded

Other Goods Available: Music Cassettes and Compact Discs
Subjects Covered: Music

Returns Procedures
Authority to Return: Neil Heyland

ACCENT EDUCATIONAL PUBLISHERS LTD
17 Isbourne Way, Winchcombe, Gloucestershire GL54 5NS
Tel: 0242 604466
Fax: 0242 604480
VAT No: 576 0048 41

Order Information

Order Dept Opening Times
Mon - Fri 9am - 5.30pm
All Dues Automatically Recorded
Representation Available

Personnel
Head of Company: Ron Gellert-Binnie (Managing Director)
Head of Accounts: Susan Blackett (Administrator)

Number of Staff: 3

Trade Terms
Cassettes 15% (special orders variable)

Other Terms: P&P charged on orders of invoice value under £10

Returns Procedures
Authority to Return: Ron Gellert-Binnie

AMBASSADOR PRODUCTIONS LTD
Providence House, 16 Hillview Avenue, Belfast, Antrim BT5 6JR
Tel: 0232 658462
Fax: 0232 659518
VAT No: 331 7347 70

Subjects Covered: Religion & Theology

BARN DANCE PUBLICATIONS LTD
62 Beechwood Road, Croydon, Surrey CR2 0AA
Tel: 081-657 2813
Fax: 081-657 8788

Personnel
Head of Company: Derek Jones

Number of titles published annually: 2
Number of Staff: 2

Complete Stocks Held of: Folk Shop, The; Hobgoblin Music; Mallinson Music
Subjects Covered: Crafts & Hobbies, Local Interest, Music, Sports & Games

Trade Terms
35%

BBC RADIO COLLECTION
Woodlands, 80 Wood Lane, London W12 0TT
Tel: 081-576 2000
Fax: 081-749 8766
Telex: 265781
Cables: BROADCAST LONDON
VAT No: 232 3276 89

Orders to
Exel Logistics Media, 3 Sheldon Way, Larkfield, Aylesford, Kent ME20 6SF
Tel: 0622 882000 (24 Hr)
Fax: 0622 718036

Order Information

Order Dept Opening Times
Mon - Fri 9am - 5pm
All Dues Automatically Recorded
Representation Available

Personnel
Head of Company: Sue Anstruther (Head of Spoken Word)
Head of Sales (Home): Barry Fletcher (UK Sales Manager)
Head of Sales (Export): Richard Gay (Export Sales Manager)

Number of titles published annually: 80
All New Titles are Bar Coded

Parent Company: BBC Enterprises Ltd

Subjects Covered: Children's Books, Drama & Plays, Fiction, Humour

Trade Terms
Standard 30% on all orders no surcharges

Girobank Number: 545 1450
Credit Cards Accepted: Access/Master, Visa, Amex

Returns Procedures
Authority to Return: Sales Representative or Sales Manager, Head Office
Address for Returns: Exel Logistics
Stock Returns: Overstocks - Authorisation from BBC Books required incorrect supply/damaged direct to Exel Logistics
Imperfect Returns: Send goods with details of fault to Exel Logistics

BERLITZ PUBLISHING CO LTD

Berlitz House, Peterley Road, Horspath, Oxford, Oxfordshire OX2 2TX
Tel: 0865 747033
Fax: 0865 779700
VAT No: 596 1055 25

Orders to
Charles Letts & Co, Thornybank Ind Est, Dalkeith, Midlothian EH22 2NE
Tel: 031-663 1971
Fax: 031-660 5435

Order Information

Order Dept Opening Times
Mon - Fri 9am - 5.30pm
Representation Available

Personnel
Head of Company: Charles Halpin
Head of Sales (Home): Jacki Heppard
Head of Accounts: William Findlay
Head of Distribution: Ann-Marie Harty

Number of Staff: 50

Other Goods Available: Language Videos
Subjects Covered: Foreign Languages, Maps, Atlases & Travel

Trade Terms
35%

Returns Procedures
Authority to Return: Charles Letts & Co

BIBLE SOCIETY (THE BRITISH & FOREIGN BIBLE SOCIETY)

Stonehill Green, Westlea, Swindon, Wiltshire SN5 7DG
Tel: 0793 513713
Tel: 0800 521229 FREE/ORDER
Fax: 0793 512539
Telex: 44283
Cables: Cables Testaments Swindon
VAT No: 243 1364 89

Order Information

Order Dept Opening Times
8.45am - 5pm
All Dues Automatically Recorded
Representation Available

Personnel
Head of Company: Neil Crosbie (Executive Director)
Head of Sales (Home): Peter Duke (Sales Manager)
Head of Accounts: Paul Clark (Finance Manager)
Head of Distribution: Veronica Pagett (Distribution Manager)

Percentage of Export Sales: 40%
Number of Staff: 135
All New Titles are Bar Coded

Selected Stock Held of: Hodder & Stoughton - NIV New Testament on cassettes; Lion - Childrens Video Bible; Profam Publications (Adventure Story Bible)
Subjects Covered: Religion & Theology

Trade Terms
35% (except on some educational materials)
Other Terms: £5 handling charge for trade orders of gross value less than £45 except when CWO

Returns Procedures
Authority to Return: Sales Department
Stock Returns: Prior permission from sales department required. Goods must be unpriced and in perfect condition
Imperfect Returns: Return stock with permission

BOND STREET MUSIC LTD

5 Wigmore Street, London W1H 9LA
Tel: 071-491 4117 24 Hours
Fax: 071-629 1966
VAT No: 340 0978 69

Order Information

Order Dept Opening Times
Mon - Fri 9am - 5.30pm
All Dues Automatically Recorded

Personnel
Head of Company: Stanley Simmonds
Head of Sales (Home): Walter Collins

Number of Staff: 5
All New Titles are Bar Coded

Complete Stocks Held of: Audio Forum; BBC Books; BBC English; Berlitz; Chivers Audio; Collins Audio; Hodder & Stoughton Languages; Hugo; Isis Audio; Linguaphone; Macmillan; Routledge; Simon & Schuster Audio; Soundings Audio
Selected Stock Held of: Harrap (Language Materials); Longman (Language Materials); Made Simple (Language Materials); Thornes, Stanley (Language Materials)

Trade Terms
33.3% on all orders
Minimum Order: £50

Returns Procedures
Stock Returns: Telephone notification - no written authorisation required

BRITISH LIBRARY NATIONAL SOUND ARCHIVE

29 Exhibition Road, London SW7 2AS
Tel: 071-589 6603
Fax: 071-823 8970

Orders to
The British Library, Publications Sales Unit, Boston Spa, Wetherby, West Yorkshire LS23 7BQ
Tel: 0937 546077
Fax: 0937 546236

Order Information

All Dues Automatically Recorded
Representation Available

Personnel
Head of Company: A P Bamford

Subjects Covered: Literature & Lit Crit, Music, Natural History, Poetry, Reference Books

Trade Terms
Credit Cards Accepted: Access/Master, Visa, Amex

Returns Procedures
Address for Returns: Publications Sales Unit

CANTO PUBLICATIONS (POETRY TAPES)
1 Market Street, Broadbottom, via Hyde, Cheshire SK14 6AX
Tel: 0457 765030

Subjects Covered: Poetry

CHILD'S PLAY
Ashworth Road, Bridgemead, Swindon, Wiltshire SN5 7YD
Tel: 0793 616286
Fax: 0793 512795
VAT No: 194 4604 47

Subjects Covered: Children's Books

Trade Terms
35%
Minimum Order: £50
Girobank Number: 2959151
Credit Cards Accepted: Access/Master, Visa

Returns Procedures
Authority to Return: Prior permission required

CHIVERS PRESS LTD
Windsor Bridge Road, Bath, Avon BA2 3AX
Tel: 0225 335336
Fax: 0225 335336
Telex: 444 633
VAT No: 318 7863 24

Order Information

Order Dept Opening Times
Mon - Fri 9am - 12.30pm 1pm - 5pm
Representation Available

Personnel
Head of Company: Roger Lewis (Managing Director)
Head of Sales (Home): Chris Fernie (Sales & Marketing Manager)
Head of Accounts: Alastair Prescott (Chief Accountant)

Number of titles published annually: 200
Number of Staff: 70

Parent Company: The Gieves Group
Subsidiary Companies: Cherrytree Press Ltd

Subjects Covered: Children's Books, Fiction, Foreign Languages

Returns Procedures
Authority to Return: Chris Fernie
Address for Returns: Customer Service Department
Stock Returns: Quote invoice and order numbers

CLIO PRESS LTD
55 St Thomas Street, Oxford, Oxfordshire OX1 1JG
Tel: 0865 250333

Fax: 0865 790358
VAT No: 196 1148 50

Order Information

Order Dept Opening Times
Mon - Fri 9am - 5pm
All Dues Automatically Recorded

Personnel
Head of Company: John Durrant (Managing Director)
Head of Sales (Home): David Meggs (Sales Manager)
Head of Accounts: Betty Smith (Financial Manager)
Head of Distribution: Lesley Chaundy (Warehouse & Distribution Manger)

Number of titles published annually: 96
Number of Staff: 30
All New Titles are Bar Coded

Parent Company: ABC Clio

Other Goods Available: Large print books, Academic Books
Subjects Covered: Most General Subjects, Biology & Zoology, Fiction

Trade Terms
25% singles 33.3% - 35% on multiple line orders
Credit Cards Accepted: Access/Master, Visa, Amex

Returns Procedures
Stock Returns: Permission required from Sales Manager

COVER TO COVER CASSETTES LTD

PO Box 112, Marlborough, Wiltshire SN8 3UG
Tel: 0264 89227 24 Hours
Fax: 0264 89203
VAT No: 398 7237 90

Orders to
Cover To Cover Ltd, Unit 23, Walworth Centre, Walworth Trading Estate, Andover, Hampshire SP10 5AP
Tel: 0264 337725 (24 Hrs)
Fax: 0264 337742

Order Information

Order Dept Opening Times
Mon - Fri 9.30am - 4.30pm
All Dues Automatically Recorded
Representation Available

Personnel
Head of Company: Helen Nicoll (Managing Director)
Head of Sales (Home): John Masters ABS Maidstone 0622 764555

Number of titles published annually: 10
Number of Staff: 4
All New Titles are Bar Coded

Subjects Covered: Children's Books, Literature & Lit Crit

Trade Terms
35% postage payable on orders under £25

Returns Procedures
Authority to Return: Firm Sale
Imperfect Returns: Return goods plus proof of purchase

CRS RECORDS

26 Crosland Road North, Lytham St Annes, Lancashire FY8 3EP
Tel: 0253 728719 24 Hours
Fax: 0253 728719
VAT No: 483 2807 32

Order Information

Order Dept Opening Times
Mon - Fri 9am - 5pm
All Dues Automatically Recorded
Representation Available

Personnel
Head of Sales (Home): Philip M Waddington (Associate Producer)

Number of titles published annually: 12
Number of Staff: 2
All New Titles are Bar Coded

Subsidiary Companies: Carma Sounds

Subjects Covered: Children's Books, Music

Trade Terms
35% Retail, 50% Wholesale
Other Terms: Carriage paid on orders over £40 (Export £80)

Returns Procedures
Imperfect Returns: Return goods with debit note

CSA TELLTAPES

101 Chamberlayne Road, London NW10 3ND
Tel: 081-960 8466
Fax: 081-968 0804
Telex: 928638 WELMAX G
VAT No: 379 5844 87

Orders to
Biblios Pub Dist, Star Road, Partridge Green, Sussex RH13 8LD
Tel: 0403 710971
Fax: 0403 711143

Order Information

All Dues Automatically Recorded
Representation Available

Personnel
Head of Company: Clive Stanhope

Number of titles published annually: 12
All New Titles are Bar Coded

Parent Company: Playbox Music Ltd

Subjects Covered: Fiction, Biology & Zoology, Humour, Poetry, Science Fiction

Trade Terms
See Biblios

DRAKE AV VIDEO

St Fagans Road, Fairwater, Cardiff, South Glamorgan CF5 3AE
Tel: 0222 560333
Fax: 0222 554909

Personnel
Head of Company: Mr R G Drake (Managing Director)
Head of Sales (Home): Mr N Drake (Marketing)

Parent Company: Drake Publishing Services Ltd

EVANGELICAL PRESS OF WALES

Bryntirion, Bridgend, Mid Glamorgan CF31 4DX
Tel: 0656 655886

Fax: 0656 656095
VAT No: 136 1308 96

Order Information

Order Dept Opening Times
Mon - Fri 9am - 1pm 2pm - 5pm
All Dues Automatically Recorded

Personnel
Head of Company: E W James
Head of Sales (Home): Matthew Evans
Head of Accounts: Patricia Layton
Head of Distribution: Jill Richards

Number of titles published annually: 10
Number of Staff: 5

Parent Company: Evangelical Movement of Wales

Selected Stock Held of: Ambassador Productions
Other Goods Available: Books & Magazines
Subjects Covered: Religion & Theology, Welsh Interest

Trade Terms
33.3% (carriage on orders under £15)

Returns Procedures
Stock Returns: By negotiation
Imperfect Returns: By negotiation

FABER & FABER

3 Queen Square, London WC1N 3AU
Tel: 071-465 0045
Fax: 071-465 0034
Fax: 071-465 0043
Telex: 299633 FABER G
VAT No: 572 9170 23

Orders to
Faber Book Services, 16 Burnt Mill, Elizabeth Way, Harlow, Essex CM20 2HX
Tel: 0279 417134
Fax: 0279 417366
24 Hour Ansafone Number: 0279 444040

Order Information

Order Dept Opening Times
Mon Fri 8.30am - 6pm
All Dues Automatically Recorded
Representation Available

Personnel
Head of Company: Matthew Evans
Head of Sales (Home): Brigid Macleod (Sales Director)
Head of Accounts: Peter Simpson (Finance Director)
Head of Distribution: Patrick Curran (Distribution Director)

Subjects Covered: Poetry

Trade Terms
Girobank Number: 557 6059 GB
Credit Cards Accepted: Access/Master, Amex, Diners, Visa

Returns Procedures
Authority to Return: Sales Reps or Tim Davies (UK Sales Manager)
Address for Returns: Faber Book Services, Burnt Mill

HARPERCOLLINS PUBLISHERS

77-85 Fulham Palace Road, Hammersmith, London W6 8JB
Tel: 081-741 7070
Fax: 081-307 4440

Telex: 25611 COLINS G
VAT No: 259 6397 06

Orders to
HarperCollins, PO Box, Glasgow, Strathclyde G4 0NB
Tel: 041-772 3200
Fax: 041-306 3119
24 Hour Ansafone Number: 041-762 0999

Order Information

Order Dept Opening Times
Mon - Fri 8.30am - 4.45pm
Representation Available

Personnel
Head of Company: Barry Winkleman/Roy Davey (Adult MD/Children's MD)
Head of Sales (Home): Iain Ogston (MD Sales)
Head of Sales (Export): Adrian Bourne (International Sales MD)

Number of titles published annually: 30
All New Titles are Bar Coded

Subjects Covered: Children's Books, Fiction, Literature & Lit Crit, Poetry

Trade Terms
35%
Other Terms: Small order surcharge: £2.50 orders net value less than £50
Girobank Number: 116 0311
Credit Cards Accepted: Access/Master, Amex, Visa

Returns Procedures
Authority to Return: Local Representative
Address for Returns: HarperCollins Publishers, Returns Dept, Westerhill Road, Bishopbriggs, Glasgow G64 2QT

HILDA KING EDUCATIONAL SERVICES

Ash Cottage, Ashwells Manor Drive, Penn, High Wycombe, Buckinghamshire HP10 8EU
Tel: 0494 813947 Tel/Fax

Order Information

Order Dept Opening Times
Mon - Fri 7.30am - 6.30pm, Sat 8am - 1pm
Representation Available

Number of titles published annually: 6

Subjects Covered: Education & Careers, English Language Training, School Textbooks

Trade Terms
17.5%-40%

KOGAN PAGE LTD

120 Pentonville Road, London N1 9JN
Tel: 071-278 0433
Fax: 071-837 6348
Telex: 263088 KOGAN G
VAT No: 417 8457 28

Order Information

Order Dept Opening Times
Mon - Fri 9.30 - 5.30pm
All Dues Automatically Recorded
Representation Available

Personnel
Head of Company: Philip Kogan (Managing Director)

Head of Sales (Home): Kate Griffin (Sales Director)
Head of Accounts: Praba Kan (Financial Director)

Number of titles published annually: 4
Number of Staff: 60
All New Titles are Bar Coded

Other Goods Available: Business & Education Books
Subjects Covered: Business & Management

Trade Terms
33.3%
Other Terms: 25% single copy order
Girobank Number: 55 6061 403
Credit Cards Accepted: Access/Master, Visa, Amex, Diners

Returns Procedures
Authority to Return: Sales Dept.
Address for Returns: Hoddle Doyle Meadows Ltd, Old Mead Lane, Eisenham, Herts CM22 6JN
Stock Returns: Authorised Returns only

LISTEN FOR PLEASURE

1/3 Uxbridge Road, Hayes, Middlesex UB4 0SY
Tel: 081-561 8722
Fax: 081-569 2163
Telex: 934614
VAT No: 194 2952 34

Orders to
EMI Music Services, Hermes Close, Tachbrook Park, Leamington Spa, Warwickshire CV34 6RP
Tel: 0926 888888
Fax: 081 479 5991

Order Information

Order Dept Opening Times
Mon - Fri 9am - 5pm
All Dues Automatically Recorded
Representation Available

Personnel
Head of Company: Roger Woodhead (General Manager)
Head of Sales (Home): Gary Howells (General Sales Manager)
Head of Accounts: Roger Aslin (Credit Control Manager)
Head of Distribution: Jim Leftwich Leamington Spa

Number of titles published annually: 25
All New Titles are Bar Coded

Parent Company: EMI Records Ltd

Complete Stocks Held of: ARGO
Subjects Covered: Biology & Zoology, Children's Books, Drama & Plays, Humour, Literature & Lit Crit

Trade Terms
30% on all orders
Minimum Order: £100 + trade price

Returns Procedures
Stock Returns: Via Salesman

MUSIC COLLECTION INTERNATIONAL LTD

Strand VCI House, 36-38 Caxton Way, Watford, Hertfordshire WD1 8UF
Tel: 0923 255558
Fax: 0923 816880

Personnel
Head of Sales (Home): Darren Ridgewell (National Sales Manager)

Other Goods Available: Music CD & Cassette
Subjects Covered: Fiction

PASTEST SERVICE
Rankin House, Parkgate Estate, Knutsford, Cheshire
WA16 8DX
Tel: 0565 755226
Fax: 0565 650264
VAT No: 349 0358 45

Order Information

Order Dept Opening Times
Mon - Fri 9am - 5pm
All Dues Automatically Recorded
Representation Available

Personnel
Head of Company: Freydis Campbell (Director)

Number of titles published annually: 6
Number of Staff: 8
All New Titles are Bar Coded

Subjects Covered: English Language Training

Trade Terms
30%
Credit Cards Accepted: Access/Master, Visa

PETERLOO POETS
2 Kelly Gardens, Calstock, Cornwall PL18 9SA
Tel: 0822 833473
VAT No: 557 6026 29

Order Information

Order Dept Opening Times
Mon - Fri 9am - 5pm
All Dues Automatically Recorded
Representation Available

Personnel
Head of Company: Harry Chambers
Head of Sales (Home): Lynn Chambers

Number of titles published annually: 2
Number of Staff: 3

Other Goods Available: The Marvell Press Philip Larkin tapes
Subjects Covered: Poetry

Trade Terms
35% on all - no surcharges for PETERLOO items
Other Terms: The Marvell Press: 25% on 1-5 items, 33.3% on 6-150 items, 35% on 151 + items
Credit Cards Accepted: Access/Master, Visa, Amex

Returns Procedures
Imperfect Returns: Send to head office

THE POETRY BUSINESS LTD
51 Byram Arcade, Westgate, Huddersfield, West Yorkshire
HD1 1ND
Tel: 0484 434840
Fax: 0484 426566

Orders to
Password (Books) Ltd, 23 New Mount Street, Manchester, M4 4DE
Tel: 061-953 4009
Fax: 061-953 4001

RANDOM HOUSE AUDIO BOOKS

Random House, 20 Vauxhall Bridge Road, London SW1V 2SA
Tel: 071-973 9000
Fax: 071-828 6681
Telex: 299080 RANDOM G
VAT No: 102 8389 80

Orders to
Grantham Services, Alma Park Trading Estate, Grantham, Lincolnshire NG31 9SD
Tel: 0476 67421
Fax: 0476 590223
24 Hour Ansafone Number: 0476 67314

Order Information

Order Dept Opening Times
Mon - Thurs 8.30am - 5pm, Fri 8.30am - 4.30pm
Representation Available

Personnel
Head of Company: Rupert Lancaster (Managing Director)
Head of Sales (Home): Dallas Manderson (Group Trade Sales Director)
Head of Sales (Export): David Parrish (Group Export Sales Director)

Number of titles published annually: 100
All New Titles are Bar Coded

Complete Stocks Held of: Tellastory
Subjects Covered: Business & Management, Children's Books, Crafts & Hobbies, Fiction, Food & Drink, Health & Beauty

Trade Terms
35%
Girobank Number: 508 7457
Credit Cards Accepted: Access/Master, Visa

SEND THE LIGHT

PO Box 300, Kingstown Broadway, Carlisle, Cumbria CA3 0QS
Tel: 0228 512512
Tel: 0800 282728 Orders
Fax: 0228 514949
Fax: 0800 282530 Orders
VAT No: 205 6950 67

Orders to
Tel: 0800 269601-5
Fax: 0800 282530

Order Information

Order Dept Opening Times
Mon - Thur 9am - 5pm Fri 9am - 4.30pm
Representation Available

Personnel
Head of Company: Keith Danby (Chief Executive)
Head of Sales (Home): Daan van Belzen (Director of Sales & Marketing)
Head of Sales (Export): Pieter Kwant (Senior Sales Manager)
Head of Accounts: Janet Busk (Director of Finance)
Head of Distribution: Bruce Beattie (General Manager)

Number of Staff: 150

Parent Company: Operation Mobilisation

Subjects Covered: Religion & Theology

Trade Terms
35% on orders over £60 retail, otherwise 5% handling min £2

Returns Procedures
Stock Returns: For all returns contact customer services on Tel 0345 056568 for authorisation

SIMON & SCHUSTER LTD
West Garden Place, Kendal Street, London W2 2AQ
Tel: 071-724 7577
Fax: 071-402 0639
Telex: 21702

Orders to
IBD, Campus 400, Maylands Avenue, Hemel Hempstead, Hertfordshire HP2 7EZ
Tel: 0442 881900
Fax: 0442 882099

Order Information

All Dues Automatically Recorded
Representation Available

Personnel
Head of Company: Nick Webb
Head of Sales (Home): Keith Barnes
Head of Sales (Export): Jonathan Atkins
Head of Accounts: Stephen Roberts
Head of Distribution: Arthur Cotton

Number of titles published annually: 65
Percentage of Export Sales: 30%
All New Titles are Bar Coded

Parent Company: Paramount Communications

Subjects Covered: Most General Subjects

Trade Terms
35%
Credit Cards Accepted: Access/Master, Visa, Amex, Diners

Returns Procedures
Authority to Return: Sales Rep
Address for Returns: IBD, Coventry Road, Magna Park, Lutterworth, Leics LE17 4XH

ALBERT SMITH HEALTH CASSETTES
183 Frinton Road, Frinton-on-Sea, Essex CO13 0PA
Tel: 0255 672031
VAT No: 418 3955 31

Order Information

Order Dept Opening Times
Mon - Sat 9am - 5.30pm
All Dues Automatically Recorded

Personnel
Head of Company: Albert Smith

Number of titles published annually: 15

Subjects Covered: Health & Beauty, Medical Sciences

Trade Terms
Trade Price given
Minimum Order: 10 cassettes
Other Terms: payment 28 days

Returns Procedures
Stock Returns: Send letter with goods
Imperfect Returns: Send letter with goods

STORYTELLER AUDIO BOOKS

19 Bergholt Crescent, London N16 5JE
Tel: 081-802 8453
Fax: 081-802 7623
VAT No: 554 0670 50

Orders to
PO Box 1301, London N16 5YS

Order Information

Order Dept Opening Times
Mon - Fri 9am - 5.30pm

Personnel
Head of Company: Yaptti Chu
Head of Accounts: Tony Millwood

Number of titles published annually: 12
Number of Staff: 2
All New Titles are Bar Coded

Parent Company: Culture Waves Ltd

Other Goods Available: Books corresponding to the tapes
Subjects Covered: Children's Books

Trade Terms
£5%, 30 Days

Returns Procedures
Stock Returns: Return goods, credit or refund if paid for
Imperfect Returns: Return goods, replaced free of charge

TALKTAPES

13 Croftdown Road, London NW5 1EL
Tel: 071-485 9981

Order Information

All Dues Automatically Recorded

Personnel
Head of Company: Michael Kendall (Proprietor)

Complete Stocks Held of: Poetry People
Subjects Covered: English Language Training, Poetry

Trade Terms
Other Terms: Carriage charges on mail orders

Returns Procedures
Stock Returns: Write in advance

TAPEWORM CHILDRENS CASSETTES

Apsley House, Apsley Road, New Malden, Surrey KT3 3NJ
Tel: 081-942 7788
Fax: 081-949 6250

All New Titles are Bar Coded

Subjects Covered: Children's Books, School Textbooks

TIME TAPES

62 Beechwood Road, South Croydon, Surrey CR2 0AA
Tel: 081-651 6080
Tel: 081-657 2813
Tel: 081-657 8788
Fax: 081-651 6080

Personnel
Head of Company: Derek Jones

Number of Staff: 2

Parent Company: Barn Dance Publications Ltd
Subjects Covered: Crafts & Hobbies, Education & Careers, Medical Sciences, Music, Sports & Games

TRAVELLERS' TALES
Great Weddington, Ash, Canterbury, Kent CT3 2AR
Tel: 0304 812531
VAT No: 443 3441 71

Personnel
Head of Company: A N Gunn

Complete Stocks Held of: Chivers; Cover to Cover; Isis; Schiltron; Soundings
Subjects Covered: Fiction

WEBUCATIONAL
PO Box 81, Wimborne, Dorset BH21 3UT
Tel: 0202 887439
Tel: 0703 333405
Fax: 0703 235128

Orders to
Webucational, 117 Athelstan Road, Bitterne, Southampton, Hampshire BH21 3UT
Tel: 0703 333405 (24 Hr)
Fax: 0703 235128

Order Information

Order Dept Opening Times
Mon - Fri 9am - 5.30pm
Representation Available

Personnel
Head of Company: Mr C Webb
Head of Sales (Export): Mr P Webb
Head of Accounts: Mrs M Hamilton
Head of Distribution: Mr P Webb

Number of titles published annually: 3
Number of Staff: 2
All New Titles are Bar Coded

Other Goods Available: Audio Tapes Only
Subjects Covered: Children's Books, Music, Education & Careers, School Textbooks, English Language Training, Fiction, Foreign Languages, Mathematics & Statistics

Trade Terms
Retail 35% discount, wholesale negotiable
Minimum Order: 10 tapes
Other Terms: Special offers published twice yearly
Credit Cards Accepted: Access/Master, Visa

Returns Procedures
Authority to Return: Firm sale only
Imperfect Returns: Return with details of fault within seven days

WHIGMALEERIE STORY CASSETTES
7 Main Street, Balerno, Edinburgh, Lothian EH14 7EQ
Tel: 031-449 5893 24 Hours
VAT No: 429 3489 21

Order Information

Order Dept Opening Times
Mon - Fri 9am - 12pm
Representation Available

Personnel
Head of Company: Lorainne Fannin/Moira Small/Pam Wardell (Partners)
Head of Sales (Home): Moira Small
Head of Accounts: Margaret Blyth

Number of titles published annually: 3
Number of Staff: 2

Subjects Covered: Children's Books, Poetry

Trade Terms
Single copy 20% CWO + 50p P&P, Multiples 35%, Orders over £20 invoice value Post Free

Returns Procedures
Authority to Return: Mrs Blyth/Mrs Small
Stock Returns: Returns accepted within 3 weeks unless SOR
Imperfect Returns: Faulty tapes will be replaced

Y LOLFA CYF

Talybont, Aberystwyth, Dyfed SY23 5HE
Tel: 0970 832304
Fax: 0970 832782
VAT No: 326 9756 20

Order Information

Order Dept Opening Times
Mon - Fri 9am - 5.15pm
All Dues Automatically Recorded
Representation Available

Personnel
Head of Company: Robat Gruffudd
Head of Accounts: Meinir Vittle (Administrator)

Number of titles published annually: 25
Number of Staff: 17

Other Goods Available: Books & Cards
Subjects Covered: Food & Drink, Politics & Current Affairs, Welsh Interest

Trade Terms
33%

Returns Procedures
Authority to Return: Prior permission required

ZEUS RECORDING CO LTD

5/34 Brunswick Terrace, Hove, East Sussex BN3 1HA
Tel: 0273 726512

Personnel
Head of Company: Basil Hope Gibsone (Company Director)
Head of Sales (Home): Z H Gibsone (Company Director)

Subjects Covered: Biology & Zoology, Poetry, Drama & Plays, Fiction, Foreign Languages, Literature & Lit Crit, Music

Trade Terms
33%
Minimum Order: 6 of any title
Other Terms: Pro-forma invoice

REMAINDER DEALERS

Notes:

This section lists companies who supply remaindered titles. If they specialise in particular subject areas, this is indicated in their entry.

AWARD PUBLICATIONS LTD
Spring House, Spring Place, Kentish Town, London NW5 3BH
Tel: 071-485 7747
Fax: 071-267 2140
VAT No: 229 3737 44

Order Information

Order Dept Opening Times
Mon - Thur 8am - 4.30pm Fri 8am - 4pm
Representation Available

Personnel
Head of Company: Ron Wilkinson
Head of Sales (Home): Anna Wilkinson
Head of Accounts: Maggie Smyth
Head of Distribution: John Crookes

Percentage of Export Sales: 40%
Number of Staff: 20

Hardback Titles in Stock: 2000
Paperback Titles in Stock: 500
Subjects Covered: Most General Subjects

Trade Terms
35% on all orders
Other Terms: Minimum carriage paid order £500 nett

BARBARA BOOKS LTD
130 Arlington Road, Camden Town, London NW1 7HP
Tel: 071-482 4581
Tel: 071-911 0445
Fax: 071-267 2536
VAT No: 381 7525 37

ROY BLOOM LTD
4/5 Academy Buildings, Fanshaw Street, London N1 6LQ
Tel: 071-729 5373 24 Hours
Fax: 071-729 2375
VAT No: 232 7150 91

Order Information

Order Dept Opening Times
Mon - Fri 9.30am - 4.30pm
Representation Available

Personnel
Head of Company: Roy Bloom (Managing Director)
Head of Sales (Home): Paul White
Head of Sales (Export): Adam Bloom (Representative)
Head of Accounts: M E Pritchard (Accounts Supervisor)

Number of Staff: 6

Hardback Titles in Stock: 800
Subjects Covered: Most General Subjects

Trade Terms
35%
Minimum Order: £100 nett; 3 copies per title
Other Terms: Negotiable for quantity

BOOK BARGAINS LTD
Liston Court, High Street, Marlow, Buckinghamshire
SL7 1ER
Tel: 0628 890022
Fax: 0628 477774

BOOKMARK INTERNATIONAL
Alpha House, Scarne Industrial Estate, Launceston, Cornwall
PL15 9HT
Tel: 0566 772709
Fax: 0566 776061
VAT No: 144 0999 53

Order Information

Order Dept Opening Times
Mon - Fri 9am - 4.30pm
Representation Available

Personnel
Head of Company: Donald Phillips
Head of Accounts: Doreen Cowling

Number of Staff: 5

Parent Company: Transglobal Exports (Western) Ltd

Hardback Titles in Stock: 200
Paperback Titles in Stock: 100
Subjects Covered: Most General Subjects

Trade Terms
Negotiable. Free delivery on orders over £75. 3% - 7 days.

BOOKMART LIMITED
Desford Road, Enderby, Leicester, Leicestershire LE9 5AD
Tel: 0533 751800
Fax: 0533 750507
VAT No: 531 9283 44

Order Information

Order Dept Opening Times
Mon - Fri 8.45am - 5pm
Representation Available

Personnel
Head of Company: P E Parkin (Managing Director)
Head of Sales (Home): P Wareing (Sales Director)
Head of Sales (Export): A P Hendry (Export Manager)

Number of Staff: 40

Subjects Covered: Most General Subjects

BOOKS & TOYS LTD
The Grange, Grange Yard, London SE1 3AG
Tel: 071-232 0565
Fax: 071-232 0113
VAT No: 207 0102 31

Order Information

Order Dept Opening Times
Mon - Fri 9am - 5.30pm
Representation Available

Personnel
Head of Company: Michael Ash (Managing Director)
Head of Sales (Home): Stephen Ash (Sales Director)
Head of Sales (Export): John Norman/Bob Siwecki (Sales Manager/Export Sales Executive)
Head of Accounts: Kevin Matthews (Finance Director)
Head of Distribution: Steve Wagstaff (Warehouse/Distribution Manager)

Percentage of Export Sales: 45%
Number of Staff: 33

Allied Companies: Universal Books Ltd

Hardback Titles in Stock: 1700
Paperback Titles in Stock: 200
Subjects Covered: Most General Subjects

Trade Terms
Minimum Order: £150.00 invoice value

Publisher, Leading Independent Supplier & Distributor of Promotional and Bargain Books to the UK Trade and International Markets

CHILDREN'S, COOKERY, GARDENING, DIY, NATURE, REFERENCE ETC

Quick efficient service   *National Salesforce*

Showrooms in London and Leicester

Bookmart Ltd., Desford Road, Enderby, Leicester LE9 5AD
Tel: 0533 751800   Fax: 0533 750507

BPL REMAINDERS

Princess House, Suite 275, 50 Eastcastle Street, London
W1N 7AP
Tel: 071-636 5070
Fax: 071-580 3001
Telex: 22303 WEBB G
VAT No: 370 7261 58

Orders to
24 Hour Ansafone Number: 0703 629639

Order Information

Order Dept Opening Times
Mon - Fri 9.30am - 4.30pm
Representation Available

Personnel
Head of Company: Kenneth Webb (Managing Director)
Head of Sales (Home): Ken Fox (Sales Manager)
Head of Accounts: Andy Mollett (Finance Director)
Head of Distribution: Francesca Ferguson (Trade Manager)

Percentage of Export Sales: 50%
Number of Staff: 10

Parent Company: Studio Editions Ltd

Hardback Titles in Stock: 150
Paperback Titles in Stock: 20
Other Goods Available: Blank Books
Subjects Covered: Most General Subjects, Crafts & Hobbies, Health & Beauty, Antiques & Collecting, DIY*, Maps, Atlases & Travel, Astrology & Magic, Education & Careers, Military, Biology & Zoology, Fashion & Costume, Photography, Children's Books, Food & Drink, Sports & Games, Cinema & Television, Gardening, Transport

Trade Terms
35%
Minimum Order: £50 nett invoice value
Other Terms: £5 order surcharge on orders below £50 net
Credit Cards Accepted: Access/Master, Visa

THE BRIDGE BOOK CO LTD

Unit 4, Goldsworth Park Trading Estate, Woking, Surrey
GU21 3BA
Tel: 0483 720505
Fax: 0483 756143

Order Information

Order Dept Opening Times
Mon - Fri 9am - 5.30pm
Representation Available

Personnel
Head of Company: M J Pemberton
Head of Sales (Home): Andrew R Hallett

Percentage of Export Sales: 40%

Paperback Titles in Stock: 2000
Subjects Covered: Most General Subjects

Trade Terms
30 days carriage paid, export - variable
Minimum Order: UK £350, Export £1500

GODFREY CAVE ASSOCIATES

42 Bloomsbury Street, London WC1B 3QJ
Tel: 071-636 9177
Fax: 071-636 9091
VAT No: 234 5696 45

Order Information

Order Dept Opening Times
Mon - Fri 9.30am - 5.30pm
Representation Available

Personnel
Head of Company: John Maxwell (Managing Director)
Head of Sales (Home): Jack Cooper (Sales Director)
Head of Accounts: Peter Cox (Accountant)
Head of Distribution: Terry Price (Trade Manager)

Number of Staff: 16

Parent Company: Penguin Books
Subsidiary Companies: Bloomsbury Books

Hardback Titles in Stock: 700
Paperback Titles in Stock: 100
Subjects Covered: Cinema & Television, Gardening, Antiques & Collecting, Crafts & Hobbies, Health & Beauty, Archaeology, DIY*, History, Astrology & Magic, Fashion & Costume, Military, Biology & Zoology, Fiction, Natural History, Children's Books, Food & Drink, Reference Books

Trade Terms
Minimum Order: £100

MIKE DAVIES BOOKS

PO Box 3, Ware, Hertfordshire SG12 0QZ
Tel: 0920 877922 24 Hours
Fax: 0920 877659
VAT No: 538 5385 02

Order Information

Order Dept Opening Times
Mon - Fri 9am - 5pm
Representation Available

Personnel
Head of Company: Mike Davies (Director)
Head of Accounts: Miss K Purcell (General Manager)

Percentage of Export Sales: 60%

Hardback Titles in Stock: 450
Paperback Titles in Stock: 50
Subjects Covered: Most General Subjects

Trade Terms
35%
Minimum Order: £100

DAVID FLATMAN LTD

36 West Shore Road, Granton East, Edinburgh, Lothian EH5 1QD
Tel: 031-551 2261 24 Hours
Fax: 031-552 1703

Order Information

Order Dept Opening Times
Mon - Fri 9am - 5pm
Representation Available

Personnel
Head of Company: David Flatman
Head of Sales (Home): Trevor Maher
Head of Accounts: Mrs C Addison

Number of Staff: 103

Subsidiary Companies: Bargain Books, Lomond Books

Subjects Covered: Most Academic Subjects, Most General Subjects

Trade Terms
Minimum Order: £50 retail
Other Terms: 33.3%, Firm 35%, CWO 38.25%

WALTER H GARDNER LTD

16 Chalton Drive, London N2 0QW
Tel: 081-458 3202

Fax: 081-458 8499
VAT No: 242 4855 26

Order Information

Order Dept Opening Times
9.30am - 5.30pm

Personnel
Head of Company: W H Gardner

Subjects Covered: Animal Care & Breeding

Trade Terms
Minimum Order: 200+ copies per titles
Other Terms: Variable depending on titles/quantities

C E HALL (MARKETING) LTD

Bridge House, Railway Terrace, Kings Langley,
Hertfordshire WD4 8BG
Tel: 0923 260355
Fax: 0923 260099
VAT No: 342 7462 57

Personnel
Head of Company: Hugh Howard (Managing Director)

HARVEYS BOOKS LTD

Magna Road, Wigston, Leicester, Leicestershire LE18 4ZH
Tel: 0533 785154 24 Hours
Fax: 0533 782534
VAT No: 115 7309 84

Order Information

Order Dept Opening Times
Mon - Fri 9am - 5.30pm
Representation Available

Personnel
Head of Company: Vance Harvey (Managing Director)
Head of Sales (Home): Andrew Tindall (Sales Director)
Head of Accounts: Stephen Taylor (Financial Controller)
Head of Distribution: Paul Bennett (Operations Manager)

Percentage of Export Sales: 40%
Number of Staff: 35

Hardback Titles in Stock: 1400
Paperback Titles in Stock: 100
Other Goods Available: Magna Art Postcard Series - 75 Titles
Subjects Covered: Most General Subjects

Trade Terms
35%
Minimum Order: £50
Other Terms: Negotiable

HOLLAND ENTERPRISES LTD

18 Bourne Court, Southend Road, Woodford Green, Essex
IG8 8HD
Tel: 081-551 7711
Fax: 081-551 1266
Telex: 911982
VAT No: 250 1604 09

Order Information

Order Dept Opening Times
Mon - Fri 9am - 5pm

Personnel
Head of Company: W C Holland

Head of Sales (Home): T C Railton
Head of Accounts: S M Holland

Percentage of Export Sales: 40%
Number of Staff: 8

Hardback Titles in Stock: 20
Paperback Titles in Stock: 200
Other Goods Available: Stationery, Pens, Gift Packs

Trade Terms
35% to 55% to wholesale and retail
Minimum Order: £700

JIM OLDROYD BOOKS
4 Meadowlands Seal, Sevenoaks, Kent TN15 0DH
Tel: 0732 62138 24 Hours
Fax: 0732 63785
VAT No: 445 7870 16

Order Information

Order Dept Opening Times
Mon - Fri 9am - 5pm
Representation Available

Percentage of Export Sales: 20%

Hardback Titles in Stock: 500
Paperback Titles in Stock: 50
Subjects Covered: Most General Subjects

Trade Terms
Minimum Order: £60 invoice value for UK

PARRAGON BOOK SERVICE
Unit A, Central Trading Estate, Bath Road, Brislington, Bristol, Avon BS4 3EH
Tel: 0272 710633
Fax: 0272 778885
VAT No: 520 0885 74

PHOENIX BOOKS
Unit 9, Bradley Trading Estate, Radcliffe Moor Road, Radcliffe, Greater Manchester BL2 6RT
Tel: 0204 370751
Fax: 0204 370752
VAT No: 519 4866 11

Order Information

Order Dept Opening Times
Mon - Fri 10am - 4pm
Representation Available

Personnel
Head of Company: Mr Andrew Walsh (Company Director)
Head of Sales (Home): Mr Cliff Hayes
Head of Accounts: Ms Dawn Robinson (Accounts Director)
Head of Distribution: Mr Jeff Wright (Warehouse Manager)

Parent Company: Aurora Enterprises Ltd

Hardback Titles in Stock: 400
Paperback Titles in Stock: 100
Subjects Covered: Most General Subjects

Trade Terms
Variable
Minimum Order: Orders under £25 subject to surcharge

H PORDES LTD
383 Cockfosters Road, Cockfosters, Hertfordshire EN4 0JS
Tel: 081-449 2524 Tel/Fax
VAT No: 232 0235 21

Order Information

Order Dept Opening Times
Mon - Sat 10.15am - 7.45pm

Personnel
Head of Company: Henry Pordes
Head of Sales (Export): Ms Malgorzata Bednarz
Head of Accounts: Tony Mackenzie

Percentage of Export Sales: 50%
Number of Staff: 4

Subjects Covered: Most Academic Subjects, Military, Antiques & Collecting, Reference Books, Archaeology, Religion & Theology, Art & Design, University Textbooks, Foreign Languages, History

Trade Terms
Single copies: 20% to 25%, 6+ copies 33.3% over 100 - 40%, over 1,000 - 46%+

RAMBORO BOOKS
Unit 5A, 202-208 New North Road, London N1 7BJ
Tel: 071-226 7777 24 Hours
Tel: 071-354 1341
Fax: 071-704 6442
Cables: DONS BAR

Order Information

Order Dept Opening Times
Mon - Friday 9am - 5pm
Representation Available

Personnel
Head of Company: Donald Murray
Head of Sales (Home): Rita Hind
Head of Sales (Export): George Pentney
Head of Accounts: Rita Hind
Head of Distribution: Tim Finch

Percentage of Export Sales: 40%

Allied Companies: Crown Publishers Ltd

Hardback Titles in Stock: 1500
Subjects Covered: Most General Subjects

Trade Terms
35% no surcharge
Minimum Order: £50
Credit Cards Accepted: Access/Master, Visa

SANDPIPER BOOKS
22A Langroyd Road, London SW17 7PL
Tel: 081-767 7421
Fax: 081-682 0280
VAT No: 372 7883 12

Order Information

Order Dept Opening Times
Mon - Fri 9am - 5.30pm

Personnel
Head of Company: Robert Collie
Head of Sales (Home): Penny Collie
Head of Sales (Export): David Lines

Percentage of Export Sales: 40%
Number of Staff: 15

Subsidiary Companies: Collie Books Ltd, Postscript Mail Order Ltd

Hardback Titles in Stock: 600
Paperback Titles in Stock: 200
Subjects Covered: Most Academic Subjects

Trade Terms
35%
Minimum Order: £50 nett invoice value

SELECTABOOK LTD

Distribution Centre, Folly Road, Roundway, Devizes, Wiltshire SN10 2HR
Tel: 0380 723000
Fax: 0380 729423
VAT No: 328 3946 33

Order Information

Order Dept Opening Times
Mon - Fri 8am - 5pm
Representation Available

Personnel
Head of Company: Mr C D Sterling
Head of Accounts: Mrs E J J Smith
Head of Distribution: Miss S J Lewis

Hardback Titles in Stock: 1000
Paperback Titles in Stock: 200
Other Goods Available: Social Stationery & Videos
Subjects Covered: Most General Subjects

Trade Terms
Minimum Order: £100
Other Terms: By arrangement

TIGER BOOKS INTERNATIONAL PLC

26A York Street, Twickenham, Middlesex TW1 3LJ
Tel: 081-892 5577
Fax: 081-891 6550
VAT No: 391 6017 54

Order Information

Order Dept Opening Times
Mon - Fri 9am - 5.30pm
Representation Available

Personnel
Head of Company: Grahame Parish (Managing Director)
Head of Sales (Home): Jenny Vaughan (Sales Director) Solihull Tel: 021-742 8696
Head of Accounts: Philip Smith (Financial Controller)

Percentage of Export Sales: 40%
Number of Staff: 16

Hardback Titles in Stock: 350
Paperback Titles in Stock: 1000
Subjects Covered: Most General Subjects

Trade Terms
Minimum Order: Hardbacks £100 at retail value Paperbacks £50 at invoice value
Other Terms: 35%, single copy or small orders 25% plus p&p
Girobank Number: 300 7960

VINE HOUSE REMAINDERS

Waldenbury, North Chailey, East Sussex BN8 4DR
Tel: 082-572 3398 24 Hours
Fax: 082-572 4188
VAT No: 475 7334 19

Order Information

Order Dept Opening Times
Mon - Fri 9am - 5.30pm

Personnel
Head of Company: Richard Squibb

Subjects Covered: Most General Subjects

Trade Terms
35%
Girobank Number: 393 3202
Credit Cards Accepted: Access/Master, Visa

W E ASSOCIATES (SWINDON) LTD

Unit 1, Alpha House, Marshgate, Stratton Road, Swindon, Wiltshire SN1 2PA
Tel: 0793 490400
Tel: 0793 538404
Fax: 0793 511408
VAT No: 200 1203 62

Order Information

Order Dept Opening Times
Mon - Fri 9am - 5pm
Representation Available

Personnel
Head of Company: Malcolm Wetherill
Head of Sales (Home): Sarah Isaac
Head of Accounts: Sue Fishlock
Head of Distribution: Malcolm Wetherill

Percentage of Export Sales: 25%
Number of Staff: 20

Hardback Titles in Stock: 500
Paperback Titles in Stock: 450
Subjects Covered: Most General Subjects

Trade Terms
Minimum Order: £100 at cost

GEOFF WEEDON BOOKS

110 Alkham Road, Maidstone, Kent ME14 5PD
Tel: 0622 761399 24 Hours
Fax: 0622 754556
VAT No: 619 0068 51

Order Information

Representation Available

Personnel
Head of Company: Geoff Weedon
Head of Accounts: Hugh Llewellyn Jones

Percentage of Export Sales: 35%
Number of Staff: 2

Hardback Titles in Stock: 150
Paperback Titles in Stock: 200
Subjects Covered: Most General Subjects

Trade Terms
Minimum Order: £50

W J WILLIAMS & SON BOOKS LTD
Ashcroft, Small Meadows, Barton-under-Needwood,
Staffordshire DE13 8BA
Tel: 0283 712948 24 Hours
Fax: 0283 716807
VAT No: 127 0414 06

Order Information

Order Dept Opening Times
Mon - Fri 9am - 5.15pm
Representation Available

Personnel
Head of Company: Anthony Williams
Head of Accounts: Margaret Thompson

Percentage of Export Sales: 20%
Number of Staff: 6

Hardback Titles in Stock: 200000

Trade Terms
35%, 40% over £150
Minimum Order: 24 books
Other Terms: By negotiation
Girobank Number: 43 376 9602

WORDSWORTH EDITIONS LTD
8B East Street, Ware, Hertfordshire SG12 9HJ
Tel: 0920 465167-9
Tel: 0920 487825
Fax: 0920 462267
VAT No: 432 2900 83

Order Information

Order Dept Opening Times
Mon - Fri 9.30am - 5pm
Representation Available

Personnel
Head of Company: Michael Trayler
Head of Accounts: Mrs Lyne
Head of Distribution: Mandy Irons

Percentage of Export Sales: 40%
Number of Staff: 7

Hardback Titles in Stock: 500
Paperback Titles in Stock: 50
Other Goods Available: Stationery
Subjects Covered: Antiques & Collecting, Humour, Architecture & Building, Literature & Lit Crit, Art & Design, Natural History, Children's Books, Reference Books, Food & Drink, Scottish Interest, History

Trade Terms
Home Orders 35% discount, 50 or more titles 40%, Export 40%
Minimum Order: £50 nett after discount
Other Terms: Single copy 20% + £2.25 post and packing

SUBJECT CATEGORY INDEX

Accountancy & Taxation
Agriculture
Animal Care & Breeding
Antiques & Collecting
Archaeology
Architecture & Building
Art & Design
Astrology & Magic
Astronomy
Biology & Zoology
Biography
Business & Management
Chemistry
Children's Books
Cinema & Television
Computing

Crafts & Hobbies
DIY
Drama & Plays
Economics
Education & Careers
Engineering
English Language Training
Environment
Fashion & Costume
Fiction
Food & Drink
Foreign Languages
Gardening
Gay & Lesbian
Geography & Geology
Health & Beauty

History
Humour
Irish Interest
Law & Criminology
Librarianship & Publishing
Literature & Lit Crit
Local Interest
Maps, Atlases & Travel
Mathematics & Statistics
Medical Sciences
Military
Music
Natural History
Nautical
Philosophy
Photography

Physics
Poetry
Politics & Current Affairs
Psychology
Reference Books
Religion & Theology
School Textbooks
Science Fiction
Scientific & Technical
Scottish Interest
Social Studies
Sports & Games
Transport
University Textbooks
Welsh Interest
Women's Studies

Most Academic Subjects

A B ACADEMIC PUB
ACADEMIC & UNIV PUB
ACADEMIC BOOK ASSOC
ADDISON-WESLEY PUB
AFRICAN BOOKS COLL
AK DISTRIBUTION
ATHLONE PRESS LTD
BANKERS BOOKS LTD
BERG PUBLISHERS LTD
BLACKIE ACAD & PROF
BLACKWELL PUB LTD
BLACKWELL SCIENTIFIC
BLAKETON HALL LTD
BMS LTD
BOOK GUILD LTD
BOOK MARKETING ASSOC
BOOK REP & DIST LTD
BOOKS FROM INDIA
BRITISH LIB MK & PUB
TREVOR BROWN ASSOC
W C BROWN PUBLISHING
CAMBRIDGE UNIV PRESS
FRANK CASS & CO LTD
CENTRAL BOOKS
CLIO PRESS LTD
CONFED BRITISH INDUS
JOHN DONALD PUB LTD
DRAKE PUB SERVICES
GERALD DUCKWORTH
DUNDURN DISTRIBUTION
ELLIS HORWOOD
EOTHEN PRESS
THE EUROSPAN GROUP
GALLERY PRESS (IR)
GARNET PUB LTD
GAZELLE BOOK SERVICE
GOLDEN COCKEREL
HARCOURT BRACE JOVAN
HEINEMANN CHILD REF
HEINEMANN EDUC
HMSO BOOKS
HODDER & STOUGHTON
IMAGES DISTRIBUTION
INT LABOUR OFFICE
INT THOMSON PUB SERV
JAI PRESS LTD
KEGAN PAUL INT
KEYDEX PUBLISHERS
KLUWER ACADEMIC PUB
LAVIS MARKETING
LONGMAN GROUP UK LTD
MCGRAW HILL BOOK CO
MACMILLAN DIST LTD
MANUTIUS PRESS
MAXWELL MACMILLAN
MULTILINGUAL MATTERS
OPEN UNIV EDUC ENT
ORION PUBLISHING
OXFORD UNIV PRESS
PENGUIN BOOKS LTD
PLENUM PUBLISHING CO
PLUTO PUBLISHING
POMEGRANATE EUROPE
ROUTLEDGE
SANGAM BOOKS LTD
SCOTTISH ACAD PRESS
SEAGULL SA
SIMON & SCHUSTER INT
SPRINGER-VERLAG
THE STOURTON PRESS
ALAN SUTTON PUB LTD
TBC DISTRIBUTION
THOEMMES PRESS
TRENTHAM BOOKS LTD
TURPIN DISTRIBUTION
UCL PRESS LTD
UNI PRESSES MARKETNG
THE USSHER PRESS
VIDEO ARTS LTD
VOLCANO PRESS LTD
JOHN WILEY & SONS
WORLD SCIENTIFIC PUB
YALE UNIV PRESS
ZED BOOKS LTD
ZENO

Most General Subjects

AFRICAN BOOKS COLL
ALIF INTERNATIONAL
ANNESS PUBLISHING
THE APPLE PRESS
AURUM PRESS LTD
BLACKSTAFF PRESS LTD
BLAKE PUBLISHING LTD
BLAKETON HALL LTD
BLOOMSBURY PUB LTD
BOOK GUILD LTD
BOOKS FROM INDIA
MARION BOYARS PUB
MARTIN BREESE PUB
CASSELL PLC
CENTRAL BOOKS
CHAPMANS PUB LTD
CHRISTCHURCH PUB LTD
CLIO PRESS LTD
LLOYD COLE
ALLAN T CONDIE PUB
CONFED BRITISH INDUS
CONSTABLE & CO LTD
COPPER BEECH PUB LTD
D SERVICES
JOHN DONALD PUB LTD
GERALD DUCKWORTH
DUNDURN DISTRIBUTION
EFFECTIVE PUBLISHING
EUROBOOK LTD
W FOULSHAM & CO LTD
FOURTH ESTATE
GALLERY PRESS (IR)
GAZELLE BOOK SERVICE
THE GLENIFFER PRESS
GRANTA EDITIONS
GWASG GWENFFRWD
HARPERCOLLINS INTER
HARPERCOLLINS TRADE
HARVEYS BOOKS LTD
HEADLINE BOOK PUB
HODDER & STOUGHTON
IMAGES DISTRIBUTION
JANUS PUBLISHING
KEYDEX PUBLISHERS
MACMILLAN DIST LTD
MAINSTREAM PUB CO
MANUTIUS PRESS
MAXWELL MACMILLAN
MERCAT PRESS
MEREHURST FAIRFAX
MERLIN PRESS
NAT EXTENSION COLL
THE O'BRIEN PRESS
ORION PUBLISHING
OXFORD UNIV PRESS
PAN MACMILLAN LTD
PAVILION BOOKS LTD
PENGUIN BOOKS LTD
PENTLAND PRESS LTD
PIATKUS BOOKS
PRINTWISE PUB LTD
PROVIDENCE BOOKS
QUILLER PRESS LTD
RANDOM HOUSE UK LTD
RANDOM HOUSE (ARROW)
RAVETTE BOOKS LTD
REED CONS BOUNTY
REED CONS MANDARIN
REED CONSUMER TRADE
ROBSON BOOKS
SANGAM BOOKS LTD
SHETLAND TIMES LTD
SIDGWICK & JACKSON
SIMON & SCHUSTER LTD
SOLO BOOKS LTD
SOUVENIR PRESS LTD
SUMMERSDALE PUB
ALAN SUTTON PUB LTD
TA HA PUBLISHERS LTD
TBC DISTRIBUTION
TRANSWORLD PUB
VENTON EDUCATIONAL
VINE HOUSE DIST
VIRAGO PRESS

Accountancy & Taxation

ACCOUNTANCY BOOKS
ACE BOOKS
PETER ANDREW PUB CO
ANGLO-GERMAN FOUND
ASHGATE PUB GROUP
BARMARICK PUB

ROGER BAYLISS
DEREK BEATTIE PUB
BLACKWELL PUB LTD
BPP PUBLISHING LTD
DR BRACEWELL-MILNES
BUILDING SOC ASSN
GRAHAM BURN PUB
BUTTERWORTH IRELAND
CCH EDITIONS
CHAPMAN & HALL
PAUL CHAPMAN PUB
CHAPMANS PUB LTD
LLOYD COLE
CORK PUBLISHING LTD
CRONER PUBLICATIONS
DP PUBLICATIONS LTD
W FOULSHAM & CO LTD
BRIAN GOOCH LTD
GRANTA EDITIONS
HLT PUBLICATIONS
IBC PUBLISHING LTD
ICC UNITED KINGDOM
JORDAN & SONS LTD
LEGALEASE
CHARLES LETTS & CO
LONGMAN LAW TAX FIN
MERCURY BOOKS
NORTHCOTE HOUSE PUB
NORTHWICK PUBLISHERS
OSBORNE BOOKS LTD
COLIN A PERRY LTD
PITMAN PUBLISHING
PROBUS EUROPE
PROFESSIONAL BK SALE
RAVENSWOOD PUB LTD
ROUTLEDGE
SMITH GRYPHON LTD
SWEET & MAXWELL LTD
TAPROBANE LTD
STANLEY THORNES PUB
TOLLEY PUBLISHING CO
WISEBUY PUBLICATIONS
WOODHEAD PUBLISHING
WOODHEAD-FAULKNER

Agriculture
ACADEMY BOOKS LTD
ASHGATE PUB GROUP
BEE BOOKS NEW & OLD
BLACKWELL PUB LTD
BLACKWELL SCIENTIFIC
BOOKS EXPRESS
BRENTHAM PRESS
THE BRITISH COUNCIL
CAB INTERNATIONAL
CHAPMAN & HALL
ELSEVIER SCIENCE PUB
FARMING PRESS BOOKS
FRIENDS OF THE EARTH
GEOGRAPHICAL PUB LTD
HGM PUBLICATIONS
HYDEN HOUSE LTD
INTERCEPT LTD
INTERMEDIATE TEC PUB
INT BEE RESEARCH ASS
LEISHMAN & TAUSSIG
LONGMAN GROUP UK LTD
MERROW PUBLISHING CO
MOSBY-YEARBOOK EUR

NATURAL HIST BOOK SV
OVERSEAS DEVEL INST
PACKARD PUB LTD
PINTER PUBLISHERS
PRISM PRESS
QUILLER PRESS LTD
RICS BOOKS
SPRINGER-VERLAG
RUDOLF STEINER PRESS
A H STOCKWELL LTD
THE TOAT PRESS

Animal Care & Breeding
ASHFORD BUCHAN
BALNAIN BOOKS
BLACKWELL SCIENTIFIC
CAB INTERNATIONAL
CARLTON BOOKS
C W DANIEL CO LTD
DAVID & CHARLES PLC
DORLING KINDERSLEY
ELLIOT RIGHT WAY
FABER & FABER
FARMING PRESS BOOKS
W & G FOYLE LTD
HARPERCOLLINS THORS
A HERIOT & CO LTD
HGM PUBLICATIONS
KENILWORTH PRESS LTD
LIVERPOOL UNIV PRESS
LONGMAN GROUP UK LTD
PORTLAND PRESS LTD
PRISM PRESS
PROMOTIONAL REPRINT
SILVER LINK PUB LTD
SMITH GRYPHON LTD
SPORTSMAN'S PRESS
TFH PUBLICATIONS
TREMATON PRESS
WHITTET BOOKS LTD

Antiques & Collecting
HARRY N ABRAMS INC
ACADEMY GROUP LTD
AIRLIFE PUBLISHING
ANTIQUE COLLECTORS
APPLEFORD PUB GROUP
B T BATSFORD LTD
BRITISH MUSEUM PRESS
CARLTON BOOKS
COLLINS & BROWN
CONSTABLE & CO LTD
DAVID & CHARLES PLC
FITZWILLIAM MUSEUM
W FOULSHAM & CO LTD
STANLEY GIBBONS PUB
GOLDEN AGE BOOKS
GUINNESS PUBLISHING
H I MARKETING
ROBERT HALE LTD
HALI PUBLICATIONS
HAN SHAN TANG LTD
HILLER AIRGUNS
HILMARTON MANOR IMAGES
KEGAN PAUL INT
CHARLES LETTS & CO
LISTER ART BOOKS
LITTLE BROWN & CO
LITTLE RED WITCH
P M LLEWELLYN CO
LYLE PUBLICATIONS
MAP COLLECTOR PUB
MARLBOROUGH BOOKS
MILESTONE PUB

MILLBANK BOOKS LTD
JOHN MURRAY PUB LTD
NEW CAVENDISH BOOKS
MICHAEL O'MARA BOOKS
PICTON PUBLISHING
PROMOTIONAL REPRINT
QUILLER PRESS LTD
REED CONSUMER ILLUS
WILLIAM REEVES LTD
RIZZOLI INT PUBNS
THE RUBICON PRESS
SCIENCE MUSEUM
SCORPION PUBLISHING
SHIRE PUBLICATIONS
SILENT BOOKS
SMITH GRYPHON LTD
SOUTHERN COLLECTORS
SPA BOOKS LTD
A H STOCKWELL LTD
I B TAURIS & CO LTD
THAMES & HUDSON LTD
TOUCAN PRESS
WHITE COCKADE PUB
PHILIP WILSON PUB
WORDSWORTH EDITIONS

Archaeology
ABCO DESIGN LTD
ACADEMIC & UNIV PUB
ARIS & PHILLIPS LTD
ASHGATE PUB GROUP
ASHMOLEAN MUSEUM PUB
B T BATSFORD LTD
BLACKWELL PUB LTD
THE BRITISH ACADEMY
BRITISH MUSEUM PRESS
CARNEGIE PUB LTD
DYLLANSOW TRURAN
EDINBURGH UNIV PRESS
FACTS ON FILE
FITZWILLIAM MUSEUM
GARNET PUB LTD
GOTHIC IMAGE PUB
ROBERT HALE LTD
HAN SHAN TANG LTD
HARVARD UNIV PRESS
HISTORICAL PUB LTD
ALISON HODGE PUB
IMMEL PUBLISHING LTD
JAMES & JAMES LTD
KEGAN PAUL INT
KINGSMEAD PRESS
KNIGHTSCROSS LTD
LA HAULE BOOKS LTD
LEISHMAN & TAUSSIG
LIVERPOOL UNIV PRESS
LUTTERWORTH PRESS
MERCIER PRESS LTD
MERLIN BOOKS LTD
HARVEY MILLER PUB
MOTILAL BOOKS
OLD VICARAGE PUB
MICHAEL O'MARA BOOKS
OPEN GATE PRESS
OPEN UNIV PRESS
ORKNEY PRESS LTD
OXBOW BOOKS
PHILLIMORE & CO LTD
PINTER PUBLISHERS
THE POUND HOUSE

PROMOTIONAL REPRINT
ROUNDHOUSE PUB LTD
ROUTLEDGE
ROYAL IRISH ACADEMY
SAGE PUBLICATIONS
SHEFFIELD ACD PRESS
SHIRE PUBLICATIONS
SOC PROM ROMAN STUDY
ALAN SUTTON PUB LTD
THAMES & HUDSON LTD
THORNHILL PRESS LTD
TOUCAN PRESS
TWELVEHEADS PRESS
UNI OF EXETER PRESS
UNI OF WALES PRESS
ZENO

Architecture & Building
HARRY N ABRAMS INC
ACADEMIC & UNIV PUB
ACADEMY GROUP LTD
AIRLIFT BOOK CO
AK DISTRIBUTION
ANNESS PUBLISHING
ANTIQUE COLLECTORS
APPLEFORD PUB GROUP
ART DATA
ASHGATE PUB GROUP
ASHGROVE PRESS
ATTIC BOOKS
BARTON PUBLISHERS
B T BATSFORD LTD
BELLEW PUBLISHING
BENN BUSINESS INFO
A & C BLACK LTD
BLACKWELL PUB LTD
BLACKWELL SCIENTIFIC
BOOK REP & DIST LTD
BURKE'S PEERAGE
BUTTERWORTH-HEINEMAN
CARNEGIE PUB LTD
CHADWYCK-HEALEY LTD
CHAPMAN & HALL
COLLINS & BROWN
COMPUTATIONAL MECH
CONSTABLE & CO LTD
CRYSTAL PALACE FOUND
DARF PUBLISHERS LTD
DAVID & CHARLES PLC
ANDRE DEUTSCH
EASON & SON LTD
EDINBURGH UNIV PRESS
AIDAN ELLIS PUB
EMAP BUSINESS PUB
FACTS ON FILE
FITZWILLIAM MUSEUM
GALE RESEARCH INT
GARNET PUB LTD
BRIAN GOOCH LTD
GRANTA EDITIONS
GREEN BOOKS
HAN SHAN TANG LTD
S HENEAGE DIST
THE HERBERT PRESS
ALISON HODGE PUB
IFS LTD
INTERMEDIATE TEC PUB
INTERNOS BOOKS
JAMES & JAMES LTD
KEGAN PAUL INT
KINGSMEAD PRESS
KUPERARD LTD
LITTLE BROWN & CO

LIVERPOOL UNIV PRESS
LONGMAN GROUP UK LTD
LUND HUMPHRIES PUB
LUTTERWORTH PRESS
MAINSTREAM PUB CO
MELIA PUB SERVICES
MILLBANK BOOKS LTD
HARVEY MILLER PUB
MIT PRESS LTD
MOMENTA PUB CO LTD
MOTILAL BOOKS
THE NATIONAL TRUST
NATIONAL TRUST (IR)
THE O'BRIEN PRESS
PACKARD PUB LTD
PHAIDON PRESS LTD
PHILLIMORE & CO LTD
PINHORNS
PINTER PUBLISHERS
PION LTD
PITKIN PICTORIALS
PRISM PRESS
QUOTES LTD
REAKTION BOOKS LTD
RIBA PUBLICATIONS
RICS BOOKS
RIZZOLI INT PUBNS
ROUNDHOUSE PUB LTD
ROUTLEDGE
THE RUBICON PRESS
SALTIRE SOCIETY
SAQI BOOKS
SB PUBLICATIONS
SCALA PUB LTD
SCARTHIN BOOKS
SCORPION PUBLISHING
SCOTTISH ACAD PRESS
SHAKTI COMMUNICATION
HILARY SHIPMAN
SHIRE PUBLICATIONS
SPA BOOKS LTD
RUDOLF STEINER PRESS
STUDIO EDITIONS LTD
THAMES & HUDSON LTD
THORNHILL PRESS LTD
TOLLEY PUBLISHING CO
VCH PUB (UK) LTD
WATERMARK PUB LTD
WHITE COCKADE PUB
PHILIP WILSON PUB
WINDSOR BOOKS INT
WORDSWORTH EDITIONS
ZENO

Art & Design
HARRY N ABRAMS INC
ACADEMIC & UNIV PUB
ACADEMY GROUP LTD
AIRLIFT BOOK CO
AK DISTRIBUTION
ALLARDYCE BARNETT
ANNESS PUBLISHING
ANTIQUE COLLECTORS
ART BOOK DIST CO
ART DATA
ART SALES INDEX LTD
ASHGATE PUB GROUP
ASHMOLEAN MUSEUM PUB
AURUM PRESS LTD
B T BATSFORD LTD
BELLEW PUBLISHING
BODLEAIN LIBRARY
BOOK BARGAINS LTD
BOOK REP & DIST LTD
THE BRITISH COUNCIL
BRITISH MUSEUM PRESS

CALOUSTE GULBENKIAN
CAMDEN PRESS
CANAL PUBLISHING CO
CANONGATE PRESS PLC
CARLTON BOOKS
CHADWYCK-HEALEY LTD
CHRISTCHURCH PUB LTD
CLEMATIS PRESS
COLLETS
COLLINS & BROWN
CONSTABLE & CO LTD
CREATIVE BOOKS INT
DAVID & CHARLES PLC
DAWSON UK LTD
THE DESIGN COUNCIL
ANDRE DEUTSCH
DRAGONS WORLD LTD
EASON & SON LTD
AIDAN ELLIS PUB
EVENLODE BOOK DIST
FABER & FABER
FARRAND PRESS
FITZWILLIAM MUSEUM
W & G FOYLE LTD
GALE RESEARCH INT
GMP PUBLISHERS LTD
GRACEWING/FOWLER
GREEN BOOKS
GRESHAM BOOKS LTD
H I MARKETING
HALI PUBLICATIONS
HAN SHAN TANG LTD
HARPERCOLLINS GENREF
HARVARD UNIV PRESS
HAWK BOOKS LTD
HAWTHORNS PUB LTD
S HENEAGE DIST
THE HERBERT PRESS
HILMARTON MANOR
HOBSONS PUBLISHING
ALISON HODGE PUB
HYPHEN PRESS
ICA PUBLISHING
IMAGES
IMMEL PUBLISHING LTD
IMPACT BOOKS
INTERNOS BOOKS
IRISH ACADEMIC PRESS
KEGAN PAUL INT
KINGSMEAD PRESS
KNOCKABOUT COMICS
LAKESIDE PUBNS
LEISHMAN & TAUSSIG
CHARLES LETTS & CO
LITTLE BROWN & CO
LITTLE RED WITCH
LONGMAN GROUP UK LTD
LUND HUMPHRIES PUB
LUTTERWORTH PRESS
MAINSTREAM PUB CO
MANCHESTER UNI PRESS
MANDRAKE
PETER MARCAN PUB
MARLBOROUGH BOOKS
MEDICI SOCIETY LTD
MELIA PUB SERVICES
MERCIER PRESS LTD
MERLIN BOOKS LTD
MERLION PUBLISHING MID
NORTHUMBERLAND
HARVEY MILLER PUB
MIT PRESS LTD
MOMENTA PUB CO LTD
JOHN MURRAY PUB LTD

PETER NAHUM
NAT GALLERY PUB LTD
NAT PORTRAIT GALLERY
ANTHONY NELSON LTD
NEWS PRODUCTIONS
MICHAEL O'MARA BOOKS
OPEN UNIV PRESS
ORIEL/WELSH ARTS CNL
PARKE SUTTON PUB LTD
PATTEN PRESS
PEVENSEY PRESS
PHAIDON PRESS LTD
PLEXUS PUBLISHING
PLUTO PUBLISHING
POLICY STUDIES INST
PREMIER BOOK MKTNG
PRISM PRESS
PROMOTIONAL REPRINT
REAKTION BOOKS LTD
REDCLIFFE PRESS LTD
REED CONSUMER ILLUS
RIZZOLI INT PUBNS
ROUNDHOUSE PUB LTD
SAREMA PRESS LTD
SCALA PUB LTD
SCORPION PUBLISHING
SCOTTISH ACAD PRESS
SHAKTI COMMUNICATION
SILENT BOOKS
SMITH SETTLE LTD
SPA BOOKS LTD
SPORTSMAN'S PRESS
RUDOLF STEINER PRESS
STOBART DAVIES LTD
STRIDE PUBLICATIONS
STUDIO EDITIONS LTD
TARQUIN PUBLICATIONS
TATE GALLERY PUB
I B TAURIS & CO LTD
TEXTILE INSTITUTE
THAMES & HUDSON LTD
STANLEY THORNES PUB
TREADWELLS ART MILL
TREFOIL PUB LTD
TURNAROUND
VCH PUB (UK) LTD
VICTORIA & ALBERT
VIRGIN PUBLISHING
VISUAL ARTS PUB
WARBURG INSTITUTE
WHITE COCKADE PUB
WHITTINGTON PRESS
PHILIP WILSON PUB
WINDSOR BOOKS INT
WOMEN'S PRESS
WORDSWORTH EDITIONS
YALE UNIV PRESS
ZENO

Astrology & Magic
AIRLIFT BOOK CO
ANNESS PUBLISHING
ASHGROVE PRESS
BARTON HOUSE PUB
BLACK FROG PRESS
BLAKE PUBLISHING LTD
BOOKSPEED
BRAINIAC BOOKS LTD
CARLTON BOOKS
CHRISTCHURCH PUB LTD
COLLINS & BROWN
CONSTABLE & CO LTD
C W DANIEL CO LTD

DORLING KINDERSLEY
ELEMENT BOOKS LTD
EVENLODE BOOK DIST
W FOULSHAM & CO LTD
GOTHIC IMAGE PUB
GUINNESS PUBLISHING
ROBERT HALE LTD
HARPERCOLLINS THORS
LENNARD ASSOCIATES
LITTLE BROWN & CO
LLANERCH PUBLISHERS
LUCIS PRESS LTD
MANDRAKE
MARLBOROUGH BOOKS
MOTILAL BOOKS
MULTIMEDIA BOOKS LTD
MICHAEL O'MARA BOOKS
PIATKUS BOOKS
PRISM PRESS
PROMOTIONAL REPRINT
REED CONSUMER ILLUS
SHAKTI COMMUNICATION
SILENT BOOKS
SMITH GRYPHON LTD
RUDOLF STEINER PRESS
TEMPLE PRESS LTD
THAMES & HUDSON LTD
VIRGIN PUBLISHING
WARBURG INSTITUTE
WHITE EAGLE PUB
WOMEN'S PRESS

Astronomy
AIRLIFT BOOK CO
BELLEW PUBLISHING
BROWN SON & FERGUSON
CARLTON BOOKS
CONSTABLE & CO LTD
DAVID & CHARLES PLC
L N FOWLER & CO LTD
W H FREEMAN & CO LTD
HARVARD UNIV PRESS
IOP PUBLISHING LTD
JONES & BARTLETT PUB
PENNY PRESS
PRISM PRESS
SHAKTI COMMUNICATION
SPRINGER-VERLAG
TARQUIN PUBLICATIONS
WORLD SCIENTIFIC PUB

Biology & Zoology
ACADEMIC & UNIV PUB
ACAIR LTD
AIRLIFT BOOK CO
AK DISTRIBUTION
ALIF INTERNATIONAL
THE AMATE PRESS
ANVIL BOOKS PUB
APPLEFORD PUB GROUP
APPLETREE PRESS LTD
ASHFORD BUCHAN
ASHGROVE PRESS
AURUM PRESS LTD
BACSA
BLACK SPRING PRESS
BLACKWELL PUB LTD
BLAKE PUBLISHING LTD
BOOK REP & DIST LTD
MARION BOYARS PUB
BRAINIAC BOOKS LTD
CALDER PUB LTD

815

CANONGATE PRESS PLC
CARCANET PRESS
CARRICK MEDIA
KYLE CATHIE LTD
CCBI PUBLICATIONS
CENTAUR PRESS LTD
CHAPMANS PUB LTD
CHRISTCHURCH PUB LTD
COLLINS & BROWN
CONSTABLE & CO LTD
DALENNAU
DARF PUBLISHERS LTD
ANDRE DEUTSCH
DYLLANSOW TRURAN
EAST WEST PUB LTD
ELAND
ELEMENT BOOKS LTD
AIDAN ELLIS PUB
EVENLODE BOOK DIST
EX LIBRIS PRESS
FABER & FABER
IAN FAULKNER PUB LTD
GALE RESEARCH INT
GERBIL BOOKS
GILL & MACMILLAN LTD
GMP PUBLISHERS LTD
GRANVILLE PUBLISHING
PETER HALBAN PUB
ROBERT HALE LTD
THE HARLEY PRESS
THOMAS HARMSWORTH
HARVARD UNIV PRESS
HAWTHORNS PUB LTD
HEADQUARTERS PUB CO
THE HERBERT PRESS
ALISON HODGE PUB
IMPACT BOOKS
INTERVARSITY PRESS
JARROLD PUBLISHING
JOHNSTON & BACON
RICHARD KAY PUB
KEGAN PAUL INT
THE KENSAL PRESS
KINGSWAY PUB
KOZMIK PRESS
JAY LANDESMAN
LAWRENCE & WISHART
LEISHMAN & TAUSSIG
LITTLE BROWN & CO
LUATH PRESS LTD
MAGNA LARGE PRINT
MAINSTREAM PUB CO
MERCIER PRESS LTD
MERLIN BOOKS LTD
MID NORTHUMBERLAND
MONARCH PUB
JOHN MURRAY PUB LTD
NAT PORTRAIT GALLERY
ANTHONY NELSON LTD
NEW FOREST LEAVES
MICHAEL O'MARA BOOKS
OMF BOOKS
OMNIBUS PRESS
PETER OWEN LTD
OWL BOOKS
PAUPERS' PRESS
COLIN A PERRY LTD
PHILLIMORE & CO LTD
PIATKUS BOOKS
PICTON PUBLISHING
PITKIN PICTORIALS
PLEXUS PUBLISHING
PLUME PRESS
PLUTO PUBLISHING

POETRY WALES PRESS
PRISM PRESS
PROSPERITY PUB
QUARTET BOOKS LTD
RAVENSWOOD PUB LTD
REINHARDT BOOKS LTD
ROBSON BOOKS
ROSEDENE PUBLISHERS
ROUNDHOUSE PUB LTD
THE ROYAL SOCIETY
THE RUBICON PRESS
SALTIRE SOCIETY
SAREMA PRESS LTD
SAWD BOOKS
SEND THE LIGHT
SHEPHEARD-WALWYN
SHIRE PUBLICATIONS
SMITH GRYPHON LTD
SMITH SETTLE LTD
COLIN SMYTHE LTD
SOLO BOOKS LTD
SPA BOOKS LTD
SPELLMOUNT LTD
SPORTSMAN'S PRESS
SQUARE ONE PUB
RUDOLF STEINER PRESS
A H STOCKWELL LTD
ALAN SUTTON PUB LTD
TABB HOUSE
I B TAURIS & CO LTD
TEECOLL PUBLICATIONS
TEMPLE PRESS LTD
THAMES & HUDSON LTD
THORNHILL PRESS LTD
TOUCAN PRESS
TRANSPORT BOOKMAN
TRIPLE CAT PUB
TRITON PUB CO LTD
UNI OF WALES PRESS
VINE HOUSE DIST
VIRAGO PRESS
VIRGIN PUBLISHING
WINDHORSE PUB
WOLFHOUND PRESS
WOMEN'S PRESS

Biography

BEE BOOKS NEW & OLD
BLACKWELL SCIENTIFIC
BRITISH ENTOMOL SOC
CAB INTERNATIONAL
CHAPMAN & HALL
CHARTWELL-BRATT
E W CLASSEY LTD
DANIELS PUBLISHING
EDINBURGH UNIV PRESS
GOWER MEDICAL PUB
HARLEY BOOKS
HARVARD UNIV PRESS
IMMEL PUBLISHING LTD
INST OF BIOLOGY
INTERCEPT LTD
INT BEE RESEARCH ASS
JONES & BARTLETT PUB
KNIGHTSCROSS LTD
LONGMAN GROUP UK LTD
MELIA PUB SERVICES
MERROW PUBLISHING CO
MOMENTA PUB CO LTD
MOSBY-YEARBOOK EUR
NATURAL HIST BOOK SV
NATURAL HIST MUSEUM
ANTHONY NELSON LTD
THOMAS NELSON & SONS

PACKARD PUB LTD
PORTLAND PRESS LTD
PROMOTIONAL REPRINT RESEARCH STUDIES LTD
RICHMOND PUB CO LTD
SCHOFIELD & SIMS LTD
SPRINGER-VERLAG
TAPROBANE LTD
TFH PUBLICATIONS
STANLEY THORNES PUB
VCH PUB (UK) LTD
WHITTET BOOKS LTD
WORLD SCIENTIFIC PUB

Business & Management

ABCO DESIGN LTD
ACADEMIC BOOK ASSOC
ACCOUNTANCY BOOKS
AIRLIFT BOOK CO
PETER ANDREW PUB CO
ANGLO-GERMAN FOUND
AP INFORMATION SERV
ASHFORD BUCHAN
ASHGATE PUB GROUP
BARMARICK PUB
BARTON HOUSE PUB
DEREK BEATTIE PUB
BELLEW PUBLISHING
BENN BUSINESS INFO
BLACKWELL PUB LTD
BOWKER-SAUR LTD
BPP PUBLISHING LTD
NICHOLAS BREALEY PUB
BREWIN BOOK DIST
BACIE
BUILDING SOC ASSN
GRAHAM BURN PUB
BUTTERWORTH-HEINEMAN
CASSELL PLC
CAVENDISH PUBLISHING
CCH EDITIONS
CEDAR TREE HOUSE
CHADWYCK-HEALEY LTD
CHAPMAN & HALL
PAUL CHAPMAN PUB
CHAPMANS PUB LTD
CHT INST PURC & SUPP
CHARTWELL-BRATT
CHRISTIAN BOOKSTALL
CLEMENT PUBS LTD
LLOYD COLE
PETER COLLIN PUB LTD
COMM RACIAL EQUALITY
CO-OPERATIVE UNION
CORK PUBLISHING LTD
CRONER PUBLICATIONS
THE DESIGN COUNCIL
DP PUBLICATIONS LTD
DUN & BRADSTREET LTD
ELC PUBLISHING LTD
ELECTRONICA BOOKS
ELLIOT RIGHT WAY
ELM PUBLICATIONS
ELSEVIER SCIENCE PUB
EUROMONITOR PLC
EVENLODE BOOK DIST
EXECUTIVE GRAPEVINE
FACTS ON FILE
THE FINANCIAL TIMES
FLAME BOOKS LTD
W FOULSHAM & CO LTD
GALE RESEARCH INT

GILL & MACMILLAN LTD
BRIAN GOOCH LTD
GRAHAM & TROTMAN LTD
HARPERCOLLINS THORS
HAWTHORN PRESS
HLT PUBLICATIONS
HOBSONS PUBLISHING
HOLLIS DIRECTORIES
HORTON PUB LTD
HOTEL & CATERING CO
HOW TO BOOKS LTD
IBC PUBLISHING LTD
IFS LTD
IMMEL PUBLISHING LTD
INDUSTRIAL SOC PRESS
INST OF MANAGEMENT
INST OF PERSONNEL MG
INT LABOUR OFFICE
INTERVARSITY PRESS
JORDAN & SONS LTD
KEAY'S PUBLICATIONS
KOGAN PAGE LTD
KUMA COMPUTERS LTD
LITTLE BROWN & CO
P M LLEWELLYN CO
LLOYD'S OF LONDON
LONGMAN GROUP UK LTD
MANAGEMENT UPDATE
MARC EUROPE
MERCURY BOOKS
MERLIN BOOKS LTD
METAL BULLETIN PLC
MILESTONE PUB
MOMENTA PUB CO LTD
JOHN MURRAY PUB LTD
NEW ERA PUB LTD
NORTHCOTE HOUSE PUB
NORTHWICK PUBLISHERS
OSBORNE BOOKS LTD
PASTEST SERVICE
PIATKUS BOOKS
PINTER PUBLISHERS
PITMAN PUBLISHING
POLICY STUDIES INST
PROBUS EUROPE
PROFESSIONAL BK SALE
RAVENSWOOD PUB LTD
REED INFO SERVICES
ROUTLEDGE
SAGE PUBLICATIONS
SAUS PUBLICATIONS
SEWELLS INT
SILVER LINK PUB LTD
SMITH GRYPHON LTD
WILLIAM SNYDER PUB
SPCK
SPOKESMAN BOOKS
SPRINGER-VERLAG
MALCOLM STEWART
SWEET & MAXWELL LTD
TELEGRAPH BOOKS
TFPL PUBLISHING
STANLEY THORNES PUB
TOLLEY PUBLISHING CO
TRADE RESEARCH PUBS
TREFOIL PUB LTD
TURNAROUND
TURPIN DISTRIBUTION
VERULAM PUB LTD
VINE HOUSE DIST
VNU BUSINESS PUB
WEAVERS PRESS PUB
WHURR PUBLISHERS LTD

JOHN WILSON BOOKS
WOODHEAD PUBLISHING
WOODHEAD-FAULKNER

Chemistry

ASHGATE PUB GROUP
BENN BUSINESS INFO
BLACKWELL SCIENTIFIC
CHAPMAN & HALL
ELSEVIER SCIENCE PUB
FMJ BOOKS
W H FREEMAN & CO LTD
INTERCEPT LTD
JAMES & JAMES LTD
JONES & BARTLETT PUB
KNIGHTSCROSS LTD
LONGMAN GROUP UK LTD
MERROW PUBLISHING CO
MICELLE PRESS
MOMENTA PUB CO LTD
MOSBY-YEARBOOK EUR
THOMAS NELSON & SONS
RESEARCH STUDIES LTD
SCHOFIELD & SIMS LTD
SPRINGER-VERLAG
STANLEY THORNES PUB
TURPIN DISTRIBUTION
VCH PUB (UK) LTD
WARD LOCK EDUC CO
WORLD SCIENTIFIC PUB

Children's Books

ABC/ALL CHILDRENS CO
HARRY N ABRAMS INC
ACAIR LTD
AFRICA CHRIST PRESS
AIRLIFT BOOK CO
ALADDIN BOOKS LTD
ALIF INTERNATIONAL
ALLARDYCE BARNETT
AMAISING PUB HOUSE
ANNUAL CONCEPTS LTD
ANVIL BOOKS LTD
APPLEFORD PUB GROUP
APPLETREE PRESS LTD
ANN ARBOR PUBLISHERS
ASHFORD BUCHAN
ATLANTIC EUROPE PUB
AUSTRALIAN CON PRESS
AWARD PUBLICATIONS
BAHAI PUBLISHING
BARNY BOOKS
BARTON HOUSE PUB
BBC BOOKS
BELLEW PUBLISHING
A & C BLACK LTD
BLACK FROG PRESS
BOOKSPEED
BOXTREE LTD
BRENTHAM PRESS
BRIGHT BOOKS LTD
BRIMAX BOOKS LTD
BROWN WATSON LTD
BUILDING BLOCKS EDUC
CAMPBELL BOOKS
CANONGATE PRESS PLC
CARLTON BOOKS
CASSELL PLC
KYLE CATHIE LTD
CHALKSOFT LTD
CHAPMANS PUB LTD
CHILDREN'S SOCIETY
CHILD'S PLAY
CHIVERS PRESS LTD
CHRISTIAN BOOK PROMO
CHURCH HOUSE PUB
CICERONE PRESS
ANTHONY CLARKE PUB
LLOYD COLE
FRANK COLEMAN PUB
CONCORDIA PUB LTD
CONSTABLE & CO LTD
CRABTREE PUBLISHING
CRESSRELLES PUB LTD
CRYSTAL PALACE FOUND
CURLEW PUBLISHING CO
DALENNAU
DAVID & CHARLES PLC
DORLING KINDERSLEY
EAGLE BOOKS
EAST WEST PUB LTD
EGMONT PUB LTD
ELITE WORDS & IMAGE
ENSIGN PUBLICATIONS
EUROBOOK LTD
EUROPEAN SCHOOLBOOKS
EVANS BROTHERS LTD
EVENLODE BOOK DIST
EXPRESS NEWSPAPERS
FABER & FABER
FIRST TIME PUB
FLORIS BOOKS
FOCUS PUBLICATIONS
FOLLOW YOUR FINGER
GAIRM PUBLICATIONS
GARNET PUB LTD
GILL & MACMILLAN LTD
GMP PUBLISHERS LTD
W F GRAHAM LTD
GRISEWOOD & DEMPSEY
GROSVENOR BOOKS
GWASG Y DREF WEN
PETER HADDOCK LTD
HARPERCOLLINS CHILD
HAWK BOOKS LTD
HAWTHORN PRESS
HEADQUARTERS PUB CO
HEINEMANN CHILD REF
HENDERSON PUB LTD
HONNO LTD
HUGHES & COLEMAN LTD
IMAGES
IMPACT BOOKS
INT BEE RESEARCH ASS
INVADER LTD
KINGSWAY PUB
KNIGHTSCROSS LTD
LADYBIRD BOOKS LTD
LAVIS MARKETING
LEARNING DEV AIDS
LEISHMAN & TAUSSIG
LIBER PRESS
LIFE EDUCATION UK
FRANCES LINCOLN PUB
LITTLE BROWN & CO
CHRIS LLOYD SALES
LONGMAN GROUP UK LTD
LUTTERWORTH PRESS
B MCCALL BARBOUR
MANOR HOUSE PUB
MEDICI SOCIETY LTD
MELIA PUB SERVICES
MERCIER PRESS LTD
MERLIN BOOKS LTD
MERLION PUBLISHING
MICHELIN TYRE PLC
MOORLEY'S PRINT PUB
MULTIMEDIA BOOKS LTD
NAT CHRIST EDUC COUN
THE NATIONAL TRUST
NEW ERA PUB LTD
NOVA DISTRIBUTION
NUTMEG PRESS
THE O'BRIEN PRESS
MICHAEL O'MARA BOOKS
OMF BOOKS
ONEWORLD PUB
ORIFLAMME PUBLISHING
PAN MACMILLAN LTD
PHAIDON PRESS LTD
PICCADILLY PRESS LTD
PLAYWRIGHTS PUB CO
POETRY WALES PRESS
PORTHILL PUBLISHERS
PROMOTIONAL REPRINT
QUAY PUBLISHING LTD
RAGGED BEARS LTD
RAMBORO BOOKS
RAVETTE BOOKS LTD
REED CONS MANDARIN
REED CONSUMER TRADE
REINHARDT BOOKS LTD
RIZZOLI INT PUBNS
ROBSON BOOKS
ST PAUL'S PUB
SAWD BOOKS
SCHOFIELD & SIMS LTD
SCHOLASTIC PUB LTD
SCRIPTURE UNION PUB
SEND THE LIGHT
SHAKTI COMMUNICATION
SHEARWATER PRESS LTD
SODANEY PUBLISHERS
SPINDLEWOOD
A H STOCKWELL LTD
STRIDE PUBLICATIONS
STUDIO EDITIONS LTD
SWEETHAWS PRESS
TABB HOUSE
TAMARIND LTD
TARQUIN PUBLICATIONS
TEENEY BOOKS LTD
THAMES & HUDSON LTD
THIMBLE PRESS
TURNAROUND
TURTON & CHAMBERS
TWO-CAN PUBLISHING
USBORNE PUB LTD
VERULAM PUB LTD
VICTORIA HOUSE PUB
VINE HOUSE DIST
VOLCANO PRESS LTD
WALKER BOOKS LTD
THE WATTS GROUP
WAYLAND (PUB) LTD
WESTERN PUB CO INC
J WHITAKER & SONS
WINDSOR BOOKS INT
WOLFHOUND PRESS
WOMEN'S PRESS
WORDSWORTH EDITIONS
WORLD LEISURE MKTG
XYLOPRESS LTD
ROY YATES BOOKS
YOUNG LIBRARY LTD

Cinema & Television

HARRY N ABRAMS INC
ACADEMIC BOOK ASSOC
ANNESS PUBLISHING
ASHGATE PUB GROUP
AURUM PRESS LTD
B T BATSFORD LTD
BENN BUSINESS INFO
BFI PUBLISHING
BLACK SPRING PRESS
BLACKWELL PUB LTD
BLAKE PUBLISHING LTD
BOXTREE LTD
MARION BOYARS PUB
BRAINIAC BOOKS LTD
THE BRITISH COUNCIL
CARLTON BOOKS
CHADWYCK-HEALEY LTD
CHAPMANS PUB LTD
CHRISTCHURCH PUB LTD
COLLINS & BROWN
CREATION PRESS
ANDRE DEUTSCH
DRAGONS WORLD LTD
FABER & FABER
FACTS ON FILE
FLICKS BOOKS
GALE RESEARCH INT
GMP PUBLISHERS LTD
GUINNESS PUBLISHING
HARVARD UNIV PRESS
HAWK BOOKS LTD
HAWTHORN PRESS
IAN HENRY PUB LTD
HOW TO BOOKS LTD
JOHN LIBBEY & CO LTD
LIBERTARIAN ALLIANCE
LITTLE BROWN & CO
MERLIN BOOKS LTD
MULTIMEDIA BOOKS LTD
NEWS PRODUCTIONS
OPEN UNIV PRESS
PLEXUS PUBLISHING
PLUTO PUBLISHING
PROMOTIONAL REPRINT
QUARTET BOOKS LTD
REED CONSUMER ILLUS
ROBSON BOOKS
ROUNDHOUSE PUB LTD
ROUTLEDGE
SAGE PUBLICATIONS
SERPENT'S TAIL
TANTIVY PRESS LTD
VERSO
VINE HOUSE DIST
VIRAGO PRESS
VIRGIN PUBLISHING

Computing

ABCO DESIGN LTD
ARIAN PUBLICATIONS
ASHGATE PUB GROUP
BERNARD BABANI LTD
BARTON HOUSE PUB
BLACK FROG PRESS
BLACKWELL PUB LTD
BLACKWELL SCIENTIFIC
BPP PUBLISHING LTD
THE BRITISH COUNCIL
BUTTERWORTH-HEINEMAN
CARLTON BOOKS
CCBI PUBLICATIONS
CHAPMAN & HALL
PAUL CHAPMAN PUB

CHARTWELL-BRATT
CLARKE ASSOCIATES
COMPUTER BOOKSHOPS
COMPUTER STEP LTD
DP PUBLICATIONS LTD
EDINBURGH UNIV PRESS
ELECTRONICA BOOKS
ELSEVIER SCIENCE PUB
EMAP BUSINESS PUB
LAWRENCE ERLBAUM ASS
W H FREEMAN & CO LTD
DAVID FULTON PUB LTD
BRIAN GOOCH LTD
DAVID HAWGOOD
IBC PUBLISHING LTD
IFS LTD
INTELLECT
IOP PUBLISHING LTD
KOGAN PAGE LTD
KUMA COMPUTERS LTD
CHARLES LETTS & CO
CHARLES LETTS & CO
LONGMAN GROUP UK LTD
MCCARTA LTD
MECHANICAL ENG PUB
MECKLER LTD
MERCURY BOOKS
MIT PRESS LTD
MOMENTA PUB CO LTD
MOSBY-YEARBOOK EUR
THOMAS NELSON & SONS
PENNY PRESS
PITMAN PUBLISHING
RESEARCH STUDIES LTD
SIGMA PRESS
SPA BOOKS LTD
SPRINGER-VERLAG
A H STOCKWELL LTD
SUMMERSDALE PUB
STANLEY THORNES PUB
V & H COMPUTER SERV
VIRGIN PUBLISHING
VITA BOOKS
VNU BUSINESS PUB
WOODHEAD PUBLISHING
WORLD LEISURE MKTG
WORLD SCIENTIFIC PUB

Crafts & Hobbies
HARRY N ABRAMS INC
AIRLIFT BOOK CO
ALADDIN BOOKS LTD
ANAYA PUBLISHERS
ANNESS PUBLISHING
APPLETREE PRESS LTD
ARGUS PUBLICATIONS
AURUM PRESS LTD
AUSTRALIAN CON PRESS
BERNARD BABANI LTD
BARN DANCE PUB LTD
B T BATSFORD LTD
RUTH BEAN PUBLISHERS
BEE BOOKS NEW & OLD
BELLEW PUBLISHING
A & C BLACK LTD
THE BLACK SWAN PRESS
BOXTREE LTD
CADOGAN BOOKS
CANONGATE PRESS PLC
CARLTON BOOKS
COLLINS & BROWN

CONSTABLE & CO LTD
CONWAY MARITIME
CREATIVE BOOKS INT
THE CROWOOD PRESS
DALESMAN PUB CO LTD
DAVID & CHARLES PLC
DORLING KINDERSLEY
DRAGONS WORLD LTD
ELEMENT BOOKS LTD
ELLIOT RIGHT WAY
FLORIS BOOKS
W FOULSHAM & CO LTD
W & G FOYLE LTD
GOLDEN AGE BOOKS
GRISEWOOD & DEMPSEY
GUILD MASTER CRAFTS
ROBERT HALE LTD
HARPERCOLLINS GENREF
HAWTHORN PRESS
THE HERBERT PRESS
ALISON HODGE PUB
IMAGES
INTERNOS BOOKS
CHARLES LETTS & CO
FRANCES LINCOLN PUB
LISTER ART BOOKS
LITTLE BROWN & CO
CHRIS LLOYD SALES
LUTTERWORTH PRESS
M & J PUBLICATIONS
MILESTONE PUB
MILLBANK BOOKS LTD
NAG PRESS
ANTHONY NELSON LTD
THE O'BRIEN PRESS
MICHAEL O'MARA BOOKS
PACKARD PUB LTD
PHAIDON PRESS LTD
PLUTO PUBLISHING
PREMIER BOOK MKTNG
PROMOTIONAL REPRINT
REED CONSUMER ILLUS
ROSEDENE PUBLISHERS
SAWD BOOKS
SMITH GRYPHON LTD
STACEY INTERNATIONAL
STOBART DAVIES LTD
A H STOCKWELL LTD
STUDIO EDITIONS LTD
TARQUIN PUBLICATIONS
TEE PUBLISHING
THAMES & HUDSON LTD
THORNHILL PRESS LTD
VERULAM PUB LTD
WORLD LEISURE MKTG

DIY
ANNESS PUBLISHING
AUTODATA LTD
BERNARD BABANI LTD
BENN BUSINESS INFO
CARLTON BOOKS
LLOYD COLE
COLLINS & BROWN
THE CROWOOD PRESS
DAVID & CHARLES PLC
DORLING KINDERSLEY
DRAGONS WORLD LTD
ELLIOT RIGHT WAY
EXPERT BOOKS
W FOULSHAM & CO LTD
W FOULSHAM & CO LTD
GUINNESS PUBLISHING
HARPERCOLLINS GENREF

J H HAYNES & CO LTD
LEADING EDGE PRESS
CHARLES LETTS & CO
FRANCES LINCOLN PUB
LITTLE BROWN & CO
PBI PUBLICATIONS
PRISM PRESS
PROMOTIONAL REPRINT
REED CONSUMER ILLUS
THOMAS REED PUB LTD
VELOCE PUBLISHING

Drama & Plays
ABSOLUTE PRESS
AK DISTRIBUTION
AMBER LANE PRESS LTD
A & C BLACK LTD
BLACK SPRING PRESS
BLACKWELL PUB LTD
BLOODAXE BOOKS
MARION BOYARS PUB
THE BRITISH COUNCIL
CALDER PUB LTD
CANONGATE PRESS PLC
CHADWYCK-HEALEY LTD
THE CHEVERELL PRESS
CRESSRELLES PUB LTD
DELECTUS BOOKS
ANDRE DEUTSCH
FABER & FABER
FOREST BOOKS
SAMUEL FRENCH LTD
GALE RESEARCH INT
GMP PUBLISHERS LTD
HANBURY PLAYS
IRON PRESS
LEISHMAN & TAUSSIG
MANCHESTER UNI PRESS
MERCIER PRESS LTD
MONARCH PUB
MOORLEY'S PRINT PUB
NAT CHRIST EDUC COUN
THOMAS NELSON & SONS
NEW PLAYWRIGHTS' NET
OBERON BOOKS LTD
THE OLEANDER PRESS
OPEN UNIV PRESS
PASSWORD (BOOKS) LTD
PAUPERS' PRESS
PEEPAL TREE BOOKS
PHAIDON PRESS LTD
PLAYWRIGHTS PUB CO
POETRY WALES PRESS
RHINEGOLD PUB LTD
ROUNDHOUSE PUB LTD
ROUTLEDGE
SHAKTI COMMUNICATION
SHEFFIELD ACD PRESS
RUDOLF STEINER PRESS
A H STOCKWELL LTD
STANLEY THORNES PUB
VERULAM PUB LTD
VIRAGO PRESS
WARD LOCK EDUC CO
WOLFHOUND PRESS
WRITERS & SCHOLARS

Economics
ACADEMIC & UNIV PUB
AK DISTRIBUTION

ALIF INTERNATIONAL
PETER ANDREW PUB CO
ANGLO-GERMAN FOUND
ASHGATE PUB GROUP
BARMARICK PUB
BLACKWELL PUB LTD
BOOK REP & DIST LTD
BOOKMARKS
BOOKS EXPRESS
MARION BOYARS PUB
BPP PUBLISHING LTD
DR BRACEWELL-MILNES
THE BRITISH ACADEMY
BRITISH NTH AMER RES
BUILDING SOC ASSN
BUTTERWORTH-HEINEMAN
FRANK CASS & CO LTD
CHADWYCK-HEALEY LTD
CHT INST PURC & SUPP
CLARIDGE PRESS
LLOYD COLE
CONSTABLE & CO LTD
CO-OPERATIVE UNION
CORK UNI PRESS
EOTHEN PRESS
FABIAN SOCIETY
FLAME BOOKS LTD
FOREST
W H FREEMAN & CO LTD
BRIAN GOOCH LTD
GRAHAM & TROTMAN LTD
GREEN BOOKS
HARVARD UNIV PRESS
HLT PUBLICATIONS
HOBSONS PUBLISHING
C HURST & CO PUB LTD
HYDATUM
IBC PUBLISHING LTD
ICC UNITED KINGDOM
INPUT-OUTPUT PUB CO
INTERMEDIATE TEC PUB
INT LABOUR OFFICE
INTERVARSITY PRESS
RICHARD KAY PUB
KEGAN PAUL INT
JESSICA KINGSLEY PUB
LAKESIDE PUBNS
LAWRENCE & WISHART
LEISHMAN & TAUSSIG
LIBERTARIAN ALLIANCE
LONGMAN GROUP UK LTD
MANCHESTER UNI PRESS
MERLIN BOOKS LTD
MILESTONE PUB
MIT PRESS LTD
MOMENTA PUB CO LTD
MOZAMBIQUE INSTITUTE
JOHN MURRAY PUB LTD
NCVO PUBLICATIONS
NORTHWICK PUBLISHERS
OSBORNE BOOKS LTD
OVERSEAS DEVEL INST
PATHFINDER PRESS
PICCADILLY PRESS LTD
PINTER PUBLISHERS
PION LTD
PITMAN PUBLISHING
PLUTO PUBLISHING
PROBUS EUROPE
PROTON PUB HOUSE LTD

ROUNDHOUSE PUB LTD
ROUTLEDGE
SAGE PUBLICATIONS
SAUS PUBLICATIONS
SCOTTISH ACAD PRESS
SHEPHEARD-WALWYN
WILLIAM SNYDER PUB
SPOKESMAN BOOKS
SPRINGER-VERLAG
THOEMMES PRESS
STANLEY THORNES PUB
TOLLEY PUBLISHING CO
TURPIN DISTRIBUTION
VERSO
WALDEN PUBLISHING
WISEBUY PUBLICATIONS
WOODHEAD PUBLISHING
WORLD SCIENTIFIC PUB

Education & Careers

AAB BRIT BOOK SEARCH
ACAIR LTD
ALIF INTERNATIONAL
ANGLO-GERMAN FOUND
AP INFORMATION SERV
ARIAN PUBLICATIONS
ASHFORD BUCHAN
B T BATSFORD LTD
BOOK REP & DIST LTD
BACIE
THE BRITISH COUNCIL
DAVID BROWN
BUILDING BLOCKS EDUC
CALOUSTE GULBENKIAN
FRANK CASS & CO LTD
CASSELL PLC
JOHN CATT EDUC LTD
CENTRAL BUREAU EDUC
PAUL CHAPMAN PUB
CHAPMANS PUB LTD
CHARTWELL-BRATT
THE CHEVERELL PRESS
FRANCIS CHICHESTER
CLARIDGE PRESS
LLOYD COLE
COMM RACIAL EQUALITY
D J COSTELLO PUB LTD
CRONER PUBLICATIONS
DANIELS PUBLISHING
THE DESIGN COUNCIL
ELLIOT RIGHT WAY
FACTS ON FILE
FLORIS BOOKS
FOLENS PUBLISHERS
FORBES PUB LTD
W FOULSHAM & CO LTD
FRAMEWORK PRESS
PETER FRANCIS PUB
FRIENDS OF THE EARTH
DAVID FULTON PUB LTD
GERBIL BOOKS
ROBERT GIBSON & SONS
GREVATT & GREVATT
HARPERCOLLINS EDUC
HAWTHORN PRESS
HAWTHORNS PUB LTD
HLT PUBLICATIONS
HOBSONS PUBLISHING
HOME & SCH COUNCIL
HOTEL & CATERING CO
HOW TO BOOKS LTD

HUMAN KINETICS PUB
IMPACT BOOKS
INST OF EDUCATION
JESSICA KINGSLEY PUB
KOGAN PAGE LTD
KUPERARD LTD
LAWRENCE & WISHART
LEARNING DEV AIDS
LEISHMAN & TAUSSIG
CHARLES LETTS & CO
LIBERTARIAN ALLIANCE
LIFE EDUCATION UK
LIVERPOOL UNIV PRESS
P M LLEWELLYN CO
LONGMAN GROUP UK LTD
MERCURY BOOKS
MOMENTA PUB CO LTD
MULTILINGUAL MATTERS
NAT CHILDRENS BUREAU
NAT INST ADULT EDUC
NORTHCOTE HOUSE PUB
ONEWORLD PUB
OPEN UNIV PRESS
ORIFLAMME PUBLISHING
OXFAM
PLUTO PUBLISHING
POSITIVE PRODUCTS
QUAY PUBLISHING LTD
REED INFO SERVICES
RHINEGOLD PUB LTD
ROUTLEDGE
SAGE PUBLICATIONS
SCHOFIELD & SIMS LTD
SCHOLASTIC PUB LTD
SCOTTISH ACAD PRESS
SFIA EDUC TRUST LTD
SPINDLEWOOD
RUDOLF STEINER PRESS
A H STOCKWELL LTD
TELEGRAPH BOOKS
TEXTILE INSTITUTE
THIMBLE PRESS
STANLEY THORNES PUB
TREADWELLS ART MILL
TROTMAN & CO LTD
TURNAROUND
UNI OF EXETER PRESS
UNI OF WALES PRESS
VACATION WORK
VERULAM PUB LTD
VOLCANO PRESS LTD
WARD LOCK EDUC CO
WAYLAND (PUB) LTD
WEAVERS PRESS PUB
WELLSWEEP PRESS
WHITING & BIRCH LTD

Engineering

AMERICAN TECH PUB
PETER ANDREW PUB CO
ARGUS PUBLICATIONS
ARTECH HOUSE
ASHGATE PUB GROUP
BERNARD BABANI LTD
BENN BUSINESS INFO
BLACKWELL PUB LTD
BLACKWELL SCIENTIFIC
BROWN SON & FERGUSON
BUTTERWORTH-HEINEMANN
CHAPMAN & HALL
CHARTWELL-BRATT
CLARKE ASSOCIATES
COMPUTATIONAL MECH
DYLLANSOW TRURAN

ELECTRONICA BOOKS
ELSEVIER SCIENCE PUB
ENTRA PUBLICATIONS
EPA PRESS
EXPERT BOOKS
FMJ BOOKS
GALE RESEARCH INT
BRIAN GOOCH LTD
IFS LTD
INST OF ELEC ENGINE
INTERMEDIATE TEC PUB
IOP PUBLISHING LTD
JAMES & JAMES LTD
KOGAN PAGE LTD
LONGMAN GROUP UK LTD
MECHANICAL ENG PUB
MIT PRESS LTD
MOMENTA PUB CO LTD
MOSBY-YEARBOOK EUR
NEWTON PUBLISHERS
PRISM PRESS
REED INFO SERVICES
THOMAS REED PUB LTD
RESEARCH STUDIES LTD
RICS BOOKS
SEMICON INDEXES
SPRINGER-VERLAG
THOMAS TELFORD LTD
STANLEY THORNES PUB
TURPIN DISTRIBUTION
VCH PUB (UK) LTD
WOODHEAD PUBLISHING
WORLD SCIENTIFIC PUB

English Language Training

AAB BRIT BOOK SEARCH
ACCENT EDUCATIONAL
ANN ARBOR PUBLISHERS
BEBC DISTRIBUTION
THE BRITISH COUNCIL
CAMBRIDGE UNIV PRESS
PETER COLLIN PUB LTD
ELM PUBLICATIONS
MARY GLASGOW PUB
INTELLECT
LANGUAGE TEACH PUB
LONGMAN GROUP UK LTD
MACMILLAN DIST LTD
THOMAS NELSON & SONS
NEW ERA PUB LTD
ORIFLAMME PUBLISHING
PACKARD PUB LTD
PANGBOURNE ENGLISH
PASTEST SERVICE
SHAKTI COMMUNICATION
STANLEY THORNES PUB
VACATION WORK
VERULAM PUB LTD
WINSLOW PRESS

Environment

HARRY N ABRAMS INC
ACADEMIC & UNIV PUB
AIRLIFT BOOK CO
AK DISTRIBUTION
ALADDIN BOOKS LTD
ANGLO-GERMAN FOUND
ARCHIVAL FACSIMILES

ASHGATE PUB GROUP
BAHAI PUBLISHING
BARTON HOUSE PUB
B T BATSFORD LTD
BLACKWELL PUB LTD
BLACKWELL SCIENTIFIC
BOOKS EXPRESS
BOOKSPEED
BOXTREE LTD
MARION BOYARS PUB
CAB INTERNATIONAL
CANONGATE PRESS PLC
CATHOLIC INSTITUTE
CHADWYCK-HEALEY LTD
CHALKSOFT LTD
PAUL CHAPMAN PUB
CHT INST PURC & SUPP
CLARKE ASSOCIATES
E W CLASSEY LTD
COLLINS & BROWN
CRONER PUBLICATIONS
ANDRE DEUTSCH
AIDAN ELLIS PUB
ELSEVIER SCIENCE PUB
EUROBOOK LTD
EX LIBRIS PRESS
FABIAN SOCIETY
FACTS ON FILE
FINDHORN PRESS
FORBES PUB LTD
W H FREEMAN & CO LTD
FRIENDS OF THE EARTH
FROGLETS PUB
DAVID FULTON PUB LTD
GAIA BOOKS LTD
GALE RESEARCH INT
GATEWAY BOOKS
GMP PUBLISHERS LTD
GOTHIC IMAGE PUB
GRAHAM & TROTMAN LTD
GRANTA EDITIONS
GREEN BOOKS
GREENCROFT BOOKS
GROTIUS PUB LTD
HARLEY BOOKS
HARPERCOLLINS THORS
HARVARD UNIV PRESS
HAWTHORN PRESS
HOBSONS PUBLISHING
ALISON HODGE PUB
HYDEN HOUSE LTD
ICC UNITED KINGDOM
IMMEL PUBLISHING LTD
IMPACT BOOKS
INTERMEDIATE TEC PUB
INT BEE RESEARCH ASS
INT LABOUR OFFICE
JAMES & JAMES LTD
JONES & BARTLETT PUB
KEGAN PAUL INT
KOGAN PAGE LTD
LAKESIDE PUBNS
LAWRENCE & WISHART
LEISHMAN & TAUSSIG
LIBERTARIAN ALLIANCE
LITTLE BROWN & CO
LIVERPOOL UNIV PRESS
LONGMAN GROUP UK LTD
LUTTERWORTH PRESS
MANCHESTER UNI PRESS
MECHANICAL ENG PUB
MINORITY RIGHTS GRP
MIT PRESS LTD

MOMENTA PUB CO LTD
MOSBY-YEARBOOK EUR
MULTILINGUAL MATTERS
NATIONAL TRUST (IR)
NATURAL HIST BOOK SV
ANTHONY NELSON LTD
THE O'BRIEN PRESS
ORKNEY PRESS LTD
OXFAM
PACKARD PUB LTD
PENNY PRESS
PINTER PUBLISHERS
PION LTD
PITMAN PUBLISHING
PLUTO PUBLISHING
POLICY STUDIES INST
PRISM PRESS
RICHMOND PUB CO LTD
ROUNDHOUSE PUB LTD
ROUTLEDGE
ROYAL IRISH ACADEMY
ST PAUL'S PUB
SHEPHEARD-WALWYN
SIGMA LEISURE
SPOKESMAN BOOKS
SPRINGER-VERLAG
SWEETHAWS PRESS
TARRAGON PRESS
I B TAURIS & CO LTD
THORNHILL PRESS LTD
TOLLEY PUBLISHING CO
TRANSPORT 2000
TURNAROUND
TURPIN DISTRIBUTION
VCH PUB (UK) LTD
VINE HOUSE DIST
WEST COUNTRY BOOKS
WORLD LEISURE MKTG
WRITERS & SCHOLARS

Fashion & Costume
HARRY N ABRAMS INC
ART DATA
B T BATSFORD LTD
RUTH BEAN PUBLISHERS
BLACKWELL SCIENTIFIC
BOOK REP & DIST LTD
BRITISH MUSEUM PRESS
CALDER PUB LTD
CARLTON BOOKS
CHRISTCHURCH PUB LTD
CONSTABLE & CO LTD
GMP PUBLISHERS LTD
GUINNESS PUBLISHING
THE HERBERT PRESS
KEGAN PAUL INT
MELIA PUB SERVICES
THE NATIONAL TRUST
PETER OWEN LTD
PARKE SUTTON PUB LTD
PLEXUS PUBLISHING
PROMOTIONAL REPRINT
QUARTET BOOKS LTD
RIZZOLI INT PUBNS
SHIRE PUBLICATIONS
SMITH GRYPHON LTD
STUDIO EDITIONS LTD
THAMES & HUDSON LTD
STANLEY THORNES PUB
TOUCAN PRESS

Fiction
AFRICA CHRIST PRESS
AIRLIFT BOOK CO

AK DISTRIBUTION
ANVIL BOOKS LTD
BALNAIN BOOKS
BARTON HOUSE PUB
BELLEW PUBLISHING
BLACK SPRING PRESS
BLAKE PUBLISHING LTD
BLOODAXE BOOKS
BOOKSPEED
BOXTREE LTD
MARION BOYARS PUB
BRAINIAC BOOKS LTD
CALDER PUB LTD
CANONGATE PRESS PLC
CARCANET PRESS
CARLTON BOOKS
J L CARR
CHAPMANS PUB LTD
CHILTON DESIGNS
CHIVERS PRESS LTD
CHRISTCHURCH PUB LTD
COLD TONNAGE BOOKS
COLLETS
CONSTABLE & CO LTD
RICHARD/ERIKA COWARD
CREATION PRESS
CURLEW PUBLISHING CO
DALENNAU
DARF PUBLISHERS LTD
DEDALUS LTD
DELAMARE PUBLISHING
DELECTUS BOOKS
ANDRE DEUTSCH
ELAND
AIDAN ELLIS PUB
EX LIBRIS PRESS
FABER & FABER
1ST WORLD PUB LTD
FOREST BOOKS
GERBIL BOOKS
GMP PUBLISHERS LTD
PETER HALBAN PUB
ROBERT HALE LTD
IAN HENRY PUB LTD
HONEYGLEN PUB LTD
HONNO LTD
IMPACT BOOKS
IRON PRESS
JOHNSTON & BACON
KINGSWAY PUB
KNIGHTSCROSS LTD
KOZMIK PRESS
LADYBIRD BOOKS LTD
LAWRENCE & WISHART
LEISHMAN & TAUSSIG
LITTLE BROWN & CO
LITTLEWOOD ARC
LLANERCH PUBLISHERS
LUATH PRESS LTD
MACMILLAN DIST LTD
MAGNA LARGE PRINT
MAINSTREAM PUB CO
MANOR HOUSE PUB
THE MENARD PRESS
MERCIER PRESS LTD
MERLIN BOOKS LTD
MILLS & BOON LTD
MONARCH PUB
MULTIMEDIA BOOKS LTD
NEW ERA PUB LTD
NOVA DISTRIBUTION
NOVEMBER BOOKS
THE O'BRIEN PRESS
OLDCASTLE BOOKS LTD
MICHAEL O'MARA BOOKS
ORIFLAMME PUBLISHING

ORKNEY PRESS LTD
PETER OWEN LTD
OWL PRESS
PASSWORD (BOOKS) LTD
PEEPAL TREE BOOKS
PIATKUS BOOKS
PLUTO PUBLISHING
PROFESSIONAL BK SALE
PROMOTIONAL REPRINT
PROSPERITY PUB
QUARTET BOOKS LTD
RAMSAY HEAD PRESS
READERS INT
REED CONS MANDARIN
REINHARDT BOOKS LTD
ROBINSON PUBLISHING
ROUNDHOUSE PUB LTD
SERPENT'S TAIL
SETTLE PRESS
SEVERN HOUSE PUB LTD
SHAKTI COMMUNICATION
SHEARWATER PRESS LTD
SILVER MOON BOOKS
SMITH GRYPHON LTD
SMITH SETTLE LTD
SPINDLEWOOD
SPORTSMAN'S PRESS
A H STOCKWELL LTD
STRIDE PUBLICATIONS
TABB HOUSE
TEMPLE PRESS LTD
TRITON PUB CO LTD
TURNAROUND
VILLIERS PUB LTD
VIRAGO PRESS
VIRGIN PUBLISHING
WEAVERS PRESS PUB
WELLSWEEP PRESS
WOLFHOUND PRESS
WOMEN'S PRESS
WRITERS & SCHOLARS
XANADU PUBLICATIONS

Food & Drink
AA PUBLISHING
ABSOLUTE PRESS
ACE BOOKS
AIRLIFT BOOK CO
ANAYA PUBLISHERS
ANNESS PUBLISHING
APPLETREE PRESS LTD
ARGUS PUBLICATIONS
AUSTRALIAN CON PRESS
BBC BOOKS
BEE BOOKS NEW & OLD
BENN BUSINESS INFO
BOXTREE LTD
BUTTERWORTH-HEINEMAN
CANONGATE PRESS PLC
CARLTON BOOKS
KYLE CATHIE LTD
CHAPMANS PUB LTD
CHRISTCHURCH PUB LTD
CHRISTIE'S WINE PUBS
COLLINS & BROWN
CONSTABLE & CO LTD
DALENNAU
DAVID & CHARLES PLC
ANDRE DEUTSCH
DORLING KINDERSLEY
ELLIOT RIGHT WAY
AIDAN ELLIS PUB
ELSEVIER SCIENCE PUB
EVENLODE BOOK DIST
FABER & FABER

FACTS ON FILE
FAMEDRAM PUB LTD
FOOD TRADE PRESS LTD
FORBES PUB LTD
W FOULSHAM & CO LTD
GAIA BOOKS LTD
GAIRM PUBLICATIONS
GARNET PUB LTD
GELOFER PRESS
GILL & MACMILLAN LTD
GRUB STREET
GUINNESS PUBLISHING
H I MARKETING
ROBERT HALE LTD
HARPERCOLLINS GENREF
HARPERCOLLINS THORS
HAWKER PUBLICATIONS
HEALTH EDUC AUTH
HOTEL & CATERING CO
IMPACT BOOKS
INTERWORLD PUB
LEON JAEGGI & SONS
JARROLD PUBLISHING
JOHNSTON & BACON
KINGSCLERE PUB LTD
LAKESIDE PUBNS
LENNARD ASSOCIATES
CHARLES LETTS & CO
FRANCES LINCOLN PUB
LITTLE BROWN & CO
P M LLEWELLYN CO
CHRIS LLOYD SALES
MAINSTREAM PUB CO
MELIA PUB SERVICES
MERROW PUBLISHING CO
MILLBANK BOOKS LTD
MULTIMEDIA BOOKS LTD
JOHN MURRAY PUB LTD
THE NATIONAL TRUST
NUTMEG PRESS
THE O'BRIEN PRESS
MICHAEL O'MARA BOOKS
PIATKUS BOOKS
PREMIER BOOK MKTNG
PRISM PRESS
PROMOTIONAL REPRINT
QUILLER PRESS LTD
REED CONSUMER ILLUS
WILLIAM REED DIR
ROBINSON PUBLISHING
ROBSON BOOKS
ROSEDENE PUBLISHERS
ROSENDALE PRESS LTD
THE RUBICON PRESS
SAWD BOOKS
SCORPION PUBLISHING
SILENT BOOKS
SMITH GRYPHON LTD
SOLO BOOKS LTD
SUMMERSDALE PUB
TABB HOUSE
TEECOLL PUBLICATIONS
TELEGRAPH BOOKS
STANLEY THORNES PUB
VERULAM PUB LTD
VINE HOUSE DIST
VIRTUE BOOKS LTD
WOLFHOUND PRESS
WORDSWORTH EDITIONS
WORLD LEISURE MKTG

Foreign Languages

ACAIR LTD
ACCENT EDUCATIONAL
ALIF INTERNATIONAL
AMCD (PUB) LTD
ARIS & PHILLIPS LTD
ASHFORD BUCHAN
BAY FOREIGN BOOKS
BBC BOOKS
BERLITZ PUBLISHING
NICHOLAS BREALEY PUB
BRIGHT BOOKS LTD
CENTRE INFO LANGUAGE
W & R CHAMBERS LTD
CHAPMANS PUB LTD
COLLETS
PETER COLLIN PUB LTD
CONSTABLE & CO LTD
CORK UNI PRESS
DARF PUBLISHERS LTD
DEDALUS LTD
DOLPHIN BOOK CO LTD
DOT PUBLICATIONS
DYLLANSOW TRURAN
ELM PUBLICATIONS
EUROPEAN SCHOOLBOOKS
W FOULSHAM & CO LTD
MARY GLASGOW PUB
HUGO'S LANGUAGE BOOK
HYDATUM
ICC UNITED KINGDOM
IMPACT BOOKS
KEGAN PAUL INT
KUPERARD LTD
LADYBIRD BOOKS LTD
LANGUAGE INFO CENTRE
LEISHMAN & TAUSSIG
CHARLES LETTS & CO
P M LLEWELLYN CO
CHRIS LLOYD SALES
LOCHEE PUB LTD
LONGMAN GROUP UK LTD
MANCHESTER UNI PRESS
MILLBANK BOOKS LTD
MOTILAL BOOKS
MULTILINGUAL MATTERS
JOHN MURRAY PUB LTD
THOMAS NELSON & SONS
OCTAGON PRESS
THE OLEANDER PRESS
PACKARD PUB LTD
PREMIER BOOK MKTNG
ROUTLEDGE
SAQI BOOKS
SCHOFIELD & SIMS LTD
SCH ORIENTAL/AFRICAN
SHAKTI COMMUNICATION
SHEARWATER PRESS LTD
SHEFFIELD ACD PRESS
SODANEY PUBLISHERS
STANLEY THORNES PUB
THORNTON'S OF OXFORD
UNI OF EXETER PRESS
VERULAM PUB LTD
VOLTAIRE FOUNDATION
ZENO

Gardening

HARRY N ABRAMS INC
ACE BOOKS
ANAYA PUBLISHERS
ANNESS PUBLISHING
ANTIQUE COLLECTORS
APPLETREE PRESS LTD
B T BATSFORD LTD
BBC BOOKS
BOOKSPEED
BURALL FLORAPRINT
CARLTON BOOKS
KYLE CATHIE LTD
CHALKSOFT LTD
CHAPMANS PUB LTD
LLOYD COLE
COLLINS & BROWN
THE CROWOOD PRESS
DAVID & CHARLES PLC
DORLING KINDERSLEY
DRAGONS WORLD LTD
ELLIOT RIGHT WAY
AIDAN ELLIS PUB
EUROBOOK LTD
EX LIBRIS PRESS
FABER & FABER
FACTS ON FILE
W FOULSHAM & CO LTD
W & G FOYLE LTD
FRIENDS OF THE EARTH
GREEN BOOKS
GRISEWOOD & DEMPSEY
ROBERT HALE LTD
HARPERCOLLINS GENREF
HARPERCOLLINS THORS
THE HERB SOCIETY
THE HERBERT PRESS
HYDEN HOUSE LTD
JARROLD PUBLISHING
LAKESIDE PUBNS
CHARLES LETTS & CO
FRANCES LINCOLN PUB
LITTLE BROWN & CO
MELIA PUB SERVICES
MOORLAND PUB CO LTD
JOHN MURRAY PUB LTD
THE NATIONAL TRUST
MICHAEL O'MARA BOOKS
PACKARD PUB LTD
PBI PUBLICATIONS
PLUTO PUBLISHING
PRISM PRESS
PROMOTIONAL REPRINT
QUILLER PRESS LTD
REED CONSUMER ILLUS
ROBSON BOOKS
ROSEDENE PUBLISHERS
SAWD BOOKS
SILENT BOOKS
SPA BOOKS LTD
A H STOCKWELL LTD
SWEETHAWS PRESS
TELEGRAPH BOOKS
THAMES & HUDSON LTD
THE TOAT PRESS
VERULAM PUB LTD
WORLD LEISURE MKTG

Gay & Lesbian

AIRLIFT BOOK CO
AK DISTRIBUTION
BOOKSPEED
MARION BOYARS PUB
BRAINIAC BOOKS LTD
CHRISTCHURCH PUB LTD
GAY LIBERATION FRONT
GMP PUBLISHERS LTD
HARPERCOLLINS THORS
HEALTH EDUC AUTH
HONNO LTD
LIBERTARIAN ALLIANCE
MONARCH PUB
OPEN UNIV PRESS
PETER OWEN LTD
PLUTO PUBLISHING
PRISM PRESS
RIVERS ORAM PRESS
ROUTLEDGE
SCARLET PRESS
SERPENT'S TAIL
SILVER MOON BOOKS
TURNAROUND
VIRAGO PRESS
WHITING & BIRCH LTD
WOMEN'S PRESS

Geography & Geology

ASHGATE PUB GROUP
ASHGROVE PRESS
ATLANTIC EUROPE PUB
BLACKWELL PUB LTD
BLACKWELL SCIENTIFIC
BOOK REP & DIST LTD
BROAD OAK PRESS
CAB INTERNATIONAL
CHADWYCK-HEALEY LTD
CHALKSOFT LTD
CHAPMAN & HALL
PAUL CHAPMAN PUB
CHARTWELL-BRATT
E W CLASSEY LTD
CORK UNI PRESS
DALESMAN PUB CO LTD
TERENCE DALTON LTD
DAVID & CHARLES PLC
DAWSON UK LTD
EUROPEAN SCHOOLBOOKS
EX LIBRIS PRESS
FACTS ON FILE
W H FREEMAN & CO LTD
DAVID FULTON PUB LTD
GALE RESEARCH INT
GARNET PUB LTD
GEOGRAPHICAL PUB LTD
GEOLOGICAL SOCIETY
MARY GLASGOW PUB
GREENCROFT BOOKS
GUINNESS PUBLISHING
HAKLUYT SOCIETY
HARPERCOLLINS GENREF
HYDATUM
JAMES & JAMES LTD
JONES & BARTLETT PUB
KEGAN PAUL INT
JESSICA KINGSLEY PUB
LEISHMAN & TAUSSIG
LIVERPOOL UNIV PRESS
LONGMAN GROUP UK LTD
MOMENTA PUB CO LTD
MOSBY-YEARBOOK EUR
NATURAL HIST BOOK SV
NATURAL HIST MUSEUM

ANTHONY NELSON LTD
THOMAS NELSON & SONS
PACKARD PUB LTD
PINTER PUBLISHERS
PION LTD
PLUTO PUBLISHING
PRISM PRESS
PROMOTIONAL REPRINT
RICS BOOKS
ROADMASTER PUB
ROUNDHOUSE PUB LTD
ROUTLEDGE
ROYAL IRISH ACADEMY
SAUS PUBLICATIONS
SCHOFIELD & SIMS LTD
SCOTTISH ACAD PRESS
SPRINGER-VERLAG
THOMAS TELFORD LTD
STANLEY THORNES PUB
THORNHILL PRESS LTD
UNI OF EXETER PRESS
UNI OF WALES PRESS
WARD LOCK EDUC CO

Health & Beauty

ACE BOOKS
ADAMSON BOOKS
AIRLIFT BOOK CO
ANAYA PUBLISHERS
PETER ANDREW PUB CO
ARIAN PUBLICATIONS
ASA SWIMMING ENT LTD
ASHGROVE PRESS
BALNAIN BOOKS
BARTON HOUSE PUB
BEACONSFIELD PUB LTD
BENN BUSINESS INFO
BLACKWELL SCIENTIFIC
BOOKSPEED
BOXTREE LTD
CAMDEN PRESS
CARLTON BOOKS
KYLE CATHIE LTD
CHAPMANS PUB LTD
CHILTON DESIGNS
CLASS PUBLISHING
LLOYD COLE
COLLINS & BROWN
C W DANIEL CO LTD
DANIELS PUBLISHING
DAVID & CHARLES PLC
DORLING KINDERSLEY
ELEMENT BOOKS LTD
ELITE WORDS & IMAGE
ELLIOT RIGHT WAY
EVENLODE BOOK DIST
FORBES PUB LTD
W FOULSHAM & CO LTD
GAIA BOOKS LTD
GMP PUBLISHERS LTD
GOTHIC IMAGE PUB
GREEN BOOKS
HARPERCOLLINS THORS
HAWKER PUBLICATIONS
HEALTH EDUC AUTH
THE HERB SOCIETY
HORTON PUB LTD
HUMAN KINETICS PUB
JARROLD PUBLISHING
KINGSCLERE PUB LTD
KNIGHTSCROSS LTD
LEISHMAN & TAUSSIG
LIFE EDUCATION UK
FRANCES LINCOLN PUB
LITTLE BROWN & CO
LONGMAN GROUP UK LTD

LUCIS PRESS LTD
MICELLE PRESS
MULTIMEDIA BOOKS
  LTD
MULTISCOPE BOOKS
NEW ERA PUB LTD
MICHAEL O'MARA
  BOOKS
PIATKUS BOOKS
PICCADILLY PRESS LTD
PREMIER BOOK MKTNG
PRISM PRESS
PROMOTIONAL
  REPRINT
REED CONSUMER ILLUS
ROBINSON PUBLISHING
ROBSON BOOKS
ROSEDENE PUBLISHERS
SERPENT'S TAIL
SETTLE PRESS
SMITH GRYPHON LTD
SPCK
SOLO BOOKS LTD
SPA BOOKS LTD
RUDOLF STEINER PRESS
TELEGRAPH BOOKS
STANLEY THORNES PUB
VIRAGO PRESS
VITA BOOKS
WHITING & BIRCH LTD
WISEBUY
  PUBLICATIONS

History

AA PUBLISHING
HARRY N ABRAMS INC
ACADEMIC & UNIV PUB
ACADEMY BOOKS LTD
AK DISTRIBUTION
ALIF INTERNATIONAL
ALLOWAY PUB LTD
ALSTON BOOKS
AMCD (PUB) LTD
AMPERSAND PRESS LTD
PETER ANDREW PUB CO
ANVIL BOOKS LTD
APPLEFORD PUB GROUP
APPLETREE PRESS LTD
ARCHIVE RESEARCH
  LTD
ASHGATE PUB GROUP
ASHGROVE PRESS
BACSA
BAHAI PUBLISHING
M & M BALDWIN
B T BATSFORD LTD
RUTH BEAN
  PUBLISHERS
BELLEW PUBLISHING
THE BLACK SWAN
  PRESS
BLACKWELL PUB LTD
BOOKMARKS
BOOKS EXPRESS
MARION BOYARS PUB
BRASSEY'S (UK) LTD
BREEDON BOOKS
BREWIN BOOK DIST
THE BRITISH ACADEMY
BRITISH MUSEUM PRESS
BROAD OAK PRESS
DAVID BROWN
BROWN SON &
  FERGUSON
CANONGATE PRESS PLC
CARNEGIE PUB LTD
FRANK CASS & CO LTD
PAUL CAVE PUB LTD
CCBI PUBLICATIONS
CHADWYCK-HEALEY
  LTD
CHALKSOFT LTD

CHAPMANS PUB LTD
CHRISTCHURCH PUB
  LTD
CICERONE PRESS
CLARIDGE PRESS
JAMES CLARKE & CO
COLLINS & BROWN
CONCORDIA PUB LTD
CONSTABLE & CO LTD
CONWAY MARITIME
CORK UNI PRESS
D J COSTELLO PUB LTD
COUNTYVISE LTD
CRANE PRESS
CRYSTAL PALACE
  FOUND
DALENNAU
DALESMAN PUB CO LTD
TERENCE DALTON LTD
DALTON WATSON
  BOOKS
DARF PUBLISHERS LTD
DAVID & CHARLES PLC
CHRISTOPHER DAVIES
DAWSON UK LTD
ANDRE DEUTSCH
DORSET PUB CO
DRAGONS WORLD LTD
DUNROD PRESS
DYLLANSOW TRURAN
EASON & SON LTD
EAST WEST PUB LTD
EDINBURGH UNIV
  PRESS
AIDAN ELLIS PUB
ELM PUBLICATIONS
ENSIGN PUBLICATIONS
EOTHEN PRESS
ERD PUBLICATIONS LTD
EUROBOOK LTD
EVENLODE BOOK DIST
EX LIBRIS PRESS
FACTS ON FILE
FARRAND PRESS
IAN FAULKNER PUB
  LTD
FIREBIRD BOOKS LTD
FOUR COURTS PRESS
FROGLETS PUB
GAIRM PUBLICATIONS
GALE RESEARCH INT
GARNET PUB LTD
GELOFER PRESS
GILL & MACMILLAN
  LTD
GMP PUBLISHERS LTD
GOTHIC IMAGE PUB
GRANTA EDITIONS
GREENCROFT BOOKS
GUINNESS PUBLISHING
HAKLUYT SOCIETY
PETER HALBAN PUB
HALFSHIRE BOOKS
J H HALL & SONS LTD
HAMBLEDON PRESS
HARVARD UNIV PRESS
DAVID HAWGOOD
HEADSTART HISTORY
IAN HENRY PUB LTD
HISTORICAL ASSN
HISTORICAL PUB LTD
ALISON HODGE PUB
HONEYGLEN PUB LTD
HONNO LTD
C HURST & CO PUB LTD
HYDATUM
IMMEL PUBLISHING
  LTD
INTERWORLD PUB
IRISH ACADEMIC PRESS
JOHNSTON & BACON
RICHARD KAY PUB
KEGAN PAUL INT

THE KENSAL PRESS
KINGSMEAD PRESS
KNIGHTSCROSS LTD
KOZMIK PRESS
KUPERARD LTD
LA HAULE BOOKS LTD
LADYBIRD BOOKS LTD
LAKESIDE PUBNS
LAWRENCE & WISHART
BILL LEESON
LEISHMAN & TAUSSIG
LIBERTARIAN
  ALLIANCE
LITTLE BROWN & CO
LIVERPOOL UNIV PRESS
LLANERCH PUBLISHERS
CHRIS LLOYD SALES
LONDON TOPOGRAPH
  SOC
LONGMAN GROUP UK
  LTD
MAINSTREAM PUB CO
MANCHESTER UNI
  PRESS
MERCAT PRESS
MERCIER PRESS LTD
MERIDIAN BOOKS
MERLIN BOOKS LTD
MOTILAL BOOKS
MOZAMBIQUE
  INSTITUTE
JOHN MURRAY PUB
  LTD
NAT PORTRAIT
  GALLERY
THE NATIONAL TRUST
ANTHONY NELSON LTD
THOMAS NELSON &
  SONS
NEW BEACON BOOKS
  LTD
NEW FOREST LEAVES
NEWTON PUBLISHERS
NUTMEG PRESS
THE O'BRIEN PRESS
OCTAGON PRESS
OLD VICARAGE PUB
MICHAEL O'MARA
  BOOKS
OMF BOOKS
OPEN GATE PRESS
OPEN UNIV PRESS
ORBACH & CHAMBERS
ORKNEY PRESS LTD
PETER OWEN LTD
OWL BOOKS
OXBOW BOOKS
PATHFINDER PRESS
PATTEN PRESS
PEEPAL TREE BOOKS
PEN & SWORD BOOKS
PENNY PRESS
COLIN A PERRY LTD
PHILLIMORE & CO LTD
PICCADILLY PRESS LTD
PICTON PUBLISHING
PINHORNS
PINTER PUBLISHERS
PITKIN PICTORIALS
PLUTO PUBLISHING
THE POUND HOUSE
POWER PUBLICATIONS
PROMOTIONAL
  REPRINT
PRYOR PUBLICATIONS
QUARTET BOOKS LTD
QUILLER PRESS LTD
QUOTES LTD
RAMSAY HEAD PRESS
REAKTION BOOKS LTD
RIVERS ORAM PRESS
ROADMASTER PUB
ROBSON BOOKS

BARRY ROSE LAW PUB
ROUNDHOUSE PUB LTD
ROUTLEDGE
ROYAL IRISH ACADEMY
THE RUBICON PRESS
RUSHWORTH LIT LTD
DAVID ST JOHN
  THOMAS
SALTIRE SOCIETY
SAQI BOOKS
SAWD BOOKS
SB PUBLICATIONS
SCARTHIN BOOKS
SCHOFIELD & SIMS LTD
SCH ORIENTAL/
  AFRICAN
SCIENCE MUSEUM
SCORPION PUBLISHING
SCOTTISH ACAD PRESS
SHEPHEARD-WALWYN
SHIRE PUBLICATIONS
SMITH SETTLE LTD
SOC PROM ROMAN
  STUDY
SOC OF GENEALOGISTS
SPA BOOKS LTD
SPELLMOUNT LTD
A H STOCKWELL LTD
ALAN SUTTON PUB LTD
I B TAURIS & CO LTD
THAMES & HUDSON
  LTD
STANLEY THORNES PUB
THORNHILL PRESS LTD
THORNTON'S OF
  OXFORD
TOUCAN PRESS
TRAIL CREST PUB
TRIGRAPH LTD
TRIPLE CAT PUB
TURNAROUND
TWELVEHEADS PRESS
UK COUN HUMAN
  RIGHTS
UNI OF EXETER PRESS
UNI OF WALES PRESS
VCH PUB (UK) LTD
VERSO
VERULAM PUB LTD
VINE HOUSE DIST
VIRAGO PRESS
VOLCANO PRESS LTD
VOLTAIRE
  FOUNDATION
WARBURG INSTITUTE
WARD LOCK EDUC CO
WHITE COCKADE PUB
WHITTET BOOKS LTD
WINDROW & GREENE
WOMEN'S PRESS
WORDSWORTH
  EDITIONS
WORLD LEISURE MKTG
WRITERS & SCHOLARS
YALE UNIV PRESS
YORICK BOOKS
ZENO

Humour

AEDIFICAMUS PRESS
AIRLIFT BOOK CO
AK DISTRIBUTION
ANNUAL CONCEPTS
  LTD
ANVIL BOOKS LTD
BBC BOOKS
BELLEW PUBLISHING
BERTIE RAMIFICATIONS
BLACK FROG PRESS
BLAKE PUBLISHING LTD
BOOKSPEED
BROADSIDE

CANONGATE PRESS PLC
CARLTON BOOKS
CHAPMANS PUB LTD
CHILTON DESIGNS
CHRISTCHURCH PUB LTD
CICERONE PRESS
CRESSRELLES PUB LTD
DALESMAN PUB CO LTD
ANDRE DEUTSCH
EGMONT PUB LTD
ELITE WORDS & IMAGE
ELLIOT RIGHT WAY
EVENLODE BOOK DIST
EXPRESS NEWSPAPERS
FAMEDRAM PUB LTD
FARMING PRESS BOOKS
FIREBIRD BOOKS LTD
1ST WORLD PUB LTD
FLAME BOOKS LTD
GERBIL BOOKS
GMP PUBLISHERS LTD
GRUB STREET
GUINNESS PUBLISHING
ROBERT HALE LTD
IDEAS UNLIMITED
IMPACT BOOKS
JARROLD PUBLISHING
KEAY'S PUBLICATIONS
KINGSWAY PUB
KNOCKABOUT COMICS
LADYBIRD BOOKS LTD
JAY LANDESMAN
LENNARD ASSOCIATES
LITTLE BROWN & CO
LITTLE RED WITCH
CHRIS LLOYD SALES
MAINSTREAM PUB CO
MARITIME BOOKS
MERCIER PRESS LTD
MILLBANK BOOKS LTD
MONARCH PUB
E J MORTEN PUB
JOHN MURRAY PUB LTD
ANTHONY NELSON LTD
NEWS PRODUCTIONS
NORHEIMSUND BOOKS
NUTMEG PRESS
THE O'BRIEN PRESS
OCTAGON PRESS
THE OLEANDER PRESS
MICHAEL O'MARA BOOKS
ORBACH & CHAMBERS
OWL PRESS
PICCADILLY PRESS LTD
PORTHILL PUBLISHERS
PRYOR PUBLICATIONS
R & B PUBLISHING
RAVETTE BOOKS LTD
ROBINSON PUBLISHING
ROBSON BOOKS
BARRY ROSE LAW PUB
SAINSBURY PUB LTD
SAWD BOOKS
SHAKTI COMMUNICATION
SILVER LINK PUB LTD
SILVEY-JEX PUB LTD
SPORTSMAN'S PRESS
A H STOCKWELL LTD
SUMMERSDALE PUB
TELEGRAPH BOOKS
TRENTHAM BOOKS LTD
VINE HOUSE DIST
VIRGIN PUBLISHING
VITA BOOKS
JOHN WILSON BOOKS
WORDSWORTH EDITIONS
WORLD LEISURE MKTG
XANADU PUBLICATIONS

Irish Interest

AIRLIFT BOOK CO
AK DISTRIBUTION
ANAYA PUBLISHERS
ANVIL BOOKS LTD
APPLETREE PRESS LTD
ASHFORD BUCHAN
AURUM PRESS LTD
B T BATSFORD LTD
BLOODAXE BOOKS
BOOKMARKS
MARION BOYARS PUB
BUTTERWORTH IRELAND
CALDER PUB LTD
CCBI PUBLICATIONS
CHAPMANS PUB LTD
CONSTABLE & CO LTD
CORK PUBLISHING LTD
CORK UNI PRESS
DALENNAU
DRAKE PUB SERVICES
EASON & SON LTD
FACTS ON FILE
FLORIS BOOKS
GILL & MACMILLAN LTD
C HURST & CO PUB LTD
IMPACT BOOKS
IRISH ACADEMIC PRESS
KINGSCLERE PUB LTD
LANGUAGE INFO CENTRE
LAWRENCE & WISHART
LITTLE BROWN & CO
MARLBOROUGH BOOKS
MERCIER PRESS LTD
JOHN MURRAY PUB LTD
NATIONAL TRUST (IR)
OBERON BOOKS LTD
THE O'BRIEN PRESS
OLDCASTLE BOOKS LTD
PASSWORD (BOOKS) LTD
PINTER PUBLISHERS
PLUTO PUBLISHING
PRISM PRESS
PROFESSIONAL BK SALE
PROMOTIONAL REPRINT
RHINEGOLD PUB LTD
ROUTLEDGE
ROYAL IRISH ACADEMY
SKELLIG PRESS
COLIN SMYTHE LTD
THAMES & HUDSON LTD
TOLLEY PUBLISHING CO
TURNAROUND
VERULAM PUB LTD
WOLFHOUND PRESS

Law & Criminology

PETER ANDREW PUB CO
APPLEFORD PUB GROUP
ASHGATE PUB GROUP
BARMARICK PUB
ROGER BAYLISS
DEREK BEATTIE PUB
BEE BOOKS NEW & OLD
BLACKSTONE PRESS LTD
BLACKWELL PUB LTD
BLACKWELL SCIENTIFIC
NICHOLAS BREALEY PUB
GRAHAM BURN PUB
BUTTERWORTH & CO LTD
BUTTERWORTH IRELAND
CAVENDISH PUBLISHING
CCH EDITIONS
CENTRAL LAW TRAINING
DEBORAH CHARLES PUB
T & T CLARK LTD
CLEMENT PUBS LTD
COMM RACIAL EQUALITY
CORK PUBLISHING LTD
CRANE PRESS
CRONER PUBLICATIONS
ELM PUBLICATIONS
FACTS ON FILE
FOURMAT PUBLISHING
GMP PUBLISHERS LTD
GRAHAM & TROTMAN LTD
W GREEN
GROTIUS PUB LTD
GUINNESS PUBLISHING
HARVARD UNIV PRESS
HLT PUBLICATIONS
HYDATUM
IBC PUBLISHING LTD
ICC UNITED KINGDOM
JORDAN & SONS LTD
KEGAN PAUL INT
LAWRENCE & WISHART
LEGAL ACTION GROUP
LEGALEASE
LIBERTARIAN ALLIANCE
LLOYD'S OF LONDON
LONGMAN GROUP UK LTD
LONGMAN LAW TAX FIN
MANDRAKE
MERCIER PRESS LTD
MINORITY RIGHTS GRP
MOMENTA PUB CO LTD
MOZAMBIQUE INSTITUTE
NORTHWICK PUBLISHERS
MICHAEL O'MARA BOOKS
OPEN UNIV PRESS
ORBACH & CHAMBERS
PINTER PUBLISHERS
PITMAN PUBLISHING
PLUTO PUBLISHING
PRISM PRESS
PROFESSIONAL BK SALE
PROSPERITY PUB
RAVENSWOOD PUB LTD
RES INS CONFLICT/TER
RICS BOOKS
ROBINSON PUBLISHING
BARRY ROSE LAW PUB
THE ROUND HALL PRESS
ROUNDHOUSE PUB LTD
ROUTLEDGE
SAGE PUBLICATIONS
SALTIRE SOCIETY
SHAW & SONS LTD
SPOKESMAN BOOKS
SPRINGER-VERLAG
SWEET & MAXWELL LTD
TEMPLE LECTURES LTD
TOLLEY PUBLISHING CO
VCH PUB (UK) LTD
OWEN WELLS PUB CO
WHITING & BIRCH LTD
XANADU PUBLICATIONS

Librarianship & Publishing

ACADEMIC BOOK ASSOC
ANGLO-GERMAN FOUND
APPLEFORD PUB GROUP
ASHGATE PUB GROUP
ASLIB
BELLEW PUBLISHING
BODLEAIN LIBRARY
BOWKER-SAUR LTD
THE BRITISH COUNCIL
BRITISH LIB DOC SUPP
BRITISH LIB NAT BIB
CAPITAL PLANNING
CHADWYCK-HEALEY LTD
CLOVER PUBLICATIONS
DAWSON UK LTD
ELM PUBLICATIONS
LAWRENCE ERLBAUM ASS
GALE RESEARCH INT
BRIAN GOOCH LTD
ROBERT HALE LTD
HOLLIS DIRECTORIES
HOW TO BOOKS LTD
IMAGES
LIBRARY & INFO UNIT
LIBRARY ASSN PUB LTD
PETER MARCAN PUB
MECKLER LTD
MOMENTA PUB CO LTD
PLUTO PUBLISHING
ROUTLEDGE
ST PAUL'S BIBLIO
TFPL PUBLISHING
THIMBLE PRESS
TURPIN DISTRIBUTION
J WHITAKER & SONS
WHITTINGTON PRESS

Literature & Lit Crit

ACADEMIC & UNIV PUB
AGENDA & EDITIONS
AIRLIFT BOOK CO
AK DISTRIBUTION
ANVIL BOOKS LTD
ARCHIVAL FACSIMILES
ARIS & PHILLIPS LTD
ASHGATE PUB GROUP
ASHGROVE PRESS
BALNAIN BOOKS
B T BATSFORD LTD
BELLEW PUBLISHING
BLACK SPRING PRESS
THE BLACK SWAN PRESS
BLACKWELL PUB LTD
BLOODAXE BOOKS
BOOK REP & DIST LTD
MARION BOYARS PUB
BRAINIAC BOOKS LTD
BRENTHAM PRESS
THE BRITISH ACADEMY
THE BRITISH COUNCIL
CALDER PUB LTD
CANONGATE PRESS PLC
CARCANET PRESS
CHADWYCK-HEALEY LTD
W & R CHAMBERS LTD
DEBORAH CHARLES PUB
CHRISTCHURCH PUB LTD
LLOYD COLE
COLLETS
COLLINS & BROWN
CONSTABLE & CO LTD

CORK UNI PRESS
DAISY BOOKS
DAWSON UK LTD
DEDALUS LTD
DELECTUS BOOKS
ANDRE DEUTSCH
DYLLANSOW TRURAN
EDINBURGH UNIV PRESS
ELEMENT BOOKS LTD
ELITE WORDS & IMAGE
AIDAN ELLIS PUB
ENITHARMON PRESS
FACTS ON FILE
IAN FAULKNER PUB LTD
GAIRM PUBLICATIONS
GALE RESEARCH INT
GALLOPING DOG PRESS
GILL & MACMILLAN LTD
GMP PUBLISHERS LTD
GRANVILLE PUBLISHING
GREEN BOOKS
PETER HALBAN PUB
ROBERT HALE LTD
HARVARD UNIV PRESS
HIPPOPOTAMUS PRESS
IMAGES
KNIGHTSCROSS LTD
LA HAULE BOOKS LTD
LANGUAGE INFO CENTRE
LEISHMAN & TAUSSIG
LIBERTARIAN ALLIANCE
LIVERPOOL UNIV PRESS
LOCHEE PUB LTD
LONDON LIMITED EDNS
LONGMAN GROUP UK LTD
LUATH PRESS LTD
MANCHESTER UNI PRESS
THE MENARD PRESS
MERCAT PRESS
MERCIER PRESS LTD
MERLIN BOOKS LTD
MID NORTHUMBERLAND
MOTILAL BOOKS
NEW BEACON BOOKS LTD
NEW CLARION PRESS
NORTHCOTE HOUSE PUB
THE O'BRIEN PRESS
OPEN UNIV PRESS
ORIEL/WELSH ARTS CNL
ORKNEY PRESS LTD
PETER OWEN LTD
PASSWORD (BOOKS) LTD
PATTEN PRESS
PAUPERS' PRESS
PEEPAL TREE BOOKS
PINTER PUBLISHERS
PLUTO PUBLISHING
POETRY WALES PRESS
PREMIER BOOK MKTNG
REDCLIFFE PRESS LTD
ROBINSON PUBLISHING
ROBSON BOOKS
BERTRAM ROTA LTD
ROUNDHOUSE PUB LTD
ROUTLEDGE
THE RUBICON PRESS
DAVID ST JOHN THOMAS
SALTIRE SOCIETY
SAQI BOOKS
SCH ORIENTAL/AFRICAN
SCOTTISH ACAD PRESS
SERPENT'S TAIL
SHEFFIELD ACD PRESS
COLIN SMYTHE LTD
SOC PROM ROMAN STUDY
TABB HOUSE
TEMPLE PRESS LTD
THAMES & HUDSON LTD
STANLEY THORNES PUB
THORNTON'S OF OXFORD
TURNAROUND
UNI OF EXETER PRESS
UNI OF WALES PRESS
VERSO
VERULAM PUB LTD
VILLIERS PUB LTD
VINE HOUSE DIST
VIRAGO PRESS
VISION PRESS LTD
VOLTAIRE FOUNDATION
WARBURG INSTITUTE
WELLSWEEP PRESS
WHITTINGTON PRESS
WOMEN'S PRESS
WOODSTOCK BOOKS
WORDSWORTH EDITIONS
WRITERS & SCHOLARS
XANADU PUBLICATIONS
YORICK BOOKS

Local Interest

AIRLIFE PUBLISHING
THE ALASTAIR PRESS
ALLOWAY PUB LTD
AMCD (PUB) LTD
AMPERSAND PRESS LTD
ASHGATE PUB GROUP
ASHGROVE PRESS
AUSTICKS PUBLICATION
M & M BALDWIN
BALNAIN BOOKS
BARN DANCE PUB LTD
B T BATSFORD LTD
BLOODAXE BOOKS
BOSSINEY BOOKS
BREEDON BOOKS
BRENTHAM PRESS
BREWIN BOOK DIST
BROADSIDE
DAVID BROWN
CANONGATE PRESS PLC
CARNEGIE PUB LTD
PAUL CAVE PUB LTD
CHAPMANS PUB LTD
CICERONE PRESS
CONSTABLE & CO LTD
COUNTRYSIDE BOOKS
COUNTYVISE LTD
CRANE PRESS
CRYSTAL PALACE FOUND
DALENNAU
DALESMAN PUB CO LTD
TERENCE DALTON LTD
C W DANIEL CO LTD
DAVID & CHARLES PLC
CHRISTOPHER DAVIES
DORSET PUB CO
DOVECOTE PRESS LTD
DYLLANSOW TRURAN
EASON & SON LTD
ENGLISH LIFE PUB
ENSIGN PUBLICATIONS
ERD PUBLICATIONS LTD
EVENLODE BOOK DIST
EX LIBRIS PRESS
FAMEDRAM PUB LTD
FOCUS PUBLICATIONS
W FOULSHAM & CO LTD
FROGLETS PUB
GALLERY PRESS
GILL & MACMILLAN LTD
GOTHIC IMAGE PUB
GREENCROFT BOOKS
ROBERT HALE LTD
HALFSHIRE BOOKS
J H HALL & SONS LTD
HARDWICK HOUSE
HAWTHORNS PUB LTD
HEADLEY BROTHERS LTD
IAN HENRY PUB LTD
HISTORICAL PUB LTD
ALISON HODGE PUB
HUTTON PRESS LTD
HYDATUM
IMAGES
JARROLD PUBLISHING
RICHARD KAY PUB
LANDSCAPE PRESS
LANDY PUBLISHING
LANGUAGE INFO CENTRE
LEADING EDGE PRESS
LONDON TOPOGRAPH SOC
LUATH PRESS LTD
MAINSTREAM PUB CO
MANAGEMENT UPDATE
MANCHESTER UNI PRESS
MANDRAKE
PETER MARCAN PUB
MERCAT PRESS
MERCIER PRESS LTD
MERESBOROUGH BOOKS
MERIDIAN BOOKS
MERLIN BOOKS LTD
MID-BORDER BOOKS
MIDDLETON PRESS
E J MORTEN PUB
THE NATIONAL TRUST
ANTHONY NELSON LTD
NUTMEG PRESS
THE O'BRIEN PRESS
OLD VICARAGE PUB
THE OLEANDER PRESS
OWL BOOKS
PHILLIMORE & CO LTD
PICTON PUBLISHING
PILGRIM PRESS LTD
PINTER PUBLISHERS
PLUME PRESS
POETRY WALES PRESS
THE POUND HOUSE
POWER PUBLICATIONS
PRINTWISE PUB LTD
PROFESSIONAL BK SALE
QUOTES LTD
REDCLIFFE PRESS LTD
ROADMASTER PUB
RUNNING ANGEL
SARSEN PUBLISHING
SAWD BOOKS
SB PUBLICATIONS
SCARTHIN BOOKS
SHEARWATER PRESS LTD
SHETLAND TIMES LTD
SHROPSHIRE BOOKS
SIGMA LEISURE
SIGMA PRESS
SILVER LINK PUB LTD
SMITH SETTLE LTD
SPA BOOKS LTD
SPELLMOUNT LTD
SPINDLEWOOD
SQUARE ONE PUB
A H STOCKWELL LTD
ALAN SUTTON PUB LTD
TABB HOUSE
THORNHILL PRESS LTD
THE TOAT PRESS
TOUCAN PRESS
TRAIL CREST PUB
TWELVEHEADS PRESS
UNI OF EXETER PRESS
UNI OF WALES PRESS
VOLCANO PRESS LTD
WEST COUNTRY BOOKS
WHITE COCKADE PUB
WILLOW PUBLISHING
WORLD LEISURE MKTG

Maps, Atlases & Travel

AA PUBLISHING
AEDIFICAMUS PRESS
AIRLIFT BOOK CO
IAN ALLAN PUBLISHING
ANNUAL CONCEPTS LTD
ARCHIVAL FACSIMILES
ARCHIVE RESEARCH LTD
ASHFORD BUCHAN
AURUM PRESS LTD
BENN BUSINESS INFO
BERLITZ PUBLISHING
A & C BLACK LTD
BOOKSPEED
BRADT PUBLICATIONS
BREWIN BOOK DIST
CADOGAN BOOKS
CALDER PUB LTD
CANAL PUBLISHING CO
CARLTON BOOKS
CENTRAL BUREAU EDUC
CHADWYCK-HEALEY LTD
CHAPMANS PUB LTD
FRANCIS CHICHESTER
CHRISTCHURCH PUB LTD
CICERONE PRESS
COLLETS
COLLINS & BROWN
THOMAS COOK PUB
CORDEE
THE CROWOOD PRESS
DALENNAU
DARF PUBLISHERS LTD
DAVID & CHARLES PLC
EAST WEST PUB LTD
ELAND
EMAP BUSINESS PUB
ENGLISH LIFE PUB
ENSIGN PUBLICATIONS
ESTATE PUBLICATIONS
EUROPEAN SCHOOLBOOKS
EVENLODE BOOK DIST
EX LIBRIS PRESS
EXPRESS NEWSPAPERS
IAN FAULKNER PUB LTD
FHG PUBLICATIONS LTD
1ST WORLD PUB LTD
FLIGHT DIRECTORIES
FOCUS PUBLICATIONS
FOLENS PUBLISHERS
W FOULSHAM & CO LTD
GARNET PUB LTD
GEOGRAPHERS' A-Z LTD
GEOPROJECTS (UK) LTD
GILL & MACMILLAN LTD
GMP PUBLISHERS LTD
GRANTA EDITIONS

GRANVILLE PUBLISHING
H I MARKETING
HAKLUYT SOCIETY
ROBERT HALE LTD
THOMAS HARMSWORTH
HARPERCOLLINS BARTH
HARPERCOLLINS GENREF
HARVEY MAP SERVICES
HOW TO BOOKS LTD
IC PUBLICATIONS LTD
IMMEL PUBLISHING LTD
IMPACT BOOKS
IMRAY LAURIE & NORIE
INTERWORLD PUB
JARROLD PUBLISHING
JERSEY ARTISTS LTD
KEGAN PAUL INT
KENSINGTON WEST LTD
KOZMIK PRESS
KUPERARD LTD
LADYBIRD BOOKS LTD
LAKESIDE PUBNS
ROGER LASCELLES
LEADING EDGE PRESS
LEISHMAN & TAUSSIG
CHARLES LETTS & CO
LITTLE BROWN & CO
P M LLEWELLYN CO
LONDON TOPOGRAPH SOC
LONELY PLANET PUB
MCCARTA LTD
MAP COLLECTOR PUB
MERIDIAN BOOKS
MICHELIN TYRE PLC
MILLBANK BOOKS LTD
MOORLAND PUB CO LTD
MULTIMEDIA BOOKS LTD
JOHN MURRAY PUB LTD
ANTHONY NELSON LTD
THOMAS NELSON & SONS
NORTHCOTE HOUSE PUB
OCTAGON PRESS
OLD VICARAGE PUB
THE OLEANDER PRESS
OMF BOOKS
ORDNANCE SURVEY
J M PEARSON & SON
PEVENSEY PRESS
PILGRIM PRESS LTD
PINTER PUBLISHERS
PITKIN PICTORIALS
POWER PUBLICATIONS
PREMIER BOOK MKTNG
PROMOTIONAL REPRINT
QUILLER PRESS LTD
R & R PUBLICATIONS
RAC PUBLISHING
REED CONSUMER ILLUS
REED CONS MANDARIN
RES INS CONFLICT/TER
RIGHT NOW BOOKS
ROSENDALE PRESS LTD
ROUNDHOUSE PUB LTD
ROYAL IRISH ACADEMY
SAGE PUBLICATIONS
SB PUBLICATIONS
SCARTHIN BOOKS
SCHOFIELD & SIMS LTD
SCOTTISH TOUR BOARD
SETTLE PRESS
SHIRE PUBLICATIONS
SIGMA LEISURE

SIGMA PRESS
SPA BOOKS LTD
STACEY INTERNATIONAL
SUMMERSDALE PUB
SUNFLOWER BOOKS
ALAN SUTTON PUB LTD
TABB HOUSE
TARQUIN PUBLICATIONS
I B TAURIS & CO LTD
TELEGRAPH BOOKS
THORNHILL PRESS LTD
TRADE & TRAVEL PUB
TRAIL CREST PUB
VACATION WORK
VINE HOUSE DIST
VIRAGO PRESS
VIRGIN PUBLISHING
WILLOWBRIDGE PUB
WINDSOR BOOKS INT
WORLD LEISURE MKTG
ZENO

Mathematics & Statistics

ABCO DESIGN LTD
BERNARD BABANI LTD
BENN BUSINESS INFO
BPP PUBLISHING LTD
THE BRITISH COUNCIL
BROWN SON & FERGUSON
CHADWYCK-HEALEY LTD
CHAPMAN & HALL
CHT INST PURC & SUPP
CHARTWELL-BRATT
CLARKE ASSOCIATES
CONSTABLE & CO LTD
W H FREEMAN & CO LTD
HAWTHORNS PUB LTD
HLT PUBLICATIONS
IOP PUBLISHING LTD
JAMES & JAMES LTD
JONES & BARTLETT PUB
LIBRARY & INFO UNIT
LONGMAN GROUP UK LTD
MOMENTA PUB CO LTD
MOSBY-YEARBOOK EUR
MOTILAL BOOKS
THOMAS NELSON & SONS
ORIFLAMME PUBLISHING
PITMAN PUBLISHING
ROYAL IRISH ACADEMY
SAGE PUBLICATIONS
SCHOFIELD & SIMS LTD
SCOTTISH ACAD PRESS
SPRINGER-VERLAG
A H STOCKWELL LTD
TARQUIN PUBLICATIONS
STANLEY THORNES PUB
TOLLEY PUBLISHING CO
TURPIN DISTRIBUTION
VCH PUB (UK) LTD
WARD LOCK EDUC CO
WORLD SCIENTIFIC PUB

Medical Sciences

ACADEMIC BOOK ASSOC
ACE BOOKS
AMERICAN PSYCH PRESS
ASHGATE PUB GROUP
ASHGROVE PRESS
AUSTICKS PUBLICATION

ROGER BAYLISS
BEACONSFIELD PUB LTD
BEBC DISTRIBUTION
BENN BUSINESS INFO
BLACKWELL SCIENTIFIC
BMJ PUBLISHING GROUP
BOOK MARKETING ASSOC
BOOKS EXPRESS
THE BRITISH COUNCIL
BRITISH LIB DOC SUPP
BUTTERWORTH-HEINEMAN
CHANGE PUBLICATIONS
CHAPMAN & HALL
CHAPMANS PUB LTD
CHARTWELL-BRATT
CHILTON DESIGNS
CHURCHILL LIVINGSTON
CLARKE ASSOCIATES
CLASS PUBLISHING
CRESSRELLES PUB LTD
DANIELS PUBLISHING
MARTIN DUNITZ LTD
FARRAND PRESS
W H FREEMAN & CO LTD
GOWER MEDICAL PUB
HARVARD UNIV PRESS
HAWKER PUBLICATIONS
HEADLEY BROTHERS LTD
HEALTH EDUC AUTH
HUMAN KINETICS PUB
HYDEN HOUSE LTD
INST HEALTH SERVICES
INTERCEPT LTD
IOP PUBLISHING LTD
JAMES & JAMES LTD
JONES & BARTLETT PUB
S KARGER AG
KLUWER ACADEMIC PUB
KNIGHTSCROSS LTD
JOHN LIBBEY & CO LTD
LIVERPOOL UNIV PRESS
MENCAP
MIT PRESS LTD
MOMENTA PUB CO LTD
MOSBY-YEARBOOK EUR
MULTISCOPE BOOKS
NEWTON PUBLISHERS
OPEN UNIV PRESS
PARKE SUTTON PUB LTD
PARTHENON PUB GROUP
PASTEST SERVICE
PATTEN PRESS
PERGAMON PRESS LTD
PHARMACEUTICAL PRESS
PION LTD
PORTLAND PRESS LTD
PRISM PRESS
PROMOTIONAL REPRINT
QUAY PUBLISHING LTD
QUEST MERIDIEN LTD
R & R PUBLICATIONS
RADCLIFFE MEDICAL
ROSEDENE PUBLISHERS
ROUTLEDGE
SAGE PUBLICATIONS
SAINSBURY PUB LTD
SCOTTISH ACAD PRESS
SPCK
SPRINGER-VERLAG
RUDOLF STEINER PRESS

A H STOCKWELL LTD
TAPROBANE LTD
TARRAGON PRESS
TEECOLL PUBLICATIONS
THORNTON'S OF OXFORD
TURPIN DISTRIBUTION
UK COUN HUMAN RIGHTS
VCH PUB (UK) LTD
VINE PUBLISHING LTD
WHITING & BIRCH LTD
WHURR PUBLISHERS LTD
WILLIAMS & WILKINS
WINSLOW PRESS
WORLD SCIENTIFIC PUB

Military

ACADEMIC & UNIV PUB
AEDIFICAMUS PRESS
ALEX AIKEN
AIRLIFE PUBLISHING
IAN ALLAN PUBLISHING
AMPERSAND PRESS LTD
APPLETREE PRESS LTD
ARGUS PUBLICATIONS
ASHFORD BUCHAN
ASHGATE PUB GROUP
BACSA
BATTLE OF BRITAIN
BOOK REP & DIST LTD
BOOKS EXPRESS
BRASSEY'S (UK) LTD
BROWN SON & FERGUSON
FRANK CASS & CO LTD
CASSELL PLC
CONSTABLE & CO LTD
CONWAY MARITIME
D J COSTELLO PUB LTD
DALTON WATSON BOOKS
DARF PUBLISHERS LTD
DAVID & CHARLES PLC
JOHN DONALD PUB LTD
DORSET PUB CO
ENSIGN PUBLICATIONS
EVENLODE BOOK DIST
FACTS ON FILE
IAN FAULKNER PUB LTD
FIREBIRD BOOKS LTD
FROGLETS PUB
GOODALL PUB LTD
GOODAY STUDIOS LTD
GREENHILL BOOKS
GRUB STREET
GUINNESS PUBLISHING
THOMAS HARMSWORTH
J H HAYNES & CO LTD
JANE'S INFO GROUP
LAKESIDE PUBNS
BILL LEESON
LINEWRIGHTS LTD
CHRIS LLOYD SALES
MARITIME BOOKS
MARLBOROUGH BOOKS
MERLIN BOOKS LTD
MIDLAND COUNTIES LTD
JOHN MURRAY PUB LTD
ANTHONY NELSON LTD
NEWTON PUBLISHERS
MICHAEL O'MARA BOOKS
ORIFLAMME PUBLISHING
ORKNEY PRESS LTD
OWL PRESS
PEN & SWORD BOOKS

COLIN A PERRY LTD
PHOTOBOOK INFO SERV
PICTON PUBLISHING
PROMOTIONAL
  REPRINT
QUOTES LTD
REED CONSUMER ILLUS
THOMAS REED PUB LTD
RES INS CONFLICT/TER
SAGE PUBLICATIONS
SAMSON BOOKS LTD
SHIRE PUBLICATIONS
SILVER LINK PUB LTD
SMITH GRYPHON LTD
SPA BOOKS LTD
SPELLMOUNT LTD
SPOKESMAN BOOKS
SQUARE ONE PUB
A H STOCKWELL LTD
ALAN SUTTON PUB LTD
THAMES & HUDSON
  LTD
THORNHILL PRESS LTD
THE TOAT PRESS
TURPIN DISTRIBUTION
UNI OF EXETER PRESS
VERULAM PUB LTD
VINE HOUSE DIST
WINDROW & GREENE

Music
ACADEMIC & UNIV PUB
ALLARDYCE BARNETT
ALSTON BOOKS
APPLEFORD PUB GROUP
APPLETREE PRESS LTD
ASHGATE PUB GROUP
BARN DANCE PUB LTD
B T BATSFORD LTD
A & C BLACK LTD
BLACK SPRING PRESS
BLACKWELL PUB LTD
BLAKE PUBLISHING LTD
BOOSEY & HAWKES LTD
MARION BOYARS PUB
BRAINIAC BOOKS LTD
BROADSIDE
CALDER PUB LTD
CARLTON BOOKS
CELEBRATION SERV
  LTD
COLLETS
COLLINS & BROWN
CONCORDIA PUB LTD
CONSTABLE & CO LTD
CORK UNI PRESS
CREATION PRESS
DALENNAU
ANDRE DEUTSCH
JOHN DONALD PUB LTD
DRAGONS WORLD LTD
DYLLANSOW TRURAN
EAST WEST PUB LTD
ELEMENT BOOKS LTD
AIDAN ELLIS PUB
FABER & FABER
FACTS ON FILE
GALE RESEARCH INT
MARY GLASGOW PUB
GUINNESS PUBLISHING
ROBERT HALE LTD
HARVARD UNIV PRESS
HYMNS ANCIENT &
  MOD
INT MUSIC PUB
KAHN & AVERILL
KINGSWAY PUB
LAMBENT BOOKS
LAWRENCE & WISHART
LEISHMAN & TAUSSIG
CHRIS LLOYD SALES

LONGMAN GROUP UK
  LTD
B MCCALL BARBOUR
MCCRIMMON
  PUBLISHING
MAINSTREAM PUB CO
PETER MARCAN PUB
KEVIN MAYHEW LTD
MERCIER PRESS LTD
MERLION PUBLISHING
METHODIST
  PUBLISHING
MOORLEY'S PRINT PUB
MUSIC PRESS
ANTHONY NELSON LTD
NOVELLO & CO LTD
NOVEMBER BOOKS
OMNIBUS PRESS
ORIEL/WELSH ARTS CNL
PEARTREE
  PUBLICATION
PICTON PUBLISHING
PLEXUS PUBLISHING
PRISM PRESS
PRITAM BOOKS
PROMOTIONAL
  REPRINT
QUARTET BOOKS LTD
WILLIAM REEVES LTD
RHINEGOLD PUB LTD
ROBSON BOOKS
ROSSLYN PUBLISHING
ROUNDHOUSE PUB LTD
SALTIRE SOCIETY
SCHOFIELD & SIMS LTD
SHAKTI
  COMMUNICATION
SHIRE PUBLICATIONS
SMITH GRYPHON LTD
STAINER & BELL LTD
TFH PUBLICATIONS
THAMES & HUDSON
  LTD
TOBIN MUSIC
VINE HOUSE DIST
VIRGIN PUBLISHING
WARD LOCK EDUC CO
WATERLOW INFO SERV
XANADU PUBLICATIONS

Natural History
ACADEMIC & UNIV PUB
AIRLIFE PUBLISHING
ALADDIN BOOKS LTD
APPLETREE PRESS LTD
ASHFORD BUCHAN
ASHGATE PUB GROUP
BBC BOOKS
BEE BOOKS NEW & OLD
A & C BLACK LTD
BLACKWELL SCIENTIFIC
BOOK REP & DIST LTD
BOOKSPEED
BOXTREE LTD
BRIGHT BOOKS LTD
BRITISH ENTOMOL SOC
CAB INTERNATIONAL
CANONGATE PRESS PLC
CARLTON BOOKS
CHALKSOFT LTD
CHILTON DESIGNS
E W CLASSEY LTD
COLLINS & BROWN
CONSTABLE & CO LTD
COUNTYVISE LTD
THE CROWOOD PRESS
DALESMAN PUB CO LTD
TERENCE DALTON LTD
DAVID & CHARLES PLC
CHRISTOPHER DAVIES
ANDRE DEUTSCH
DORLING KINDERSLEY

AIDAN ELLIS PUB
ENSIGN PUBLICATIONS
EUROBOOK LTD
EX LIBRIS PRESS
FACTS ON FILE
W H FREEMAN & CO
  LTD
GAIA BOOKS LTD
GREEN BOOKS
GRISEWOOD &
  DEMPSEY
GUINNESS PUBLISHING
ROBERT HALE LTD
HARLEY BOOKS
HARPERCOLLINS
  GENREF
HARVARD UNIV PRESS
THE HERB SOCIETY
THE HERBERT PRESS
ALISON HODGE PUB
IMMEL PUBLISHING
  LTD
IMPACT BOOKS
INT BEE RESEARCH ASS
JARROLD PUBLISHING
JOHNSTON & BACON
KEGAN PAUL INT
KNIGHTSCROSS LTD
LAKESIDE PUBNS
LEISHMAN & TAUSSIG
CHARLES LETTS & CO
LITTLE BROWN & CO
LLOYD'S OF LONDON
MELIA PUB SERVICES
MERROW PUBLISHING
  CO
MILLBANK BOOKS LTD
MIT PRESS LTD
MOMENTA PUB CO LTD
MOORLAND PUB CO
  LTD
MULTIMEDIA BOOKS
  LTD
NATURAL HIST BOOK
  SV
NATURAL HIST
  MUSEUM
ANTHONY NELSON LTD
THE O'BRIEN PRESS
OCTAGON PRESS
ORKNEY PRESS LTD
PACKARD PUB LTD
PENNY PRESS
PION LTD
PRISM PRESS
PROMOTIONAL
  REPRINT
PRYOR PUBLICATIONS
QUOTES LTD
REED CONSUMER ILLUS
RICHMOND PUB CO LTD
ROBINSON PUBLISHING
ROBSON BOOKS
ROUNDHOUSE PUB LTD
SAINSBURY PUB LTD
SHIRE PUBLICATIONS
SIGMA PRESS
SMITH GRYPHON LTD
SPORTSMAN'S PRESS
SPRINGER-VERLAG
STACEY
  INTERNATIONAL
STOBART DAVIES LTD
ORIEL STRINGER
SWEETHAWS PRESS
TABB HOUSE
TFH PUBLICATIONS
THAMES & HUDSON
  LTD
VERULAM PUB LTD
WEST COUNTRY BOOKS
WHITTET BOOKS LTD

WORDSWORTH
  EDITIONS
WORLD LEISURE MKTG

Nautical
AEDIFICAMUS PRESS
AIRLIFE PUBLISHING
ASHGATE PUB GROUP
BARKER & HOWARD
  LTD
BARNACLE MARINE
  LTD
A & C BLACK LTD
BROWN SON &
  FERGUSON
CONSTABLE & CO LTD
CONWAY MARITIME
THE CROWOOD PRESS
DAVID & CHARLES PLC
JOHN DONALD PUB LTD
DYLLANSOW TRURAN
AIDAN ELLIS PUB
ENSIGN PUBLICATIONS
FABER & FABER
FERNHURST BOOKS
J H HAYNES & CO LTD
IMRAY LAURIE & NORIE
JANE'S INFO GROUP
KEGAN PAUL INT
BILL LEESON
CHRIS LLOYD SALES
MARITIME BOOKS
MERLIN BOOKS LTD
MILLBANK BOOKS LTD
ANTHONY NELSON LTD
ORKNEY PRESS LTD
PHOTOBOOK INFO SERV
PROMOTIONAL
  REPRINT
QUOTES LTD
THOMAS REED PUB LTD
ROUNDHOUSE PUB LTD
SB PUBLICATIONS
SHIP PICTORIAL PUB
SILVER LINK PUB LTD
SPELLMOUNT LTD
SQUARE ONE PUB
A H STOCKWELL LTD
UNI OF EXETER PRESS
VINE HOUSE DIST
WILLOWBRIDGE PUB
WITHERBY & CO LTD

Philosophy
ACADEMIC & UNIV PUB
ACADEMY GROUP LTD
AGORA BOOKS
AIRLIFT BOOK CO
AK DISTRIBUTION
ALIF INTERNATIONAL
THE AMATE PRESS
APPLEFORD PUB GROUP
ARIS & PHILLIPS LTD
ASHGATE PUB GROUP
ASHGROVE PRESS
BARTON HOUSE PUB
BESHARA
  PUBLICATIONS
BIBLIAGORA
BLACKWELL PUB LTD
BOOK REP & DIST LTD
MARION BOYARS PUB
THE BRITISH ACADEMY
KYLE CATHIE LTD
CCBI PUBLICATIONS
CENTAUR PRESS LTD
DEBORAH CHARLES
  PUB
CHARTWELL-BRATT
CLARIDGE PRESS
LLOYD COLE

CONSTABLE & CO LTD
CRANSWICK PRESS
EAST WEST PUB LTD
EDINBURGH UNIV PRESS
ELEMENT BOOKS LTD
AIDAN ELLIS PUB
EVENLODE BOOK DIST
FOREST
L N FOWLER & CO LTD
GATEWAY BOOKS
GMP PUBLISHERS LTD
GOTHIC IMAGE PUB
GRACEWING/FOWLER
HARVARD UNIV PRESS
HEADQUARTERS PUB CO
HONEYGLEN PUB LTD
HYDEN HOUSE LTD
ICA PUBLISHING
INDEXREACH LTD
INTELLECT
INTERVARSITY PRESS
JONES & BARTLETT PUB
RICHARD KAY PUB
KEGAN PAUL INT
KNIGHTSCROSS LTD
LEISHMAN & TAUSSIG
LIBERTARIAN ALLIANCE
LLANERCH PUBLISHERS
BARRY LONG FOUND
LONGMAN GROUP UK LTD
LUCIS PRESS LTD
MANCHESTER UNI PRESS
MERCIER PRESS LTD
MERLIN BOOKS LTD
MIT PRESS LTD
MOMENTA PUB CO LTD
MOTILAL BOOKS
OCTAGON PRESS
ONEWORLD PUB
OPEN GATE PRESS
OPEN UNIV PRESS
PALLADIO PRESS
PATHFINDER PRESS
PAUPERS' PRESS
PLUTO PUBLISHING
PREMIER BOOK MKTNG
PRISM PRESS
PROMETHEUS BOOKS UK
QUARTET BOOKS LTD
ROUTLEDGE
SCOTTISH ACAD PRESS
SEND THE LIGHT
SHAKTI COMMUNICATION
SHARE INTERNATIONAL
SHEPHEARD-WALWYN
SPRINGER-VERLAG
RUDOLF STEINER PRESS
TABB HOUSE
TAPROBANE LTD
TEMPLE PRESS LTD
THAMES & HUDSON LTD
THOEMMES PRESS
TURNAROUND
TURPIN DISTRIBUTION
UNI OF WALES PRESS
VCH PUB (UK) LTD
VERITAS PUBLICATIONS
VERSO
VILLIERS PUB LTD
VOLTAIRE FOUNDATION
WARBURG INSTITUTE
WINDHORSE PUB
WISDOM BOOKS
ZENO

Photography
HARRY N ABRAMS INC
AIRLIFE PUBLISHING
AIRLIFT BOOK CO
ANAYA PUBLISHERS
ART DATA
AURUM PRESS LTD
BELLEW PUBLISHING
BFP BOOKS
BLACKWELL PUB LTD
BLOODAXE BOOKS
BOXTREE LTD
THE BRITISH COUNCIL
BUTTERWORTH-HEINEMAN
CALDER PUB LTD
CANONGATE PRESS PLC
CARLTON BOOKS
ZELDA CHEATLE PRESS
LLOYD COLE
COLLINS & BROWN
CONSTABLE & CO LTD
CORNERHOUSE PUB
DALENNAU
DALESMAN PUB CO LTD
DAVID & CHARLES PLC
ANDRE DEUTSCH
DORLING KINDERSLEY
DRAGONS WORLD LTD
AIDAN ELLIS PUB
ENSIGN PUBLICATIONS
EVENLODE BOOK DIST
GARNET PUB LTD
GMP PUBLISHERS LTD
GREY EDITIONS
GUINNESS PUBLISHING
H I MARKETING
J H HAYNES & CO LTD
THE HERBERT PRESS
HILMARTON MANOR
ALISON HODGE PUB
ICA PUBLISHING
IMPACT BOOKS
INTERNOS BOOKS
KOZMIK PRESS
LITTLE BROWN & CO
MELIA PUB SERVICES
MULTIMEDIA BOOKS LTD
NAT PORTRAIT GALLERY
NEWS PRODUCTIONS
PHAIDON PRESS LTD
PLEXUS PUBLISHING
PROMOTIONAL REPRINT
QUARTET BOOKS LTD
QUILLER PRESS LTD
REAKTION BOOKS LTD
REED CONSUMER ILLUS
THOMAS REED PUB LTD
RIVERS ORAM PRESS
RIZZOLI INT PUBNS
ROUNDHOUSE PUB LTD
A H STOCKWELL LTD
THAMES & HUDSON LTD
TURNAROUND
VINE HOUSE DIST
VIRAGO PRESS
VIRGIN PUBLISHING
WATERMARK PUB LTD
WEST COUNTRY BOOKS
WINDSOR BOOKS INT
WOLFHOUND PRESS

Physics
BROWN SON & FERGUSON
CHAPMAN & HALL
CHARTWELL-BRATT
CLARKE ASSOCIATES
CONSTABLE & CO LTD
DANIELS PUBLISHING
IOP PUBLISHING LTD
JAMES & JAMES LTD
JONES & BARTLETT PUB
KNIGHTSCROSS LTD
LONGMAN GROUP UK LTD
MANDRAKE
MOMENTA PUB CO LTD
THOMAS NELSON & SONS
PRISM PRESS
SCHOFIELD & SIMS LTD
SCOTTISH ACAD PRESS
SPRINGER-VERLAG
STANLEY THORNES PUB
TURPIN DISTRIBUTION
VCH PUB (UK) LTD
WARD LOCK EDUC CO
WORLD SCIENTIFIC PUB

Poetry
ACAIR LTD
AGENDA & EDITIONS
AGORA BOOKS
AIRLIFT BOOK CO
AK DISTRIBUTION
ALLARDYCE BARNETT
ALLOWAY PUB LTD
THE AMATE PRESS
ANVIL PRESS POETRY
APPLETREE PRESS LTD
ASHGROVE PRESS
AURUM PRESS LTD
BELLEW PUBLISHING
BERTIE RAMIFICATIONS
BLACKWELL PUB LTD
BLOODAXE BOOKS
BOOK MARKETING ASSOC
MARION BOYARS PUB
BROWN SON & FERGUSON
CALDER PUB LTD
CANONGATE PRESS PLC
CARCANET PRESS
J L CARR
KYLE CATHIE LTD
CCBI PUBLICATIONS
CHADWYCK-HEALEY LTD
CHAPMANS PUB LTD
CHRISTCHURCH PUB LTD
ANTHONY CLARKE PUB
LLOYD COLE
CORK UNI PRESS
CREATION PRESS
CURLEW PUBLISHING CO
DAISY BOOKS
DALENNAU
THE DEDALUS PR (IR)
ANDRE DEUTSCH
DOWNLANDER PUB
DYLLANSOW TRURAN
EDINBURGH UNIV PRESS
EFFECTIVE PUBLISHING
ELEMENT BOOKS LTD
ENITHARMON PRESS
EVENLODE BOOK DIST
FABER & FABER
FOREST BOOKS
GAIRM PUBLICATIONS
GALLOPING DOG PRESS
GMP PUBLISHERS LTD
GREVATT & GREVATT
ROBERT HALE LTD
HEADQUARTERS PUB CO
HIPPOPOTAMUS PRESS
IRON PRESS
JARROLD PUBLISHING
KEGAN PAUL INT
KOZMIK PRESS
KROPOTKIN'S PUB
JAY LANDESMAN
LANGUAGE INFO CENTRE
LEISHMAN & TAUSSIG
LITTLEWOOD ARC
LLANERCH PUBLISHERS
LONGMAN GROUP UK LTD
LUATH PRESS LTD
B MCCALL BARBOUR
MANDEVILLE PRESS
THE MENARD PRESS
MERCIER PRESS LTD
MERLIN BOOKS LTD
MID NORTHUMBERLAND
MOORLEY'S PRINT PUB
E J MORTEN PUB
NAT POETRY FOUND
THOMAS NELSON & SONS
NEW BEACON BOOKS LTD
OCTAGON PRESS
THE OLEANDER PRESS
MICHAEL O'MARA BOOKS
ORIEL/WELSH ARTS CNL
ORKNEY PRESS LTD
PASSWORD (BOOKS) LTD
PEEPAL TREE BOOKS
PETERLOO POETS
PIG PRESS
PLAYWRIGHTS PUB CO
POETRY WALES PRESS
RAMSAY HEAD PRESS
BERTRAM ROTA LTD
ROUTLEDGE
SALTIRE SOCIETY
SCEPTRE PRESS LTD
SCHOFIELD & SIMS LTD
SCORPION PUBLISHING
SHAKTI COMMUNICATION
COLIN SMYTHE LTD
A H STOCKWELL LTD
STRIDE PUBLICATIONS
TABB HOUSE
TEMPLE PRESS LTD
STANLEY THORNES PUB
THORNHILL PRESS LTD
THORNTON'S OF OXFORD
TOUCAN PRESS
TRIPLE CAT PUB
TURNAROUND
VIRAGO PRESS
WELLSWEEP PRESS
WINDHORSE PUB
WOLFHOUND PRESS
YORICK BOOKS
ZENO

Politics & Current Affairs
ACADEMIC & UNIV PUB
AK DISTRIBUTION
ALIF INTERNATIONAL
AMNESTY PUBLICATIONS
ANGLO-GERMAN FOUND
APPLEFORD PUB GROUP
APPLETREE PRESS LTD

ARCHIVE RESEARCH LTD
ASHGATE PUB GROUP
ASHGROVE PRESS
AUSTICKS PUBLICATION
BELLEW PUBLISHING
BLACKWELL PUB LTD
BLOODAXE BOOKS
BOOK REP & DIST LTD
BOOKMARKS
BOOKSPEED
BOWKER-SAUR LTD
BOXTREE LTD
MARION BOYARS PUB
BRASSEY'S (UK) LTD
BRENTHAM PRESS
BRITISH NTH AMER RES
CAMDEN PRESS
CANONGATE PRESS PLC
CARNEGIE PUB LTD
FRANK CASS & CO LTD
CATHOLIC INSTITUTE
CAVENDISH PUBLISHING
CCBI PUBLICATIONS
CHADWYCK-HEALEY LTD
W & R CHAMBERS LTD
CHAPMANS PUB LTD
CHARTWELL-BRATT
CHRISTCHURCH PUB LTD
CLARIDGE PRESS
LLOYD COLE
COLLINS & BROWN
COMM RACIAL EQUALITY
CONSERVATIVE CENTRAL
CORK UNI PRESS
DOD'S PARLIAMENTARY
DUNROD PRESS
EDINBURGH UNIV PRESS
EOTHEN PRESS
EUROPA PUBS LTD
EUROPEAN SCHOOLBOOKS
FABER & FABER
FABIAN SOCIETY
FACTS ON FILE
FOREST
GATEWAY BOOKS
GILL & MACMILLAN LTD
GMP PUBLISHERS LTD
GOODAY STUDIOS LTD
GREEN BOOKS
GROSVENOR BOOKS
HARVARD UNIV PRESS
HLT PUBLICATIONS
C HURST & CO PUB LTD
ICC UNITED KINGDOM
INDEXREACH LTD
INTERVARSITY PRESS
RICHARD KAY PUB
KEGAN PAUL INT
JESSICA KINGSLEY PUB
KROPOTKIN'S PUB
KUPERARD LTD
LAKESIDE PUBNS
LATIN AMERICA BUREAU
LAWRENCE & WISHART
LEADING EDGE PRESS
LEISHMAN & TAUSSIG
LIBERTARIAN ALLIANCE
LONGMAN GROUP UK LTD
MANCHESTER UNI PRESS

THE MENARD PRESS
MERCIER PRESS LTD
MERLIN BOOKS LTD
MINORITY RIGHTS GRP
MIT PRESS LTD
MOZAMBIQUE INSTITUTE
JOHN MURRAY PUB LTD
NCVO PUBLICATIONS
NEW BEACON BOOKS LTD
NEW CLARION PRESS
THE O'BRIEN PRESS
ONEWORLD PUB
OPEN GATE PRESS
OPEN UNIV PRESS
ORBACH & CHAMBERS
OVERSEAS DEVEL INST
OXFAM
PATHFINDER PRESS
PAUPERS' PRESS
PINTER PUBLISHERS
PLUTO PUBLISHING
POLICY STUDIES INST
PRISM PRESS
QUARTET BOOKS LTD
RES INS CONFLICT/TER
RIVERS ORAM PRESS
ROUNDHOUSE PUB LTD
ROUTLEDGE
SAGE PUBLICATIONS
SAQI BOOKS
SCARLET PRESS
SCORPION PUBLISHING
SHEPHEARD-WALWYN
HILARY SHIPMAN
SPOKESMAN BOOKS
I B TAURIS & CO LTD
STANLEY THORNES PUB
THORNTON'S OF OXFORD
TURNAROUND
TURPIN DISTRIBUTION
UK COUN HUMAN RIGHTS
UNI OF EXETER PRESS
UNI OF WALES PRESS
VERSO
VIRAGO PRESS
VOLCANO PRESS LTD
WHITING & BIRCH LTD
WORLD LEISURE MKTG
WRITERS & SCHOLARS
ZENO

Psychology
ACADEMIC & UNIV PUB
AGORA BOOKS
AIRLIFT BOOK CO
AK DISTRIBUTION
AMERICAN PSYCH PRESS
ASHGROVE PRESS
BARTON HOUSE PUB
BLACKWELL PUB LTD
BLACKWELL SCIENTIFIC
BOOK REP & DIST LTD
MARION BOYARS PUB
BRITISH PSYCH SOC
CHANGE PUBLICATIONS
CHAPMAN & HALL
CHILTON DESIGNS
LLOYD COLE
CONSTABLE & CO LTD
CORK UNI PRESS
DANIELS PUBLISHING
ELEMENT BOOKS LTD
ELLIOT RIGHT WAY
ELM PUBLICATIONS
LAWRENCE ERLBAUM ASS

EVENLODE BOOK DIST
FINDHORN PRESS
FOREST
L N FOWLER & CO LTD
W H FREEMAN & CO LTD
GATEWAY BOOKS
GMP PUBLISHERS LTD
GOTHIC IMAGE PUB
HARVARD UNIV PRESS
HAWTHORN PRESS
HUMAN KINETICS PUB
ICA PUBLISHING
INTELLECT
ARTHUR JAMES LTD
H KARNAC BOOKS LTD
KEGAN PAUL INT
JESSICA KINGSLEY PUB
KOGAN PAGE LTD
KUPERARD LTD
LAMBENT BOOKS
LIBERTARIAN ALLIANCE
LIFESPACE PUBLISHING
LONGMAN GROUP UK LTD
MIT PRESS LTD
MOMENTA PUB CO LTD
MONARCH PUB
E J MORTEN PUB
MULTILINGUAL MATTERS
MULTIMEDIA BOOKS LTD
OCTAGON PRESS
ONEWORLD PUB
OPEN GATE PRESS
OPEN UNIV PRESS
ORBACH & CHAMBERS
PIATKUS BOOKS
PITMAN PUBLISHING
PLUTO PUBLISHING
PRISM PRESS
PROTON PUB HOUSE LTD
PSYCHOLOGY NEWS
ROSENDALE PRESS LTD
ROUTLEDGE
SAGE PUBLICATIONS
SPCK
SOLOMON INT PUB CO
SPRINGER-VERLAG
A H STOCKWELL LTD
TAPROBANE LTD
THAMES & HUDSON LTD
TURNAROUND
TURPIN DISTRIBUTION
VERITAS PUBLICATIONS
VINE PUBLISHING LTD
VIRAGO PRESS
WHITING & BIRCH LTD
WHURR PUBLISHERS LTD
WINSLOW PRESS

Reference Books
AA PUBLISHING
ACE BOOKS
ADAMSON BOOKS
AEROSPACE PROFILES
AIRLIFT BOOK CO
AMERICAN TECH PUB
ANTIQUE COLLECTORS
APPLEFORD PUB GROUP
ASHFORD BUCHAN
ASHGATE PUB GROUP
ASLIB
ATLANTIC EUROPE PUB
AUTODATA LTD
BERNARD BABANI LTD
BACSA

BELLEW PUBLISHING
BENN BUSINESS INFO
A & C BLACK LTD
BLACKWELL PUB LTD
BOOK REP & DIST LTD
BOOKSELLERS ASSOC
BOOKSPEED
BOWKER-SAUR LTD
BOXTREE LTD
BRASSEY'S (UK) LTD
NICHOLAS BREALEY PUB
THE BRITISH COUNCIL
BURKE'S PEERAGE
CAMBRIDGE UNIV PRESS
CARCANET PRESS
CARLTON BOOKS
CARRICK MEDIA
KYLE CATHIE LTD
CBD RESEARCH LTD
CCBI PUBLICATIONS
CHADWYCK-HEALEY LTD
W & R CHAMBERS LTD
CHAPMAN & HALL
CHARTWELL-BRATT
CHRISTIAN BOOKSTALL
CHURCH HOUSE PUB
CLARKE ASSOCIATES
JAMES CLARKE & CO
CLEMENT PUBS LTD
LLOYD COLE
PETER COLLIN PUB LTD
CONSTABLE & CO LTD
CONWAY MARITIME
CRONER PUBLICATIONS
CRYSTAL PALACE FOUND
DAVID & CHARLES PLC
DAWSON UK LTD
DEBRETTS PEERAGE LTD
ANDRE DEUTSCH
DORLING KINDERSLEY
DRAGONS WORLD LTD
DUN & BRADSTREET LTD
DYLLANSOW TRURAN
EAGLE BOOKS
ECONOMIST BOOKS
ELC PUBLISHING LTD
ELLIOT RIGHT WAY
AIDAN ELLIS PUB
ELSEVIER SCIENCE PUB
EMAP BUSINESS PUB
ENCYC BRITANNICA LTD
EUROMONITOR PLC
EUROPA PUBS LTD
EUROPEAN SCHOOLBOOKS
EXECUTIVE GRAPEVINE
FACTS ON FILE
1ST WORLD PUB LTD
FLIGHT DIRECTORIES
W FOULSHAM & CO LTD
GAIRM PUBLICATIONS
GALE RESEARCH INT
GMP PUBLISHERS LTD
BRIAN GOOCH LTD
GRAHAM & TROTMAN LTD
GREENCROFT BOOKS
GRISEWOOD & DEMPSEY
GUINNESS PUBLISHING
H I MARKETING
ROBERT HALE LTD
HALI PUBLICATIONS
HARLEY BOOKS
THOMAS HARMSWORTH

HARPERCOLLINS BARTH
HARPERCOLLINS GENREF
HARVARD UNIV PRESS
HEALTH EDUC AUTH
HGM PUBLICATIONS
HILLER AIRGUNS
HILMARTON MANOR ALISON HODGE PUB
HOLLIS DIRECTORIES
HOW TO BOOKS LTD
IBC PUBLISHING LTD
IC PUBLICATIONS LTD
ICC UNITED KINGDOM IMAGES
INT BEE RESEARCH ASS
INT LABOUR OFFICE
IOP PUBLISHING LTD
LEON JAEGGI & SONS
JOHNSTON & BACON
JONES & BARTLETT PUB
RICHARD JOSEPH PUB
KEGAN PAUL INT
KOGAN PAGE LTD
LADYBIRD BOOKS LTD
LEGALEASE
LEISHMAN & TAUSSIG
LLANERCH PUBLISHERS
LONGMAN GROUP UK LTD
MACMILLAN DIST LTD
MARC EUROPE
PETER MARCAN PUB
MECHANICAL ENG PUB
MERROW PUBLISHING CO
METAL BULLETIN PLC
MIT PRESS LTD
MOMENTA PUB CO LTD
MOTILAL BOOKS
MULTIMEDIA BOOKS LTD
NAG PRESS
NATURAL HIST BOOK SV
NCVO PUBLICATIONS
ANTHONY NELSON LTD
THE OLEANDER PRESS
MICHAEL O'MARA BOOKS
ORBACH & CHAMBERS
PHARMACEUTICAL PRESS
PICTON PUBLISHING
PILLAR PUBLICATIONS
PINHORNS
PINTER PUBLISHERS
PITMAN PUBLISHING
PRISM PRESS
PROMOTIONAL REPRINT
QUILLER PRESS LTD
RAMBORO BOOKS
REED CONSUMER ILLUS
REED INFO SERVICES
RHINEGOLD PUB LTD
RICHMOND PUB CO LTD
ROUNDHOUSE PUB LTD
ROUTLEDGE
SAGE PUBLICATIONS
DAVID ST JOHN THOMAS
ST PAUL'S BIBLIO
SCARLET PRESS
SCHOFIELD & SIMS LTD
SCORPION PUBLISHING
SEMICON INDEXES
SEND THE LIGHT
SHIRE PUBLICATIONS
SILVER LINK PUB LTD
WILLIAM SNYDER PUB
SPRINGER-VERLAG

STACEY INTERNATIONAL
I B TAURIS & CO LTD
TELEGRAPH BOOKS
TFPL PUBLISHING
THAMES & HUDSON LTD
THORNHILL PRESS LTD
TOLLEY PUBLISHING CO
TOUCAN PRESS
TURNAROUND
VACATION WORK
VCH PUB (UK) LTD
VERBATIM
VERULAM PUB LTD
VIRGIN PUBLISHING
VISUAL ARTS PUB
WATERLOW INFO SERV
THE WATTS GROUP
OWEN WELLS PUB CO
WEST COUNTRY BOOKS
J WHITAKER & SONS
JOHN WILSON BOOKS
JOHN WISDEN & CO LTD
WISEBUY PUBLICATIONS
WITHERBY & CO LTD
WORDSWORTH EDITIONS
WORLD BOOK CHILD INT
WORLD LEISURE MKTG ZENO

Religion & Theology

ACADEMIC & UNIV PUB
AFRICA CHRIST PRESS
AGORA BOOKS
AIRLIFT BOOK CO
ALIF INTERNATIONAL
THE AMATE PRESS
AMBASSADOR PROD LTD
APPLEFORD PUB GROUP
ARCHIVAL FACSIMILES
ARIS & PHILLIPS LTD
ASHGROVE PRESS
AUKANA TRUST
BAHAI PUBLISHING
BANNER OF TRUTH
BELLEW PUBLISHING
BESHARA PUBLICATIONS
BIBLE READING FELLOW
BIBLE SOCIETY
A & C BLACK LTD
BLACKWELL PUB LTD
THE BRITISH ACADEMY
BUDDHIST PUB GROUP
CARCANET PRESS
CARGATE PRESS
CARLTON BOOKS
CASSELL PLC
KYLE CATHIE LTD
CATHOLIC INSTITUTE
CCBI PUBLICATIONS
CELEBRATION SERV LTD
W & R CHAMBERS LTD
CHARTWELL-BRATT
CHRISTIAN BOOK PROMO
CHRISTIAN BOOKSTALL
CHRISTIAN LIT CRUS
CHURCH HOUSE PUB
CHURCH LIT ASSN
CLARIDGE PRESS
T & T CLARK LTD
ANTHONY CLARKE PUB
JAMES CLARKE & CO

COLUMBA BOOK SERVICE
CONCORDIA PUB LTD
CONSTABLE & CO LTD
CRANSWICK PRESS
DARTON LONGMAN TODD
DAVID & CHARLES PLC
EAST WEST PUB LTD
EFFECTIVE PUBLISHING
ELEMENT BOOKS LTD
EUROBOOK LTD
EVANGELICAL PRESS
EVANGELICAL PR WALES
EVENLODE BOOK DIST
FAMILY PUBLICATIONS
FINDHORN PRESS
FLORIS BOOKS
FOUR COURTS PRESS
GILL & MACMILLAN LTD
GO TEACH PUB
GOLDEN AGE BOOKS
GOODAY STUDIOS LTD
GRACEWING/FOWLER
GRESHAM BOOKS LTD
GREVATT & GREVATT
GROSVENOR BOOKS
GROVE BOOKS LTD
H I MARKETING
PETER HALBAN PUB
HARPERCOLLINS RELIG
HEADQUARTERS PUB CO
HUGHES & COLEMAN LTD
HYMNS ANCIENT & MOD
INTERVARSITY PRESS
ISLAMIC TEXTS SOC
JAMES & JAMES LTD
ARTHUR JAMES LTD
JAY BOOKS
JEWISH CHRONICLE PUB
KEGAN PAUL INT
KINGSWAY PUB
KNIGHTSCROSS LTD
KUPERARD LTD
LEISHMAN & TAUSSIG
LLANERCH PUBLISHERS
P M LLEWELLYN CO
LOCHEE PUB LTD
LONGMAN GROUP UK LTD
LUTTERWORTH PRESS
B MCCALL BARBOUR
MCCRIMMON PUBLISHING
KEVIN MAYHEW LTD
MERCIER PRESS LTD
JOHN METCALFE PUB
METHODIST PUBLISHING
MINORITY RIGHTS GRP
MONARCH PUB
MOORLEY'S PRINT PUB
MOTILAL BOOKS
NAT CHRIST EDUC COUN
ANTHONY NELSON LTD
THOMAS NELSON & SONS
NORHEIMSUND BOOKS
NOVA DISTRIBUTION
OCTAGON PRESS
THE OFFICE LONDON
OMF BOOKS
ONEWORLD PUB
OPEN BIBLE TRUST
OPEN UNIV PRESS
PALLADIO PRESS

PEARTREE PUBLICATION
PLUTO PUBLISHING
PRISM PRESS
PRITAM BOOKS
PROMETHEUS BOOKS UK
QUAKER HOME SERVICE
GEORGE RONALD PUB
ROUNDHOUSE PUB LTD
ROUTLEDGE
RUSHWORTH LIT LTD
SAGE PUBLICATIONS
SAINT ANDREW PRESS
ST PAUL'S PUB
SCHOFIELD & SIMS LTD
SCH ORIENTAL/ AFRICAN
SCM PRESS LTD
SCOTTISH ACAD PRESS
SCRIPTURE GIFT MISS
SCRIPTURE PRESS
SCRIPTURE UNION PUB
SEND THE LIGHT
SHAKTI COMMUNICATION
SHARE INTERNATIONAL
SHARON PUBLICATIONS
SHEED & WARD LTD
SHEFFIELD ACD PRESS
SHEPHEARD-WALWYN
SLG PRESS
SPCK
STACEY INTERNATIONAL
A H STOCKWELL LTD
STRIDE PUBLICATIONS
TA HA PUBLISHERS LTD
TAPROBANE LTD
TEECOLL PUBLICATIONS
TEMPLE PRESS LTD
THAMES & HUDSON LTD
THARPA PUBLICATIONS
THEOSOPHICAL PUB LTD
STANLEY THORNES PUB
UNI OF EXETER PRESS
UNI OF WALES PRESS
VCH PUB (UK) LTD
VERITAS PUBLICATIONS
VILLIERS PUB LTD
VINE PUBLISHING LTD
VOLCANO PRESS LTD
WARD LOCK EDUC CO
J WHITAKER & SONS
WHITE EAGLE PUB
WINDHORSE PUB
WISDOM BOOKS
WOMEN'S PRESS
WORD PUBLISHING
ZENO

School Textbooks

ABCO DESIGN LTD
ACCENT EDUCATIONAL
ALIF INTERNATIONAL
ANN ARBOR PUBLISHERS
BARN DANCE PUB LTD
BRIGHT BOOKS LTD
CAMBRIDGE UNIV PRESS
CARCANET PRESS
CASSELL PLC
CAUSEWAY PRESS LTD
CHALKSOFT LTD
CHARTWELL-BRATT
CHILDREN'S SOCIETY
DALENNAU
DANIELS PUBLISHING

DP PUBLICATIONS LTD
DYLLANSOW TRURAN
EDUC CO OF IRELAND
ELM PUBLICATIONS
LAWRENCE ERLBAUM ASS
EUROPEAN SCHOOLBOOKS
EVANS BROTHERS LTD
FOLENS PUBLISHERS
FORBES PUB LTD
FRAMEWORK PRESS
GAIRM PUBLICATIONS
GILL & MACMILLAN LTD
GINN & CO LTD
MARY GLASGOW PUB
GRACEWING/FOWLER
GREENCROFT BOOKS
HARPERCOLLINS EDUC
HEALTH EDUC AUTH
HLT PUBLICATIONS
HYMNS ANCIENT & MOD
KNIGHTSCROSS LTD
LEARNING DEV AIDS
LEISHMAN & TAUSSIG
LIFE EDUCATION UK
LONGMAN GROUP UK LTD
MANCHESTER UNI PRESS
KEVIN MAYHEW LTD
JOHN MURRAY PUB LTD
NAT CHRIST EDUC COUN
THOMAS NELSON & SONS
JAMES NISBET & CO
NORTHWICK PUBLISHERS
ORIFLAMME PUBLISHING
PENNY PRESS
POETRY WALES PRESS
PRITAM BOOKS
THOMAS REED PUB LTD
RICHMOND PUB CO LTD
ROUTLEDGE
SCHOFIELD & SIMS LTD
SCHOLASTIC PUB LTD
SODANEY PUBLISHERS
TARQUIN PUBLICATIONS
STANLEY THORNES PUB
WARD LOCK EDUC CO
J WHITAKER & SONS

Science Fiction
BOXTREE LTD
BRAINIAC BOOKS LTD
CANONGATE PRESS PLC
COLD TONNAGE BOOKS
CONSTABLE & CO LTD
GMP PUBLISHERS LTD
KINGSWAY PUB
LITTLE BROWN & CO
NEW ERA PUB LTD
ORIFLAMME PUBLISHING
ORKNEY PRESS LTD
PAUPERS' PRESS
ROBINSON PUBLISHING
SEVERN HOUSE PUB LTD
COLIN SMYTHE LTD
A H STOCKWELL LTD
VINE HOUSE DIST
VIRGIN PUBLISHING
WELLSWEEP PRESS
WOLFHOUND PRESS

WOMEN'S PRESS
XANADU PUBLICATIONS

Scientific & Technical
ABCO DESIGN LTD
ACADEMIC BOOK ASSOC
AMERICAN TECH PUB
ARCHIVAL FACSIMILES
ARIAN PUBLICATIONS
ASHGATE PUB GROUP
ASLIB
BERNARD BABANI LTD
ROGER BAYLISS
BENN BUSINESS INFO
BLACKWELL SCIENTIFIC
BOOKS EXPRESS
BOWKER-SAUR LTD
BRITISH CERAMIC RES
THE BRITISH COUNCIL
BUTTERWORTH-HEINEMAN
CAB INTERNATIONAL
CHALKSOFT LTD
CHAPMAN & HALL
CHARTWELL-BRATT
CHILTON DESIGNS
CLARKE ASSOCIATES
COMPUTATIONAL MECH
COMPUTER STEP LTD
CONSTABLE & CO LTD
CRONER PUBLICATIONS
MARTIN DUNITZ LTD
ELECTRONICA BOOKS
ELSEVIER SCIENCE PUB
FACTS ON FILE
FLORIS BOOKS
FMJ BOOKS
FORBES PUB LTD
W H FREEMAN & CO LTD
FRIENDS OF THE EARTH
GALE RESEARCH INT
GATEWAY BOOKS
BRIAN GOOCH LTD
HAWK BOOKS LTD
HAWKER PUBLICATIONS
HEALTH EDUC AUTH
IFS LTD
INST OF ELEC ENGINE
INTELLECT
INTERCEPT LTD
INTERMEDIATE TEC PUB
INT BEE RESEARCH ASS
IOP PUBLISHING LTD
JAMES & JAMES LTD
JAY BOOKS
JONES & BARTLETT PUB
JESSICA KINGSLEY PUB
KNIGHTSCROSS LTD
KOGAN PAGE LTD
LAVIS MARKETING
LIBERTARIAN ALLIANCE
LIVERPOOL UNIV PRESS
LONGMAN GROUP UK LTD
MANDRAKE
MECHANICAL ENG PUB
MECKLER LTD
MERROW PUBLISHING CO
MICELLE PRESS
MIT PRESS LTD
MOMENTA PUB CO LTD
MOSBY-YEARBOOK EUR
NATURAL HIST BOOK SV
NEWTON PUBLISHERS

PARTHENON PUB GROUP
PENNY PRESS
PERGAMON PRESS LTD
PION LTD
PITMAN PUBLISHING
PORTLAND PRESS LTD
PRISM PRESS
RADCLIFFE MEDICAL
RADIO SOCIETY OF GB
RESEARCH STUDIES LTD
RICHMOND PUB CO LTD
RICS BOOKS
THE ROYAL SOCIETY
SCHOFIELD & SIMS LTD
SCIENCE MUSEUM
SCIENCE REVIEWS LTD
SCI & TECH BOOK SVCE
SCOTTISH ACAD PRESS
SEMICON INDEXES
WILLIAM SNYDER PUB
SPRINGER-VERLAG
RUDOLF STEINER PRESS
TARRAGON PRESS
THOMAS TELFORD LTD
TEXTILE INSTITUTE
STANLEY THORNES PUB
TURPIN DISTRIBUTION
VCH PUB (UK) LTD
VINE PUBLISHING LTD
WARD LOCK EDUC CO
WITHERBY & CO LTD
WOODHEAD PUBLISHING
WORLD SCIENTIFIC PUB

Scottish Interest
ACAIR LTD
AIRLIFE PUBLISHING
AK DISTRIBUTION
ALLOWAY PUB LTD
ALSTON BOOKS
APPLEFORD PUB GROUP
APPLETREE PRESS LTD
ASHFORD BUCHAN
BALNAIN BOOKS
B T BATSFORD LTD
BELLEW PUBLISHING
BENN BUSINESS INFO
BOOKSPEED
CALDER PUB LTD
CANONGATE PRESS PLC
CARCANET PRESS
CARRICK MEDIA
CCBI PUBLICATIONS
W & R CHAMBERS LTD
CHAPMANS PUB LTD
CHRISTCHURCH PUB LTD
CLAN BOOKS
CONSTABLE & CO LTD
CORDEE
JOHN DONALD PUB LTD
EDINBURGH UNIV PRESS
FAMEDRAM PUB LTD
FLORIS BOOKS
GAIRM PUBLICATIONS
ROBERT HALE LTD
HILMARTON MANOR
JARROLD PUBLISHING
JOHNSTON & BACON
KINGSCLERE PUB LTD
LANGUAGE INFO CENTRE
LITTLE BROWN & CO
LLANERCH PUBLISHERS
LOCHEE PUB LTD
LUATH PRESS LTD
MAINSTREAM PUB CO
MERCAT PRESS

JOHN MURRAY PUB LTD
OBERON BOOKS LTD
ORKNEY PRESS LTD
PINTER PUBLISHERS
PLUTO PUBLISHING
RAMSAY HEAD PRESS
ROBINSON PUBLISHING
ROUTLEDGE
SALTIRE SOCIETY
SCOTTISH ACAD PRESS
SCOTTISH TOUR BOARD
SHEPHEARD-WALWYN
SHIRE PUBLICATIONS
SPA BOOKS LTD
THAMES & HUDSON LTD
TRIPLE CAT PUB
WHITE COCKADE PUB
WORDSWORTH EDITIONS
GORDON WRIGHT PUB
XYLOPRESS LTD

Social Studies
ACADEMIC & UNIV PUB
ACE BOOKS
AK DISTRIBUTION
AMNESTY PUBLICATIONS
ANGLO-GERMAN FOUND
APPLETREE PRESS LTD
ASHGATE PUB GROUP
ASHGROVE PRESS
BARMARICK PUB
B T BATSFORD LTD
BLACKWELL PUB LTD
BOOK REP & DIST LTD
BOOKSPEED
MARION BOYARS PUB
BRASSEY'S (UK) LTD
THE BRITISH ACADEMY
CALDER PUB LTD
CALOUSTE GULBENKIAN
FRANK CASS & CO LTD
CAVENDISH PUBLISHING
CENTAUR PRESS LTD
CHALKSOFT LTD
DEBORAH CHARLES PUB
CHILDREN'S SOCIETY
CHILTON DESIGNS
COMM RACIAL EQUALITY
CRYSTAL PALACE FOUND
EDINBURGH UNIV PRESS
ELM PUBLICATIONS
EOTHEN PRESS
FABIAN SOCIETY
FAMILY POLICY ST CEN
FAMILY PUBLICATIONS
FOREST
GALE RESEARCH INT
GREENCROFT BOOKS
GROSVENOR BOOKS
HARVARD UNIV PRESS
HAWTHORN PRESS
HEALTH EDUC AUTH
HISTORICAL PUB LTD
HLT PUBLICATIONS
HONEYGLEN PUB LTD
HORTON PUB LTD
C HURST & CO PUB LTD
ARTHUR JAMES LTD
KEGAN PAUL INT
JESSICA KINGSLEY PUB
KINGSWAY PUB

KOGAN PAGE LTD
JAY LANDESMAN
LEISHMAN & TAUSSIG
JOHN LIBBEY & CO LTD
LIVERPOOL UNIV PRESS
MANCHESTER UNI PRESS
MOMENTA PUB CO LTD
MOTILAL BOOKS
MOZAMBIQUE INSTITUTE
NAT CHILDRENS BUREAU
NCVO PUBLICATIONS
THOMAS NELSON & SONS
NEW CLARION PRESS
NORTHCOTE HOUSE PUB
NOVEMBER BOOKS
OCTAGON PRESS
OPEN GATE PRESS
OPEN UNIV PRESS
OVERSEAS DEVEL INST
OXFAM
PATHFINDER PRESS
PATTEN PRESS
PAUPERS' PRESS
PEEPAL TREE BOOKS
PINTER PUBLISHERS
PION LTD
PLUTO PUBLISHING
POLICY STUDIES INST
PRISM PRESS
PROTON PUB HOUSE LTD
RADCLIFFE MEDICAL
RIVERS ORAM PRESS
ROUNDHOUSE PUB LTD
ROUTLEDGE
SAGE PUBLICATIONS
SARSEN PUBLISHING
SAUS PUBLICATIONS
SCOTTISH ACAD PRESS
SERPENT'S TAIL
HILARY SHIPMAN
SILENT BOOKS
SOCIAL CARE ASSN LTD
SPOKESMAN BOOKS
TAPROBANE LTD
STANLEY THORNES PUB
TURNAROUND
TURPIN DISTRIBUTION
UNI OF EXETER PRESS
VCH PUB (UK) LTD
VIRAGO PRESS
WARD LOCK EDUC CO
OWEN WELLS PUB CO
WHITE COCKADE PUB
WHITING & BIRCH LTD
WINSLOW PRESS

Sports & Games
AA PUBLISHING
AEDIFICAMUS PRESS
AESCULUS PRESS
AIRLIFE PUBLISHING
ANAYA PUBLISHERS
PETER ANDREW PUB CO
ANNUAL CONCEPTS LTD
ASA SWIMMING ENT LTD
ASHFORD BUCHAN
AURUM PRESS LTD
BALNAIN BOOKS
BARN DANCE PUB LTD
B T BATSFORD LTD
BIBLIAGORA
A & C BLACK LTD
BLACK FROG PRESS
BOXTREE LTD

BREEDON BOOKS
CANONGATE PRESS PLC
CARLTON BOOKS
CHAPMANS PUB LTD
CHILTON DESIGNS
CICERONE PRESS
CORDEE
PAUL H CROMPTON LTD
THE CROWOOD PRESS
CRYSTAL PALACE FOUND
DALESMAN PUB CO LTD
JOHN DONALD PUB LTD
ELLIOT RIGHT WAY
EMAP BUSINESS PUB
EQUESTRIAN MANG CON
EXPRESS NEWSPAPERS
FABER & FABER
FERNHURST BOOKS
FHG PUBLICATIONS LTD
FOLENS PUBLISHERS
W FOULSHAM & CO LTD
GOODALL PUB LTD
GUINNESS PUBLISHING
ROBERT HALE LTD
THOMAS HARMSWORTH
HARVEY MAP SERVICES
HEALTH EDUC AUTH
HILLER AIRGUNS
HUMAN KINETICS PUB
IMRAY LAURIE & NORIE
JARROLD PUBLISHING
JONES & BARTLETT PUB
KENSINGTON WEST LTD
KIME PUBLISHING
LENNARD ASSOCIATES
LITTLE BROWN & CO
LITTLE RED WITCH
CHRIS LLOYD SALES
MAINSTREAM PUB CO
MARLBOROUGH BOOKS
JOHN MURRAY PUB LTD
THOMAS NELSON & SONS
OLDCASTLE BOOKS LTD
PACKARD PUB LTD
PINTER PUBLISHERS
PISCES ANGLING PUB
PORTHILL PUBLISHERS
PREMIER BOOK MKTNG
PROMOTIONAL REPRINT
QUOTES LTD
R & B PUBLISHING
REED CONSUMER ILLUS
THOMAS REED PUB LTD
ROBSON BOOKS
RONALDSON PUB
SB PUBLICATIONS
SCARLET PRESS
SIGMA LEISURE
SMITH GRYPHON LTD
SPELLMOUNT LTD
SPORTSMAN'S PRESS
A H STOCKWELL LTD
TELEGRAPH BOOKS
THORNHILL PRESS LTD
TRAIL CREST PUB
VINE HOUSE DIST
VIRGIN PUBLISHING
JOHN WISDEN & CO LTD
WORLD LEISURE MKTG

Transport
ACADEMY BOOKS LTD
ACE BOOKS
AIRLIFE PUBLISHING
IAN ALLAN PUBLISHING
ANNUAL CONCEPTS LTD

ARGUS PUBLICATIONS
MARTIN BAIRSTOW
M & M BALDWIN
BAY VIEW BOOKS LTD
ROGER BAYLISS
BENN BUSINESS INFO
BREEDON BOOKS
BREWIN BOOK DIST
BROWN SON & FERGUSON
CAPITAL TRANSPORT
CARNEGIE PUB LTD
CHAPMAN & HALL
CHAPMANS PUB LTD
CHRISTCHURCH PUB LTD
CONWAY MARITIME
THOMAS COOK PUB
COUNTRYSIDE BOOKS
COUNTYVISE LTD
CRONER PUBLICATIONS
THE CROWOOD PRESS
DALTON WATSON BOOKS
DAVID & CHARLES PLC
ELLIOT RIGHT WAY
EMAP BUSINESS PUB
ENSIGN PUBLICATIONS
EX LIBRIS PRESS
EXPERT BOOKS
FAMEDRAM PUB LTD
FERNHURST BOOKS
FLIGHT DIRECTORIES
FRIENDS OF THE EARTH
GRANTA EDITIONS
GUINNESS PUBLISHING
H I MARKETING
J H HAYNES & CO LTD
IAN HENRY PUB LTD
HISTORICAL PUB LTD
HUTTON PRESS LTD
ICC UNITED KINGDOM
IMRAY LAURIE & NORIE
JANE'S INFO GROUP
JARROLD PUBLISHING
JERSEY ARTISTS LTD
KINGSMEAD PRESS
LANDSCAPE PRESS
LAWRENCE & WISHART
LEADING EDGE PRESS
LEISHMAN & TAUSSIG
LINEWRIGHTS LTD
CHRIS LLOYD SALES
LONDON TRANSPORT
MECHANICAL ENG PUB
MERLIN BOOKS LTD
MIDDLETON PRESS
MIDLAND COUNTIES LTD
MOMENTA PUB CO LTD
MOTOR RACING PUB LTD
MULTIMEDIA BOOKS LTD
NEWTON PUBLISHERS
OAKWOOD PRESS
ORIFLAMME PUBLISHING
J M PEARSON & SON
PHOTOBOOK INFO SERV
PICTON PUBLISHING
PINTER PUBLISHERS
PION LTD
PLATFORM 5 PUB LTD
POLICY STUDIES INST
THE POUND HOUSE
PROMOTIONAL REPRINT
QUOTES LTD
THOMAS REED PUB LTD
ROADMASTER PUB

ROUNDOAK PUBLISHING
DAVID ST JOHN THOMAS
SB PUBLICATIONS
SEWELLS INT
SHIRE PUBLICATIONS
SILVER LINK PUB LTD
WILLIAM SNYDER PUB
ALAN SUTTON PUB LTD
TRANSPORT BOOKMAN
TRANSPORT PUB CO LTD
TRANSPORT 2000
TWELVEHEADS PRESS
VELOCE PUBLISHING
VINE HOUSE DIST
WINDROW & GREENE
WITHERBY & CO LTD
WORLD LEISURE MKTG

University Textbooks
ABCO DESIGN LTD
ACCENT EDUCATIONAL
PETER ANDREW PUB CO
APPLEFORD PUB GROUP
ARIS & PHILLIPS LTD
ASHGATE PUB GROUP
BLACKWELL PUB LTD
BLACKWELL SCIENTIFIC
BLOODAXE BOOKS
BOOK REP & DIST LTD
BUTTERWORTH & CO LTD
CAB INTERNATIONAL
CANONGATE PRESS PLC
CARCANET PRESS
CAUSEWAY PRESS LTD
CAVENDISH PUBLISHING
CHANGE PUBLICATIONS
PAUL CHAPMAN PUB
DEBORAH CHARLES PUB
CHARTWELL-BRATT
CLASS PUBLISHING
ELM PUBLICATIONS
EOTHEN PRESS
LAWRENCE ERLBAUM ASS
EUROPEAN SCHOOLBOOKS
FORBES PUB LTD
W H FREEMAN & CO LTD
GAIRM PUBLICATIONS
GERBIL BOOKS
GILL & MACMILLAN LTD
GOWER MEDICAL PUB
GROTIUS PUB LTD
HARPERCOLLINS EDUC
HARPERCOLLINS HARCOL
HARVARD UNIV PRESS
HEALTH EDUC AUTH
HLT PUBLICATIONS
HUMAN KINETICS PUB
C HURST & CO PUB LTD
ICC UNITED KINGDOM
INT BEE RESEARCH ASS
INTERVARSITY PRESS
IOP PUBLISHING LTD
JONES & BARTLETT PUB
JESSICA KINGSLEY PUB
KNIGHTSCROSS LTD
KOGAN PAGE LTD
LA HAULE BOOKS LTD
LAWRENCE & WISHART
LEISHMAN & TAUSSIG

LONGMAN GROUP UK LTD
MACMILLAN DIST LTD
MANCHESTER UNI PRESS
MERROW PUBLISHING CO
MIT PRESS LTD
MOMENTA PUB CO LTD
MULTILINGUAL MATTERS
NATURAL HIST BOOK SV
OPEN UNIV PRESS
OVERSEAS DEVEL INST
PACKARD PUB LTD
PINTER PUBLISHERS
PITMAN PUBLISHING
PLUTO PUBLISHING
PORTLAND PRESS LTD
RICHMOND PUB CO LTD
ROUNDHOUSE PUB LTD
ROUTLEDGE
ROYAL IRISH ACADEMY
SAGE PUBLICATIONS
SALTIRE SOCIETY
SPRINGER-VERLAG
SWEET & MAXWELL LTD
I B TAURIS & CO LTD
TEXTILE INSTITUTE
THORNTON'S OF OXFORD
UNI OF WALES PRESS
WORLD SCIENTIFIC PUB

Welsh Interest

ACADEMY BOOKS LTD
APPLEFORD PUB GROUP
APPLETREE PRESS LTD
ATTIC BOOKS
CARCANET PRESS
CCBI PUBLICATIONS
DALENNAU
CHRISTOPHER DAVIES
DRAKE PUB SERVICES
DYLLANSOW TRURAN
EVANGELICAL PR WALES
FOCUS PUBLICATIONS
GREENCROFT BOOKS
GWASG Y DREF WEN
ROBERT HALE LTD
HARDWICK HOUSE
HONNO LTD
JARROLD PUBLISHING
LANGUAGE INFO CENTRE
LEADING EDGE PRESS
LLANERCH PUBLISHERS
ANTHONY NELSON LTD
ORIEL/WELSH ARTS CNL
POETRY WALES PRESS
THE POUND HOUSE QUOTES LTD
ROBINSON PUBLISHING
SB PUBLICATIONS
SPREAD EAGLE PUB
THORNHILL PRESS LTD
UNI OF WALES PRESS
WELSH BOOKS COUNCIL

Women's Studies

ACADEMIC & UNIV PUB
AK DISTRIBUTION
ALIF INTERNATIONAL
APPLEFORD PUB GROUP
BAHAI PUBLISHING
BARMARICK PUB
BLOODAXE BOOKS
BOOK REP & DIST LTD
BOOKMARKS
BOOKSPEED
MARION BOYARS PUB
CANONGATE PRESS PLC
KYLE CATHIE LTD
CCBI PUBLICATIONS
CHADWYCK-HEALEY LTD
CHAPMANS PUB LTD
DEBORAH CHARLES PUB
LLOYD COLE
DALENNAU
EDINBURGH UNIV PRESS
ELEMENT BOOKS LTD
ELM PUBLICATIONS
LAWRENCE ERLBAUM ASS
FOREST
GALE RESEARCH INT
GOTHIC IMAGE PUB
GRACEWING/FOWLER
THE HARLEY PRESS
HARPERCOLLINS THORS
HARVARD UNIV PRESS
HAWTHORN PRESS
HEALTH EDUC AUTH
HONEYGLEN PUB LTD
HONNO LTD
ICA PUBLISHING
INT LABOUR OFFICE
INTERVARSITY PRESS
KINGSCLERE PUB LTD
KINGSWAY PUB
KUPERARD LTD
LAVIS MARKETING
LAWRENCE & WISHART
LEISHMAN & TAUSSIG
LIBERTARIAN ALLIANCE
LITTLE BROWN & CO
LONGMAN GROUP UK LTD
MINORITY RIGHTS GRP
NEW BEACON BOOKS LTD
NEW CLARION PRESS
OPEN GATE PRESS
OPEN UNIV PRESS
OXFAM
PATHFINDER PRESS
PATTEN PRESS
PIATKUS BOOKS
PICCADILLY PRESS LTD
PLUTO PUBLISHING
POLICY STUDIES INST
PRISM PRESS
READERS INT
RIVERS ORAM PRESS
ROUNDHOUSE PUB LTD
ROUTLEDGE
SAGE PUBLICATIONS
SAQI BOOKS
SAUS PUBLICATIONS
SCARLET PRESS
SERPENT'S TAIL
TAPROBANE LTD
I B TAURIS & CO LTD
TREADWELLS ART MILL
TRENTHAM BOOKS LTD
TURNAROUND
VERSO
VIRAGO PRESS
VOLCANO PRESS LTD
WHITE COCKADE PUB
WOLFHOUND PRESS
WOMEN'S PRESS
WRITERS & SCHOLARS
XANADU PUBLICATIONS

AMENDMENTS FORM

Company Name: _____ Page Number: _____

PLEASE NOTE AMENDMENTS BELOW

Company Name: _____

Address: _____

_____

Tel: _____ Fax: _____

Orders to: _____

Other changes: _____

_____

_____

_____

From: _____ Date: _____

Please return to: Sydney Davies, Booksellers Association, Minster House, 272 Vauxhall Bridge Road, London SW1V 1BA.

AMENDMENTS FORM

Company Name: _____ Page Number: _____

PLEASE NOTE AMENDMENTS BELOW

Company Name: _____

Address: _____

_____

Tel: _____ Fax: _____

Orders to: _____

Other changes: _____

_____

_____

_____

From: _____ Date: _____

Please return to: Sydney Davies, Booksellers Association, Minster House,
272 Vauxhall Bridge Road, London SW1V 1BA.

ORDER FORM

KEEP UP TO DATE...

People and companies are constantly on the move in the book industry. To help you keep up, this Directory is published annually.

To make sure you receive future editions 'hot off the press', simply fill in the standing order form below and return it to:

Publications Department, Booksellers Association Service House, 272 Vauxhall Bridge Road, London, SW1V 1BA.

☐ Please send me _____ copies of the 1994 of the Directory of Book Publishers, Distributors and Wholesalers. Please also send me all future editions until further notice.

☐ Please send me details of the 1994 Directory prior to publication.

Name: _____

Position: _____

Company: _____

Address: _____

_____

_____

Signature: _____ Date: _____